DATE DUE

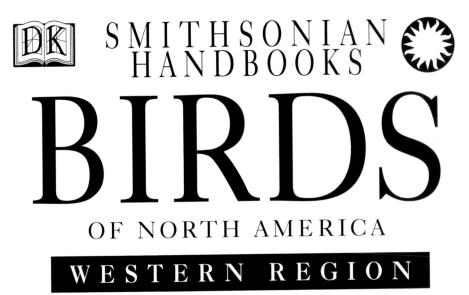

SMITHSONIAN
HANDBOOKS

BIRDS

OF NORTH AMERICA

WESTERN REGION

Fred J. Alsop III

SMITHSONIAN HANDBOOKS

BIRDS

OF NORTH AMERICA

WESTERN REGION

Fred J. Alsop III

LONDON, NEW YORK, SYDNEY, DEHLI, PARIS
MUNICH, AND JOHANNESBURG

Editor-in-Chief Russell Greenberg, Ph.D.
Director of the Migratory Bird Center at the National Zoological Park

Senior Editor Jill Hamilton
Editorial Director LaVonne Carlson
Art Director Tina Vaughan
Publisher Sean Moore
Production Director David Proffit

Produced by Southern Lights Custom Publishing
Managing Editor Shelley DeLuca
Production Director Lee Howard
Graphic Design Miles Parsons, Tim Kolankiewicz, Scott Fuller
President Ellen Sullivan

First American Edition, 2001
2 4 6 8 10 9 7 5 3 1

Published in the United States by
DK Publishing, Inc.
95 Madison Avenue
New York, New York 10016

DK Publishing, Inc. offers special discounts for bulk purchases for sales promotions or
premiums. Specific, large-quantity needs can be met with special editions, including personalized
covers,excerpts of existing guides, and corporate imprints. For more information, contact
Special Markets Department, DK Publishing, Inc.,
95 Madison Avenue, New York, NY 10016; Fax: 800-600-9098.

Library of Congress Cataloging-in-Publication Data

Birds of North America: West – 1st American ed.
p. cm.
ISBN 0-7894-7157-4 (alk.paper)
1. Birds—West (U.S.)—Identification. 2. Birds—Canada, Western—Identification. I.
DK Publishing, Inc.

QL683.W4 B52 2001
598'.0978—dc21
00-047414

Printed and bound in the United States by R. R. Donnelley & Sons Co..
Color reproduction by Colourscan, Singapore.
See our complete catalog at
www.dk.com

CONTENTS

INTRODUCTION

Birdwatching, or birding as it is now commonly called, is practiced by more than 60 million North Americans – making it the single largest hobby on the continent. North America is an exciting place to go birding because it holds billions of birds representing more than 900 species that are permanent or summer residents, visit regularly, or stray occasionally to the continent.

AVIAN DIVERSITY
Having attained the power of flight more than 150 million years ago, birds might be expected to be uniformly distributed in every corner of the earth. But they are not. They are bound to the earth by the habitats to which they have adapted and limited by geographical barriers as well as the history of their lineage.

Different species are often associated with major plant communities, or biomes, that provide them with critical habitat requirements for part or all of their annual cycle. Polar regions of permanent ice and snow are home to Ivory Gulls; the arctic tundra to Snowy Owls,

The SPOTTED OWL inhabits old-growth forests and wooded canyons.

ptarmigans, jaegers, Gyrfalcons, and countless shorebirds in summer. The great block of northern coniferous forests provide seeds for crossbills, grosbeaks, finches, and nuthatches; in summer, insects for flycatchers, vireos, and warblers abound.

Deciduous forests, southern pine forests, grasslands, and deserts all hold particular species of birds different from those in other biomes. Other species, such as herons, are adapted for freshwater ponds, lakes, rivers, and streams; still others for marshes and seashores as well as the open ocean.

The SPOT-BILLED DUCK, an Asian species, visits the Alaskan islands.

BIRDWATCHING IN WESTERN NORTH AMERICA

The avian diversity of Western North America is reflected in the more than 780 species of birds that have been recorded roughly west of the 100th meridian, the approximate north-south line used as a division in creating this book as a western edition. Within the western half of the continent are spectacular mountain ranges, vast grasslands, hot and cold deserts, chapparral, boreal forests, tundra, glaciers, and ice fields. Flycatchers and hummingbirds reach their greatest Northern Hemisphere diversity here.

The VERMILION FLYCATCHER thrives in arid and semiarid habitats.

Many birdwatchers practice their hobby close to their own backyards. They learn to recognize the species they see most often and occasionally identify a "new" species for the yard, perhaps even photograph the birds they see. Many take their birding to the field. Some are so passionate that they travel North America identifying as many species as they can, often covering many miles on short notice to observe a newly discovered vagrant.

Not even the most ardent birder has seen all of the more than 920 species now accepted as having occurred in North America. But that is part of the fun and challenge of birding. It holds something for every level of interest, and the amateur birder stands as much chance as the professional of making a discovery that sheds important light on the field of ornithology.

MALLARDS are found almost anywhere there is shallow freshwater, including the mountains of the Southwest.

HOW THIS BOOK WORKS

Until now, no tool for identifying birds has also provided access to information on behavior, nesting, flight patterns, and similar birds in a compact and user-friendly format. Written for the novice as well as the experienced birder, this book showcases in individual page profiles each of the 696 species of birds documented for western North America. The species are in taxonomic order and include all those known to breed west of the 100th meridian in North America north of Mexico, or adjacent islands

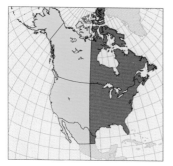

and seas within 200 miles of the coast, and all species documented as regular visitors or casual vagrants by the American Ornithologists' Union (AOU) and the American Birding Association (ABA). Only those species listed on the current AOU *Check-list of North American Birds* (7th edition, 1998 and its 42nd Supplement, 2000) and the ABA 1998–99 ABA *Check-list Report*, *Birding* 31: 518–524 are included. Additionally listed are more than 80 rare species that have been recorded as accidental visitors to the western half of the continent. This list begins on page 734. Other species that have been seen but not yet accepted by the AOU or ABA are not included. Also excluded are a host of introduced exotic species that are living in the wild, mostly in southern California and southern Florida, that are not yet recognized by either the AOU or the ABA as having viable breeding populations in North America.

FINDING YOUR BIRD

To find a bird, you can scan the pages of the book, or look up either scientific name or common name in the index. The species are in taxonomic order, beginning with the non-passerines such as grebes, loons, ducks, hawks, owls, doves, hummingbirds, and

woodpeckers. They are followed by the passerines, the perching or songbirds, which begin on page 428. Once you have found your bird's species profile, it will help you identify the bird as well as provide ready reference to its natural history.

LEAST GREBE (non-passerine)
Birds that do not perch and sing are in the first part of this book.

TOWNSEND'S WARBLER (passerine)
Birds that do perch and sing are in the second part of this book.

Scientific family name •

Scientific name of species •

Average length from tip of bill to tip of tail •

Average length between tips of open wings •

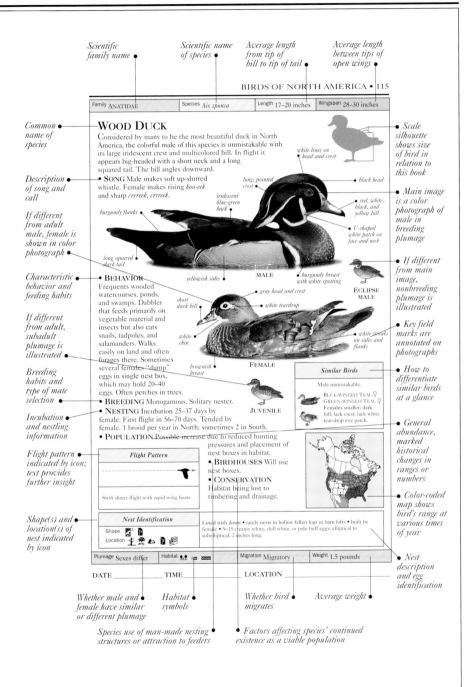

BIRDS OF NORTH AMERICA • 115

Family ANATIDAE | Species *Aix sponsa* | Length 17–20 inches | Wingspan 28–30 inches

Common • name of species

WOOD DUCK

Considered by many to be the most beautiful duck in North America, the colorful male of this species is unmistakable with its large iridescent crest and multicolored bill. In flight it appears big-headed with a short neck and a long squared tail. The bill angles downward.

• **SONG** Male makes soft up-slurred whistle. Female makes rising *hoo-eek* and sharp *crrreek, crrreek.*

Description • of song and call

If different from adult male, female is shown in color photograph •

white lines on head and crest

long, pointed crest

iridescent blue-green back

black head

burgundy flanks

red, white, black, and yellow bill

U-shaped white patch on face and neck

long squared dark tail

yellowish sides

MALE

burgundy breast with white spotting

ECLIPSE MALE

Scale • silhouette shows size of bird in relation to this book

Main image • is a color photograph of male in breeding plumage

If different • from main image, nonbreeding plumage is illustrated

Characteristic • behavior and feeding habits

• **BEHAVIOR** Frequents wooded watercourses, ponds, and swamps. Dabbler that feeds primarily on vegetable material and insects but also eats snails, tadpoles, and salamanders. Walks easily on land and often forages there. Sometimes several females "dump" eggs in single nest box, which may hold 20–40 eggs. Often perches in trees.

If different from adult, subadult plumage is illustrated •

Breeding habits and type of mate selection •

Incubation and nestling information

short dark bill

white chin

brownish breast

gray head and crest

white teardrop

FEMALE

white streaks on sides and flanks

JUVENILE

Key field • marks are annotated on photographs

How to • differentiate similar birds at a glance

Similar Birds

Male unmistakable.

BLUE-WINGED TEAL ♀
GREEN-WINGED TEAL ♀
Females smaller; dark bill; lack crest; lack white tear-drop eye patch.

• **BREEDING** Monogamous. Solitary nester.
• **NESTING** Incubation 25–37 days by female. First flight in 56–70 days. Tended by female. 1 brood per year in North; sometimes 2 in South.
• **POPULATION** Possible increase due to reduced hunting pressures and placement of nest boxes in habitat.

General • abundance, marked historical changes in ranges or numbers

Flight pattern • indicated by icon; text provides further insight

Flight Pattern

Swift direct flight with rapid wing beats.

• **BIRDHOUSES** Will use nest boxes.
• **CONSERVATION** Habitat being lost to timbering and drainage.

Color-coded • map shows bird's range at various times of year

Shape(s) and • location(s) of nest indicated by icon

Nest Identification

Shape
Location

Lined with down • rarely nests in hollow fallen logs or barn lofts • built by female • 9–15 creamy white, dull white, or pale buff eggs; elliptical to subelliptical, 2 inches long.

Nest • description and egg identification

Plumage Sexes differ | Habitat | Migration Migratory | Weight 1.5 pounds

DATE _____ TIME _____ LOCATION _____

Whether male and • female have similar or different plumage

Habitat • symbols

Whether bird • migrates

Average weight •

Species use of man-made nesting • structures or attraction to feeders

Factors affecting species' continued • existence as a viable population

GUIDE TO VISUAL REFERENCES

PHOTOGRAPHS

Because users of this guide will be viewing these birds in backyards, woodlands, and other natural environments, realistic photographs are used as visual reference. Some rare and seldom-photographed species are illustrated. Unless otherwise noted, the primary image shows the male bird in breeding plumage. If the adult female has significantly different plumage from the male a second image depicts the female in breeding plumage. If field marks are not visible in a photograph they are described in the accompanying text.

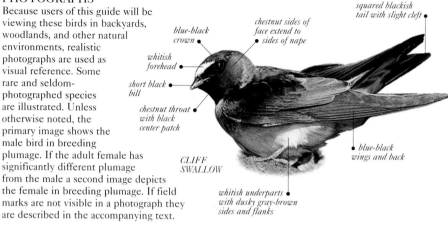

squared blackish tail with slight cleft •

chestnut sides of face extend to • sides of nape

blue-black crown •

whitish forehead •

short black bill •

chestnut throat with black center patch •

• blue-black wings and back

CLIFF SWALLOW

whitish underparts • with dusky gray-brown sides and flanks

ILLUSTRATIONS

Many birds also have other plumages, including the winter plumage, which are depicted in illustrations. The plumage of the immature if different from both adults also is illustrated. Some species have different color morphs, which are also illustrated.

LIGHT MORPH JUVENILE WINTER PLUMAGE WHITE MORPH

SIMILAR BIRDS

In many cases it can be difficult to distinguish between certain birds in the field. Thus species accounts feature a list of similar birds with accompanying text that identifies distinct features and behavior that clearly set them apart. Male and female symbols indicate the sex of the bird that could be mistaken for the species being profiled.

Similar Birds
CAVE SWALLOW Pale cinnamon-buff throat; cinnamon forehead; richer cinnamon-rust rump.

DISTRIBUTION MAP

Each species profile has a map showing where the bird is likely to be seen either all year long (permanent resident), in the breeding season (summer resident), or in the winter (winter resident). The maps depict only those parts of each species' range within North America and up to approximately 100 miles offshore north of central Mexico to the northern borders of Canada.

 permanent resident   summer resident   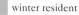 winter resident

SCALE SILHOUETTES
These show the silhouette of the bird overlaid proportionally on a copy of this book.

NEST IDENTIFICATION
The Nest Identification box provides icons describing nest shape and location.

Flight Pattern
Swift graceful flight alternating several deep, rapid wing beats with long elliptical glides with sharp sweeping upturns at the end. Soars on thermals and updrafts.

FLIGHT PATTERN
Each bird's flight pattern is shown in its species profile by an icon. For more information on flight patterns, see page 20.

Nest Identification	Pellets of clay or mud, with lining of grasses, down, and feathers • usually under eaves of buildings or under dams or bridges; sometimes on ridges of canyons; rarely on trunk of conifer tree under overhanging branch • built by both sexes • 3–6 white, cream, or pinkish eggs, marked with browns; oval to long oval, 0.8 x 0.5 inches.
Shape	
Location	

Shape						Location						
Burrow Excavated	Burrow Preformed	Crevice	Deep Cup	Floating	Man-made	Bank	Building	Bridge	Cave	Chimney	Cliff	Conifer
None	Open Cup	Pendant	Platform	Saucer	Scrape	Deciduous	Floating	Grass	Gravel Roof	Hollow Log	Man-made	Pebbles
Shallow	Sphere	Tree Cavity Primary	Tree Cavity Secondary			Reed/Cattails	Shrub	Snag	Bare Soil	Stump		

HABITAT
At the bottom of each species account is a set of icons representing all the habitat types in the order in which the bird is found, from the most to the least likely.

forest: coniferous, broadleaf, temperate, or tropical

open forest; more space between the trees, tundra forest, semiopen areas

forest edge, oak and riparian

grassland with scattered trees (includes farmland, citrus groves, orchards)

bushes, shrubs, thickets and undergrowth; tropical lowland

areas of scrub vegetation, frequently with thorns

open landscapes: grassland, tundra, savanna, coastal ponds/sloughs – salt, brackish or freshwater, coastal marshes, coastal wetlands, salt marshes, prairie potholes

semidesert

desert

lakes, rivers and vicinity, sandspits, mudflats, ponds

upland streams and vicinity

open sea, low flat islands

rocky or sandy seashore, bay islands, coastal islands, shallow coastal habitats, coastal bays, coastal mangroves, tidal flats, sand spits, mudflats

freshwater marshes, swamps

rocky places or cliffs (both on the coast and inland)

mountains, wooded canyons

ANATOMY OF BIRDS

Birds are the most diverse terrestrial vertebrates with more than 9,800 extant species. Mammals are the only other homeothermic group with whom they share the planet. Yet, although mammal species number less than half that of birds, the mammals are much more varied in body shape and size. Mammals vary in form from primates to giraffes to armadillos, with specialists in running, hopping, flying, swimming, burrowing, digging, and climbing. Birds, however, all look like birds – with the same basic architecture, a body shape dictated by the demands of flight.

FEATHERS

Birds have three basic types of feathers: down, contour, and flight (wing and tail) feathers. Down feathers are next to the bird's skin for insulation. The contour is the most commonly recognized feather and the one that covers most of the bird's body. Typical contour feathers consist of a central shaft or quill and the flattened portion or vane. Contour feathers that extend beyond the wings and tail are the flight feathers.

DOWN   CONTOUR   FLIGHT
(WING AND TAIL)

BONES

In most species both the wings and the legs must be strong enough to transport the full weight of the bird, yet light enough to fly. Some bones have been fused and some bear internal struts. Ribs are overlapped for strength; others are hollowed, thinned, and reduced in numbers for lightness. In flying birds, and those flightless birds like penguins that use flipperlike forelimbs to "fly" under-water, the sternum, or breastbone, bears a thin knifelike keel to which the large flight muscles of the breast, the pectoral muscles, are attached.

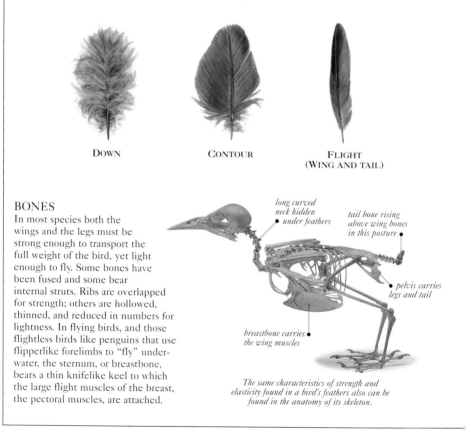

long curved neck hidden under feathers

tail bone rising above wing bones in this posture

pelvis carries legs and tail

breastbone carries the wing muscles

The same characteristics of strength and elasticity found in a bird's feathers also can be found in the anatomy of its skeleton.

BILLS

Birds' bills are composed of a horny sheath overlying a bony core. The entire lightweight structure has evolved in countless ways to the specialized needs of its owner, from seed-cracking to nectar probing and from fish-catching to fruit-picking. Birds also use their bills to build nests, preen, and court. Bills may change in size and/or color in breeding season.

The ROSEATE SPOONBILL uses its spoon-shaped bill to scoop food from water.

The NORTHERN CARDINAL uses its conical bill to crunch seeds.

The RUBY-THROATED HUMMINGBIRD uses its long needlelike bill to probe into flowers for nectar.

The RED CROSSBILL's bill features mandibles crossed at the tips that are ideal for digging the seeds out of pinecones.

LEGS AND FEET

The legs of birds are thin, strong, and springy, and in most species lack feathers on their distal parts where they are instead covered with scales. Muscles, which are concentrated on the portion of the leg nearest the body, control the extremities with a series of tendons. Toes generally number four with three forward and one opposable toe pointed backward, but some North American birds have only three. Toes are covered by scales and have claws at their tips which in birds of prey are enlarged into strong talons.

The AMERICAN ROBIN has a typical bird's foot: four toes with three forward and one back.

Some, like the HAIRY WOODPECKER, have two toes forward and two back.

The MALLARD has three webbed toes and one vestigial toe in back.

The DOUBLE-CRESTED CORMORANT has four webbed toes.

The BALD EAGLE has claws enlarged and elongated into talons.

WINGS AND TAILS

The shapes of wings and tails are an adaptation to where and how a bird flies. Look carefully at flight silhouettes: forest raptors (a) have rounded wings for living in dense vegetation; swallows (b) have narrow tapering wings. The tapering wings and narrow tail of a falcon (c) contrast with the broad splayed wings and broad tail of an eagle (d), which allow an eagle to soar. Terns (e) have long elegant wings; albatross wings (f) are very long, with an extended inner section for flying over water like a sailplane.

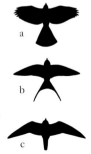

TOPOGRAPHY OF A BIRD

A s you consult the species profiles in this book you will encounter a
number of ornithological terms that describe the "landscape," or groups
of feathers, of a bird's body. Learning these terms will help you use your
field guide and, when you look at living birds, prompt you to see more detail
with each sighting.

TIPS FOR THE FIELD
1. Start by looking at the bird's head. Note its bill and the markings on its face.
2. Get a feel for the bird's overall shape and size and note body markings.
3. Note shapes and markings of tail and wings.
4. Watch it fly and note markings visible in flight.

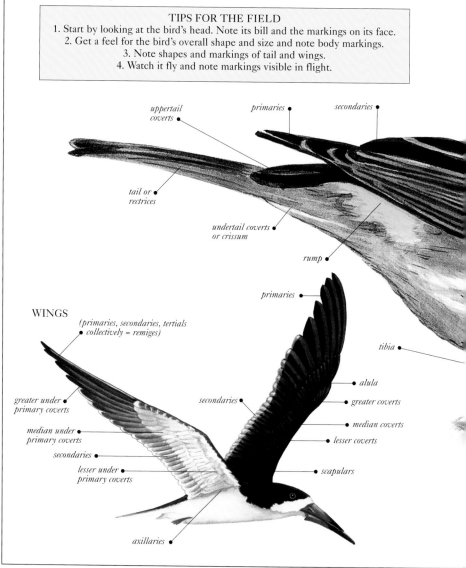

uppertail coverts

primaries

secondaries

tail or rectrices

undertail coverts or crissum

rump

primaries

WINGS
(primaries, secondaries, tertials collectively = remiges)

tibia

greater under primary coverts

secondaries

alula

greater coverts

median under primary coverts

median coverts

lesser coverts

secondaries

lesser under primary coverts

scapulars

axillaries

HEAD

median crown stripe

lateral crown stripe

supraloral area

supercilium (superciliary stripe)

postocular stripe

lore

mustache

submustachial stripe

malar stripe

ear patch (auricular)

crown

ear covert or auricular

nape

back

tertials

forehead

lore

upper mandible

lower mandible

chin

throat

side of neck

breast

scapulars

side

belly

tarsus or tibiotarsus

flank

VARIATIONS WITHIN SPECIES

Birds are the most colorful of all terrestrial vertebrates. Their coloration varies widely not only from species to species but within species. Often plumage colors differ between the sexes, between adults and their young, and from season to season. All of these different color patterns increase the challenge of identification for the birder.

MALE/FEMALE VARIATIONS

Within a species, adult males often differ in color and pattern of plumage, and sometimes in size, from adult females.

MALE   FEMALE   JUVENILE

PAINTED BUNTINGS have three distinct plumages.

JUVENILE PLUMAGE VARIATIONS

On an individual bird, color changes occur when feathers molt, or drop from their follicles to be replaced by new feathers. In its life span a bird will molt many times. After its first molt, when it loses its natal down, the bird will attain its *juvenile plumage*. This will be its first plumage with contour and flight feathers. This plumage often does not resemble that of either adult and is worn briefly for a few weeks or months. For the purposes of this book the term "juvenile" is used to refer to subadult plumaged birds that may, or may not, be sexually mature.

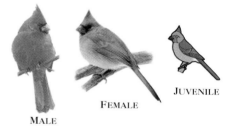

MALE   FEMALE   JUVENILE

Male and female NORTHERN CARDINALS have different plumages, while juveniles resemble females.

OTHER SUBADULT PLUMAGES

Although in many species, such as the bunting and cardinal, the juvenile attains adult plumage after its first year, there are species in which it takes the juvenile longer to do this. It may take juveniles of some species two years or more. These individuals may experience what are known as first, second, or even third winter or summer plumages before attaining the plumage of adult birds. The Ring-billed Gull is one such example.

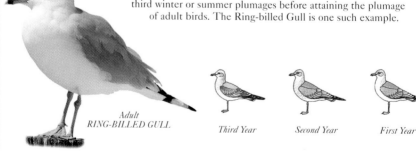

Adult
RING-BILLED GULL

Third Year   *Second Year*   *First Year*

SEASONAL VARIATIONS IN ADULT BIRDS

Most adult birds have two molts a year with a complete molt of all feathers after the breeding season and a partial molt in late winter/early spring in which only the head and body feathers are replaced.

INDIGO BUNTING
in winter plumage

MALLARD in
breeding plumage

MALLARD in
eclipse plumage

INDIGO BUNTING
in breeding plumage

The late winter or early spring molt produces the brighter plumage associated with many breeding birds and is called the *breeding plumage* or *alternate plumage.* Male ducks undergo a molt just after the nesting season begins and get a fresh coat of feathers that is drab like the female's called an *eclipse plumage.* Fall molts produce a plumage called *winter plumage, fall plumage,* or *basic plumage.*

OTHER VARIATIONS

Some genetic variations in color and pattern can be seen among populations representing different geographical races of a species. These races are also referred to as subspecies.

SLATE-
COLORED
JUNCO

OREGON
JUNCO

PINK-SIDED
JUNCO

WHITE-WINGED
JUNCO

GRAY-HEADED
JUNCO

The DARK-EYED JUNCO has five adult plumage variations associated with different geographical regions.

Hybrids between species may produce birds that share some characteristics of each parent but still have a very different appearance.

Some species have two or more color phases or morphs.

LAWRENCE'S
WARBLER

BREWSTER'S
WARBLER

Results from crosses between Golden-winged Warblers and
Blue-winged Warblers and their offspring.

The EASTERN SCREECH-OWL has red, gray,
and brown morphs.

HOW TO IDENTIFY BIRDS

Birds that come to backyard feeders often stay long enough for you to study them in detail, but not all birds are so cooperative and often a fleeting glimpse is all you get. Learn to get the best look you can under the conditions and to see the entire bird well. First impressions of a bird, especially a new species for you, will give you clues for comparing it with birds you already know. What you are looking for are field marks, those physical clues that include size, shape, color patterns, and behavior, and also the habitat the bird is in and the sounds it may make.

Learn to routinely and quickly look at the details of the head; markings on the body, wings, and tail; and the shapes of the bird's parts.

HEAD
Is the crown:

striped

streaked

capped

crested

Look for other markings on the face such as:

superciliary stripes

eye lines

eye rings

spectacles

mustache marks

malar marks

ear patches

a mask through
the eye

BODY PLUMAGE
Are the underparts:

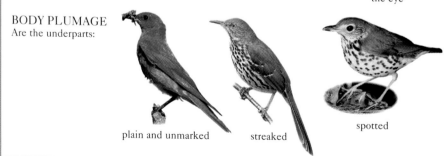

plain and unmarked

streaked

spotted

TAIL
Is the tail:

forked

rounded

fan-shaped

wedge-shaped

pointed

notched

square

short

long

MARKINGS
Does it have distinctive wing or tail markings such as:

bars

bands

spots

contrasting colors

BILL
Is the bill:

cone-shaped

needlelike

hooked

decurved

spatulate

long or short

SONG
Many expert birders rely on their ears as much as their eyes to identify birds. Any of the many cassette tapes, CDs, or videos can help you learn the songs, calls, and other sounds birds make.

BEHAVIOR
The behavior of the bird will also provide clues to its identity. Does it bob, wag, or pump its tail either up and down or back and forth? Note its flight pattern. Does it back down a tree or go headfirst? For more information on Behavior, see page 22.

IDENTIFYING BIRDS IN FLIGHT

How a bird flies – the speed of the wing stroke as well as the pattern – can often help you recognize a species.

Direct – steady flight with regular wing beats, along a constant line; typical of most species, including waterfowl, herons, doves, crows, shorebirds, and many songbirds.

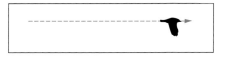

Dynamic soaring – glides over water "downhill" with the wind to its back and when close to the surface quickly turns 180 degrees back into the wind. There the bird is lifted back up to near the original height upon which it turns back and soars "downhill" again. Characteristic of many pelagic species, including albatrosses, shearwaters, and petrels.

Flap and glide – alternates a burst of several wing beats with a short or long level glide. Many birds of prey, both hawks and owls, use this flight pattern as do Black Vultures, ibis, and pelicans.

Flightless – many species living in environments free of predators have given up the energy-demanding activity of flight. The only flightless North American species, the Great Auk, was hunted to extinction in 1844.

Glide – wings are held fully or partially extended as the bird loses altitude. Many birds glide down to a landing, or from perch to perch. Hawks may glide from the top of one thermal to the bottom of the next in migration.

Hawking – flying up from the ground or down from an aerial perch to seize a flying insect and looping back down to the same or nearby perch. Characteristic of flycatchers and other small, active insect-eating birds such as warblers, the Cedar Waxwing, and several species of woodpeckers.

Hovering – rapid wingbeats while the bird remains suspended in one spot over the ground or water. Typical of hummingbirds, kingfishers, American Kestrel, Osprey, Rough-legged Hawk and many small birds that hover briefly to glean food from vegetation.

Mothlike – an erratic, sometimes bouncy, slow flight seen in nightjars, a few storm-petrels, and in the display flights of some small birds.

Skims – the flight pattern of the Black Skimmer in which the bird flies a steady course with its lower mandible cleaving the surface of still water as it feeds.

Static soaring – requires about a twentieth of the energy of flapping flight. Birds soar on rising heated columns of air, thermals, or on deflected currents and updrafts. Large hawks, eagles, vultures, storks, White Pelicans, and gulls soar this way.

Straight line formation – an energy-saving style of flight used by some larger birds such as cormorants, pelicans, ibis, some waterfowl, and others. Birds may fly one behind the other, or abreast as do some scoters and eiders.

Undulating – some small birds conserve energy by rising on one or more wing beats and then folding the wings to the body and swooping down to the next wing beat. Characteristic of woodpeckers, finches, and chickadees.

V formation – an energy-saving flight style used by some larger birds, including ducks, geese, cranes, and cormorants.

Zigzag – a pattern used by birds flushed from the ground as a way to elude predators. The Common Snipe and several species of quail are good examples.

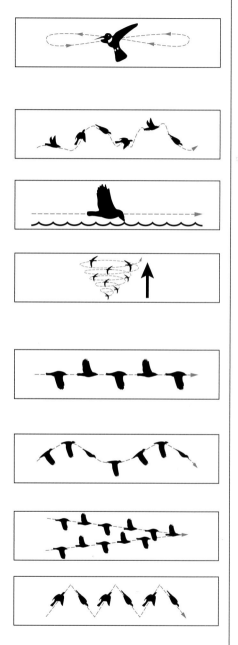

BEHAVIOR

A large portion of the bird behavior we admire is instinctive and associated with particular species and families. So as you look for field marks, notice the bird's body language. It will give you many clues to its identity.

TAIL MOVEMENT
Some birds flip their tails as they move or perch. The tail may be cocked at an angle over the back, fanned open or closed, wagged, bobbed, or pumped up or down. Some birds constantly bob their bodies up and down as they walk or stand; others bob or jerk occasionally, while others sway back and forth as they walk.

BEWICK'S WREN holds its tail high above its back as it hops, often flicking it from side to side.

BODY MOVEMENT
Some birds hop like a sparrow. Some run or walk. They may climb trees straight up, hitch up or back down them, walk headfirst down them, or cling upside down. Many birds wade like herons and egrets, or swim like ducks and geese. Some aquatic species feed by dabbling or tipping up their bodies with their heads and necks beneath the surface. Others dive completely below the surface.

The PAINTED REDSTART spreads its tail, flashing the white outer tail feathers.

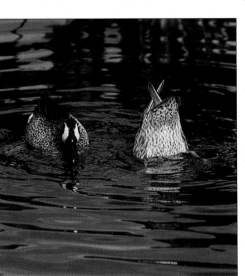

The BLUE-WINGED TEAL dabbles for food.

The TRICOLORED HERON wades.

FORAGING

Notice whether the bird forages on the ground, in the treetops, or at the mid-story level. Shorebirds may stay on the dry sand or away from the water's edge on a mudflat, or they may wade in the shallows, while some species may wade up to their bellies. Some shorebirds pick at their food while others drill and probe rapidly in the mud.

A juvenile WHITE IBIS probes with its bill for food in shallow water.

These MOURNING DOVES are foraging on the ground.

DISPLAY BEHAVIORS

Many species exhibit distinctive display behaviors during breeding season. They may dance like Prairie-Chickens, cranes, or Western Grebes; skylark like sparrows or buntings; or put on the aerial shows of woodcock and snipe. Many species, especially ground-nesters, will try to lead intruders away from the nest with distraction displays including the broken-wing or crippled-bird act.

The GREAT EGRET flashes its long white plumes in courtship display.

ABUNDANCE AND DISTRIBUTION

What does it mean when someone says a bird is "common" or that a species is "abundant" or "rare?" To appreciate a bird species' presence (or lack of it) in a given region you need to consider the factors of habitat, geographical range, and season of the year. Keep in mind that the distribution and abundance of birds, among the most mobile of the earth's creatures, are not static and the boundaries of populations often change. Birds are easily impacted by changes in climate and habitat brought about by natural or human causes, with seasonal migrations being the most obvious result. Thus knowing the seasonal occurrence of a bird is important in confirming its identification. The range maps in this guide are color-coded to provide you with this information. You can get even more specific information from local checklists, local bird books, websites, and local birders.

Abundant means a species is so conspicuous that birders usually observe more than 25 individuals daily in proper habitat and season.

EUROPEAN STARLING

Common means birders are likely to see 5–25 individuals daily in proper habitat and season.

BLACK-CAPPED CHICKADEE

Fairly common means a species is common enough that birders should observe at least one individual daily in proper habitat and season.

Uncommon species can be widespread but may not be observed by birders searching for it in proper habitat and season.

YELLOW-THROATED VIREO

LONG-EARED OWL

Casual means a bird that wanders into North America at infrequent intervals and is not observed annually, but exhibits a pattern of occurrence over several decades.

Rare can mean either that the species is widely distributed outside North America but exists in low numbers here, or that the entire population is small and local.

ANTILLEAN NIGHTHAWK

WHITE-THROATED ROBIN

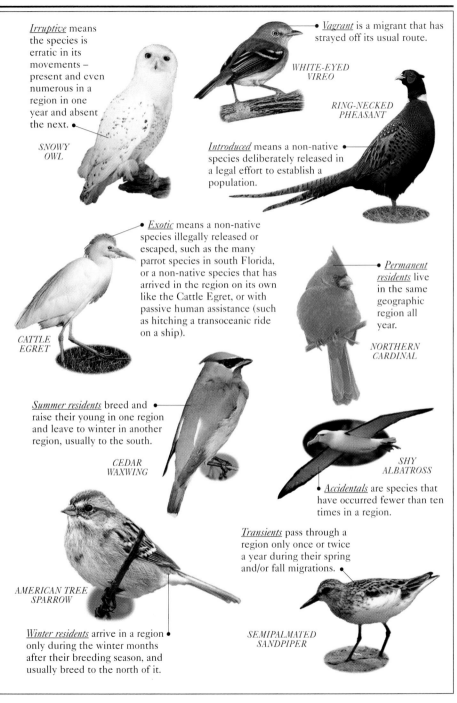

Irruptive means the species is erratic in its movements – present and even numerous in a region in one year and absent the next.

SNOWY OWL

Vagrant is a migrant that has strayed off its usual route.

WHITE-EYED VIREO

RING-NECKED PHEASANT

Introduced means a non-native species deliberately released in a legal effort to establish a population.

Exotic means a non-native species illegally released or escaped, such as the many parrot species in south Florida, or a non-native species that has arrived in the region on its own like the Cattle Egret, or with passive human assistance (such as hitching a transoceanic ride on a ship).

CATTLE EGRET

Permanent residents live in the same geographic region all year.

NORTHERN CARDINAL

Summer residents breed and raise their young in one region and leave to winter in another region, usually to the south.

CEDAR WAXWING

SHY ALBATROSS

Accidentals are species that have occurred fewer than ten times in a region.

Transients pass through a region only once or twice a year during their spring and/or fall migrations.

AMERICAN TREE SPARROW

Winter residents arrive in a region only during the winter months after their breeding season, and usually breed to the north of it.

SEMIPALMATED SANDPIPER

WATCHING BIRDS IN THE BACKYARD

If you provide suitable food, shelter, and water, birds will come to your backyard. If you offer a variety of these necessities you will attract a greater diversity of birds. Place your feeders, nesting boxes, and birdbaths where the birds will feel safe from people and animals and where you can see the birds as you go about your daily routine.

FOOD AND FEEDERS

Many people enjoy feeding birds year-round. Basic types of feeders include platform feeders, hopper feeders, tube feeders, ball feeders, window feeders, fruit feeders, nectar feeders, and suet feeders. Standard foods include black (oil) sunflower seed (the best single seed), striped sunflower seed, hulled sunflower (chips/hearts) seed, niger (called "thistle") seed, safflower seed, white proso millet seed, red millet seed, milo seed, corn (whole kernel, shelled, and cracked), peanuts, peanut butter, suet and suet mixes, fruits, and nectar.

HOUSE FINCHES and a NORTHERN CARDINAL find food and shelter.

AMERICAN GOLDFINCHES at a tube feeder.

A female RED-BELLIED WOODPECKER finds suet in a wire cage feeder.

WATER

Birds need water as much as they need food. If you include even one dependable source of water in your yard you will attract a great variety of birds to drink, bathe, and cool off. If there is a running water or dripping water element even more species will come.

There are many styles of water containers to choose from but the only requirement is: Maintain a stable supply of clean water in a shallow container no deeper than three inches.

NORTHERN CARDINAL at a traditional birdbath.

"Hotel" for PURPLE MARTINS.

Two types of nest boxes you can make yourself.

SHELTER AND NEST BOXES

Planting trees, shrubs, and other vegetation not only provides food for birds but shelter and nesting places. Many species will use nest boxes. Others will use nesting shelves or ledges, and larger species will use raised nesting platforms. Nesting boxes can be made of wood, aluminum, or plastic; natural gourds are often used for martins and swallows.

Urban nest for MOURNING DOVES.

WATCHING BIRDS IN THE FIELD

Very little gear is needed to watch birds, other than your own curiosity. Two indispensable items are a good pair of binoculars and a good field guide. Birding with experienced birders who know the area is also valuable in getting you off to a good start. It is a good idea to keep a small notebook handy. Later you may want to add a camera and telephoto lens; a spotting scope with tripod becomes a good investment for the more serious birder.

A long-lens camera and binoculars allow birders to photograph and see birds that might otherwise be missed.

BINOCULARS
Look for magnifying ranges from
7x to 10x power.

BINOCULARS

Look for magnifying ranges from 7x to 10x power. The outside diameter of the lenses that are farthest from your eyes (the objective lenses) should range from 35mm to 50mm. The power of magnification and the diameter of the objective lenses (the latter helps determine light-gathering ability) are combined and stamped on the binoculars as two numbers such as: 7 x 35, 7 x 50, or 8 x 42. Small compact binoculars such as 8 x 23 are lightweight and tempting to carry in the field, but the small size of the objective lenses limits the amount of light they can gather, making birdwatching under low light difficult.

BASIC PHOTOGRAPHY EQUIPMENT

The best camera body for bird photography is a 35mm single lens reflex (SLR). This camera allows you to view the subject directly through the lens. Many birds move quickly so your camera should have a fast shutter speed of at least 1/500 sec or higher, and the films you use with natural light should have high exposure speeds in the range of 200–400 ISO (ASA). A telephoto lens will allow you to photograph a larger image; you will need one in the 300mm to 500mm range. A sturdy tripod is required for sharp exposures. Use blinds to conceal yourself from the bird and let you get much closer. Automobiles will work as long as you stay inside.

TRIPOD
*To improve the sharpness
of your exposures.*

CAMERA
35mm single lens reflex (SLR).

TELEPHOTO LENS
*Look for a lens in the 300 mm to
500mm range.*

A temporary moveable blind in the form of a simple tent can conceal birders enough to put wary birds at ease.

HOW TO BE A BETTER BIRDER

There are many ways to improve your birding skills and increase your enjoyment of birdwatching.

STUDY AT HOME
Time spent at home studying your field guide will make a big difference. Find local checklists of birds, or state and regional bird books, that provide even more specific information about the birds in your area. Listen to recordings of bird songs and calls.

Patience is one of a birder's most important skills.

IMPROVE YOUR FIELD SKILLS
Birds have keen color eyesight and hearing. They are frightened by sudden movements, loud noises, and bright clothing that does not "blend" with the background. Experienced birders move deliberately, stalking quietly. They converse in low tones and stand patiently.

Birds are curious and attracted to sounds. When you make "pishing" noises (forcing air out through clenched teeth as if saying "pish, pish, pish"), or "squeaking" (making a high-pitched squeak by sucking air through closely pursed lips, a sound that can be amplified by "kissing" the back of your hand) many birds' curiosity will be piqued and they will come closer. Often they produce alarm notes or assembly calls, causing even more birds to come out where you can see them.

KEEP A RECORD
Keeping good records of the birds you see will help you learn when seasonal species are present and how abundant they may be. There is still much science does not know about birds, particularly about behavior and abundance in some habitats, and the amateur birder can make valuable contributions.

PRACTICE BIRDING ETHICS

Birding is not without its responsibility to the welfare of the bird. The American Birding Association has compiled a Code of Ethics for its members. (Copies can be obtained by writing to the ABA at the address below.) Their basic message is that birders' actions should not endanger the welfare of birds or other wildlife; they should not harm the natural environment; and birders must always respect the rights of others, especially their rights to privacy and private property rights.

A female feeds baby bluebirds.

The welfare of fledgling SCREECH-OWLS like these depends on birders who practice good ethics.

BIRD PROTECTION IN BREEDING SEASON

Remember that birds are sensitive to disturbance. Nothing should be done that will frighten them or alter the surroundings of their nest. Once frightened, they may abandon the nest, and this could set their breeding back a whole year.

JOIN A CLUB

Every state and province has established bird clubs. Many local clubs are associated with state, provincial, or regional ornithological societies that network activities, have regular meetings, and publish newsletters. You can locate your nearest bird clubs on the internet, or though the Conservation Directory of the National Wildlife Federation, your state conservation or wildlife department, local library, or newspaper.

Birding organizations exist on the national and international level as well. Some national organizations and their publications are:
• American Birding Association, PO Box 6599, Colorado Springs, CO 80934; *Birding.*
• American Ornithologists' Union, *The Auk;* Association of Field Ornithologists, *Journal of Field Ornithology;* Cooper Ornithological Society, *The Condor;* Wilson Ornithological Society, *Wilson Bulletin.* All can be contacted c/o Ornithological Societies of North America, 810E, 10th Street, Lawrence, KS 66044.
• Laboratory of Ornithology at Cornell University, 159 Sapsucker Woods Road, Ithaca, NY 14850; *Living Bird* quarterly.
• National Audubon Society, 700 Broadway, New York, NY 10003.

CONSERVATION

We are lucky that here in North America we have lost relatively few bird species to extinction. Laws to protect some species were passed as early as the late 1700s, but even then some came too late or were not enforced. Today, all species of birds native to North America are protected by state, provincial, and federal laws and cannot be collected or held in captivity without a legal permit (introduced, non-native species are not so protected). Some species, considered game species, are managed and can be legally harvested during hunting seasons.

Still, many species of North American birds are in decline. Several species require management because their populations have become dangerously low. These species are given additional protection and listed by state, provincial, or federal authorities as "threatened" or "endangered." The bird conservation effort across America is joined by organizations such as the National Audubon Society, the American Bird Conservancy, and

The WOOD STORK is declining due to habitat destruction and the disruption of water flow through southern Florida.

Partners in Flight. The latter group is an Americas-wide coalition of more than 160 organizations and government agencies. Many of our continent's birds have not fared well at the hands of man. They have been persecuted as pests, victimized by wanton shooting, deprived of habitat, subjected to poisons, forced into competition by introduced species,

Some populations of LEAST TERN are endangered due to human disturbance of nesting areas.

The SPECTACLED EIDER has seen major decline in recent years due to the introduction of firearms into its limited nesting range.

and preyed upon by brood parasites. Many of the species that nest in North America, particularly songbirds and shorebirds, are neotropical migrants wintering in other countries where they are exposed to similar stresses, often with less protection.

Birds and other wildlife need our help now more than ever before. Conservation requires the support of every citizen to prevent the continued loss of our natural heritage.

The CALIFORNIA CONDOR is now nearly extinct in the wild due to hunting and lead poisoning.

LAUGHING GULLS and BROWN PELICANS live side by side with America's offshore oil industry.

EXTINCTION

The North American continent north of Mexico hosts more than 700 species of native nesting birds. Direct persecution and indirect population stresses caused by loss of required habitat – both factors generated by humans – have resulted in a small percentage that are now either extinct or on the very brink of extinction. Likewise, many other species are declining and some are in serious trouble. The first to go was the Great Auk, the only flightless species on the continent, after centuries of unregulated exploitation. Many of these species were abundant, and some, like the Passenger Pigeon, were among the most numerous species in North America. Often sheer numbers made them easy to kill in quantity and their marketing profitable. Improvements in firearms and transportation, plus the conversion of the vast eastern forests into farmland, hastened the decline of these species.

Today we are more enlightened. We have enacted laws and extended efforts to save species. There are preservation success stories with species like Peregrine Falcons, Bald Eagles, Brown Pelicans, Ospreys, Whooping Cranes, and Trumpeter Swans. But, there is still much to do as human populations continue to alter critical habitats.

The Eskimo Curlew, Ivory-billed Woodpecker, and Bachman's Warbler are considered probably extinct. The four species on the pages that follow, the Labrador Duck, Great Auk, Passenger Pigeon, and Carolina Parakeet, are now classified as extinct.

Family SCOLOPACIDAE	Species *Numenius borealis*	Length 14 inches	Wingspan 23–27 inches

ESKIMO CURLEW

Once among the most numerous shorebirds in North America, this bird was rare by the 20th century due to unrestricted shooting during fall migration on the North Atlantic Coast, on the wintering grounds in Argentina, and in spring migration in Texas and on the Great Plains. Gregarious by nature, large flocks attracted market and sport hunters, who killed them by the wagonload and shipped them to eastern cities. Most records in the 20th century were in spring on the Texas coast; the last specimen was recorded in Barbados in 1963, and the last sight records were in 1982 in Canada.

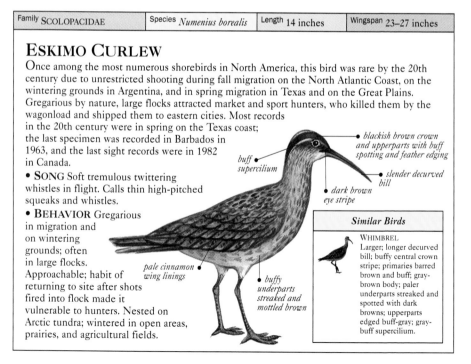

blackish brown crown and upperparts with buff spotting and feather edging

buff supercilium

slender decurved bill

dark brown eye stripe

• **SONG** Soft tremulous twittering whistles in flight. Calls thin high-pitched squeaks and whistles.

• **BEHAVIOR** Gregarious in migration and on wintering grounds; often in large flocks. Approachable; habit of returning to site after shots fired into flock made it vulnerable to hunters. Nested on Arctic tundra; wintered in open areas, prairies, and agricultural fields.

pale cinnamon wing linings

buffy underparts streaked and mottled brown

Similar Birds

WHIMBREL
Larger; longer decurved bill; buffy central crown stripe; primaries barred brown and buff; gray-brown body; paler underparts streaked and spotted with dark browns; upperparts edged buff-gray; gray-buff supercilium.

| Family PICIDAE | Species *Campephilus principalis* | Length 19.5 inches | Wingspan 30–32 inches |

IVORY-BILLED WOODPECKER

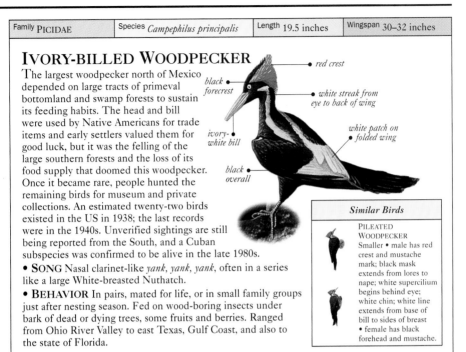

red crest

black forecrest

white streak from eye to back of wing

white patch on folded wing

ivory-white bill

black overall

The largest woodpecker north of Mexico depended on large tracts of primeval bottomland and swamp forests to sustain its feeding habits. The head and bill were used by Native Americans for trade items and early settlers valued them for good luck, but it was the felling of the large southern forests and the loss of its food supply that doomed this woodpecker. Once it became rare, people hunted the remaining birds for museum and private collections. An estimated twenty-two birds existed in the US in 1938; the last records were in the 1940s. Unverified sightings are still being reported from the South, and a Cuban subspecies was confirmed to be alive in the late 1980s.

• **SONG** Nasal clarinet-like *yank, yank, yank*, often in a series like a large White-breasted Nuthatch.

• **BEHAVIOR** In pairs, mated for life, or in small family groups just after nesting season. Fed on wood-boring insects under bark of dead or dying trees, some fruits and berries. Ranged from Ohio River Valley to east Texas, Gulf Coast, and also to the state of Florida.

Similar Birds

PILEATED WOODPECKER Smaller • male has red crest and mustache mark; black mask extends from lores to nape; white supercilium begins behind eye; white chin; white line extends from base of bill to sides of breast • female has black forehead and mustache.

| Family PARULIDAE | Species *Vermivora bachmanii* | Length 4.25–4.75 inches | Wingspan 6.75–7.5 inches |

BACHMAN'S WARBLER

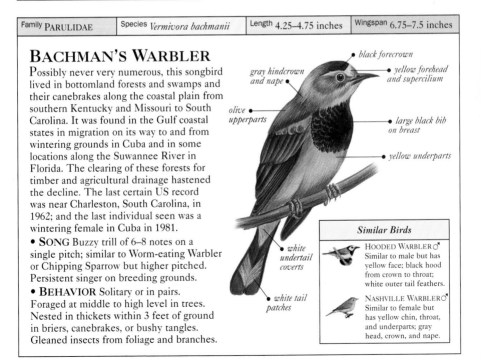

black forecrown

gray hindcrown and nape

yellow forehead and supercilium

olive upperparts

large black bib on breast

yellow underparts

white undertail coverts

white tail patches

Possibly never very numerous, this songbird lived in bottomland forests and swamps and their canebrakes along the coastal plain from southern Kentucky and Missouri to South Carolina. It was found in the Gulf coastal states in migration on its way to and from wintering grounds in Cuba and in some locations along the Suwannee River in Florida. The clearing of these forests for timber and agricultural drainage hastened the decline. The last certain US record was near Charleston, South Carolina, in 1962; and the last individual seen was a wintering female in Cuba in 1981.

• **SONG** Buzzy trill of 6–8 notes on a single pitch; similar to Worm-eating Warbler or Chipping Sparrow but higher pitched. Persistent singer on breeding grounds.

• **BEHAVIOR** Solitary or in pairs. Foraged at middle to high level in trees. Nested in thickets within 3 feet of ground in briers, canebrakes, or bushy tangles. Gleaned insects from foliage and branches.

Similar Birds

HOODED WARBLER ♂ Similar to male but has yellow face; black hood from chin to throat; white outer tail feathers.

NASHVILLE WARBLER ♂ Similar to female but has yellow chin, throat, and underparts; gray head, crown, and nape.

Family ANATIDAE	Species *Camptorhynchus labradorius*	Length 20 inches	Wingspan 30–32 inches

LABRADOR DUCK

This small duck was thought to have nested on islands on the south coast of the Labrador Peninsula. It was market hunted into the 1860s even though its flesh was not relished and specimens often spoiled. The last recorded individual was shot off the coast of Long Island in 1875.

- **SONG** Unrecorded.
- **BEHAVIOR** Wary, quick to fly on whistling wings. Small flocks of 7–10 in winter. Leathery spoonlike expansion at end of upper mandible and prominent vertical lamellae in the lower mandible were used to sift shellfish from mud or sand. Reported to have fed on marine invertebrates and seaweed. Nested on tundra islands; wintered at sea frequenting sandy bays and coastal estuaries along North Atlantic Coast.

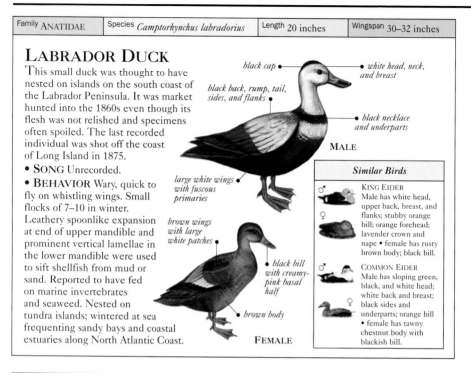

black cap

white head, neck, and breast

black back, rump, tail, sides, and flanks

black necklace and underparts

MALE

large white wings with fuscous primaries

brown wings with large white patches

black bill with creamy-pink basal half

brown body

FEMALE

Similar Birds

♂ KING EIDER
♀ Male has white head, upper back, breast, and flanks; stubby orange bill; orange forehead; lavender crown and nape • female has rusty brown body; black bill.

♂ COMMON EIDER
Male has sloping green, black, and white head; white back and breast; black sides and
♀ underparts; orange bill • female has tawny chestnut body with blackish bill.

Family ALCIDAE	Species *Pinguinus impennis*	Length 28–30 inches	Wingspan 23–25 inches

GREAT AUK

The largest alcid was the original penguin and the only flightless species on the continent in historical times. Widespread in the 16th and 17th centuries, it was recorded as breeding on islands from Scotland and Sweden to the Gulf of St. Lawrence and the Canadian Maritimes. Once numerous, centuries of raids on its colonies by sailors and fisherman who took adults and young for food brought it to extinction. Wintering along the Atlantic Coast occasionally as far south as Florida, the last known pair was captured at their nest on Eldey Rock off the coast of Iceland on June 3, 1844.

- **SONG** Generally silent except when alarmed in breeding colonies. Croak or guttural gurgling.
- **BEHAVIOR** Flightless. Gregarious; in flocks or small groups at sea. Nested in large colonies on isolated rocky islands in North Atlantic. Widespread at sea in the nonbreeding season in winter. Walked upright on land standing erect. Used short wings to move swiftly underwater, steering with its feet, diving down to an estimated 250 feet to feed on fish.

large arched black bill crossed by numerous vertical white lines

large white oval in front of eye

short white postocular spot

white underparts from upper breast to tip of undertail coverts

brownish black wings with white tips to secondaries

brownish black upperparts and tail

Similar Birds

RAZORBILL
Much smaller; single vertical line near tip of bill; white line from base of bill to eye; white underparts ascend to point on throat; black upperparts, tail, and wings; white trailing edge on secondary feathers.

| Family COLUMBIDAE | Species *Ectopistes migratorius* | Length 16 inches | Wingspan 24–25.5 inches |

PASSENGER PIGEON

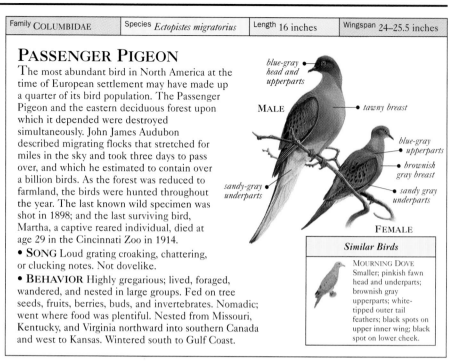

blue-gray head and upperparts

MALE

tawny breast

blue-gray upperparts

brownish gray breast

sandy-gray underparts

sandy gray underparts

FEMALE

The most abundant bird in North America at the time of European settlement may have made up a quarter of its bird population. The Passenger Pigeon and the eastern deciduous forest upon which it depended were destroyed simultaneously. John James Audubon described migrating flocks that stretched for miles in the sky and took three days to pass over, and which he estimated to contain over a billion birds. As the forest was reduced to farmland, the birds were hunted throughout the year. The last known wild specimen was shot in 1898; and the last surviving bird, Martha, a captive reared individual, died at age 29 in the Cincinnati Zoo in 1914.

• **SONG** Loud grating croaking, chattering, or clucking notes. Not dovelike.

• **BEHAVIOR** Highly gregarious; lived, foraged, wandered, and nested in large groups. Fed on tree seeds, fruits, berries, buds, and invertebrates. Nomadic; went where food was plentiful. Nested from Missouri, Kentucky, and Virginia northward into southern Canada and west to Kansas. Wintered south to Gulf Coast.

Similar Birds

MOURNING DOVE
Smaller; pinkish fawn head and underparts; brownish gray upperparts; white-tipped outer tail feathers; black spots on upper inner wing; black spot on lower cheek.

| Family PSITTACIDAE | Species *Conuropsis carloinesis* | Length 16 inches | Wingspan 24–26 inches |

CAROLINA PARAKEET

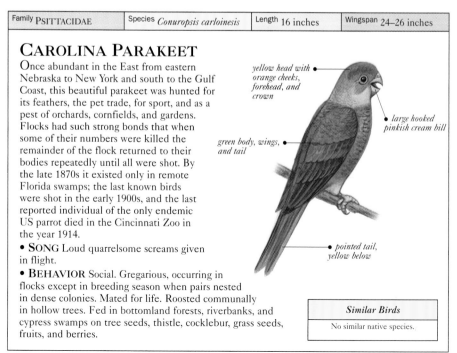

yellow head with orange cheeks, forehead, and crown

large hooked pinkish cream bill

green body, wings, and tail

pointed tail, yellow below

Once abundant in the East from eastern Nebraska to New York and south to the Gulf Coast, this beautiful parakeet was hunted for its feathers, the pet trade, for sport, and as a pest of orchards, cornfields, and gardens. Flocks had such strong bonds that when some of their numbers were killed the remainder of the flock returned to their bodies repeatedly until all were shot. By the late 1870s it existed only in remote Florida swamps; the last known birds were shot in the early 1900s, and the last reported individual of the only endemic US parrot died in the Cincinnati Zoo in the year 1914.

• **SONG** Loud quarrelsome screams given in flight.

• **BEHAVIOR** Social. Gregarious, occurring in flocks except in breeding season when pairs nested in dense colonies. Mated for life. Roosted communally in hollow trees. Fed in bottomland forests, riverbanks, and cypress swamps on tree seeds, thistle, cocklebur, grass seeds, fruits, and berries.

Similar Birds

No similar native species.

Family GAVIIDAE	Species *Gavia stellata*	Length 24–27 inches	Wingspan 42–45 inches

RED-THROATED LOON

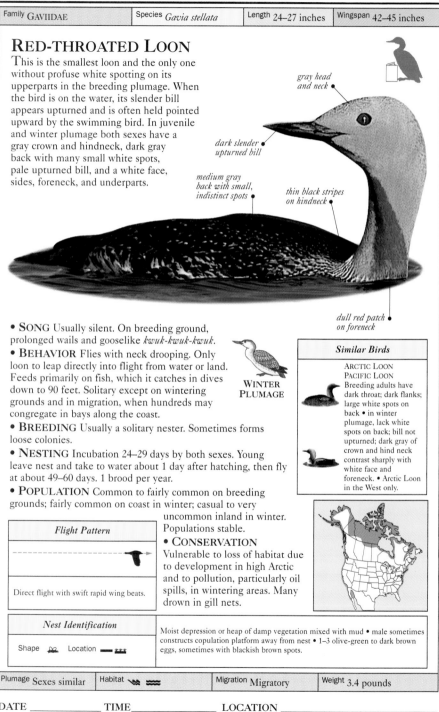

This is the smallest loon and the only one without profuse white spotting on its upperparts in the breeding plumage. When the bird is on the water, its slender bill appears upturned and is often held pointed upward by the swimming bird. In juvenile and winter plumage both sexes have a gray crown and hindneck, dark gray back with many small white spots, pale upturned bill, and a white face, sides, foreneck, and underparts.

gray head and neck

dark slender upturned bill

medium gray back with small, indistinct spots

thin black stripes on hindneck

dull red patch on foreneck

- **SONG** Usually silent. On breeding ground, prolonged wails and gooselike *kwuk-kwuk-kwuk*.
- **BEHAVIOR** Flies with neck drooping. Only loon to leap directly into flight from water or land. Feeds primarily on fish, which it catches in dives down to 90 feet. Solitary except on wintering grounds and in migration, when hundreds may congregate in bays along the coast.
- **BREEDING** Usually a solitary nester. Sometimes forms loose colonies.
- **NESTING** Incubation 24–29 days by both sexes. Young leave nest and take to water about 1 day after hatching, then fly at about 49–60 days. 1 brood per year.
- **POPULATION** Common to fairly common on breeding grounds; fairly common on coast in winter; casual to very uncommon inland in winter. Populations stable.
- **CONSERVATION** Vulnerable to loss of habitat due to development in high Arctic and to pollution, particularly oil spills, in wintering areas. Many drown in gill nets.

WINTER PLUMAGE

Similar Birds

ARCTIC LOON
PACIFIC LOON
Breeding adults have dark throat; dark flanks; large white spots on back • in winter plumage, lack white spots on back; bill not upturned; dark gray of crown and hind neck contrast sharply with white face and foreneck. • Arctic Loon in the West only.

Flight Pattern
Direct flight with swift rapid wing beats.

Nest Identification	
Shape ♒ Location ▬ ⁂	Moist depression or heap of damp vegetation mixed with mud • male sometimes constructs copulation platform away from nest • 1–3 olive-green to dark brown eggs, sometimes with blackish brown spots.

Plumage Sexes similar	Habitat 〰 〰	Migration Migratory	Weight 3.4 pounds

DATE _____ TIME_____ LOCATION _____

Family GAVIIDAE	Species *Gavia arctica*	Length 28 inches	Wingspan 45–49 inches

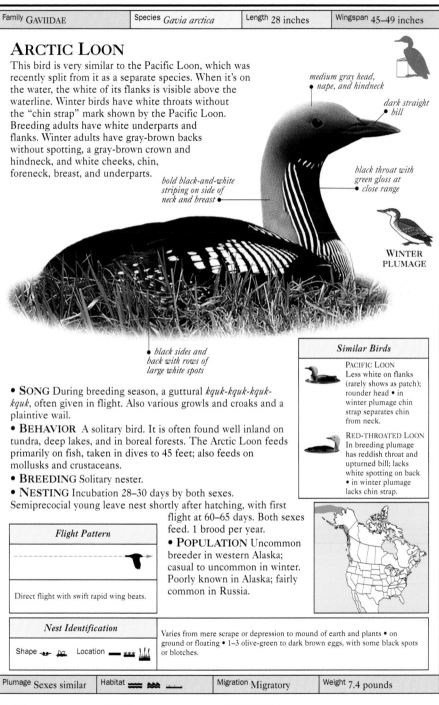

ARCTIC LOON

This bird is very similar to the Pacific Loon, which was recently split from it as a separate species. When it's on the water, the white of its flanks is visible above the waterline. Winter birds have white throats without the "chin strap" mark shown by the Pacific Loon. Breeding adults have white underparts and flanks. Winter adults have gray-brown backs without spotting, a gray-brown crown and hindneck, and white cheeks, chin, foreneck, breast, and underparts.

medium gray head, nape, and hindneck

dark straight bill

black throat with green gloss at close range

bold black-and-white striping on side of neck and breast

WINTER PLUMAGE

black sides and back with rows of large white spots

- **SONG** During breeding season, a guttural *kquk-kquk-kquk-kquk*, often given in flight. Also various growls and croaks and a plaintive wail.
- **BEHAVIOR** A solitary bird. It is often found well inland on tundra, deep lakes, and in boreal forests. The Arctic Loon feeds primarily on fish, taken in dives to 45 feet; also feeds on mollusks and crustaceans.
- **BREEDING** Solitary nester.
- **NESTING** Incubation 28–30 days by both sexes. Semiprecocial young leave nest shortly after hatching, with first flight at 60–65 days. Both sexes feed. 1 brood per year.
- **POPULATION** Uncommon breeder in western Alaska; casual to uncommon in winter. Poorly known in Alaska; fairly common in Russia.

Similar Birds

PACIFIC LOON
Less white on flanks (rarely shows as patch); rounder head • in winter plumage chin strap separates chin from neck.

RED-THROATED LOON
In breeding plumage has reddish throat and upturned bill; lacks white spotting on back • in winter plumage lacks chin strap.

Flight Pattern

Direct flight with swift rapid wing beats.

Nest Identification

Shape ⚬ Location ▬ ▬ Varies from mere scrape or depression to mound of earth and plants • on ground or floating • 1–3 olive-green to dark brown eggs, with some black spots or blotches.

Plumage Sexes similar	Habitat ≈≈ ⋙ ⌣	Migration Migratory	Weight 7.4 pounds

DATE _____ TIME_____ LOCATION _____

Family GAVIIDAE	Species *Gavia pacifica*	Length 26 inches	Wingspan 43–48 inches

PACIFIC LOON

Until recently this species was considered a race of the Arctic Loon, which it closely resembles. The Pacific Loon flies with its head and neck held straight. When swimming it holds its dark slender bill level. Winter adults have dark gray upperparts and a thin dark strap that reaches around the chin. Underparts are white year-round.

pale gray head, nape, and hindneck

dark slender bill

black sides of neck with white stripes

black back with rows of large white spots

WINTER PLUMAGE

white underparts

black sides and flanks

• **SONG** Generally silent. On breeding grounds, variety of guttural quacks and croaks, and a long drawn-out *ah-hah-awee*.
• **BEHAVIOR** Migrates in flocks, unlike other loons. Feeds primarily on fish but takes some crustaceans and mollusks. Nests on freshwater lakes and islands from tundra to boreal forests.
• **BREEDING** Solitary. Monogamous.
• **NESTING** Incubation 23–25 days by both sexes, but female does more. Young leave nest shortly after hatching. First flight at 60–65 days. 1 brood per year.
• **POPULATION** Common to fairly common on tundra breeding grounds. During winter, uncommon on the West Coast, casual on the East Coast, and rare inland. Stable.

• **CONSERVATION** Affected by encroachment of humans on breeding grounds. Vulnerable to the pollution of its wintering areas, including oil spills. Also vulnerable to drowning in gill nets.

Similar Birds
ARCTIC LOON More white on flanks • breeding adults have dark chin • in winter lacks chin strap. • in the West only.
RED-THROATED LOON Breeding adults have red foreneck; lacks large white spots on back; bill is upturned.

Flight Pattern
Direct flight with rapid wing beats.

Nest Identification	
Shape ⚬ ⚬⚬ Location ▬ ▬▬▬	Heap of vegetation pulled up around nest • edge of water on ground • built by both sexes • 1–3 brownish eggs with blackish brown spots.

Plumage Sexes similar	Habitat ≋ ⌣ ≋	Migration Migratory	Weight 3.7 pounds

DATE _____ TIME_____ LOCATION _____

Family GAVIIDAE	Species *Gavia immer*	Length 28–36 inches	Wingspan 50–58 inches

COMMON LOON

Frequenting quiet lakes and usually sleeping on the water, this large bird rarely comes on land except to nest. It must run at least 20 yards across water to gain enough momentum to fly. Loons require such pristine conditions to nest that their presence as a nesting bird is a good indicator of the wilderness condition of a lake and the frequency of human activity on it. Winter adults have gray or brown upperparts; an irregular or broken pattern on the head to the base of the eye and the sides of the neck; white underparts, chin, and foreneck; a blue-gray bill; and a white eye ring.

glossy black head with greenish sheen

red-brown eyes

stout, straight black bill

checkered black-and-white back

glossy black throat

broken white neck collar

white breast and belly

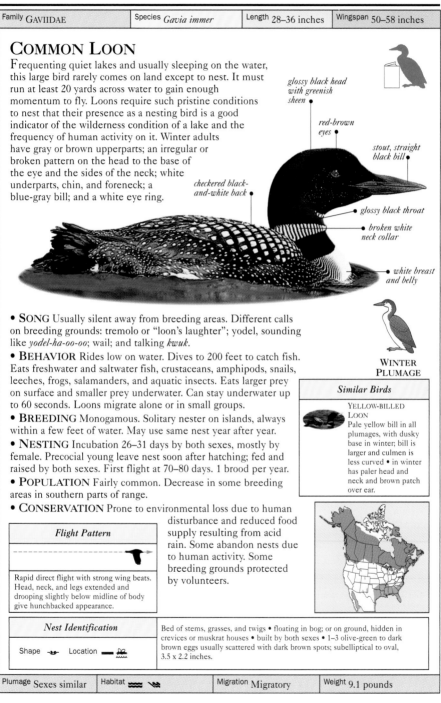

WINTER PLUMAGE

- **SONG** Usually silent away from breeding areas. Different calls on breeding grounds: tremolo or "loon's laughter"; yodel, sounding like *yodel-ha-oo-oo*; wail; and talking *kwuk*.
- **BEHAVIOR** Rides low on water. Dives to 200 feet to catch fish. Eats freshwater and saltwater fish, crustaceans, amphipods, snails, leeches, frogs, salamanders, and aquatic insects. Eats larger prey on surface and smaller prey underwater. Can stay underwater up to 60 seconds. Loons migrate alone or in small groups.
- **BREEDING** Monogamous. Solitary nester on islands, always within a few feet of water. May use same nest year after year.
- **NESTING** Incubation 26–31 days by both sexes, mostly by female. Precocial young leave nest soon after hatching; fed and raised by both sexes. First flight at 70–80 days. 1 brood per year.
- **POPULATION** Fairly common. Decrease in some breeding areas in southern parts of range.
- **CONSERVATION** Prone to environmental loss due to human disturbance and reduced food supply resulting from acid rain. Some abandon nests due to human activity. Some breeding grounds protected by volunteers.

Similar Birds

YELLOW-BILLED LOON
Pale yellow bill in all plumages, with dusky base in winter; bill is larger and culmen is less curved • in winter has paler head and neck and brown patch over ear.

Flight Pattern
Rapid direct flight with strong wing beats. Head, neck, and legs extended and drooping slightly below midline of body give hunchbacked appearance.

Nest Identification	
Shape Location	Bed of stems, grasses, and twigs • floating in bog; or on ground, hidden in crevices or muskrat houses • built by both sexes • 1–3 olive-green to dark brown eggs usually scattered with dark brown spots; subelliptical to oval, 3.5 x 2.2 inches.

Plumage Sexes similar	Habitat	Migration Migratory	Weight 9.1 pounds

DATE _____ TIME_____ LOCATION _____

Family GAVIIDAE	Species *Gavia adamsii*	Length 30–36 inches	Wingspan 54–60 inches

YELLOW-BILLED LOON

Once considered a weather prophet in Eskimo folklore, this loon is the largest of its species and has the northernmost range of any loon. Swimming with its head tilted slightly upward, this bird sometimes carries its young on its back. Winter plumage shows a tan crown with a white face and a dark ear patch.

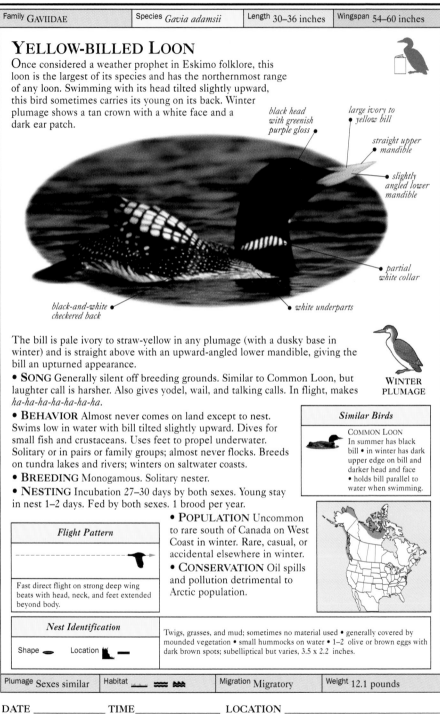

black head with greenish purple gloss

large ivory to yellow bill

straight upper mandible

slightly angled lower mandible

partial white collar

black-and-white checkered back

white underparts

The bill is pale ivory to straw-yellow in any plumage (with a dusky base in winter) and is straight above with an upward-angled lower mandible, giving the bill an upturned appearance.

WINTER PLUMAGE

- **SONG** Generally silent off breeding grounds. Similar to Common Loon, but laughter call is harsher. Also gives yodel, wail, and talking calls. In flight, makes *ha-ha-ha-ha-ha-ha-ha*.
- **BEHAVIOR** Almost never comes on land except to nest. Swims low in water with bill tilted slightly upward. Dives for small fish and crustaceans. Uses feet to propel underwater. Solitary or in pairs or family groups; almost never flocks. Breeds on tundra lakes and rivers; winters on saltwater coasts.
- **BREEDING** Monogamous. Solitary nester.
- **NESTING** Incubation 27–30 days by both sexes. Young stay in nest 1–2 days. Fed by both sexes. 1 brood per year.

Similar Birds

COMMON LOON
In summer has black bill • in winter has dark upper edge on bill and darker head and face • holds bill parallel to water when swimming.

- **POPULATION** Uncommon to rare south of Canada on West Coast in winter. Rare, casual, or accidental elsewhere in winter.
- **CONSERVATION** Oil spills and pollution detrimental to Arctic population.

Flight Pattern
Fast direct flight on strong deep wing beats with head, neck, and feet extended beyond body.

Nest Identification	
Shape ⬡ Location 🪺 ▬	Twigs, grasses, and mud; sometimes no material used • generally covered by mounded vegetation • small hummocks on water • 1–2 olive or brown eggs with dark brown spots; subelliptical but varies, 3.5 x 2.2 inches.

Plumage Sexes similar	Habitat 〜〜 ≈≈	Migration Migratory	Weight 12.1 pounds

DATE _____ TIME_____ LOCATION _____

Family PODICIPEDIDAE	Species *Tachybaptus dominicus*	Length 9–10 inches	Wingspan 20 inches

LEAST GREBE

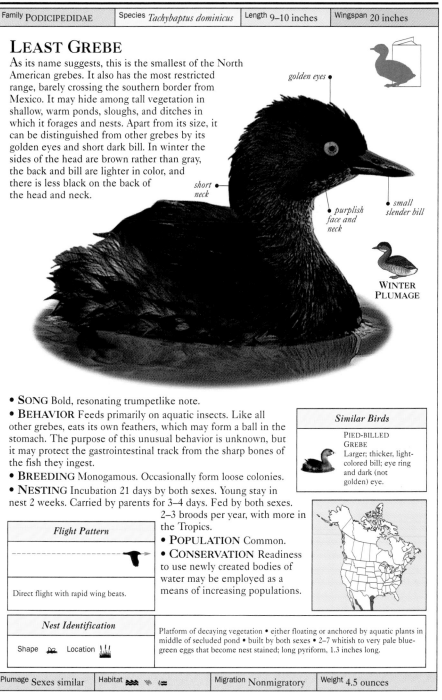

As its name suggests, this is the smallest of the North American grebes. It also has the most restricted range, barely crossing the southern border from Mexico. It may hide among tall vegetation in shallow, warm ponds, sloughs, and ditches in which it forages and nests. Apart from its size, it can be distinguished from other grebes by its golden eyes and short dark bill. In winter the sides of the head are brown rather than gray, the back and bill are lighter in color, and there is less black on the back of the head and neck.

golden eyes •

short • neck

• *purplish face and neck*

• *small slender bill*

WINTER PLUMAGE

• **SONG** Bold, resonating trumpetlike note.
• **BEHAVIOR** Feeds primarily on aquatic insects. Like all other grebes, eats its own feathers, which may form a ball in the stomach. The purpose of this unusual behavior is unknown, but it may protect the gastrointestinal track from the sharp bones of the fish they ingest.
• **BREEDING** Monogamous. Occasionally form loose colonies.
• **NESTING** Incubation 21 days by both sexes. Young stay in nest 2 weeks. Carried by parents for 3–4 days. Fed by both sexes. 2–3 broods per year, with more in the Tropics.
• **POPULATION** Common.
• **CONSERVATION** Readiness to use newly created bodies of water may be employed as a means of increasing populations.

Similar Birds

PIED-BILLED GREBE
Larger; thicker, light-colored bill; eye ring and dark (not golden) eye.

Flight Pattern
Direct flight with rapid wing beats.

Nest Identification	
Shape 🐚 Location 🌿	Platform of decaying vegetation • either floating or anchored by aquatic plants in middle of secluded pond • built by both sexes • 2–7 whitish to very pale blue-green eggs that become nest stained; long pyriform, 1.3 inches long.

Plumage Sexes similar	Habitat 〰 🌿 🌾	Migration Nonmigratory	Weight 4.5 ounces

DATE _____ TIME_____ LOCATION _____

| Family PODICIPEDIDAE | Species *Podilymbus podiceps* | Length 12–15 inches | Wingspan 22.5 inches |

PIED-BILLED GREBE

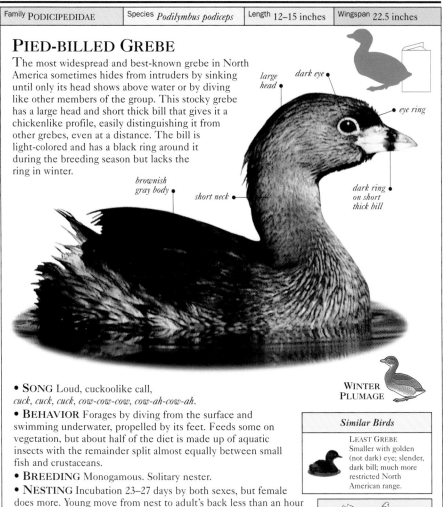

The most widespread and best-known grebe in North America sometimes hides from intruders by sinking until only its head shows above water or by diving like other members of the group. This stocky grebe has a large head and short thick bill that gives it a chickenlike profile, easily distinguishing it from other grebes, even at a distance. The bill is light-colored and has a black ring around it during the breeding season but lacks the ring in winter.

large head
dark eye
eye ring
brownish gray body
short neck
dark ring on short thick bill

WINTER PLUMAGE

- **SONG** Loud, cuckoolike call, *cuck, cuck, cuck, cow-cow-cow, cow-ah-cow-ah*.
- **BEHAVIOR** Forages by diving from the surface and swimming underwater, propelled by its feet. Feeds some on vegetation, but about half of the diet is made up of aquatic insects with the remainder split almost equally between small fish and crustaceans.
- **BREEDING** Monogamous. Solitary nester.
- **NESTING** Incubation 23–27 days by both sexes, but female does more. Young move from nest to adult's back less than an hour after hatching. Nest use stops in 24–42 days. First flight at 35–37 days. Young fed by both sexes. 1–2 broods per year.
- **POPULATION** Very common in range.
- **CONSERVATION** May be declining due to habitat loss.

Similar Birds

LEAST GREBE
Smaller with golden (not dark) eye; slender, dark bill; much more restricted North American range.

Flight Pattern
Direct flight with rapid wing beats.

Nest Identification	
Shape 🪺 Location 🌾	Platform of decaying vegetation • inconspicuously anchored to vegetation in open water among reeds or rushes • built by both sexes • 2–10 pale bluish white or nest-stained eggs; elliptical to subelliptical, 1.7 inches long.

| Plumage Sexes similar | Habitat 〰️ 〜 | Migration Some migrate | Weight 15.6 ounces |

DATE _____ TIME_____ LOCATION _____

Family PODICIPEDIDAE	Species *Podiceps auritus*	Length 12–15 inches	Wingspan 24 inches

HORNED GREBE

The "horns" for which this bird is named are actually tufts of golden feathers above and behind the eyes, that are present only during the bird's breeding season. In summer the reddish neck of the Horned Grebe distinguishes it from the Eared Grebe, which shares much of the breeding range. The Horned Grebe's life is tied to water, breeding in freshwater habitats and often spending the winter both in freshwater and in saltwater.

• **SONG** This grebe gives an abrasive *keark, keark* or *yark, yark*. It also makes a repeated prattling sound followed by shrill screams.

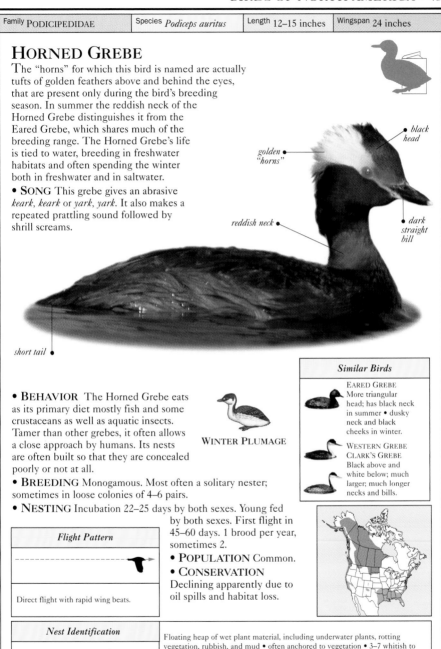

golden "horns"

black head

reddish neck

dark straight bill

short tail

• **BEHAVIOR** The Horned Grebe eats as its primary diet mostly fish and some crustaceans as well as aquatic insects. Tamer than other grebes, it often allows a close approach by humans. Its nests are often built so that they are concealed poorly or not at all.

WINTER PLUMAGE

• **BREEDING** Monogamous. Most often a solitary nester; sometimes in loose colonies of 4–6 pairs.

• **NESTING** Incubation 22–25 days by both sexes. Young fed by both sexes. First flight in 45–60 days. 1 brood per year, sometimes 2.

• **POPULATION** Common.

• **CONSERVATION** Declining apparently due to oil spills and habitat loss.

Similar Birds

EARED GREBE
More triangular head; has black neck in summer • dusky neck and black cheeks in winter.

WESTERN GREBE
CLARK'S GREBE
Black above and white below; much larger; much longer necks and bills.

Flight Pattern
Direct flight with rapid wing beats.

Nest Identification	
Shape 🪺 Location 🌿	Floating heap of wet plant material, including underwater plants, rotting vegetation, rubbish, and mud • often anchored to vegetation • 3–7 whitish to very pale green eggs, usually nest-stained; 1.7 inches long.

Plumage Sexes similar	Habitat 〰 〰 🌿	Migration Migratory	Weight 1 pound

DATE _____ TIME_____ LOCATION _____

Family PODICIPEDIDAE	Species *Podiceps grisegena*	Length 17–21 inches	Wingspan 30–32 inches

RED-NECKED GREBE

Slightly smaller than the Western and Clark's grebes, this bird's neck is much thicker in appearance. In flight it is the only grebe that shows white leading and trailing edges on the inner wing. Although it requires large bodies of freshwater for breeding, most of the population spends the winter months on saltwater.

- **SONG** On breeding ground, utters drawling cries and *crick-crick*; during courtship both sexes make loonlike calls of *ah-ooo, ah-ooo, ah-ooo, ah-ah-ah-ah-ah*.
- **BEHAVIOR** Feeds primarily on small fish and crustaceans that it gathers in dives to 25–30 feet. One of

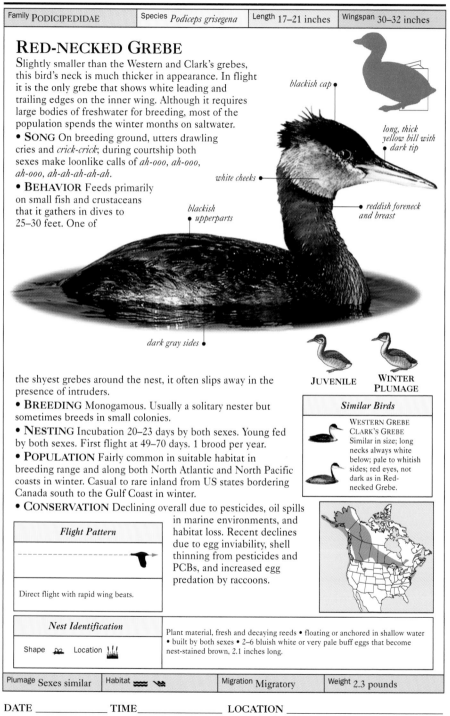

blackish cap

long, thick yellow bill with dark tip

white cheeks

reddish foreneck and breast

blackish upperparts

dark gray sides

JUVENILE   WINTER PLUMAGE

the shyest grebes around the nest, it often slips away in the presence of intruders.

- **BREEDING** Monogamous. Usually a solitary nester but sometimes breeds in small colonies.
- **NESTING** Incubation 20–23 days by both sexes. Young fed by both sexes. First flight at 49–70 days. 1 brood per year.
- **POPULATION** Fairly common in suitable habitat in breeding range and along both North Atlantic and North Pacific coasts in winter. Casual to rare inland from US states bordering Canada south to the Gulf Coast in winter.
- **CONSERVATION** Declining overall due to pesticides, oil spills in marine environments, and habitat loss. Recent declines due to egg inviability, shell thinning from pesticides and PCBs, and increased egg predation by raccoons.

Similar Birds

WESTERN GREBE
CLARK'S GREBE
Similar in size; long necks always white below; pale to whitish sides; red eyes, not dark as in Red-necked Grebe.

Flight Pattern

Direct flight with rapid wing beats.

Nest Identification

Shape   Location

Plant material, fresh and decaying reeds • floating or anchored in shallow water • built by both sexes • 2–6 bluish white or very pale buff eggs that become nest-stained brown, 2.1 inches long.

Plumage Sexes similar	Habitat	Migration Migratory	Weight 2.3 pounds

DATE _____ TIME_____ LOCATION _____

| Family PODICIPEDIDAE | Species *Podiceps nigricollis* | Length 12–13 inches | Wingspan 22.5 inches |

EARED GREBE

The "ear" for which this bird is named is a wide golden tuft of feathers behind the eyes, present only in breeding plumage. It has a more triangular-shaped head than other grebes and is the only one that has a black neck during breeding season. The neck remains dusky gray in winter – a good field mark. The slender, dark bill appears slightly upturned.

triangular-shaped head

golden "ears"

black neck

slender, dark upturned bill

WINTER PLUMAGE

SONG Utters soft *poo-eee-chk* in courtship. Also has grating shrieks.
• **BEHAVIOR** Pairs and family groups during the nesting season but often nests in dense colonies of up to several hundred pairs. Breeding pairs have several mutual displays, including an upright "penguin dance" side-by-side on the water. Forages by diving and swimming underwater for aquatic insects, which make up most of its summer diet. Many winter in marine environments, where shrimplike crustaceans become their principal food. A gregarious bird that often gathers in large flocks in winter. Tends to ride higher on the water than the somewhat similar Horned Grebe.
• **BREEDING** Monogamous. Colonial.
• **NESTING** Incubation 20–22 days by both sexes. Young leave nest after last egg hatches. Fed by both sexes. Become independent 21 days after hatching. 1 brood per year, sometimes 2.
• **POPULATION** Common. Becoming increasingly more common in the East in winter. Numbers concentrated on lakes in Great Basin during migration.

Similar Birds

HORNED GREBE
Reddish neck in summer • white in winter plumage; white cheeks (not blackish like Eared Grebe) in winter • gold feathers in breeding plumage are restricted to "horns" above and behind the eye, not over the ears.

Flight Pattern
Direct flight with rapid wing beats.

Nest Identification	
Shape ⌒ Location ⌇⌇⌇	Made from fresh and decayed vegetation • floating but anchored by standing vegetation • built by both sexes • 1–9 whitish or bluish white eggs that become nest-stained brown, 1.7 inches long.

| Plumage Sexes similar | Habitat ⌇≈ ≈≈ | Migration Migratory | Weight 10.3 ounces |

DATE _____ TIME_____ LOCATION _____

| Family PODICIPEDIDAE | Species *Aechmophorus occidentalis* | Length 22–29 inches | Wingspan 31–40 inches |

WESTERN GREBE

Identical in shape and size to Clark's Grebe, the Western Grebe shares much of the same range. It has a long swanlike neck and a slender, greenish yellow bill. Like all other grebes, it has feet modified for swimming, and the toes are lobed, not webbed as in waterfowl. Fish make up most of its diet.

• **SONG** Bold *crick-kreek*. Grating, whistled *c-r-r-ee-er-r-ee*.

• **BEHAVIOR** Both Western and Clark's Grebes have a structure in

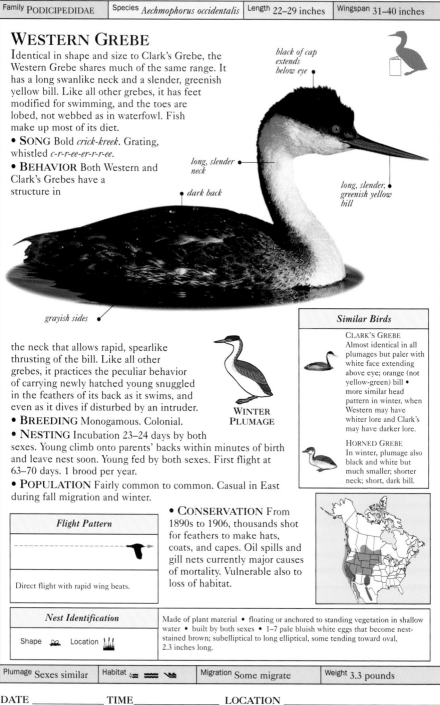

black of cap extends below eye

long, slender neck

dark back

long, slender, greenish yellow bill

grayish sides

the neck that allows rapid, spearlike thrusting of the bill. Like all other grebes, it practices the peculiar behavior of carrying newly hatched young snuggled in the feathers of its back as it swims, and even as it dives if disturbed by an intruder.

WINTER PLUMAGE

• **BREEDING** Monogamous. Colonial.

• **NESTING** Incubation 23–24 days by both sexes. Young climb onto parents' backs within minutes of birth and leave nest soon. Young fed by both sexes. First flight at 63–70 days. 1 brood per year.

• **POPULATION** Fairly common to common. Casual in East during fall migration and winter.

• **CONSERVATION** From 1890s to 1906, thousands shot for feathers to make hats, coats, and capes. Oil spills and gill nets currently major causes of mortality. Vulnerable also to loss of habitat.

Similar Birds

CLARK'S GREBE
Almost identical in all plumages but paler with white face extending above eye; orange (not yellow-green) bill • more similar head pattern in winter, when Western may have whiter lore and Clark's may have darker lore.

HORNED GREBE
In winter, plumage also black and white but much smaller; shorter neck; short, dark bill.

Flight Pattern

Direct flight with rapid wing beats.

Nest Identification

Shape 🐦 Location ⚭

Made of plant material • floating or anchored to standing vegetation in shallow water • built by both sexes • 1–7 pale bluish white eggs that become nest-stained brown; subelliptical to long elliptical, some tending toward oval, 2.3 inches long.

| Plumage Sexes similar | Habitat 🏞 〰 🐟 | Migration Some migrate | Weight 3.3 pounds |

Family PODICIPEDIDAE	Species *Aechmophorus clarkii*	Length 26 inches	Wingspan 30–40 inches

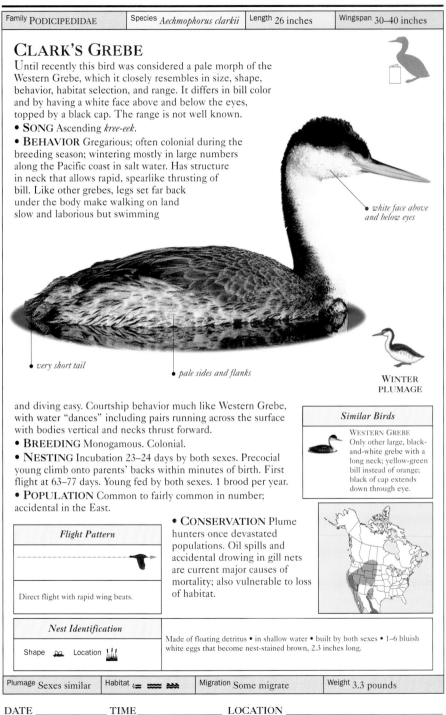

CLARK'S GREBE

Until recently this bird was considered a pale morph of the Western Grebe, which it closely resembles in size, shape, behavior, habitat selection, and range. It differs in bill color and by having a white face above and below the eyes, topped by a black cap. The range is not well known.
- **SONG** Ascending *kree-eek*.
- **BEHAVIOR** Gregarious; often colonial during the breeding season; wintering mostly in large numbers along the Pacific coast in salt water. Has structure in neck that allows rapid, spearlike thrusting of bill. Like other grebes, legs set far back under the body make walking on land slow and laborious but swimming

• *white face above and below eyes*

• *very short tail*

• *pale sides and flanks*

WINTER PLUMAGE

and diving easy. Courtship behavior much like Western Grebe, with water "dances" including pairs running across the surface with bodies vertical and necks thrust forward.
- **BREEDING** Monogamous. Colonial.
- **NESTING** Incubation 23–24 days by both sexes. Precocial young climb onto parents' backs within minutes of birth. First flight at 63–77 days. Young fed by both sexes. 1 brood per year.
- **POPULATION** Common to fairly common in number; accidental in the East.
- **CONSERVATION** Plume hunters once devastated populations. Oil spills and accidental drowing in gill nets are current major causes of mortality; also vulnerable to loss of habitat.

Similar Birds
WESTERN GREBE Only other large, black-and-white grebe with a long neck; yellow-green bill instead of orange; black of cap extends down through eye.

Flight Pattern
Direct flight with rapid wing beats.

Nest Identification	
Shape Location	Made of floating detritus • in shallow water • built by both sexes • 1–6 bluish white eggs that become nest-stained brown, 2.3 inches long.

Plumage Sexes similar	Habitat	Migration Some migrate	Weight 3.3 pounds

DATE _____ TIME_____ LOCATION _____

Family DIOMEDEIDAE	Species *Phoebastria immutabilis*	Length 35 inches	Wingspan 78–82 inches

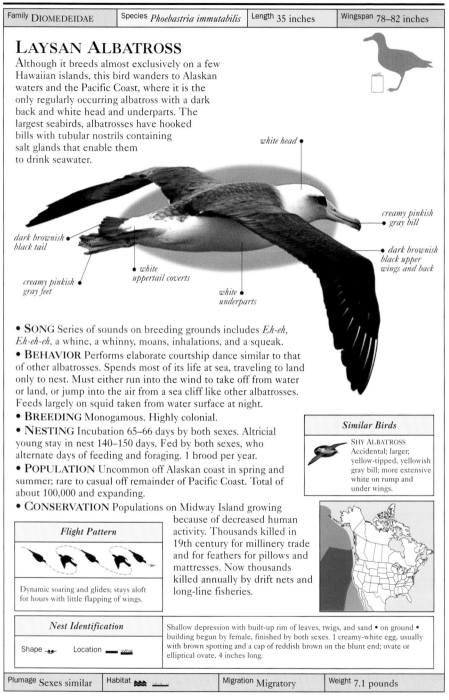

LAYSAN ALBATROSS

Although it breeds almost exclusively on a few Hawaiian islands, this bird wanders to Alaskan waters and the Pacific Coast, where it is the only regularly occurring albatross with a dark back and white head and underparts. The largest seabirds, albatrosses have hooked bills with tubular nostrils containing salt glands that enable them to drink seawater.

white head

creamy pinkish gray bill

dark brownish black tail

dark brownish black upper wings and back

creamy pinkish gray feet

white uppertail coverts

white underparts

• **SONG** Series of sounds on breeding grounds includes *Eh-eh*, *Eh-eh-eh*, a whine, a whinny, moans, inhalations, and a squeak.
• **BEHAVIOR** Performs elaborate courtship dance similar to that of other albatrosses. Spends most of its life at sea, traveling to land only to nest. Must either run into the wind to take off from water or land, or jump into the air from a sea cliff like other albatrosses. Feeds largely on squid taken from water surface at night.
• **BREEDING** Monogamous. Highly colonial.
• **NESTING** Incubation 65–66 days by both sexes. Altricial young stay in nest 140–150 days. Fed by both sexes, who alternate days of feeding and foraging. 1 brood per year.
• **POPULATION** Uncommon off Alaskan coast in spring and summer; rare to casual off remainder of Pacific Coast. Total of about 100,000 and expanding.
• **CONSERVATION** Populations on Midway Island growing because of decreased human activity. Thousands killed in 19th century for millinery trade and for feathers for pillows and mattresses. Now thousands killed annually by drift nets and long-line fisheries.

Similar Birds
SHY ALBATROSS Accidental; larger; yellow-tipped, yellowish gray bill; more extensive white on rump and under wings.

Flight Pattern
Dynamic soaring and glides; stays aloft for hours with little flapping of wings.

Nest Identification	Shallow depression with built-up rim of leaves, twigs, and sand • on ground • building begun by female, finished by both sexes. 1 creamy-white egg, usually with brown spotting and a cap of reddish brown on the blunt end; ovate or elliptical ovate, 4 inches long.
Shape ⬤ Location ▬▬	

Plumage Sexes similar	Habitat ≈≈	Migration Migratory	Weight 7.1 pounds

DATE _____ TIME_____ LOCATION _____

Family DIOMEDEIDAE	Species *Phoebastria nigripes*	Length 32 inches	Wingspan 70–80 inches

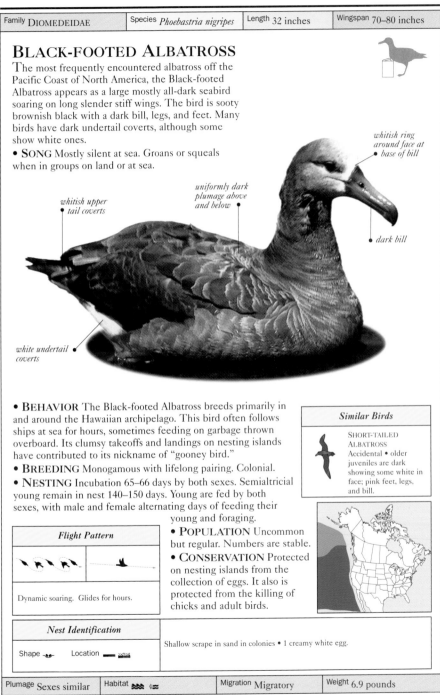

BLACK-FOOTED ALBATROSS

The most frequently encountered albatross off the Pacific Coast of North America, the Black-footed Albatross appears as a large mostly all-dark seabird soaring on long slender stiff wings. The bird is sooty brownish black with a dark bill, legs, and feet. Many birds have dark undertail coverts, although some show white ones.

• **SONG** Mostly silent at sea. Groans or squeals when in groups on land or at sea.

whitish ring around face at base of bill

uniformly dark plumage above and below

whitish upper tail coverts

dark bill

white undertail coverts

• **BEHAVIOR** The Black-footed Albatross breeds primarily in and around the Hawaiian archipelago. This bird often follows ships at sea for hours, sometimes feeding on garbage thrown overboard. Its clumsy takeoffs and landings on nesting islands have contributed to its nickname of "gooney bird."

• **BREEDING** Monogamous with lifelong pairing. Colonial.

• **NESTING** Incubation 65–66 days by both sexes. Semialtricial young remain in nest 140–150 days. Young are fed by both sexes, with male and female alternating days of feeding their young and foraging.

• **POPULATION** Uncommon but regular. Numbers are stable.

• **CONSERVATION** Protected on nesting islands from the collection of eggs. It also is protected from the killing of chicks and adult birds.

Similar Birds

SHORT-TAILED ALBATROSS
Accidental • older juveniles are dark showing some white in face; pink feet, legs, and bill.

Flight Pattern

Dynamic soaring. Glides for hours.

Nest Identification

Shape ⚬ Location ▬

Shallow scrape in sand in colonies • 1 creamy white egg.

Plumage Sexes similar	Habitat	Migration Migratory	Weight 6.9 pounds

DATE _____ TIME_____ LOCATION _____

Family PROCELLARIIDAE	Species *Fulmarus glacialis*	Length 19 inches	Wingspan 42 inches

NORTHERN FULMAR

When threatened by an enemy or handled by a person, the Northern Fulmar discharges a foul-smelling oil from its stomach by spitting. This audacious bird follows fishing boats, often closely, to take advantage of refuse. The light morph is superficially gull-like in appearance, but its stiff-winged flight is like a shearwater's. It is mostly gray above with a white chest and belly; the dark color morph is gray overall. Fulmars are rarely seen from shore away from the breeding colonies, except during storms.

• **SONG** When feeding, makes chucking and grunting noises. During breeding season makes variety of guttural calls.

• **BEHAVIOR** Gregarious. Highly pelagic; may not come ashore until 3–4 years old. Grabs food with beak from just below surface and eats on the water. Sometimes makes shallow dives, using wings and feet for propulsion. Eats variety of fish, crustaceans, squid, marine worms, and carrion. Feeds alone, in pairs, or in flocks. Drinks seawater by sucking it up dove-fashion. In flight carries wings stiffly and wheels up in arcs over waves by taking advantage of winds.

• **BREEDING** Monogamous. Colonial.

• **NESTING** Incubation 52–53 days by both sexes. Semialtricial young fed by both sexes. First flight at 46–51 days. 1 brood per year.

• **POPULATION** Common; abundant in some places. In winter found at sea off both coasts.

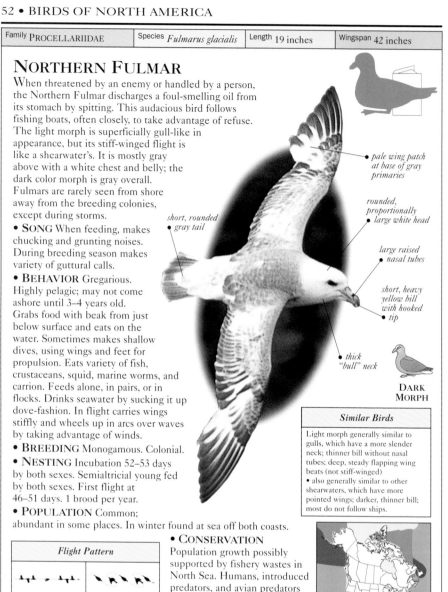

pale wing patch at base of gray primaries

rounded, proportionally large white head

large raised nasal tubes

short, heavy yellow bill with hooked tip

thick "bull" neck

short, rounded gray tail

DARK MORPH

Similar Birds

Light morph generally similar to gulls, which have a more slender neck; thinner bill without nasal tubes; deep, steady flapping wing beats (not stiff-winged)
• also generally similar to other shearwaters, which have more pointed wings; darker, thinner bill; most do not follow ships.

• **CONSERVATION** Population growth possibly supported by fishery wastes in North Sea. Humans, introduced predators, and avian predators take a toll, but humans are major predator for meat, eggs, and feathers.

Flight Pattern
Flap and glide flight on bowed wings with bursts of stiff wing beats alternating with periods of effortless banking and gliding.

Nest Identification	
Shape	Slight depression on ground • sometimes layered with pebbles • may be built by both sexes • 1 white or off-white egg, often nest-stained and occasionally marked with reddish brown; subelliptical, 2.9 inches long.
Location	

Plumage Sexes similar	Habitat	Migration Migratory	Weight 21.5 ounces

DATE _____ TIME_____ LOCATION _____

Family PROCELLARIIDAE	Species *Pterodroma ultima*	Length 15–16 inches	Wingspan 38 inches

MURPHY'S PETREL

Since it prefers to live on open tropical seas, Murphy's Petrel is usually about forty miles away from shore when it is spotted. It does not hold its wings as stiffly as do other gadfly petrels, and its flight is rapid and vigorous with great wheeling arcs that carry it well above the horizon. In flight Murphy's Petrel appears entirely dark with a faint M pattern across its wings and back. Note the white flash on the underwings at the base of the primaries, the pale legs and feet, and – visible only at close range – the black toes with distal webbing.

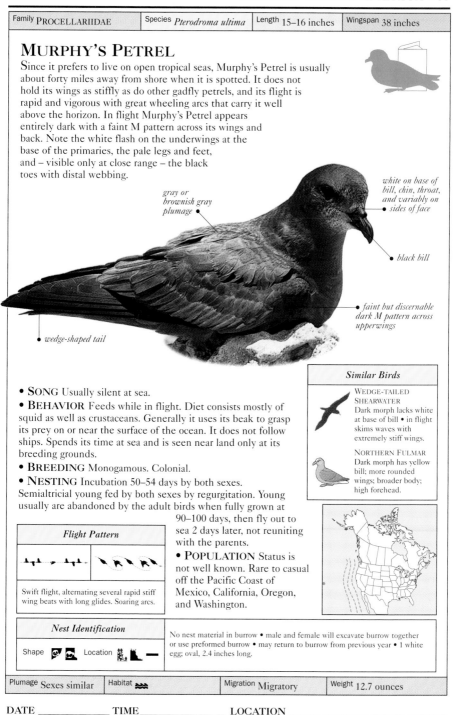

gray or brownish gray plumage

white on base of bill, chin, throat, and variably on sides of face

black bill

faint but discernable dark M pattern across upperwings

wedge-shaped tail

- **SONG** Usually silent at sea.
- **BEHAVIOR** Feeds while in flight. Diet consists mostly of squid as well as crustaceans. Generally it uses its beak to grasp its prey on or near the surface of the ocean. It does not follow ships. Spends its time at sea and is seen near land only at its breeding grounds.
- **BREEDING** Monogamous. Colonial.
- **NESTING** Incubation 50–54 days by both sexes. Semialtricial young fed by both sexes by regurgitation. Young usually are abandoned by the adult birds when fully grown at 90–100 days, then fly out to sea 2 days later, not reuniting with the parents.
- **POPULATION** Status is not well known. Rare to casual off the Pacific Coast of Mexico, California, Oregon, and Washington.

Similar Birds

WEDGE-TAILED SHEARWATER
Dark morph lacks white at base of bill • in flight skims waves with extremely stiff wings.

NORTHERN FULMAR
Dark morph has yellow bill; more rounded wings; broader body; high forehead.

Flight Pattern
Swift flight, alternating several rapid stiff wing beats with long glides. Soaring arcs.

Nest Identification	
Shape	Location	No nest material in burrow • male and female will excavate burrow together or use preformed burrow • may return to burrow from previous year • 1 white egg; oval, 2.4 inches long.

Plumage Sexes similar	Habitat	Migration Migratory	Weight 12.7 ounces

DATE _____ TIME_____ LOCATION _____

Family PROCELLARIIDAE	Species *Pterodroma inexpectata*	Length 13–14 inches	Wingspan 27–33 inches

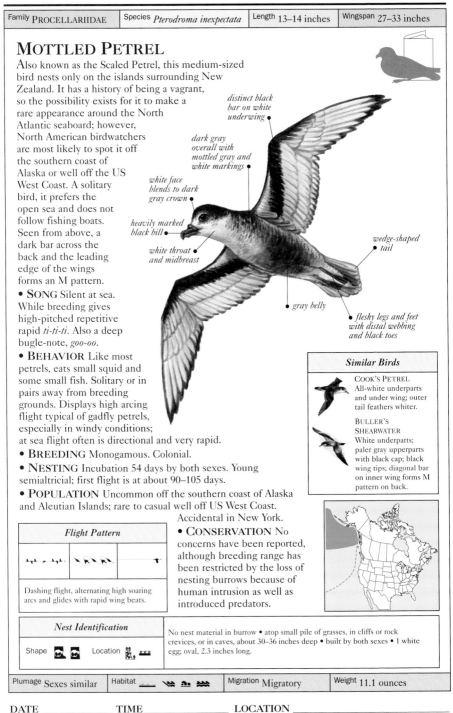

MOTTLED PETREL

Also known as the Scaled Petrel, this medium-sized bird nests only on the islands surrounding New Zealand. It has a history of being a vagrant, so the possibility exists for it to make a rare appearance around the North Atlantic seaboard; however, North American birdwatchers are most likely to spot it off the southern coast of Alaska or well off the US West Coast. A solitary bird, it prefers the open sea and does not follow fishing boats. Seen from above, a dark bar across the back and the leading edge of the wings forms an M pattern.

distinct black bar on white underwing

dark gray overall with mottled gray and white markings

white face blends to dark gray crown

heavily marked black bill

white throat and midbreast

wedge-shaped tail

gray belly

fleshy legs and feet with distal webbing and black toes

• **SONG** Silent at sea. While breeding gives high-pitched repetitive rapid *ti-ti-ti*. Also a deep bugle-note, *goo-oo*.

• **BEHAVIOR** Like most petrels, eats small squid and some small fish. Solitary or in pairs away from breeding grounds. Displays high arcing flight typical of gadfly petrels, especially in windy conditions; at sea flight often is directional and very rapid.

• **BREEDING** Monogamous. Colonial.

• **NESTING** Incubation 54 days by both sexes. Young semialtricial; first flight is at about 90–105 days.

• **POPULATION** Uncommon off the southern coast of Alaska and Aleutian Islands; rare to casual well off US West Coast. Accidental in New York.

• **CONSERVATION** No concerns have been reported, although breeding range has been restricted by the loss of nesting burrows because of human intrusion as well as introduced predators.

Similar Birds

COOK'S PETREL
All-white underparts and under wing; outer tail feathers whiter.

BULLER'S SHEARWATER
White underparts; paler gray upperparts with black cap; black wing tips; diagonal bar on inner wing forms M pattern on back.

Flight Pattern

Dashing flight, alternating high soaring arcs and glides with rapid wing beats.

Nest Identification

Shape ◨ ◪   Location ▓ ♠

No nest material in burrow • atop small pile of grasses, in cliffs or rock crevices, or in caves, about 30–36 inches deep • built by both sexes • 1 white egg; oval, 2.3 inches long.

Plumage Sexes similar	Habitat ⌇ 🌊 ⌇ 🌊	Migration Migratory	Weight 11.1 ounces

DATE _____ TIME _____ LOCATION _____

Family PROCELLARIIDAE	Species *Pterodroma cookii*	Length 10.5 inches	Wingspan 25–26 inches

COOK'S PETREL

This petrel breeds on the islands off New Zealand but migrates regularly to Pacific waters near North America, where it is among the most numerous *Pterodroma* petrels seen in summer off the California coast. It is named for the English explorer Captain James Cook, who navigated around the world and explored New Zealand. This bird is rarely seen because it prefers the open seas. In flight it appears long-winged and long-tailed with a distinctive dark M across its upperwings; it has white outer tail feathers with black-tipped central tail feathers.

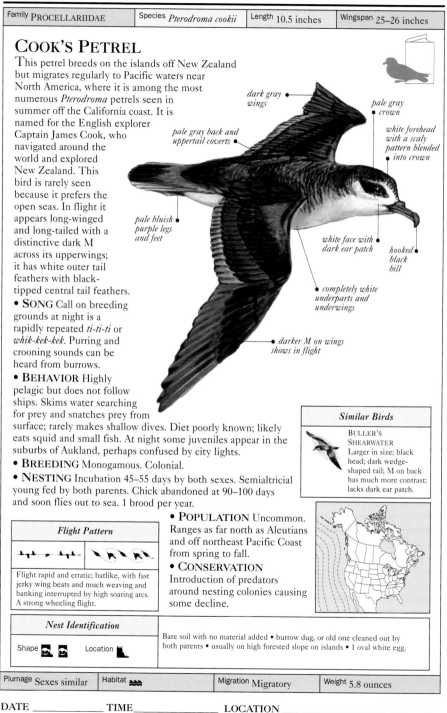

dark gray wings

pale gray crown

pale gray back and uppertail coverts

white forehead with a scaly pattern blended into crown

pale bluish purple legs and feet

white face with dark ear patch

hooked black bill

completely white underparts and underwings

darker M on wings shows in flight

• **SONG** Call on breeding grounds at night is a rapidly repeated *ti-ti-ti* or *whik-kek-kek*. Purring and crooning sounds can be heard from burrows.

• **BEHAVIOR** Highly pelagic but does not follow ships. Skims water searching for prey and snatches prey from surface; rarely makes shallow dives. Diet poorly known; likely eats squid and small fish. At night some juveniles appear in the suburbs of Aukland, perhaps confused by city lights.

• **BREEDING** Monogamous. Colonial.

• **NESTING** Incubation 45–55 days by both sexes. Semialtricial young fed by both parents. Chick abandoned at 90–100 days and soon flies out to sea. 1 brood per year.

• **POPULATION** Uncommon. Ranges as far north as Aleutians and off northeast Pacific Coast from spring to fall.

• **CONSERVATION** Introduction of predators around nesting colonies causing some decline.

Similar Birds

BULLER'S SHEARWATER Larger in size; black head; dark wedge-shaped tail; M on back has much more contrast; lacks dark ear patch.

Flight Pattern

Flight rapid and erratic; batlike, with fast jerky wing beats and much weaving and banking interrupted by high soaring arcs. A strong wheeling flight.

Nest Identification

Shape — Location —

Bare soil with no material added • burrow dug, or old one cleaned out by both parents • usually on high forested slope on islands • 1 oval white egg.

Plumage Sexes similar	Habitat ≈≈	Migration Migratory	Weight 5.8 ounces

DATE _____ TIME_____ LOCATION _____

Family PROCELLARIIDAE	Species *Pterodroma longirostris*	Length 12 inches	Wingspan 30 inches

STEJNEGER'S PETREL

This bird breeds on the Juan Fernandez Islands off the coast of Chile and off the islands of New Zealand (*P. l. pycrofti*). In the fall, birdwatchers from California may be able to spot this petrel flying well off the coast. It is known to associate with Cook's Petrel. In flight this petrel appears mostly white on the underparts, and the upperparts are a deep gray-brown, contrasting with the black cap and hindneck. The upperwing is a deep brownish gray, with the blackish greater coverts and outer primaries forming an M pattern linked across the lower back. The tail is a uniform brownish gray, darkest at the tip and with narrow white mottling on the outer web of the outermost feathers. In flight from below, underwings show narrow black margins; legs and feet are bluish. Juveniles are similar to adults but have grayer upperparts, contrasting more sharply with the dark half hood.

brownish gray wings with blackish greater coverts and outer primaries

gray-brown upperparts

dark brownish gray tail, mottled white on outer web of outer tail feathers

blackish head, nape, and upper back

white underparts

black bill

• **SONG** Usually silent at sea. Vocalizations around nesting colony unrecorded.
• **BEHAVIOR** Solitary at sea away from breeding grounds or flies in company of other petrels and shearwaters. Skims water for squid and small fish. Rarely dives for food. Does not follow ships. Activities around nesting colonies are primarily nocturnal.
• **BREEDING** Monogamous. Colonial.
• **NESTING** Breeding biology poorly known; incubation estimated at 51–54 days by both sexes. Semialtricial young stay in nest estimated 90–100 days; fed by both sexes. 1 brood per year.

Similar Birds

COOK'S PETREL
More extensive white edging on tail; paler frosty gray crown, nape, and upperparts lack contrast between crown and neck.

• **POPULATION** Accidental to casual in fall in pelagic waters off coast of southern California.
• **CONSERVATION** Vulnerable to destruction of eggs, young, and adult birds by introduced predators on its nesting islands.

Flight Pattern

Flight is rapid, erratic, and batlike, with fast jerky wing beats followed by banking and arcing glides; soars in high wheeling arcs as wind speeds increase.

Nest Identification

Shape 〇 〇 〇   Location 🏝 ⛰

No nest material • bare soil in burrow or crevice on island; burrow excavated or cleaned out by both sexes • one white egg; oval, 1.9 x 1.3 inches.

Plumage Sexes similar	Habitat 〰 〰	Migration Migratory	Weight Undetermined

DATE _____ TIME_____ LOCATION _____

Family PROCELLARIIDAE	Species *Calonectris leucomelas*	Length 19 inches	Wingspan 48 inches

STREAKED SHEARWATER

This Eurasian species is rare in North America. It is most likely to be seen in Hawaii and, occasionally, off the coast of California in autumn. This shearwater is the most abundant breeding seabird in Japan. Its dark grayish brown upperparts have a pale feather edging that gives a scaled effect. White fringes on long uppertail coverts may form an indistinct band over the tail. The pale head is lightly streaked and may look white at a distance; this attribute, coupled with the stiff-winged flight, may suggest a light morph fulmar.

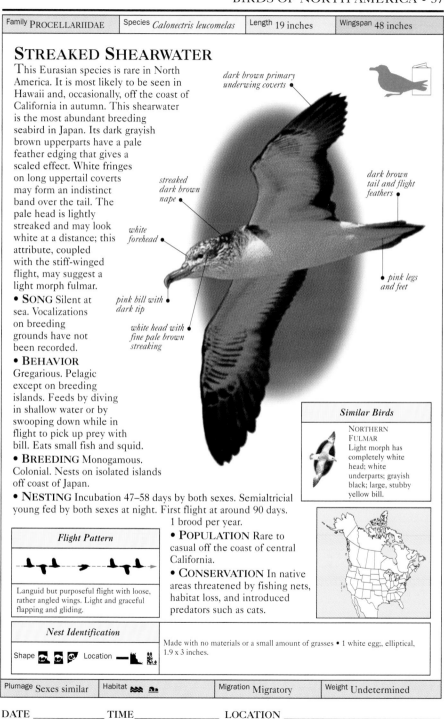

dark brown primary underwing coverts

streaked dark brown nape

white forehead

dark brown tail and flight feathers

pink legs and feet

pink bill with dark tip

white head with fine pale brown streaking

• **SONG** Silent at sea. Vocalizations on breeding grounds have not been recorded.

• **BEHAVIOR** Gregarious. Pelagic except on breeding islands. Feeds by diving in shallow water or by swooping down while in flight to pick up prey with bill. Eats small fish and squid.

• **BREEDING** Monogamous. Colonial. Nests on isolated islands off coast of Japan.

• **NESTING** Incubation 47–58 days by both sexes. Semialtricial young fed by both sexes at night. First flight at around 90 days. 1 brood per year.

• **POPULATION** Rare to casual off the coast of central California.

• **CONSERVATION** In native areas threatened by fishing nets, habitat loss, and introduced predators such as cats.

Similar Birds

NORTHERN FULMAR
Light morph has completely white head; white underparts; grayish black; large, stubby yellow bill.

Flight Pattern

Languid but purposeful flight with loose, rather angled wings. Light and graceful flapping and gliding.

Nest Identification

Shape | Location —

Made with no materials or a small amount of grasses • 1 white egg;, elliptical, 1.9 x 3 inches.

Plumage Sexes similar	Habitat	Migration Migratory	Weight Undetermined

DATE _____ TIME_____ LOCATION _____

Family PROCELLARIIDAE	Species *Puffinus creatopus*	Length 19 inches	Wingspan 43 inches

PINK-FOOTED SHEARWATER

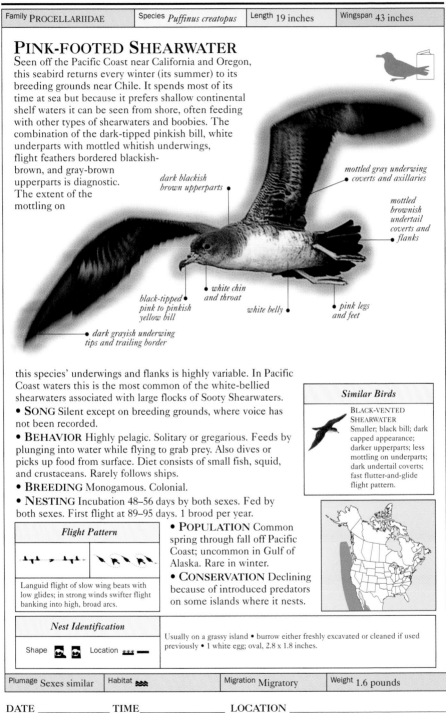

Seen off the Pacific Coast near California and Oregon, this seabird returns every winter (its summer) to its breeding grounds near Chile. It spends most of its time at sea but because it prefers shallow continental shelf waters it can be seen from shore, often feeding with other types of shearwaters and boobies. The combination of the dark-tipped pinkish bill, white underparts with mottled whitish underwings, flight feathers bordered blackish-brown, and gray-brown upperparts is diagnostic. The extent of the mottling on

dark blackish brown upperparts

mottled gray underwing coverts and axillaries

mottled brownish undertail coverts and flanks

black-tipped pink to pinkish yellow bill

white chin and throat

white belly

pink legs and feet

dark grayish underwing tips and trailing border

this species' underwings and flanks is highly variable. In Pacific Coast waters this is the most common of the white-bellied shearwaters associated with large flocks of Sooty Shearwaters.

• **SONG** Silent except on breeding grounds, where voice has not been recorded.

• **BEHAVIOR** Highly pelagic. Solitary or gregarious. Feeds by plunging into water while flying to grab prey. Also dives or picks up food from surface. Diet consists of small fish, squid, and crustaceans. Rarely follows ships.

• **BREEDING** Monogamous. Colonial.

• **NESTING** Incubation 48–56 days by both sexes. Fed by both sexes. First flight at 89–95 days. 1 brood per year.

• **POPULATION** Common spring through fall off Pacific Coast; uncommon in Gulf of Alaska. Rare in winter.

• **CONSERVATION** Declining because of introduced predators on some islands where it nests.

Similar Birds

BLACK-VENTED SHEARWATER
Smaller; black bill; dark capped appearance; darker upperparts; less mottling on underparts; dark undertail coverts; fast flutter-and-glide flight pattern.

Flight Pattern

Languid flight of slow wing beats with low glides; in strong winds swifter flight banking into high, broad arcs.

Nest Identification

Shape ◗ ◗   Location ⁙ ▬

Usually on a grassy island • burrow either freshly excavated or cleaned if used previously • 1 white egg; oval, 2.8 x 1.8 inches.

Plumage Sexes similar	Habitat 〰	Migration Migratory	Weight 1.6 pounds

DATE _____ TIME_____ LOCATION _____

Family PROCELLARIIDAE	Species *Puffinus carneipes*	Length 19–20 inches	Wingspan 39–43 inches

FLESH-FOOTED SHEARWATER

This large dark seabird spends more time near shore than most pelagic birds. Nesting on islands off New Zealand and Australia, stragglers make rare visits to North America and can be spotted off the Pacific Coast from Alaska to California. This adept diver often joins flocks of terns and gulls. In flight it appears brownish black with a creamy pink bill, legs, and feet. In good light the bases of the underwing primaries look silvery.

silvery to light brown bases of underwing primaries

dark brown overall

large creamy pink bill with dark tip

creamy pink legs and feet

• **SONG** Usually silent except on breeding grounds, where it makes a distinct mewing call. Also gives brief series of *gug gug gugs*, expanding to *ku koo ah*, which leads into shrieking.

• **BEHAVIOR** Gregarious. Feeds in open companies with other species but forms rafts at dusk off breeding grounds and when food is concentrated. Usually forages for food by diving from water's surface. Also feeds by skimming surface, extending pink feet to tread water between shallow belly flops. Eats fish and squid. Often follows fishing trawlers. Sometimes dives for bait on fishing lines.

• **BREEDING** Monogamous. Colonial.

• **NESTING** Incubation by both sexes, but period of time unknown. Young stay in nest 92 days. Fed by both sexes. First flight at 89–95 days. 1 brood per year.

Similar Birds

SOOTY SHEARWATER
Black bill; light underwings; blackish gray legs and feet; faster wing beats.

SHORT-TAILED SHEARWATER
Smaller; black bill; all dark, but sometimes with pale, often concentrated, underwing linings that form a panel; sometimes has whitish chin; blackish gray feet and legs.

• **POPULATION** Rare in summer and fall off the West Coast from California to Alaska.

• **CONSERVATION** Vulnerable to pollution of marine environment, oil spills, and introduction of predators at nesting colonies.

Flight Pattern

Slow flight with stiff-winged flapping and gliding near water surface. In higher flight soars and arcs, wheeling on stiff wings.

Nest Identification

Shape ▪ Location ▪ ▬

Scrape of vegetation in dry burrow lined with grass roots, feathers, and rush stems • at end of tunnel 3–6 feet long * from near sea level to high on hills • 1 white egg, 2.9 x 1.8 inches.

Plumage Sexes similar	Habitat 〰	Migration Migratory	Weight 1.3 pounds

DATE _____ TIME_____ LOCATION _____

Family PROCELLARIIDAE	Species *Puffinus pacificus*	Length 17–19 inches	Wingspan 38–41 inches

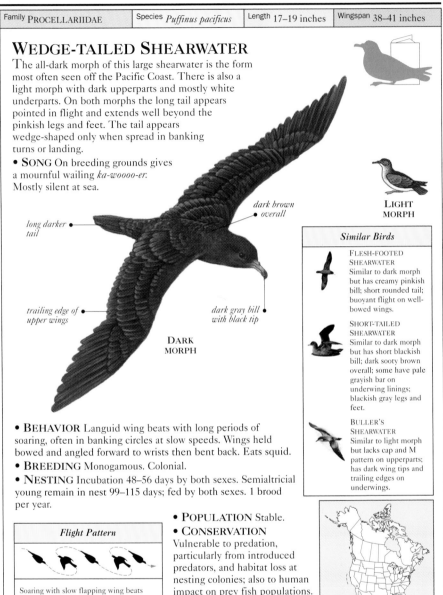

WEDGE-TAILED SHEARWATER

The all-dark morph of this large shearwater is the form most often seen off the Pacific Coast. There is also a light morph with dark upperparts and mostly white underparts. On both morphs the long tail appears pointed in flight and extends well beyond the pinkish legs and feet. The tail appears wedge-shaped only when spread in banking turns or landing.

• **SONG** On breeding grounds gives a mournful wailing *ka-woooo-er.* Mostly silent at sea.

long darker tail

dark brown overall

LIGHT MORPH

trailing edge of upper wings

dark gray bill with black tip

DARK MORPH

Similar Birds

FLESH-FOOTED SHEARWATER
Similar to dark morph but has creamy pinkish bill; short rounded tail; buoyant flight on well-bowed wings.

SHORT-TAILED SHEARWATER
Similar to dark morph but has short blackish bill; dark sooty brown overall; some have pale grayish bar on underwing linings; blackish gray legs and feet.

BULLER'S SHEARWATER
Similar to light morph but lacks cap and M pattern on upperparts; has dark wing tips and trailing edges on underwings.

• **BEHAVIOR** Languid wing beats with long periods of soaring, often in banking circles at slow speeds. Wings held bowed and angled forward to wrists then bent back. Eats squid.
• **BREEDING** Monogamous. Colonial.
• **NESTING** Incubation 48–56 days by both sexes. Semialtricial young remain in nest 99–115 days; fed by both sexes. 1 brood per year.

• **POPULATION** Stable.
• **CONSERVATION** Vulnerable to predation, particularly from introduced predators, and habitat loss at nesting colonies; also to human impact on prey fish populations.

Flight Pattern

Soaring with slow flapping wing beats followed by upward glide.

Nest Identification

Shape ▢ ▢   Location ▬▬▆

Lined with plant material • in ground in shaded area • built by both sexes • will nest above ground when burrows are scarce • 1 white egg, often nest-stained; long oval, 2.5 inches long.

Plumage Sexes similar	Habitat 〰〰 〰	Migration Migratory	Weight 13.7 ounces

DATE _____ TIME_____ LOCATION _____

Family PROCELLARIIDAE	Species *Puffinus bulleri*	Length 16 inches	Wingspan 38 inches

BULLER'S SHEARWATER

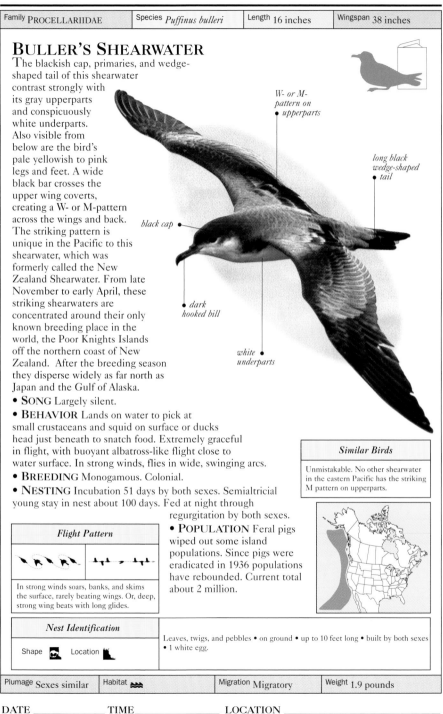

The blackish cap, primaries, and wedge-shaped tail of this shearwater contrast strongly with its gray upperparts and conspicuously white underparts. Also visible from below are the bird's pale yellowish to pink legs and feet. A wide black bar crosses the upper wing coverts, creating a W- or M-pattern across the wings and back. The striking pattern is unique in the Pacific to this shearwater, which was formerly called the New Zealand Shearwater. From late November to early April, these striking shearwaters are concentrated around their only known breeding place in the world, the Poor Knights Islands off the northern coast of New Zealand. After the breeding season they disperse widely as far north as Japan and the Gulf of Alaska.

W- or M-pattern on upperparts

long black wedge-shaped tail

black cap

dark hooked bill

white underparts

• **SONG** Largely silent.
• **BEHAVIOR** Lands on water to pick at small crustaceans and squid on surface or ducks head just beneath to snatch food. Extremely graceful in flight, with buoyant albatross-like flight close to water surface. In strong winds, flies in wide, swinging arcs.
• **BREEDING** Monogamous. Colonial.
• **NESTING** Incubation 51 days by both sexes. Semialtricial young stay in nest about 100 days. Fed at night through regurgitation by both sexes.
• **POPULATION** Feral pigs wiped out some island populations. Since pigs were eradicated in 1936 populations have rebounded. Current total about 2 million.

Similar Birds

Unmistakable. No other shearwater in the eastern Pacific has the striking M pattern on upperparts.

Flight Pattern

In strong winds soars, banks, and skims the surface, rarely beating wings. Or, deep, strong wing beats with long glides.

Nest Identification

Shape   Location

Leaves, twigs, and pebbles • on ground • up to 10 feet long • built by both sexes • 1 white egg.

Plumage Sexes similar	Habitat	Migration Migratory	Weight 1.9 pounds

DATE _____ TIME_____ LOCATION _____

Family PROCELLARIIDAE	Species *Puffinus griseus*	Length 18–20 inches	Wingspan 37–43 inches

SOOTY SHEARWATER

A common summer visitor off both the Atlantic and Pacific Coasts, this stocky short-necked sooty brown bird is probably the best-known shearwater in North American waters. It normally feeds well offshore, but during strong onshore winds hundreds of birds may be seen by observers from the shoreline. Look for the long slender dark wings with silvery gray underwing coverts. Some birds may have a white underwing lining. Legs and feet are blackish.

silvery gray underwing coverts

long slender dark wings

long dark bill

dark sooty brown plumage, darkest on tail and primaries

• **SONG** The Sooty Shearwater is silent except for noisy squeals when squabbling for food. Also makes inhaled and exhaled *koo-wah-koo-wah-koo-wah* when on breeding grounds.

• **BEHAVIOR** This bird often gathers in large flocks. Does not follow ships like some other seabirds, but is attracted to fishing trawlers. Flies with long glides on long narrow slightly swept-back wings. Sometimes makes short dives for fish, squid, and crustaceans. May plunge to dive on open wings from several feet above water.

• **BREEDING** Colonial. The Sooty Shearwater nests on various isolated islands in the southern oceans.

• **NESTING** Incubation 52–56 days by both sexes. Semialtricial young remain in nest for about 97 days. Adults usually leave at night. Young fed by both sexes at night.

• **POPULATION** The Sooty Shearwater is an abundant bird, with a total population of more than 10 million.

Similar Birds

SHORT-TAILED SHEARWATER
Shorter bill; less contrasting grayer underwing linings often restricted to a panel on the median secondary coverts and extending slightly onto the inner median primary coverts; underwings may be dark overall, lacking pale panels • only in the West.

Flight Pattern

Strong direct flapping alternating with long glides.

Nest Identification

Shape ⬛ ⬛   Location 🪨 🪨

Made of leaves and grass • up to 10 feet long • built by both sexes • 1 white egg; elliptical, 1.9 x 3 inches.

Plumage Sexes similar	Habitat 〰️ 🐚	Migration Migratory	Weight 1.8 pounds

DATE _____ TIME_____ LOCATION _____

Family PROCELLARIIDAE	Species *Puffinus tenuirostris*	Length 16–17 inches	Wingspan 38–39 inches

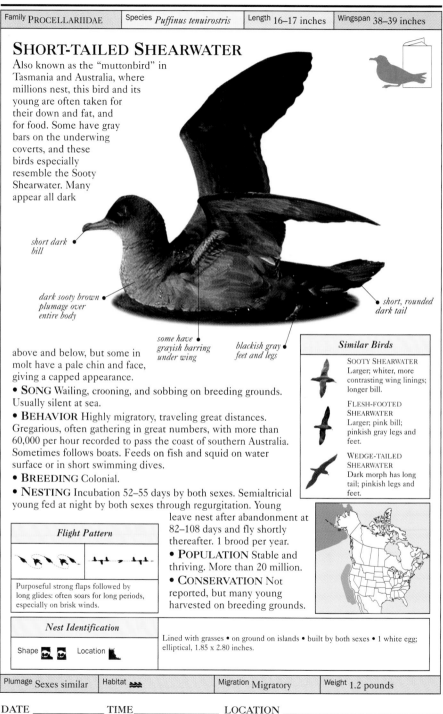

SHORT-TAILED SHEARWATER

Also known as the "muttonbird" in Tasmania and Australia, where millions nest, this bird and its young are often taken for their down and fat, and for food. Some have gray bars on the underwing coverts, and these birds especially resemble the Sooty Shearwater. Many appear all dark

short dark bill

dark sooty brown plumage over entire body

short, rounded dark tail

some have grayish barring under wing

blackish gray feet and legs

above and below, but some in molt have a pale chin and face, giving a capped appearance.

• **SONG** Wailing, crooning, and sobbing on breeding grounds. Usually silent at sea.

• **BEHAVIOR** Highly migratory, traveling great distances. Gregarious, often gathering in great numbers, with more than 60,000 per hour recorded to pass the coast of southern Australia. Sometimes follows boats. Feeds on fish and squid on water surface or in short swimming dives.

• **BREEDING** Colonial.

• **NESTING** Incubation 52–55 days by both sexes. Semialtricial young fed at night by both sexes through regurgitation. Young leave nest after abandonment at 82–108 days and fly shortly thereafter. 1 brood per year.

• **POPULATION** Stable and thriving. More than 20 million.

• **CONSERVATION** Not reported, but many young harvested on breeding grounds.

Similar Birds

SOOTY SHEARWATER
Larger; whiter, more contrasting wing linings; longer bill.

FLESH-FOOTED SHEARWATER
Larger; pink bill; pinkish gray legs and feet.

WEDGE-TAILED SHEARWATER
Dark morph has long tail; pinkish legs and feet.

Flight Pattern

Purposeful strong flaps followed by long glides: often soars for long periods, especially on brisk winds.

Nest Identification

Shape | Location

Lined with grasses • on ground on islands • built by both sexes • 1 white egg; elliptical, 1.85 x 2.80 inches.

Plumage Sexes similar	Habitat	Migration Migratory	Weight 1.2 pounds

DATE _____ TIME_____ LOCATION _____

Family PROCELLARIIDAE	Species *Puffinus opisthomelas*	Length 13–14 inches	Wingspan 30–35 inches

BLACK-VENTED SHEARWATER

Unlike most shearwaters, this bird sometimes can be seen from shore. It feeds relatively close to the coast and dives with its wings partially opened. Formerly considered a subspecies of the Manx Shearwater, it occasionally follows ships. In flight the white flanks extend around the sides of the rump, giving the appearance of a narrow white patch on each side of the uppertail – a good field mark. The upperwing is blackish brown, and the underwing is white with a black tip and narrow trailing edge. Legs and feet are blackish with purplish webbing.

- **SONG** Largely silent at sea.
- **BEHAVIOR** Swims well. Dives into water to feed; sometimes "flies" underwater, using wings to help it swim. Feeds no more than 10 miles from the shore. Eats a variety of fish, crustaceans, and squid. Nocturnal around nesting colonies.

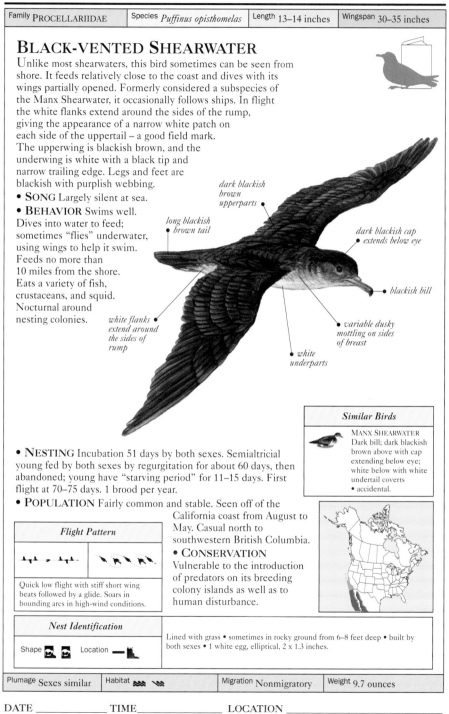

dark blackish brown upperparts

long blackish brown tail

dark blackish cap extends below eye

blackish bill

variable dusky mottling on sides of breast

white flanks extend around the sides of rump

white underparts

Similar Birds

MANX SHEARWATER
Dark bill; dark blackish brown above with cap extending below eye; white below with white undertail coverts
• accidental.

- **NESTING** Incubation 51 days by both sexes. Semialtricial young fed by both sexes by regurgitation for about 60 days, then abandoned; young have "starving period" for 11–15 days. First flight at 70–75 days. 1 brood per year.
- **POPULATION** Fairly common and stable. Seen off of the California coast from August to May. Casual north to southwestern British Columbia.
- **CONSERVATION** Vulnerable to the introduction of predators on its breeding colony islands as well as to human disturbance.

Flight Pattern

Quick low flight with stiff short wing beats followed by a glide. Soars in bounding arcs in high-wind conditions.

Nest Identification

Shape ⬛ ⬛ Location ▬ ⬛

Lined with grass • sometimes in rocky ground from 6–8 feet deep • built by both sexes • 1 white egg, elliptical, 2 x 1.3 inches.

Plumage Sexes similar	Habitat 〰〰 〰	Migration Nonmigratory	Weight 9.7 ounces

DATE _____ TIME_____ LOCATION _____

Family HYDROBATIDAE	Species *Oceanodroma furcata*	Length 8–9 inches	Wingspan 18 inches

FORK-TAILED STORM-PETREL

As the only blue-gray storm-petrel in its range, this bird contrasts strongly with all its darker brownish black congeners. The forked tail appears long in flight. All tail feathers are narrowly tipped white, and a white outer web, the outermost vane of the outer tail feathers, borders its entire length. At a distance in bright sunlight, the bird appears almost white, so when sitting on the water it might be confused with a phalarope. It has pale bluish pearl-gray underparts, and its legs are dark in color. Juvenile plumage is similar to that of the adult. In Alaska these cold-water birds are commonly found near the shore, especially in fall, and near air holes after the water is covered with ice.

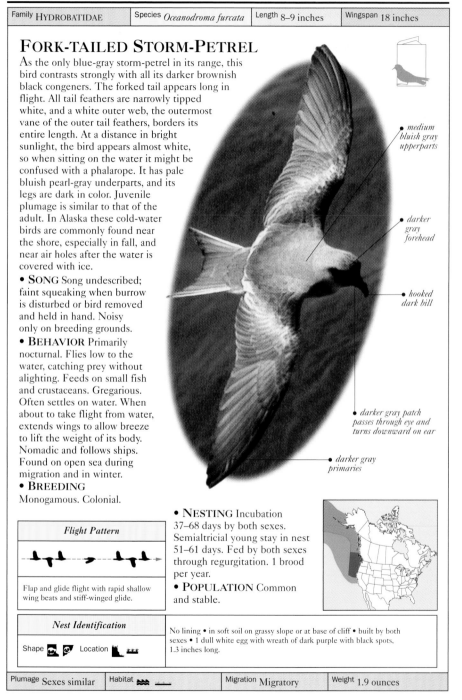

• medium bluish gray upperparts

• darker gray forehead

• hooked dark bill

• darker gray patch passes through eye and turns downward on ear

• darker gray primaries

• **SONG** Song undescribed; faint squeaking when burrow is disturbed or bird removed and held in hand. Noisy only on breeding grounds.
• **BEHAVIOR** Primarily nocturnal. Flies low to the water, catching prey without alighting. Feeds on small fish and crustaceans. Gregarious. Often settles on water. When about to take flight from water, extends wings to allow breeze to lift the weight of its body. Nomadic and follows ships. Found on open sea during migration and in winter.
• **BREEDING** Monogamous. Colonial.

• **NESTING** Incubation 37–68 days by both sexes. Semialtricial young stay in nest 51–61 days. Fed by both sexes through regurgitation. 1 brood per year.
• **POPULATION** Common and stable.

Flight Pattern
Flap and glide flight with rapid shallow wing beats and stiff-winged glide.

Nest Identification	
Shape ▨ ◨ Location ▮ ✸✸	No lining • in soft soil on grassy slope or at base of cliff • built by both sexes • 1 dull white egg with wreath of dark purple with black spots, 1.3 inches long.

Plumage Sexes similar	Habitat ≈≈ ⌇	Migration Migratory	Weight 1.9 ounces

DATE _____ TIME_____ LOCATION _____

| Family HYDROBATIDAE | Species *Oceanodroma leucorhoa* | Length 8–9 inches | Wingspan 18–19 inches |

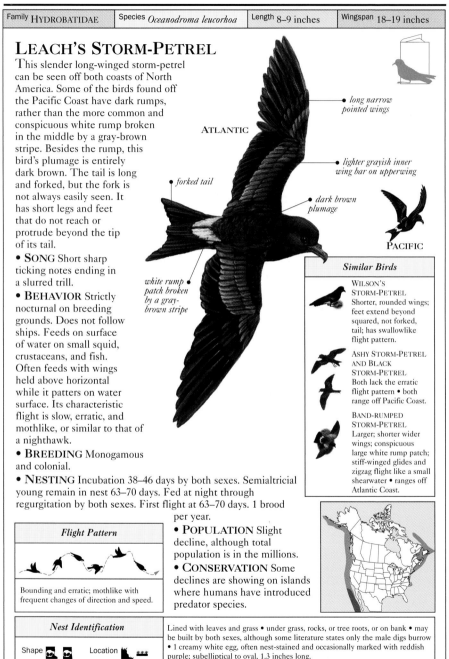

LEACH'S STORM-PETREL

This slender long-winged storm-petrel can be seen off both coasts of North America. Some of the birds found off the Pacific Coast have dark rumps, rather than the more common and conspicuous white rump broken in the middle by a gray-brown stripe. Besides the rump, this bird's plumage is entirely dark brown. The tail is long and forked, but the fork is not always easily seen. It has short legs and feet that do not reach or protrude beyond the tip of its tail.

- **SONG** Short sharp ticking notes ending in a slurred trill.
- **BEHAVIOR** Strictly nocturnal on breeding grounds. Does not follow ships. Feeds on surface of water on small squid, crustaceans, and fish. Often feeds with wings held above horizontal while it patters on water surface. Its characteristic flight is slow, erratic, and mothlike, or similar to that of a nighthawk.
- **BREEDING** Monogamous and colonial.
- **NESTING** Incubation 38–46 days by both sexes. Semialtricial young remain in nest 63–70 days. Fed at night through regurgitation by both sexes. First flight at 63–70 days. 1 brood per year.
- **POPULATION** Slight decline, although total population is in the millions.
- **CONSERVATION** Some declines are showing on islands where humans have introduced predator species.

ATLANTIC

long narrow pointed wings

lighter grayish inner wing bar on upperwing

forked tail

dark brown plumage

PACIFIC

white rump patch broken by a gray-brown stripe

Similar Birds

WILSON'S STORM-PETREL Shorter, rounded wings; feet extend beyond squared, not forked, tail; has swallowlike flight pattern.

ASHY STORM-PETREL AND BLACK STORM-PETREL Both lack the erratic flight pattern • both range off Pacific Coast.

BAND-RUMPED STORM-PETREL Larger; shorter wider wings; conspicuous large white rump patch; stiff-winged glides and zigzag flight like a small shearwater • ranges off Atlantic Coast.

Flight Pattern
Bounding and erratic; mothlike with frequent changes of direction and speed.

Nest Identification	
Shape ◗ ◗ Location 🌿 ✹✹✹	Lined with leaves and grass • under grass, rocks, or tree roots, or on bank • may be built by both sexes, although some literature states only the male digs burrow • 1 creamy white egg, often nest-stained and occasionally marked with reddish purple; subelliptical to oval, 1.3 inches long.

| Plumage Sexes similar | Habitat ≈≈≈ ⌇ | Migration Migratory | Weight 1.2 ounces |

DATE _____ TIME_____ LOCATION _____

Family HYDROBATIDAE	Species *Oceanodroma homochroa*	Length 7–8 inches	Wingspan 17 inches

ASHY STORM-PETREL

The smallest of the all-dark, forked-tailed storm-petrels off the Pacific Coast, this bird's short wings give it a chunky appearance. Coupled with its normally slow fluttering flight and shallow wing beats, this helps distinguish it from other dark storm-petrels in its range.

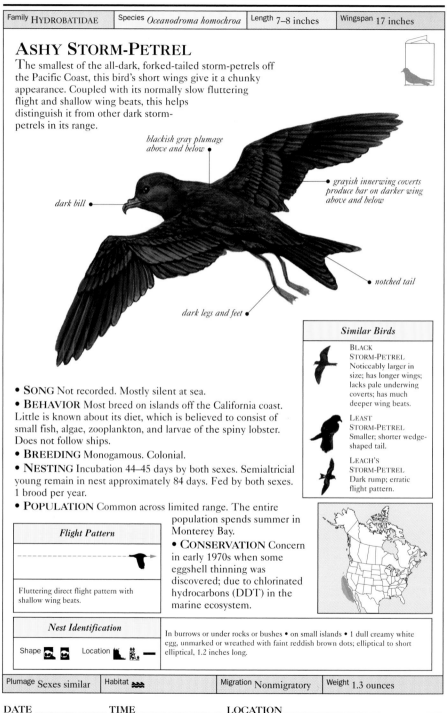

blackish gray plumage above and below

grayish innerwing coverts produce bar on darker wing above and below

dark bill

notched tail

dark legs and feet

Similar Birds

BLACK STORM-PETREL Noticeably larger in size; has longer wings; lacks pale underwing coverts; has much deeper wing beats.

LEAST STORM-PETREL Smaller; shorter wedge-shaped tail.

LEACH'S STORM-PETREL Dark rump; erratic flight pattern.

- **SONG** Not recorded. Mostly silent at sea.
- **BEHAVIOR** Most breed on islands off the California coast. Little is known about its diet, which is believed to consist of small fish, algae, zooplankton, and larvae of the spiny lobster. Does not follow ships.
- **BREEDING** Monogamous. Colonial.
- **NESTING** Incubation 44–45 days by both sexes. Semialtricial young remain in nest approximately 84 days. Fed by both sexes. 1 brood per year.
- **POPULATION** Common across limited range. The entire population spends summer in Monterey Bay.
- **CONSERVATION** Concern in early 1970s when some eggshell thinning was discovered; due to chlorinated hydrocarbons (DDT) in the marine ecosystem.

Flight Pattern

Fluttering direct flight pattern with shallow wing beats.

Nest Identification

Shape   Location

In burrows or under rocks or bushes • on small islands • 1 dull creamy white egg, unmarked or wreathed with faint reddish brown dots; elliptical to short elliptical, 1.2 inches long.

Plumage Sexes similar	Habitat	Migration Nonmigratory	Weight 1.3 ounces

DATE _____ TIME_____ LOCATION _____

| Family HYDROBATIDAE | Species *Oceanodroma tethys* | Length 6.5–7.25 inches | Wingspan 13.25–15 inches |

WEDGE-RUMPED STORM-PETREL

From August to January this small seabird is casual off the California coast before it returns to the Galapagos Islands and islands off the coast of Peru to nest. In flight, it shows the largest white rump of any storm-petrel, often appearing as if its entire rump and tail were white. Juveniles resemble adults.

blackish brown overall

large white triangle on rump and uppertail coverts extends to lateral tail coverts and flanks

short notched black tail

black bill

black legs and feet

paler brown greater secondary coverts on upper wing form diagonal bar

long pointed wings

• **SONG** Gives low soft growling calls around the breeding colony. Also utters *chirka*. Silent at sea.

• **BEHAVIOR** Solitary or in pairs or small groups in nonbreeding season. Large numbers at breeding colonies are active both day and night. It is the only storm-petrel to visit nesting burrows in daylight. On its way to and from its nesting burrows in the volcanic crevices of the breeding colony, this bird often is attacked by Short-eared Owls on the Galapagos Islands. Feeds far out at sea. Flies over water, swooping down to pick up food in skipping bounding flight, with legs trailing on surface. Does not patter feet on water as do some other storm-petrels. Occasionally follows ships. Eats mollusks, small crustaceans, plankton, and small fishes.

• **BREEDING** Monogamous. Colonial. Male and female mate for life.

• **NESTING** Incubation 41–42 days by both sexes. Semialtricial young stay in nest 63–70 days, fed by regurgitation and tended by both sexes. 1 brood per year.

• **POPULATION** Casual off the Pacific Coast north to the central California coast in fall and winter seasons.

• **CONSERVATION** Vulnerable to introduced predators in vicinity of nesting colonies and to pollution of marine environments.

Similar Birds

LEACH'S STORM-PETREL
Larger; deeper fork in tail; smaller white rump patch, often divided in middle, reduced or absent in some birds off southern California coast; longer more pointed wings; bounding nighthawklike flight.

WILSON'S STORM-PETREL
Larger; U-shaped white rump patch only reaches middle of black tail; yellow-webbed black feet trail beyond tail; more fluttery and erratic flight.

Flight Pattern

Swift forceful direct flight with deep wing beats and much twisting and banking; often high above the surface of the water.

Nest Identification

Shape

Location

No nest materials • in crevices of rocks or burrow or on ground under shrub, 2–3 feet deep • cleaned out or dug by both sexes • 1 white egg; elliptical to subelliptical, 1.1 inches long.

| Plumage Sexes similar | Habitat | Migration Migratory | Weight 0.8 ounce |

DATE _____ TIME_____ LOCATION _____

Family HYDROBATIDAE	Species *Oceanodroma melania*	Length 9 inches	Wingspan 18–20 inches

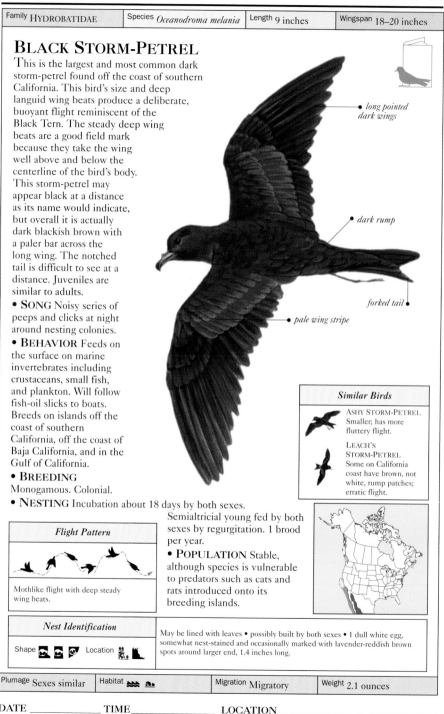

BLACK STORM-PETREL

This is the largest and most common dark storm-petrel found off the coast of southern California. This bird's size and deep languid wing beats produce a deliberate, buoyant flight reminiscent of the Black Tern. The steady deep wing beats are a good field mark because they take the wing well above and below the centerline of the bird's body. This storm-petrel may appear black at a distance as its name would indicate, but overall it is actually dark blackish brown with a paler bar across the long wing. The notched tail is difficult to see at a distance. Juveniles are similar to adults.

long pointed dark wings

dark rump

forked tail

pale wing stripe

- **SONG** Noisy series of peeps and clicks at night around nesting colonies.
- **BEHAVIOR** Feeds on the surface on marine invertebrates including crustaceans, small fish, and plankton. Will follow fish-oil slicks to boats. Breeds on islands off the coast of southern California, off the coast of Baja California, and in the Gulf of California.
- **BREEDING** Monogamous. Colonial.
- **NESTING** Incubation about 18 days by both sexes. Semialtricial young fed by both sexes by regurgitation. 1 brood per year.
- **POPULATION** Stable, although species is vulnerable to predators such as cats and rats introduced onto its breeding islands.

Similar Birds

ASHY STORM-PETREL
Smaller; has more fluttery flight.

LEACH'S STORM-PETREL
Some on California coast have brown, not white, rump patches; erratic flight.

Flight Pattern

Mothlike flight with deep steady wing beats.

Nest Identification

Shape   Location

May be lined with leaves • possibly built by both sexes • 1 dull white egg, somewhat nest-stained and occasionally marked with lavender-reddish brown spots around larger end, 1.4 inches long.

Plumage Sexes similar	Habitat	Migration Migratory	Weight 2.1 ounces

DATE _____ TIME_____ LOCATION _____

Family HYDROBATIDAE	Species *Oceanodroma microsoma*	Length 5–6 inches	Wingspan 12 inches

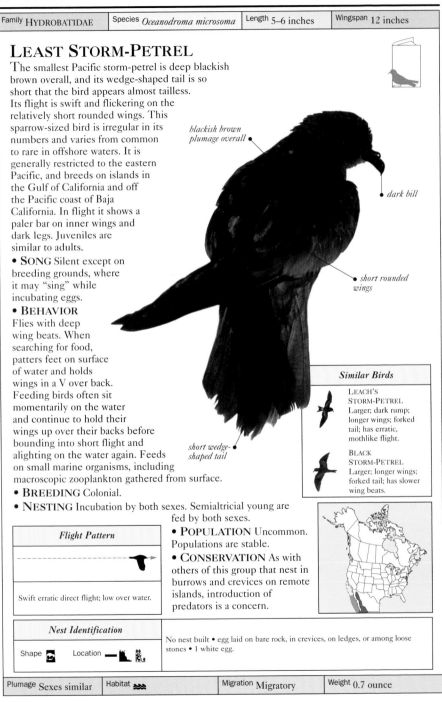

LEAST STORM-PETREL

The smallest Pacific storm-petrel is deep blackish brown overall, and its wedge-shaped tail is so short that the bird appears almost tailless. Its flight is swift and flickering on the relatively short rounded wings. This sparrow-sized bird is irregular in its numbers and varies from common to rare in offshore waters. It is generally restricted to the eastern Pacific, and breeds on islands in the Gulf of California and off the Pacific coast of Baja California. In flight it shows a paler bar on inner wings and dark legs. Juveniles are similar to adults.

blackish brown plumage overall

dark bill

short rounded wings

• **SONG** Silent except on breeding grounds, where it may "sing" while incubating eggs.

• **BEHAVIOR** Flies with deep wing beats. When searching for food, patters feet on surface of water and holds wings in a V over back. Feeding birds often sit momentarily on the water and continue to hold their wings up over their backs before bounding into short flight and alighting on the water again. Feeds on small marine organisms, including macroscopic zooplankton gathered from surface.

short wedge-shaped tail

Similar Birds

LEACH'S STORM-PETREL
Larger; dark rump; longer wings; forked tail; has erratic, mothlike flight.

BLACK STORM-PETREL
Larger; longer wings; forked tail; has slower wing beats.

• **BREEDING** Colonial.

• **NESTING** Incubation by both sexes. Semialtricial young are fed by both sexes.

• **POPULATION** Uncommon. Populations are stable.

• **CONSERVATION** As with others of this group that nest in burrows and crevices on remote islands, introduction of predators is a concern.

Flight Pattern

Swift erratic direct flight; low over water.

Nest Identification

Shape ▨   Location ▬ ◣ ▦

No nest built • egg laid on bare rock, in crevices, on ledges, or among loose stones • 1 white egg.

Plumage Sexes similar	Habitat ≈≈≈	Migration Migratory	Weight 0.7 ounce

DATE _____ TIME_____ LOCATION _____

Family PHAETHONTIDAE	Species *Phaethon rubricauda*	Length 18–36 inches	Wingspan 44 inches

RED-TAILED TROPICBIRD

Breeding on islands in the Pacific and Indian Oceans this seabird is rare off California. In a unique "bicycling" flight display a pair hovers in the wind with one bird above the other; the top bird drops as the lower bird climbs, and both resume hovering.

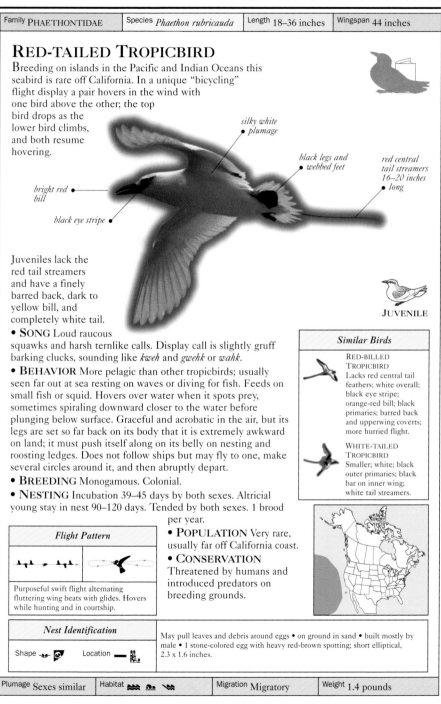

silky white plumage

black legs and webbed feet

red central tail streamers 16–20 inches long

bright red bill

black eye stripe

Juveniles lack the red tail streamers and have a finely barred back, dark to yellow bill, and completely white tail.

JUVENILE

- **SONG** Loud raucous squawks and harsh ternlike calls. Display call is slightly gruff barking clucks, sounding like *kweh* and *gwehk* or *wahk*.
- **BEHAVIOR** More pelagic than other tropicbirds; usually seen far out at sea resting on waves or diving for fish. Feeds on small fish or squid. Hovers over water when it spots prey, sometimes spiraling downward closer to the water before plunging below surface. Graceful and acrobatic in the air, but its legs are set so far back on its body that it is extremely awkward on land; it must push itself along on its belly on nesting and roosting ledges. Does not follow ships but may fly to one, make several circles around it, and then abruptly depart.
- **BREEDING** Monogamous. Colonial.
- **NESTING** Incubation 39–45 days by both sexes. Altricial young stay in nest 90–120 days. Tended by both sexes. 1 brood per year.
- **POPULATION** Very rare, usually far off California coast.
- **CONSERVATION** Threatened by humans and introduced predators on breeding grounds.

Similar Birds

RED-BILLED TROPICBIRD
Lacks red central tail feathers; white overall; black eye stripe; orange-red bill; black primaries; barred back and upperwing coverts; more hurried flight.

WHITE-TAILED TROPICBIRD
Smaller; white; black outer primaries; black bar on inner wing; white tail streamers.

Flight Pattern

Purposeful swift flight alternating fluttering wing beats with glides. Hovers while hunting and in courtship.

Nest Identification

Shape

Location

May pull leaves and debris around eggs • on ground in sand • built mostly by male • 1 stone-colored egg with heavy red-brown spotting; short elliptical, 2.3 x 1.6 inches.

Plumage Sexes similar	Habitat	Migration Migratory	Weight 1.4 pounds

DATE _____ TIME_____ LOCATION _____

Family SULIDAE	Species *Sula dactylatra*	Length 26–34 inches	Wingspan 60–62 inches

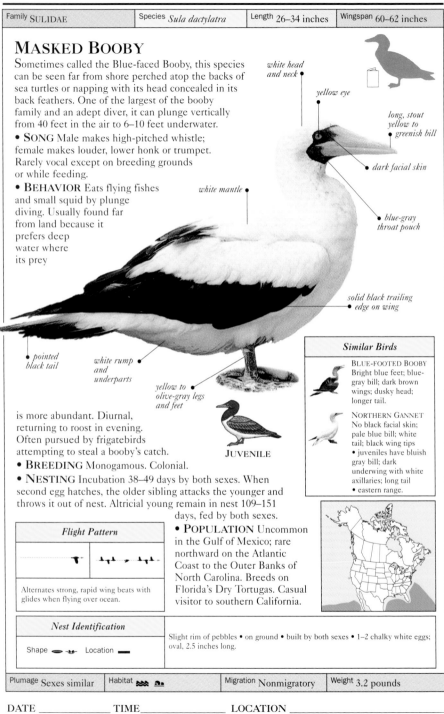

MASKED BOOBY

Sometimes called the Blue-faced Booby, this species can be seen far from shore perched atop the backs of sea turtles or napping with its head concealed in its back feathers. One of the largest of the booby family and an adept diver, it can plunge vertically from 40 feet in the air to 6–10 feet underwater.

• **SONG** Male makes high-pitched whistle; female makes louder, lower honk or trumpet. Rarely vocal except on breeding grounds or while feeding.

• **BEHAVIOR** Eats flying fishes and small squid by plunge diving. Usually found far from land because it prefers deep water where its prey

white head and neck

yellow eye

long, stout yellow to greenish bill

dark facial skin

white mantle

blue-gray throat pouch

solid black trailing edge on wing

pointed black tail

white rump and underparts

yellow to olive-gray legs and feet

JUVENILE

is more abundant. Diurnal, returning to roost in evening. Often pursued by frigatebirds attempting to steal a booby's catch.

• **BREEDING** Monogamous. Colonial.

• **NESTING** Incubation 38–49 days by both sexes. When second egg hatches, the older sibling attacks the younger and throws it out of nest. Altricial young remain in nest 109–151 days, fed by both sexes.

• **POPULATION** Uncommon in the Gulf of Mexico; rare northward on the Atlantic Coast to the Outer Banks of North Carolina. Breeds on Florida's Dry Tortugas. Casual visitor to southern California.

Similar Birds

BLUE-FOOTED BOOBY
Bright blue feet; blue-gray bill; dark brown wings; dusky head; longer tail.

NORTHERN GANNET
No black facial skin; pale blue bill; white tail; black wing tips • juveniles have bluish gray bill; dark underwing with white axillaries; long tail • eastern range.

Flight Pattern

Alternates strong, rapid wing beats with glides when flying over ocean.

Nest Identification

Shape — Location ▬

Slight rim of pebbles • on ground • built by both sexes • 1–2 chalky white eggs; oval, 2.5 inches long.

Plumage Sexes similar	Habitat 〰	Migration Nonmigratory	Weight 3.2 pounds

DATE _____ TIME_____ LOCATION _____

Family SULIDAE	Species *Sula nebouxii*	Length 32 inches	Wingspan 60–62 inches

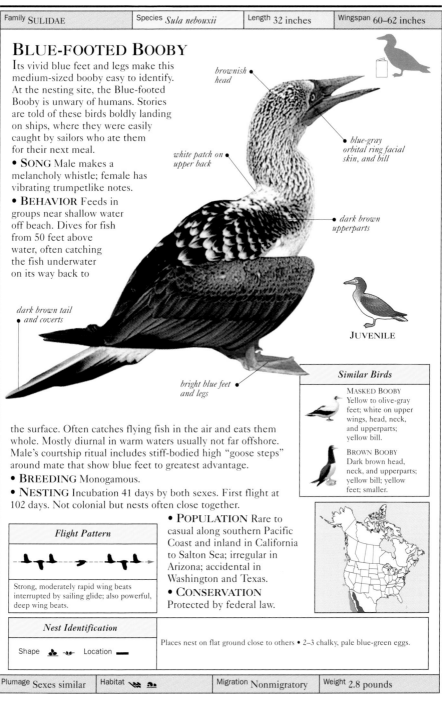

BLUE-FOOTED BOOBY

Its vivid blue feet and legs make this medium-sized booby easy to identify. At the nesting site, the Blue-footed Booby is unwary of humans. Stories are told of these birds boldly landing on ships, where they were easily caught by sailors who ate them for their next meal.

• **SONG** Male makes a melancholy whistle; female has vibrating trumpetlike notes.

• **BEHAVIOR** Feeds in groups near shallow water off beach. Dives for fish from 50 feet above water, often catching the fish underwater on its way back to

brownish head

blue-gray orbital ring facial skin, and bill

white patch on upper back

dark brown upperparts

dark brown tail and coverts

JUVENILE

bright blue feet and legs

Similar Birds

MASKED BOOBY
Yellow to olive-gray feet; white on upper wings, head, neck, and upperparts; yellow bill.

BROWN BOOBY
Dark brown head, neck, and upperparts; yellow bill; yellow feet; smaller.

the surface. Often catches flying fish in the air and eats them whole. Mostly diurnal in warm waters usually not far offshore. Male's courtship ritual includes stiff-bodied high "goose steps" around mate that show blue feet to greatest advantage.

• **BREEDING** Monogamous.

• **NESTING** Incubation 41 days by both sexes. First flight at 102 days. Not colonial but nests often close together.

• **POPULATION** Rare to casual along southern Pacific Coast and inland in California to Salton Sea; irregular in Arizona; accidental in Washington and Texas.

• **CONSERVATION** Protected by federal law.

Flight Pattern
Strong, moderately rapid wing beats interrupted by sailing glide; also powerful, deep wing beats.

Nest Identification
Shape · · Location ▬

Places nest on flat ground close to others • 2–3 chalky, pale blue-green eggs.

Plumage Sexes similar	Habitat	Migration Nonmigratory	Weight 2.8 pounds

DATE _____ TIME_____ LOCATION _____

Family SULIDAE	Species *Sula leucogaster*	Length 26–29 inches	Wingspan 52–59 inches

BROWN BOOBY

Because of its habit of landing aboard ships and not trying to escape, sailors nicknamed this bird "booby," meaning "dunce" in Spanish. The Brown Booby is one of the most common boobies and prefers to feed and travel in large flocks. The female can be distinguished from the male by its yellow (rather than blue) orbital ring and yellow bill. Males of the subspecies *brewsteri*, rarely observed in North America, have white foreheads and whitish tan heads and necks. Juveniles have gray facial skin and underparts, and underwings washed with dusky brown.

blue orbital ring

bluish gray bill

dark brown overall

JUVENILE

sharp demarcation between brown neck and white underparts

blackish brown upperwing

- **SONG** Usually silent at sea. On breeding grounds, a harsh honking. Also gives harsh brays and a hoarse hissing whistle.
- **BEHAVIOR** Gregarious. Marine and pelagic but often seen from shore. Eats parrot fishes, mullets, flatfishes, and halfbeaks. Feeds inshore more often than other boobies by making shallow plunging dives from 30–50 feet

dark brown wedge-shaped tail

yellowish legs and feet

Similar Birds

RED-FOOTED BOOBY Brown morph and juvenile similar • brown overall; brown underwing; gray to pinkish bill, legs, and feet.

BLUE-FOOTED BOOBY Juvenile similar • white patch at base of neck; white rump.

MASKED BOOBY Juvenile similar • brown coloring extends only to throat; has complete white collar.

NORTHERN GANNET Juvenile similar • larger; dark gray upperparts with light spots and spangling; grayish underparts • eastern range.

above the water. Prefers to perch rather than sit on the water and comes ashore at night to roost in trees, shrubs, wharfs, buildings, etc. Attracted to ships and will perch in their rigging.

- **BREEDING** Monogamous. Colonial.
- **NESTING** Incubation 40–47 days by both sexes. Altricial young stay in or near nest; fed by both sexes. First flight at 84–119 days. 1 brood per year.
- **POPULATION** Casual to rare in South Florida and Florida Keys, Gulf Coast, and Gulf of California. Accidental elsewhere. Wide range of nesting sites has kept population stable.
- **CONSERVATION** Vulnerable to breeding colony disturbances as well as introduced predators.

Flight Pattern
Strong, moderately rapid wing beats interrupted by sailing glide; also powerful, deep wing beats.

Nest Identification	
Shape ᴗ Location	Grass, twigs, and debris • on ground • 1-3 whitish to pale blue-green eggs with chalky coating, often nest stained; ovate to elliptical ovate, 2.4 x 1.6 inches.

Plumage Sexes differ	Habitat	Migration Nonmigratory	Weight 2.4 pounds

DATE _____ TIME_____ LOCATION _____

Family SULIDAE	Species *Sula sula*	Length 26–28 inches	Wingspan 53–60 inches

RED-FOOTED BOOBY

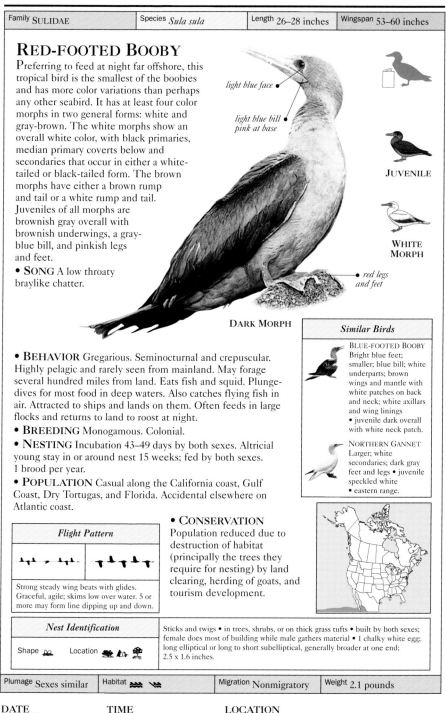

Preferring to feed at night far offshore, this tropical bird is the smallest of the boobies and has more color variations than perhaps any other seabird. It has at least four color morphs in two general forms: white and gray-brown. The white morphs show an overall white color, with black primaries, median primary coverts below and secondaries that occur in either a white-tailed or black-tailed form. The brown morphs have either a brown rump and tail or a white rump and tail. Juveniles of all morphs are brownish gray overall with brownish underwings, a gray-blue bill, and pinkish legs and feet.

• **SONG** A low throaty braylike chatter.

light blue face

*light blue bill
pink at base*

JUVENILE

WHITE MORPH

*red legs
and feet*

DARK MORPH

• **BEHAVIOR** Gregarious. Seminocturnal and crepuscular. Highly pelagic and rarely seen from mainland. May forage several hundred miles from land. Eats fish and squid. Plunge-dives for most food in deep waters. Also catches flying fish in air. Attracted to ships and lands on them. Often feeds in large flocks and returns to land to roost at night.

• **BREEDING** Monogamous. Colonial.

• **NESTING** Incubation 43–49 days by both sexes. Altricial young stay in or around nest 15 weeks; fed by both sexes. 1 brood per year.

• **POPULATION** Casual along the California coast, Gulf Coast, Dry Tortugas, and Florida. Accidental elsewhere on Atlantic coast.

Similar Birds

BLUE-FOOTED BOOBY
Bright blue feet; smaller; blue bill; white underparts; brown wings and mantle with white patches on back and neck; white axillars and wing linings
• juvenile dark overall with white neck patch.

NORTHERN GANNET
Larger; white secondaries; dark gray feet and legs • juvenile speckled white
• eastern range.

• **CONSERVATION** Population reduced due to destruction of habitat (principally the trees they require for nesting) by land clearing, herding of goats, and tourism development.

Flight Pattern

Strong steady wing beats with glides. Graceful, agile; skims low over water. 5 or more may form line dipping up and down.

Nest Identification

Shape   Location

Sticks and twigs • in trees, shrubs, or on thick grass tufts • built by both sexes; female does most of building while male gathers material • 1 chalky white egg; long elliptical or long to short subelliptical, generally broader at one end; 2.5 x 1.6 inches.

Plumage Sexes similar	Habitat	Migration Nonmigratory	Weight 2.1 pounds

DATE _____ TIME_____ LOCATION _____

Family PELECANIDAE	Species *Pelecanus erythrorhynchos*	Length 60–63 inches	Wingspan 96–110 inches

AMERICAN WHITE PELICAN

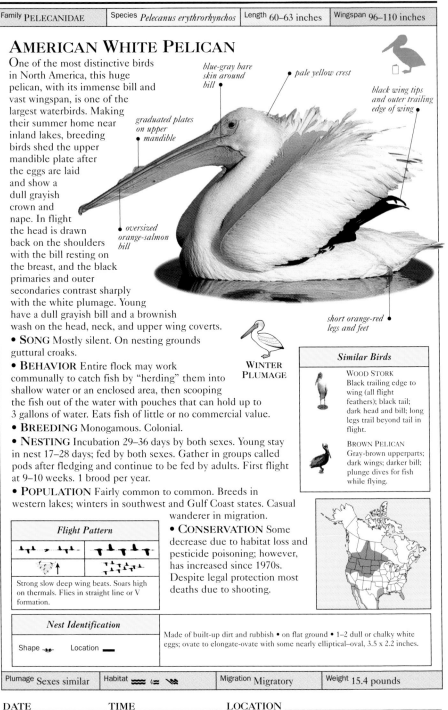

One of the most distinctive birds in North America, this huge pelican, with its immense bill and vast wingspan, is one of the largest waterbirds. Making their summer home near inland lakes, breeding birds shed the upper mandible plate after the eggs are laid and show a dull grayish crown and nape. In flight the head is drawn back on the shoulders with the bill resting on the breast, and the black primaries and outer secondaries contrast sharply with the white plumage. Young have a dull grayish bill and a brownish wash on the head, neck, and upper wing coverts.

blue-gray bare skin around bill

pale yellow crest

black wing tips and outer trailing edge of wing

graduated plates on upper mandible

oversized orange-salmon bill

short orange-red legs and feet

WINTER PLUMAGE

• **SONG** Mostly silent. On nesting grounds guttural croaks.

• **BEHAVIOR** Entire flock may work communally to catch fish by "herding" them into shallow water or an enclosed area, then scooping the fish out of the water with pouches that can hold up to 3 gallons of water. Eats fish of little or no commercial value.

• **BREEDING** Monogamous. Colonial.

• **NESTING** Incubation 29–36 days by both sexes. Young stay in nest 17–28 days; fed by both sexes. Gather in groups called pods after fledging and continue to be fed by adults. First flight at 9–10 weeks. 1 brood per year.

• **POPULATION** Fairly common to common. Breeds in western lakes; winters in southwest and Gulf Coast states. Casual wanderer in migration.

Similar Birds

WOOD STORK Black trailing edge to wing (all flight feathers); black tail; dark head and bill; long legs trail beyond tail in flight.

BROWN PELICAN Gray-brown upperparts; dark wings; darker bill; plunge dives for fish while flying.

• **CONSERVATION** Some decrease due to habitat loss and pesticide poisoning; however, has increased since 1970s. Despite legal protection most deaths due to shooting.

Flight Pattern

Strong slow deep wing beats. Soars high on thermals. Flies in straight line or V formation.

Nest Identification

Shape ••• Location ▬

Made of built-up dirt and rubbish • on flat ground • 1–2 dull or chalky white eggs; ovate to elongate-ovate with some nearly elliptical–oval, 3.5 x 2.2 inches.

Plumage Sexes similar	Habitat ～～ ⧗ ⧠	Migration Migratory	Weight 15.4 pounds

DATE _____ TIME_____ LOCATION _____

Family PELECANIDAE	Species *Pelecanus occidentalis*	Length 48–50 inches	Wingspan 78–84 inches

BROWN PELICAN

Louisiana's state bird is the smallest of the world's pelicans. Strictly a marine bird, it almost faced extinction because of pesticides and hydrocarbons that led to the thinning of its eggshells and reproductive failure in many colonies in the 1960s and 1970s. The population is now recovering, although it is still listed as threatened. It is rarely seen inland except around the Salton Sea. The color of its gular pouch varies from red in the West to blackish in the East. Young birds are brownish with a whitish belly.

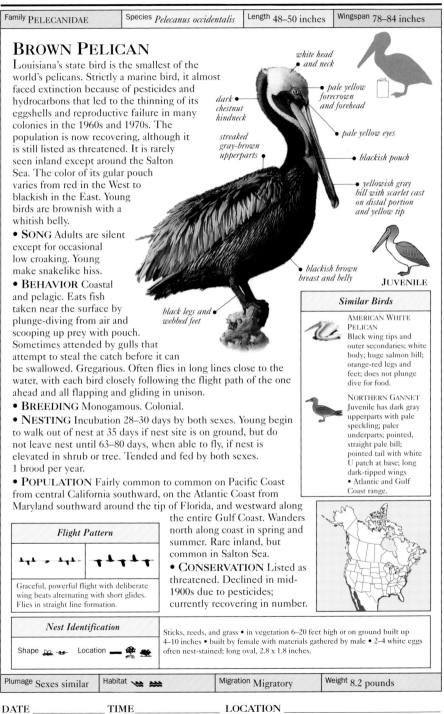

white head and neck

pale yellow forecrown and forehead

dark chestnut hindneck

pale yellow eyes

streaked gray-brown upperparts

blackish pouch

yellowish gray bill with scarlet cast on distal portion and yellow tip

blackish brown breast and belly

JUVENILE

black legs and webbed feet

- **SONG** Adults are silent except for occasional low croaking. Young make snakelike hiss.
- **BEHAVIOR** Coastal and pelagic. Eats fish taken near the surface by plunge-diving from air and scooping up prey with pouch. Sometimes attended by gulls that attempt to steal the catch before it can be swallowed. Gregarious. Often flies in long lines close to the water, with each bird closely following the flight path of the one ahead and all flapping and gliding in unison.
- **BREEDING** Monogamous. Colonial.
- **NESTING** Incubation 28–30 days by both sexes. Young begin to walk out of nest at 35 days if nest site is on ground, but do not leave nest until 63–80 days, when able to fly, if nest is elevated in shrub or tree. Tended and fed by both sexes. 1 brood per year.
- **POPULATION** Fairly common to common on Pacific Coast from central California southward, on the Atlantic Coast from Maryland southward around the tip of Florida, and westward along the entire Gulf Coast. Wanders north along coast in spring and summer. Rare inland, but common in Salton Sea.
- **CONSERVATION** Listed as threatened. Declined in mid-1900s due to pesticides; currently recovering in number.

Similar Birds

AMERICAN WHITE PELICAN
Black wing tips and outer secondaries; white body; huge salmon bill; orange-red legs and feet; does not plunge dive for food.

NORTHERN GANNET
Juvenile has dark gray upperparts with pale speckling; paler underparts; pointed, straight pale bill; pointed tail with white U patch at base; long dark-tipped wings
• Atlantic and Gulf Coast range.

Flight Pattern

Graceful, powerful flight with deliberate wing beats alternating with short glides. Flies in straight line formation.

Nest Identification

Shape ◡◡ ↝   Location ▬ 🌳 🌳

Sticks, reeds, and grass • in vegetation 6–20 feet high or on ground built up 4–10 inches • built by female with materials gathered by male • 2–4 white eggs often nest-stained; long oval, 2.8 x 1.8 inches.

Plumage Sexes similar	Habitat 〰 〰	Migration Migratory	Weight 8.2 pounds

DATE _____ TIME_____ LOCATION _____

Family PHALACROCORACIDAE	Species *Phalacrocorax penicillatus*	Length 35 inches	Wingspan 49 inches

BRANDT'S CORMORANT

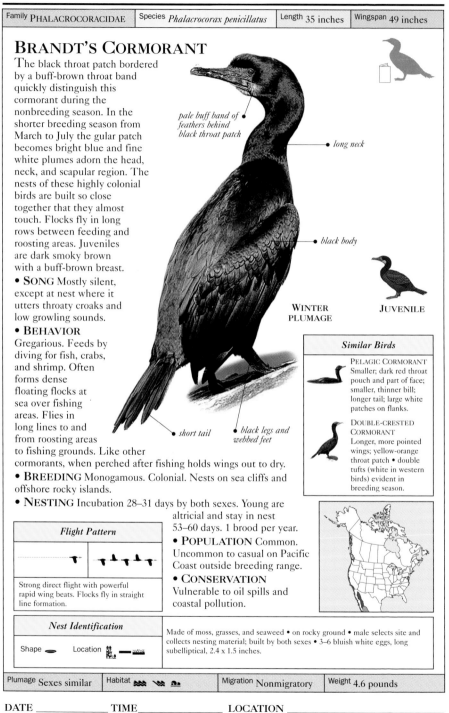

The black throat patch bordered by a buff-brown throat band quickly distinguish this cormorant during the nonbreeding season. In the shorter breeding season from March to July the gular patch becomes bright blue and fine white plumes adorn the head, neck, and scapular region. The nests of these highly colonial birds are built so close together that they almost touch. Flocks fly in long rows between feeding and roosting areas. Juveniles are dark smoky brown with a buff-brown breast.

• **SONG** Mostly silent, except at nest where it utters throaty croaks and low growling sounds.

• **BEHAVIOR** Gregarious. Feeds by diving for fish, crabs, and shrimp. Often forms dense floating flocks at sea over fishing areas. Flies in long lines to and from roosting areas to fishing grounds. Like other cormorants, when perched after fishing holds wings out to dry.

• **BREEDING** Monogamous. Colonial. Nests on sea cliffs and offshore rocky islands.

• **NESTING** Incubation 28–31 days by both sexes. Young are altricial and stay in nest 53–60 days. 1 brood per year.

• **POPULATION** Common. Uncommon to casual on Pacific Coast outside breeding range.

• **CONSERVATION** Vulnerable to oil spills and coastal pollution.

pale buff band of feathers behind black throat patch

long neck

black body

WINTER PLUMAGE

JUVENILE

short tail

black legs and webbed feet

Similar Birds

PELAGIC CORMORANT Smaller; dark red throat pouch and part of face; smaller, thinner bill; longer tail; large white patches on flanks.

DOUBLE-CRESTED CORMORANT Longer, more pointed wings; yellow-orange throat patch • double tufts (white in western birds) evident in breeding season.

Flight Pattern

Strong direct flight with powerful rapid wing beats. Flocks fly in straight line formation.

Nest Identification

Shape ⬧   Location 🪺 ▬ ⬠

Made of moss, grasses, and seaweed • on rocky ground • male selects site and collects nesting material; built by both sexes • 3–6 bluish white eggs, long subelliptical, 2.4 x 1.5 inches.

Plumage Sexes similar	Habitat ≈≈ ≈≈ ♒	Migration Nonmigratory	Weight 4.6 pounds

DATE _____ TIME_____ LOCATION _____

Family PHALACROCORACIDAE	Species *Phalacrocorax brasilianus*	Length 23–29 inches	Wingspan 40 inches

NEOTROPIC CORMORANT

Primarily found along the Mexican border, Neotropic Cormorants can be spotted perched on fence posts or in trees. This small slender cormorant with a long tail frequently holds its neck in an S-shape. The throat pouch is yellow-brown and has a white edge when the bird is breeding. It inhabits freshwater, brackish water, or saltwater. Juveniles are brownish in color.

- **SONG** Low gutteral piglike grunts.
- **BEHAVIOR** With eyes adapted for underwater as well as aerial vision, all cormorants swim well and dive for fish from the surface. Occasionally hunts cooperatively, beating the water with its wings, confusing fish. Also eats amphibians and crustaceans. Often perches upon leaving water and holds wings and tail open in "spread eagle" fashion to dry them. Unlike other North American cormorants, often perches on wires.
- **BREEDING** Monogamous. Colonial.
- **NESTING** Incubation 25–30 days by both sexes. Altricial young fed by both sexes; swim and dive at 8 weeks, feed until 11 weeks, and become independent at 12 weeks. 1 brood per year.

long hooked bill

pointed posterior edge of brownish yellow throat skin reaches behind eye

brownish upperparts scaled black

pointed feathers on back and scapulars

white tufts on the sides of the head in breeding plumage

black overall

long slender body

JUVENILE

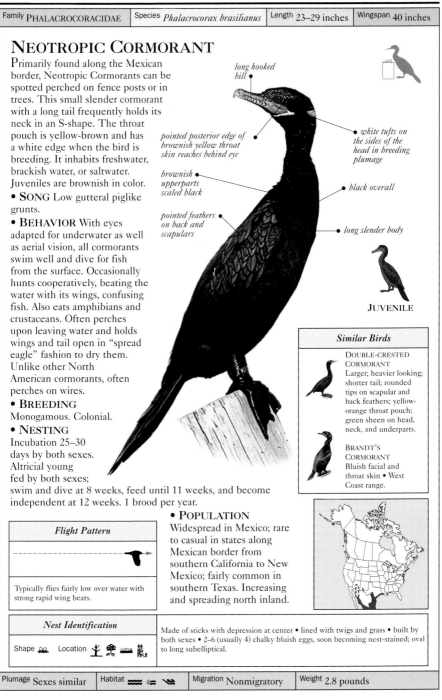

Similar Birds

DOUBLE-CRESTED CORMORANT
Larger; heavier looking; shorter tail; rounded tips on scapular and back feathers; yellow-orange throat pouch; green sheen on head, neck, and underparts.

BRANDT'S CORMORANT
Bluish facial and throat skin • West Coast range.

Flight Pattern

Typically flies fairly low over water with strong rapid wing beats.

- **POPULATION** Widespread in Mexico; rare to casual in states along Mexican border from southern California to New Mexico; fairly common in southern Texas. Increasing and spreading north inland.

Nest Identification

Shape ⌒ Location 🌲 🏛 〰 🎋

Made of sticks with depression at center • lined with twigs and grass • built by both sexes • 2–6 (usually 4) chalky bluish eggs, soon becoming nest-stained; oval to long subelliptical.

Plumage Sexes similar	Habitat 〰 〰 〰	Migration Nonmigratory	Weight 2.8 pounds

DATE _____ TIME_____ LOCATION _____

Family PHALACROCORACIDAE	Species *Phalacrocorax auritus*	Length 32 inches	Wingspan 52 inches

DOUBLE-CRESTED CORMORANT

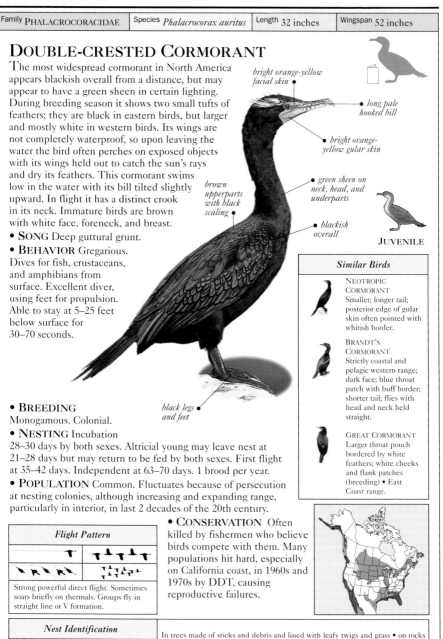

The most widespread cormorant in North America appears blackish overall from a distance, but may appear to have a green sheen in certain lighting. During breeding season it shows two small tufts of feathers; they are black in eastern birds, but larger and mostly white in western birds. Its wings are not completely waterproof, so upon leaving the water the bird often perches on exposed objects with its wings held out to catch the sun's rays and dry its feathers. This cormorant swims low in the water with its bill tilted slightly upward. In flight it has a distinct crook in its neck. Immature birds are brown with white face, foreneck, and breast.

bright orange-yellow facial skin

long pale hooked bill

bright orange-yellow gular skin

brown upperparts with black scaling

green sheen on neck, head, and underparts

blackish overall

JUVENILE

• **SONG** Deep guttural grunt.
• **BEHAVIOR** Gregarious. Dives for fish, crustaceans, and amphibians from surface. Excellent diver, using feet for propulsion. Able to stay at 5–25 feet below surface for 30–70 seconds.

black legs and feet

• **BREEDING** Monogamous. Colonial.
• **NESTING** Incubation 28–30 days by both sexes. Altricial young may leave nest at 21–28 days but may return to be fed by both sexes. First flight at 35–42 days. Independent at 63–70 days. 1 brood per year.
• **POPULATION** Common. Fluctuates because of persecution at nesting colonies, although increasing and expanding range, particularly in interior, in last 2 decades of the 20th century.

• **CONSERVATION** Often killed by fishermen who believe birds compete with them. Many populations hit hard, especially on California coast, in 1960s and 1970s by DDT, causing reproductive failures.

Similar Birds

NEOTROPIC CORMORANT
Smaller; longer tail; posterior edge of gular skin often pointed with whitish border.

BRANDT'S CORMORANT
Strictly coastal and pelagic western range; dark face; blue throat patch with buff border; shorter tail; flies with head and neck held straight.

GREAT CORMORANT
Larger throat pouch bordered by white feathers; white cheeks and flank patches (breeding) • East Coast range.

Flight Pattern

Strong powerful direct flight. Sometimes soars briefly on thermals. Groups fly in straight line or V formation.

Nest Identification

Shape   Location

In trees made of sticks and debris and lined with leafy twigs and grass • on rocks often made of seaweed and trash gathered at water's edge • near water • built by female • 2 nest-stained bluish white eggs; long subelliptical, 2.4 x 1.5 inches.

Plumage Sexes similar	Habitat	Migration Migratory	Weight 4.0 pounds

DATE _____ TIME_____ LOCATION _____

Family PHALACROCORACIDAE	Species *Phalacrocorax urile*	Length 29–34 inches	Wingspan 46–48 inches

RED-FACED CORMORANT

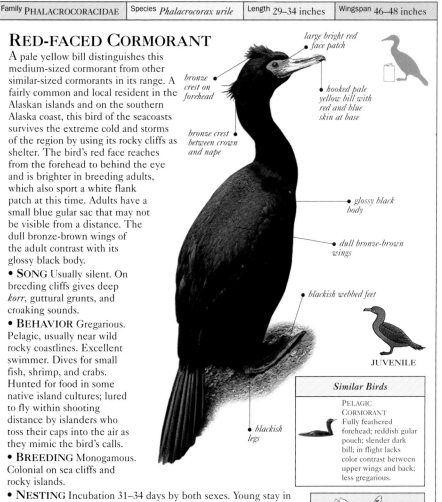

large bright red
face patch

bronze
crest on
forehead

hooked pale
yellow bill with
red and blue
skin at base

bronze crest
between crown
and nape

glossy black
body

dull bronze-brown
wings

blackish webbed feet

JUVENILE

blackish
legs

A pale yellow bill distinguishes this medium-sized cormorant from other similar-sized cormorants in its range. A fairly common and local resident in the Alaskan islands and on the southern Alaska coast, this bird of the seacoasts survives the extreme cold and storms of the region by using its rocky cliffs as shelter. The bird's red face reaches from the forehead to behind the eye and is brighter in breeding adults, which also sport a white flank patch at this time. Adults have a small blue gular sac that may not be visible from a distance. The dull bronze-brown wings of the adult contrast with its glossy black body.

• **SONG** Usually silent. On breeding cliffs gives deep *korr*, guttural grunts, and croaking sounds.

• **BEHAVIOR** Gregarious. Pelagic, usually near wild rocky coastlines. Excellent swimmer. Dives for small fish, shrimp, and crabs. Hunted for food in some native island cultures; lured to fly within shooting distance by islanders who toss their caps into the air as they mimic the bird's calls.

• **BREEDING** Monogamous. Colonial on sea cliffs and rocky islands.

• **NESTING** Incubation 31–34 days by both sexes. Young stay in nest 50–60 days, fed by both sexes. 1 brood per year.

• **POPULATION** Rare to locally common. Found only on Alaskan waters in North America. Population expanding in Aleutian Islands.

Similar Birds

PELAGIC
CORMORANT
Fully feathered
forehead; reddish gular
pouch; slender dark
bill; in flight lacks
color contrast between
upper wings and back;
less gregarious.

Flight Pattern

Strong powerful direct flight. Flies in straight line formation.

Nest Identification

Shape   Location

Made of seaweed, algae, grasses, and moss • on bare ground on ridge, ledge, or shelf of cliff • built by both sexes • 3–4 pale blue eggs, often nest-stained; long oval, 2.4 inches long.

Plumage Sexes similar	Habitat	Migration Nonmigratory	Weight 5.6 pounds

DATE _____ TIME_____ LOCATION _____

Family PHALACROCORACIDAE	Species *Phalacrocorax pelagicus*	Length 26–29 inches	Wingspan 40 inches

PELAGIC CORMORANT

The distinctive white patches on its flanks and short double crest during breeding season distinguish the Pelagic Cormorant from other Pacific Coast cormorants except for the Red-faced Cormorant in Alaska. Its small size and short neck are good additional field marks, and no other cormorant in its range has a slender black bill. Near the base of the bill is a blackish area of bare skin and reddish throat pouch. Slender white streaks appear on the bird's neck only when it is breeding. Juveniles are dark sooty brown.

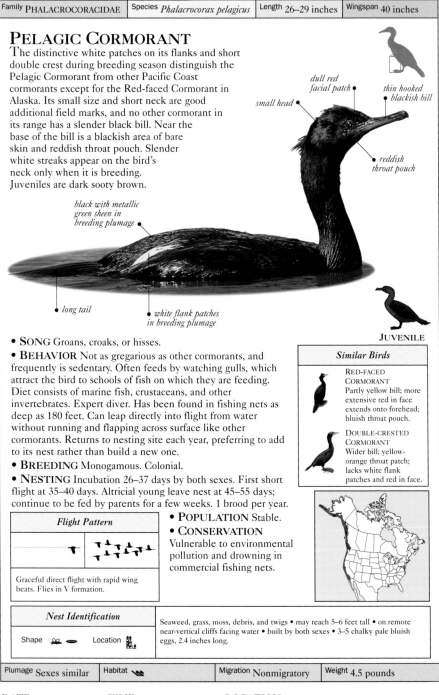

dull red facial patch

small head

thin hooked blackish bill

reddish throat pouch

black with metallic green sheen in breeding plumage

long tail

white flank patches in breeding plumage

JUVENILE

- **SONG** Groans, croaks, or hisses.
- **BEHAVIOR** Not as gregarious as other cormorants, and frequently is sedentary. Often feeds by watching gulls, which attract the bird to schools of fish on which they are feeding. Diet consists of marine fish, crustaceans, and other invertebrates. Expert diver. Has been found in fishing nets as deep as 180 feet. Can leap directly into flight from water without running and flapping across surface like other cormorants. Returns to nesting site each year, preferring to add to its nest rather than build a new one.
- **BREEDING** Monogamous. Colonial.
- **NESTING** Incubation 26–37 days by both sexes. First short flight at 35–40 days. Altricial young leave nest at 45–55 days; continue to be fed by parents for a few weeks. 1 brood per year.
- **POPULATION** Stable.
- **CONSERVATION** Vulnerable to environmental pollution and drowning in commercial fishing nets.

Similar Birds

RED-FACED CORMORANT Partly yellow bill; more extensive red in face; bluish throat pouch.

DOUBLE-CRESTED CORMORANT Wider bill; yellow-orange throat patch; lacks white flank patches and red in face.

Flight Pattern

Graceful direct flight with rapid wing beats. Flies in V formation.

Nest Identification

Shape

Location

Seaweed, grass, moss, debris, and twigs • may reach 5–6 feet tall • on remote near-vertical cliffs facing water • built by both sexes • 3–5 chalky pale bluish eggs, 2.4 inches long.

Plumage Sexes similar	Habitat	Migration Nonmigratory	Weight 4.5 pounds

DATE _____ TIME_____ LOCATION _____

Family ANHINGIDAE	Species *Anhinga anhinga*	Length 35 inches	Wingspan 45–48 inches

ANHINGA

Although clumsy on perches and slow on the ground, the Anhinga is a graceful flier capable of soaring to great heights. It's also called the snakebird because of its long thin neck and small narrow head, which appears serpentine when this bird swims with its body submerged to the neck. Water turkey, its other common name, comes from the long buff-tipped tail.

• SONG Mostly silent. Low grunt similar to that of the cormorant. When quarreling makes distinct rapid clicking sound, *guk-guk-guk-guk-guk*.

• BEHAVIOR Swims underwater and uses sharply pointed bill to spear fish. Eats small to

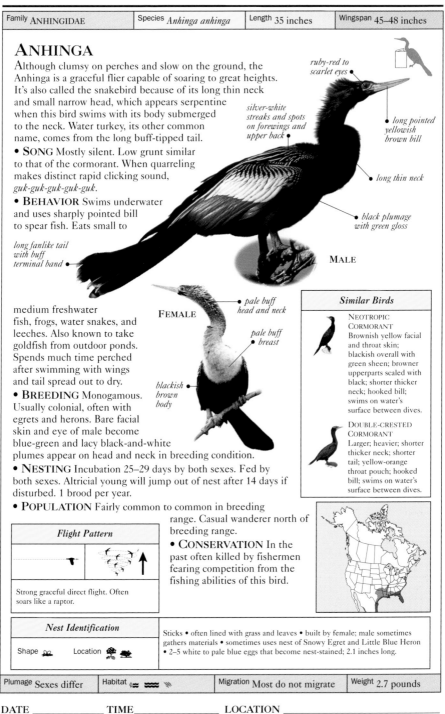

ruby-red to scarlet eyes

silver-white streaks and spots on forewings and upper back

long pointed yellowish brown bill

long thin neck

black plumage with green gloss

long fanlike tail with buff terminal band

MALE

medium freshwater fish, frogs, water snakes, and leeches. Also known to take goldfish from outdoor ponds. Spends much time perched after swimming with wings and tail spread out to dry.

FEMALE

pale buff head and neck

pale buff breast

blackish brown body

• BREEDING Monogamous. Usually colonial, often with egrets and herons. Bare facial skin and eye of male become blue-green and lacy black-and-white plumes appear on head and neck in breeding condition.

• NESTING Incubation 25–29 days by both sexes. Fed by both sexes. Altricial young will jump out of nest after 14 days if disturbed. 1 brood per year.

• POPULATION Fairly common to common in breeding range. Casual wanderer north of breeding range.

• CONSERVATION In the past often killed by fishermen fearing competition from the fishing abilities of this bird.

Similar Birds

NEOTROPIC CORMORANT
Brownish yellow facial and throat skin; blackish overall with green sheen; browner upperparts scaled with black; shorter thicker neck; hooked bill; swims on water's surface between dives.

DOUBLE-CRESTED CORMORANT
Larger; heavier; shorter thicker neck; shorter tail; yellow-orange throat pouch; hooked bill; swims on water's surface between dives.

Flight Pattern

Strong graceful direct flight. Often soars like a raptor.

Nest Identification

Shape   Location

Sticks • often lined with grass and leaves • built by female; male sometimes gathers materials • sometimes uses nest of Snowy Egret and Little Blue Heron • 2–5 white to pale blue eggs that become nest-stained; 2.1 inches long.

Plumage Sexes differ	Habitat	Migration Most do not migrate	Weight 2.7 pounds

DATE _____ TIME_____ LOCATION _____

Family FREGATIDAE	Species *Fregata magnificens*	Length 37–41 inches	Wingspan 82–94 inches

MAGNIFICENT FRIGATEBIRD

The male has a most striking courtship display when he inflates his throat sac into a huge brilliant red balloon. In flight it looks almost sinister with its black plumage, long thin crooked wings, and deeply forked tail often folded into a point. Juveniles are black without gloss and have a white head, neck, sides, breast, and belly. Even when not nesting, flocks of these birds often gather at their permanent roosts in treetops, or on high cliffs.

straight hooked gray bill

entirely black with purple gloss on head and back

bright red pouch usually shows as red patch on throat when not distended

MALE

JUVENILE

- **SONG** Clacks bill; nasal *kack* or *ka-ack*; soft chippering at nesting grounds. Silent at sea.
- **BEHAVIOR** Soars over sea to find food. Dives for prey and catches it in bill from surface. Eats fish, crustaceans, and jellyfish. Attacks other large seabirds in flight until they drop or disgorge their catch, which the frigatebird then catches in midair. Roosts communally and is gregarious.
- **BREEDING** Monogamous. Colonial.
- **NESTING** Incubation 40–50 days by both sexes. Fed by both sexes. First flight at 20–24 weeks. Young never left unguarded because other birds in colony may eat eggs and hatchlings. Most females do not breed every year.
- **POPULATION** Total difficult to monitor. Rare to casual on Salton Sea and along California coast to Washington. Breeds on Dry Tortugas off Florida Keys. Fairly common to casual along Gulf of Mexico, Florida coasts, and north to North Carolina. Rare straggler north to Maritimes and inland, especially after storms.

straight hooked gray bill

white breast and sides

FEMALE

black without gloss

long, narrow pointed wings

long deeply forked tail

Similar Birds

GREAT FRIGATEBIRD ♂
Male has pale brownish alar bar; scalloped pale grayish axillars; green gloss on head and back • female has gray-white throat, breast, and upper belly; red orbital ring; broader black belly patch • juvenile has white head, neck, and breast; neck and head tinged with rust-brown.

- **CONSERVATION** Frigatebirds are legally protected, but they are still killed in the nest by local people, who hunt at night with flashlights and clubs. Some years no young survive.

Flight Pattern

Very high effortless soaring flight. Extremely graceful and buoyant in the air.

Nest Identification

Shape   Location

Made of sticks, twigs, grass, and reeds • in mangroves, trees, or bushes, 2–20 feet above ground • built by female with materials gathered by male, who often steals from neighbors' nests • 1 white egg; rarely 2.

Plumage Sexes differ	Habitat	Migration Nonmigratory	Weight 2.8 pounds

DATE _____ TIME_____ LOCATION _____

Family ARDEIDAE	Species *Botaurus lentiginosus*	Length 23 inches	Wingspan 42–50 inches

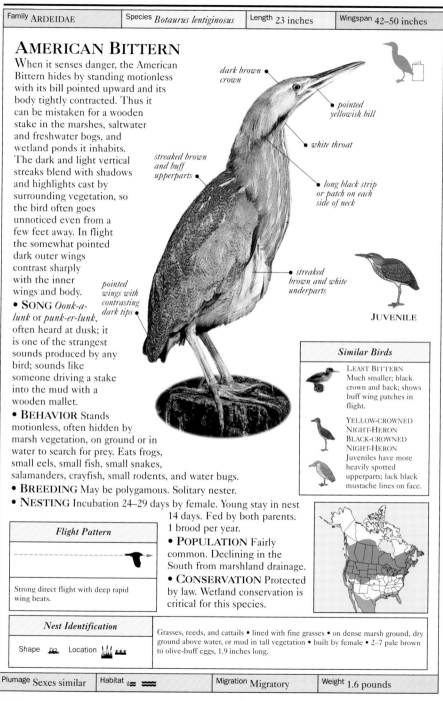

AMERICAN BITTERN

When it senses danger, the American Bittern hides by standing motionless with its bill pointed upward and its body tightly contracted. Thus it can be mistaken for a wooden stake in the marshes, saltwater and freshwater bogs, and wetland ponds it inhabits. The dark and light vertical streaks blend with shadows and highlights cast by surrounding vegetation, so the bird often goes unnoticed even from a few feet away. In flight the somewhat pointed dark outer wings contrast sharply with the inner wings and body.

dark brown crown

pointed yellowish bill

white throat

streaked brown and buff upperparts

long black strip or patch on each side of neck

pointed wings with contrasting dark tips

streaked brown and white underparts

JUVENILE

• **SONG** *Oonk-a-lunk* or *punk-er-lunk*, often heard at dusk; it is one of the strangest sounds produced by any bird; sounds like someone driving a stake into the mud with a wooden mallet.

• **BEHAVIOR** Stands motionless, often hidden by marsh vegetation, on ground or in water to search for prey. Eats frogs, small eels, small fish, small snakes, salamanders, crayfish, small rodents, and water bugs.

• **BREEDING** May be polygamous. Solitary nester.

• **NESTING** Incubation 24–29 days by female. Young stay in nest 14 days. Fed by both parents. 1 brood per year.

• **POPULATION** Fairly common. Declining in the South from marshland drainage.

• **CONSERVATION** Protected by law. Wetland conservation is critical for this species.

Similar Birds

LEAST BITTERN Much smaller; black crown and back; shows buff wing patches in flight.

YELLOW-CROWNED NIGHT-HERON BLACK-CROWNED NIGHT-HERON Juveniles have more heavily spotted upperparts; lack black mustache lines on face.

Flight Pattern

Strong direct flight with deep rapid wing beats.

Nest Identification

Shape ⚬⚬ Location 🌿🌿🌿

Grasses, reeds, and cattails • lined with fine grasses • on dense marsh ground, dry ground above water, or mud in tall vegetation • built by female • 2–7 pale brown to olive-buff eggs, 1.9 inches long.

Plumage Sexes similar	Habitat 〜 〜	Migration Migratory	Weight 1.6 pounds

DATE _____ TIME_____ LOCATION _____

Family ARDEIDAE	Species *Ixobrychus exilis*	Length 11–14 inches	Wingspan 16–18 inches

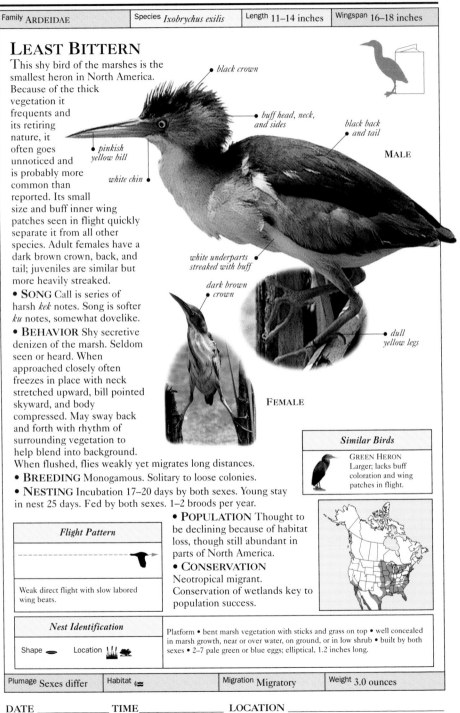

LEAST BITTERN

This shy bird of the marshes is the smallest heron in North America. Because of the thick vegetation it frequents and its retiring nature, it often goes unnoticed and is probably more common than reported. Its small size and buff inner wing patches seen in flight quickly separate it from all other species. Adult females have a dark brown crown, back, and tail; juveniles are similar but more heavily streaked.

- **SONG** Call is series of harsh *kek* notes. Song is softer *ku* notes, somewhat dovelike.
- **BEHAVIOR** Shy secretive denizen of the marsh. Seldom seen or heard. When approached closely often freezes in place with neck stretched upward, bill pointed skyward, and body compressed. May sway back and forth with rhythm of surrounding vegetation to help blend into background. When flushed, flies weakly yet migrates long distances.
- **BREEDING** Monogamous. Solitary to loose colonies.
- **NESTING** Incubation 17–20 days by both sexes. Young stay in nest 25 days. Fed by both sexes. 1–2 broods per year.
- **POPULATION** Thought to be declining because of habitat loss, though still abundant in parts of North America.
- **CONSERVATION** Neotropical migrant. Conservation of wetlands key to population success.

black crown

buff head, neck, and sides

black back and tail

MALE

pinkish yellow bill

white chin

white underparts streaked with buff

dark brown crown

dull yellow legs

FEMALE

Similar Birds

GREEN HERON Larger; lacks buff coloration and wing patches in flight.

Flight Pattern

Weak direct flight with slow labored wing beats.

Nest Identification

Shape 〜 Location 🌾🐢

Platform • bent marsh vegetation with sticks and grass on top • well concealed in marsh growth, near or over water, on ground, or in low shrub • built by both sexes • 2–7 pale green or blue eggs; elliptical, 1.2 inches long.

Plumage Sexes differ	Habitat 🌾	Migration Migratory	Weight 3.0 ounces

DATE _____ TIME_____ LOCATION _____

| Family ARDEIDAE | Species *Ardea herodias* | Length 46–52 inches | Wingspan 77–82 inches |

GREAT BLUE HERON

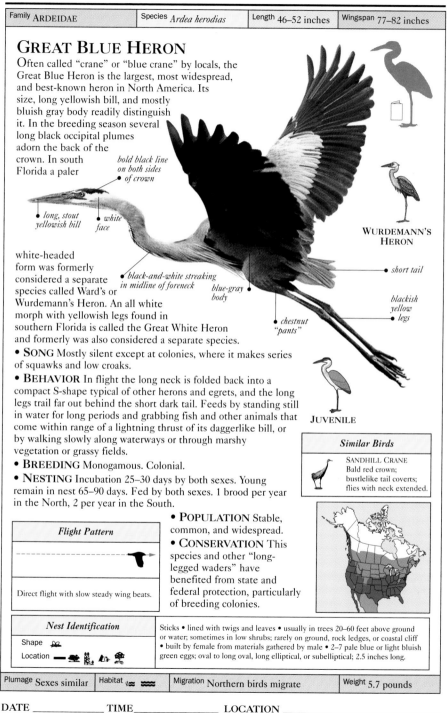

Often called "crane" or "blue crane" by locals, the Great Blue Heron is the largest, most widespread, and best-known heron in North America. Its size, long yellowish bill, and mostly bluish gray body readily distinguish it. In the breeding season several long black occipital plumes adorn the back of the crown. In south Florida a paler

bold black line on both sides of crown

long, stout yellowish bill

white face

white-headed form was formerly considered a separate species called Ward's or Wurdemann's Heron. An all white morph with yellowish legs found in southern Florida is called the Great White Heron and formerly was also considered a separate species.

black-and-white streaking in midline of foreneck

blue-gray body

chestnut "pants"

WURDEMANN'S HERON

short tail

blackish yellow legs

• **SONG** Mostly silent except at colonies, where it makes series of squawks and low croaks.

• **BEHAVIOR** In flight the long neck is folded back into a compact S-shape typical of other herons and egrets, and the long legs trail far out behind the short dark tail. Feeds by standing still in water for long periods and grabbing fish and other animals that come within range of a lightning thrust of its daggerlike bill, or by walking slowly along waterways or through marshy vegetation or grassy fields.

JUVENILE

• **BREEDING** Monogamous. Colonial.

• **NESTING** Incubation 25–30 days by both sexes. Young remain in nest 65–90 days. Fed by both sexes. 1 brood per year in the North, 2 per year in the South.

Similar Birds
SANDHILL CRANE Bald red crown; bustlelike tail coverts; flies with neck extended.

• **POPULATION** Stable, common, and widespread.

• **CONSERVATION** This species and other "long-legged waders" have benefited from state and federal protection, particularly of breeding colonies.

Flight Pattern
Direct flight with slow steady wing beats.

Nest Identification	
Shape	Sticks • lined with twigs and leaves • usually in trees 20–60 feet above ground or water; sometimes in low shrubs; rarely on ground, rock ledges, or coastal cliff • built by female from materials gathered by male • 2–7 pale blue or light bluish green eggs; oval to long oval, long elliptical, or subelliptical; 2.5 inches long.
Location	

| Plumage Sexes similar | Habitat | Migration Northern birds migrate | Weight 5.7 pounds |

Family ARDEIDAE	Species *Ardea alba*	Length 37–41 inches	Wingspan 55 inches

GREAT EGRET

The largest white egret found over most of its range can be distinguished from other white egrets and juvenile herons by its size, yellow bill, and black legs and feet. This tall, slender-necked bird develops long trains of lacy plumes on its back that extend beyond the tail when breeding, and its yellow bill appears more orange in color.

- **SONG** Bold throaty croaking or repeated *cuk, cuk*.
- **BEHAVIOR** Prefers to feed in open areas from salt marshes to freshwater habitats.

black legs and feet

yellow bill

white plumage

Diurnal in its activities, it flies singly or in groups to communal roosts in trees for the night. Feeds on wide variety of small aquatic animals and animals found in wetland environs, from fish to frogs, snakes, crayfish, and large insects.

- **BREEDING** Monogamous. Colonial, usually with other species of herons, egrets, ibis, and other similar species.
- **NESTING** Incubation 23–26 days by both sexes. Young stay in nest 21 days. Fed by both sexes. 1 brood per year.
- **POPULATION** Decimated by plume hunters in late 1800s. Protected since early 20th century. In recent decades breeding range has expanded northward.
- **CONSERVATION** With full protection in North America, species is increasing. Still, factors such as polluted waters, coastal development, and draining of wetlands negatively impact egrets.

Similar Birds

GREAT BLUE HERON Wurdemann's Heron (morph) larger with yellowish legs and feet.

SNOWY EGRET Smaller; dark bill.

REDDISH EGRET White morph smaller with dark bill.

LITTLE BLUE HERON Juvenile smaller with dark bill.

CATTLE EGRET Much smaller; yellow legs and feet.

Flight Pattern

Buoyant direct flight with deep steady wing beats.

Nest Identification

Shape   Location

Made of sticks • unlined or lined with fine material • in tree or shrub, usually 10–40 feet above ground • built by both sexes • 1–6 pale blue-green or light blue eggs, 2.2 inches long.

Plumage Sexes similar	Habitat	Migration Some migrate	Weight 2.0 pounds

DATE _____ TIME_____ LOCATION _____

Family ARDEIDAE	Species *Egretta thula*	Length 22–27 inches	Wingspan 38–45 inches

SNOWY EGRET

This is perhaps the most beautiful of all North American egrets and herons in its nuptial plumage, and the daintiest with or without it. This energetic medium-sized white egret has black legs and bright yellow "slippers." Slaughtered by the thousands for its soft, lacy breeding finery, it was the most persecuted of all egrets by plume hunters in the late 19th and early 20th century.

• **SONG** Generally silent. Vocalizations are harsh squawks.

• **BEHAVIOR** Most active heron when feeding. Rushes after prey in manner of Reddish Egret. Often sticks one foot forward in water and rapidly vibrates it to startle prey. Crustaceans, insects, and fish are important components of diet.

• **BREEDING** Monogamous. Colonial, often nests in mixed colonies with other herons and egrets.

• **NESTING** Incubation 20–24 days by both sexes. Young stay in nest 30 days. Fed by both sexes. 1 brood per year.

• **POPULATION** Increasing. Range expanding northward.

yellow eyes

long, slender black bill

yellow lores

white plumage

WINTER PLUMAGE

Similar Birds

CATTLE EGRET
Stockier; shorter neck; yellow bill and legs.

GREAT EGRET
Much larger; yellow bill; black feet.

LITTLE BLUE HERON
Juvenile has greenish legs; gray bill with black tip.

bright yellow feet

black legs

Flight Pattern

Buoyant flight with steady fast wing beats.

• **CONSERVATION**
Seemingly thriving today, but almost extirpated in the early 20th century by demand for its "cross aigrettes" for ladies' fashions.

Nest Identification

Shape   Location

Made of sticks • lined with fine twigs and rushes • in short tree or shrub, 5–10 feet high • sometimes on ground • built by both sexes • 2–6 pale blue-green eggs, 1.7 inches long.

Plumage Sexes similar	Habitat	Migration Migratory	Weight 13.1 ounces

DATE _____ TIME_____ LOCATION _____

Family ARDEIDAE	Species *Egretta caerulea*	Length 24–29 inches	Wingspan 40–41 inches

LITTLE BLUE HERON

Adults appear entirely dark at a distance, but at closer range they are slate-colored with a purplish maroon head and neck. This is the only dark heron species in North America in which the juvenile is white. The juvenile begins molting into adult plumage in its first spring and gradually acquires more blue-gray feathers, achieving a calico appearance in the transition from white to slate gray.

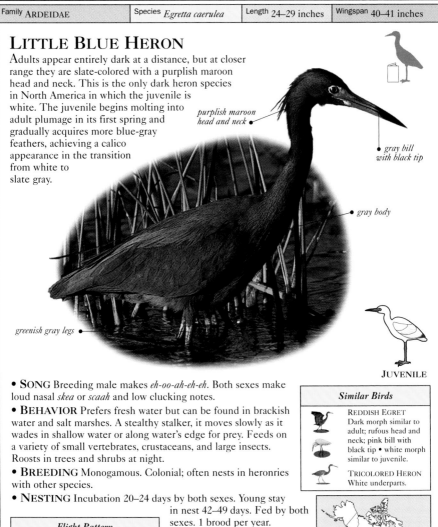

purplish maroon head and neck

gray bill with black tip

gray body

greenish gray legs

JUVENILE

- **SONG** Breeding male makes *eh-oo-ah-eh-eh*. Both sexes make loud nasal *skea* or *scaah* and low clucking notes.
- **BEHAVIOR** Prefers fresh water but can be found in brackish water and salt marshes. A stealthy stalker, it moves slowly as it wades in shallow water or along water's edge for prey. Feeds on a variety of small vertebrates, crustaceans, and large insects. Roosts in trees and shrubs at night.
- **BREEDING** Monogamous. Colonial; often nests in heronries with other species.
- **NESTING** Incubation 20–24 days by both sexes. Young stay in nest 42–49 days. Fed by both sexes. 1 brood per year.
- **POPULATION** Increasing and expanding.
- **CONSERVATION** Responding to protection of nesting colonies.

Similar Birds

REDDISH EGRET Dark morph similar to adult; rufous head and neck; pink bill with black tip • white morph similar to juvenile.

TRICOLORED HERON White underparts.

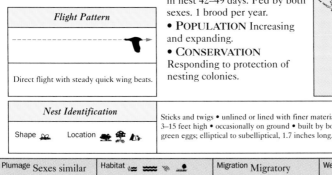

Flight Pattern

Direct flight with steady quick wing beats.

Nest Identification

Shape   Location

Sticks and twigs • unlined or lined with finer material • usually in tree or shrub, 3–15 feet high • occasionally on ground • built by both sexes • 1–6 pale blue-green eggs; elliptical to subelliptical, 1.7 inches long.

Plumage Sexes similar	Habitat	Migration Migratory	Weight 12.9 ounces

DATE _____ TIME_____ LOCATION _____

Family ARDEIDAE	Species *Egretta tricolor*	Length 24–26 inches	Wingspan 36 inches

TRICOLORED HERON

Our only large dark heron with white underparts can be found in salty coastal marshes to inland freshwater. Its long, slender neck and long, thin bill make it seem larger and skinnier than other medium-sized herons. *Tricolored* refers to the dark upperparts, white underparts, and reddish brown stripes on the foreneck. In breeding plumage there are white plumes on the back of the crown and shaggy purplish or tan feathers on the lower neck, crown, and back.

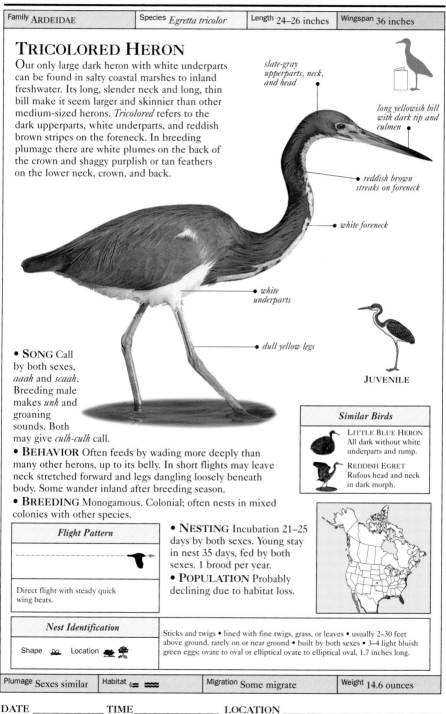

slate-gray upperparts, neck, and head

long yellowish bill with dark tip and culmen

reddish brown streaks on foreneck

white foreneck

white underparts

dull yellow legs

JUVENILE

• **SONG** Call by both sexes, *aaah* and *scaah*. Breeding male makes *unh* and groaning sounds. Both may give *culh-culh* call.

• **BEHAVIOR** Often feeds by wading more deeply than many other herons, up to its belly. In short flights may leave neck stretched forward and legs dangling loosely beneath body. Some wander inland after breeding season.

• **BREEDING** Monogamous. Colonial; often nests in mixed colonies with other species.

Similar Birds

LITTLE BLUE HERON
All dark without white underparts and rump.

REDDISH EGRET
Rufous head and neck in dark morph.

• **NESTING** Incubation 21–25 days by both sexes. Young stay in nest 35 days, fed by both sexes. 1 brood per year.

• **POPULATION** Probably declining due to habitat loss.

Flight Pattern

Direct flight with steady quick wing beats.

Nest Identification

Shape   Location

Sticks and twigs • lined with fine twigs, grass, or leaves • usually 2–30 feet above ground, rarely on or near ground • built by both sexes • 3–4 light bluish green eggs; ovate to oval or elliptical ovate to elliptical oval, 1.7 inches long.

Plumage Sexes similar	Habitat	Migration Some migrate	Weight 14.6 ounces

DATE _____ TIME_____ LOCATION _____

Family ARDEIDAE	Species *Bubulcus ibis*	Length 19–21 inches	Wingspan 36–38 inches

CATTLE EGRET

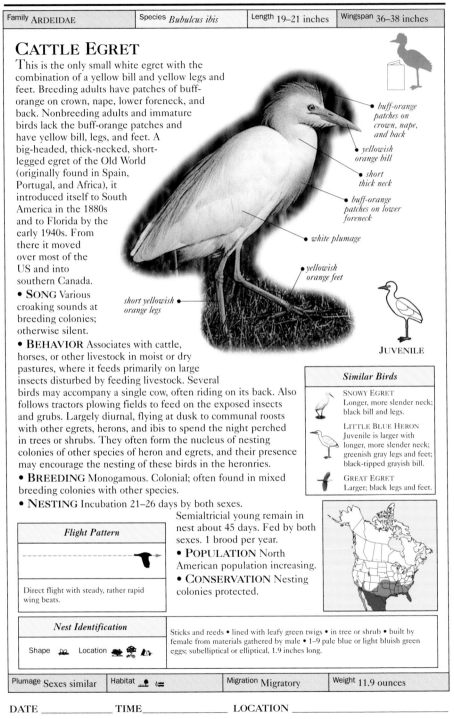

This is the only small white egret with the combination of a yellow bill and yellow legs and feet. Breeding adults have patches of buff-orange on crown, nape, lower foreneck, and back. Nonbreeding adults and immature birds lack the buff-orange patches and have yellow bill, legs, and feet. A big-headed, thick-necked, short-legged egret of the Old World (originally found in Spain, Portugal, and Africa), it introduced itself to South America in the 1880s and to Florida by the early 1940s. From there it moved over most of the US and into southern Canada.

• **buff-orange patches on crown, nape, and back**

• **yellowish orange bill**

• **short thick neck**

• **buff-orange patches on lower foreneck**

• **white plumage**

• **yellowish orange feet**

short yellowish orange legs •

• **SONG** Various croaking sounds at breeding colonies; otherwise silent.

JUVENILE

• **BEHAVIOR** Associates with cattle, horses, or other livestock in moist or dry pastures, where it feeds primarily on large insects disturbed by feeding livestock. Several birds may accompany a single cow, often riding on its back. Also follows tractors plowing fields to feed on the exposed insects and grubs. Largely diurnal, flying at dusk to communal roosts with other egrets, herons, and ibis to spend the night perched in trees or shrubs. They often form the nucleus of nesting colonies of other species of heron and egrets, and their presence may encourage the nesting of these birds in the heronries.

• **BREEDING** Monogamous. Colonial; often found in mixed breeding colonies with other species.

• **NESTING** Incubation 21–26 days by both sexes. Semialtricial young remain in nest about 45 days. Fed by both sexes. 1 brood per year.

• **POPULATION** North American population increasing.

• **CONSERVATION** Nesting colonies protected.

Similar Birds

SNOWY EGRET Longer, more slender neck; black bill and legs.

LITTLE BLUE HERON Juvenile is larger with longer, more slender neck; greenish gray legs and feet; black-tipped grayish bill.

GREAT EGRET Larger; black legs and feet.

Flight Pattern

Direct flight with steady, rather rapid wing beats.

Nest Identification

Shape ☙ Location 🌳 🌲 ⛰

Sticks and reeds • lined with leafy green twigs • in tree or shrub • built by female from materials gathered by male • 1–9 pale blue or light bluish green eggs; subelliptical or elliptical, 1.9 inches long.

Plumage Sexes similar	Habitat 🏞 〰	Migration Migratory	Weight 11.9 ounces

DATE _____ TIME_____ LOCATION _____

Family ARDEIDAE	Species *Butorides virescens*	Length 18–22 inches	Wingspan 26 inches

GREEN HERON

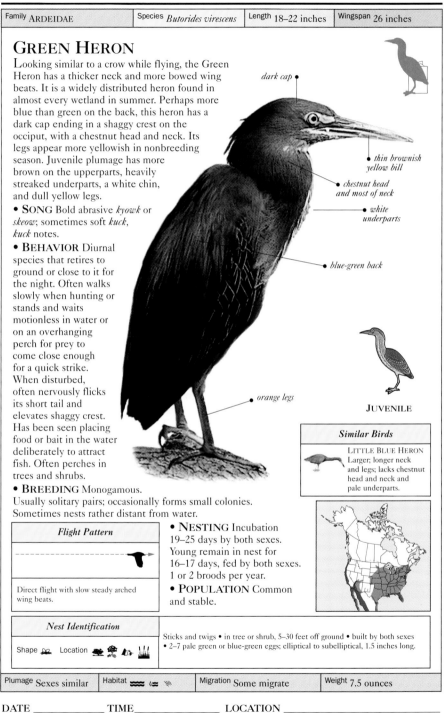

Looking similar to a crow while flying, the Green Heron has a thicker neck and more bowed wing beats. It is a widely distributed heron found in almost every wetland in summer. Perhaps more blue than green on the back, this heron has a dark cap ending in a shaggy crest on the occiput, with a chestnut head and neck. Its legs appear more yellowish in nonbreeding season. Juvenile plumage has more brown on the upperparts, heavily streaked underparts, a white chin, and dull yellow legs.

- **SONG** Bold abrasive *kyowk* or *skeow*; sometimes soft *kuck*, *kuck* notes.
- **BEHAVIOR** Diurnal species that retires to ground or close to it for the night. Often walks slowly when hunting or stands and waits motionless in water or on an overhanging perch for prey to come close enough for a quick strike. When disturbed, often nervously flicks its short tail and elevates shaggy crest. Has been seen placing food or bait in the water deliberately to attract fish. Often perches in trees and shrubs.
- **BREEDING** Monogamous. Usually solitary pairs; occasionally forms small colonies. Sometimes nests rather distant from water.

dark cap

thin brownish yellow bill

chestnut head and most of neck

white underparts

blue-green back

orange legs

JUVENILE

Similar Birds

LITTLE BLUE HERON Larger; longer neck and legs; lacks chestnut head and neck and pale underparts.

Flight Pattern

Direct flight with slow steady arched wing beats.

- **NESTING** Incubation 19–25 days by both sexes. Young remain in nest for 16–17 days, fed by both sexes. 1 or 2 broods per year.
- **POPULATION** Common and stable.

Nest Identification

Shape ☌ 〰 Location 🪹 🏠 🔺 🌾

Sticks and twigs • in tree or shrub, 5–30 feet off ground • built by both sexes • 2–7 pale green or blue-green eggs; elliptical to subelliptical, 1.5 inches long.

Plumage Sexes similar	Habitat 〰 〰 〰	Migration Some migrate	Weight 7.5 ounces

DATE _____ TIME_____ LOCATION _____

Family ARDEIDAE	Species *Nycticorax nycticorax*	Length 25–28 inches	Wingspan 44–45 inches

BLACK-CROWNED NIGHT-HERON

The scientific name of this bird means "Night Raven," and it refers to the nature of the bird, as does the common name of Night-Heron. A stocky bird with short legs and a thick, short neck, it prowls freshwater pools, marshes, and streams and coastal estuaries across much of North America. In flight the toes often protrude beyond the short tail. Juvenile plumage shows brown above with white spots and streaking, buff-brown below with dark brown spots and streaking. Juveniles have a yellowish bill with a dark tip and greenish yellow legs and feet.

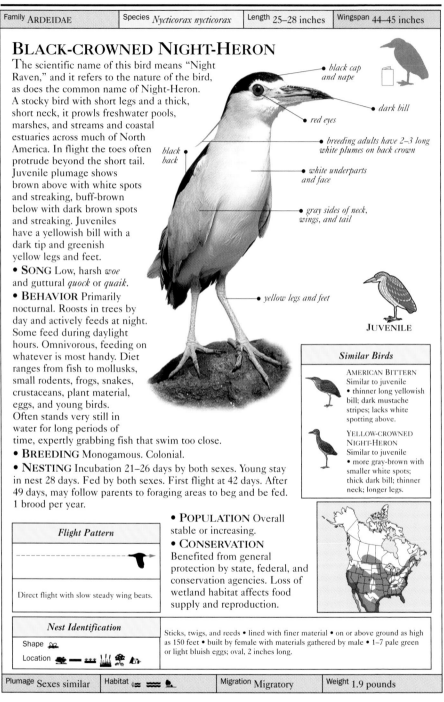

black cap and nape

dark bill

red eyes

breeding adults have 2–3 long white plumes on back crown

black back

white underparts and face

gray sides of neck, wings, and tail

yellow legs and feet

JUVENILE

- **SONG** Low, harsh *woe* and guttural *quock* or *quaik*.
- **BEHAVIOR** Primarily nocturnal. Roosts in trees by day and actively feeds at night. Some feed during daylight hours. Omnivorous, feeding on whatever is most handy. Diet ranges from fish to mollusks, small rodents, frogs, snakes, crustaceans, plant material, eggs, and young birds. Often stands very still in water for long periods of time, expertly grabbing fish that swim too close.
- **BREEDING** Monogamous. Colonial.
- **NESTING** Incubation 21–26 days by both sexes. Young stay in nest 28 days. Fed by both sexes. First flight at 42 days. After 49 days, may follow parents to foraging areas to beg and be fed. 1 brood per year.

Similar Birds

AMERICAN BITTERN
Similar to juvenile
• thinner long yellowish bill; dark mustache stripes; lacks white spotting above.

YELLOW-CROWNED NIGHT-HERON
Similar to juvenile
• more gray-brown with smaller white spots; thick dark bill; thinner neck; longer legs.

- **POPULATION** Overall stable or increasing.
- **CONSERVATION** Benefited from general protection by state, federal, and conservation agencies. Loss of wetland habitat affects food supply and reproduction.

Flight Pattern

Direct flight with slow steady wing beats.

Nest Identification

Shape

Location

Sticks, twigs, and reeds • lined with finer material • on or above ground as high as 150 feet • built by female with materials gathered by male • 1–7 pale green or light bluish eggs; oval, 2 inches long.

Plumage Sexes similar	Habitat	Migration Migratory	Weight 1.9 pounds

DATE _____ TIME_____ LOCATION _____

Family THRESKIORNITHIDAE	Species *Eudocimus albus*	Length 21–27 inches	Wingspan 38 inches

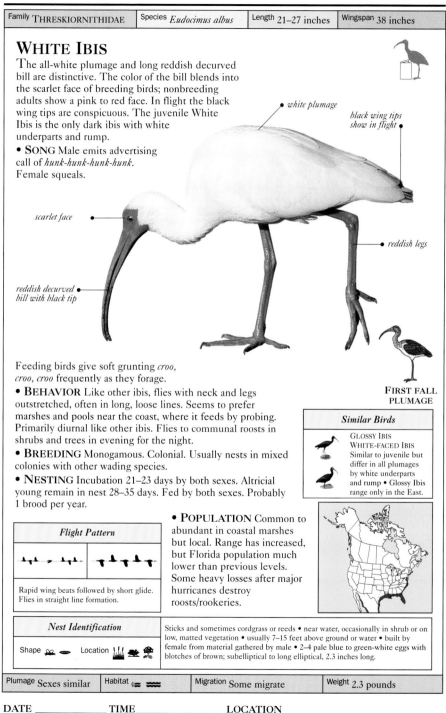

WHITE IBIS

The all-white plumage and long reddish decurved bill are distinctive. The color of the bill blends into the scarlet face of breeding birds; nonbreeding adults show a pink to red face. In flight the black wing tips are conspicuous. The juvenile White Ibis is the only dark ibis with white underparts and rump.

• **SONG** Male emits advertising call of *hunk-hunk-hunk-hunk*. Female squeals.

white plumage

black wing tips show in flight

scarlet face

reddish legs

reddish decurved bill with black tip

Feeding birds give soft grunting *croo, croo, croo* frequently as they forage.

• **BEHAVIOR** Like other ibis, flies with neck and legs outstretched, often in long, loose lines. Seems to prefer marshes and pools near the coast, where it feeds by probing. Primarily diurnal like other ibis. Flies to communal roosts in shrubs and trees in evening for the night.

• **BREEDING** Monogamous. Colonial. Usually nests in mixed colonies with other wading species.

• **NESTING** Incubation 21–23 days by both sexes. Altricial young remain in nest 28–35 days. Fed by both sexes. Probably 1 brood per year.

FIRST FALL PLUMAGE

Similar Birds

GLOSSY IBIS
WHITE-FACED IBIS
Similar to juvenile but differ in all plumages by white underparts and rump • Glossy Ibis range only in the East.

• **POPULATION** Common to abundant in coastal marshes but local. Range has increased, but Florida population much lower than previous levels. Some heavy losses after major hurricanes destroy roosts/rookeries.

Flight Pattern

Rapid wing beats followed by short glide. Flies in straight line formation.

Nest Identification

Shape ◠ ⌒   Location ⫲ ♣ ♠

Sticks and sometimes cordgrass or reeds • near water, occasionally in shrub or on low, matted vegetation • usually 7–15 feet above ground or water • built by female from material gathered by male • 2–4 pale blue to green-white eggs with blotches of brown; subelliptical to long elliptical, 2.3 inches long.

Plumage Sexes similar	Habitat ⫽ ≈≈	Migration Some migrate	Weight 2.3 pounds

DATE _____ TIME_____ LOCATION _____

| Family THRESKIORNITHIDAE | Species *Plegadis chihi* | Length 20–26 inches | Wingspan 36–38 inches |

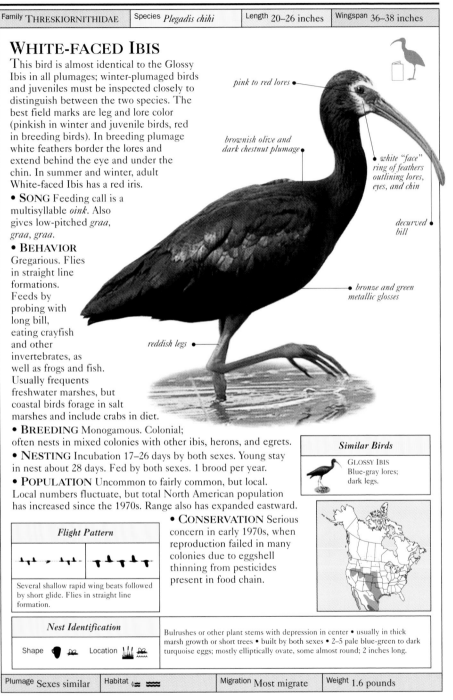

WHITE-FACED IBIS

This bird is almost identical to the Glossy Ibis in all plumages; winter-plumaged birds and juveniles must be inspected closely to distinguish between the two species. The best field marks are leg and lore color (pinkish in winter and juvenile birds, red in breeding birds). In breeding plumage white feathers border the lores and extend behind the eye and under the chin. In summer and winter, adult White-faced Ibis has a red iris.

- **SONG** Feeding call is a multisyllable *oink*. Also gives low-pitched *graa, graa, graa.*
- **BEHAVIOR** Gregarious. Flies in straight line formations. Feeds by probing with long bill, eating crayfish and other invertebrates, as well as frogs and fish. Usually frequents freshwater marshes, but coastal birds forage in salt marshes and include crabs in diet.
- **BREEDING** Monogamous. Colonial; often nests in mixed colonies with other ibis, herons, and egrets.
- **NESTING** Incubation 17–26 days by both sexes. Young stay in nest about 28 days. Fed by both sexes. 1 brood per year.
- **POPULATION** Uncommon to fairly common, but local. Local numbers fluctuate, but total North American population has increased since the 1970s. Range also has expanded eastward.
- **CONSERVATION** Serious concern in early 1970s, when reproduction failed in many colonies due to eggshell thinning from pesticides present in food chain.

pink to red lores

brownish olive and dark chestnut plumage

white "face" ring of feathers outlining lores, eyes, and chin

decurved bill

bronze and green metallic glosses

reddish legs

Similar Birds

GLOSSY IBIS
Blue-gray lores; dark legs.

Flight Pattern

Several shallow rapid wing beats followed by short glide. Flies in straight line formation.

Nest Identification

Shape   Location

Bulrushes or other plant stems with depression in center • usually in thick marsh growth or short trees • built by both sexes • 2–5 pale blue-green to dark turquoise eggs; mostly elliptically ovate, some almost round; 2 inches long.

| Plumage Sexes similar | Habitat | Migration Most migrate | Weight 1.6 pounds |

DATE _____ TIME_____ LOCATION _____

Family THRESKIORNITHIDAE	Species *Ajaia ajaia*	Length 30–40 inches	Wingspan 50–53 inches

ROSEATE SPOONBILL

The only spoonbill native to North America, this is also the only large pink wading bird normally found on our southern coasts. Adults and juveniles alike are unmistakable with large spatulate bills. In flight the adult bird looks almost entirely pink and flies with its neck and legs extended. During breeding season the head sometimes becomes a copper-buff color. Juveniles are pale whitish overall.

• **SONG** Soft quacking sounds when disturbed.

• **BEHAVIOR** Feeds while wading in shallow water by rhythmically sweeping its spoonbill back and forth. Sensitive nerve endings snap bill shut

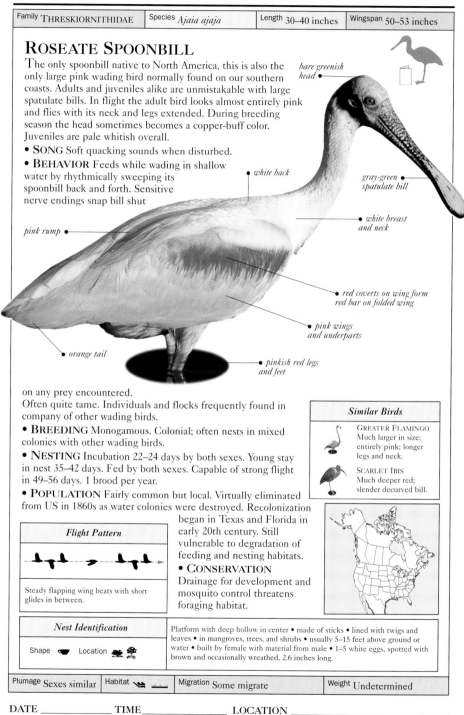

bare greenish head

gray-green spatulate bill

white back

white breast and neck

pink rump

red coverts on wing form red bar on folded wing

pink wings and underparts

orange tail

pinkish red legs and feet

on any prey encountered. Often quite tame. Individuals and flocks frequently found in company of other wading birds.

• **BREEDING** Monogamous. Colonial; often nests in mixed colonies with other wading birds.

• **NESTING** Incubation 22–24 days by both sexes. Young stay in nest 35–42 days. Fed by both sexes. Capable of strong flight in 49–56 days. 1 brood per year.

• **POPULATION** Fairly common but local. Virtually eliminated from US in 1860s as water colonies were destroyed. Recolonization began in Texas and Florida in early 20th century. Still vulnerable to degradation of feeding and nesting habitats.

• **CONSERVATION** Drainage for development and mosquito control threatens foraging habitat.

Similar Birds

GREATER FLAMINGO Much larger in size; entirely pink; longer legs and neck.

SCARLET IBIS Much deeper red; slender decurved bill.

Flight Pattern

Steady flapping wing beats with short glides in between.

Nest Identification

Shape ⬛ Location 🌳 🌳

Platform with deep hollow in center • made of sticks • lined with twigs and leaves • in mangroves, trees, and shrubs • usually 5–15 feet above ground or water • built by female with material from male • 1–5 white eggs, spotted with brown and occasionally wreathed, 2.6 inches long.

Plumage Sexes similar	Habitat	Migration Some migrate	Weight Undetermined

DATE _____ TIME_____ LOCATION _____

Family CICONIIDAE	Species *Mycteria americana*	Length 35–45 inches	Wingspan 65 inches

WOOD STORK

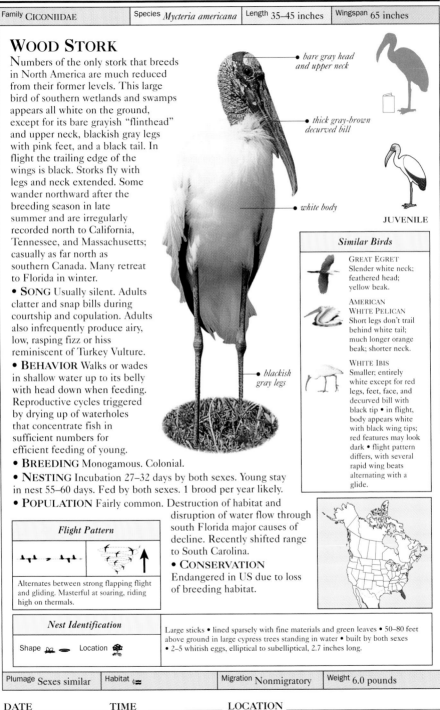

Numbers of the only stork that breeds in North America are much reduced from their former levels. This large bird of southern wetlands and swamps appears all white on the ground, except for its bare grayish "flinthead" and upper neck, blackish gray legs with pink feet, and a black tail. In flight the trailing edge of the wings is black. Storks fly with legs and neck extended. Some wander northward after the breeding season in late summer and are irregularly recorded north to California, Tennessee, and Massachusetts; casually as far north as southern Canada. Many retreat to Florida in winter.

• **SONG** Usually silent. Adults clatter and snap bills during courtship and copulation. Adults also infrequently produce airy, low, rasping fizz or hiss reminiscent of Turkey Vulture.

• **BEHAVIOR** Walks or wades in shallow water up to its belly with head down when feeding. Reproductive cycles triggered by drying up of waterholes that concentrate fish in sufficient numbers for efficient feeding of young.

• **BREEDING** Monogamous. Colonial.

• **NESTING** Incubation 27–32 days by both sexes. Young stay in nest 55–60 days. Fed by both sexes. 1 brood per year likely.

• **POPULATION** Fairly common. Destruction of habitat and disruption of water flow through south Florida major causes of decline. Recently shifted range to South Carolina.

• **CONSERVATION** Endangered in US due to loss of breeding habitat.

*Labels on main image:*
- bare gray head and upper neck
- thick gray-brown decurved bill
- white body
- blackish gray legs

JUVENILE

Similar Birds

GREAT EGRET Slender white neck; feathered head; yellow beak.

AMERICAN WHITE PELICAN Short legs don't trail behind white tail; much longer orange beak; shorter neck.

WHITE IBIS Smaller; entirely white except for red legs, feet, face, and decurved bill with black tip • in flight, body appears white with black wing tips; red features may look dark • flight pattern differs, with several rapid wing beats alternating with a glide.

Flight Pattern

Alternates between strong flapping flight and gliding. Masterful at soaring, riding high on thermals.

Nest Identification

Shape ⌒⌒ ⌒ Location 🌳

Large sticks • lined sparsely with fine materials and green leaves • 50–80 feet above ground in large cypress trees standing in water • built by both sexes • 2–5 whitish eggs, elliptical to subelliptical, 2.7 inches long.

Plumage Sexes similar	Habitat 🌿	Migration Nonmigratory	Weight 6.0 pounds

DATE _____ TIME_____ LOCATION _____

| Family CATHARTIDAE | Species *Coragyps atratus* | Length 23–27 inches | Wingspan 54–60 inches |

BLACK VULTURE

Alternating between several quick flaps and a short sail on flat wings, this bird seems to labor on the wing more than the Turkey Vulture that it superficially resembles. In flight the wings are wide, with the six outermost primaries showing white bases beneath. The tail of this vulture is short and squared, barely extending beyond the wing, and the feet often protrude beyond it.

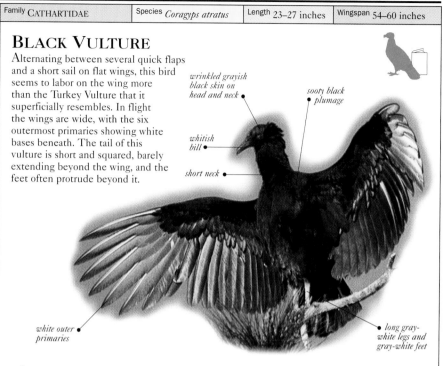

wrinkled grayish black skin on head and neck

sooty black plumage

whitish bill

short neck

white outer primaries

long gray-white legs and gray-white feet

- **SONG** Usually silent, but when competing for food it makes grumbling, barking, and hissing noises.
- **BEHAVIOR** Solitary or found in small to large groups. Often roosts communally. Diet consists primarily of carrion. Aggressive in nature for a vulture, it often dominates carrion when other species are present. Sometimes attacks and kills prey. It spreads its wings when on the roost, especially in the morning, to catch the ultraviolet rays of the sun.
- **BREEDING** Monogamous. Colonial.
- **NESTING** Incubation 37–48 days by both sexes. Semialtricial young remain in nest 80–94 days, and are fed by both sexes. 1 brood per year.
- **POPULATION** Fairly common to common. Decline in the Southeast has been due to the loss of safe nesting habitat. Overall, there has been a slight increase in the Northeast as range has expanded.

Similar Birds

TURKEY VULTURE
Bare red head (black on juvenile); long rectangular tail; 2-toned wings from below (black in front, silver-gray trailing edge); holds wings in dihedral when soaring.

Flight Pattern

Several quick deep wing beats followed by a glide; soars on thermals.

Nest Identification

Shape

Location

No nest • lives in dark recesses or under cover in caves, hollow logs, stumps, tree trunks, or abandoned buildings • 2 light grayish green or bluish white eggs, usually marked with brown or lavender; elliptical ovate or elongate ovate, 3 inches long.

| Plumage Sexes similar | Habitat | Migration Some migrate | Weight 4.8 pounds |

DATE _____ TIME_____ LOCATION _____

Family CATHARTIDAE	Species *Cathartes aura*	Length 26–32 inches	Wingspan 68–72 inches

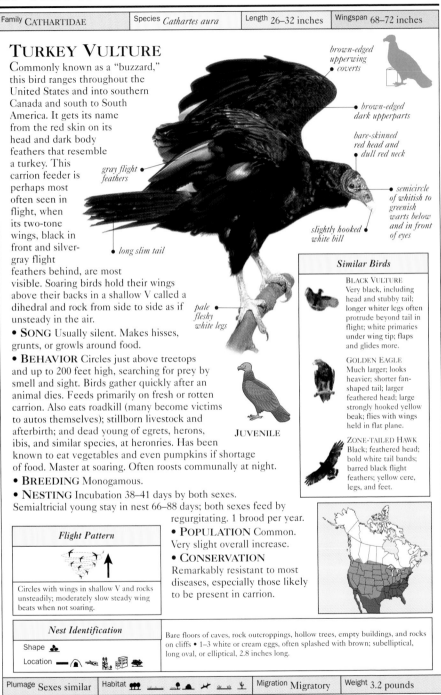

TURKEY VULTURE

Commonly known as a "buzzard," this bird ranges throughout the United States and into southern Canada and south to South America. It gets its name from the red skin on its head and dark body feathers that resemble a turkey. This carrion feeder is perhaps most often seen in flight, when its two-tone wings, black in front and silver-gray flight feathers behind, are most visible. Soaring birds hold their wings above their backs in a shallow V called a dihedral and rock from side to side as if unsteady in the air.

brown-edged upperwing coverts

brown-edged dark upperparts

bare-skinned red head and dull red neck

gray flight feathers

semicircle of whitish to greenish warts below and in front of eyes

slightly hooked white bill

long slim tail

pale fleshy white legs

- **SONG** Usually silent. Makes hisses, grunts, or growls around food.
- **BEHAVIOR** Circles just above treetops and up to 200 feet high, searching for prey by smell and sight. Birds gather quickly after an animal dies. Feeds primarily on fresh or rotten carrion. Also eats roadkill (many become victims to autos themselves); stillborn livestock and afterbirth; and dead young of egrets, herons, ibis, and similar species, at heronries. Has been known to eat vegetables and even pumpkins if shortage of food. Master at soaring. Often roosts communally at night.
- **BREEDING** Monogamous.
- **NESTING** Incubation 38–41 days by both sexes. Semialtricial young stay in nest 66–88 days; both sexes feed by regurgitating. 1 brood per year.
- **POPULATION** Common. Very slight overall increase.
- **CONSERVATION** Remarkably resistant to most diseases, especially those likely to be present in carrion.

JUVENILE

Similar Birds

BLACK VULTURE
Very black, including head and stubby tail; longer whiter legs often protrude beyond tail in flight; white primaries under wing tip; flaps and glides more.

GOLDEN EAGLE
Much larger; looks heavier; shorter fan-shaped tail; larger feathered head; large strongly hooked yellow beak; flies with wings held in flat plane.

ZONE-TAILED HAWK
Black; feathered head; bold white tail bands; barred black flight feathers; yellow cere, legs, and feet.

Flight Pattern

Circles with wings in shallow V and rocks unsteadily; moderately slow steady wing beats when not soaring.

Nest Identification

Shape ♣

Location ▬ ◮ ⬟ 🏠 🏢 ♣

Bare floors of caves, rock outcroppings, hollow trees, empty buildings, and rocks on cliffs • 1–3 white or cream eggs, often splashed with brown; subelliptical, long oval, or elliptical, 2.8 inches long.

Plumage Sexes similar	Habitat 🌳🌳 ⌂ ⌂ ★ 🏠 🌿 🌿 🌿	Migration Migratory	Weight 3.2 pounds

DATE _____ TIME_____ LOCATION _____

Family CATHARTIDAE	Species *Gymnogyps californianus*	Length 43–55 inches	Wingspan 8–9.5 feet

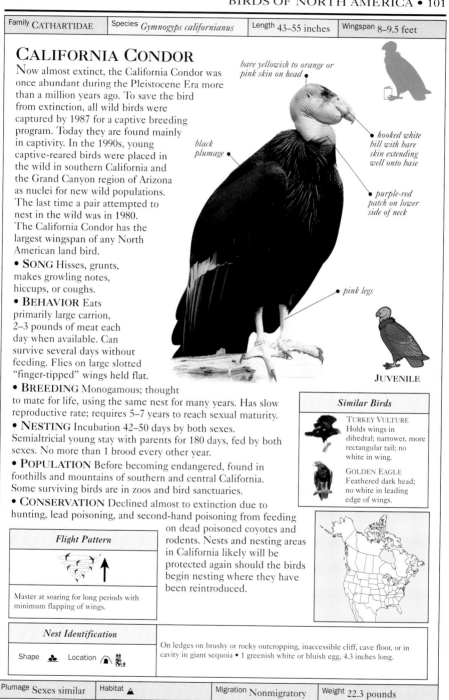

CALIFORNIA CONDOR

Now almost extinct, the California Condor was once abundant during the Pleistocene Era more than a million years ago. To save the bird from extinction, all wild birds were captured by 1987 for a captive breeding program. Today they are found mainly in captivity. In the 1990s, young captive-reared birds were placed in the wild in southern California and the Grand Canyon region of Arizona as nuclei for new wild populations. The last time a pair attempted to nest in the wild was in 1980. The California Condor has the largest wingspan of any North American land bird.

bare yellowish to orange or pink skin on head

black plumage

hooked white bill with bare skin extending well onto base

purple-red patch on lower side of neck

pink legs

JUVENILE

• **SONG** Hisses, grunts, makes growling notes, hiccups, or coughs.

• **BEHAVIOR** Eats primarily large carrion, 2–3 pounds of meat each day when available. Can survive several days without feeding. Flies on large slotted "finger-tipped" wings held flat.

• **BREEDING** Monogamous; thought to mate for life, using the same nest for many years. Has slow reproductive rate; requires 5–7 years to reach sexual maturity.

• **NESTING** Incubation 42–50 days by both sexes. Semialtricial young stay with parents for 180 days, fed by both sexes. No more than 1 brood every other year.

• **POPULATION** Before becoming endangered, found in foothills and mountains of southern and central California. Some surviving birds are in zoos and bird sanctuaries.

• **CONSERVATION** Declined almost to extinction due to hunting, lead poisoning, and second-hand poisoning from feeding on dead poisoned coyotes and rodents. Nests and nesting areas in California likely will be protected again should the birds begin nesting where they have been reintroduced.

Similar Birds

TURKEY VULTURE
Holds wings in dihedral; narrower, more rectangular tail; no white in wing.

GOLDEN EAGLE
Feathered dark head; no white in leading edge of wings.

Flight Pattern

Master at soaring for long periods with minimum flapping of wings.

Nest Identification

Shape 🐾   Location 🏔️ 🪹

On ledges on brushy or rocky outcropping, inaccessible cliff, cave floor, or in cavity in giant sequoia • 1 greenish white or bluish egg, 4.3 inches long.

Plumage Sexes similar	Habitat ▲	Migration Nonmigratory	Weight 22.3 pounds

DATE _____ TIME_____ LOCATION _____

Family ANATIDAE	Species *Dendrocygna autumnalis*	Length 19–22 inches	Wingspan 34–36 inches

BLACK-BELLIED WHISTLING-DUCK

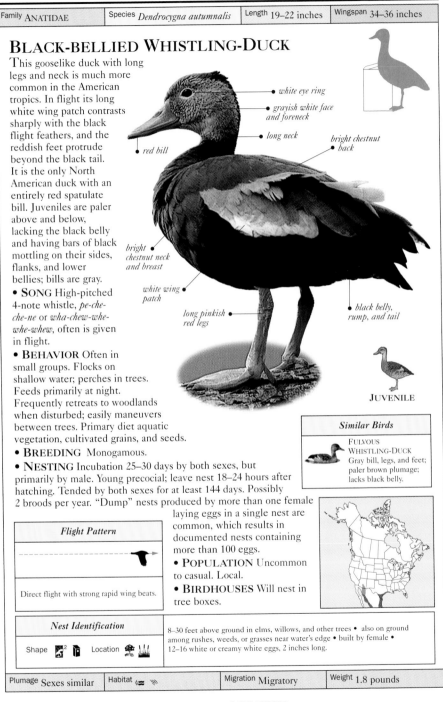

This gooselike duck with long legs and neck is much more common in the American tropics. In flight its long white wing patch contrasts sharply with the black flight feathers, and the reddish feet protrude beyond the black tail. It is the only North American duck with an entirely red spatulate bill. Juveniles are paler above and below, lacking the black belly and having bars of black mottling on their sides, flanks, and lower bellies; bills are gray.

• **SONG** High-pitched 4-note whistle, *pe-che-che-ne* or *wha-chew-whe-whe-whew*, often is given in flight.

• **BEHAVIOR** Often in small groups. Flocks on shallow water; perches in trees. Feeds primarily at night. Frequently retreats to woodlands when disturbed; easily maneuvers between trees. Primary diet aquatic vegetation, cultivated grains, and seeds.

• **BREEDING** Monogamous.

• **NESTING** Incubation 25–30 days by both sexes, but primarily by male. Young precocial; leave nest 18–24 hours after hatching. Tended by both sexes for at least 144 days. Possibly 2 broods per year. "Dump" nests produced by more than one female laying eggs in a single nest are common, which results in documented nests containing more than 100 eggs.

• **POPULATION** Uncommon to casual. Local.

• **BIRDHOUSES** Will nest in tree boxes.

Labels on image:
- white eye ring
- grayish white face and foreneck
- long neck
- bright chestnut back
- red bill
- bright chestnut neck and breast
- white wing patch
- long pinkish red legs
- black belly, rump, and tail

JUVENILE

Similar Birds

FULVOUS WHISTLING-DUCK
Gray bill, legs, and feet; paler brown plumage; lacks black belly.

Flight Pattern

Direct flight with strong rapid wing beats.

Nest Identification

Shape | Location

8–30 feet above ground in elms, willows, and other trees • also on ground among rushes, weeds, or grasses near water's edge • built by female • 12–16 white or creamy white eggs, 2 inches long.

Plumage Sexes similar	Habitat	Migration Migratory	Weight 1.8 pounds

DATE _____ TIME_____ LOCATION _____

| Family ANATIDAE | Species *Dendrocygna bicolor* | Length 18–21 inches | Wingspan 36 inches |

FULVOUS WHISTLING-DUCK

In its upright stance with its long legs and neck, this duck is somewhat gooselike in appearance. One of the most widely distributed waterfowl in the world, this rich fulvous brown duck resembles no other North American duck on land or water. It flies with a noticeable droop in its long neck and with legs and feet extended beyond the tail. Its white rump patch contrasts against the black tail.

tawny-fulvous head and neck

dark cap and line extending down midline of hindneck

brownish black back with feathers edged tawny-brown

grayish blue bill

black tail

white rump

white slashes on sides

tawny-fulvous underparts

• **SONG** High squeaking 2-syllable whistle, *pe-chee*, usually is given while bird is in flight.
• **BEHAVIOR** Feeds at night. Walks on land. Eats grass and weed seeds. Forages in fields for waste grain; seems to be particularly fond of rice. Roosts by day in dense vegetation. Often found in large flocks.
• **BREEDING** Monogamous.
• **NESTING** Incubation 24–26 days by both sexes. Young stay in nest 55–63 days. Young tended by both sexes but find own food. 1 brood per year.
• **POPULATION** Uncommon to fairly common locally. Decline in Southwest; increase in Southeast.
• **CONSERVATION** Considered a "pest" species by some rice farmers in the South.

Similar Birds
BLACK-BELLIED WHISTLING-DUCK ♂ Bold white wing stripe in flight; black belly; red bill, legs, and feet.

Flight Pattern
Direct heronlike flight with slow deep wing beats.

Nest Identification	
Shape	Woven grass, sedges, and cattails • no down added • on ground next to water or in dense marsh just above water in bulrushes or dense beds of cattails • rarely in tree cavity • built by female • 12–14 white or buff-white eggs; bluntly ovate, short ovate, or oval; 2.1 inches in diameter.
Location	

| Plumage Sexes similar | Habitat | Migration Migratory | Weight 1.6 pounds |

DATE _____ TIME_____ LOCATION _____

Family ANATIDAE	Species *Anser fabalis*	Length 28–35 inches	Wingspan 53–64 inches

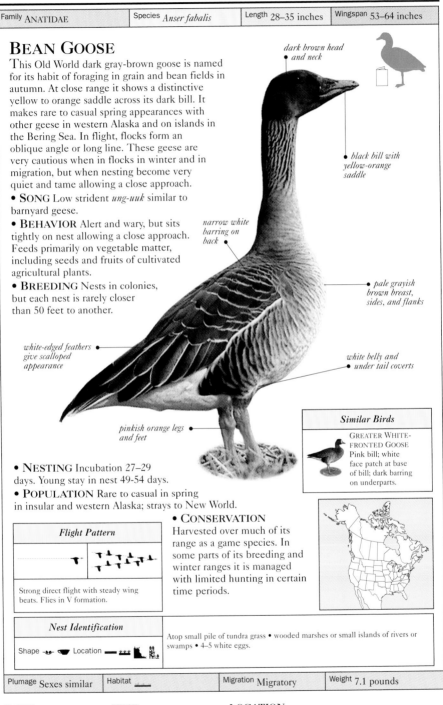

BEAN GOOSE

This Old World dark gray-brown goose is named for its habit of foraging in grain and bean fields in autumn. At close range it shows a distinctive yellow to orange saddle across its dark bill. It makes rare to casual spring appearances with other geese in western Alaska and on islands in the Bering Sea. In flight, flocks form an oblique angle or long line. These geese are very cautious when in flocks in winter and in migration, but when nesting become very quiet and tame allowing a close approach.

- **SONG** Low strident *ung-uuk* similar to barnyard geese.
- **BEHAVIOR** Alert and wary, but sits tightly on nest allowing a close approach. Feeds primarily on vegetable matter, including seeds and fruits of cultivated agricultural plants.
- **BREEDING** Nests in colonies, but each nest is rarely closer than 50 feet to another.

dark brown head and neck

black bill with yellow-orange saddle

narrow white barring on back

pale grayish brown breast, sides, and flanks

white-edged feathers give scalloped appearance

white belly and under tail coverts

pinkish orange legs and feet

- **NESTING** Incubation 27–29 days. Young stay in nest 49-54 days.
- **POPULATION** Rare to casual in spring in insular and western Alaska; strays to New World.
- **CONSERVATION** Harvested over much of its range as a game species. In some parts of its breeding and winter ranges it is managed with limited hunting in certain time periods.

Similar Birds

GREATER WHITE-FRONTED GOOSE Pink bill; white face patch at base of bill; dark barring on underparts.

Flight Pattern

Strong direct flight with steady wing beats. Flies in V formation.

Nest Identification

Shape ᴗ ⬛ Location ⬛⬛⬛

Atop small pile of tundra grass • wooded marshes or small islands of rivers or swamps • 4–5 white eggs.

Plumage Sexes similar	Habitat ___	Migration Migratory	Weight 7.1 pounds

DATE _____ TIME_____ LOCATION _____

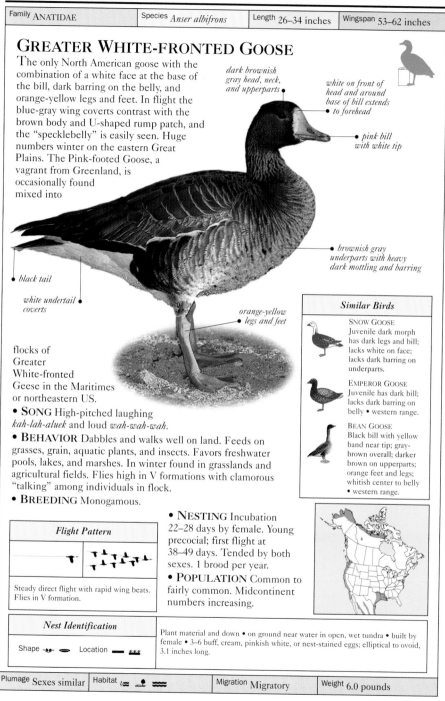

Family ANATIDAE	Species *Anser albifrons*	Length 26–34 inches	Wingspan 53–62 inches

GREATER WHITE-FRONTED GOOSE

The only North American goose with the combination of a white face at the base of the bill, dark barring on the belly, and orange-yellow legs and feet. In flight the blue-gray wing coverts contrast with the brown body and U-shaped rump patch, and the "specklebelly" is easily seen. Huge numbers winter on the eastern Great Plains. The Pink-footed Goose, a vagrant from Greenland, is occasionally found mixed into

dark brownish gray head, neck, and upperparts

white on front of head and around base of bill extends to forehead

pink bill with white tip

brownish gray underparts with heavy dark mottling and barring

black tail

white undertail coverts

orange-yellow legs and feet

flocks of Greater White-fronted Geese in the Maritimes or northeastern US.

• **SONG** High-pitched laughing *kah-lah-aluek* and loud *wah-wah-wah*.

• **BEHAVIOR** Dabbles and walks well on land. Feeds on grasses, grain, aquatic plants, and insects. Favors freshwater pools, lakes, and marshes. In winter found in grasslands and agricultural fields. Flies high in V formations with clamorous "talking" among individuals in flock.

• **BREEDING** Monogamous.

Similar Birds

SNOW GOOSE
Juvenile dark morph has dark legs and bill; lacks white on face; lacks dark barring on underparts.

EMPEROR GOOSE
Juvenile has dark bill; lacks dark barring on belly • western range.

BEAN GOOSE
Black bill with yellow band near tip; gray-brown overall; darker brown on upperparts; orange feet and legs; whitish center to belly • western range.

• **NESTING** Incubation 22–28 days by female. Young precocial; first flight at 38–49 days. Tended by both sexes. 1 brood per year.

• **POPULATION** Common to fairly common. Midcontinent numbers increasing.

Flight Pattern

Steady direct flight with rapid wing beats. Flies in V formation.

Nest Identification

Shape ⌣ ⬯ Location ▬ ✻✻✻

Plant material and down • on ground near water in open, wet tundra • built by female • 3–6 buff, cream, pinkish white, or nest-stained eggs; elliptical to ovoid, 3.1 inches long.

Plumage Sexes similar	Habitat	Migration Migratory	Weight 6.0 pounds

DATE _____ TIME_____ LOCATION _____

Family ANATIDAE	Species *Chen canagica*	Length 26–30 inches	Wingspan 48–56 inches

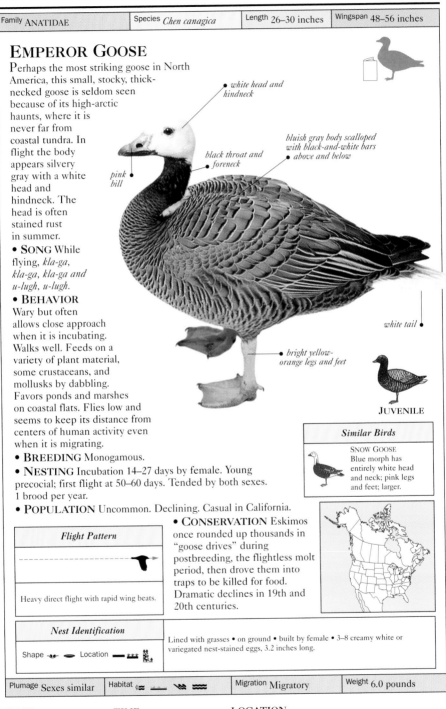

EMPEROR GOOSE

Perhaps the most striking goose in North America, this small, stocky, thick-necked goose is seldom seen because of its high-arctic haunts, where it is never far from coastal tundra. In flight the body appears silvery gray with a white head and hindneck. The head is often stained rust in summer.

white head and hindneck

black throat and foreneck

bluish gray body scalloped with black-and-white bars above and below

pink bill

white tail

bright yellow-orange legs and feet

JUVENILE

• **SONG** While flying, *kla-ga, kla-ga, kla-ga* and *u-lugh, u-lugh.*

• **BEHAVIOR** Wary but often allows close approach when it is incubating. Walks well. Feeds on a variety of plant material, some crustaceans, and mollusks by dabbling. Favors ponds and marshes on coastal flats. Flies low and seems to keep its distance from centers of human activity even when it is migrating.

• **BREEDING** Monogamous.

• **NESTING** Incubation 14–27 days by female. Young precocial; first flight at 50–60 days. Tended by both sexes. 1 brood per year.

• **POPULATION** Uncommon. Declining. Casual in California.

Similar Birds

SNOW GOOSE
Blue morph has entirely white head and neck; pink legs and feet; larger.

• **CONSERVATION** Eskimos once rounded up thousands in "goose drives" during postbreeding, the flightless molt period, then drove them into traps to be killed for food. Dramatic declines in 19th and 20th centuries.

Flight Pattern
Heavy direct flight with rapid wing beats.

Nest Identification	
Shape ⌄ ⌐ Location ▬ ⌗ ⌗	Lined with grasses • on ground • built by female • 3–8 creamy white or variegated nest-stained eggs, 3.2 inches long.

Plumage Sexes similar	Habitat	Migration Migratory	Weight 6.0 pounds

DATE _____ TIME_____ LOCATION _____

Family ANATIDAE	Species *Chen caerulescens*	Length 25–31 inches	Wingspan 53–60 inches

SNOW GOOSE

This species comprises two color morphs that, until the last quarter of the 20th century, were considered separate species: Snow Goose for the white morph and Blue Goose for the dark or blue morph. The plumage of the white morph is entirely white in adults except for black primary feathers. Blue morph adults have a white head and neck with a dusky gray-brown body and white tail coverts.

• **SONG** Shrill falsetto notes and occasional softened honk. High-pitched nasal barking continuously in chorus in flight.

• **BEHAVIOR** Flies in bunched flocks or in broad U formations. Dabbler that walks easily on land. Grazes on tender shoots, waste grain, and other vegetable matter. Color morphs tend to segregate on breeding grounds, but mixed partners sometimes do pair and nest.

• **BREEDING** Monogamous. Colonial; densities of up to 1,200 pairs per square mile.

• **NESTING** Incubation 23–25 days by female. Precocial young leave nest soon after hatching, tended by both parents. First flight at 38–49 days. 1 brood per year.

• **POPULATION** Very common to abundant. Increasing overall, with blue morph increasing and white morph decreasing because of selection by predators on breeding grounds and hunters on wintering grounds.

• **CONSERVATION** Some management in certain areas of breeding range to prevent overpopulation and destruction of habitat by increased populations.

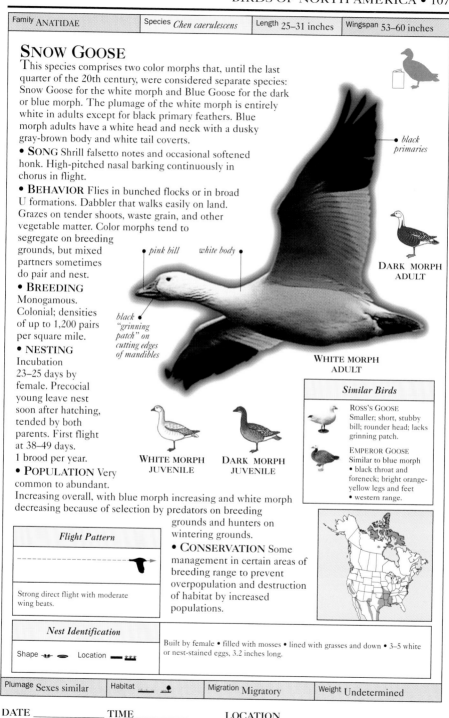

black primaries

DARK MORPH ADULT

pink bill

white body

black "grinning patch" on cutting edges of mandibles

WHITE MORPH ADULT

WHITE MORPH JUVENILE

DARK MORPH JUVENILE

Similar Birds

ROSS'S GOOSE
Smaller; short, stubby bill; rounder head; lacks grinning patch.

EMPEROR GOOSE
Similar to blue morph
• black throat and foreneck; bright orange-yellow legs and feet
• western range.

Flight Pattern
Strong direct flight with moderate wing beats.

Nest Identification	
Shape 〜 ⬤　Location ▬ ✲✲✲	Built by female • filled with mosses • lined with grasses and down • 3–5 white or nest-stained eggs, 3.2 inches long.

Plumage Sexes similar	Habitat	Migration Migratory	Weight Undetermined

DATE _____ TIME _____ LOCATION _____

Family ANATIDAE	Species *Chen rossii*	Length 21–26 inches	Wingspan 47–54 inches

ROSS'S GOOSE

Often seen with the Snow Goose, North America's smallest goose is said to have a gentle expression. Like the Snow Goose, Ross's Goose has both a white morph and a very uncommon blue morph. It can be distinguished from the Snow Goose from a distance by its smaller size and shorter neck and at closer range by its stubby triangular bill, which lacks the "grinning patch." In flight it has faster wing beats than the Snow Goose.

round head

short neck

stubby, triangular, deep pinkish red bill with warty bluish base

black wing tips

snow-white body

WHITE MORPH

BLUE MORPH

• **SONG** Low throaty *kug* or weak *kek, kek* or *ke-gak, ke-gak*. Similar to call of smaller races of Canada Goose.
• **BEHAVIOR** Eats fresh grasses and grains. Often can be seen feeding with Snow Geese.
• **BREEDING** Monogamous. Colonial.
• **NESTING** Incubation 21–24 days by female. Tended by both sexes. First flight at 40–45 days. 1 brood per year.
• **POPULATION** Rare to uncommon in migration and outside its wintering grounds in California, New Mexico, and the states along the lower Mississippi River. Fairly common on its breeding grounds.

Similar Birds

SNOW GOOSE
Longer neck and bill; has "grinning patch" on cutting edge of bill; flatter head; rusty stains often visible on face in summer; slower wing beats.

• **CONSERVATION** Numbers were decimated by market hunting, especially in California, until it was regulated early in the 20th century. Populations increased in the last half of the 20th century.

Flight Pattern

Rapid direct flight with strong wing beats. Flies in V formation.

Nest Identification

Shape   Location

Soft grasses, moss, and twigs • lined with small amount of down • built by female • 4–5 white eggs; subelliptical, 2.9 x 1.9 inches.

Plumage Sexes similar	Habitat	Migration Migratory	Weight 3.7 pounds

DATE _____ TIME_____ LOCATION _____

Family ANATIDAE	Species *Branta canadensis*	Length 25–45 inches	Wingspan 75 inches

CANADA GOOSE

Found in every province and state at some time of the year, this is the most common, familiar, and widespread goose in North America. Breeding programs in the 20th century established or reestablished populations in the southern part of the range. Size varies tremendously over the vast range, from 22-inch Mallard-sized arctic birds to giant geese reaching 45 inches and weighing 24 pounds.

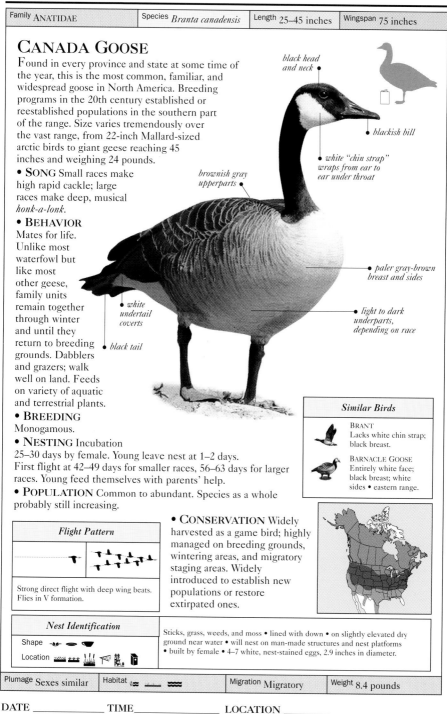

black head and neck

blackish bill

white "chin strap" wraps from ear to ear under throat

brownish gray upperparts

paler gray-brown breast and sides

light to dark underparts, depending on race

white undertail coverts

black tail

• **SONG** Small races make high rapid cackle; large races make deep, musical *honk-a-lonk*.

• **BEHAVIOR** Mates for life. Unlike most waterfowl but like most other geese, family units remain together through winter and until they return to breeding grounds. Dabblers and grazers; walk well on land. Feeds on variety of aquatic and terrestrial plants.

• **BREEDING** Monogamous.

• **NESTING** Incubation 25–30 days by female. Young leave nest at 1–2 days. First flight at 42–49 days for smaller races, 56–63 days for larger races. Young feed themselves with parents' help.

• **POPULATION** Common to abundant. Species as a whole probably still increasing.

• **CONSERVATION** Widely harvested as a game bird; highly managed on breeding grounds, wintering areas, and migratory staging areas. Widely introduced to establish new populations or restore extirpated ones.

Similar Birds

BRANT
Lacks white chin strap; black breast.

BARNACLE GOOSE
Entirely white face; black breast; white sides • eastern range.

Flight Pattern	
Strong direct flight with deep wing beats. Flies in V formation.	

Nest Identification	
Shape	
Location	

Sticks, grass, weeds, and moss • lined with down • on slightly elevated dry ground near water • will nest on man-made structures and nest platforms • built by female • 4–7 white, nest-stained eggs, 2.9 inches in diameter.

Plumage Sexes similar	Habitat	Migration Migratory	Weight 8.4 pounds

DATE _____ TIME_____ LOCATION _____

Family ANATIDAE	Species *Branta bernicla*	Length 22–26 inches	Wingspan 43–48 inches

BRANT

A tundra species most often seen wintering along sea coasts, this small short-necked goose is not much larger than a Mallard. The two races in North America differ in appearance. Both have dark brown backs, but whereas the western bird has a dark belly, the eastern form has a paler one and its white patches do not meet at the front of the neck. In both plumages the white rump is conspicuous in flight.

- **SONG** Call is throaty drawled *c-r-r-onk, crr-ronk.*
- **BEHAVIOR** Often flies low in ragged bunches with position of birds changing often and without appearance of a leader. Incubating

white scalloped patch on sides of upper neck

blackish bill

black head, neck, and breast

white rump, upper tail and under tail coverts

blackish legs and feet

black tail

dusky brown bars on sides and flanks

birds sit tightly on nest and lie low with neck and head stretched flat, blending with surrounding tundra. Relatively tame. Feeds primarily on vegetable matter.

- **BREEDING** Monogamous. Mates for life. Forms loose colonies.
- **NESTING** Incubation 22–26 days by female. First flight at 40–50 days. Tended by both sexes.
- **POPULATION** Common and local. May be declining.
- **CONSERVATION** A die-off of eelgrass, a major source of food for the Brant, on the Atlantic Coast in the 1930s had serious impact on population. No long-term damage reported, because the Brant switched to another food source. Eelgrass made a partial recovery.

Similar Birds

CANADA GOOSE
Larger; longer neck; large white "chin strap"; pale brown breast.

BARNACLE GOOSE
Whitish face and sides • eastern range.

Flight Pattern

Heavy direct flight with strong wing beats. Flies in straight line formation.

Nest Identification

Shape   Location

Shallow bowl of grass and other materials • heavily lined with down • on small island in tundra pond, usually 1–5 miles from coast • built by female • 1–7 creamy white or buff eggs; subelliptical to elliptical, 2.9 inches in diameter.

Plumage Sexes similar	Habitat	Migration Migratory	Weight 3.0 pounds

DATE _____ TIME_____ LOCATION _____

Family ANATIDAE	Species *Cygnus olor*	Length 56–62 inches	Wingspan 7–8 feet

MUTE SWAN

Affluent residents and urban parks introduced this European swan to the environs of the Hudson River and Long Island through gardens, pools, and ponds. It has become established primarily along the north Atlantic Coast from southern New England to Virginia and secondarily around the Great Lakes (where there are now coordinated efforts to reduce its numbers). Adults, with their graceful S-curved necks, erected wing feathers, and black-knobbed orange bills, are unmistakable on the water.

naked black lores

all-white plumage

orange bill with large black basal knob

long neck often held in S curve

• **SONG** Variety of hisses, barks, and snorts. Generally silent although not really "mute."

• **BEHAVIOR** Decorative and graceful on water but awkward on land. Feeds by thrusting its long neck down to collect aquatic plants from bottom or tips up. Aggressive in defense of territory, it attempts to drive away any large bird or animal (humans and dogs included). Prefers freshwater, salt marshes, and protected bays.

JUVENILE

• **BREEDING** Monogamous. Forms long-term pair bonds. Pair defends large territory. Rarely nests in colonies.

• **NESTING** Incubation 35–38 days by both sexes, but female does more. Precocial young tended by both sexes but feed themselves. First flight at 100–155 days.

• **POPULATION** Introduced, naturalized, and locally common. Increasing by expansion from contiguous areas of release.

• **CONSERVATION** Exotic species; native of Eurasia. Efforts to systematically remove or reduce populations in some areas because of fear of competition with native species.

Similar Birds

TUNDRA SWAN
Winters in range of introduction • black bill without knob; naked yellow lores (not all birds); holds neck straight upright and bill parallel to water; does not elevate secondaries when swimming.

Flight Pattern

Direct flight with strong steady wing beats.

Nest Identification

Shape ___ Location ___

Plant material in mound • lined with down • on shoreline, small island, or mound built up in shallows • built by both sexes • 4–8 light gray or bluish green eggs; subelliptical, 4.5 inches long.

Plumage Sexes similar	Habitat ___	Migration Nonmigratory	Weight 26.0 pounds

DATE _____ TIME_____ LOCATION _____

Family ANATIDAE	Species *Cygnus buccinator*	Length 58–72 inches	Wingspan 6–8.5 feet

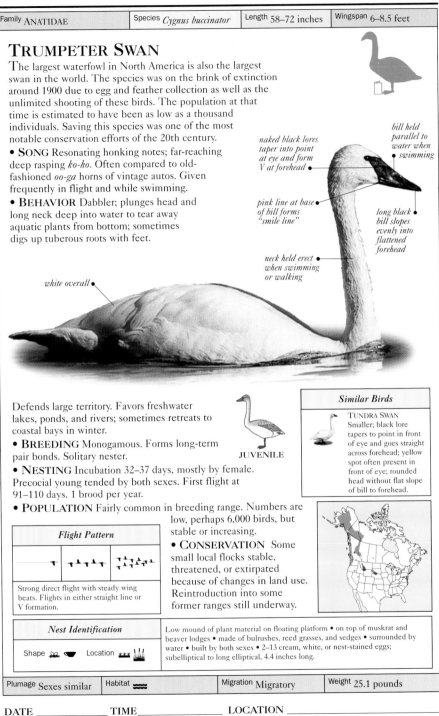

TRUMPETER SWAN

The largest waterfowl in North America is also the largest swan in the world. The species was on the brink of extinction around 1900 due to egg and feather collection as well as the unlimited shooting of these birds. The population at that time is estimated to have been as low as a thousand individuals. Saving this species was one of the most notable conservation efforts of the 20th century.

- **SONG** Resonating honking notes; far-reaching deep rasping *ko-ho*. Often compared to old-fashioned *oo-ga* horns of vintage autos. Given frequently in flight and while swimming.
- **BEHAVIOR** Dabbler; plunges head and long neck deep into water to tear away aquatic plants from bottom; sometimes digs up tuberous roots with feet.

naked black lores taper into point at eye and form V at forehead

bill held parallel to water when swimming

pink line at base of bill forms "smile line"

long black bill slopes evenly into flattened forehead

neck held erect when swimming or walking

white overall

Defends large territory. Favors freshwater lakes, ponds, and rivers; sometimes retreats to coastal bays in winter.

- **BREEDING** Monogamous. Forms long-term pair bonds. Solitary nester.

JUVENILE

- **NESTING** Incubation 32–37 days, mostly by female. Precocial young tended by both sexes. First flight at 91–110 days. 1 brood per year.
- **POPULATION** Fairly common in breeding range. Numbers are low, perhaps 6,000 birds, but stable or increasing.
- **CONSERVATION** Some small local flocks stable, threatened, or extirpated because of changes in land use. Reintroduction into some former ranges still underway.

Similar Birds

TUNDRA SWAN
Smaller; black lore tapers to point in front of eye and goes straight across forehead; yellow spot often present in front of eye; rounded head without flat slope of bill to forehead.

Flight Pattern

Strong direct flight with steady wing beats. Flights in either straight line or V formation.

Nest Identification

Shape 🥚 🦢   Location 🌾 🏔️

Low mound of plant material on floating platform • on top of muskrat and beaver lodges • made of bulrushes, reed grasses, and sedges • surrounded by water • built by both sexes • 2–13 cream, white, or nest-stained eggs; subelliptical to long elliptical, 4.4 inches long.

Plumage Sexes similar	Habitat 〰️	Migration Migratory	Weight 25.1 pounds

DATE _____ TIME_____ LOCATION _____

Family ANATIDAE	Species *Cygnus columbianus*	Length 47–58 inches	Wingspan 6–7 feet

TUNDRA SWAN

The most common and widespread swan in North America, this species breeds on arctic tundra and winters principally on the Atlantic and Pacific Coasts. Wintering concentrations on some coastal bays and lakes are spectacular in scope and activity. Swans are often associated with water; they are exceptionally fast swimmers. When flying they are large spectacular birds with long triangular wings, snow white to the tips of all flight feathers. The thin outstreached neck appears like a line more than half the length of the body, with a black point at the end.

yellow to orange spot in front of eye (most birds)

black bill with slightly concave profile to rounded head

black lores pointed to just in front of eye make straight line across forehead

• **SONG** Clamoring notes or yodeling; soft musical laughter, *wow-HOW-ow*, heavily accented on second syllable; repeated *who-who's*.

• **BEHAVIOR** Dabbler; plunges long neck and head beneath water to pick aquatic

entirely white body

JUVENILE

vegetation and dig up roots of submerged plants. Like other swans, runs across water beating its wings to achieve takeoff. Once in flight flies with neck and head thrust straight forward and feet protruding beneath tail.

• **BREEDING** The Tundra Swan is monogamous. It finds a mate and pairs for life. It is also known to be a solitary nester that is widespread over the tundra.

• **NESTING** Incubation 31–40 days, mostly by female. Precocial young tended by both sexes. First flight at 60–70 days. 1 brood per year.

• **POPULATION** Common on breeding range. Common to rare on wintering range. Increasing.

Similar Birds

TRUMPETER SWAN ♀ ♂ Larger; bill slopes into flat forehead; no yellow spot in front of eye; black lores taper to point touching eye and form V across forehead; pink "smile line."

Flight Pattern

Strong direct flight with steady wing beats. Flies in straight line or V formation.

Nest Identification

Shape ♀♀ ◥ Location ▬ ♣♣♣

Low mound of plant material such as mosses, dried grasses, and sedges • near lake or other open water on ridge or island • built by both sexes, but male does more • 4–5 creamy white or nest-stained eggs; elliptically ovate, 4.2 inches long.

Plumage Sexes similar	Habitat ▬ ◟◞ ≈≈	Migration Migratory	Weight 15.7 pounds

Family ANATIDAE	Species *Cygnus cygnus*	Length 60 inches	Wingspan 7–8 feet

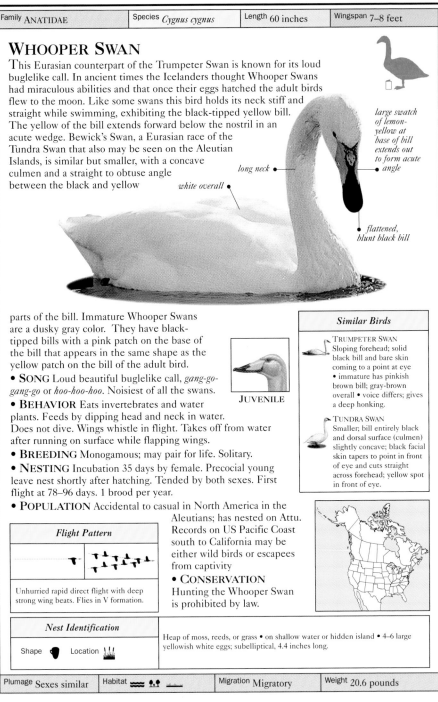

WHOOPER SWAN

This Eurasian counterpart of the Trumpeter Swan is known for its loud buglelike call. In ancient times the Icelanders thought Whooper Swans had miraculous abilities and that once their eggs hatched the adult birds flew to the moon. Like some swans this bird holds its neck stiff and straight while swimming, exhibiting the black-tipped yellow bill. The yellow of the bill extends forward below the nostril in an acute wedge. Bewick's Swan, a Eurasian race of the Tundra Swan that also may be seen on the Aleutian Islands, is similar but smaller, with a concave culmen and a straight to obtuse angle between the black and yellow

large swatch of lemon-yellow at base of bill extends out to form acute angle

long neck

white overall

flattened, blunt black bill

parts of the bill. Immature Whooper Swans are a dusky gray color. They have black-tipped bills with a pink patch on the base of the bill that appears in the same shape as the yellow patch on the bill of the adult bird.

JUVENILE

- **SONG** Loud beautiful buglelike call, *gang-go-gang-go* or *hoo-hoo-hoo*. Noisiest of all the swans.
- **BEHAVIOR** Eats invertebrates and water plants. Feeds by dipping head and neck in water. Does not dive. Wings whistle in flight. Takes off from water after running on surface while flapping wings.
- **BREEDING** Monogamous; may pair for life. Solitary.
- **NESTING** Incubation 35 days by female. Precocial young leave nest shortly after hatching. Tended by both sexes. First flight at 78–96 days. 1 brood per year.
- **POPULATION** Accidental to casual in North America in the Aleutians; has nested on Attu. Records on US Pacific Coast south to California may be either wild birds or escapees from captivity
- **CONSERVATION** Hunting the Whooper Swan is prohibited by law.

Similar Birds

TRUMPETER SWAN
Sloping forehead; solid black bill and bare skin coming to a point at eye • immature has pinkish brown bill; gray-brown overall • voice differs; gives a deep honking.

TUNDRA SWAN
Smaller; bill entirely black and dorsal surface (culmen) slightly concave; black facial skin tapers to point in front of eye and cuts straight across forehead; yellow spot in front of eye.

Flight Pattern

Unhurried rapid direct flight with deep strong wing beats. Flies in V formation.

Nest Identification

Shape · Location

Heap of moss, reeds, or grass • on shallow water or hidden island • 4–6 large yellowish white eggs; subelliptical, 4.4 inches long.

Plumage Sexes similar	Habitat	Migration Migratory	Weight 20.6 pounds

DATE _____ TIME_____ LOCATION _____

Family ANATIDAE	Species *Aix sponsa*	Length 17–20 inches	Wingspan 28–30 inches

WOOD DUCK

Considered by many to be the most beautiful duck in North America, the colorful male of this species is unmistakable with its large iridescent crest and multicolored bill. In flight it appears big-headed with a short neck and a long squared tail. The bill angles downward.

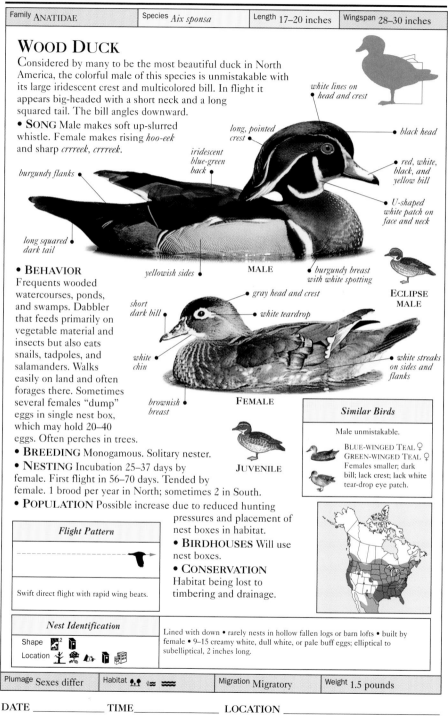

white lines on head and crest

- **SONG** Male makes soft up-slurred whistle. Female makes rising *hoo-eek* and sharp *crrreek, crrreek*.

long, pointed crest

black head

iridescent blue-green back

red, white, black, and yellow bill

burgundy flanks

U-shaped white patch on face and neck

long squared dark tail

yellowish sides

MALE

burgundy breast with white spotting

ECLIPSE MALE

- **BEHAVIOR** Frequents wooded watercourses, ponds, and swamps. Dabbler that feeds primarily on vegetable material and insects but also eats snails, tadpoles, and salamanders. Walks easily on land and often forages there. Sometimes several females "dump" eggs in single nest box, which may hold 20–40 eggs. Often perches in trees.

short dark bill

gray head and crest

white teardrop

white chin

white streaks on sides and flanks

brownish breast

FEMALE

- **BREEDING** Monogamous. Solitary nester.
- **NESTING** Incubation 25–37 days by female. First flight in 56–70 days. Tended by female. 1 brood per year in North; sometimes 2 in South.

JUVENILE

- **POPULATION** Possible increase due to reduced hunting pressures and placement of nest boxes in habitat.
- **BIRDHOUSES** Will use nest boxes.
- **CONSERVATION** Habitat being lost to timbering and drainage.

Similar Birds

Male unmistakable.

BLUE-WINGED TEAL ♀
GREEN-WINGED TEAL ♀
Females smaller; dark bill; lack crest; lack white tear-drop eye patch.

Flight Pattern

Swift direct flight with rapid wing beats.

Nest Identification

Shape

Location

Lined with down • rarely nests in hollow fallen logs or barn lofts • built by female • 9–15 creamy white, dull white, or pale buff eggs; elliptical to subelliptical, 2 inches long.

Plumage Sexes differ	Habitat	Migration Migratory	Weight 1.5 pounds

DATE _____ TIME_____ LOCATION _____

Family ANATIDAE	Species *Anas strepera*	Length 18–23 inches	Wingspan 31–36 inches

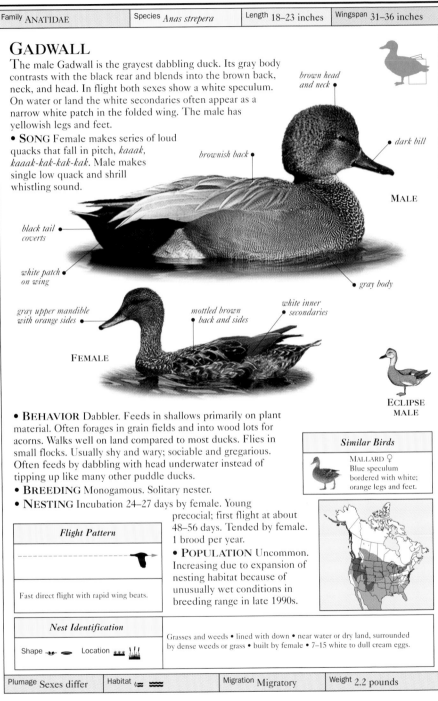

GADWALL

The male Gadwall is the grayest dabbling duck. Its gray body contrasts with the black rear and blends into the brown back, neck, and head. In flight both sexes show a white speculum. On water or land the white secondaries often appear as a narrow white patch in the folded wing. The male has yellowish legs and feet.

- **SONG** Female makes series of loud quacks that fall in pitch, *kaaak, kaaak-kak-kak-kak*. Male makes single low quack and shrill whistling sound.

brown head and neck

dark bill

brownish back

MALE

black tail coverts

white patch on wing

gray upper mandible with orange sides

mottled brown back and sides

white inner secondaries

gray body

FEMALE

ECLIPSE MALE

- **BEHAVIOR** Dabbler. Feeds in shallows primarily on plant material. Often forages in grain fields and into wood lots for acorns. Walks well on land compared to most ducks. Flies in small flocks. Usually shy and wary; sociable and gregarious. Often feeds by dabbling with head underwater instead of tipping up like many other puddle ducks.
- **BREEDING** Monogamous. Solitary nester.
- **NESTING** Incubation 24–27 days by female. Young precocial; first flight at about 48–56 days. Tended by female. 1 brood per year.
- **POPULATION** Uncommon. Increasing due to expansion of nesting habitat because of unusually wet conditions in breeding range in late 1990s.

Similar Birds

MALLARD ♀
Blue speculum bordered with white; orange legs and feet.

Flight Pattern
Fast direct flight with rapid wing beats.

Nest Identification	
Shape 〜 ⬭ Location 🌿🌿 🌾🌾	Grasses and weeds • lined with down • near water or dry land, surrounded by dense weeds or grass • built by female • 7–15 white to dull cream eggs.

Plumage Sexes differ	Habitat 〜 〜	Migration Migratory	Weight 2.2 pounds

DATE _____ TIME_____ LOCATION _____

Family ANATIDAE	Species *Anas falcata*	Length 18–21 inches	Wingspan 30–33 inches

FALCATED DUCK

This Eurasian bird is named for the male's long sickle-shaped tertials that overhang the tail. Both males and females have a big-headed appearance because of the male's large crest and the female's smaller one. In flight the dark gray-green speculum has a white border.

• **SONG** Low-pitched trilled, unique whistle begins with a quiet whistle and ends with a wavering *uit-trrrrr*. Female quacks much like a Gadwall.

• **BEHAVIOR** Highly gregarious, often forming large flocks on wintering grounds in the Old World. Usually found on freshwater, principally on small taiga lakes, rivers, channels, and swamps. Feeds by dabbling but also goes into agricultural stubble fields, where it feeds on waste grains.

• **BREEDING** Monogamous. Solitary.

• **NESTING** Incubation 24–25 days by female. Precocial young leave nest within a day of hatching.

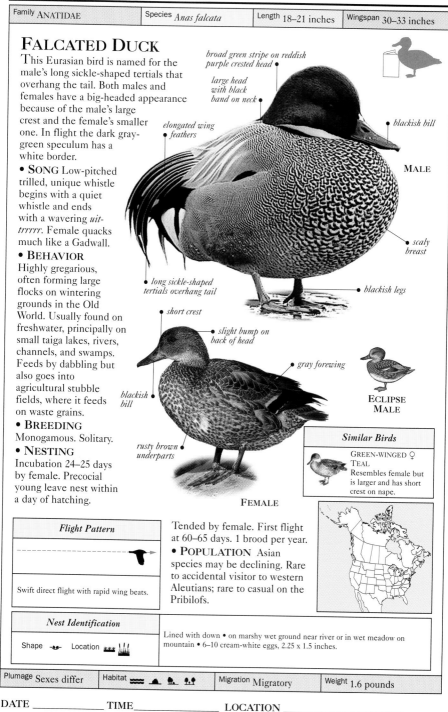

broad green stripe on reddish purple crested head •

large head with black band on neck •

elongated wing • feathers

blackish bill •

MALE

• scaly breast

long sickle-shaped • tertials overhang tail

blackish legs •

short crest •

• slight bump on back of head

• gray forewing

blackish • bill

rusty brown • underparts

ECLIPSE MALE

FEMALE

Similar Birds

GREEN-WINGED ♀ TEAL
Resembles female but is larger and has short crest on nape.

Tended by female. First flight at 60–65 days. 1 brood per year.

• **POPULATION** Asian species may be declining. Rare to accidental visitor to western Aleutians; rare to casual on the Pribilofs.

Flight Pattern
Swift direct flight with rapid wing beats.

Nest Identification	
Shape 🦆 Location ✶✶✶ 🌿🌿	Lined with down • on marshy wet ground near river or in wet meadow on mountain • 6–10 cream-white eggs, 2.25 x 1.5 inches.

Plumage Sexes differ	Habitat 〰️ 🔺 🏞️ 👣	Migration Migratory	Weight 1.6 pounds

DATE _____ TIME_____ LOCATION _____

Family ANATIDAE	Species *Anas penelope*	Length 18–20 inches	Wingspan 30–32 inches

EURASIAN WIGEON

Although the Eurasian Wigeon is not known to nest on this continent, this dabbling duck has been a rare but regular visitor in winter on both coasts in North America for the last forty to fifty years. The adult female has a cinnamon-buff head in contrast to the male's reddish head. The female also has two morphs: rufous and gray. In flight it is best distinguished from the American Wigeon by its dusky axillars and underwing linings.

buff crown

reddish head

gray overall

creamy forehead cap

blue-gray bill

brownish rose breast

white patch on forewings

MALE

ECLIPSE MALE

cinnamon-buff head

white belly

FEMALE

- **SONG** Male makes wild musical whistle, *whee-oo*, and short cheeping note. Female makes hoarse croak and sharp quack when alarmed.
- **BEHAVIOR** Highly gregarious after breeding season, often forming large flocks on the Eurasian wintering grounds. Dabbles in mud or tips up in shallow water to eat favorite foods: pond weeds, eelgrass, and other aquatic plants. Eats seeds but prefers leaves, stems, and buds. Also eats snails, beetles, and crickets. Walks well on land and often forages in fields and wooded lots some distance from water.
- **BREEDING** Monogamous. Semicolonial.
- **NESTING** Incubation 24–25 days by female. Precocial young leave nest shortly after hatching and find own food but still tended by female. First flight at 60–70 days.
- **POPULATION** Rare to uncommon visitor on both coasts but more common on the West Coast. Rare inland.

Similar Birds

♂ AMERICAN WIGEON Larger • male has gray head with wide green postocular patch; bright white crown; wine sides; white underwing linings show in flight • female generally grayer with white underwing linings.

Flight Pattern
Swift direct flight with rapid wing beats.

Nest Identification	
Shape ⚬ ⬭ Location ⫿⫿ ✦✦✦ ❧	Lined with grass and large amount of down • built in depression on ground, well hidden in tall grass • 7–9 whitish or pale buff or cream-white eggs • eggs identical to those of American Wigeon.

Plumage Sexes differ	Habitat 〰️ 〰️ 〰️	Migration Migratory	Weight 1.8 pounds

DATE _____ TIME_____ LOCATION _____

Family ANATIDAE	Species *Anas americana*	Length 18–23 inches	Wingspan 30–35 inches

AMERICAN WIGEON

This species is identified in flight by the bold white patches on its forewings, which are gray on females, and the white underwing linings. The male has a conspicuous white forehead and crown, leading hunters to nickname it "baldpate." Both males and females are more rusty brown on their breast and sides than other dabbling ducks. Legs and feet are gray. In flight females show a white belly and undertail coverts and a green speculum.

• **SONG** Throaty whistle, *whew, whew, whew.* Female makes weak guttural quack.

gray head with wide green postocular stripe

white forehead and crown

black tail and undertail coverts

MALE

black-tipped blue-gray bill

white of underparts extends onto flanks

• **BEHAVIOR** Dabbler. Flies in tight flocks that may twist and turn like those of teals. Eats plant material. Will graze on shore and in fields. Often feeds in shallow water with other duck species. Wary; takes flight quickly when it is disturbed.

gray bill with black tip

gray head and neck

brown back with rusty shoulders

reddish brown breast and sides

ECLIPSE MALE

rufous-brown breast, sides, and flanks

FEMALE

Similar Birds

♂ EURASIAN WIGEON Rufous-brown head; creamy buff forehead and crown; gray sides and back • female shows dusky underwing linings in flight; gray-morph has brownish gray head, throat, and breast; rufous morph has rufous head, neck, throat, and breast.

• **BREEDING** Monogamous. Solitary. Nests on dry land, sometimes far from water; often on small islands.

• **NESTING** Incubation 22–25 days by female. Precocial young stay in nest 45–63 days. Fed by female. 1 brood per year.

• **POPULATION** Common and apparently stable. Breeding range expanding eastward in Canada and northeastern US. Increase has been due to wet conditions as well as increase in nesting sites.

• **CONSERVATION** No issues at present; carefully monitored and managed.

Flight Pattern
Swift direct flight with strong wing beats.

Nest Identification	
Shape ⌣ Location ✦✦✦	Grasses and weeds lined with down • on dry land, sometimes on island • built by female • 6–12 white to creamy white eggs; elliptical, 2.1 inches in diameter.

Plumage Sexes differ	Habitat ⌁ ≈≈ ⌁	Migration Migratory	Weight 1.7 pounds

DATE _____ TIME_____ LOCATION _____

Family ANATIDAE	Species *Anas rubripes*	Length 19–24 inches	Wingspan 33–36 inches

AMERICAN BLACK DUCK

The darkest dabbling duck on the water looks almost black at a distance, with a paler head and foreneck. In flight the white wing linings contrast boldly with the dark body and wings. The purplish blue speculum is bordered with black, and the posterior border often has a narrow white edge. It is as large as a Mallard. Into the 1940s this was the most abundant duck in eastern and central North America and was the most heavily hunted without noticable decline in numbers. Today it seems to be losing steadily to years of heavy hunting preasure and increasing displacement by Mallards.

greenish bill with black flecking

yellow bill

FEMALE

brownish black body

pale brownish gray head and foreneck

brownish black body

MALE

- **SONG** Typical female gives loud duck quack; male makes lower croak.
- **BEHAVIOR** Dabbler. Very alert and wary; one of the quickest ducks into the air when disturbed, thrusting upward energetically off water or land. Feeds in shallow water, taking mostly plant materials in winter and a variety of aquatic insects in summer.
- **BREEDING** Monogamous. Solitary nester. Sometimes hybridizes with Mallard.
- **NESTING** Incubation 23–33 days by female. Young stay in nest 58–63 days. Fed by female. 1 brood per year.
- **POPULATION** Fairly common.
- **CONSERVATION** Management warranted due to decline in numbers, which may be caused by changes to its habitat and deforestation. Both of these circumstances seem to favor Mallards, which tend to replace Black Ducks where the two species coexist.

Similar Birds

MALLARD ♀
Female lacks contrast between head and body; paler brown; yellow-orange bill with blackish mottling; bright orange feet; metallic blue speculum bordered with a white front and back; white tail.

Flight Pattern

Swift direct flight with strong wing beats.

Nest Identification

Shape

Location

Shallow depression with plant material added • lined with down • on ground among clumps of dense vegetation • sometimes in raised situation, as on top of stump • built by female • 6–12 creamy white to greenish buff eggs.

Plumage Sexes differ	Habitat 〰〰 ⍦ ⍮	Migration Migratory	Weight 3.1 pounds

Family ANATIDAE	Species *Anas platyrhynchos*	Length 23 inches	Wingspan 30–40 inches

MALLARD

One of the best-known waterfowl in the world, the Mallard can be found almost anywhere shallow freshwater occurs. Some even reside in salt marshes and bays. The male is larger than the female. Many domesticated forms are entirely white with an orange bill, legs, and feet.

yellow bill

shiny green head

white collar

gray-brown back

metallic blue-violet speculum with white borders

2 curled-up black tail feathers

purple-chestnut breast

white sides and underparts

white tail

orange feet and legs

MALE

ECLIPSE MALE

orange and brown mottled bill

metallic blue-violet speculum with white borders

white tail

orange feet and legs

FEMALE

- **SONG** Female makes loud *quack-quack-quack, quack, quack-quack,* descending in scale. Male sounds double note and low reedy *kwek-kwek-kwek.*

- **BEHAVIOR** Generally found in shallow freshwater, where it dabbles primarily for plant food, also taking insects, mollusks, and crustaceans. Sometimes dives underwater. Walks well and often forages on shore in fields and woodlots. Leaps directly into flight from water. Frequently hybridizes.

- **BREEDING** Monogamous. Solitary nester.

- **NESTING** Incubation 26–30 days by female. Young leave nest soon after hatching. 1 brood per year.

- **POPULATION** Common to abundant.

- **FEEDERS** Corn or grains. In city parks some are tame enough to be hand-fed by humans.

- **CONSERVATION** One of the ducks harvested in greatest numbers by waterfowl hunters. Prone to lead poisoning from ingesting spent lead shot with food from bottom ooze.

Similar Birds

Female resembles many other female ducks, but blue speculum bordered white is unique.

NORTHERN SHOVELER ♂
Long dark bill; white breast; chestnut sides.

COMMON MERGANSER ♂
Narrow red bill; puffy or crested head.

RED-BREASTED MERGANSER ♂
Narrow red bill; puffy or crested head.

Flight Pattern

Swift direct flight with strong wing beats.

Nest Identification

Shape

Location

Shallow pool of plant material gathered at the site, lined with down • may be more than 1 mile from water, usually on ground among concealing vegetation • built by female • 5–14 greenish buff or grayish buff eggs, 2.3 inches long.

Plumage Sexes differ	Habitat	Migration Migratory	Weight 2.4 pounds

DATE _____ TIME_____ LOCATION _____

Family ANATIDAE	Species *Anas poecilorhyncha*	Length 22 inches	Wingspan 30–33 inches

SPOT-BILLED DUCK

This Asian native is named for the red spotting on the base of its bill, but the

buff face with black stripe through eyes to crown

blackish brown crown

black bill with yellow tip

subspecies, *A.p. zonorhyncha*, that actually reaches this continent in Alaska lacks them. Rather, look for the yellow-tipped bill on this Mallard-sized duck that otherwise resembles a female Mallard or an American Black Duck at a distance.

buff-brown, gray, and black mottling overall

orange feet and legs

blue speculum

white tertials produce white wing spot on folded wing

Like all dabbling ducks, it can spring directly into flight from the water without a running start. In flight it shows white underwing linings and a lighter colored belly that contrast sharply with its dark body and flight feathers.

- **SONG** Has not been described.
- **BEHAVIOR** Gregarious in nonbreeding season. Feeds in typical dabbling duck fashion with head in water and tail pointed upward. Sometimes skims food from surface. Eats aquatic plants, seeds, and snails. Walks easily on land and often rests or forages on shore.
- **BREEDING** Monogamous.
- **NESTING** Incubation 26–30 days by female. Young precocial. Female leads young to water shortly after hatching but tends them until first flight at 49–60 days. 1 brood per year.
- **POPULATION** Casual to accidental on islands off mainland Alaska. Fairly common to common in native Asian range.
- **CONSERVATION** Hunted over much of breeding and winter ranges.

Similar Birds

MALLARD ♀
Female has yellow-orange bill with dark mottling; metallic blue speculum with white border on both sides.

AMERICAN BLACK DUCK
Blackish brown overall; paler face and foreneck; yellow bill with no black tip; darker tertials; purple-blue speculum with black border; red-brown feet and legs.

Flight Pattern

Swift powerful direct flight with rapid wing beats.

Nest Identification

Shape ⌒ ⬯   Location ✦✦✦ ⍦⍦⍦

Lined with feathers and down • on dry ground atop thick pile of moss or grasses • built by female • 7–10 eggs; oval to long oval, 2.3 x 1.7 inches.

Plumage Sexes similar	Habitat 〰 〰	Migration Migratory	Weight Undetermined

DATE _____ TIME_____ LOCATION _____

| Family ANATIDAE | Species *Anas discors* | Length 14–16 inches | Wingspan 23–31 inches |

BLUE-WINGED TEAL

One of the smallest ducks in North America travels great distances between breeding and wintering grounds, as much as 7,000 miles. Both sexes have a large pale blue patch on the forewings and a long metallic green speculum that is visible when wings are spread. Males in breeding colors have a gray-violet head bordered by a bold white facial crescent.

gray-violet head

short dark bill

white crescent on face

MALE

tawny brown body with dark spotting

yellowish legs and feet

white flank patch

pale grayish brown head

brown body with dark chevron-shaped spots

FEMALE

- **SONG** In flight, the male often makes a high sibilant *tseel*. The female makes *wak* quacking sound.
- **BEHAVIOR** Very fast taking off from the water, this bird flies quickly and rapidly, often twisting and turning in small compact flocks. Plants make up the bulk of its diet. Often forages in shallow waters. One of the earliest ducks to migrate southward to wintering areas. More than 90 percent of population winters south of US border. Tame, often allowing close approach.
- **BREEDING** Monogamous. Solitary nester.
- **NESTING** Incubation 22–27 days by female. First flight at 35–49 days. Tended by female. 1 brood per year.
- **POPULATION** Fairly common in the East; uncommon in the West. Apparently stable.
- **CONSERVATION** Most Blue-Winged Teals winter south of US borders, so Latin American cooperation is needed to further conservation efforts.

Similar Birds

NORTHERN SHOVELER ♀
Much larger; spatulate bill.

GREEN-WINGED TEAL ♀
Larger bill; lacks white undertail coverts and blue forewing patch in flight.

CINNAMON TEAL ♀
Longer bill; richer brown; less distinct eye line.

Flight Pattern
Fast direct flight with steady wing beats.

Nest Identification	Shallow depression with some grass or weeds added • lined with down • on ground in prairie, hayfield, or coastal meadow • built by female • 6–15 white, olive-white, dull white, or tinged olive eggs; ovate to elliptical ovate, 1.8 inches in diameter.
Shape ➛ ➛ ➛ Location ━ ✿✿ 𝟏𝟏𝟏	

| Plumage Sexes differ | Habitat 🌾 〰〰 | Migration Migratory | Weight 14.4 ounces |

DATE _____ TIME_____ LOCATION _____

| Family ANATIDAE | Species *Anas cyanoptera* | Length 14–17 inches | Wingspan 24–30 inches |

CINNAMON TEAL

The male, with its rich cinnamon hues, is one of the most recognizable ducks in western North America. The female's warm earth tones blend well with the cattails and reeds that surround its home. The Cinnamon Teal and the Ruddy Duck are the only waterfowl to breed in both North and South America. In flight the upper forewing features a large pale powder-blue patch and the speculum is metallic green with a white border. Juveniles and eclipse males resemble females.

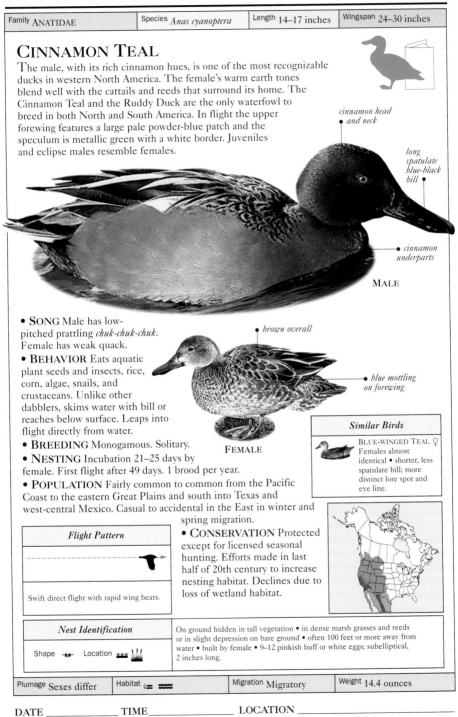

cinnamon head and neck

long spatulate blue-black bill

cinnamon underparts

MALE

brown overall

blue mottling on forewing

FEMALE

- **SONG** Male has low-pitched prattling *chuk-chuk-chuk*. Female has weak quack.
- **BEHAVIOR** Eats aquatic plant seeds and insects, rice, corn, algae, snails, and crustaceans. Unlike other dabblers, skims water with bill or reaches below surface. Leaps into flight directly from water.
- **BREEDING** Monogamous. Solitary.
- **NESTING** Incubation 21–25 days by female. First flight after 49 days. 1 brood per year.
- **POPULATION** Fairly common to common from the Pacific Coast to the eastern Great Plains and south into Texas and west-central Mexico. Casual to accidental in the East in winter and spring migration.
- **CONSERVATION** Protected except for licensed seasonal hunting. Efforts made in last half of 20th century to increase nesting habitat. Declines due to loss of wetland habitat.

Similar Birds

BLUE-WINGED TEAL ♀ Females almost identical • shorter, less spatulate bill; more distinct lore spot and eye line.

Flight Pattern

Swift direct flight with rapid wing beats.

| *Nest Identification* | On ground hidden in tall vegetation • in dense marsh grasses and reeds or in slight depression on bare ground • often 100 feet or more away from water • built by female • 9–12 pinkish buff or white eggs; subelliptical, 2 inches long. |
| Shape — Location | |

| Plumage Sexes differ | Habitat | Migration Migratory | Weight 14.4 ounces |

DATE _____ TIME_____ LOCATION _____

Family ANATIDAE	Species *Anas clypeata*	Length 17–20 inches	Wingspan 27–33 inches

NORTHERN SHOVELER

No duck in North America has a bigger bill. The large, spatulate bill is longer than the head, giving the bird a front heavy look. In flight both sexes show large powder-blue patches on the forewing and a metallic green speculum. Both males and females have bright orange legs and feet.

black head with green gloss

MALE

large spoon-shaped black bill

white tail feathers (most)

black undertail and uppertail coverts

white flank spot

blue patch on folded wing

orange legs and feet

rich chestnut sides and belly

white breast

ECLIPSE MALE

grayish bill mottled orange

mottled brown

FEMALE

Similar Birds

MALLARD
Male has green head but has chestnut breast; white sides; lacks blue patch on forewing • female has smaller bill; lacks blue on front of wing.

BLUE-WINGED TEAL
Smaller; shows pale blue forewing patch in flight • male has brown body; gray head; white crescent on front of face; small black bill • female is brown overall; small black bill.

• **SONG** In courtship male utters guttural *who, who, who* or *took, took, took*. Female utters feeble quack and descending *WACK-wack-wack-wa-wa*.

• **BEHAVIOR** Frequently swims with head held low, bill partly submerged, straining water for small aquatic plants and animals through the comblike teeth along sides of bill. Animals make up approximately one-third of its diet. Swift flight into air by leaping off water. Rapid, sometimes darting, teal-like flight.

• **BREEDING** Monogamous. Solitary nester.

• **NESTING** Incubation 21–27 days by female. Precocial young leave nest within a few hours of hatching. First flight at 38–66 days. Tended by female. 1 brood per year.

• **POPULATION** Common to abundant. Increasing due to wet conditions in breeding range.

Flight Pattern
Strong direct flight with rapid wing beats.

Nest Identification	
Shape 🦆 ⬭ Location ⁂	Partly filled with dried grasses and weeds • lined with down • close to water, generally in area of short grass, or far from water on high dry ground of prairies • built by female • 6–19 olive-buff or greenish gray eggs; elliptical, 2 inches long.

Plumage Sexes differ	Habitat 🌾 〰️ 🔺 🌱	Migration Migratory	Weight 1.4 pounds

DATE _____ TIME_____ LOCATION _____

Family ANATIDAE	Species *Anas acuta*	Length 21–29 inches	Wingspan 29–35 inches

NORTHERN PINTAIL

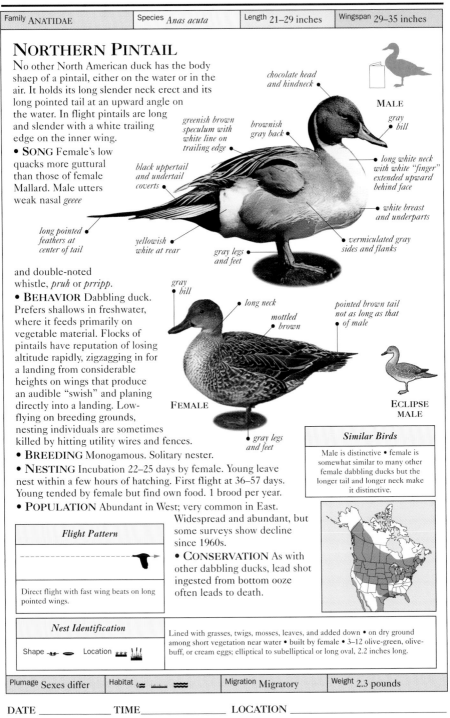

No other North American duck has the body shaep of a pintail, either on the water or in the air. It holds its long slender neck erect and its long pointed tail at an upward angle on the water. In flight pintails are long and slender with a white trailing edge on the inner wing.

• **SONG** Female's low quacks more guttural than those of female Mallard. Male utters weak nasal *geeee*

chocolate head and hindneck

MALE

greenish brown speculum with white line on trailing edge

brownish gray back

gray bill

black uppertail and undertail coverts

long white neck with white "finger" extended upward behind face

white breast and underparts

long pointed feathers at center of tail

yellowish white at rear

gray legs and feet

vermiculated gray sides and flanks

and double-noted whistle, *pruh* or *prripp*.

gray bill

long neck

mottled brown

pointed brown tail not as long as that of male

• **BEHAVIOR** Dabbling duck. Prefers shallows in freshwater, where it feeds primarily on vegetable material. Flocks of pintails have reputation of losing altitude rapidly, zigzagging in for a landing from considerable heights on wings that produce an audible "swish" and planing directly into a landing. Low-flying on breeding grounds, nesting individuals are sometimes killed by hitting utility wires and fences.

FEMALE

ECLIPSE MALE

gray legs and feet

Similar Birds

Male is distinctive • female is somewhat similar to many other female dabbling ducks but the longer tail and longer neck make it distinctive.

• **BREEDING** Monogamous. Solitary nester.

• **NESTING** Incubation 22–25 days by female. Young leave nest within a few hours of hatching. First flight at 36–57 days. Young tended by female but find own food. 1 brood per year.

• **POPULATION** Abundant in West; very common in East. Widespread and abundant, but some surveys show decline since 1960s.

• **CONSERVATION** As with other dabbling ducks, lead shot ingested from bottom ooze often leads to death.

Flight Pattern

Direct flight with fast wing beats on long pointed wings.

Nest Identification

Shape — —   Location ▪▪▪ ⩗⩗

Lined with grasses, twigs, mosses, leaves, and added down • on dry ground among short vegetation near water • built by female • 3–12 olive-green, olive-buff, or cream eggs; elliptical to subelliptical or long oval, 2.2 inches long.

Plumage Sexes differ	Habitat ⩗ ⩘ ⩯	Migration Migratory	Weight 2.3 pounds

DATE _____ TIME_____ LOCATION _____

Family ANATIDAE	Species *Anas formosa*	Length 16 inches	Wingspan 20–25 inches

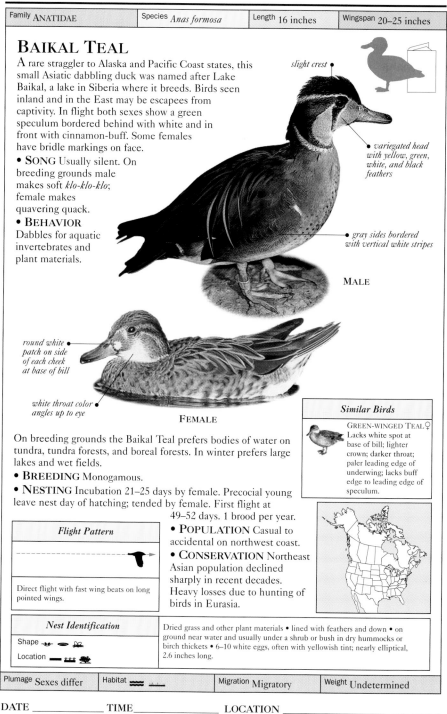

BAIKAL TEAL

A rare straggler to Alaska and Pacific Coast states, this small Asiatic dabbling duck was named after Lake Baikal, a lake in Siberia where it breeds. Birds seen inland and in the East may be escapees from captivity. In flight both sexes show a green speculum bordered behind with white and in front with cinnamon-buff. Some females have bridle markings on face.

• **SONG** Usually silent. On breeding grounds male makes soft *klo-klo-klo*; female makes quavering quack.

• **BEHAVIOR** Dabbles for aquatic invertebrates and plant materials.

slight crest

variegated head with yellow, green, white, and black feathers

gray sides bordered with vertical white stripes

MALE

round white patch on side of each cheek at base of bill

white throat color angles up to eye

FEMALE

On breeding grounds the Baikal Teal prefers bodies of water on tundra, tundra forests, and boreal forests. In winter prefers large lakes and wet fields.

• **BREEDING** Monogamous.

• **NESTING** Incubation 21–25 days by female. Precocial young leave nest day of hatching; tended by female. First flight at 49–52 days. 1 brood per year.

• **POPULATION** Casual to accidental on northwest coast.

• **CONSERVATION** Northeast Asian population declined sharply in recent decades. Heavy losses due to hunting of birds in Eurasia.

Similar Birds

GREEN-WINGED TEAL ♀
Lacks white spot at base of bill; lighter crown; darker throat; paler leading edge of underwing; lacks buff edge to leading edge of speculum.

Flight Pattern
Direct flight with fast wing beats on long pointed wings.

Nest Identification	
Shape	Dried grass and other plant materials • lined with feathers and down • on ground near water and usually under a shrub or bush in dry hummocks or birch thickets • 6–10 white eggs, often with yellowish tint; nearly elliptical, 2.6 inches long.
Location	

Plumage Sexes differ	Habitat	Migration Migratory	Weight Undetermined

DATE _____ TIME_____ LOCATION _____

Family ANATIDAE	Species *Anas crecca*	Length 12–16 inches	Wingspan 20–25 inches

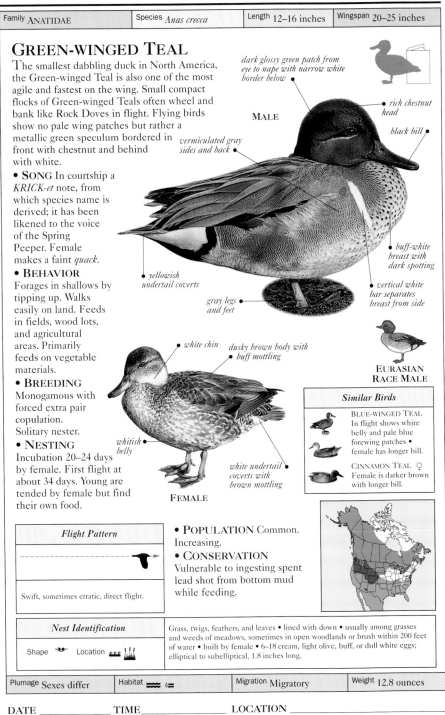

GREEN-WINGED TEAL

The smallest dabbling duck in North America, the Green-winged Teal is also one of the most agile and fastest on the wing. Small compact flocks of Green-winged Teals often wheel and bank like Rock Doves in flight. Flying birds show no pale wing patches but rather a metallic green speculum bordered in front with chestnut and behind with white.

dark glossy green patch from eye to nape with narrow white border below

MALE

vermiculated gray sides and back

rich chestnut head

black bill

buff-white breast with dark spotting

vertical white bar separates breast from side

- **SONG** In courtship a *KRICK-et* note, from which species name is derived; it has been likened to the voice of the Spring Peeper. Female makes a faint *quack*.
- **BEHAVIOR** Forages in shallows by tipping up. Walks easily on land. Feeds in fields, wood lots, and agricultural areas. Primarily feeds on vegetable materials.
- **BREEDING** Monogamous with forced extra pair copulation. Solitary nester.
- **NESTING** Incubation 20–24 days by female. First flight at about 34 days. Young are tended by female but find their own food.

yellowish undertail coverts

gray legs and feet

white chin

dusky brown body with buff mottling

EURASIAN RACE MALE

whitish belly

white undertail coverts with brown mottling

FEMALE

Similar Birds

BLUE-WINGED TEAL
In flight shows white belly and pale blue forewing patches • female has longer bill.

CINNAMON TEAL ♀
Female is darker brown with longer bill.

Flight Pattern	
Swift, sometimes erratic, direct flight.	

- **POPULATION** Common. Increasing.
- **CONSERVATION** Vulnerable to ingesting spent lead shot from bottom mud while feeding.

Nest Identification	
Shape 〰 Location ▸▸▸ ⅗⅗	Grass, twigs, feathers, and leaves • lined with down • usually among grasses and weeds of meadows, sometimes in open woodlands or brush within 200 feet of water • built by female • 6–18 cream, light olive, buff, or dull white eggs; elliptical to subelliptical, 1.8 inches long.

Plumage Sexes differ	Habitat 〰 ⩫	Migration Migratory	Weight 12.8 ounces

DATE _____ TIME_____ LOCATION _____

Family ANATIDAE	Species *Aythya valisineria*	Length 19–24 inches	Wingspan 28–36 inches

CANVASBACK

A sloping profile from the front of its crown to the tip of its long dark bill distinguishes this bird. It is one of the largest and heaviest ducks in North America. At a distance the male appears white with a black rear and breast. The long neck and head are rich rust-red. The female is grayer with a rusty tint to the neck and head.

• **SONG** Male makes grunt or croak; female makes quack.

• **BEHAVIOR** A wary species that often rafts well away from the shoreline. Flies high, frequently in formations. Dives

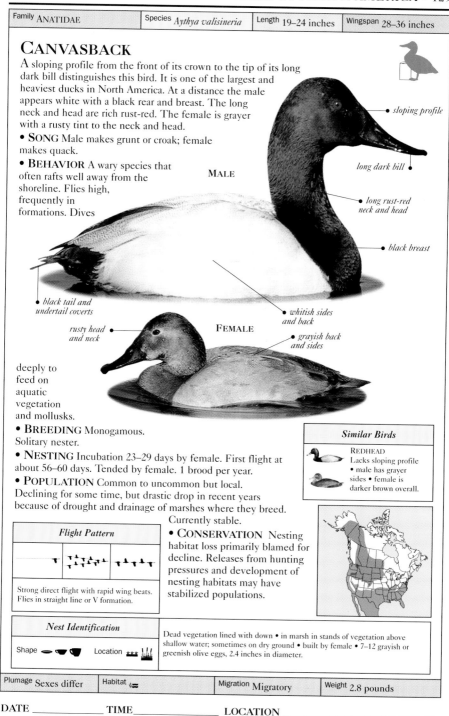

sloping profile

MALE

long dark bill

long rust-red neck and head

black breast

black tail and undertail coverts

whitish sides and back

rusty head and neck

FEMALE

grayish back and sides

deeply to feed on aquatic vegetation and mollusks.

• **BREEDING** Monogamous. Solitary nester.

• **NESTING** Incubation 23–29 days by female. First flight at about 56–60 days. Tended by female. 1 brood per year.

• **POPULATION** Common to uncommon but local. Declining for some time, but drastic drop in recent years because of drought and drainage of marshes where they breed. Currently stable.

• **CONSERVATION** Nesting habitat loss primarily blamed for decline. Releases from hunting pressures and development of nesting habitats may have stabilized populations.

Similar Birds

REDHEAD
Lacks sloping profile • male has grayer sides • female is darker brown overall.

Flight Pattern

Strong direct flight with rapid wing beats. Flies in straight line or V formation.

Nest Identification

Shape ⬭ ◗ ◖   Location ✶✶✶ ⋓⋓

Dead vegetation lined with down • in marsh in stands of vegetation above shallow water; sometimes on dry ground • built by female • 7–12 grayish or greenish olive eggs, 2.4 inches in diameter.

Plumage Sexes differ	Habitat	Migration Migratory	Weight 2.8 pounds

DATE _____ TIME_____ LOCATION _____

Family ANATIDAE	Species *Aythya americana*	Length 18–22 inches	Wingspan 29–35 inches

REDHEAD

A diving duck of freshwater marshes in summer, this bird congregates in large numbers on marine bays, estuaries, and big lakes in winter. The male's golden yellow eye is the most striking of North American waterfowl. In flight both sexes show a broad gray trailing edge to the wing.

• **SONG** Silent most of year. During courtship male utters mewing sounds, *whee-ough* or *keyair*. Also makes low trilling *rrrrrr*. Female has grating *squak*.

• **BEHAVIOR** Diving duck. Crepuscular activities, including flight and feeding. Some feeding at night.

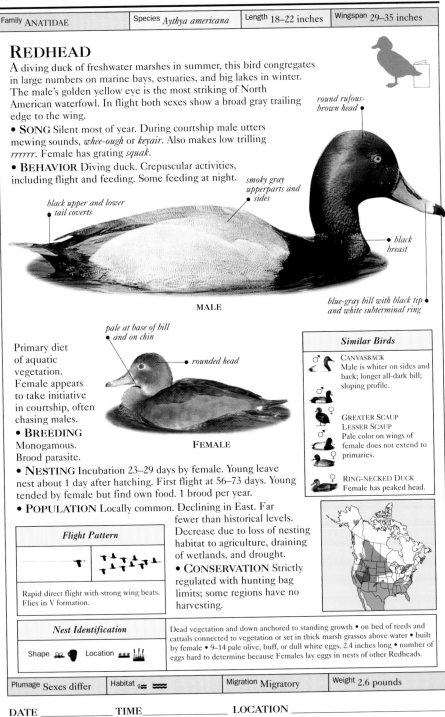

round rufous-brown head

smoky gray upperparts and sides

black upper and lower tail coverts

black breast

MALE

blue-gray bill with black tip and white subterminal ring

pale at base of bill and on chin

rounded head

Primary diet of aquatic vegetation. Female appears to take initiative in courtship, often chasing males.

• **BREEDING** Monogamous. Brood parasite.

FEMALE

Similar Birds

CANVASBACK
Male is whiter on sides and back; longer all-dark bill; sloping profile.

GREATER SCAUP
LESSER SCAUP
Pale color on wings of female does not extend to primaries.

RING-NECKED DUCK
Female has peaked head.

• **NESTING** Incubation 23–29 days by female. Young leave nest about 1 day after hatching. First flight at 56–73 days. Young tended by female but find own food. 1 brood per year.

• **POPULATION** Locally common. Declining in East. Far fewer than historical levels. Decrease due to loss of nesting habitat to agriculture, draining of wetlands, and drought.

• **CONSERVATION** Strictly regulated with hunting bag limits; some regions have no harvesting.

Flight Pattern

Rapid direct flight with strong wing beats. Flies in V formation.

Nest Identification

Shape   Location

Dead vegetation and down anchored to standing growth • on bed of reeds and cattails connected to vegetation or set in thick marsh grasses above water • built by female • 9–14 pale olive, buff, or dull white eggs, 2.4 inches long • number of eggs hard to determine because Females lay eggs in nests of other Redheads.

Plumage Sexes differ	Habitat	Migration Migratory	Weight 2.6 pounds

DATE _____ TIME_____ LOCATION _____

Family ANATIDAE	Species *Aythya ferina*	Length 18–22 inches	Wingspan 29–35 inches

COMMON POCHARD

Although the Common Pochard is not common in North America, it has been recorded in increasing numbers on the Pribilof Islands since 1957. This duck, which nests in Eurasia, is an adept diver, capable of diving as deep as ten feet below the water's surface. However, the heavy body requires these ducks to take a running start across the water in order to fly. In flight both sexes show a gray trailing edge to the wing.
• **SONG** Usually silent. In courtship male gives a whistle. Female utters shrieking hoarse *karrr*.

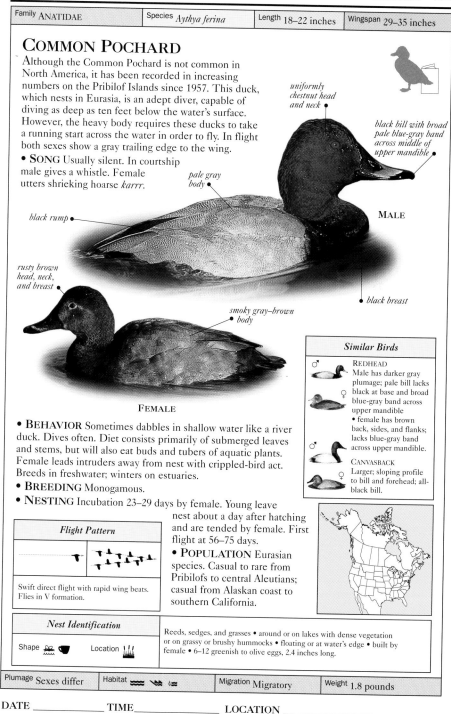

uniformly chestnut head and neck

black bill with broad pale blue-gray band across middle of upper mandible

MALE

pale gray body

black rump

rusty brown head, neck, and breast

smoky gray–brown body

black breast

FEMALE

• **BEHAVIOR** Sometimes dabbles in shallow water like a river duck. Dives often. Diet consists primarily of submerged leaves and stems, but will also eat buds and tubers of aquatic plants. Female leads intruders away from nest with crippled-bird act. Breeds in freshwater; winters on estuaries.
• **BREEDING** Monogamous.
• **NESTING** Incubation 23–29 days by female. Young leave nest about a day after hatching and are tended by female. First flight at 56–75 days.
• **POPULATION** Eurasian species. Casual to rare from Pribilofs to central Aleutians; casual from Alaskan coast to southern California.

Similar Birds

♂ REDHEAD
Male has darker gray plumage; pale bill lacks black at base and broad blue-gray band across upper mandible
♀ • female has brown back, sides, and flanks; lacks blue-gray band across upper mandible.

CANVASBACK
Larger; sloping profile to bill and forehead; all-black bill.

Flight Pattern

Swift direct flight with rapid wing beats. Flies in V formation.

Nest Identification

Shape | Location

Reeds, sedges, and grasses • around or on lakes with dense vegetation or on grassy or brushy hummocks • floating or at water's edge • built by female • 6–12 greenish to olive eggs, 2.4 inches long.

Plumage Sexes differ	Habitat	Migration Migratory	Weight 1.8 pounds

DATE _____ TIME _____ LOCATION _____

Family ANATIDAE	Species *Aythya collaris*	Length 14–18 inches	Wingspan 24–30 inches

RING-NECKED DUCK

This puffy-headed diving duck with a peaked crown prefers small freshwater ponds, wooded lakes, and swamps. On water the male appears dark with whitish gray sides separated from the black breast by a white crescent that is clearly discernible at a distance. Both sexes have a white ring on the bill, white bellies, bluish gray legs and feet, and show a gray wing stripe in flight. The cinnamon ring at the base of the neck, which gives the duck its name, is a poor field mark, seen only at close range in good light.

peaked black head with purplish gloss

MALE

blue-gray bill with black tip and broad white subterminal ring

pale gray sides and flanks

black back, tail coverts, and tail

black neck and breast

- **SONG**
Generally silent. Male makes a faint wheezy whistle; female makes harsh *deeeer*.

peaked head

white eye ring and thin postocular stripe

FEMALE

pale face at base of bill, chin, and throat

- **BEHAVIOR**
Swims lightly with head up. Excellent diver. Aquatic plants more than 80 percent of diet. Feeds on bottom as deep as 40 feet below surface.
- **BREEDING** Monogamous. Solitary nester.
- **NESTING** Incubation 25–29 days by female. Young leave nest in 12–24 hours. First flight after 49–56 days. Young tended by female but find own food. 1 brood per year.

Similar Birds

GREATER SCAUP
LESSER SCAUP
White wing stripe • male has gray back • female has white ring around bill.

TUFTED DUCK
Males have white flanks • head rounded with tuft on back of crown; both sexes lack broad white band on bill • female lacks pale eye line; has shorter tuft on crown.

- **POPULATION** Fairly common and widespread. Stable or increasing.
- **CONSERVATION** As with other ducks that feed on the bottom, may ingest lead shot and be susceptible to lead poisoning.

Flight Pattern
Direct flight with rapid wing beats in loose flocks.

Nest Identification	Grasses, sedges, and weeds • lined with down and marsh plants • on dry hammock, clump of brush, or floating mat of vegetation, close to open water or just above water in marsh border of pond or slough • built by female • 6–14 olive, gray, olive-brown, or green-buff eggs; elliptical to oval, 2.3 inches long.
Shape ⌣ ⌣ ⌣ Location ᪥᪥᪥ ⋔⋔	

Plumage Sexes differ	Habitat 〜 〜	Migration Migratory	Weight 1.6 pounds

DATE _____ TIME_____ LOCATION _____

Family ANATIDAE	Species *Aythya fuligula*	Length 18–22 inches	Wingspan 30–35 inches

TUFTED DUCK

Superficially like a Ring-necked Duck with a long crested tuft, this Old World duck is accidental to casual in North America, except on the western coast of Alaska, where it is a regular visitor. At a distance the breeding male appears black with white sides and flanks. In flight both sexes show a broad white wing stripe that extends onto the inner primaries.

rounded black head with purple gloss

yellow eye

gray bill with black tip

long, loose crested tuft on back of head

black neck and breast

black back, tail coverts, and tail

MALE

sometimes whitish at base of bill

short tuft

white sides, flanks, and belly

FEMALE

Similar Birds

RING-NECKED DUCK
Male has gray sides and flanks; white crescent separates black breast from gray side • both sexes have gray wing stripe.

GREATER SCAUP
LESSER SCAUP
Males have gray backs • females have bolder white face patches at base of bill.

- **SONG** Usually silent. Various soft growling notes and low whistles.
- **BEHAVIOR** Excellent diver. Prefers freshwater lakes and reservoirs but can be found in coastal marshes, bays, and estuaries in company of other diving ducks. Feeds on plants, crustaceans, mollusks, and aquatic insects.
- **BREEDING** Monogamous. Sometimes forms loose colonies.
- **NESTING** Incubation 23–28 days. First flight within 45–50 days. Young tended by female. 1 brood per year.
- **POPULATION** Uncommon to rare. Not known to breed in North America; a visitor during migration and winter.

Flight Pattern
Swift direct flight with steady wing beats.

Nest Identification	
Shape	Location	Grasses and dark gray down • hidden in reeds or under bushes close to water • 7–10 yellow, brown, or greenish eggs.

Plumage Sexes differ	Habitat	Migration Migratory	Weight 1.5 pounds

DATE _____ TIME_____ LOCATION _____

Family ANATIDAE	Species *Aythya marila*	Length 15–20 inches	Wingspan 30–34 inches

GREATER SCAUP

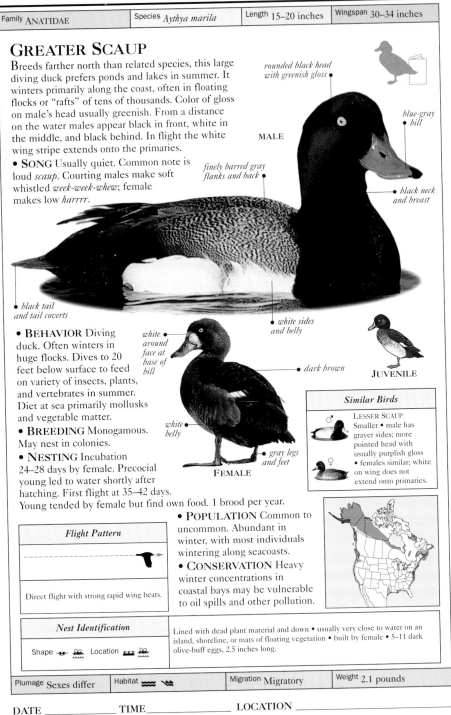

Breeds farther north than related species, this large diving duck prefers ponds and lakes in summer. It winters primarily along the coast, often in floating flocks or "rafts" of tens of thousands. Color of gloss on male's head usually greenish. From a distance on the water males appear black in front, white in the middle, and black behind. In flight the white wing stripe extends onto the primaries.

rounded black head with greenish gloss

MALE

blue-gray bill

finely barred gray flanks and back

black neck and breast

• **SONG** Usually quiet. Common note is loud *scaup*. Courting males make soft whistled *week-week-whew*; female makes low *harrrr*.

black tail and tail coverts

white around face at base of bill

white sides and belly

dark brown

JUVENILE

• **BEHAVIOR** Diving duck. Often winters in huge flocks. Dives to 20 feet below surface to feed on variety of insects, plants, and vertebrates in summer. Diet at sea primarily mollusks and vegetable matter.

white belly

gray legs and feet

FEMALE

• **BREEDING** Monogamous. May nest in colonies.

• **NESTING** Incubation 24–28 days by female. Precocial young led to water shortly after hatching. First flight at 35–42 days. Young tended by female but find own food. 1 brood per year.

Similar Birds

LESSER SCAUP
Smaller • male has grayer sides; more pointed head with usually purplish gloss • females similar; white on wing does not extend onto primaries.

• **POPULATION** Common to uncommon. Abundant in winter, with most individuals wintering along seacoasts.

• **CONSERVATION** Heavy winter concentrations in coastal bays may be vulnerable to oil spills and other pollution.

Flight Pattern

Direct flight with strong rapid wing beats.

Nest Identification

Shape —   Location

Lined with dead plant material and down • usually very close to water on an island, shoreline, or mats of floating vegetation • built by female • 5–11 dark olive-buff eggs, 2.5 inches long.

Plumage Sexes differ	Habitat	Migration Migratory	Weight 2.1 pounds

Family ANATIDAE	Species *Aythya affinis*	Length 15–18 inches	Wingspan 24–33 inches

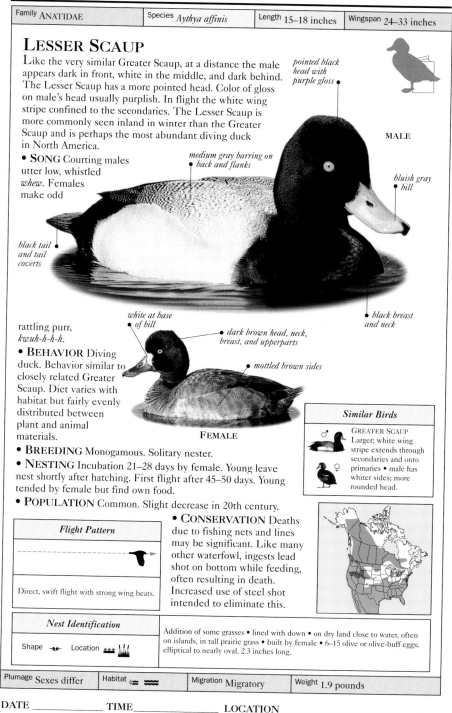

LESSER SCAUP

Like the very similar Greater Scaup, at a distance the male appears dark in front, white in the middle, and dark behind. The Lesser Scaup has a more pointed head. Color of gloss on male's head usually purplish. In flight the white wing stripe confined to the secondaries. The Lesser Scaup is more commonly seen inland in winter than the Greater Scaup and is perhaps the most abundant diving duck in North America.

pointed black head with purple gloss

MALE

• **SONG** Courting males utter low, whistled *whew.* Females make odd

medium gray barring on back and flanks

bluish gray bill

black tail and tail coverts

rattling purr, *kwuh-h-h-h.*

white at base of bill

black breast and neck

dark brown head, neck, breast, and upperparts

• **BEHAVIOR** Diving duck. Behavior similar to closely related Greater Scaup. Diet varies with habitat but fairly evenly distributed between plant and animal materials.

mottled brown sides

FEMALE

• **BREEDING** Monogamous. Solitary nester.

• **NESTING** Incubation 21–28 days by female. Young leave nest shortly after hatching. First flight after 45–50 days. Young tended by female but find own food.

• **POPULATION** Common. Slight decrease in 20th century.

• **CONSERVATION** Deaths due to fishing nets and lines may be significant. Like many other waterfowl, ingests lead shot on bottom while feeding, often resulting in death. Increased use of steel shot intended to eliminate this.

Similar Birds

♂ **GREATER SCAUP** Larger; white wing stripe extends through secondaries and onto primaries • male has whiter sides; more rounded head.
♀

Flight Pattern
Direct, swift flight with strong wing beats.

Nest Identification	
Shape ～ Location ✳✳ ⱴⱴ	Addition of some grasses • lined with down • on dry land close to water, often on islands, in tall prairie grass • built by female • 6–15 olive or olive-buff eggs; elliptical to nearly oval, 2.3 inches long.

Plumage Sexes differ	Habitat ⱴ ～	Migration Migratory	Weight 1.9 pounds

DATE _____ TIME_____ LOCATION _____

Family ANATIDAE	Species *Polysticta stelleri*	Length 17–19 inches	Wingspan 28–30 inches

STELLER'S EIDER

The smallest eider (about the size of a Surf Scoter), the Steller's Eider is rarely found outside Alaska. The male is the only eider with bright, buffy underparts. It has a short bill and does not have the stout chunky appearance of other eiders. Its white head, back, and sides are adorned with a black line down the center of the back, rear, and tail. Legs and feet are blue-gray like its bill, and its wings make a whistling sound when the bird is in flight. On the back of its white head the male has a green "bump" of feathers with a black

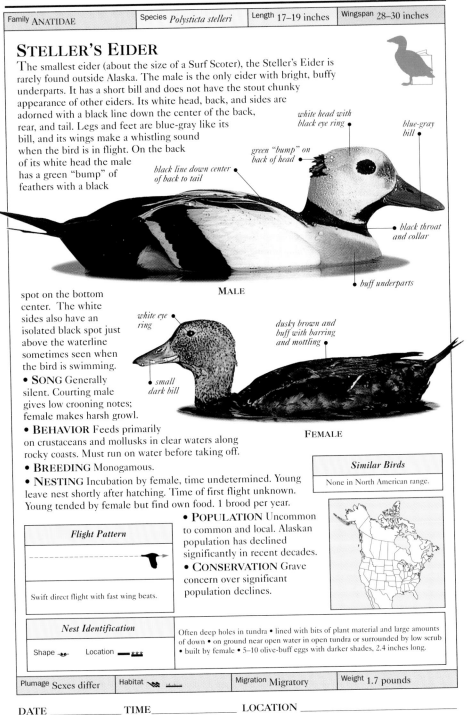

white head with black eye ring

blue-gray bill

green "bump" on back of head

black line down center of back to tail

black throat and collar

buff underparts

MALE

white eye ring

small dark bill

dusky brown and buff with barring and mottling

FEMALE

spot on the bottom center. The white sides also have an isolated black spot just above the waterline sometimes seen when the bird is swimming.

• **SONG** Generally silent. Courting male gives low crooning notes; female makes harsh growl.

• **BEHAVIOR** Feeds primarily on crustaceans and mollusks in clear waters along rocky coasts. Must run on water before taking off.

• **BREEDING** Monogamous.

• **NESTING** Incubation by female, time undetermined. Young leave nest shortly after hatching. Time of first flight unknown. Young tended by female but find own food. 1 brood per year.

• **POPULATION** Uncommon to common and local. Alaskan population has declined significantly in recent decades.

• **CONSERVATION** Grave concern over significant population declines.

Similar Birds
None in North American range.

Flight Pattern
Swift direct flight with fast wing beats.

Nest Identification	
Shape	Location	Often deep holes in tundra • lined with bits of plant material and large amounts of down • on ground near open water in open tundra or surrounded by low scrub • built by female • 5–10 olive-buff eggs with darker shades, 2.4 inches long.

Plumage Sexes differ	Habitat	Migration Migratory	Weight 1.7 pounds

DATE _____ TIME_____ LOCATION _____

| Family ANATIDAE | Species *Somateria fischeri* | Length 20–23 inches | Wingspan 35–36 inches |

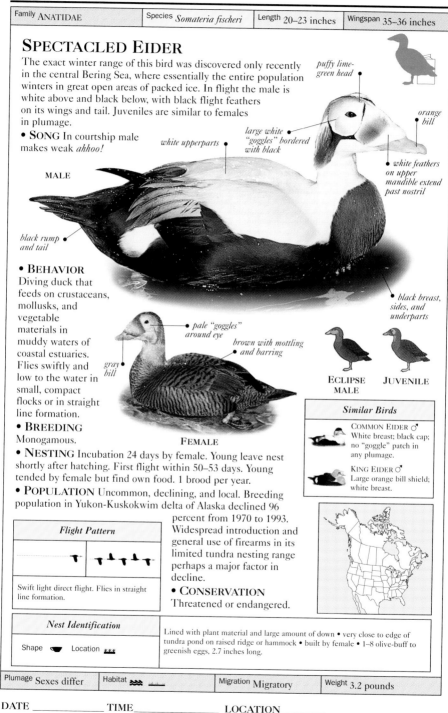

SPECTACLED EIDER

The exact winter range of this bird was discovered only recently in the central Bering Sea, where essentially the entire population winters in great open areas of packed ice. In flight the male is white above and black below, with black flight feathers on its wings and tail. Juveniles are similar to females in plumage.

puffy lime-green head

orange bill

large white "goggles" bordered with black

white upperparts

white feathers on upper mandible extend past nostril

- **SONG** In courtship male makes weak *ahhoo!*

MALE

black rump and tail

- **BEHAVIOR**
Diving duck that feeds on crustaceans, mollusks, and vegetable materials in muddy waters of coastal estuaries. Flies swiftly and low to the water in small, compact flocks or in straight line formation.

black breast, sides, and underparts

pale "goggles" around eye

brown with mottling and barring

gray bill

ECLIPSE MALE   **JUVENILE**

- **BREEDING**
Monogamous.

FEMALE

Similar Birds

COMMON EIDER ♂
White breast; black cap; no "goggle" patch in any plumage.

KING EIDER ♂
Large orange bill shield; white breast.

- **NESTING** Incubation 24 days by female. Young leave nest shortly after hatching. First flight within 50–53 days. Young tended by female but find own food. 1 brood per year.
- **POPULATION** Uncommon, declining, and local. Breeding population in Yukon-Kuskokwim delta of Alaska declined 96 percent from 1970 to 1993. Widespread introduction and general use of firearms in its limited tundra nesting range perhaps a major factor in decline.

Flight Pattern

Swift light direct flight. Flies in straight line formation.

- **CONSERVATION**
Threatened or endangered.

Nest Identification	
Shape ⬗ Location ♦♦♦	Lined with plant material and large amount of down • very close to edge of tundra pond on raised ridge or hammock • built by female • 1–8 olive-buff to greenish eggs, 2.7 inches long.

| Plumage Sexes differ | Habitat ≈≈ ⌐ | Migration Migratory | Weight 3.2 pounds |

DATE _____ TIME_____ LOCATION _____

Family ANATIDAE	Species *Somateria spectabilis*	Length 18–25 inches	Wingspan 35–40 inches

KING EIDER

In its breeding plumage, the male of this chunky sea duck is spectacular. It appears black above and behind, and white in front, with a large blue-gray cap, greenish cheeks, and a large orange knob at the base of the bill. In flight it appears mostly black and white with a black back and large white wing patches.

• **SONG** During courtship male makes soft dovelike cooing in threes, *urrr-urrr-URR!*

blue-gray crown, back of head, and nape

greenish cheeks

large orange basal knob outlined in black

MALE

orange bill

black rump and tail

white to creamy white breast, neck, and chin

white flank spot

concave slope of dark bill to head

black sides, flanks, and belly

FEMALE

Female makes low *kuck* or *kwack*; also guttural croaking, *gag, gag, gag.*

ECLIPSE MALE   JUVENILE

• **BEHAVIOR** Often fly in big flocks abreast, not one behind the other. Favors rocky shores and reefs. Dives to depths of 180 feet to feed on mollusks and crustaceans, its primary food.

rufous-brown body

dark chevron on sides and flanks

Similar Birds

♂ COMMON EIDER
Black cap; white back • female has
♀ sloping profile and barred sides.

♂ SPECTACLED EIDER
Black breast and spectacles; white
♀ back • female has pale spectacles.

• **BREEDING** Monogamous. Solitary nester.

• **NESTING** Incubation 22–24 days by female. Precocial young leave nest shortly after hatching. First flight at 30–50 days. Young tended by female but find own food. 1 brood per year.

• **POPULATION** Common to abundant in breeding range. Uncommon in winter in south Alaska, Great Lakes, or New York, but wintering population in Great Lakes is increasing. Abundant in its remote northern range. Population totals several million. Casual on East and West Coasts.

Flight Pattern

Swift direct flight with rapid wing beats. Flies in straight line formation.

Nest Identification	
Shape ⚬ ⚬ Location ▬ ♦♦♦	Lined with bits of plant material and large amounts of down • on raised dry ground not far from water • built by female • 3–7 olive, buff, or pale olive eggs; 2.7 inches long.

Plumage Sexes differ	Habitat 〰 〰	Migration Migratory	Weight 3.7 pounds

DATE _____ TIME_____ LOCATION _____

Family ANATIDAE	Species *Somateria mollissima*	Length 23–27 inches	Wingspan 35–42 inches

COMMON EIDER

The largest sea duck is best known for the female's soft down, used for its softness and insulation in pillows, comforters, sleeping bags and jackets. Eiders use the down to line their nests. Rather than killing the eider, humans have learned to take the down a few days after the young leave the nest. To make a pound requires down from 35–40 nests. Juveniles are similar to females. Western females are duller brown; western males have a yellow-orange bill, and most

white head with black cap

feathers extend along side of bill

gray to green bill turns yellow-orange in summer

white back

EASTERN MALE

black tail

2 pale green patches on back of head

white back

black sides

have a narrow black V on the throat.

sloping profile

feathers extend along side of bill

light brown with heavy dark brown barring

ECLIPSE MALE

• **SONG** Male makes pigeonlike *cooo* or hoarse *kor-er-korkorr-kor*; also moans. Female makes hoarse quacking sound. Silent in winter.

EASTERN FEMALE

Similar Birds

KING EIDER Male has black back; blue-gray crown; lacks sloping profile • female has chevron pattern and lacks sloping profile.

SPECTACLED EIDER Male has large white "goggles" with black border • female has pale brown "goggles."

• **BEHAVIOR** Feeds at low tide by day. Dives only 33–60 feet deep. Uses wings to swim underwater and can fly straight out of water. Breaks shellfish shells with gizzard.

• **BREEDING** Monogamous. Nests in colonies.

• **NESTING** Incubation 25–30 days by female. Young led to water by female after hatching. Female feeds young with help of another female. First flight at about 56 days. 1 brood per year.

• **POPULATION** Abundant to common; somewhat local.

• **CONSERVATION** Local populations vulnerable to oil spills and other forms of pollution. Females still pursued for valuable down. Heavily hunted in the Arctic.

Flight Pattern
Rapid direct flight, often low over water.

Nest Identification	
Shape ⚬ ⚬ Location 🪺 🪺 🪺	On bed of twigs, mosses, grass, and seaweed with large amounts of female down used for lining and wrapped around and under nest • sheltered by rocks or plants on ground • built by female • 3–5 light olive, brownish olive, or gray-olive eggs, 3 inches long.

Plumage Sexes differ	Habitat 〰	Migration Some migrate	Weight 4.9 pounds

DATE _____ TIME _____ LOCATION _____

| Family ANATIDAE | Species *Histrionicus histrionicus* | Length 15–21 inches | Wingspan 24–28 inches |

HARLEQUIN DUCK

The male of this small diving duck appears entirely dark from a distance, but at close range the plumage consists of a wild pattern of bold white and black crescents, lines, and spots. Females are dark grayish brown with stubby bills and three white spots on each side of the face. Juveniles are similar to females.

• SONG Usually silent. In courtship male gives mouselike squeak. Both sexes have low croaking calls.

white triangle extends into chestnut line bordering black crown

white spot and vertical crescent on back of head

short bluish black bill

black tail coverts

long pointed black tail

numerous white lines on body

rich chestnut sides

MALE

three white spots on head

dark brownish gray overall

JUVENILE

• BEHAVIOR Favors fast-flowing mountain streams or isolated pools during breeding season. Found along rocky turbulent seacoasts in winter. Dives for food, swimming underwater using both wings and feet. May walk on bottom of mountain stream with head down feeding on aquatic insects. Mollusks and crustaceans form bulk of winter diet.

FEMALE

Similar Birds

Male is unmistakable.

BUFFLEHEAD ♀
Smaller • female has single white spot on face.

• BREEDING Monogamous.
• NESTING Incubation 27–30 days by female. Young leave nest shortly after hatching. First flight at 35–42 days. Young tended by female but find own food. 1 brood per year.
• POPULATION Common in the West; uncommon in the East. Stable in the Northwest, but has declined there during the past century.

Flight Pattern

Rapid direct flight, often low over water.

Nest Identification

Shape   Location

Grasses, twigs, and weeds lined with down • on ground close to water, well hidden among rocks, under brush, or in hollow tree • built by female • 3–10 pale buff or cream eggs, 2.3 inches long.

| Plumage Sexes differ | Habitat | Migration Migratory | Weight 1.5 pounds |

DATE _____ TIME_____ LOCATION _____

Family ANATIDAE	Species *Melanitta perspicillata*	Length 17–21 inches	Wingspan 30–36 inches

SURF SCOTER

The male's black-and-white head pattern has given it the nickname "skunk head." The bill of both sexes is swollen at its base, and that of the male is a bright combination of red, orange, black, and white. The bill and forehead form a slope similar to that of the Canvasback. In flight the wings are dark and have no pattern.

• **SONG** Usually silent but sometimes makes low throaty notes. During courtship male whistles and has gurgling call.

• **BEHAVIOR** Very common along the coasts in winter, where it often feeds beyond the

white patch on forehead

white eye

sloping profile

white patch on nape

multicolored bill

all black body

MALE

2 whitish patches on side of head

swollen greenish black bill

pale whitish patch on nape

dusky brown body

surf line by diving for food, primarily mollusks and crustaceans. Occurs in rafts offshore with other two scoters. Long strings of scoters may be seen as they move along the coast in winter.

FEMALE

Similar Birds

WHITE-WINGED ♀ SCOTER
Female has white wing patch.

BLACK SCOTER
Lacks head pattern
• female has pale face and foreneck.

• **BREEDING** Monogamous.

• **NESTING** Incubation by female. Young leave nest shortly after hatching. First flight within 55 days. Fed by female. 1 brood per year.

• **POPULATION** Common to abundant. May have declined, but now stable and numerous. Declining in the West; the cause is unknown, but hunting is a possibility.

Flight Pattern
Rapid direct flight with strong wing beats. Flies in straight line formation.

Nest Identification
Shape Location	Lined with down and weeds • on ground, often some distance from water, and well hidden under low tree branches or grass clumps • built by female • 5–8 pale buff, pinkish, or buff-white eggs, 2.4 inches long.

Plumage Sexes differ	Habitat	Migration Migratory	Weight 2.2 pounds

DATE _____ TIME_____ LOCATION _____

| Family ANATIDAE | Species *Melanitta fusca* | Length 19–24 inches | Wingspan 33–41 inches |

WHITE-WINGED SCOTER

The largest of the scoters is the only one with a white speculum, which is seen easily in flight but may show as a white patch in the folded wing or be concealed. Scoters may fly in bunched flocks, long lines, or V formations. Winter duck hunters along the Atlantic Coast discovered that when these ducks were flying too high overhead or too distant to shoot, they often would come closer when shouted at loudly.

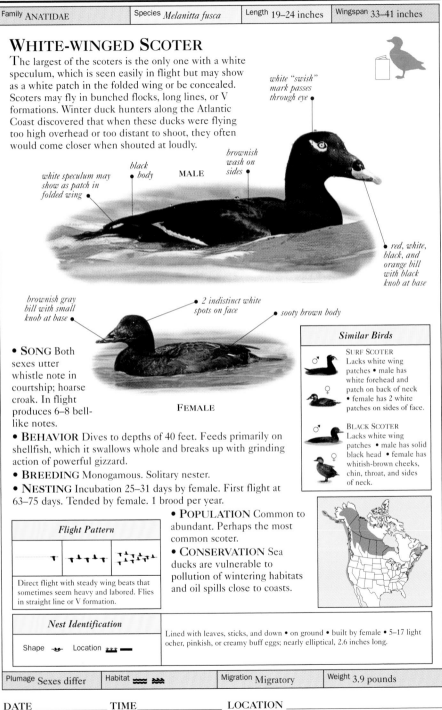

white "swish" mark passes through eye

brownish wash on sides

black body **MALE**

white speculum may show as patch in folded wing

red, white, black, and orange bill with black knob at base

brownish gray bill with small knob at base

2 indistinct white spots on face

sooty brown body

FEMALE

• **SONG** Both sexes utter whistle note in courtship; hoarse croak. In flight produces 6–8 bell-like notes.

Similar Birds

SURF SCOTER
Lacks white wing patches • male has white forehead and patch on back of neck • female has 2 white patches on sides of face.

BLACK SCOTER
Lacks white wing patches • male has solid black head • female has whitish-brown cheeks, chin, throat, and sides of neck.

• **BEHAVIOR** Dives to depths of 40 feet. Feeds primarily on shellfish, which it swallows whole and breaks up with grinding action of powerful gizzard.
• **BREEDING** Monogamous. Solitary nester.
• **NESTING** Incubation 25–31 days by female. First flight at 63–75 days. Tended by female. 1 brood per year.

• **POPULATION** Common to abundant. Perhaps the most common scoter.
• **CONSERVATION** Sea ducks are vulnerable to pollution of wintering habitats and oil spills close to coasts.

Flight Pattern

Direct flight with steady wing beats that sometimes seem heavy and labored. Flies in straight line or V formation.

Nest Identification

Shape ⚮   Location ⁂ ▬

Lined with leaves, sticks, and down • on ground • built by female • 5–17 light ocher, pinkish, or creamy buff eggs; nearly elliptical, 2.6 inches long.

| Plumage Sexes differ | Habitat ≈≈≈ ⧼⧼⧼ | Migration Migratory | Weight 3.9 pounds |

DATE _____ TIME_____ LOCATION _____

Family ANATIDAE	Species *Melanitta nigra*	Length 17–21 inches	Wingspan 30–35 inches

BLACK SCOTER

One of the large sea ducks, most birds of this species are seen on wintering grounds along both coasts. The male is the only all-black duck in North America. In flight both sexes show a silvery gray sheen on the flight feathers that contrasts with the black linings of the underwings. Wings make a whistling sound in flight. Males often winter further north than females, keeping in tight-knit flocks on the water. Adult males have brownish black feet and legs.

all-black plumage

yellow-orange knob on black bill

MALE

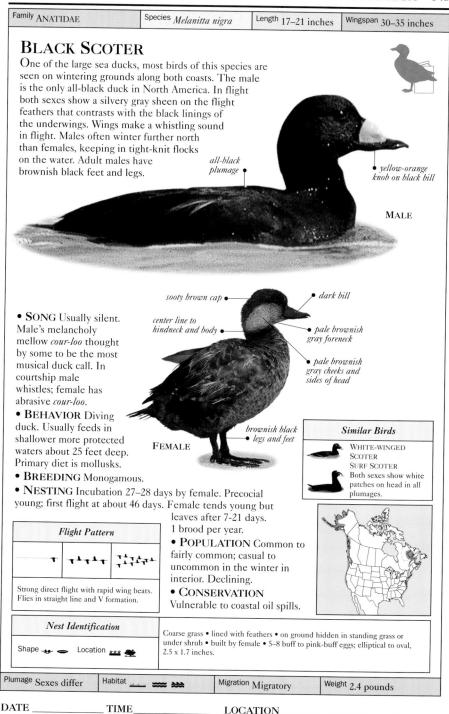

sooty brown cap

dark bill

center line to hindneck and body

pale brownish gray foreneck

pale brownish gray cheeks and sides of head

brownish black legs and feet

FEMALE

• **SONG** Usually silent. Male's melancholy mellow *cour-loo* thought by some to be the most musical duck call. In courtship male whistles; female has abrasive *cour-loo*.

• **BEHAVIOR** Diving duck. Usually feeds in shallower more protected waters about 25 feet deep. Primary diet is mollusks.

• **BREEDING** Monogamous.

• **NESTING** Incubation 27–28 days by female. Precocial young; first flight at about 46 days. Female tends young but leaves after 7-21 days. 1 brood per year.

• **POPULATION** Common to fairly common; casual to uncommon in the winter in interior. Declining.

• **CONSERVATION** Vulnerable to coastal oil spills.

Similar Birds

WHITE-WINGED SCOTER
SURF SCOTER
Both sexes show white patches on head in all plumages.

Flight Pattern

Strong direct flight with rapid wing beats. Flies in straight line and V formation.

Nest Identification

Shape ⚊ ⬭   Location ⬚⬚⬚ ⬥

Coarse grass • lined with feathers • on ground hidden in standing grass or under shrub • built by female • 5–8 buff to pink-buff eggs; elliptical to oval, 2.5 x 1.7 inches.

Plumage Sexes differ	Habitat ⬚⬚ ≈≈ ≋	Migration Migratory	Weight 2.4 pounds

DATE _____ TIME_____ LOCATION _____

Family ANATIDAE	Species *Clangula hyemalis*	Length 15–22 inches	Wingspan 26–31 inches

LONG-TAILED DUCK

Both the genus name and the former common name of Oldsquaw refer to the almost continuous chatter of this long-tailed sea duck. It is the only duck that undergoes two complete brilliant molts annually, plus an eclipse plumage. Winter males have a mostly white body with brownish black patches on the face, breast, and back, and a long black tail. Winter females appear similar but have a paler head. In flight both sexes show uniform dark wings without markings.

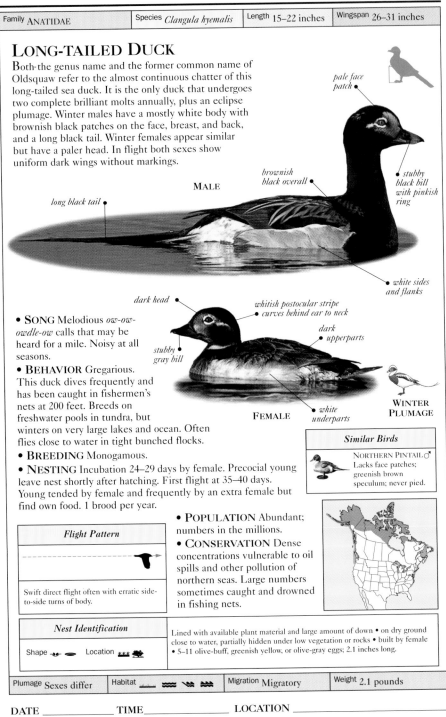

pale face patch

MALE

brownish black overall

stubby black bill with pinkish ring

long black tail

white sides and flanks

dark head

whitish postocular stripe curves behind ear to neck

dark upperparts

stubby gray bill

FEMALE

white underparts

WINTER PLUMAGE

• **SONG** Melodious *ow-ow-owdle-ow* calls that may be heard for a mile. Noisy at all seasons.

• **BEHAVIOR** Gregarious. This duck dives frequently and has been caught in fishermen's nets at 200 feet. Breeds on freshwater pools in tundra, but winters on very large lakes and ocean. Often flies close to water in tight bunched flocks.

• **BREEDING** Monogamous.

• **NESTING** Incubation 24–29 days by female. Precocial young leave nest shortly after hatching. First flight at 35–40 days. Young tended by female and frequently by an extra female but find own food. 1 brood per year.

Similar Birds

NORTHERN PINTAIL♂
Lacks face patches; greenish brown speculum; never pied.

• **POPULATION** Abundant; numbers in the millions.

• **CONSERVATION** Dense concentrations vulnerable to oil spills and other pollution of northern seas. Large numbers sometimes caught and drowned in fishing nets.

Flight Pattern
Swift direct flight often with erratic side-to-side turns of body.

Nest Identification	Lined with available plant material and large amount of down • on dry ground close to water, partially hidden under low vegetation or rocks • built by female • 5–11 olive-buff, greenish yellow, or olive-gray eggs; 2.1 inches long.
Shape ⬳ ⬲ Location ⬳ ⬲	

Plumage Sexes differ	Habitat	Migration Migratory	Weight 2.1 pounds

DATE _____ TIME_____ LOCATION _____

Family ANATIDAE	Species *Bucephala albeola*	Length 13–16 inches	Wingspan 20–24 inches

BUFFLEHEAD

The name of this large-headed duck, which means buffalo-headed or ox-headed, belies the Bufflehead's agility in flying, swimming, and diving. It is the smallest diving duck, but it is one of the best divers. In flight the male's pink legs and feet are bright against white underparts, and a white patch crosses the entire inner wing; female shows white in the secondaries only. These birds nest only in North America.

- **SONG** Squeaky whistle and low squealing or growling call.

large white patch from eye to crown

large dark head with green to purple gloss in good light

black back

In courtship makes loud grating or chattering noise. Female has a harsh quack, *ec-ec-ec* and buzzy *cuc-cuc-cuc*.

MALE

mostly white body

small bill

- **BEHAVIOR** Can take off directly from water unlike other diving ducks. Uses feet to swim underwater. Dives in groups for safety, leaving "lookouts" on surface. Eats aquatic insects, larvae, snails, small fish, and aquatic plant seeds. On saltwater eats shrimp and other crustaceans, shellfish, and snails. Male performs head-bobbing display in courtship.

small white cheek patch

gray-brown body

white underparts

FEMALE

Similar Birds

HOODED MERGANSER ♂
Larger; brown sides; spikelike bill; large crest that can be fanned or lowered.

RUDDY DUCK ♂
Winter male resembles female Bufflehead
- longer bill and tail; large white cheek patch.

- **BREEDING** Monogamous. Solitary nester.
- **NESTING** Incubation 28–33 days by female. Young leave nest by jumping out of tree cavity within 1 day of hatching. Tended by female. First flight at 50–55 days. 1 brood per year.

- **POPULATION** Common but has declined.
- **BIRDHOUSES** Will use nest boxes located near water.
- **CONSERVATION** Much less numerous now due to unrestricted shooting in the 20th century and loss of habitat.

Flight Pattern

Swift direct flight with rapid wing beats.

Nest Identification

Shape 🗝² Location 🌱 🐝 ⛰ 🏠

No material added to nest • will use wooden box placed in tree • 8–10 ivory-yellow, light olive-buff, or cream to pale buff eggs; elliptical to oval in shape, 2 x 1.5 inches.

Plumage Sexes differ	Habitat 〰	Migration Migratory	Weight 1.0 pound

DATE _____ TIME_____ LOCATION _____

Family ANATIDAE	Species *Bucephala clangula*	Length 16–20 inches	Wingspan 25–32 inches

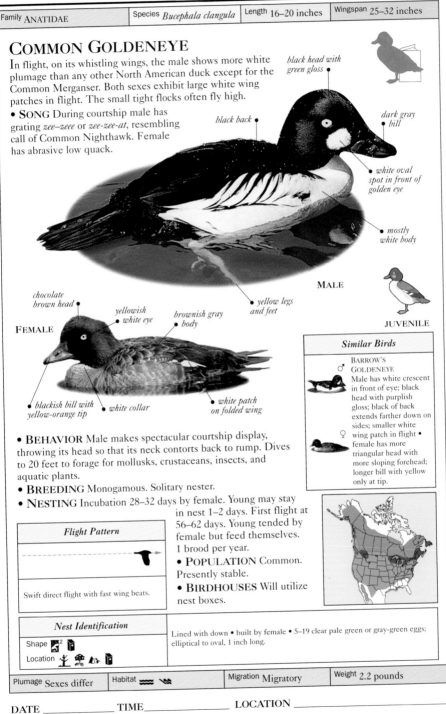

COMMON GOLDENEYE

In flight, on its whistling wings, the male shows more white plumage than any other North American duck except for the Common Merganser. Both sexes exhibit large white wing patches in flight. The small tight flocks often fly high.

• **SONG** During courtship male has grating *zee–zeee* or *zee-zee-at*, resembling call of Common Nighthawk. Female has abrasive low quack.

black head with green gloss

black back

dark gray bill

white oval spot in front of golden eye

mostly white body

MALE

chocolate brown head

yellowish white eye

brownish gray body

yellow legs and feet

JUVENILE

FEMALE

blackish bill with yellow-orange tip

white collar

white patch on folded wing

Similar Birds

BARROW'S GOLDENEYE
♂ Male has white crescent in front of eye; black head with purplish gloss; black of back extends farther down on sides; smaller white wing patch in flight • ♀ female has more triangular head with more sloping forehead; longer bill with yellow only at tip.

• **BEHAVIOR** Male makes spectacular courtship display, throwing its head so that its neck contorts back to rump. Dives to 20 feet to forage for mollusks, crustaceans, insects, and aquatic plants.
• **BREEDING** Monogamous. Solitary nester.
• **NESTING** Incubation 28–32 days by female. Young may stay in nest 1–2 days. First flight at 56–62 days. Young tended by female but feed themselves. 1 brood per year.
• **POPULATION** Common. Presently stable.
• **BIRDHOUSES** Will utilize nest boxes.

Flight Pattern
Swift direct flight with fast wing beats.

Nest Identification	
Shape	Lined with down • built by female • 5–19 clear pale green or gray-green eggs; elliptical to oval, 1 inch long.
Location	

Plumage Sexes differ	Habitat	Migration Migratory	Weight 2.2 pounds

DATE _____ TIME_____ LOCATION _____

Family ANATIDAE	Species *Bucephala islandica*	Length 16–20 inches	Wingspan 30 inches

BARROW'S GOLDENEYE

In summer this puffy-headed duck plays in mountain streams and rides currents in large rivers. In winter it generally is found on saltwater along the coasts. The forehead rises abruptly from a short triangular bill to a crown that appears flattened, and the nape is puffy. Female bill color varies with season and may be mostly dark with a yellow tip in the winter; the amount of yellow gradually increases to the point the bill may be entirely yellow or have dark

puffy black head with purplish sheen

golden eye

black of back extends as bar on sides in front of wing

white crescent on face

black tail

MALE

white spots on scapulars

JUVENILE

brown head

golden eye

FEMALE

darker gray-brown back

mottling at the base when breeding.

• **SONG** Makes low grating croaks. During courtship male utters kittenlike squeals and muted grunts.

grayish brown mottling on breast

grayish brown mottling on sides and flanks

Similar Birds

COMMON GOLDENEYE Male has large white spot on face, not crescent; more pointed head with greenish gloss; mostly white scapulars, not spotted • female has longer, more slender bill with yellow restricted to tip; more gently sloped forehead.

• **BEHAVIOR** Flies close to surface of water for some time after the running takeoff typical of diving ducks. Not as gregarious as many other waterfowl. Relatively tame. In western mountains may nest as high as 10,000 feet above sea level.

• **BREEDING** Monogamous.

Flight Pattern

Swift direct flight; wings make whistling noise.

• **NESTING** Incubation 28–34 days by female. Young stay in nest 1–2 days. First flight at 56 days. Young tended by female but find own food. 1 brood per year.

• **POPULATION** Uncommon to fairly common.

Nest Identification

Shape | Location

Up to 50 feet off ground in large tree cavity, rock crevice, or abandoned building; also in burrow or on ground under bushes • built by female • 5–15 pale olive or blue-green eggs, 2.4 inches long.

Plumage Sexes differ	Habitat	Migration Migratory	Weight 2.4 pounds

DATE _____ TIME_____ LOCATION _____

Family ANATIDAE	Species *Lophodytes cucullatus*	Length 16–19 inches	Wingspan 24–26 inches

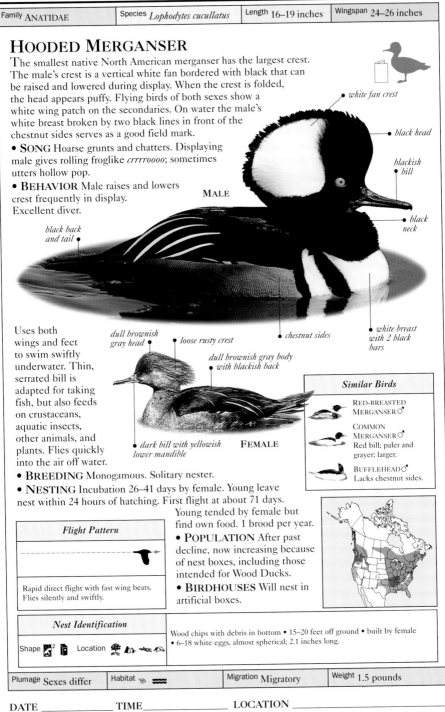

HOODED MERGANSER

The smallest native North American merganser has the largest crest. The male's crest is a vertical white fan bordered with black that can be raised and lowered during display. When the crest is folded, the head appears puffy. Flying birds of both sexes show a white wing patch on the secondaries. On water the male's white breast broken by two black lines in front of the chestnut sides serves as a good field mark.

• **SONG** Hoarse grunts and chatters. Displaying male gives rolling froglike *crrrroooo*; sometimes utters hollow pop.

• **BEHAVIOR** Male raises and lowers crest frequently in display. Excellent diver.

white fan crest

black head

blackish bill

black neck

MALE

black back and tail

black neck

black back and tail

Uses both wings and feet to swim swiftly underwater. Thin, serrated bill is adapted for taking fish, but also feeds on crustaceans, aquatic insects, other animals, and plants. Flies quickly into the air off water.

dull brownish gray head

loose rusty crest

dull brownish gray body with blackish back

chestnut sides

white breast with 2 black bars

dark bill with yellowish lower mandible

FEMALE

Similar Birds

RED-BREASTED MERGANSER ♂

COMMON MERGANSER ♂
Red bill; paler and grayer; larger.

BUFFLEHEAD ♂
Lacks chestnut sides.

• **BREEDING** Monogamous. Solitary nester.

• **NESTING** Incubation 26–41 days by female. Young leave nest within 24 hours of hatching. First flight at about 71 days. Young tended by female but find own food. 1 brood per year.

• **POPULATION** After past decline, now increasing because of nest boxes, including those intended for Wood Ducks.

• **BIRDHOUSES** Will nest in artificial boxes.

Flight Pattern

Rapid direct flight with fast wing beats. Flies silently and swiftly.

Nest Identification

Shape ▨² ▯   Location 🪹 🌿 🪿 🦆

Wood chips with debris in bottom • 15–20 feet off ground • built by female • 6–18 white eggs, almost spherical; 2.1 inches long.

Plumage Sexes differ	Habitat 〰️ 〰️	Migration Migratory	Weight 1.5 pounds

DATE _____ TIME_____ LOCATION _____

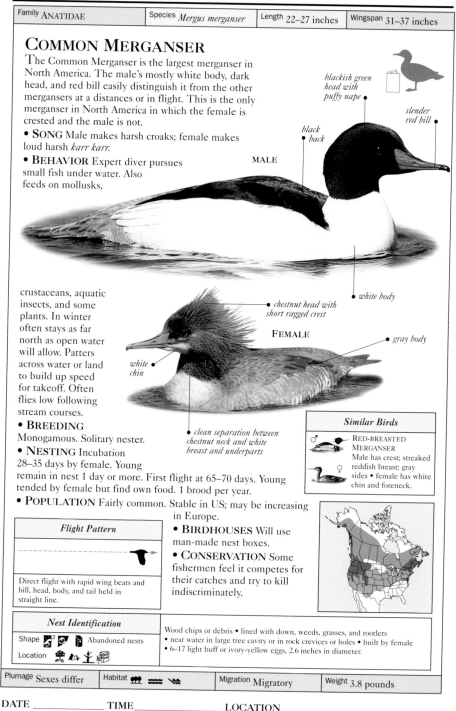

Family ANATIDAE	Species *Mergus merganser*	Length 22–27 inches	Wingspan 31–37 inches

COMMON MERGANSER

The Common Merganser is the largest merganser in North America. The male's mostly white body, dark head, and red bill easily distinguish it from the other mergansers at a distances or in flight. This is the only merganser in North America in which the female is crested and the male is not.

• **SONG** Male makes harsh croaks; female makes loud harsh *karr karr*.

• **BEHAVIOR** Expert diver pursues small fish under water. Also feeds on mollusks,

blackish green head with puffy nape

black back

slender red bill

MALE

white body

crustaceans, aquatic insects, and some plants. In winter often stays as far north as open water will allow. Patters across water or land to build up speed for takeoff. Often flies low following stream courses.

chestnut head with short ragged crest

FEMALE

gray body

white chin

• **BREEDING** Monogamous. Solitary nester.

• **NESTING** Incubation 28–35 days by female. Young remain in nest 1 day or more. First flight at 65–70 days. Young tended by female but find own food. 1 brood per year.

clean separation between chestnut neck and white breast and underparts

Similar Birds

♂ **RED-BREASTED MERGANSER** Male has crest; streaked reddish breast; gray sides • female has white chin and foreneck.

• **POPULATION** Fairly common. Stable in US; may be increasing in Europe.

• **BIRDHOUSES** Will use man-made nest boxes.

• **CONSERVATION** Some fishermen feel it competes for their catches and try to kill indiscriminately.

Flight Pattern

Direct flight with rapid wing beats and bill, head, body, and tail held in straight line.

Nest Identification

Shape ⬧² ⬧ ⬧ Abandoned nests

Location 🌳 🪨 ⚓ 🏚

Wood chips or debris • lined with down, weeds, grasses, and rootlets • near water in large tree cavity or in rock crevices or holes • built by female • 6–17 light buff or ivory-yellow eggs, 2.6 inches in diameter.

Plumage Sexes differ	Habitat 🌲 〰 🌾	Migration Migratory	Weight 3.8 pounds

DATE _____ TIME_____ LOCATION _____

Family ANATIDAE	Species *Mergus serrator*	Length 16–26 inches	Wingspan 31–35 inches

RED-BREASTED MERGANSER

One of the fastest flying ducks, this species has been clocked at 100 mph. In flight males show a large white square on the inner wing; females have white secondaries only. Both sexes have a ragged crest. It is often seen from the shore along seacoasts in winter.

• **SONG** Generally silent. Female makes harsh *krrr-Krrr* and hoarse croaks. Courting male makes catlike *yeow*.

rakish crest

blackish head with green gloss

MALE

narrow hooked serrated red bill

black upperparts

streaked chestnut breast to waterline

reddish legs and feet

vermiculated gray sides and flanks

reddish bill

rusty brown crest, head, and neck

grayish brown upperparts

whitish chin, throat, and foreneck

• **BEHAVIOR**
Swift on the wing.
To take off, runs
with wings flapping
across either water or land. Dives to forage for animal food. Principal diet is fish. Mergansers sometimes form a line to drive fish into shallow water to catch them.

FEMALE

Similar Birds

♂ COMMON MERGANSER
Male has white underparts and breast; lacks crest.
♀ • female has clean-cut line between rusty neck and white breast.

• **BREEDING** Monogamous.
• **NESTING** Incubation 29–35 days by female. Young leave nest within 1 day of hatching. First flight after 59 days. Young tended by female but find own food. 1 brood per year.
• **POPULATION** Widespread and common. Coastal wintering habitat vulnerable to pollution and oil spills.

Flight Pattern

Fast direct flight with rapid wing beats.

Nest Identification	
Shape ⌒ ⌒ Location ▬ ᳱᳱᳱ ⏃⏃ 🌲	Lined with down • on ground in sheltered spot; sometimes in hollow stump, under rocks, or in shallow burrow • built by female • sometimes eggs laid in nests of Mallard, Gadwall, or Lesser Scaup • 5–16 olive-buff or green-buff eggs, 2.5 inches long.

Plumage Sexes differ	Habitat ᳱᳱ ᳽ ᷂ ᳵ	Migration Migratory	Weight 2.5 pounds

DATE _____ TIME_____ LOCATION _____

Family ANATIDAE	Species *Oxyura jamaicensis*	Length 14–16 inches	Wingspan 21–24 inches

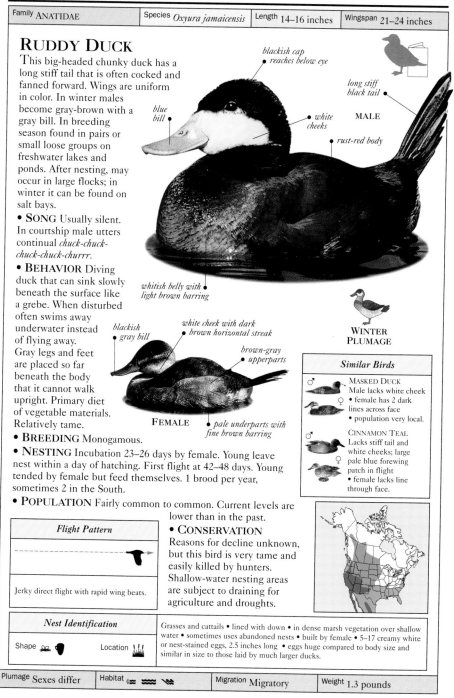

RUDDY DUCK

This big-headed chunky duck has a long stiff tail that is often cocked and fanned forward. Wings are uniform in color. In winter males become gray-brown with a gray bill. In breeding season found in pairs or small loose groups on freshwater lakes and ponds. After nesting, may occur in large flocks; in winter it can be found on salt bays.

- **SONG** Usually silent. In courtship male utters continual *chuck-chuck-chuck-chuck-churrr*.
- **BEHAVIOR** Diving duck that can sink slowly beneath the surface like a grebe. When disturbed often swims away underwater instead of flying away. Gray legs and feet are placed so far beneath the body that it cannot walk upright. Primary diet of vegetable materials. Relatively tame.
- **BREEDING** Monogamous.
- **NESTING** Incubation 23–26 days by female. Young leave nest within a day of hatching. First flight at 42–48 days. Young tended by female but feed themselves. 1 brood per year, sometimes 2 in the South.
- **POPULATION** Fairly common to common. Current levels are lower than in the past.
- **CONSERVATION** Reasons for decline unknown, but this bird is very tame and easily killed by hunters. Shallow-water nesting areas are subject to draining for agriculture and droughts.

blackish cap reaches below eye

long stiff black tail

blue bill

white cheeks

MALE

rust-red body

whitish belly with light brown barring

blackish gray bill

white cheek with dark brown horizontal streak

brown-gray upperparts

WINTER PLUMAGE

FEMALE *pale underparts with fine brown barring*

Similar Birds

♂ MASKED DUCK
Male lacks white cheek
♀ • female has 2 dark lines across face
• population very local.

♂ CINNAMON TEAL
Lacks stiff tail and white cheeks; large
♀ pale blue forewing patch in flight
• female lacks line through face.

Flight Pattern
Jerky direct flight with rapid wing beats.

Nest Identification	
Shape	Location	Grasses and cattails • lined with down • in dense marsh vegetation over shallow water • sometimes uses abandoned nests • built by female • 5–17 creamy white or nest-stained eggs, 2.5 inches long • eggs huge compared to body size and similar in size to those laid by much larger ducks.

Plumage Sexes differ	Habitat	Migration Migratory	Weight 1.3 pounds

DATE _____ TIME_____ LOCATION _____

Family ACCIPITRIDAE	Species *Pandion haliaetus*	Length 21–24 inches	Wingspan 54–72 inches

OSPREY

A kindred of other diurnal birds of prey, the Osprey is so didstinctive it is sometimes placed in it own family. Its large size and uniquely curved claws allow the Osprey to carry a large fish a considerable distance to feed to its young in the nest. Occasionally an eagle dives upon an Osprey carrying a fish, forces a release, and catches the fish for itself before the fish hits the water.

dark brown upperparts with purplish gloss

mostly white head

broad black mark through cheeks and sides of neck

• **SONG** Series of loud whistled *kyews* or melodious whistle of *chewk-chewk-chewk* or *cheap-cheap-cheap*.

clear white belly

long tail with narrow black bars

toes equal in length on claws curved into one-third of a circle

• **BEHAVIOR** Eats mainly fish. Dives into water to catch prey from 30–100 feet above surface. Holds fish with both feet, stops to shake water out of feathers, points fish head forward to decrease wind resistance, and carries to perch or to feed young. Often flies with distinctive crook or kink in wing bent at wrist, which has a black patch.

• **BREEDING** Monogamous. Colonial or solitary nester.

• **NESTING** Incubation 32–43 days by both sexes; however, female does more, while male brings food. Young stay in nest 48–59 days. Fed by both parents. 1 brood per year.

JUVENILE

Similar Birds

BALD EAGLE
Entirely white head and tail; crown held flat; dark underparts and underwings • juvenile has entirely dark head and patchy tannish white underwings.

• **POPULATION** Uncommon inland; fairly common in coastal range.

• **BIRDHOUSES** Osprey will build nest on man-made cartwheel on pole or on platforms built in marshes.

• **CONSERVATION** Endangered in 1950s because of chemical pollution (especially DDT), but has since made a comeback, at least partly by transplanting young into areas where entire populations had been extirpated.

Flight Pattern
Deep, slow wing beats alternate with glides; sometimes soars on thermals.

Nest Identification	
Shape Location	Sticks, sod, cow dung, seaweed, rubbish, and similar material • up to 200 feet above ground in dead or live trees near or over water, or atop telephone poles or bridges • built by both sexes • Usually 3 white or pinkish eggs marked with brown and olive, 2.4 x 1 inches long.

Plumage Sexes similar	Habitat	Migration Migratory	Weight 3.1 pounds

DATE _____ TIME_____ LOCATION _____

Family ACCIPITRIDAE	Species *Elanus leucurus*	Length 15–17 inches	Wingspan 40–42 inches

WHITE-TAILED KITE

Sometimes called the white hawk, the White-tailed Kite soars and glides like a small gull. When seen from a distance, this gregarious bird appears completely white. Previously called the Black-shouldered Kite, the white linings of the underwing are broken distally by a black "thumb" mark on the wrist. It is the only North American kite to hover while hunting, with tail down and often with legs dangling, over savanna, riparian woodland, marshes, grassy foothills, or the cultivated fields it searches for food. It is a master at soaring on thermals and glides long distances after reaching considerable heights. Juveniles' underparts and head are lightly streaked with rufous.

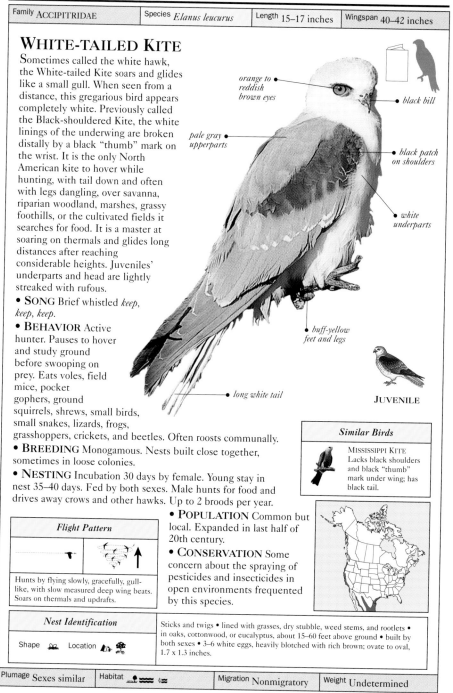

orange to reddish brown eyes

black bill

pale gray upperparts

black patch on shoulders

white underparts

buff-yellow feet and legs

long white tail

JUVENILE

- **SONG** Brief whistled *keep, keep, keep.*
- **BEHAVIOR** Active hunter. Pauses to hover and study ground before swooping on prey. Eats voles, field mice, pocket gophers, ground squirrels, shrews, small birds, small snakes, lizards, frogs, grasshoppers, crickets, and beetles. Often roosts communally.
- **BREEDING** Monogamous. Nests built close together, sometimes in loose colonies.
- **NESTING** Incubation 30 days by female. Young stay in nest 35–40 days. Fed by both sexes. Male hunts for food and drives away crows and other hawks. Up to 2 broods per year.
- **POPULATION** Common but local. Expanded in last half of 20th century.
- **CONSERVATION** Some concern about the spraying of pesticides and insecticides in open environments frequented by this species.

Similar Birds

MISSISSIPPI KITE
Lacks black shoulders and black "thumb" mark under wing; has black tail.

Flight Pattern

Hunts by flying slowly, gracefully, gull-like, with slow measured deep wing beats. Soars on thermals and updrafts.

Nest Identification

Shape   Location

Sticks and twigs • lined with grasses, dry stubble, weed stems, and rootlets • in oaks, cottonwood, or eucalyptus, about 15–60 feet above ground • built by both sexes • 3–6 white eggs, heavily blotched with rich brown; ovate to oval, 1.7 x 1.3 inches.

Plumage Sexes similar	Habitat	Migration Nonmigratory	Weight Undetermined

DATE _____ TIME_____ LOCATION _____

Family ACCIPITRIDAE	Species *Ictinia mississippiensis*	Length 13–17 inches	Wingspan 34–37 inches

MISSISSIPPI KITE

Far from shy, the Mississippi Kite has been seen chasing bats into caves and flying around horseback riders and cattle to catch insects. This bird is not territorial; several might perch together in trees, even during nesting season. They also gather at communal perches and foraging areas, and often soar communally while hunting insects. As many as 20 birds have been recorded following a herd of livestock for flushed insects. The Mississippi Kite never hovers and has a smooth graceful flight with its white secondary feathers showing.

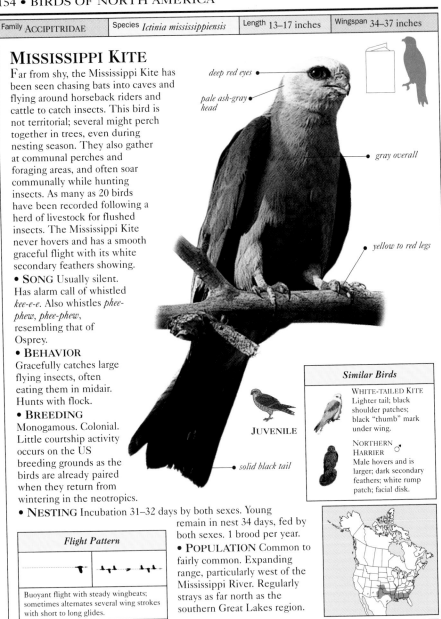

deep red eyes

pale ash-gray head

gray overall

yellow to red legs

JUVENILE

solid black tail

- **SONG** Usually silent. Has alarm call of whistled *kee-e-e*. Also whistles *phee-phew, phee-phew*, resembling that of Osprey.
- **BEHAVIOR** Gracefully catches large flying insects, often eating them in midair. Hunts with flock.
- **BREEDING** Monogamous. Colonial. Little courtship activity occurs on the US breeding grounds as the birds are already paired when they return from wintering in the neotropics.

Similar Birds

WHITE-TAILED KITE
Lighter tail; black shoulder patches; black "thumb" mark under wing.

NORTHERN HARRIER ♂
Male hovers and is larger; dark secondary feathers; white rump patch; facial disk.

- **NESTING** Incubation 31–32 days by both sexes. Young remain in nest 34 days, fed by both sexes. 1 brood per year.
- **POPULATION** Common to fairly common. Expanding range, particularly west of the Mississippi River. Regularly strays as far north as the southern Great Lakes region.

Flight Pattern

Buoyant flight with steady wingbeats; sometimes alternates several wing strokes with short to long glides.

Nest Identification

Shape ● ～ ♑   Location 🐦

Sticks and twigs • lined with green leaves and Spanish moss (where available) • in upper branches, small forks, and occasionally on horizontal lines, 30–135 feet above ground • built by both sexes • 1–3 white or bluish white eggs, unmarked or faintly spotted, often nest-stained.

Plumage Sexes similar	Habitat 🌳 🌿 🏔 〜 ⚊	Migration Migratory	Weight 12.6 ounces

DATE _____ TIME_____ LOCATION _____

Family ACCIPITRIDAE	Species *Haliaeetus leucocephalus*	Length 34–43 inches	Wingspan 6–8 feet

BALD EAGLE

The national bird of the United States has an awe-inspiring wingspan and striking white head and tail that make adults easy to identify. Big concentrations of these huge birds can be seen perched in trees and resting on sandbars when salmon run in rivers of the Northwest. Juveniles can be recognized by their large size; dark brown head, tail, and body; mottled white patches on underwings and underparts; grayish eyes; and light yellow feet.

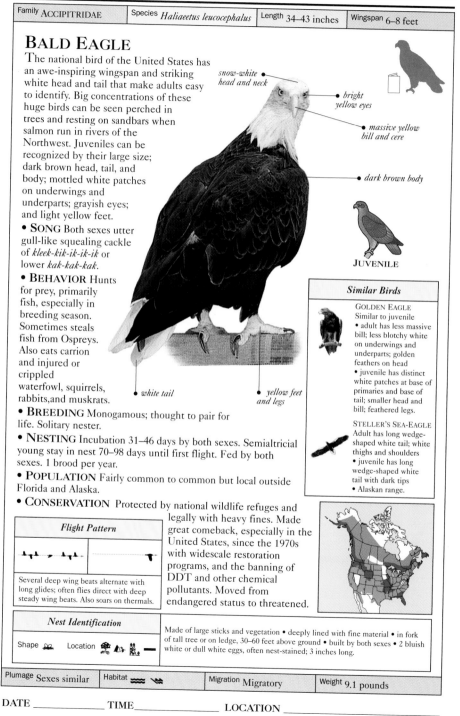

snow-white head and neck

bright yellow eyes

massive yellow bill and cere

dark brown body

JUVENILE

white tail

yellow feet and legs

• **SONG** Both sexes utter gull-like squealing cackle of *kleek-kik-ik-ik-ik* or lower *kak-kak-kak*.

• **BEHAVIOR** Hunts for prey, primarily fish, especially in breeding season. Sometimes steals fish from Ospreys. Also eats carrion and injured or crippled waterfowl, squirrels, rabbits, and muskrats.

• **BREEDING** Monogamous; thought to pair for life. Solitary nester.

• **NESTING** Incubation 31–46 days by both sexes. Semialtricial young stay in nest 70–98 days until first flight. Fed by both sexes. 1 brood per year.

• **POPULATION** Fairly common to common but local outside Florida and Alaska.

• **CONSERVATION** Protected by national wildlife refuges and legally with heavy fines. Made great comeback, especially in the United States, since the 1970s with widescale restoration programs, and the banning of DDT and other chemical pollutants. Moved from endangered status to threatened.

Similar Birds

GOLDEN EAGLE
Similar to juvenile
• adult has less massive bill; less blotchy white on underwings and underparts; golden feathers on head
• juvenile has distinct white patches at base of primaries and base of tail; smaller head and bill; feathered legs.

STELLER'S SEA-EAGLE
Adult has long wedge-shaped white tail; white thighs and shoulders
• juvenile has long wedge-shaped white tail with dark tips
• Alaskan range.

Flight Pattern

Several deep wing beats alternate with long glides; often flies direct with deep steady wing beats. Also soars on thermals.

Nest Identification

Shape   Location

Made of large sticks and vegetation • deeply lined with fine material • in fork of tall tree or on ledge, 30–60 feet above ground • built by both sexes • 2 bluish white or dull white eggs, often nest-stained; 3 inches long.

Plumage Sexes similar	Habitat	Migration Migratory	Weight 9.1 pounds

DATE _____ TIME_____ LOCATION _____

Family ACCIPITRIDAE	Species *Haliaeetus albicilla*	Length 31–40 inches	Wingspan 6–8 feet

WHITE-TAILED EAGLE

Sometimes referred to as an erne, the White-tailed Eagle is the fourth-largest eagle in the world and is only a little smaller than Steller's Sea-Eagle. Bird-watchers in North America sometimes can spy this native of Eurasia and Greenland on the Aleutian Island Attu, where it has nested, or on other Aleutian Islands. Eastern records of its appearance exist from just after the turn of the 20th century along the north Atlantic Coast. Juveniles have darker plumage than adults and a mottled white base of the tail.

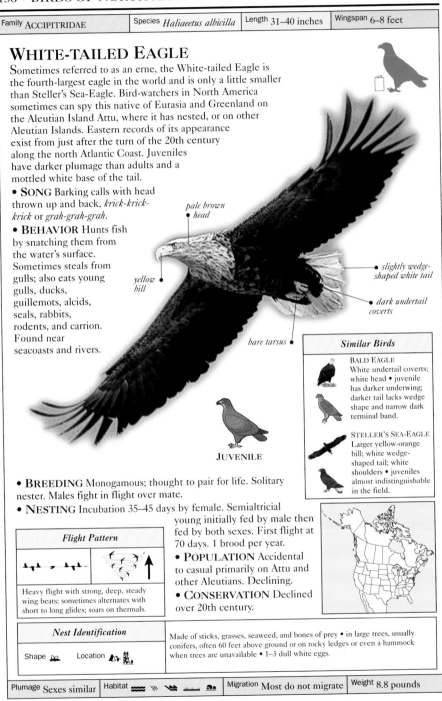

pale brown head

yellow bill

bare tarsus

slightly wedge-shaped white tail

dark undertail coverts

JUVENILE

- **SONG** Barking calls with head thrown up and back, *krick-krick-krick* or *grah-grah-grah*.
- **BEHAVIOR** Hunts fish by snatching them from the water's surface. Sometimes steals from gulls; also eats young gulls, ducks, guillemots, alcids, seals, rabbits, rodents, and carrion. Found near seacoasts and rivers.

Similar Birds

BALD EAGLE
White undertail coverts; white head • juvenile has darker underwing; darker tail lacks wedge shape and narrow dark terminal band.

STELLER'S SEA-EAGLE
Larger yellow-orange bill; white wedge-shaped tail; white shoulders • juveniles almost indistinguishable in the field.

- **BREEDING** Monogamous; thought to pair for life. Solitary nester. Males fight in flight over mate.
- **NESTING** Incubation 35–45 days by female. Semialtricial young initially fed by male then fed by both sexes. First flight at 70 days. 1 brood per year.
- **POPULATION** Accidental to casual primarily on Attu and other Aleutians. Declining.
- **CONSERVATION** Declined over 20th century.

Flight Pattern

Heavy flight with strong, deep, steady wing beats; sometimes alternates with short to long glides; soars on thermals.

Nest Identification

Shape ⌒⌒   Location 🌲▲ 🪨

Made of sticks, grasses, seaweed, and bones of prey • in large trees, usually conifers, often 60 feet above ground or on rocky ledges or even a hammock when trees are unavailable • 1–3 dull white eggs.

Plumage Sexes similar	Habitat 〜〜 🌿 🦆 ⛰ ⌒	Migration Most do not migrate	Weight 8.8 pounds

DATE _____ TIME_____ LOCATION _____

Family ACCIPITRIDAE	Species *Haliaeetus pelagicus*	Length 42–45 inches	Wingspan 7–8 feet

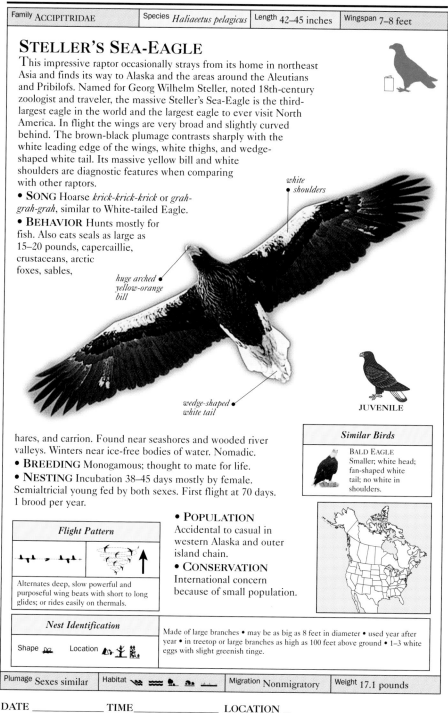

STELLER'S SEA-EAGLE

This impressive raptor occasionally strays from its home in northeast Asia and finds its way to Alaska and the areas around the Aleutians and Pribilofs. Named for Georg Wilhelm Steller, noted 18th-century zoologist and traveler, the massive Steller's Sea-Eagle is the third-largest eagle in the world and the largest eagle to ever visit North America. In flight the wings are very broad and slightly curved behind. The brown-black plumage contrasts sharply with the white leading edge of the wings, white thighs, and wedge-shaped white tail. Its massive yellow bill and white shoulders are diagnostic features when comparing with other raptors.

white
shoulders

• **SONG** Hoarse *krick-krick-krick* or *grah-grah-grah*, similar to White-tailed Eagle.

• **BEHAVIOR** Hunts mostly for fish. Also eats seals as large as 15–20 pounds, capercaillie, crustaceans, arctic foxes, sables,

huge arched
yellow-orange
bill

wedge-shaped
white tail

JUVENILE

hares, and carrion. Found near seashores and wooded river valleys. Winters near ice-free bodies of water. Nomadic.

• **BREEDING** Monogamous; thought to mate for life.

• **NESTING** Incubation 38–45 days mostly by female. Semialtricial young fed by both sexes. First flight at 70 days. 1 brood per year.

Similar Birds

BALD EAGLE
Smaller; white head; fan-shaped white tail; no white in shoulders.

• **POPULATION** Accidental to casual in western Alaska and outer island chain.

• **CONSERVATION** International concern because of small population.

Flight Pattern

Alternates deep, slow powerful and purposeful wing beats with short to long glides; or rides easily on thermals.

Nest Identification	
Shape ⌒ Location 🔺⚘🌿	Made of large branches • may be as big as 8 feet in diameter • used year after year • in treetop or large branches as high as 100 feet above ground • 1–3 white eggs with slight greenish tinge.

Plumage Sexes similar	Habitat 〰🌊🐟🐾	Migration Nonmigratory	Weight 17.1 pounds

DATE _____ TIME_____ LOCATION _____

Family ACCIPITRIDAE	Species *Circus cyaneus*	Length 16–24 inches	Wingspan 38–48 inches

NORTHERN HARRIER

Its owl-like facial disk and white rump patch, which is prominent in flight, set the Northern Harrier apart from all other North American falconiformes. Males take several years to acquire their gray-plumaged upperparts. Their wings are long with black-tipped trailing edges, and the outermost four or five primaries are black.

gray upperparts

chestnut spotting on throat and breast

MALE

- **SONG** Shrill calls *kek, kek, kek* or *keee, keee, keee*, especially around the nest.
- **BEHAVIOR** Hunts using low slow flight that consists of alternately flapping and gliding with the wings held in a shallow V above the back. Often quarters back and forth over low vegetation and can turn and drop rapidly on prey that it may detect initially by sound. Feeds on small mammals, especially rodents up to the size of a small rabbit, frogs, snakes, small birds, carrion, and large insects. Sometimes hunts the edges of grass fires to capture prey driven out by the flames. Courtship flight of males is thrillingly acrobatic.

black wing tips and secondary tips

whitish underparts

very long tail

JUVENILE

- **BREEDING** Some pairs monogamous; some males are polygamous with up to 3 mates. Solitary nester. Both sexes very vocal with high-pitched screams when defending nest.
- **NESTING** Incubation 31–32 days by female. Semi-altricial young stay in nest 30–35 days, fed by both sexes. 1 brood per year.
- **POPULATION** Common but declining.

disk of feathers around face

brown upperparts

FEMALE

Similar Birds

ROUGH-LEGGED HAWK
Base of tail (not rump) white; broad blackish subterminal band on tail • does not course low over fields but hunts from perch or by hovering.

- **CONSERVATION** Populations have declined everywhere on its breeding range because of the loss of marshland habitat as well as pesticides. Formerly, many were lost to shooting.

Flight Pattern

Several deep wing beats alternate with glides.

Nest Identification

Shape   Location

Sticks and grass lined with fine material • usually placed on the ground • may be 5 feet above water or marshy terrain • built by both sexes, but female does most construction • 3–9 bluish white eggs, sometimes spotted with brown, 1.8 inches long.

Plumage Sexes differ	Habitat	Migration Some migrate	Weight 12.6 ounces

DATE _____ TIME_____ LOCATION _____

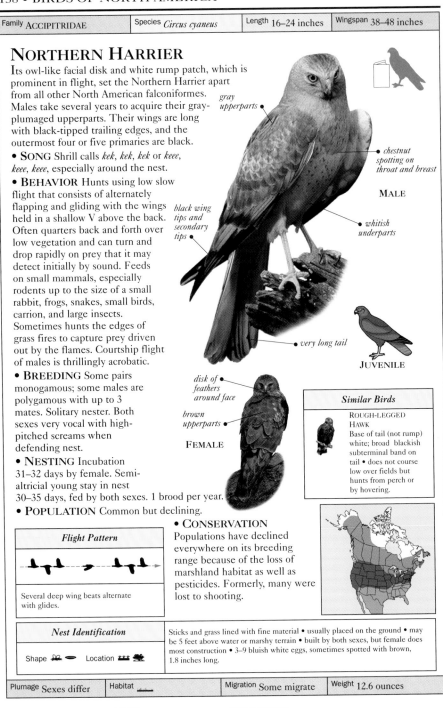

Family ACCIPITRIDAE	Species *Accipiter striatus*	Length 10–14 inches	Wingspan 20–28 inches

SHARP-SHINNED HAWK

A territorial bird, the Sharp-shinned Hawk occasionally strikes humans in defense of its nest. Its name describes its flattened, thin tarsus or shank. This is the smallest of the North American accipiters; the female is larger than the male. The head and neck seem small for its long, slender body. Its long tail has three to four narrow black crossbars, and is squared or notched on the tip. Juveniles have brown upperparts and white underparts with heavy brown streaking.

• **SONG** When disturbed utters *kek-kek-kek* or *kik-kik-kik*. Call is melancholy cry.

• **BEHAVIOR** Eats mostly small birds, including songbirds, taken off ground or twigs, or in air. Also eats small mammals (including bats), reptiles, grasshoppers, and other larger insects.

• **BREEDING** Monogamous. Solitary nester.

• **NESTING** Incubation 32–35 days by female. Semialtricial young stay in nest 23–27 days. Fed by both sexes. 1 brood per year.

• **POPULATION** Common to fairly common.

• **FEEDERS** Often attracted to concentrations of small birds

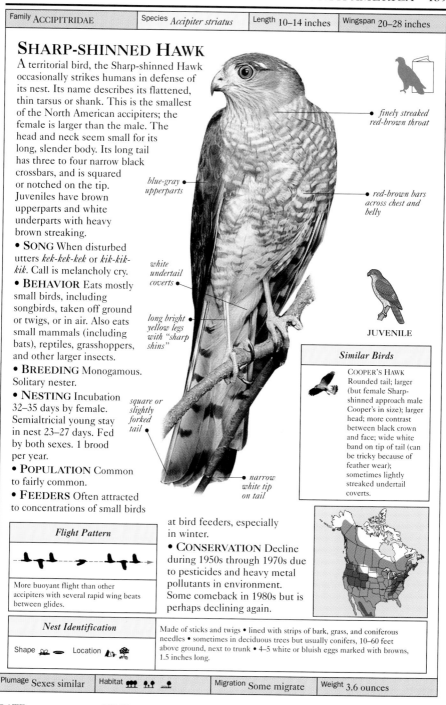

finely streaked red-brown throat

blue-gray upperparts

red-brown bars across chest and belly

white undertail coverts

long bright yellow legs with "sharp shins"

JUVENILE

square or slightly forked tail

narrow white tip on tail

Similar Birds

COOPER'S HAWK
Rounded tail; larger (but female Sharp-shinned approach male Cooper's in size); larger head; more contrast between black crown and face; wide white band on tip of tail (can be tricky because of feather wear); sometimes lightly streaked undertail coverts.

at bird feeders, especially in winter.

• **CONSERVATION** Decline during 1950s through 1970s due to pesticides and heavy metal pollutants in environment. Some comeback in 1980s but is perhaps declining again.

Flight Pattern
More buoyant flight than other accipiters with several rapid wing beats between glides.

Nest Identification	
Shape Location	Made of sticks and twigs • lined with strips of bark, grass, and coniferous needles • sometimes in deciduous trees but usually conifers, 10–60 feet above ground, next to trunk • 4–5 white or bluish eggs marked with browns, 1.5 inches long.

Plumage Sexes similar	Habitat	Migration Some migrate	Weight 3.6 ounces

DATE _____ TIME_____ LOCATION _____

Family ACCIPITRIDAE	Species *Accipiter cooperii*	Length 14–21 inches	Wingspan 27–36 inches

COOPER'S HAWK

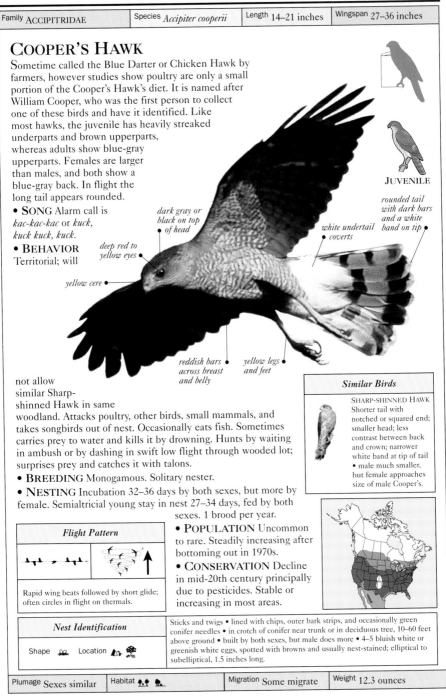

Sometime called the Blue Darter or Chicken Hawk by farmers, however studies show poultry are only a small portion of the Cooper's Hawk's diet. It is named after William Cooper, who was the first person to collect one of these birds and have it identified. Like most hawks, the juvenile has heavily streaked underparts and brown upperparts, whereas adults show blue-gray upperparts. Females are larger than males, and both show a blue-gray back. In flight the long tail appears rounded.

- **SONG** Alarm call is *kac-kac-kac* or *kuck, kuck kuck, kuck.*
- **BEHAVIOR** Territorial; will

dark gray or black on top of head

deep red to yellow eyes

yellow cere

reddish bars across breast and belly

yellow legs and feet

white undertail coverts

JUVENILE

rounded tail with dark bars and a white band on tip

not allow similar Sharp-shinned Hawk in same woodland. Attacks poultry, other birds, small mammals, and takes songbirds out of nest. Occasionally eats fish. Sometimes carries prey to water and kills it by drowning. Hunts by waiting in ambush or by dashing in swift low flight through wooded lot; surprises prey and catches it with talons.

- **BREEDING** Monogamous. Solitary nester.
- **NESTING** Incubation 32–36 days by both sexes, but more by female. Semialtricial young stay in nest 27–34 days, fed by both sexes. 1 brood per year.
- **POPULATION** Uncommon to rare. Steadily increasing after bottoming out in 1970s.
- **CONSERVATION** Decline in mid-20th century principally due to pesticides. Stable or increasing in most areas.

Similar Birds

SHARP-SHINNED HAWK
Shorter tail with notched or squared end; smaller head; less contrast between back and crown; narrower white band at tip of tail • male much smaller, but female approaches size of male Cooper's.

Flight Pattern

Rapid wing beats followed by short glide; often circles in flight on thermals.

Nest Identification

Shape   Location

Sticks and twigs • lined with chips, outer bark strips, and occasionally green conifer needles • in crotch of conifer near trunk or in deciduous tree, 10–60 feet above ground • built by both sexes, but male does more • 4–5 bluish white or greenish white eggs, spotted with browns and usually nest-stained; elliptical to subelliptical, 1.5 inches long.

Plumage Sexes similar	Habitat	Migration Some migrate	Weight 12.3 ounces

DATE _____ TIME _____ LOCATION _____

Family *ACCIPITRIDAE*	Species *Accipiter gentilis*	Length 19–27 inches	Wingspan 40–47 inches

NORTHERN GOSHAWK

An agile and proficient flier, the Northern Goshawk is not afraid to catch prey near humans when it is hungry. This bold hawk has been known to attack duck decoys. It appears pale gray at a distance, and in flight the shorter tail and longer, broad wings (for an accipiter) give the superficial appearance of a Red-tailed Hawk. The female is the larger and dominant partner in a pair.

distinct white eyebrow over each eye widens posteriorly

black crown

wedge-shaped black postocular stripe

orange-red eyes

blue-gray back

white underparts with gray mottling

relatively long rounded wings

JUVENILE

long rounded to wedge-shaped tail

fluffy white undertail coverts

- **SONG** Alarm call is harsher and deeper than Cooper's Hawk, *kac-kac-kac* or *kuk, kuk, kuk*. Female utters high-pitched melancholy whine, *kee-a-ah*, reminiscent of the Red-shouldered Hawk.

- **BEHAVIOR** Eats snowshoe hare, lemmings, and grouse; migrates south in irruptive numbers when their prey populations crash. Also eats small to medium mammals, large and small birds (including ducks and crows), and some large insects. Dives and kills prey on ground or in air with deadly grip of talons. Female very defensive of nest site to the point of attacking intruders, including humans.

- **BREEDING** Monogamous. Solitary nester.

- **NESTING** Incubation 36–42 days by both sexes, but female does more. Semialtricial young stay in nest 41–43 days. Fed by both sexes. First flight at 45 days. 1 brood per year.

- **POPULATION** Uncommon to rare.

- **CONSERVATION** Expanding range. Possible increase in the Northeast during recent decades. Southwestern mountain populations may be threatened by loss of habitat.

Similar Birds

COOPER'S HAWK Shorter wings; longer tail; darker blue-gray upperparts; barred rusty underparts.

Flight Pattern

Several strong rapid wing beats interspersed with glides; soars on thermals.

Nest Identification

Shape ___ Location ___

Sticks and twigs • lined with bark strips, evergreen sprigs, grass, and feathers • in fork of branch or trunk of tree, 20–75 feet above ground • built by both sexes, but male does more • 3–4 bluish or off-white eggs, occasionally nest-stained or spotted with brown; slightly elongate elliptical or oval, 2.3 inches long.

Plumage Sexes similar	Habitat	Migration Migratory	Weight 2.0 pounds

DATE _____ TIME_____ LOCATION _____

Family ACCIPITRIDAE	Species *Asturina nitida*	Length 16–18 inches	Wingspan 32–38 inches

GRAY HAWK

This stout little hawk is an uncommon and local resident of
low-lying woodlands along streams in south Texas and a
summer visitor to Arizona. It is not an accipiter as formerly
thought but actually a small buteolike hawk. Juveniles are
rusty or sooty brown with brown-streaked pale to buff
underparts and have narrow dusky bars on the tail. In
flight adults show whitish underparts with gray
barring, rounded wing tips, a black tail with
numerous white bands, and a white rump.

• **SONG** Loud descending mournful
whistles, often in series of 3–7,
wheeeooo; plaintive *cree-ee-ee*.

• **BEHAVIOR** Often perches
conspicuously on roadside
utility poles, wires, posts,
and trees. Darts to ground
for swift-running lizards.
Picks up prey in talons.
Also eats snakes,
rabbits, small
rodents, some
birds, fish,
and beetles.

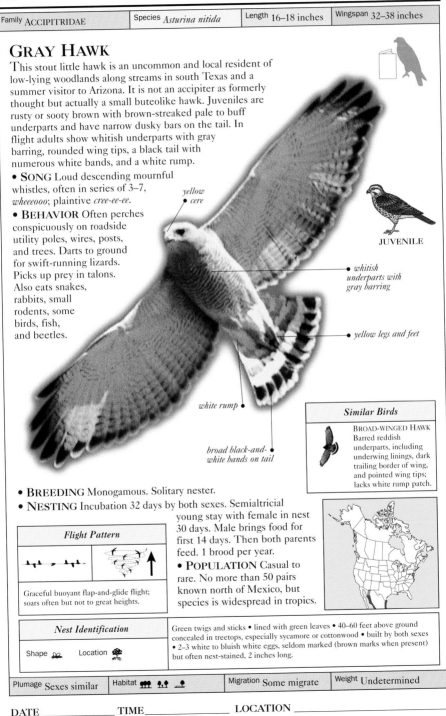

yellow cere

JUVENILE

whitish underparts with gray barring

yellow legs and feet

white rump

broad black-and-white bands on tail

Similar Birds

BROAD-WINGED HAWK
Barred reddish
underparts, including
underwing linings, dark
trailing border of wing,
and pointed wing tips;
lacks white rump patch.

• **BREEDING** Monogamous. Solitary nester.

• **NESTING** Incubation 32 days by both sexes. Semialtricial
young stay with female in nest
30 days. Male brings food for
first 14 days. Then both parents
feed. 1 brood per year.

• **POPULATION** Casual to
rare. No more than 50 pairs
known north of Mexico, but
species is widespread in tropics.

Flight Pattern

Graceful buoyant flap-and-glide flight;
soars often but not to great heights.

Nest Identification

Shape   Location

Green twigs and sticks • lined with green leaves • 40–60 feet above ground
concealed in treetops, especially sycamore or cottonwood • built by both sexes
• 2–3 white to bluish white eggs, seldom marked (brown marks when present)
but often nest-stained, 2 inches long.

Plumage Sexes similar	Habitat	Migration Some migrate	Weight Undetermined

DATE _____ TIME _____ LOCATION _____

| Family ACCIPITRIDAE | Species *Buteogallus anthracinus* | Length 20–23 inches | Wingspan 48–50 inches |

COMMON BLACK-HAWK

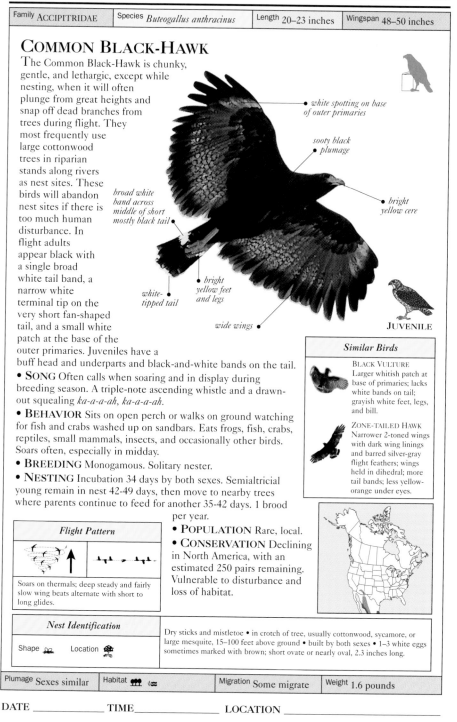

The Common Black-Hawk is chunky, gentle, and lethargic, except while nesting, when it will often plunge from great heights and snap off dead branches from trees during flight. They most frequently use large cottonwood trees in riparian stands along rivers as nest sites. These birds will abandon nest sites if there is too much human disturbance. In flight adults appear black with a single broad white tail band, a narrow white terminal tip on the very short fan-shaped tail, and a small white patch at the base of the outer primaries. Juveniles have a buff head and underparts and black-and-white bands on the tail.

white spotting on base of outer primaries

sooty black plumage

bright yellow cere

broad white band across middle of short mostly black tail

bright yellow feet and legs

white-tipped tail

wide wings

JUVENILE

• **SONG** Often calls when soaring and in display during breeding season. A triple-note ascending whistle and a drawn-out squealing *ka-a-a-ah, ka-a-a-ah*.
• **BEHAVIOR** Sits on open perch or walks on ground watching for fish and crabs washed up on sandbars. Eats frogs, fish, crabs, reptiles, small mammals, insects, and occasionally other birds. Soars often, especially in midday.
• **BREEDING** Monogamous. Solitary nester.
• **NESTING** Incubation 34 days by both sexes. Semialtricial young remain in nest 42-49 days, then move to nearby trees where parents continue to feed for another 35-42 days. 1 brood per year.
• **POPULATION** Rare, local.
• **CONSERVATION** Declining in North America, with an estimated 250 pairs remaining. Vulnerable to disturbance and loss of habitat.

Similar Birds

BLACK VULTURE
Larger whitish patch at base of primaries; lacks white bands on tail; grayish white feet, legs, and bill.

ZONE-TAILED HAWK
Narrower 2-toned wings with dark wing linings and barred silver-gray flight feathers; wings held in dihedral; more tail bands; less yellow-orange under eyes.

Flight Pattern

Soars on thermals; deep steady and fairly slow wing beats alternate with short to long glides.

Nest Identification

Shape   Location

Dry sticks and mistletoe • in crotch of tree, usually cottonwood, sycamore, or large mesquite, 15–100 feet above ground • built by both sexes • 1–3 white eggs sometimes marked with brown; short ovate or nearly oval, 2.3 inches long.

| Plumage Sexes similar | Habitat | Migration Some migrate | Weight 1.6 pounds |

DATE _____ TIME_____ LOCATION _____

Family ACCIPITRIDAE	Species *Parabuteo unicinctus*	Length 17–24 inches	Wingspan 46 inches

HARRIS'S HAWK

Named after a friend of John James Audubon, Edward Harris, Harris's Hawk is rather tame. This dark sooty brown hawk has beautiful markings, including rufous-chestnut shoulders, underwing linings, and thighs, and a boldly marked black-and-white tail set off by a white rump and white tail coverts. Once called the Bay-winged Hawk, the juvenile has streaked underparts, a white rump, and rusty shoulders not as deeply colored as those of the adult.

• **SONG** Loud harsh nasal screams of *jaaahrr*, sounding similar to a Barn Owl.

• **BEHAVIOR** Often perches conspicuously near roads on utility

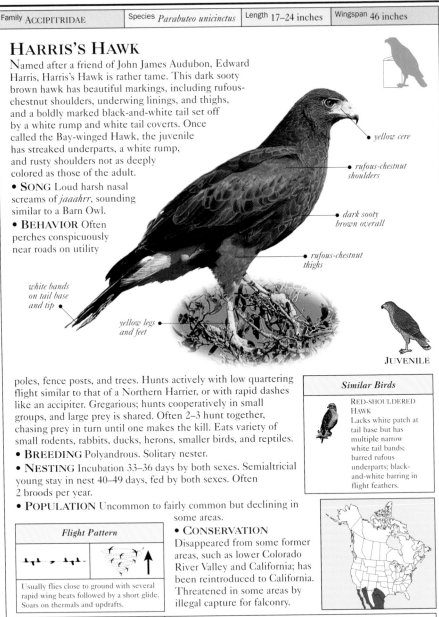

yellow cere

rufous-chestnut shoulders

dark sooty brown overall

rufous-chestnut thighs

white bands on tail base and tip

yellow legs and feet

JUVENILE

poles, fence posts, and trees. Hunts actively with low quartering flight similar to that of a Northern Harrier, or with rapid dashes like an accipiter. Gregarious; hunts cooperatively in small groups, and large prey is shared. Often 2–3 hunt together, chasing prey in turn until one makes the kill. Eats variety of small rodents, rabbits, ducks, herons, smaller birds, and reptiles.

• **BREEDING** Polyandrous. Solitary nester.

• **NESTING** Incubation 33–36 days by both sexes. Semialtricial young stay in nest 40–49 days, fed by both sexes. Often 2 broods per year.

• **POPULATION** Uncommon to fairly common but declining in some areas.

• **CONSERVATION** Disappeared from some former areas, such as lower Colorado River Valley and California; has been reintroduced to California. Threatened in some areas by illegal capture for falconry.

Similar Birds

RED-SHOULDERED HAWK
Lacks white patch at tail base but has multiple narrow white tail bands; barred rufous underparts; black-and-white barring in flight feathers.

Flight Pattern

Usually flies close to ground with several rapid wing beats followed by a short glide. Soars on thermals and updrafts.

Nest Identification

Shape   Location

Sticks, twigs, and roots • lined with green mesquite, green shoots and leaves, grass, bark, and roots • in cactus 10–30 feet above ground • built by both sexes, but female does more • 2–4 white or bluish eggs, half marked with browns and lavender; short subelliptical to elongated, 2.1 inches long.

Plumage Sexes similar	Habitat	Migration Nonmigratory	Weight 1.6 pounds

DATE _____ TIME_____ LOCATION _____

Family ACCIPITRIDAE	Species *Buteo lineatus*	Length 17–24 inches	Wingspan 32–50 inches

RED-SHOULDERED HAWK

This bird uses the same territory for years, and even succeeding generations may return to the same territory. The longest recorded continuous use of the same territory is forty-five years. Five races (*lineatus, alleni, extimus, elagans,* and *texanus*) show variations in color and size but all have barred rusty underparts, reddish wing linings, and shoulders with banded tails. In flight the long black tail displays numerous narrow white bands on adults and juveniles. Flight feathers are spotted and barred black and white and show a pale "window" at the base of the outer primaries. Male is larger than female.

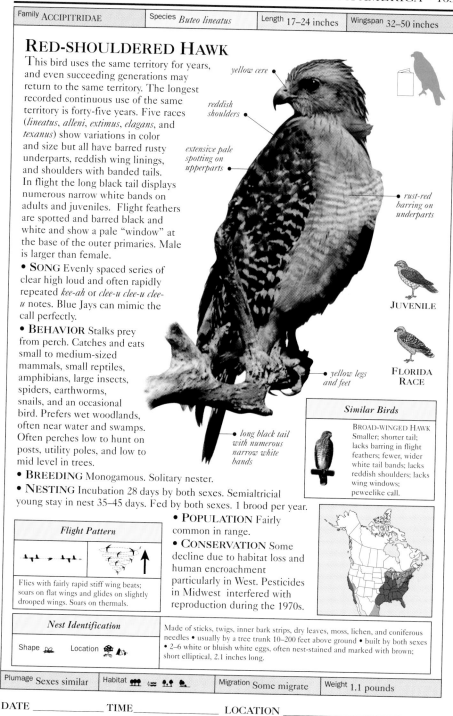

yellow cere

reddish shoulders

extensive pale spotting on upperparts

rust-red barring on underparts

JUVENILE

yellow legs and feet

FLORIDA RACE

- **SONG** Evenly spaced series of clear high loud and often rapidly repeated *kee-ah* or *clee-u clee-u clee-u* notes. Blue Jays can mimic the call perfectly.

- **BEHAVIOR** Stalks prey from perch. Catches and eats small to medium-sized mammals, small reptiles, amphibians, large insects, spiders, earthworms, snails, and an occasional bird. Prefers wet woodlands, often near water and swamps. Often perches low to hunt on posts, utility poles, and low to mid level in trees.

- **BREEDING** Monogamous. Solitary nester.

- **NESTING** Incubation 28 days by both sexes. Semialtricial young stay in nest 35–45 days. Fed by both sexes. 1 brood per year.

long black tail with numerous narrow white bands

Similar Birds

BROAD-WINGED HAWK Smaller; shorter tail; lacks barring in flight feathers; fewer, wider white tail bands; lacks reddish shoulders; lacks wing windows; peweelike call.

- **POPULATION** Fairly common in range.

- **CONSERVATION** Some decline due to habitat loss and human encroachment particularly in West. Pesticides in Midwest interfered with reproduction during the 1970s.

Flight Pattern

Flies with fairly rapid stiff wing beats; soars on flat wings and glides on slightly drooped wings. Soars on thermals.

Nest Identification

Shape 〰 Location 🌳🔺

Made of sticks, twigs, inner bark strips, dry leaves, moss, lichen, and coniferous needles • usually by a tree trunk 10–200 feet above ground • built by both sexes • 2–6 white or bluish white eggs, often nest-stained and marked with brown; short elliptical, 2.1 inches long.

Plumage Sexes similar	Habitat 🌳 〰 🌾 ⛰	Migration Some migrate	Weight 1.1 pounds

DATE _____ TIME_____ LOCATION _____

Family ACCIPITRIDAE	Species *Buteo platypterus*	Length 13–19 inches	Wingspan 32–39 inches

BROAD-WINGED HAWK

The smallest of the North American buteos is similar in size to a stocky crow. These birds, which migrate in flocks of thousands, make up the bulk of hawk flights in September in the East. This peaceful bird is one of the tamest hawks. In flight the tips of the flight feathers appear dark, producing a black border along the trailing edge of the wing, and the underwing linings vary from white to rusty-buff. The black-and-white bands in the tail are approximately equal in width. Juveniles are similar to adults but appear more washed out and have fainter tail bands; underparts are pale with heavy dark streaking.

dark brown upperparts

brown underparts with red barring

- **SONG** Thin shrill whistle, *peeteeee* or *peweeeeeeeeee*, often given in flight and similar to the high plaintive whistled note of an Eastern Wood-Pewee.
- **BEHAVIOR** Perches to watch for prey from utility poles and wires or near water along edge of woods. Hunts along wooded roads under the tree canopy. Swoops down to grab prey with talons. Eats amphibians, reptiles, small rodents, shrews, rabbits, some small birds, large insects, and insect larvae.

large black-and-white bands on tail

JUVENILE

- **BREEDING** Monogamous. Solitary nester.
- **NESTING** Incubation 28–32 days by both sexes, but mostly by female. Semialtricial young stay in nest 29–35 days, fed by both sexes. 1 brood per year.
- **POPULATION** Common in eastern US and southern Canada west to a portion of eastern British Columbia. Rare in winter in California and Florida.
- **CONSERVATION** Large numbers once shot during migration, particularly along mountainous ridges in the East. Now protected by law. Neotropical migrant.

Similar Birds

RED-SHOULDERED HAWK
Larger in size; narrower, more rounded wings with barred and spotted black-and-white flight feathers; buff to rusty-red wing linings; longer, narrower tail with white bands much narrower than dark ones.

Flight Pattern

Several rapid shallow wing beats followed by a glide. Soars on thermals and updrafts.

Nest Identification	Sticks, twigs, and dead leaves • lined with inner bark strips with lichen, outer bark chips, evergreen sprigs, and green leaves • in crotch of deciduous tree, 30–50 feet above ground • built by both sexes in slow process that takes 3–5 weeks • 2–4 white or bluish white eggs sometimes marked with brown; short elliptical, 1.9 inches long.
Shape ～ Location 🕸	

Plumage Sexes similar	Habitat 🌳 🌿	Migration Migratory	Weight 14.8 ounces

DATE _____ TIME_____ LOCATION _____

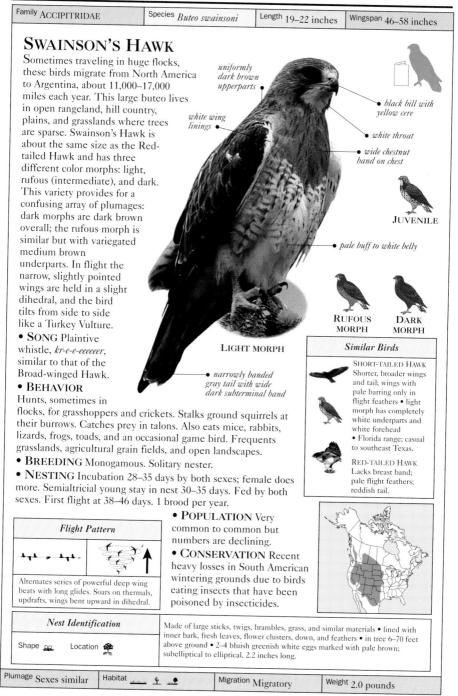

Family ACCIPITRIDAE	Species *Buteo swainsoni*	Length 19–22 inches	Wingspan 46–58 inches

SWAINSON'S HAWK

Sometimes traveling in huge flocks, these birds migrate from North America to Argentina, about 11,000–17,000 miles each year. This large buteo lives in open rangeland, hill country, plains, and grasslands where trees are sparse. Swainson's Hawk is about the same size as the Red-tailed Hawk and has three different color morphs: light, rufous (intermediate), and dark. This variety provides for a confusing array of plumages: dark morphs are dark brown overall; the rufous morph is similar but with variegated medium brown underparts. In flight the narrow, slightly pointed wings are held in a slight dihedral, and the bird tilts from side to side like a Turkey Vulture.

• **SONG** Plaintive whistle, *kr-e-e-eeeeer*, similar to that of the Broad-winged Hawk.

• **BEHAVIOR** Hunts, sometimes in flocks, for grasshoppers and crickets. Stalks ground squirrels at their burrows. Catches prey in talons. Also eats mice, rabbits, lizards, frogs, toads, and an occasional game bird. Frequents grasslands, agricultural grain fields, and open landscapes.

• **BREEDING** Monogamous. Solitary nester.

• **NESTING** Incubation 28–35 days by both sexes; female does more. Semialtricial young stay in nest 30–35 days. Fed by both sexes. First flight at 38–46 days. 1 brood per year.

• **POPULATION** Very common to common but numbers are declining.

• **CONSERVATION** Recent heavy losses in South American wintering grounds due to birds eating insects that have been poisoned by insecticides.

uniformly dark brown upperparts

white wing linings

black bill with yellow cere

white throat

wide chestnut band on chest

JUVENILE

pale buff to white belly

RUFOUS MORPH

DARK MORPH

LIGHT MORPH

narrowly banded gray tail with wide dark subterminal band

Similar Birds

SHORT-TAILED HAWK Shorter, broader wings and tail; wings with pale barring only in flight feathers • light morph has completely white underparts and white forehead • Florida range; casual to southeast Texas.

RED-TAILED HAWK Lacks breast band; pale flight feathers; reddish tail.

Flight Pattern

Alternates series of powerful deep wing beats with long glides. Soars on thermals, updrafts, wings bent upward in dihedral.

Nest Identification

Shape ⌒⌒   Location 🜨

Made of large sticks, twigs, brambles, grass, and similar materials • lined with inner bark, fresh leaves, flower clusters, down, and feathers • in tree 6–70 feet above ground • 2–4 bluish greenish white eggs marked with pale brown; subelliptical to elliptical, 2.2 inches long.

Plumage Sexes similar	Habitat	Migration Migratory	Weight 2.0 pounds

DATE _____ TIME_____ LOCATION _____

| Family ACCIPITRIDAE | Species *Buteo albonotatus* | Length 18–21 inches | Wingspan 47–53 inches |

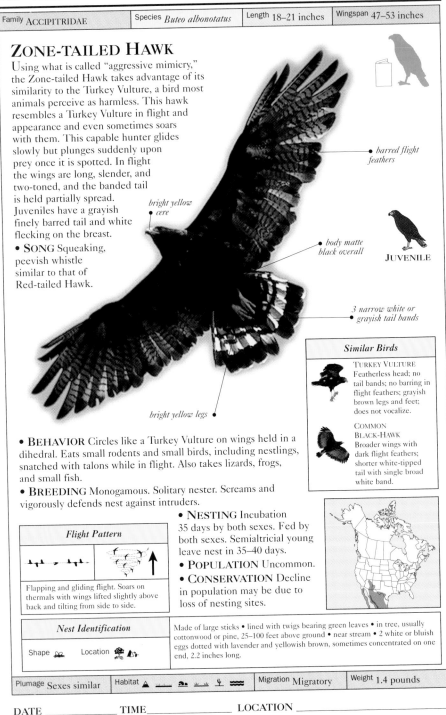

ZONE-TAILED HAWK

Using what is called "aggressive mimicry," the Zone-tailed Hawk takes advantage of its similarity to the Turkey Vulture, a bird most animals perceive as harmless. This hawk resembles a Turkey Vulture in flight and appearance and even sometimes soars with them. This capable hunter glides slowly but plunges suddenly upon prey once it is spotted. In flight the wings are long, slender, and two-toned, and the banded tail is held partially spread. Juveniles have a grayish finely barred tail and white flecking on the breast.
• **SONG** Squeaking, peevish whistle similar to that of Red-tailed Hawk.

barred flight feathers

bright yellow cere

body matte black overall

JUVENILE

3 narrow white or grayish tail bands

bright yellow legs

Similar Birds

TURKEY VULTURE
Featherless head; no tail bands; no barring in flight feathers; grayish brown legs and feet; does not vocalize.

COMMON BLACK-HAWK
Broader wings with dark flight feathers; shorter white-tipped tail with single broad white band.

• **BEHAVIOR** Circles like a Turkey Vulture on wings held in a dihedral. Eats small rodents and small birds, including nestlings, snatched with talons while in flight. Also takes lizards, frogs, and small fish.
• **BREEDING** Monogamous. Solitary nester. Screams and vigorously defends nest against intruders.

• **NESTING** Incubation 35 days by both sexes. Fed by both sexes. Semialtricial young leave nest in 35–40 days.
• **POPULATION** Uncommon.
• **CONSERVATION** Decline in population may be due to loss of nesting sites.

Flight Pattern

Flapping and gliding flight. Soars on thermals with wings lifted slightly above back and tilting from side to side.

Nest Identification	
Shape	Location	Made of large sticks • lined with twigs bearing green leaves • in tree, usually cottonwood or pine, 25–100 feet above ground • near stream • 2 white or bluish eggs dotted with lavender and yellowish brown, sometimes concentrated on one end, 2.2 inches long.

| Plumage Sexes similar | Habitat | Migration Migratory | Weight 1.4 pounds |

Family ACCIPITRIDAE	Species *Buteo jamaicensis*	Length 19–25 inches	Wingspan 46–58 inches

RED-TAILED HAWK

This hawk is found in more habitats than any other North American buteo and, consequently, is the most common hawk on the continent. This species has five races: a pale pink-tailed Great Plains race known as "Krider's Red-tailed," *krideri;* the eastern *borealis,* the southwestern *fuertesi;* the western, *calurus;* and the rare "Harlan's Hawk" or *harlani,* once considered a separate species, which is very dark with a white-based tail. All adults show a dark brownish mantle in flight and dark brown bar on leading edge of underwing. All juveniles have a dark brown tail with a black band. Because it perches low on woodland edges and along roadsides this is one of the most conspicuous and easily observed hawks.

• reddish tail ranges from pale buff-pink to deep rufous-red

• whitish flight feathers with pale barring

• pale wing linings

• large bill with yellow cere

• white belly with broad band of dark streaking

EASTERN ADULT
BOREALIS

• **SONG** Harsh descending slurred *keeeeer-r-r.* Also rasping hissing screamy, *p-s-s-s, kree-kree ree-e-e.*
• **BEHAVIOR** Across its vast range takes a wide variety of prey Eats small to medium mammals, reptiles, amphibians, grasshoppers, spiders, earthworms, crustaceans, some fish, and an occasional small bird or bat.. Carries small prey to perch; partially eats large prey on ground.
• **BREEDING** Monogamous; may mate for life. Solitary nester.
• **NESTING** Incubation 28–35 days by both sexes; more by female. Semialtricial young stay in nest 42–46 days. Fed by both sexes. 1 brood per year.

HARLAN'S HAWK

KRIDER'S RED-TAILED

Similar Birds
ROUGH-LEGGED HAWK Smaller bill and feet; feathered legs; white rump; white tail with multiple dark bands; black belly (light morph).
SWAINSON'S HAWK Multiple tail bands; dark flight feathers; pale wing linings; brown chest (light morph).

• **POPULATION** Very common. Some decline due to habitat loss.
• **CONSERVATION** Some eggshell thinning. Many still killed illegally, and some are accidentally killed by cars.

Flight Pattern	

Several rapid strong wing beats followed by a glide. Soars well on thermals and sometimes hangs on updrafts.

Nest Identification	
Shape 🐦 Location 🌳🏢🌿 🪵	Sticks and twigs • lined with inner bark strips, evergreen sprigs, and green leaves • in crotch of large tree, on cliff ledge, or on artificial structure, as high as 120 feet above ground • built by both sexes • 2–3 white or bluish white eggs sometimes spotted brown, 2.4 inches long.

Plumage Sexes similar	Habitat 🌲 🌿🌿 🌱 ─── ⚘ ⚘ ⚘	Migration Migratory	Weight 2.3 pounds

DATE _____ TIME_____ LOCATION _____

Family ACCIPITRIDAE	Species *Buteo regalis*	Length 22–28 inches	Wingspan 56 inches

FERRUGINOUS HAWK

One of the largest and most powerful buteos, this hawk is true to its Latin species name, meaning kingly or royal. This bird has light, dark, and reddish morphs; the light morph is the most common. Dark morphs are dark rufous to dark brown overall. In flight all three hold the long pointed wings in a dihedral, and show a white patch at base of primaries from above. The light morph appears almost completely white from below except for the reddish legs, which form a rusty red V beneath the body.

- **SONG** Alarm call of *kree-a* or *kaah kaah*.

- **BEHAVIOR** Eats mainly ground squirrels; spots them from perch, flies high in air, and swoops down to catch them. Also hunts prairie dogs, rabbits, small rodents, snakes, lizards, small to medium birds, and large insects. One of the few large hawks that hovers. Prefers open country, where it often hunts from low perches on fence posts, utility poles, or small trees.

- **BREEDING** Monogamous. Solitary nester.

- **NESTING** Incubation 31–33 days by both sexes, but female does more. Semialtricial young stay in nest 40–50 days; for first 21 days female stays on nest while male hunts, then both sexes hunt. First flight at 38–50 days. 1 brood per year.

- **POPULATION** Uncommon to fairly common. Rare to casual in migration or winter to states bordered by the Mississippi River and occasionally Florida.

- **CONSERVATION** Threatened and declining due to illegal shooting and loss of habitat. Some are accidentally killed by cars.

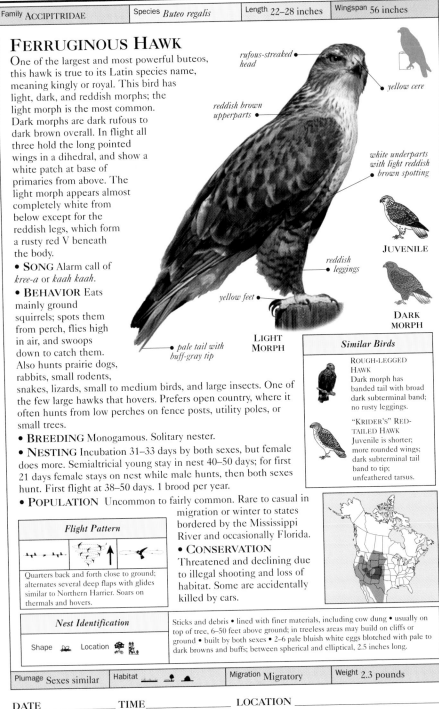

rufous-streaked head

yellow cere

reddish brown upperparts

white underparts with light reddish brown spotting

JUVENILE

reddish leggings

DARK MORPH

yellow feet

LIGHT MORPH

pale tail with buff-gray tip

Similar Birds

ROUGH-LEGGED HAWK
Dark morph has banded tail with broad dark subterminal band; no rusty leggings.

"KRIDER'S" RED-TAILED HAWK
Juvenile is shorter; more rounded wings; dark subterminal tail band to tip; unfeathered tarsus.

Flight Pattern

Quarters back and forth close to ground; alternates several deep flaps with glides similar to Northern Harrier. Soars on thermals and hovers.

Nest Identification	Sticks and debris • lined with finer materials, including cow dung • usually on top of tree, 6–50 feet above ground; in treeless areas may build on cliffs or ground • built by both sexes • 2–6 pale bluish white eggs blotched with pale to dark browns and buffs; between spherical and elliptical, 2.5 inches long.
Shape Location	

Plumage Sexes similar	Habitat	Migration Migratory	Weight 2.3 pounds

DATE _____ TIME_____ LOCATION _____

Family *ACCIPITRIDAE*	Species *Buteo lagopus*	Length 18–24 inches	Wingspan 48–56 inches

ROUGH-LEGGED HAWK

Named for the feathered shanks of its legs, this big high-soaring hawk of the open country often is seen perched on fence posts or dead trees. It flies low on long, thin pointed wings and is one of the few large hawks that regularly hovers. In flight the light morph's long grayish white tail with a broad dark subterminal band and white tail coverts contrast sharply with its black belly and dark back.

- **SONG** Usually silent in winter. Circling pairs in breeding season give melancholy whistle.
- **BEHAVIOR** Eats mostly small rodents and large insects. Usually catches prey on ground. Often hunts from low perch or by standing on ground on a mound or other elevation. When hunting in flight, flies low over open vegetation, quartering slowly back and forth, alternately flapping and gliding or hovering before plunging feet-first on prey. Irruptive flights when prey populations crash bring many south in winter.
- **BREEDING** Monogamous. Pairs have been recorded to remain together for many years.
- **NESTING** Incubation 28–31 days by female. Young leave nest at about 41 days and spend 21–42 days in Arctic after fledging and before migrating south for winter.
- **POPULATION** Common in breeding range; uncommon to fairly common with erratic numbers on wintering grounds.
- **CONSERVATION** Enormous numbers once were shot in western US because of tameness. In the West many killed while feeding on animal carcasses on highways.

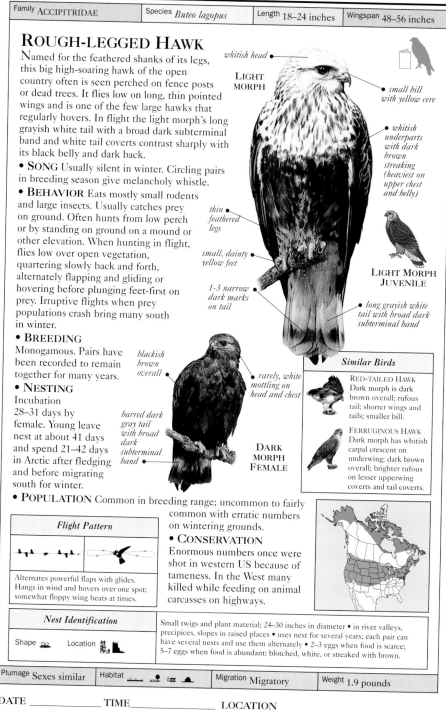

LIGHT MORPH

whitish head

small bill with yellow cere

whitish underparts with dark brown streaking (heaviest on upper chest and belly)

thin feathered legs

small, dainty yellow feet

1–3 narrow dark marks on tail

LIGHT MORPH JUVENILE

long grayish white tail with broad dark subterminal band

blackish brown overall

barred dark gray tail with broad dark subterminal band

rarely, white mottling on head and chest

DARK MORPH FEMALE

Similar Birds

RED-TAILED HAWK Dark morph is dark brown overall; rufous tail; shorter wings and tails; smaller bill.

FERRUGINOUS HAWK Dark morph has whitish carpal crescent on underwing; dark brown overall; brighter rufous on lesser upperwing coverts and tail coverts.

Flight Pattern

Alternates powerful flaps with glides. Hangs in wind and hovers over one spot; somewhat floppy wing beats at times.

Nest Identification

Shape 〰 Location 🪨🌲

Small twigs and plant material; 24–30 inches in diameter • in river valleys, precipices, slopes in raised places • uses nest for several years; each pair can have several nests and use them alternately • 2–3 eggs when food is scarce; 5–7 eggs when food is abundant; blotched, white, or streaked with brown.

Plumage Sexes similar	Habitat	Migration Migratory	Weight 1.9 pounds

DATE _____ TIME_____ LOCATION _____

Family ACCIPITRIDAE	Species *Aquila chrysaetos*	Length 33–38 inches	Wingspan 6–8 feet

GOLDEN EAGLE

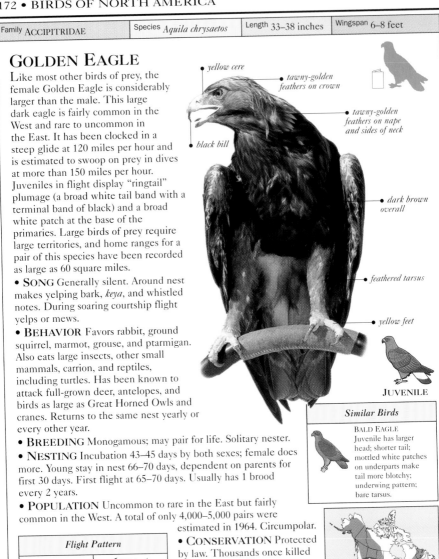

yellow cere

tawny-golden feathers on crown

tawny-golden feathers on nape and sides of neck

black bill

dark brown overall

feathered tarsus

yellow feet

JUVENILE

Like most other birds of prey, the female Golden Eagle is considerably larger than the male. This large dark eagle is fairly common in the West and rare to uncommon in the East. It has been clocked in a steep glide at 120 miles per hour and is estimated to swoop on prey in dives at more than 150 miles per hour. Juveniles in flight display "ringtail" plumage (a broad white tail band with a terminal band of black) and a broad white patch at the base of the primaries. Large birds of prey require large territories, and home ranges for a pair of this species have been recorded as large as 60 square miles.

• **SONG** Generally silent. Around nest makes yelping bark, *keya*, and whistled notes. During soaring courtship flight yelps or mews.

• **BEHAVIOR** Favors rabbit, ground squirrel, marmot, grouse, and ptarmigan. Also eats large insects, other small mammals, carrion, and reptiles, including turtles. Has been known to attack full-grown deer, antelopes, and birds as large as Great Horned Owls and cranes. Returns to the same nest yearly or every other year.

• **BREEDING** Monogamous; may pair for life. Solitary nester.

• **NESTING** Incubation 43–45 days by both sexes; female does more. Young stay in nest 66–70 days, dependent on parents for first 30 days. First flight at 65–70 days. Usually has 1 brood every 2 years.

• **POPULATION** Uncommon to rare in the East but fairly common in the West. A total of only 4,000–5,000 pairs were estimated in 1964. Circumpolar.

Similar Birds

BALD EAGLE
Juvenile has larger head; shorter tail; mottled white patches on underparts make tail more blotchy; underwing pattern; bare tarsus.

• **CONSERVATION** Protected by law. Thousands once killed by ranchers in efforts to protect livestock from potential predation. Also killed in collisions with aircraft. Protected areas established.

Flight Pattern

Alternates deep slow powerful wing beats with glides or rides easily on thermals.

Nest Identification	Sticks woven with brush and leaves • lined with fine material • located 10–100 feet high in trees • 8–10 feet across and 3–4 feet deep • built by both sexes • 2 white or creamy buff eggs marked with brown or reddish brown, 2.9 inches long.
Shape Location	

Plumage Sexes similar	Habitat ▲ ___	Migration Some migrate	Weight 3.5 pounds

DATE _____ TIME_____ LOCATION _____

Family FALCONIDAE	Species *Caracara plancus*	Length 20–25 inches	Wingspan 45–48 inches

CRESTED CARACARA

This large vulturelike raptor often walks on the ground on long legs in search of prey. Its black crown and short crest above the red to yellowish bare skin of the face are distinctive. In flight its flat profile, broad wings, and fanned tail are ravenlike. Flying birds also show white patches at the wing tips, a white head and breast, and a white tail with a broad black terminal band.

- **SONG** In breeding season makes loud *wick-wick-wick-wick-querrr*, throwing its head backward over its back on the last note. Harsh grating rattle. Usually silent.
- **BEHAVIOR** Makes head-throwing display. Only member of Falconidae that actually collects materials and builds nest. Often scavenges with vultures, where it may dominate the carcass. Feeds on variety of animal material, from large insects, reptiles, mammals, birds, amphibians, and fish to carrion.
- **BREEDING** Monogamous. Solitary nester.
- **NESTING** Incubation 28–33 days by both sexes. Semialtricial young stay in nest 30–60 days. Fed by both sexes. 1–2 broods per year.
- **POPULATION** Fairly common in Texas; rare to casual and local in Arizona; rare in Louisiana; fairly common and local in Florida. Has declined throughout range. Florida population stable; Texas population increasing and expanding; Arizona population stable.
- **CONSERVATION** Considered threatened federally and in Florida.

black crown and crest

creamy white sides of head and neck

long neck

red to yellow bare skin on face from nostril to eye

thick whitish bill

white breast with black bars not visible in flight

black body

JUVENILE

long yellow legs and feet

creamy white under tail coverts

Similar Birds

BLACK VULTURE Black head and beak; only creamy white on wing tips.

Flight Pattern

Strong steady deep wing beats; often alternates series of wing beats with long to short glides. Sometimes soars on thermals.

Nest Identification

Shape ◡ ♥   Location 🌴 🌵 ⛰ 🌳

Made of sticks, vines, and twigs • lined with fine material • 15–30 feet above ground in palmetto or giant cacti • built by both sexes • 1–4 white or pinkish white eggs marked with browns, rarely unmarked; ovate to broadly oval or subspherical, slightly pointed at one end; 2.3 inches long.

Plumage Sexes similar	Habitat ⌐ 🌵	Migration Nonmigratory	Weight 2.1 pounds

DATE _____ TIME_____ LOCATION _____

Family FALCONIDAE	Species *Falco tinnunculus*	Length 12–16 inches	Wingspan 27–30 inches

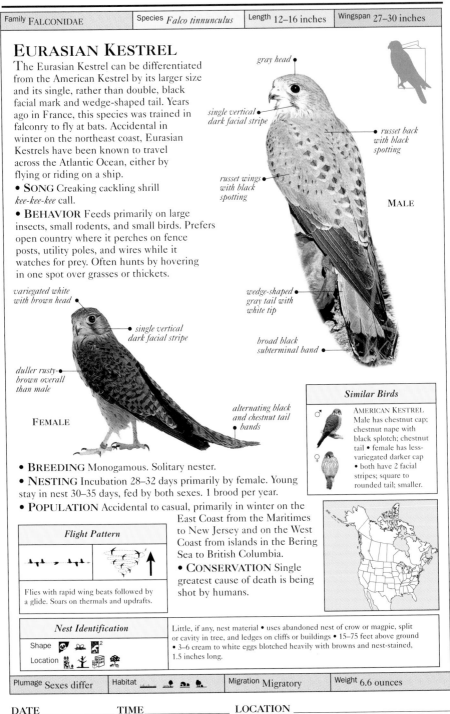

EURASIAN KESTREL

The Eurasian Kestrel can be differentiated from the American Kestrel by its larger size and its single, rather than double, black facial mark and wedge-shaped tail. Years ago in France, this species was trained in falconry to fly at bats. Accidental in winter on the northeast coast, Eurasian Kestrels have been known to travel across the Atlantic Ocean, either by flying or riding on a ship.

gray head

single vertical dark facial stripe

russet back with black spotting

russet wings with black spotting

MALE

• **SONG** Creaking cackling shrill *kee-kee-kee* call.
• **BEHAVIOR** Feeds primarily on large insects, small rodents, and small birds. Prefers open country where it perches on fence posts, utility poles, and wires while it watches for prey. Often hunts by hovering in one spot over grasses or thickets.

variegated white with brown head

single vertical dark facial stripe

wedge-shaped gray tail with white tip

broad black subterminal band

duller rusty-brown overall than male

FEMALE

alternating black and chestnut tail bands

Similar Birds

♂ AMERICAN KESTREL
Male has chestnut cap; chestnut nape with black splotch; chestnut tail • female has less-variegated darker cap
♀ • both have 2 facial stripes; square to rounded tail; smaller.

• **BREEDING** Monogamous. Solitary nester.
• **NESTING** Incubation 28–32 days primarily by female. Young stay in nest 30–35 days, fed by both sexes. 1 brood per year.
• **POPULATION** Accidental to casual, primarily in winter on the East Coast from the Maritimes to New Jersey and on the West Coast from islands in the Bering Sea to British Columbia.
• **CONSERVATION** Single greatest cause of death is being shot by humans.

Flight Pattern
Flies with rapid wing beats followed by a glide. Soars on thermals and updrafts.

Nest Identification	
Shape	Little, if any, nest material • uses abandoned nest of crow or magpie, split or cavity in tree, and ledges on cliffs or buildings • 15–75 feet above ground • 3–6 cream to white eggs blotched heavily with browns and nest-stained, 1.5 inches long.
Location	

Plumage Sexes differ	Habitat	Migration Migratory	Weight 6.6 ounces

DATE _____ TIME_____ LOCATION _____

Family FALCONIDAE	Species *Falco sparverius*	Length 9–12 inches	Wingspan 20–25 inches

AMERICAN KESTREL

The smallest most common North American falcon is found all over the continent and north to the tree line in summer. It is sometimes called the Sparrow Hawk, a misnomer as the bird is neither a hawk nor does its diet include a significant amount of sparrows or other small birds. In flight it shows the typical long tail and long pointed wings of a falcon. A bird of the open country, it often is seen perched on wires along roadsides.

- **SONG** Alarm call a loud quick *klee-klee-klee* or *killy, killy, killy*.
- **BEHAVIOR** When perched bobs tail. Hunts rodents and insects from perch or hovers. Also eats bats, small birds, small reptiles, and frogs. Not dependent on drinking water in desert because it extracts water from its diet.
- **BREEDING** Monogamous. Solitary nester. During courtship male brings food and feeds female in the air.
- **NESTING** Incubation 29–31 days by both sexes, mostly by female. Semialtricial young stay in nest 30–31 days, fed by female. Male calls female from nest to feed. 1 brood per year, sometimes 2 in the South.
- **POPULATION** Common.
- **BIRDHOUSES** Readily nests in bird boxes built especially for kestrels. Occasionally attracted to bird feeders to prey on birds.

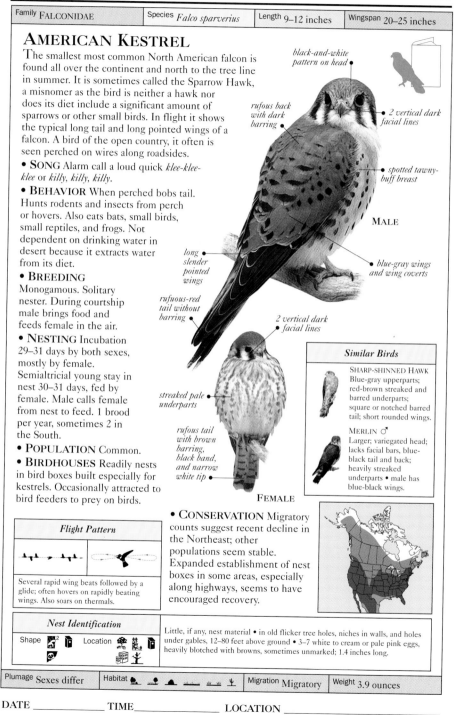

black-and-white pattern on head

rufous back with dark barring

2 vertical dark facial lines

spotted tawny-buff breast

MALE

long slender pointed wings

blue-gray wings and wing coverts

rufous-red tail without barring

2 vertical dark facial lines

streaked pale underparts

rufous tail with brown barring, black band, and narrow white tip

FEMALE

Similar Birds

SHARP-SHINNED HAWK
Blue-gray upperparts; red-brown streaked and barred underparts; square or notched barred tail; short rounded wings.

MERLIN ♂
Larger; variegated head; lacks facial bars, blue-black tail and back; heavily streaked underparts • male has blue-black wings.

- **CONSERVATION** Migratory counts suggest recent decline in the Northeast; other populations seem stable. Expanded establishment of nest boxes in some areas, especially along highways, seems to have encouraged recovery.

Flight Pattern

Several rapid wing beats followed by a glide; often hovers on rapidly beating wings. Also soars on thermals.

Nest Identification

Shape [icons] Location [icons]

Little, if any, nest material • in old flicker tree holes, niches in walls, and holes under gables, 12–80 feet above ground • 3–7 white to cream or pale pink eggs, heavily blotched with browns, sometimes unmarked; 1.4 inches long.

Plumage Sexes differ	Habitat [icons]	Migration Migratory	Weight 3.9 ounces

DATE _____ TIME_____ LOCATION _____

Family FALCONIDAE	Species *Falco columbarius*	Length 11–13 inches	Wingspan 23–26 inches

MERLIN

This medium-sized falcon of northern coniferous forests hunts the openings in parklike grasslands, bogs, and shrubby barrens. In flight it shows the distinctive falcon "jiz" of long pointed wings and a long tail with a big-headed, powerful look, and it displays impressive bursts of speed when in pursuit of prey. Geographic variation in color exists, from pale prairie birds to dark Pacific Northwest forms.

• **SONG** *Ki-ki-kee, kek-kek-kek* rapidly repeated.

• **BEHAVIOR** A relatively tame bird, allowing close approach. Defensive of nest; often attacks intruders, including humans. The Merlin flies close to the ground and catches prey with bursts of speed while in pursuit, rather than by diving or hovering. It is a bird that often hunts from an open perch. Primary diet of small birds, mammals, and large insects. May frequent cities in winter.

• **BREEDING** Monogamous. Solitary nester.

• **NESTING** Incubation 28–32 days mostly by female. Semialtricial young stay in nest 25–35 days. Fed by both sexes. 1 brood per year.

• **POPULATION** Uncommon.

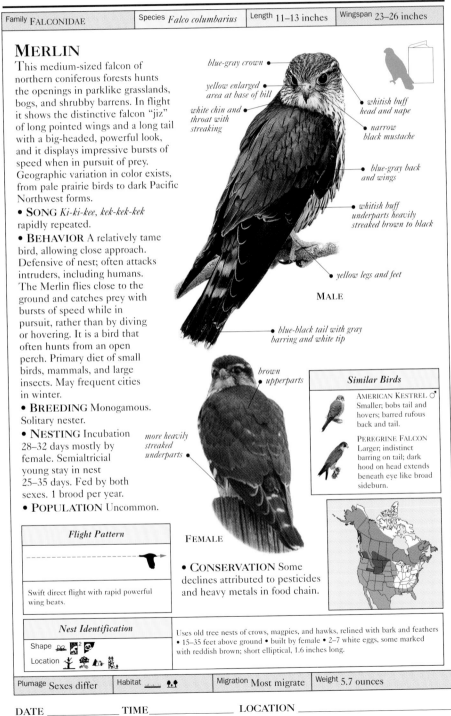

blue-gray crown •

yellow enlarged • area at base of bill

white chin and • throat with streaking

• whitish buff head and nape

• narrow black mustache

• blue-gray back and wings

• whitish buff underparts heavily streaked brown to black

• yellow legs and feet

MALE

• blue-black tail with gray barring and white tip

brown • upperparts

more heavily streaked underparts •

FEMALE

Similar Birds

AMERICAN KESTREL ♂
Smaller; bobs tail and hovers; barred rufous back and tail.

PEREGRINE FALCON
Larger; indistinct barring on tail; dark hood on head extends beneath eye like broad sideburn.

Flight Pattern

Swift direct flight with rapid powerful wing beats.

• **CONSERVATION** Some declines attributed to pesticides and heavy metals in food chain.

Nest Identification

Shape

Location

Uses old tree nests of crows, magpies, and hawks, relined with bark and feathers • 15–35 feet above ground • built by female • 2–7 white eggs, some marked with reddish brown; short elliptical, 1.6 inches long.

Plumage Sexes differ	Habitat	Migration Most migrate	Weight 5.7 ounces

DATE _____ TIME_____ LOCATION _____

Family FALCONIDAE	Species *Falco subbuteo*	Length 12 inches	Wingspan 30 inches

EURASIAN HOBBY

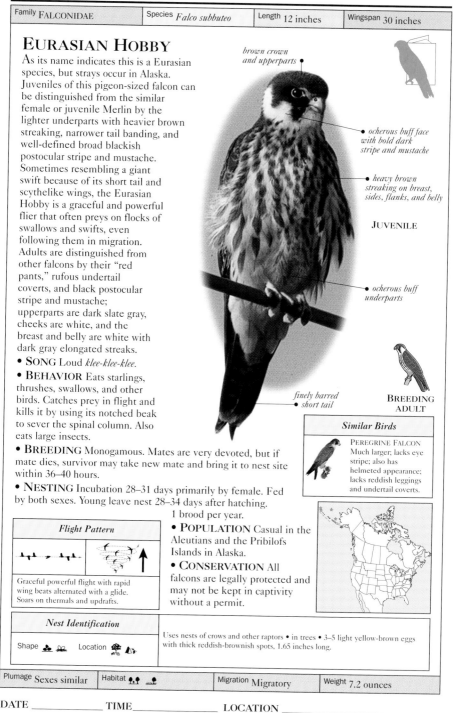

As its name indicates this is a Eurasian species, but strays occur in Alaska. Juveniles of this pigeon-sized falcon can be distinguished from the similar female or juvenile Merlin by the lighter underparts with heavier brown streaking, narrower tail banding, and well-defined broad blackish postocular stripe and mustache. Sometimes resembling a giant swift because of its short tail and scythelike wings, the Eurasian Hobby is a graceful and powerful flier that often preys on flocks of swallows and swifts, even following them in migration. Adults are distinguished from other falcons by their "red pants," rufous undertail coverts, and black postocular stripe and mustache; upperparts are dark slate gray, cheeks are white, and the breast and belly are white with dark gray elongated streaks.

- **SONG** Loud *klee-klee-klee.*
- **BEHAVIOR** Eats starlings, thrushes, swallows, and other birds. Catches prey in flight and kills it by using its notched beak to sever the spinal column. Also eats large insects.
- **BREEDING** Monogamous. Mates are very devoted, but if mate dies, survivor may take new mate and bring it to nest site within 36–40 hours.
- **NESTING** Incubation 28–31 days primarily by female. Fed by both sexes. Young leave nest 28–34 days after hatching. 1 brood per year.
- **POPULATION** Casual in the Aleutians and the Pribilofs Islands in Alaska.
- **CONSERVATION** All falcons are legally protected and may not be kept in captivity without a permit.

brown crown and upperparts

ocherous buff face with bold dark stripe and mustache

heavy brown streaking on breast, sides, flanks, and belly

JUVENILE

ocherous buff underparts

finely barred short tail

BREEDING ADULT

Similar Birds

PEREGRINE FALCON Much larger; lacks eye stripe; also has helmeted appearance; lacks reddish leggings and undertail coverts.

Flight Pattern

Graceful powerful flight with rapid wing beats alternated with a glide. Soars on thermals and updrafts.

Nest Identification

Shape · · Location · ·

Uses nests of crows and other raptors • in trees • 3–5 light yellow-brown eggs with thick reddish-brownish spots, 1.65 inches long.

Plumage Sexes similar	Habitat	Migration Migratory	Weight 7.2 ounces

DATE _____ TIME_____ LOCATION _____

Family FALCONIDAE	Species *Falco femoralis*	Length 15–18 inches	Wingspan 40–48 inches

APLOMADO FALCON

This raptor is similar in size to the Prairie Falcon. The Aplomado Falcon formerly ranged into the southern US along the Mexican border from Texas to Arizona, and was fairly common in open desert and grasslands in the summer prior to the 1880s. By the early part of the 20th century it had all but disappeared. Continuing casual records probably represent birds from the population that still can be found near Chihuahua, Mexico. In flight this falcon shows dark underwings and cinnamon-orange thigh "britches" and undertail coverts.

- **SONG** Shrieking *keeh-keeh-keeh* and an abrasive single-note *keeh* or *kiih*.
- **BEHAVIOR** Found in open grasslands, savanna, and marshy habitats, where it often hunts from a perch on a pole, short tree, or shrub. Often lands on the ground. Hovers. Feeds primarily on large insects and small birds, both of which it often catches in flight. Sometimes this raptor will work grassfires, catching prey that is driven from its grassland cover by the flames.
- **BREEDING** Monogamous.
- **NESTING** Possibly 1 brood per year.
- **POPULATION** Casual to rare. Essentially extirpated from US range and declining in the northern part of Mexico.
- **CONSERVATION** Endangered subspecies. Restoration being attempted in southeast Texas, where introduced birds are successfully breeding.

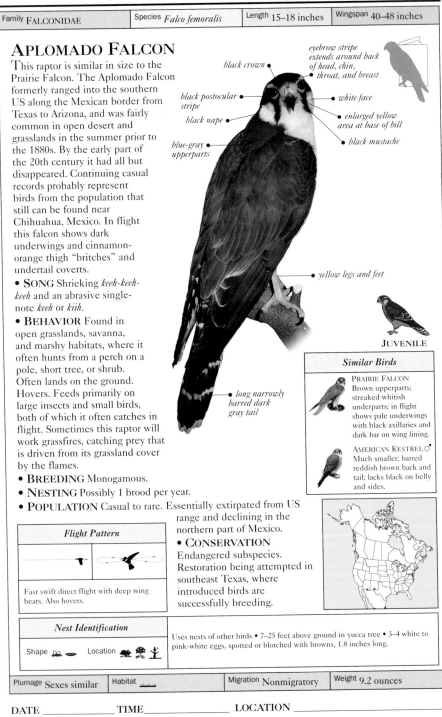

black crown

eyebrow stripe extends around back of head, chin, throat, and breast

black postocular stripe

white face

black nape

enlarged yellow area at base of bill

black mustache

blue-gray upperparts

yellow legs and feet

JUVENILE

long narrowly barred dark gray tail

Similar Birds

PRAIRIE FALCON
Brown upperparts; streaked whitish underparts; in flight shows pale underwings with black axillaries and dark bar on wing lining.

AMERICAN KESTREL ♂
Much smaller; barred reddish brown back and tail; lacks black on belly and sides.

Flight Pattern
Fast swift direct flight with deep wing beats. Also hovers.

Nest Identification	
Shape	Location	Uses nests of other birds • 7–25 feet above ground in yucca tree • 3–4 white to pink-white eggs, spotted or blotched with browns, 1.8 inches long.

Plumage Sexes similar	Habitat	Migration Nonmigratory	Weight 9.2 ounces

DATE _____ TIME_____ LOCATION _____

Family FALCONIDAE	Species *Falco rusticolus*	Length 20–25 inches	Wingspan 48–64 inches

GYRFALCON

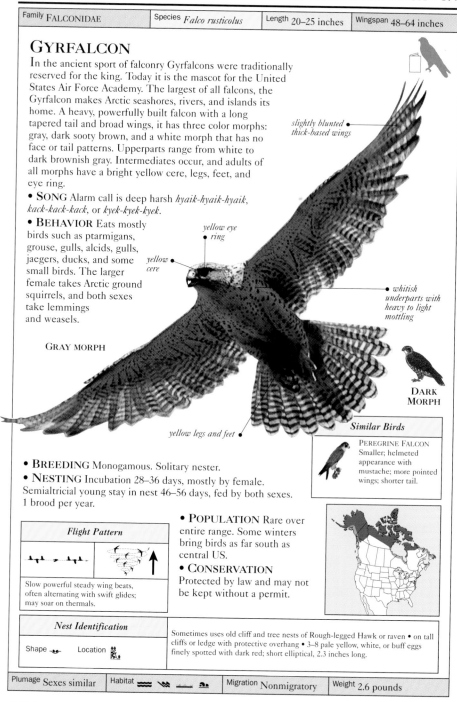

In the ancient sport of falconry Gyrfalcons were traditionally reserved for the king. Today it is the mascot for the United States Air Force Academy. The largest of all falcons, the Gyrfalcon makes Arctic seashores, rivers, and islands its home. A heavy, powerfully built falcon with a long tapered tail and broad wings, it has three color morphs: gray, dark sooty brown, and a white morph that has no face or tail patterns. Upperparts range from white to dark brownish gray. Intermediates occur, and adults of all morphs have a bright yellow cere, legs, feet, and eye ring.

• **SONG** Alarm call is deep harsh *hyaik-hyaik-hyaik*, *kack-kack-kack*, or *kyek-kyek-kyek*.

• **BEHAVIOR** Eats mostly birds such as ptarmigans, grouse, gulls, alcids, gulls, jaegers, ducks, and some small birds. The larger female takes Arctic ground squirrels, and both sexes take lemmings and weasels.

GRAY MORPH

slightly blunted thick-based wings

yellow eye ring

yellow cere

whitish underparts with heavy to light mottling

DARK MORPH

yellow legs and feet

Similar Birds

PEREGRINE FALCON
Smaller; helmeted appearance with mustache; more pointed wings; shorter tail.

• **BREEDING** Monogamous. Solitary nester.
• **NESTING** Incubation 28–36 days, mostly by female. Semialtricial young stay in nest 46–56 days, fed by both sexes. 1 brood per year.

• **POPULATION** Rare over entire range. Some winters bring birds as far south as central US.
• **CONSERVATION** Protected by law and may not be kept without a permit.

Flight Pattern
Slow powerful steady wing beats, often alternating with swift glides; may soar on thermals.

Nest Identification	
Shape Location	Sometimes uses old cliff and tree nests of Rough-legged Hawk or raven • on tall cliffs or ledge with protective overhang • 3–8 pale yellow, white, or buff eggs finely spotted with dark red; short elliptical, 2.3 inches long.

Plumage Sexes similar	Habitat	Migration Nonmigratory	Weight 2.6 pounds

DATE _____ TIME_____ LOCATION _____

Family FALCONIDAE	Species *Falco peregrinus*	Length 16–20 inches	Wingspan 43–46 inches

PEREGRINE FALCON

A peregrine in a stoop is one of the fastest birds in the world, reaching speeds of 175 mph or more.

• **SONG** Usually silent. On breeding grounds makes loud *witchew, witchew, witchew*. When disturbed gives loud repeated *cack, cack, cack, cack*.

• **BEHAVIOR** Prefers open areas with good vantage points on which to perch, often near water. Feeds almost exclusively on birds it takes in the air after a steep swift dive from above them. Wanders widely after nesting season, following prey south as far as southern South America. Faithful to nesting sites and aeries, some of which have been used by generations of peregrines for centuries. Lives on buildings in large cities.

• **BREEDING** Monogamous. Solitary nester.

• **NESTING** Incubation 28–32 days mostly by female. Semialtricial young stay in nest 35–42 days. Fed by both sexes. 1 brood per year.

• **POPULATION** Common to fairly common on tundra; fairly common in migration; uncommon to rare as breeding bird in US. Increasing since continental lows suffered in 1960s and 1970s.

• **CONSERVATION** Federally listed as threatened. Regulation of DDT along with captive breeding and release program have sparked comeback.

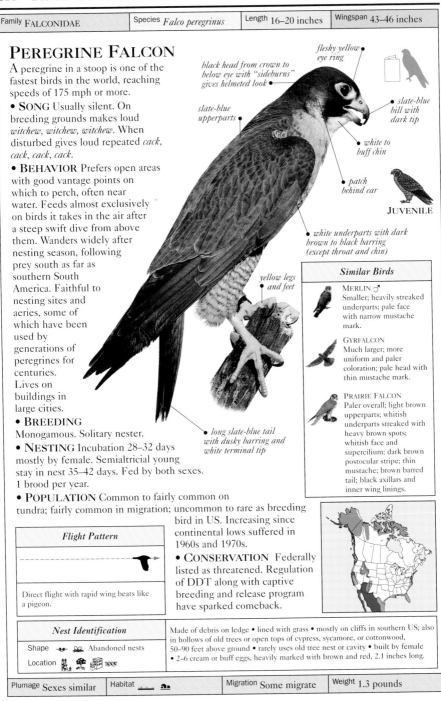

fleshy yellow eye ring

black head from crown to below eye with "sideburns" gives helmeted look

slate-blue upperparts

slate-blue bill with dark tip

white to buff chin

patch behind ear

JUVENILE

white underparts with dark brown to black barring (except throat and chin)

yellow legs and feet

long slate-blue tail with dusky barring and white terminal tip

Similar Birds

MERLIN ♂
Smaller; heavily streaked underparts; pale face with narrow mustache mark.

GYRFALCON
Much larger; more uniform and paler coloration; pale head with thin mustache mark.

PRAIRIE FALCON
Paler overall; light brown upperparts; whitish underparts streaked with heavy brown spots; whitish face and supercilium; dark brown postocular stripe; thin mustache; brown barred tail; black axillars and inner wing linings.

Flight Pattern

Direct flight with rapid wing beats like a pigeon.

Nest Identification

Shape — Abandoned nests

Location

Made of debris on ledge • lined with grass • mostly on cliffs in southern US; also in hollows of old trees or open tops of cypress, sycamore, or cottonwood, 50–90 feet above ground • rarely uses old tree nest or cavity • built by female • 2–6 cream or buff eggs, heavily marked with brown and red, 2.1 inches long.

Plumage Sexes similar	Habitat	Migration Some migrate	Weight 1.3 pounds

DATE _____ TIME_____ LOCATION _____

Family FALCONIDAE	Species *Falco mexicanus*	Length 15–19 inches	Wingspan 40–42 inches

PRAIRIE FALCON

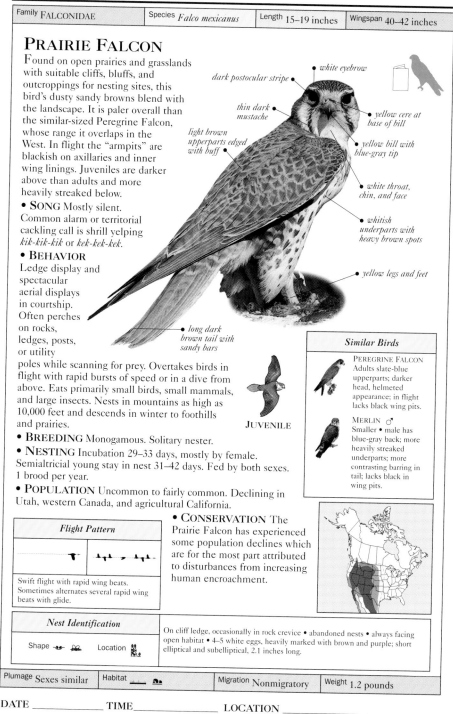

Found on open prairies and grasslands with suitable cliffs, bluffs, and outcroppings for nesting sites, this bird's dusty sandy browns blend with the landscape. It is paler overall than the similar-sized Peregrine Falcon, whose range it overlaps in the West. In flight the "armpits" are blackish on axillaries and inner wing linings. Juveniles are darker above than adults and more heavily streaked below.

- **SONG** Mostly silent. Common alarm or territorial cackling call is shrill yelping *kik-kik-kik* or *kek-kek-kek*.
- **BEHAVIOR** Ledge display and spectacular aerial displays in courtship. Often perches on rocks, ledges, posts, or utility poles while scanning for prey. Overtakes birds in flight with rapid bursts of speed or in a dive from above. Eats primarily small birds, small mammals, and large insects. Nests in mountains as high as 10,000 feet and descends in winter to foothills and prairies.
- **BREEDING** Monogamous. Solitary nester.
- **NESTING** Incubation 29–33 days, mostly by female. Semialtricial young stay in nest 31–42 days. Fed by both sexes. 1 brood per year.
- **POPULATION** Uncommon to fairly common. Declining in Utah, western Canada, and agricultural California.
- **CONSERVATION** The Prairie Falcon has experienced some population declines which are for the most part attributed to disturbances from increasing human encroachment.

dark postocular stripe
white eyebrow
thin dark mustache
light brown upperparts edged with buff
yellow cere at base of bill
yellow bill with blue-gray tip
white throat, chin, and face
whitish underparts with heavy brown spots
yellow legs and feet
long dark brown tail with sandy bars

JUVENILE

Similar Birds

PEREGRINE FALCON
Adults slate-blue upperparts; darker head, helmeted appearance; in flight lacks black wing pits.

MERLIN ♂
Smaller • male has blue-gray back; more heavily streaked underparts; more contrasting barring in tail; lacks black in wing pits.

Flight Pattern
Swift flight with rapid wing beats. Sometimes alternates several rapid wing beats with glide.

Nest Identification	
Shape Location	On cliff ledge, occasionally in rock crevice • abandoned nests • always facing open habitat • 4–5 white eggs, heavily marked with brown and purple; short elliptical and subelliptical, 2.1 inches long.

Plumage Sexes similar	Habitat	Migration Nonmigratory	Weight 1.2 pounds

DATE _____ TIME_____ LOCATION _____

Family PHASIANIDAE	Species *Alectoris chukar*	Length 14 inches	Wingspan 20–23 inches

CHUKAR

This bird was first introduced from Eurasia into the western United States and southwestern Canada as a game bird in the 1930s. Males are slightly larger than females and carry a small spur on each leg, but are otherwise similar. Adults show bold blackish brown flank and side bars. Juveniles lack flank barring and are scaly on the sides with mottling and spots on the upperparts.

• **SONG** Series of loud rapid *chuck chuck chuck chuck* notes that inspired its name; also a shrill *whitoo* alarm note.

• **BEHAVIOR** Spends most of breeding season on the ground in pairs; in flocks or coveys of 6–40 birds the rest of the year. Roosts on the ground, sometimes sleeping in a "wagon-wheel" configuration similar to the bobwhite. Usually escapes danger by running.

• **BREEDING** Monogamous. A few males reported to be polygamous.

• **NESTING** Incubation 22–24 days by female. Precocial young; first flight at about 14 days. 1 brood per year.

• **POPULATION** Common, but can vary dramatically from year to year. Winters with heavy prolonged snow covering food can cause major drops in local populations.

• **FEEDERS** May feed on small grain seeds on ground; more commonly attracted to permanent sources of water such as farm ponds and cattle tanks.

• **CONSERVATION** Managed as a game species where population is established.

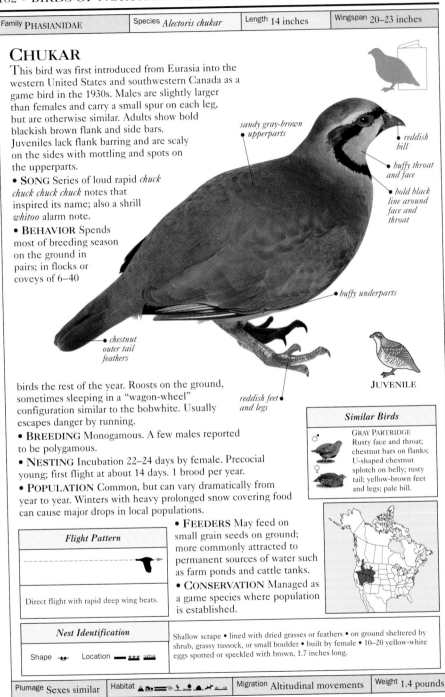

sandy gray-brown upperparts

reddish bill

buffy throat and face

bold black line around face and throat

buffy underparts

chestnut outer tail feathers

reddish feet and legs

JUVENILE

Similar Birds

GRAY PARTRIDGE Rusty face and throat; chestnut bars on flanks; U-shaped chestnut splotch on belly; rusty tail; yellow-brown feet and legs; pale bill.

Flight Pattern

Direct flight with rapid deep wing beats.

Nest Identification

Shape — Location

Shallow scrape • lined with dried grasses or feathers • on ground sheltered by shrub, grassy tussock, or small boulder • built by female • 10–20 yellow-white eggs spotted or speckled with brown, 1.7 inches long.

Plumage Sexes similar	Habitat	Migration Altitudinal movements	Weight 1.4 pounds

DATE _____ TIME_____ LOCATION _____

Family PHASIANIDAE	Species *Tetraogallus himalayensis*	Length 28 inches	Wingspan 34–38 inches

HIMALAYAN SNOWCOCK

This sturdily built Asian ground dweller can be seen in North America only in the Ruby Mountains of northeastern Nevada, where it has been successfully introduced in the alpine and subalpine regions. The Himalayan Snowcock has an unusual pattern of feeding: it flies down the mountain each morning and walks back up the hill, eating along the way. It can be recognized by its whitish face and throat with chestnut stripes, and the distinctive brown streaky collar around its neck. It does not take flight very often; when it does the overall brownish body of this bird is set off by the contrast of the white face and foreneck and the undertail coverts.

tan streaking on upperparts

whitish face and throat outlined with chestnut stripes

brown collar around neck

gray-brown overall

white undertail coverts

• **SONG** Gives a melodic whistle or cry of *gul-gul-gul.*

• **BEHAVIOR** Forages for and eats parts of grassy and shrubby plants, bulbs of various kinds, flowers, an assortment of insects, thin branchlets, and seeds. It is an extremely wary species. It exhibits the rather unusual behavior of foraging for food on the ground, usually in small flocks of birds, moving along the slopes of the mountains where it lives at a slow and steady pace. Rarely does the Himalayan Snowcock run; even when disturbed or pushed, it will determinedly walk away and, upon reaching a bluff or outcropping, launch itself into flight. When birds fly downslope to forage every morning they start by leaping, flapping into the air, then gliding down the slope, keeping quite close to the ground on set and seldom-flapping wings.

• **BREEDING** Monogamous. Solitary.

Similar Birds
BLUE GROUSE Male has sooty gray plumage; orange-yellow combs above eye; whitish undertail coverts; dark gray-tipped tail • female has mottled brown upperparts and underparts; grayish belly; dark tail shows gray tips.

• **NESTING** Incubation by female. The young of this bird are precocial and tended by the female. 1 brood per year.

• **POPULATION** The Himalayan Snowcock has been introduced into North America and is a rare species.

Flight Pattern
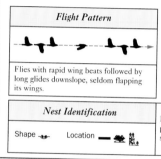
Flies with rapid wing beats followed by long glides downslope, seldom flapping its wings.

Nest Identification	
Shape ◦⦁ Location ━ 🌳 🪨	Lined with grass, twigs, and feathers • on ground, under overhanging rock, in pine tree, or in niche of cliff • 7–11 brownish gray or grayish ocher eggs with small and large brown spots.

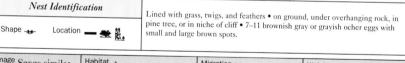

Plumage Sexes similar	Habitat ▲	Migration Nonmigratory	Weight 5.4 pounds

DATE _____ TIME_____ LOCATION _____

Family PHASIANIDAE	Species *Perdix perdix*	Length 12 inches	Wingspan 18–22 inches

GRAY PARTRIDGE

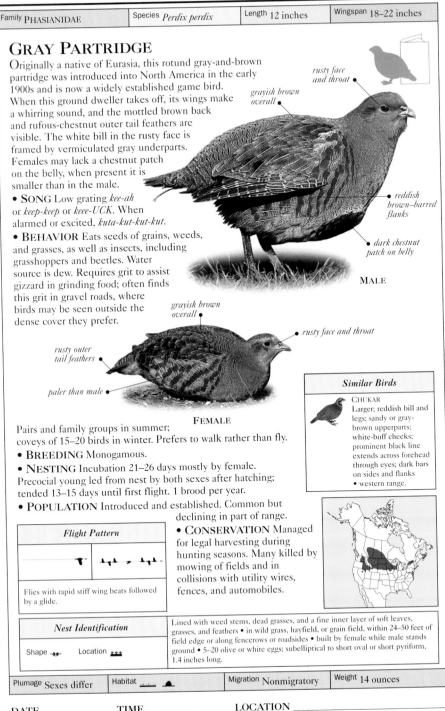

Originally a native of Eurasia, this rotund gray-and-brown partridge was introduced into North America in the early 1900s and is now a widely established game bird. When this ground dweller takes off, its wings make a whirring sound, and the mottled brown back and rufous-chestnut outer tail feathers are visible. The white bill in the rusty face is framed by vermiculated gray underparts. Females may lack a chestnut patch on the belly, when present it is smaller than in the male.

rusty face and throat

grayish brown overall

reddish brown–barred flanks

dark chestnut patch on belly

MALE

• **SONG** Low grating *kee-ah* or *keep-keep* or *keee-UCK*. When alarmed or excited, *kuta-kut-kut-kut*.

• **BEHAVIOR** Eats seeds of grains, weeds, and grasses, as well as insects, including grasshoppers and beetles. Water source is dew. Requires grit to assist gizzard in grinding food; often finds this grit in gravel roads, where birds may be seen outside the dense cover they prefer.

grayish brown overall

rusty face and throat

rusty outer tail feathers

paler than male

FEMALE

Pairs and family groups in summer; coveys of 15–20 birds in winter. Prefers to walk rather than fly.

• **BREEDING** Monogamous.

• **NESTING** Incubation 21–26 days mostly by female. Precocial young led from nest by both sexes after hatching; tended 13–15 days until first flight. 1 brood per year.

• **POPULATION** Introduced and established. Common but declining in part of range.

• **CONSERVATION** Managed for legal harvesting during hunting seasons. Many killed by mowing of fields and in collisions with utility wires, fences, and automobiles.

Similar Birds

CHUKAR
Larger; reddish bill and legs; sandy or gray-brown upperparts; white-buff cheeks; prominent black line extends across forehead through eyes; dark bars on sides and flanks • western range.

Flight Pattern

Flies with rapid stiff wing beats followed by a glide.

Nest Identification	Lined with weed stems, dead grasses, and a fine inner layer of soft leaves, grasses, and feathers • in wild grass, hayfield, or grain field, within 24–50 feet of field edge or along fencerows or roadsides • built by female while male stands ground • 5–20 olive or white eggs; subelliptical to short oval or short pyriform, 1.4 inches long.
Shape 🥚 Location ♣♣♣	

Plumage Sexes differ	Habitat 〰〰 ▲	Migration Nonmigratory	Weight 14 ounces

DATE _____ TIME_____ LOCATION _____

Family PHASIANIDAE	Species *Phasianus colchicus*	Length 21–36 inches	Wingspan 32 inches

RING-NECKED PHEASANT

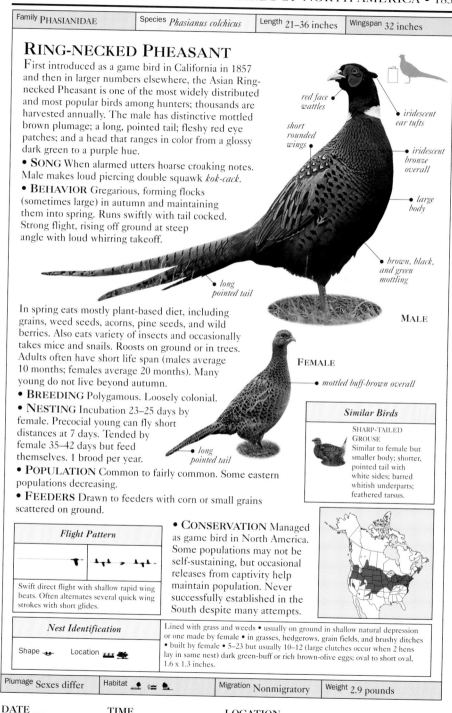

First introduced as a game bird in California in 1857 and then in larger numbers elsewhere, the Asian Ring-necked Pheasant is one of the most widely distributed and most popular birds among hunters; thousands are harvested annually. The male has distinctive mottled brown plumage; a long, pointed tail; fleshy red eye patches; and a head that ranges in color from a glossy dark green to a purple hue.

- **SONG** When alarmed utters hoarse croaking notes. Male makes loud piercing double squawk *kok-cack*.
- **BEHAVIOR** Gregarious, forming flocks (sometimes large) in autumn and maintaining them into spring. Runs swiftly with tail cocked. Strong flight, rising off ground at steep angle with loud whirring takeoff.

red face wattles

short rounded wings

iridescent ear tufts

iridescent bronze overall

large body

brown, black, and green mottling

long pointed tail

MALE

In spring eats mostly plant-based diet, including grains, weed seeds, acorns, pine seeds, and wild berries. Also eats variety of insects and occasionally takes mice and snails. Roosts on ground or in trees. Adults often have short life span (males average 10 months; females average 20 months). Many young do not live beyond autumn.

- **BREEDING** Polygamous. Loosely colonial.
- **NESTING** Incubation 23–25 days by female. Precocial young can fly short distances at 7 days. Tended by female 35–42 days but feed themselves. 1 brood per year.
- **POPULATION** Common to fairly common. Some eastern populations decreasing.
- **FEEDERS** Drawn to feeders with corn or small grains scattered on ground.

FEMALE

mottled buff-brown overall

long pointed tail

Similar Birds

SHARP-TAILED GROUSE Similar to female but smaller body; shorter, pointed tail with white sides; barred whitish underparts; feathered tarsus.

- **CONSERVATION** Managed as game bird in North America. Some populations may not be self-sustaining, but occasional releases from captivity help maintain population. Never successfully established in the South despite many attempts.

Flight Pattern
Swift direct flight with shallow rapid wing beats. Often alternates several quick wing strokes with short glides.

Nest Identification	
Shape	Location	Lined with grass and weeds • usually on ground in shallow natural depression or one made by female • in grasses, hedgerows, grain fields, and brushy ditches • built by female • 5–23 but usually 10–12 (large clutches occur when 2 hens lay in same nest) dark green-buff or rich brown-olive eggs; oval to short oval, 1.6 x 1.3 inches.

Plumage Sexes differ	Habitat	Migration Nonmigratory	Weight 2.9 pounds

DATE _____ TIME_____ LOCATION _____

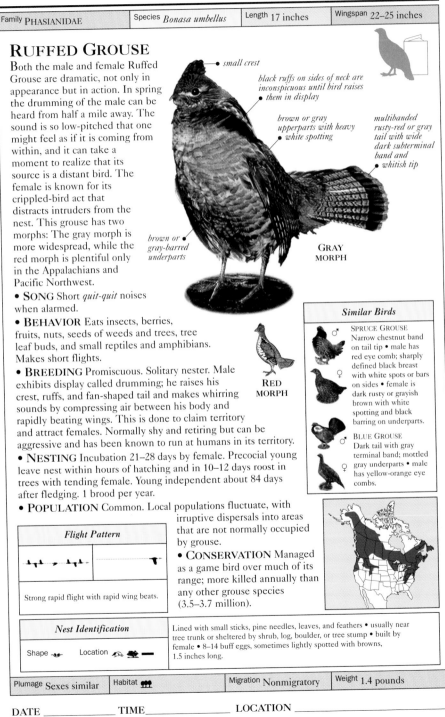

| Family PHASIANIDAE | Species *Bonasa umbellus* | Length 17 inches | Wingspan 22–25 inches |

RUFFED GROUSE

Both the male and female Ruffed Grouse are dramatic, not only in appearance but in action. In spring the drumming of the male can be heard from half a mile away. The sound is so low-pitched that one might feel as if it is coming from within, and it can take a moment to realize that its source is a distant bird. The female is known for its crippled-bird act that distracts intruders from the nest. This grouse has two morphs: The gray morph is more widespread, while the red morph is plentiful only in the Appalachians and Pacific Northwest.

• **SONG** Short *quit-quit* noises when alarmed.

• **BEHAVIOR** Eats insects, berries, fruits, nuts, seeds of weeds and trees, tree leaf buds, and small reptiles and amphibians. Makes short flights.

• **BREEDING** Promiscuous. Solitary nester. Male exhibits display called drumming; he raises his crest, ruffs, and fan-shaped tail and makes whirring sounds by compressing air between his body and rapidly beating wings. This is done to claim territory and attract females. Normally shy and retiring but can be aggressive and has been known to run at humans in its territory.

• **NESTING** Incubation 21–28 days by female. Precocial young leave nest within hours of hatching and in 10–12 days roost in trees with tending female. Young independent about 84 days after fledging. 1 brood per year.

• **POPULATION** Common. Local populations fluctuate, with irruptive dispersals into areas that are not normally occupied by grouse.

• **CONSERVATION** Managed as a game bird over much of its range; more killed annually than any other grouse species (3.5–3.7 million).

small crest

black ruffs on sides of neck are inconspicuous until bird raises them in display

brown or gray upperparts with heavy white spotting

multibanded rusty-red or gray tail with wide dark subterminal band and whitish tip

brown or gray-barred underparts

GRAY MORPH

RED MORPH

Similar Birds

SPRUCE GROUSE
Narrow chestnut band on tail tip • male has red eye comb; sharply defined black breast with white spots or bars on sides • female is dark rusty or grayish brown with white spotting and black barring on underparts.

BLUE GROUSE
Dark tail with gray terminal band; mottled gray underparts • male has yellow-orange eye combs.

Flight Pattern	
Strong rapid flight with rapid wing beats.	

Nest Identification	Lined with small sticks, pine needles, leaves, and feathers • usually near tree trunk or sheltered by shrub, log, boulder, or tree stump • built by female • 8–14 buff eggs, sometimes lightly spotted with browns, 1.5 inches long.
Shape ⌣ Location 🌿🌲 ▬	

| Plumage Sexes similar | Habitat 🌳 | Migration Nonmigratory | Weight 1.4 pounds |

DATE _____ TIME_____ LOCATION _____

Family PHASIANIDAE	Species *Centrocercus urophasianus*	Length 21–30 inches	Wingspan 28–38 inches

GREATER SAGE-GROUSE

This plump chickenlike bird is the largest of the North American grouse. It also has one of the most spectacular mating displays of all grouse. The male struts; rapidly inflates and deflates the air sacs of its breast, producing loud, far-carrying, bubbling, popping sounds; and spreads its pointed tail feathers. The much smaller female appears similar to the male but lacks eye combs, white ruff feathers on the breast, and the black bib on the throat.

long stiff spikelike tail feathers

yellow eye comb

black throat and bib

MALE

white breast ruff

mottled gray-brown overall

black belly

- **SONG** Flushing note, *kuk kuk kuk.* In courtship display male makes bubbling, popping sound with air sacs.
- **BEHAVIOR** Eats soft evergreen leaves, shoots of plain sagebrush, blossoms, leaves, pods, buds, and insects. Prefers to walk but when flushed rises rapidly in flight; usually doesn't fly far.
- **BREEDING** Promiscuous. Social. Males display together at traditional communal dancing areas called leks. Females attracted to the leks mate with only 1 or 2 males.
- **NESTING** Incubation 25–27 days by female. Precocial young stay with female. First flight at 7–14 days.

white throat

FEMALE

black belly

Similar Birds

SHARP-TAILED GROUSE Smaller; narrow pointed tail; white belly and undertail coverts; scaled spotted pale underparts.

GUNNISON SAGE-GROUSE Paler tail with more white barring • male has more prominent crown plumes.

- **POPULATION** Seems to have disappeared over much of range because of land clearing and overgrazing.
- **CONSERVATION** Managed as a game bird.

Flight Pattern
Rises with rapid wing beats (female slips from side to side), then alternates series of rapid flaps with glides.

Nest Identification	
Shape 〜 Location 🌿	Lined with grass and sage leaves • concealed under sagebrush • built by female • 6–9 pale green eggs evenly marked with brown spots and dots; short elliptical to oval, 2.2 inches long.

Plumage Sexes differ	Habitat 🌿	Migration Nonmigratory	Weight 7.0 pounds

DATE _____ TIME_____ LOCATION _____

Family PHASIANIDAE	Species *Centrocercus minimus*	Length 19–22 inches	Wingspan 25–34 inches

GUNNISON SAGE-GROUSE

Not recognized as a species until the 1990s, this grouse was formally split from the larger Greater Sage-Grouse in 2000. It is separated by range, voice, breeding display, and on a genetic basis as a distinct species. It is found locally in southeastern Utah and principally in the Gunnison Basin of southwestern Colorado, but populations have declined and some have been extirpated from their former range in northeast Arizona, northern New Mexico, Utah, Colorado, and the Kansas-Oklahoma border. Females are smaller than males and have a mottled brown body, pale lores, white eye ring, and thin postocular stripe; the whitish chin and throat are connected to a white bar crossing the ear patch. Females also have a black belly, and the long pointed tail, which is paler than the rump, is barred with dark and light brown. Juveniles resemble females.

long, stiff spiked tail feathers •

white bands in tail •

long filoplumes on neck •

yellow eye combs •

mottled gray-brown overall

black face, chin, throat, and bib •

white ruff on • neck and breast

black belly •

- **SONG** Low clucking notes; alarm call is rapid *tuck-a-tuck*. Lek display includes series of sounds followed by 3 quick loud pops as air is forced out of inflated air sacs, followed by 6 more pops.
- **BEHAVIOR** Solitary or in small groups except during mating season, when males display in leks. Eats sagebrush leaves, buds, blossoms, and seeds; some insects during brood rearing. Terrestrial; spends most of time on ground in vegetation. Usually runs from danger. Seldom found away from sagebrush.
- **BREEDING** Promiscuous; social displays at leks. Filoplumes erected on neck in courtship display. Solitary nester.
- **NESTING** Incubation 22–27 days by female. Precocial young tended by female. First flight at 8–14 days. 1 brood per year.
- **POPULATION** Locally common to fairly common. Endemic to sagebrush communities.
- **CONSERVATION** Managed as game bird before recognized as a species. Current attempts are to stabilize populations and halt decline due to overgrazing, development, and overhunting.

Similar Birds
GREATER SAGE-GROUSE Larger but less pronounced filoplumes on nape and neck; more brown in tail; less white in tail feathers with irregularly mottled pattern.

Flight Pattern

When flushed rises directly on rapid wing beats; then alternates series of quick beats with glides. Usually does not fly far.

Nest Identification

Shape ⌣ Location ▬ 🌿 ✦✦✦

Lined (often poorly) with grass, sedge leaves; concealed beneath sagebrush or in grasses; built by female; 5–9 pale green to brownish eggs marked uniformly with brown spots and small dots; short elliptical to oval, 2.0 inches long.

Plumage Sexes differ	Habitat ⤳ ▬▬	Migration Nonmigratory	Weight 4.6 pounds

DATE _____ TIME_____ LOCATION _____

Family PHASIANIDAE	Species *Falcipennis canadensis*	Length 16 inches	Wingspan 23 inches

SPRUCE GROUSE

Also known as the Black Grouse, this bird is mainly a tree dweller. Sometimes called a "fool hen" because it seems fearless of man, it is an easy target for hunters. Franklin's Grouse, a subspecies in the northern Rockies and Cascades, lacks the chestnut band on the tail tip, and the uppertail coverts have white tips. In all other forms the tail has a dark tip and chestnut band. When flying over his territory, the male Franklin's Grouse makes a "wind cracking" sound with his wings to mark his claim.

• **SONG** Usually silent. Males make low hooting sounds. Makes clucking noise around intruders.

• **BEHAVIOR** Arboreal. Tame. Eats buds and needles of conifers, seeds of weeds and grasses, berries, mushrooms, fern fronds, some insects. Forages along wooded roadsides.

• **BREEDING** Promiscuous. Solitary nester.

• **NESTING** Incubation 17–24 days by female. Precocial young abandon nest upon hatching and can take short weak flights at 7–10 days. Young tended by female. 1 brood per year.

• **POPULATION** Common. Local populations fluctuate. Southern edge of range may have seen slight decline, but still common in far north.

• **CONSERVATION** Managed as a game bird.

crimson comb
of bare skin
above eyes

black chin,
throat, and
foreneck

white spots
along sides of
neck and breast

black
breast

mottled gray
upperparts

blackish tail
with chestnut
terminal band

MALE

lacks red
comb and
white spots

mottled brownish
or grayish

dark barring
and white
spotting on
underparts

FEMALE

Similar Birds

RUFFED GROUSE
Slightly larger; slight crest; dark subterminal tail band; dark patch on side of neck • male lacks red eye comb; slight crest; pale chin; barred pale breast; finely barred gray or reddish brown tail with dark subterminal band.

BLUE GROUSE
Dusky or sooty in color; broad pale band at tip of blackish tail; mottled gray underparts • male has yellow or orange comb above eyes • western range.

Flight Pattern

Strong rapid flight with series of rapid stiff wing beats alternating with short glides on downward-pointed wings.

Nest Identification

Shape   Location ▬

Lined with dry grasses, leaves, twigs, and a few feathers • under low branch of spruce or bushes • built by female • 5–10 beautiful cinnamon to pink-buff or cream-buff eggs, usually marked with large rich brown spots and blotches, some thickly and evenly covered with small spots or dots; oval to short oval, 1.7 inches long.

Plumage Sexes differ	Habitat 🐦	Migration Migratory	Weight 1.1 pounds

DATE _____ TIME_____ LOCATION _____

| Family PHASIANIDAE | Species *Lagopus lagopus* | Length 15–17 inches | Wingspan 20–22.5 inches |

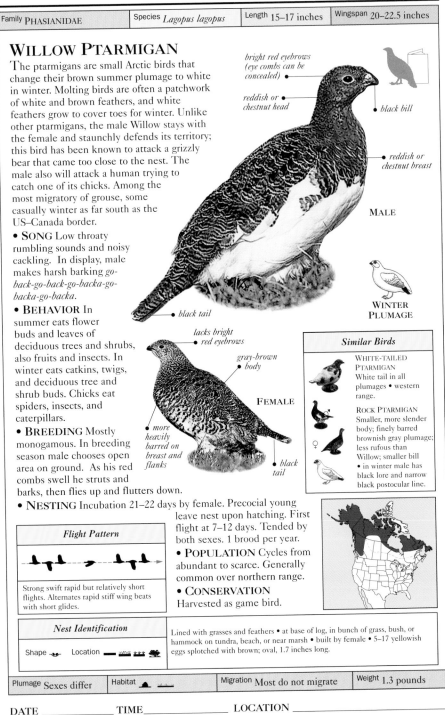

WILLOW PTARMIGAN

The ptarmigans are small Arctic birds that change their brown summer plumage to white in winter. Molting birds are often a patchwork of white and brown feathers, and white feathers grow to cover toes for winter. Unlike other ptarmigans, the male Willow stays with the female and staunchly defends its territory; this bird has been known to attack a grizzly bear that came too close to the nest. The male also will attack a human trying to catch one of its chicks. Among the most migratory of grouse, some casually winter as far south as the US–Canada border.

• **SONG** Low throaty rumbling sounds and noisy cackling. In display, male makes harsh barking *go-back-go-back-go-backa-go-backa-go-backa*.

• **BEHAVIOR** In summer eats flower buds and leaves of deciduous trees and shrubs, also fruits and insects. In winter eats catkins, twigs, and deciduous tree and shrub buds. Chicks eat spiders, insects, and caterpillars.

• **BREEDING** Mostly monogamous. In breeding season male chooses open area on ground. As his red combs swell he struts and barks, then flies up and flutters down.

• **NESTING** Incubation 21–22 days by female. Precocial young leave nest upon hatching. First flight at 7–12 days. Tended by both sexes. 1 brood per year.

• **POPULATION** Cycles from abundant to scarce. Generally common over northern range.

• **CONSERVATION** Harvested as game bird.

bright red eyebrows (eye combs can be concealed)

reddish or chestnut head

black bill

reddish or chestnut breast

MALE

black tail

WINTER PLUMAGE

lacks bright red eyebrows

gray-brown body

FEMALE

more heavily barred on breast and flanks

black tail

Similar Birds

WHITE-TAILED PTARMIGAN
White tail in all plumages • western range.

ROCK PTARMIGAN
Smaller, more slender body; finely barred brownish gray plumage; less rufous than Willow; smaller bill • in winter male has black lore and narrow black postocular line.

Flight Pattern

Strong swift rapid but relatively short flights. Alternates rapid stiff wing beats with short glides.

Nest Identification

Shape 〰 Location ▬ ▬ ▬ ▬

Lined with grasses and feathers • at base of log, in bunch of grass, bush, or hammock on tundra, beach, or near marsh • built by female • 5–17 yellowish eggs splotched with brown; oval, 1.7 inches long.

| Plumage Sexes differ | Habitat ▲ ▬▬ | Migration Most do not migrate | Weight 1.3 pounds |

DATE _____ TIME_____ LOCATION _____

Family PHASIANIDAE	Species *Lagopus mutus*	Length 13–15 inches	Wingspan 17–20 inches

ROCK PTARMIGAN

This bird is perhaps the hardiest of the ptarmigans. It lives year-round in the cold northern mountain regions of Greenland and arctic North America. These birds have been seen flying directly into snowbanks to sleep. As do other species of ptarmigans, the Rock Ptarmigan develops two different plumages to match the predominant colors of the season: white in winter and brown in summer. Winter males retain their red combs and show a black line running from the bill through the eye. Birds experience great and varying amounts of white patches in individual plumages during the sequence of the molt.

small red combs over eyes

MALE

mottled, barred brownish gray plumage

black tail

feathers on entire leg to toe

mottled, barred blackish-brown on brownish-buff plumage

short black bill

WINTER PLUMAGE

feathers on entire leg to toe

white wing feathers

FEMALE

- **SONG** Low growls and croaks and noisy cackles.
- **BEHAVIOR** In summer eats spiders, insects, leaves, buds, fruits, seeds, and mosses. In winter finds food on top of snow such as twigs, buds, and seeds. Unusually resilient for a grouse in flight, it can travel up to a mile before alighting.
- **BREEDING** Monogamous. Colonial. Male defends small territory on breeding ground; displays with swollen red combs to attract females and drive away rival males.
- **NESTING** Incubation 21–24 days by female. Precocial young remain in nest 10–16 days, fed by female. 1 brood per year.
- **POPULATION** Common on tundra. Casual in winter south into taiga. Accidental elsewhere.
- **CONSERVATION** Harvested as a game bird.

Similar Birds

WILLOW PTARMIGAN
Darker; less gray-brown summer plumage • male has rufous-brown plumage; larger bill.

WHITE-TAILED PTARMIGAN
White tail; smaller • western range.

Flight Pattern

Strong swift takeoff; in flight alternates several quick wing beats with glides on down-bowed wings.

Nest Identification

Shape ⚬ Location ▬

Lined with grass, moss, and a few feathers • built by female • 6–13 buff or cinnamon eggs marked with dark browns and blacks; subelliptical, 1.6 inches long.

Plumage Sexes differ	Habitat ⌣	Migration Nonmigratory	Weight 14.9 ounces

DATE _____ TIME _____ LOCATION _____

Family PHASIANIDAE	Species *Lagopus leucurus*	Length 12–13 inches	Wingspan 16–17 inches

WHITE-TAILED PTARMIGAN

Making its home in high mountain peaks, this bird is the only ptarmigan to nest south of Canada. It is the smallest of the ptarmigans, distinguishable from others by its white tail. This bird of high-elevation alpine and subalpine tundra lives most of its life above the timberline. Small numbers have been successfully introduced into suitable habitat in Utah and the Sierras of eastern California and western Nevada. The plumage is molted three times annually and those who have seen this bird in its high mountain home know how well it matches the background in a habitat that seemingly offers little concealment. In winter the bird is entirely white except for its black eyes and bill and the small red comb arcing above the eye, while in other seasons it is a patchwork of white and mottled browns.

red comb over eye

back, neck, head, and breast are mottled brown, white, and black

MALE

white wings

white underparts and legs

white tail and rump

WINTER PLUMAGE

- **SONG** Soft clucking and mellow hooting.
- **BEHAVIOR** In winter eats buds and twigs of alpine shrubs and dwarf trees, alder catkins, and conifer needles and buds. In spring and summer eats leaves, flowers of herbaceous alpine plants, berries, buds of willows, some grit, seeds, and insects. Social in nonbreeding season, with dozens roosting together. Can fly up to a mile before alighting.
- **BREEDING** Monogamous.
- **NESTING** Incubation 22–24 days by female. Precocial young leave nest upon hatching. First flight at 7–21 days. Tended by female. 1 brood per year.
- **POPULATION** Common above tree line but local.
- **CONSERVATION** Harvested as a game bird.

Similar Birds

WILLOW PTARMIGAN
ROCK PTARMIGAN
Larger in size; black on tail in all plumages.

Flight Pattern

Strong, swift, and rapid, but relatively short, flight; rises with explosive roar of wings; alternates wing beats with short glides.

Nest Identification

Shape 〜 Location ▬ 〰 ✲✲✲

Lined with grasses, lichen, small leaves, and feathers • in fine grasses of steep slopes or between rocks above timberline, 10,000–14,000 feet above ground • built by female • 3–9 pink or buff eggs with brown blotches or fine dots, 1.7 inches long.

Plumage Sexes similar	Habitat ▬ ▲	Migration Nonmigratory	Weight 12.7 ounces

DATE _____ TIME_____ LOCATION _____

Family PHASIANIDAE	Species *Dendragapus obscurus*	Length 18–21 inches	Wingspan 24–28 inches

BLUE GROUSE

During courtship this fowl-like bird will perch, inflate its colorful air sac, and make owl-like calls or moans that can be heard two hundred yards away. The Blue Grouse of coastal areas has a yellow neck sac and a gray band at the end of its tail. Although nonmigratory, populations move up and down mountain slopes annually, spending summer in mixed deciduous forests at lower elevations and winter in conifers higher up the slope.

orange to yellowish comb of bare skin above eyes

slightly crested head

purplish red to yellow neck sac surrounded by white-based feathers

MALE

dark tail

gray or sooty overall plumage

- **SONG** Series of hoots.
- **BEHAVIOR** Feeds along edges of coniferous forests. Eats berries, tree buds, tender twigs, leaves, conifer needles, seeds, and insects. Relatively tame; allows close approach. Solitary and arboreal. In courtship display male retracts white-based feathers to reveal neck sac.
- **BREEDING** Promiscuous. Solitary nester.
- **NESTING** Incubation 25–26 days by female. Precocial young leave nest soon after hatching. First flight at 7–10 days. Tended by female. After breeding male often moves to alpine meadows while female keeps incubating at nest on lower slopes; female and young follow 30–60 days later. 1 brood per year.

dark upperparts with brown mottling

gray underparts

FEMALE

Similar Birds

RUFFED GROUSE
Finely barred gray to rusty brown tail with dark subterminal band (broken in female); lacks eye combs.

♂ SPRUCE GROUSE
Male has sharply defined black breast with white spots or bars on side • female has dark barring and white spotting on underparts
♀ • both sexes have chestnut band on tail tip (except birds in northern Rockies and Cascades).

- **POPULATION** A fairly common species.
- **CONSERVATION** Affected by forest management; may increase after clear-cuts but declines as forest grows up. Seems to fare best in original old-growth forests.

Flight Pattern

Strong rapid direct flight; alternates series of rapid stiff wing beats with glides.

Nest Identification

Shape ⚬ Location ▬

Conifer needles, grasses, and leaves • sheltered by log or rock, or near base of tree • built by female • 7–16 pink-buff eggs finely dotted with brown or sometimes unmarked; short subelliptical, 2 inches long.

Plumage Sexes differ	Habitat 🌲 🌿	Migration Nonmigratory	Weight 2.6 pounds

DATE _____ TIME_____ LOCATION _____

Family PHASIANIDAE	Species *Tympanuchus phasianellus*	Length 16–19 inches	Wingspan 21–25 inches

SHARP-TAILED GROUSE

This gregarious bird performs fascinating extravagant mating rituals in spring at communal leks where the male "dances," with tail spread, purple neck sac exposed, and quills rattling; and fights with other males. Often seen on prairies in summer, the Sharp-tailed Grouse gets its name from its narrow pointed tail. There is a small stiff crest on the top of the head. In flight adults can be distinguished from female Ring-necked Pheasants by the white feathers on the side of the tail.

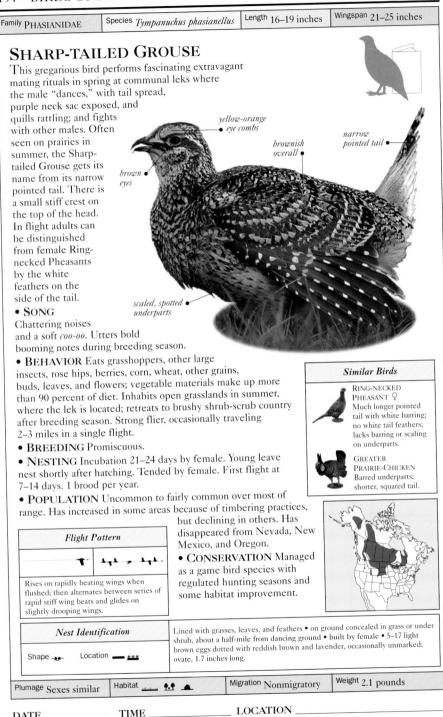

yellow-orange eye combs

brownish overall

narrow pointed tail

brown eyes

scaled, spotted underparts

- **SONG**
Chattering noises and a soft *coo-oo*. Utters bold booming notes during breeding season.
- **BEHAVIOR** Eats grasshoppers, other large insects, rose hips, berries, corn, wheat, other grains, buds, leaves, and flowers; vegetable materials make up more than 90 percent of diet. Inhabits open grasslands in summer, where the lek is located; retreats to brushy shrub-scrub country after breeding season. Strong flier, occasionally traveling 2–3 miles in a single flight.
- **BREEDING** Promiscuous.
- **NESTING** Incubation 21–24 days by female. Young leave nest shortly after hatching. Tended by female. First flight at 7–14 days. 1 brood per year.
- **POPULATION** Uncommon to fairly common over most of range. Has increased in some areas because of timbering practices, but declining in others. Has disappeared from Nevada, New Mexico, and Oregon.
- **CONSERVATION** Managed as a game bird species with regulated hunting seasons and some habitat improvement.

Similar Birds

RING-NECKED PHEASANT ♀ Much longer pointed tail with white barring; no white tail feathers; lacks barring or scaling on underparts.

GREATER PRAIRIE-CHICKEN Barred underparts; shorter, squared tail.

Flight Pattern

Rises on rapidly beating wings when flushed; then alternates between series of rapid stiff wing beats and glides on slightly drooping wings.

Nest Identification

Shape ⌣⌣   Location ▬ ✳✳✳

Lined with grasses, leaves, and feathers • on ground concealed in grass or under shrub, about a half-mile from dancing ground • built by female • 5–17 light brown eggs dotted with reddish brown and lavender, occasionally unmarked; ovate, 1.7 inches long.

Plumage Sexes similar	Habitat ▬ ♠♠ ▲	Migration Nonmigratory	Weight 2.1 pounds

DATE _____ TIME_____ LOCATION _____

Family PHASIANIDAE	Species *Tympanuchus cupido*	Length 17–18 inches	Wingspan 28 inches

GREATER PRAIRIE-CHICKEN

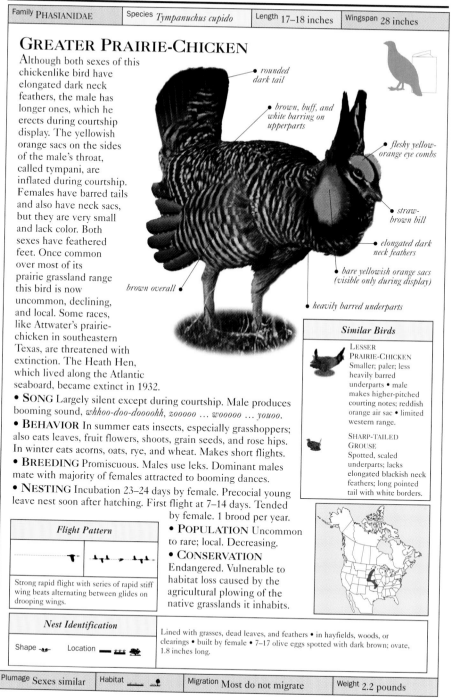

Although both sexes of this chickenlike bird have elongated dark neck feathers, the male has longer ones, which he erects during courtship display. The yellowish orange sacs on the sides of the male's throat, called tympani, are inflated during courtship. Females have barred tails and also have neck sacs, but they are very small and lack color. Both sexes have feathered feet. Once common over most of its prairie grassland range this bird is now uncommon, declining, and local. Some races, like Attwater's prairie-chicken in southeastern Texas, are threatened with extinction. The Heath Hen, which lived along the Atlantic seaboard, became extinct in 1932.

- **SONG** Largely silent except during courtship. Male produces booming sound, *whhoo-doo-doooohh, zooooo … wooooo … youoo.*
- **BEHAVIOR** In summer eats insects, especially grasshoppers; also eats leaves, fruit flowers, shoots, grain seeds, and rose hips. In winter eats acorns, oats, rye, and wheat. Makes short flights.
- **BREEDING** Promiscuous. Males use leks. Dominant males mate with majority of females attracted to booming dances.
- **NESTING** Incubation 23–24 days by female. Precocial young leave nest soon after hatching. First flight at 7–14 days. Tended by female. 1 brood per year.
- **POPULATION** Uncommon to rare; local. Decreasing.
- **CONSERVATION** Endangered. Vulnerable to habitat loss caused by the agricultural plowing of the native grasslands it inhabits.

Labels on image:
- rounded dark tail
- brown, buff, and white barring on upperparts
- fleshy yellow-orange eye combs
- straw-brown bill
- elongated dark neck feathers
- bare yellowish orange sacs (visible only during display)
- heavily barred underparts
- brown overall

Similar Birds

LESSER PRAIRIE-CHICKEN
Smaller; paler; less heavily barred underparts • male makes higher-pitched courting notes; reddish orange air sac • limited western range.

SHARP-TAILED GROUSE
Spotted, scaled underparts; lacks elongated blackish neck feathers; long pointed tail with white borders.

Flight Pattern

Strong rapid flight with series of rapid stiff wing beats alternating between glides on drooping wings.

Nest Identification

Shape ⚬ Location ▬ ⚬⚬⚬ 🌿

Lined with grasses, dead leaves, and feathers • in hayfields, woods, or clearings • built by female • 7–17 olive eggs spotted with dark brown; ovate, 1.8 inches long.

Plumage Sexes similar	Habitat	Migration Most do not migrate	Weight 2.2 pounds

DATE _____ TIME_____ LOCATION _____

Family PHASIANIDAE	Species *Tympanuchus pallidicinctus*	Length 16 inches	Wingspan 28 inches

LESSER PRAIRIE-CHICKEN

The Lesser Prairie-Chicken resembles the Greater Prairie-Chicken but is smaller in size, paler in color, and has dull red instead of orange air sacs. Having a more limited range than its relative, it chooses to live in short-grass prairies with scattered trees, especially shinnery oak, sagebrush, and other deciduous trees. Females are very similar in appearance to the males but have a barred brown tail instead of a black one, and they lack the male's yellow eyebrow combs and neck sacs.

dull red air sacs (visible only during display)

blackish tail

fine buff, brown, and white barring on upperparts

yellow eye combs

blackish neck feathers

brown overall

barred underparts

- **SONG** Booming often described as gobbling, bubbling, or even yodeling.
- **BEHAVIOR** Eats grasshoppers, other insects, leaves, flowers, shoots, seeds, grain, acorns, corn, oats, wheat, and rye. Males concentrate on leks during breeding season, booming and displaying to attract females. Dominant males breed with majority of females attending lek displays. Prefers short-grass prairies and more brushy cover than Greater Prairie-Chicken. Usually walks rather than flies. Makes relatively short flights.
- **BREEDING** Polygamous; promiscuous.
- **NESTING** Incubation 22–24 days by female. Precocial young leave nest soon after hatching. First flight at 7–10 days. Tended by female. 1 brood per year.
- **POPULATION** Uncommon to rare. Declining. Extirpated from much of former range.
- **CONSERVATION** Threatened due to conversion of habitat to farmland. Listed federally as a Threatened Wildlife species.

Similar Birds

GREATER PRAIRIE-CHICKEN
Larger; yellow-orange air sacs; heavier barring on underparts.

SHARP-TAILED GROUSE
Scaled, spotted underparts; pointed mostly white tail; has less prominent yellow eye combs.

Flight Pattern

Strong rapid flight; in flight often alternates several rapid wing beats with short glides.

Nest Identification

Shape 〰️   Location 🌾🌿

Lined with grasses • on ground often at base of sagebrush or concealed in grass or shrubs • built by female • 11–13 whitish to buff eggs, sometimes finely spotted with pale brown or olive; ovate, 1.6 inches long.

Plumage Sexes similar	Habitat 🦗 ⋯ 🌲	Migration Nonmigratory	Weight 1.7 pounds

DATE _____ TIME_____ LOCATION _____

Family PHASIANIDAE	Species *Meleagris gallopavo*	Length 37–46 inches	Wingspan 4–5 feet

WILD TURKEY

The largest game bird in North America, the Wild Turkey once was so widespread it was considered for the US national emblem. Male turkeys gobble year round, but in spring they are easily startled and will gobble at any abrupt noise. Today this unmistakable symbol of a US national holiday is becoming common again due to conservation efforts and its own adjustments to changes in its original woodland habitat.

bare blue and pink head

large iridescent dark body glistens with greens and bronzes

red wattles

MALE

- **SONG** Gobbling may be heard up to a mile away and is easily imitated, with bird often responding to it. Several different clucking calls given by both sexes: *cluk, cluck, cut, putt,* and others.

white-barred flight feathers

- **BEHAVIOR** Powerful muscular gizzard can grind hardest foods. Eats nuts, seeds, large insects, frogs, lizards, wild fruits, and grapes. Flies to tree roosts for the night. Male displays by strutting with tail spread, wings drooped to ground, bare skin of head intensified in color, and frequent gobbling.

proportionally smaller head

blackish breast tuft or "beard"

lacks breast tuft (small "beard" present in some older females)

spurred pinkish legs

- **BREEDING** Polygamous.
- **NESTING** Incubation 27–28 days by female. First flight in about 14 days. Tended by female. 1 brood per year.

duller in color and less iridescent than male

smaller than male

FEMALE

- **POPULATION** Rare to fairly common. Wild birds unlikely in areas of human habitation, though widely domesticated. Increasing.

medium-length broad tail

- **CONSERVATION** Trap and transfer programs have helped reestablish some populations. Increased comeback of blocks of forest interspersed with agricultural areas, as well as wildlife management programs, have helped increase populations.

Flight Pattern
Swift powerful flight for short distances with rapid wing beats and deep strokes; often glides after several series of wing beats.

Nest Identification	
Shape Location ▬	Lined with a few dead leaves and grass • on ground concealed under shrub or in grass • built by female • 8–20 white to cream or buff eggs, sometimes blotched or spotted with brown or red, 2.5 inches long.

Plumage Sexes differ	Habitat	Migration Nonmigratory	Weight 16.3 pounds

DATE _____ TIME_____ LOCATION _____

Family ODONTOPHORIDAE	Species *Oreortyx pictus*	Length 10.5–11.5 inches	Wingspan 14–16.5 inches

MOUNTAIN QUAIL

The largest and perhaps most striking of native North American quail is a swift runner and can often escape its pursuers by dashing across the ground, even on the steepest slopes and in the thickest cover, at speeds up to 12 miles per hour. The female is similar to the male but has duller coloring and shorter head plumes. Immature birds have long plumes, but show a black throat with a white border, white chin, pale gray breast, upper belly scalloped with white feather edging, and white flecking on earth-brown upperparts.

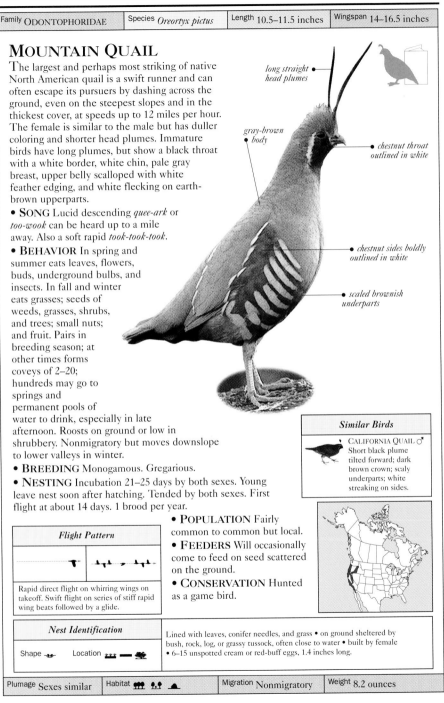

long straight head plumes

gray-brown body

chestnut throat outlined in white

chestnut sides boldly outlined in white

scaled brownish underparts

• **SONG** Lucid descending *quee-ark* or *too-wook* can be heard up to a mile away. Also a soft rapid *took-took-took*.

• **BEHAVIOR** In spring and summer eats leaves, flowers, buds, underground bulbs, and insects. In fall and winter eats grasses; seeds of weeds, grasses, shrubs, and trees; small nuts; and fruit. Pairs in breeding season; at other times forms coveys of 2–20; hundreds may go to springs and permanent pools of water to drink, especially in late afternoon. Roosts on ground or low in shrubbery. Nonmigratory but moves downslope to lower valleys in winter.

• **BREEDING** Monogamous. Gregarious.

• **NESTING** Incubation 21–25 days by both sexes. Young leave nest soon after hatching. Tended by both sexes. First flight at about 14 days. 1 brood per year.

Similar Birds

CALIFORNIA QUAIL ♂
Short black plume tilted forward; dark brown crown; scaly underparts; white streaking on sides.

• **POPULATION** Fairly common to common but local.

• **FEEDERS** Will occasionally come to feed on seed scattered on the ground.

• **CONSERVATION** Hunted as a game bird.

Flight Pattern

Rapid direct flight on whirring wings on takeoff. Swift flight on series of stiff rapid wing beats followed by a glide.

Nest Identification

Shape   Location

Lined with leaves, conifer needles, and grass • on ground sheltered by bush, rock, log, or grassy tussock, often close to water • built by female • 6–15 unspotted cream or red-buff eggs, 1.4 inches long.

Plumage Sexes similar	Habitat	Migration Nonmigratory	Weight 8.2 ounces

DATE _____ TIME_____ LOCATION _____

Family ODONTOPHORIDAE	Species *Callipepla squamata*	Length 10 inches	Wingspan 13–14 inches

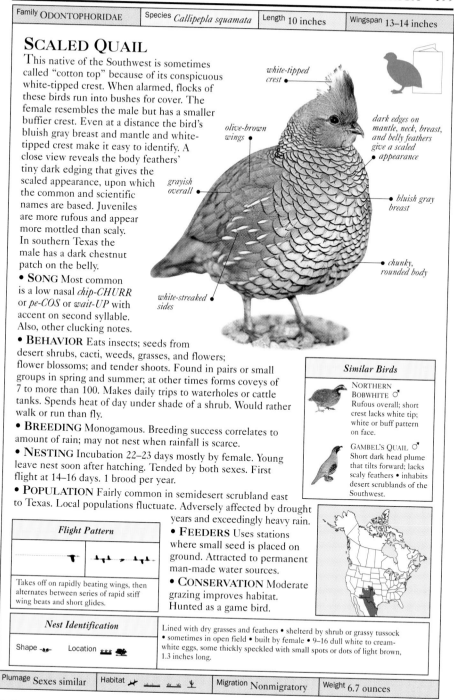

SCALED QUAIL

This native of the Southwest is sometimes called "cotton top" because of its conspicuous white-tipped crest. When alarmed, flocks of these birds run into bushes for cover. The female resembles the male but has a smaller buffier crest. Even at a distance the bird's bluish gray breast and mantle and white-tipped crest make it easy to identify. A close view reveals the body feathers' tiny dark edging that gives the scaled appearance, upon which the common and scientific names are based. Juveniles are more rufous and appear more mottled than scaly. In southern Texas the male has a dark chestnut patch on the belly.

white-tipped crest

olive-brown wings

grayish overall

dark edges on mantle, neck, breast, and belly feathers give a scaled appearance

bluish gray breast

chunky, rounded body

white-streaked sides

- **SONG** Most common is a low nasal *chip-CHURR* or *pe-COS* or *wait-UP* with accent on second syllable. Also, other clucking notes.
- **BEHAVIOR** Eats insects; seeds from desert shrubs, cacti, weeds, grasses, and flowers; flower blossoms; and tender shoots. Found in pairs or small groups in spring and summer; at other times forms coveys of 7 to more than 100. Makes daily trips to waterholes or cattle tanks. Spends heat of day under shade of a shrub. Would rather walk or run than fly.
- **BREEDING** Monogamous. Breeding success correlates to amount of rain; may not nest when rainfall is scarce.
- **NESTING** Incubation 22–23 days mostly by female. Young leave nest soon after hatching. Tended by both sexes. First flight at 14–16 days. 1 brood per year.
- **POPULATION** Fairly common in semidesert scrubland east to Texas. Local populations fluctuate. Adversely affected by drought years and exceedingly heavy rain.
- **FEEDERS** Uses stations where small seed is placed on ground. Attracted to permanent man-made water sources.
- **CONSERVATION** Moderate grazing improves habitat. Hunted as a game bird.

Similar Birds

NORTHERN BOBWHITE ♂
Rufous overall; short crest lacks white tip; white or buff pattern on face.

GAMBEL'S QUAIL ♂
Short dark head plume that tilts forward; lacks scaly feathers • inhabits desert scrublands of the Southwest.

Flight Pattern

Takes off on rapidly beating wings, then alternates between series of rapid stiff wing beats and short glides.

Nest Identification

Shape 〰 Location ✻✻✻ 🌿

Lined with dry grasses and feathers • shelterd by shrub or grassy tussock • sometimes in open field • built by female • 9–16 dull white to cream-white eggs, some thickly speckled with small spots or dots of light brown, 1.3 inches long.

Plumage Sexes similar	Habitat ⤲ 〰 ⚊ ⚊ ⚊ ↓	Migration Nonmigratory	Weight 6.7 ounces

DATE _____ TIME_____ LOCATION _____

Family ODONTOPHORIDAE	Species *Callipepla californica*	Length 10 inches	Wingspan 14–16 inches

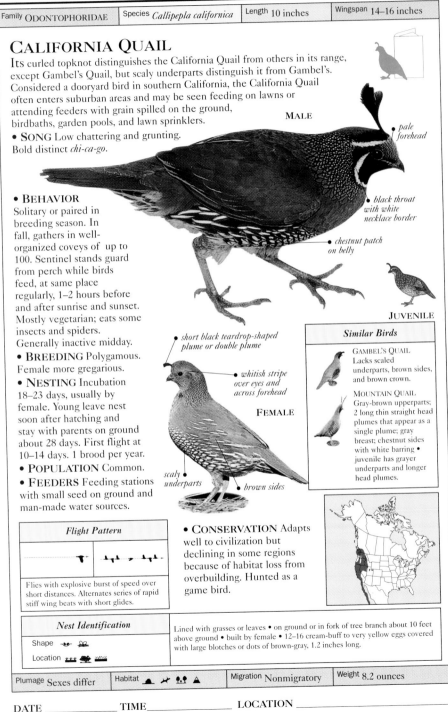

CALIFORNIA QUAIL

Its curled topknot distinguishes the California Quail from others in its range, except Gambel's Quail, but scaly underparts distinguish it from Gambel's. Considered a dooryard bird in southern California, the California Quail often enters suburban areas and may be seen feeding on lawns or attending feeders with grain spilled on the ground, birdbaths, garden pools, and lawn sprinklers.

MALE

• **SONG** Low chattering and grunting. Bold distinct *chi-ca-go.*

pale forehead

• **BEHAVIOR**
Solitary or paired in breeding season. In fall, gathers in well-organized coveys of up to 100. Sentinel stands guard from perch while birds feed, at same place regularly, 1–2 hours before and after sunrise and sunset. Mostly vegetarian; eats some insects and spiders. Generally inactive midday.

black throat with white necklace border

chestnut patch on belly

JUVENILE

• **BREEDING** Polygamous. Female more gregarious.
• **NESTING** Incubation 18–23 days, usually by female. Young leave nest soon after hatching and stay with parents on ground about 28 days. First flight at 10–14 days. 1 brood per year.
• **POPULATION** Common.
• **FEEDERS** Feeding stations with small seed on ground and man-made water sources.

short black teardrop-shaped plume or double plume

whitish stripe over eyes and across forehead

FEMALE

scaly underparts

brown sides

Similar Birds

GAMBEL'S QUAIL
Lacks scaled underparts, brown sides, and brown crown.

MOUNTAIN QUAIL
Gray-brown upperparts; 2 long thin straight head plumes that appear as a single plume; gray breast; chestnut sides with white barring • juvenile has grayer underparts and longer head plumes.

Flight Pattern

Flies with explosive burst of speed over short distances. Alternates series of rapid stiff wing beats with short glides.

• **CONSERVATION** Adapts well to civilization but declining in some regions because of habitat loss from overbuilding. Hunted as a game bird.

Nest Identification

Shape

Location

Lined with grasses or leaves • on ground or in fork of tree branch about 10 feet above ground • built by female • 12–16 cream-buff to very yellow eggs covered with large blotches or dots of brown-gray, 1.2 inches long.

Plumage Sexes differ	Habitat	Migration Nonmigratory	Weight 8.2 ounces

DATE _____ TIME_____ LOCATION _____

Family ODONTOPHORIDAE	Species *Callipepla gambelii*	Length 11 inches	Wingspan 14–16 inches

GAMBEL'S QUAIL

The pleasant call of the male is is a familiar sound of the desert often heard in old western films. Named after William Gambel, an early field collector of birds in southern California, this is the most hunted game bird in parts of Arizona, Nevada, New Mexico, and California. The combination of a comma-shaped black head plume and black belly patch makes the male unmistakable. The female lacks the scaly underparts characteristic of other quail in its range.

- **SONG** Low grunting sounds similar to piglets. Also melancholy *quoit* or *oit* and loud grating 4-note *chi-CA-go-go*.
- **BEHAVIOR** Prefers to walk or run rather than fly. Leaves roost in shrubs in early morning. Large groups gather at drinking places, then feed for several hours in good weather; rests in midday heat. Eats mainly plant materials, but also insects, spiders, and small reptiles. Makes location call if mate leaves visual range. Highly gregarious outside breeding season; forms large coveys in autumn and winter.
- **BREEDING** Monogamous. Gregarious.
- **NESTING** Incubation 21–24 days by female. Young leave nest shortly after hatching; tended by both sexes. First flight at 10 days. When family moves on ground, male takes lead while female brings up rear. 1–2 broods per year.
- **POPULATION** Common. Dry years often result in poor reproduction, but population has remained stable overall.
- **FEEDERS** Attends stations with small seeds scattered on ground and permanent man-made pools of water, lawn sprinklers, and cattle tanks.

black plume

chestnut crown

black forehead, face, chin, and throat with white outline

chestnut sides

MALE

JUVENILE

russet crown

scaly pattern on upperparts

black crest ends in teardrop

sandy-buff underparts

FEMALE

Similar Birds

CALIFORNIA QUAIL
♂ Male has chestnut patch center of belly; less russet crown; scaly underparts; pale forehead • female has scaly belly pattern; darker brown flanks; brownish gray breast.
♀

SCALED QUAIL
Broad white-tipped crest; lacks teardrop-shaped head plume; body appears scaly • male lacks black in face and on belly.

Flight Pattern

Flies with explosive burst of speed over short distances. Alternates series of rapid stiff wing beats with short glides.

Nest Identification

Shape — Location

Lined with grasses, sticks, and feathers • on ground sheltered by grassy tussock or desert shrub • built by female • 9–14 dull white, buff, or pink-buff eggs irregularly blotched, spotted, or dotted with purples and browns, 1.2 inches long.

Plumage Sexes differ	Habitat ⚑	Migration Nonmigratory	Weight 6.0 ounces

DATE _____ TIME_____ LOCATION _____

Family ODONTOPHORIDAE	Species *Colinus virginianus*	Length 9–10 inches	Wingspan 14–16 inches

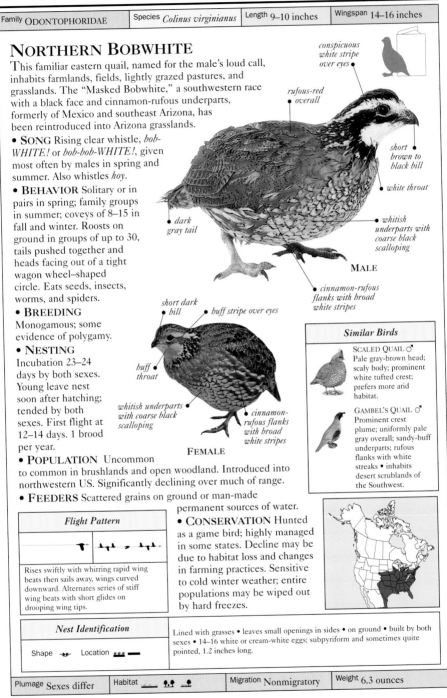

NORTHERN BOBWHITE

This familiar eastern quail, named for the male's loud call, inhabits farmlands, fields, lightly grazed pastures, and grasslands. The "Masked Bobwhite," a southwestern race with a black face and cinnamon-rufous underparts, formerly of Mexico and southeast Arizona, has been reintroduced into Arizona grasslands.

• **SONG** Rising clear whistle, *bob-WHITE!* or *bob-bob-WHITE!*, given most often by males in spring and summer. Also whistles *hoy*.

• **BEHAVIOR** Solitary or in pairs in spring; family groups in summer; coveys of 8–15 in fall and winter. Roosts on ground in groups of up to 30, tails pushed together and heads facing out of a tight wagon wheel–shaped circle. Eats seeds, insects, worms, and spiders.

• **BREEDING** Monogamous; some evidence of polygamy.

• **NESTING** Incubation 23–24 days by both sexes. Young leave nest soon after hatching; tended by both sexes. First flight at 12–14 days. 1 brood per year.

• **POPULATION** Uncommon to common in brushlands and open woodland. Introduced into northwestern US. Significantly declining over much of range.

• **FEEDERS** Scattered grains on ground or man-made permanent sources of water.

• **CONSERVATION** Hunted as a game bird; highly managed in some states. Decline may be due to habitat loss and changes in farming practices. Sensitive to cold winter weather; entire populations may be wiped out by hard freezes.

conspicuous white stripe over eyes

rufous-red overall

short brown to black bill

white throat

whitish underparts with coarse black scalloping

dark gray tail

MALE

cinnamon-rufous flanks with broad white stripes

short dark bill

buff stripe over eyes

buff throat

whitish underparts with coarse black scalloping

cinnamon-rufous flanks with broad white stripes

FEMALE

Similar Birds

SCALED QUAIL ♂
Pale gray-brown head; scaly body; prominent white tufted crest; prefers more arid habitat.

GAMBEL'S QUAIL ♂
Prominent crest plume; uniformly pale gray overall; sandy-buff underparts; rufous flanks with white streaks • inhabits desert scrublands of the Southwest.

Flight Pattern

Rises swiftly with whirring rapid wing beats then sails away, wings curved downward. Alternates series of stiff wing beats with short glides on drooping wing tips.

Nest Identification

Shape — Location —

Lined with grasses • leaves small openings in sides • on ground • built by both sexes • 14–16 white or cream-white eggs; subpyriform and sometimes quite pointed, 1.2 inches long.

Plumage Sexes differ	Habitat	Migration Nonmigratory	Weight 6.3 ounces

DATE _____ TIME_____ LOCATION _____

Family ODONTOPHORIDAE	Species *Cyrtonyx montezumae*	Length 8–9 inches	Wingspan 12–14 inches

MONTEZUMA QUAIL

This quail's arched claws help it walk easily over steep rocky places in mountainous open oak grasslands. It is a plump, short-tailed, secretive quail. The male has a bold pattern with white spots on the sides and flanks, a striking black-and-white pattern on its "clown face," and a soft pale brown crest. Females are brown with white, black, and brown mottling and streaking. Juveniles are paler brown with heavy black mottling on the underparts.

• **SONG** Bold tremulous descending whistle resembling that of the Eastern Screech-Owl.

• **BEHAVIOR** Prefers grasslands in pine-oak or juniper-oak open forests in mountains and foothills. Scratches on ground to uncover plant bulbs. Eats nuts of oak and pine, fruits of juniper, seeds of grasses, weeds, buds, tender leaves, blossoms, and insects. Tame. Often sits low and explodes into flight practically beneath one's feet. Moves in pairs or families.

• **BREEDING** Monogamous.

• **NESTING** Incubation 25–26 days by both sexes. Precocial young leave nest soon after hatching. First flight at about 10 days. Tended by both sexes. 1 brood per year.

• **POPULATION** Uncommon to rare and local. Has disappeared or become scarce in parts of the Southwest due to overgrazing by livestock. This also may be occuring in Mexico, but the bird's status there is not well known.

• **FEEDERS** Attends feeders with small seeds scattered on ground and permanent man-made water sources in proper habitat.

• **CONSERVATION** Concern over population declines, though still considered a game bird in some areas.

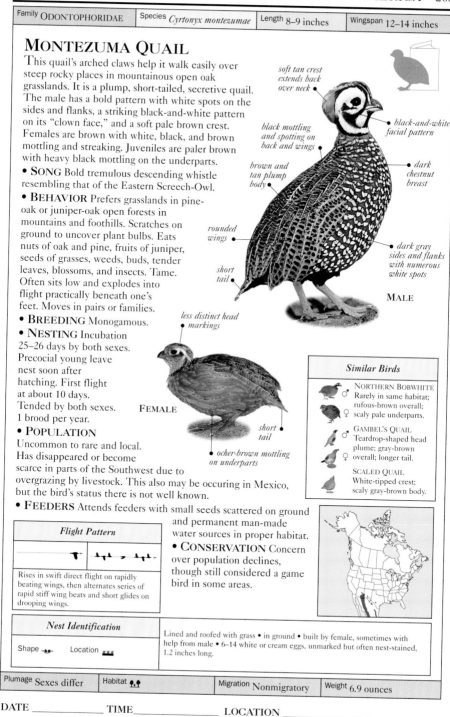

soft tan crest extends back over neck

black mottling and spotting on back and wings

black-and-white facial pattern

brown and tan plump body

dark chestnut breast

rounded wings

short tail

dark gray sides and flanks with numerous white spots

MALE

less distinct head markings

FEMALE

short tail

ocher-brown mottling on underparts

Similar Birds

NORTHERN BOBWHITE
Rarely in same habitat; rufous-brown overall; scaly pale underparts.

GAMBEL'S QUAIL
Teardrop-shaped head plume; gray-brown overall; longer tail.

SCALED QUAIL
White-tipped crest; scaly gray-brown body.

Flight Pattern

Rises in swift direct flight on rapidly beating wings, then alternates series of rapid stiff wing beats and short glides on drooping wings.

Nest Identification

Shape ⌣ Location ⋯

Lined and roofed with grass • in ground • built by female, sometimes with help from male • 6–14 white or cream eggs, unmarked but often nest-stained, 1.2 inches long.

Plumage Sexes differ	Habitat 🌾🌱		Migration Nonmigratory	Weight 6.9 ounces

DATE _____ TIME _____ LOCATION _____

| Family RALLIDAE | Species *Coturnicops noveboracensis* | Length 6–7.25 inches | Wingspan 10–13 inches |

YELLOW RAIL

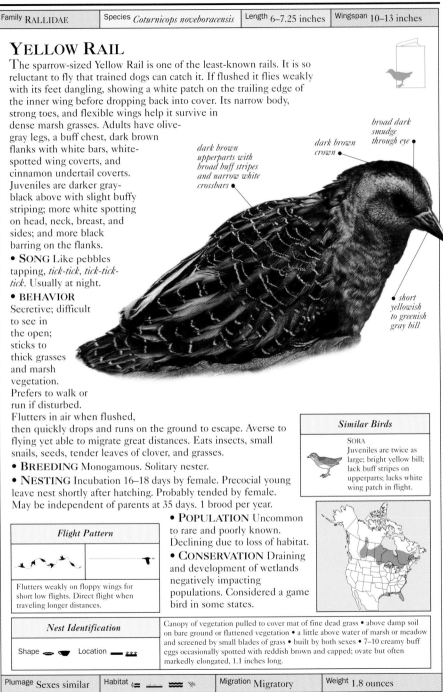

The sparrow-sized Yellow Rail is one of the least-known rails. It is so reluctant to fly that trained dogs can catch it. If flushed it flies weakly with its feet dangling, showing a white patch on the trailing edge of the inner wing before dropping back into cover. Its narrow body, strong toes, and flexible wings help it survive in dense marsh grasses. Adults have olive-gray legs, a buff chest, dark brown flanks with white bars, white-spotted wing coverts, and cinnamon undertail coverts. Juveniles are darker gray-black above with slight buffy striping; more white spotting on head, neck, breast, and sides; and more black barring on the flanks.

dark brown upperparts with broad buff stripes and narrow white crossbars

dark brown crown

broad dark smudge through eye

short yellowish to greenish gray bill

• **SONG** Like pebbles tapping, *tick-tick, tick-tick-tick.* Usually at night.

• **BEHAVIOR** Secretive; difficult to see in the open; sticks to thick grasses and marsh vegetation. Prefers to walk or run if disturbed. Flutters in air when flushed, then quickly drops and runs on the ground to escape. Averse to flying yet able to migrate great distances. Eats insects, small snails, seeds, tender leaves of clover, and grasses.

• **BREEDING** Monogamous. Solitary nester.

• **NESTING** Incubation 16–18 days by female. Precocial young leave nest shortly after hatching. Probably tended by female. May be independent of parents at 35 days. 1 brood per year.

Similar Birds

SORA
Juveniles are twice as large; bright yellow bill; lack buff stripes on upperparts; lacks white wing patch in flight.

• **POPULATION** Uncommon to rare and poorly known. Declining due to loss of habitat.

• **CONSERVATION** Draining and development of wetlands negatively impacting populations. Considered a game bird in some states.

Flight Pattern

Flutters weakly on floppy wings for short low flights. Direct flight when traveling longer distances.

Nest Identification

Shape ◔ ◑   Location ▬ ✴✴✴

Canopy of vegetation pulled to cover mat of fine dead grass • above damp soil on bare ground or flattened vegetation • a little above water of marsh or meadow and screened by small blades of grass • built by both sexes • 7–10 creamy buff eggs occasionally spotted with reddish brown and capped; ovate but often markedly elongated, 1.1 inches long.

| Plumage Sexes similar | Habitat | Migration Migratory | Weight 1.8 ounces |

DATE _____ TIME_____ LOCATION _____

Family RALLIDAE	Species *Laterallus jamaicensis*	Length 6 inches	Wingspan 10.5–11.5 inches

BLACK RAIL

The smallest and perhaps most secretive member of the rail family, this bird was first recorded on the island of Jamaica and is extremely difficult to find. Its range is not well known, and small populations and individual records scattered widely across the United States provide our only information. If glimpsed, it appears like a rodent scampering. Its flight is faint and shaky with legs dangling,

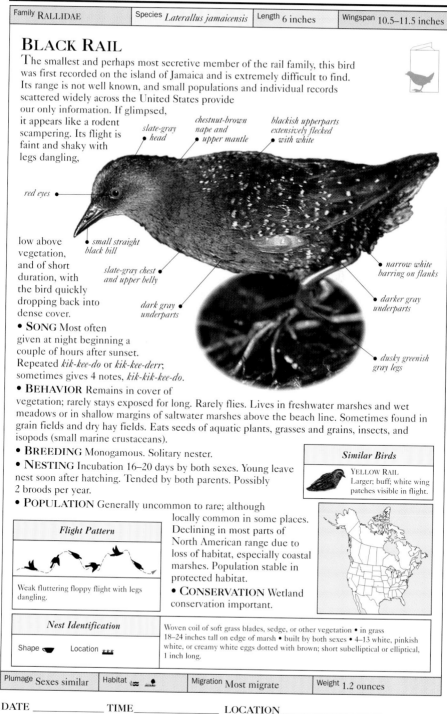

slate-gray head

chestnut-brown nape and upper mantle

blackish upperparts extensively flecked with white

red eyes

small straight black bill

low above vegetation, and of short duration, with the bird quickly dropping back into dense cover.

slate-gray chest and upper belly

dark gray underparts

narrow white barring on flanks

darker gray underparts

dusky greenish gray legs

• **SONG** Most often given at night beginning a couple of hours after sunset. Repeated *kik-kee-do* or *kik-kee-derr*; sometimes gives 4 notes, *kik-kik-kee-do*.

• **BEHAVIOR** Remains in cover of vegetation; rarely stays exposed for long. Rarely flies. Lives in freshwater marshes and wet meadows or in shallow margins of saltwater marshes above the beach line. Sometimes found in grain fields and dry hay fields. Eats seeds of aquatic plants, grasses and grains, insects, and isopods (small marine crustaceans).

• **BREEDING** Monogamous. Solitary nester.

• **NESTING** Incubation 16–20 days by both sexes. Young leave nest soon after hatching. Tended by both parents. Possibly 2 broods per year.

• **POPULATION** Generally uncommon to rare; although locally common in some places. Declining in most parts of North American range due to loss of habitat, especially coastal marshes. Population stable in protected habitat.

• **CONSERVATION** Wetland conservation important.

Similar Birds

YELLOW RAIL Larger; buff; white wing patches visible in flight.

Flight Pattern

Weak fluttering floppy flight with legs dangling.

Nest Identification

Shape ⌐ Location ⁂

Woven coil of soft grass blades, sedge, or other vegetation • in grass 18–24 inches tall on edge of marsh • built by both sexes • 4–13 white, pinkish white, or creamy white eggs dotted with brown; short subelliptical or elliptical, 1 inch long.

Plumage Sexes similar	Habitat	Migration Most migrate	Weight 1.2 ounces

DATE _____ TIME_____ LOCATION _____

Family RALLIDAE	Species *Rallus longirostris*	Length 14–16 inches	Wingspan 19–21 inches

CLAPPER RAIL

gray-brown
overall

gray or gray-
brown cheeks

long thin slightly
down-curved bill

very short tail
with white
undertail coverts

gray to brown
flanks with
white barring

whitish or
buff underparts

JUVENILE

As with most rails the Clapper Rail is more often heard than seen. It is named for its noisy rattling call which is said to sound like old-time clappers. Abrupt noises cause these birds to cry in unison; noisiest at night. This large rail is locally known as "marsh hen" and often leaves the cover of the salt marshes it inhabits to work the muddy flats at low tide. As it walks it bobs its head and flips its short tail exposing white undertail coverts.

• SONG A series of grating *kek-kek-kek* notes, accelerating then dropping off. Given most often at dusk on moonlit nights or when suddenly disturbed by loud noise. One call stimulates another; the calls travel like a wave through the marsh.

• BEHAVIOR Feeds mostly in the open at low tide on mudflats. At other times forages concealed in salt marsh vegetation. Eats crabs and other crustaceans, worms, amphibians, reptiles, mollusks, small fish, and aquatic insects.

• BREEDING Monogamous. Solitary nester.

• NESTING Incubation 20–23 days by both sexes. Precocial young abandon nest soon after hatching. Tended by both sexes. Independent after 35–42 days. First flight at 63–70 days. Possibly 2 broods per year.

• POPULATION Common in coastal salt marshes but declining on West Coast and in some places in the East. Casual on Atlantic Coast to the Maritimes.

• CONSERVATION The inland freshwater race on the lower Colorado River is considered endangered. Also endangered on the West Coast due to habitat loss and perhaps introduced predators.

Similar Birds

KING RAIL
Favors freshwater marshes; bolder black-and-white bars on flanks; bright rufous-brown neck and chest; tawny-buff cheeks; buff-edged back feathers; brown wing coverts; voice differs.

VIRGINIA RAIL
One-third the size; darker overall; blue-gray auriculars; bright rufous upperwing coverts.

Flight Pattern

Low fluttering flight over short distances with legs dangling.

Nest Identification

Shape ⬬   Location 🪨 🌿 🌾

Basket of aquatic vegetation and tide-deposited materials • elevated on firm bank or under small bush • built by both sexes, but male does more • 5–12 buff or olive-buff eggs marked with brown; subelliptical to long subelliptical to ovate, 1.7 inches long.

Plumage Sexes similar	Habitat 🌊 ⎯⎯	Migration Migratory	Weight 11.4 ounces

DATE _____ TIME_____ LOCATION _____

Family RALLIDAE	Species *Rallus limicola*	Length 9–10 inches	Wingspan 13–14.5 inches

VIRGINIA RAIL

Like all rails, the Virginia Rail generally does not fly when it is being pursued but will run swiftly through the marsh grasses. Note its gray cheeks and the reddish bill and legs. Flanks, lower belly, and undertail coverts are barred with black and white. In flight the wings show chestnut in the leading edge. Although this bird prefers freshwater and brackish marshes, it often inhabits salt marshes in winter. Juveniles have dark blackish brown upperparts and black, gray, and white mottling and barring on underparts.

blue-gray face

blackish crown

whitish to pale chin

slightly down-curved, long, slender reddish bill

cinnamon-rufous throat and breast

reddish legs and feet

JUVENILE

• SONG Resembles the clicking of keys on an old typewriter, *kid-ick, kid-ick, kid-ick* or *tic-tic-tic*. Also makes *kik, kik, kik, ki-queea* "kicker" call and descending series of piglike grunts and other odd calls.
• BEHAVIOR Somewhat secretive and terrestrial. Feeds primarily on insects but also takes aquatic animals, including worms, spiders, crustaceans, and small fish. Diet is varied, especially in winter, with duckweed and seeds of marsh grasses, rushes, and sedges.
• BREEDING Monogamous.
• NESTING Incubation 18–20 days by both sexes. Young leave nest soon after hatching. Tended by both parents. First flight at about 25 days. Possibly 2 broods per year.

Similar Birds

KING RAIL
About twice the size • olive-brown head; brown to gray cheeks; cinnamon-rufous underparts; black-and-white barring on flanks.

CLAPPER RAIL
Larger; grayish body; cinnamon to gray underparts; black-and-white barring on flanks; prefers salt marshes.

• POPULATION Fairly common to uncommon. Declining but still widespread despite loss of wetland habitat.
• CONSERVATION Still hunted as a game bird in some states. Wetland protection and management is crucial.

Flight Pattern

Weak brief fluttering flight with long legs dangling.

Nest Identification

Shape ⬥   Location ⁂ ⅏

Pile of matted reeds and layers of coarse aquatic vegetation and grass • in tussock or clumped vegetation • built by both sexes • 5–13 off-white or buff eggs spotted with brown and often wreathed; oval to short oval, 1.3 inches long.

Plumage Sexes similar	Habitat 〰 ▃▃	Migration Migratory	Weight 3.1 ounces

DATE _____ TIME_____ LOCATION _____

Family RALLIDAE	Species *Porzana carolina*	Length 8–10 inches	Wingspan 12–14.5 inches

SORA

In late summer large numbers of these birds gather in marshes to feed and build up fat reserves before migrating; they seem especially fond of smartweed seeds and wild rice. Like all rails, the Sora migrates at night, and for a group that hardly distinguishes itself in the air, this species may cover almost 3,000 miles between wintering and breeding grounds. It is identifiable by its short yellow bill framed with black feathers around its base, black throat, and black center in the upper breast. Small and plump, it is one of the most common North American rails. Juveniles lack the black on the face and underparts and, with their buff coloration, sometimes are confused with the much smaller Yellow Rail.

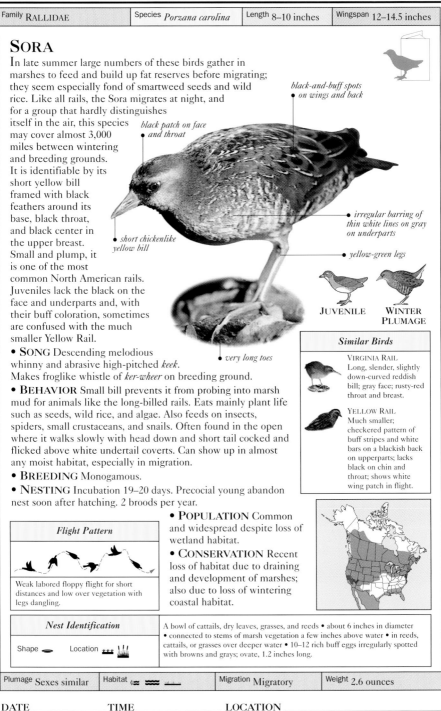

black-and-buff spots on wings and back

black patch on face and throat

irregular barring of thin white lines on gray on underparts

yellow-green legs

short chickenlike yellow bill

very long toes

JUVENILE   **WINTER PLUMAGE**

Similar Birds

VIRGINIA RAIL
Long, slender, slightly down-curved reddish bill; gray face; rusty-red throat and breast.

YELLOW RAIL
Much smaller; checkered pattern of buff stripes and white bars on a blackish back on upperparts; lacks black on chin and throat; shows white wing patch in flight.

• **SONG** Descending melodious whinny and abrasive high-pitched *keek*. Makes froglike whistle of *ker-wheer* on breeding ground.
• **BEHAVIOR** Small bill prevents it from probing into marsh mud for animals like the long-billed rails. Eats mainly plant life such as seeds, wild rice, and algae. Also feeds on insects, spiders, small crustaceans, and snails. Often found in the open where it walks slowly with head down and short tail cocked and flicked above white undertail coverts. Can show up in almost any moist habitat, especially in migration.
• **BREEDING** Monogamous.
• **NESTING** Incubation 19–20 days. Precocial young abandon nest soon after hatching. 2 broods per year.
• **POPULATION** Common and widespread despite loss of wetland habitat.
• **CONSERVATION** Recent loss of habitat due to draining and development of marshes; also due to loss of wintering coastal habitat.

Flight Pattern

Weak labored floppy flight for short distances and low over vegetation with legs dangling.

Nest Identification

Shape ⬯   Location ⚶ ⫰⫰

A bowl of cattails, dry leaves, grasses, and reeds • about 6 inches in diameter • connected to stems of marsh vegetation a few inches above water • in reeds, cattails, or grasses over deeper water • 10–12 rich buff eggs irregularly spotted with browns and grays; ovate, 1.2 inches long.

Plumage Sexes similar	Habitat	Migration Migratory	Weight 2.6 ounces

DATE _____ TIME_____ LOCATION _____

Family RALLIDAE	Species *Gallinula chloropus*	Length 14 inches	Wingspan 20–23 inches

COMMON MOORHEN

This is a fairly tame chickenlike bird of freshwater marshes, ponds, and lakes with heavy stands of cattails, rushes, sedges, and other aquatic vegetation.

• **SONG** No musical sounds are produced. Vocalizations range from explosive, froglike *hups* to loud, chickenlike grunts, clucks, and squeaks along with drawn-out whines and rapid *thicket-thicket-thicket* calls.

• **BEHAVIOR** This noisy bird of the wetlands, unlike most of the rail family, is often seen in the open walking over or climbing through aquatic vegetation. It swims with a pumping back-and-forth motion of its head and neck. When walking it often flicks its tail up and down, flashing the white undertail coverts with their dark center. Usually found in medium to large groups in which individuals can be aggressive toward other members in disputes over food, mates, or nesting areas. Feeds on aquatic vegetation, snails, grasshoppers, and other invertebrates.

• **BREEDING** Monogamous. Solitary to semicolonial, some cooperative breeding.

• **NESTING** Incubation 18–22 days by both sexes. Precocial young stay in nest 40–50 days, fed by both parents and extra birds. 1–3 broods per year.

• **POPULATION** Common, but loss of wetlands has resulted in decline, especially in northern range. Still widespread; may be common in good marsh habitat.

blackish head and neck

brownish olive back

white "line" on side

red frontal shield

red bill with yellow tip

red garter

yellow-green legs

yellow feet

JUVENILE

WINTER PLUMAGE

Similar Birds

AMERICAN COOT
White bill; slate-gray back; no white band on flanks.

Flight Pattern
- - - - - - - - - - - →
Swift and strong direct flight when moving long distance. Weak and fluttering flight when moving very short distance.

Nest Identification	
Shape ☕ Location 🌿 🌿 🪨	Often with ramp of vegetation • made of bleached aquatic vegetation lined with grass • on ground near water or low shrub over water • built by both sexes • 2–13 cinnamon or buff eggs spotted with reddish brown or olive and overlaid with scattered fine dots, 1.7 inches long.

Plumage Sexes similar	Habitat 〰 〰	Migration Some migrate	Weight 12.0 ounces

DATE _____ TIME_____ LOCATION_____

Family RALLIDAE	Species *Fulica americana*	Length 15 inches	Wingspan 23–28 inches

AMERICAN COOT

This close relative of the gallinules and moorhens lives on open water and is often mistaken for a duck. It pumps its small head back and forth like a chicken when walking or swimming and usually travels and feeds in flocks. A common and widely distributed species over much of North America, the American Coot is easily distinguished by its overall slate-gray plumage, which is

gray-black head and neck

reddish brown frontal shield

slate-gray body

short white bill

JUVENILE

blacker on the head and neck, its white bill, and small reddish brown frontal shield. Juveniles are similar to adults but paler, particularly on the underparts, with a darker bill.

• **SONG** Grunts, grating quacks, and hoarse chatters of *ke-yik* and *k-rrk!* or *krek!* Drawling *k-yew-r* and laughing *wah wahk* or *kuk-kuk-kuk-kuk-kuk.*
• **BEHAVIOR** Feeds by immersing head and neck in shallows with body and tail tipped up. May also pick food off surface. Dives 10–25 feet deep for fronds, leaves, seeds, and roots of aquatic plants, which make up most of diet. Also eats insects, amphibians, mollusks, and small fish. Runs with wings flapping rapidly to gain flight from water. Often aggressive toward other waterbirds, chasing them nosily from its vicinity.
• **BREEDING** Monogamous. Pairs display in front of each other on water in courtship. Male also chases female across surface of water.
• **NESTING** Incubation 21–25 days by both sexes. Precocial young abandon nest shortly after hatching and drying off. Tended by both sexes. First flight at 49–56 days. 1–2 broods per year.
• **POPULATION** Common to abundant. Has decreased in the East in recent years.

Similar Birds

COMMON MOORHEN Red shield; yellow-tipped red bill; brown back; white-tipped flank feathers form line between flank and back • juvenile paler with white flank stripe.

PURPLE GALLINULE Dark bluish purple head, neck, and underparts; greenish brown back; yellow-tipped red bill; pale blue shield • juvenile has olive-brown upperparts; pale brown underparts; dull yellowish bill.

Flight Pattern

Fairly swift direct flight with rapid wing beats and feet protruding beyond tail.

Nest Identification

Shape ⌒⌒ Location ⌒⌒ 🌾

Made of dead stems • lined with finer material • floating and anchored to vegetation • built by both sexes • 2–12 pinkish buff eggs marked with blackish brown, 1.9 inches long.

Plumage Sexes similar	Habitat 〰〰 〰	Migration Migratory	Weight 1.6 pounds

DATE _____ TIME_____ LOCATION _____

Family GRUIDAE	Species *Grus canadensis*	Length 34–48 inches	Wingspan 73–90 inches

SANDHILL CRANE

The five North American subspecies of this crane (plus one in Cuba) differ in size and intensity of coloration. The small southern sedentary populations are the most threatened. On the ground cranes look stately with long necks, heavy straight bills, long legs, "bustle" of tertials drooping over the tail, and upright stance. In flight they are distinguished from herons because the neck and head are extended and the slow downward wing beat is jerked quickly upward. This bird may probe for food in mud that contains iron, which deposits on the bill and stains the feathers rusty-brown when the bird preens.

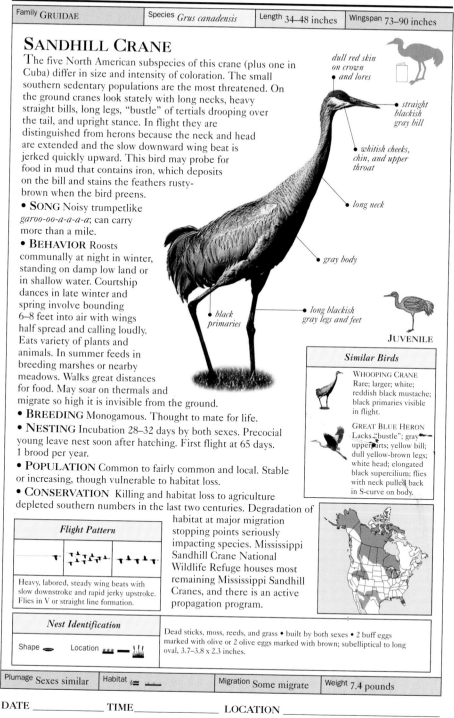

dull red skin on crown and lores

straight blackish gray bill

whitish cheeks, chin, and upper throat

long neck

gray body

black primaries

long blackish gray legs and feet

JUVENILE

• **SONG** Noisy trumpetlike *garoo-oo-a-a-a-a*; can carry more than a mile.

• **BEHAVIOR** Roosts communally at night in winter, standing on damp low land or in shallow water. Courtship dances in late winter and spring involve bounding 6–8 feet into air with wings half spread and calling loudly. Eats variety of plants and animals. In summer feeds in breeding marshes or nearby meadows. Walks great distances for food. May soar on thermals and migrate so high it is invisible from the ground.

• **BREEDING** Monogamous. Thought to mate for life.

• **NESTING** Incubation 28–32 days by both sexes. Precocial young leave nest soon after hatching. First flight at 65 days. 1 brood per year.

• **POPULATION** Common to fairly common and local. Stable or increasing, though vulnerable to habitat loss.

• **CONSERVATION** Killing and habitat loss to agriculture depleted southern numbers in the last two centuries. Degradation of habitat at major migration stopping points seriously impacting species. Mississippi Sandhill Crane National Wildlife Refuge houses most remaining Mississippi Sandhill Cranes, and there is an active propagation program.

Similar Birds

WHOOPING CRANE Rare; larger; white; reddish black mustache; black primaries visible in flight.

GREAT BLUE HERON Lacks "bustle"; gray upperparts; yellow bill; dull yellow-brown legs; white head; elongated black supercilium; flies with neck pulled back in S-curve on body.

Flight Pattern
Heavy, labored, steady wing beats with slow downstroke and rapid jerky upstroke. Flies in V or straight line formation.

Nest Identification	
Shape ➝ Location	Dead sticks, moss, reeds, and grass • built by both sexes • 2 buff eggs marked with olive or 2 olive eggs marked with brown; subelliptical to long oval, 3.7–3.8 x 2.3 inches.

Plumage Sexes similar	Habitat	Migration Some migrate	Weight 7.4 pounds

DATE _____ TIME_____ LOCATION _____

Family GRUIDAE	Species *Grus americana*	Length 52 inches	Wingspan 87 inches

WHOOPING CRANE

The stately Whooping Crane is the tallest bird in North America and one of the most endangered. By 1941 only fifteen individuals wintering on the Texas coast were left in the wild. The breeding grounds of these birds were unknown until 1954 when they were discovered in Wood Buffalo National Park in Alberta in central Canada. Intensive conservation and management programs have slowly increased this flock to more than one hundred fifty individuals. The juvenile is white with a rusty red head and neck and has rusty red feathers scattered over rest of its body.

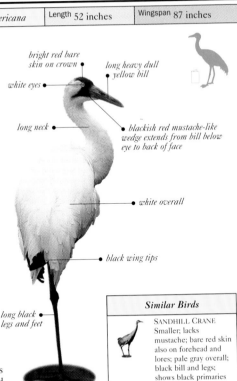

bright red bare skin on crown

long heavy dull yellow bill

white eyes

long neck

blackish red mustache-like wedge extends from bill below eye to back of face

white overall

black wing tips

long black legs and feet

• **SONG** Piercing trumpetlike *ker-loo ker-lee-loo* that can be heard for more than 2 miles. This volume is achieved by the 5-foot-long trachea coiled within the keel of the breast bone.

• **BEHAVIOR** Eats fish, frogs, small mammals, mollusks, crustaceans, corn, other grains, and roots of water plants.

• **BREEDING** Monogamous; mates for life. In courtship dance, one of pair begins by lowering head and flapping wings. Bird leaps 3 feet in air with head back, bill pointed skyward, neck arched over back, legs stiff, and wings flapping. Mate runs forward a few steps, pumping head up and down and flapping wings. Then both leap into air and bounce up and down. The silent dance ends as suddenly as it begins. On wintering grounds do not form flocks but maintain family groups of 3–4 birds and hold winter territory.

• **NESTING** Incubation 29–35 days by both sexes. Precocial young abandon nest soon after hatching; tended by both parents. First flight at approximately 80–90 days. 1 brood per year.

• **POPULATION** Increasing. Populations introduced in Idaho and Florida.

• **CONSERVATION** Endangered, but public education as well as intensive management and protection programs, slowly succeeding.

Similar Birds

SANDHILL CRANE Smaller; lacks mustache; bare red skin also on forehead and lores; pale gray overall; black bill and legs; shows black primaries in flight.

AMERICAN WHITE PELICAN Larger; white with black outer secondaries, primaries, and upper primary coverts; short legs; flies with neck folded and long yellow-orange bill resting on breast.

Flight Pattern

Typical crane flight of slow downward wing beat with powerful flick or jerk on upbeat. Flies in V formation in migration.

Nest Identification

Shape ⌒ Location ▬ ✹✹✹ ⊎

Soft or coarse grass, reeds, or sod • built on a mound by both sexes • 1–3 cream-olive buff eggs marked with brown; ovate or elliptical ovate, 3.9 x 2.5 inches.

Plumage Sexes similar	Habitat ◢◤	Migration Migratory	Weight 12.8 pounds

Family CHARADRIIDAE	Species *Pluvialis squatarola*	Length 11.5–13 inches	Wingspan 22–25 inches

BLACK-BELLIED PLOVER

The largest of the North American plovers, this stocky bird has a cautious nature and tends to travel in flocks, which helped it survive during a period when many plovers were destroyed by market hunters. This is the grayest of all the New World plovers in both breeding and winter plumages. In flight it shows a bold white wing stripe, white uppertail coverts, and black axillars. Seen on

white stripe over eyes extends down sides of neck

gray-white crown and forehead

short stout black bill

gray-spotted black upperparts

black face, chin, and throat

black breast and belly

mudflats in winter, this bird is distinguished by its larger size, stout black bill, and gray plumage.

snow-white tail coverts

WINTER PLUMAGE

- **SONG** Long melancholy triple-note whistle, *tlee-oo-eee* or *pee-oo-ee*, with second note lower-pitched.
- **BEHAVIOR** Feeds along seacoasts on broad tidal sand, mudflats, or in salt marshes. Eats marine worms, insects, small mollusks, and crustaceans.
- **BREEDING** Monogamous.
- **NESTING** Incubation 26–27 days by both sexes. Young precocial; leave nest soon after hatching. Tended by both sexes for 14 days, then by male only. First flight at 23–35 days. 1 brood per year.
- **POPULATION** Uncommon to common migrant on both coasts and in Great Lakes; uncommon to rare elsewhere in interior. On tundra breeding grounds cycles between uncommon, common, and rare. Difficult to detect population trends.
- **CONSERVATION** Stopover staging areas for foraging migrants important to population stability.

Similar Birds

AMERICAN GOLDEN-PLOVER
Winter adults and juveniles are smaller; long primary projection beyond tertials and tail; dusky underwings and axillars; in flight show uniform upperparts with indistinct, narrow whitish wing stripe.

PACIFIC GOLDEN-PLOVER
Winter adults and juveniles are smaller; smaller black bill; buff cast to plumage; buff spots and bars on underparts.

Flight Pattern
Strong direct flight with rapid wing beats.

Nest Identification	
Shape	Location

Tundra moss • lined with dried grasses, moss, and lichens • on dry ground with good visibility • male begins scrape; lined by female • 3–5 gray, green, whitish, or brown eggs spotted and scrawled with dark brown and black, 2 inches long.

Plumage Sexes similar	Habitat	Migration Migratory	Weight 7.8 ounces

DATE _____ TIME_____ LOCATION _____

Family CHARADRIIDAE	Species *Pluvialis dominica*	Length 10–11 inches	Wingspan 18–22.5 inches

AMERICAN GOLDEN-PLOVER

This expert long-distance migrant flies at a rate of sixty miles per hour and covers thousands of miles per year between Arctic tundra nesting grounds and winter quarters as far away as Argentina. Once an abundant bird, the American Golden-Plover was almost eradicted by market hunters during the late 1800s. Winter adults and

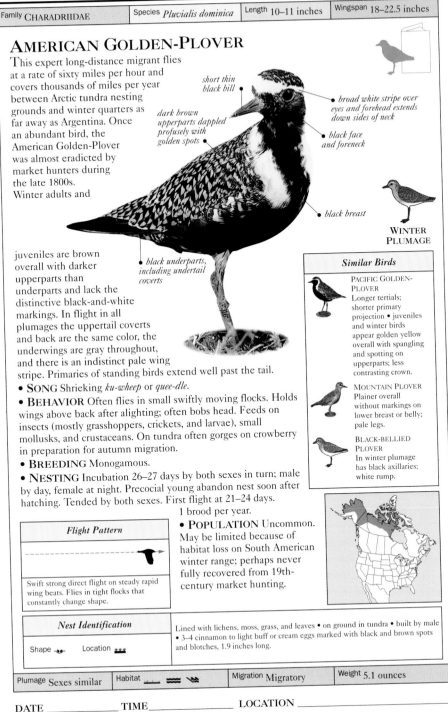

short thin black bill

dark brown upperparts dappled profusely with golden spots

broad white stripe over eyes and forehead extends down sides of neck

black face and foreneck

black breast

WINTER PLUMAGE

black underparts, including undertail coverts

juveniles are brown overall with darker upperparts than underparts and lack the distinctive black-and-white markings. In flight in all plumages the uppertail coverts and back are the same color, the underwings are gray throughout, and there is an indistinct pale wing stripe. Primaries of standing birds extend well past the tail.

- **SONG** Shrieking *ku-wheep* or *quee-dle*.
- **BEHAVIOR** Often flies in small swiftly moving flocks. Holds wings above back after alighting; often bobs head. Feeds on insects (mostly grasshoppers, crickets, and larvae), small mollusks, and crustaceans. On tundra often gorges on crowberry in preparation for autumn migration.
- **BREEDING** Monogamous.
- **NESTING** Incubation 26–27 days by both sexes in turn; male by day, female at night. Precocial young abandon nest soon after hatching. Tended by both sexes. First flight at 21–24 days. 1 brood per year.
- **POPULATION** Uncommon. May be limited because of habitat loss on South American winter range; perhaps never fully recovered from 19th-century market hunting.

Similar Birds

PACIFIC GOLDEN-PLOVER
Longer tertials; shorter primary projection • juveniles and winter birds appear golden yellow overall with spangling and spotting on upperparts; less contrasting crown.

MOUNTAIN PLOVER
Plainer overall without markings on lower breast or belly; pale legs.

BLACK-BELLIED PLOVER
In winter plumage has black axillaries; white rump.

Flight Pattern
Swift strong direct flight on steady rapid wing beats. Flies in tight flocks that constantly change shape.

Nest Identification	
Shape ～ Location ＊＊＊	Lined with lichens, moss, grass, and leaves • on ground in tundra • built by male • 3–4 cinnamon to light buff or cream eggs marked with black and brown spots and blotches, 1.9 inches long.

Plumage Sexes similar	Habitat ▃▃ ～ ✧	Migration Migratory	Weight 5.1 ounces

DATE _____ TIME_____ LOCATION _____

Family CHARADRIIDAE	Species *Pluvialis fulva*	Length 9.75 inches	Wingspan 18 inches

PACIFIC GOLDEN-PLOVER

The smallest of the Golden-Plovers is most likely to be seen in the Pacific Coast states of North America in winter. It breeds on the coast and river valleys of northwestern Alaska and winters in southern Asia and on many Pacific islands, including the Hawaiian Islands – a feat requiring pinpoint navigational skills. If grassland or coastal roosting sites are unavailable, these plovers may roost on flat roofs of buildings. In winter plumage bird has mottled tawny-buff and brown upperparts, and whitish buff underparts with spots and bars.

• **SONG** Repeated, plaintive *teee-chewee*; also loud *chu-wheet*.

• **BEHAVIOR** Eats variety of invertebrates, seeds, and berries. Feeds in small flocks, often associating with other shorebirds. Makes short runs and stops and quickly stabs at ground during feeding.

• **BREEDING** Monogamous.

• **NESTING** Incubation 25 days by both sexes. Precocial young abandon nest shortly after hatching. Tended by both sexes but find own food. First flight at 26–28 days.

• **POPULATION** Uncommon to casual along Pacific Coast in winter. Common to fairly common on breeding grounds in western Alaska and Siberia.

white line extends from forehead over eye and behind face; along side of neck, sides, and flanks; and onto undertail coverts

thick black bill

black face and throat

bright golden spangling and spotting on upperparts

MALE

black underparts to undertail coverts

white on flanks and undertail coverts

long grayish black legs

WINTER PLUMAGE

dusky-black postocular stripe and rear edge of ear coverts

FEMALE

face, chin, throat, and upper neck white with tiny black flecking

more extensive white feathering on sides, flanks, and undertail coverts

Similar Birds

AMERICAN GOLDEN-PLOVER
In winter dark streaking and tipping on breast feathers is broader and forms mottled or barred pattern; duller in color; primaries extend well beyond tail when standing; shorter bill and legs • in breeding plumage white stripe stops on side of neck; black undertail coverts.

Flight Pattern
Swift direct flight with rapid steady wing beats.

Nest Identification	
Shape ⌣ Location ▬ ▰▰▰	Lined with lichens, moss, grass, and dead leaves • built by male • 4 whitish to buff, cinnamon-buff, creamy buff, greenish buff, or ivory-yellow eggs heavily marked with dark black or brown; ovate pyriform, 1.9 inches long.

Plumage Sexes differ	Habitat ▬	Migration Migratory	Weight 5.4 ounces

DATE _____ TIME_____ LOCATION _____

Family CHARADRIIDAE	Species *Charadrius mongolus*	Length 7–8 inches	Wingspan 15–16 inches

MONGOLIAN PLOVER

Sometimes called the Lesser Sandplover. Like other plovers this bird uses a distraction display to lure intruders away from its eggs. The broad cinnamon breast, which separates its white throat from its belly, is narrower and darker in winter. In winter birds are grayish with white underparts, gray patches on each side of the breast, dark lores, and a smudge on the ear. Females resemble males but have duller plumage. Juveniles are similar to winter adults but have a buff breast band.

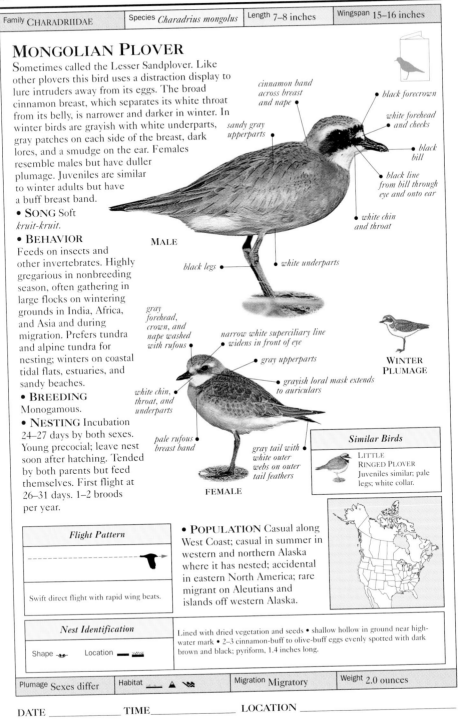

cinnamon band across breast and nape

black forecrown

white forehead and cheeks

sandy gray upperparts

black bill

black line from bill through eye and onto ear

white chin and throat

MALE

black legs

white underparts

• **SONG** Soft *kruit-kruit*.
• **BEHAVIOR** Feeds on insects and other invertebrates. Highly gregarious in nonbreeding season, often gathering in large flocks on wintering grounds in India, Africa, and Asia and during migration. Prefers tundra and alpine tundra for nesting; winters on coastal tidal flats, estuaries, and sandy beaches.
• **BREEDING** Monogamous.
• **NESTING** Incubation 24–27 days by both sexes. Young precocial; leave nest soon after hatching. Tended by both parents but feed themselves. First flight at 26–31 days. 1–2 broods per year.

gray forehead, crown, and nape washed with rufous

narrow white superciliary line widens in front of eye

gray upperparts

grayish loral mask extends to auriculars

WINTER PLUMAGE

white chin, throat, and underparts

pale rufous breast band

gray tail with white outer webs on outer tail feathers

FEMALE

Similar Birds

LITTLE RINGED PLOVER Juveniles similar; pale legs; white collar.

Flight Pattern

Swift direct flight with rapid wing beats.

• **POPULATION** Casual along West Coast; casual in summer in western and northern Alaska where it has nested; accidental in eastern North America; rare migrant on Aleutians and islands off western Alaska.

Nest Identification	
Shape	Location	Lined with dried vegetation and seeds • shallow hollow in ground near high-water mark • 2–3 cinnamon-buff to olive-buff eggs evenly spotted with dark brown and black; pyriform, 1.4 inches long.

Plumage Sexes differ	Habitat	Migration Migratory	Weight 2.0 ounces

DATE _____ TIME_____ LOCATION _____

Family CHARADRIIDAE	Species *Charadrius alexandrinus*	Length 6–7 inches	Wingspan 13.5 inches

SNOWY PLOVER

The smallest and whitest of the North American plovers inhabits barren sandy beaches. Unlike all other "ringed" plovers in North America, breast band is never complete. Females and juveniles resemble males except for

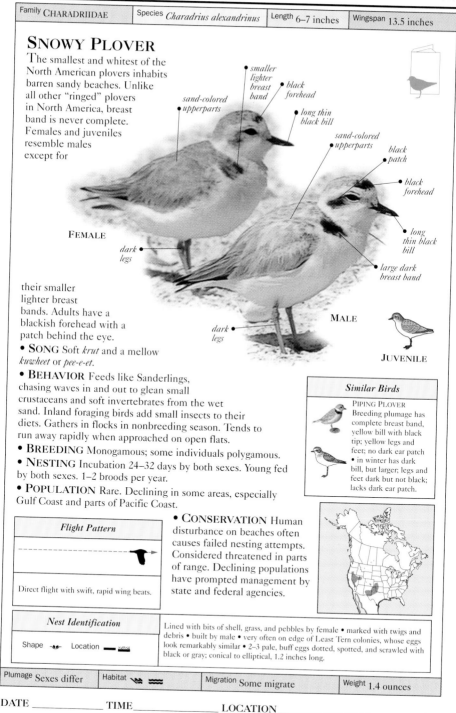

smaller lighter breast band

black forehead

sand-colored upperparts

long thin black bill

sand-colored upperparts

black patch

black forehead

long thin black bill

large dark breast band

FEMALE

dark legs

dark legs

MALE

JUVENILE

their smaller lighter breast bands. Adults have a blackish forehead with a patch behind the eye.

- **SONG** Soft *krut* and a mellow *kuwheet* or *pee-e-et*.
- **BEHAVIOR** Feeds like Sanderlings, chasing waves in and out to glean small crustaceans and soft invertebrates from the wet sand. Inland foraging birds add small insects to their diets. Gathers in flocks in nonbreeding season. Tends to run away rapidly when approached on open flats.
- **BREEDING** Monogamous; some individuals polygamous.
- **NESTING** Incubation 24–32 days by both sexes. Young fed by both sexes. 1–2 broods per year.
- **POPULATION** Rare. Declining in some areas, especially Gulf Coast and parts of Pacific Coast.
- **CONSERVATION** Human disturbance on beaches often causes failed nesting attempts. Considered threatened in parts of range. Declining populations have prompted management by state and federal agencies.

Similar Birds

PIPING PLOVER
Breeding plumage has complete breast band, yellow bill with black tip; yellow legs and feet; no dark ear patch.
• in winter has dark bill, but larger; legs and feet dark but not black; lacks dark ear patch.

Flight Pattern

Direct flight with swift, rapid wing beats.

Nest Identification

Shape ⚬   Location ▬ ▬

Lined with bits of shell, grass, and pebbles by female • marked with twigs and debris • built by male • very often on edge of Least Tern colonies, whose eggs look remarkably similar • 2–3 pale, buff eggs dotted, spotted, and scrawled with black or gray; conical to elliptical, 1.2 inches long.

Plumage Sexes differ	Habitat ≈≈	Migration Some migrate	Weight 1.4 ounces

DATE _____ TIME_____ LOCATION _____

Family CHARADRIIDAE	Species *Charadrius wilsonia*	Length 7–8 inches	Wingspan 14–16 inches

WILSON'S PLOVER

Like other plovers, if a human intrudes upon its nest, the female will dash around, pretending to scrape various nests, to distract the trespasser. Both sexes perform the "crippled bird" act to lure predators away from the nest. This coastal species flies effortlessly, yet if presented with danger on land it usually runs down the beach instead of flying. The duller-colored female is similar to the male but has a brown neck band, forecrown, and lores. Juveniles resemble females, but have scalier upperparts.

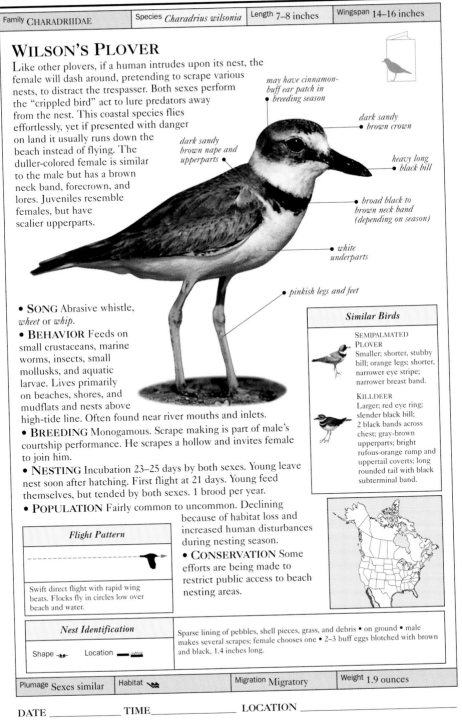

may have cinnamon-buff ear patch in breeding season

dark sandy brown crown

dark sandy brown nape and upperparts

heavy long black bill

broad black to brown neck band (depending on season)

white underparts

pinkish legs and feet

- **SONG** Abrasive whistle, *wheet* or *whip*.
- **BEHAVIOR** Feeds on small crustaceans, marine worms, insects, small mollusks, and aquatic larvae. Lives primarily on beaches, shores, and mudflats and nests above high-tide line. Often found near river mouths and inlets.
- **BREEDING** Monogamous. Scrape making is part of male's courtship performance. He scrapes a hollow and invites female to join him.
- **NESTING** Incubation 23–25 days by both sexes. Young leave nest soon after hatching. First flight at 21 days. Young feed themselves, but tended by both sexes. 1 brood per year.
- **POPULATION** Fairly common to uncommon. Declining because of habitat loss and increased human disturbances during nesting season.
- **CONSERVATION** Some efforts are being made to restrict public access to beach nesting areas.

Similar Birds

SEMIPALMATED PLOVER
Smaller; shorter, stubby bill; orange legs; shorter, narrower eye stripe; narrower breast band.

KILLDEER
Larger; red eye ring; slender black bill; 2 black bands across chest; gray-brown upperparts; bright rufous-orange rump and uppertail coverts; long rounded tail with black subterminal band.

Flight Pattern

Swift direct flight with rapid wing beats. Flocks fly in circles low over beach and water.

Nest Identification

Shape ⸺ Location ⸺

Sparse lining of pebbles, shell pieces, grass, and debris • on ground • male makes several scrapes; female chooses one • 2–3 buff eggs blotched with brown and black, 1.4 inches long.

Plumage Sexes similar	Habitat ⸺	Migration Migratory	Weight 1.9 ounces

DATE _____ TIME_____ LOCATION _____

Family CHARADRIIDAE	Species *Charadrius hiaticula*	Length 7.5 inches	Wingspan 15 inches

COMMON RINGED PLOVER

Small, bulky, and sporting a single band across its breast, the Common Ringed Plover is almost indistinguishable from the Semipalmated Plover. Morphologically, there is no easy way to distinguish the two species unless you have them in hand (this species has little or no webbing between the toes), but they have very different

well-defined white superciliary stripe

white forehead

brown upperparts

orange-yellow bill with black tip

single dark breast band

white underparts

orange-yellow legs and feet

voices. Female is similar to male but has brownish ear coverts and a blackish brown breast band year-round. In North America the Common Ringed Plover is normally found only in the extreme northeastern Arctic. In the fall these birds return via Greenland to the Old World to winter in Africa.

• **SONG** A soft fluted disyllabic *tu-lee* or *too-ie*.

• **BEHAVIOR** Gregarious. Frequents coastal mudflats and sandy, pebbly seashores. Eats worms, aquatic insects, crustaceans, and mollusks. Normally wary and alert but sometimes allows fairly close approach. Performs vigorous distraction display with "crippled bird" act to lead intruders away from nest. In winter may occur inland on lakeshores and river banks, or in cultivated fields and meadows

• **BREEDING** Monogamous. Gregarious.

• **NESTING** Incubation 23–25 days by both sexes. Precocial young leave nest shortly after hatching. Tended by both sexes. First flight at 24 days. 1–2 broods per year.

• **POPULATION** Breeds in eastern Arctic. Casual to rare spring migrant on western Alaskan islands.

Similar Birds

SEMIPALMATED PLOVER
Shorter bill; webbing between toes; thinner breast band; smaller auricular patch; shorter superciliary line.

LITTLE RINGED PLOVER
Smaller; lacks clear wing bar; thick bright yellow eye ring; dull pink legs; narrower breast band.

Flight Pattern

Direct flight with rapid wing beats.

Nest Identification

Shape — Location —

Depression in beach sand • lined with bits of shells and driftwood, small pebbles, and rabbit droppings • above high-water mark on seashore • 3–4 buff eggs lightly spotted with brown or black, elliptical, 1.3 inches long.

Plumage Sexes similar	Habitat	Migration Migratory	Weight 1.0 ounce

DATE _____ TIME _____ LOCATION _____

Family CHARADRIIDAE	Species *Charadrius semipalmatus*	Length 7 inches	Wingspan 14–15.25 inches

SEMIPALMATED PLOVER

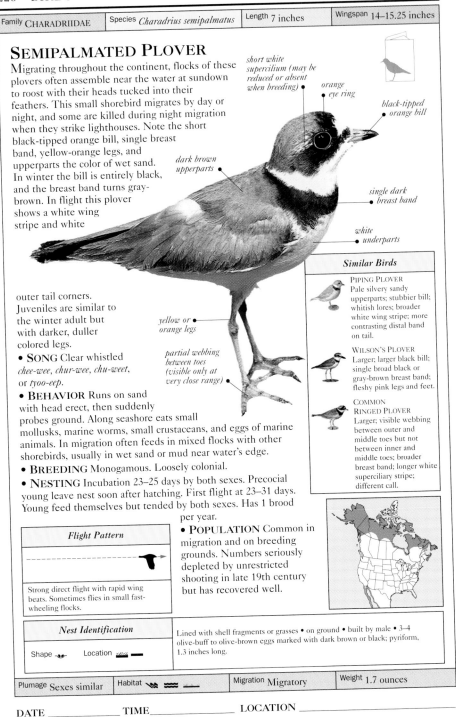

Migrating throughout the continent, flocks of these plovers often assemble near the water at sundown to roost with their heads tucked into their feathers. This small shorebird migrates by day or night, and some are killed during night migration when they strike lighthouses. Note the short black-tipped orange bill, single breast band, yellow-orange legs, and upperparts the color of wet sand. In winter the bill is entirely black, and the breast band turns gray-brown. In flight this plover shows a white wing stripe and white

short white superciliun (may be reduced or absent when breeding)

orange eye ring

black-tipped orange bill

dark brown upperparts

single dark breast band

white underparts

outer tail corners. Juveniles are similar to the winter adult but with darker, duller colored legs.

yellow or orange legs

partial webbing between toes (visible only at very close range)

- **SONG** Clear whistled *chee-wee, chur-wee, chu-weet,* or *tyoo-eep.*
- **BEHAVIOR** Runs on sand with head erect, then suddenly probes ground. Along seashore eats small mollusks, marine worms, small crustaceans, and eggs of marine animals. In migration often feeds in mixed flocks with other shorebirds, usually in wet sand or mud near water's edge.
- **BREEDING** Monogamous. Loosely colonial.
- **NESTING** Incubation 23–25 days by both sexes. Precocial young leave nest soon after hatching. First flight at 23–31 days. Young feed themselves but tended by both sexes. Has 1 brood per year.
- **POPULATION** Common in migration and on breeding grounds. Numbers seriously depleted by unrestricted shooting in late 19th century but has recovered well.

Similar Birds

PIPING PLOVER
Pale silvery sandy upperparts; stubbier bill; whitish lores; broader white wing stripe; more contrasting distal band on tail.

WILSON'S PLOVER
Larger; larger black bill; single broad black or gray-brown breast band; fleshy pink legs and feet.

COMMON RINGED PLOVER
Larger; visible webbing between outer and middle toes but not between inner and middle toes; broader breast band; longer white superciliary stripe; different call.

Flight Pattern
Strong direct flight with rapid wing beats. Sometimes flies in small fast-wheeling flocks.

Nest Identification	Lined with shell fragments or grasses • on ground • built by male • 3–4 olive-buff to olive-brown eggs marked with dark brown or black; pyriform, 1.3 inches long.
Shape ⚬ Location ⚬⚬	

Plumage Sexes similar	Habitat	Migration Migratory	Weight 1.7 ounces

DATE _____ TIME_____ LOCATION _____

Family CHARADRIIDAE	Species *Charadrius melodus*	Length 7.25 inches	Wingspan 14–15.5 inches

PIPING PLOVER

This plover is difficult to spot until it moves, as its plumage blends in with the dry summer sand along the Atlantic Coast and south shores of the Great Lakes region. Endemic to central and eastern North America, and once common on beaches, this bird is now endangered because of human activity and disturbance during nesting season. Note the dry sand color of the upperparts, the yellow legs, and in flight the white wing stripe and white rump with contrasting black tail tip. Winter plumaged birds have a blackish orange bill, darker duller orange legs, and the sandy breast band may be broken. Juveniles are similar to winter adults.

white forehead and lores

sandy buff overall

orange bill with black tip

narrow blackish breast band (may be incomplete in females and East Coast birds)

yellow-orange legs and feet

white underparts

WINTER PLUMAGE

- **SONG** Clear *peep-lo*.
- **BEHAVIOR** Gregarious in post-breeding seasons, but territorial when nesting. Sprints, then stops to inspect sand with head cocked to one side; picks food off ground. Eats fly larvae, beetles, crustaceans, and marine worms. Often feeds higher on the beach (where upperparts more closely match sand) than other small plovers. In migration feeds in mixed flocks with other shorebirds.
- **BREEDING** Monogamous. Loosely colonial. Territorial during breeding season.
- **NESTING** Incubation 26–28 days by both sexes. Precocial young stay in nest 20–35 days. Fed by both sexes. Has 1 brood per year.
- **POPULATION** Uncommon to rare and declining in many parts of range, especially in Midwest and Great Lakes. Uncommon migrant inland.
- **CONSERVATION** Endangered; almost eliminated as a breeder in Great Lakes region due to human activity on beaches. Irregular pattern of water release from dams affects nesting on interior rivers.

Similar Birds

SEMIPALMATED PLOVER
Dark brown upperparts the color of wet sand; dark rump in flight.

SNOWY PLOVER
Smaller; long dark legs; slim dark bill; lateral dark breast patches; lacks white rump patch in flight.

Flight Pattern

Wild direct flight with twists and turns and rapid steady wing beats; often in small flocks.

Nest Identification

Shape ⚬ Location ▬▬

Lined with broken shells, small stones, or driftwood • on sandy shore of lake or ocean well above high-water mark • built by both sexes • 3–4 pale buff eggs blotched with black and dark brown; short oval to short pyriform, 1.2 inches long.

Plumage Sexes similar	Habitat 〰 ▬	Migration Migratory	Weight 1.9 ounces

DATE _____ TIME _____ LOCATION _____

Family CHARADRIIDAE	Species *Charadrius dubius*	Length 6 inches	Wingspan 11 inches

LITTLE RINGED PLOVER

A common and widespread Old World shorebird, the Little Ringed Plover is a casual spring migrant in the western Aleutians. It is similar in appearance, but smaller than the New World's Semipalmated Plover. The thinner black bill easily distinguishes it from its North American relative. In flight, unlike most small plovers, it shows

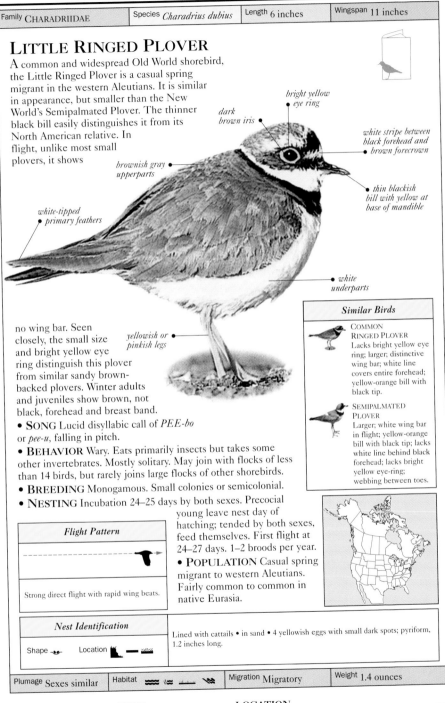

bright yellow eye ring

dark brown iris

white stripe between black forehead and brown forecrown

brownish gray upperparts

thin blackish bill with yellow at base of mandible

white-tipped primary feathers

white underparts

yellowish or pinkish legs

no wing bar. Seen closely, the small size and bright yellow eye ring distinguish this plover from similar sandy brown-backed plovers. Winter adults and juveniles show brown, not black, forehead and breast band.

- **SONG** Lucid disyllabic call of *PEE-bo* or *pee-u*, falling in pitch.
- **BEHAVIOR** Wary. Eats primarily insects but takes some other invertebrates. Mostly solitary. May join with flocks of less than 14 birds, but rarely joins large flocks of other shorebirds.
- **BREEDING** Monogamous. Small colonies or semicolonial.
- **NESTING** Incubation 24–25 days by both sexes. Precocial young leave nest day of hatching; tended by both sexes, feed themselves. First flight at 24–27 days. 1–2 broods per year.
- **POPULATION** Casual spring migrant to western Aleutians. Fairly common to common in native Eurasia.

Similar Birds

COMMON RINGED PLOVER
Lacks bright yellow eye ring; larger; distinctive wing bar; white line covers entire forehead; yellow-orange bill with black tip.

SEMIPALMATED PLOVER
Larger; white wing bar in flight; yellow-orange bill with black tip; lacks white line behind black forehead; lacks bright yellow eye-ring; webbing between toes.

Flight Pattern

Strong direct flight with rapid wing beats.

Nest Identification

Shape — Location

Lined with cattails • in sand • 4 yellowish eggs with small dark spots; pyriform, 1.2 inches long.

Plumage Sexes similar	Habitat	Migration Migratory	Weight 1.4 ounces

DATE _____ TIME_____ LOCATION _____

Family CHARADRIIDAE	Species *Charadrius vociferus*	Length 9–10.5 inches	Wingspan 19–21 inches

KILLDEER

Named for its distinctive call, this bird is the largest of the ringed plovers and the only double-banded plover within its range. Perhaps the most familiar shorebird in North America, in summer it is found across almost the entire continent south of the tundra. In flight note the long pointed wings with long white stripe and the rufous-gold rump and long tail with subterminal black tail band. Juveniles are similar in appearance but have only one black band across the chest.

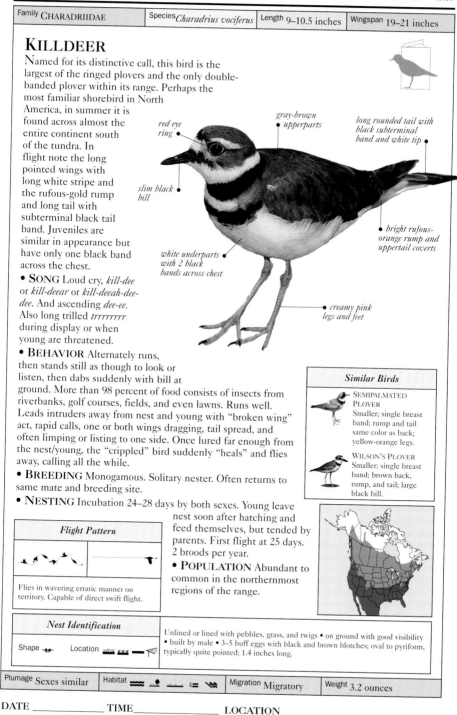

gray-brown
upperparts

long rounded tail with
black subterminal
band and white tip

red eye
ring

slim black
bill

bright rufous-
orange rump and
uppertail coverts

white underparts
with 2 black
bands across chest

creamy pink
legs and feet

• **SONG** Loud cry, *kill-dee* or *kill-deear* or *kill-deeah-dee-dee*. And ascending *dee-ee*. Also long trilled *trrrrrrrr* during display or when young are threatened.

• **BEHAVIOR** Alternately runs, then stands still as though to look or listen, then dabs suddenly with bill at ground. More than 98 percent of food consists of insects from riverbanks, golf courses, fields, and even lawns. Runs well. Leads intruders away from nest and young with "broken wing" act, rapid calls, one or both wings dragging, tail spread, and often limping or listing to one side. Once lured far enough from the nest/young, the "crippled" bird suddenly "heals" and flies away, calling all the while.

• **BREEDING** Monogamous. Solitary nester. Often returns to same mate and breeding site.

• **NESTING** Incubation 24–28 days by both sexes. Young leave nest soon after hatching and feed themselves, but tended by parents. First flight at 25 days. 2 broods per year.

• **POPULATION** Abundant to common in the northernmost regions of the range.

Similar Birds

SEMIPALMATED PLOVER
Smaller; single breast band; rump and tail same color as back; yellow-orange legs.

WILSON'S PLOVER
Smaller; single breast band; brown back, rump, and tail; large black bill.

Flight Pattern

Flies in wavering erratic manner on territory. Capable of direct swift flight.

Nest Identification

Shape   Location

Unlined or lined with pebbles, grass, and twigs • on ground with good visibility • built by male • 3–5 buff eggs with black and brown blotches; oval to pyriform, typically quite pointed; 1.4 inches long.

Plumage Sexes similar	Habitat	Migration Migratory	Weight 3.2 ounces

DATE _____ TIME_____ LOCATION _____

Family CHARADRIIDAE	Species *Charadrius montanus*	Length 9 inches	Wingspan 17.5–19.5 inches

MOUNTAIN PLOVER

This fast-running pale brown plover is one of few shorebirds that lives in dry regions away from water. Its sand-colored back and buffy white underparts and breast help distinguish this large plover and also blend it perfectly into the arid grasslands it calls home. In flight note the black-tipped tail, thin white wing stripe, and the white undersides of the wings. In winter the sandy buff breast is more extensive.

black frontal crown bar

black forecrown has white forehead stripe over eyes

black lores

sandy brown back

slim blackish or brownish bill

sandy buff breast

- **SONG** Variable. Slightly rasping dry *krehrr*, a clipped dry *kep*, and a slightly reedy *krrip* or *krreek*.
- **BEHAVIOR** Eats grasshoppers, beetles, flies, crickets, and other insects. Protective of its eggs. Will fly up into the face of cattle or other intruder or try to lure them away with the crippled-bird

fairly long pale brownish yellow legs

black tail band with white border

display. Forms small flocks on the wintering grounds.
- **BREEDING** Mostly monogamous; some polygamous.
- **NESTING** Incubation 28–31 days by both sexes. After laying first set of eggs, which are incubated by male, female lays and incubates second set. First flight at 33–34 days. Precocial young feed themselves, tended by both sexes. 2 broods per year.
- **POPULATION** Uncommon to casual.
- **CONSERVATION** Has disappeared from much of former breeding range due to the land's conversion to farmland and range land for cattle that often overgraze it. Decline also linked to decline of prairie dog population, because plovers use the mounds around the entrances to old prairie dog burrows for nests.

Similar Birds

AMERICAN GOLDEN-PLOVER
Winter adult and juvenile • slightly larger; darker legs; darker gray plumage conspicuously spotted and notched on upperparts; dull brownish gray underwings and auxiliaries; lacks black and white on tail.

Flight Pattern

Short flights on breeding grounds with few rapid wing flutters between short glides. Direct flight with rapid steady wing beats for longer distances or in migration.

Nest Identification

Shape ➣   Location ▬

Scant lining of rootlets and dried grass, often added during incubation • flat open ground between hummocks, occasionally amid cacti or scattered shrubs • built by male • 2–4 olive-buff eggs, with many black marks and wreathed; blunt pyriform, 1.5 inches long.

Plumage Sexes similar	Habitat ♠ ⌐	Migration Migratory	Weight 3.6 ounces

DATE _____ TIME_____ LOCATION _____

Family CHARADRIIDAE	Species *Charadrius morinellus*	Length 8.5 inches	Wingspan 17 inches

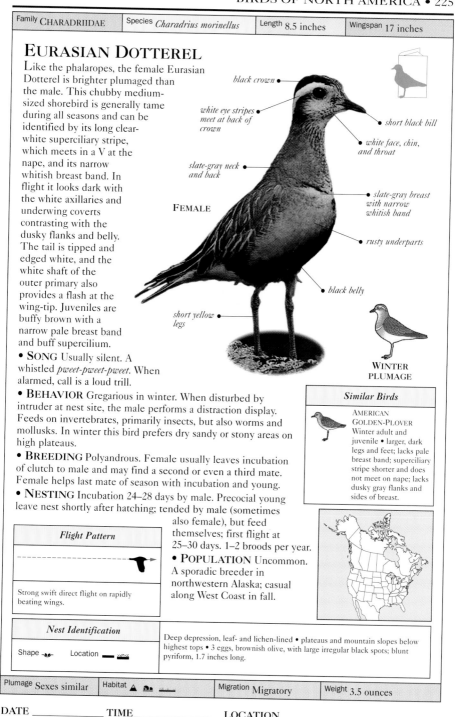

EURASIAN DOTTEREL

Like the phalaropes, the female Eurasian Dotterel is brighter plumaged than the male. This chubby medium-sized shorebird is generally tame during all seasons and can be identified by its long clear-white superciliary stripe, which meets in a V at the nape, and its narrow whitish breast band. In flight it looks dark with the white axillaries and underwing coverts contrasting with the dusky flanks and belly. The tail is tipped and edged white, and the white shaft of the outer primary also provides a flash at the wing-tip. Juveniles are buffy brown with a narrow pale breast band and buff supercilium.

black crown •

white eye stripes meet at back of crown •

slate-gray neck and back •

FEMALE

• short black bill

• white face, chin, and throat

• slate-gray breast with narrow whitish band

• rusty underparts

• black belly

short yellow • legs

WINTER PLUMAGE

• **SONG** Usually silent. A whistled *pweet-pweet-pweet*. When alarmed, call is a loud trill.
• **BEHAVIOR** Gregarious in winter. When disturbed by intruder at nest site, the male performs a distraction display. Feeds on invertebrates, primarily insects, but also worms and mollusks. In winter this bird prefers dry sandy or stony areas on high plateaus.
• **BREEDING** Polyandrous. Female usually leaves incubation of clutch to male and may find a second or even a third mate. Female helps last mate of season with incubation and young.
• **NESTING** Incubation 24–28 days by male. Precocial young leave nest shortly after hatching; tended by male (sometimes also female), but feed themselves; first flight at 25–30 days. 1–2 broods per year.
• **POPULATION** Uncommon. A sporadic breeder in northwestern Alaska; casual along West Coast in fall.

Similar Birds

AMERICAN GOLDEN-PLOVER Winter adult and juvenile • larger, dark legs and feet; lacks pale breast band; superciliary stripe shorter and does not meet on nape; lacks dusky gray flanks and sides of breast.

Flight Pattern

- - - - - - - - - - - ➤

Strong swift direct flight on rapidly beating wings.

Nest Identification

Shape 🐦 Location ▬ ▥

Deep depression, leaf- and lichen-lined • plateaus and mountain slopes below highest tops • 3 eggs, brownish olive, with large irregular black spots; blunt pyriform, 1.7 inches long.

Plumage Sexes similar	Habitat ▲ 🐚 ▬	Migration Migratory	Weight 3.5 ounces

DATE _____ TIME_____ LOCATION _____

Family HAEMATOPODIDAE	Species *Haematopus palliatus*	Length 18–20 inches	Wingspan 30–36 inches

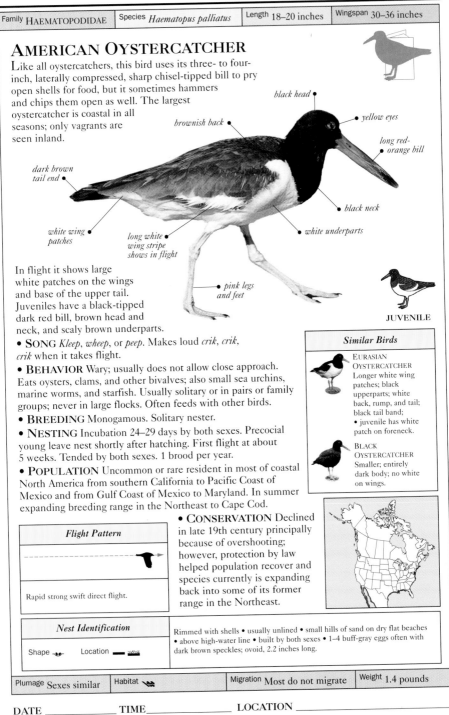

AMERICAN OYSTERCATCHER

Like all oystercatchers, this bird uses its three- to four-inch, laterally compressed, sharp chisel-tipped bill to pry open shells for food, but it sometimes hammers and chips them open as well. The largest oystercatcher is coastal in all seasons; only vagrants are seen inland.

black head •
• yellow eyes
brownish back •
long red-orange bill
dark brown tail end •
• black neck
white wing patches
long white wing stripe shows in flight
• white underparts
• pink legs and feet

In flight it shows large white patches on the wings and base of the upper tail. Juveniles have a black-tipped dark red bill, brown head and neck, and scaly brown underparts.

JUVENILE

- **SONG** *Kleep*, *wheep*, or *peep*. Makes loud *crik*, *crik*, *crik* when it takes flight.
- **BEHAVIOR** Wary; usually does not allow close approach. Eats oysters, clams, and other bivalves; also small sea urchins, marine worms, and starfish. Usually solitary or in pairs or family groups; never in large flocks. Often feeds with other birds.
- **BREEDING** Monogamous. Solitary nester.
- **NESTING** Incubation 24–29 days by both sexes. Precocial young leave nest shortly after hatching. First flight at about 5 weeks. Tended by both sexes. 1 brood per year.
- **POPULATION** Uncommon or rare resident in most of coastal North America from southern California to Pacific Coast of Mexico and from Gulf Coast of Mexico to Maryland. In summer expanding breeding range in the Northeast to Cape Cod.
- **CONSERVATION** Declined in late 19th century principally because of overshooting; however, protection by law helped population recover and species currently is expanding back into some of its former range in the Northeast.

Similar Birds

EURASIAN OYSTERCATCHER Longer white wing patches; black upperparts; white back, rump, and tail; black tail band;
• juvenile has white patch on foreneck.

BLACK OYSTERCATCHER Smaller; entirely dark body; no white on wings.

Flight Pattern

Rapid strong swift direct flight.

Nest Identification

Shape 🐦   Location ▬ 🐚

Rimmed with shells • usually unlined • small hills of sand on dry flat beaches • above high-water line • built by both sexes • 1–4 buff-gray eggs often with dark brown speckles; ovoid, 2.2 inches long.

Plumage Sexes similar	Habitat 〰	Migration Most do not migrate	Weight 1.4 pounds

DATE _____ TIME_____ LOCATION _____

Family HAEMOTOPODIDAE	Species *Haematopus bachmani*	Length 17.5 inches	Wingspan 30–35 inches

BLACK OYSTERCATCHER

John James Audubon gave this oystercatcher its species name to honor his friend, Reverend John Bachman of Charleston, South Carolina. This stocky bird's mostly blackish brown coloring can make it difficult to spot against the dark rocks along the Pacific Coast. Juveniles are browner and have an orange-based dusky bill. In flight this large shorebird appears entirely dark without any white in the wings or tail.

yellow eyes

orange eye ring

long straight bright red-orange bill

- **SONG** Loud *keee*, *kee-ah* and a rapid series of *tees*, *whee-whee-tee-tee-tee*.
- **BEHAVIOR** Relatively tame. Usually found singly or in small groups. Eats mussels and marine worms, but feeds primarily on limpets and other shellfish that it pries open with its flattened bill. Often feeds on surf-hammered rocks, rocky reefs at low tide, or mudflats.

black or blackish brown overall

pink feet and legs

- **BREEDING** Monogamous. Performs piping display, where birds run side by side with heads down and bills pointing forward.
- **NESTING** Incubation 24–36 days by both sexes. Young leave nest soon after hatching. Tended by both sexes. First flight at 30–35 days or more. 1 brood per year.
- **POPULATION** Still widespread along the Pacific Coast from Baja California to the Aleutian Islands and numerous in some areas of range.
- **CONSERVATION** Vulnerable to disturbance at nesting sites. All oystercatchers are protected by federal law.

Similar Birds

AMERICAN OYSTERCATCHER White underparts, wing bars, and tail base.

Flight Pattern

Rapid direct flight with slight shallow wing beats

Nest Identification

Shape ⚬ Location ⬡

Sparsely lined with pebbles and shells • on beach in small pebbles above high-water mark • built by both sexes • 1–4 pale buff to olive eggs spotted and scrawled with brown and black; ovate to pyriform, 2.2 inches long.

Plumage Sexes similar	Habitat ⬡	Migration Nonmigratory	Weight 1.3 pounds

DATE _____ TIME_____ LOCATION _____

| Family RECURVIROSTRIDAE | Species *Himantopus mexicanus* | Length 14–15.5 inches | Wingspan 25–27 inches |

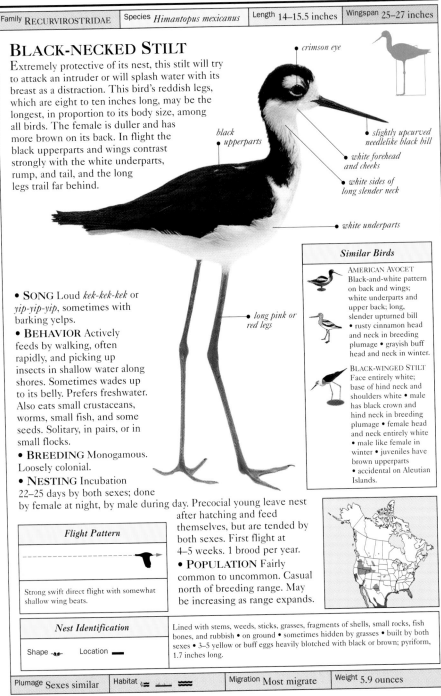

BLACK-NECKED STILT

Extremely protective of its nest, this stilt will try to attack an intruder or will splash water with its breast as a distraction. This bird's reddish legs, which are eight to ten inches long, may be the longest, in proportion to its body size, among all birds. The female is duller and has more brown on its back. In flight the black upperparts and wings contrast strongly with the white underparts, rump, and tail, and the long legs trail far behind.

• *crimson eye*

black upperparts

• *slightly upcurved needlelike black bill*

• *white forehead and cheeks*

• *white sides of long slender neck*

• *white underparts*

• *long pink or red legs*

Similar Birds

AMERICAN AVOCET
Black-and-white pattern on back and wings; white underparts and upper back; long, slender upturned bill • rusty cinnamon head and neck in breeding plumage • grayish buff head and neck in winter.

BLACK-WINGED STILT
Face entirely white; base of hind neck and shoulders white • male has black crown and hind neck in breeding plumage • female head and neck entirely white • male like female in winter • juveniles have brown upperparts • accidental on Aleutian Islands.

• **SONG** Loud *kek-kek-kek* or *yip-yip-yip*, sometimes with barking yelps.
• **BEHAVIOR** Actively feeds by walking, often rapidly, and picking up insects in shallow water along shores. Sometimes wades up to its belly. Prefers freshwater. Also eats small crustaceans, worms, small fish, and some seeds. Solitary, in pairs, or in small flocks.
• **BREEDING** Monogamous. Loosely colonial.
• **NESTING** Incubation 22–25 days by both sexes; done by female at night, by male during day. Precocial young leave nest after hatching and feed themselves, but are tended by both sexes. First flight at 4–5 weeks. 1 brood per year.
• **POPULATION** Fairly common to uncommon. Casual north of breeding range. May be increasing as range expands.

Flight Pattern
Strong swift direct flight with somewhat shallow wing beats.

Nest Identification	
Shape	Location ▬	Lined with stems, weeds, sticks, grasses, fragments of shells, small rocks, fish bones, and rubbish • on ground • sometimes hidden by grasses • built by both sexes • 3–5 yellow or buff eggs heavily blotched with black or brown; pyriform, 1.7 inches long.

| Plumage Sexes similar | Habitat | Migration Most migrate | Weight 5.9 ounces |

DATE _____ TIME_____ LOCATION _____

Family RECURVIROSTRIDAE	Species *Recurvirostra americana*	Length 18–20 inches	Wingspan 27–38 inches

AMERICAN AVOCET

The tallest in its family, this graceful long-legged bird is the world's only avocet with distinct basic and alternate plumages. Winter (basic) plumage shows a gray head and neck, while breeding adults show rusty cinnamon on the head and neck. Females are similar to males but have a shorter and more upward-curved bill. In flight both sexes show a bold black-and-white pattern on the upperparts and black wing tips, primary coverts, and scapular bars.

rusty cinnamon head and neck

black-and-white upperparts

whitish scapulars

long slender upcurved black bill

white underparts

long blue-gray legs

- **SONG** Loud *wheet* or *pleeet*.
- **BEHAVIOR** Eats primarily insects, shrimp, and other crustaceans but also takes other aquatic invertebrates. Prefers to feed in flocks, sometimes with more than 100 birds walking shoulder to shoulder. Sometimes feeds in water up to its belly with bill in water. In shallow water brings food to surface by sweeping its open bill back and forth in the water. In deep water may feed like a dabbling duck by tipping over.
- **BREEDING** Monogamous. Loosely colonial. Pairs perform elaborate courtship display and group rituals.
- **NESTING** Incubation 22–29 days by both sexes. Precocial young leave nest soon after hatching. Tended by both sexes but feed themselves. First flight at 28–35 days. 1 brood per year.
- **POPULATION** The American Avocet is fairly common; stable and possibly increasing west of the Great Plains; uncommon and local in the East, where it is an uncommon transient in summer and a coastal species in winter.
- **CONSERVATION** Protected by law and currently making a comeback after overhunting in the 19th and early 20th centuries.

WINTER PLUMAGE

Similar Birds

BLACK-NECKED STILT
Slightly upcurved black bill; black upperparts; white underparts; long reddish legs and feet.

Flight Pattern
Strong direct flight with neck extended slightly forward and long legs trailing behind tail.

Nest Identification	
Shape ⚲ Location ▬ ♁♁♁	Lined with dry grasses and mud chips • on flat ground or marsh near water • built by both sexes • 3–4 olive-buff eggs blotched with brown and black; pyriform to long pyriform, 2 inches long.

Plumage Sexes similar	Habitat ≈≈ ⚲ ⤳ ⟆	Migration Migratory	Weight 11.1 ounces

DATE _____ TIME_____ LOCATION _____

Family JACANIDAE	Species *Jacana spinosa*	Length 9 inches	Wingspan 17–18 inches

NORTHERN JACANA

An extremely territorial and aggressive bird, this jacana prefers freshwater ponds and marshes with heavy vegetation, a habitat for which it is well suited as it has extremely long toes with long nails to support it on the soft mud and delicate aquatic vegetation. During courtship display both sexes lift their wings and flaunt the green-yellow wing patches beneath them, revealing an unusual long yellowish spur at the bend of the wing. The female jacana is similar to the male, but larger. In flight the yellow flight feathers contrast with the dark brownish body, and the long legs trail or dangle behind. Juveniles have brown upperparts and white underparts with a black postocular stripe extending along the side of the neck.

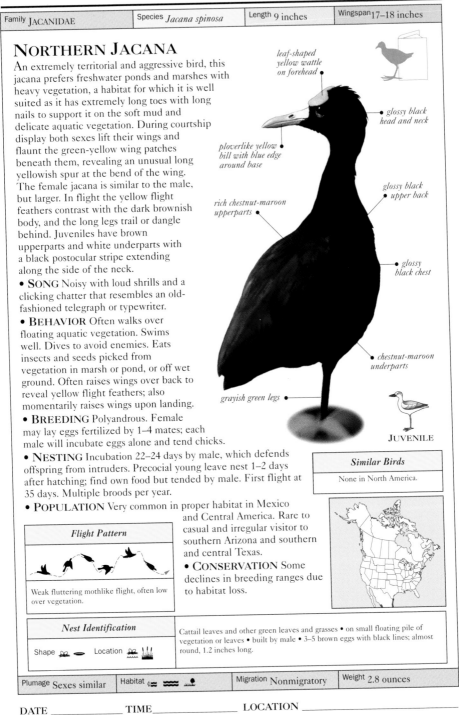

leaf-shaped yellow wattle on forehead

glossy black head and neck

ploverlike yellow bill with blue edge around base

rich chestnut-maroon upperparts

glossy black upper back

glossy black chest

chestnut-maroon underparts

grayish green legs

JUVENILE

- **SONG** Noisy with loud shrills and a clicking chatter that resembles an old-fashioned telegraph or typewriter.
- **BEHAVIOR** Often walks over floating aquatic vegetation. Swims well. Dives to avoid enemies. Eats insects and seeds picked from vegetation in marsh or pond, or off wet ground. Often raises wings over back to reveal yellow flight feathers; also momentarily raises wings upon landing.
- **BREEDING** Polyandrous. Female may lay eggs fertilized by 1–4 mates; each male will incubate eggs alone and tend chicks.
- **NESTING** Incubation 22–24 days by male, which defends offspring from intruders. Precocial young leave nest 1–2 days after hatching; find own food but tended by male. First flight at 35 days. Multiple broods per year.
- **POPULATION** Very common in proper habitat in Mexico and Central America. Rare to casual and irregular visitor to southern Arizona and southern and central Texas.
- **CONSERVATION** Some declines in breeding ranges due to habitat loss.

Similar Birds

None in North America.

Flight Pattern

Weak fluttering mothlike flight, often low over vegetation.

Nest Identification

Shape   Location

Cattail leaves and other green leaves and grasses • on small floating pile of vegetation or leaves • built by male • 3–5 brown eggs with black lines; almost round, 1.2 inches long.

Plumage Sexes similar	Habitat	Migration Nonmigratory	Weight 2.8 ounces

DATE _____ TIME_____ LOCATION _____

Family SCOLOPACIDAE	Species *Tringa melanoleuca*	Length 14 inches	Wingspan 23–26 inches

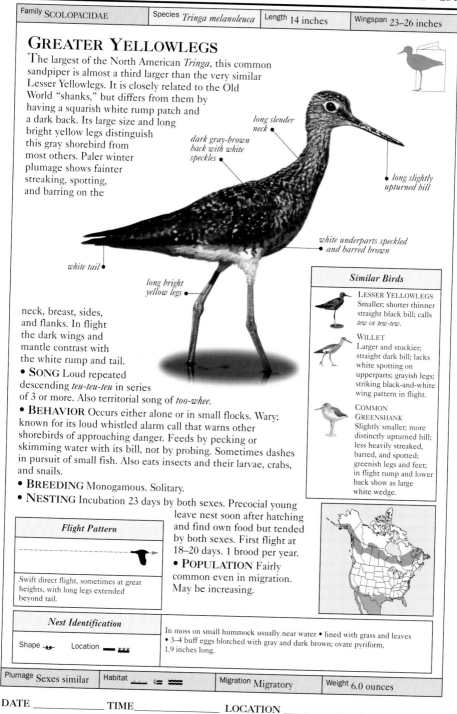

GREATER YELLOWLEGS

The largest of the North American *Tringa*, this common sandpiper is almost a third larger than the very similar Lesser Yellowlegs. It is closely related to the Old World "shanks," but differs from them by having a squarish white rump patch and a dark back. Its large size and long bright yellow legs distinguish this gray shorebird from most others. Paler winter plumage shows fainter streaking, spotting, and barring on the

long slender neck

dark gray-brown back with white speckles

long slightly upturned bill

white underparts speckled and barred brown

white tail

long bright yellow legs

neck, breast, sides, and flanks. In flight the dark wings and mantle contrast with the white rump and tail.

• **SONG** Loud repeated descending *teu-teu-teu* in series of 3 or more. Also territorial song of *too-whee*.

• **BEHAVIOR** Occurs either alone or in small flocks. Wary; known for its loud whistled alarm call that warns other shorebirds of approaching danger. Feeds by pecking or skimming water with its bill, not by probing. Sometimes dashes in pursuit of small fish. Also eats insects and their larvae, crabs, and snails.

• **BREEDING** Monogamous. Solitary.

• **NESTING** Incubation 23 days by both sexes. Precocial young leave nest soon after hatching and find own food but tended by both sexes. First flight at 18–20 days. 1 brood per year.

• **POPULATION** Fairly common even in migration. May be increasing.

Similar Birds

LESSER YELLOWLEGS
Smaller; shorter thinner straight black bill; calls *tew* or *tew-tew*.

WILLET
Larger and stockier; straight dark bill; lacks white spotting on upperparts; grayish legs; striking black-and-white wing pattern in flight.

COMMON GREENSHANK
Slightly smaller; more distinctly upturned bill; less heavily streaked, barred, and spotted; greenish legs and feet; in flight white rump and lower back show as large white wedge.

Flight Pattern

Swift direct flight, sometimes at great heights, with long legs extended beyond tail.

Nest Identification

Shape ⸱⸱⸱ Location ▬ ⸱⸱⸱

In moss on small hummock usually near water • lined with grass and leaves • 3–4 buff eggs blotched with gray and dark brown; ovate pyriform, 1.9 inches long.

Plumage Sexes similar	Habitat ⸱⸱⸱ ⸱⸱⸱ ≈≈≈	Migration Migratory	Weight 6.0 ounces

DATE _____ TIME_____ LOCATION _____

Family SCOLOPACIDAE	Species *Tringa flavipes*	Length 10.5 inches	Wingspan 19–22 inches

LESSER YELLOWLEGS

Often seen walking gracefully on mudflats or shores, this sandpiper is tame and approachable. It is best distinguished from the Greater Yellowlegs by its smaller size and its bill, which is completely straight and only one-third the length of its cousin's bill, as well as by its different voice. Winter plumage is grayer and paler overall with little or no streaking. In flight the dark wings and back contrast sharply with the white tail and rump.

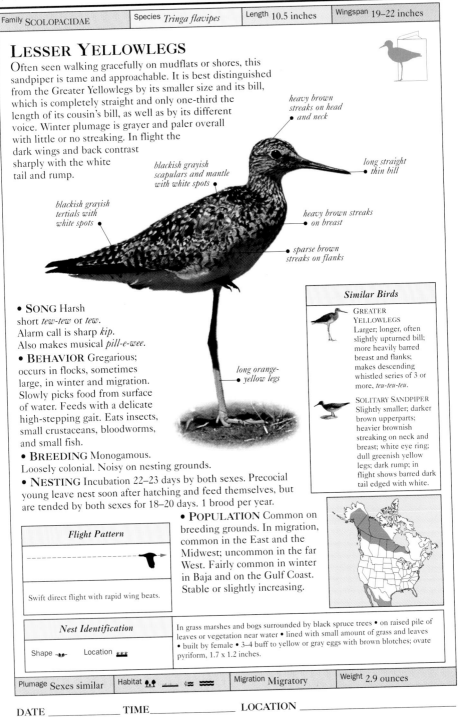

heavy brown streaks on head and neck

long straight thin bill

blackish grayish scapulars and mantle with white spots

blackish grayish tertials with white spots

heavy brown streaks on breast

sparse brown streaks on flanks

long orange-yellow legs

• **SONG** Harsh short *tew-tew* or *tew*. Alarm call is sharp *kip*. Also makes musical *pill-e-wee*.
• **BEHAVIOR** Gregarious; occurs in flocks, sometimes large, in winter and migration. Slowly picks food from surface of water. Feeds with a delicate high-stepping gait. Eats insects, small crustaceans, bloodworms, and small fish.
• **BREEDING** Monogamous. Loosely colonial. Noisy on nesting grounds.
• **NESTING** Incubation 22–23 days by both sexes. Precocial young leave nest soon after hatching and feed themselves, but are tended by both sexes for 18–20 days. 1 brood per year.
• **POPULATION** Common on breeding grounds. In migration, common in the East and the Midwest; uncommon in the far West. Fairly common in winter in Baja and on the Gulf Coast. Stable or slightly increasing.

Similar Birds

GREATER YELLOWLEGS Larger; longer, often slightly upturned bill; more heavily barred breast and flanks; makes descending whistled series of 3 or more, *teu-teu-teu*.

SOLITARY SANDPIPER Slightly smaller; darker brown upperparts; heavier brownish streaking on neck and breast; white eye ring; dull greenish yellow legs; dark rump; in flight shows barred dark tail edged with white.

Flight Pattern

Swift direct flight with rapid wing beats.

Nest Identification

Shape ⚬⚬⚬ Location ⚬⚬⚬

In grass marshes and bogs surrounded by black spruce trees • on raised pile of leaves or vegetation near water • lined with small amount of grass and leaves • built by female • 3–4 buff to yellow or gray eggs with brown blotches; ovate pyriform, 1.7 x 1.2 inches.

Plumage Sexes similar	Habitat 🏞	Migration Migratory	Weight 2.9 ounces

DATE _____ TIME_____ LOCATION _____

Family SCOLOPACIDAE	Species *Tringa erythropus*	Length 12.5 inches	Wingspan 23–25 inches

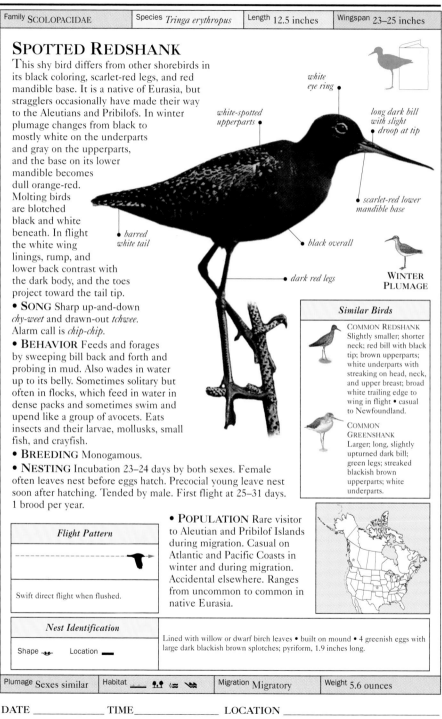

SPOTTED REDSHANK

This shy bird differs from other shorebirds in its black coloring, scarlet-red legs, and red mandible base. It is a native of Eurasia, but stragglers occasionally have made their way to the Aleutians and Pribilofs. In winter plumage changes from black to mostly white on the underparts and gray on the upperparts, and the base on its lower mandible becomes dull orange-red. Molting birds are blotched black and white beneath. In flight the white wing linings, rump, and lower back contrast with the dark body, and the toes project toward the tail tip.

white eye ring

white-spotted upperparts

long dark bill with slight droop at tip

scarlet-red lower mandible base

barred white tail

black overall

dark red legs

WINTER PLUMAGE

• **SONG** Sharp up-and-down *chy-weet* and drawn-out *tchwee*. Alarm call is *chip-chip*.
• **BEHAVIOR** Feeds and forages by sweeping bill back and forth and probing in mud. Also wades in water up to its belly. Sometimes solitary but often in flocks, which feed in water in dense packs and sometimes swim and upend like a group of avocets. Eats insects and their larvae, mollusks, small fish, and crayfish.
• **BREEDING** Monogamous.
• **NESTING** Incubation 23–24 days by both sexes. Female often leaves nest before eggs hatch. Precocial young leave nest soon after hatching. Tended by male. First flight at 25–31 days. 1 brood per year.

Similar Birds

COMMON REDSHANK
Slightly smaller; shorter neck; red bill with black tip; brown upperparts; white underparts with streaking on head, neck, and upper breast; broad white trailing edge to wing in flight • casual to Newfoundland.

COMMON GREENSHANK
Larger; long, slightly upturned dark bill; green legs; streaked blackish brown upperparts; white underparts.

• **POPULATION** Rare visitor to Aleutian and Pribilof Islands during migration. Casual on Atlantic and Pacific Coasts in winter and during migration. Accidental elsewhere. Ranges from uncommon to common in native Eurasia.

Flight Pattern
Swift direct flight when flushed.

Nest Identification	
Shape ↝ Location ▬	Lined with willow or dwarf birch leaves • built on mound • 4 greenish eggs with large dark blackish brown splotches; pyriform, 1.9 inches long.

Plumage Sexes similar	Habitat	Migration Migratory	Weight 5.6 ounces

DATE _____ TIME_____ LOCATION _____

Family SCOLOPACIDAE	Species *Tringa glareola*	Length 8 inches	Wingspan 16 inches

WOOD SANDPIPER

One of the most numerous and widespread *Tringa* sandpipers, this tall, lithe bird is also a champion long-distance flier. It is a fairly common spring visitor and irregular breeder on the outer Aleutian Islands and is rare to

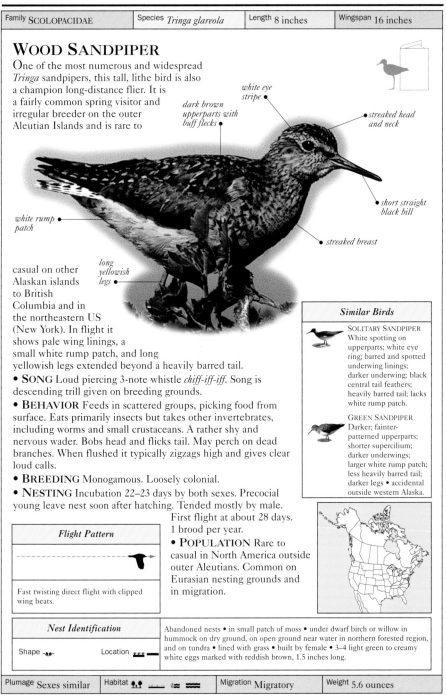

white eye stripe

dark brown upperparts with buff flecks

streaked head and neck

short straight black bill

white rump patch

streaked breast

casual on other Alaskan islands to British Columbia and in the northeastern US (New York). In flight it shows pale wing linings, a small white rump patch, and long yellowish legs extended beyond a heavily barred tail.

long yellowish legs

- **SONG** Loud piercing 3-note whistle *chiff-iff-iff*. Song is descending trill given on breeding grounds.
- **BEHAVIOR** Feeds in scattered groups, picking food from surface. Eats primarily insects but takes other invertebrates, including worms and small crustaceans. A rather shy and nervous wader. Bobs head and flicks tail. May perch on dead branches. When flushed it typically zigzags high and gives clear loud calls.
- **BREEDING** Monogamous. Loosely colonial.
- **NESTING** Incubation 22–23 days by both sexes. Precocial young leave nest soon after hatching. Tended mostly by male. First flight at about 28 days. 1 brood per year.
- **POPULATION** Rare to casual in North America outside outer Aleutians. Common on Eurasian nesting grounds and in migration.

Similar Birds

SOLITARY SANDPIPER
White spotting on upperparts; white eye ring; barred and spotted underwing linings; darker underwing; black central tail feathers; heavily barred tail; lacks white rump patch.

GREEN SANDPIPER
Darker; fainter-patterned upperparts; shorter supercilium; darker underwings; larger white rump patch; less heavily barred tail; darker legs • accidental outside western Alaska.

Flight Pattern
Fast twisting direct flight with clipped wing beats.

Nest Identification	
Shape ⌣ Location ••• ▬	Abandoned nests • in small patch of moss • under dwarf birch or willow in hummock on dry ground, on open ground near water in northern forested region, and on tundra • lined with grass • built by female • 3–4 light green to creamy white eggs marked with reddish brown, 1.5 inches long.

Plumage Sexes similar	Habitat ••• ⌣ ⌣	Migration Migratory	Weight 5.6 ounces

DATE _____ TIME_____ LOCATION _____

Family SCOLOPACIDAE	Species *Tringa solitaria*	Length 8–9 inches	Wingspan 15–17 inches

SOLITARY SANDPIPER

As its name suggests, this sandpiper is often seen alone or in small loose groups in its habitat of freshwater lakes, ponds, marshes, and rivers. This shorebird is not wary around humans and often exhibits an up-and-down bobbing or jerking motion with its head and body similar to a Spotted Sandpiper's bobbing. In flight the dark

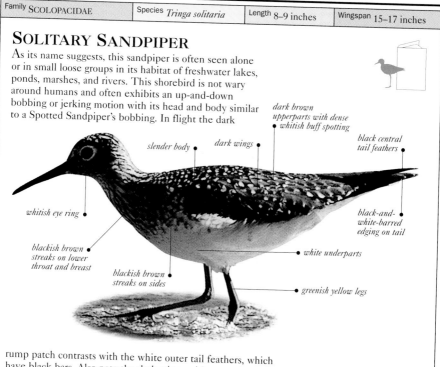

dark brown upperparts with dense whitish buff spotting

black central tail feathers

slender body

dark wings

black-and-white-barred edging on tail

whitish eye ring

blackish brown streaks on lower throat and breast

blackish brown streaks on sides

white underparts

greenish yellow legs

rump patch contrasts with the white outer tail feathers, which have black bars. Also note the dark wings without a wing stripe, dark underwings.

- **SONG** High shrill *pit-peet-wheet* or *peet*.
- **BEHAVIOR** Searches for food by stirring up water, especially in stagnant pools, with bill and feet. Picks food from surface or probes with bill. Eats insects and insect larvae, small fish, small crustaceans, and other invertebrates. Somewhat aggressive toward other birds when feeding. Migrates singly or in small groups. Upon landing holds wings above back before folding.
- **BREEDING** Monogamous.
- **NESTING** Incubation 23–24 days by female. Precocial young leave nest soon after hatching and are tended by female. First flight at 17–20 days. 1 brood per year.
- **POPULATION** Fairly common on breeding grounds; fairly common and widespread in migration. Seems stable.

Similar Birds

SPOTTED SANDPIPER Smaller; less upright stance; teeters body; yellowish or creamy pink legs; pink bill with dark tip; white supercilium; white wing stripe; shallow stiff wing beats • spotted underparts in summer.

Flight Pattern

Often zigzags on takeoff; light buoyant swallowlike direct flight.

Nest Identification

Shape

Location

Female strengthens abandoned nest with other material • most often in conifers, 4–40 feet above ground • 4–5 olive eggs marked with brown, usually in wreath shape; pyriform to oval, 1.5 x 1.1 inches.

Plumage Sexes similar	Habitat	Migration Migratory	Weight 1.7 ounces

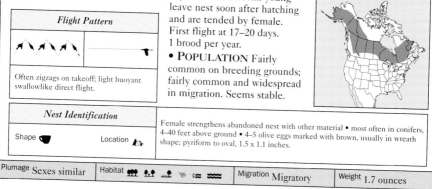

DATE _____ TIME_____ LOCATION _____

| Family SCOLOPACIDAE | Species *Catoptrophorus semipalmatus* | Length 13–16 inches | Wingspan 24–31 inches |

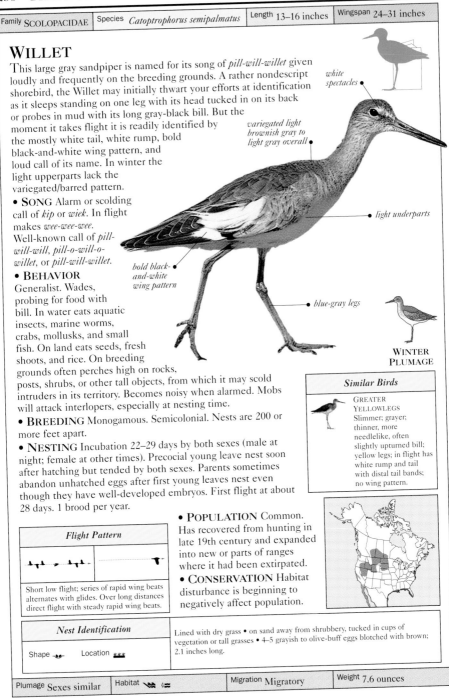

WILLET

This large gray sandpiper is named for its song of *pill-will-willet* given loudly and frequently on the breeding grounds. A rather nondescript shorebird, the Willet may initially thwart your efforts at identification as it sleeps standing on one leg with its head tucked in on its back or probes in mud with its long gray-black bill. But the moment it takes flight it is readily identified by the mostly white tail, white rump, bold black-and-white wing pattern, and loud call of its name. In winter the light upperparts lack the variegated/barred pattern.

white spectacles

variegated light brownish gray to light gray overall

light underparts

bold black-and-white wing pattern

blue-gray legs

WINTER PLUMAGE

- **SONG** Alarm or scolding call of *kip* or *wiek*. In flight makes *wee-wee-wee*. Well-known call of *pill-will-will, pill-o-will-o-willet*, or *pill-will-willet*.
- **BEHAVIOR** Generalist. Wades, probing for food with bill. In water eats aquatic insects, marine worms, crabs, mollusks, and small fish. On land eats seeds, fresh shoots, and rice. On breeding grounds often perches high on rocks, posts, shrubs, or other tall objects, from which it may scold intruders in its territory. Becomes noisy when alarmed. Mobs will attack interlopers, especially at nesting time.
- **BREEDING** Monogamous. Semicolonial. Nests are 200 or more feet apart.
- **NESTING** Incubation 22–29 days by both sexes (male at night; female at other times). Precocial young leave nest soon after hatching but tended by both sexes. Parents sometimes abandon unhatched eggs after first young leaves nest even though they have well-developed embryos. First flight at about 28 days. 1 brood per year.

Similar Birds

GREATER YELLOWLEGS Slimmer; grayer; thinner, more needlelike, often slightly upturned bill; yellow legs; in flight has white rump and tail with distal tail bands; no wing pattern.

- **POPULATION** Common. Has recovered from hunting in late 19th century and expanded into new or parts of ranges where it had been extirpated.
- **CONSERVATION** Habitat disturbance is beginning to negatively affect population.

Flight Pattern
Short low flight; series of rapid wing beats alternates with glides. Over long distances direct flight with steady rapid wing beats.

Nest Identification	Lined with dry grass • on sand away from shrubbery, tucked in cups of vegetation or tall grasses • 4–5 grayish to olive-buff eggs blotched with brown; 2.1 inches long.
Shape 🪶 Location ✦✦✦	

| Plumage Sexes similar | Habitat 🌊 〰 | Migration Migratory | Weight 7.6 ounces |

DATE _____ TIME_____ LOCATION _____

Family SCOLOPACIDAE	Species *Heteroscelus incanus*	Length 11 inches	Wingspan 22 inches

WANDERING TATTLER

An Alaskan breeder, the Wandering Tattler flies long distances during migration to some of the most isolated Pacific islands and as far away as Australia. Although this bird often allows a close approach, an identifiable behavior is its tendency to crouch rather than fly when in danger. In flight it differs from most other shorebirds that

inhabit rocky coasts by its unmarked completely dark upperparts. Like many other shorebird species, the female is larger than the male.

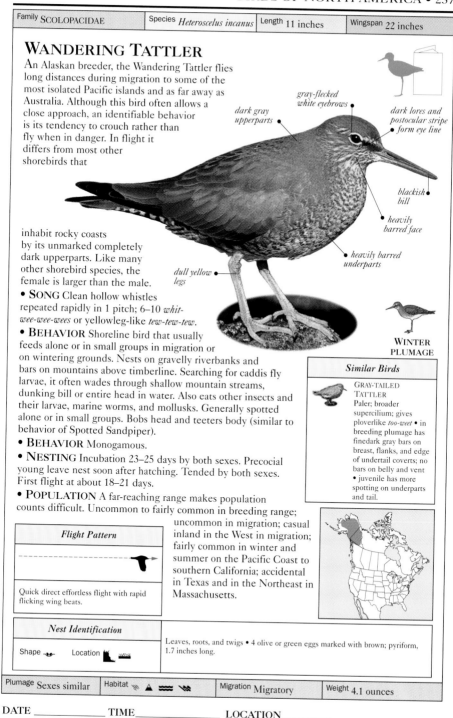

gray-flecked white eyebrows

dark gray upperparts

dark lores and postocular stripe form eye line

blackish bill

heavily barred face

heavily barred underparts

dull yellow legs

WINTER PLUMAGE

- **SONG** Clean hollow whistles repeated rapidly in 1 pitch; 6–10 *whit-wee-wee-wees* or yellowleg-like *tew-tew-tew*.
- **BEHAVIOR** Shoreline bird that usually feeds alone or in small groups in migration or on wintering grounds. Nests on gravelly riverbanks and bars on mountains above timberline. Searching for caddis fly larvae, it often wades through shallow mountain streams, dunking bill or entire head in water. Also eats other insects and their larvae, marine worms, and mollusks. Generally spotted alone or in small groups. Bobs head and teeters body (similar to behavior of Spotted Sandpiper).
- **BEHAVIOR** Monogamous.
- **NESTING** Incubation 23–25 days by both sexes. Precocial young leave nest soon after hatching. Tended by both sexes. First flight at about 18–21 days.
- **POPULATION** A far-reaching range makes population counts difficult. Uncommon to fairly common in breeding range; uncommon in migration; casual inland in the West in migration; fairly common in winter and summer on the Pacific Coast to southern California; accidental in Texas and in the Northeast in Massachusetts.

Similar Birds

GRAY-TAILED TATTLER
Paler; broader supercilium; gives ploverlike *too-weet* • in breeding plumage has fine dark gray bars on breast, flanks, and edge of undertail coverts; no bars on belly and vent • juvenile has more spotting on underparts and tail.

Flight Pattern
Quick direct effortless flight with rapid flicking wing beats.

Nest Identification	
Shape Location	Leaves, roots, and twigs • 4 olive or green eggs marked with brown; pyriform, 1.7 inches long.

Plumage Sexes similar	Habitat	Migration Migratory	Weight 4.1 ounces

DATE _____ TIME_____ LOCATION _____

Family SCOLOPACIDAE	Species *Heteroscelus brevipes*	Length 10 inches	Wingspan 20 inches

GRAY-TAILED TATTLER

The Gray-tailed Tattler closely resembles the Wandering Tattler and the two were once thought to be the same species. However, the Gray-tailed Tattler is only a rare visitor to North America from its Siberian nesting grounds. The first nest was not found in northeast Siberia until 1959. Often allowing humans to come quite near, it sometimes squats low to the ground rather than taking flight when approached. The female is similar to the male but is larger in size and, like him, shows thin white barring on the uppertail coverts in breeding plumage. Barring on the breast and sides fades in winter plumage. Juveniles are similar to winter adults, but show whitish buff spots on the upperparts and white edging on the tail.

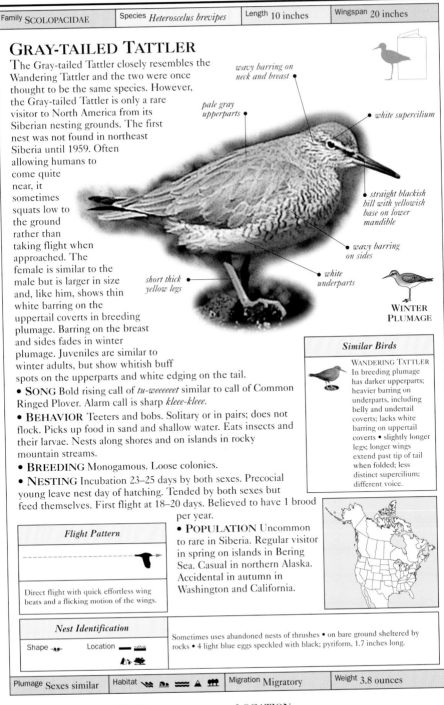

wavy barring on neck and breast

pale gray upperparts

white supercilium

straight blackish bill with yellowish base on lower mandible

wavy barring on sides

short thick yellow legs

white underparts

WINTER PLUMAGE

- **SONG** Bold rising call of *tu-weeeeeet* similar to call of Common Ringed Plover. Alarm call is sharp *kleee-kleee.*
- **BEHAVIOR** Teeters and bobs. Solitary or in pairs; does not flock. Picks up food in sand and shallow water. Eats insects and their larvae. Nests along shores and on islands in rocky mountain streams.
- **BREEDING** Monogamous. Loose colonies.
- **NESTING** Incubation 23–25 days by both sexes. Precocial young leave nest day of hatching. Tended by both sexes but feed themselves. First flight at 18–20 days. Believed to have 1 brood per year.
- **POPULATION** Uncommon to rare in Siberia. Regular visitor in spring on islands in Bering Sea. Casual in northern Alaska. Accidental in autumn in Washington and California.

Similar Birds

WANDERING TATTLER
In breeding plumage has darker upperparts; heavier barring on underparts, including belly and undertail coverts; lacks white barring on uppertail coverts • slightly longer legs; longer wings extend past tip of tail when folded; less distinct supercilium; different voice.

Flight Pattern

Direct flight with quick effortless wing beats and a flicking motion of the wings.

Nest Identification

Shape 〰   Location ▬ ▨

Sometimes uses abandoned nests of thrushes • on bare ground sheltered by rocks • 4 light blue eggs speckled with black; pyriform, 1.7 inches long.

Plumage Sexes similar	Habitat	Migration Migratory	Weight 3.8 ounces

DATE _____ TIME_____ LOCATION _____

Family SCOLOPACIDAE	Species *Actitis hypoleucos*	Length 8 inches	Wingspan 15 inches

COMMON SANDPIPER

This thrush-sized bird lives near the cold, swift inland streams and lakes of Europe and Asia. During migration, however, it makes regular trips to coastal Alaska and islands in the Bering Sea, including the Aleutians and Pribilofs. Usually seen alone, this sandpiper bobs and teeters constantly, especially when

greenish brown crown and nape with fine dark brown streaks

greenish brown upperparts with dark brown streaking

dark brownish bill

narrow dark barring on upper breast

white underparts

grayish to dull straw-colored feet

landing; it actually appears to be off balance while walking. Adults and juveniles are similar to winter-plumaged Spotted Sandpipers, but they lack any spotting on the underparts and have noticeably longer tails. In flight the white wing stripe extends farther out the wing and shows a longer white trailing edge to the wing.

• **SONG** High-pitched fluted call of *twee-wee-wee*. When perched sings twittering *tee-t-t-t-t*. During breeding cries a loud *hee-deedeedee*.

• **BEHAVIOR** Solitary, or in pairs or small flocks. Feeds slowly and deliberately. Eats various small invertebrates, especially insects. Forages in shallow water or on edges of shore or sometimes feeds along roadsides or grasslands. Perches readily on posts, limbs, or boats. Flies low over water with shallow, stiff wing beats and glides.

• **BREEDING** Monogamous. Solitary, but sometimes breeds in small colonies.

• **NESTING** Incubation 21–22 days by both sexes. Precocial young leave nest soon after hatching. Tended by both sexes but feed themselves. First flight at 26–28 days. 1 brood per year.

• **POPULATION** Rare but regular visitor to the islands off the coast of Alaska and to Alaska's Seward Peninsula.

Similar Birds

SPOTTED SANDPIPER
When breeding has spotted underparts; longer yellow legs; shorter tail; pinkish bill with dark tip; grayer upperparts; shorter white wing stripe; shorter white trailing edge of inner wing
• winter birds lack spotted underparts
• different voice.

Flight Pattern

Flies low over water with shallow stiff wing beats and glides. In migration, swift direct flight with rapid wing beats.

Nest Identification

Shape ᴗ   Location ▬ ᨿ ⚹⚹

Lined with dried grasses and plant material • on ground near grassy area, trees, or shrubs • built by female • 4 pinkish gray eggs with brownish red speckles; pyriform, 1.4 inches long.

Plumage Sexes similar	Habitat ꕥ ≋ ⬚ ꕥ ▂	Migration Migratory	Weight 1.8 ounces

DATE _____ TIME_____ LOCATION _____

Family SCOLOPACIDAE	Species *Actitis macularia*	Length 7.5 inches	Wingspan 13–14 inches

SPOTTED SANDPIPER

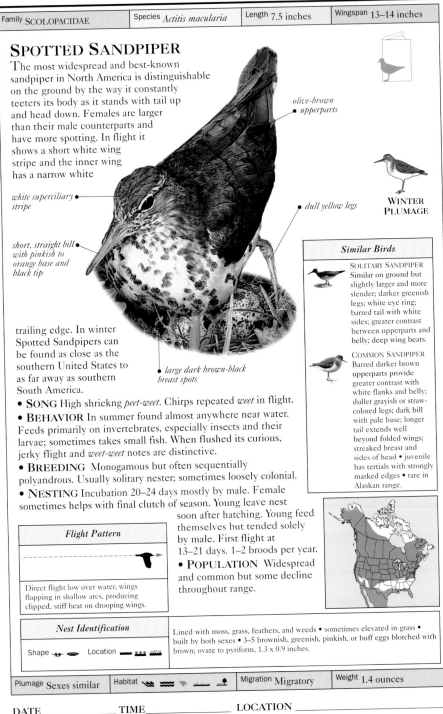

The most widespread and best-known sandpiper in North America is distinguishable on the ground by the way it constantly teeters its body as it stands with tail up and head down. Females are larger than their male counterparts and have more spotting. In flight it shows a short white wing stripe and the inner wing has a narrow white

olive-brown upperparts

white superciliary stripe

short, straight bill with pinkish to orange base and black tip

dull yellow legs

WINTER PLUMAGE

trailing edge. In winter Spotted Sandpipers can be found as close as the southern United States to as far away as southern South America.

large dark brown-black breast spots

Similar Birds

SOLITARY SANDPIPER Similar on ground but slightly larger and more slender; darker greenish legs; white eye ring; barred tail with white sides; greater contrast between upperparts and belly; deep wing beats.

COMMON SANDPIPER Barred darker brown upperparts provide greater contrast with white flanks and belly; duller grayish or straw-colored legs; dark bill with pale base; longer tail extends well beyond folded wings; streaked breast and sides of head • juvenile has tertials with strongly marked edges • rare in Alaskan range.

- **SONG** High shriekng *peet-weet*. Chirps repeated *weet* in flight.
- **BEHAVIOR** In summer found almost anywhere near water. Feeds primarily on invertebrates, especially insects and their larvae; sometimes takes small fish. When flushed its curious, jerky flight and *weet-weet* notes are distinctive.
- **BREEDING** Monogamous but often sequentially polyandrous. Usually solitary nester; sometimes loosely colonial.
- **NESTING** Incubation 20–24 days mostly by male. Female sometimes helps with final clutch of season. Young leave nest soon after hatching. Young feed themselves but tended solely by male. First flight at 13–21 days. 1–2 broods per year.
- **POPULATION** Widespread and common but some decline throughout range.

Flight Pattern

Direct flight low over water, wings flapping in shallow arcs, producing clipped, stiff beat on drooping wings.

Nest Identification

Shape ⌒ ⌒　　Location ▬ ▰▰▰ ▨

Lined with moss, grass, feathers, and weeds • sometimes elevated in grass • built by both sexes • 3–5 brownish, greenish, pinkish, or buff eggs blotched with brown; ovate to pyriform, 1.3 x 0.9 inches.

Plumage Sexes similar	Habitat ⌇⌇ ≈≈ ⩲ ▬ ⚲	Migration Migratory	Weight 1.4 ounces

DATE _____ TIME_____ LOCATION _____

Family SCOLOPACIDAE	Species *Bartramia longicauda*	Length 12 inches	Wingspan 17–20 inches

UPLAND SANDPIPER

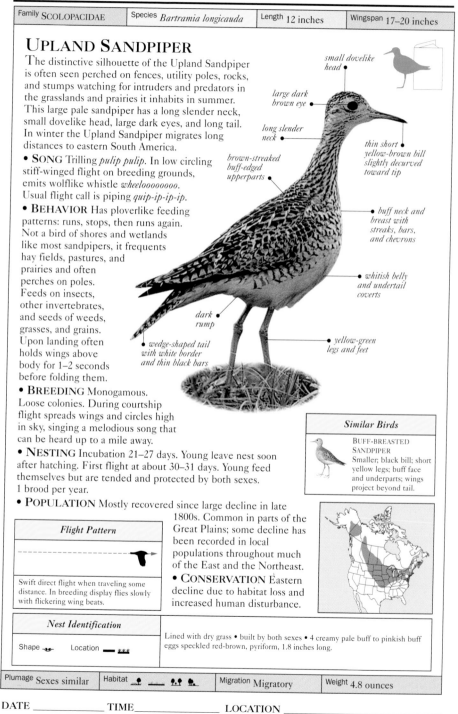

The distinctive silhouette of the Upland Sandpiper is often seen perched on fences, utility poles, rocks, and stumps watching for intruders and predators in the grasslands and prairies it inhabits in summer. This large pale sandpiper has a long slender neck, small dovelike head, large dark eyes, and long tail. In winter the Upland Sandpiper migrates long distances to eastern South America.

• **SONG** Trilling *pulip pulip*. In low circling stiff-winged flight on breeding grounds, emits wolflike whistle *wheelooooooooo*. Usual flight call is piping *quip-ip-ip-ip*.

• **BEHAVIOR** Has ploverlike feeding patterns: runs, stops, then runs again. Not a bird of shores and wetlands like most sandpipers, it frequents hay fields, pastures, and prairies and often perches on poles. Feeds on insects, other invertebrates, and seeds of weeds, grasses, and grains. Upon landing often holds wings above body for 1–2 seconds before folding them.

• **BREEDING** Monogamous. Loose colonies. During courtship flight spreads wings and circles high in sky, singing a melodious song that can be heard up to a mile away.

• **NESTING** Incubation 21–27 days. Young leave nest soon after hatching. First flight at about 30–31 days. Young feed themselves but are tended and protected by both sexes. 1 brood per year.

• **POPULATION** Mostly recovered since large decline in late 1800s. Common in parts of the Great Plains; some decline has been recorded in local populations throughout much of the East and the Northeast.

• **CONSERVATION** Eastern decline due to habitat loss and increased human disturbance.

Labels on illustration:
- small dovelike head
- large dark brown eye
- long slender neck
- thin short yellow-brown bill slightly decurved toward tip
- brown-streaked buff-edged upperparts
- buff neck and breast with streaks, bars, and chevrons
- whitish belly and undertail coverts
- dark rump
- wedge-shaped tail with white border and thin black bars
- yellow-green legs and feet

Similar Birds

BUFF-BREASTED SANDPIPER Smaller; black bill; short yellow legs; buff face and underparts; wings project beyond tail.

Flight Pattern

Swift direct flight when traveling some distance. In breeding display flies slowly with flickering wing beats.

Nest Identification

Shape ••   Location ▬ ***

Lined with dry grass • built by both sexes • 4 creamy pale buff to pinkish buff eggs speckled red-brown, pyriform, 1.8 inches long.

Plumage Sexes similar	Habitat	Migration Migratory	Weight 4.8 ounces

DATE _____ TIME_____ LOCATION _____

Family SCOLOPACIDAE	Species *Numenius phaeopus*	Length 17–18 inches	Wingspan 31–33 inches

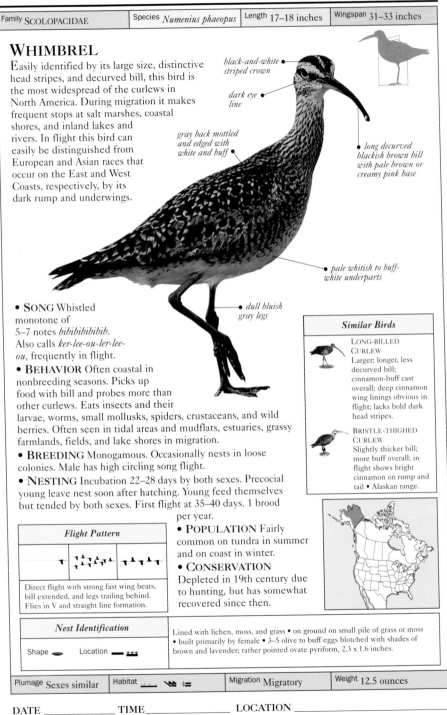

WHIMBREL

Easily identified by its large size, distinctive head stripes, and decurved bill, this bird is the most widespread of the curlews in North America. During migration it makes frequent stops at salt marshes, coastal shores, and inland lakes and rivers. In flight this bird can easily be distinguished from European and Asian races that occur on the East and West Coasts, respectively, by its dark rump and underwings.

black-and-white striped crown

dark eye line

gray back mottled and edged with white and buff

long decurved blackish brown bill with pale brown or creamy pink base

pale whitish to buff-white underparts

dull bluish gray legs

• **SONG** Whistled monotone of 5–7 notes *bibibibibibib*. Also calls *ker-lee-ou-ler-lee-ou*, frequently in flight.
• **BEHAVIOR** Often coastal in nonbreeding seasons. Picks up food with bill and probes more than other curlews. Eats insects and their larvae, worms, small mollusks, spiders, crustaceans, and wild berries. Often seen in tidal areas and mudflats, estuaries, grassy farmlands, fields, and lake shores in migration.
• **BREEDING** Monogamous. Occasionally nests in loose colonies. Male has high circling song flight.
• **NESTING** Incubation 22–28 days by both sexes. Precocial young leave nest soon after hatching. Young feed themselves but tended by both sexes. First flight at 35–40 days. 1 brood per year.
• **POPULATION** Fairly common on tundra in summer and on coast in winter.
• **CONSERVATION** Depleted in 19th century due to hunting, but has somewhat recovered since then.

Similar Birds

LONG-BILLED CURLEW
Larger; longer, less decurved bill; cinnamon-buff cast overall; deep cinnamon wing linings obvious in flight; lacks bold dark head stripes.

BRISTLE-THIGHED CURLEW
Slightly thicker bill; more buff overall; in flight shows bright cinnamon on rump and tail • Alaskan range.

Flight Pattern

Direct flight with strong fast wing beats, bill extended, and legs trailing behind. Flies in V and straight line formation.

Nest Identification

Shape ⬤   Location ⚬⚬⚬

Lined with lichen, moss, and grass • on ground on small pile of grass or moss • built primarily by female • 3–5 olive to buff eggs blotched with shades of brown and lavender; rather pointed ovate pyriform, 2.3 x 1.6 inches.

Plumage Sexes similar	Habitat	Migration Migratory	Weight 12.5 ounces

DATE _____ TIME_____ LOCATION _____

Family SCOLOPACIDAE	Species *Numenius tahitiensis*	Length 17–18 inches	Wingspan 32–34.5 inches

BRISTLE-THIGHED CURLEW

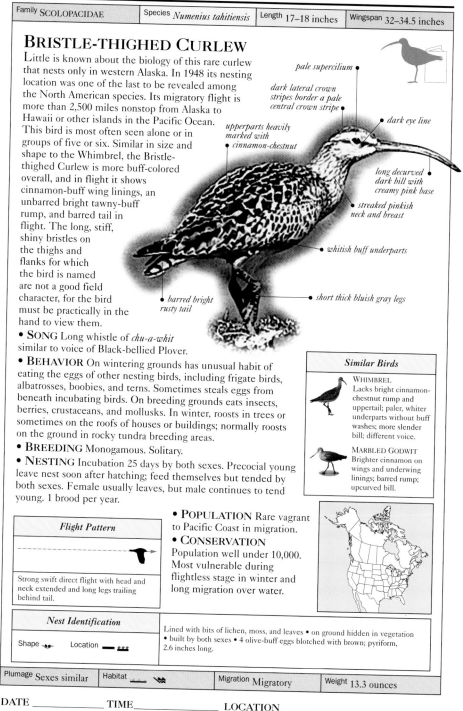

Little is known about the biology of this rare curlew that nests only in western Alaska. In 1948 its nesting location was one of the last to be revealed among the North American species. Its migratory flight is more than 2,500 miles nonstop from Alaska to Hawaii or other islands in the Pacific Ocean. This bird is most often seen alone or in groups of five or six. Similar in size and shape to the Whimbrel, the Bristle-thighed Curlew is more buff-colored overall, and in flight it shows cinnamon-buff wing linings, an unbarred bright tawny-buff rump, and barred tail in flight. The long, stiff, shiny bristles on the thighs and flanks for which the bird is named are not a good field character, for the bird must be practically in the hand to view them.

pale supercilium

dark lateral crown stripes border a pale central crown stripe

upperparts heavily marked with cinnamon-chestnut

dark eye line

long decurved dark bill with creamy pink base

streaked pinkish neck and breast

whitish buff underparts

barred bright rusty tail

short thick bluish gray legs

• **SONG** Long whistle of *chu-a-whit* similar to voice of Black-bellied Plover.
• **BEHAVIOR** On wintering grounds has unusual habit of eating the eggs of other nesting birds, including frigate birds, albatrosses, boobies, and terns. Sometimes steals eggs from beneath incubating birds. On breeding grounds eats insects, berries, crustaceans, and mollusks. In winter, roosts in trees or sometimes on the roofs of houses or buildings; normally roosts on the ground in rocky tundra breeding areas.
• **BREEDING** Monogamous. Solitary.
• **NESTING** Incubation 25 days by both sexes. Precocial young leave nest soon after hatching; feed themselves but tended by both sexes. Female usually leaves, but male continues to tend young. 1 brood per year.
• **POPULATION** Rare vagrant to Pacific Coast in migration.
• **CONSERVATION** Population well under 10,000. Most vulnerable during flightless stage in winter and long migration over water.

Similar Birds

WHIMBREL
Lacks bright cinnamon-chestnut rump and uppertail; paler, whiter underparts without buff washes; more slender bill; different voice.

MARBLED GODWIT
Brighter cinnamon on wings and underwing linings; barred rump; upcurved bill.

Flight Pattern

Strong swift direct flight with head and neck extended and long legs trailing behind tail.

Nest Identification

Shape ᴥ Location ━ ✦✦✦

Lined with bits of lichen, moss, and leaves • on ground hidden in vegetation • built by both sexes • 4 olive-buff eggs blotched with brown; pyriform, 2.6 inches long.

Plumage Sexes similar	Habitat ▲▲ ❧	Migration Migratory	Weight 13.3 ounces

DATE _____ TIME_____ LOCATION _____

Family SCOLOPACIDAE	Species *Numenius madagascariensis*	Length 22–26 inches	Wingspan 32–35 inches

FAR EASTERN CURLEW

Its remarkably long bill, nearly half the length of its body, and distinct night call of *ker-lew*, help identify this large shorebird. Flying from wintering areas in Australia to nesting areas in Siberia, strays sometimes appear on the Pribilofs and Aleutians during spring and summer; it is accidental in British Columbia. In flight it shows a dark rump and white underwings. The axillaries have dark barring and a blackish patch on the outer part of the leading edge of the wing. The rump is dark.

• **SONG** Contact call is *coor-ee*. Alarm call of *ker ker-ee-ker-ee*. Night call sounds like bird's name, *ker-lew*.

• **BEHAVIOR** Wary; solitary to large and somewhat dispersed flocks. Active and vocal at night. Sometimes roosts in tall trees or shrubs. Uses beak to probe for burrowing prey. Also picks prey from the surface. Eats crustaceans, marine worms, insects and insect larvae, and other invertebrates.

• **BREEDING** Monogamous. Colonial.

• **NESTING** Incubation 27–29 days by both sexes. Precocial young tended by both parents; leave nest soon after hatching. First flight at 32–38 days. 1 brood per year.

buffy brown head with dark brown streaks

long decurved bill

brown wings mottled with white

blue-gray legs

Similar Birds

LONG-BILLED CURLEW
Cinnamon overall, including underwings.

• **POPULATION** Casual on Aleutians and Pribilofs in spring and summer. Accidental in coastal British Columbia. Fairly common to common in breeding range of southeastern Eurasia. Perhaps declining on winter grounds in Australia.

Flight Pattern

Steady strong direct flight on rapidly beating wings. Flies in straight line or V formation when in flocks or migrating.

Nest Identification

Shape ⌣ Location ▬

Lined with leaves and grasses • on knoll or dry hill • 4 olive-green eggs marked with brown to greenish brown blotches; oval to short elliptical, 2.8 inches long.

Plumage Sexes similar	Habitat	Migration Migratory	Weight 1.7 pounds

DATE _____ TIME_____ LOCATION _____

Family SCOLOPACIDAE	Species *Numenius americanus*	Length 23 inches	Wingspan 36–40 inches

LONG-BILLED CURLEW

The largest North American member of the sandpiper family has a very long, slender decurved bill. The male claims and defends large territories with a flapping gliding flight. After courtship and mating, these birds usually nest in dry uplands often near rivers but sometimes rangelands or farmlands. As with other curlews the female is larger than the male. It is distinguished in flight by the long decurved bill and cinnamon underwing linings.

indistinct eye line

cinnamon-brown upperparts

long decurved bill

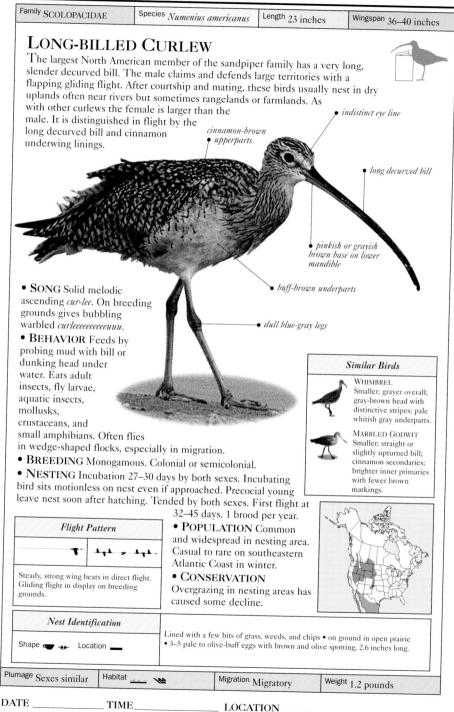

pinkish or grayish brown base on lower mandible

buff-brown underparts

dull blue-gray legs

- **SONG** Solid melodic ascending *cur-lee*. On breeding grounds gives bubbling warbled *curleeeeeeeeeeuuu*.
- **BEHAVIOR** Feeds by probing mud with bill or dunking head under water. Eats adult insects, fly larvae, aquatic insects, mollusks, crustaceans, and small amphibians. Often flies in wedge-shaped flocks, especially in migration.
- **BREEDING** Monogamous. Colonial or semicolonial.
- **NESTING** Incubation 27–30 days by both sexes. Incubating bird sits motionless on nest even if approached. Precocial young leave nest soon after hatching. Tended by both sexes. First flight at 32–45 days. 1 brood per year.
- **POPULATION** Common and widespread in nesting area. Casual to rare on southeastern Atlantic Coast in winter.
- **CONSERVATION** Overgrazing in nesting areas has caused some decline.

Similar Birds

WHIMBREL
Smaller; grayer overall; gray-brown head with distinctive stripes; pale whitish gray underparts.

MARBLED GODWIT
Smaller; straight or slightly upturned bill; cinnamon secondaries; brighter inner primaries with fewer brown markings.

Flight Pattern

Steady, strong wing beats in direct flight. Gliding flight in display on breeding grounds.

Nest Identification

Shape ⌒ ↘   Location ▬

Lined with a few bits of grass, weeds, and chips • on ground in open prairie • 3–5 pale to olive-buff eggs with brown and olive spotting, 2.6 inches long.

Plumage Sexes similar	Habitat	Migration Migratory	Weight 1.2 pounds

DATE _____ TIME_____ LOCATION _____

Family SCOLOPACIDAE	Species *Limosa limosa*	Length 16 inches	Wingspan 30 inches

BLACK-TAILED GODWIT

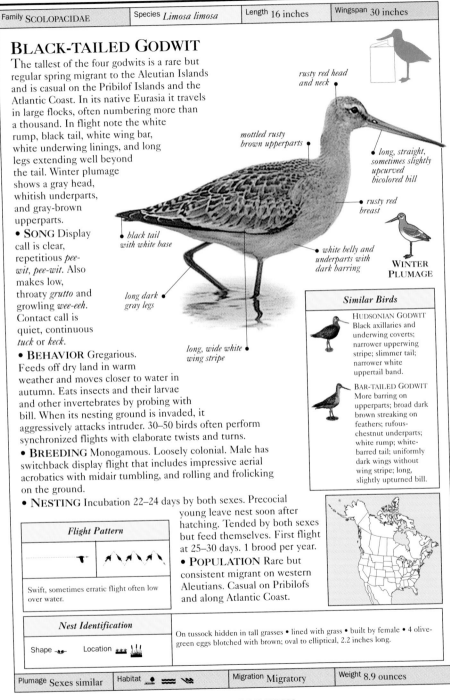

The tallest of the four godwits is a rare but regular spring migrant to the Aleutian Islands and is casual on the Pribilof Islands and the Atlantic Coast. In its native Eurasia it travels in large flocks, often numbering more than a thousand. In flight note the white rump, black tail, white wing bar, white underwing linings, and long legs extending well beyond the tail. Winter plumage shows a gray head, whitish underparts, and gray-brown upperparts.

rusty red head and neck

mottled rusty brown upperparts

long, straight, sometimes slightly upcurved bicolored bill

rusty red breast

black tail with white base

white belly and underparts with dark barring

WINTER PLUMAGE

long dark gray legs

long, wide white wing stripe

- **SONG** Display call is clear, repetitious *pee-wit, pee-wit*. Also makes low, throaty *grutto* and growling *wee-eeh*. Contact call is quiet, continuous *tuck* or *keck*.
- **BEHAVIOR** Gregarious. Feeds off dry land in warm weather and moves closer to water in autumn. Eats insects and their larvae and other invertebrates by probing with bill. When its nesting ground is invaded, it aggressively attacks intruder. 30–50 birds often perform synchronized flights with elaborate twists and turns.
- **BREEDING** Monogamous. Loosely colonial. Male has switchback display flight that includes impressive aerial acrobatics with midair tumbling, and rolling and frolicking on the ground.
- **NESTING** Incubation 22–24 days by both sexes. Precocial young leave nest soon after hatching. Tended by both sexes but feed themselves. First flight at 25–30 days. 1 brood per year.
- **POPULATION** Rare but consistent migrant on western Aleutians. Casual on Pribilofs and along Atlantic Coast.

Similar Birds

HUDSONIAN GODWIT
Black axillaries and underwing coverts; narrower upperwing stripe; slimmer tail; narrower white uppertail band.

BAR-TAILED GODWIT
More barring on upperparts; broad dark brown streaking on feathers; rufous-chestnut underparts; white rump; white-barred tail; uniformly dark wings without wing stripe; long, slightly upturned bill.

Flight Pattern

Swift, sometimes erratic flight often low over water.

Nest Identification

Shape ⚬⚬   Location ⚬⚬⚬ ⅏

On tussock hidden in tall grasses • lined with grass • built by female • 4 olive-green eggs blotched with brown; oval to elliptical, 2.2 inches long.

Plumage Sexes similar	Habitat 🌿 〰 🦆	Migration Migratory	Weight 8.9 ounces

DATE _____ TIME_____ LOCATION _____

Family SCOLOPACIDAE	Species *Limosa haemastica*	Length 15 inches	Wingspan 27 inches

HUDSONIAN GODWIT

On the shores of James Bay in Canada, thousands of these birds can be seen migrating together in late August. The male godwit is quiet during migration but has a noisy, complex display flight during breeding. The female is larger and duller with less barring. Both sexes are distinctive in flight with a white rump, a black tail with white base, a white wing stripe, and dusky black wing linings and axillaries. In winter the bird has a gray back and neck and whitish underparts.

brownish black back with white-tipped feathers giving scaly appearance

long pointed slightly upcurved creamy pink bill with black tip

black barring overall

dark chestnut underparts

dark blue-gray legs

black-and-white tail

WINTER PLUMAGE

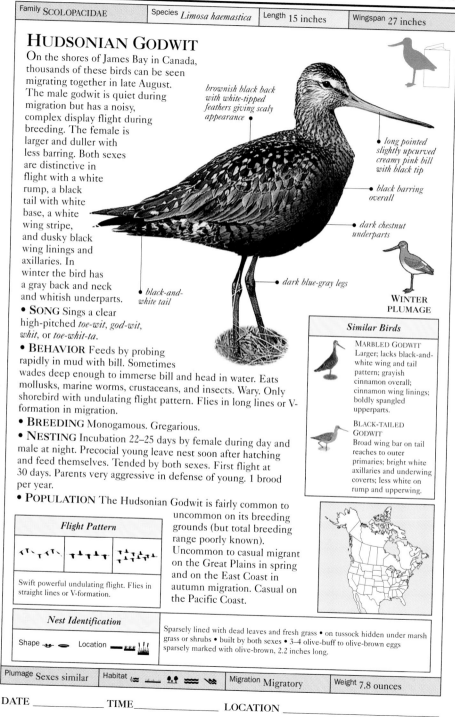

• **SONG** Sings a clear high-pitched *toe-wit, god-wit, whit*, or *toe-whit-ta*.

• **BEHAVIOR** Feeds by probing rapidly in mud with bill. Sometimes wades deep enough to immerse bill and head in water. Eats mollusks, marine worms, crustaceans, and insects. Wary. Only shorebird with undulating flight pattern. Flies in long lines or V-formation in migration.

• **BREEDING** Monogamous. Gregarious.

• **NESTING** Incubation 22–25 days by female during day and male at night. Precocial young leave nest soon after hatching and feed themselves. Tended by both sexes. First flight at 30 days. Parents very aggressive in defense of young. 1 brood per year.

• **POPULATION** The Hudsonian Godwit is fairly common to uncommon on its breeding grounds (but total breeding range poorly known). Uncommon to casual migrant on the Great Plains in spring and on the East Coast in autumn migration. Casual on the Pacific Coast.

Similar Birds

MARBLED GODWIT Larger; lacks black-and-white wing and tail pattern; grayish cinnamon overall; cinnamon wing linings; boldly spangled upperparts.

BLACK-TAILED GODWIT Broad wing bar on tail reaches to outer primaries; bright white axillaries and underwing coverts; less white on rump and upperwing.

Flight Pattern
Swift powerful undulating flight. Flies in straight lines or V-formation.

Nest Identification	
Shape ⌣ ⬭ Location ▬ ✦✦✦ ⩘⩗⩘	Sparsely lined with dead leaves and fresh grass • on tussock hidden under marsh grass or shrubs • built by both sexes • 3–4 olive-buff to olive-brown eggs sparsely marked with olive-brown, 2.2 inches long.

Plumage Sexes similar	Habitat	Migration Migratory	Weight 7.8 ounces

DATE _____ TIME_____ LOCATION _____

Family SCOLOPACIDAE	Species *Limosa lapponica*	Length 16 inches	Wingspan 28 inches

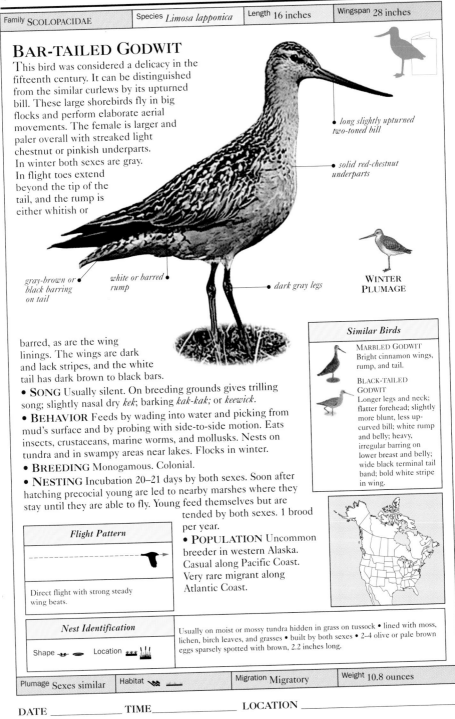

BAR-TAILED GODWIT

This bird was considered a delicacy in the fifteenth century. It can be distinguished from the similar curlews by its upturned bill. These large shorebirds fly in big flocks and perform elaborate aerial movements. The female is larger and paler overall with streaked light chestnut or pinkish underparts. In winter both sexes are gray. In flight toes extend beyond the tip of the tail, and the rump is either whitish or

long slightly upturned two-toned bill

solid red-chestnut underparts

gray-brown or black barring on tail

white or barred rump

dark gray legs

WINTER PLUMAGE

barred, as are the wing linings. The wings are dark and lack stripes, and the white tail has dark brown to black bars.

• **SONG** Usually silent. On breeding grounds gives trilling song; slightly nasal dry *kek*; barking *kak-kak*; or *keewick*.
• **BEHAVIOR** Feeds by wading into water and picking from mud's surface and by probing with side-to-side motion. Eats insects, crustaceans, marine worms, and mollusks. Nests on tundra and in swampy areas near lakes. Flocks in winter.
• **BREEDING** Monogamous. Colonial.
• **NESTING** Incubation 20–21 days by both sexes. Soon after hatching precocial young are led to nearby marshes where they stay until they are able to fly. Young feed themselves but are tended by both sexes. 1 brood per year.
• **POPULATION** Uncommon breeder in western Alaska. Casual along Pacific Coast. Very rare migrant along Atlantic Coast.

Similar Birds

MARBLED GODWIT
Bright cinnamon wings, rump, and tail.

BLACK-TAILED GODWIT
Longer legs and neck; flatter forehead; slightly more blunt, less up-curved bill; white rump and belly; heavy, irregular barring on lower breast and belly; wide black terminal tail band; bold white stripe in wing.

Flight Pattern

Direct flight with strong steady wing beats.

Nest Identification

Shape ⌣ ⬭   Location ▦▦▦ ⩗⩗⩗

Usually on moist or mossy tundra hidden in grass on tussock • lined with moss, lichen, birch leaves, and grasses • built by both sexes • 2–4 olive or pale brown eggs sparsely spotted with brown, 2.2 inches long.

Plumage Sexes similar	Habitat 〰 ▬	Migration Migratory	Weight 10.8 ounces

DATE _____ TIME_____ LOCATION _____

Family SCOLOPACIDAE	Species *Limosa fedoa*	Length 18–20 inches	Wingspan 32 inches

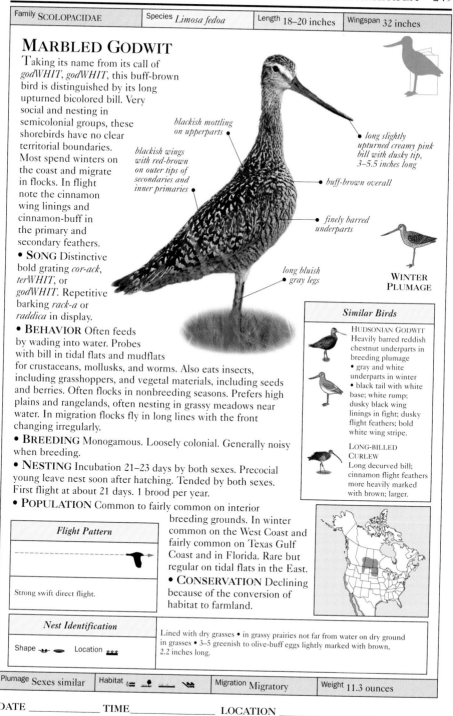

MARBLED GODWIT

Taking its name from its call of *godWHIT, godWHIT*, this buff-brown bird is distinguished by its long upturned bicolored bill. Very social and nesting in semicolonial groups, these shorebirds have no clear territorial boundaries. Most spend winters on the coast and migrate in flocks. In flight note the cinnamon wing linings and cinnamon-buff in the primary and secondary feathers.

blackish mottling on upperparts

blackish wings with red-brown on outer tips of secondaries and inner primaries

long slightly upturned creamy pink bill with dusky tip, 3–5.5 inches long

buff-brown overall

finely barred underparts

long bluish gray legs

WINTER PLUMAGE

• **SONG** Distinctive bold grating *cor-ack, terWHIT*, or *godWHIT*. Repetitive barking *rack-a* or *raddica* in display.

• **BEHAVIOR** Often feeds by wading into water. Probes with bill in tidal flats and mudflats for crustaceans, mollusks, and worms. Also eats insects, including grasshoppers, and vegetal materials, including seeds and berries. Often flocks in nonbreeding seasons. Prefers high plains and rangelands, often nesting in grassy meadows near water. In migration flocks fly in long lines with the front changing irregularly.

• **BREEDING** Monogamous. Loosely colonial. Generally noisy when breeding.

• **NESTING** Incubation 21–23 days by both sexes. Precocial young leave nest soon after hatching. Tended by both sexes. First flight at about 21 days. 1 brood per year.

• **POPULATION** Common to fairly common on interior breeding grounds. In winter common on the West Coast and fairly common on Texas Gulf Coast and in Florida. Rare but regular on tidal flats in the East.

• **CONSERVATION** Declining because of the conversion of habitat to farmland.

Similar Birds

HUDSONIAN GODWIT
Heavily barred reddish chestnut underparts in breeding plumage
• gray and white underparts in winter
• black tail with white base; white rump; dusky black wing linings in fight; dusky flight feathers; bold white wing stripe.

LONG-BILLED CURLEW
Long decurved bill; cinnamon flight feathers more heavily marked with brown; larger.

Flight Pattern
Strong swift direct flight.

Nest Identification	
Shape ᘛ ⬭ Location ▲▲▲	Lined with dry grasses • in grassy prairies not far from water on dry ground in grasses • 3–5 greenish to olive-buff eggs lightly marked with brown, 2.2 inches long.

Plumage Sexes similar	Habitat	Migration Migratory	Weight 11.3 ounces

DATE _____ TIME_____ LOCATION _____

Family SCOLOPACIDAE	Species *Arenaria interpres*	Length 9–10 inches	Wingspan 17–18 inches

RUDDY TURNSTONE

The alarm cry of this stout little ploverlike shorebird alerts other birds to possible danger. It often is seen probing the drift line on beaches, even cleaning up leftovers from beach picnics. Some will take bread from a human hand. In flight the vividly patterned body and wings are unmistakable in bold rusty reds, blacks, and white. Winter plumage shows a brown-and-white face, dull brown wings and back, and a brown bib but retains the striking white stripes on the wings, back, and tail.

black-and-white face

short pointed dark bill tilts up at tip

black, white, and rusty red harlequin-patterned wings and back

white chin

black bib on breast

white underparts

short orange-red legs (duller in winter)

WINTER PLUMAGE

• **SONG** Low guttural rattle. Alarm call is *chick-ik* or *kewk*. Flight call is *ket-ah-kek* or *kit-it-it*. While feeding gives contact call of *tut*.
• **BEHAVIOR** Roots through seaweed and tips over stones, shells, and other things washed up onto shore. Feeds on insects, mollusks, crustaceans and their eggs, worms, and bird eggs. Sometimes eats discards of birds such as oystercatchers, including carrion. May eat coconut meat as well. Forages alone or in small flocks often mixed with other shorebirds. Other shorebirds may nest near Turnstones to gain protection from predators.
• **BREEDING** Monogamous.
• **NESTING** Incubation 21–24 days by both sexes, but female does more. Precocial young leave nest soon after hatching but feed themselves. Tended by both sexes, but female leaves before first flight at 19–21 days. 1 brood per year.

Similar Birds

BLACK TURNSTONE
Dark chin; lacks chestnut or rust coloring; dark reddish brown legs • Alaskan and West Coast range.

• **POPULATION** Common and widespread on tundra breeding grounds and on coasts in winter. Casual to rare inland in migration, except around the Great Lakes where the species is more common.

Flight Pattern
Swift direct flight with rapid wing beats.

Nest Identification	Lined with bits of dry plants, withered leaves, moss, grass, or seaweed • in open tundra • built by female • 2–4 olive-green to olive-buff eggs marked with browns and blacks, 1.6 inches long.
Shape ⚬ Location ⦁⦁⦁ ▬	

Plumage Sexes similar	Habitat ___	Migration Migratory	Weight 3.9 ounces

DATE _____ TIME_____ LOCATION _____

| Family SCOLOPACIDAE | Species *Arenaria melanocephala* | Length 9 inches | Wingspan 17–18 inches |

BLACK TURNSTONE

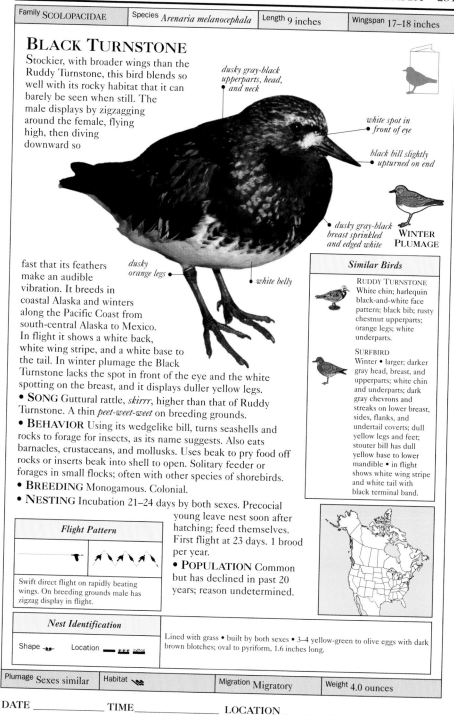

Stockier, with broader wings than the Ruddy Turnstone, this bird blends so well with its rocky habitat that it can barely be seen when still. The male displays by zigzagging around the female, flying high, then diving downward so

dusky gray-black upperparts, head, and neck

white spot in front of eye

black bill slightly upturned on end

dusky gray-black breast sprinkled and edged white

WINTER PLUMAGE

fast that its feathers make an audible vibration. It breeds in coastal Alaska and winters along the Pacific Coast from south-central Alaska to Mexico. In flight it shows a white back, white wing stripe, and a white base to the tail. In winter plumage the Black Turnstone lacks the spot in front of the eye and the white spotting on the breast, and it displays duller yellow legs.

dusky orange legs

white belly

• **SONG** Guttural rattle, *skirrr*, higher than that of Ruddy Turnstone. A thin *peet-weet-weet* on breeding grounds.
• **BEHAVIOR** Using its wedgelike bill, turns seashells and rocks to forage for insects, as its name suggests. Also eats barnacles, crustaceans, and mollusks. Uses beak to pry food off rocks or inserts beak into shell to open. Solitary feeder or forages in small flocks; often with other species of shorebirds.
• **BREEDING** Monogamous. Colonial.
• **NESTING** Incubation 21–24 days by both sexes. Precocial young leave nest soon after hatching; feed themselves. First flight at 23 days. 1 brood per year.
• **POPULATION** Common but has declined in past 20 years; reason undetermined.

Similar Birds

RUDDY TURNSTONE
White chin; harlequin black-and-white face pattern; black bib; rusty chestnut upperparts; orange legs; white underparts.

SURFBIRD
Winter • larger; darker gray head, breast, and upperparts; white chin and underparts; dark gray chevrons and streaks on lower breast, sides, flanks, and undertail coverts; dull yellow legs and feet; stouter bill has dull yellow base to lower mandible • in flight shows white wing stripe and white tail with black terminal band.

Flight Pattern

Swift direct flight on rapidly beating wings. On breeding grounds male has zigzag display in flight.

Nest Identification

Shape ⚲   Location ▬ ⚶⚶⚶ ⚶⚶⚶

Lined with grass • built by both sexes • 3–4 yellow-green to olive eggs with dark brown blotches; oval to pyriform, 1.6 inches long.

| Plumage Sexes similar | Habitat 〰 | Migration Migratory | Weight 4.0 ounces |

DATE _____ TIME_____ LOCATION _____

| Family SCOLOPACIDAE | Species *Aphriza virgata* | Length 10 inches | Wingspan 20 inches |

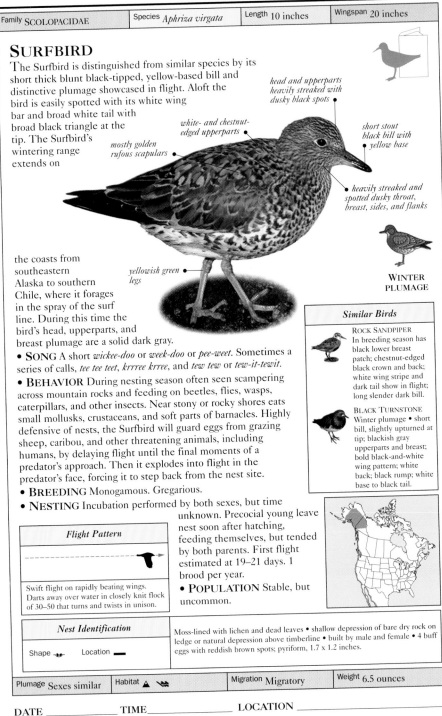

SURFBIRD

The Surfbird is distinguished from similar species by its short thick blunt black-tipped, yellow-based bill and distinctive plumage showcased in flight. Aloft the bird is easily spotted with its white wing bar and broad white tail with broad black triangle at the tip. The Surfbird's wintering range extends on the coasts from southeastern Alaska to southern Chile, where it forages in the spray of the surf line. During this time the bird's head, upperparts, and breast plumage are a solid dark gray.

head and upperparts heavily streaked with dusky black spots

white- and chestnut-edged upperparts

mostly golden rufous scapulars

short stout black bill with yellow base

heavily streaked and spotted dusky throat, breast, sides, and flanks

yellowish green legs

WINTER PLUMAGE

- **SONG** A short *wickee-doo* or *week-doo* or *pee-weet*. Sometimes a series of calls, *tee tee teet*, *krrree krree*, and *tew tew* or *tew-it-tewit*.
- **BEHAVIOR** During nesting season often seen scampering across mountain rocks and feeding on beetles, flies, wasps, caterpillars, and other insects. Near stony or rocky shores eats small mollusks, crustaceans, and soft parts of barnacles. Highly defensive of nests, the Surfbird will guard eggs from grazing sheep, caribou, and other threatening animals, including humans, by delaying flight until the final moments of a predator's approach. Then it explodes into flight in the predator's face, forcing it to step back from the nest site.
- **BREEDING** Monogamous. Gregarious.
- **NESTING** Incubation performed by both sexes, but time unknown. Precocial young leave nest soon after hatching, feeding themselves, but tended by both parents. First flight estimated at 19–21 days. 1 brood per year.
- **POPULATION** Stable, but uncommon.

Similar Birds

ROCK SANDPIPER
In breeding season has black lower breast patch; chestnut-edged black crown and back; white wing stripe and dark tail show in flight; long slender dark bill.

BLACK TURNSTONE
Winter plumage • short bill, slightly upturned at tip; blackish gray upperparts and breast; bold black-and-white wing pattern; white back; black rump; white base to black tail.

Flight Pattern

Swift flight on rapidly beating wings. Darts away over water in closely knit flock of 30–50 that turns and twists in unison.

Nest Identification

Shape ⌣ Location ▬

Moss-lined with lichen and dead leaves • shallow depression of bare dry rock on ledge or natural depression above timberline • built by male and female • 4 buff eggs with reddish brown spots; pyriform, 1.7 x 1.2 inches.

| Plumage Sexes similar | Habitat ▲ 🦅 | Migration Migratory | Weight 6.5 ounces |

DATE _____ TIME _____ LOCATION _____

Family SCOLOPACIDAE	Species *Calidris tenuirostris*	Length 11 inches	Wingspan 22 inches

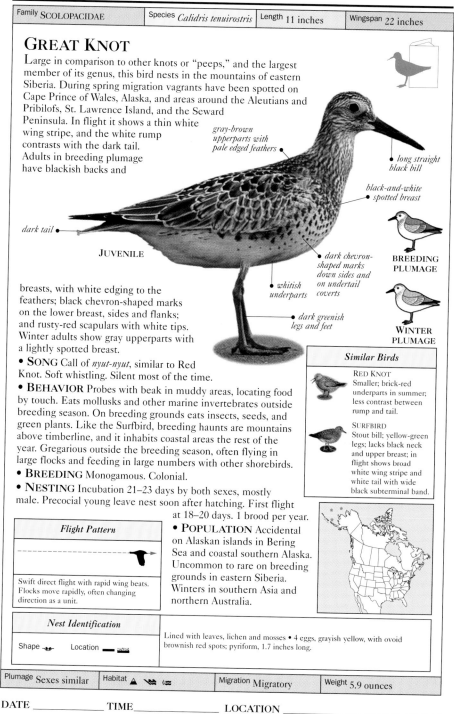

GREAT KNOT

Large in comparison to other knots or "peeps," and the largest member of its genus, this bird nests in the mountains of eastern Siberia. During spring migration vagrants have been spotted on Cape Prince of Wales, Alaska, and areas around the Aleutians and Pribilofs, St. Lawrence Island, and the Seward Peninsula. In flight it shows a thin white wing stripe, and the white rump contrasts with the dark tail. Adults in breeding plumage have blackish backs and

gray-brown upperparts with pale edged feathers

long straight black bill

black-and-white spotted breast

dark tail

JUVENILE

dark chevron-shaped marks down sides and on undertail coverts

BREEDING PLUMAGE

whitish underparts

dark greenish legs and feet

WINTER PLUMAGE

breasts, with white edging to the feathers; black chevron-shaped marks on the lower breast, sides and flanks; and rusty-red scapulars with white tips. Winter adults show gray upperparts with a lightly spotted breast.

- **SONG** Call of *nyut-nyut*, similar to Red Knot. Soft whistling. Silent most of the time.
- **BEHAVIOR** Probes with beak in muddy areas, locating food by touch. Eats mollusks and other marine invertebrates outside breeding season. On breeding grounds eats insects, seeds, and green plants. Like the Surfbird, breeding haunts are mountains above timberline, and it inhabits coastal areas the rest of the year. Gregarious outside the breeding season, often flying in large flocks and feeding in large numbers with other shorebirds.
- **BREEDING** Monogamous. Colonial.
- **NESTING** Incubation 21–23 days by both sexes, mostly male. Precocial young leave nest soon after hatching. First flight at 18–20 days. 1 brood per year.
- **POPULATION** Accidental on Alaskan islands in Bering Sea and coastal southern Alaska. Uncommon to rare on breeding grounds in eastern Siberia. Winters in southern Asia and northern Australia.

Similar Birds

RED KNOT
Smaller; brick-red underparts in summer; less contrast between rump and tail.

SURFBIRD
Stout bill; yellow-green legs; lacks black neck and upper breast; in flight shows broad white wing stripe and white tail with wide black subterminal band.

Flight Pattern

Swift direct flight with rapid wing beats. Flocks move rapidly, often changing direction as a unit.

Nest Identification

Shape   Location

Lined with leaves, lichen and mosses • 4 eggs, grayish yellow, with ovoid brownish red spots; pyriform, 1.7 inches long.

Plumage Sexes similar	Habitat	Migration Migratory	Weight 5.9 ounces

DATE _____ TIME_____ LOCATION _____

Family SCOLOPACIDAE	Species *Calidris canutus*	Length 10–11 inches	Wingspan 20 inches

RED KNOT

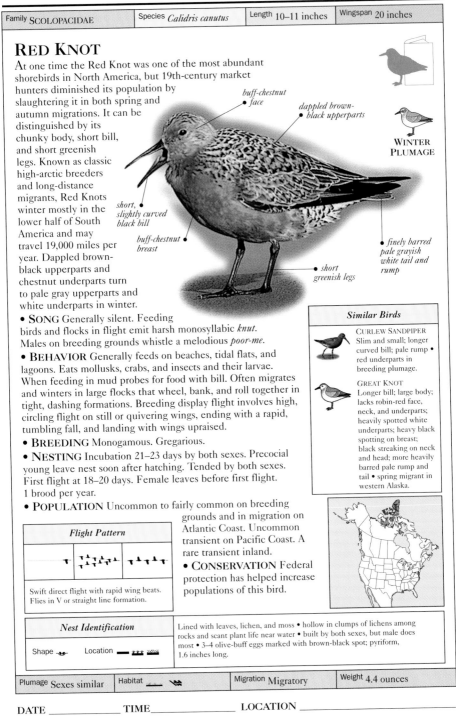

At one time the Red Knot was one of the most abundant shorebirds in North America, but 19th-century market hunters diminished its population by slaughtering it in both spring and autumn migrations. It can be distinguished by its chunky body, short bill, and short greenish legs. Known as classic high-arctic breeders and long-distance migrants, Red Knots winter mostly in the lower half of South America and may travel 19,000 miles per year. Dappled brown-black upperparts and chestnut underparts turn to pale gray upperparts and white underparts in winter.

buff-chestnut face

dappled brown-black upperparts

WINTER PLUMAGE

short, slightly curved black bill

buff-chestnut breast

finely barred pale grayish white tail and rump

short greenish legs

• **SONG** Generally silent. Feeding birds and flocks in flight emit harsh monosyllabic *knut*. Males on breeding grounds whistle a melodious *poor-me*.
• **BEHAVIOR** Generally feeds on beaches, tidal flats, and lagoons. Eats mollusks, crabs, and insects and their larvae. When feeding in mud probes for food with bill. Often migrates and winters in large flocks that wheel, bank, and roll together in tight, dashing formations. Breeding display flight involves high, circling flight on still or quivering wings, ending with a rapid, tumbling fall, and landing with wings upraised.
• **BREEDING** Monogamous. Gregarious.
• **NESTING** Incubation 21–23 days by both sexes. Precocial young leave nest soon after hatching. Tended by both sexes. First flight at 18–20 days. Female leaves before first flight. 1 brood per year.
• **POPULATION** Uncommon to fairly common on breeding grounds and in migration on Atlantic Coast. Uncommon transient on Pacific Coast. A rare transient inland.
• **CONSERVATION** Federal protection has helped increase populations of this bird.

Similar Birds

CURLEW SANDPIPER
Slim and small; longer curved bill; pale rump • red underparts in breeding plumage.

GREAT KNOT
Longer bill; large body; lacks robin-red face, neck, and underparts; heavily spotted white underparts; heavy black spotting on breast; black streaking on neck and head; more heavily barred pale rump and tail • spring migrant in western Alaska.

Flight Pattern

Swift direct flight with rapid wing beats. Flies in V or straight line formation.

Nest Identification	Lined with leaves, lichen, and moss • hollow in clumps of lichens among rocks and scant plant life near water • built by both sexes, but male does most • 3–4 olive-buff eggs marked with brown-black spot; pyriform, 1.6 inches long.
Shape ⚬ Location ▬ ⁂ ▨	

Plumage Sexes similar	Habitat ⌇ ❧	Migration Migratory	Weight 4.4 ounces

DATE _____ TIME_____ LOCATION _____

| Family SCOLOPACIDAE | Species *Calidris alba* | Length 8 inches | Wingspan 15 inches |

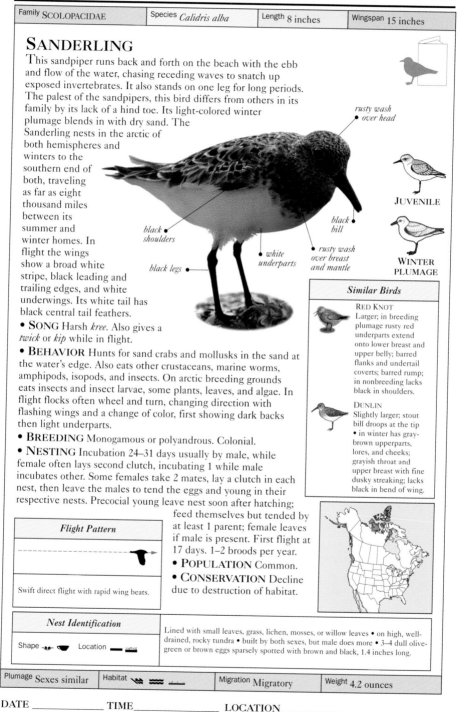

SANDERLING

This sandpiper runs back and forth on the beach with the ebb and flow of the water, chasing receding waves to snatch up exposed invertebrates. It also stands on one leg for long periods. The palest of the sandpipers, this bird differs from others in its family by its lack of a hind toe. Its light-colored winter plumage blends in with dry sand. The Sanderling nests in the arctic of both hemispheres and winters to the southern end of both, traveling as far as eight thousand miles between its summer and winter homes. In flight the wings show a broad white stripe, black leading and trailing edges, and white underwings. Its white tail has black central tail feathers.

rusty wash over head

JUVENILE

WINTER PLUMAGE

black shoulders

black legs

white underparts

black bill

rusty wash over breast and mantle

• **SONG** Harsh *kree*. Also gives a *twick* or *kip* while in flight.

• **BEHAVIOR** Hunts for sand crabs and mollusks in the sand at the water's edge. Also eats other crustaceans, marine worms, amphipods, isopods, and insects. On arctic breeding grounds eats insects and insect larvae, some plants, leaves, and algae. In flight flocks often wheel and turn, changing direction with flashing wings and a change of color, first showing dark backs then light underparts.

• **BREEDING** Monogamous or polyandrous. Colonial.

• **NESTING** Incubation 24–31 days usually by male, while female often lays second clutch, incubating 1 while male incubates other. Some females take 2 mates, lay a clutch in each nest, then leave the males to tend the eggs and young in their respective nests. Precocial young leave nest soon after hatching; feed themselves but tended by at least 1 parent; female leaves if male is present. First flight at 17 days. 1–2 broods per year.

• **POPULATION** Common.

• **CONSERVATION** Decline due to destruction of habitat.

Similar Birds

RED KNOT
Larger; in breeding plumage rusty red underparts extend onto lower breast and upper belly; barred flanks and undertail coverts; barred rump; in nonbreeding lacks black in shoulders.

DUNLIN
Slightly larger; stout bill droops at the tip
• in winter has gray-brown upperparts, lores, and cheeks; grayish throat and upper breast with fine dusky streaking; lacks black in bend of wing.

Flight Pattern

Swift direct flight with rapid wing beats.

Nest Identification

Shape ⌣ ⌣   Location ▬ ▬

Lined with small leaves, grass, lichen, mosses, or willow leaves • on high, well-drained, rocky tundra • built by both sexes, but male does more • 3–4 dull olive-green or brown eggs sparsely spotted with brown and black, 1.4 inches long.

| Plumage Sexes similar | Habitat ⩲ ⩲ ⌣ | Migration Migratory | Weight 4.2 ounces |

DATE _____ TIME_____ LOCATION _____

Family SCOLOPACIDAE	Species *Calidris pusilla*	Length 6.5 inches	Wingspan 11–13 inches

SEMIPALMATED SANDPIPER

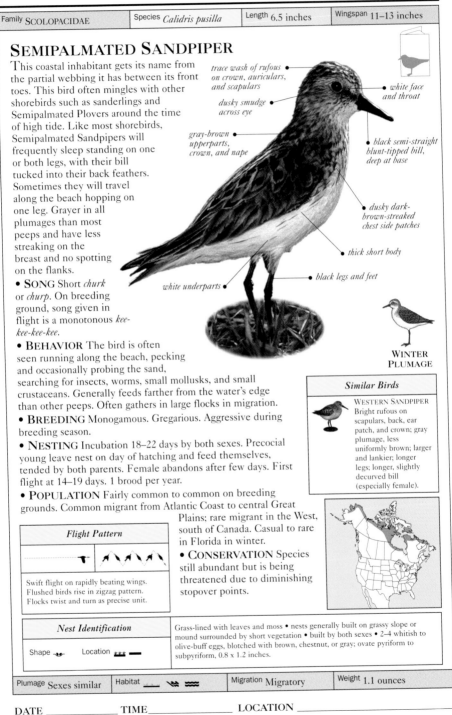

This coastal inhabitant gets its name from the partial webbing it has between its front toes. This bird often mingles with other shorebirds such as sanderlings and Semipalmated Plovers around the time of high tide. Like most shorebirds, Semipalmated Sandpipers will frequently sleep standing on one or both legs, with their bill tucked into their back feathers. Sometimes they will travel along the beach hopping on one leg. Grayer in all plumages than most peeps and have less streaking on the breast and no spotting on the flanks.

trace wash of rufous on crown, auriculars, and scapulars

dusky smudge across eye

gray-brown upperparts, crown, and nape

white face and throat

black semi-straight blunt-tipped bill, deep at base

dusky dark-brown-streaked chest side patches

thick short body

black legs and feet

white underparts

WINTER PLUMAGE

- **SONG** Short *churk* or *churp*. On breeding ground, song given in flight is a monotonous *kee-kee-kee-kee*.
- **BEHAVIOR** The bird is often seen running along the beach, pecking and occasionally probing the sand, searching for insects, worms, small mollusks, and small crustaceans. Generally feeds farther from the water's edge than other peeps. Often gathers in large flocks in migration.
- **BREEDING** Monogamous. Gregarious. Aggressive during breeding season.
- **NESTING** Incubation 18–22 days by both sexes. Precocial young leave nest on day of hatching and feed themselves, tended by both parents. Female abandons after few days. First flight at 14–19 days. 1 brood per year.
- **POPULATION** Fairly common to common on breeding grounds. Common migrant from Atlantic Coast to central Great Plains; rare migrant in the West, south of Canada. Casual to rare in Florida in winter.
- **CONSERVATION** Species still abundant but is being threatened due to diminishing stopover points.

Similar Birds

WESTERN SANDPIPER Bright rufous on scapulars, back, ear patch, and crown; gray plumage, less uniformly brown; larger and lankier; longer legs; longer, slightly decurved bill (especially female).

Flight Pattern

Swift flight on rapidly beating wings. Flushed birds rise in zigzag pattern. Flocks twist and turn as precise unit.

Nest Identification	Grass-lined with leaves and moss • nests generally built on grassy slope or mound surrounded by short vegetation • built by both sexes • 2–4 whitish to olive-buff eggs, blotched with brown, chestnut, or gray; ovate pyriform to subpyriform, 0.8 x 1.2 inches.
Shape �= Location ⬩⬩⬩ ▬	

Plumage Sexes similar	Habitat ___ ⬤⬤ ≈≈	Migration Migratory	Weight 1.1 ounces

DATE _____ TIME_____ LOCATION _____

Family SCOLOPACIDAE	Species *Calidris mauri*	Length 6–7 inches	Wingspan 12–14 inches

WESTERN SANDPIPER

A long-distance migrant, the Western Sandpiper flies southeast and remains on North and South American coasts during the winter months. It is the western relative of the Semipalmated Sandpiper, which it closely resembles

bright rufous crown

rufous base of scapulars

bright rufous ear patches

long tapered black bill slightly drooped at the tip

arrow-shaped spots on sides

partially webbed toes

black legs and feet

WINTER PLUMAGE

except for a longer bill that usually appears slightly drooped at the tip. In breeding plumage it has arrow-shaped spots on the sides and breast and rufous on the crown, ear patches, and scapulars. In winter plumage it is one of the palest "peeps," with almost no contrast in the faintly mottled upperparts.

- **SONG** High raspy *jeet* or *cheet*.
- **BEHAVIOR** Often can be identified by a distinctive feeding pattern: while snatching invertebrates it occasionally eats with its head immersed in the water. Feeds primarily on insects but also takes small crustaceans, mollusks, and worms. In migration and on wintering grounds, often occurs in large flocks. Coastal outside breeding season, but fairly common inland in migration.
- **BREEDING** Monogamous. Colonial. Highly gregarious.
- **NESTING** Incubation 18–21 days by both sexes. Precocial young leave nest a few hours after hatching. Female departs, but male tends young. Young feed themselves. First flight at 17–21 days. 1 brood per year.
- **POPULATION** Common to abundant on breeding grounds; common in migration and on US coastal wintering grounds.
- **CONSERVATION** Abundant but still vulnerable to habitat loss at stopover points.

Similar Birds

SEMIPALMATED SANDPIPER
Shorter bill without drooped tip; duller in color; less rufous; faint or nonexistent mantle and scapular lines; dark brown upperparts edged with buff; makes harsh *churk*.

LEAST SANDPIPER
Smaller; brown wash on head, head, neck, and breast with dark brown streaking; yellow-green legs and feet.

Flight Pattern

Swift direct flight with rapid wing beats. Large tight flocks twist and turn in coordinated movements.

Nest Identification

Shape ⚬ Location ✦

Lined with leaves, grass, and lichens • slightly elevated on moist or dry tundra near water • male hollows out several sites; female chooses one and lines nest • 3–5 whitish brown eggs marked with red-brown spots; pyriform, 0.87 x 1.2 inches.

Plumage Sexes similar	Habitat	Migration Migratory	Weight 0.8 ounce

DATE _____ TIME_____ LOCATION _____

Family SCOLOPACIDAE	Species *Calidris ruficollis*	Length 6.25 inches	Wingspan 11–12 inches

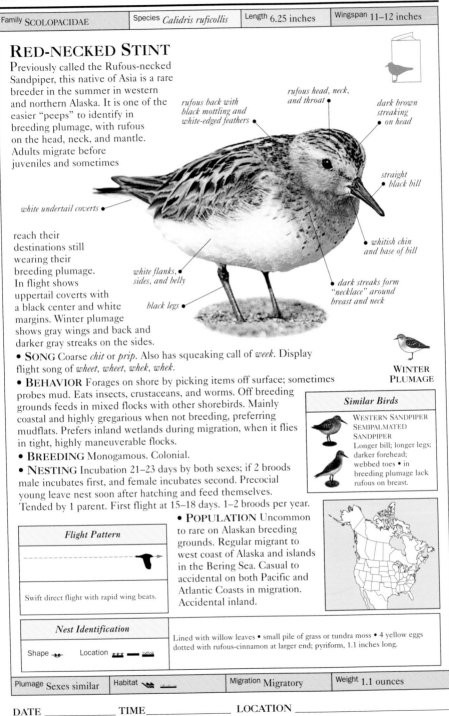

RED-NECKED STINT

Previously called the Rufous-necked Sandpiper, this native of Asia is a rare breeder in the summer in western and northern Alaska. It is one of the easier "peeps" to identify in breeding plumage, with rufous on the head, neck, and mantle. Adults migrate before juveniles and sometimes

rufous back with black mottling and white-edged feathers

rufous head, neck, and throat

dark brown streaking on head

straight black bill

white undertail coverts

whitish chin and base of bill

reach their destinations still wearing their breeding plumage. In flight shows uppertail coverts with a black center and white margins. Winter plumage shows gray wings and back and darker gray streaks on the sides.

white flanks, sides, and belly

black legs

dark streaks form "necklace" around breast and neck

- **SONG** Coarse *chit* or *prip*. Also has squeaking call of *week*. Display flight song of *wheet, wheet, whek, whek*.
- **BEHAVIOR** Forages on shore by picking items off surface; sometimes probes mud. Eats insects, crustaceans, and worms. Off breeding grounds feeds in mixed flocks with other shorebirds. Mainly coastal and highly gregarious when not breeding, preferring mudflats. Prefers inland wetlands during migration, when it flies in tight, highly maneuverable flocks.
- **BREEDING** Monogamous. Colonial.
- **NESTING** Incubation 21–23 days by both sexes; if 2 broods male incubates first, and female incubates second. Precocial young leave nest soon after hatching and feed themselves. Tended by 1 parent. First flight at 15–18 days. 1–2 broods per year.

WINTER PLUMAGE

Similar Birds

WESTERN SANDPIPER
SEMIPALMATED SANDPIPER
Longer bill; longer legs; darker forehead; webbed toes • in breeding plumage lack rufous on breast.

- **POPULATION** Uncommon to rare on Alaskan breeding grounds. Regular migrant to west coast of Alaska and islands in the Bering Sea. Casual to accidental on both Pacific and Atlantic Coasts in migration. Accidental inland.

Flight Pattern

Swift direct flight with rapid wing beats.

Nest Identification

Shape Location

Lined with willow leaves • small pile of grass or tundra moss • 4 yellow eggs dotted with rufous-cinnamon at larger end; pyriform, 1.1 inches long.

Plumage Sexes similar	Habitat	Migration Migratory	Weight 1.1 ounces

DATE _____ TIME _____ LOCATION _____

Family SCOLOPACIDAE	Species *Calidris minuta*	Length 6 inches	Wingspan 11–12 inches

LITTLE STINT

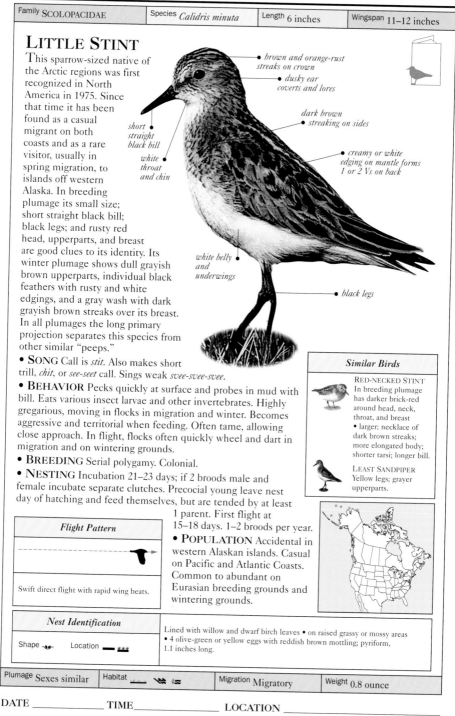

This sparrow-sized native of the Arctic regions was first recognized in North America in 1975. Since that time it has been found as a casual migrant on both coasts and as a rare visitor, usually in spring migration, to islands off western Alaska. In breeding plumage its small size; short straight black bill; black legs; and rusty red head, upperparts, and breast are good clues to its identity. Its winter plumage shows dull grayish brown upperparts, individual black feathers with rusty and white edgings, and a gray wash with dark grayish brown streaks over its breast. In all plumages the long primary projection separates this species from other similar "peeps."

brown and orange-rust streaks on crown

dusky ear coverts and lores

dark brown streaking on sides

short straight black bill

white throat and chin

creamy or white edging on mantle forms 1 or 2 Vs on back

white belly and underwings

black legs

- **SONG** Call is *stit*. Also makes short trill, *chit*, or *see-seet* call. Sings weak *svee-svee-svee*.
- **BEHAVIOR** Pecks quickly at surface and probes in mud with bill. Eats various insect larvae and other invertebrates. Highly gregarious, moving in flocks in migration and winter. Becomes aggressive and territorial when feeding. Often tame, allowing close approach. In flight, flocks often quickly wheel and dart in migration and on wintering grounds.
- **BREEDING** Serial polygamy. Colonial.
- **NESTING** Incubation 21–23 days; if 2 broods male and female incubate separate clutches. Precocial young leave nest day of hatching and feed themselves, but are tended by at least 1 parent. First flight at 15–18 days. 1–2 broods per year.
- **POPULATION** Accidental in western Alaskan islands. Casual on Pacific and Atlantic Coasts. Common to abundant on Eurasian breeding grounds and wintering grounds.

Similar Birds

RED-NECKED STINT
In breeding plumage has darker brick-red around head, neck, throat, and breast
- larger; necklace of dark brown streaks; more elongated body; shorter tarsi; longer bill.

LEAST SANDPIPER
Yellow legs; grayer upperparts.

Flight Pattern
Swift direct flight with rapid wing beats.

Nest Identification	
Shape ⚬ Location ▬ ✳✳✳	Lined with willow and dwarf birch leaves • on raised grassy or mossy areas • 4 olive-green or yellow eggs with reddish brown mottling; pyriform, 1.1 inches long.

Plumage Sexes similar	Habitat ▬▬ 🦆 ⟆	Migration Migratory	Weight 0.8 ounce

Family SCOLOPACIDAE	Species *Calidris subminuta*	Length 5–6 inches	Wingspan 11–12 inches

LONG-TOED STINT

Longer toes, particularly middle and hind digits, easily distinguish this East Asian shorebird from other stints and "peeps." However, this is a very difficult characteristic to see in the field. More useful field marks are the long neck, rufous cap, white superciliary stripe, and dark forehead extending to the base of the bill, sometimes joining the dusky lores. The legs and feet are yellow-green. Juveniles are similar to breeding adults, which have a buffy wash on the breast and a dark eye stripe expanding into a dark auricular patch. A long-distance migrant, this bird winters on the coasts of India, Asia, and Australia. In flight it shows a narrow white wing stripe and a gray tail with dark central tail feathers.

dark rufous-brown-streaked crown

gray-brown and rufous-buff-edged upperparts

thin blackish bill

green base to lower mandible

gray-brown-streaked breast and neck

white underparts

JUVENILE

• **SONG** Slow repeated *roer*. Most common call is soft bubbling brief *prrt*, *chrrup*, or *chulip*. Other calls include grating *tik-tik-tik*.

• **BEHAVIOR** Frequents grassy swampy regions and alpine tundra. Feeds in small flocks or alone, either slowly and mouselike or actively with quick little runs. Eats a variety of invertebrates in vegetation at water's edge. Lures intruders from nest with intensive distraction display. When alarmed, freezes crouched flat or stands upright with neck extended.

• **BREEDING** Monogamous. Colonial. Displaying male circles high while singing.

• **NESTING** Incubation 18–22 days by both sexes. Precocial young leave nest few hours after hatching and feed themselves. Female often deserts, leaving male to care for young. First flight at 17–21 days. 1 brood per year.

• **POPULATION** Uncommon to rare in native Eurasia. Casual in migration to islands in Bering Sea; fairly common in spring migration on outer Aleutians. Rare to accidental on West Coast and elsewhere.

• **CONSERVATION** Common to fairly common, though vulnerable to habitat loss at stopover grounds.

Similar Birds

LITTLE STINT
Smaller and darker black legs; shorter toes; similar coloring; short straight bill; rufous upperparts and sides of breast, with dark spotting pattern; white underparts.

LEAST SANDPIPER
Closely resembles; mouselike bird; medium-length slightly decurved bill; gray-brown head, chest, and upperparts; white underparts; indistinct whitish supercilium; yellow legs and feet.

Flight Pattern

Swift direct flight with rapid wing beats. If flushed rises quickly with fast jerking flight, wing beats weak and fluttery.

Nest Identification

Shape ___ Location ▬

Grass- and leaf-lined with sedges and lichen • on slightly elevated moist to dry tundra by water, usually under shrub • male builds several scrapes, female chooses one and lines • 3–5 whitish brown eggs, marked with red-brown spots; pyriform to subpyriform, 1.2 x 0.9 inches.

Plumage Sexes similar	Habitat	Migration Migratory	Weight 1.1 ounces

DATE _____ TIME_____ LOCATION _____

Family SCOLOPACIDAE	Species *Calidris minutilla*	Length 6 inches	Wingspan 11–12 inches

LEAST SANDPIPER

During migration a small sandpiper on the edge of an inland pool or wet area is likely to be this species. The Least Sandpiper is the smallest of the native North American sandpipers and among the smallest waders

streaked dark neck

brown-gray upperparts

slender slightly decurved dark bill

streaked dark breast

white belly

white undertail coverts

pale green-yellow legs

WINTER PLUMAGE

in the world. These tame birds will walk close to humans along the shore. With a buff-brown wash on its streaked breast, it is one of the brownest and darkest of the "peeps." The legs and feet are dull yellowish or greenish yellow rather than black like those of most small North American sandpipers.

• **SONG** High *kneet* or *knee-eet*.

• **BEHAVIOR** Usually found in wet habitats where it obtains food by picking small animals from surface of mud and by probing mud for insects, insect larvae, and small crustaceans. Gregarious, occurring in small to large flocks. Often mixes and forages with other species of shorebirds, especially in migration and on wintering grounds. Relatively tame. Migrates at night. When flushed often rises quickly in zigzag fashion.

• **BREEDING** Monogamous. Colonial. Male announces territory by singing continuously, often for several minutes, in display flight.

• **NESTING** Incubation 19–23 days by both sexes (female at night; male during day; male does more). Precocial young leave nest day of hatching and feed themselves. Tended by both sexes. First flight at 14–16 days. 1 brood per year.

• **POPULATION** Common.

Similar Birds

SEMIPALMATED SANDPIPER
Slightly larger; straighter bill; whiter face, throat, and chest; black legs.

WESTERN SANDPIPER
Larger; long bill is heavier at base and slightly downcurved at tip; rustier back, ear patch, and crown; black legs • in breeding plumage has more heavily streaked breast.

Flight Pattern

Swift direct flight with rapid wing beats. When flushed often rises quickly in zigzag fashion.

Nest Identification

Shape ⚬ Location ••• ▬

Lined with grass and dry leaves • on small pile of grass or moss near water • male begins building; female finishes • 3–4 olive, pinkish, or buff eggs with dark brown spots; ovate pyriform, 1.2 x 0.85 inches.

Plumage Sexes similar	Habitat ▲♠ ▬ ▬ ▬	Migration Migratory	Weight 0.8 ounce

DATE _____ TIME_____ LOCATION _____

Family SCOLOPACIDAE	Species *Calidris fuscicollis*	Length 7–8 inches	Wingspan 14–16.5 inches

WHITE-RUMPED SANDPIPER

The white rump, best seen in flight, can sometimes be glimpsed on a standing bird when it spreads its wings slightly. At rest the wing tips extend well beyond the tail. In flight the rump is a distinctive field mark shared by only one other small sandpiper, the Curlew Sandpiper (a casual to rare Eurasian species). A long-distance champion flier, this bird migrates from the Canadian Arctic to southern South America, a distance of more than eight thousand miles. It appears larger in flight than it does on the ground. Crown and back are rusty.

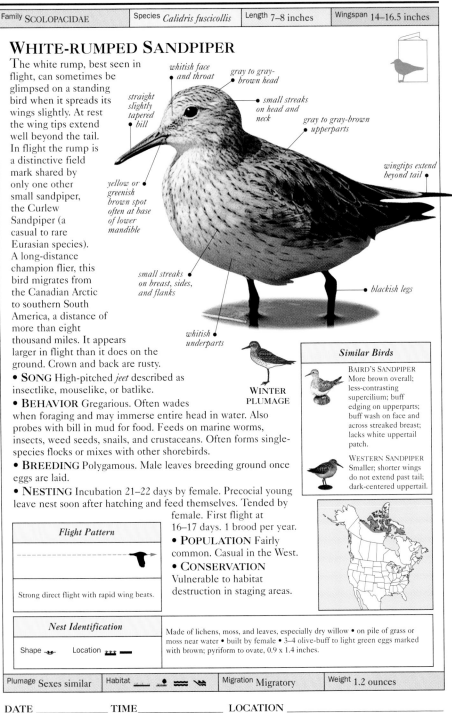

whitish face and throat

gray to gray-brown head

straight slightly tapered bill

small streaks on head and neck

gray to gray-brown upperparts

wingtips extend beyond tail

yellow or greenish brown spot often at base of lower mandible

small streaks on breast, sides, and flanks

blackish legs

whitish underparts

WINTER PLUMAGE

• **SONG** High-pitched *jeet* described as insectlike, mouselike, or batlike.
• **BEHAVIOR** Gregarious. Often wades when foraging and may immerse entire head in water. Also probes with bill in mud for food. Feeds on marine worms, insects, weed seeds, snails, and crustaceans. Often forms single-species flocks or mixes with other shorebirds.
• **BREEDING** Polygamous. Male leaves breeding ground once eggs are laid.
• **NESTING** Incubation 21–22 days by female. Precocial young leave nest soon after hatching and feed themselves. Tended by female. First flight at 16–17 days. 1 brood per year.
• **POPULATION** Fairly common. Casual in the West.
• **CONSERVATION** Vulnerable to habitat destruction in staging areas.

Similar Birds

BAIRD'S SANDPIPER
More brown overall; less-contrasting supercilium; buff edging on upperparts; buff wash on face and across streaked breast; lacks white uppertail patch.

WESTERN SANDPIPER
Smaller; shorter wings do not extend past tail; dark-centered uppertail.

Flight Pattern
Strong direct flight with rapid wing beats.

Nest Identification	
Shape ⌣ Location ⁂ ▬	Made of lichens, moss, and leaves, especially dry willow • on pile of grass or moss near water • built by female • 3–4 olive-buff to light green eggs marked with brown; pyriform to ovate, 0.9 x 1.4 inches.

Plumage Sexes similar	Habitat	Migration Migratory	Weight 1.2 ounces

DATE _____ TIME_____ LOCATION _____

Family SCOLOPACIDAE	Species *Calidris bairdii*	Length 7.5 inches	Wingspan 15–16.5 inches

BAIRD'S SANDPIPER

In early autumn large flocks of these thrush-sized birds gather on the Great Plains and fly to South America. Although they often join other small sandpipers during migration, these birds will separate from those flocks and feed by themselves. This buff sandpiper has black legs and long wings that protrude well beyond the tip of the tail when standing. Its rump and uppertail are broadly dark-centered with very narrow whitish sides. Winter plumage shows more gray and less streaking, but the combination of short bill, short legs, and long wings distinguish it.

buff head with fine streaks

indistinct pale eye stripe

streaked back with scaly appearance

straight dark bill slightly drooped at tip

buff breast with fine streaks

wingtips extend beyond tail

blackish legs and feet

white underparts

WINTER PLUMAGE

• **SONG** Low raspy *kreep* or *preeet*.
• **BEHAVIOR** Fairly tame. Essentially an inland species in migration. On migration prefers to feed in higher and dryer areas than other small sandpipers. Runs across mud and through shallow water, picking up bits of food. Does not probe with bill. Eats algae, amphipods, insects, and insect larvae. Sometimes flies in mixed flocks with other shorebirds.
• **BREEDING** Monogamous. Less gregarious than most other birds in genus.
• **NESTING** Incubation 19–22 days by both sexes. Precocial young leave nest soon after hatching. Tended by both sexes. First flight at 16–20 days. 1 brood per year.
• **POPULATION** Fairly common inland; uncommon on both coasts in migration.
• **CONSERVATION** Vulnerable to habitat changes on staging areas.

Similar Birds

WHITE-RUMPED SANDPIPER Brighter breeding and juvenile plumage with rusty wash on crown and back • grayer nonbreeding plumage • streaking on underparts to flanks; lacks buff wash on head and breast; white tail base.

LEAST SANDPIPER Smaller; shorter, thinner bill; dull yellow legs.

Flight Pattern
Swift direct flight with rapid wing beats.

Nest Identification	
Shape	Location

No nest material • under low plants or moss-covered rocks or on small pile of grass • 4 pink to olive-buff eggs marked with dark browns; pyriform, 0.9 x 1.4 inches.

Plumage Sexes similar	Habitat	Migration Migratory	Weight 1.4 ounces

DATE _____ TIME_____ LOCATION _____

Family SCOLOPACIDAE	Species *Calidris melanotos*	Length 8–9 inches	Wingspan 15–16 inches

PECTORAL SANDPIPER

This bird is named for the two saclike structures under the neck and breast of the male. During courtship the male inflates these sacs, thus enhancing the appearance of the heavy streaking on its breast. The streaking ends abruptly in a sharp line, separating it from the snow-white belly. During flight the sacs pump up and down in rhythm with the bird's hooting calls. In flight this bird shows a blackish brown rump and tail. Males and females are similar but the male has darker brown streaking on the throat and breast with white mottling. Winter plumage is pale brown overall.

dark brown crown with black, chestnut, and pale olive-brown stripes

white stripe over each eye

thin white stripes on back and scapulars

slender black bill with greenish yellow base to lower mandible

streaked brown breast

scapular, tertial, and mantle feathers have blackish brown centers with chestnut to buff fringes

whitish underparts

greenish yellow legs

• **SONG** Low reedy *churk* or *churrrt*. Male has hooting courtship call; murmuring foghornlike *khoor, khoor*; or loud coarse *gr, gr, gr* repeated several times per second.

• **BEHAVIOR** Forages in vegetation. Feeds by pecking and shallow probing. Eats insects and larvae, small crustaceans, spiders, seeds, and amphipods. In migration prefers meadows, marshes, pond edges, tidal flats, and mudflats. Usually in small flocks of 20–40 birds. Relatively tame. May fly short distance, then pitch back into grass.

• **BREEDING** Promiscuous. Males mate several times. Females visit territories of other males. Males leave territories prior to hatching of eggs.

• **NESTING** Incubation 19–23 days by female. Precocial young leave nest soon after hatching and feed themselves, tended by female. First flight at 18–21 days. 1 brood per year.

• **POPULATION** Fairly common to common on breeding grounds and in migration on East Coast and in Midwest; uncommon from Great Plains to West Coast.

Similar Birds

SHARP-TAILED SANDPIPER
Lacks sharply defined streaked breast; buff wash across breast • in breeding plumage has streaking on crissum, sides, and flanks • juvenile has buff-orange breast and rusty crown.

RUFF ♀
Larger; longer neck; gray-brown breast with heavy spotting and blotches; in flight shows large white ovals on uppertail and stronger wing bars.

Flight Pattern

Swift direct flight with rapid wing beats. When flushed climbs with zigzag flight.

Nest Identification

Shape ◖   Location ••• ▬

Grass and leaves • on dry ground near water • built by female • whitish to olive-buff eggs splotched with dark browns; pyriform to oval, 1.5 x 1.0 inches.

Plumage Sexes similar	Habitat ⸺ ≈≈≈ ⸽≈	Migration Migratory	Weight 3.5 ounces

DATE _____ TIME_____ LOCATION _____

Family SCOLOPACIDAE	Species *Calidris acuminata*	Length 8.5 inches	Wingspan 17 inches

SHARP-TAILED SANDPIPER

This native of Eurasian tundra regions is a casual to uncommon spring migrant and common autumn migrant in western Alaska, and is a rare autumn migrant along the Pacific Coast to California. These sandpipers usually travel in the company of other shorebirds. In flight it shows mostly white underwing coverts and axillaries, white lateral uppertail coverts with dark shaft streaks, and

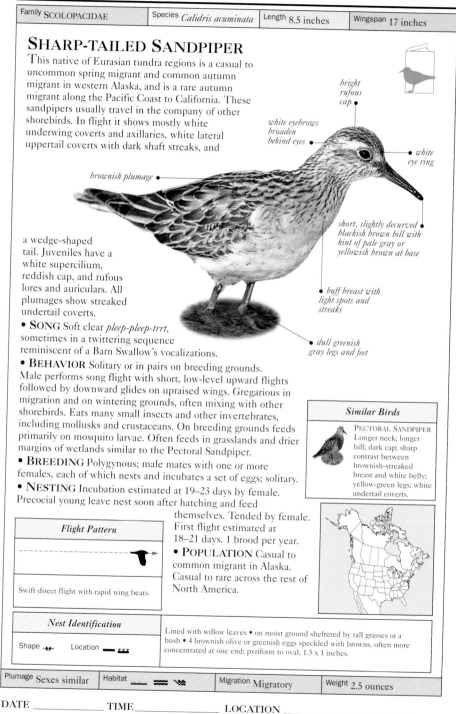

bright rufous cap

white eyebrows broaden behind eyes

white eye ring

brownish plumage

short, slightly decurved blackish brown bill with hint of pale gray or yellowish brown at base

buff breast with light spots and streaks

dull greenish gray legs and feet

a wedge-shaped tail. Juveniles have a white supercilium, reddish cap, and rufous lores and auriculars. All plumages show streaked undertail coverts.

• **SONG** Soft clear *pleep-pleep-trrt*, sometimes in a twittering sequence reminiscent of a Barn Swallow's vocalizations.

• **BEHAVIOR** Solitary or in pairs on breeding grounds. Male performs song flight with short, low-level upward flights followed by downward glides on upraised wings. Gregarious in migration and on wintering grounds, often mixing with other shorebirds. Eats many small insects and other invertebrates, including mollusks and crustaceans. On breeding grounds feeds primarily on mosquito larvae. Often feeds in grasslands and drier margins of wetlands similar to the Pectoral Sandpiper.

• **BREEDING** Polygynous; male mates with one or more females, each of which nests and incubates a set of eggs; solitary.

• **NESTING** Incubation estimated at 19–23 days by female. Precocial young leave nest soon after hatching and feed themselves. Tended by female. First flight estimated at 18–21 days. 1 brood per year.

• **POPULATION** Casual to common migrant in Alaska. Casual to rare across the rest of North America.

Similar Birds

PECTORAL SANDPIPER Longer neck; longer bill; dark cap; sharp contrast between brownish-streaked breast and white belly; yellow-green legs; white undertail coverts.

Flight Pattern
Swift direct flight with rapid wing beats.

Nest Identification	
Shape ⬤ Location ▬ ⁂	Lined with willow leaves • on moist ground sheltered by tall grasses or a bush • 4 brownish olive or greenish eggs speckled with browns, often more concentrated at one end; pyriform to oval, 1.5 x 1 inches.

Plumage Sexes similar	Habitat ≈ 🌾	Migration Migratory	Weight 2.5 ounces

DATE _____ TIME_____ LOCATION _____

Family SCOLOPACIDAE	Species *Calidris ptilocnemis*	Length 9 inches	Wingspan 14–15.5 inches

ROCK SANDPIPER

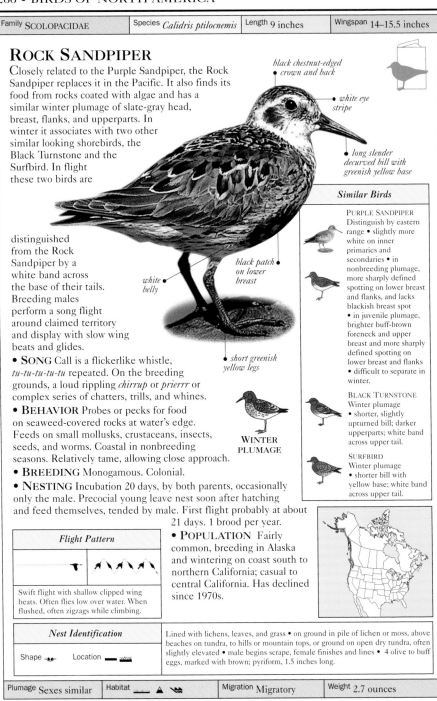

Closely related to the Purple Sandpiper, the Rock Sandpiper replaces it in the Pacific. It also finds its food from rocks coated with algae and has a similar winter plumage of slate-gray head, breast, flanks, and upperparts. In winter it associates with two other similar looking shorebirds, the Black Turnstone and the Surfbird. In flight these two birds are distinguished from the Rock Sandpiper by a white band across the base of their tails. Breeding males perform a song flight around claimed territory and display with slow wing beats and glides.

black chestnut-edged crown and back

white eye stripe

long slender decurved bill with greenish yellow base

black patch on lower breast

white belly

short greenish yellow legs

WINTER PLUMAGE

Similar Birds

PURPLE SANDPIPER
Distinguish by eastern range • slightly more white on inner primaries and secondaries • in nonbreeding plumage, more sharply defined spotting on lower breast and flanks, and lacks blackish breast spot • in juvenile plumage, brighter buff-brown foreneck and upper breast and more sharply defined spotting on lower breast and flanks • difficult to separate in winter.

BLACK TURNSTONE
Winter plumage • shorter, slightly upturned bill; darker upperparts; white band across upper tail.

SURFBIRD
Winter plumage • shorter bill with yellow base; white band across upper tail.

- **SONG** Call is a flickerlike whistle, *tu-tu-tu-tu-tu* repeated. On the breeding grounds, a loud rippling *chirrup* or *prierrr* or complex series of chatters, trills, and whines.
- **BEHAVIOR** Probes or pecks for food on seaweed-covered rocks at water's edge. Feeds on small mollusks, crustaceans, insects, seeds, and worms. Coastal in nonbreeding seasons. Relatively tame, allowing close approach.
- **BREEDING** Monogamous. Colonial.
- **NESTING** Incubation 20 days, by both parents, occasionally only the male. Precocial young leave nest soon after hatching and feed themselves, tended by male. First flight probably at about 21 days. 1 brood per year.
- **POPULATION** Fairly common, breeding in Alaska and wintering on coast south to northern California; casual to central California. Has declined since 1970s.

Flight Pattern

Swift flight with shallow clipped wing beats. Often flies low over water. When flushed, often zigzags while climbing.

Nest Identification

Shape · Location

Lined with lichens, leaves, and grass • on ground in pile of lichen or moss, above beaches on tundra, to hills or mountain tops, or ground on open dry tundra, often slightly elevated • male begins scrape, female finishes and lines • 4 olive to buff eggs, marked with brown; pyriform, 1.5 inches long.

Plumage Sexes similar	Habitat ▲	Migration Migratory	Weight 2.7 ounces

DATE _____ TIME_____ LOCATION _____

Family SCOLOPACIDAE	Species *Calidris alpina*	Length 7.5–8.5 inches	Wingspan 14.5–15.75 inches

DUNLIN

Impressive fliers, these small brown sandpipers are able to migrate at speeds of more than a hundred miles per hour and travel in flocks that can be so large they look like a swarm of insects. Once known as the Red-backed Sandpiper, the breeding bird is unmistakable with its long sturdy droop-tipped bill, rusty red upperparts, and black belly patch. Females are similar to males but have brown napes. When feeding it often gives the appearance of being hunchbacked.

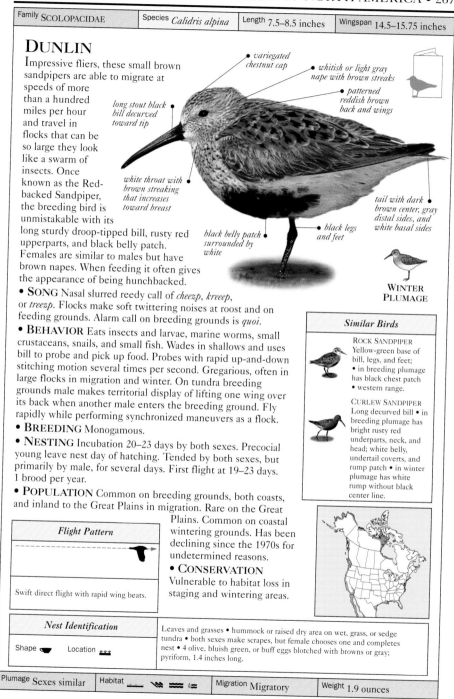

variegated chestnut cap

whitish or light gray nape with brown streaks

patterned reddish brown back and wings

long stout black bill decurved toward tip

white throat with brown streaking that increases toward breast

tail with dark brown center, gray distal sides, and white basal sides

black belly patch surrounded by white

black legs and feet

WINTER PLUMAGE

- **SONG** Nasal slurred reedy call of *cheezp, kreeep,* or *treezp.* Flocks make soft twittering noises at roost and on feeding grounds. Alarm call on breeding grounds is *quoi.*
- **BEHAVIOR** Eats insects and larvae, marine worms, small crustaceans, snails, and small fish. Wades in shallows and uses bill to probe and pick up food. Probes with rapid up-and-down stitching motion several times per second. Gregarious, often in large flocks in migration and winter. On tundra breeding grounds male makes territorial display of lifting one wing over its back when another male enters the breeding ground. Fly rapidly while performing synchronized maneuvers as a flock.
- **BREEDING** Monogamous.
- **NESTING** Incubation 20–23 days by both sexes. Precocial young leave nest day of hatching. Tended by both sexes, but primarily by male, for several days. First flight at 19–23 days. 1 brood per year.
- **POPULATION** Common on breeding grounds, both coasts, and inland to the Great Plains in migration. Rare on the Great Plains. Common on coastal wintering grounds. Has been declining since the 1970s for undetermined reasons.
- **CONSERVATION** Vulnerable to habitat loss in staging and wintering areas.

Similar Birds

ROCK SANDPIPER Yellow-green base of bill, legs, and feet;
- in breeding plumage has black chest patch
- western range.

CURLEW SANDPIPER Long decurved bill • in breeding plumage has bright rusty red underparts, neck, and head; white belly, undertail coverts, and rump patch • in winter plumage has white rump without black center line.

Flight Pattern
Swift direct flight with rapid wing beats.

Nest Identification	
Shape ⌣ Location ⁂	Leaves and grasses • hummock or raised dry area on wet, grass, or sedge tundra • both sexes make scrapes, but female chooses one and completes nest • 4 olive, bluish green, or buff eggs blotched with browns or gray; pyriform, 1.4 inches long.

Plumage Sexes similar	Habitat	Migration Migratory	Weight 1.9 ounces

DATE _____ TIME_____ LOCATION _____

Family SCOLOPACIDAE	Species *Calidris ferruginea*	Length 7.5–8.5 inches	Wingspan 14.5–16.5 inches

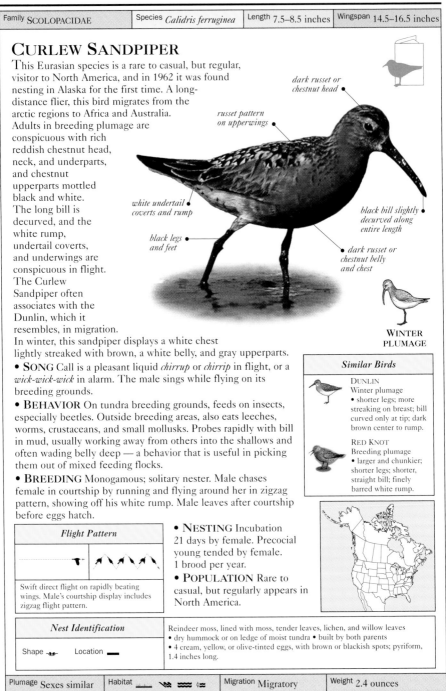

CURLEW SANDPIPER

This Eurasian species is a rare to casual, but regular, visitor to North America, and in 1962 it was found nesting in Alaska for the first time. A long-distance flier, this bird migrates from the arctic regions to Africa and Australia. Adults in breeding plumage are conspicuous with rich reddish chestnut head, neck, and underparts, and chestnut upperparts mottled black and white. The long bill is decurved, and the white rump, undertail coverts, and underwings are conspicuous in flight. The Curlew Sandpiper often associates with the Dunlin, which it resembles, in migration. In winter, this sandpiper displays a white chest lightly streaked with brown, a white belly, and gray upperparts.

dark russet or chestnut head

russet pattern on upperwings

white undertail coverts and rump

black legs and feet

black bill slightly decurved along entire length

dark russet or chestnut belly and chest

WINTER PLUMAGE

• **SONG** Call is a pleasant liquid *chirrup* or *chirrip* in flight, or a *wick-wick-wick* in alarm. The male sings while flying on its breeding grounds.

• **BEHAVIOR** On tundra breeding grounds, feeds on insects, especially beetles. Outside breeding areas, also eats leeches, worms, crustaceans, and small mollusks. Probes rapidly with bill in mud, usually working away from others into the shallows and often wading belly deep — a behavior that is useful in picking them out of mixed feeding flocks.

• **BREEDING** Monogamous; solitary nester. Male chases female in courtship by running and flying around her in zigzag pattern, showing off his white rump. Male leaves after courtship before eggs hatch.

Similar Birds

DUNLIN
Winter plumage
• shorter legs; more streaking on breast; bill curved only at tip; dark brown center to rump.

RED KNOT
Breeding plumage
• larger and chunkier; shorter legs; shorter, straight bill; finely barred white rump.

Flight Pattern

Swift direct flight on rapidly beating wings. Male's courtship display includes zigzag flight pattern.

• **NESTING** Incubation 21 days by female. Precocial young tended by female. 1 brood per year.

• **POPULATION** Rare to casual, but regularly appears in North America.

Nest Identification	
Shape 〜 Location ▬	Reindeer moss, lined with moss, tender leaves, lichen, and willow leaves • dry hummock or on ledge of moist tundra • built by both parents • 4 cream, yellow, or olive-tinted eggs, with brown or blackish spots; pyriform, 1.4 inches long.

Plumage Sexes similar	Habitat 〜 〜 〜	Migration Migratory	Weight 2.4 ounces

DATE _____ TIME_____ LOCATION _____

Family SCOLOPACIDAE	Species *Calidris himantopus*	Length 7.5–8.5 inches	Wingspan 15.5–17 inches

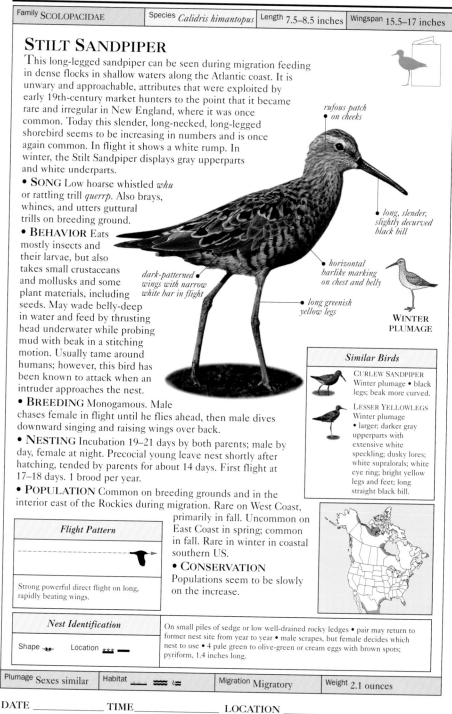

STILT SANDPIPER

This long-legged sandpiper can be seen during migration feeding in dense flocks in shallow waters along the Atlantic coast. It is unwary and approachable, attributes that were exploited by early 19th-century market hunters to the point that it became rare and irregular in New England, where it was once common. Today this slender, long-necked, long-legged shorebird seems to be increasing in numbers and is once again common. In flight it shows a white rump. In winter, the Stilt Sandpiper displays gray upperparts and white underparts.

- **SONG** Low hoarse whistled *whu* or rattling trill *querrp*. Also brays, whines, and utters guttural trills on breeding ground.
- **BEHAVIOR** Eats mostly insects and their larvae, but also takes small crustaceans and mollusks and some plant materials, including seeds. May wade belly-deep in water and feed by thrusting head underwater while probing mud with beak in a stitching motion. Usually tame around humans; however, this bird has been known to attack when an intruder approaches the nest.
- **BREEDING** Monogamous. Male chases female in flight until he flies ahead, then male dives downward singing and raising wings over back.
- **NESTING** Incubation 19–21 days by both parents; male by day, female at night. Precocial young leave nest shortly after hatching, tended by parents for about 14 days. First flight at 17–18 days. 1 brood per year.
- **POPULATION** Common on breeding grounds and in the interior east of the Rockies during migration. Rare on West Coast, primarily in fall. Uncommon on East Coast in spring; common in fall. Rare in winter in coastal southern US.
- **CONSERVATION** Populations seem to be slowly on the increase.

rufous patch on cheeks

long, slender, slightly decurved black bill

horizontal barlike marking on chest and belly

dark-patterned wings with narrow white bar in flight

long greenish yellow legs

WINTER PLUMAGE

Similar Birds

CURLEW SANDPIPER
Winter plumage • black legs; beak more curved.

LESSER YELLOWLEGS
Winter plumage • larger; darker gray upperparts with extensive white speckling; dusky lores; white supralorals; white eye ring; bright yellow legs and feet; long straight black bill.

Flight Pattern
Strong powerful direct flight on long, rapidly beating wings.

Nest Identification	
Shape Location	On small piles of sedge or low well-drained rocky ledges • pair may return to former nest site from year to year • male scrapes, but female decides which nest to use • 4 pale green to olive-green or cream eggs with brown spots; pyriform, 1.4 inches long.

Plumage Sexes similar	Habitat	Migration Migratory	Weight 2.1 ounces

DATE _____ TIME_____ LOCATION _____

Family SCOLOPACIDAE	Species *Tryngites subruficollis*	Length 7.5–8.25 inches	Wingspan 16–17 inches

BUFF-BREASTED SANDPIPER

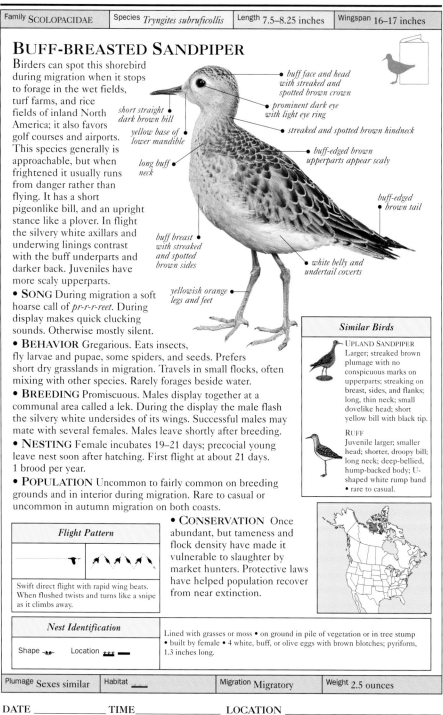

Birders can spot this shorebird during migration when it stops to forage in the wet fields, turf farms, and rice fields of inland North America; it also favors golf courses and airports. This species generally is approachable, but when frightened it usually runs from danger rather than flying. It has a short pigeonlike bill, and an upright stance like a plover. In flight the silvery white axillars and underwing linings contrast with the buff underparts and darker back. Juveniles have more scaly upperparts.

short straight dark brown bill

yellow base of lower mandible

long buff neck

buff breast with streaked and spotted brown sides

yellowish orange legs and feet

buff face and head with streaked and spotted brown crown

prominent dark eye with light eye ring

streaked and spotted brown hindneck

buff-edged brown upperparts appear scaly

buff-edged brown tail

white belly and undertail coverts

• SONG During migration a soft hoarse call of *pr-r-r-reet*. During display makes quick clucking sounds. Otherwise mostly silent.

• BEHAVIOR Gregarious. Eats insects, fly larvae and pupae, some spiders, and seeds. Prefers short dry grasslands in migration. Travels in small flocks, often mixing with other species. Rarely forages beside water.

• BREEDING Promiscuous. Males display together at a communal area called a lek. During the display the male flash the silvery white undersides of its wings. Successful males may mate with several females. Males leave shortly after breeding.

• NESTING Female incubates 19–21 days; precocial young leave nest soon after hatching. First flight at about 21 days. 1 brood per year.

• POPULATION Uncommon to fairly common on breeding grounds and in interior during migration. Rare to casual or uncommon in autumn migration on both coasts.

• CONSERVATION Once abundant, but tameness and flock density have made it vulnerable to slaughter by market hunters. Protective laws have helped population recover from near extinction.

Similar Birds

UPLAND SANDPIPER
Larger; streaked brown plumage with no conspicuous marks on upperparts; streaking on breast, sides, and flanks; long, thin neck; small dovelike head; short yellow bill with black tip.

RUFF
Juvenile larger; smaller head; shorter, droopy bill; long neck; deep-bellied; hump-backed body; U-shaped white rump band • rare to casual.

Flight Pattern

Swift direct flight with rapid wing beats. When flushed twists and turns like a snipe as it climbs away.

Nest Identification

Lined with grasses or moss • on ground in pile of vegetation or in tree stump • built by female • 4 white, buff, or olive eggs with brown blotches; pyriform, 1.3 inches long.

Shape ↝   Location ⁎⁎⁎ ▬

Plumage Sexes similar	Habitat ⌣⌣	Migration Migratory	Weight 2.5 ounces

DATE _____ TIME_____ LOCATION _____

Family SCOLOPACIDAE	Species *Limnodromus griseus*	Length 10.5–12 inches	Wingspan 18–22 inches

SHORT-BILLED DOWITCHER

This snipelike sandpiper is commonly seen in open marshes and mudflats during migration. Dowitchers are known by the long bill, a white wedge from the barred tail to the back that is only visible in flight, and a light belly. Although its call differs from that of the Long-billed Dowitcher, they are difficult to distinguish in the field because of the variety of

white superciliary stripe

dark brownish upperparts with rufous-buff-edged feathers

chunky body

whitish chin

long blackish brown bill

barred tail

white to cinnamon-red breast with heavy brownish spotting or barring

short greenish legs

WINTER PLUMAGE

breeding plumages in its three races and the overlap in bill length between the two species. Juveniles are the easiest to separate by plumage from August to October. Winter plumage is gray overall. The female is similar to the male but larger.

• **SONG** Generally silent. Utters clear mellow or abrasive *chi-too-too* or *kee-you*. Also sings *tiddle-whee*, especially in spring.

• **BEHAVIOR** Gregarious; feeds and roosts in large flocks and associates with other species. Eats mostly insects, also eggs of king or horseshoe crabs. Probes with fast up-and-down motion of bill. Often submerges head in water. May freeze in standing position when approached. Often flies at considerable heights.

• **BREEDING** Monogamous. Colonial. Male displays with a hovering flight song over breeding territory.

• **NESTING** Incubation 21 days by female, sometimes by both sexes. Precocial young leave nest soon after hatching. Tended by male but feed themselves. 1 brood per year.

• **POPULATION** Common.

Similar Birds

LONG-BILLED DOWITCHER
Slightly larger; longer legs; darker overall; darker tail with white bars narrower than dark bars; different voice • females may have longer bill than males • in breeding plumage lacks white underparts.

Flight Pattern

Strong swift direct flight with rapid wing beats.

Nest Identification

Shape — Location

Sticks, leaves, and grasses * on ground in small pile of grass or moss • built by both sexes • 4 buff-green or brownish eggs speckled and blotched with brown; pyriform, 1.6 x 1.1 inches.

Plumage Sexes similar	Habitat	Migration Migratory	Weight 3.8 ounces

DATE _____ TIME_____ LOCATION _____

| Family SCOLOPACIDAE | Species *Limnodromus scolopaceus* | Length 11–12.5 inches | Wingspan 18–20 inches |

LONG-BILLED DOWITCHER

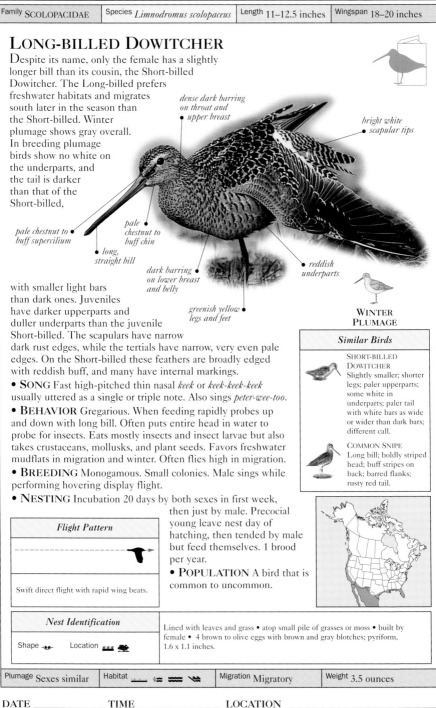

Despite its name, only the female has a slightly longer bill than its cousin, the Short-billed Dowitcher. The Long-billed prefers freshwater habitats and migrates south later in the season than the Short-billed. Winter plumage shows gray overall. In breeding plumage birds show no white on the underparts, and the tail is darker than that of the Short-billed,

dense dark barring on throat and upper breast

bright white scapular tips

pale chestnut to buff supercilium

pale chestnut to buff chin

long, straight bill

dark barring on lower breast and belly

reddish underparts

greenish yellow legs and feet

WINTER PLUMAGE

with smaller light bars than dark ones. Juveniles have darker upperparts and duller underparts than the juvenile Short-billed. The scapulars have narrow dark rust edges, while the tertials have narrow, very even pale edges. On the Short-billed these feathers are broadly edged with reddish buff, and many have internal markings.

• **SONG** Fast high-pitched thin nasal *keek* or *keek-keek-keek* usually uttered as a single or triple note. Also sings *peter-wee-too*.

• **BEHAVIOR** Gregarious. When feeding rapidly probes up and down with long bill. Often puts entire head in water to probe for insects. Eats mostly insects and insect larvae but also takes crustaceans, mollusks, and plant seeds. Favors freshwater mudflats in migration and winter. Often flies high in migration.

• **BREEDING** Monogamous. Small colonies. Male sings while performing hovering display flight.

• **NESTING** Incubation 20 days by both sexes in first week, then just by male. Precocial young leave nest day of hatching, then tended by male but feed themselves. 1 brood per year.

• **POPULATION** A bird that is common to uncommon.

Similar Birds

SHORT-BILLED DOWITCHER
Slightly smaller; shorter legs; paler upperparts; some white in underparts; paler tail with white bars as wide or wider than dark bars; different call.

COMMON SNIPE
Long bill; boldly striped head; buff stripes on back; barred flanks; rusty red tail.

Flight Pattern
Swift direct flight with rapid wing beats.

Nest Identification	Lined with leaves and grass • atop small pile of grasses or moss • built by female • 4 brown to olive eggs with brown and gray blotches; pyriform, 1.6 x 1.1 inches.
Shape 〜 Location 🌿🌳	

| Plumage Sexes similar | Habitat 〜〜 | Migration Migratory | Weight 3.5 ounces |

DATE _____ TIME_____ LOCATION _____

Family SCOLOPACIDAE	Species *Gallinago gallinago*	Length 10–11 inches	Wingspan 17–20 inches

COMMON SNIPE

Identified by its extremely long, straight bill and longitudinal stripes on its head, this bird typically can be found in freshwater marshes and swamps and in the vicinity of lakes and rivers. It generally frequents open landscapes.

• **SONG** On breeding grounds gives *wheat-wheat-wheat-wheat*. Nonvocal, winnowing, territorial advertisement, *whoo-whoo-whoo-whoo*, produced in flight by rushing air vibrating two outermost tail feathers that are modified to produce this sound.

eyes set far back on head

longitudinal stripes on head

long flexible bill

buff-edged stripes on back

barring on flanks

greenish legs and feet

• **BEHAVIOR**
Sits tight in wet boggy areas and blends into background, flushing only when approached closely. When flushed, flies in zigzag pattern emitting sudden, rasping *skaipe* vocalization. Feeds principally on insects, insect larvae, and earthworms taken from mud by probing with its long bill.

• **BREEDING** Solitary nester.

• **NESTING** Incubation 18–20 days by female. Precocial young leave nest within hours of hatching. First flight at 14–20 days. 1 brood per year.

• **POPULATION** Significant decline in US from 1980 to 1995. Breeds in northern US, Canada, and Eurasia. Winters as far south as northern South America and central Africa.

• **CONSERVATION** Lands have been managed primarily to increase populations for hunting. It is highly questionable whether the Common Snipe should retain its status as a game bird species.

Similar Birds

AMERICAN WOODCOCK Chunkier; bars on crown, not longitudinal stripes; no barring on flanks; cinnamon-buff underparts, including wing linings.

LONG-BILLED DOWITCHER SHORT-BILLED DOWITCHER Lack head striping; barring or spotting on longer neck.

Flight Pattern
Zigzag flight on takeoff followed by direct flight with rapid wing beats.

Nest Identification	
Shape — Location —	Scrape • 2–4 olive-brown or pale olive-brown eggs covered with mostly brown and black dark spots and blotches, slightly glossy finish; 1.3 x 1.1 inches.

Plumage Sexes similar	Habitat	Migration Migratory	Weight 4.5 ounces

DATE _____ TIME_____ LOCATION _____

Family SCOLOPACIDAE	Species *Scolopax minor*	Length 10.5–11 inches	Wingspan 18 inches

AMERICAN WOODCOCK

The long bill of this upland shorebird is sensitive and flexible, allowing it to feel for worms in deep soil. Woodcocks are rarely seen during the day unless flushed and escaping straightaway in flight on twittering rounded wings. Chunky, short-necked, and short-legged, its plumage matches the dead leaves of the forest floor and old fields where it roosts by day.

• **SONG** Generally silent. In spring, male on display ground has nasal call of *peeant*, similar to that of the Common Nighthawk. During display flights male produces a musical twittering with wings and a liquid, bubbling song from high overhead.

• **BEHAVIOR** Crepuscular and nocturnal.

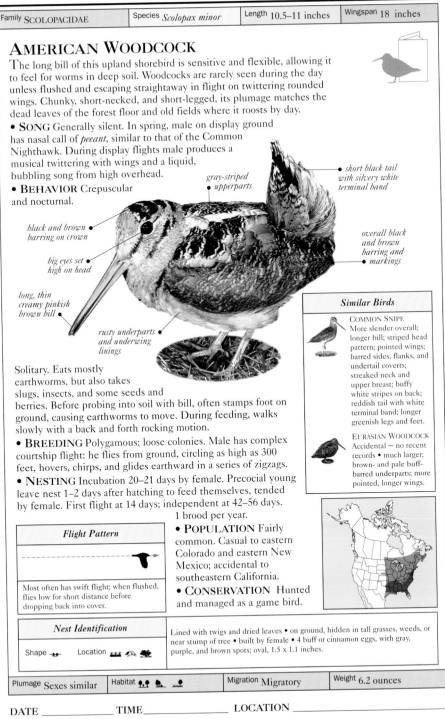

gray-striped upperparts

short black tail with silvery white terminal band

black and brown barring on crown

big eyes set high on head

overall black and brown barring and markings

long, thin creamy pinkish brown bill

rusty underparts and underwing linings

Solitary. Eats mostly earthworms, but also takes slugs, insects, and some seeds and berries. Before probing into soil with bill, often stamps foot on ground, causing earthworms to move. During feeding, walks slowly with a back and forth rocking motion.

• **BREEDING** Polygamous; loose colonies. Male has complex courtship flight: he flies from ground, circling as high as 300 feet, hovers, chirps, and glides earthward in a series of zigzags.

• **NESTING** Incubation 20–21 days by female. Precocial young leave nest 1–2 days after hatching to feed themselves, tended by female. First flight at 14 days; independent at 42–56 days. 1 brood per year.

• **POPULATION** Fairly common. Casual to eastern Colorado and eastern New Mexico; accidental to southeastern California.

• **CONSERVATION** Hunted and managed as a game bird.

Similar Birds

COMMON SNIPE
More slender overall; longer bill; striped head pattern; pointed wings; barred sides, flanks, and undertail coverts; streaked neck and upper breast; buffy white stripes on back; reddish tail with white terminal band; longer greenish legs and feet.

EURASIAN WOODCOCK
Accidental — no recent records • much larger; brown- and pale buff-barred underparts; more pointed, longer wings.

Flight Pattern

Most often has swift flight; when flushed, flies low for short distance before dropping back into cover.

Nest Identification

Shape

Location

Lined with twigs and dried leaves • on ground, hidden in tall grasses, weeds, or near stump of tree • built by female • 4 buff or cinnamon eggs, with gray, purple, and brown spots; oval, 1.5 x 1.1 inches.

Plumage Sexes similar	Habitat	Migration Migratory	Weight 6.2 ounces

DATE _____ TIME_____ LOCATION _____

Family SCOLOPACIDAE	Species *Phalaropus tricolor*	Length 8–9.5 inches	Wingspan 14.5–16 inches

WILSON'S PHALAROPE

Phalaropes have devised a terrific way to get plankton and other food to the water's surface for harvest. They spin like tops – as fast as 60 times per minute – creating small whirlpools that pull food to the surface where they can pick it up with their long slender bills. In flight, wings lack striping, and uppertail coverts are white. This is the only phalarope confined to inland habitats and restricted to the Western Hemisphere.

long needle-shaped bill

brownish black upperparts are duller than female's

MALE

white underparts

white chin and cheeks

JUVENILE

dull yellow legs and feet with narrow lateral membranes

- **SONG** Generally silent. Breeding call of *nya* sounds like a toy whistle. Occasional flight call a low croaking *aangh*.
- **BEHAVIOR** Tame. Solitary, pairs, small flocks. Eats insects, larvae, crustaceans, marsh plant seeds. Probes mud in shallow water, sometimes with head submerged. Spins and dabbles. Seen following shoveler ducks to pick stirred-up prey from surface. Sometimes snags insects from air. Often walks in vegetation, picking prey from ground and plants.

pale gray crown

white mark above eye

broad black stripe extends down neck, fading to reddish chestnut

WINTER PLUMAGE

gray wing coverts and wings

orange wash forms partial necklace on pale gray neck

black legs and feet

FEMALE

Similar Birds

LESSER YELLOWLEGS Larger; darker upperparts; streaked breast and belly; lightly barred tail; canary-yellow legs.

RED-NECKED PHALAROPE Smaller; shorter bill; black ear patch even in winter plumage; strongly streaked upperparts; dark gray rump; white wing stripe.

- **BREEDING** May be polyandrous. Loose colonies. Female courts male by swimming beside him and chasing off other females; eventually male makes sexual advances. Male develops incubation patches.
- **NESTING** Incubation 18–21 days by male. Precocial young leave nest day of hatching. Tended by male but feed themselves. First flight at 16–18 days. 1 or more broods per year.
- **POPULATION** Abundant to common in the West, although declining slightly. Uncommon to rare or casual in the East.
- **CONSERVATION** Drainage of marshes has caused loss of nesting areas; protection of such areas is needed.

Flight Pattern

Swift direct flight with rapid wing beats.

Nest Identification

Shape ⚬ Location ▬ ✱✱✱ ⱮⱮ

Lined with grass • female may start, but built mostly by male • 4 buff eggs with brown blotches; pyriform, 1.3 inches long.

Plumage Sexes differ	Habitat ▬ ▬ ≈≈	Migration Migratory	Weight 2.4 ounces

DATE _____ TIME_____ LOCATION _____

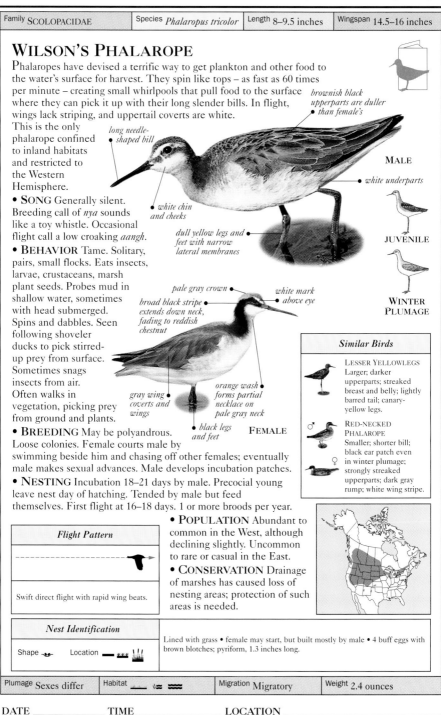

Family SCOLOPACIDAE	Species *Phalaropus lobatus*	Length 7.75–8 inches	Wingspan 14–15 inches

RED-NECKED PHALAROPE

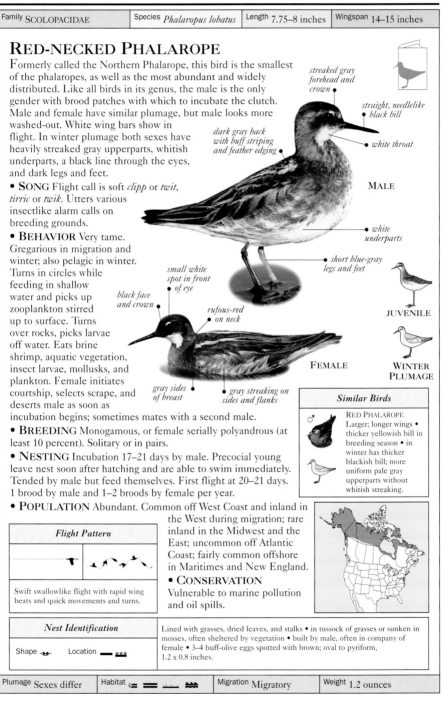

Formerly called the Northern Phalarope, this bird is the smallest of the phalaropes, as well as the most abundant and widely distributed. Like all birds in its genus, the male is the only gender with brood patches with which to incubate the clutch. Male and female have similar plumage, but male looks more washed-out. White wing bars show in flight. In winter plumage both sexes have heavily streaked gray upperparts, whitish underparts, a black line through the eyes, and dark legs and feet.

streaked gray forehead and crown

straight, needlelike black bill

white throat

dark gray back with buff striping and feather edging

MALE

white underparts

• **SONG** Flight call is soft *clipp* or *twit, tirric* or *twik*. Utters various insectlike alarm calls on breeding grounds.

• **BEHAVIOR** Very tame. Gregarious in migration and winter; also pelagic in winter. Turns in circles while feeding in shallow water and picks up zooplankton stirred up to surface. Turns over rocks, picks larvae off water. Eats brine shrimp, aquatic vegetation, insect larvae, mollusks, and plankton. Female initiates courtship, selects scrape, and deserts male as soon as incubation begins; sometimes mates with a second male.

small white spot in front of eye

black face and crown

rufous-red on neck

short blue-gray legs and feet

JUVENILE

FEMALE

gray sides of breast

gray streaking on sides and flanks

WINTER PLUMAGE

• **BREEDING** Monogamous, or female serially polyandrous (at least 10 percent). Solitary or in pairs.

• **NESTING** Incubation 17–21 days by male. Precocial young leave nest soon after hatching and are able to swim immediately. Tended by male but feed themselves. First flight at 20–21 days. 1 brood by male and 1–2 broods by female per year.

• **POPULATION** Abundant. Common off West Coast and inland in the West during migration; rare inland in the Midwest and the East; uncommon off Atlantic Coast; fairly common offshore in Maritimes and New England.

• **CONSERVATION** Vulnerable to marine pollution and oil spills.

Similar Birds
RED PHALAROPE Larger; longer wings • thicker yellowish bill in breeding season • in winter has thicker blackish bill; more uniform pale gray upperparts without whitish streaking.

Flight Pattern

Swift swallowlike flight with rapid wing beats and quick movements and turns.

Nest Identification

Shape   Location

Lined with grasses, dried leaves, and stalks • in tussock of grasses or sunken in mosses, often sheltered by vegetation • built by male, often in company of female • 3–4 buff-olive eggs spotted with brown; oval to pyriform, 1.2 x 0.8 inches.

Plumage Sexes differ	Habitat	Migration Migratory	Weight 1.2 ounces

DATE _____ TIME_____ LOCATION _____

Family SCOLOPACIDAE	Species *Phalaropus fulicaria*	Length 8–9 inches	Wingspan 14–16 inches

RED PHALAROPE

Of all phalaropes, the Red is most pelagic, nests farthest north, and migrates farthest south. It breeds well north of the Arctic Circle and winters at sea off both Atlantic and Pacific Coasts. Its bill is shorter and thicker than that of other phalaropes. In flight it shows a white wing stripe, a uniformly gray back (in winter), and brownish legs and feet.

black wing tips

• **SONG** Bell-like *clink-clink.* Also a shrieking shrill *wit-wit* and *tink* or *tsik.*

MALE

• *white face*

• **BEHAVIOR** Tame. Solitary or in small flocks; at sea occasionally in very large flocks. Pelagic in winter. Swims readily. Wades into water to feed; finds food on surface and in shallow water. Swims and spins often, picking up planktonic food particles with its bill from the surface. Eats small insects, fish, and aquatic invertebrates.

black crown and forehead

black at base of bill

dark gray upperparts have feathers fringed with rufous-buff

yellowish bill with black tip

JUVENILE

• **BREEDING** Female polyandrous; male promiscuous. Semicolonial. Female selects territory, leaves area shortly after laying eggs; and sometimes mates again.

WINTER PLUMAGE

• *chestnut-red underparts*

• **NESTING** Incubation 18–20 days by male. Precocial young leave nest soon after hatching. Tended by male but feed themselves. First flight at 16–20 days. 1 brood per year by male and 2 broods by female.

• *more brightly colored*

FEMALE

• *chestnut-red underparts*

Similar Birds

♂ **RED-NECKED PHALAROPE**
Thinner, needlelike bill; smaller • in winter plumage is darker with heavily striped back; blacker crown; more contrasting wing stripe.

• **POPULATION** Abundant on breeding grounds. In winter and migration fairly common off the West Coast; uncommon off the East Coast. Rare inland.

Flight Pattern

Swift direct flight with rapid wing beats.

• **CONSERVATION** Accidents occur during migration, such as collisions with lighthouses. Storms at sea can blow birds inland. Vulnerable to oil spills.

Nest Identification

Shape • Location

Domed with grass • lined with grasses and other fine materials • on ground near water • built by male • 3–4 olive-green eggs blotched with black or brown; oval to pyriform, 1.2 x 0.9 inches.

Plumage Sexes differ	Habitat	Migration Migratory	Weight 1.8 ounces

DATE _____ TIME_____ LOCATION _____

Family LARIDAE	Species *Stercorarius maccormicki*	Length 21 inches	Wingspan 52 inches

SOUTH POLAR SKUA

Rarely seen from shore, this skua spends much of its time at sea, scavenging around fishing boats and chasing gulls and shearwaters. It nests along the coast of Antarctica but winters (our summer) in northern oceans; vagrants have been spotted in the Aleutians and once in North Dakota. They may be seen well off the Atlantic and Pacific coasts from May to November. In flight, the South Polar Skua looks stout-bodied and chunky, with a "hunched shoulder" appearance. The smallest of the skuas, this bird has a smaller head than the Great Skua; both a light and dark morph with gradations in between may range from almost white-bodied to blackish. The intermediate morph has a medium-brown nape and underparts.

white base to primaries forms bar on middle of forewing

• **SONG** Usually silent away from breeding areas. Gull-like *scoo-ah*.

brown unstreaked mantle

• **BEHAVIOR** Solitary outside breeding season. Aggressive hunter. Eats fish, penguin eggs, lemmings, and carrion. Shakes birds with its bill

short broad tail

broad rounded wings

PALE MORPH

to make them let go of their prey then seizes it. Dives into water from air to catch fish. Tends fishing trawlers. Defensive at nest; often flies straight at the head of a human intruder.

• **BREEDING** Monogamous; small colonies. Male feeds female during courtship.

• **NESTING** Incubation 24–34 days by both parents; female does more. Young semiprecocial; one nestling may be forced by its sibling to leave nest shortly after hatching; usually dies. The remaining one is fed by both parents by regurgitation. First flight at 49–59 days. 1 brood per year.

Similar Birds
GREAT SKUA Larger; reddish streaking on upperparts; lacks pale nape • eastern range.

• **POPULATION** Casual May to November well offshore on both Pacific and Atlantic Coasts, as postbreeding birds disperse northward from Antarctica.

Flight Pattern

Strong swift direct flight with constant shallow wing beats.

Nest Identification

Shape 🦅   Location 🪨 ▬

Moss or bare soil • on rocky slopes, bottom of hill • male begins nest, female completes • 1–3 yellow to green or brown eggs marked with purples and browns; short elliptical, 2.4 inches long.

Plumage Sexes similar	Habitat 〰️ 〰️ ▬	Migration Migratory	Weight 2.5 pounds

DATE _____ TIME_____ LOCATION _____

Family LARIDAE	Species *Stercorarius pomarinus*	Length 20–23 inches	Wingspan 48 inches

POMARINE JAEGER

The largest and strongest jaeger is about the size of a Ring-billed or Heermann's Gull, with a bulky body, thick neck, and wide-based wings. Like many of the skuas, its nesting is related to lemming populations on the Arctic tundra. When the brown lemming is numerous these seabirds nest, and when the rodent is not abundant they may not breed at all.

It has a light color morph and a more rare dark morph. Adults

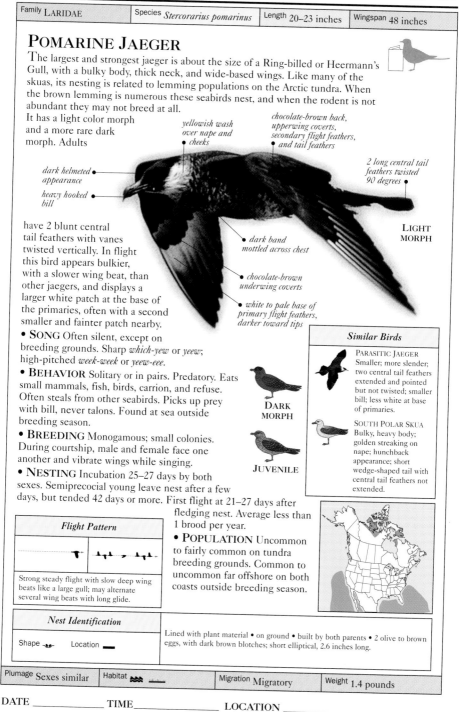

yellowish wash over nape and cheeks

chocolate-brown back, upperwing coverts, secondary flight feathers, and tail feathers

2 long central tail feathers twisted 90 degrees

dark helmeted appearance

heavy hooked bill

LIGHT MORPH

have 2 blunt central tail feathers with vanes twisted vertically. In flight this bird appears bulkier, with a slower wing beat, than other jaegers, and displays a larger white patch at the base of the primaries, often with a second smaller and fainter patch nearby.

dark band mottled across chest

chocolate-brown underwing coverts

white to pale base of primary flight feathers, darker toward tips

• **SONG** Often silent, except on breeding grounds. Sharp *which-yew* or *yeew*; high-pitched *week-week* or *yeew-eee.*

• **BEHAVIOR** Solitary or in pairs. Predatory. Eats small mammals, fish, birds, carrion, and refuse. Often steals from other seabirds. Picks up prey with bill, never talons. Found at sea outside breeding season.

DARK MORPH

• **BREEDING** Monogamous; small colonies. During courtship, male and female face one another and vibrate wings while singing.

• **NESTING** Incubation 25–27 days by both sexes. Semiprecocial young leave nest after a few days, but tended 42 days or more. First flight at 21–27 days after fledging nest. Average less than 1 brood per year.

JUVENILE

Similar Birds

PARASITIC JAEGER Smaller; more slender; two central tail feathers extended and pointed but not twisted; smaller bill; less white at base of primaries.

SOUTH POLAR SKUA Bulky, heavy body; golden streaking on nape; hunchback appearance; short wedge-shaped tail with central tail feathers not extended.

Flight Pattern

Strong steady flight with slow deep wing beats like a large gull; may alternate several wing beats with long glide.

• **POPULATION** Uncommon to fairly common on tundra breeding grounds. Common to uncommon far offshore on both coasts outside breeding season.

Nest Identification

Shape ⬩   Location ▬

Lined with plant material • on ground • built by both parents • 2 olive to brown eggs, with dark brown blotches; short elliptical, 2.6 inches long.

Plumage Sexes similar	Habitat 〰 ⸺	Migration Migratory	Weight 1.4 pounds

DATE _____ TIME_____ LOCATION _____

Family LARIDAE	Species *Stercorarius parasiticus*	Length 15–21 inches	Wingspan 36 inches

PARASITIC JAEGER

This skua can sometimes be seen from shore, intruding upon migrating flocks of terns and stealing food from other seabirds. It has two distinct color morphs, light and dark, and many intermediates. Falconlike in pursuit, it is about the size of a Laughing or Mew Gull and normally flies with quick wing beats broken by short glides. It is not known to breed until three to five years of age.

• **SONG** Usually silent when not on breeding grounds. Yelping notes and rising *skooo-a* or *ka-aaow*.

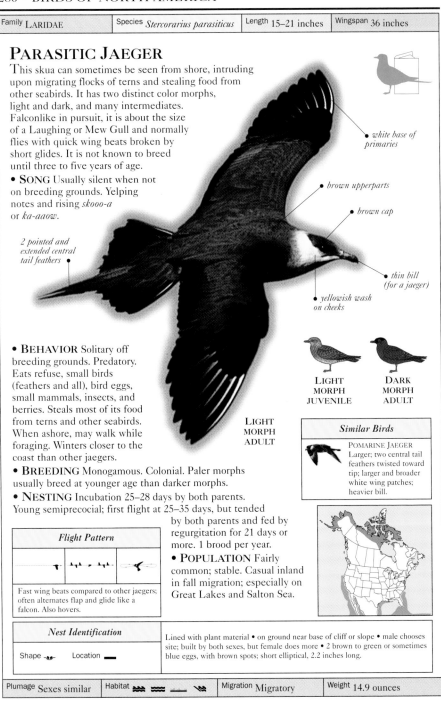

• white base of primaries

• brown upperparts

• brown cap

2 pointed and extended central tail feathers •

• thin bill (for a jaeger)

• yellowish wash on cheeks

• **BEHAVIOR** Solitary off breeding grounds. Predatory. Eats refuse, small birds (feathers and all), bird eggs, small mammals, insects, and berries. Steals most of its food from terns and other seabirds. When ashore, may walk while foraging. Winters closer to the coast than other jaegers.

• **BREEDING** Monogamous. Colonial. Paler morphs usually breed at younger age than darker morphs.

• **NESTING** Incubation 25–28 days by both parents. Young semiprecocial; first flight at 25–35 days, but tended by both parents and fed by regurgitation for 21 days or more. 1 brood per year.

• **POPULATION** Fairly common; stable. Casual inland in fall migration; especially on Great Lakes and Salton Sea.

LIGHT MORPH JUVENILE

DARK MORPH ADULT

LIGHT MORPH ADULT

Similar Birds

POMARINE JAEGER Larger; two central tail feathers twisted toward tip; larger and broader white wing patches; heavier bill.

Flight Pattern

Fast wing beats compared to other jaegers; often alternates flap and glide like a falcon. Also hovers.

Nest Identification

Shape 〰 Location ▬

Lined with plant material • on ground near base of cliff or slope • male chooses site; built by both sexes, but female does more • 2 brown to green or sometimes blue eggs, with brown spots; short elliptical, 2.2 inches long.

Plumage Sexes similar	Habitat 〰 〰 〰 〰	Migration Migratory	Weight 14.9 ounces

DATE _____ TIME_____ LOCATION _____

Family LARIDAE	Species *Stercorarius longicaudus*	Length 20–23 inches	Wingspan 30–33 inches

LONG-TAILED JAEGER

Distinguished by its eight- to ten-inch central tail feathers, this jaeger is rarely seen from land outside breeding season in the Arctic. These birds migrate in family groups to the central Pacific and south Atlantic in winter, but their route is unknown. The smallest of the jaegers, it is the least likely to steal food from other seabirds and is highly dependent on the tundra's small rodent populations in summer. In flight adults do not show a breast band, as do other jaegers. They have light grayish brown upperparts and long slender wings without a white patch at the base of the primaries (shafts of three outer primaries are white) and a slender body. Juveniles have a short tail and a white patch at the base of the primaries under the wing.

yellow cheeks

black cap

dark brown flight feathers contrast with gray coverts

white collar

blue-gray legs and feet

long pointed inner tail feathers

• **SONG** While flying, *pheu-pheu-pheu.* When irritated utters *kr-r-r-r; kr-r-r-r; kir-kri-kri.*

• **BEHAVIOR** In summer eats mostly lemmings and other small rodents, but also takes birds, eggs, insects, carrion, and berries. In winter eats fish, squid, carrion, and refuse. Uses beak to pick up food. Catches insects and other prey in flight. Often flies low over land or water. Most pelagic jaeger in postbreeding season.

DARK MORPH JUVENILE

LIGHT MORPH JUVENILE

• **BREEDING** Monogamous. Colonial. Does not breed until 3–4 years old. Courtship display features zigzag chasing flight. During courtship, male feeds female from the ground.

• **NESTING** Incubation 23–25 days by both sexes. Young semiprecocial; first flight at 22–27 days, but both sexes tend and feed by regurgitation for 7–21 days. 1 brood per year unless lemmings are scarce, then birds will not breed at all.

Similar Birds

PARASITIC JAEGER
Larger; black legs; larger white patch on outer wings; grayish breast band; short, pointed central tail feathers.

• **POPULATION** Common on tundra breeding grounds. Trends stable. Disperses widely at sea outside breeding season. Fairly common to uncommon off West Coast; casual in Gulf of Mexico and on East Coast. Rare to accidental inland.

Flight Pattern

Light floating buoyant ternlike flight is graceful compared with other jaegers. Hovers before dipping to pick up prey.

Nest Identification

Shape _____   Location _____

Lined with grasses, moss, and leaves • on ground near edge of slope • built mostly by female • 2 brown to olive eggs with dark brown and gray blotches; short elliptical, 2.2 inches long.

Plumage Sexes similar	Habitat	Migration Migratory	Weight 9.9 ounces

DATE _____ TIME_____ LOCATION _____

Family LARIDAE	Species *Larus atricilla*	Length 15–17 inches	Wingspan 40–42 inches

LAUGHING GULL

Named for its laughterlike call, this gull was threatened by the feather trade in the early 20th century. Now this coastal inhabitant forms colonies with thousands of nests. A distinguishing habit is its tendency to steal food from the Brown Pelican by snatching it out of the pelican's pouch after it surfaces with a catch. This three-year gull passes through two different winter plumages prior to attaining adult plumage. Adults have a white tail year round. In winter adults the black head is replaced by a gray smudge on the nape, and the bill, legs, and feet are dull blackish.

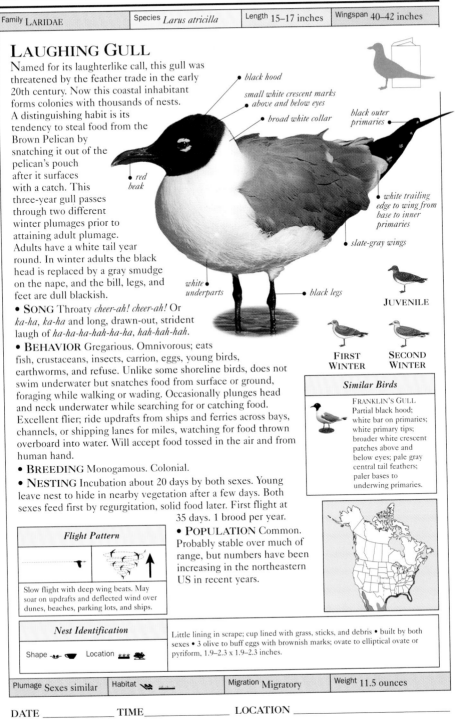

black hood

small white crescent marks above and below eyes

broad white collar

black outer primaries

red beak

white trailing edge to wing from base to inner primaries

slate-gray wings

white underparts

black legs

JUVENILE

FIRST WINTER

SECOND WINTER

Similar Birds

FRANKLIN'S GULL
Partial black hood; white bar on primaries; white primary tips; broader white crescent patches above and below eyes; pale gray central tail feathers; paler bases to underwing primaries.

• **SONG** Throaty *cheer-ah! cheer-ah!* Or *ka-ha, ka-ha* and long, drawn-out, strident laugh of *ha-ha-ha-hah-ha-ha, hah-hah-hah.*

• **BEHAVIOR** Gregarious. Omnivorous; eats fish, crustaceans, insects, carrion, eggs, young birds, earthworms, and refuse. Unlike some shoreline birds, does not swim underwater but snatches food from surface or ground, foraging while walking or wading. Occasionally plunges head and neck underwater while searching for or catching food. Excellent flier; ride updrafts from ships and ferries across bays, channels, or shipping lanes for miles, watching for food thrown overboard into water. Will accept food tossed in the air and from human hand.

• **BREEDING** Monogamous. Colonial.

• **NESTING** Incubation about 20 days by both sexes. Young leave nest to hide in nearby vegetation after a few days. Both sexes feed first by regurgitation, solid food later. First flight at 35 days. 1 brood per year.

• **POPULATION** Common. Probably stable over much of range, but numbers have been increasing in the northeastern US in recent years.

Flight Pattern

Slow flight with deep wing beats. May soar on updrafts and deflected wind over dunes, beaches, parking lots, and ships.

Nest Identification

Shape 〜 ◡   Location 🌿 🪺

Little lining in scrape; cup lined with grass, sticks, and debris • built by both sexes • 3 olive to buff eggs with brownish marks; ovate to elliptical ovate or pyriform, 1.9–2.3 x 1.9–2.3 inches.

Plumage Sexes similar	Habitat 〜 ▬	Migration Migratory	Weight 11.5 ounces

DATE _____ TIME_____ LOCATION _____

Family LARIDAE	Species *Larus pipixcan*	Length 13–15 inches	Wingspan 36 inches

FRANKLIN'S GULL

Often called the Prairie Dove, this three-year gull is sometimes spotted on farmland, following plows to feed on grubs and other insects. The bird has a characteristic black hood in summer, but in winter its head is white with the reduced dusky hood covering its eye and reaching from midcrown to nape. In flight, it differs from the similar Laughing Gull by a white bar and large white tips on primaries and a paler surface on the underwing primaries.

• **SONG** A shrill *kuk-kuk-kuk*, with *weeh-ah, weeh-ah* occasionally interjected.

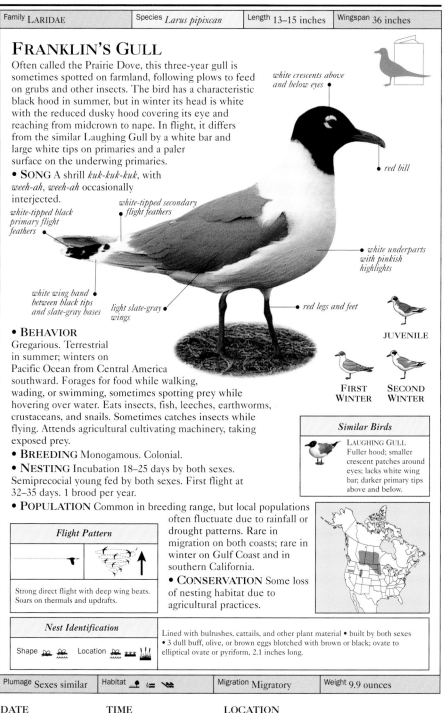

white crescents above and below eyes

red bill

white-tipped secondary flight feathers

white-tipped black primary flight feathers

white underparts with pinkish highlights

white wing band between black tips and slate-gray bases

light slate-gray wings

red legs and feet

JUVENILE

FIRST WINTER

SECOND WINTER

• **BEHAVIOR** Gregarious. Terrestrial in summer; winters on Pacific Ocean from Central America southward. Forages for food while walking, wading, or swimming, sometimes spotting prey while hovering over water. Eats insects, fish, leeches, earthworms, crustaceans, and snails. Sometimes catches insects while flying. Attends agricultural cultivating machinery, taking exposed prey.

• **BREEDING** Monogamous. Colonial.

• **NESTING** Incubation 18–25 days by both sexes. Semiprecocial young fed by both sexes. First flight at 32–35 days. 1 brood per year.

• **POPULATION** Common in breeding range, but local populations often fluctuate due to rainfall or drought patterns. Rare in migration on both coasts; rare in winter on Gulf Coast and in southern California.

• **CONSERVATION** Some loss of nesting habitat due to agricultural practices.

Similar Birds

LAUGHING GULL
Fuller hood; smaller crescent patches around eyes; lacks white wing bar; darker primary tips above and below.

Flight Pattern

Strong direct flight with deep wing beats. Soars on thermals and updrafts.

Nest Identification

Shape   Location

Lined with bulrushes, cattails, and other plant material • built by both sexes • 3 dull buff, olive, or brown eggs blotched with brown or black; ovate to elliptical ovate or pyriform, 2.1 inches long.

Plumage Sexes similar	Habitat	Migration Migratory	Weight 9.9 ounces

DATE _____ TIME_____ LOCATION _____

Family LARIDAE	Species *Larus philadelphia*	Length 12–14 inches	Wingspan 33–36 inches

BONAPARTE'S GULL

This is one of the smallest gulls in North America and the smallest native species. It is named for French zoologist Charles Lucien Bonaparte, a nephew of Napoleon. In winter plumage it shows a plain white head without the black hood, leaving only a distinctive black spot between the eye and ear. In flight, note a white wedge on the leading edge of the outer wing, black tips on the primaries, and pale underwings. This is a two-year gull.

blackish hood

gray back and wings

black bill

black-tipped primaries

white wedge on wing

orange legs

white underparts

JUVENILE

WINTER PLUMAGE

• **SONG** Shrieking whistles and a call of *cheeer*.
• **BEHAVIOR** Gregarious. Eats mostly insects on summer breeding grounds, where it sometimes hawks flying insects. In winter eats fish, crustaceans, and marine worms. Catches fish by wading in water as well as by diving. Forages on ground for insects and also catches them in flight. Its habit of nesting in trees is most unusual among gulls.
• **BREEDING** Monogamous. Solitary or small colonial.
• **NESTING** Incubation 24 days by both sexes. Not known when semiprecocial young first fly, but known to be fed by both parents while in nest. 1 brood per year.
• **POPULATION** Stable. Common in migration and winter on Great Lakes and on Pacific, Atlantic, and Gulf Coasts. Uncommon migrant inland in the West.

Similar Birds
BLACK-HEADED GULL Dark brown-black hood; red bill; dark underside of primaries.

Flight Pattern

Light and buoyant direct flight is ternlike, with rapid wing beats.

Nest Identification

Shape   Location

Sticks lined with moss and grasses; abandoned nests lined with hay and moss • coniferous tree, 4–20 feet above ground • built by both sexes • 2–4 olive to buff eggs, marked with brown blotches; ovate to elliptical-ovate, 2 inches long.

Plumage Sexes similar	Habitat	Migration Migratory	Weight 7.5 ounces

DATE _____ TIME_____ LOCATION _____

Family LARIDAE	Species *Larus heermanni*	Length 18–21 inches	Wingspan 48–51 inches

HEERMANN'S GULL

The overall dark coloring distinguishes this gull from others and makes it one of the easiest gulls in the West to identify. No other Pacific Coast gull combines the characteristics of white head, dark gray body, black tail with white tip, and red bill. When perched, the wing tips protrude well beyond the tip of the tail, covering the bird's pale gray rump and uppertail coverts. This somewhat aggressive bird is common along the Pacific Coast and spends most of its time at sea. First and second winter birds are very dark. This is a four-year gull.

• **SONG** A whiny *whee-ee*. While flying, repeatedly utters *cow-auk, cow-eek*.

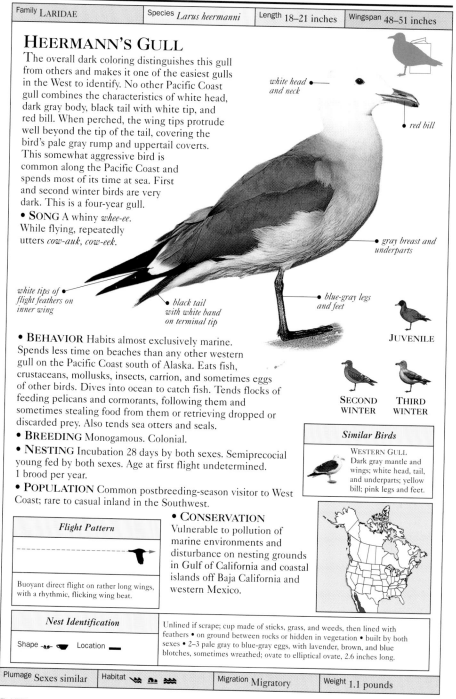

white head and neck

red bill

gray breast and underparts

white tips of flight feathers on inner wing

black tail with white band on terminal tip

blue-gray legs and feet

JUVENILE

SECOND WINTER

THIRD WINTER

• **BEHAVIOR** Habits almost exclusively marine. Spends less time on beaches than any other western gull on the Pacific Coast south of Alaska. Eats fish, crustaceans, mollusks, insects, carrion, and sometimes eggs of other birds. Dives into ocean to catch fish. Tends flocks of feeding pelicans and cormorants, following them and sometimes stealing food from them or retrieving dropped or discarded prey. Also tends sea otters and seals.

• **BREEDING** Monogamous. Colonial.

• **NESTING** Incubation 28 days by both sexes. Semiprecocial young fed by both sexes. Age at first flight undetermined. 1 brood per year.

• **POPULATION** Common postbreeding-season visitor to West Coast; rare to casual inland in the Southwest.

• **CONSERVATION** Vulnerable to pollution of marine environments and disturbance on nesting grounds in Gulf of California and coastal islands off Baja California and western Mexico.

Similar Birds

WESTERN GULL
Dark gray mantle and wings; white head, tail, and underparts; yellow bill; pink legs and feet.

Flight Pattern

Buoyant direct flight on rather long wings, with a rhythmic, flicking wing beat.

Nest Identification

Shape ⚬ ⚬   Location ▬

Unlined if scrape; cup made of sticks, grass, and weeds, then lined with feathers • on ground between rocks or hidden in vegetation • built by both sexes • 2–3 pale gray to blue-gray eggs, with lavender, brown, and blue blotches, sometimes wreathed; ovate to elliptical ovate, 2.6 inches long.

Plumage Sexes similar	Habitat 〰 ⬛ 〰	Migration Migratory	Weight 1.1 pounds

DATE _____ TIME_____ LOCATION _____

Family LARIDAE	Species *Larus crassirostris*	Length 18–19 inches	Wingspan 47–48 inches

BLACK-TAILED GULL

Easily identified with its combination of yellow bill with red tip and black subterminal band, yellow eyes with red orbital ring, and broad black tail band, this Asian straggler has been spotted on rare occasion in San Diego Bay, California. It is also casual in coastal Alaska and in northeastern North America as far south as Virginia.

yellow iris with red orbital ring

white head, neck, breast, and underparts

large yellow bill with black ring above red tip

light charcoal-gray wings and back

long wings

broad black subterminal band and white terminal band on tail

white-based tail with white uppertail coverts

short yellow legs and feet

JUVENILE

SECOND WINTER

THIRD WINTER

Since these three-year gulls are nomadic but nonmigratory, it is difficult to understand how they find their way to North America. Winter adults have a brownish gray–streaked head and nape.

- **SONG** Very low *kaoo-kaoo.*
- **BEHAVIOR** Gregarious. Frequents seashores, where it feeds on small fish, especially smelt and greenlings. Also eats insects, crustaceans, carrion, and refuse. Like most gulls, catches insects and other food in flight. Often forages while wading, swimming, and walking.
- **BREEDING** Monogamous. Colonial.
- **NESTING** Incubation 24–27 days by both sexes. Semiprecocial young known to be fed by both sexes, but it is not known how long they stay in nest. First flight at 30–40 days. 1 brood per year.
- **POPULATION** Accidental to casual in North America. Common in Asia.

Similar Birds

BAND-TAILED GULL
Darker blackish upperwings and mantle; dark eyes with yellow orbital ring; longer legs.

Flight Pattern
Strong direct flight with deep wing beats.

Nest Identification	
Shape ⬤ Location ▬	Dry grass • on ledges, slopes, and small cliffs hidden by vegetation • built by both sexes • 2–3 greenish to ocherish eggs with dark spots; oval to elliptical oval, 2.6 inches long.

Plumage Sexes similar	Habitat	Migration Nonmigratory/nomadic	Weight 1.3 pounds

DATE _____ TIME_____ LOCATION _____

Family LARIDAE	Species *Larus canus*	Length 16–18 inches	Wingspan 43 inches

MEW GULL

Heard from the tops of conifers with its catlike *mee-you*, the Mew Gull is common along the Pacific coast. It breeds along the coast and on lakes in the interior of extreme northwestern North America. Separated from similar gulls by the short unmarked yellow bill and the white spots (mirrors) in the black-tipped primaries. Winter adults have a white head washed with brown and a

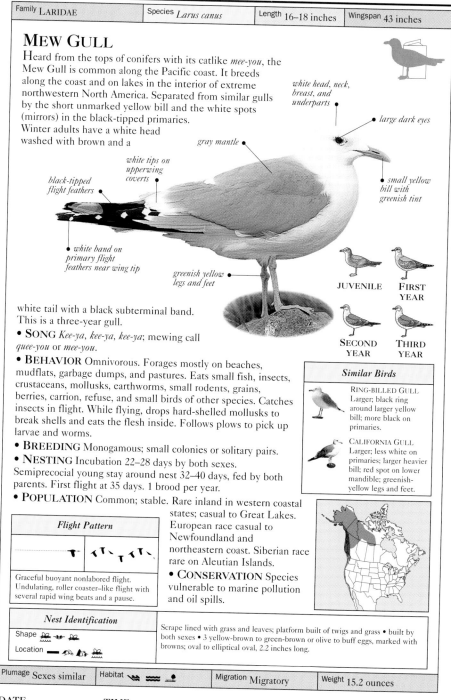

white head, neck, breast, and underparts

large dark eyes

gray mantle

white tips on upperwing coverts

black-tipped flight feathers

small yellow bill with greenish tint

white band on primary flight feathers near wing tip

greenish yellow legs and feet

JUVENILE · FIRST YEAR

SECOND YEAR · THIRD YEAR

white tail with a black subterminal band. This is a three-year gull.

- **SONG** *Kee-ya, kee-ya, kee-ya*; mewing call *quee-you* or *mee-you.*
- **BEHAVIOR** Omnivorous. Forages mostly on beaches, mudflats, garbage dumps, and pastures. Eats small fish, insects, crustaceans, mollusks, earthworms, small rodents, grains, berries, carrion, refuse, and small birds of other species. Catches insects in flight. While flying, drops hard-shelled mollusks to break shells and eats the flesh inside. Follows plows to pick up larvae and worms.
- **BREEDING** Monogamous; small colonies or solitary pairs.
- **NESTING** Incubation 22–28 days by both sexes. Semiprecocial young stay around nest 32–40 days, fed by both parents. First flight at 35 days. 1 brood per year.
- **POPULATION** Common; stable. Rare inland in western coastal states; casual to Great Lakes. European race casual to Newfoundland and northeastern coast. Siberian race rare on Aleutian Islands.
- **CONSERVATION** Species vulnerable to marine pollution and oil spills.

Similar Birds

RING-BILLED GULL
Larger; black ring around larger yellow bill; more black on primaries.

CALIFORNIA GULL
Larger; less white on primaries; larger heavier bill; red spot on lower mandible; greenish-yellow legs and feet.

Flight Pattern

Graceful buoyant nonlabored flight. Undulating, roller coaster–like flight with several rapid wing beats and a pause.

Nest Identification

Shape

Location

Scrape lined with grass and leaves; platform built of twigs and grass • built by both sexes • 3 yellow-brown to green-brown or olive to buff eggs, marked with browns; oval to elliptical oval, 2.2 inches long.

Plumage Sexes similar	Habitat	Migration Migratory	Weight 15.2 ounces

DATE _____ TIME_____ LOCATION _____

| Family LARIDAE | Species *Larus delawarensis* | Length 18–19 inches | Wingspan 48 inches |

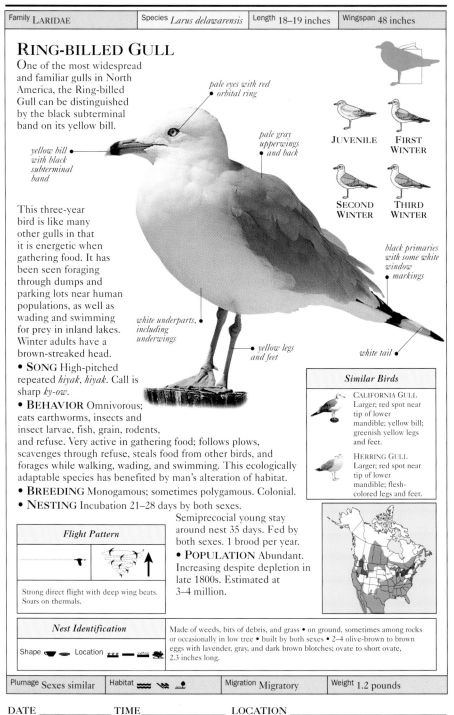

RING-BILLED GULL

One of the most widespread and familiar gulls in North America, the Ring-billed Gull can be distinguished by the black subterminal band on its yellow bill.

pale eyes with red orbital ring

yellow bill with black subterminal band

pale gray upperwings and back

JUVENILE   FIRST WINTER

SECOND WINTER   THIRD WINTER

This three-year bird is like many other gulls in that it is energetic when gathering food. It has been seen foraging through dumps and parking lots near human populations, as well as wading and swimming for prey in inland lakes. Winter adults have a brown-streaked head.

black primaries with some white window markings

white underparts, including underwings

yellow legs and feet

white tail

• SONG High-pitched repeated *hiyak, hiyak*. Call is sharp *ky-ow*.

• BEHAVIOR Omnivorous; eats earthworms, insects and insect larvae, fish, grain, rodents, and refuse. Very active in gathering food; follows plows, scavenges through refuse, steals food from other birds, and forages while walking, wading, and swimming. This ecologically adaptable species has benefited by man's alteration of habitat.

• BREEDING Monogamous; sometimes polygamous. Colonial.

• NESTING Incubation 21–28 days by both sexes. Semiprecocial young stay around nest 35 days. Fed by both sexes. 1 brood per year.

• POPULATION Abundant. Increasing despite depletion in late 1800s. Estimated at 3–4 million.

Similar Birds

CALIFORNIA GULL
Larger; red spot near tip of lower mandible; yellow bill; greenish yellow legs and feet.

HERRING GULL
Larger; red spot near tip of lower mandible; flesh-colored legs and feet.

Flight Pattern

Strong direct flight with deep wing beats. Soars on thermals.

Nest Identification

Shape ⬛ ⬤   Location ⁂ ▬ ▥

Made of weeds, bits of debris, and grass • on ground, sometimes among rocks or occasionally in low tree • built by both sexes • 2–4 olive-brown to brown eggs with lavender, gray, and dark brown blotches; ovate to short ovate, 2.3 inches long.

| Plumage Sexes similar | Habitat ▬ ⬗ ⬤ | Migration Migratory | Weight 1.2 pounds |

DATE _____ TIME_____ LOCATION _____

Family LARIDAE	Species *Larus californicus*	Length 21–22 inches	Wingspan 48–54 inches

CALIFORNIA GULL

The monument to the gull in Salt Lake City was inspired by the California Gull, because it saved the crops of the Mormon settlers from the grasshopper plague of 1848. Today, this four-year gull is the state bird of Utah. It builds its nests close to freshwater marshes and lakes, but at other times, it is frequently seen on inland fields and nearby farms, foraging through trash and eating insects. In flight, note that adults have

white head, neck, and breast

gray back and upperwings

yellow bill with red and black spot on lower mandible

black-tipped wings with white windows

white underparts and tail

greenish yellow to gray-green legs and feet

DARK JUVENILE

FIRST WINTER

SECOND WINTER

a dusky gray stripe on the trailing edge of the underwing. Winter adults have brownish streaking on the head and hindneck.

• **SONG** Has soft call of *kow-kow-kow, kee-ou,* or *klee-ah.* Has alarm call of *yowww;* also a quiet repeated *waaaaaaaah.*

• **BEHAVIOR** Primarily an inland species during summer months. Feeds on a host of agricultural pests, from grasshoppers and many other insects to rodents. Also takes fish, eggs and young from other birds, worms, spiders, refuse, and carrion. Like most gulls it is an active forager.

• **BREEDING** Monogamous. Colonial.

• **NESTING** Incubation 23–27 days by both sexes. Semiprecocial young tended by both sexes; it is not known how long they stay in nest. First flight at about 45 days. 1 brood per year.

• **POPULATION** Increasing. Abundant. Casual on Gulf Coast and East Coast in winter.

• **CONSERVATION** Vulnerable to human disturbance at nesting colonies on large western lakes and pollution of lakes and habitat loss. Mono Lake has 50,000 seriously threatened pairs.

Similar Birds

RING-BILLED GULL
Smaller; black ring around beak; lighter eyes; lacks dusky trailing edge to underwing.

HERRING GULL
Larger; red spot only on lower mandible; yellow eye; creamy pink legs and feet; lacks dusky trailing edge to underwing; lighter gray back and upperwings.

Flight Pattern
Strong direct flight with deep wing beats. Soars on thermals and updrafts.

Nest Identification	
Shape ⌒ ⌄ Location ▬	Twigs, dried feathers, bits of debris, grass, and weeds; 14–18 inches • on ground • built by both sexes • 2–3 olive-buff eggs, often blotched with deep grays and browns; oval to short oval; if third egg is laid, shape is short, subelliptical; 2.8 inches long.

Plumage Sexes similar	Habitat ≈ ⌂ ⌇	Migration Migratory	Weight 1.4 pounds

DATE _____ TIME_____ LOCATION _____

| Family LARIDAE | Species *Larus argentatus* | Length 22–26 inches | Wingspan 54–58 inches |

HERRING GULL

After facing a serious decrease in population in the 19th century, the Herring Gull has recovered and is once again numerous along the Atlantic Coast. Its range continues to expand, making it the most widespread and best-known gull in North America. This four-year gull usually nests on the ground, but when humans intrude, it will

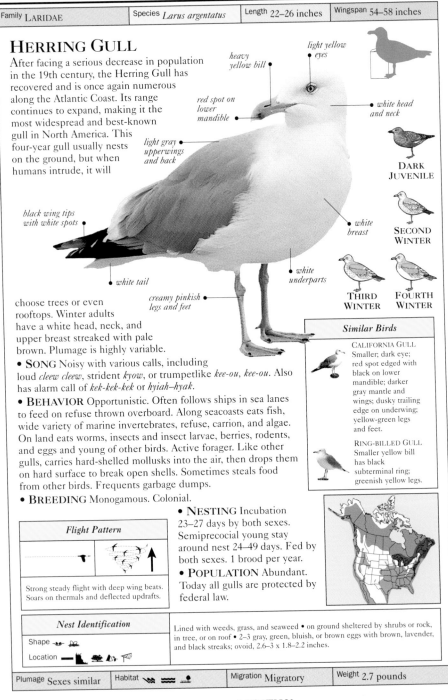

light yellow eyes

heavy yellow bill

red spot on lower mandible

white head and neck

light gray upperwings and back

DARK JUVENILE

black wing tips with white spots

white breast

SECOND WINTER

white tail

white underparts

creamy pinkish legs and feet

THIRD WINTER **FOURTH WINTER**

choose trees or even rooftops. Winter adults have a white head, neck, and upper breast streaked with pale brown. Plumage is highly variable.

• **SONG** Noisy with various calls, including loud *cleew cleew*, strident *kyow*, or trumpetlike *kee-ou, kee-ou*. Also has alarm call of *kek-kek-kek* or *hyiah–hyak*.

• **BEHAVIOR** Opportunistic. Often follows ships in sea lanes to feed on refuse thrown overboard. Along seacoasts eats fish, wide variety of marine invertebrates, refuse, carrion, and algae. On land eats worms, insects and insect larvae, berries, rodents, and eggs and young of other birds. Active forager. Like other gulls, carries hard-shelled mollusks into the air, then drops them on hard surface to break open shells. Sometimes steals food from other birds. Frequents garbage dumps.

• **BREEDING** Monogamous. Colonial.

Similar Birds

CALIFORNIA GULL Smaller; dark eye; red spot edged with black on lower mandible; darker gray mantle and wings; dusky trailing edge on underwing; yellow-green legs and feet.

RING-BILLED GULL Smaller yellow bill has black subterminal ring; greenish yellow legs.

• **NESTING** Incubation 23–27 days by both sexes. Semiprecocial young stay around nest 24–49 days. Fed by both sexes. 1 brood per year.

• **POPULATION** Abundant. Today all gulls are protected by federal law.

Flight Pattern
Strong steady flight with deep wing beats. Soars on thermals and deflected updrafts.

Nest Identification	
Shape	Lined with weeds, grass, and seaweed • on ground sheltered by shrubs or rock, in tree, or on roof • 2–3 gray, green, bluish, or brown eggs with brown, lavender, and black streaks; ovoid, 2.6–3 x 1.8–2.2 inches.
Location	

| Plumage Sexes similar | Habitat | Migration Migratory | Weight 2.7 pounds |

DATE _____ TIME_____ LOCATION _____

Family LARIDAE	Species *Larus thayeri*	Length 23–25 inches	Wingspan 55 inches

THAYER'S GULL

This graceful dovelike bird is a little smaller than the Herring Gull, the species from which it was recently split and the one its behavior most resembles. Spending most of its time in the Canadian Arctic, this bird may nest in colonies with other gulls but more often

reddish purple eye ring around gray to mottled brown eyes •

white head and neck •

medium gray wings and back •

smallish yellow bill gently curved • on top

• red spot on lower mandible

restricted black • primary tips

• white breast and underparts

JUVENILE

• white tail

• dark pink legs

SECOND WINTER

THIRD WINTER

nests on cliff ledges. Note the dark eye color and paler wing tips, especially on underside of the gray primaries. Winter adults have pale brown streaking on the head, neck, and upper breast. A four-year bird, it is difficult to separate from the Herring Gull, and its taxonomy is still disputed: Some still consider it a race of the Herring Gull, while others think it is a subspecies of the Iceland Gull.

• **SONG** A familiar *kee-yow*; a loud *kuc-kuc-kuc-kuc-kuckle-kuckle* or *hiyak, hiyak, hiyak-hiyak*. Mewing squeals.

• **BEHAVIOR** Eats small fish, mollusks, crustaceans, carrion, refuse, berries, and young and eggs of other birds. Finds food by diving in shallow water, plunging while flying, and foraging while walking on shore.

• **BREEDING** Monogamous. Colonial.

• **NESTING** Incubation 23–27 days by both sexes. Semiprecocial young stay around nest 24–29 days. Fed by both sexes. 1 brood per year.

• **POPULATION** Uncommon. Winters primarily on West Coast. Rare to casual on Great Lakes, East Coast, and in interior in winter.

Similar Birds

HERRING GULL
Larger; yellow eyes with orange orbital ring; lighter gray mantle; darker-tipped primaries on upperparts and underparts; paler legs and feet; heavier bill.

ICELAND GULL
Lighter gray mantle; usually yellow (sometimes brown) eyes; translucent pale wing tips.

Flight Pattern

Strong direct flight with steady deep wing beats. Sometimes soars on thermals or updrafts.

Nest Identification

Shape ⚬ ⚬   Location ▨

Lined with weeds, grasses, and leaves • on bare ground sheltered by rock or shrubbery • built by both sexes • 2–3 gray, green, or brown eggs; ovate, 2.8 x 2.1 inches.

Plumage Sexes similar	Habitat ▨ ▨ ▨	Migration Migratory	Weight 2.4 pounds

DATE _____ TIME_____ LOCATION _____

Family LARIDAE	Species *Larus glaucoides*	Length 23–25 inches	Wingspan 54 inches

ICELAND GULL

Restricted to the North Atlantic Ocean where it
is in the company of larger, more robust gulls,
this highly variable four-year gull spends its
summers on the coasts of northeastern
Canada and Greenland. It has two
morphs: the typical form, which
nests in Greenland and has white
wing-tips, and the Kumlien's,
which nests in Canada and
has gray wing-tips. The
pale primaries look
translucent in

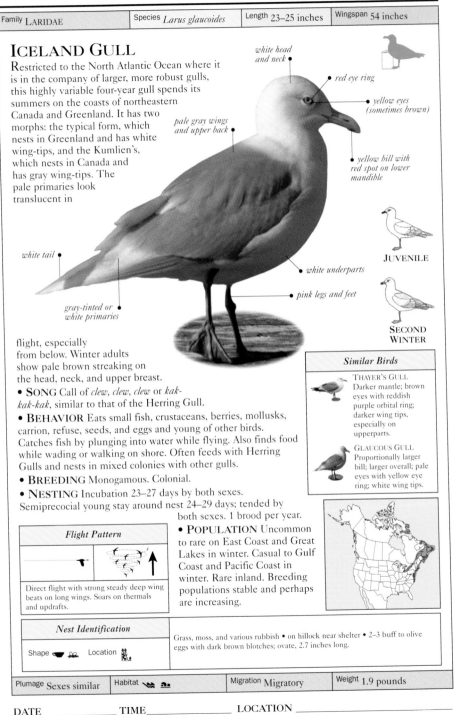

*white head
and neck*

red eye ring

*yellow eyes
(sometimes brown)*

*pale gray wings
and upper back*

*yellow bill with
red spot on lower
mandible*

white tail

white underparts

pink legs and feet

*gray-tinted or
white primaries*

JUVENILE

**SECOND
WINTER**

flight, especially
from below. Winter adults
show pale brown streaking on
the head, neck, and upper breast.

• **SONG** Call of *clew, clew, clew* or *kak-
kak-kak*, similar to that of the Herring Gull.

• **BEHAVIOR** Eats small fish, crustaceans, berries, mollusks,
carrion, refuse, seeds, and eggs and young of other birds.
Catches fish by plunging into water while flying. Also finds food
while wading or walking on shore. Often feeds with Herring
Gulls and nests in mixed colonies with other gulls.

• **BREEDING** Monogamous. Colonial.

• **NESTING** Incubation 23–27 days by both sexes.
Semiprecocial young stay around nest 24–29 days; tended by
both sexes. 1 brood per year.

• **POPULATION** Uncommon
to rare on East Coast and Great
Lakes in winter. Casual to Gulf
Coast and Pacific Coast in
winter. Rare inland. Breeding
populations stable and perhaps
are increasing.

Similar Birds

THAYER'S GULL
Darker mantle; brown
eyes with reddish
purple orbital ring;
darker wing tips,
especially on
upperparts.

GLAUCOUS GULL
Proportionally larger
bill; larger overall; pale
eyes with yellow eye
ring; white wing tips.

Flight Pattern

Direct flight with strong steady deep wing
beats on long wings. Soars on thermals
and updrafts.

Nest Identification

Shape ⌒ ☌   Location 🪨

Grass, moss, and various rubbish • on hillock near shelter • 2–3 buff to olive
eggs with dark brown blotches; ovate, 2.7 inches long.

Plumage Sexes similar	Habitat 〰️ ⚓	Migration Migratory	Weight 1.9 pounds

DATE _____ TIME_____ LOCATION _____

Family LARIDAE	Species *Larus fuscus*	Length 21–22 inches	Wingspan 54 inches

LESSER BLACK-BACKED GULL

This European gull is wintering in increasing numbers in North America. It is similar to the Western Gull and the Great Black-Backed Gull. Smaller than either of those gulls, it has yellow, not pink, feet and legs. Winter adults have a brown streaked head and neck. This four-year gull's behavior and voice resembles other gulls.

pale yellow eyes with red orbital ring

white head and neck

yellow bill with red spot on lower mandible

dark slate-gray or black mantle

white chest, belly, and underparts

JUVENILE

yellow legs and feet

white tail and rump

SECOND WINTER   THIRD WINTER

• **SONG** A loud *kyow* and a wide range of other calls, including *yuk-yuk-yuck-yuckle-yuckle* or *hiyak, hiyak, hiyak, hiyak-hiyak.*

• **BEHAVIOR** Eats small fish, seaweed, wide variety of marine invertebrates, insects, refuse, carrion, and eggs and young of other birds. Finds food by wading, swimming, and plunging to ocean's surface while flying. Also steals food from other birds. Scavenges.

• **BREEDING** Monogamous. Colonial.

• **NESTING** Incubation 24–27 days by both sexes. Semiprecocial young climb out of nest after a few days and explore surrounding area. Fed by both sexes. First flight at 30–40 days. 1 brood per year.

• **POPULATION** Rare to uncommon in eastern North America; casual in the interior around the Great Lakes and on the West Coast to Alaska. Common to fairly common in western Europe and Eurasia.

Similar Birds

GREAT BLACK-BACKED GULL
Larger; pink legs and feet; darker wings and mantle.

WESTERN GULL
Larger; pink legs and feet.

Flight Pattern

Direct flight with strong steady, deep wing beats on long wings. Sometimes soars on thermals and updrafts.

Nest Identification	Lined with dry lichens, dry vegetation, and feathers • built by both sexes • on ground near grassy shore or hidden in grasses and rocks • 3 brown or olive to blue-green eggs usually blotched with dark brown; size varies but most are ovoid, 2.7 inches long.
Shape 🐦 Location ━ 🪺 🏝	

Plumage Sexes similar	Habitat 〰〰	Migration Migratory	Weight 1.7 pounds

DATE _____ TIME_____ LOCATION _____

Family LARIDAE	Species *Larus schistisagus*	Length 25–27 inches	Wingspan 58 inches

SLATY-BACKED GULL

This four-year Asian gull spends most of its time near the Bering Sea, but occasionally wanders to the islands near Alaska. It is similar to but smaller than the Atlantic Coast's Great Black-backed Gull. In flight note the dark slate-gray mantle and wings, the broad

white head and neck

yellow eyes with reddish purple to pink orbital ring

short, massive yellow bill with red spot on lower mandible

dark slate-gray mantle

white trailing edge on wings

white breast and underparts

whitish markings on base of outer 4–5 primaries

white rump and tail

grayish black primaries

bright pink legs and feet

JUVENILE

white trailing edge to the wing that extends into the primaries, gray wing-tips on underparts (not black as in other larger dark-mantled gulls of the region), and white band that separates the tips of the outer four or five primaries from the dark mantle. Winter adults have pale brown streaking on the white head and neck.

SECOND SUMMER   SECOND WINTER

• **SONG** Laughing call, *ka-hah-gah-gah*. Also loud *yeah, yeah* similar to Great Black-backed Gull.
• **BEHAVIOR** Feeds at low tide while walking or swimming. Also swoops down to water from flight. Eats mollusks, fish, carrion, berries, and small mammals. Prefers sandy shores and steep ridges of cliffs. Nonmigratory but nomadic.
• **BREEDING** Monogamous. Colonial.
• **NESTING** Incubation 26–28 days by both sexes. Young semiprecocial; first flight at 49–56 days. 1 brood per year.
• **POPULATION** Rare in coastal Alaska; rare to casual in winter on northern Pacific Coast; casual to uncommon around islands in Bering Sea; accidental in US in Midwest, Texas, and Northeast.

Similar Birds

WESTERN GULL
Underside of wings darker gray; black primaries have white tips only. Northern birds have darker eyes; paler pink legs and feet.

Flight Pattern

Strong steady direct flight with deep wing beats. Sometimes soars.

Nest Identification

Shape   Location

Lined with dried grasses, seaweed, and feathers • on ground hidden in grasses and usually sheltered by rock or cliff • built by both sexes • 2–3 ocherish or olive-buff eggs spotted with brown or black; ovate, 2.8 x 2 inches.

Plumage Sexes similar	Habitat	Migration Nonmigratory	Weight 2.9 pounds

DATE _____ TIME_____ LOCATION _____

Family LARIDAE	Species *Larus livens*	Length 27 inches	Wingspan 60 inches

YELLOW-FOOTED GULL

A native of Mexico, this large three-year gull reaches maturity in its third year but gains its yellow legs and feet in its second winter. It is distinguished from the Western Gull by its yellow rather than pinkish feet. The male has a white rump and tail. This gull can be seen around the Salton Sea after breeding season in summer, with a few birds remaining into winter.
• SONG Quick *quock, kuck, kuck, kuck*, similar to the call of the Western Gull but lower in pitch.

white head and neck

yellow eyes with pink orbital ring

thick yellow bill with red spot on lower mandible

slate-gray back and wings

white rump and tail

white breast and underparts

yellow legs and feet

JUVENILE

FIRST SUMMER

SECOND WINTER

• BEHAVIOR Eats fish, crustaceans, mollusks, eggs and young of other birds, carrion, and refuse. Feeds while wading in water. Also catches prey while flying.
• BREEDING Monogamous. Colonial.
• NESTING Incubation 28 days by both sexes. Semiprecocial young fed by both sexes. First flight at 30-35 days. Typically 1 brood per year.
• POPULATION Stable. Breeds in Mexico in the Gulf of California. Common vagrant in summer around Salton Sea where a few winter. Casual in southern California.
• CONSERVATION Susceptible to pollution and human intrusion into its breeding area.

Similar Birds

WESTERN GULL
Pink legs and feet; slimmer bill.

Flight Pattern

Strong steady flight with deep wing beats. Often soars on thermals or updrafts.

Nest Identification

Shape ✿ Location ▬

Lined with grass, seaweed, and feathers • on ground above high watermark • built by both sexes • 2–3 pale olive to buff eggs marked with dark brown; ellipsoid to ovoid, 2.9 x 1.9 inches.

Plumage Sexes similar	Habitat 🌾	Migration Nonmigratory	Weight 2.9 pounds

DATE _____ TIME_____ LOCATION _____

Family LARIDAE	Species *Larus occidentalis*	Length 24–27 inches	Wingspan 54–58 inches

WESTERN GULL

Rarely seen far inland from shore and residing almost exclusively on the Pacific Coast, this four-year gull often lives near nesting colonies of other birds and sea lions because it includes in its diet various types of eggs, small birds, and carrion. Two races exist: the northern *occidentalis* and southern *wymani*; *occidentalis* has a paler mantle and slightly darker eyes. In flight shows a white trailing edge on its wings, a dark slate-gray mantle, and a white tail, tail coverts, and rump. Winter adults of the

white head and neck

gray-brown eyes (paler in southern birds)

large yellow bill with red spot on lower mandible

JUVENILE

white trailing edge on wings

white chest and belly

white tail

pinkish legs and feet

SECOND WINTER

northern form have moderate brown streaking on their heads; southern birds show faint streaking.

THIRD WINTER

• **SONG** Rapid call of *quock, kuk, kuk, kuk.*
• **BEHAVIOR** Inhabits coastal areas. Eats fish, a great variety of marine invertebrates, carrion, refuse, small mammals, and eggs and young of other birds. Catches fish by diving from the air to the water's surface, or by wading in water. Harasses cormorants and pelicans to force them to disgorge their catch. Drops hard shellfish in flight to ground to break shell. Follows fishing boats. Commonly found around seacoast towns and on wharves, jetties, docks, pillions, buildings, and moored ships.
• **BREEDING** Monogamous. Colonial. On offshore islands.
• **NESTING** Incubation 25–32 days by both sexes, mostly female. Semiprecocial young stay around nest 29–32 days. Fed by both sexes. 1 brood per year.

Similar Birds

YELLOW-FOOTED GULL
Slightly larger; yellow legs and feet; lighter mantle.

GLAUCOUS-WINGED GULL
Lighter mantle; gray primaries; dark eyes with red orbital ring.

• **POPULATION** Common. Stable along Pacific Coast from Baja to southern British Columbia. Casual north to southern Alaska. Rare inland.
• **CONSERVATION** Vulnerable to pollution of coastal marine environment.

Flight Pattern

Direct flight with strong steady wing beats. Often soars to great heights on updrafts along coastal sea cliffs.

Nest Identification

Shape ⌣
Location

Moss, weeds, and grass • on ground near ridge of rock or sand • built by both sexes • 1–6 buff to olive-gray eggs with dark brown blotches; ellipsoid to ovoid, 2.6–3 inches x 1.9–2 inches.

Plumage Sexes similar	Habitat	Migration Nonmigratory	Weight 2.2 pounds

DATE _____ TIME_____ LOCATION _____

Family LARIDAE	Species *Larus glaucescens*	Length 24–27 inches	Wingspan 54–58 inches

GLAUCOUS-WINGED GULL

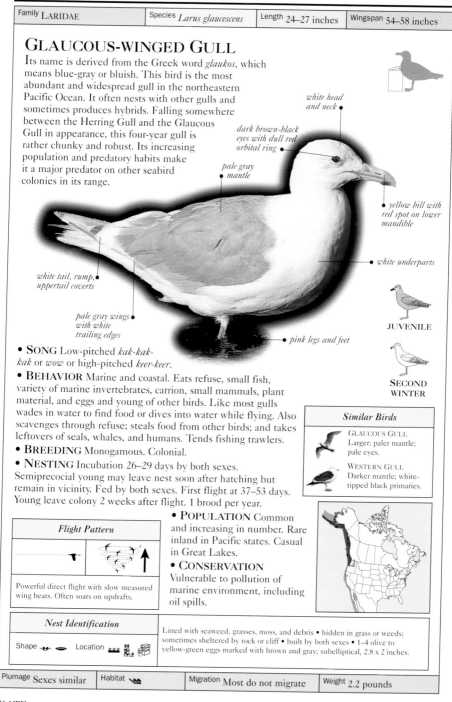

Its name is derived from the Greek word *glaukos*, which means blue-gray or bluish. This bird is the most abundant and widespread gull in the northeastern Pacific Ocean. It often nests with other gulls and sometimes produces hybrids. Falling somewhere between the Herring Gull and the Glaucous Gull in appearance, this four-year gull is rather chunky and robust. Its increasing population and predatory habits make it a major predator on other seabird colonies in its range.

white head and neck

dark brown-black eyes with dull red orbital ring

pale gray mantle

yellow bill with red spot on lower mandible

white underparts

white tail, rump, uppertail coverts

pale gray wings with white trailing edges

pink legs and feet

JUVENILE

SECOND WINTER

• **SONG** Low-pitched *kak-kak-kak* or *wow* or high-pitched *keer-keer.*
• **BEHAVIOR** Marine and coastal. Eats refuse, small fish, variety of marine invertebrates, carrion, small mammals, plant material, and eggs and young of other birds. Like most gulls wades in water to find food or dives into water while flying. Also scavenges through refuse; steals food from other birds; and takes leftovers of seals, whales, and humans. Tends fishing trawlers.
• **BREEDING** Monogamous. Colonial.
• **NESTING** Incubation 26–29 days by both sexes. Semiprecocial young may leave nest soon after hatching but remain in vicinity. Fed by both sexes. First flight at 37–53 days. Young leave colony 2 weeks after flight. 1 brood per year.

Similar Birds

GLAUCOUS GULL
Larger; paler mantle; pale eyes.

WESTERN GULL
Darker mantle; white-tipped black primaries.

• **POPULATION** Common and increasing in number. Rare inland in Pacific states. Casual in Great Lakes.
• **CONSERVATION** Vulnerable to pollution of marine environment, including oil spills.

Flight Pattern

Powerful direct flight with slow measured wing beats. Often soars on updrafts.

Nest Identification

Shape ﹏ ⬤   Location ⏙ 🪨 🏚

Lined with seaweed, grasses, moss, and debris • hidden in grass or weeds; sometimes sheltered by rock or cliff • built by both sexes • 1–4 olive to yellow-green eggs marked with brown and gray; subelliptical, 2.8 x 2 inches.

Plumage Sexes similar	Habitat 〰	Migration Most do not migrate	Weight 2.2 pounds

DATE _____ TIME_____ LOCATION _____

Family LARIDAE	Species *Larus hyperboreus*	Length 26–30 inches	Wingspan 56–60 inches

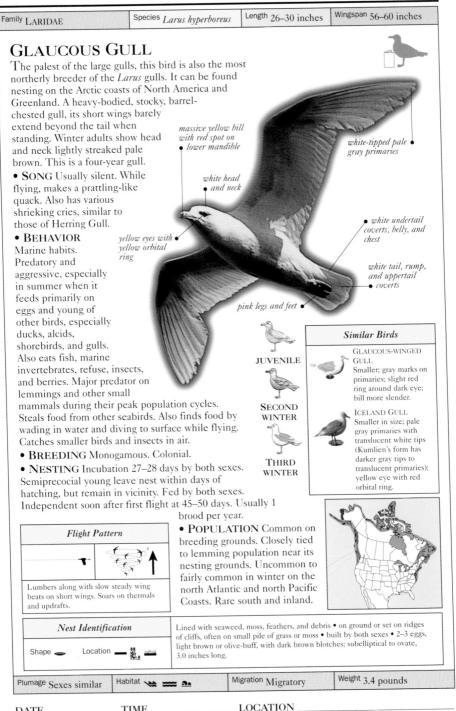

GLAUCOUS GULL

The palest of the large gulls, this bird is also the most northerly breeder of the *Larus* gulls. It can be found nesting on the Arctic coasts of North America and Greenland. A heavy-bodied, stocky, barrel-chested gull, its short wings barely extend beyond the tail when standing. Winter adults show head and neck lightly streaked pale brown. This is a four-year gull.

- **SONG** Usually silent. While flying, makes a prattling-like quack. Also has various shrieking cries, similar to those of Herring Gull.
- **BEHAVIOR** Marine habits. Predatory and aggressive, especially in summer when it feeds primarily on eggs and young of other birds, especially ducks, alcids, shorebirds, and gulls. Also eats fish, marine invertebrates, refuse, insects, and berries. Major predator on lemmings and other small mammals during their peak population cycles. Steals food from other seabirds. Also finds food by wading in water and diving to surface while flying. Catches smaller birds and insects in air.
- **BREEDING** Monogamous. Colonial.
- **NESTING** Incubation 27–28 days by both sexes. Semiprecocial young leave nest within days of hatching, but remain in vicinity. Fed by both sexes. Independent soon after first flight at 45–50 days. Usually 1 brood per year.
- **POPULATION** Common on breeding grounds. Closely tied to lemming population near its nesting grounds. Uncommon to fairly common in winter on the north Atlantic and north Pacific Coasts. Rare south and inland.

massive yellow bill with red spot on lower mandible

white head and neck

white-tipped pale gray primaries

white undertail coverts, belly, and chest

white tail, rump, and uppertail coverts

yellow eyes with yellow orbital ring

pink legs and feet

JUVENILE

SECOND WINTER

THIRD WINTER

Similar Birds

GLAUCOUS-WINGED GULL
Smaller; gray marks on primaries; slight red ring around dark eye; bill more slender.

ICELAND GULL
Smaller in size; pale gray primaries with translucent white tips (Kumlien's form has darker gray tips to translucent white primaries); yellow eye with red orbital ring.

Flight Pattern

Lumbers along with slow steady wing beats on short wings. Soars on thermals and updrafts.

Nest Identification

Shape ⌒   Location

Lined with seaweed, moss, feathers, and debris • on ground or set on ridges of cliffs, often on small pile of grass or moss • built by both sexes • 2–3 eggs, light brown or olive-buff, with dark brown blotches; subelliptical to ovate, 3.0 inches long.

Plumage Sexes similar	Habitat	Migration Migratory	Weight 3.4 pounds

DATE _____ TIME_____ LOCATION _____

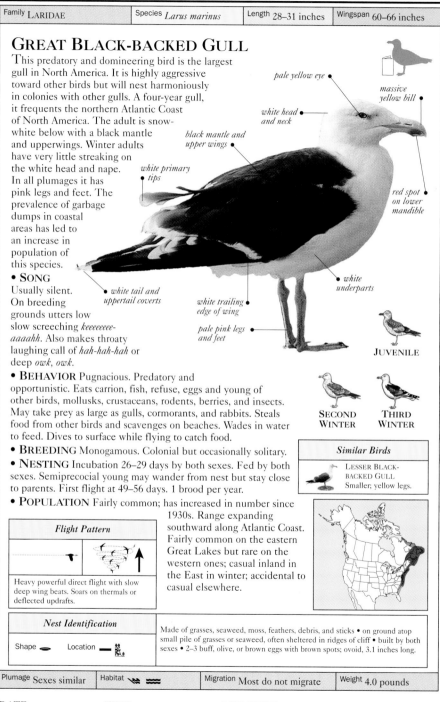

Family LARIDAE	Species *Larus marinus*	Length 28–31 inches	Wingspan 60–66 inches

GREAT BLACK-BACKED GULL

This predatory and domineering bird is the largest gull in North America. It is highly aggressive toward other birds but will nest harmoniously in colonies with other gulls. A four-year gull, it frequents the northern Atlantic Coast of North America. The adult is snow-white below with a black mantle and upperwings. Winter adults have very little streaking on the white head and nape. In all plumages it has pink legs and feet. The prevalence of garbage dumps in coastal areas has led to an increase in population of this species.

pale yellow eye

massive yellow bill

white head and neck

black mantle and upper wings

white primary tips

red spot on lower mandible

white underparts

• **SONG** Usually silent. On breeding grounds utters low slow screeching *keeeeeeee-aaaahh*. Also makes throaty laughing call of *hah-hah-hah* or deep *owk, owk*.

white tail and uppertail coverts

white trailing edge of wing

pale pink legs and feet

JUVENILE

• **BEHAVIOR** Pugnacious. Predatory and opportunistic. Eats carrion, fish, refuse, eggs and young of other birds, mollusks, crustaceans, rodents, berries, and insects. May take prey as large as gulls, cormorants, and rabbits. Steals food from other birds and scavenges on beaches. Wades in water to feed. Dives to surface while flying to catch food.

SECOND WINTER

THIRD WINTER

• **BREEDING** Monogamous. Colonial but occasionally solitary.

• **NESTING** Incubation 26–29 days by both sexes. Fed by both sexes. Semiprecocial young may wander from nest but stay close to parents. First flight at 49–56 days. 1 brood per year.

Similar Birds

LESSER BLACK-BACKED GULL
Smaller; yellow legs.

• **POPULATION** Fairly common; has increased in number since 1930s. Range expanding southward along Atlantic Coast. Fairly common on the eastern Great Lakes but rare on the western ones; casual inland in the East in winter; accidental to casual elsewhere.

Flight Pattern

Heavy powerful direct flight with slow deep wing beats. Soars on thermals or deflected updrafts.

Nest Identification

Shape — Location —

Made of grasses, seaweed, moss, feathers, debris, and sticks • on ground atop small pile of grasses or seaweed, often sheltered in ridges of cliff • built by both sexes • 2–3 buff, olive, or brown eggs with brown spots; ovoid, 3.1 inches long.

Plumage Sexes similar	Habitat 〰〰 〰〰	Migration Most do not migrate	Weight 4.0 pounds

DATE _____ TIME_____ LOCATION _____

Family LARIDAE	Species *Xema sabini*	Length 13–14 inches	Wingspan 33–36 inches

SABINE'S GULL

This two-year gull summers near the Arctic coasts of North America, but after nesting season it is rarely spotted from shore because it spends most of its time at sea. Nesting in the tundra, parents are very protective of the nest and will attack intruders or use silent distraction methods to lure them away. In flight birds have a striking black, white, and gray wing pattern; black primaries; and a gray mantle separated by a wide white triangle on the back of the wing. It is the only North American

dark slate-gray partial hood

black bill with yellow tip

black ring separates gray hood from white neck

black primaries with white tips

blackish brown eye with red orbital ring

forked white tail

gull with a distinctly forked tail. Winter adults have a white head with dusky gray on the back of the crown and nape.

- **SONG** Short, harsh ternlike cry of *creeeeee*.
- **BEHAVIOR** Largely pelagic. Eats insects, fish, crustaceans, mollusks, and marine worms in breeding season; otherwise, eats mostly fish. Runs along mudflats like a plover searching for food. Also feeds by dipping to water's surface from flight and foraging while swimming.
- **BREEDING** Monogamous. Small colonies. Often in company of Arctic Terns.
- **NESTING** Incubation 23–26 days by both sexes. Semiprecocial young. Shortly after hatching, nestlings led to water by parents. Young feed themselves. First flight at about 35 days. 1 brood per year.

JUVENILE   WINTER ADULT

Similar Birds

BONAPARTE'S GULL
Black bill; black hood; orange legs and feet; white outer primaries form triangle at wing tip; square tail.

- **POPULATION** Common on breeding grounds. Winters at sea mainly in Southern Hemisphere. Common migrant well off West Coast; casual on and off East Coast. Rare to casual in migration in interior of the West and on Great Lakes.

Flight Pattern

Ternlike airy flight with continuous wing beats, a few glides, and numerous dives. Also hovers.

Nest Identification

Shape ⬯   Location ▬ ✦✦✦

Seaweed, grasses, moss, and feathers • on ground atop pile of vegetation near water • may be built by both sexes • 1–3 olive-buff eggs spotted with darker olive-brown and occasionally wreathed; ovate to subelliptical, 1.8 inches long.

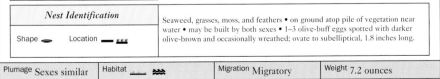

Plumage Sexes similar	Habitat ▬ ≈≈	Migration Migratory	Weight 7.2 ounces

DATE _____ TIME _____ LOCATION _____

Family LARIDAE	Species *Rissa tridactyla*	Length 16–17 inche	Wingspan 36 inches

BLACK-LEGGED KITTIWAKE

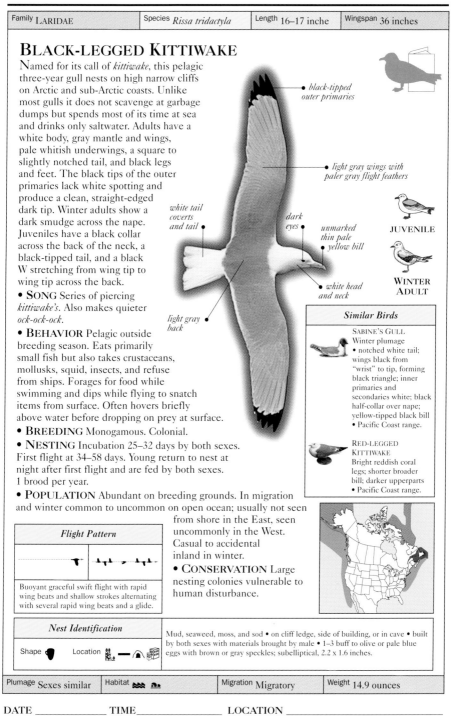

Named for its call of *kittiwake*, this pelagic three-year gull nests on high narrow cliffs on Arctic and sub-Arctic coasts. Unlike most gulls it does not scavenge at garbage dumps but spends most of its time at sea and drinks only saltwater. Adults have a white body, gray mantle and wings, pale whitish underwings, a square to slightly notched tail, and black legs and feet. The black tips of the outer primaries lack white spotting and produce a clean, straight-edged dark tip. Winter adults show a dark smudge across the nape. Juveniles have a black collar across the back of the neck, a black-tipped tail, and a black W stretching from wing tip to wing tip across the back.

• black-tipped outer primaries

• light gray wings with paler gray flight feathers

white tail coverts and tail

dark eyes

unmarked thin pale yellow bill

JUVENILE

• white head and neck

WINTER ADULT

light gray back

• **SONG** Series of piercing *kittiwake's*. Also makes quieter *ock-ock-ock*.

• **BEHAVIOR** Pelagic outside breeding season. Eats primarily small fish but also takes crustaceans, mollusks, squid, insects, and refuse from ships. Forages for food while swimming and dips while flying to snatch items from surface. Often hovers briefly above water before dropping on prey at surface.

• **BREEDING** Monogamous. Colonial.

• **NESTING** Incubation 25–32 days by both sexes. First flight at 34–58 days. Young return to nest at night after first flight and are fed by both sexes. 1 brood per year.

• **POPULATION** Abundant on breeding grounds. In migration and winter common to uncommon on open ocean; usually not seen from shore in the East, seen uncommonly in the West. Casual to accidental inland in winter.

• **CONSERVATION** Large nesting colonies vulnerable to human disturbance.

Similar Birds

SABINE'S GULL
Winter plumage
• notched white tail; wings black from "wrist" to tip, forming black triangle; inner primaries and secondaries white; black half-collar over nape; yellow-tipped black bill
• Pacific Coast range.

RED-LEGGED KITTIWAKE
Bright reddish coral legs; shorter broader bill; darker upperparts
• Pacific Coast range.

Flight Pattern

Buoyant graceful swift flight with rapid wing beats and shallow strokes alternating with several rapid wing beats and a glide.

Nest Identification

Shape — Location

Mud, seaweed, moss, and sod • on cliff ledge, side of building, or in cave • built by both sexes with materials brought by male • 1–3 buff to olive or pale blue eggs with brown or gray speckles; subelliptical, 2.2 x 1.6 inches.

Plumage Sexes similar	Habitat	Migration Migratory	Weight 14.9 ounces

DATE _____ TIME_____ LOCATION _____

Family LARIDAE	Species *Rissa brevirostris*	Length 14–16 inches	Wingspan 33 inches

RED-LEGGED KITTIWAKE

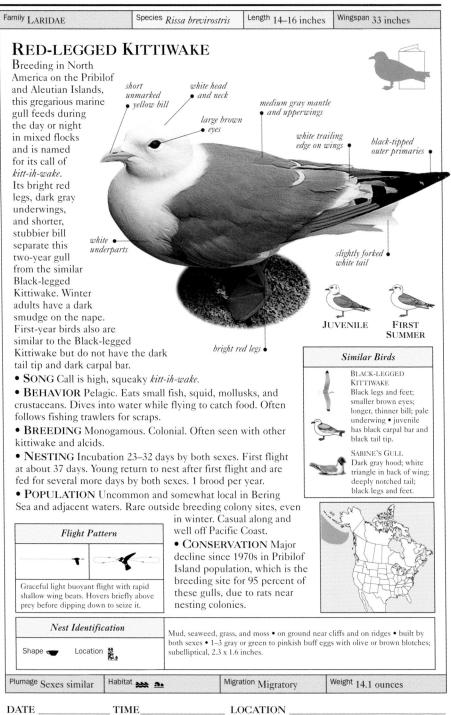

Breeding in North America on the Pribilof and Aleutian Islands, this gregarious marine gull feeds during the day or night in mixed flocks and is named for its call of *kitt-ih-wake*. Its bright red legs, dark gray underwings, and shorter, stubbier bill separate this two-year gull from the similar Black-legged Kittiwake. Winter adults have a dark smudge on the nape. First-year birds also are similar to the Black-legged Kittiwake but do not have the dark tail tip and dark carpal bar.

short unmarked yellow bill
white head and neck
medium gray mantle and upperwings
large brown eyes
white trailing edge on wings
black-tipped outer primaries
white underparts
slightly forked white tail
bright red legs

JUVENILE   FIRST SUMMER

- **SONG** Call is high, squeaky *kitt-ih-wake*.
- **BEHAVIOR** Pelagic. Eats small fish, squid, mollusks, and crustaceans. Dives into water while flying to catch food. Often follows fishing trawlers for scraps.
- **BREEDING** Monogamous. Colonial. Often seen with other kittiwake and alcids.
- **NESTING** Incubation 23–32 days by both sexes. First flight at about 37 days. Young return to nest after first flight and are fed for several more days by both sexes. 1 brood per year.
- **POPULATION** Uncommon and somewhat local in Bering Sea and adjacent waters. Rare outside breeding colony sites, even in winter. Casual along and well off Pacific Coast.
- **CONSERVATION** Major decline since 1970s in Pribilof Island population, which is the breeding site for 95 percent of these gulls, due to rats near nesting colonies.

Similar Birds

BLACK-LEGGED KITTIWAKE
Black legs and feet; smaller brown eyes; longer, thinner bill; pale underwing • juvenile has black carpal bar and black tail tip.

SABINE'S GULL
Dark gray hood; white triangle in back of wing; deeply notched tail; black legs and feet.

Flight Pattern

Graceful light buoyant flight with rapid shallow wing beats. Hovers briefly above prey before dipping down to seize it.

Nest Identification

Shape 🥄   Location 🪺

Mud, seaweed, grass, and moss • on ground near cliffs and on ridges • built by both sexes • 1–3 gray or green to pinkish buff eggs with olive or brown blotches; subelliptical, 2.3 x 1.6 inches.

Plumage Sexes similar	Habitat 〰️ 🪨	Migration Migratory	Weight 14.1 ounces

DATE _____ TIME_____ LOCATION _____

Family LARIDAE	Species *Rhodostethia rosea*	Length 13–14 inches	Wingspan 33 inches

ROSS'S GULL

Sometimes called the Rosy Gull because of its pinkish underparts. It is rarely seen by most birders as it spends most of its time confined in the Arctic Circle. The only known nesting area in North America is near Churchill, Manitoba where the species has nested since 1980. In winter plumage the black collar fades away to a small dark ear spot. In flight look for long pointed wings, darker below than above with white trailing edges and the long wedge-shaped tail. Juveniles have paler legs and feet, a black ear spot, and a black tail tip; a combination of dark brown outer primaries and carpal bar form a W across the wings and mantle.

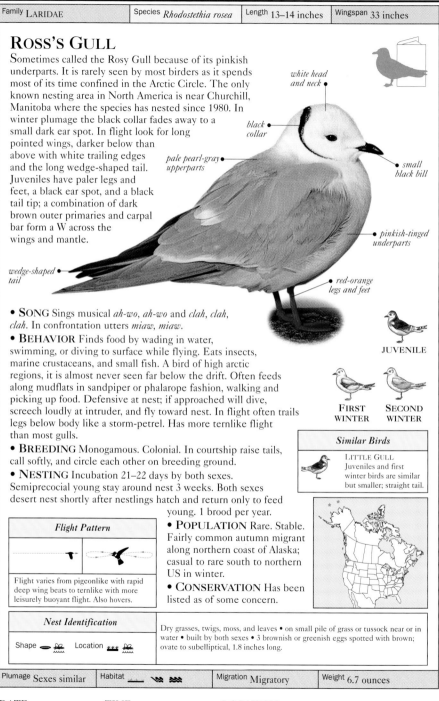

white head and neck

black collar

pale pearl-gray upperparts

small black bill

pinkish-tinged underparts

wedge-shaped tail

red-orange legs and feet

JUVENILE

FIRST WINTER

SECOND WINTER

- **SONG** Sings musical *ah-wo*, *ah-wo* and *clah*, *clah*, *clah*. In confrontation utters *miaw*, *miaw*.
- **BEHAVIOR** Finds food by wading in water, swimming, or diving to surface while flying. Eats insects, marine crustaceans, and small fish. A bird of high arctic regions, it is almost never seen far below the drift. Often feeds along mudflats in sandpiper or phalarope fashion, walking and picking up food. Defensive at nest; if approached will dive, screech loudly at intruder, and fly toward nest. In flight often trails legs below body like a storm-petrel. Has more ternlike flight than most gulls.
- **BREEDING** Monogamous. Colonial. In courtship raise tails, call softly, and circle each other on breeding ground.
- **NESTING** Incubation 21–22 days by both sexes. Semiprecocial young stay around nest 3 weeks. Both sexes desert nest shortly after nestlings hatch and return only to feed young. 1 brood per year.
- **POPULATION** Rare. Stable. Fairly common autumn migrant along northern coast of Alaska; casual to rare south to northern US in winter.
- **CONSERVATION** Has been listed as of some concern.

Similar Birds

LITTLE GULL
Juveniles and first winter birds are similar but smaller; straight tail.

Flight Pattern

Flight varies from pigeonlike with rapid deep wing beats to ternlike with more leisurely buoyant flight. Also hovers.

Nest Identification

Shape   Location

Dry grasses, twigs, moss, and leaves • on small pile of grass or tussock near or in water • built by both sexes • 3 brownish or greenish eggs spotted with brown; ovate to subelliptical, 1.8 inches long.

Plumage Sexes similar	Habitat	Migration Migratory	Weight 6.7 ounces

DATE _____ TIME_____ LOCATION _____

Family LARIDAE	Species *Pagophila eburnea*	Length 15–17 inches	Wingspan 37 inches

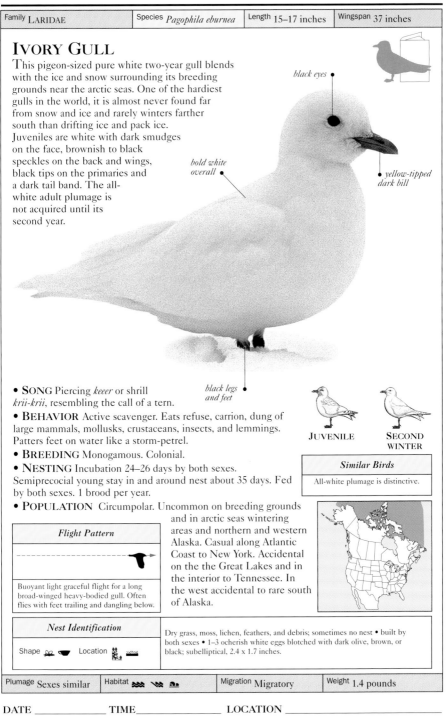

IVORY GULL

This pigeon-sized pure white two-year gull blends with the ice and snow surrounding its breeding grounds near the arctic seas. One of the hardiest gulls in the world, it is almost never found far from snow and ice and rarely winters farther south than drifting ice and pack ice. Juveniles are white with dark smudges on the face, brownish to black speckles on the back and wings, black tips on the primaries and a dark tail band. The all-white adult plumage is not acquired until its second year.

black eyes

bold white overall

yellow-tipped dark bill

black legs and feet

• **SONG** Piercing *keeer* or shrill *krii-krii*, resembling the call of a tern.
• **BEHAVIOR** Active scavenger. Eats refuse, carrion, dung of large mammals, mollusks, crustaceans, insects, and lemmings. Patters feet on water like a storm-petrel.
• **BREEDING** Monogamous. Colonial.
• **NESTING** Incubation 24–26 days by both sexes. Semiprecocial young stay in and around nest about 35 days. Fed by both sexes. 1 brood per year.
• **POPULATION** Circumpolar. Uncommon on breeding grounds and in arctic seas wintering areas and northern and western Alaska. Casual along Atlantic Coast to New York. Accidental on the the Great Lakes and in the interior to Tennessee. In the west accidental to rare south of Alaska.

JUVENILE SECOND WINTER

Similar Birds

All-white plumage is distinctive.

Flight Pattern

Buoyant light graceful flight for a long broad-winged heavy-bodied gull. Often flies with feet trailing and dangling below.

Nest Identification	Dry grass, moss, lichen, feathers, and debris; sometimes no nest • built by both sexes • 1–3 ocherish white eggs blotched with dark olive, brown, or black; subelliptical, 2.4 x 1.7 inches.
Shape ‿ ◡ Location ⚏ ▚	

Plumage Sexes similar	Habitat ≈≈ ✈ ☁	Migration Migratory	Weight 1.4 pounds

DATE _____ TIME_____ LOCATION _____

Family LARIDAE	Species *Sterna nilotica*	Length 13–14 inches	Wingspan 33–34 inches

GULL-BILLED TERN

The whitest of the North American tern species was almost exterminated in the early 1900s due to the demand for their eggs as a delicacy and their feathers to adorn women's hats. Gull-billed Terns are common summer residents in California and along the Atlantic Coast. Some remain on the Gulf Coast during winter months. In summer adults have a black cap that extends below the eyes and down the nape and pale gray upperparts that are darker at the wing tips. At a distance it appears white with rather broad, rounded wings, a heavy body, and a moderately forked tail. In winter the head is white with faint dusky streaking on the nape. Juveniles have dusky streaking on the pale upperparts and a brownish bill.

black crown and nape

pale gray upperparts

stout black bill

white underparts

broad wings with darker tips

long black legs and feet

stocky body

JUVENILE

WINTER PLUMAGE

• **SONG** Raspy sharp *ge-rek* or dry raspy *kay-tih-DID* or *kay-DID*. Young give faint high-pitched *peep peep* call.
• **BEHAVIOR** Flies over farm fields or marshes to catch insects, its main diet. Over water sometimes swoops to surface to catch small prey. Also eats earthworms, frogs, and crustaceans.
• **BREEDING** Monogamous. Colonial and/or solitary. Pairs sometimes nest at edge of other tern species' colonies.
• **NESTING** Incubation 22–23 days by both sexes. Semiprecocial young may leave nest a few days after hatching and hide in dense plant cover. Fed by both sexes. First flight at 28–35 days. Young may remain with parents for 90 days or more and migrate with them. 1 brood per year.
• **POPULATION** Fairly common but local. Less common on Atlantic Coast. Casual to accidental in interior except in Salton Sea.
• **CONSERVATION** Species has never recovered from near extermination in early 1900s.

Similar Birds

SANDWICH TERN
Slender black bill with yellow tip; deeper fork in tail; longer, more slender, more pointed wings with darker outer primaries; more slender body.

FORSTER'S TERN
White underparts; pale gray upperparts; more slender body; slender, more pointed wings; deeply forked tail; mostly orange bill, legs, and feet.

Flight Pattern

Direct flight with easy, graceful shallow wing beats.

Nest Identification

Shape ⚲   Location ▬ ▬ 🌿 🌿 🌿 🎋

On open ground; often concealed in detritus among shells • lined with plant material and debris; rimmed with sand, shells, sticks, and grass • built by both sexes • 1–4 pink-buff to yellowish eggs lightly spotted with dark brown; oval and well-rounded at small end, 1.9 x 1.3 inches.

Plumage Sexes similar	Habitat	Migration Migratory	Weight 8.2 ounces

DATE _____ TIME_____ LOCATION _____

Family LARIDAE	Species *Sterna caspia*	Length 19–23 inches	Wingspan 50–55 inches

CASPIAN TERN

The largest and least sociable tern is easily distinguished by its large size, stout red-orange bill, and tail forked to a quarter of its length. In flight the underside of the outer primaries are dark. Caspian Terns are known for their predatory feeding habits, sometimes stealing catches from other seabirds and eating eggs and young of other terns and gulls. Many Caspian Terns migrate to coastal regions during winter months, moving as far south as the West Indies and the northern regions of South America. Some remain in coastal locales year-round. Juveniles and winter adults have a streaked dusky-and-white cap that extends below the eye.

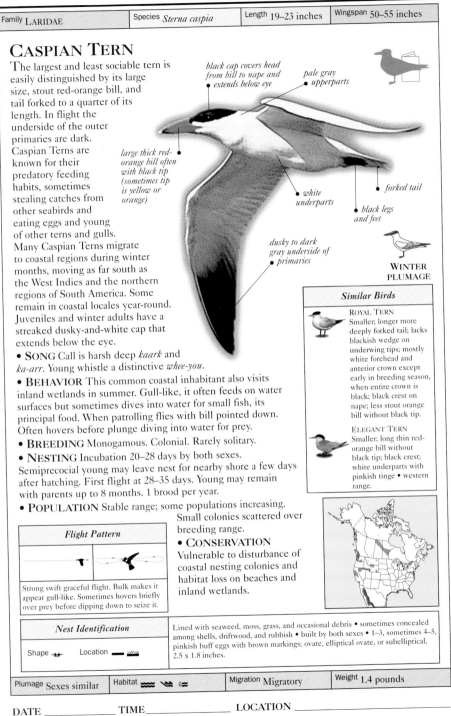

black cap covers head from bill to nape and extends below eye

pale gray upperparts

large thick red-orange bill often with black tip (sometimes tip is yellow or orange)

white underparts

forked tail

black legs and feet

dusky to dark gray underside of primaries

WINTER PLUMAGE

Similar Birds

ROYAL TERN
Smaller; longer more deeply forked tail; lacks blackish wedge on underwing tips; mostly white forehead and anterior crown except early in breeding season, when entire crown is black; black crest on nape; less stout orange bill without black tip.

ELEGANT TERN
Smaller; long red-orange bill without black tip; black crest; white underparts with pinkish tinge • western range.

• **SONG** Call is harsh deep *kaark* and *ka-arr*. Young whistle a distinctive *whee-you*.
• **BEHAVIOR** This common coastal inhabitant also visits inland wetlands in summer. Gull-like, it often feeds on water surfaces but sometimes dives into water for small fish, its principal food. When patrolling flies with bill pointed down. Often hovers before plunge diving into water for prey.
• **BREEDING** Monogamous. Colonial. Rarely solitary.
• **NESTING** Incubation 20–28 days by both sexes. Semiprecocial young may leave nest for nearby shore a few days after hatching. First flight at 28–35 days. Young may remain with parents up to 8 months. 1 brood per year.
• **POPULATION** Stable range; some populations increasing. Small colonies scattered over breeding range.
• **CONSERVATION** Vulnerable to disturbance of coastal nesting colonies and habitat loss on beaches and inland wetlands.

Flight Pattern

Strong swift graceful flight. Bulk makes it appear gull-like. Sometimes hovers briefly over prey before dipping down to seize it.

Nest Identification	Lined with seaweed, moss, grass, and occasional debris • sometimes concealed among shells, driftwood, and rubbish • built by both sexes • 1–3, sometimes 4–5, pinkish buff eggs with brown markings; ovate, elliptical ovate, or subelliptical, 2.5 x 1.8 inches.
Shape 👣 Location ▬ 〰️	

Plumage Sexes similar	Habitat 〰️ 🦆 〰️	Migration Migratory	Weight 1.4 pounds

DATE _____ TIME_____ LOCATION _____

| Family LARIDAE | Species *Sterna maxima* | Length 18–21 inches | Wingspan 42–44 inches |

ROYAL TERN

pumpkin-orange to yellow-orange bill

black head and crest

pale gray mantle

The second-largest tern in North America sometimes is seen snatching food from the Brown Pelican's pouch. Briefly in spring and early summer adults have a shaggy black crown from bill to nape; the rest of the year the forehead and forecrown are white. In flight birds show a tail forked to about half its length, pale underwings to the tips of dusky outermost primaries, and an orange bill. Juveniles look like winter adults but have more faint streaking on the upperparts and yellowish or orange feet and legs.

black legs and feet

white body

WINTER PLUMAGE

• **SONG** Large repertoire of calls includes bleating *ee-ah* and melodic trilled whistle, *tourreee*. In nesting areas often squawks *quak, kak,* or *kowk.*

• **BEHAVIOR** Plunge dives, from a hover 40–60 feet above ocean or inlets, and goes below surface for a catch. Eats mostly fish but also takes marine invertebrates, including shrimp and squid. When not feeding often loafs on sandbars, beaches, or mudflats with other species of terns and gulls.

• **BREEDING** Monogamous. Colonial. Often nests in mixed colonies with other species of terns.

• **NESTING** Incubation 20–31 days by both sexes. Young semiprecocial; upon leaving nest a few days after hatching, young often gather in creche, where they recognize parents by voice and beg for food. First flight at 28–35 days. May remain with parents up to 8 months or longer and migrate with them.

• **POPULATION** Declining. Has declined in California since 1950. Fairly common in breeding range; uncommon to rare north of it in late summer on Atlantic Coast. Fairly common in winter in southern California; rare to accidental inland from coasts.

• **CONSERVATION** Vulnerable to disturbance on nesting beaches by humans and wild and domestic predators.

Similar Birds

ELEGANT TERN
Smaller body; more slender reddish orange bill that appears slightly drooped at tip; longer shaggy crest extends down nape;
• western range.

CASPIAN TERN
Larger body; black cap extends below eyes; lacks white forehead; thicker bright red bill; tail not as deeply forked; dark underside and pale upperside on primaries.

Flight Pattern

Direct flight with deep, more rangy, continual slow wing beats. Hovers briefly before plunge diving for prey.

Nest Identification

Shape ⌣   Location 〰

Sometimes sparsely lined with debris • built by both sexes • 1–2, sometimes 3–4, whitish buff to brown eggs with reddish brown markings, occasionally wreathed; ovate to elliptical ovate, 2.5 inches long.

| Plumage Sexes similar | Habitat 〰 〰 | Migration Migratory | Weight 1.0 pound |

DATE _____ TIME_____ LOCATION _____

Family LARIDAE	Species *Sterna elegans*	Length 16–17 inches	Wingspan 34 inches

ELEGANT TERN

This medium-sized coastal inhabitant can be identified by its long, deep red-orange bill, which, unlike similar species, lacks a black tip. In flight it shows a white rump. This native of Mexico breeds as far north as southern California but moves north along the

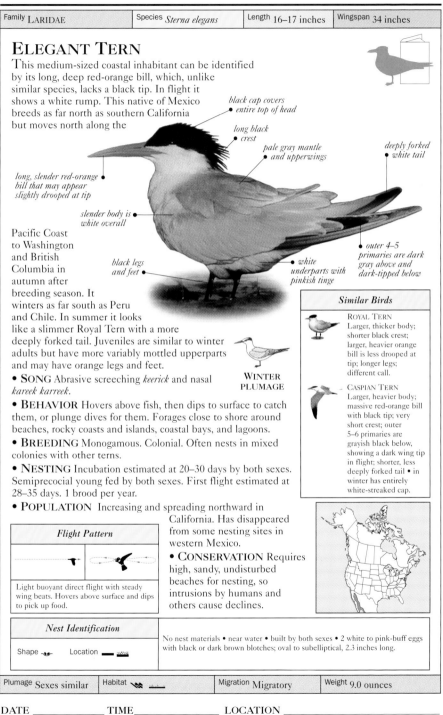

black cap covers entire top of head

long black crest

pale gray mantle and upperwings

deeply forked white tail

long, slender red-orange bill that may appear slightly drooped at tip

slender body is white overall

Pacific Coast to Washington and British Columbia in autumn after breeding season. It winters as far south as Peru and Chile. In summer it looks like a slimmer Royal Tern with a more deeply forked tail. Juveniles are similar to winter adults but have more variably mottled upperparts and may have orange legs and feet.

black legs and feet

white underparts with pinkish tinge

outer 4–5 primaries are dark gray above and dark-tipped below

WINTER PLUMAGE

• **SONG** Abrasive screeching *keerick* and nasal *kareek karreek*.

• **BEHAVIOR** Hovers above fish, then dips to surface to catch them, or plunge dives for them. Forages close to shore around beaches, rocky coasts and islands, coastal bays, and lagoons.

• **BREEDING** Monogamous. Colonial. Often nests in mixed colonies with other terns.

• **NESTING** Incubation estimated at 20–30 days by both sexes. Semiprecocial young fed by both sexes. First flight estimated at 28–35 days. 1 brood per year.

• **POPULATION** Increasing and spreading northward in California. Has disappeared from some nesting sites in western Mexico.

• **CONSERVATION** Requires high, sandy, undisturbed beaches for nesting, so intrusions by humans and others cause declines.

Similar Birds

ROYAL TERN
Larger, thicker body; shorter black crest; larger, heavier orange bill is less drooped at tip; longer legs; different call.

CASPIAN TERN
Larger, heavier body; massive red-orange bill with black tip; very short crest; outer 5–6 primaries are grayish black below, showing a dark wing tip in flight; shorter, less deeply forked tail • in winter has entirely white-streaked cap.

Flight Pattern

Light buoyant direct flight with steady wing beats. Hovers above surface and dips to pick up food.

Nest Identification

Shape — Location —
No nest materials • near water • built by both sexes • 2 white to pink-buff eggs with black or dark brown blotches; oval to subelliptical, 2.3 inches long.

Plumage Sexes similar	Habitat	Migration Migratory	Weight 9.0 ounces

DATE _____ TIME_____ LOCATION _____

Family LARIDAE	Species *Sterna hirundo*	Length 13–16 inches	Wingspan 30–31 inches

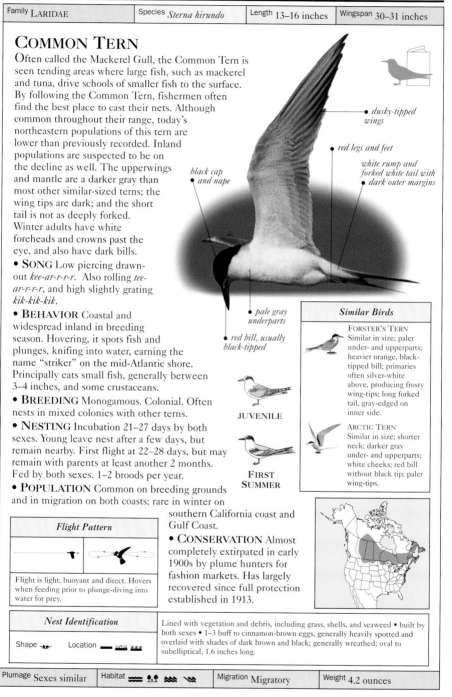

COMMON TERN

Often called the Mackerel Gull, the Common Tern is seen tending areas where large fish, such as mackerel and tuna, drive schools of smaller fish to the surface. By following the Common Tern, fishermen often find the best place to cast their nets. Although common throughout their range, today's northeastern populations of this tern are lower than previously recorded. Inland populations are suspected to be on the decline as well. The upperwings and mantle are a darker gray than most other similar-sized terns; the wing tips are dark; and the short tail is not as deeply forked. Winter adults have white foreheads and crowns past the eye, and also have dark bills.

• **SONG** Low piercing drawn-out *kee-ar-r-r-r*. Also rolling *tee-ar-r-r-r*, and high slightly grating *kik-kik-kik*.

• **BEHAVIOR** Coastal and widespread inland in breeding season. Hovering, it spots fish and plunges, knifing into water, earning the name "striker" on the mid-Atlantic shore. Principally eats small fish, generally between 3–4 inches, and some crustaceans.

• **BREEDING** Monogamous. Colonial. Often nests in mixed colonies with other terns.

• **NESTING** Incubation 21–27 days by both sexes. Young leave nest after a few days, but remain nearby. First flight at 22–28 days, but may remain with parents at least another 2 months. Fed by both sexes. 1–2 broods per year.

• **POPULATION** Common on breeding grounds and in migration on both coasts; rare in winter on southern California coast and Gulf Coast.

• **CONSERVATION** Almost completely extirpated in early 1900s by plume hunters for fashion markets. Has largely recovered since full protection established in 1913.

dusky-tipped wings

red legs and feet

white rump and forked white tail with dark outer margins

black cap and nape

pale gray underparts

red bill, usually black-tipped

JUVENILE

FIRST SUMMER

Similar Birds

FORSTER'S TERN
Similar in size; paler under- and upperparts; heavier orange, black-tipped bill; primaries often silver-white above, producing frosty wing-tips; long forked tail, gray-edged on inner side.

ARCTIC TERN
Similar in size; shorter neck; darker gray under- and upperparts; white cheeks; red bill without black tip; paler wing-tips.

Flight Pattern

Flight is light, buoyant and direct. Hovers when feeding prior to plunge-diving into water for prey.

Nest Identification

Shape ⚬ Location ▬ ▨ ♦♦

Lined with vegetation and debris, including grass, shells, and seaweed • built by both sexes • 1–3 buff to cinnamon-brown eggs, generally heavily spotted and overlaid with shades of dark brown and black; generally wreathed; oval to subelliptical, 1.6 inches long.

Plumage Sexes similar	Habitat ～～ 🐟 ～～ ～	Migration Migratory	Weight 4.2 ounces

DATE _____ TIME_____ LOCATION _____

| Family LARIDAE | Species *Sterna paradisaea* | Length 14–17 inches | Wingspan 29–33 inches |

ARCTIC TERN

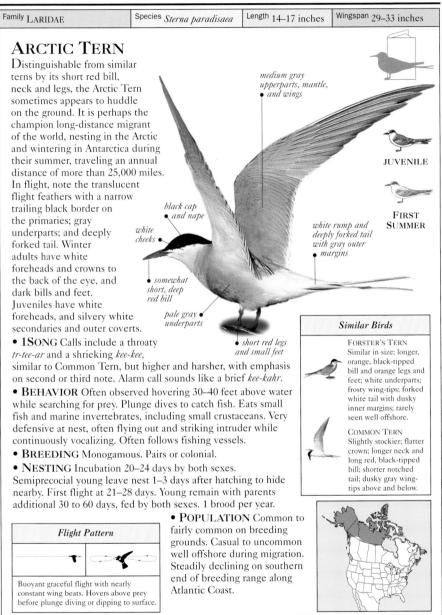

Distinguishable from similar terns by its short red bill, neck and legs, the Arctic Tern sometimes appears to huddle on the ground. It is perhaps the champion long-distance migrant of the world, nesting in the Arctic and wintering in Antarctica during their summer, traveling an annual distance of more than 25,000 miles. In flight, note the translucent flight feathers with a narrow trailing black border on the primaries; gray underparts; and deeply forked tail. Winter adults have white foreheads and crowns to the back of the eye, and dark bills and feet. Juveniles have white foreheads, and silvery white secondaries and outer coverts.

medium gray upperparts, mantle, and wings

black cap and nape

white cheeks

white rump and deeply forked tail with gray outer margins

JUVENILE

FIRST SUMMER

somewhat short, deep red bill

pale gray underparts

short red legs and small feet

• **1SONG** Calls include a throaty *tr-tee-ar* and a shrieking *kee-kee,* similar to Common Tern, but higher and harsher, with emphasis on second or third note. Alarm call sounds like a brief *kee-kahr.*
• **BEHAVIOR** Often observed hovering 30–40 feet above water while searching for prey. Plunge dives to catch fish. Eats small fish and marine invertebrates, including small crustaceans. Very defensive at nest, often flying out and striking intruder while continuously vocalizing. Often follows fishing vessels.
• **BREEDING** Monogamous. Pairs or colonial.
• **NESTING** Incubation 20–24 days by both sexes. Semiprecocial young leave nest 1–3 days after hatching to hide nearby. First flight at 21–28 days. Young remain with parents additional 30 to 60 days, fed by both sexes. 1 brood per year.
• **POPULATION** Common to fairly common on breeding grounds. Casual to uncommon well offshore during migration. Steadily declining on southern end of breeding range along Atlantic Coast.

Similar Birds

FORSTER'S TERN
Similar in size; longer, orange, black-tipped bill and orange legs and feet; white underparts; frosty wing-tips; forked white tail with dusky inner margins; rarely seen well offshore.

COMMON TERN
Slightly stockier; flatter crown; longer neck and long red, black-tipped bill; shorter notched tail; dusky gray wing-tips above and below.

Flight Pattern

Buoyant graceful flight with nearly constant wing beats. Hovers above prey before plunge diving or dipping to surface.

Nest Identification

Shape ⸝⸝⸝   Location ▬ ▬ ≈≈≈ ★★★

Vegetation lined with debris, occasionally grass and shells • built by both sexes • 1–3 buff to pale olive eggs, blotched with black and brown markings; oval to subelliptical, 1.6 inches long.

| Plumage Sexes similar | Habitat ▬ ▬ ≈≈ ≈≈≈ | Migration Migratory | Weight 3.8 ounces |

DATE _____ TIME_____ LOCATION _____

Family LARIDAE	Species *Sterna forsteri*	Length 14–15 inches	Wingspan 30–31 inches

FORSTER'S TERN

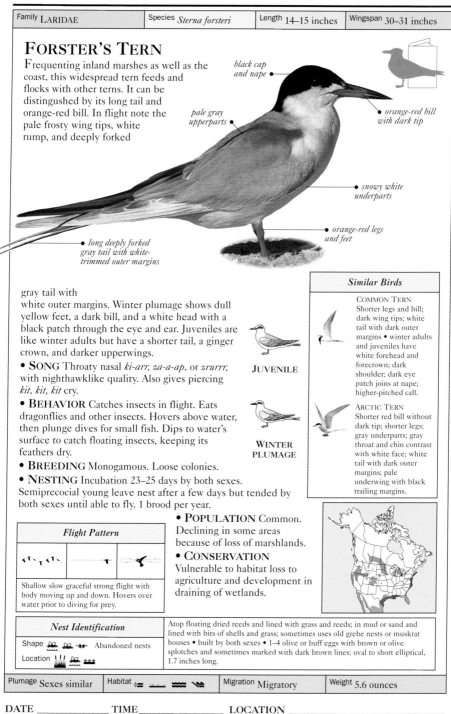

Frequenting inland marshes as well as the coast, this widespread tern feeds and flocks with other terns. It can be distinguished by its long tail and orange-red bill. In flight note the pale frosty wing tips, white rump, and deeply forked

black cap and nape

pale gray upperparts

orange-red bill with dark tip

snowy white underparts

orange-red legs and feet

long deeply forked gray tail with white-trimmed outer margins

gray tail with white outer margins. Winter plumage shows dull yellow feet, a dark bill, and a white head with a black patch through the eye and ear. Juveniles are like winter adults but have a shorter tail, a ginger crown, and darker upperwings.

- **SONG** Throaty nasal *ki-arr, za-a-ap,* or *zrurr,* with nighthawklike quality. Also gives piercing *kit, kit, kit* cry.
- **BEHAVIOR** Catches insects in flight. Eats dragonflies and other insects. Hovers above water, then plunge dives for small fish. Dips to water's surface to catch floating insects, keeping its feathers dry.
- **BREEDING** Monogamous. Loose colonies.
- **NESTING** Incubation 23–25 days by both sexes. Semiprecocial young leave nest after a few days but tended by both sexes until able to fly. 1 brood per year.
- **POPULATION** Common. Declining in some areas because of loss of marshlands.
- **CONSERVATION** Vulnerable to habitat loss to agriculture and development in draining of wetlands.

JUVENILE

WINTER PLUMAGE

Similar Birds

COMMON TERN
Shorter legs and bill; dark wing tips; white tail with dark outer margins • winter adults and juveniles have white forehead and forecrown; dark shoulder; dark eye patch joins at nape; higher-pitched call.

ARCTIC TERN
Shorter red bill without dark tip; shorter legs; gray underparts; gray throat and chin contrast with white face; white tail with dark outer margins; pale underwing with black trailing margins.

Flight Pattern

Shallow slow graceful strong flight with body moving up and down. Hovers over water prior to diving for prey.

Nest Identification

Shape [icons]   Abandoned nests

Location [icons]

Atop floating dried reeds and lined with grass and reeds; in mud or sand and lined with bits of shells and grass; sometimes uses old grebe nests or muskrat houses • built by both sexes • 1–4 olive or buff eggs with brown or olive splotches and sometimes marked with dark brown lines; oval to short elliptical, 1.7 inches long.

Plumage Sexes similar	Habitat [icons]	Migration Migratory	Weight 5.6 ounces

DATE _____ TIME_____ LOCATION _____

Family LARIDAE	Species *Sterna antillarum*	Length 8–9 inches	Wingspan 20 inches

LEAST TERN

The smallest North American tern has a graceful airy flight. Like other terns, it is very protective of its nest and will divebomb intruders, screeching and releasing droppings. The female is similar to the male but smaller. The small size; yellow-orange bill, legs, and feet; black lores, crown, and nape; and white forehead distinguish this species. Winter adults show a dark bill and dusky-streaked whitish crown. Juveniles are similar to winter adults but have darker outer wings and a dusky carpal bar on the leading edge of the inner wings.

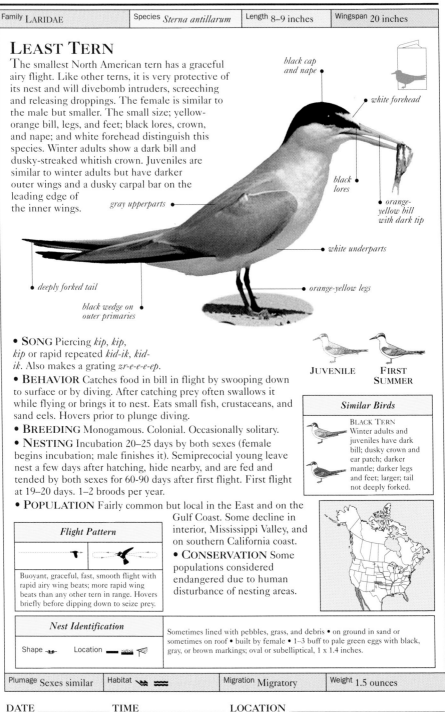

black cap and nape

white forehead

black lores

orange-yellow bill with dark tip

gray upperparts

white underparts

deeply forked tail

black wedge on outer primaries

orange-yellow legs

JUVENILE   FIRST SUMMER

• **SONG** Piercing *kip, kip, kip* or rapid repeated *kid-ik, kid-ik*. Also makes a grating *zr-e-e-e-ep.*
• **BEHAVIOR** Catches food in bill in flight by swooping down to surface or by diving. After catching prey often swallows it while flying or brings it to nest. Eats small fish, crustaceans, and sand eels. Hovers prior to plunge diving.
• **BREEDING** Monogamous. Colonial. Occasionally solitary.
• **NESTING** Incubation 20–25 days by both sexes (female begins incubation; male finishes it). Semiprecocial young leave nest a few days after hatching, hide nearby, and are fed and tended by both sexes for 60-90 days after first flight. First flight at 19–20 days. 1–2 broods per year.
• **POPULATION** Fairly common but local in the East and on the Gulf Coast. Some decline in interior, Mississippi Valley, and on southern California coast.
• **CONSERVATION** Some populations considered endangered due to human disturbance of nesting areas.

Similar Birds
BLACK TERN Winter adults and juveniles have dark bill; dusky crown and ear patch; darker mantle; darker legs and feet; larger; tail not deeply forked.

Flight Pattern
Buoyant, graceful, fast, smooth flight with rapid airy wing beats; more rapid wing beats than any other tern in range. Hovers briefly before dipping down to seize prey.

Nest Identification	
Shape Location	Sometimes lined with pebbles, grass, and debris • on ground in sand or sometimes on roof • built by female • 1–3 buff to pale green eggs with black, gray, or brown markings; oval or subelliptical, 1 x 1.4 inches.

Plumage Sexes similar	Habitat	Migration Migratory	Weight 1.5 ounces

DATE _____ TIME_____ LOCATION _____

Family LARIDAE	Species *Sterna aleutica*	Length 13–15 inches	Wingspan 29–32 inches

ALEUTIAN TERN

First discovered in 1868 on Kodiak Island, this tern was not spotted on the Aleutian Islands until 1962, despite its name. The Aleutian Tern often flocks with Arctic Terns and sometimes can be seen off the coast of British Columbia in spring. Its mantle and upperwings are darker lead-gray than other terns of the region and contrast with the white underparts, short tail, and rump. It has a black crown, nape, and lores and a white forehead; the trailing edges of the secondaries produce a dark gray bar bordered with white. Juveniles have brown upperparts with buff feather edging and a reddish bill, legs, and feet. Winter adults show white streaking on the crown.

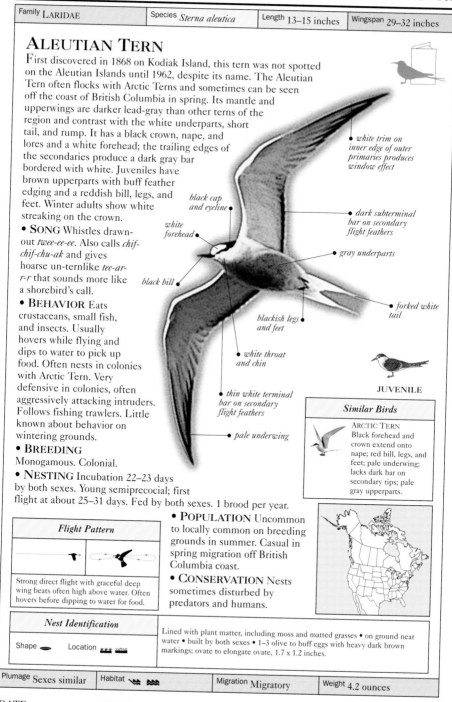

white trim on inner edge of outer primaries produces window effect

black cap and eyeline

white forehead

dark subterminal bar on secondary flight feathers

gray underparts

black bill

forked white tail

blackish legs and feet

white throat and chin

thin white terminal bar on secondary flight feathers

pale underwing

JUVENILE

- **SONG** Whistles drawn-out *twee-ee-ee*. Also calls *chif-chif-chu-ak* and gives hoarse un-ternlike *tee-ar-r-r* that sounds more like a shorebird's call.
- **BEHAVIOR** Eats crustaceans, small fish, and insects. Usually hovers while flying and dips to water to pick up food. Often nests in colonies with Arctic Tern. Very defensive in colonies, often aggressively attacking intruders. Follows fishing trawlers. Little known about behavior on wintering grounds.
- **BREEDING** Monogamous. Colonial.
- **NESTING** Incubation 22–23 days by both sexes. Young semiprecocial; first flight at about 25–31 days. Fed by both sexes. 1 brood per year.

Similar Birds
ARCTIC TERN Black forehead and crown extend onto nape; red bill, legs, and feet; pale underwing; lacks dark bar on secondary tips; pale gray upperparts.

- **POPULATION** Uncommon to locally common on breeding grounds in summer. Casual in spring migration off British Columbia coast.
- **CONSERVATION** Nests sometimes disturbed by predators and humans.

Flight Pattern

Strong direct flight with graceful deep wing beats often high above water. Often hovers before dipping to water for food.

Nest Identification

Shape ⬤   Location ☀☀☀ ≋

Lined with plant matter, including moss and matted grasses • on ground near water • built by both sexes • 1–3 olive to buff eggs with heavy dark brown markings; ovate to elongate ovate, 1.7 x 1.2 inches.

Plumage Sexes similar	Habitat ≋ ≋	Migration Migratory	Weight 4.2 ounces

DATE _____ TIME_____ LOCATION _____

Family LARIDAE	Species *Chlidonias niger*	Length 9–10 inches	Wingspan 20–24 inches

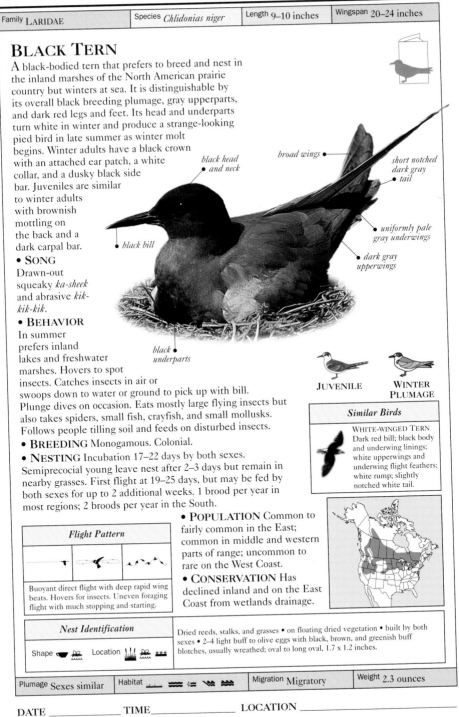

BLACK TERN

A black-bodied tern that prefers to breed and nest in the inland marshes of the North American prairie country but winters at sea. It is distinguishable by its overall black breeding plumage, gray upperparts, and dark red legs and feet. Its head and underparts turn white in winter and produce a strange-looking pied bird in late summer as winter molt begins. Winter adults have a black crown with an attached ear patch, a white collar, and a dusky black side bar. Juveniles are similar to winter adults with brownish mottling on the back and a dark carpal bar.

black head and neck

broad wings

short notched dark gray tail

uniformly pale gray underwings

dark gray upperwings

black bill

black underparts

- **SONG**
Drawn-out squeaky *ka-sheek* and abrasive *kik-kik-kik*.
- **BEHAVIOR**
In summer prefers inland lakes and freshwater marshes. Hovers to spot insects. Catches insects in air or swoops down to water or ground to pick up with bill. Plunge dives on occasion. Eats mostly large flying insects but also takes spiders, small fish, crayfish, and small mollusks. Follows people tilling soil and feeds on disturbed insects.
- **BREEDING** Monogamous. Colonial.
- **NESTING** Incubation 17–22 days by both sexes. Semiprecocial young leave nest after 2–3 days but remain in nearby grasses. First flight at 19–25 days, but may be fed by both sexes for up to 2 additional weeks. 1 brood per year in most regions; 2 broods per year in the South.
- **POPULATION** Common to fairly common in the East; common in middle and western parts of range; uncommon to rare on the West Coast.
- **CONSERVATION** Has declined inland and on the East Coast from wetlands drainage.

JUVENILE

WINTER PLUMAGE

Similar Birds

WHITE-WINGED TERN
Dark red bill; black body and underwing linings; white upperwings and underwing flight feathers; white rump; slightly notched white tail.

Flight Pattern

Buoyant direct flight with deep rapid wing beats. Hovers for insects. Uneven foraging flight with much stopping and starting.

Nest Identification

Shape Location

Dried reeds, stalks, and grasses • on floating dried vegetation • built by both sexes • 2–4 light buff to olive eggs with black, brown, and greenish buff blotches, usually wreathed; oval to long oval, 1.7 x 1.2 inches.

Plumage Sexes similar	Habitat	Migration Migratory	Weight 2.3 ounces

DATE _____ TIME_____ LOCATION _____

Family LARIDAE	Species *Rynchops niger*	Length 18–19 inches	Wingspan 42–50 inches

BLACK SKIMMER

This crow-sized bird's Spanish name, *rayador*, is derived from the word *rayar*, for its habit of making lines in the ground by skimming sand around the nest with its long bill. The Black Skimmer is the largest of the world's three species and, like them, has unique compressed, knifelike mandibles, with the lower one one-third longer than the upper one. This long-winged bird has black upperparts, white underparts, a black rump and a slightly notched tail. Winter adults have a white collar. Juveniles are similar to winter adults but they have mottled brown upperparts. Nestlings are camouflaged by their buff coloring, which blends with the seashore. The lower and upper mandibles are similar in length until young are almost fully grown.

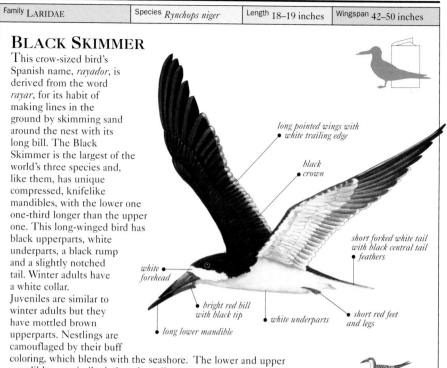

long pointed wings with white trailing edge

black crown

short forked white tail with black central tail feathers

white forehead

bright red bill with black tip

white underparts

short red feet and legs

long lower mandible

JUVENILE

• **SONG** Low throaty bark of *kak-kak-kak, kuk-kuk-kuk*, or *yap-yap-yap*. Pairs sometimes sing together, *kow-kow* or *keow-keow*.

• **BEHAVIOR** Crepuscular and partially nocturnal. Often begins foraging in late evening when waters are calmer and prey rises to surface. Flies low and skims water with lower mandible to locate prey by touch, which snaps the bill shut. Grasps small fish and crustaceans with upper mandible, tilts head, and swallows while still flying. Spends much of day loafing on beaches.

• **BREEDING** Monogamous. Small colonies.

• **NESTING** Incubation 21–23 days by both sexes. Semiprecocial young remain in nest area 23–25 days. Fed by both sexes. 1 brood per year.

• **POPULATION** Common in coastal areas. Casual to accidental inland; birds are often driven there by storms.

• **CONSERVATION** Vulnerable to disturbance of nesting colonies. Eggs and young often trampled by dogs or humans, especially runners on beach.

Flight Pattern
Graceful buoyant direct flight with measured wing beats. In perfect synchrony flocks wheel, twist, and glide.

Nest Identification
Shape ᵔ Location ▬ ▬

No materials added • on upper beach above high tidemark • built by both sexes • 4–5 bluish white or pinkish white eggs with brown, lilac, and gray blotches; round ovate to elongated ovate, 1.3 inches long.

Plumage Sexes similar	Habitat ➤ ≋	Migration Some migrate	Weight 12.3 ounces

DATE _____ TIME_____ LOCATION _____

Family ALCIDAE	Species *Alle alle*	Length 8.5 inches	Wingspan 13 inches

DOVEKIE

The smallest Atlantic alcid, this little auk, with its chubby body and proportionally large head, nests and breeds above the Arctic Circle but winters off the northern Atlantic Coast. Although it is a food source for arctic foxes, gyrfalcons, some gulls, and even large fish, it remains abundant in its habitat. It has black upperparts, white underparts, a short black bill, and waterproof plumage. In flight the underwings show black.

short neck

black head

black upperparts

stubby black bill

black upper breast and throat

white on remaining underparts

short blackish gray legs and feet set back on body

Winter plumage shows completely white underparts with a white stripe curving up toward the top of the head.

- **SONG** Silent at sea. Various shrill chatters and squeaks in nesting colony.
- **BEHAVIOR** Dives for food and flies underwater using its wings. Eats small saltwater crustaceans and small freshwater fish. Often found at sea in huge flocks. Disperses widely at sea outside breeding season.
- **BREEDING** Monogamous. Colonial.
- **NESTING** Incubation 24–28 days by both sexes. Semiprecocial young stay in nest 26–31 days. Fed by both sexes. 1 brood per year.
- **POPULATION** Abundant on breeding grounds, where colonies may number in the millions. Winters irregularly offshore to North Carolina and rarely to Florida. Casual inland after winter storms.
- **CONSERVATION** All auks are protected by law, but young and eggs are still harvested for food. Vulnerable to oil spills.

WINTER PLUMAGE

Similar Birds

COMMON MURRE
Much larger; longer bill; longer neck.

Flight Pattern

Rapid direct flight with fast whirring wing beats low over water..

Nest Identification

Shape | Location

Nothing added • on bare ground hidden in crannies of rocky cliffs • 1 bluish white or green egg, usually unmarked; oval to long elliptical, 1.9 inches long.

Plumage Sexes similar	Habitat	Migration Nonmigratory	Weight 5.7 ounces

DATE _____ TIME_____ LOCATION _____

Family ALCIDAE	Species *Uria aalge*	Length 17.5 inches	Wingspan 28–30 inches

COMMON MURRE

This large-bodied, crow-sized seabird is one of the most adept divers in the alcid family and is capable of diving to depths of more than 240 feet. Like all murres its pear-shaped egg is adapted to turn in a circle rather than roll off the precipitous cliffs where these birds nest. It has dark sooty brown upperparts, including the neck and head; a long thin black bill; and white underparts. Some Atlantic birds have a narrow white eye ring and stripe extending behind eye, but most East Coast birds and all Pacific Coast birds lack the eye adornment. Winter and juvenile birds show a white throat and cheeks and a black postocular stripe.

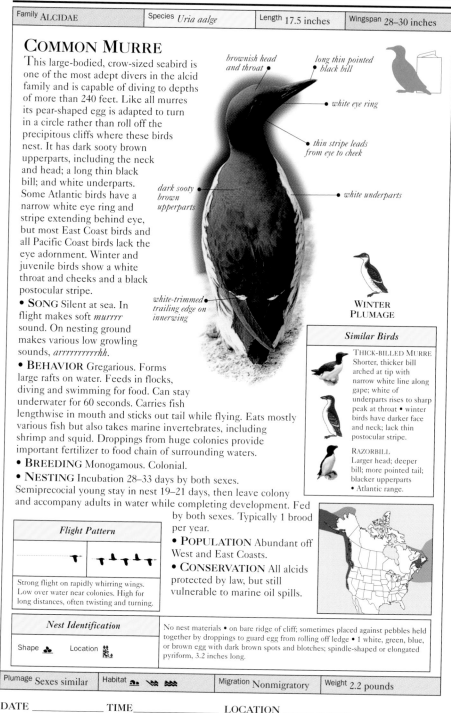

brownish head and throat

long thin pointed black bill

white eye ring

thin stripe leads from eye to cheek

dark sooty brown upperparts

white underparts

white-trimmed trailing edge on innerwing

WINTER PLUMAGE

• **SONG** Silent at sea. In flight makes soft *murrrr* sound. On nesting ground makes various low growling sounds, *arrrrrrrrrrhh*.
• **BEHAVIOR** Gregarious. Forms large rafts on water. Feeds in flocks, diving and swimming for food. Can stay underwater for 60 seconds. Carries fish lengthwise in mouth and sticks out tail while flying. Eats mostly various fish but also takes marine invertebrates, including shrimp and squid. Droppings from huge colonies provide important fertilizer to food chain of surrounding waters.
• **BREEDING** Monogamous. Colonial.
• **NESTING** Incubation 28–33 days by both sexes. Semiprecocial young stay in nest 19–21 days, then leave colony and accompany adults in water while completing development. Fed by both sexes. Typically 1 brood per year.
• **POPULATION** Abundant off West and East Coasts.
• **CONSERVATION** All alcids protected by law, but still vulnerable to marine oil spills.

Similar Birds

THICK-BILLED MURRE
Shorter, thicker bill arched at tip with narrow white line along gape; white of underparts rises to sharp peak at throat • winter birds have darker face and neck; lack thin postocular stripe.

RAZORBILL
Larger head; deeper bill; more pointed tail; blacker upperparts • Atlantic range.

Flight Pattern
Strong flight on rapidly whirring wings. Low over water near colonies. High for long distances, often twisting and turning.

Nest Identification	
Shape 🐾 Location 🐦	No nest materials • on bare ridge of cliff; sometimes placed against pebbles held together by droppings to guard egg from rolling off ledge • 1 white, green, blue, or brown egg with dark brown spots and blotches; spindle-shaped or elongated pyriform, 3.2 inches long.

Plumage Sexes similar	Habitat 🐚 🌊 🌊	Migration Nonmigratory	Weight 2.2 pounds

DATE _____ TIME_____ LOCATION _____

Family ALCIDAE	Species *Uria lomvia*	Length 18 inches	Wingspan 28–32 inches

THICK-BILLED MURRE

Although considered one of the most common seabirds in the Northern Hemisphere, the Thick-billed Murre is threatened by fishing practices and pollution. It is still much more numerous than its close relatives, the Common Murre and Razorbill. Its bill is shorter and broader than that of the similar Common Murre, and most birds sport a narrow white line along its gape. In winter, white chin and foreneck extends onto the face to just under the eye. Juveniles are similar to winter

short thick black bill with white line on cutting edge of upper mandible

black head and neck

sooty black upperparts

white chest rises to a point on black throat

white underparts

WINTER PLUMAGE

adults but have browner upperparts.
• **SONG** Silent at sea. Noisy around breeding colonies. Call sounds like *arrr* or *arra* in a deep hoarse voice; similar to Common Murre but harsher and lower.

dark yellowish brown legs and feet

• **BEHAVIOR** Gregarious. Forms large rafts on water. Stands upright on rocks like a penguin. Forages while swimming, sometimes diving as deep as 200 feet and using wings to "fly" underwater. Eats fish, crustaceans, marine worms, and squid.
• **BREEDING** Monogamous. Colonial.
• **NESTING** Incubation 28–35 days by both sexes. Semiprecocial young stay in nest 16–30 days; leave colony when about a third grown, and remain with parents. Fed by both sexes. 1 brood per year.

Similar Birds

COMMON MURRE
Longer, thinner bill; lacks white gape line; white of upper breast meets throat in inverted U; occasional white eye ring; brown upperparts • in winter shows more white on face and dark postocular line.

RAZORBILL
Thicker, arching bill with vertical white line across it near tip; longer tail • darker face in winter • Atlantic range.

• **POPULATION** Common to abundant on breeding grounds. Casual, widely dispersed, off coasts rest of year. Declining.
• **CONSERVATION** Affected by oil spills, marine pollution, and entanglement or drowning in commercial fishing nets.

Flight Pattern

Strong rapid flight low over water on short whirring wings, often with much twisting and turning of body. Groups fly in lines.

Nest Identification

Shape 🐾   Location 🪹

No nest material • 1 whitish, tan, blue, or green egg with brown and black markings; spindle-shaped or elongated pyriform, 3.2 inches long.

Plumage Sexes similar	Habitat 〰〰 🐚	Migration Nonmigratory	Weight 2.1 pounds

DATE _____ TIME_____ LOCATION _____

Family ALCIDAE	Species *Cepphus grylle*	Length 12–14 inches	Wingspan 23 inches

BLACK GUILLEMOT

A shoreline inhabitant, the Black Guillemot is usually observed closer to shore than most other alcids, especially in the North Atlantic. While its population is widely dispersed, it is not as gregarious as other birds in its family. Black Guillemots sometimes can be spotted coaxing their young to fly off cliffs, dangling prey just beyond reach for encouragement. In flight note the large white wing patch, white axillaries, and white underwing linings. The inside of this bird's mouth is bright coral orange. Winter adults and juveniles are white with mottled black upperparts.

• **SONG** Weak, high-pitched whistle of *peeee*.

• **BEHAVIOR** Not gregarious but may occur in small flocks; usually in pairs or alone. Eats rock eels, small fish, mollusks, crustaceans, insects, marine worms, and some vegetation. Often surface dives 30–100 feet underwater to forage for food under loose stones while swimming with wings. In flight flashes white patches and dangles red feet behind tail.

black bill

black plumage

large white shoulder patch

WINTER PLUMAGE

• **BREEDING** Monogamous. Semicolonial to colonial (colonies of only a few pairs).

• **NESTING** Incubation 23–39 days by both sexes. Semiprecocial young stay in nest 35 days. Fed by both sexes. 1 brood per year.

• **POPULATION** Fairly common on breeding grounds; disperses after breeding.

• **CONSERVATION** Introduction of predators to nesting areas poses danger, but birds still numerous, Geographically dispersed nesting areas help offset the threat. Vulnerable to oil spills.

Similar Birds

PIGEON GUILLEMOT Dusky wing linings and axillaries; black bar on white shoulder patch.
• Pacific Coast range.

Flight Pattern

Direct flight with rapid wing beats low over water.

Nest Identification

Shape ☑ ⌁ Location ▓ ▬

Made of debris and small stones • often near driftwood • built by both sexes • 1–2 white eggs, sometimes tinted with bluish green, with black, brown, and gray markings; long elliptical to pyriform, 2.3 inches long.

Plumage Sexes similar	Habitat ≈≈ ⌁	Migration Most do not migrate	Weight 14.3 ounces

DATE _____ TIME_____ LOCATION _____

| Family ALCIDAE | Species *Cepphus columba* | Length 13–14 inches | Wingspan 23 inches |

PIGEON GUILLEMOT

This western species, like other alcids, "flies" underwater as it searches for food, swimming with its wings. During breeding season flocks of these birds participate in a complicated water dance, gathering in lines above the water, then diving under the surface and playing tag with one another. This coastal species often can be spotted from shore. Look for the large white wing patch bisected by a black bar or wedge. In flight the axillars and underwings are dusky gray. Winter adults are white with black mottling on the upperparts, hindneck, and crown. Juveniles are similar to winter adults but duskier.

black bill

black plumage

large white wing patch bisected by black bar

WINTER PLUMAGE

reddish legs and feet

• **SONG** Usually silent at sea. Nesting birds give weak hissing whistle *peeeeee*.
• **BEHAVIOR** Semigregarious. Occurs alone or in pairs or small groups. Dives underwater to feed on small fish at bottom. Also eats mollusks, crustaceans, and marine worms.
• **BREEDING** Monogamous. Small colonies or individual.
• **NESTING** Incubation 29–32 days by both sexes. Semiprecocial young stay in nest 29–39 days. Fed by both sexes. 1 brood per year.
• **POPULATION** Fairly common along northern Pacific Coast from Alaska to southern California. Winter distribution poorly known.
• **CONSERVATION** Declining because of pollution, oil spills, and warming climatic trends.

Similar Birds

BLACK GUILLEMOT White underwing lining; solid white wing patch.

Flight Pattern

Strong swift direct flight low over water, often in wide circle, wings beating rapidly.

Nest Identification

Shape — Location

Made of rock chips, pebbles, and debris • on bare rock, in deserted holes of puffins and rabbits, under railroad ties, or on buildings and wharves • built by both sexes • 1–2 off-white, pale bluish, or very pale yellow eggs with gray and dark brown blotches; conical to pyriform, rounder toward end, 2.4 inches long.

| Plumage Sexes similar | Habitat | Migration Nonmigratory | Weight 1.1 pounds |

DATE _____ TIME_____ LOCATION _____

Family ALCIDAE	Species *Brachyramphus perdix*	Length 11.5 inches	Wingspan 18 inches

LONG-BILLED MURRELET

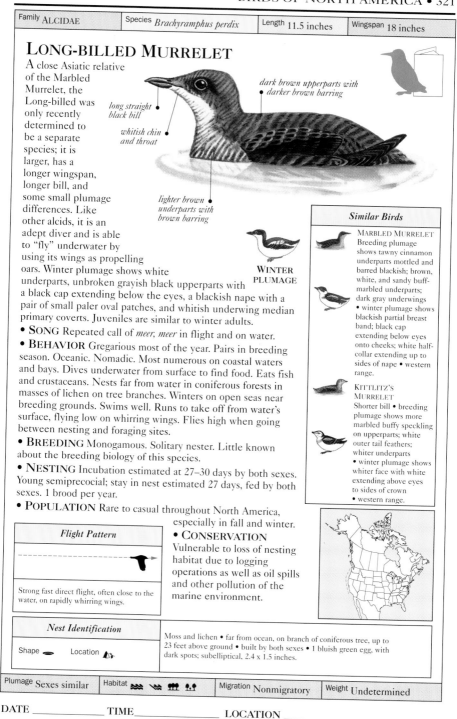

A close Asiatic relative of the Marbled Murrelet, the Long-billed was only recently determined to be a separate species; it is larger, has a longer wingspan, longer bill, and some small plumage differences. Like other alcids, it is an adept diver and is able to "fly" underwater by using its wings as propelling oars. Winter plumage shows white underparts, unbroken grayish black upperparts with a black cap extending below the eyes, a blackish nape with a pair of small paler oval patches, and whitish underwing median primary coverts. Juveniles are similar to winter adults.

long straight black bill

whitish chin and throat

dark brown upperparts with darker brown barring

lighter brown underparts with brown barring

WINTER PLUMAGE

- **SONG** Repeated call of *meer, meer* in flight and on water.
- **BEHAVIOR** Gregarious most of the year. Pairs in breeding season. Oceanic. Nomadic. Most numerous on coastal waters and bays. Dives underwater from surface to find food. Eats fish and crustaceans. Nests far from water in coniferous forests in masses of lichen on tree branches. Winters on open seas near breeding grounds. Swims well. Runs to take off from water's surface, flying low on whirring wings. Flies high when going between nesting and foraging sites.
- **BREEDING** Monogamous. Solitary nester. Little known about the breeding biology of this species.
- **NESTING** Incubation estimated at 27–30 days by both sexes. Young semiprecocial; stay in nest estimated 27 days, fed by both sexes. 1 brood per year.
- **POPULATION** Rare to casual throughout North America, especially in fall and winter.
- **CONSERVATION** Vulnerable to loss of nesting habitat due to logging operations as well as oil spills and other pollution of the marine environment.

Similar Birds

MARBLED MURRELET Breeding plumage shows tawny cinnamon underparts mottled and barred blackish; brown, white, and sandy buff-marbled underparts; dark gray underwings • winter plumage shows blackish partial breast band; black cap extending below eyes onto cheeks; white half-collar extending up to sides of nape • western range.

KITTLITZ'S MURRELET Shorter bill • breeding plumage shows more marbled buffy speckling on upperparts; white outer tail feathers; whiter underparts • winter plumage shows whiter face with white extending above eyes to sides of crown • western range.

Flight Pattern

Strong fast direct flight, often close to the water, on rapidly whirring wings.

Nest Identification

Shape ⌒ Location 🌿

Moss and lichen • far from ocean, on branch of coniferous tree, up to 23 feet above ground • built by both sexes • 1 bluish green egg, with dark spots; subelliptical, 2.4 x 1.5 inches.

Plumage Sexes similar	Habitat 〰〰 〰 🌲 ⚘	Migration Nonmigratory	Weight Undetermined

DATE _____ TIME_____ LOCATION _____

Family ALCIDAE	Species *Brachyramphus marmoratus*	Length 10 inches	Wingspan 16 inches

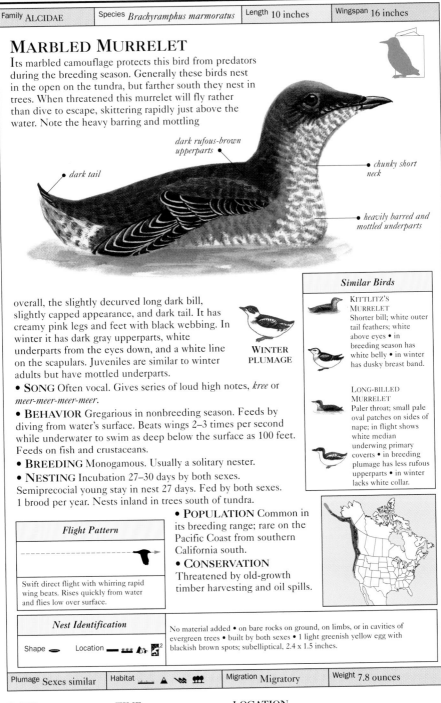

MARBLED MURRELET

Its marbled camouflage protects this bird from predators during the breeding season. Generally these birds nest in the open on the tundra, but farther south they nest in trees. When threatened this murrelet will fly rather than dive to escape, skittering rapidly just above the water. Note the heavy barring and mottling

dark rufous-brown upperparts •

• dark tail

• chunky short neck

• heavily barred and mottled underparts

Similar Birds

KITTLITZ'S MURRELET
Shorter bill; white outer tail feathers; white above eyes • in breeding season has white belly • in winter has dusky breast band.

LONG-BILLED MURRELET
Paler throat; small pale oval patches on sides of nape; in flight shows white median underwing primary coverts • in breeding plumage has less rufous upperparts • in winter lacks white collar.

overall, the slightly decurved long dark bill, slightly capped appearance, and dark tail. It has creamy pink legs and feet with black webbing. In winter it has dark gray upperparts, white underparts from the eyes down, and a white line on the scapulars. Juveniles are similar to winter adults but have mottled underparts.

WINTER PLUMAGE

• **SONG** Often vocal. Gives series of loud high notes, *kree* or *meer-meer-meer-meer*.
• **BEHAVIOR** Gregarious in nonbreeding season. Feeds by diving from water's surface. Beats wings 2–3 times per second while underwater to swim as deep below the surface as 100 feet. Feeds on fish and crustaceans.
• **BREEDING** Monogamous. Usually a solitary nester.
• **NESTING** Incubation 27–30 days by both sexes. Semiprecocial young stay in nest 27 days. Fed by both sexes. 1 brood per year. Nests inland in trees south of tundra.
• **POPULATION** Common in its breeding range; rare on the Pacific Coast from southern California south.
• **CONSERVATION** Threatened by old-growth timber harvesting and oil spills.

Flight Pattern
Swift direct flight with whirring rapid wing beats. Rises quickly from water and flies low over surface.

Nest Identification	
Shape ⌒ Location ▬ ▦ ⛰ 🌲	No material added • on bare rocks on ground, on limbs, or in cavities of evergreen trees • built by both sexes • 1 light greenish yellow egg with blackish brown spots; subelliptical, 2.4 x 1.5 inches.

Plumage Sexes similar	Habitat	Migration Migratory	Weight 7.8 ounces

DATE _____ TIME_____ LOCATION _____

Family ALCIDAE	Species *Brachyramphus brevirostris*	Length 9.5 inches	Wingspan 14.5 inches

KITTLITZ'S MURRELET

Little is known about this bird named after F.H. Kittlitz, a German scientist who was part of a Russian expedition to Kamchatka. This small murrelet summers along the Alaskan coast. Note the short bill and extensively mottled underparts. In flight look for the white outer tail feathers, white belly, and brownish legs and feet. Winter plumage is black and white overall with a black cap, white face, white-striped edging on the scapulars, an almost completely white collar, and a dark gray breast band. Juveniles are similar to winter adults but have dusky mottling on white plumage.

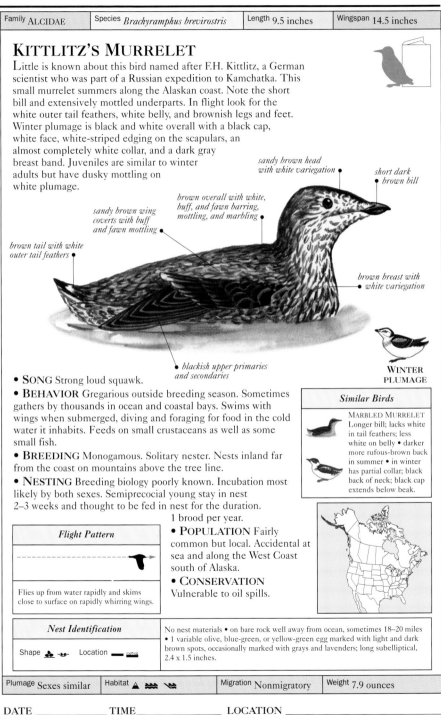

sandy brown head with white variegation

short dark brown bill

brown overall with white, buff, and fawn barring, mottling, and marbling

sandy brown wing coverts with buff and fawn mottling

brown tail with white outer tail feathers

brown breast with white variegation

blackish upper primaries and secondaries

WINTER PLUMAGE

• **SONG** Strong loud squawk.

• **BEHAVIOR** Gregarious outside breeding season. Sometimes gathers by thousands in ocean and coastal bays. Swims with wings when submerged, diving and foraging for food in the cold water it inhabits. Feeds on small crustaceans as well as some small fish.

• **BREEDING** Monogamous. Solitary nester. Nests inland far from the coast on mountains above the tree line.

• **NESTING** Breeding biology poorly known. Incubation most likely by both sexes. Semiprecocial young stay in nest 2–3 weeks and thought to be fed in nest for the duration. 1 brood per year.

Similar Birds
MARBLED MURRELET Longer bill; lacks white in tail feathers; less white on belly • darker more rufous-brown back in summer • in winter has partial collar; black back of neck; black cap extends below beak.

• **POPULATION** Fairly common but local. Accidental at sea and along the West Coast south of Alaska.

• **CONSERVATION** Vulnerable to oil spills.

Flight Pattern

Flies up from water rapidly and skims close to surface on rapidly whirring wings.

Nest Identification	
Shape 🐦 🐤 Location ▬ 〰	No nest materials • on bare rock well away from ocean, sometimes 18–20 miles • 1 variable olive, blue-green, or yellow-green egg marked with light and dark brown spots, occasionally marked with grays and lavenders; long subelliptical, 2.4 x 1.5 inches.

Plumage Sexes similar	Habitat ▲ 〰 〰	Migration Nonmigratory	Weight 7.9 ounces

DATE _____ TIME_____ LOCATION _____

Family ALCIDAE	Species *Synthliboramphus hypoleucus*	Length 10 inches	Wingspan 16 inches

XANTUS'S MURRELET

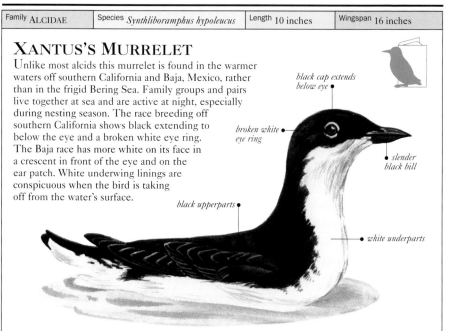

Unlike most alcids this murrelet is found in the warmer waters off southern California and Baja, Mexico, rather than in the frigid Bering Sea. Family groups and pairs live together at sea and are active at night, especially during nesting season. The race breeding off southern California shows black extending to below the eye and a broken white eye ring. The Baja race has more white on its face in a crescent in front of the eye and on the ear patch. White underwing linings are conspicuous when the bird is taking off from the water's surface.

black cap extends below eye

broken white eye ring

slender black bill

black upperparts

white underparts

• **SONG** During nesting season gives high-pitched chattering whistle, generally at night. Makes fluting notes year-round.

• **BEHAVIOR** Usually stays at sea in daytime but moves closer to shore at night. Swims low in water, keeping the white sides and flanks beneath the water and the head held aloft on the extended neck, unlike other murrelets. Often forages in pairs. Dives and swims underwater using wings to propel itself. Eats small crustaceans; while nesting eats small fish. When pursued avoids diving unless wounded but flushes into rapid flight.

• **BREEDING** Monogamous. Colonial.

• **NESTING** Pairs return to same nest site year after year. Incubation 27–44 days by both sexes. Precocial young leave nest a few days after hatching by jumping from as high as 200 feet. Fed by both sexes at sea, where they remain in family groups. 1 brood per year but sometimes lays second clutch if first is lost.

Similar Birds
CRAVERI'S MURRELET Dusky underwing linings; partial black breast collar; longer, thinner bill; black extends from head to under bill.

• **POPULATION** Uncommon to fairly common. Rare in late summer to fall to Oregon; casual farther north.

• **CONSERVATION** Vulnerable to pollution of marine environments, including oil spills.

Flight Pattern
Swift direct flight with rapid, whirring wing beats close to water. Very fast off the water.

Nest Identification	
Shape	Location

No material added • in rock crevices, under thick bushes, or on bare ground • sometimes uses abandoned nests • 2 (rarely 1) blue or green eggs marked with brown spots or solid brown; subelliptical to oval, 2.1 inches long.

Plumage Sexes similar	Habitat	Migration Nonmigratory	Weight 5.9 ounces

DATE _____ TIME _____ LOCATION _____

Family ALCIDAE	Species *Synthliboramphus craveri*	Length 8.5 inches	Wingspan 13.5 inches

CRAVERI'S MURRELET

Like the similar Xantus's Murrelet, this small murrelet prefers warm waters. Its nesting is restricted to the islands of the Gulf of California and Baja but is a regular visitor August through October in the waters off southern California. Active at night, this bird often can be heard chattering as it romps in its burrow. In flight look for the dusky underwing coverts and dark spur of a breast band on the otherwise white underparts. It does

blackish brown upperparts and upperwing surface

black of cap and face extends under bill

black bill

JUVENILE

not experience a marked seasonal change in plumage. Adults have blackish brown upperparts and upperwings, a slightly longer bill, and are pure white below.

• **SONG** Call is insectlike chattering. Makes harsh trills when agitated.

• **BEHAVIOR** Frequents open waters and is not usually seen from shore. Eats crustaceans and small fish. Surface dives and swims swiftly underwater, propelling itself with its wings to catch food. Solitary or in pairs, family groups, or small flocks.

• **BREEDING** Monogamous. Colonial.

• **NESTING** Incubation 27–44 days by both sexes. Adults lead precocial young from nest 1–2 days after hatching to find their way down the cliffs to swim. Tended by both sexes. 1 brood per year; if first clutch is destroyed, a second may be laid.

• **POPULATION** Common to fairly common around breeding islands. Regular off southern California coast in late summer and autumn; casual in central California; rare in Oregon.

• **CONSERVATION** Vulnerable to disturbances and introduced predators on nesting islands and pollution of marine environments and oil spills.

Similar Birds

XANTUS'S MURRELET
White underwing linings; white chin; shorter thicker bill
• more white on face of Baja race.

Flight Pattern

Rapid takeoff and low direct flight over water with rapid wing beats.

Nest Identification

Shape

Location

No nest material • in rock crevices on bare ground under vegetation or rocky debris • 2 white, yellow-tinted, olive, or brown eggs with brown markings; long subelliptical, 2.3 x 1.4 inches.

Plumage Sexes similar	Habitat	Migration Nonmigratory	Weight 5.3 ounces

DATE _____ TIME _____ LOCATION _____

| Family ALCIDAE | Species *Synthliboramphus antiquus* | Length 10 inches | Wingspan 16 inches |

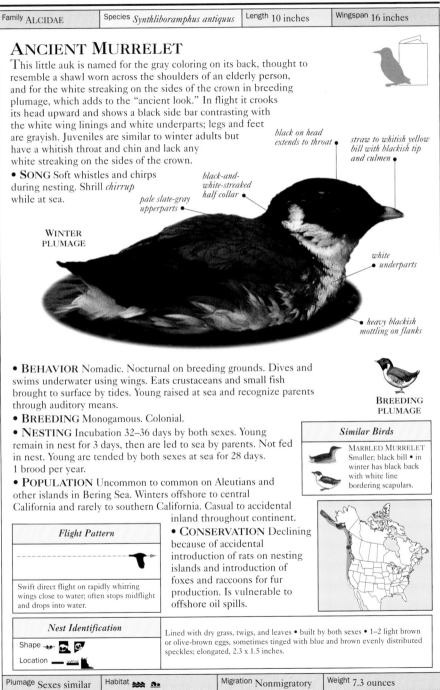

ANCIENT MURRELET

This little auk is named for the gray coloring on its back, thought to resemble a shawl worn across the shoulders of an elderly person, and for the white streaking on the sides of the crown in breeding plumage, which adds to the "ancient look." In flight it crooks its head upward and shows a black side bar contrasting with the white wing linings and white underparts; legs and feet are grayish. Juveniles are similar to winter adults but have a whitish throat and chin and lack any white streaking on the sides of the crown.

black on head extends to throat

straw to whitish yellow bill with blackish tip and culmen

• **SONG** Soft whistles and chirps during nesting. Shrill *chirrup* while at sea.

black-and-white-streaked half collar

pale slate-gray upperparts

WINTER PLUMAGE

white underparts

heavy blackish mottling on flanks

• **BEHAVIOR** Nomadic. Nocturnal on breeding grounds. Dives and swims underwater using wings. Eats crustaceans and small fish brought to surface by tides. Young raised at sea and recognize parents through auditory means.

BREEDING PLUMAGE

• **BREEDING** Monogamous. Colonial.

• **NESTING** Incubation 32–36 days by both sexes. Young remain in nest for 3 days, then are led to sea by parents. Not fed in nest. Young are tended by both sexes at sea for 28 days. 1 brood per year.

• **POPULATION** Uncommon to common on Aleutians and other islands in Bering Sea. Winters offshore to central California and rarely to southern California. Casual to accidental inland throughout continent.

Similar Birds
MARBLED MURRELET Smaller; black bill • in winter has black back with white line bordering scapulars.

• **CONSERVATION** Declining because of accidental introduction of rats on nesting islands and introduction of foxes and raccoons for fur production. Is vulnerable to offshore oil spills.

Flight Pattern
Swift direct flight on rapidly whirring wings close to water; often stops midflight and drops into water.

Nest Identification	
Shape	Lined with dry grass, twigs, and leaves • built by both sexes • 1–2 light brown or olive-brown eggs, sometimes tinged with blue and brown evenly distributed speckles; elongated, 2.3 x 1.5 inches.
Location	

| Plumage Sexes similar | Habitat | Migration Nonmigratory | Weight 7.3 ounces |

DATE _____ TIME_____ LOCATION _____

Family ALCIDAE	Species *Ptychoramphus aleuticus*	Length 9 inches	Wingspan 13.5 inches

CASSIN'S AUKLET

After hiding by day on its breeding islands, this bird is busy at night, constructing burrows for its nest or renovating a used one. The male and female take turns digging, stopping to bow to one another. It may take sixty days to dig a new burrow. One of the most widespread and abundant of the northeast Pacific alcids, it is a chunky little seabird with brownish gray upperparts and paler gray-brown underparts. At close range the short thick bill shows a light spot at the base. In flight the underwings are gray-brown, and the belly is whitish. Juveniles are

light yellowish eyes

darker gray-brown head

white crescent patch above eye

dark gray back and upperwings

short stout black bill with white spot on base of lower mandible

mostly gray-brown overall, with paler underparts

lighter in color with dark eyes, whiter throats, and browner wings and tails.

rounded wings

WINTER PLUMAGE

- **SONG** Silent at sea. In breeding colonies, this bird gives a faint croaking *kreek*.
- **BEHAVIOR** Gregarious throughout the year. Nocturnal during breeding season. Highly pelagic. Feeds far offshore, often in large flocks. Forages for food in deep waters, diving 120 feet or more below the surface and using wings to swim while submerged. Feeds day and night on planktonic crustaceans, small fish, and squid.
- **BREEDING** Monogamous. Colonial.
- **NESTING** Incubation 37–42 days by both parents. Young semiprecocial; stay in nest 37 days, fed by both parents through regurgitation. Occasionally 2 broods per year.
- **POPULATION** Common to abundant in its range.
- **CONSERVATION** Vulnerable to oil spills. Declining local populations due to introduction of predators to nesting sites.

Similar Birds

MARBLED MURRELET
Summer only
- browner, darker belly; longer, thinner bill; longer pointed wings.

LEAST AUKLET
Red bill; black back; variegated white-and-gray underparts; wide breast band.

NOTE In winter in southern parts of its range, Cassin's Auklet is the only small grayish brown alcid.

Flight Pattern
Rapid direct flight very low on short rounded wings. Rises swiftly from surface after pattering across water.

Nest Identification

Shape ▢ ▢ ▢   Location ▬

No materials used • built by both sexes • 1 creamy white egg, sometimes tinted blue or green, becoming nest-stained; ovate, 1.9 inches long.

Plumage Sexes similar	Habitat ≋ ≋ ⚓	Migration Northern birds migrate	Weight 6.6 ounces

DATE _____ TIME_____ LOCATION _____

Family ALCIDAE	Species *Aethia psittacula*	Length 10 inches	Wingspan 15.5 inches

PARAKEET AUKLET

A shy and rather solitary bird, this is the only red-billed auklet south of Alaska (in winter it inhabits California waters). The winter plumage shows a dull orange-red bill and white underparts, including the throat. The laterally compressed upturned red bill, pale yellowish white plume behind the pale eye, and dark upperparts identify this species.

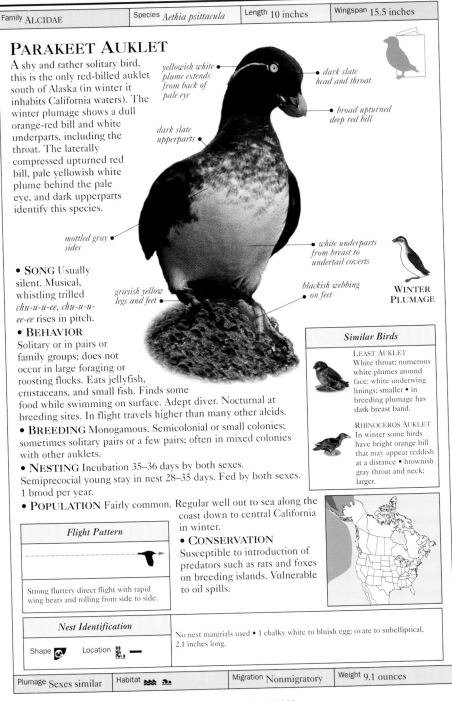

yellowish white plume extends from back of pale eye

dark slate head and throat

broad upturned deep red bill

dark slate upperparts

mottled gray sides

grayish yellow legs and feet

white underparts from breast to undertail coverts

blackish webbing on feet

WINTER PLUMAGE

- **SONG** Usually silent. Musical, whistling trilled *chu-u-u-ee, chu-u-u-ee-ee* rises in pitch.
- **BEHAVIOR** Solitary or in pairs or family groups; does not occur in large foraging or roosting flocks. Eats jellyfish, crustaceans, and small fish. Finds some food while swimming on surface. Adept diver. Nocturnal at breeding sites. In flight travels higher than many other alcids.
- **BREEDING** Monogamous. Semicolonial or small colonies; sometimes solitary pairs or a few pairs; often in mixed colonies with other auklets.
- **NESTING** Incubation 35–36 days by both sexes. Semiprecocial young stay in nest 28–35 days. Fed by both sexes. 1 brood per year.
- **POPULATION** Fairly common. Regular well out to sea along the coast down to central California in winter.
- **CONSERVATION** Susceptible to introduction of predators such as rats and foxes on breeding islands. Vulnerable to oil spills.

Similar Birds

LEAST AUKLET
White throat; numerous white plumes around face; white underwing linings; smaller • in breeding plumage has dark breast band.

RHINOCEROS AUKLET
In winter some birds have bright orange bill that may appear reddish at a distance • brownish gray throat and neck; larger.

Flight Pattern

Strong fluttery direct flight with rapid wing beats and rolling from side to side.

Nest Identification

Shape ● Location ●

No nest materials used • 1 chalky white to bluish egg; ovate to subelliptical, 2.1 inches long.

Plumage Sexes similar	Habitat ～～ ●●	Migration Nonmigratory	Weight 9.1 ounces

DATE _____ TIME_____ LOCATION _____

Family ALCIDAE	Species *Aethia pusilla*	Length 6 inches	Wingspan 9.5 inches

LEAST AUKLET

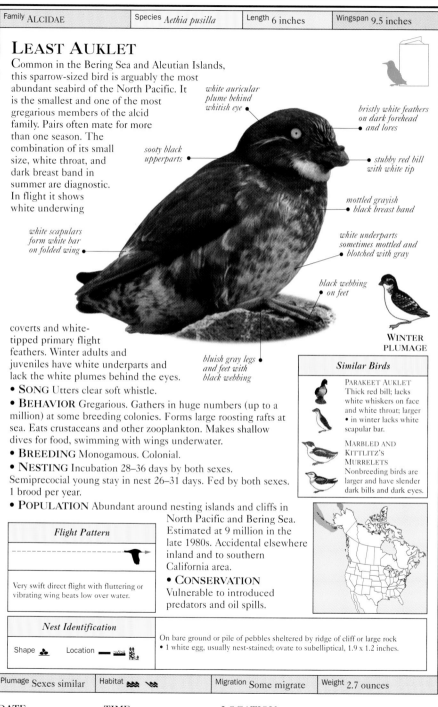

Common in the Bering Sea and Aleutian Islands, this sparrow-sized bird is arguably the most abundant seabird of the North Pacific. It is the smallest and one of the most gregarious members of the alcid family. Pairs often mate for more than one season. The combination of its small size, white throat, and dark breast band in summer are diagnostic. In flight it shows white underwing

white auricular plume behind whitish eye

bristly white feathers on dark forehead and lores

sooty black upperparts

stubby red bill with white tip

mottled grayish black breast band

white scapulars form white bar on folded wing

white underparts sometimes mottled and blotched with gray

black webbing on feet

WINTER PLUMAGE

coverts and white-tipped primary flight feathers. Winter adults and juveniles have white underparts and lack the white plumes behind the eyes.

bluish gray legs and feet with black webbing

• **SONG** Utters clear soft whistle.

• **BEHAVIOR** Gregarious. Gathers in huge numbers (up to a million) at some breeding colonies. Forms large roosting rafts at sea. Eats crustaceans and other zooplankton. Makes shallow dives for food, swimming with wings underwater.

• **BREEDING** Monogamous. Colonial.

• **NESTING** Incubation 28–36 days by both sexes. Semiprecocial young stay in nest 26–31 days. Fed by both sexes. 1 brood per year.

• **POPULATION** Abundant around nesting islands and cliffs in North Pacific and Bering Sea. Estimated at 9 million in the late 1980s. Accidental elsewhere inland and to southern California area.

• **CONSERVATION** Vulnerable to introduced predators and oil spills.

Similar Birds

PARAKEET AUKLET
Thick red bill; lacks white whiskers on face and white throat; larger
• in winter lacks white scapular bar.

MARBLED AND KITTLITZ'S MURRELETS
Nonbreeding birds are larger and have slender dark bills and dark eyes.

Flight Pattern

Very swift direct flight with fluttering or vibrating wing beats low over water.

Nest Identification

Shape [icon]   Location [icon]

On bare ground or pile of pebbles sheltered by ridge of cliff or large rock
• 1 white egg, usually nest-stained; ovate to subelliptical, 1.9 x 1.2 inches.

Plumage Sexes similar	Habitat [icons]	Migration Some migrate	Weight 2.7 ounces

DATE _____ TIME_____ LOCATION _____

Family ALCIDAE	Species *Aethia pygmaea*	Length 7 inches	Wingspan 11 inches

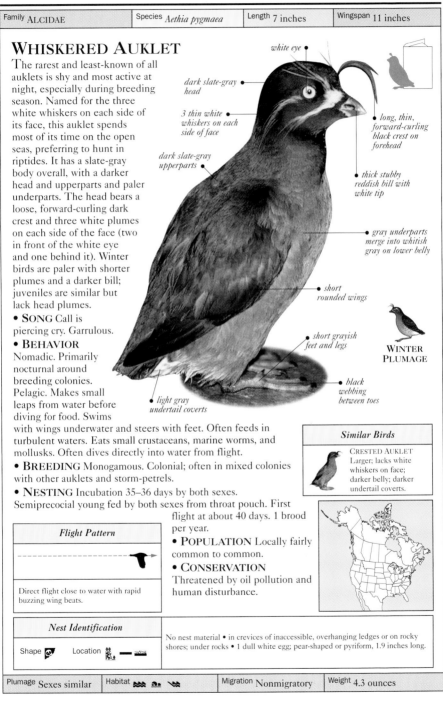

WHISKERED AUKLET

The rarest and least-known of all auklets is shy and most active at night, especially during breeding season. Named for the three white whiskers on each side of its face, this auklet spends most of its time on the open seas, preferring to hunt in riptides. It has a slate-gray body overall, with a darker head and upperparts and paler underparts. The head bears a loose, forward-curling dark crest and three white plumes on each side of the face (two in front of the white eye and one behind it). Winter birds are paler with shorter plumes and a darker bill; juveniles are similar but lack head plumes.

white eye

dark slate-gray head

3 thin white whiskers on each side of face

dark slate-gray upperparts

long, thin, forward-curling black crest on forehead

thick stubby reddish bill with white tip

gray underparts merge into whitish gray on lower belly

short rounded wings

short grayish feet and legs

WINTER PLUMAGE

black webbing between toes

light gray undertail coverts

• **SONG** Call is piercing cry. Garrulous.
• **BEHAVIOR** Nomadic. Primarily nocturnal around breeding colonies. Pelagic. Makes small leaps from water before diving for food. Swims with wings underwater and steers with feet. Often feeds in turbulent waters. Eats small crustaceans, marine worms, and mollusks. Often dives directly into water from flight.
• **BREEDING** Monogamous. Colonial; often in mixed colonies with other auklets and storm-petrels.
• **NESTING** Incubation 35–36 days by both sexes. Semiprecocial young fed by both sexes from throat pouch. First flight at about 40 days. 1 brood per year.
• **POPULATION** Locally fairly common to common.
• **CONSERVATION** Threatened by oil pollution and human disturbance.

Similar Birds

CRESTED AUKLET
Larger; lacks white whiskers on face; darker belly; darker undertail coverts.

Flight Pattern

Direct flight close to water with rapid buzzing wing beats.

Nest Identification

Shape Location

No nest material • in crevices of inaccessible, overhanging ledges or on rocky shores; under rocks • 1 dull white egg; pear-shaped or pyriform, 1.9 inches long.

Plumage Sexes similar	Habitat	Migration Nonmigratory	Weight 4.3 ounces

DATE _____ TIME_____ LOCATION _____

Family ALCIDAE	Species *Aethia cristatella*	Length 9 inches	Wingspan 14 inches

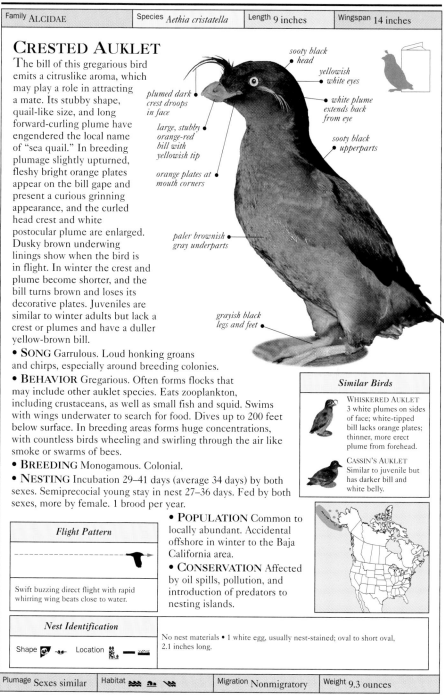

CRESTED AUKLET

The bill of this gregarious bird emits a citruslike aroma, which may play a role in attracting a mate. Its stubby shape, quail-like size, and long forward-curling plume have engendered the local name of "sea quail." In breeding plumage slightly upturned, fleshy bright orange plates appear on the bill gape and present a curious grinning appearance, and the curled head crest and white postocular plume are enlarged. Dusky brown underwing linings show when the bird is in flight. In winter the crest and plume become shorter, and the bill turns brown and loses its decorative plates. Juveniles are similar to winter adults but lack a crest or plumes and have a duller yellow-brown bill.

sooty black head

yellowish white eyes

plumed dark crest droops in face

white plume extends back from eye

large, stubby orange-red bill with yellowish tip

sooty black upperparts

orange plates at mouth corners

paler brownish gray underparts

grayish black legs and feet

• SONG Garrulous. Loud honking groans and chirps, especially around breeding colonies.
• BEHAVIOR Gregarious. Often forms flocks that may include other auklet species. Eats zooplankton, including crustaceans, as well as small fish and squid. Swims with wings underwater to search for food. Dives up to 200 feet below surface. In breeding areas forms huge concentrations, with countless birds wheeling and swirling through the air like smoke or swarms of bees.
• BREEDING Monogamous. Colonial.
• NESTING Incubation 29–41 days (average 34 days) by both sexes. Semiprecocial young stay in nest 27–36 days. Fed by both sexes, more by female. 1 brood per year.
• POPULATION Common to locally abundant. Accidental offshore in winter to the Baja California area.
• CONSERVATION Affected by oil spills, pollution, and introduction of predators to nesting islands.

Similar Birds

WHISKERED AUKLET
3 white plumes on sides of face; white-tipped bill lacks orange plates; thinner, more erect plume from forehead.

CASSIN'S AUKLET
Similar to juvenile but has darker bill and white belly.

Flight Pattern

Swift buzzing direct flight with rapid whirring wing beats close to water.

Nest Identification

Shape 🐦 ⚓   Location 🌿 ▬ 🪺

No nest materials • 1 white egg, usually nest-stained; oval to short oval, 2.1 inches long.

Plumage Sexes similar	Habitat 〰️ 🐚 🦅	Migration Nonmigratory	Weight 9.3 ounces

DATE _____ TIME_____ LOCATION _____

Family ALCIDAE	Species *Cerorhinca monocerata*	Length 15 inches	Wingspan 22 inches

RHINOCEROS AUKLET

Named for the unusual hornlike protrusion on its bill during breeding season, this bird digs and nests in burrows to which it returns each year along with its same mate. In flight it appears puffinlike but has more pointed wings, a whitish belly that blends into a darker breast and upperparts, and dark brownish gray underwings. In winter this bird lacks the horn on its upper mandible, and the color of its bill and plumes fade.

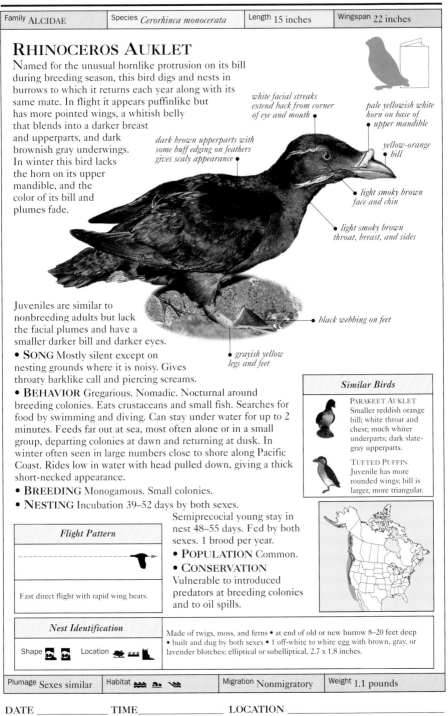

white facial streaks extend back from corner of eye and mouth

pale yellowish white horn on base of upper mandible

dark brown upperparts with some buff edging on feathers gives scaly appearance

yellow-orange bill

light smoky brown face and chin

light smoky brown throat, breast, and sides

black webbing on feet

grayish yellow legs and feet

Juveniles are similar to nonbreeding adults but lack the facial plumes and have a smaller darker bill and darker eyes.

• **SONG** Mostly silent except on nesting grounds where it is noisy. Gives throaty barklike call and piercing screams.

• **BEHAVIOR** Gregarious. Nomadic. Nocturnal around breeding colonies. Eats crustaceans and small fish. Searches for food by swimming and diving. Can stay under water for up to 2 minutes. Feeds far out at sea, most often alone or in a small group, departing colonies at dawn and returning at dusk. In winter often seen in large numbers close to shore along Pacific Coast. Rides low in water with head pulled down, giving a thick short-necked appearance.

• **BREEDING** Monogamous. Small colonies.

• **NESTING** Incubation 39–52 days by both sexes. Semiprecocial young stay in nest 48–55 days. Fed by both sexes. 1 brood per year.

• **POPULATION** Common.

• **CONSERVATION** Vulnerable to introduced predators at breeding colonies and to oil spills.

Similar Birds

PARAKEET AUKLET
Smaller reddish orange bill; white throat and chest; much whiter underparts; dark slate-gray upperparts.

TUFTED PUFFIN
Juvenile has more rounded wings; bill is larger, more triangular.

Flight Pattern

Fast direct flight with rapid wing beats.

Nest Identification

Shape ◼◼   Location 🌿 🌿🌿 🪨

Made of twigs, moss, and ferns • at end of old or new burrow 8–20 feet deep • built and dug by both sexes • 1 off-white to white egg with brown, gray, or lavender blotches; elliptical or subelliptical, 2.7 x 1.8 inches.

Plumage Sexes similar	Habitat 〰️ 🌊 〰️	Migration Nonmigratory	Weight 1.1 pounds

DATE _____ TIME_____ LOCATION _____

Family ALCIDAE	Species *Fratercula corniculata*	Length 15 inches	Wingspan 22–23 inches

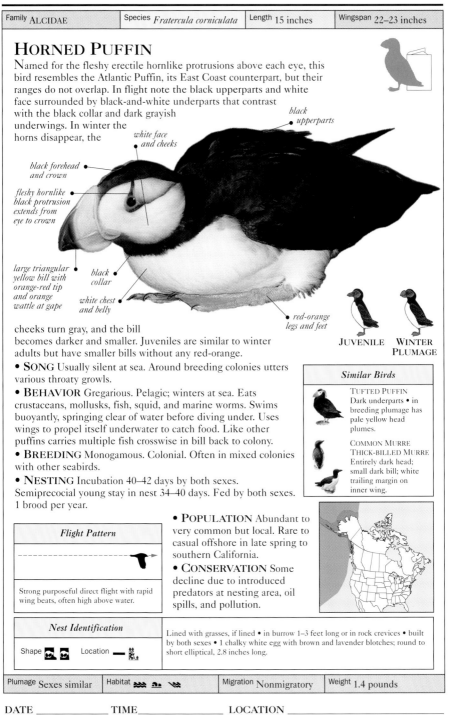

HORNED PUFFIN

Named for the fleshy erectile hornlike protrusions above each eye, this bird resembles the Atlantic Puffin, its East Coast counterpart, but their ranges do not overlap. In flight note the black upperparts and white face surrounded by black-and-white underparts that contrast with the black collar and dark grayish underwings. In winter the horns disappear, the

white face and cheeks

black upperparts

black forehead and crown

fleshy hornlike black protrusion extends from eye to crown

large triangular yellow bill with orange-red tip and orange wattle at gape

black collar

white chest and belly

red-orange legs and feet

cheeks turn gray, and the bill becomes darker and smaller. Juveniles are similar to winter adults but have smaller bills without any red-orange.

JUVENILE   WINTER
PLUMAGE

• **SONG** Usually silent at sea. Around breeding colonies utters various throaty growls.

• **BEHAVIOR** Gregarious. Pelagic; winters at sea. Eats crustaceans, mollusks, fish, squid, and marine worms. Swims buoyantly, springing clear of water before diving under. Uses wings to propel itself underwater to catch food. Like other puffins carries multiple fish crosswise in bill back to colony.

• **BREEDING** Monogamous. Colonial. Often in mixed colonies with other seabirds.

• **NESTING** Incubation 40–42 days by both sexes. Semiprecocial young stay in nest 34–40 days. Fed by both sexes. 1 brood per year.

Similar Birds

TUFTED PUFFIN
Dark underparts • in breeding plumage has pale yellow head plumes.

COMMON MURRE
THICK-BILLED MURRE
Entirely dark head; small dark bill; white trailing margin on inner wing.

• **POPULATION** Abundant to very common but local. Rare to casual offshore in late spring to southern California.

• **CONSERVATION** Some decline due to introduced predators at nesting area, oil spills, and pollution.

Flight Pattern

Strong purposeful direct flight with rapid wing beats, often high above water.

Nest Identification

Shape 🐚 🐚   Location ▬ 🪺

Lined with grasses, if lined • in burrow 1–3 feet long or in rock crevices • built by both sexes • 1 chalky white egg with brown and lavender blotches; round to short elliptical, 2.8 inches long.

Plumage Sexes similar	Habitat 〰 🦆 〰	Migration Nonmigratory	Weight 1.4 pounds

Family ALCIDAE		Species *Fratercula cirrhata*	Length 15.5 inches	Wingspan 23–24 inches

TUFTED PUFFIN

The largest of the puffins is distinguished by its odd-looking head plumes in breeding season. The combination of a massive red, orange, and yellow bill; long ivory-yellow head tufts; white face; and stout black body is unmistakable. Though it always nests in colonies, it travels and feeds alone at sea. In flight birds show grayish wing linings. In winter the plumes disappear, the bill becomes smaller and duller, and the overall plumage, including the face, becomes blackish gray-brown. Juveniles are smaller and darker and have small dull yellow bills.

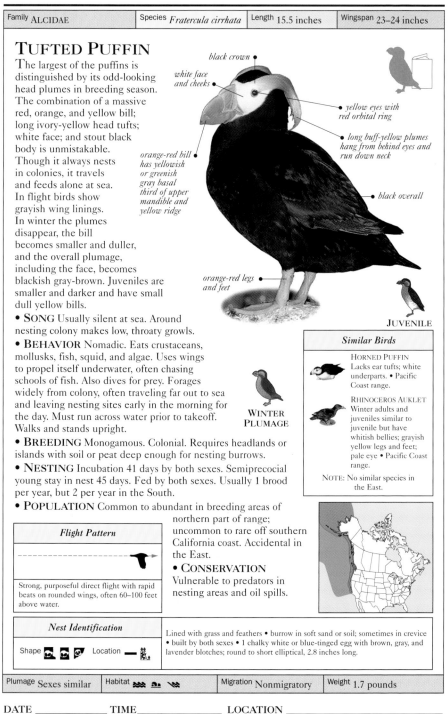

black crown

white face and cheeks

yellow eyes with red orbital ring

long buff-yellow plumes hang from behind eyes and run down neck

orange-red bill has yellowish or greenish gray basal third of upper mandible and yellow ridge

black overall

orange-red legs and feet

JUVENILE

- **SONG** Usually silent at sea. Around nesting colony makes low, throaty growls.
- **BEHAVIOR** Nomadic. Eats crustaceans, mollusks, fish, squid, and algae. Uses wings to propel itself underwater, often chasing schools of fish. Also dives for prey. Forages widely from colony, often traveling far out to sea and leaving nesting sites early in the morning for the day. Must run across water prior to takeoff. Walks and stands upright.
- **BREEDING** Monogamous. Colonial. Requires headlands or islands with soil or peat deep enough for nesting burrows.
- **NESTING** Incubation 41 days by both sexes. Semiprecocial young stay in nest 45 days. Fed by both sexes. Usually 1 brood per year, but 2 per year in the South.
- **POPULATION** Common to abundant in breeding areas of northern part of range; uncommon to rare off southern California coast. Accidental in the East.
- **CONSERVATION** Vulnerable to predators in nesting areas and oil spills.

WINTER PLUMAGE

Similar Birds

HORNED PUFFIN
Lacks ear tufts; white underparts. • Pacific Coast range.

RHINOCEROS AUKLET
Winter adults and juveniles similar to juvenile but have whitish bellies; grayish yellow legs and feet; pale eye • Pacific Coast range.

NOTE: No similar species in the East.

Flight Pattern

Strong, purposeful direct flight with rapid beats on rounded wings, often 60–100 feet above water.

Nest Identification

Shape 🐚 🐚 🐚 Location ▬ 🏞

Lined with grass and feathers • burrow in soft sand or soil; sometimes in crevice • built by both sexes • 1 chalky white or blue-tinged egg with brown, gray, and lavender blotches; round to short elliptical, 2.8 inches long.

Plumage Sexes similar	Habitat 🌊 🏞 🌾	Migration Nonmigratory	Weight 1.7 pounds

DATE _____ TIME_____ LOCATION _____

Family COLUMBIDAE	Species *Columba livia*	Length 13–14 inches	Wingspan 24–25 inches

ROCK DOVE

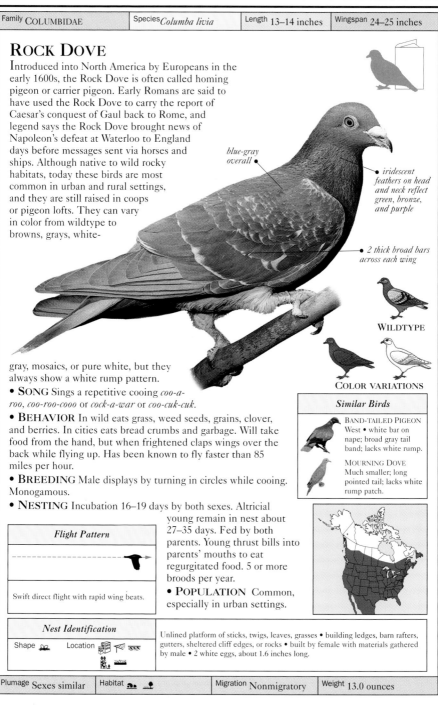

Introduced into North America by Europeans in the early 1600s, the Rock Dove is often called homing pigeon or carrier pigeon. Early Romans are said to have used the Rock Dove to carry the report of Caesar's conquest of Gaul back to Rome, and legend says the Rock Dove brought news of Napoleon's defeat at Waterloo to England days before messages sent via horses and ships. Although native to wild rocky habitats, today these birds are most common in urban and rural settings, and they are still raised in coops or pigeon lofts. They can vary in color from wildtype to browns, grays, white-

blue-gray overall •

• *iridescent feathers on head and neck reflect green, bronze, and purple*

• *2 thick broad bars across each wing*

WILDTYPE

gray, mosaics, or pure white, but they always show a white rump pattern.

COLOR VARIATIONS

- **SONG** Sings a repetitive cooing *coo-a-roo, coo-roo-cooo* or *cock-a-war* or *coo-cuk-cuk*.
- **BEHAVIOR** In wild eats grass, weed seeds, grains, clover, and berries. In cities eats bread crumbs and garbage. Will take food from the hand, but when frightened claps wings over the back while flying up. Has been known to fly faster than 85 miles per hour.
- **BREEDING** Male displays by turning in circles while cooing. Monogamous.
- **NESTING** Incubation 16–19 days by both sexes. Altricial young remain in nest about 27–35 days. Fed by both parents. Young thrust bills into parents' mouths to eat regurgitated food. 5 or more broods per year.
- **POPULATION** Common, especially in urban settings.

Similar Birds

BAND-TAILED PIGEON
West • white bar on nape; broad gray tail band; lacks white rump.

MOURNING DOVE
Much smaller; long pointed tail; lacks white rump patch.

Flight Pattern

Swift direct flight with rapid wing beats.

Nest Identification

Shape   Location

Unlined platform of sticks, twigs, leaves, grasses • building ledges, barn rafters, gutters, sheltered cliff edges, or rocks • built by female with materials gathered by male • 2 white eggs, about 1.6 inches long.

Plumage Sexes similar	Habitat	Migration Nonmigratory	Weight 13.0 ounces

DATE _____ TIME_____ LOCATION _____

Family COLUMBIDAE	Species *Columba fasciata*	Length 14–15 inches	Wingspan 25 inches

BAND-TAILED PIGEON

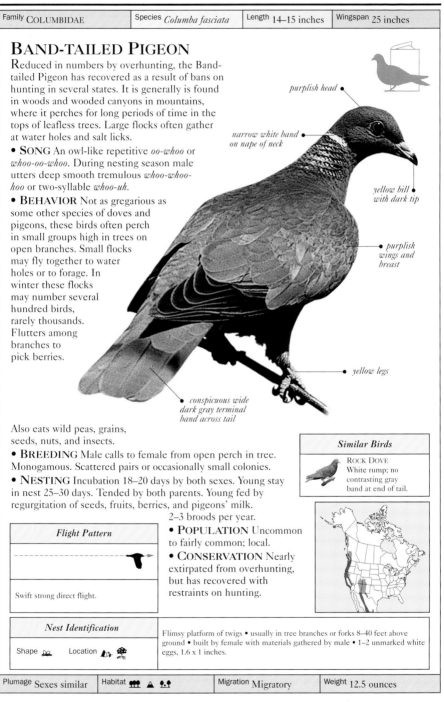

Reduced in numbers by overhunting, the Band-tailed Pigeon has recovered as a result of bans on hunting in several states. It is generally is found in woods and wooded canyons in mountains, where it perches for long periods of time in the tops of leafless trees. Large flocks often gather at water holes and salt licks.

purplish head

narrow white band on nape of neck

yellow bill with dark tip

purplish wings and breast

yellow legs

conspicuous wide dark gray terminal band across tail

• **SONG** An owl-like repetitive *oo-whoo* or *whoo-oo-whoo*. During nesting season male utters deep smooth tremulous *whoo-whoo-hoo* or two-syllable *whoo-uh*.

• **BEHAVIOR** Not as gregarious as some other species of doves and pigeons, these birds often perch in small groups high in trees on open branches. Small flocks may fly together to water holes or to forage. In winter these flocks may number several hundred birds, rarely thousands. Flutters among branches to pick berries.

Also eats wild peas, grains, seeds, nuts, and insects.

• **BREEDING** Male calls to female from open perch in tree. Monogamous. Scattered pairs or occasionally small colonies.

• **NESTING** Incubation 18–20 days by both sexes. Young stay in nest 25–30 days. Tended by both parents. Young fed by regurgitation of seeds, fruits, berries, and pigeons' milk. 2–3 broods per year.

• **POPULATION** Uncommon to fairly common; local.

• **CONSERVATION** Nearly extirpated from overhunting, but has recovered with restraints on hunting.

Similar Birds

ROCK DOVE
White rump; no contrasting gray band at end of tail.

Flight Pattern

Swift strong direct flight.

Nest Identification

Shape ⌣ Location 🏔️ 🌲

Flimsy platform of twigs • usually in tree branches or forks 8–40 feet above ground • built by female with materials gathered by male • 1–2 unmarked white eggs, 1.6 x 1 inches.

Plumage Sexes similar	Habitat 🌳 ▲ 🌾	Migration Migratory	Weight 12.5 ounces

DATE _____ TIME_____ LOCATION _____

Family COLUMBIDAE	Species *Streptopelia decaocto*	Length 12.5 inches	Wingspan 18–19 inches

EURASIAN COLLARED-DOVE

This large dove, a native of Eurasia, was introduced into the Bahama Islands in 1974. By the end of the 1970s, it had found its way to Florida, where it could be seen feeding in backyard gardens, towns, and parks. By the beginning of the new millennium this now established exotic had spread up the Atlantic Coast to North Carolina, across the Gulf Coast to Texas, and up the Mississippi River to Tennessee, with records in Oklahoma and Pennsylvania. Although similar to other doves

pale gray-pink head, neck, and breast

black bill

very pale buff upperparts

black "half-moon" trimmed with white on nape

pink legs and feet

in its habits, this dove is less shy around people and prefers life in and around human habitation. In flight, it shows a two-toned tail, gray base, and white-tipped blackish primaries.

• **SONG** Soft, continual cooing *hoo-hoooo-hoo* with emphasis on the second syllable; also a complaining *mair*.

• **BEHAVIOR** Solitary; pairs and family groups, but not in large flocks. Feeds close to houses; trusting of human contact. Eats mostly grain and seeds. Feeds on lawns, roadsides, feed mills, farms, and agricultural areas.

• **BREEDING** Monogamous. Male gives displays and coos while perched in tree or roof.

• **NESTING** Incubation 14–18 days by both sexes. Young stay in nest 15–20 days, fed and tended by both parents for an additional week. Up to 6 broods per year in Europe, possibly same in Florida.

• **POPULATION** Fairly common to common. Spreading quickly in southeastern US cities, villages, and gardens.

• **FEEDERS** Attracted to feeding stations, bird feeders, birdbaths, and garden pools.

Similar Birds

MOURNING DOVE
Smaller; pinkish fawn head and underparts; pinkish iridescence on neck; black spot on auriculars; brownish gray upperparts and unmarked nape; long, pointed tail with white tips and black subteminal band on all but two central feathers; black spots on upper inner wing • wings make whistling sound in flight.

Flight Pattern

Swift strong direct flight on rapidly beating wings.

Nest Identification

Shape Location

Twigs and dry stalks • in tree, shrub, and balconies or eves of houses, 6–7 feet above ground • male collects materials, female builds • 2 pure white eggs; oval to elliptical, 1.2 inches.

Plumage Sexes similar	Habitat	Migration Nonmigratory	Weight 5.4 ounces

DATE _____ TIME_____ LOCATION _____

| Family COLUMBIDAE | Species *Streptopelia chinensis* | Length 12–13 inches | Wingspan 17–19 inches |

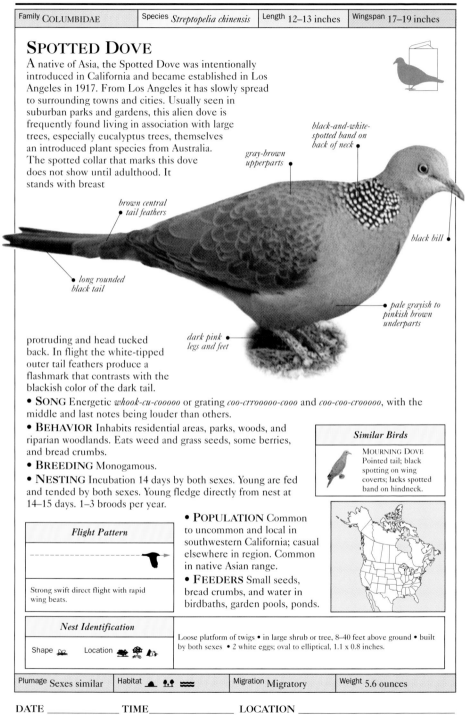

SPOTTED DOVE

A native of Asia, the Spotted Dove was intentionally introduced in California and became established in Los Angeles in 1917. From Los Angeles it has slowly spread to surrounding towns and cities. Usually seen in suburban parks and gardens, this alien dove is frequently found living in association with large trees, especially eucalyptus trees, themselves an introduced plant species from Australia. The spotted collar that marks this dove does not show until adulthood. It stands with breast

black-and-white-spotted band on back of neck

gray-brown upperparts

brown central tail feathers

black bill

long rounded black tail

pale grayish to pinkish brown underparts

dark pink legs and feet

protruding and head tucked back. In flight the white-tipped outer tail feathers produce a flashmark that contrasts with the blackish color of the dark tail.

• **SONG** Energetic *whook-cu-cooooo* or grating *coo-crrooooo-cooo* and *coo-coo-crooooo*, with the middle and last notes being louder than others.

• **BEHAVIOR** Inhabits residential areas, parks, woods, and riparian woodlands. Eats weed and grass seeds, some berries, and bread crumbs.

• **BREEDING** Monogamous.

• **NESTING** Incubation 14 days by both sexes. Young are fed and tended by both sexes. Young fledge directly from nest at 14–15 days. 1–3 broods per year.

Similar Birds

MOURNING DOVE
Pointed tail; black spotting on wing coverts; lacks spotted band on hindneck.

• **POPULATION** Common to uncommon and local in southwestern California; casual elsewhere in region. Common in native Asian range.

• **FEEDERS** Small seeds, bread crumbs, and water in birdbaths, garden pools, ponds.

Flight Pattern

Strong swift direct flight with rapid wing beats.

Nest Identification

Shape | Location

Loose platform of twigs • in large shrub or tree, 8–40 feet above ground • built by both sexes • 2 white eggs; oval to elliptical, 1.1 x 0.8 inches.

| Plumage Sexes similar | Habitat | Migration Migratory | Weight 5.6 ounces |

DATE _____ TIME_____ LOCATION _____

| Family COLUMBIDAE | Species *Zenaida asiatica* | Length 11–12 inches | Wingspan 17–18 inches |

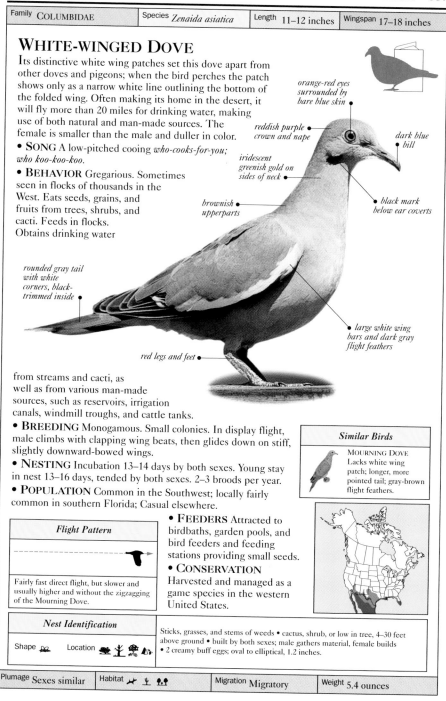

WHITE-WINGED DOVE

Its distinctive white wing patches set this dove apart from other doves and pigeons; when the bird perches the patch shows only as a narrow white line outlining the bottom of the folded wing. Often making its home in the desert, it will fly more than 20 miles for drinking water, making use of both natural and man-made sources. The female is smaller than the male and duller in color.

orange-red eyes surrounded by bare blue skin

reddish purple crown and nape

dark blue bill

iridescent greenish gold on sides of neck

black mark below ear coverts

brownish upperparts

• **SONG** A low-pitched cooing *who-cooks-for-you; who koo-koo-koo.*
• **BEHAVIOR** Gregarious. Sometimes seen in flocks of thousands in the West. Eats seeds, grains, and fruits from trees, shrubs, and cacti. Feeds in flocks. Obtains drinking water

rounded gray tail with white corners, black-trimmed inside

large white wing bars and dark gray flight feathers

red legs and feet

from streams and cacti, as well as from various man-made sources, such as reservoirs, irrigation canals, windmill troughs, and cattle tanks.
• **BREEDING** Monogamous. Small colonies. In display flight, male climbs with clapping wing beats, then glides down on stiff, slightly downward-bowed wings.
• **NESTING** Incubation 13–14 days by both sexes. Young stay in nest 13–16 days, tended by both sexes. 2–3 broods per year.
• **POPULATION** Common in the Southwest; locally fairly common in southern Florida; Casual elsewhere.

Similar Birds

MOURNING DOVE Lacks white wing patch; longer, more pointed tail; gray-brown flight feathers.

• **FEEDERS** Attracted to birdbaths, garden pools, and bird feeders and feeding stations providing small seeds.
• **CONSERVATION** Harvested and managed as a game species in the western United States.

Flight Pattern

Fairly fast direct flight, but slower and usually higher and without the zigzagging of the Mourning Dove.

Nest Identification

Shape ⌒ Location 🌿🌱🪴🍃

Sticks, grasses, and stems of weeds • cactus, shrub, or low in tree, 4–30 feet above ground • built by both sexes; male gathers material, female builds • 2 creamy buff eggs; oval to elliptical, 1.2 inches.

| Plumage Sexes similar | Habitat 🌿🌱🍃 | Migration Migratory | Weight 5.4 ounces |

DATE _____ TIME_____ LOCATION _____

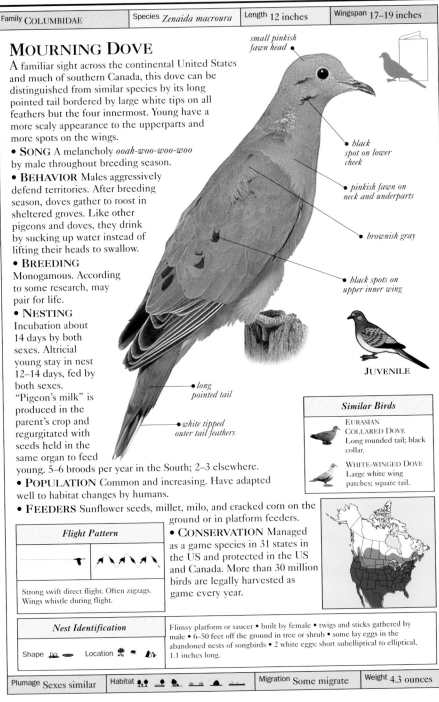

Family COLUMBIDAE	Species *Zenaida macroura*	Length 12 inches	Wingspan 17–19 inches

MOURNING DOVE

small pinkish fawn head •

A familiar sight across the continental United States and much of southern Canada, this dove can be distinguished from similar species by its long pointed tail bordered by large white tips on all feathers but the four innermost. Young have a more scaly appearance to the upperparts and more spots on the wings.

• **SONG** A melancholy *ooah-woo-woo-woo* by male throughout breeding season.

• **BEHAVIOR** Males aggressively defend territories. After breeding season, doves gather to roost in sheltered groves. Like other pigeons and doves, they drink by sucking up water instead of lifting their heads to swallow.

• **BREEDING** Monogamous. According to some research, may pair for life.

• **NESTING** Incubation about 14 days by both sexes. Altricial young stay in nest 12–14 days, fed by both sexes. "Pigeon's milk" is produced in the parent's crop and regurgitated with seeds held in the same organ to feed young. 5–6 broods per year in the South; 2–3 elsewhere.

• **POPULATION** Common and increasing. Have adapted well to habitat changes by humans.

• **FEEDERS** Sunflower seeds, millet, milo, and cracked corn on the ground or in platform feeders.

• **CONSERVATION** Managed as a game species in 31 states in the US and protected in the US and Canada. More than 30 million birds are legally harvested as game every year.

• black spot on lower cheek

• pinkish fawn on neck and underparts

• brownish gray

• black spots on upper inner wing

JUVENILE

• long pointed tail

• white tipped outer tail feathers

Similar Birds

EURASIAN COLLARED DOVE Long rounded tail; black collar.

WHITE-WINGED DOVE Large white wing patches; square tail.

Flight Pattern

Strong swift direct flight. Often zigzags. Wings whistle during flight.

Nest Identification

Shape ♒ ⬭   Location 🌳 ▪ 🌲

Flimsy platform or saucer • built by female • twigs and sticks gathered by male • 6–50 feet off the ground in tree or shrub • some lay eggs in the abandoned nests of songbirds • 2 white eggs; short subelliptical to elliptical, 1.1 inches long.

Plumage Sexes similar	Habitat 🌿🌾 🌱 🌳 🌾 🌾 ⛰ 🌾	Migration Some migrate	Weight 4.3 ounces

DATE _____ TIME_____ LOCATION _____

Family COLUMBIDAE	Species *Columbina inca*	Length 7.5–8 inches	Wingspan 12–13 inches

INCA DOVE

During autumn large flocks of these small birds can be seen huddled together for warmth on clotheslines or fences. Choosing to make its home near human habitation, this tame dove feeds in parks, barnyards,

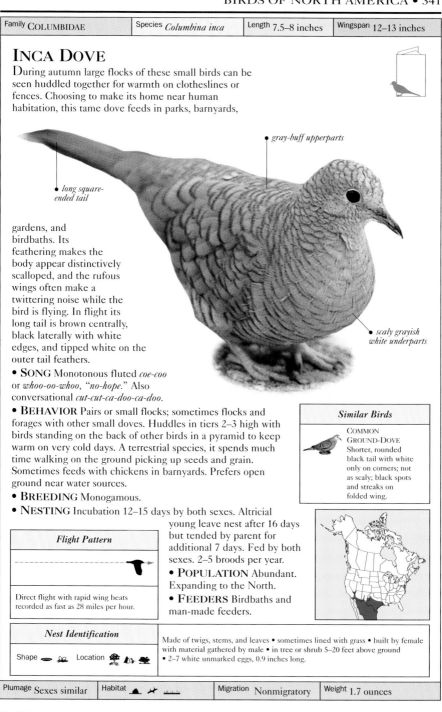

• *gray-buff upperparts*

• *long square-ended tail*

• *scaly grayish white underparts*

gardens, and birdbaths. Its feathering makes the body appear distinctively scalloped, and the rufous wings often make a twittering noise while the bird is flying. In flight its long tail is brown centrally, black laterally with white edges, and tipped white on the outer tail feathers.

• **SONG** Monotonous fluted *coe-coo* or *whoo-oo-whoo*, "*no-hope*." Also conversational *cut-cut-ca-doo-ca-doo*.

• **BEHAVIOR** Pairs or small flocks; sometimes flocks and forages with other small doves. Huddles in tiers 2–3 high with birds standing on the back of other birds in a pyramid to keep warm on very cold days. A terrestrial species, it spends much time walking on the ground picking up seeds and grain. Sometimes feeds with chickens in barnyards. Prefers open ground near water sources.

• **BREEDING** Monogamous.

• **NESTING** Incubation 12–15 days by both sexes. Altricial young leave nest after 16 days but tended by parent for additional 7 days. Fed by both sexes. 2–5 broods per year.

• **POPULATION** Abundant. Expanding to the North.

• **FEEDERS** Birdbaths and man-made feeders.

Similar Birds

COMMON GROUND-DOVE Shorter, rounded black tail with white only on corners; not as scaly; black spots and streaks on folded wing.

Flight Pattern

Direct flight with rapid wing beats recorded as fast as 28 miles per hour.

Nest Identification

Shape — Location

Made of twigs, stems, and leaves • sometimes lined with grass • built by female with material gathered by male • in tree or shrub 5–20 feet above ground • 2–7 white unmarked eggs, 0.9 inches long.

Plumage Sexes similar	Habitat	Migration Nonmigratory	Weight 1.7 ounces

DATE _____ TIME _____ LOCATION _____

Family COLUMBIDAE	Species *Columbina passerina*	Length 6–7 inches	Wingspan 8.75–10 inches

COMMON GROUND-DOVE

The Common Ground-Dove is about the size of a sparrow and often can be seen perched on fences, roofs of buildings, and trees. Known as tame, this bird sometimes will not fly away until almost stepped upon. The female is grayer than the male and more uniformly colored. In flight this small dove has flashing rufous-red primaries and wing linings and a black tail with white corners.

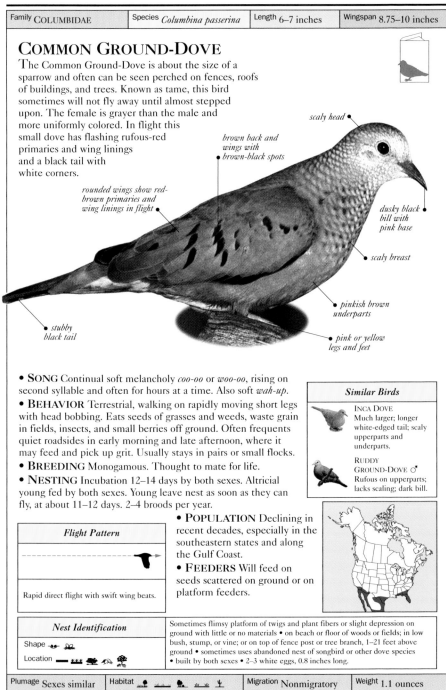

scaly head

brown back and wings with brown-black spots

rounded wings show red-brown primaries and wing linings in flight

dusky black bill with pink base

scaly breast

pinkish brown underparts

stubby black tail

pink or yellow legs and feet

• **SONG** Continual soft melancholy *coo-oo* or *woo-oo*, rising on second syllable and often for hours at a time. Also soft *wah-up*.

• **BEHAVIOR** Terrestrial, walking on rapidly moving short legs with head bobbing. Eats seeds of grasses and weeds, waste grain in fields, insects, and small berries off ground. Often frequents quiet roadsides in early morning and late afternoon, where it may feed and pick up grit. Usually stays in pairs or small flocks.

• **BREEDING** Monogamous. Thought to mate for life.

• **NESTING** Incubation 12–14 days by both sexes. Altricial young fed by both sexes. Young leave nest as soon as they can fly, at about 11–12 days. 2–4 broods per year.

• **POPULATION** Declining in recent decades, especially in the southeastern states and along the Gulf Coast.

• **FEEDERS** Will feed on seeds scattered on ground or on platform feeders.

Similar Birds

INCA DOVE
Much larger; longer white-edged tail; scaly upperparts and underparts.

RUDDY GROUND-DOVE ♂
Rufous on upperparts; lacks scaling; dark bill.

Flight Pattern

Rapid direct flight with swift wing beats.

Nest Identification	Sometimes flimsy platform of twigs and plant fibers or slight depression on ground with little or no materials • on beach or floor of woods or fields; in low bush, stump, or vine; or on top of fence post or tree branch, 1–21 feet above ground • sometimes uses abandoned nest of songbird or other dove species • built by both sexes • 2–3 white eggs, 0.8 inches long.
Shape	
Location	

Plumage Sexes similar	Habitat	Migration Nonmigratory	Weight 1.1 ounces

DATE _____ TIME _____ LOCATION _____

| Family COLUMBIDAE | Species *Columbina talpacoti* | Length 6–7 inches | Wingspan 9–10 inches |

RUDDY GROUND-DOVE

This gregarious dove enjoys the company of other birds. Often, as many as forty doves will gather facing the same direction and pick up seeds from the ground, moving in step with one another. Although primarily a Mexican and Central and South American native, in recent years it has strayed into Texas, Arizona, and California. In flight, note the rufous or brown upperparts, black outer tail feathers, and rusty red primaries (compare with Common Ground-Dove).

• **SONG** A *wooh* or *woop.* Sometimes, a soft *per-woop, per-woop.*

blue-gray crown and nape

rufous upperparts

grayish bill with dark tip

ruddy wine-colored face and neck

scattered black spots and bars on lower scapulars and wing coverts

wine-colored underparts

MALE

dark gray-brown crown, nape, and upperparts

grayish face, neck, and underparts

FEMALE

long tail with black outer tail feathers

• **BEHAVIOR** Feeds from ground, eating seeds; also takes berries. Often seen on roads, possibly gathering grit. Often in pairs or groups of 10–20. Sometimes in large flocks with other species, including Inca Dove and Common Ground-Dove. Roosts gregariously in dense foliage.

• **BREEDING** Monogamous. Colonial.

• **NESTING** Incubation 12–13 days by both sexes; female at night, male during day. Altricial young stay in nest 12–14 days, fed by both sexes. 2 or more broods per year.

• **POPULATION** Casual in the US from southern California to southeastern Texas close to Mexican border. Common throughout most of its semitropical and tropical breeding range.

• **FEEDERS** Attracted to feeding stations with small grain, especially if scattered on the ground. Also attracted to birdbaths and garden pools.

Similar Birds

COMMON GROUND-DOVE
Scaled appearance on head and breast; black bill with pink base; brown upperparts; pinkish brown underparts; outermost tail feathers narrowly tipped white.

Flight Pattern

Fast low direct flight on flashing rufous-red wings.

Nest Identification

Shape   Location

Twigs and grass • tree or bush, 3–35 feet above ground • built by both sexes • 2 white eggs; oval to elliptical, 0.9 x 0.7 inches.

| Plumage Sexes differ | Habitat | Migration Nonmigratory | Weight 1.7 ounces |

DATE _____ TIME_____ LOCATION _____

Family COLUMBIDAE	Species *Leptotila verreauxi*	Length 11–12 inches	Wingspan 17–18 inches

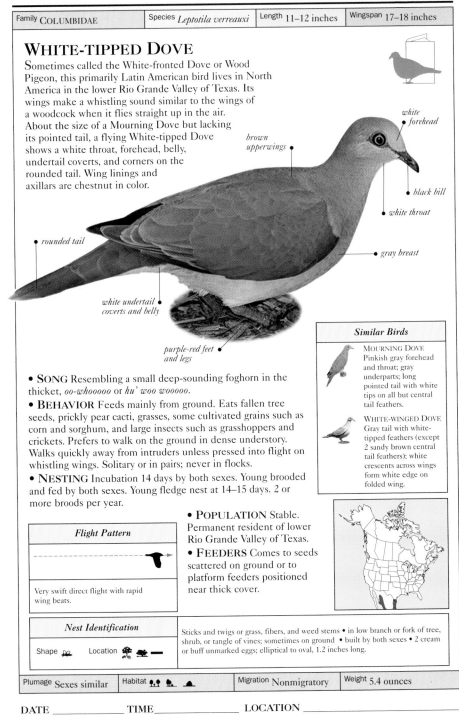

WHITE-TIPPED DOVE

Sometimes called the White-fronted Dove or Wood Pigeon, this primarily Latin American bird lives in North America in the lower Rio Grande Valley of Texas. Its wings make a whistling sound similar to the wings of a woodcock when it flies straight up in the air. About the size of a Mourning Dove but lacking its pointed tail, a flying White-tipped Dove shows a white throat, forehead, belly, undertail coverts, and corners on the rounded tail. Wing linings and axillars are chestnut in color.

white forehead

brown upperwings

black bill

white throat

gray breast

rounded tail

white undertail coverts and belly

purple-red feet and legs

Similar Birds

MOURNING DOVE Pinkish gray forehead and throat; gray underparts; long pointed tail with white tips on all but central tail feathers.

WHITE-WINGED DOVE Gray tail with white-tipped feathers (except 2 sandy brown central tail feathers); white crescents across wings form white edge on folded wing.

• **SONG** Resembling a small deep-sounding foghorn in the thicket, *oo-whooooo* or *hu' woo wooooo*.

• **BEHAVIOR** Feeds mainly from ground. Eats fallen tree seeds, prickly pear cacti, grasses, some cultivated grains such as corn and sorghum, and large insects such as grasshoppers and crickets. Prefers to walk on the ground in dense understory. Walks quickly away from intruders unless pressed into flight on whistling wings. Solitary or in pairs; never in flocks.

• **NESTING** Incubation 14 days by both sexes. Young brooded and fed by both sexes. Young fledge nest at 14–15 days. 2 or more broods per year.

• **POPULATION** Stable. Permanent resident of lower Rio Grande Valley of Texas.

• **FEEDERS** Comes to seeds scattered on ground or to platform feeders positioned near thick cover.

Flight Pattern

Very swift direct flight with rapid wing beats.

Nest Identification

Shape   Location

Sticks and twigs or grass, fibers, and weed stems • in low branch or fork of tree, shrub, or tangle of vines; sometimes on ground • built by both sexes • 2 cream or buff unmarked eggs; elliptical to oval, 1.2 inches long.

Plumage Sexes similar	Habitat	Migration Nonmigratory	Weight 5.4 ounces

DATE _____ TIME_____ LOCATION _____

Family PSITTACIDAE	Species *Rhynchopsitta pachyrhyncha*	Length 15–16.5 inches	Wingspan 25–26 inches

THICK-BILLED PARROT

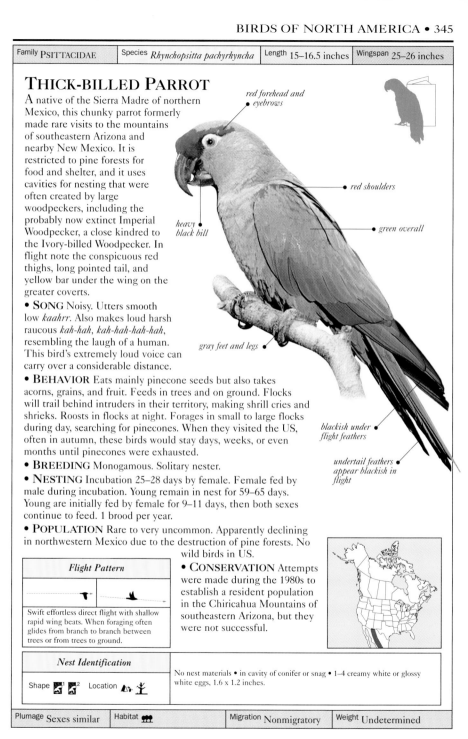

red forehead and eyebrows

red shoulders

green overall

heavy black bill

gray feet and legs

blackish under flight feathers

undertail feathers appear blackish in flight

A native of the Sierra Madre of northern Mexico, this chunky parrot formerly made rare visits to the mountains of southeastern Arizona and nearby New Mexico. It is restricted to pine forests for food and shelter, and it uses cavities for nesting that were often created by large woodpeckers, including the probably now extinct Imperial Woodpecker, a close kindred to the Ivory-billed Woodpecker. In flight note the conspicuous red thighs, long pointed tail, and yellow bar under the wing on the greater coverts.

• **SONG** Noisy. Utters smooth low *kaahrr*. Also makes loud harsh raucous *kah-hah, kah-hah-hah-hah*, resembling the laugh of a human. This bird's extremely loud voice can carry over a considerable distance.

• **BEHAVIOR** Eats mainly pinecone seeds but also takes acorns, grains, and fruit. Feeds in trees and on ground. Flocks will trail behind intruders in their territory, making shrill cries and shrieks. Roosts in flocks at night. Forages in small to large flocks during day, searching for pinecones. When they visited the US, often in autumn, these birds would stay days, weeks, or even months until pinecones were exhausted.

• **BREEDING** Monogamous. Solitary nester.

• **NESTING** Incubation 25–28 days by female. Female fed by male during incubation. Young remain in nest for 59–65 days. Young are initially fed by female for 9–11 days, then both sexes continue to feed. 1 brood per year.

• **POPULATION** Rare to very uncommon. Apparently declining in northwestern Mexico due to the destruction of pine forests. No wild birds in US.

• **CONSERVATION** Attempts were made during the 1980s to establish a resident population in the Chiricahua Mountains of southeastern Arizona, but they were not successful.

Flight Pattern
Swift effortless direct flight with shallow rapid wing beats. When foraging often glides from branch to branch between trees or from trees to ground.

Nest Identification
Shape ▨¹ ▨² Location ▲ 🌲

No nest materials • in cavity of conifer or snag • 1–4 creamy white or glossy white eggs, 1.6 x 1.2 inches.

Plumage Sexes similar	Habitat 🌿		Migration Nonmigratory	Weight Undetermined

DATE _____ TIME_____ LOCATION _____

Family PSITTACIDAE	Species *Brotogeris versicolurus*	Length 8–9 inches	Wingspan 13–14 inches

WHITE-WINGED PARAKEET

Sometimes called the Canary-winged Parakeet, this South American native makes its home in the forest, including parklands. The only noted established populations from released or escaped birds in North America peaked in Miami and in California in the mid-20th century; they have since declined. In flight, note the long pointed green tail, the colorful wing pattern of a green wedge in the forewing, yellow greater secondary and primary coverts, white secondaries and inner primaries, and blue-green outer primaries. This bird is also easy to identify in flight from below by its translucent white flight feathers.

pale teardrop-shaped eye ring

green overall

hooked pinkish yellow to yellow-tinged pale brown bill

yellow-and-white border on folded wing

- **SONG** Garrulous. While flying or perched gives a rapid repetition of shrieking metallic notes. When feeding has various chatters, chirps, and low muttering calls.
- **BEHAVIOR** Gregarious; occurs in flocks of 8–10 birds, sometimes up to 50. Flocks break up into pairs during breeding season. Eats seeds, berries, fruit, blossoms, and buds of fruit and other trees. Presence difficult to overlook because of its noisy vocalizations

long pointed green tail

grayish pink legs and feet

but difficult to see when perched because the dark green plumage blends well with the foliage. Frequents areas around human habitation in urban and suburban areas with tropical and subtropical ornamental plantings.

- **BREEDING** Monogamous. Solitary.
- **NESTING** Incubation 26 days by female. Altricial young stay in nest 56 days, fed by both sexes. 1 brood per year.
- **POPULATION** Exotic. Introduced into southern California and southern Florida, where they are now established, but declining from peaks in the 1970s and 1980s. Being replaced by Yellow-chevroned Parakeet, also introduced, which now outnumbers the White-winged Parakeet.
- **FEEDERS** Attends feeders providing seeds and/or fruits. Comes to birdbaths, pools, and ponds to drink.
- **CONSERVATION** No efforts in US because it is not a native species.

Similar Birds
An introduced species in south Florida, the Yellow-chevroned Parakeet is growing in number; it differs only in that it lacks white patches in the wing.

Flight Pattern

Swift direct flight on rapidly beating wings.

Nest Identification

Shape 🛏️²   Location 🌳 🌿 🌱

No nesting materials • in tree • 5 dull white or pure white eggs; slightly ovate, 0.9 x 0.7 inches.

Plumage Sexes similar	Habitat 🌿🌿 🌱	Migration Nonmigratory	Weight 1.9 ounces

DATE _____ TIME_____ LOCATION _____

Family CUCULIDAE	Species *Cuculus canorus*	Length 13 inches	Wingspan 29 inches

COMMON CUCKOO

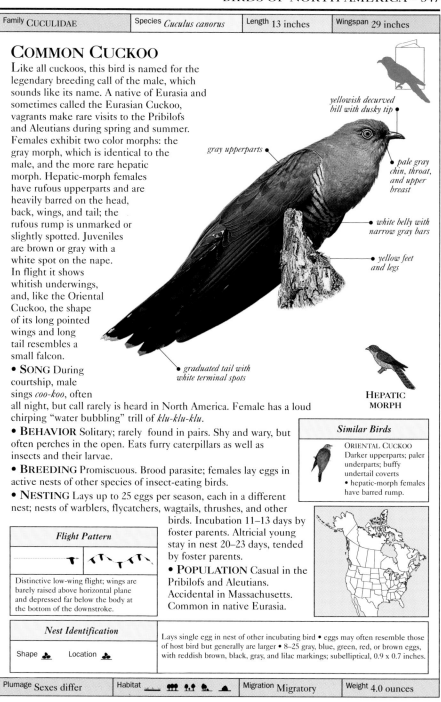

Like all cuckoos, this bird is named for the legendary breeding call of the male, which sounds like its name. A native of Eurasia and sometimes called the Eurasian Cuckoo, vagrants make rare visits to the Pribilofs and Aleutians during spring and summer. Females exhibit two color morphs: the gray morph, which is identical to the male, and the more rare hepatic morph. Hepatic-morph females have rufous upperparts and are heavily barred on the head, back, wings, and tail; the rufous rump is unmarked or slightly spotted. Juveniles are brown or gray with a white spot on the nape. In flight it shows whitish underwings, and, like the Oriental Cuckoo, the shape of its long pointed wings and long tail resembles a small falcon.

yellowish decurved bill with dusky tip

gray upperparts

pale gray chin, throat, and upper breast

white belly with narrow gray bars

yellow feet and legs

graduated tail with white terminal spots

HEPATIC MORPH

- **SONG** During courtship, male sings *coo-koo*, often all night, but call rarely is heard in North America. Female has a loud chirping "water bubbling" trill of *klu-klu-klu*.
- **BEHAVIOR** Solitary; rarely found in pairs. Shy and wary, but often perches in the open. Eats furry caterpillars as well as insects and their larvae.
- **BREEDING** Promiscuous. Brood parasite; females lay eggs in active nests of other species of insect-eating birds.
- **NESTING** Lays up to 25 eggs per season, each in a different nest; nests of warblers, flycatchers, wagtails, thrushes, and other birds. Incubation 11–13 days by foster parents. Altricial young stay in nest 20–23 days, tended by foster parents.
- **POPULATION** Casual in the Pribilofs and Aleutians. Accidental in Massachusetts. Common in native Eurasia.

Similar Birds

ORIENTAL CUCKOO
Darker upperparts; paler underparts; buffy undertail coverts
- hepatic-morph females have barred rump.

Flight Pattern
Distinctive low-wing flight; wings are barely raised above horizontal plane and depressed far below the body at the bottom of the downstroke.

Nest Identification	
Shape 🔸 Location 🔸	Lays single egg in nest of other incubating bird • eggs may often resemble those of host bird but generally are larger • 8–25 gray, blue, green, red, or brown eggs, with reddish brown, black, gray, and lilac markings; subelliptical, 0.9 x 0.7 inches.

Plumage Sexes differ	Habitat	Migration Migratory	Weight 4.0 ounces

DATE _____ TIME_____ LOCATION _____

Family CUCULIDAE	Species *Cuculus saturatus*	Length 12.5 inches	Wingspan 28 inches

ORIENTAL CUCKOO

This bird is a native of Europe and Asia and makes rare visits to the Pribilofs and western Aleutians. The female has two color morphs: gray and hepatic. The gray-morph female is similar to the male. The hepatic-morph female has rusty brown upperparts, with heavy barring on the head, back, rump, and tail. Oriental Cuckoos often perch with their wings slightly dropped, while they slowly raise and lower the tail. In flight, note the buff belly barred with dark gray and pale rufous underwings. Like the Common Cuckoo, these birds resemble a small falcon in flight because of the shape of the long wings and tail.

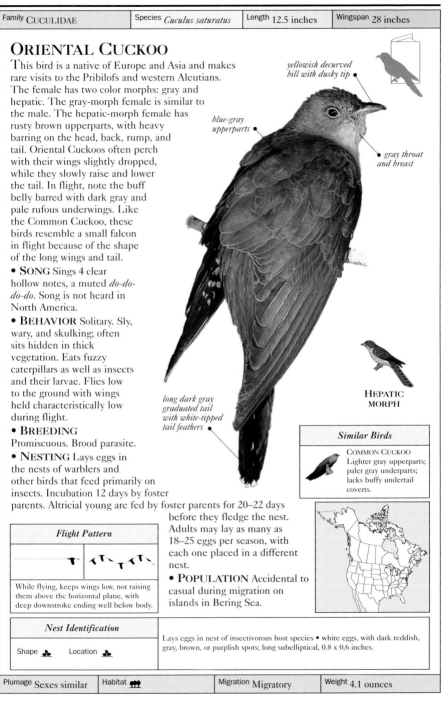

yellowish decurved bill with dusky tip

blue-gray upperparts

gray throat and breast

long dark gray graduated tail with white-tipped tail feathers

HEPATIC MORPH

- **SONG** Sings 4 clear hollow notes, a muted *do-do-do-do*. Song is not heard in North America.
- **BEHAVIOR** Solitary. Sly, wary, and skulking; often sits hidden in thick vegetation. Eats fuzzy caterpillars as well as insects and their larvae. Flies low to the ground with wings held characteristically low during flight.
- **BREEDING** Promiscuous. Brood parasite.
- **NESTING** Lays eggs in the nests of warblers and other birds that feed primarily on insects. Incubation 12 days by foster parents. Altricial young are fed by foster parents for 20–22 days before they fledge the nest. Adults may lay as many as 18–25 eggs per season, with each one placed in a different nest.
- **POPULATION** Accidental to casual during migration on islands in Bering Sea.

Similar Birds

COMMON CUCKOO
Lighter gray upperparts; paler gray underparts; lacks buffy undertail coverts.

Flight Pattern

While flying, keeps wings low, not raising them above the horizontal plane, with deep downstroke ending well below body.

Nest Identification

Shape ♣   Location ♣

Lays eggs in nest of insectivorous host species • white eggs, with dark reddish, gray, brown, or purplish spots; long subelliptical, 0.8 x 0.6 inches.

Plumage Sexes similar	Habitat 🐾	Migration Migratory	Weight 4.1 ounces

DATE _____ TIME_____ LOCATION _____

Family CUCULIDAE	Species *Coccyzus erythropthalmus*	Length 11–12 inches	Wingspan 15–17 inches

BLACK-BILLED CUCKOO

This shy bird spends most of its time skulking in deep wooded forests. In rare instances, instead of incubating its own eggs it will lay its eggs in the nests of Yellow-billed Cuckoos, Gray Catbirds, Wood Thrushes, Yellow Warblers, or Chipping Sparrows. In flight note the long tail, which has small crescent-shaped white spots on the tips of all but the two central tail feathers, and the uniformly grayish brown wings and back. Juveniles are similar to adults but have a buff eye ring, paler undertail, and buff wash on the underparts, especially the undertail coverts.

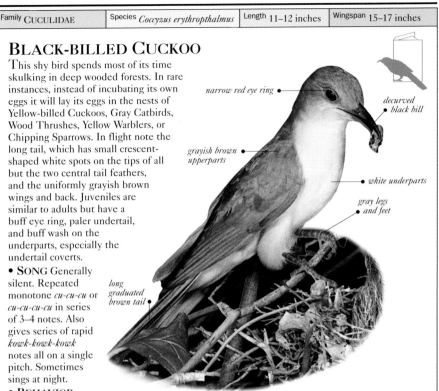

narrow red eye ring

grayish brown upperparts

decurved black bill

white underparts

gray legs and feet

long graduated brown tail

• **SONG** Generally silent. Repeated monotone *cu-cu-cu* or *cu-cu-cu-cu* in series of 3–4 notes. Also gives series of rapid *kowk-kowk-kowk* notes all on a single pitch. Sometimes sings at night.

• **BEHAVIOR** Skulks through thick vegetation in shrubs and trees. Often sits quietly on branch scanning in all directions before changing perches. Eats primarily caterpillars, especially hairy tent caterpillars, and other insects; occasionally eats small mollusks, fish, and some wild fruits. Often found in damp thickets and wet places. Engages in courtship feeding.

• **BREEDING** Monogamous.

• **NESTING** Incubation 10–14 days by both sexes. Altricial young stay in nest 7–9 days; fed by both sexes. Young leave nest before they can fly and climb around on nest tree or shrub for about 14 days. 1 brood per year.

• **POPULATION** Uncommon to fairly common. Somewhat dependant on caterpillar populations; larger clutches laid when food is plentiful.

Similar Birds

YELLOW-BILLED CUCKOO
Yellow bill with dark tip; rufous primaries contrast with wing coverts and upperparts; larger white spots on undertail.

Flight Pattern

Often flies low and makes short flights from one tree to the next.

Nest Identification

Shape 🪹 ⬭   Location 🌳 🌿

Dried twigs • lined with fresh grass, leaves, pine needles, catkins, and vegetation • in tree or shrub 2–20 feet above ground • 2–5 blue-green eggs with dark blotches, 1.1 x 0.8 inches.

Plumage Sexes similar	Habitat 🌳🌳 ▲ 🌱	Migration Migratory	Weight 3.6 ounces

DATE _____ TIME_____ LOCATION _____

| Family CUCULIDAE | Species *Coccyzus americanus* | Length 11–13 inches | Wingspan 15–17 inches |

YELLOW-BILLED CUCKOO

Like most of the cuckoos, this bird prefers to perch unobtrusively in thick forests or shrubs. Many rural people know this bird as the "Rain Crow." Sometimes it lays its eggs in nests of the Black-billed Cuckoo but rarely in nests of other birds. It is often a casualty at "tower kills" while migrating at night. In flight, note the long tail and the contrast of rufous primaries against gray-brown wing coverts and upperparts. The juvenile shows a paler undertail pattern, and the lower mandible may not be yellow.

decurved bill with dark upper mandible and tip

grayish brown upperparts

rufous wings

lower yellow mandible

white underparts

gray feet and legs

large white spots on black undertail

• SONG Often silent; song heard more often in summer. A monotonous throaty *ka-ka-ka-ka-kow-kow-kow-kow-kowlp—kowlp——kowl*, pruning down and slowing at the end.

• BEHAVIOR Slips quietly and somewhat stealthily through tangles; flies easily from tree to tree. Often sits motionless on an interior branch and slowly surveys the surrounding vegetation. Eats mostly hairy caterpillars; also insects, larvae, and small fruits and berries. Sometimes eats small frogs and lizards and the eggs of other birds. Engages in courtship feeding in which the male lands by perched female, climbs on her shoulder, and places food in her bill.

• BREEDING Monogamous. Solitary nester.

• NESTING Incubation 9–11 days by both sexes. Altricial young stay in nest 7–9 days, fed by both sexes. Young leave nest before able to fly but remain in vicinity, climbing in branches; fed by parent for about 14 more days. 1 brood per year.

• POPULATION Uncommon to common. Somewhat dependent on caterpillar population; species produces greater number of eggs when plentiful.

• CONSERVATION Neotropical migrant that has declined significantly over much of its range.

Similar Birds

BLACK-BILLED CUCKOO
Entirely black bill; red eye ring; no rufous in wing; gray underside of tail with smaller crescent-shaped white spots; voice differs.

MANGROVE CUCKOO
Gray-brown wings and coverts; black mask extends past eye; tawny-buff lower breast, sides, belly, flanks, and undertail coverts; decurved black bill, yellow at base of lower mandible • limited range in Florida; accidental on Gulf Coast.

Flight Pattern

Direct flight with slow light steady wing beats; often flies low from tree to tree with flash of rufous in wings.

Nest Identification

Shape ⌒ ⌣　Location 🌳 🌿

Small sticks, with lining of leaves, grasses, mosses, bits of fabric, and catkins from oaks and willow trees • so flimsy eggs can sometimes be seen from beneath • in tree or shrub, 2–12 feet above ground • built by both sexes • 1–5 pale bluish green eggs that fade to light greenish yellow, unmarked; elliptical to cylindrical, 1.2 x 0.9 inches.

| Plumage Sexes similar | Habitat | Migration Migratory | Weight 3.6 ounces |

DATE _____ TIME_____ LOCATION _____

| Family CUCULIDAE | Species *Geococcyx californianus* | Length 20–24 inches | Wingspan 32 inches |

GREATER ROADRUNNER

Able to run up to 15 miles per hour, this bird generally seems to prefer sprinting rather than flying. Because this large slender member of the cuckoo family habitually stays on the ground, it can be difficult to see. Centuries ago, it was sometimes called the Ground Cuckoo because it would run along paths in front of horse-drawn carriages. This shy solitary bird is the state bird of New Mexico. Look for the large streaked body, shaggy crest, and long tail that shows white tips when it is spread. In flight, the short, rounded wings reveal a white crescent in the primaries. Sometimes visible is a patch of bare skin around and behind the eye that shades from blue proximally to red to orange distally.

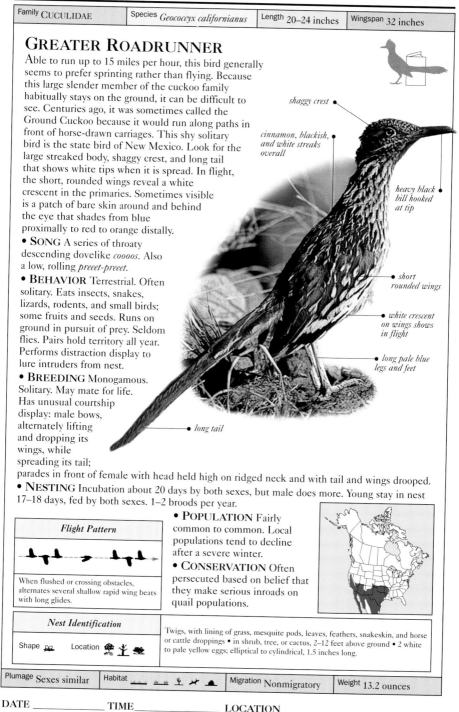

shaggy crest

cinnamon, blackish, and white streaks overall

heavy black bill hooked at tip

short rounded wings

white crescent on wings shows in flight

long pale blue legs and feet

long tail

• **SONG** A series of throaty descending dovelike *coooos*. Also a low, rolling *preeet-preeet*.

• **BEHAVIOR** Terrestrial. Often solitary. Eats insects, snakes, lizards, rodents, and small birds; some fruits and seeds. Runs on ground in pursuit of prey. Seldom flies. Pairs hold territory all year. Performs distraction display to lure intruders from nest.

• **BREEDING** Monogamous. Solitary. May mate for life. Has unusual courtship display: male bows, alternately lifting and dropping its wings, while spreading its tail; parades in front of female with head held high on ridged neck and with tail and wings drooped.

• **NESTING** Incubation about 20 days by both sexes, but male does more. Young stay in nest 17–18 days, fed by both sexes. 1–2 broods per year.

• **POPULATION** Fairly common to common. Local populations tend to decline after a severe winter.

• **CONSERVATION** Often persecuted based on belief that they make serious inroads on quail populations.

Flight Pattern	
When flushed or crossing obstacles, alternates several shallow rapid wing beats with long glides.	

Nest Identification	
Shape 🪹 Location 🌳 🌿 🌲	Twigs, with lining of grass, mesquite pods, leaves, feathers, snakeskin, and horse or cattle droppings • in shrub, tree, or cactus, 2–12 feet above ground • 2 white to pale yellow eggs; elliptical to cylindrical, 1.5 inches long.

| Plumage Sexes similar | Habitat | Migration Nonmigratory | Weight 13.2 ounces |

DATE _____ TIME_____ LOCATION _____

Family CUCULIDAE	Species *Crotophaga sulcirostris*	Length 12–14 inches	Wingspan 16–18 inches

GROOVE-BILLED ANI

Easily distinguished as an ani by its black plumage and its parrotlike bill, this member of the cuckoo family often sleeps at night in communal roosts in trees as many as thirty to forty birds. During breeding season, three to four pairs of birds build and share one nest. The laterally compressed black bill has a series of three to four parallel grooves in the upper mandible that are difficult to see except at close range. It shows paler scalloping on the chest and back.
• SONG Sings a liquid *TEE-hoe* with first upslurred note

curved ridge on top of bill, lower than crown

parallel grooves on upper mandible

black overall with shimmering purple and green overtones

long tail

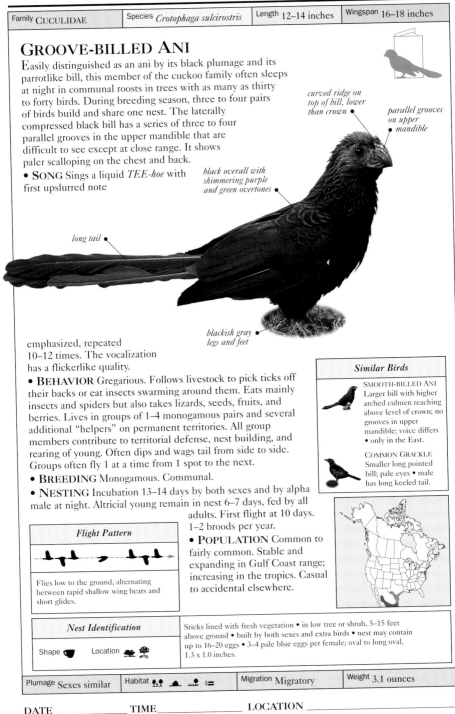

blackish gray legs and feet

emphasized, repeated 10–12 times. The vocalization has a flickerlike quality.
• BEHAVIOR Gregarious. Follows livestock to pick ticks off their backs or eat insects swarming around them. Eats mainly insects and spiders but also takes lizards, seeds, fruits, and berries. Lives in groups of 1–4 monogamous pairs and several additional "helpers" on permanent territories. All group members contribute to territorial defense, nest building, and rearing of young. Often dips and wags tail from side to side. Groups often fly 1 at a time from 1 spot to the next.
• BREEDING Monogamous. Communal.
• NESTING Incubation 13–14 days by both sexes and by alpha male at night. Altricial young remain in nest 6–7 days, fed by all adults. First flight at 10 days. 1–2 broods per year.
• POPULATION Common to fairly common. Stable and expanding in Gulf Coast range; increasing in the tropics. Casual to accidental elsewhere.

Similar Birds

SMOOTH-BILLED ANI
Larger bill with higher arched culmen reaching above level of crown; no grooves in upper mandible; voice differs
• only in the East.

COMMON GRACKLE
Smaller long pointed bill; pale eyes • male has long keeled tail.

Flight Pattern

Flies low to the ground, alternating between rapid shallow wing beats and short glides.

Nest Identification

Shape   Location

Sticks lined with fresh vegetation • in low tree or shrub, 5–15 feet above ground • built by both sexes and extra birds • nest may contain up to 16–20 eggs • 3–4 pale blue eggs per female; oval to long oval, 1.3 x 1.0 inches.

Plumage Sexes similar	Habitat	Migration Migratory	Weight 3.1 ounces

DATE _____ TIME_____ LOCATION _____

Family TYTONIDAE	Species *Tyto alba*	Length 14–20 inches	Wingspan 43–47 inches

BARN OWL

Associating more closely with man than any other owl, the nearly cosmopolitan Barn Owl often roosts and nests in buildings and hunts in areas cleared for agriculture, particularly meadows and pastures. It is perhaps the most distinctive looking owl with its long legs and heart-shaped "monkey" face. The unexpected gasping screech of this owl nearby in the darkness can raise the hair on the back of one's head. Like other species of owls it can locate and capture its prey in total darkness using its hearing alone. This is accomplished with asymetrically positioned ear openings, and the aid of the facial disks.

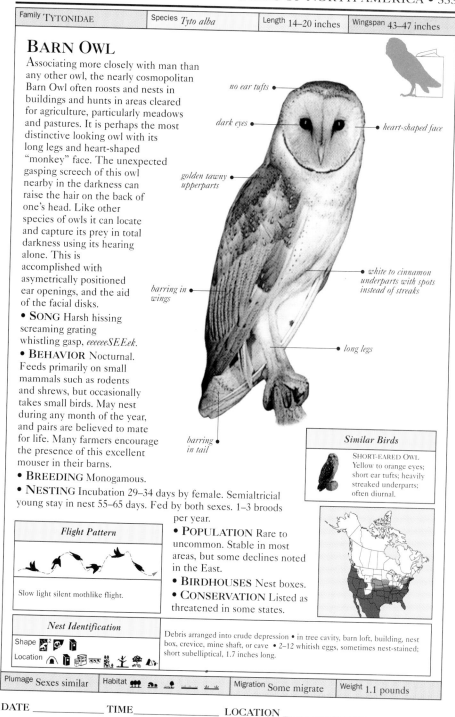

- no ear tufts
- dark eyes
- heart-shaped face
- golden tawny upperparts
- white to cinnamon underparts with spots instead of streaks
- barring in wings
- long legs
- barring in tail

- **SONG** Harsh hissing screaming grating whistling gasp, *eeeeeSEEek.*
- **BEHAVIOR** Nocturnal. Feeds primarily on small mammals such as rodents and shrews, but occasionally takes small birds. May nest during any month of the year, and pairs are believed to mate for life. Many farmers encourage the presence of this excellent mouser in their barns.
- **BREEDING** Monogamous.
- **NESTING** Incubation 29–34 days by female. Semialtricial young stay in nest 55–65 days. Fed by both sexes. 1–3 broods per year.

Similar Birds

SHORT-EARED OWL Yellow to orange eyes; short ear tufts; heavily streaked underparts; often diurnal.

- **POPULATION** Rare to uncommon. Stable in most areas, but some declines noted in the East.
- **BIRDHOUSES** Nest boxes.
- **CONSERVATION** Listed as threatened in some states.

Flight Pattern

Slow light silent mothlike flight.

Nest Identification

Shape

Location

Debris arranged into crude depression • in tree cavity, barn loft, building, nest box, crevice, mine shaft, or cave • 2–12 whitish eggs, sometimes nest-stained; short subelliptical, 1.7 inches long.

Plumage Sexes similar	Habitat	Migration Some migrate	Weight 1.1 pounds

DATE _____ TIME _____ LOCATION _____

Family STRIGIDAE	Species *Otus flammeolus*	Length 6–7 inches	Wingspan 13 inches

FLAMMULATED OWL

One of the smallest owls in North America, the Flammulated Owl is also the only small owl with dark, not yellow, eyes. This owl's ear tufts are minute and hardly noticeable. The Flammulated Owl has two color phases, reddish and gray, with the former more common in the southeastern part of the bird's range. The natural history of this diminutive North American owl is poorly known.

small ear tufts

dark eyes

reddish brown facial disk

tawny scapular bar

grayish brown body

REDDISH FORM

- **SONG** *Boo-BOOT* with emphasis on the second note of the song. A series of single paired low hoarse hollow hoots is given repeatedly at intervals of 2–3 seconds.

- **BEHAVIOR** Little is known. The bird is nocturnal. It feeds primarily on insects, including moths taken in flight and arachnids such as spiders and scorpions gleaned from the ground or the foliage of trees in its habitat. Sometimes will take as its prey various small mammals or other birds. It frequents primarily open pine and oak forests and spruce-fir forests in mountains as high that are 8,000 feet.

- **BREEDING** Monogamous. Sometimes has been observed living in loose colonies.

- **NESTING** Incubation 21–26 days by female. Semialtricial young remain in nest about 25 days. Young are fed by both sexes. 1 brood per year.

- **POPULATION** Widespread and common in range, though slight declines are possible. Highly migratory; strays have made it to Florida and the Gulf Coast.

Similar Birds

NORTHERN PYGMY-OWL
Thinner; longer tail; white underparts with heavy streaking; lacks ear tufts; yellow eyes; black nape patches; chiefly diurnal.

WESTERN SCREECH-OWL
Yellow eyes; lacks brown bar in scapulars; has different voice.

WHISKERED SCREECH-OWL
Longer ear tufts; yellow eyes; different voice.

NOTE: These are all permanent residents of the woodlands in the West. There are no similar birds ranging in the East.

Flight Pattern

Slow light steady wing beats.

Nest Identification

Shape Location

Old woodpecker hole • no lining • 15–40 feet above ground • 2–4 white or creamy white eggs; about oval, 1.1 inches long.

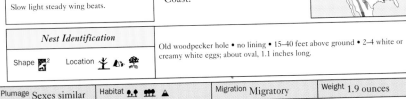

Plumage Sexes similar	Habitat	Migration Migratory	Weight 1.9 ounces

DATE _____ TIME _____ LOCATION _____

Family STRIGIDAE	Species *Otus kennicottii*	Length 8–10 inches	Wingspan 18–24 inches

WESTERN SCREECH-OWL

This small tufted owl, the western counterpart of the Eastern Screech-Owl, is found in a wide variety of habitats, from wooded canyons, riparian thickets, and deserts to orchards and the suburbs. It is more often heard than seen. Over most of its range its plumage is generally gray, but Pacific Coast birds are more brownish in color.

ear tufts

gray to brown upperparts with vermiculations and streaking

yellow eyes

dark bill

large white spots on scapulars

heavily streaked and lightly barred underparts

• **SONG** Repeated brief whistles accelerating in tempo in the pattern of a dropped ball bouncing to a stop; a short trill followed by a drawn-out trill.

• **BEHAVIOR** Nocturnal; becomes active at dusk. Feeds on variety of small mammals, birds, reptiles, large insects, and arachnids, but the primary food is large insects. Small mammals carried to the nest to feed the young often are decapitated by the adults. Surplus food is cached in winter roosting cavities. Roosts by day in cavities or thick vegetation. Sedentary, often staying in the same home range throughout the year; males may defend a territory for as long as 10 months. Courtship begins as early as February when the male begins calling each night shortly after sunset to attract a mate. The calls cease when a pair is formed.

• **BREEDING** Monogamous.

• **NESTING** Incubation 21–30 days by female. Semialtricial young stay in nest about 28 days, fed by both sexes. 1 brood per year.

• **POPULATION** Common; widely distributed over range.

• **BIRDHOUSES** Will use man-made nest boxes.

Similar Birds

EASTERN SCREECH-OWL
May have rufous-red plumage; pale bill; different voice.

WHISKERED SCREECH-OWL
Pale bill; different voice; bolder streaking on underparts.

FLAMMULATED OWL
Dark eyes; brown bar in scapulars; different voice.

Flight Pattern

Buoyant silent flight with rapid wing beats.

Nest Identification

Shape

Location

Natural hole in tree or woodpecker hole • may use old magpie nests • no lining added • 5–35 feet off ground • 2–6 white eggs, 1.4 inches long.

Plumage Sexes similar	Habitat	Migration Nonmigratory	Weight 5.4 ounces

DATE _____ TIME_____ LOCATION _____

Family STRIGIDAE	Species *Otus asio*	Length 8–10 inches	Wingspan 18–24 inches

EASTERN SCREECH-OWL

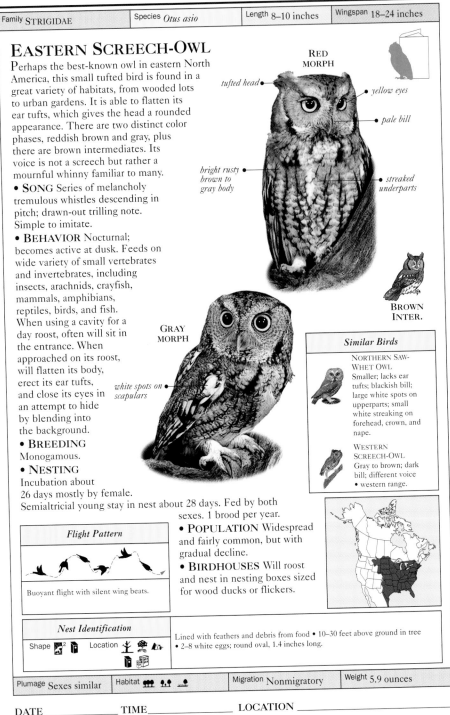

RED MORPH

tufted head

yellow eyes

pale bill

bright rusty brown to gray body

streaked underparts

BROWN INTER.

GRAY MORPH

white spots on scapulars

Perhaps the best-known owl in eastern North America, this small tufted bird is found in a great variety of habitats, from wooded lots to urban gardens. It is able to flatten its ear tufts, which gives the head a rounded appearance. There are two distinct color phases, reddish brown and gray, plus there are brown intermediates. Its voice is not a screech but rather a mournful whinny familiar to many.

• **SONG** Series of melancholy tremulous whistles descending in pitch; drawn-out trilling note. Simple to imitate.

• **BEHAVIOR** Nocturnal; becomes active at dusk. Feeds on wide variety of small vertebrates and invertebrates, including insects, arachnids, crayfish, mammals, amphibians, reptiles, birds, and fish. When using a cavity for a day roost, often will sit in the entrance. When approached on its roost, will flatten its body, erect its ear tufts, and close its eyes in an attempt to hide by blending into the background.

• **BREEDING** Monogamous.

• **NESTING** Incubation about 26 days mostly by female. Semialtricial young stay in nest about 28 days. Fed by both sexes. 1 brood per year.

• **POPULATION** Widespread and fairly common, but with gradual decline.

• **BIRDHOUSES** Will roost and nest in nesting boxes sized for wood ducks or flickers.

Similar Birds

NORTHERN SAW-WHET OWL Smaller; lacks ear tufts; blackish bill; large white spots on upperparts; small white streaking on forehead, crown, and nape.

WESTERN SCREECH-OWL Gray to brown; dark bill; different voice • western range.

Flight Pattern

Buoyant flight with silent wing beats.

Nest Identification

Shape — Location

Lined with feathers and debris from food • 10–30 feet above ground in tree • 2–8 white eggs; round oval, 1.4 inches long.

Plumage Sexes similar	Habitat	Migration Nonmigratory	Weight 5.9 ounces

DATE _____ TIME_____ LOCATION _____

Family STRIGIDAE	Species *Otus trichopsis*	Length 6–8 inches	Wingspan 16–18 inches

WHISKERED SCREECH-OWL

More often heard than seen in the wooded mountain canyons it prefers, this small owl with ear tufts looks much like the Western Screech-Owl, whose range it overlaps. Therefore it is best to distinguish the Whiskered Screech-Owl by voice as well as by elevation, as it is generally

ear tufts

yellow eyes

pale bill

heavily streaked and mottled gray-brown upperparts

large white spots on scapulars

found higher in the mountains at 4,000–6,000 feet.

• **SONG** Brief series of one-pitch whistles, *boot-boot-boot-boot*. Also has irregular hoots that sound similar to Morse code.

• **BEHAVIOR** Nocturnal. Retires by day to concealed perch, often on limb sitting close to tree trunk. Takes prey with feet from ground or foliage. Feeds primarily on insects and other invertebrates, including spiders and centipedes. Responds well to imitation of call, often coming very close to investigate source.

• **BREEDING** Monogamous.

• **NESTING** Incubation 21–30 days by female. Semialtricial young stay in nest about 28 days; fed by both sexes. 1 brood per year.

• **POPULATION** Fairly common to common. Locally common and stable in limited US range.

grayish white underparts with bold barring and vermiculations

Similar Birds

WESTERN SCREECH-OWL
Different voice; dark bill; streaking on underparts not as bold.

FLAMMULATED OWL
Different voice; shorter ear tufts; dark eyes.

Flight Pattern

Mothlike flight with rapid silent wing beats.

Nest Identification

Shape   Location

In tree cavity or abandoned woodpecker hole • remnant lining material • 10–30 feet above ground • 2–4 white eggs, 1.3 inches long.

Plumage Sexes similar	Habitat	Migration Nonmigratory	Weight 3.0 ounces

DATE _____ TIME_____ LOCATION _____

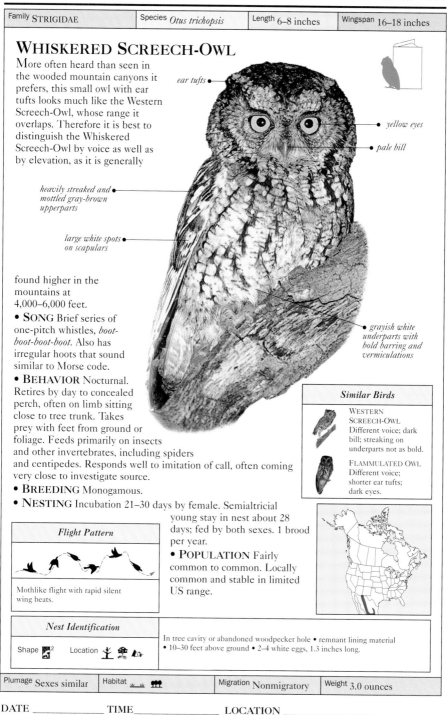

Family STRIGIDAE	Species *Bubo virginianus*	Length 18–25 inches	Wingspan 36–60 inches

GREAT HORNED OWL

The most widespread owl in North America and perhaps the most powerful, this owl often attacks animals much larger and heavier than itself, including domestic cats, skunks, and porcupines. Its color varies regionally from pale arctic birds to dark northwestern ones.

large "horns" on head

yellow eyes

rusty facial disks

white chin and throat

mottled barred brownish gray upperparts

• **SONG** Series of 3–8 bold deep hoots, with the second and third hoots often running together, *Whoo! Whoo-whoo-whoo! Whoo! Whoo!* Often described as "You awake? Me too!" Female's hooting is higher in pitch.

• **BEHAVIOR** Chiefly nocturnal; becomes active at dusk. Sometimes hunts during the day. Takes wide variety of vertebrates; primarily feeds on mammals, but also eats birds, reptiles, and amphibians. Often aggressively defends nest and young to the point of striking humans who venture too close.

• **BREEDING** Monogamous. One of the earliest nesting species, with eggs laid in winter.

• **NESTING** Incubation 28–35 days mostly by female. Young stay in nest 35–45 days. Fed by both sexes. 1 brood per year.

• **POPULATION** Fairly common to common. Widespread.

• **BIRDHOUSES** Accepts artificial nesting platforms.

• **CONSERVATION** Many are killed by hunters and farmers.

Similar Birds

LONG-EARED OWL
Smaller and thinner; ear tufts closer together; vertical streaking, not horizontal barring, on underparts.

GREAT GRAY OWL
Larger; lacks ear tufts; large grayish white facial disks ringed with dark brown concentric circles; brown upperparts barred with dark browns and white; whitish underparts barred and streaked with browns; yellowish bill; long brownish tail barred with dark browns and white.

Flight Pattern

Direct flap-and-glide flight with strong, silent wing beats.

Nest Identification

Shape

Location

Abandoned nest of larger bird • large cavities, broken-off snags, buildings, ledges • 20–60 feet above ground • 1–5 dull whitish eggs; elliptical, 2.7 inches long.

Plumage Sexes similar	Habitat	Migration Nonmigratory	Weight 3.0 pounds

DATE _____ TIME _____ LOCATION _____

Family STRIGIDAE	Species *Nyctea scandiaca*	Length 20–27 inches	Wingspan 54–66 inches

SNOWY OWL

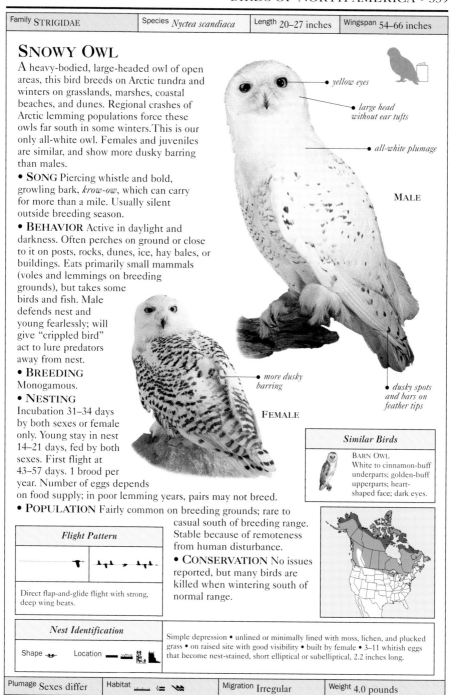

A heavy-bodied, large-headed owl of open areas, this bird breeds on Arctic tundra and winters on grasslands, marshes, coastal beaches, and dunes. Regional crashes of Arctic lemming populations force these owls far south in some winters. This is our only all-white owl. Females and juveniles are similar, and show more dusky barring than males.

- **SONG** Piercing whistle and bold, growling bark, *krow-ow*, which can carry for more than a mile. Usually silent outside breeding season.
- **BEHAVIOR** Active in daylight and darkness. Often perches on ground or close to it on posts, rocks, dunes, ice, hay bales, or buildings. Eats primarily small mammals (voles and lemmings on breeding grounds), but takes some birds and fish. Male defends nest and young fearlessly; will give "crippled bird" act to lure predators away from nest.
- **BREEDING** Monogamous.
- **NESTING** Incubation 31–34 days by both sexes or female only. Young stay in nest 14–21 days, fed by both sexes. First flight at 43–57 days. 1 brood per year. Number of eggs depends on food supply; in poor lemming years, pairs may not breed.
- **POPULATION** Fairly common on breeding grounds; rare to casual south of breeding range. Stable because of remoteness from human disturbance.
- **CONSERVATION** No issues reported, but many birds are killed when wintering south of normal range.

yellow eyes

large head without ear tufts

all-white plumage

MALE

more dusky barring

FEMALE

dusky spots and bars on feather tips

Similar Birds

BARN OWL
White to cinnamon-buff underparts; golden-buff upperparts; heart-shaped face; dark eyes.

Flight Pattern

Direct flap-and-glide flight with strong, deep wing beats.

Nest Identification

Shape ﹏ Location ▬ ▦ ▓ ▮

Simple depression • unlined or minimally lined with moss, lichen, and plucked grass • on raised site with good visibility • built by female • 3–11 whitish eggs that become nest-stained, short elliptical or subelliptical, 2.2 inches long.

Plumage Sexes differ	Habitat ﹏ ﹏ ≈ ≋	Migration Irregular	Weight 4.0 pounds

DATE _____ TIME_____ LOCATION _____

Family STRIGIDAE	Species *Surnia ulula*	Length 14–17 inches	Wingspan 33 inches

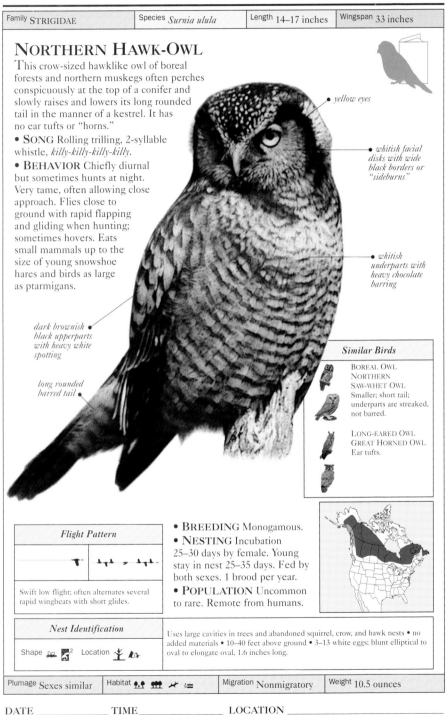

NORTHERN HAWK-OWL

This crow-sized hawklike owl of boreal forests and northern muskegs often perches conspicuously at the top of a conifer and slowly raises and lowers its long rounded tail in the manner of a kestrel. It has no ear tufts or "horns."

• **SONG** Rolling trilling, 2-syllable whistle, *killy-killy-killy-killy.*

• **BEHAVIOR** Chiefly diurnal but sometimes hunts at night. Very tame, often allowing close approach. Flies close to ground with rapid flapping and gliding when hunting; sometimes hovers. Eats small mammals up to the size of young snowshoe hares and birds as large as ptarmigans.

yellow eyes

whitish facial disks with wide black borders or "sideburns"

whitish underparts with heavy chocolate barring

dark brownish black upperparts with heavy white spotting

long rounded barred tail

Similar Birds

BOREAL OWL
NORTHERN
SAW-WHET OWL
Smaller; short tail; underparts are streaked, not barred.

LONG-EARED OWL
GREAT HORNED OWL
Ear tufts.

Flight Pattern

Swift low flight; often alternates several rapid wingbeats with short glides.

• **BREEDING** Monogamous.
• **NESTING** Incubation 25–30 days by female. Young stay in nest 25–35 days. Fed by both sexes. 1 brood per year.
• **POPULATION** Uncommon to rare. Remote from humans.

Nest Identification

Shape ⌒⌒ 🔲² Location 🌲 🪹

Uses large cavities in trees and abandoned squirrel, crow, and hawk nests • no added materials • 10–40 feet above ground • 3–13 white eggs; blunt elliptical to oval to elongate oval, 1.6 inches long.

Plumage Sexes similar	Habitat 🌿 🌳 ✈ 〰	Migration Nonmigratory	Weight 10.5 ounces

DATE _____ TIME_____ LOCATION _____

Family STRIGIDAE	Species *Glaucidium gnoma*	Length 6–7 inches	Wingspan 15 inches

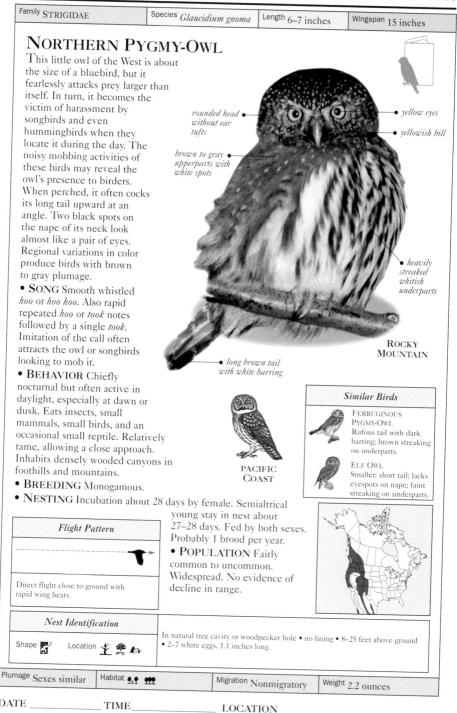

NORTHERN PYGMY-OWL

This little owl of the West is about the size of a bluebird, but it fearlessly attacks prey larger than itself. In turn, it becomes the victim of harassment by songbirds and even hummingbirds when they locate it during the day. The noisy mobbing activities of these birds may reveal the owl's presence to birders. When perched, it often cocks its long tail upward at an angle. Two black spots on the nape of its neck look almost like a pair of eyes. Regional variations in color produce birds with brown to gray plumage.

rounded head without ear tufts

yellow eyes

yellowish bill

brown to gray upperparts with white spots

heavily streaked whitish underparts

ROCKY MOUNTAIN

long brown tail with white barring

• **SONG** Smooth whistled *hoo* or *hoo hoo*. Also rapid repeated *hoo* or *took* notes followed by a single *took*. Imitation of the call often attracts the owl or songbirds looking to mob it.

• **BEHAVIOR** Chiefly nocturnal but often active in daylight, especially at dawn or dusk. Eats insects, small mammals, small birds, and an occasional small reptile. Relatively tame, allowing a close approach. Inhabits densely wooded canyons in foothills and mountains.

• **BREEDING** Monogamous.

• **NESTING** Incubation about 28 days by female. Semialtrical young stay in nest about 27–28 days. Fed by both sexes. Probably 1 brood per year.

• **POPULATION** Fairly common to uncommon. Widespread. No evidence of decline in range.

PACIFIC COAST

Similar Birds

FERRUGINOUS PYGMY-OWL
Rufous tail with dark barring; brown streaking on underparts.

ELF OWL
Smaller; short tail; lacks eyespots on nape; faint streaking on underparts.

Flight Pattern
Direct flight close to ground with rapid wing beats.

Nest Identification	
Shape	Location	In natural tree cavity or woodpecker hole • no lining • 8–25 feet above ground • 2–7 white eggs, 1.1 inches long.

Plumage Sexes similar	Habitat	Migration Nonmigratory	Weight 2.2 ounces

DATE _____ TIME_____ LOCATION _____

Family STRIGIDAE	Species *Glaucidium brasilianum*	Length 6–7 inches	Wingspan 15 inches

FERRUGINOUS PYGMY-OWL

This very small long-tailed owl inhabits cottonwood riparian, mesquite thicket, and saguaro desert habitats. A bold little predator, it is often noisily mobbed by other birds. Its streaked head lacks ear tufts, and it often can be seen nervously flicking its long barred rufous tail. Like the Northern Pygmy-Owl, two black spots on the nape of its neck resemble a pair of eyes.

• **SONG** Fluted notes, *puk-puk-puk*; rapid, repeated *took* up to 50–60 times.

yellow eyes

streaked head without ear tufts

reddish brown upperparts

whitish buff underparts with brown streaking

long barred reddish tail

• **BEHAVIOR** Diurnal, but often most active at dusk and at dawn (crepuscular). Often roosts in dense cover. Frequently gets mobbed by songbirds, which attracts attention to the little owl. Feeds primarily on large insects and arachnids, also taking some small vertebrates. Male feeds female and young in nest cavity.

• **BREEDING** Monogamous.

• **NESTING** Incubation about 28 days by female. Young remain in nest 27–30 days. Fed by both sexes. 1 brood per year.

• **POPULATION** Uncommon. Endangered or threatened in limited range in US. Widespread in tropics.

• **CONSERVATION** Concern over small populations.

Similar Birds

ELF OWL
Smaller; short tail; no eye spots on nape; faint streaking on underparts; facial disk has black border.

NORTHERN PYGMY-OWL
Brown tail with white barring; heavy blackish brown streaking on underparts • inhabits denser forests at higher elevations; not found in deserts; inhabits montane and foothill woodlands in the West.

Flight Pattern

Rapid direct flight with unmuffled wing beats.

Nest Identification

Shape ▨² Location 🌵 ⸷

In tree cavity or cactus; usually in old woodpecker hole • no material added • 10–30 feet above ground • 3–5 white eggs, 1.1 inches long.

Plumage Sexes similar	Habitat ⸷ ⸷ 🌵	Migration Nonmigratory	Weight 2.2 ounces

| Family STRIGIDAE | Species *Micrathene whitneyi* | Length 5–6 inches | Wingspan 15 inches |

ELF OWL

At about the size of a chunky sparrow, this is the smallest owl in the world. It can be recognized by its size, small round head, lack of ear tufts, and short tail. This species is perhaps more often heard than seen.

• **SONG** Puppylike chuckling and yips; erratic series of high chirps, and chattering notes. Amazingly loud for such a small owl.

• **BEHAVIOR** Nocturnal; becomes active at dusk. Roosts and nests in woodpecker holes and in natural cavities in trees, saguaro, and utility poles. Feeds primarily on insects, arachnids

no ear tufts

yellow eyes

mottled grayish brown body

white spotting on scapulars

whitish underparts with ochre-brown streaking

short tail

(including scorpions), and some small vertebrates. Catches some insects in flight with its feet.

• **BREEDING** Monogamous.

• **NESTING** Incubation 24 days by female. Young stay in nest 28 days. Fed by both sexes. 1 brood per year.

• **POPULATION** Fairly common to common. Scarce along lower Colorado River and in southern Texas; still abundant in southern Arizona; almost eliminated in California.

• **BIRDHOUSES** Will occasionally roost and nest in man-made boxes.

Similar Birds

FERRUGINOUS PYGMY-OWL NORTHERN PYGMY-OWL Longer tails; black eyespots on nape; heavily streaked underparts; diurnal • Northern Pygmy-Owl inhabits montane and foothill woodlands in the West.

Flight Pattern

Mothlike flight with silent wing beats; sometimes hovers and hawks.

Nest Identification

Shape ▨² ◧   Location ⚘ ⚘ ◧

In old woodpecker hole in tree, utility pole, or cactus • no lining added • 15–50 feet above ground in sycamores or 10–30 feet above ground in saguaros • 1–5 white eggs, 1.1 inches long.

| Plumage Sexes similar | Habitat ⚘ ▲ ♣ | Migration Migratory | Weight 1.4 ounces |

DATE _____ TIME_____ LOCATION _____

Family STRIGIDAE	Species *Athene cunicularia*	Length 9–11 inches	Wingspan 20–24 inches

BURROWING OWL

This long-legged, short-tailed little owl inhabits grassland and prairies, but in its range it also can be found in similar habitats near humans such as golf courses and airports. In the West the Burrowing Owl often is associated with prairie dog towns, and the historical poisoning of the prairie dogs also brought declines in the owl's populations. The owls use an abandoned burrow for their nest and daytime roost, usually after some additional digging to enlarge and reshape it.

• **SONG** High melancholy cry, *coo-coo-roo* or *co-hoo;* twittering series of *chack* notes. If disturbed in nest, young give alarm that mimics the buzzing of a rattlesnake.

• **BEHAVIOR** Terrestrial. Primarily nocturnal and crepuscular. Perches on ground, fence posts, utility wires, rocks, or mounds near burrow during day. Inhabits open country where it feeds primarily on large insects, some of which it catches in flight, and small mammals.

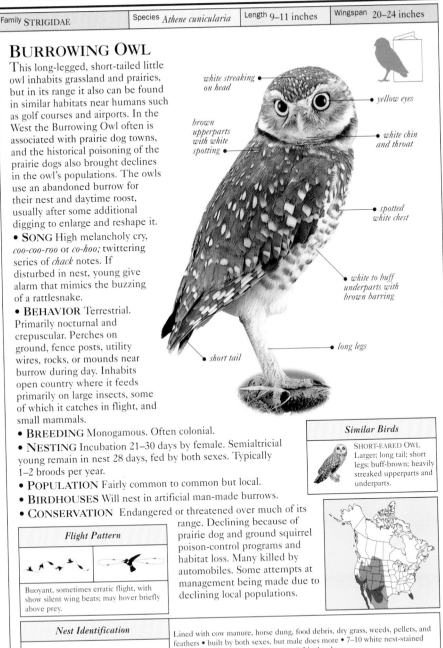

white streaking on head

brown upperparts with white spotting

short tail

yellow eyes

white chin and throat

spotted white chest

white to buff underparts with brown barring

long legs

• **BREEDING** Monogamous. Often colonial.

• **NESTING** Incubation 21–30 days by female. Semialtricial young remain in nest 28 days, fed by both sexes. Typically 1–2 broods per year.

• **POPULATION** Fairly common to common but local.

• **BIRDHOUSES** Will nest in artificial man-made burrows.

• **CONSERVATION** Endangered or threatened over much of its range. Declining because of prairie dog and ground squirrel poison-control programs and habitat loss. Many killed by automobiles. Some attempts at management being made due to declining local populations.

Similar Birds

SHORT-EARED OWL
Larger; long tail; short legs; buff-brown; heavily streaked upperparts and underparts.

Flight Pattern

Buoyant, sometimes erratic flight, with show silent wing beats; may hover briefly above prey.

Nest Identification

Shape 🦉 🦉   Location ▬

Lined with cow manure, horse dung, food debris, dry grass, weeds, pellets, and feathers • built by both sexes, but male does more • 7–10 white nest-stained eggs (4–6 in Florida); round to ovate, 1.2 inches long.

Plumage Sexes similar	Habitat ▬ 🌱	Migration Some migrate	Weight 5.3 ounces

DATE _____ TIME_____ LOCATION _____

Family STRIGIDAE	Species *Strix occidentalis*	Length 16–19 inches	Wingspan 45–48 inches

SPOTTED OWL

Although it is the western counterpart of the Barred Owl in shape, size, and habitat preference, this owl lacks the barring and streaking of that species. Its dark brown plumage is heavily spotted with white on the underparts and upperparts. This secretive bird inhabits dense, moist old-growth forests and deeply wooded canyons.

• *large, puffy head without ear tufts*

• *dark eyes*

• *rich dark brown and liberally spotted white overall*

• **SONG** 3–4 barking notes, *Whoo-whoo-hoo-hoo*. Also gives low, hollow, ascending whistle, sounding like *coooo-wee*.

• **BEHAVIOR** Nocturnal and seldom seen. Perches inconspicuously in dense cover during the day. Feeds primarily on small mammals, some birds, and large insects. Hybridizes with Barred Owl, which is becoming more common in its northwestern range.

• **BREEDING** Monogamous.

• **NESTING** Incubation 28–32 days by female. Young stay in nest 34–36 days. Fed by both sexes. 1 brood per year.

• **POPULATION** Rare to uncommon. Listed as endangered in the Pacific Northwest and threatened in the Southwest. Does poorly in second-growth forests.

• **CONSERVATION** Federally protected. Affected by loss of old-growth forest habitat from logging and by hybridization with expanding populations of Barred Owl.

Similar Birds

BARRED OWL
Barred chest and upper breast; streaked underparts.

GREAT GRAY OWL
Larger; grayer; streaked underparts; yellow eyes.

Flight Pattern

Short flights with quick wing strokes; longer flights series of silent strong wing beats followed by short glides.

Nest Identification

Shape

Location

Simple scrape • hollow in tree, cave, or crevice • on cliff or in tree 30–160 feet above ground • sometimes uses abandoned nests • built by female • 1–4 white eggs with faint tinge of buff; elliptical, 2 inches long.

Plumage Sexes similar	Habitat	Migration Nonmigratory	Weight 1.3 pounds

DATE _____ TIME_____ LOCATION _____

Family STRIGIDAE	Species *Strix varia*	Length 17–24 inches	Wingspan 50–60 inches

BARRED OWL

The "hoot owl" of southern swamps, this puffy-headed owl can also be found in woodlands. It lacks ear tufts, is stoutly built, and is heavily streaked, spotted, and variegated brown, buff, and white. This is one of only three large owls with dark eyes in North America.

• **SONG** Usually 8 or more drawn-out notes, *"Who cooks for you; who cooks for you-all?"* Call is drawn-out, descending *hoooAwllll.* Group of 2 or more owls make a loud, excited caterwauling. Often heard in daytime. Responds readily to imitations of its call by coming closer and often calling back.

• **BEHAVIOR** Mostly nocturnal and crepuscular but often active in daylight. Prefers deep woods; inhabits conifer, riparian, and swampy habitats. Feeds on wide variety of animals, including small mammals, birds, frogs, salamanders, lizards, snakes, fish, large insects, crabs, and crayfish.

• **BREEDING** Monogamous. Thought to pair for life.

• **NESTING.** Incubation 28–33 days by female. Young stay in nest 42 days. Fed by both sexes. 1 brood per year.

• **POPULATION** Very common to common and widespread. Swamp habitat population in the South has diminished. Range increasing now in the Northwest, where hybridizes with Spotted Owl.

large, round head

dark eyes

horizontal barring on upper breast

heavily streaked paler underparts

brown upperparts with heavy white spotting

long barred tail

Similar Birds

GREAT GRAY OWL
Much larger and grayer; yellow eyes.

SPOTTED OWL
White spotting on underparts, not barring or streaking • western range.

Flight Pattern

Short flights with steady, shallow wing beats, longer flights on silent rapid wing strokes followed by short glide.

Nest Identification

Shape ▨ ▣ ▱ Location ⚘ ⚘ ⚘

In the East uses abandoned nests • 15–80 feet above ground in tree • 2–3 white eggs, 2 inches long.

Plumage Sexes similar	Habitat 🌲 🍂 〰	Migration Nonmigratory	Weight 1.4 pounds

DATE _____ TIME _____ LOCATION _____

Family STRIGIDAE	Species *Strix nebulosa*	Length 24–33 inches	Wingspan 54–60 inches

GREAT GRAY OWL

Although this is the largest North American owl, the Great Horned Owl is heavier. Long-tailed and large-headed, the Great Gray Owl has huge facial disks crossed by a series of dark gray concentric circles that make the yellow eyes seem small. It inhabits deep boreal forests and open muskeg bogs.

• **SONG** A bold, deep, booming *hoo-hoo-hooo*; also utters single-note hoots.

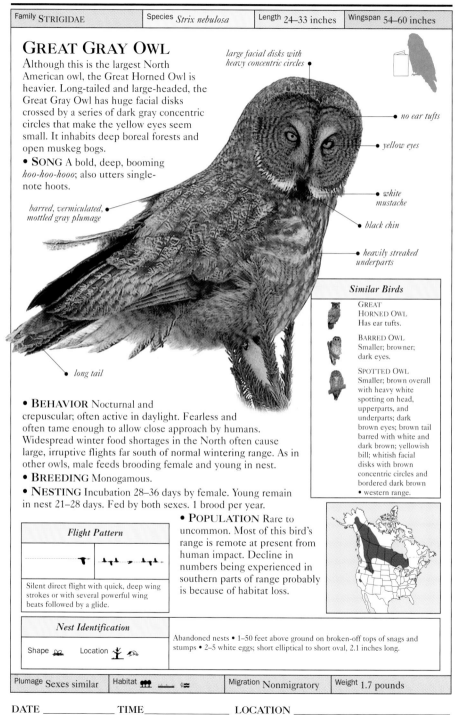

large facial disks with heavy concentric circles

no ear tufts

yellow eyes

white mustache

black chin

heavily streaked underparts

barred, vermiculated, mottled gray plumage

long tail

• **BEHAVIOR** Nocturnal and crepuscular; often active in daylight. Fearless and often tame enough to allow close approach by humans. Widespread winter food shortages in the North often cause large, irruptive flights far south of normal wintering range. As in other owls, male feeds brooding female and young in nest.

• **BREEDING** Monogamous.

• **NESTING** Incubation 28–36 days by female. Young remain in nest 21–28 days. Fed by both sexes. 1 brood per year.

• **POPULATION** Rare to uncommon. Most of this bird's range is remote at present from human impact. Decline in numbers being experienced in southern parts of range probably is because of habitat loss.

Similar Birds

GREAT HORNED OWL
Has ear tufts.

BARRED OWL
Smaller; browner; dark eyes.

SPOTTED OWL
Smaller; brown overall with heavy white spotting on head, upperparts, and underparts; dark brown eyes; brown tail barred with white and dark brown; yellowish bill; whitish facial disks with brown concentric circles and bordered dark brown
• western range.

Flight Pattern

Silent direct flight with quick, deep wing strokes or with several powerful wing beats followed by a glide.

Nest Identification

Shape 🦆   Location 🌳 🦆

Abandoned nests • 1–50 feet above ground on broken-off tops of snags and stumps • 2–5 white eggs; short elliptical to short oval, 2.1 inches long.

Plumage Sexes similar	Habitat 🐾 ⋯ 🌿	Migration Nonmigratory	Weight 1.7 pounds

DATE _____ TIME_____ LOCATION _____

Family STRIGIDAE	Species *Asio otus*	Length 13–16 inches	Wingspan 36–42 inches

LONG-EARED OWL

The most slender and most nocturnal of the large owls is perhaps the most overlooked. It is hard to detect because of its cryptic coloration, shy habits, and the ability to "freeze" against a perch with body flattened. This owl often uses the same winter perch day after day, resulting in a large accumulation of pellets and droppings beneath it; this telltale evidence can be used to locate the roosting owl above. Although the female is larger, both sexes appear similar. Frequents a wide range of habitats, from desert oases to riparian thickets to dense coniferous woodlands.

long close-set blackish ear tufts

yellow eyes

mottled brown

rusty facial disks

mottled buffy-white with heavy vertical streaking

• **SONG** Melodic low hoots, *quoo-quoo-quoo*, and long *hoos*. Sometimes sounds like a barking, whining puppy. Virtually mute outside breeding season.

• **BEHAVIOR** Nocturnal. Roosts perched close to tree trunk in thick cover during day. Hunts over open fields and marshes. Feeds primarily on mouse-size mammals; sometimes takes small birds. Often gregarious on roosts in winter. Accumulated pellet contents below roost can reveal local diet, as the undigested bones, teeth, and exoskeletons of its prey are compacted within them. Chooses abandoned nest of squirrel, crow, hawk, or heron as its own nesting site.

long tail

Similar Birds

GREAT HORNED OWL
Much larger, stouter build; ear tufts farther apart on head; horizontal barring beneath (not vertical streaking).

SHORT-EARED OWL
Buffier below; shorter ear tufts; diurnal.

• **BREEDING** Monogamous.

Flight Pattern

Buoyant silent wing beats. Ear tufts flattened back on head in flight.

• **NESTING** Incubation 26–28 days by female. Semialtricial young stay in nest 23–26 days, fed by both sexes. 1 brood per year.

• **POPULATION** Uncommon to locally common; may be more common than suspected.

Nest Identification

Shape 🪺   Location 🌳🌲🪨

Typically does not build nest • uses abandoned nests; sometimes tree cavity • suspected of sometimes evicting crow • 4–30 feet above ground in a tree • 2–10 white eggs; elliptical, 1.6 inches long.

Plumage Sexes similar	Habitat 🌳 🌿 ⚘	Migration Northern birds migrate	Weight 8.6 ounces

DATE _____ TIME_____ LOCATION _____

Family STRIGIDAE	Species *Asio flammeus*	Length 13–17 inches	Wingspan 38–44 inches

SHORT-EARED OWL

A big-headed, short-necked owl of grasslands and marshes, this bird is often seen quartering low over vegetation during the day. With tawny to buff-brown plumage, it shows large buff wing patches on the upperwing and a dark "wrist" mark on the underwing in flight. The ear tufts are very small and difficult to see unless the bird is perched. It has a streaked buff to whitish belly and white undertail coverts with faint streaking. Its diurnal activities make it frequently visible.

dark facial disks that become paler farther from the center

short ear tufts

yellow to orange eyes

heavily streaked head

tawny to buff-brown

heavily streaked upper breast

• **SONG** On breeding grounds this owl gives a loud *eeee-yerp*; a high-pitched grating *waowk, waowk, waowk*, like the barking of a dog; or a *toot-toot-toot-toot-toot*. When on its wintering grounds, the Short-eared Owl usually remains silent.

• **BEHAVIOR** Nocturnal and crepuscular; may hunt in late afternoons or on overcast days. Flies back and forth low over the ground, dropping feet first with wings held high onto prey. May perch on post or shrub to watch for prey. Feeds primarily on small rodents but also takes some small birds of open habitats and large insects. Uses crippled-bird display to lure intruders away from the nest or young on the ground.

• **BREEDING** Monogamous. Sometimes forms small colonies.

• **NESTING** Incubation 24–37 days by female. Semialtricial young stay in nest 21–36 days. Fed by both sexes. Typically 1 brood per year.

• **POPULATION** Fairly common. It has disappeared in parts of its southern range because of habitat loss.

• **CONSERVATION** The main conservation concern for this owl is a degree of habitat loss to agriculture and also loss due to killing by shooting.

Similar Birds

LONG-EARED OWL
Smaller buff upperwing and black wrist patches; heavily barred underparts; large ear tufts; nocturnal.

Flight Pattern

Buoyant erratic flight with flopping wing beats.

Nest Identification

Shape 🪶 ⬤ ⬛   Location 🌱 🌾

Shallow depression • lined with grass and feathers • on ground • built by female • 3–11 white eggs that become nest-stained; short elliptical, 1.5 inches long.

Plumage Sexes similar	Habitat 〰️ 🌾	Migration Some migrate	Weight 11.1 ounces

DATE _____ TIME_____ LOCATION _____

Family STRIGIDAE	Species *Aegolius funereus*	Length 8–12 inches	Wingspan 20–26 inches

BOREAL OWL

flat-topped head

This small flat-headed owl is seldom seen because it is strictly nocturnal and sits concealed close to the trunk of a thick conifer when on its daytime perch. Its white facial disks are bordered with black. During irruptive flight in winter, when this owl comes far south of its normal winter range into the middle and eastern US, most individuals seem to be females and many are found seeking shelter in buildings. Juveniles are similar to adults on the upperparts, but they are a rich chocolate brown below with a dark brown facial disk, whitish upturned mustache, and a white wedge between the eyes that spreads above them on the forehead.

whitish gray facial disks with black border

deep brown upperparts with heavy white spotting

yellow eyes

pale bill

whitish underparts with heavy chocolate streaking

• **SONG** Resembles high-pitched ringing *ting, ting, ting, ting.* Brief series of tremulous *hoo* notes.

• **BEHAVIOR** Nocturnal. Solitary. Prefers thick old growth coniferous forests. Feeds primarily on small rodents and other small mammals, rarely on small birds. Males cease singing after they are mated.

• **BREEDING** Polygamous.

• **NESTING** Incubation 26–37 days by both sexes. Semialtricial young stay in nest 28–36 days. Fed by female with food brought by male. 1 brood per year.

JUVENILE

Similar Birds

NORTHERN SAW-WHET OWL
Smaller; dark bill; white streaked head, not spotted • juvenile has tawny-cinnamon underparts without streaking.

• **POPULATION** Uncommon. Northern populations in no danger; status of western populations not well known, but the Boreal Owl is vulnerable to logging operations.

• **BIRDHOUSES** Will use man-made nest boxes.

Flight Pattern

Short flights on rapidly beating wings; longer ones more buoyant with shallow somewhat fluttering silent wing beats.

Nest Identification

Shape [ ] Location [ ]

In tree cavity, usually a woodpecker hole • no lining added • 20–80 feet above ground • 2–6 white eggs, 1.3 inches long.

Plumage Sexes similar	Habitat	Migration Irregular	Weight 3.6 ounces

DATE _____ TIME_____ LOCATION _____

Family STRIGIDAE	Species *Aegolius acadicus*	Length 7–8 inches	Wingspan 17–20 inches

NORTHERN SAW-WHET OWL

The incessant call of the male Northern Saw-whet Owl during breeding season sounds like a saw being sharpened or whetted. Some winters numbers of this little owl are found well south of the normal breeding range. This species is one of the smallest owls. Note the lack of ear tufts, dark bill, and white eyebrows. Females are larger than males. Juveniles have tawny-cinnamon underparts, chocolate-brown upperparts with white spotting, and a bold white Y from beak to eyebrows.

brown forehead and crown with liberal white streaking

pale buff to brownish facial disks

whitish eyebrows

white patch between eyes

blackish bill

chestnut-brown upperparts with heavy white and buff spotting

white underparts with reddish brown and dark brown blotches and streaks

unmarked white undertail coverts

JUVENILE

• **SONG** Repeated 1-note whistle of *too, too, too, too, too* or *sch-whet, sch-whet,* sometimes for hours at a time. Sings during breeding season only; singing decreases after mate is attracted. Voice may carry 0.5 mile or more.

• **BEHAVIOR** Solitary or in pairs. Eats small rodents, large insects, birds, and bats. Hunts primarily at night. Perches low, searching for prey, then flies down and snatches it with talons. Territorial birds often respond to imitations of their call by speeding up the rate of their calling; often attracted to playbacks of their call.

• **BREEDING** Monogamous. Solitary.

• **NESTING** Incubation 26–29 days by female. Semialtricial young stay in nest 27–34 days. Fed by both sexes: Male brings food, then female feeds young for about first 18 days. 1 brood per year.

• **POPULATION** Fairly common. Declining.

Similar Birds
BOREAL OWL Larger; white face with blackish border; darker brown head with contrasting white spots; pale bill.

• **BIRDHOUSES** Uses nest boxes about the size of Wood Duck boxes.

• **CONSERVATION** Declining in parts of range due to habitat loss from logging, air pollution, and adelgid tree kills in high peaks of southern Appalachians.

Flight Pattern
Silent buoyant direct flight with fluttering wing beats.

Nest Identification	
Shape	Location	No nest materials • in tree cavity, abandoned woodpecker hole, or nesting box, 14–60 feet above ground • 4–7 white eggs; oval to ovate, 1.2 inches long.

Plumage Sexes similar	Habitat	Migration Most do not migrate	Weight 2.6 ounces

DATE _____ TIME_____ LOCATION _____

Family CAPRIMULGIDAE	Species *Chordeiles acutipennis*	Length 8–9 inches	Wingspan 20–23 inches

LESSER NIGHTHAWK

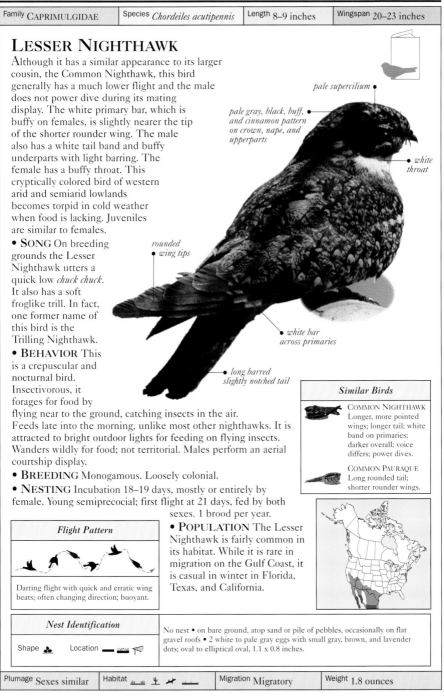

Although it has a similar appearance to its larger cousin, the Common Nighthawk, this bird generally has a much lower flight and the male does not power dive during its mating display. The white primary bar, which is buffy on females, is slightly nearer the tip of the shorter rounder wing. The male also has a white tail band and buffy underparts with light barring. The female has a buffy throat. This cryptically colored bird of western arid and semiarid lowlands becomes torpid in cold weather when food is lacking. Juveniles are similar to females.

- **SONG** On breeding grounds the Lesser Nighthawk utters a quick low *chuck chuck*. It also has a soft froglike trill. In fact, one former name of this bird is the Trilling Nighthawk.
- **BEHAVIOR** This is a crepuscular and nocturnal bird. Insectivorous, it forages for food by flying near to the ground, catching insects in the air. Feeds late into the morning, unlike most other nighthawks. It is attracted to bright outdoor lights for feeding on flying insects. Wanders wildly for food; not territorial. Males perform an aerial courtship display.
- **BREEDING** Monogamous. Loosely colonial.
- **NESTING** Incubation 18–19 days, mostly or entirely by female. Young semiprecocial; first flight at 21 days, fed by both sexes. 1 brood per year.
- **POPULATION** The Lesser Nighthawk is fairly common in its habitat. While it is rare in migration on the Gulf Coast, it is casual in winter in Florida, Texas, and California.

pale supercilium

pale gray, black, buff, and cinnamon pattern on crown, nape, and upperparts

white throat

rounded wing tips

white bar across primaries

long barred slightly notched tail

Similar Birds

COMMON NIGHTHAWK
Longer, more pointed wings; longer tail; white band on primaries; darker overall; voice differs; power dives.

COMMON PAURAQUE
Long rounded tail; shorter rounder wings.

Flight Pattern

Darting flight with quick and erratic wing beats; often changing direction; buoyant.

Nest Identification

Shape • Location

No nest • on bare ground, atop sand or pile of pebbles, occasionally on flat gravel roofs • 2 white to pale gray eggs with small gray, brown, and lavender dots; oval to elliptical oval, 1.1 x 0.8 inches.

Plumage Sexes similar	Habitat	Migration Migratory	Weight 1.8 ounces

DATE _____ TIME_____ LOCATION _____

Family CAPRIMULGIDAE	Species *Chordeiles minor*	Length 8–10 inches	Wingspan 21–24 inches

COMMON NIGHTHAWK

Like all members of the nightjar family, the adult bird flutters its gular pouch during intense heat to cool itself. The eggs and nestlings are sometimes carried to another location if temperatures become extreme. The female is similar to the male, but has a buffy, rather than white, throat and lacks the white tail band. Juveniles also lack this tail band. Note the long pointed wings with the white bar through the primaries, and the mothlike flight of the "bullbat," which is the colloquial name used for this nighthawk in the South. Although predominantly grayish brown overall, there is much color variation over the large North American range.

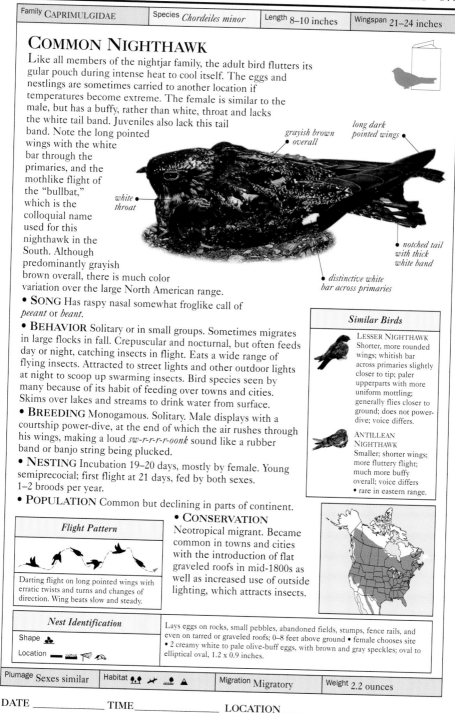

grayish brown overall

long dark pointed wings

white throat

notched tail with thick white band

distinctive white bar across primaries

- **SONG** Has raspy nasal somewhat froglike call of *peeant* or *beant.*
- **BEHAVIOR** Solitary or in small groups. Sometimes migrates in large flocks in fall. Crepuscular and nocturnal, but often feeds day or night, catching insects in flight. Eats a wide range of flying insects. Attracted to street lights and other outdoor lights at night to scoop up swarming insects. Bird species seen by many because of its habit of feeding over towns and cities. Skims over lakes and streams to drink water from surface.
- **BREEDING** Monogamous. Solitary. Male displays with a courtship power-dive, at the end of which the air rushes through his wings, making a loud *sw-r-r-r-oonk* sound like a rubber band or banjo string being plucked.
- **NESTING** Incubation 19–20 days, mostly by female. Young semiprecocial; first flight at 21 days, fed by both sexes. 1–2 broods per year.
- **POPULATION** Common but declining in parts of continent.
- **CONSERVATION** Neotropical migrant. Became common in towns and cities with the introduction of flat graveled roofs in mid-1800s as well as increased use of outside lighting, which attracts insects.

Similar Birds

LESSER NIGHTHAWK Shorter, more rounded wings; whitish bar across primaries slightly closer to tip; paler upperparts with more uniform mottling; generally flies closer to ground; does not power-dive; voice differs.

ANTILLEAN NIGHTHAWK Smaller; shorter wings; more fluttery flight; much more buffy overall; voice differs • rare in eastern range.

Flight Pattern

Darting flight on long pointed wings with erratic twists and turns and changes of direction. Wing beats slow and steady.

Nest Identification	
Shape ♣	Lays eggs on rocks, small pebbles, abandoned fields, stumps, fence rails, and even on tarred or graveled roofs; 0–8 feet above ground • female chooses site • 2 creamy white to pale olive-buff eggs, with brown and gray speckles; oval to elliptical oval, 1.2 x 0.9 inches.
Location ▬ ▬ ⚘ ⌂	

Plumage Sexes similar	Habitat	Migration Migratory	Weight 2.2 ounces

DATE _____ TIME_____ LOCATION _____

| Family CAPRIMULGIDAE | Species *Nyctidromus albicollis* | Length 10–11 inches | Wingspan 21–23 inches |

COMMON PAURAQUE

A primarily tropical nightjar that reaches the northern limit of its range in south Texas, the Common Pauaque is very busy at night when it can be heard singing for hours. The name "pauraque" is an imitation of the Spanish rendering of its call. It flies low to the ground and sometimes feeds for insects in the beams of automobile headlights. In flight, note the white bar crossing the primaries and the

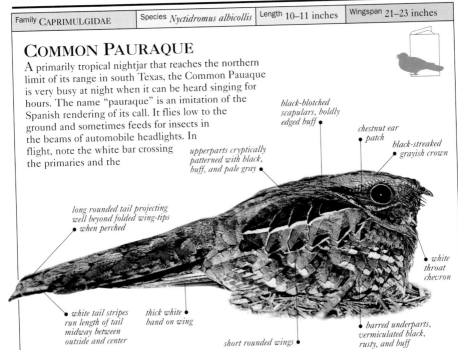

black-blotched scapulars, boldly edged buff

chestnut ear patch

black-streaked grayish crown

upperparts cryptically patterned with black, buff, and pale gray

long rounded tail projecting well beyond folded wing-tips when perched

white throat chevron

white tail stripes run length of tail midway between outside and center

thick white band on wing

short rounded wings

barred underparts, vermiculated black, rusty, and buff

white tail patches on the long rounded tail. The female resembles the male but with a pale buff to cinnamon bar on the primaries and buffy tail patches on just the outside tip of the tail. Easily overlooked when not calling. On the daytime ground roost the camouflaged birds are almost invisible against the dead leaf background until flushed.

- **SONG** Call is a slightly burry low *purrr* or a high *wheer*. Song is a loud whistled *puc, puc, puc, puc p'weeEER*, sounding like *who-who-who-are-you?*
- **BEHAVIOR** Solitary. Crepuscular and nocturnal. Sings most often on moonlit nights. Perches low or hunts from ground for insects, then catches in flight. Eats a variety of flying insects. Typically flies close to ground. Roosts on ground during day.
- **BREEDING** Monogamous. Solitary.

Similar Birds
COMMON NIGHTHAWK LESSER NIGHTHAWK Long, pointed wings; long, notched tail; voices differ.

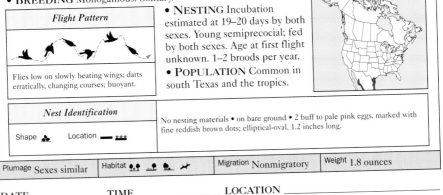

Flight Pattern

Flies low on slowly beating wings; darts erratically, changing courses; buoyant.

- **NESTING** Incubation estimated at 19–20 days by both sexes. Young semiprecocial; fed by both sexes. Age at first flight unknown. 1–2 broods per year.
- **POPULATION** Common in south Texas and the tropics.

Nest Identification	
Shape ♣ Location ▬ ▬ ★★★	No nesting materials • on bare ground • 2 buff to pale pink eggs, marked with fine reddish brown dots; elliptical-oval, 1.2 inches long.

| Plumage Sexes similar | Habitat 🌿🌸 🌿 🌲 ✈ | Migration Nonmigratory | Weight 1.8 ounces |

DATE _____ TIME_____ LOCATION _____

Family CAPRIMULGIDAE	Species *Phalaenoptilus nuttallii*	Length 7–8 inches	Wingspan 11–13 inches

COMMON POORWILL

The smallest of the North American nightjars, this bird is the western counterpart of the eastern Whip-poor-will. It primarily feeds at night. Though all but its southernmost population migrates, the Common Poorwill is the only bird known to hibernate. It sometimes returns to the same rock crevice each winter. In flight, note its small size, short, rounded wings that

mixed mottled brownish gray to pale gray plumage

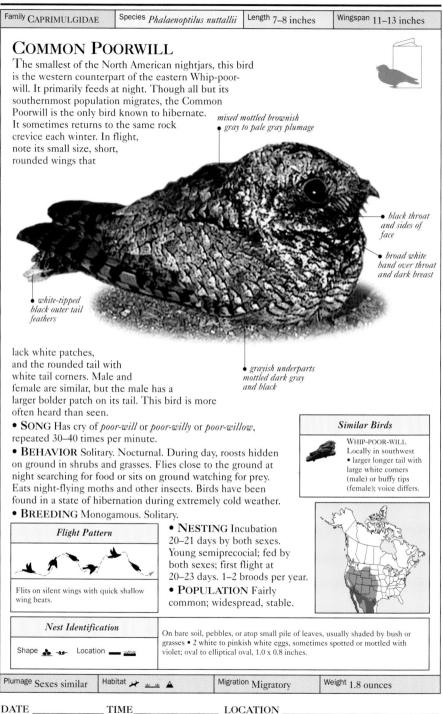

black throat and sides of face

broad white band over throat and dark breast

white-tipped black outer tail feathers

lack white patches, and the rounded tail with white tail corners. Male and female are similar, but the male has a larger bolder patch on its tail. This bird is more often heard than seen.

grayish underparts mottled dark gray and black

• **SONG** Has cry of *poor-will* or *poor-willy* or *poor-willow*, repeated 30–40 times per minute.

• **BEHAVIOR** Solitary. Nocturnal. During day, roosts hidden on ground in shrubs and grasses. Flies close to the ground at night searching for food or sits on ground watching for prey. Eats night-flying moths and other insects. Birds have been found in a state of hibernation during extremely cold weather.

• **BREEDING** Monogamous. Solitary.

• **NESTING** Incubation 20–21 days by both sexes. Young semiprecocial; fed by both sexes; first flight at 20–23 days. 1–2 broods per year.

• **POPULATION** Fairly common; widespread, stable.

Similar Birds

WHIP-POOR-WILL
Locally in southwest
• larger longer tail with large white corners (male) or buffy tips (female); voice differs.

Flight Pattern

Flits on silent wings with quick shallow wing beats.

Nest Identification

Shape ⬤ ⚬ Location ▬ ▬

On bare soil, pebbles, or atop small pile of leaves, usually shaded by bush or grasses • 2 white to pinkish white eggs, sometimes spotted or mottled with violet; oval to elliptical oval, 1.0 x 0.8 inches.

Plumage Sexes similar	Habitat	Migration Migratory	Weight 1.8 ounces

DATE _____ TIME_____ LOCATION _____

Family CAPRIMULGIDAE	Species *Caprimulgus carolinensis*	Length 11–13 inches	Wingspan 24.5–25.5 inches

CHUCK-WILL'S-WIDOW

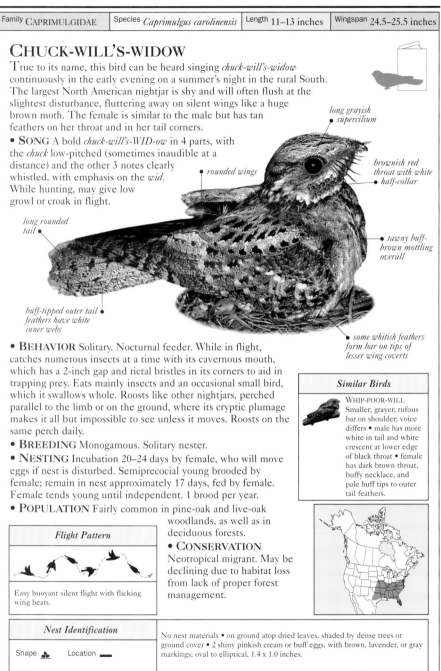

True to its name, this bird can be heard singing *chuck-will's-widow* continuously in the early evening on a summer's night in the rural South. The largest North American nightjar is shy and will often flush at the slightest disturbance, fluttering away on silent wings like a huge brown moth. The female is similar to the male but has tan feathers on her throat and in her tail corners.

• SONG A bold *chuck-will's-WID-ow* in 4 parts, with the *chuck* low-pitched (sometimes inaudible at a distance) and the other 3 notes clearly whistled, with emphasis on the *wid*. While hunting, may give low growl or croak in flight.

long grayish supercilium

brownish red throat with white half-collar

rounded wings

long rounded tail

tawny buff-brown mottling overall

buff-tipped outer tail feathers have white inner webs

some whitish feathers form bar on tips of lesser wing coverts

• BEHAVIOR Solitary. Nocturnal feeder. While in flight, catches numerous insects at a time with its cavernous mouth, which has a 2-inch gap and rictal bristles in its corners to aid in trapping prey. Eats mainly insects and an occasional small bird, which it swallows whole. Roosts like other nightjars, perched parallel to the limb or on the ground, where its cryptic plumage makes it all but impossible to see unless it moves. Roosts on the same perch daily.

• BREEDING Monogamous. Solitary nester.

• NESTING Incubation 20–24 days by female, who will move eggs if nest is disturbed. Semiprecocial young brooded by female; remain in nest approximately 17 days, fed by female. Female tends young until independent. 1 brood per year.

• POPULATION Fairly common in pine-oak and live-oak woodlands, as well as in deciduous forests.

• CONSERVATION Neotropical migrant. May be declining due to habitat loss from lack of proper forest management.

Similar Birds

WHIP-POOR-WILL
Smaller; grayer; rufous bar on shoulder; voice differs • male has more white in tail and white crescent at lower edge of black throat • female has dark brown throat, buffy necklace, and pale buff tips to outer tail feathers.

Flight Pattern

Easy buoyant silent flight with flicking wing beats.

Nest Identification

Shape 🌿   Location ▬

No nest materials • on ground atop dried leaves, shaded by dense trees or ground cover • 2 shiny pinkish cream or buff eggs, with brown, lavender, or gray markings; oval to elliptical, 1.4 x 1.0 inches.

Plumage Sexes similar	Habitat 🌿 🌲	Migration Migratory	Weight 4.2 ounces

DATE _____ TIME_____ LOCATION _____

Family CAPRIMULGIDAE	Species *Caprimulgus ridgwayi*	Length 8–9 inches	Wingspan 15 inches

BUFF-COLLARED NIGHTJAR

This quiet bird is a rare visitor to the desert canyons of extreme southwestern New Mexico and southeastern Arizona. The female is similar to the male, but her brownish gray tail has a cinnamon trim whereas the male's has white. The ecology and breeding biology of this nightjar is essentially unknown.

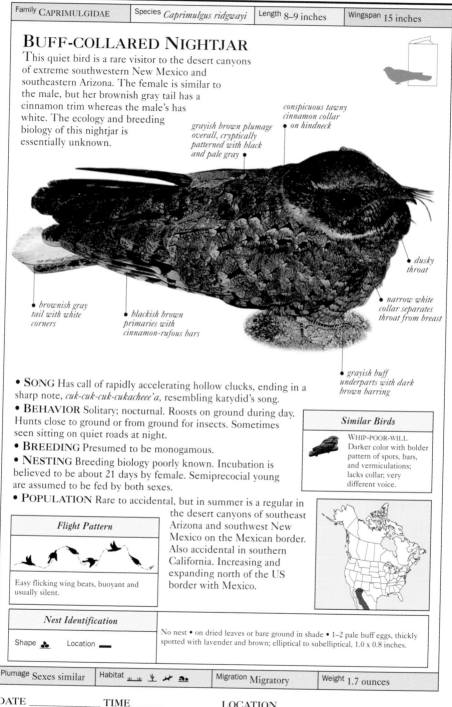

grayish brown plumage overall, cryptically patterned with black and pale gray

conspicuous tawny cinnamon collar on hindneck

dusky throat

narrow white collar separates throat from breast

brownish gray tail with white corners

blackish brown primaries with cinnamon-rufous bars

grayish buff underparts with dark brown barring

- **SONG** Has call of rapidly accelerating hollow clucks, ending in a sharp note, *cuk-cuk-cuk-cukacheee'a*, resembling katydid's song.
- **BEHAVIOR** Solitary; nocturnal. Roosts on ground during day. Hunts close to ground or from ground for insects. Sometimes seen sitting on quiet roads at night.
- **BREEDING** Presumed to be monogamous.
- **NESTING** Breeding biology poorly known. Incubation is believed to be about 21 days by female. Semiprecocial young are assumed to be fed by both sexes.
- **POPULATION** Rare to accidental, but in summer is a regular in the desert canyons of southeast Arizona and southwest New Mexico on the Mexican border. Also accidental in southern California. Increasing and expanding north of the US border with Mexico.

Similar Birds

WHIP-POOR-WILL
Darker color with bolder pattern of spots, bars, and vermiculations; lacks collar; very different voice.

Flight Pattern

Easy flicking wing beats, buoyant and usually silent.

Nest Identification

Shape 🐾   Location ▬

No nest • on dried leaves or bare ground in shade • 1–2 pale buff eggs, thickly spotted with lavender and brown; elliptical to subelliptical, 1.0 x 0.8 inches.

Plumage Sexes similar	Habitat ᴗ ᴗ ⚲ ✈ ⌂	Migration Migratory	Weight 1.7 ounces

DATE _____ TIME_____ LOCATION _____

Family CAPRIMULGIDAE	Species *Caprimulgus vociferus*	Length 9–10 inches	Wingspan 16–19.5 inches

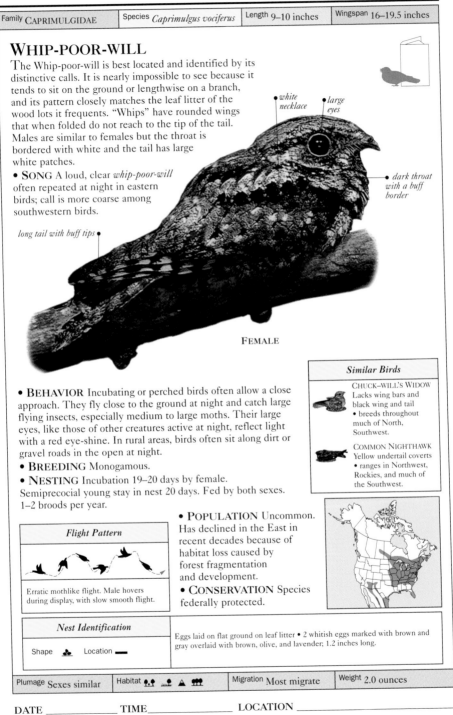

WHIP-POOR-WILL

The Whip-poor-will is best located and identified by its distinctive calls. It is nearly impossible to see because it tends to sit on the ground or lengthwise on a branch, and its pattern closely matches the leaf litter of the wood lots it frequents. "Whips" have rounded wings that when folded do not reach to the tip of the tail. Males are similar to females but the throat is bordered with white and the tail has large white patches.

• **SONG** A loud, clear *whip-poor-will* often repeated at night in eastern birds; call is more coarse among southwestern birds.

white necklace

large eyes

dark throat with a buff border

long tail with buff tips

FEMALE

• **BEHAVIOR** Incubating or perched birds often allow a close approach. They fly close to the ground at night and catch large flying insects, especially medium to large moths. Their large eyes, like those of other creatures active at night, reflect light with a red eye-shine. In rural areas, birds often sit along dirt or gravel roads in the open at night.

• **BREEDING** Monogamous.

• **NESTING** Incubation 19–20 days by female. Semiprecocial young stay in nest 20 days. Fed by both sexes. 1–2 broods per year.

Similar Birds

CHUCK–WILL'S WIDOW
Lacks wing bars and black wing and tail
• breeds throughout much of North, Southwest.

COMMON NIGHTHAWK
Yellow undertail coverts
• ranges in Northwest, Rockies, and much of the Southwest.

• **POPULATION** Uncommon. Has declined in the East in recent decades because of habitat loss caused by forest fragmentation and development.

• **CONSERVATION** Species federally protected.

Flight Pattern

Erratic mothlike flight. Male hovers during display, with slow smooth flight.

Nest Identification	
Shape 🐾 Location ▬	Eggs laid on flat ground on leaf litter • 2 whitish eggs marked with brown and gray overlaid with brown, olive, and lavender; 1.2 inches long.

Plumage Sexes similar	Habitat 🌿 🌱 ⛰ 🌲	Migration Most migrate	Weight 2.0 ounces

DATE _____ TIME_____ LOCATION _____

Family APODIDAE	Species *Cypseloides niger*	Length 7–7.5 inches	Wingspan 15 inches

BLACK SWIFT

The largest of the North American swifts, the Black Swift is rarely seen away from nesting sites because it spends most of its time thousands of feet in the air, traveling over the lofty mountains and canyons of its habitat. Flocks of these strong fast high-flying birds will follow storm clouds for more than three hundred miles to feed where insects gather in the warm air mass. In flight, juveniles of this species show faintly blacker underwing linings.
- **SONG** Heard infrequently. A harsh clear call of *ci-chi-chi-chit* or *plik-plik-plik-plik-plik*.
- **BEHAVIOR** Gregarious. Flies and travels in flocks, although the flocks often are small.

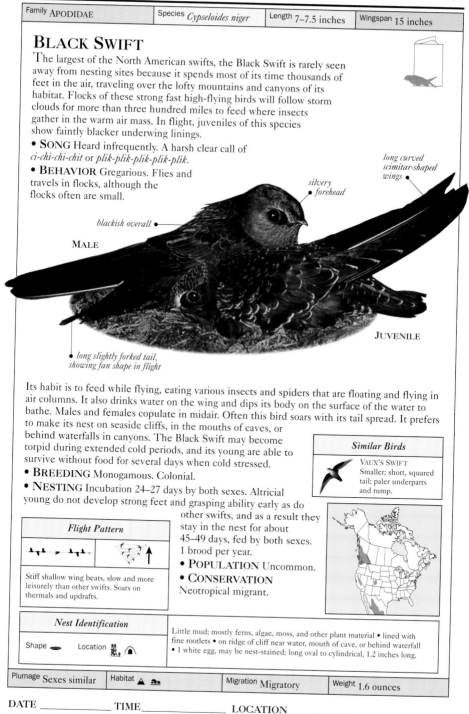

long curved
scimitar-shaped
wings

silvery
• forehead

blackish overall •

MALE

JUVENILE

• long slightly forked tail,
showing fan shape in flight

Its habit is to feed while flying, eating various insects and spiders that are floating and flying in air columns. It also drinks water on the wing and dips its body on the surface of the water to bathe. Males and females copulate in midair. Often this bird soars with its tail spread. It prefers to make its nest on seaside cliffs, in the mouths of caves, or behind waterfalls in canyons. The Black Swift may become torpid during extended cold periods, and its young are able to survive without food for several days when cold stressed.
- **BREEDING** Monogamous. Colonial.
- **NESTING** Incubation 24–27 days by both sexes. Altricial young do not develop strong feet and grasping ability early as do other swifts, and as a result they stay in the nest for about 45–49 days, fed by both sexes. 1 brood per year.
- **POPULATION** Uncommon.
- **CONSERVATION** Neotropical migrant.

Similar Birds

VAUX'S SWIFT
Smaller; short, squared
tail; paler underparts
and rump.

Flight Pattern

Stiff shallow wing beats, slow and more
leisurely than other swifts. Soars on
thermals and updrafts.

Nest Identification

Shape ⬡   Location 🪨 ⌒

Little mud; mostly ferns, algae, moss, and other plant material • lined with
fine rootlets • on ridge of cliff near water, mouth of cave, or behind waterfall
• 1 white egg, may be nest-stained; long oval to cylindrical, 1.2 inches long.

Plumage Sexes similar	Habitat 🔺 🐚	Migration Migratory	Weight 1.6 ounces

DATE _____ TIME_____ LOCATION _____

Family APODIDAE	Species *Chaetura pelagica*	Length 5.5 inches	Wingspan 12–12.75 inches

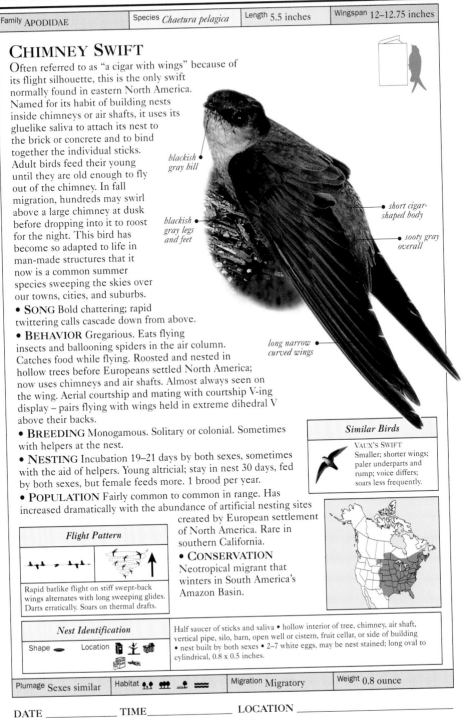

CHIMNEY SWIFT

Often referred to as "a cigar with wings" because of its flight silhouette, this is the only swift normally found in eastern North America. Named for its habit of building nests inside chimneys or air shafts, it uses its gluelike saliva to attach its nest to the brick or concrete and to bind together the individual sticks. Adult birds feed their young until they are old enough to fly out of the chimney. In fall migration, hundreds may swirl above a large chimney at dusk before dropping into it to roost for the night. This bird has become so adapted to life in man-made structures that it now is a common summer species sweeping the skies over our towns, cities, and suburbs.

blackish gray bill

blackish gray legs and feet

short cigar-shaped body

sooty gray overall

long narrow curved wings

- **SONG** Bold chattering; rapid twittering calls cascade down from above.
- **BEHAVIOR** Gregarious. Eats flying insects and ballooning spiders in the air column. Catches food while flying. Roosted and nested in hollow trees before Europeans settled North America; now uses chimneys and air shafts. Almost always seen on the wing. Aerial courtship and mating with courtship V-ing display – pairs flying with wings held in extreme dihedral V above their backs.
- **BREEDING** Monogamous. Solitary or colonial. Sometimes with helpers at the nest.
- **NESTING** Incubation 19–21 days by both sexes, sometimes with the aid of helpers. Young altricial; stay in nest 30 days, fed by both sexes, but female feeds more. 1 brood per year.
- **POPULATION** Fairly common to common in range. Has increased dramatically with the abundance of artificial nesting sites created by European settlement of North America. Rare in southern California.
- **CONSERVATION** Neotropical migrant that winters in South America's Amazon Basin.

Similar Birds

VAUX'S SWIFT
Smaller; shorter wings; paler underparts and rump; voice differs; soars less frequently.

Flight Pattern

Rapid batlike flight on stiff swept-back wings alternates with long sweeping glides. Darts erratically. Soars on thermal drafts.

Nest Identification	
Shape	Location	Half saucer of sticks and saliva • hollow interior of tree, chimney, air shaft, vertical pipe, silo, barn, open well or cistern, fruit cellar, or side of building • nest built by both sexes • 2–7 white eggs, may be nest stained; long oval to cylindrical, 0.8 x 0.5 inches.

Plumage Sexes similar	Habitat	Migration Migratory	Weight 0.8 ounce

DATE _____ TIME_____ LOCATION _____

Family APODIDAE	Species *Chaetura vauxi*	Length 4–4.5 inches	Wingspan 11.5 inches

VAUX'S SWIFT

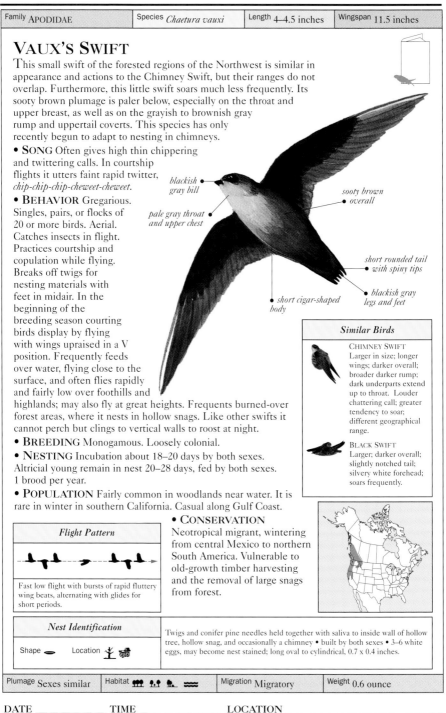

This small swift of the forested regions of the Northwest is similar in appearance and actions to the Chimney Swift, but their ranges do not overlap. Furthermore, this little swift soars much less frequently. Its sooty brown plumage is paler below, especially on the throat and upper breast, as well as on the grayish to brownish gray rump and uppertail coverts. This species has only recently begun to adapt to nesting in chimneys.

• **SONG** Often gives high thin chippering and twittering calls. In courtship flights it utters faint rapid twitter, *chip-chip-chip-cheweet-cheweet.*

• **BEHAVIOR** Gregarious. Singles, pairs, or flocks of 20 or more birds. Aerial. Catches insects in flight. Practices courtship and copulation while flying. Breaks off twigs for nesting materials with feet in midair. In the beginning of the breeding season courting birds display by flying with wings upraised in a V position. Frequently feeds over water, flying close to the surface, and often flies rapidly and fairly low over foothills and highlands; may also fly at great heights. Frequents burned-over forest areas, where it nests in hollow snags. Like other swifts it cannot perch but clings to vertical walls to roost at night.

• **BREEDING** Monogamous. Loosely colonial.

• **NESTING** Incubation about 18–20 days by both sexes. Altricial young remain in nest 20–28 days, fed by both sexes. 1 brood per year.

• **POPULATION** Fairly common in woodlands near water. It is rare in winter in southern California. Casual along Gulf Coast.

• **CONSERVATION** Neotropical migrant, wintering from central Mexico to northern South America. Vulnerable to old-growth timber harvesting and the removal of large snags from forest.

blackish gray bill

pale gray throat and upper chest

sooty brown overall

short rounded tail with spiny tips

short cigar-shaped body

blackish gray legs and feet

Similar Birds

CHIMNEY SWIFT
Larger in size; longer wings; darker overall; broader darker rump; dark underparts extend up to throat. Louder chattering call; greater tendency to soar; different geographical range.

BLACK SWIFT
Larger; darker overall; slightly notched tail; silvery white forehead; soars frequently.

Flight Pattern

Fast low flight with bursts of rapid fluttery wing beats, alternating with glides for short periods.

Nest Identification

Shape ⌒   Location 🌱 🏠

Twigs and conifer pine needles held together with saliva to inside wall of hollow tree, hollow snag, and occasionally a chimney • built by both sexes • 3–6 white eggs, may become nest stained; long oval to cylindrical, 0.7 x 0.4 inches.

Plumage Sexes similar	Habitat 🐾 🍂 🦌 ~~~	Migration Migratory	Weight 0.6 ounce

DATE _____ TIME _____ LOCATION _____

| Family APODIDAE | Species *Hirundapus caudacutus* | Length 7.5–8.5 inches | Wingspan 20 inches |

WHITE-THROATED NEEDLETAIL

This large powerful swift may be one of the world's fastest-flying birds. A native of Eurasia, it sometimes visits the outer Aleutians in the springtime. In flight its extensive white undertail coverts and short rounded tail, combined with its thick body, white forehead and throat, set it apart from other swifts. Seen from above in flight it shows white patches on the tertials and a light brown back with a pale patch fading almost to white. Viewed at very close range the needlelike quills projecting beyond each feather in the tail are visible.

• **SONG** A rapid high-pitched chitter, given most often when birds are chasing each other.

• **BEHAVIOR** Gregarious. Flies and forages in large flocks and seems to be in the air constantly. Roosting habits poorly known. Catches food in flight. Diet consists almost entirely of flying insects. Flight typically consists of upward flutters or downward swoops, comprising several quick stiff wing strokes followed by fast raking and twisting glides. Frequently soars. Inhabits skies over cities, timbered ridges, and hilltops.

• **BREEDING** Monogamous. Colonial.

• **NESTING** Breeding biology poorly known. Estimated incubation 17–23 days by both sexes. Young altricial; brooded by female; remain in nest estimated 45–55 days, fed by both sexes. 1 brood per year.

• **POPULATION** Casual in spring on Alaska's outer Aleutian Islands.

• **CONSERVATION** Vulnerable to habitat loss due to logging operations in mature forests with trees that have hollows suitable for nesting.

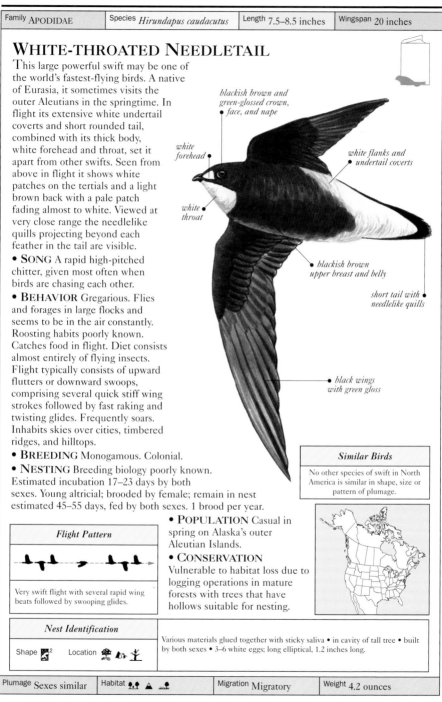

blackish brown and green-glossed crown, face, and nape

white forehead

white flanks and undertail coverts

white throat

blackish brown upper breast and belly

short tail with needlelike quills

black wings with green gloss

Similar Birds

No other species of swift in North America is similar in shape, size or pattern of plumage.

Flight Pattern

Very swift flight with several rapid wing beats followed by swooping glides.

Nest Identification

Shape ▨² Location 🌲 🏔 ✝

Various materials glued together with sticky saliva • in cavity of tall tree • built by both sexes • 3–6 white eggs; long elliptical, 1.2 inches long.

| Plumage Sexes similar | Habitat 🏙 ⛰ 🌳 | Migration Migratory | Weight 4.2 ounces |

DATE _____ TIME_____ LOCATION _____

Family APODIDAE	Species *Apus pacificus*	Length 7.75 inches	Wingspan 19–21 inches

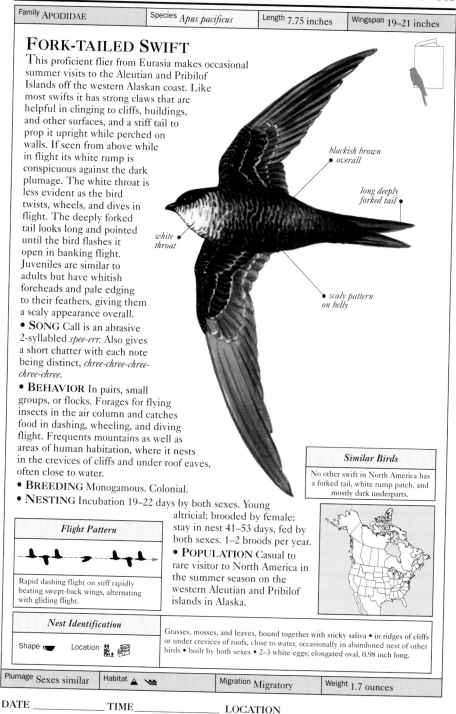

FORK-TAILED SWIFT

This proficient flier from Eurasia makes occasional summer visits to the Aleutian and Pribilof Islands off the western Alaskan coast. Like most swifts it has strong claws that are helpful in clinging to cliffs, buildings, and other surfaces, and a stiff tail to prop it upright while perched on walls. If seen from above while in flight its white rump is conspicuous against the dark plumage. The white throat is less evident as the bird twists, wheels, and dives in flight. The deeply forked tail looks long and pointed until the bird flashes it open in banking flight. Juveniles are similar to adults but have whitish foreheads and pale edging to their feathers, giving them a scaly appearance overall.

blackish brown overall

long deeply forked tail

white throat

scaly pattern on belly

• **SONG** Call is an abrasive 2-syllabled *spee-err*. Also gives a short chatter with each note being distinct, *chree-chree-chree-chree-chree*.

• **BEHAVIOR** In pairs, small groups, or flocks. Forages for flying insects in the air column and catches food in dashing, wheeling, and diving flight. Frequents mountains as well as areas of human habitation, where it nests in the crevices of cliffs and under roof eaves, often close to water.

• **BREEDING** Monogamous. Colonial.

• **NESTING** Incubation 19–22 days by both sexes. Young altricial; brooded by female; stay in nest 41–53 days, fed by both sexes. 1–2 broods per year.

• **POPULATION** Casual to rare visitor to North America in the summer season on the western Aleutian and Pribilof islands in Alaska.

Similar Birds

No other swift in North America has a forked tail, white rump patch, and mostly dark underparts.

Flight Pattern

Rapid dashing flight on stiff rapidly beating swept-back wings, alternating with gliding flight.

Nest Identification

Shape ⌒   Location 🏠🪨

Grasses, mosses, and leaves, bound together with sticky saliva • in ridges of cliffs or under crevices of roofs, close to water, occasionally in abandoned nest of other birds • built by both sexes • 2–3 white eggs; elongated oval, 0.98 inch long.

Plumage Sexes similar	Habitat ⛰🌊	Migration Migratory	Weight 1.7 ounces

DATE _____ TIME_____ LOCATION _____

Family APODIDAE	Species *Aeronautes saxatalis*	Length 6–7 inches	Wingspan 13–14 inches

WHITE-THROATED SWIFT

Possibly the most rapid flying North American bird, the White-throated Swift has been seen fleeing from Peregrine Falcons at estimated speeds of more than 200 mph. This darting black-and-white swift is associated with steep cliff faces in mountain canyons and on the coast; recently it has started to nest under freeway overpasses and bridges. In flight from below it shows white underparts from the chin to midline at the end of the belly, a large white oval patch on each flank that is visible from above and below, and a long, forked tail that often looks pointed in flight when not spread.

• **SONG** 2–3 birds flying together utter piercing laughing *he he he he*. Distinctive high liquid to slightly screechy twittering and trilling calls.

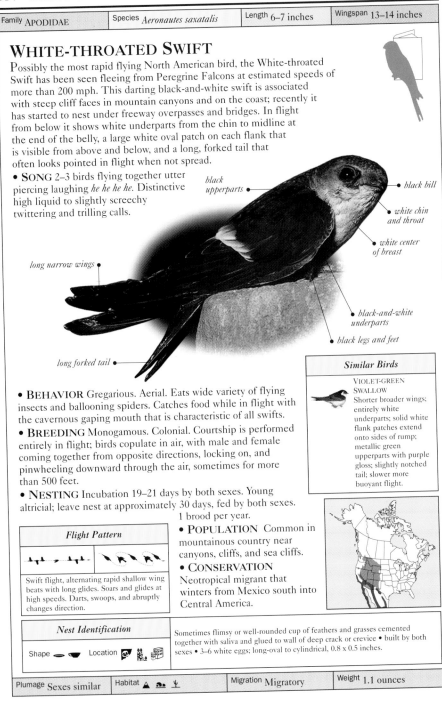

black upperparts

black bill

white chin and throat

white center of breast

long narrow wings

black-and-white underparts

black legs and feet

long forked tail

• **BEHAVIOR** Gregarious. Aerial. Eats wide variety of flying insects and ballooning spiders. Catches food while in flight with the cavernous gaping mouth that is characteristic of all swifts.
• **BREEDING** Monogamous. Colonial. Courtship is performed entirely in flight; birds copulate in air, with male and female coming together from opposite directions, locking on, and pinwheeling downward through the air, sometimes for more than 500 feet.
• **NESTING** Incubation 19–21 days by both sexes. Young altricial; leave nest at approximately 30 days, fed by both sexes. 1 brood per year.

Similar Birds

VIOLET-GREEN SWALLOW Shorter broader wings; entirely white underparts; solid white flank patches extend onto sides of rump; metallic green upperparts with purple gloss; slightly notched tail; slower more buoyant flight.

• **POPULATION** Common in mountainous country near canyons, cliffs, and sea cliffs.
• **CONSERVATION** Neotropical migrant that winters from Mexico south into Central America.

Flight Pattern

Swift flight, alternating rapid shallow wing beats with long glides. Soars and glides at high speeds. Darts, swoops, and abruptly changes direction.

Nest Identification

Shape ☛ ⬭   Location 🪺 🏚 🏛

Sometimes flimsy or well-rounded cup of feathers and grasses cemented together with saliva and glued to wall of deep crack or crevice • built by both sexes • 3–6 white eggs; long-oval to cylindrical, 0.8 x 0.5 inches.

Plumage Sexes similar	Habitat ⛰ 🏞 ⚓	Migration Migratory	Weight 1.1 ounces

DATE _____ TIME_____ LOCATION _____

Family TROCHILIDAE	Species *Cynanthus latirostris*	Length 3–4 inches	Wingspan 5–6 inches

BROAD-BILLED HUMMINGBIRD

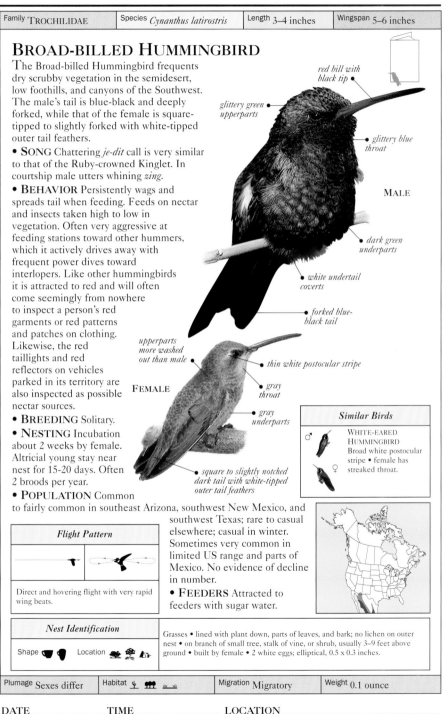

The Broad-billed Hummingbird frequents dry scrubby vegetation in the semidesert, low foothills, and canyons of the Southwest. The male's tail is blue-black and deeply forked, while that of the female is square-tipped to slightly forked with white-tipped outer tail feathers.

- **SONG** Chattering *je-dit* call is very similar to that of the Ruby-crowned Kinglet. In courtship male utters whining *zing*.
- **BEHAVIOR** Persistently wags and spreads tail when feeding. Feeds on nectar and insects taken high to low in vegetation. Often very aggressive at feeding stations toward other hummers, which it actively drives away with frequent power dives toward interlopers. Like other hummingbirds it is attracted to red and will often come seemingly from nowhere to inspect a person's red garments or red patterns and patches on clothing. Likewise, the red taillights and red reflectors on vehicles parked in its territory are also inspected as possible nectar sources.
- **BREEDING** Solitary.
- **NESTING** Incubation about 2 weeks by female. Altricial young stay near nest for 15-20 days. Often 2 broods per year.
- **POPULATION** Common to fairly common in southeast Arizona, southwest New Mexico, and southwest Texas; rare to casual elsewhere; casual in winter. Sometimes very common in limited US range and parts of Mexico. No evidence of decline in number.
- **FEEDERS** Attracted to feeders with sugar water.

red bill with black tip
glittery green upperparts
glittery blue throat

MALE

dark green underparts
white undertail coverts
forked blue-black tail

upperparts more washed out than male
thin white postocular stripe

FEMALE

gray throat
gray underparts
square to slightly notched dark tail with white-tipped outer tail feathers

Similar Birds

♂ **WHITE-EARED HUMMINGBIRD** Broad white postocular stripe • female has ♀ streaked throat.

Flight Pattern

Direct and hovering flight with very rapid wing beats.

Nest Identification

Shape ◗ ◖ Location 🌳 🌲 🏠

Grasses • lined with plant down, parts of leaves, and bark; no lichen on outer nest • on branch of small tree, stalk of vine, or shrub, usually 3–9 feet above ground • built by female • 2 white eggs; elliptical, 0.5 x 0.3 inches.

Plumage Sexes differ	Habitat ↡ 🐾 ↟ ↟	Migration Migratory	Weight 0.1 ounce

Family TROCHILIDAE	Species *Hylocharis leucotis*	Length 3–4 inches	Wingspan 4–5 inches

WHITE-EARED HUMMINGBIRD

The only small hummingbird occurring somewhat regularly in North America with a bold white postocular stripe that contrasts sharply with its dark head. The much larger Blue-throated Hummingbird also has similar head markings. The upperparts are dark green, the underparts are green and white, and the black-tipped red bill is rather short. It is principally a mountain species; look for it near low banks of flowers in clearings in open oak and oak-pine woodlands.

• **SONG** Display call is series of bell-like *tink tink* notes. Also gives bold, metallic twittering calls.

• **BEHAVIOR** Feeds and perches low to midlevel. Eats primarily nectar along with some small insects and spiders. Little is known of the biology of this small hummer in its limited US range.

• **BREEDING** Solitary.

• **NESTING** Incubation 14–16 days by female. Young stay in nest 23–26 days.

• **POPULATION** Casual to rare in limited and local US range. Widespread and locally very common

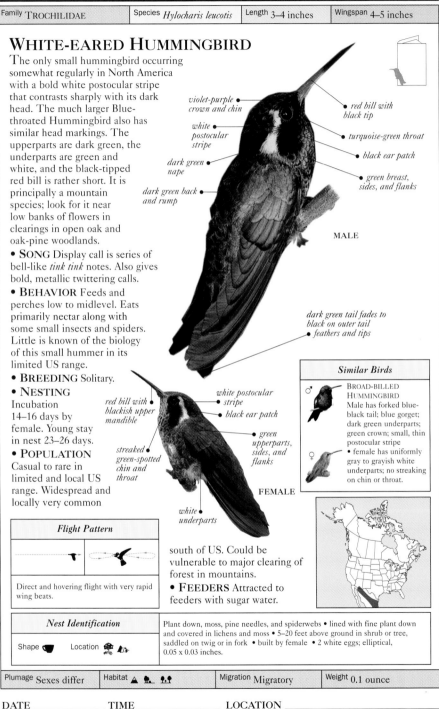

violet-purple crown and chin

red bill with black tip

white postocular stripe

turquoise-green throat

black ear patch

dark green nape

green breast, sides, and flanks

dark green back and rump

MALE

dark green tail fades to black on outer tail feathers and tips

red bill with blackish upper mandible

white postocular stripe

black ear patch

green upperparts, sides, and flanks

streaked green-spotted chin and throat

FEMALE

white underparts

Similar Birds

♂ BROAD-BILLED HUMMINGBIRD Male has forked blue-black tail; blue gorget; dark green underparts; green crown; small, thin postocular stripe
♀ • female has uniformly gray to grayish white underparts; no streaking on chin or throat.

Flight Pattern

Direct and hovering flight with very rapid wing beats.

south of US. Could be vulnerable to major clearing of forest in mountains.

• **FEEDERS** Attracted to feeders with sugar water.

Nest Identification

Shape ⬥   Location 🪺 🌲

Plant down, moss, pine needles, and spiderwebs • lined with fine plant down and covered in lichens and moss • 5–20 feet above ground in shrub or tree, saddled on twig or in fork • built by female • 2 white eggs; elliptical, 0.05 x 0.03 inches.

Plumage Sexes differ	Habitat 🔺 🌿 🌾	Migration Migratory	Weight 0.1 ounce

DATE _____ TIME _____ LOCATION _____

Family TROCHILIDAE	Species *Hylocharis xantusii*	Length 3–4 inches	Wingspan 4.5 inches

XANTUS'S HUMMINGBIRD

This very small greenish hummingbird with cinnamon-buff underparts and rufous in the tail is rarely seen outside the mountains of southern Baja California. Males have a black forehead and black line through the eye, providing sharp contrast with the white postocular stripe.

• **SONG** Raspy twitter or warble. Also gives high-pitched metallic sounding *chi-tiik* or *ti-tink*.

• **BEHAVIOR** Feeds on nectar and insects at low

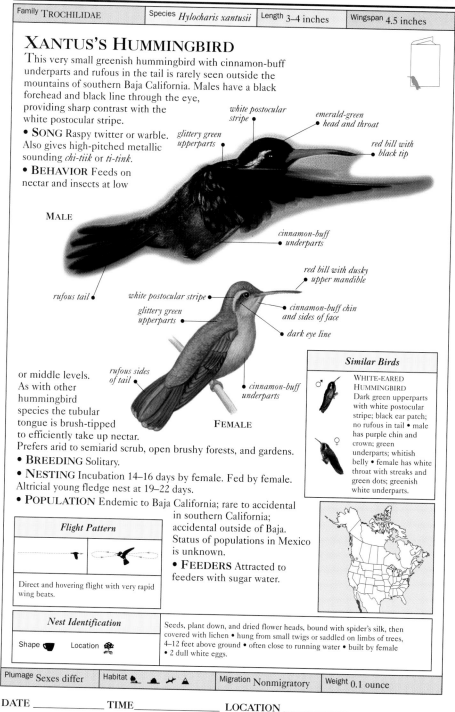

white postocular stripe

emerald-green head and throat

glittery green upperparts

red bill with black tip

MALE

cinnamon-buff underparts

red bill with dusky upper mandible

rufous tail

white postocular stripe

glittery green upperparts

cinnamon-buff chin and sides of face

dark eye line

rufous sides of tail

cinnamon-buff underparts

FEMALE

or middle levels. As with other hummingbird species the tubular tongue is brush-tipped to efficiently take up nectar. Prefers arid to semiarid scrub, open brushy forests, and gardens.

• **BREEDING** Solitary.

• **NESTING** Incubation 14–16 days by female. Fed by female. Altricial young fledge nest at 19–22 days.

• **POPULATION** Endemic to Baja California; rare to accidental in southern California; accidental outside of Baja. Status of populations in Mexico is unknown.

• **FEEDERS** Attracted to feeders with sugar water.

Similar Birds

WHITE-EARED HUMMINGBIRD
Dark green upperparts with white postocular stripe; black ear patch; no rufous in tail • male has purple chin and crown; green underparts; whitish belly • female has white throat with streaks and green dots; greenish white underparts.

Flight Pattern

Direct and hovering flight with very rapid wing beats.

Nest Identification

Shape   Location

Seeds, plant down, and dried flower heads, bound with spider's silk, then covered with lichen • hung from small twigs or saddled on limbs of trees, 4–12 feet above ground • often close to running water • built by female • 2 dull white eggs.

Plumage Sexes differ	Habitat	Migration Nonmigratory	Weight 0.1 ounce

DATE _____ TIME_____ LOCATION _____

Family TROCHILIDAE	Species *Amazilia beryllina*	Length 3.75–4.25 inches	Wingspan 5.25 inches

BERYLLINE HUMMINGBIRD

This infrequent visitor from Mexico sometimes can be seen in summer in the mountains of southeast Arizona in open oak forests, woodland edges, and scrub vegetation. It is glittery metallic green with rufous in the wings and tail, unlike any other western hummingbird. (Only the Buff-bellied Hummingbird that ranges into the Lower Rio Grande Valley of south Texas is also mostly green overall with a chestnut tail, but it does not have chestnut in its wings). Males show a cinnamon belly and undertail coverts. Adult females are similar to males but are duller in color and have a pale gray belly and undertail coverts. Juveniles resemble the female but the throat and chest are buffy-cinnamon with some greenish mottling on the sides. This species is known to have nested on occasion in the Huachuca Mountains.

glittery green head and nape

black bill with reddish base to lower mandible

glittery green back

glittery green throat and breast

rufous-brown wings

rufous-brown tail

• **SONG** Varied. Series of hoarse high twitters *sirr*; *kirr-I-rr*, *kirr-I-rr*. Also gives buzzing *drrzzzzt*.

• **BEHAVIOR** Feeds on nectar and insects; often dominates other feeding hummingbirds diving at them and chasing them from the flowers in hot pursuit. Perches low to high. May bathe by hovering with its breast and belly against a leaf wet with dew. Perches low to high.

• **BREEDING** Solitary.

• **NESTING** Incubation probably 2 weeks by female. Altricial young stay in nest 18–20 days, fed by female.

• **POPULATION** Rare to casual visitor to southeast Arizona; this bird is both common and widespread in Mexico.

• **FEEDERS** Will come to nectar feeders.

• **CONSERVATION** In Mexico vulnerable to loss of habitat when lower mountain slopes are cleared.

Similar Birds

BUFF-BELLIED HUMMINGBIRD
Buff-cinnamon belly; no rufous shows in wings; red mandibles have black tip
• accidental outside lower Rio Grande Valley of Texas.

Flight Pattern	
Direct and hovering flight with rapid wing beats.	

Nest Identification	
Shape	Location	Plant fibers and spiderwebs covered with lichens • in tree or shrub, 17–25 feet above ground on horizontal branch or vertical fork • probably built by female alone • 2 white eggs.

Plumage Sexes similar	Habitat	Migration Nonmigratory	Weight 0.2 ounce

| Family TROCHILIDAE | Species *Amazilia violiceps* | Length 4.25–4.5 inches | Wingspan 5.5 inches |

VIOLET-CROWNED HUMMINGBIRD

The only hummingbird in North America with a violet crown and completely white underparts made its first US nesting record in Guadalupe Canyon, which straddles the border between New Mexico and Arizona. The Violet-crowned Hummingbird is one of the rarest of the breeding North American hummingbirds. The female is similar to the male but has a dull greenish blue crown. Juveniles resemble females. It prefers riparian groves and arid and semiarid open woodlands. Most observations of this species in the US are made at nectar feeders in southeastern Arizona, where the birds may feed in the company of other species of hummingbirds.

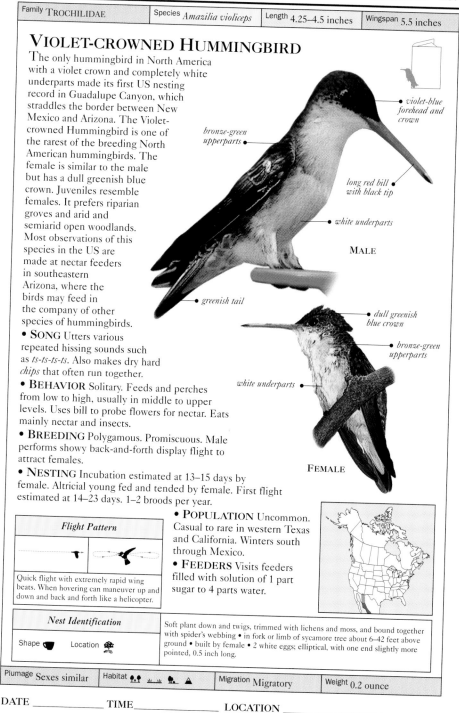

violet-blue forehead and crown

bronze-green upperparts

long red bill with black tip

white underparts

MALE

greenish tail

dull greenish blue crown

bronze-green upperparts

white underparts

FEMALE

- **SONG** Utters various repeated hissing sounds such as *ts-ts-ts-ts*. Also makes dry hard *chips* that often run together.
- **BEHAVIOR** Solitary. Feeds and perches from low to high, usually in middle to upper levels. Uses bill to probe flowers for nectar. Eats mainly nectar and insects.
- **BREEDING** Polygamous. Promiscuous. Male performs showy back-and-forth display flight to attract females.
- **NESTING** Incubation estimated at 13–15 days by female. Altricial young fed and tended by female. First flight estimated at 14–23 days. 1–2 broods per year.
- **POPULATION** Uncommon. Casual to rare in western Texas and California. Winters south through Mexico.
- **FEEDERS** Visits feeders filled with solution of 1 part sugar to 4 parts water.

Flight Pattern
Quick flight with extremely rapid wing beats. When hovering can maneuver up and down and back and forth like a helicopter.

Nest Identification	Soft plant down and twigs, trimmed with lichens and moss, and bound together with spider's webbing • in fork or limb of sycamore tree about 6–42 feet above ground • built by female • 2 white eggs; elliptical, with one end slightly more pointed, 0.5 inch long.
Shape ☕ Location 🐦	

| Plumage Sexes similar | Habitat 🌿🌿 🐦 ⛰ | Migration Migratory | Weight 0.2 ounce |

DATE _____ TIME_____ LOCATION _____

Family TROCHILIDAE	Species *Lampornis clemenciae*	Length 5–5.5 inches	Wingspan 7 inches

BLUE-THROATED HUMMINGBIRD

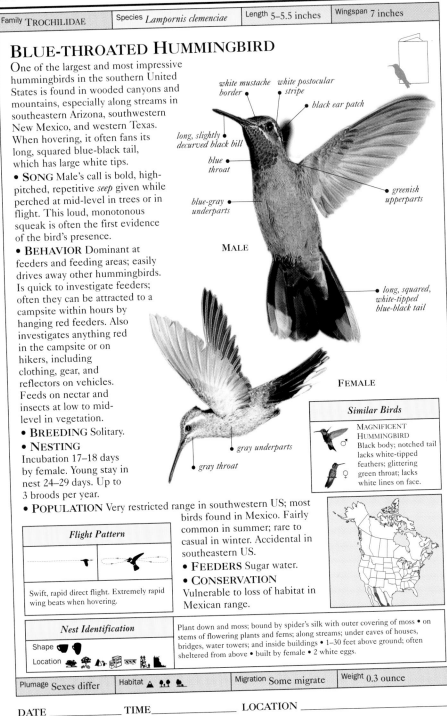

One of the largest and most impressive hummingbirds in the southern United States is found in wooded canyons and mountains, especially along streams in southeastern Arizona, southwestern New Mexico, and western Texas. When hovering, it often fans its long, squared blue-black tail, which has large white tips.

• **SONG** Male's call is bold, high-pitched, repetitive *seep* given while perched at mid-level in trees or in flight. This loud, monotonous squeak is often the first evidence of the bird's presence.

• **BEHAVIOR** Dominant at feeders and feeding areas; easily drives away other hummingbirds. Is quick to investigate feeders; often they can be attracted to a campsite within hours by hanging red feeders. Also investigates anything red in the campsite or on hikers, including clothing, gear, and reflectors on vehicles. Feeds on nectar and insects at low to mid-level in vegetation.

• **BREEDING** Solitary.

• **NESTING** Incubation 17–18 days by female. Young stay in nest 24–29 days. Up to 3 broods per year.

• **POPULATION** Very restricted range in southwestern US; most birds found in Mexico. Fairly common in summer; rare to casual in winter. Accidental in southeastern US.

• **FEEDERS** Sugar water.

• **CONSERVATION** Vulnerable to loss of habitat in Mexican range.

white mustache border • white postocular stripe

black ear patch

long, slightly decurved black bill

blue throat

blue-gray underparts

greenish upperparts

MALE

long, squared, white-tipped blue-black tail

FEMALE

gray underparts

gray throat

Similar Birds

MAGNIFICENT HUMMINGBIRD
♂ Black body; notched tail lacks white-tipped feathers; glittering
♀ green throat; lacks white lines on face.

Flight Pattern

Swift, rapid direct flight. Extremely rapid wing beats when hovering.

Nest Identification

Shape

Location

Plant down and moss; bound by spider's silk with outer covering of moss • on stems of flowering plants and ferns; along streams; under eaves of houses, bridges, water towers; and inside buildings • 1–30 feet above ground; often sheltered from above • built by female • 2 white eggs.

Plumage Sexes differ	Habitat	Migration Some migrate	Weight 0.3 ounce

Family TROCHILIDAE	Species *Eugenes fulgens*	Length 4.5–5.25 inches	Wingspan 7 inches

MAGNIFICENT HUMMINGBIRD

Large for a hummingbird, it appears all black at a distance, but when the male turns in sunlight the crown flashes deep purple and the chin and throat glitter green. The bill is long and black, and the male's dark green tail is deeply forked. It is often found in deciduous woods along streams or on pine-oak mountain slopes.

• **SONG** Main call is grating *tcheep*. Also has squeaky scratchy twittering song.

• **BEHAVIOR** Aggressively defends feeding areas. Feeds on nectar, insects, and spiders. Hawks insects in flight and gleans them from foliage. Often sits on exposed, rather high perches. Attracted to the color red.

• **BREEDING** Solitary.

• **NESTING** Incubation about 16 days by female. Fed by female. Young fledge at 20–24 days. Probably 1 brood per year.

• **POPULATION** Common to fairly common in southwest Texas, southwest New Mexico, and southeast Arizona in summer; rare to casual elsewhere. Stable in restricted US range. Some declines in Mexico due to habitat loss.

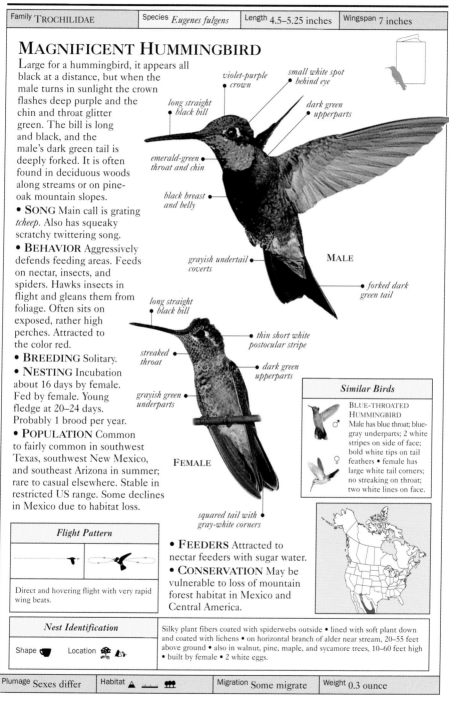

violet-purple crown
small white spot behind eye
long straight black bill
dark green upperparts
emerald-green throat and chin
black breast and belly
grayish undertail coverts
MALE
forked dark green tail

long straight black bill
thin short white postocular stripe
streaked throat
dark green upperparts
grayish green underparts
FEMALE
squared tail with gray-white corners

Similar Birds

BLUE-THROATED HUMMINGBIRD
♂ Male has blue throat; blue-gray underparts; 2 white stripes on side of face; bold white tips on tail feathers • female has ♀ large white tail corners; no streaking on throat; two white lines on face.

Flight Pattern

Direct and hovering flight with very rapid wing beats.

• **FEEDERS** Attracted to nectar feeders with sugar water.

• **CONSERVATION** May be vulnerable to loss of mountain forest habitat in Mexico and Central America.

Nest Identification

Shape 🌰   Location 🌿 🔼

Silky plant fibers coated with spiderwebs outside • lined with soft plant down and coated with lichens • on horizontal branch of alder near stream, 20–55 feet above ground • also in walnut, pine, maple, and sycamore trees, 10–60 feet high • built by female • 2 white eggs.

Plumage Sexes differ	Habitat ▲ ⸗ 🌳	Migration Some migrate	Weight 0.3 ounce

DATE _____ TIME _____ LOCATION _____

Family TROCHILIDAE	Species *Heliomaster constantii*	Length 4–5 inches	Wingspan 5–6 inches

PLAIN-CAPPED STARTHROAT

A casual stray from Mexico, this large hummingbird has greenish gray to golden green upperparts, grayish white underparts, and a white rump patch. The black bill is long and straight, and the long squared tail has white-tipped corners. The upper throat is sooty-gray but the lower gorget is rose-red to orange-red in good light. It might be confused with the more common Blue-throated Hummingbird, but note the Starthroat's longer and bolder white mustache and the white patch on its back. Although most often seen at feeders, it sometimes can be spotted feeding on agave blossoms, and any large hummer feeding on these semidesert flowers in summer in southern Arizona should be checked for this species. Females are similar to males but have a whitish gray throat.

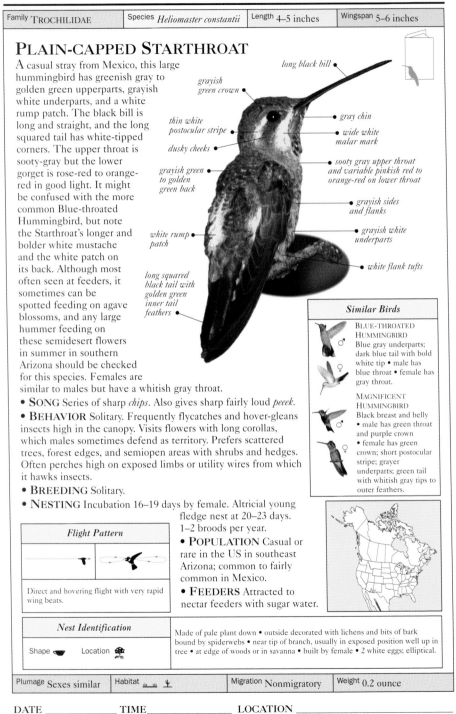

long black bill

grayish green crown

gray chin

thin white postocular stripe

wide white malar mark

dusky cheeks

grayish green to golden green back

sooty gray upper throat and variable pinkish red to orange-red on lower throat

grayish sides and flanks

white rump patch

grayish white underparts

white flank tufts

long squared black tail with golden green inner tail feathers

Similar Birds

BLUE-THROATED HUMMINGBIRD
♂ Blue gray underparts; dark blue tail with bold white tip • male has blue throat • female has gray throat.

MAGNIFICENT HUMMINGBIRD
♂ Black breast and belly • male has green throat and purple crown
♀ • female has green crown; short postocular stripe; grayer underparts; green tail with whitish gray tips to outer feathers.

• **SONG** Series of sharp *chips*. Also gives sharp fairly loud *peeek*.
• **BEHAVIOR** Solitary. Frequently flycatches and hover-gleans insects high in the canopy. Visits flowers with long corollas, which males sometimes defend as territory. Prefers scattered trees, forest edges, and semiopen areas with shrubs and hedges. Often perches high on exposed limbs or utility wires from which it hawks insects.
• **BREEDING** Solitary.
• **NESTING** Incubation 16–19 days by female. Altricial young fledge nest at 20–23 days. 1–2 broods per year.
• **POPULATION** Casual or rare in the US in southeast Arizona; common to fairly common in Mexico.
• **FEEDERS** Attracted to nectar feeders with sugar water.

Flight Pattern
Direct and hovering flight with very rapid wing beats.

Nest Identification	
Shape ⌒ Location 🪹	Made of pale plant down • outside decorated with lichens and bits of bark bound by spiderwebs • near tip of branch, usually in exposed position well up in tree • at edge of woods or in savanna • built by female • 2 white eggs; elliptical.

Plumage Sexes similar	Habitat ⏐⏐ ⏐⏐ ⚘	Migration Nonmigratory	Weight 0.2 ounce

DATE _____ TIME _____ LOCATION _____

Family TROCHILIDAE	Species *Calothorax lucifer*	Length 3–4 inches	Wingspan 4–5 inches

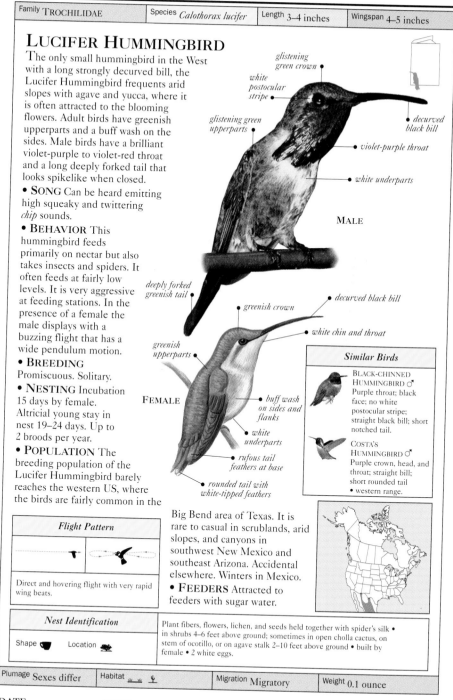

LUCIFER HUMMINGBIRD

The only small hummingbird in the West with a long strongly decurved bill, the Lucifer Hummingbird frequents arid slopes with agave and yucca, where it is often attracted to the blooming flowers. Adult birds have greenish upperparts and a buff wash on the sides. Male birds have a brilliant violet-purple to violet-red throat and a long deeply forked tail that looks spikelike when closed.

- **SONG** Can be heard emitting high squeaky and twittering *chip* sounds.
- **BEHAVIOR** This hummingbird feeds primarily on nectar but also takes insects and spiders. It often feeds at fairly low levels. It is very aggressive at feeding stations. In the presence of a female the male displays with a buzzing flight that has a wide pendulum motion.
- **BREEDING** Promiscuous. Solitary.
- **NESTING** Incubation 15 days by female. Altricial young stay in nest 19–24 days. Up to 2 broods per year.
- **POPULATION** The breeding population of the Lucifer Hummingbird barely reaches the western US, where the birds are fairly common in the Big Bend area of Texas. It is rare to casual in scrublands, arid slopes, and canyons in southwest New Mexico and southeast Arizona. Accidental elsewhere. Winters in Mexico.
- **FEEDERS** Attracted to feeders with sugar water.

glistening green crown

white postocular stripe

glistening green upperparts

decurved black bill

violet-purple throat

white underparts

MALE

deeply forked greenish tail

greenish crown

decurved black bill

greenish upperparts

white chin and throat

FEMALE

buff wash on sides and flanks

white underparts

rufous tail feathers at base

rounded tail with white-tipped feathers

Similar Birds

BLACK-CHINNED HUMMINGBIRD ♂ Purple throat; black face; no white postocular stripe; straight black bill; short notched tail.

COSTA'S HUMMINGBIRD ♂ Purple crown, head, and throat; straight bill; short rounded tail • western range.

Flight Pattern

Direct and hovering flight with very rapid wing beats.

Nest Identification

Shape ◖ Location ⬥

Plant fibers, flowers, lichen, and seeds held together with spider's silk • in shrubs 4–6 feet above ground; sometimes in open cholla cactus, on stem of ocotillo, or on agave stalk 2–10 feet above ground • built by female • 2 white eggs.

Plumage Sexes differ	Habitat ⚊⚊ ⚘	Migration Migratory	Weight 0.1 ounce

DATE _____ TIME_____ LOCATION _____

Family TROCHILIDAE	Species *Archilochus colubris*	Length 3–3.75 inches	Wingspan 4.25–4.5 inches

RUBY-THROATED HUMMINGBIRD

The only hummer known by most Easterners has a range that covers most of eastern North America. This is the hummingbird that frequents Eastern gardens and feeders. Both sexes have glittering green crown and upperparts, and the underparts are grayish to white. Males have black faces and a deep red to orange-red throat, or gorget. The humming of its wings is clearly discernible from some distance.

- **SONG** Series of rapid squeaky *chipping* notes.
- **BEHAVIOR** Feeds primarily on nectar but takes some insects and spiders, also sap from sapsucker drill wells. In courtship flight male makes huge a 180-degree arc back and forth, emitting a buzzing sound at its lowest point. Males often arrive on breeding grounds well ahead of females. These birds are strongly attracted to the color red, as are many other hummers.
- **BREEDING** Solitary.
- **NESTING** Incubation 11–16 days by female. Altricial young stay in nest 20–22 days. Fed by female. 1–3 broods per year.
- **POPULATION** Common to fairly common in breeding range. A few winter regularly in south Florida. Rare elsewhere.
- **FEEDERS** Red columbine in spring; saliva, trumpet or coral honeysuckle, and bee balm later in year. Also jewelweed, phlox, petunias, lilies, trumpet creeper, Siberian peatree, nasturtium, cone-shaped red flowers (wild and domesticated), and sugar water.
- **CONSERVATION** Red food dyes added to sugar water may harm birds. Sometimes attracted to red supporting insulators on electrical fences, then killed.

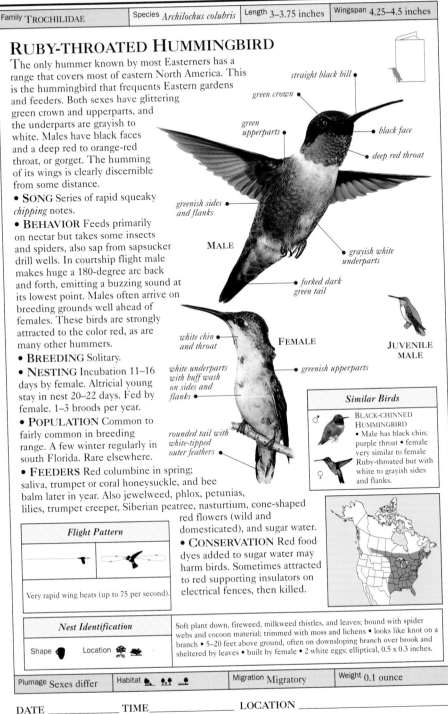

straight black bill
green crown
green upperparts
black face
deep red throat
greenish sides and flanks
MALE
grayish white underparts
forked dark green tail
white chin and throat
FEMALE
greenish upperparts
JUVENILE MALE
white underparts with buff wash on sides and flanks
rounded tail with white-tipped outer feathers

Similar Birds

♂ BLACK-CHINNED HUMMINGBIRD
- Male has black chin; purple throat • female very similar to female Ruby-throated but with white to grayish sides and flanks.
♀

Flight Pattern	

Very rapid wing beats (up to 75 per second).

Nest Identification	
Shape Location	Soft plant down, fireweed, milkweed thistles, and leaves; bound with spider webs and cocoon material; trimmed with moss and lichens • looks like knot on a branch • 5–20 feet above ground, often on downsloping branch over brook and sheltered by leaves • built by female • 2 white eggs; elliptical, 0.5 x 0.3 inches.

Plumage Sexes differ	Habitat	Migration Migratory	Weight 0.1 ounce

DATE _____ TIME_____ LOCATION _____

Family TROCHILIDAE	Species *Archilochus alexandri*	Length 3.5–3.75 inches	Wingspan 4–5 inches

BLACK-CHINNED HUMMINGBIRD

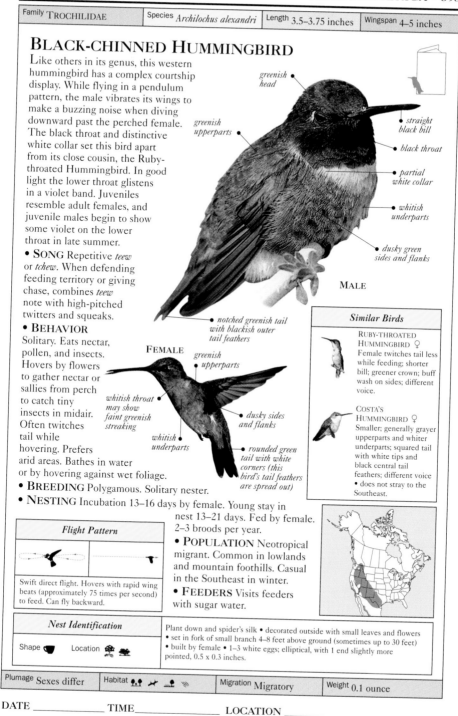

Like others in its genus, this western hummingbird has a complex courtship display. While flying in a pendulum pattern, the male vibrates its wings to make a buzzing noise when diving downward past the perched female. The black throat and distinctive white collar set this bird apart from its close cousin, the Ruby-throated Hummingbird. In good light the lower throat glistens in a violet band. Juveniles resemble adult females, and juvenile males begin to show some violet on the lower throat in late summer.

- **SONG** Repetitive *teew* or *tchew*. When defending feeding territory or giving chase, combines *teew* note with high-pitched twitters and squeaks.
- **BEHAVIOR** Solitary. Eats nectar, pollen, and insects. Hovers by flowers to gather nectar or sallies from perch to catch tiny insects in midair. Often twitches tail while hovering. Prefers arid areas. Bathes in water or by hovering against wet foliage.
- **BREEDING** Polygamous. Solitary nester.
- **NESTING** Incubation 13–16 days by female. Young stay in nest 13–21 days. Fed by female. 2–3 broods per year.
- **POPULATION** Neotropical migrant. Common in lowlands and mountain foothills. Casual in the Southeast in winter.
- **FEEDERS** Visits feeders with sugar water.

greenish head

greenish upperparts

straight black bill

black throat

partial white collar

whitish underparts

dusky green sides and flanks

MALE

notched greenish tail with blackish outer tail feathers

FEMALE

greenish upperparts

whitish throat may show faint greenish streaking

whitish underparts

dusky sides and flanks

rounded green tail with white corners (this bird's tail feathers are spread out)

Similar Birds

RUBY-THROATED HUMMINGBIRD ♀ Female twitches tail less while feeding; shorter bill; greener crown; buff wash on sides; different voice.

COSTA'S HUMMINGBIRD ♀ Smaller; generally grayer upperparts and whiter underparts; squared tail with white tips and black central tail feathers; different voice.
- does not stray to the Southeast.

Flight Pattern

Swift direct flight. Hovers with rapid wing beats (approximately 75 times per second) to feed. Can fly backward.

Nest Identification	
Shape 🪺 Location 🌿 🌳	Plant down and spider's silk • decorated outside with small leaves and flowers • set in fork of small branch 4–8 feet above ground (sometimes up to 30 feet) • built by female • 1–3 white eggs; elliptical, with 1 end slightly more pointed, 0.5 x 0.3 inches.

Plumage Sexes differ	Habitat 🌾 ⤴ 🌿 〰	Migration Migratory	Weight 0.1 ounce

DATE _____ TIME_____ LOCATION _____

Family TROCHILIDAE	Species *Calypte anna*	Length 3.5–4 inches	Wingspan 4.75 inches

ANNA'S HUMMINGBIRD

Able to adapt to suburban habitat, this hummingbird is expanding geographically and becoming more numerous. Although predominantly nonmigratory, some have been reported to migrate. It eats more insects and spiders than any other hummingbird. The male, which often vocalizes while perched, is the only North American hummingbird with rose-red crown and throat. Juveniles are similar to females, but juvenile males have some red on the crown as well as the throat.

- **SONG** Sharp squeaky call, *chick*. Chase calls are rapid, high-pitched rattles. Song is garbled mixture of coarse squeaky notes, usually delivered from a perch.
- **BEHAVIOR** Solitary. Eats nectar, insects, spiders, and sap from sapsucker drill wells. Hovers to gather nectar from flowers. Catches insects in midair and plucks spiders and insects from spider webs. Often bathes by hovering against rain- or dew-covered foliage. Male displays for female in a high arc, making explosive *chirp* at the bottom after a rapid dive. Often found in gardens and attending ornamental plantings in yards.
- **BREEDING** Polygamous. Solitary.
- **NESTING** Incubation 14–19 days by female. Altricial young stay in nest 18–23 days, fed by female. 2–3 broods per year.
- **POPULATION** Abundant; increasing. Vagrants get to coastal Alaska in summer; casual to accidental in the East in winter.
- **FEEDERS** Sugar-water.
- **CONSERVATION** Neotropical migrant wintering south to central Baja and northwestern Mexico.

rose-red head, throat, and sides of neck

short straight black bill

MALE

grayish underparts with greenish tint to sides, flanks, and belly

slightly notched, dark green tail with blackish outer tail feathers

JUVENILE MALE

straight black bill

green crown, nape, and upperparts

red flecks or spot on throat

FEMALE

pale gray underparts

rounded green tail with white tips on outer three feathers

Similar Birds

BLACK-CHINNED HUMMINGBIRD ♀
COSTA'S HUMMINGBIRD ♀
Smaller; whitish underparts; lack red markings on throat • Costa's winters only as far east as west Texas.

Flight Pattern

Flies forward, backward, up, down, and side to side on rapidly beating wings as it feeds. Swift darting flight from place to place. Wing beats a blur.

Nest Identification

Shape ◗   Location 🌳🌿

Plant down bound with spider silk and lined with plant down and feathers • on small tree branch, on ledge of cliff, or sometimes on utility wire • 1.5–30 feet above ground • built by female • 1–3 white eggs; elliptical oval or subelliptical, with similar curvatures at each end, 0.5 x 0.3 inches.

Plumage Sexes differ	Habitat 🌿🍃 ✈ 🏔 ⚘ ⚘ 🌾	Migration Nonmigratory	Weight 0.1 ounce

Family TROCHILIDAE	Species *Calypte costae*	Length 3.5 inches	Wingspan 4.5 inches

COSTA'S HUMMINGBIRD

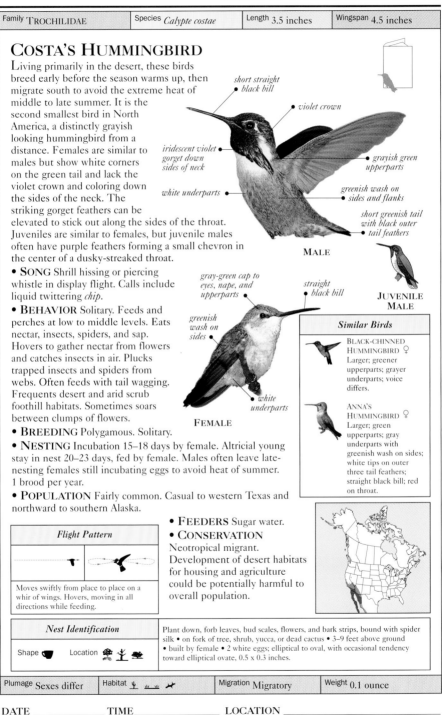

Living primarily in the desert, these birds breed early before the season warms up, then migrate south to avoid the extreme heat of middle to late summer. It is the second smallest bird in North America, a distinctly grayish looking hummingbird from a distance. Females are similar to males but show white corners on the green tail and lack the violet crown and coloring down the sides of the neck. The striking gorget feathers can be elevated to stick out along the sides of the throat. Juveniles are similar to females, but juvenile males often have purple feathers forming a small chevron in the center of a dusky-streaked throat.

short straight black bill

violet crown

iridescent violet gorget down sides of neck

grayish green upperparts

white underparts

greenish wash on sides and flanks

short greenish tail with black outer tail feathers

MALE

gray-green cap to eyes, nape, and upperparts

straight black bill

JUVENILE MALE

greenish wash on sides

• **SONG** Shrill hissing or piercing whistle in display flight. Calls include liquid twittering *chip*.

• **BEHAVIOR** Solitary. Feeds and perches at low to middle levels. Eats nectar, insects, spiders, and sap. Hovers to gather nectar from flowers and catches insects in air. Plucks trapped insects and spiders from webs. Often feeds with tail wagging. Frequents desert and arid scrub foothill habitats. Sometimes soars between clumps of flowers.

white underparts

FEMALE

Similar Birds

BLACK-CHINNED HUMMINGBIRD ♀
Larger; greener upperparts; grayer underparts; voice differs.

ANNA'S HUMMINGBIRD ♀
Larger; green upperparts; gray underparts with greenish wash on sides; white tips on outer three tail feathers; straight black bill; red on throat.

• **BREEDING** Polygamous. Solitary.
• **NESTING** Incubation 15–18 days by female. Altricial young stay in nest 20–23 days, fed by female. Males often leave late-nesting females still incubating eggs to avoid heat of summer. 1 brood per year.
• **POPULATION** Fairly common. Casual to western Texas and northward to southern Alaska.

• **FEEDERS** Sugar water.
• **CONSERVATION** Neotropical migrant. Development of desert habitats for housing and agriculture could be potentially harmful to overall population.

Flight Pattern

Moves swiftly from place to place on a whir of wings. Hovers, moving in all directions while feeding.

Nest Identification

Shape ▽   Location 🪹 🌱 🌳

Plant down, forb leaves, bud scales, flowers, and bark strips, bound with spider silk • on fork of tree, shrub, yucca, or dead cactus • 3–9 feet above ground • built by female • 2 white eggs; elliptical to oval, with occasional tendency toward elliptical ovate, 0.5 x 0.3 inches.

Plumage Sexes differ	Habitat ⚤ 🌾 🌿 ✈	Migration Migratory	Weight 0.1 ounce

DATE _____ TIME_____ LOCATION _____

Family TROCHILIDAE	Species *Stellula calliope*	Length 2.75–3.25 inches	Wingspan 4.25 inches

CALLIOPE HUMMINGBIRD

This is the smallest bird north of Mexico. As the female incubates her eggs in the extreme cold of the high mountains, she does not become torpid but is able to maintain her body heat from the insulation in the nest and by remaining at rest. In addition to the small size, note the short black bill and the short tail.

• **SONG** Relatively silent. High shrill sharp chips, *si tsi-tsi, tsi-tsi*, repeated.

• **BEHAVIOR** Solitary. Often dominated by other hummingbirds at flowers. Hovers over low flowers to feed and snatches insects in midair. Plucks insects and spiders from web and also drinks sap from holes drilled by sapsuckers. Hardy; inhabits open coniferous, montane forests and mountain meadows. Courting males fly in huge U-shaped pattern in front of the female, rising as high as 65 feet before darting back down to repeat the pattern. Gives high-pitched *bzzt* note at bottom of dive.

• **BREEDING** Polygamous. Solitary.

• **NESTING** Incubation 15–16 days by female. Young stay in nest 18–23 days, fed by female. 1 brood per year, although may possibly have 2 broods.

• **POPULATION** Common. Rare in the Southeast in fall and in winter.

• **FEEDERS** Will come to feeders filled with sugar water.

• **CONSERVATION** Neotropical migrant. Vulnerable to loss of habitat.

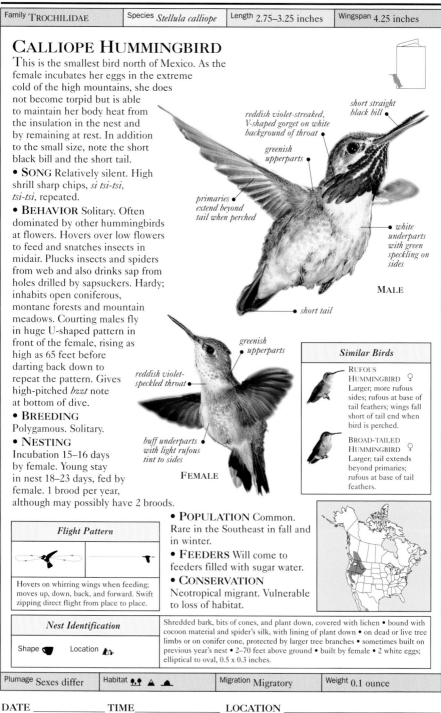

reddish violet-streaked, V-shaped gorget on white background of throat

greenish upperparts

short straight black bill

primaries extend beyond tail when perched

white underparts with green speckling on sides

MALE

short tail

greenish upperparts

reddish violet-speckled throat

buff underparts with light rufous tint to sides

FEMALE

Similar Birds

RUFOUS HUMMINGBIRD ♀
Larger; more rufous sides; rufous at base of tail feathers; wings fall short of tail end when bird is perched.

BROAD-TAILED HUMMINGBIRD ♀
Larger; tail extends beyond primaries; rufous at base of tail feathers.

Flight Pattern

Hovers on whirring wings when feeding; moves up, down, back, and forward. Swift zipping direct flight from place to place.

Nest Identification	Shredded bark, bits of cones, and plant down, covered with lichen • bound with cocoon material and spider's silk, with lining of plant down • on dead or live tree limbs or on conifer cone, protected by larger tree branches • sometimes built on previous year's nest • 2–70 feet above ground • built by female • 2 white eggs; elliptical to oval, 0.5 x 0.3 inches.
Shape ◥ Location 🐾	

Plumage Sexes differ	Habitat 🌿 ⛰ 🌲	Migration Migratory	Weight 0.1 ounce

DATE _____ TIME_____ LOCATION _____

Family TROCHILIDAE	Species *Selasphorus platycercus*	Length 4–4.5 inches	Wingspan 5 inches

BROAD-TAILED HUMMINGBIRD

The male's wings produce a unique trilling sound when the bird is in flight. The buzzing whistle sound is produced by air rushing through the slots created by the finely tapered tips of the male's outer primaries. Dwelling in the Rocky Mountains and outlying mountain ranges, it can be seen bathing in the shallow waters of mountain streams or defending its territory of flower patches from other hummingbirds. When perched the wings extend beyond the tail tip.

• **SONG** Fairly sharp but not hard, repeated *chip; chitter chitter chitter*; no song. In display makes high thin slurred *szzzzzziiuu*.

• **BEHAVIOR** Solitary. Feeds and perches at low to middle levels in open pine and pine-oak woodlands and edges. Eats nectar, insects, spiders, and sap. Hovers with tail closed, rarely flashed open or wagged, to feed on nectar and catch insects in flight. Plucks insects and spiders from spider webs. Like other hummers, eats sap from holes drilled by sapsuckers. In display flight male flies in U-shaped pattern in front of female, diving 30–50 feet; both sexes may ascend together to 90–100 feet, with one 4–5 feet beneath the other, before diving back down again.

• **BREEDING** Promiscuous. Solitary nester.

• **NESTING** Incubation 14–17 days by female. Young stay in nest 21–26 days. Fed by female. 1–2 broods per year.

• **POPULATION** Common in summer in mountains. Casual in autumn and winter in Gulf Coast states.

• **FEEDERS** Sugar water.

• **CONSERVATION** Neotropical migrant.

rose-red gorget

iridescent green upperparts

long straight black bill

green sides

gray underparts gradually become white near throat

MALE

green upperparts

bronze dots on throat

buff underparts

FEMALE

white-tipped outer tail feathers have rufous base

rufous sides

Similar Birds

CALLIOPE HUMMINGBIRD ♀ Female is smaller; wing tips extend beyond short tail; lighter rufous tint on sides; no rufous in bases of tail feathers; shorter bill.

Flight Pattern

Hovers when feeding, moving in all directions in a blur of rapidly beating wings. Swift dashing direct flight from point to point.

Nest Identification

Shape   Location

Plant down and bound with spider webs; exterior made of lichens, bark shreds, and leaves • on horizontal tree branch or occasionally in fork; often near or over mountain streams; 4–15 feet above ground • built by female • 2 white eggs; elliptical-oval or subelliptical, 0.5 x 0.34 inches.

Plumage Sexes differ	Habitat	Migration Migratory	Weight 0.1 ounce

DATE _____ TIME_____ LOCATION _____

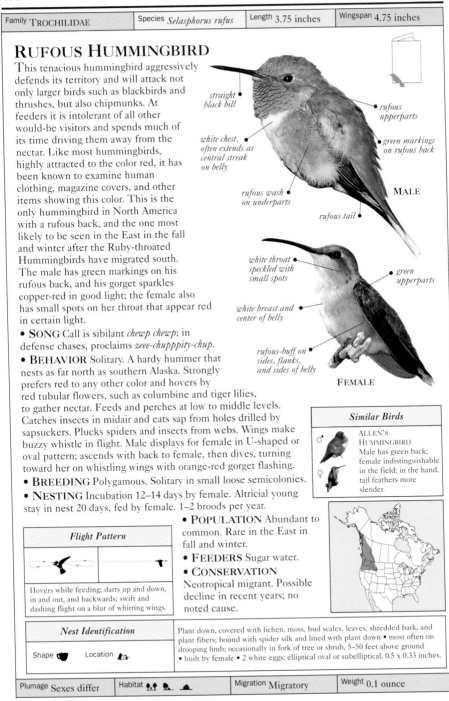

| Family TROCHILIDAE | Species *Selasphorus rufus* | Length 3.75 inches | Wingspan 4.75 inches |

RUFOUS HUMMINGBIRD

This tenacious hummingbird aggressively defends its territory and will attack not only larger birds such as blackbirds and thrushes, but also chipmunks. At feeders it is intolerant of all other would-be visitors and spends much of its time driving them away from the nectar. Like most hummingbirds, highly attracted to the color red, it has been known to examine human clothing, magazine covers, and other items showing this color. This is the only hummingbird in North America with a rufous back, and the one most likely to be seen in the East in the fall and winter after the Ruby-throated Hummingbirds have migrated south. The male has green markings on his rufous back, and his gorget sparkles copper-red in good light; the female also has small spots on her throat that appear red in certain light.

straight black bill

white chest, often extends as central streak on belly

rufous wash on underparts

rufous upperparts

green markings on rufous back

MALE

rufous tail

white throat speckled with small spots

green upperparts

white breast and center of belly

rufous-buff on sides, flanks, and sides of belly

FEMALE

• **SONG** Call is sibilant *chewp chewp*; in defense chases, proclaims *zeee-chupppity-chup*.
• **BEHAVIOR** Solitary. A hardy hummer that nests as far north as southern Alaska. Strongly prefers red to any other color and hovers by red tubular flowers, such as columbine and tiger lilies, to gather nectar. Feeds and perches at low to middle levels. Catches insects in midair and eats sap from holes drilled by sapsuckers. Plucks spiders and insects from webs. Wings make buzzy whistle in flight. Male displays for female in U-shaped or oval pattern; ascends with back to female, then dives, turning toward her on whistling wings with orange-red gorget flashing.
• **BREEDING** Polygamous. Solitary in small loose semicolonies.
• **NESTING** Incubation 12–14 days by female. Altricial young stay in nest 20 days, fed by female. 1–2 broods per year.

Similar Birds

ALLEN'S HUMMINGBIRD
Male has green back; female indistinguishable in the field; in the hand, tail feathers more slender.

• **POPULATION** Abundant to common. Rare in the East in fall and winter.
• **FEEDERS** Sugar water.
• **CONSERVATION** Neotropical migrant. Possible decline in recent years; no noted cause.

Flight Pattern

Hovers while feeding; darts up and down, in and out, and backwards; swift and dashing flight on a blur of whirring wings.

Nest Identification	
Shape	Location	Plant down, covered with lichen, moss, bud scales, leaves, shredded bark, and plant fibers; bound with spider silk and lined with plant down • most often on drooping limb; occasionally in fork of tree or shrub, 5–50 feet above ground • built by female • 2 white eggs; elliptical oval or subelliptical, 0.5 x 0.33 inches.

| Plumage Sexes differ | Habitat | Migration Migratory | Weight 0.1 ounce |

DATE _____ TIME_____ LOCATION _____

Family TROCHILIDAE	Species *Selasphorus sasin*	Length 3.75 inches	Wingspan 4.75 inches

ALLEN'S HUMMINGBIRD

When defending its territory this diminutive bird will attack many birds, including large hawks. Highly adaptable, it can be found in suburban gardens and parks in its range. Males appear similar to the Rufous Hummingbird but have a green back; females and juveniles are inseparable from the Rufous in the field. Allen's is often found in drier habitats, including chaparral and thickets, than the Rufous.

• **SONG** Utters sharp *chip* or series of *chips* similar to voice of Rufous Hummingbird.

• **BEHAVIOR** Solitary. Gathers nectar from flowers and catches insects in midair. Also plucks insects and spiders from webs. Eats sap from sapsucker holes. In courtship display male flies in J-shaped pattern: He ascends 75–80 feet and dives on whistling wings to the level of the perched female, then ascends about 25 feet on the other side of the arc and hovers, with his gorget glittering in the sun. Begins with pendulum-like, side-to-side display. Males may depart breeding areas a month or more before females depart.

• **BREEDING** Promiscuous. Solitary nester. Semicolonial, with nests often clustered.

• **NESTING** Incubation 15–22 days by female. Young stay in nest 22–25 days. Fed by female. 2 broods per year.

• **POPULATION** Common to fairly common. Casual to rare vagrant in the East in autumn migration and winter.

• **FEEDERS** Sugar water.

• **CONSERVATION** Declining because of habitat loss.

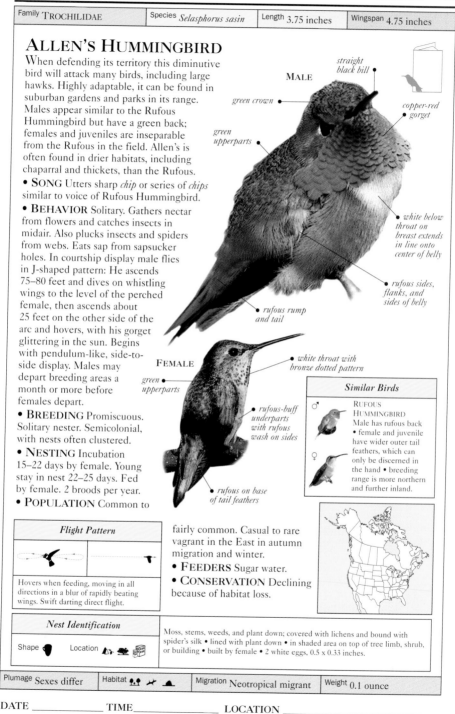

MALE

straight black bill

green crown

copper-red gorget

green upperparts

white below throat on breast extends in line onto center of belly

rufous sides, flanks, and sides of belly

rufous rump and tail

FEMALE

green upperparts

white throat with bronze dotted pattern

rufous-buff underparts with rufous wash on sides

rufous on base of tail feathers

Similar Birds

RUFOUS HUMMINGBIRD
Male has rufous back • female and juvenile have wider outer tail feathers, which can only be discerned in the hand • breeding range is more northern and further inland.

Flight Pattern

Hovers when feeding, moving in all directions in a blur of rapidly beating wings. Swift darting direct flight.

Nest Identification

Shape Location

Moss, stems, weeds, and plant down; covered with lichens and bound with spider's silk • lined with plant down • in shaded area on top of tree limb, shrub, or building • built by female • 2 white eggs, 0.5 x 0.33 inches.

Plumage Sexes differ	Habitat	Migration Neotropical migrant	Weight 0.1 ounce

DATE _____ TIME_____ LOCATION _____

| Family TROGONIDAE | Species *Trogon elegans* | Length 11–12.5 inches | Wingspan 18–22 inches |

ELEGANT TROGON

More often heard than seen, this bird has a habit of sitting practically motionless for long periods of time in or just below the canopy. Its posture is erect, with the long tail pointing straight down. Plumage features a unique combination of pink (female) to deep red (male) underparts and a tail that is white below with narrow black vermiculations and black terminal band.

- **SONG** Series of hoarse, throaty, downslurred *k'row'hr* notes repeated 5–10 times, then a pause before the next series.
- **BEHAVIOR** Often sits quietly for long periods in sycamores and oaks in wooded mountain canyons, particularly in the vicinity of streams. Feeds on insects, berries, and fruits, which it often gathers by sallying or by hovering beneath vegetation. Often vocal in early morning, with calls carrying long distances in mountain canyons. Often allows fairly close approach.
- **BREEDING** Monogamous. Solitary.
- **NESTING** Incubation 22–23 days by both sexes. Altricial young stay in nest 20–23 days. Fed by both sexes.
- **POPULATION** US population small and local. Accidental to casual in south Texas.
- **CONSERVATION** Vulnerable to habitat loss by deforestation, as well as to disturbance by observers while nesting, especially if playback voice recordings are used to attract territorial birds.

red ring around eye

deep glistening green head, breast, and upperparts

short, thick yellow bill

white band separates breast from belly

MALE

deep red belly, sides, flanks, and undertail coverts

brown head and upperparts

white undertail with blackish gray vermiculations

pale brownish white lower breast

downward-curved white patch behind eye

brown upper breast

black terminal band

white bar crosses breast

pinkish belly, sides, flanks, and undertail coverts

FEMALE

Similar Birds

EARED TROGON
Larger; dark bill; larger patch of white on blue-black tail; no white band across breast • no white patch behind ear of female • does not stray into southeast Texas.

Flight Pattern

Slow undulating flight, but rapid when bird is pressed.

Nest Identification

Shape ▨² Location 🌳 🪹 🕳

Hay, straw, trash, mosses, wool, feathers, and thistle down with little or no lining • inside natural cavity of large streamside trees such as sycamores or in deserted woodpecker hole • 12–40 feet above ground • 3–4 white eggs; rounded ovate to oval; 1.14 x 0.9 inches.

| Plumage Sexes differ | Habitat 🌿 | Migration Most do not migrate | Weight 2.4 ounces |

DATE _____ TIME_____ LOCATION _____

Family TROGONIDAE	Species *Euptilotis neoxenus*	Length 13–14.25 inches	Wingspan 20–24 inches

EARED TROGON

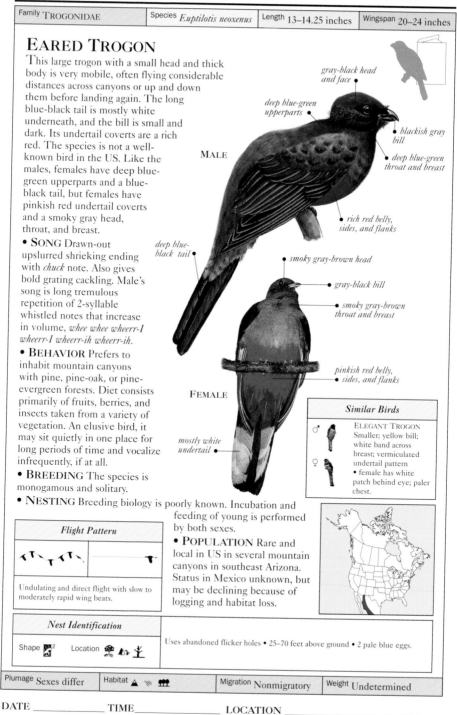

This large trogon with a small head and thick body is very mobile, often flying considerable distances across canyons or up and down them before landing again. The long blue-black tail is mostly white underneath, and the bill is small and dark. Its undertail coverts are a rich red. The species is not a well-known bird in the US. Like the males, females have deep blue-green upperparts and a blue-black tail, but females have pinkish red undertail coverts and a smoky gray head, throat, and breast.

gray-black head and face

deep blue-green upperparts

MALE

blackish gray bill

deep blue-green throat and breast

rich red belly, sides, and flanks

deep blue-black tail

smoky gray-brown head

gray-black bill

smoky gray-brown throat and breast

pinkish red belly, sides, and flanks

FEMALE

mostly white undertail

• **SONG** Drawn-out upslurred shrieking ending with *chuck* note. Also gives bold grating cackling. Male's song is long tremulous repetition of 2-syllable whistled notes that increase in volume, *whee whee wheerr-I wheerr-I wheerr-ih wheerr-ih.*

• **BEHAVIOR** Prefers to inhabit mountain canyons with pine, pine-oak, or pine-evergreen forests. Diet consists primarily of fruits, berries, and insects taken from a variety of vegetation. An elusive bird, it may sit quietly in one place for long periods of time and vocalize infrequently, if at all.

• **BREEDING** The species is monogamous and solitary.

• **NESTING** Breeding biology is poorly known. Incubation and feeding of young is performed by both sexes.

• **POPULATION** Rare and local in US in several mountain canyons in southeast Arizona. Status in Mexico unknown, but may be declining because of logging and habitat loss.

Similar Birds

♂ ELEGANT TROGON Smaller; yellow bill; white band across breast; vermiculated undertail pattern
♀ • female has white patch behind eye; paler chest.

Flight Pattern

Undulating and direct flight with slow to moderately rapid wing beats.

Nest Identification

Shape   Location   Uses abandoned flicker holes • 25–70 feet above ground • 2 pale blue eggs.

Plumage Sexes differ	Habitat	Migration Nonmigratory	Weight Undetermined

DATE _____ TIME_____ LOCATION _____

Family ALCEDINIDAE	Species *Ceryle torquata*	Length 16.5 inches	Wingspan 24–29 inches

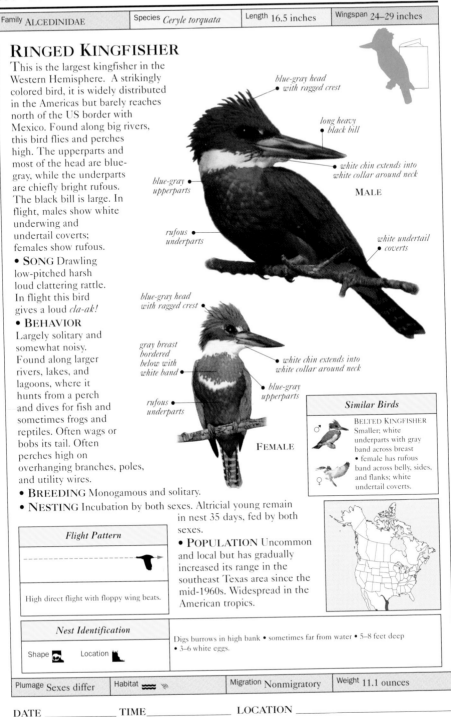

RINGED KINGFISHER

This is the largest kingfisher in the Western Hemisphere. A strikingly colored bird, it is widely distributed in the Americas but barely reaches north of the US border with Mexico. Found along big rivers, this bird flies and perches high. The upperparts and most of the head are blue-gray, while the underparts are chiefly bright rufous. The black bill is large. In flight, males show white underwing and undertail coverts; females show rufous.

• **SONG** Drawling low-pitched harsh loud clattering rattle. In flight this bird gives a loud *cla-ak!*

• **BEHAVIOR** Largely solitary and somewhat noisy. Found along larger rivers, lakes, and lagoons, where it hunts from a perch and dives for fish and sometimes frogs and reptiles. Often wags or bobs its tail. Often perches high on overhanging branches, poles, and utility wires.

blue-gray head with ragged crest

long heavy black bill

white chin extends into white collar around neck

MALE

blue-gray upperparts

rufous underparts

white undertail coverts

blue-gray head with ragged crest

gray breast bordered below with white band

white chin extends into white collar around neck

blue-gray upperparts

rufous underparts

FEMALE

Similar Birds

BELTED KINGFISHER Smaller; white underparts with gray band across breast • female has rufous band across belly, sides, and flanks; white undertail coverts.

• **BREEDING** Monogamous and solitary.

• **NESTING** Incubation by both sexes. Altricial young remain in nest 35 days, fed by both sexes.

• **POPULATION** Uncommon and local but has gradually increased its range in the southeast Texas area since the mid-1960s. Widespread in the American tropics.

Flight Pattern

High direct flight with floppy wing beats.

Nest Identification

Shape ▨   Location ▮

Digs burrows in high bank • sometimes far from water • 5–8 feet deep • 3–6 white eggs.

Plumage Sexes differ	Habitat 〰 〰	Migration Nonmigratory	Weight 11.1 ounces

DATE _____ TIME_____ LOCATION _____

Family ALCEDINIDAE	Species *Ceryle alcyon*	Length 11–14.5 inches	Wingspan 22–26 inches

BELTED KINGFISHER

Widely distributed and common along freshwater bodies of water as well as the coast, this is the only kingfisher across most of its range, except along the Mexican border. It is one of the few North American birds in which the female is more colorful than the male. The male has blue-gray upperparts with a blue-gray band across the breast and appears big-headed with its large bill and ragged crest. In flight it shows a white patch on the upperwing at the base of the primaries.

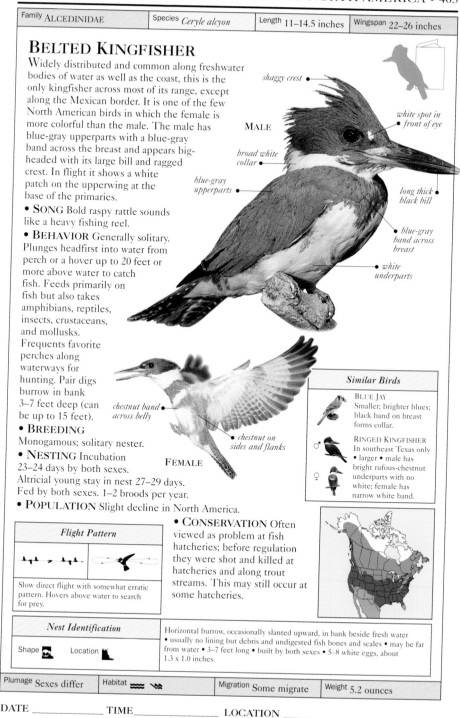

shaggy crest

MALE

white spot in front of eye

broad white collar

blue-gray upperparts

long thick black bill

blue-gray band across breast

white underparts

• **SONG** Bold raspy rattle sounds like a heavy fishing reel.
• **BEHAVIOR** Generally solitary. Plunges headfirst into water from perch or a hover up to 20 feet or more above water to catch fish. Feeds primarily on fish but also takes amphibians, reptiles, insects, crustaceans, and mollusks. Frequents favorite perches along waterways for hunting. Pair digs burrow in bank 3–7 feet deep (can be up to 15 feet).

chestnut band across belly

chestnut on sides and flanks

FEMALE

• **BREEDING** Monogamous; solitary nester.
• **NESTING** Incubation 23–24 days by both sexes. Altricial young stay in nest 27–29 days. Fed by both sexes. 1–2 broods per year.
• **POPULATION** Slight decline in North America.

Similar Birds

BLUE JAY
Smaller; brighter blues; black band on breast forms collar.

RINGED KINGFISHER
In southeast Texas only • larger • male has bright rufous-chestnut underparts with no white; female has narrow white band.

• **CONSERVATION** Often viewed as problem at fish hatcheries; before regulation they were shot and killed at hatcheries and along trout streams. This may still occur at some hatcheries.

Flight Pattern

Slow direct flight with somewhat erratic pattern. Hovers above water to search for prey.

Nest Identification

Shape ▢   Location ▲

Horizontal burrow, occasionally slanted upward, in bank beside fresh water • usually no lining but debris and undigested fish bones and scales • may be far from water • 3–7 feet long • built by both sexes • 5–8 white eggs, about 1.3 x 1.0 inches.

Plumage Sexes differ	Habitat 〰 〰	Migration Some migrate	Weight 5.2 ounces

DATE _____ TIME_____ LOCATION _____

Family ALCEDINIDAE	Species *Chloroceryle americana*	Length 8.75 inches	Wingspan 11–13 inches

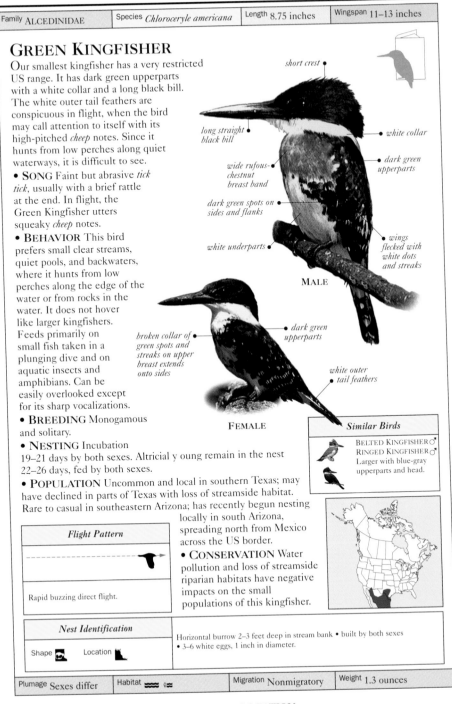

GREEN KINGFISHER

Our smallest kingfisher has a very restricted US range. It has dark green upperparts with a white collar and a long black bill. The white outer tail feathers are conspicuous in flight, when the bird may call attention to itself with its high-pitched *cheep* notes. Since it hunts from low perches along quiet waterways, it is difficult to see.

• **SONG** Faint but abrasive *tick tick*, usually with a brief rattle at the end. In flight, the Green Kingfisher utters squeaky *cheep* notes.

• **BEHAVIOR** This bird prefers small clear streams, quiet pools, and backwaters, where it hunts from low perches along the edge of the water or from rocks in the water. It does not hover like larger kingfishers. Feeds primarily on small fish taken in a plunging dive and on aquatic insects and amphibians. Can be easily overlooked except for its sharp vocalizations.

• **BREEDING** Monogamous and solitary.

• **NESTING** Incubation 19–21 days by both sexes. Altricial young remain in the nest 22–26 days, fed by both sexes.

• **POPULATION** Uncommon and local in southern Texas; may have declined in parts of Texas with loss of streamside habitat. Rare to casual in southeastern Arizona; has recently begun nesting locally in south Arizona, spreading north from Mexico across the US border.

• **CONSERVATION** Water pollution and loss of streamside riparian habitats have negative impacts on the small populations of this kingfisher.

short crest

long straight black bill

wide rufous-chestnut breast band

dark green spots on sides and flanks

white underparts

white collar

dark green upperparts

wings flecked with white dots and streaks

MALE

broken collar of green spots and streaks on upper breast extends onto sides

dark green upperparts

white outer tail feathers

FEMALE

Similar Birds
BELTED KINGFISHER ♂ RINGED KINGFISHER ♂ Larger with blue-gray upperparts and head.

Flight Pattern

Rapid buzzing direct flight.

Nest Identification

Shape ▢   Location ▢

Horizontal burrow 2–3 feet deep in stream bank • built by both sexes • 3–6 white eggs, 1 inch in diameter.

Plumage Sexes differ	Habitat 〰 ⫴	Migration Nonmigratory	Weight 1.3 ounces

DATE _____ TIME_____ LOCATION _____

Family PICIDAE	Species *Melanerpes lewis*	Length 10–11.5 inches	Wingspan 20–21 inches

LEWIS'S WOODPECKER

Discovered by and named for Meriwether Lewis of the Lewis and Clark expedition of 1803–1806, this bird often is mistaken for a crow in flight because of its overall blackish appearance and its direct flight pattern, which is unlike most woodpeckers. It is the only North American woodpecker that is mostly black with iridescent green highlights and a pinkish belly. In flight it shows a blackish green crissum. The female is similar to the male but smaller. Juveniles have a brownish head and underparts and lack the gray collar, red face, and pink belly.

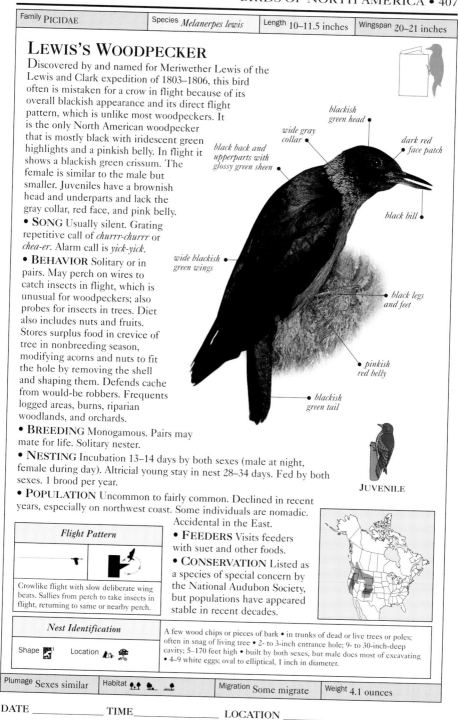

blackish green head

wide gray collar

dark red face patch

black back and upperparts with glossy green sheen

black bill

wide blackish green wings

black legs and feet

pinkish red belly

blackish green tail

JUVENILE

• **SONG** Usually silent. Grating repetitive call of *churrr-churrr* or *chea-er*. Alarm call is *yick-yick*.

• **BEHAVIOR** Solitary or in pairs. May perch on wires to catch insects in flight, which is unusual for woodpeckers; also probes for insects in trees. Diet also includes nuts and fruits. Stores surplus food in crevice of tree in nonbreeding season, modifying acorns and nuts to fit the hole by removing the shell and shaping them. Defends cache from would-be robbers. Frequents logged areas, burns, riparian woodlands, and orchards.

• **BREEDING** Monogamous. Pairs may mate for life. Solitary nester.

• **NESTING** Incubation 13–14 days by both sexes (male at night, female during day). Altricial young stay in nest 28–34 days. Fed by both sexes. 1 brood per year.

• **POPULATION** Uncommon to fairly common. Declined in recent years, especially on northwest coast. Some individuals are nomadic. Accidental in the East.

• **FEEDERS** Visits feeders with suet and other foods.

• **CONSERVATION** Listed as a species of special concern by the National Audubon Society, but populations have appeared stable in recent decades.

Flight Pattern
Crowlike flight with slow deliberate wing beats. Sallies from perch to take insects in flight, returning to same or nearby perch.

Nest Identification	
Shape ▨ Location ▲▲ 🌲	A few wood chips or pieces of bark • in trunks of dead or live trees or poles; often in snag of living tree • 2- to 3-inch entrance hole; 9- to 30-inch-deep cavity; 5–170 feet high • built by both sexes, but male does most of excavating • 4–9 white eggs; oval to elliptical, 1 inch in diameter.

Plumage Sexes similar	Habitat ♠♠ ♠♠ ♠	Migration Some migrate	Weight 4.1 ounces

DATE _____ TIME_____ LOCATION _____

| Family PICIDAE | Species *Melanerpes erythrocephalus* | Length 8.5–9.25 inches | Wingspan 16–18 inches |

RED-HEADED WOODPECKER

The ecological eastern counterpart of Lewis's Woodpecker, this is the only woodpecker in the East with an entirely red head. Unlike many other woodpeckers, the Red-headed Woodpecker catches most of its food in flight, from the ground, or by gleaning it from tree trunks and limbs; it rarely bores holes in trees to probe for insects. The male does, however, vigorously drill its nest cavity with the aid of its mate. In flight the white underparts, white rump, and large white secondary patches contrast sharply with the black tail, wings, and back. Juveniles have brownish black upperparts and brown heads.

- **SONG** Fairly noisy. In breeding season has bold grating *queark* or *queer, queer, queer*. Also sounds like a chicken clucking, *kerr-uck, kerr-uck*.
- **BEHAVIOR** Solitary or in pairs. Eats various insects, spiders, millipedes, and centipedes; sometimes takes eggs and young of other birds, mice, corn, grains, various nuts, and berries. Often hunts from low perches, flying to ground to pick up prey or nut. Caches acorns and nuts, removing shells and storing the meat for winter.
- **BREEDING** Monogamous. Solitary nester.
- **NESTING** Incubation 12–14 days by both sexes. Altricial young stay in nest 27–31 days. Fed by both sexes. 1–2 broods per year.
- **POPULATION** Uncommon and declining. Casual to accidental west of the Rocky Mountains.
- **FEEDERS AND BIRDHOUSES** Suet, sunflower seeds, cracked corn, raisins, nuts, and bread. Some will nest in birdhouse built for woodpeckers.
- **CONSERVATION** Listed as species of special concern by National Audubon Society. Decline in past century due to habitat loss, collisions with automobiles, and competition for nesting cavities with European Starling. Creosote-coated utility poles are lethal to eggs and young.

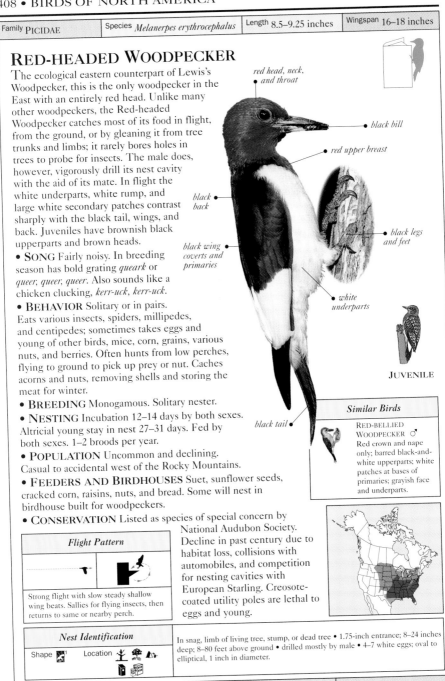

red head, neck, and throat

black bill

red upper breast

black back

black legs and feet

black wing coverts and primaries

white underparts

JUVENILE

black tail

Similar Birds

RED-BELLIED WOODPECKER ♂ Red crown and nape only; barred black-and-white upperparts; white patches at bases of primaries; grayish face and underparts.

Flight Pattern

Strong flight with slow steady shallow wing beats. Sallies for flying insects, then returns to same or nearby perch.

Nest Identification

Shape ___   Location ___

In snag, limb of living tree, stump, or dead tree • 1.75-inch entrance; 8–24 inches deep; 8–80 feet above ground • drilled mostly by male • 4–7 white eggs; oval to elliptical, 1 inch in diameter.

| Plumage Sexes similar | Habitat ___ | Migration Some migrate | Weight 2.5 ounces |

DATE _____ TIME _____ LOCATION _____

Family PICIDAE	Species *Melanerpes formicivorus*	Length 9 inches	Wingspan 17 inches

ACORN WOODPECKER

This noisy sociable woodpecker is found where oaks are plentiful in the southwestern US and along the Pacific Coast from Baja California to Washington. Its colorful face pattern is clownlike, with bright contrasting splashes of white, black, red, and yellow set around a pale yellow-white eye. In flight white patches show on each wing and the rump. In appearance, the females differ from the male only in their bicolor crown, which is black in front and red in the back.

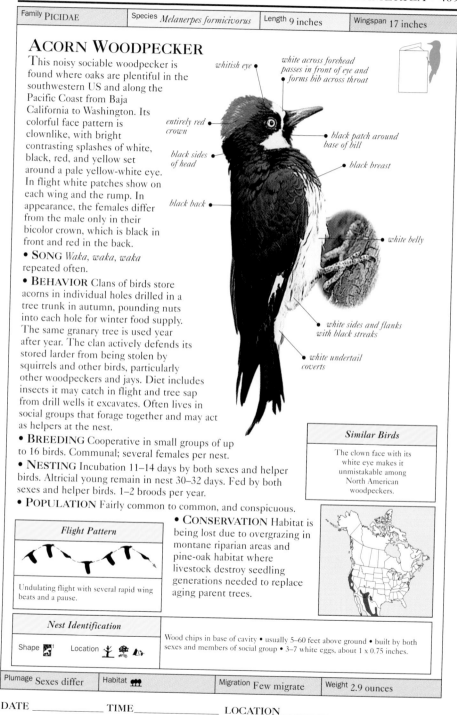

whitish eye

white across forehead passes in front of eye and forms bib across throat

entirely red crown

black sides of head

black back

black patch around base of bill

black breast

white belly

white sides and flanks with black streaks

white undertail coverts

• **SONG** *Waka, waka, waka* repeated often.

• **BEHAVIOR** Clans of birds store acorns in individual holes drilled in a tree trunk in autumn, pounding nuts into each hole for winter food supply. The same granary tree is used year after year. The clan actively defends its stored larder from being stolen by squirrels and other birds, particularly other woodpeckers and jays. Diet includes insects it may catch in flight and tree sap from drill wells it excavates. Often lives in social groups that forage together and may act as helpers at the nest.

• **BREEDING** Cooperative in small groups of up to 16 birds. Communal; several females per nest.

• **NESTING** Incubation 11–14 days by both sexes and helper birds. Altricial young remain in nest 30–32 days. Fed by both sexes and helper birds. 1–2 broods per year.

• **POPULATION** Fairly common to common, and conspicuous.

Similar Birds

The clown face with its white eye makes it unmistakable among North American woodpeckers.

• **CONSERVATION** Habitat is being lost due to overgrazing in montane riparian areas and pine-oak habitat where livestock destroy seedling generations needed to replace aging parent trees.

Flight Pattern

Undulating flight with several rapid wing beats and a pause.

Nest Identification

Shape   Location

Wood chips in base of cavity • usually 5–60 feet above ground • built by both sexes and members of social group • 3–7 white eggs, about 1 x 0.75 inches.

Plumage Sexes differ	Habitat	Migration Few migrate	Weight 2.9 ounces

DATE _____ TIME_____ LOCATION _____

| Family PICIDAE | Species *Melanerpes uropygialis* | Length 8–10 inches | Wingspan 15–18 inches |

GILA WOODPECKER

An important member of the cactus-scrub community, the Gila Woodpecker's abandoned nesting and roost holes are used by other birds, reptiles, and small mammals. This is the only "zebra-backed" woodpecker in its range with black-and-white barring on all its upperparts down through its two central tail feathers. In flight a white patch shows at the base of the primary wing feathers near the tip.

• **SONG** Trilled *churr* and loud abrasive high-pitched *yip* or *pit*, often in series.

• **BEHAVIOR** Hawks for insects. Noisy, conspicuous bird that attracts attention.

• **BREEDING** Monogamous. Solitary nester.

• **NESTING** Incubation 12–14 days by both sexes. Young stay in nest 4 weeks. Fed by both parents for many weeks after leaving nest. 2–3 broods each year. Accepts presence of people and often nests close to human dwellings.

• **POPULATION** This bird's numbers are not known to be decreasing in Arizona; however, significant population reductions have been recorded in the California deserts.

• **FEEDERS** Will attend feeders for suet or other meat, as well as for fruits ranging from grapes to watermelon.

red cap

fawn-gray head

MALE

fawn-gray underparts

black-and-white barring on upperparts

black-and-white barring

FEMALE

Flight Pattern

Undulating flight with several wing beats and a pause.

Nest Identification

Shape   Location

Most often in saguaro cactus • 15–25 feet above ground • built by both sexes • 3–5 white eggs, 1 inch in diameter.

| Plumage Sexes differ | Habitat | Migration Mostly nonmigratory | Weight 2.5 ounces |

DATE _____ TIME_____ LOCATION _____

Family PICIDAE	Species *Melanerpes aurifrons*	Length 8.5–10 inches	Wingspan 16–18 inches

GOLDEN-FRONTED WOODPECKER

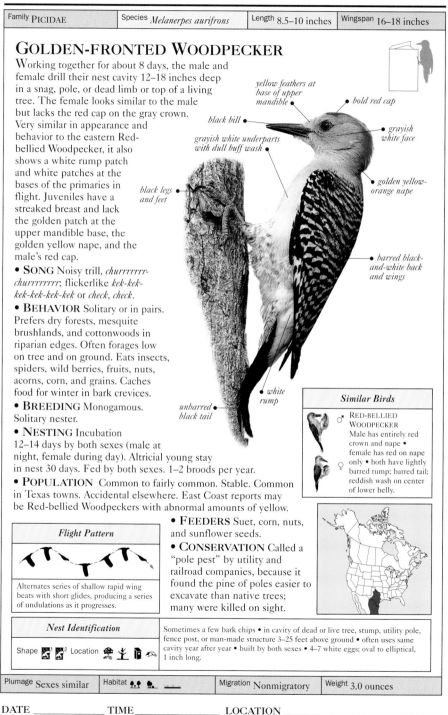

Working together for about 8 days, the male and female drill their nest cavity 12–18 inches deep in a snag, pole, or dead limb or top of a living tree. The female looks similar to the male but lacks the red cap on the gray crown. Very similar in appearance and behavior to the eastern Red-bellied Woodpecker, it also shows a white rump patch and white patches at the bases of the primaries in flight. Juveniles have a streaked breast and lack the golden patch at the upper mandible base, the golden yellow nape, and the male's red cap.

yellow feathers at base of upper mandible
bold red cap
black bill
grayish white face
grayish white underparts with dull buff wash
golden yellow-orange nape
black legs and feet
barred black-and-white back and wings
white rump
unbarred black tail

• **SONG** Noisy trill, *churrrrrrr-churrrrrrrr*; flickerlike *kek-kek-kek-kek-kek-kek* or *check, check.*

• **BEHAVIOR** Solitary or in pairs. Prefers dry forests, mesquite brushlands, and cottonwoods in riparian edges. Often forages low on tree and on ground. Eats insects, spiders, wild berries, fruits, nuts, acorns, corn, and grains. Caches food for winter in bark crevices.

• **BREEDING** Monogamous. Solitary nester.

• **NESTING** Incubation 12–14 days by both sexes (male at night, female during day). Altricial young stay in nest 30 days. Fed by both sexes. 1–2 broods per year.

• **POPULATION** Common to fairly common. Stable. Common in Texas towns. Accidental elsewhere. East Coast reports may be Red-bellied Woodpeckers with abnormal amounts of yellow.

• **FEEDERS** Suet, corn, nuts, and sunflower seeds.

• **CONSERVATION** Called a "pole pest" by utility and railroad companies, because it found the pine of poles easier to excavate than native trees; many were killed on sight.

Similar Birds

♂ **RED-BELLIED WOODPECKER** Male has entirely red crown and nape • female has red on nape only • both have lightly barred rump; barred tail; reddish wash on center of lower belly. ♀

Flight Pattern

Alternates series of shallow rapid wing beats with short glides, producing a series of undulations as it progresses.

Nest Identification

Shape [icons] Location [icons]

Sometimes a few bark chips • in cavity of dead or live tree, stump, utility pole, fence post, or man-made structure 3–25 feet above ground • often uses same cavity year after year • built by both sexes • 4–7 white eggs; oval to elliptical, 1 inch long.

Plumage Sexes similar	Habitat [icons]	Migration Nonmigratory	Weight 3.0 ounces

DATE _____ TIME_____ LOCATION _____

Family PICIDAE	Species *Melanerpes carolinus*	Length 9–10.5 inches	Wingspan 15–18 inches

RED-BELLIED WOODPECKER

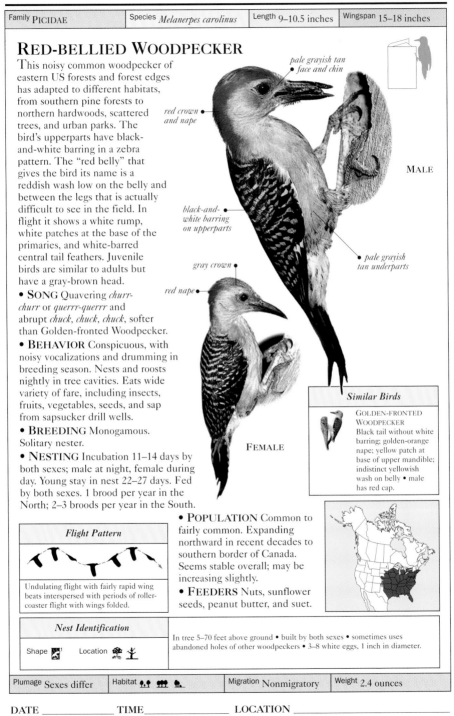

This noisy common woodpecker of eastern US forests and forest edges has adapted to different habitats, from southern pine forests to northern hardwoods, scattered trees, and urban parks. The bird's upperparts have black-and-white barring in a zebra pattern. The "red belly" that gives the bird its name is a reddish wash low on the belly and between the legs that is actually difficult to see in the field. In flight it shows a white rump, white patches at the base of the primaries, and white-barred central tail feathers. Juvenile birds are similar to adults but have a gray-brown head.

- **SONG** Quavering *churr-churr* or *querrr-querrr* and abrupt *chuck, chuck, chuck*, softer than Golden-fronted Woodpecker.
- **BEHAVIOR** Conspicuous, with noisy vocalizations and drumming in breeding season. Nests and roosts nightly in tree cavities. Eats wide variety of fare, including insects, fruits, vegetables, seeds, and sap from sapsucker drill wells.
- **BREEDING** Monogamous. Solitary nester.
- **NESTING** Incubation 11–14 days by both sexes; male at night, female during day. Young stay in nest 22–27 days. Fed by both sexes. 1 brood per year in the North; 2–3 broods per year in the South.

pale grayish tan face and chin

red crown and nape

MALE

black-and-white barring on upperparts

gray crown

red nape

pale grayish tan underparts

FEMALE

Similar Birds

GOLDEN-FRONTED WOODPECKER
Black tail without white barring; golden-orange nape; yellow patch at base of upper mandible; indistinct yellowish wash on belly • male has red cap.

- **POPULATION** Common to fairly common. Expanding northward in recent decades to southern border of Canada. Seems stable overall; may be increasing slightly.
- **FEEDERS** Nuts, sunflower seeds, peanut butter, and suet.

Flight Pattern

Undulating flight with fairly rapid wing beats interspersed with periods of roller-coaster flight with wings folded.

Nest Identification

Shape / Location

In tree 5–70 feet above ground • built by both sexes • sometimes uses abandoned holes of other woodpeckers • 3–8 white eggs, 1 inch in diameter.

Plumage Sexes differ	Habitat	Migration Nonmigratory	Weight 2.4 ounces

DATE _____ TIME_____ LOCATION _____

Family PICIDAE	Species *Sphyrapicus thyroideus*	Length 9 inches	Wingspan 17 inches

WILLIAMSON'S SAPSUCKER

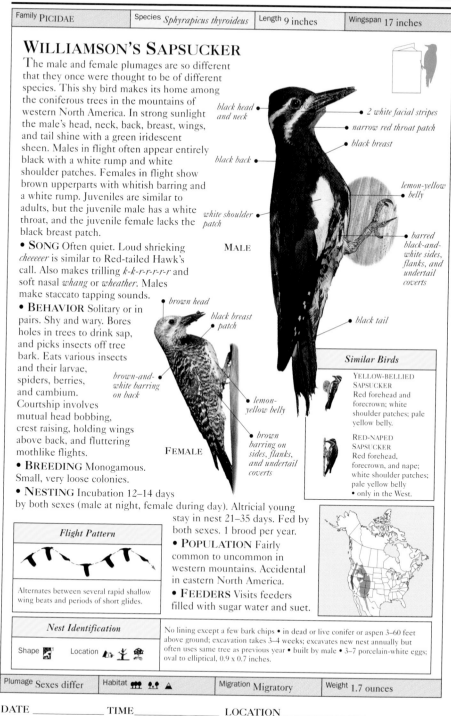

The male and female plumages are so different that they once were thought to be of different species. This shy bird makes its home among the coniferous trees in the mountains of western North America. In strong sunlight the male's head, neck, back, breast, wings, and tail shine with a green iridescent sheen. Males in flight often appear entirely black with a white rump and white shoulder patches. Females in flight show brown upperparts with whitish barring and a white rump. Juveniles are similar to adults, but the juvenile male has a white throat, and the juvenile female lacks the black breast patch.

black head and neck
2 white facial stripes
narrow red throat patch
black breast
black back
lemon-yellow belly
white shoulder patch
MALE
barred black-and-white sides, flanks, and undertail coverts

• **SONG** Often quiet. Loud shrieking *cheeeeer* is similar to Red-tailed Hawk's call. Also makes trilling *k-k-r-r-r-r-r* and soft nasal *whang* or *wheather*. Males make staccato tapping sounds.

• **BEHAVIOR** Solitary or in pairs. Shy and wary. Bores holes in trees to drink sap, and picks insects off tree bark. Eats various insects and their larvae, spiders, berries, and cambium. Courtship involves mutual head bobbing, crest raising, holding wings above back, and fluttering mothlike flights.

brown head
black breast patch
black tail
brown-and-white barring on back
lemon-yellow belly
FEMALE
brown barring on sides, flanks, and undertail coverts

Similar Birds

YELLOW-BELLIED SAPSUCKER
Red forehead and forecrown; white shoulder patches; pale yellow belly.

RED-NAPED SAPSUCKER
Red forehead, forecrown, and nape; white shoulder patches; pale yellow belly
• only in the West.

• **BREEDING** Monogamous. Small, very loose colonies.

• **NESTING** Incubation 12–14 days by both sexes (male at night, female during day). Altricial young stay in nest 21–35 days. Fed by both sexes. 1 brood per year.

• **POPULATION** Fairly common to uncommon in western mountains. Accidental in eastern North America.

• **FEEDERS** Visits feeders filled with sugar water and suet.

Flight Pattern

Alternates between several rapid shallow wing beats and periods of short glides.

Nest Identification

Shape   Location

No lining except a few bark chips • in dead or live conifer or aspen 3–60 feet above ground; excavation takes 3–4 weeks; excavates new nest annually but often uses same tree as previous year • built by male • 3–7 porcelain-white eggs; oval to elliptical, 0.9 x 0.7 inches.

Plumage Sexes differ	Habitat	Migration Migratory	Weight 1.7 ounces

DATE _____ TIME_____ LOCATION _____

| Family PICIDAE | Species *Sphyrapicus varius* | Length 8–9 inches | Wingspan 16–18 inches |

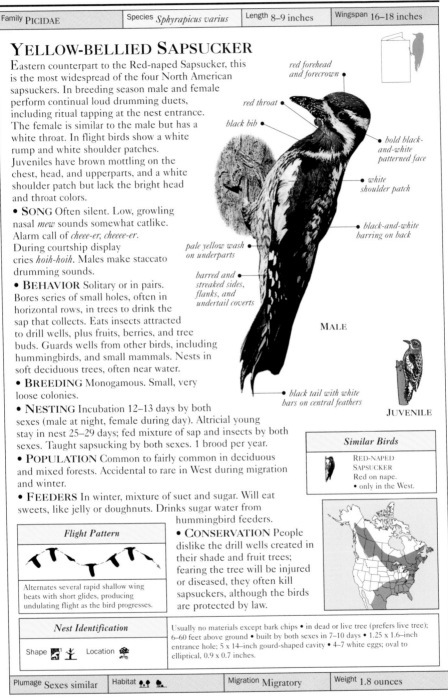

YELLOW-BELLIED SAPSUCKER

Eastern counterpart to the Red-naped Sapsucker, this is the most widespread of the four North American sapsuckers. In breeding season male and female perform continual loud drumming duets, including ritual tapping at the nest entrance. The female is similar to the male but has a white throat. In flight birds show a white rump and white shoulder patches. Juveniles have brown mottling on the chest, head, and upperparts, and a white shoulder patch but lack the bright head and throat colors.

red forehead and forecrown

red throat

black bib

bold black-and-white patterned face

white shoulder patch

black-and-white barring on back

pale yellow wash on underparts

barred and streaked sides, flanks, and undertail coverts

MALE

black tail with white bars on central feathers

JUVENILE

• **SONG** Often silent. Low, growling nasal *mew* sounds somewhat catlike. Alarm call of *cheee-er, cheeee-er*. During courtship display cries *hoih-hoih*. Males make staccato drumming sounds.

• **BEHAVIOR** Solitary or in pairs. Bores series of small holes, often in horizontal rows, in trees to drink the sap that collects. Eats insects attracted to drill wells, plus fruits, berries, and tree buds. Guards wells from other birds, including hummingbirds, and small mammals. Nests in soft deciduous trees, often near water.

• **BREEDING** Monogamous. Small, very loose colonies.

• **NESTING** Incubation 12–13 days by both sexes (male at night, female during day). Altricial young stay in nest 25–29 days; fed mixture of sap and insects by both sexes. Taught sapsucking by both sexes. 1 brood per year.

• **POPULATION** Common to fairly common in deciduous and mixed forests. Accidental to rare in West during migration and winter.

• **FEEDERS** In winter, mixture of suet and sugar. Will eat sweets, like jelly or doughnuts. Drinks sugar water from hummingbird feeders.

Similar Birds

RED-NAPED SAPSUCKER
Red on nape.
• only in the West.

• **CONSERVATION** People dislike the drill wells created in their shade and fruit trees; fearing the tree will be injured or diseased, they often kill sapsuckers, although the birds are protected by law.

Flight Pattern

Alternates several rapid shallow wing beats with short glides, producing undulating flight as the bird progresses.

Nest Identification

Shape 🪹 ⚘ Location 🌳

Usually no materials except bark chips • in dead or live tree (prefers live tree); 6–60 feet above ground • built by both sexes in 7–10 days • 1.25 x 1.6–inch entrance hole; 5 x 14–inch gourd-shaped cavity • 4–7 white eggs; oval to elliptical, 0.9 x 0.7 inches.

| Plumage Sexes similar | Habitat 🌿🌲 | Migration Migratory | Weight 1.8 ounces |

DATE _____ TIME_____ LOCATION _____

Family PICIDAE	Species *Sphyrapicus nuchalis*	Length 8–9 inches	Wingspan 16–18 inches

RED-NAPED SAPSUCKER

South and west of the Rocky Mountains, this is the counterpart to the Yellow-bellied Sapsucker, which it very much resembles. Adept at drilling sap wells, these birds carry sap in their crops to feed their nestlings and teach them to "sapsuck" shortly after fledging. Its white rump patch is conspicuous in flight. Females are similar to males but usually have a whitish chin with variable amounts of red on the throat. Juveniles lack the red head and have brown-mottled upperparts and underparts, but do have the white shoulder patch.

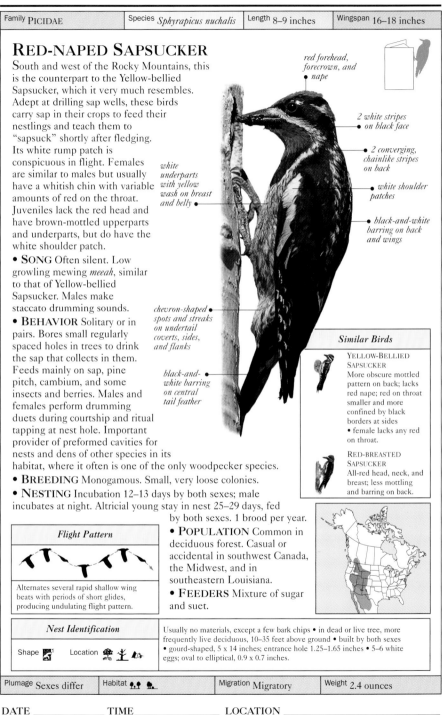

red forehead, forecrown, and nape

2 white stripes on black face

2 converging, chainlike stripes on back

white shoulder patches

black-and-white barring on back and wings

white underparts with yellow wash on breast and belly

chevron-shaped spots and streaks on undertail coverts, sides, and flanks

black-and-white barring on central tail feather

- **SONG** Often silent. Low growling mewing *meeah*, similar to that of Yellow-bellied Sapsucker. Males make staccato drumming sounds.
- **BEHAVIOR** Solitary or in pairs. Bores small regularly spaced holes in trees to drink the sap that collects in them. Feeds mainly on sap, pine pitch, cambium, and some insects and berries. Males and females perform drumming duets during courtship and ritual tapping at nest hole. Important provider of preformed cavities for nests and dens of other species in its habitat, where it often is one of the only woodpecker species.
- **BREEDING** Monogamous. Small, very loose colonies.
- **NESTING** Incubation 12–13 days by both sexes; male incubates at night. Altricial young stay in nest 25–29 days, fed by both sexes. 1 brood per year.
- **POPULATION** Common in deciduous forest. Casual or accidental in southwest Canada, the Midwest, and in southeastern Louisiana.
- **FEEDERS** Mixture of sugar and suet.

Similar Birds

YELLOW-BELLIED SAPSUCKER
More obscure mottled pattern on back; lacks red nape; red on throat smaller and more confined by black borders at sides
- female lacks any red on throat.

RED-BREASTED SAPSUCKER
All-red head, neck, and breast; less mottling and barring on back.

Flight Pattern

Alternates several rapid shallow wing beats with periods of short glides, producing undulating flight pattern.

Nest Identification

Shape | Location

Usually no materials, except a few bark chips • in dead or live tree, more frequently live deciduous, 10–35 feet above ground • built by both sexes • gourd-shaped, 5 x 14 inches; entrance hole 1.25–1.65 inches • 5–6 white eggs; oval to elliptical, 0.9 x 0.7 inches.

Plumage Sexes differ	Habitat	Migration Migratory	Weight 2.4 ounces

DATE _____ TIME_____ LOCATION _____

Family PICIDAE	Species *Sphyrapicus ruber*	Length 8–9 inches	Wingspan 16–18 inches

RED-BREASTED SAPSUCKER

Its bold red hood makes this bird easy to spot as it drills sap wells in trees along the Pacific Coast. It is one of few woodpecker species with identical male and female plumages. This bird often hybridizes with the Red-naped Sapsucker. The amount of white to yellow spotting and barring on the back varies; the southern subspecies has much more white. In flight look for the white rump and white shoulder patches. Juveniles are brownish with little or no red on the head, neck, and breast.

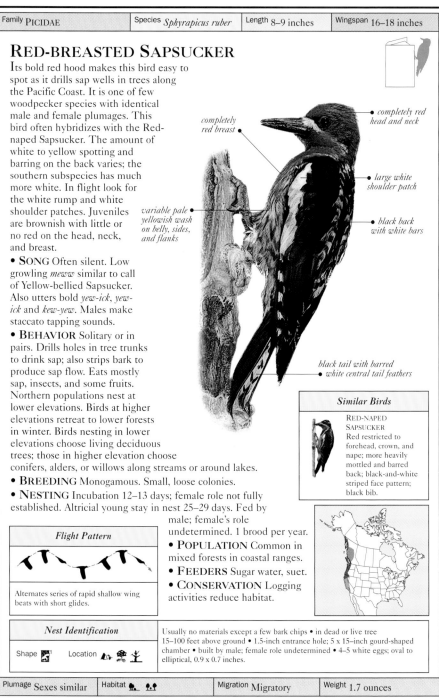

completely red breast

completely red head and neck

large white shoulder patch

variable pale yellowish wash on belly, sides, and flanks

black back with white bars

black tail with barred white central tail feathers

- **SONG** Often silent. Low growling *meww* similar to call of Yellow-bellied Sapsucker. Also utters bold *yew-ick*, *yew-ick* and *kew-yew*. Males make staccato tapping sounds.
- **BEHAVIOR** Solitary or in pairs. Drills holes in tree trunks to drink sap; also strips bark to produce sap flow. Eats mostly sap, insects, and some fruits. Northern populations nest at lower elevations. Birds at higher elevations retreat to lower forests in winter. Birds nesting in lower elevations choose living deciduous trees; those in higher elevation choose conifers, alders, or willows along streams or around lakes.
- **BREEDING** Monogamous. Small, loose colonies.
- **NESTING** Incubation 12–13 days; female role not fully established. Altricial young stay in nest 25–29 days. Fed by male; female's role undetermined. 1 brood per year.
- **POPULATION** Common in mixed forests in coastal ranges.
- **FEEDERS** Sugar water, suet.
- **CONSERVATION** Logging activities reduce habitat.

Similar Birds

RED-NAPED SAPSUCKER Red restricted to forehead, crown, and nape; more heavily mottled and barred back; black-and-white striped face pattern; black bib.

Flight Pattern

Alternates series of rapid shallow wing beats with short glides.

Nest Identification	Usually no materials except a few bark chips • in dead or live tree 15–100 feet above ground • 1.5-inch entrance hole; 5 x 15–inch gourd-shaped chamber • built by male; female role undetermined • 4–5 white eggs; oval to elliptical, 0.9 x 0.7 inches.
Shape ▨ᵈ Location ⬛ 🌳 🌲	

Plumage Sexes similar	Habitat 🌳 🏞	Migration Migratory	Weight 1.7 ounces

DATE _____ TIME _____ LOCATION _____

Family PICIDAE	Species *Picoides scalaris*	Length 7.25 inches	Wingspan 11–12 inches

LADDER-BACKED WOODPECKER

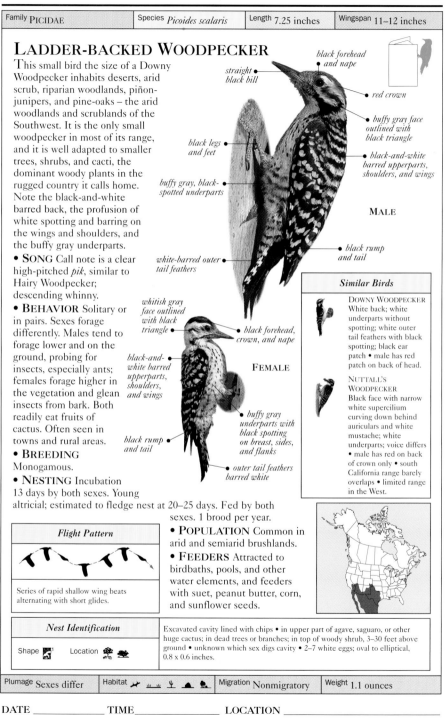

This small bird the size of a Downy Woodpecker inhabits deserts, arid scrub, riparian woodlands, piñon-junipers, and pine-oaks – the arid woodlands and scrublands of the Southwest. It is the only small woodpecker in most of its range, and it is well adapted to smaller trees, shrubs, and cacti, the dominant woody plants in the rugged country it calls home. Note the black-and-white barred back, the profusion of white spotting and barring on the wings and shoulders, and the buffy gray underparts.

• **SONG** Call note is a clear high-pitched *pik*, similar to Hairy Woodpecker; descending whinny.

• **BEHAVIOR** Solitary or in pairs. Sexes forage differently. Males tend to forage lower and on the ground, probing for insects, especially ants; females forage higher in the vegetation and glean insects from bark. Both readily eat fruits of cactus. Often seen in towns and rural areas.

• **BREEDING** Monogamous.

• **NESTING** Incubation 13 days by both sexes. Young altricial; estimated to fledge nest at 20–25 days. Fed by both sexes. 1 brood per year.

• **POPULATION** Common in arid and semiarid brushlands.

• **FEEDERS** Attracted to birdbaths, pools, and other water elements, and feeders with suet, peanut butter, corn, and sunflower seeds.

black forehead and nape
straight black bill
red crown
buffy gray face outlined with black triangle
black-and-white barred upperparts, shoulders, and wings
black legs and feet
buffy gray, black-spotted underparts

MALE

black rump and tail
white-barred outer tail feathers

whitish gray face outlined with black triangle
black-and-white barred upperparts, shoulders, and wings
black forehead, crown, and nape

FEMALE

buffy gray underparts with black spotting on breast, sides, and flanks
black rump and tail
outer tail feathers barred white

Similar Birds

DOWNY WOODPECKER
White back; white underparts without spotting; white outer tail feathers with black spotting; black ear patch • male has red patch on back of head.

NUTTALL'S WOODPECKER
Black face with narrow white supercilium curving down behind auriculars and white mustache; white underparts; voice differs • male has red on back of crown only • south California range barely overlaps • limited range in the West.

Flight Pattern

Series of rapid shallow wing beats alternating with short glides.

Nest Identification

Shape | Location

Excavated cavity lined with chips • in upper part of agave, saguaro, or other huge cactus; in dead trees or branches; in top of woody shrub, 3–30 feet above ground • unknown which sex digs cavity • 2–7 white eggs; oval to elliptical, 0.8 x 0.6 inches.

Plumage Sexes differ	Habitat	Migration Nonmigratory	Weight 1.1 ounces

DATE _____ TIME_____ LOCATION _____

| Family PICIDAE | Species *Picoides nuttallii* | Length 7.5 inches | Wingspan 13.5 inches |

NUTTALL'S WOODPECKER

In the spring, the sound of courtship drumming against the timber carries across the chaparral region of California, where this small woodpecker makes its home. A characteristic bird of the California foothills, it is the only black-and-white "zebra-backed" woodpecker west of the Sierra Mountains that has a black-and-white-striped face. The outer tail feathers are white with black spotting. The female is similar to the male, but lacks the red occipital patch.

black forecrown

white nasal bristles

short black bill

red occipital patch

white chin, throat, and underparts

black ear patches

spotted sides

black-and-white zebralike stripes on body

barred flanks and crissum

• SONG A low, hoarse, sharp *pa-teck* or *pr-dik* may be repeated in a series or run into a rolling chatter as *prrrrrrrt*. Also utters an abrasive thin *quee-quee-quee-queep*.
• BEHAVIOR Solitary or in pairs. Forages for insects off trunks and branches, probing into cavities. Often flies up to alight upside down on the underside of a limb, nimbly turning and gleaning from beneath the limb like a nuthatch. Often peels bits of bark off tree instead of excavating cavities. Eats insects and their larvae; also eats wild berries, acorns, sap, and some grain. Pairs remain on territory year-round and sometimes drive off other woodpeckers, including flickers, from favored trees. Frequents chaparral, oak woodlands, and riparian areas with big sycamores.
• BREEDING Monogamous.
• NESTING Incubation about 14 days by both sexes, but mostly by male, including all nocturnal incubation and brooding. Altricial young remain in nest 26–28 days, fed by both sexes. 1 brood per year.
• POPULATION Common to fairly common.

Similar Birds

♂ LADDER-BACKED WOODPECKER
Buffy nasal bristles; red crown; black patch on nape; black-outlined ear patch; gray-buff underparts; spotted breast and sides
• female has black crown.
♀

Flight Pattern

Alternates several rapid wing beats with short glides.

Nest Identification

Shape   Location

No nest materials except a few bark chips • in tree, 2–60 feet above ground; sometimes in fence post or utility pole • 3–6 white eggs; oval to elliptical, 0.9 x 0.7 inches.

| Plumage Sexes differ | Habitat | Migration Nonmigratory | Weight 1.3 ounces |

DATE _____ TIME_____ LOCATION _____

| Family PICIDAE | Species *Picoides pubescens* | Length 6.75–7 inches | Wingspan 11–12 inches |

DOWNY WOODPECKER

The smallest woodpecker in North America is found across most of the continent, ranging from coast to coast and from the northern tree line south to the Gulf and the deserts and dry grasslands just north of the Mexican border. The combination of small size, white back, and small stubby bill distinguishes this common woodpecker. The female differs from the male only in that it lacks the red occipital patch. In the Pacific Northwest these birds show pale brownish gray underparts and back.

• **SONG** Downslurred soft high-pitched whinny. Call is flat *pik* or *pick* and not as high-pitched as that given by the Hairy Woodpecker.

• **BEHAVIOR** Both sexes drum on dead limbs or tree trunks with good resonating qualities or on utility poles, buildings, or other man-made objects to advertise their presence and proclaim territorial rights. Eats primarily insects and their larvae and eggs, but also takes seeds, nuts, berries (including those of poison ivy), spiders, and snails. The agility that comes with its small size allows it to feed on smaller branches and farther out on their tips than other woodpeckers. Roosts in cavities at night.

• **BREEDING** Monogamous.

• **NESTING** Incubation 12 days by both sexes (male at night). Young stay in nest 20–25 days. Fed by both sexes. 1 brood per year, possibly 2 in the South.

• **POPULATION** Widespread and common. Species can be found almost anywhere there are trees.

• **FEEDERS AND BIRDHOUSES** Will come to feeders for suet, peanut butter, sunflower seeds, and bread. Will nest in bird box designed for it.

Labels on illustration:
white face
short stubby black bill shorter than depth of head
red occipital patch
black malar mark
wedge-shaped black postocular stripe
black nape and shoulders
white back
black wings with white spotting
white underparts
3 outermost tail feathers of black tail are white with dark spots or bars

Similar Birds

HAIRY WOODPECKER Larger; longer bill; white outer feathers of black tail lack spots or bars; call is *peek*.

Flight Pattern

Undulating flight with rapid wing beats alternating with pauses on folded wings, which produces bouncing flight.

Nest Identification

Shape — Location —

Excavated in dead tree trunk or branch; pair usually leaves chips in bottom • usually 12–30 feet above ground, sometimes 5–60 feet • built by both sexes • 3–7 white eggs, 0.8 inch in diameter.

| Plumage Sexes similar | Habitat | Migration Nonmigratory | Weight 1.0 ounce |

DATE _____ TIME _____ LOCATION _____

Family PICIDAE	Species *Picoides villosus*	Length 8.5–10.5 inches	Wingspan 15–17.5 inches

HAIRY WOODPECKER

The Hairy Woodpecker and the Northern Flicker are the two most widely distributed woodpeckers in North America. This woodpecker is found almost anywhere forests exist. Similar in appearance to the smaller Downy Woodpecker, it is noisier but less confiding in humans and does not often allow a close approach before it flies away. Learning its high-pitched *peek* call note will make this shy bird easier to locate. Look for a white back when bird is in flight. The only difference between male and female birds is that the female lacks the red occipital patch. Birds in the Pacific Northwest show pale brownish gray underparts.

long black bill is nearly as long as head is deep

red occipital patch

white face with black malar mark and wedge-shaped postocular stripe

black nape and shoulders

white underparts

black wings with white spotting/barring

black tail with 3 entirely white outermost feathers on each side

- **SONG** Loud downslurred whinny reminiscent of Belted Kingfisher's rattle. Call is bold, grating, sharp *peek*.
- **BEHAVIOR** Roosts in cavities at night. Feeds primarily on wood-boring insects and their larvae, other insects, nuts, seeds, and from the drill wells of sapsuckers. Both sexes drum to advertise presence and maintain territory.
- **BREEDING** Monogamous. Some individuals known to remain with same mate for at least 4 years.
- **NESTING** Incubation 11–15 days by both sexes (male at night). Altricial young remain in nest 28–30 days. Fed by both sexes. 1 brood per year unless nest is robbed or disturbed.
- **POPULATION** Fairly common, but sometimes local, over most of range. Sometimes more common in northern hardwood and boreal forests; rare in the Deep South and in Florida.
- **FEEDERS** Sometimes comes for sunflower seeds, nuts, fruits, peanut butter, and suet.

Similar Birds

DOWNY WOODPECKER
Smaller; shorter, stubby bill (length much less than depth of head); white outer tailfeathers with dark spots/bars.

THREE-TOED WOODPECKER
Black-and-white barring on back; dark barred sides • male has yellow crown.

Flight Pattern

Undulating flight with rapid wing beats alternating with pauses on folded wings, which produces bouncing flight.

Nest Identification

Shape 🪺   Location 🌲 🌿 🦅

4–60 feet above ground • built by both sexes • 3–6 white eggs, 1 inch in diameter.

Plumage Sexes differ	Habitat 🌿 🌳	Migration Most do not migrate	Weight 2.5 ounces

DATE _____ TIME_____ LOCATION _____

| Family PICIDAE | Species *Picoides arizonae* | Length 7–8 inches | Wingspan 14–15 inches |

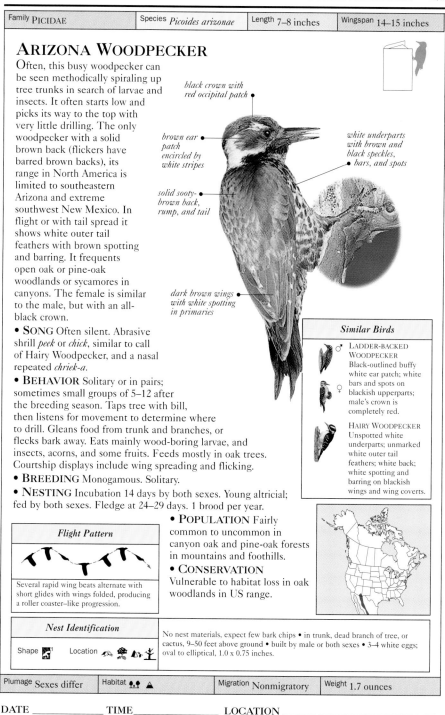

ARIZONA WOODPECKER

Often, this busy woodpecker can be seen methodically spiraling up tree trunks in search of larvae and insects. It often starts low and picks its way to the top with very little drilling. The only woodpecker with a solid brown back (flickers have barred brown backs), its range in North America is limited to southeastern Arizona and extreme southwest New Mexico. In flight or with tail spread it shows white outer tail feathers with brown spotting and barring. It frequents open oak or pine-oak woodlands or sycamores in canyons. The female is similar to the male, but with an all-black crown.

black crown with red occipital patch

brown ear patch encircled by white stripes

white underparts with brown and black speckles, bars, and spots

solid sooty-brown back, rump, and tail

dark brown wings with white spotting in primaries

• **SONG** Often silent. Abrasive shrill *peek* or *chick*, similar to call of Hairy Woodpecker, and a nasal repeated *chriek-a*.

• **BEHAVIOR** Solitary or in pairs; sometimes small groups of 5–12 after the breeding season. Taps tree with bill, then listens for movement to determine where to drill. Gleans food from trunk and branches, or flecks bark away. Eats mainly wood-boring larvae, and insects, acorns, and some fruits. Feeds mostly in oak trees. Courtship displays include wing spreading and flicking.

• **BREEDING** Monogamous. Solitary.

• **NESTING** Incubation 14 days by both sexes. Young altricial; fed by both sexes. Fledge at 24–29 days. 1 brood per year.

Similar Birds

♂ **LADDER-BACKED WOODPECKER** Black-outlined buffy white ear patch; white bars and spots on blackish upperparts; male's crown is completely red.

♀ **HAIRY WOODPECKER** Unspotted white underparts; unmarked white outer tail feathers; white back; white spotting and barring on blackish wings and wing coverts.

• **POPULATION** Fairly common to uncommon in canyon oak and pine-oak forests in mountains and foothills.

• **CONSERVATION** Vulnerable to habitat loss in oak woodlands in US range.

Flight Pattern

Several rapid wing beats alternate with short glides with wings folded, producing a roller coaster–like progression.

Nest Identification

Shape | Location

No nest materials, expect few bark chips • in trunk, dead branch of tree, or cactus, 9–50 feet above ground • built by male or both sexes • 3–4 white eggs; oval to elliptical, 1.0 x 0.75 inches.

| Plumage Sexes differ | Habitat | Migration Nonmigratory | Weight 1.7 ounces |

DATE _____ TIME_____ LOCATION _____

Family PICIDAE	Species *Picoides albolarvatus*	Length 9 inches	Wingspan 17 inches

WHITE-HEADED WOODPECKER

The only North American woodpecker with a white head, this bird makes its home in the coniferous forests of the mountains of the western United States. Sometimes it can be observed perching upside-down or sideways, nuthatchlike, on tree trunks or branches. The female is similar to the male, but lacks the red patch on the back of her head. In flight the white head and white patches in the primaries contrast with the black body.

• **SONG** Calls include a sharp *pee-dink* or *pee-dee-dink*. Also utters abrasive *chick* or *ick*, and a rattle that descends at the end, similar to that of a Downy Woodpecker.

• **BEHAVIOR** Solitary or in pairs. Gleans insects off pinecones, branches, and trunks of trees. Wedges bark off trees to expose food or sometimes flycatches. Eats a variety of insects and their larvae, spiders, seeds, and berries. In the southern part of the range, more than half the diet may be made up of pinecone seeds. Males and females tend to forage separately in winter, partitioning the resources, with females feeding low on ponderosa pine and incense cedar, while males forage higher in the same trees and additionally on Coulter pines.

• **BREEDING** Monogamous.

• **NESTING** Incubation 14 days by both sexes. Young altricial; stay in nest 26 days before first flight, fed by both sexes. 1 brood per year.

white head, throat, and upper breast

narrow red patch on back of head

small black bill

black postocular stripe

black body

large white wing patch at base of primaries

Similar Birds

The entirely white head is unique among North American woodpeckers.

• **POPULATION** Fairly common in mountainous conifer forests from 4,000–9,000 feet; rare and local in the northern parts of the range.

• **CONSERVATION** Vulnerable to logging operations.

Flight Pattern

Relatively slow flight, alternating several deep rapid wing beats and short glides with wings partially folded to sides.

Nest Identification

Shape [symbol] Location [symbols]

A few bark chips • tree stump or tree, 4–25 feet above ground; sometimes bores several cavities in one trunk • built by both sexes • 3–7 white eggs; oval to elliptical, 1.0 x 0.8 inches.

Plumage Sexes similar	Habitat [symbols]	Migration Nonmigratory	Weight 2.2 ounces

DATE _____ TIME_____ LOCATION _____

Family PICIDAE	Species *Picoides tridactylus*	Length 8–9 inches	Wingspan 14–16 inches

THREE-TOED WOODPECKER

Formerly called Northern Three-toed Woodpecker. Black-and-white barring on sides and flanks, with black-and-white-barred back, set it apart from similar species. Barring on the back varies with geography, with Rocky Mountain birds having almost white backs and birds in the Northeast having mostly black backs with thin white bars. Not as active as many birds in its family; easily overlooked, spending long periods of time simply clinging to the trunk of a tree. The female is similar to the male but has a speckled crown, rather than a yellow cap. Juveniles are duller, with yellow spotting on the crown which later disappears in females.

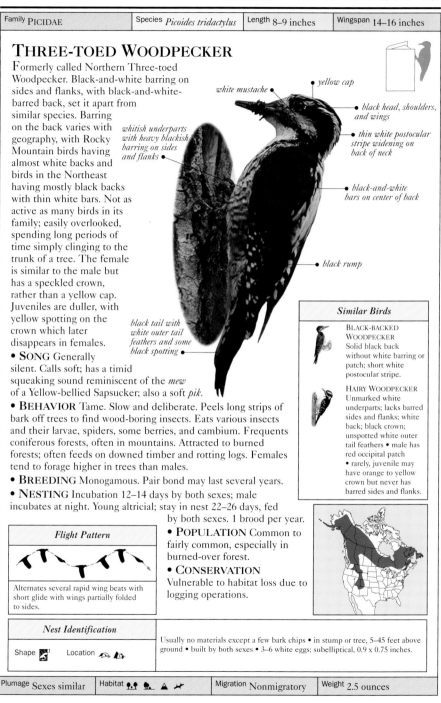

white mustache

yellow cap

black head, shoulders, and wings

thin white postocular stripe widening on back of neck

black-and-white bars on center of back

whitish underparts with heavy blackish barring on sides and flanks

black rump

black tail with white outer tail feathers and some black spotting

• **SONG** Generally silent. Calls soft; has a timid squeaking sound reminiscent of the *mew* of a Yellow-bellied Sapsucker; also a soft *pik.*

• **BEHAVIOR** Tame. Slow and deliberate. Peels long strips of bark off trees to find wood-boring insects. Eats various insects and their larvae, spiders, some berries, and cambium. Frequents coniferous forests, often in mountains. Attracted to burned forests; often feeds on downed timber and rotting logs. Females tend to forage higher in trees than males.

• **BREEDING** Monogamous. Pair bond may last several years.

• **NESTING** Incubation 12–14 days by both sexes; male incubates at night. Young altricial; stay in nest 22–26 days, fed by both sexes. 1 brood per year.

Similar Birds

BLACK-BACKED WOODPECKER Solid black back without white barring or patch; short white postocular stripe.

HAIRY WOODPECKER Unmarked white underparts; lacks barred sides and flanks; white back; black crown; unspotted white outer tail feathers • male has red occipital patch • rarely, juvenile may have orange to yellow crown but never has barred sides and flanks.

• **POPULATION** Common to fairly common, especially in burned-over forest.

• **CONSERVATION** Vulnerable to habitat loss due to logging operations.

Flight Pattern

Alternates several rapid wing beats with short glide with wings partially folded to sides.

Nest Identification

Shape | Location

Usually no materials except a few bark chips • in stump or tree, 5–45 feet above ground • built by both sexes • 3–6 white eggs; subelliptical, 0.9 x 0.75 inches.

Plumage Sexes similar	Habitat	Migration Nonmigratory	Weight 2.5 ounces

DATE _____ TIME_____ LOCATION _____

Family PICIDAE	Species *Picoides arcticus*	Length 9.5 inches	Wingspan 17 inches

BLACK-BACKED WOODPECKER

yellow cap on
black head

long stout
black bill

white
mustache mark

solid black back
and wings

white
underparts

heavily barred flanks

black tail with
unmarked white
outer tail feathers

Formerly called the Black-backed Three-toed Woodpecker, this species shares the anatomical distinction of three toes with the Three-toed Woodpecker. It is closely related to the latter species but is distinguished by its black back, the lack of a long white postocular stripe and the male's more solidly yellow cap. Both species often leave behind rows of bark-stripped conifers in the boreal pine forests of North America they frequent. Both are attracted to burned-over forests, areas of windfall, and swampy areas with standing dead trees. The female has a solid black head, without the yellow cap of the male.

• SONG Often silent and easily overlooked. Call is a single-note, abrasive sharp *pick* or *chik*, similar to Three-toed or Hairy Woodpeckers, but lower in pitch. Sometimes repeated rapidly in a series.

• BEHAVIOR Solitary or in pairs. Tame; deliberate in its movements. Somewhat nomadic and may erupt in numbers where insect outbreaks provide abundant food source. Peels large pieces of bark off trunk of tree to find wood-boring insects. Eats a variety of insects, including ants; also takes spiders, cambium, wild fruits, and nuts.

• BREEDING Monogamous.

• NESTING Incubation 12–14 days by both sexes, but mostly by female. Young altricial; stay in nest 25 days, fed by both sexes. 1 brood per year.

• POPULATION Uncommon to fairly common; sometimes local. In the East, may wander south of breeding range during winter.

• CONSERVATION Vulnerable to habitat loss due to logging operations.

Similar Birds

THREE-TOED WOODPECKER
Black-and-white barring down center of back; much longer white postocular stripe.

HAIRY WOODPECKER
White back; wider, longer white postocular stripe; unmarked white underparts, including sides and flanks; white spots and barring on wings and wing coverts; •male has red occipital patch.

Flight Pattern

Alternates between several rapid wing beats and short glides with wings partially folded to sides.

Nest Identification

Shape [icon] Location [icons]

Cavity lined with chips • excavated in dead stubs or trunks of dead trees, 2–80 feet above ground, usually within opening in forest; sloped entry used as doorstep • built by both sexes, mostly by male • 2–6 white eggs; subelliptical, 0.9 x 0.75 inches.

Plumage Sexes similar	Habitat [icons]	Migration Nonmigratory	Weight 2.5 ounces

DATE _____ TIME_____ LOCATION _____

Family PICIDAE	Species *Colaptes auratus*	Length 12.75–14 inches	Wingspan 19–21 inches

NORTHERN FLICKER

This large woodpecker is often found in open spaces where it spends considerable time on the ground foraging for ants. Two distinct geographical groups, which were considered separate species until the early 1980s, occur: in the East and Northwest, Yellow-shafted Flicker has yellow underwings and undertail, and a black mustache; and, in the West, Red-shafted Flicker has bright salmon-red to red-orange underwings and undertail, and a red mustache. Although the two forms have similar bodies, the Red-shafted form shows a different pattern on its head with colors that are basically reversed from those of the Yellow-shafted form: a gray face and brown forehead, crown, and nape with no red crescent. Females are similar to males, lacking only the mustache. All birds have brown backs and wings with dark barring, a black crescent bib, buff to grayish underparts with heavy spotting, and a white rump patch.

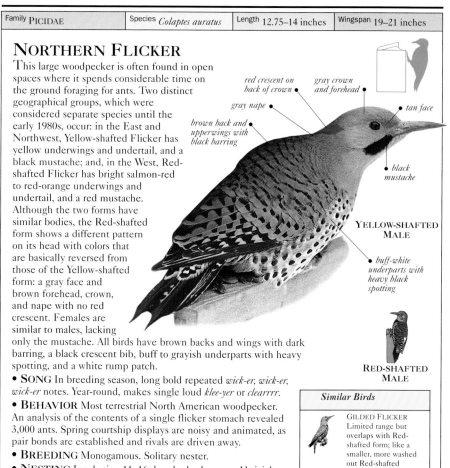

red crescent on back of crown
gray crown and forehead
gray nape
tan face
brown back and upperwings with black barring
black mustache

YELLOW-SHAFTED MALE

buff-white underparts with heavy black spotting

RED-SHAFTED MALE

• **SONG** In breeding season, long bold repeated *wick-er, wick-er, wick-er* notes. Year-round, makes single loud *klee-yer* or *clearrrr*.
• **BEHAVIOR** Most terrestrial North American woodpecker. An analysis of the contents of a single flicker stomach revealed 3,000 ants. Spring courtship displays are noisy and animated, as pair bonds are established and rivals are driven away.
• **BREEDING** Monogamous. Solitary nester.
• **NESTING** Incubation 11–16 days by both sexes. Altricial young stay in nest 4 weeks, fed by both sexes. Usually 1 brood per year, sometimes 2 in the South.
• **POPULATION** Yellow-shafted form common. Red-shafted form is fairly common to common. Both thought to be declining.
• **BIRDHOUSES** Nests in houses and boxes.
• **CONSERVATION** Declining. Introduced European Starlings successfully compete for nest sites.

Similar Birds

GILDED FLICKER Limited range but overlaps with Red-shafted form; like a smaller, more washed out Red-shafted Flicker; yellow wash under wings and tail • only in the West.

Flight Pattern

Several rapid wing beats followed by a pause with wings folded at sides produces up-and-down flight pattern.

Nest Identification

Shape | Location | In snag, poles, posts, buildings, nest boxes, and banks (sometimes driving out the kingfisher or Bank Swallow tenants) • 6–20 feet above ground, sometimes higher • built by both sexes • sometimes uses same nest hole for second season • 3–12 white eggs; oval to short-oval; 1.1 x 0.8 inches.

Plumage Sexes differ	Habitat	Migration Most do not migrate	Weight 4.8 ounces

DATE _____ TIME _____ LOCATION _____

Family PICIDAE	Species *Colaptes chrysoides*	Length 10.5–12 inches	Wingspan 18 inches

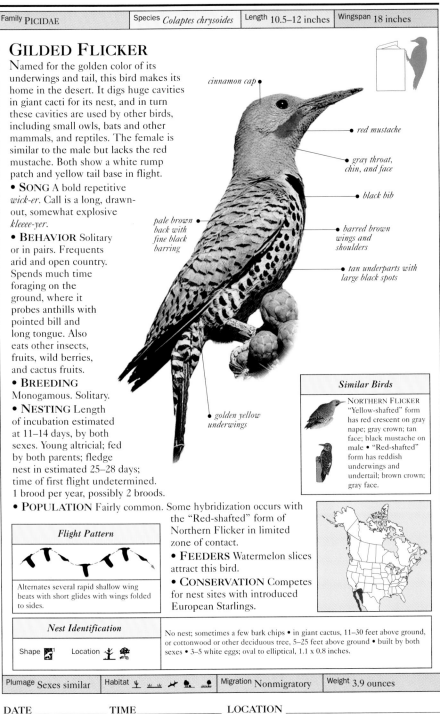

GILDED FLICKER

Named for the golden color of its underwings and tail, this bird makes its home in the desert. It digs huge cavities in giant cacti for its nest, and in turn these cavities are used by other birds, including small owls, bats and other mammals, and reptiles. The female is similar to the male but lacks the red mustache. Both show a white rump patch and yellow tail base in flight.

- **SONG** A bold repetitive *wick-er.* Call is a long, drawn-out, somewhat explosive *kleeee-yer.*
- **BEHAVIOR** Solitary or in pairs. Frequents arid and open country. Spends much time foraging on the ground, where it probes anthills with pointed bill and long tongue. Also eats other insects, fruits, wild berries, and cactus fruits.
- **BREEDING** Monogamous. Solitary.
- **NESTING** Length of incubation estimated at 11–14 days, by both sexes. Young altricial; fed by both parents; fledge nest in estimated 25–28 days; time of first flight undetermined. 1 brood per year, possibly 2 broods.
- **POPULATION** Fairly common. Some hybridization occurs with the "Red-shafted" form of Northern Flicker in limited zone of contact.
- **FEEDERS** Watermelon slices attract this bird.
- **CONSERVATION** Competes for nest sites with introduced European Starlings.

cinnamon cap

red mustache

gray throat, chin, and face

black bib

pale brown back with fine black barring

barred brown wings and shoulders

tan underparts with large black spots

golden yellow underwings

Similar Birds

NORTHERN FLICKER "Yellow-shafted" form has red crescent on gray nape; gray crown; tan face; black mustache on male • "Red-shafted" form has reddish underwings and undertail; brown crown; gray face.

Flight Pattern

Alternates several rapid shallow wing beats with short glides with wings folded to sides.

Nest Identification

Shape ⬛ Location 🌵 🌳

No nest; sometimes a few bark chips • in giant cactus, 11–30 feet above ground, or cottonwood or other deciduous tree, 5–25 feet above ground • built by both sexes • 3–5 white eggs; oval to elliptical, 1.1 x 0.8 inches.

Plumage Sexes similar	Habitat 🌾 ⚘ 🌿 🌲 🏞	Migration Nonmigratory	Weight 3.9 ounces

DATE _____ TIME_____ LOCATION _____

| Family PICIDAE | Species *Dryocopus pileatus* | Length 16.5–19.5 inches | Wingspan 27–30 inches |

PILEATED WOODPECKER

These crow-sized woodpeckers drum on trees to claim territory and attract a mate; the loud heavy sound is as if the tree is being hit with a wooden mallet. Each member of a mated pair excavates several roosting cavities and may retire for the evening in one of them. The male roosts in the current nesting cavity before the eggs are laid and afterward incubates them there at night. In flight both sexes show a large white patch at the base of the primaries and they also show white underwing linings.

red crest extending from forehead to nape

large black bill

scarlet mustache

white chin

white line from base of bill crosses face to back of neck and extends down neck to side

solid black back

- **SONG** Location call to mate is a deliberate loud *cuck, cuck, cuck.* Both sexes have a call of *yucka, yucka, yucka,* similar to a flicker, that changes in pitch, loudness, and in its cadence.
- **BEHAVIOR** Solitary or in pairs. Loud and often conspicuous. Bores deep into trees and peels off large strips of bark for food. Also digs on ground and on fallen logs. Eats ants, beetles, and a variety of other insects, especially tree-boring ones, acorns, beechnuts, seeds of tree cones, nuts, and various fruits.
- **BREEDING** Monogamous.
- **NESTING** Incubation 15–18 days by both sexes, mostly male. Young altricial; brooded by female; stay in nest 26–28 days, fed by both sexes. 1 brood per year.
- **POPULATION** Common to fairly common in the Southeast; uncommon and local elsewhere.
- **FEEDERS** Mixture of melted suet, pecans, and walnut meats.

MALE

black forehead

black mustache

FEMALE

Similar Birds

♂ **IVORY-BILLED WOODPECKER** Probably extinct • larger; two white stripes on back extending from sides of neck; white secondaries make white patch on back when wings fold; black chin; ivory-white bill; in flight, shows white secondaries and tips of inner primaries; white lining onedge of underwing • female has black crest.

- **CONSERVATION** Vulnerable to habitat loss and forest fragmentation. Sharp decline in early 20th century, but has adapted to habitat changes. Competes for excavated nesting cavities with European Starlings.

Flight Pattern

Strong powerful wing beats when traveling distances; alternates rapid wing strokes with brief periods of wings folded to sides on short flights beneath the canopy.

Nest Identification

Shape | Location

Few wood chips • dead or live tree in shaded area, 15–85 feet above ground • excavated by both sexes; female sometimes does more • 3–8 white eggs; oval to elliptical, 1.3 x 1.0 inches.

| Plumage Sexes differ | Habitat | Migration Nonmigratory | Weight 10.9 ounces |

DATE _____ TIME_____ LOCATION _____

Family TYRANNIDAE	Species *Camptostoma imberbe*	Length 4.5 inches	Wingspan 7 inches

NORTHERN BEARDLESS-TYRANNULET

As it is difficult to spot, this bird is best located by its high, thin voice. The male tends to sing from high perches in tall trees. Once spotted, this little flycatcher can be somewhat difficult to identify, especially if the crest is not raised and apparent. In conjunction with its voice, crest, and small size, other characteristics are the bird's fairly upright posture and wagging tail.

crown with bushy crest

faint whitish eyebrow

indistinct eye ring

nape sometimes lighter than crown

gray-olive upperparts

two buff-colored wing bars

small slightly curved bill with dusky tip and creamy-pink base

dull white or pale yellow underparts

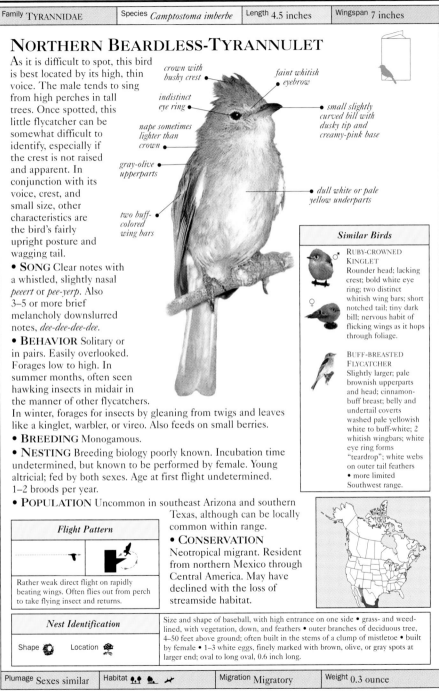

• **SONG** Clear notes with a whistled, slightly nasal *peeert* or *pee-yerp*. Also 3–5 or more brief melancholy downslurred notes, *dee-dee-dee-dee*.

• **BEHAVIOR** Solitary or in pairs. Easily overlooked. Forages low to high. In summer months, often seen hawking insects in midair in the manner of other flycatchers. In winter, forages for insects by gleaning from twigs and leaves like a kinglet, warbler, or vireo. Also feeds on small berries.

• **BREEDING** Monogamous.

• **NESTING** Breeding biology poorly known. Incubation time undetermined, but known to be performed by female. Young altricial; fed by both sexes. Age at first flight undetermined. 1–2 broods per year.

• **POPULATION** Uncommon in southeast Arizona and southern Texas, although can be locally common within range.

• **CONSERVATION** Neotropical migrant. Resident from northern Mexico through Central America. May have declined with the loss of streamside habitat.

Similar Birds

♂ **RUBY-CROWNED KINGLET**
Rounder head; lacking crest; bold white eye ring; two distinct whitish wing bars; short notched tail; tiny dark bill; nervous habit of flicking wings as it hops through foliage.

BUFF-BREASTED FLYCATCHER
Slightly larger; pale brownish upperparts and head; cinnamon-buff breast; belly and undertail coverts washed pale yellowish white to buff-white; 2 whitish wingbars; white eye ring forms "teardrop"; white webs on outer tail feathers • more limited Southwest range.

Flight Pattern

Rather weak direct flight on rapidly beating wings. Often flies out from perch to take flying insect and returns.

Nest Identification

Shape 🥚   Location 🌿

Size and shape of baseball, with high entrance on one side • grass- and weed-lined, with vegetation, down, and feathers • outer branches of deciduous tree, 4–50 feet above ground; often built in the stems of a clump of mistletoe • built by female • 1–3 white eggs, finely marked with brown, olive, or gray spots at larger end; oval to long oval, 0.6 inch long.

Plumage Sexes similar	Habitat 🌳🌿	Migration Migratory	Weight 0.3 ounce

DATE _____ TIME_____ LOCATION _____

Family TYRANNIDAE	Species *Contopus cooperi*	Length 7.5 inches	Wingspan 13 inches

OLIVE-SIDED FLYCATCHER

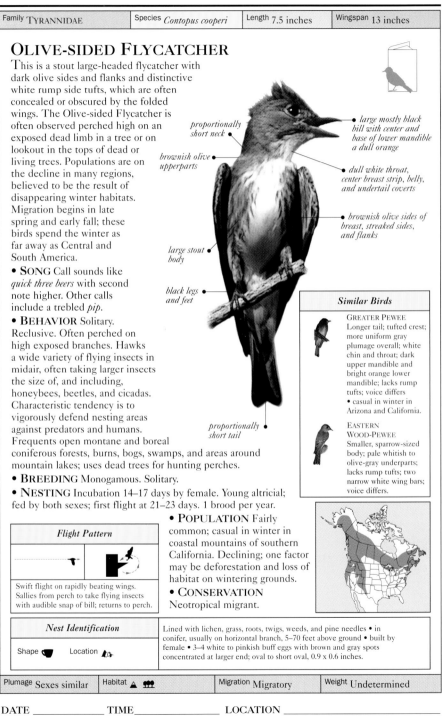

This is a stout large-headed flycatcher with dark olive sides and flanks and distinctive white rump side tufts, which are often concealed or obscured by the folded wings. The Olive-sided Flycatcher is often observed perched high on an exposed dead limb in a tree or on lookout in the tops of dead or living trees. Populations are on the decline in many regions, believed to be the result of disappearing winter habitats. Migration begins in late spring and early fall; these birds spend the winter as far away as Central and South America.

proportionally short neck

brownish olive upperparts

large mostly black bill with center and base of lower mandible a dull orange

dull white throat, center breast strip, belly, and undertail coverts

brownish olive sides of breast, streaked sides, and flanks

large stout body

black legs and feet

- **SONG** Call sounds like *quick three beers* with second note higher. Other calls include a trebled *pip*.

- **BEHAVIOR** Solitary. Reclusive. Often perched on high exposed branches. Hawks a wide variety of flying insects in midair, often taking larger insects the size of, and including, honeybees, beetles, and cicadas. Characteristic tendency is to vigorously defend nesting areas against predators and humans. Frequents open montane and boreal coniferous forests, burns, bogs, swamps, and areas around mountain lakes; uses dead trees for hunting perches.

proportionally short tail

- **BREEDING** Monogamous. Solitary.

- **NESTING** Incubation 14–17 days by female. Young altricial; fed by both sexes; first flight at 21–23 days. 1 brood per year.

- **POPULATION** Fairly common; casual in winter in coastal mountains of southern California. Declining; one factor may be deforestation and loss of habitat on wintering grounds.

- **CONSERVATION** Neotropical migrant.

Similar Birds

GREATER PEWEE
Longer tail; tufted crest; more uniform gray plumage overall; white chin and throat; dark upper mandible and bright orange lower mandible; lacks rump tufts; voice differs.
• casual in winter in Arizona and California.

EASTERN WOOD-PEWEE
Smaller, sparrow-sized body; pale whitish to olive-gray underparts; lacks rump tufts; two narrow white wing bars; voice differs.

Flight Pattern

Swift flight on rapidly beating wings. Sallies from perch to take flying insects with audible snap of bill; returns to perch.

Nest Identification

Shape — Location —

Lined with lichen, grass, roots, twigs, weeds, and pine needles • in conifer, usually on horizontal branch, 5–70 feet above ground • built by female • 3–4 white to pinkish buff eggs with brown and gray spots concentrated at larger end; oval to short oval, 0.9 x 0.6 inches.

Plumage Sexes similar	Habitat ▲ 🐾	Migration Migratory	Weight Undetermined

DATE _____ TIME _____ LOCATION _____

Family TYRANNIDAE	Species *Contopus pertinax*	Length 8 inches	Wingspan 13.5 inches

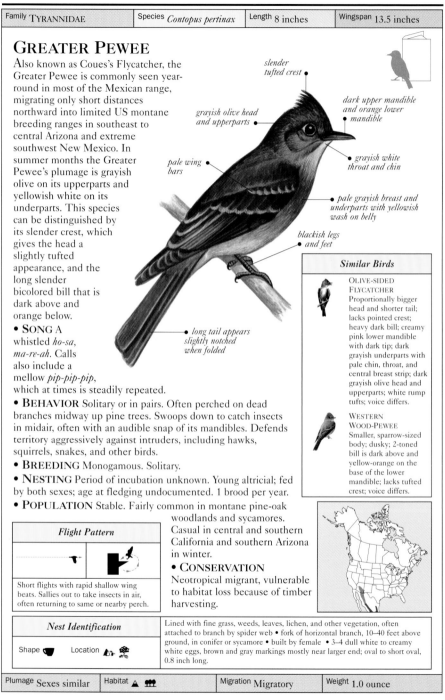

GREATER PEWEE

Also known as Coues's Flycatcher, the Greater Pewee is commonly seen year-round in most of the Mexican range, migrating only short distances northward into limited US montane breeding ranges in southeast to central Arizona and extreme southwest New Mexico. In summer months the Greater Pewee's plumage is grayish olive on its upperparts and yellowish white on its underparts. This species can be distinguished by its slender crest, which gives the head a slightly tufted appearance, and the long slender bicolored bill that is dark above and orange below.

slender tufted crest

grayish olive head and upperparts

dark upper mandible and orange lower mandible

pale wing bars

grayish white throat and chin

pale grayish breast and underparts with yellowish wash on belly

blackish legs and feet

long tail appears slightly notched when folded

• **SONG** A whistled *ho-sa, ma-re-ah.* Calls also include a mellow *pip-pip-pip*, which at times is steadily repeated.

• **BEHAVIOR** Solitary or in pairs. Often perched on dead branches midway up pine trees. Swoops down to catch insects in midair, often with an audible snap of its mandibles. Defends territory aggressively against intruders, including hawks, squirrels, snakes, and other birds.

• **BREEDING** Monogamous. Solitary.

• **NESTING** Period of incubation unknown. Young altricial; fed by both sexes; age at fledging undocumented. 1 brood per year.

• **POPULATION** Stable. Fairly common in montane pine-oak woodlands and sycamores. Casual in central and southern California and southern Arizona in winter.

• **CONSERVATION** Neotropical migrant, vulnerable to habitat loss because of timber harvesting.

Similar Birds

OLIVE-SIDED FLYCATCHER
Proportionally bigger head and shorter tail; lacks pointed crest; heavy dark bill; creamy pink lower mandible with dark tip; dark grayish underparts with pale chin, throat, and central breast strip; dark grayish olive head and upperparts; white rump tufts; voice differs.

WESTERN WOOD-PEWEE
Smaller, sparrow-sized body; dusky; 2-toned bill is dark above and yellow-orange on the base of the lower mandible; lacks tufted crest; voice differs.

Flight Pattern

Short flights with rapid shallow wing beats. Sallies out to take insects in air, often returning to same or nearby perch.

Nest Identification

Shape ☞ Location 🌳🌿

Lined with fine grass, weeds, leaves, lichen, and other vegetation, often attached to branch by spider web • fork of horizontal branch, 10–40 feet above ground, in conifer or sycamore • built by female • 3–4 dull white to creamy white eggs, brown and gray markings mostly near larger end; oval to short oval, 0.8 inch long.

Plumage Sexes similar	Habitat 🔺 🌾	Migration Migratory	Weight 1.0 ounce

DATE _____ TIME_____ LOCATION _____

Family TYRANNIDAE	Species *Contopus sordidulus*	Length 6.25 inches	Wingspan 10.5 inches

WESTERN WOOD-PEWEE

The western counterpart to the Eastern Wood-Pewee is similar in appearance but has a different call. Like other pewees, its wings quiver when it lands, but it does not wag its tail. This sparrow-sized flycatcher is dark and dusky overall and inhabits riparian woodlands and open, mixed conifer and hardwood forests in the mountains. Note the two thin wing bars and the lack of an eye ring.

dark grayish brown overall

dark bill

yellow-orange on base of lower mandible

2 thin white bars on wings

paler underparts

blackish feet and legs

• **SONG** On breeding grounds sings *tswee-tee-teet.* Also has soft, nasal whistle *peeer* or *peeyee,* given throughout the year. Often vocalizes before daylight; in evenings sometimes sings until after dark.

• **BEHAVIOR** Solitary. Stays quietly hidden in trees or perched in open view until it spots food, then flies out and snatches insect. Eats wide variety of small to medium flying insects, some spiders, and a few wild berries.

• **BREEDING** Monogamous.

• **NESTING** Incubation 12–13 days by female. Altricial young. Fed by both sexes. First flight at 14–18 days. 1 brood per year.

• **POPULATION** Common to abundant in some areas but declining in parts of California. Casual in the East in migration.

• **CONSERVATION** Neotropical migrant. This bird is vulnerable to deforestation on its wintering grounds.

Similar Birds

GREATER PEWEE
Tufted crest; larger; larger bill; dark upperparts; yellow-orange underparts; indistinct wing bars; different call • casual in winter in Arizona and California.

EASTERN WOOD-PEWEE
More olive upperparts; less dusky underparts; pale bill; different voice.

Flight Pattern

Weak fluttering direct flight with shallow wing beats. Sallies from perch to catch insects, returning to same or nearby perch.

Nest Identification

Shape ◣   Location 🔺 🌲

Grass, plant fibers, and plant down • decorated outside with gray moss, leaves, and sometimes lichen • bound to branch with spider webs • in trees, usually conifer, on horizontal branch 15–75 feet above ground • built by female • 2–4 whitish to creamy eggs blotched with brown and lavender, often concentrated toward larger end; oval to short oval, 0.7 inch long.

Plumage Sexes similar	Habitat 🌿 🌳	Migration Migratory	Weight 0.5 ounce

DATE _____ TIME_____ LOCATION _____

Family TYRANNIDAE	Species *Contopus virens*	Length 6.25 inches	Wingspan 10.5 inches

EASTERN WOOD-PEWEE

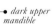

Although this bird is very difficult to distinguish visually from its western counterpart, the Western Wood-Pewee, their ranges barely overlap and their voices differ. Like most flycatchers, it tends to perch on an open lookout among thick trees or shrubs, sailing into the open only to feed. It is often first detected by its voice, because it often calls its distinctive *pee-a-wee* while perched, awaiting its next chance at a flying insect. Juveniles are similar to adults but both upper and lower mandibles showing dark coloration.

dark grayish olive upperparts

• *dark upper mandible*

• *yellow-orange lower mandible*

• *whitish throat, center breast, and belly*

• *2 thin whitish wing bars*

• *pale dusky olive sides and flanks*

• *pale underparts washed yellowish*

• *black feet and legs*

- **SONG** During the day whistles distinctive, slow plaintive *pee-a-wee*, with second note lower; on second or third repeat, often followed by *pee-yeer*; second note lower. At dusk and early dawn, sings *ah-de-deee*.
- **BEHAVIOR** Solitary. Perches on open and/or dead branches in trees to spot prey; flies out to catch food. Eats a wide variety of flying insects, including beetles, flies, moths, wasps, and bees. Takes some spiders and a few berries. Like other flycatchers, it often defends its territory even from larger birds by flying at them and pecking at their backs.
- **BREEDING** Monogamous.
- **NESTING** Incubation 12–13 days by female. Young altricial; stay in nest 14–18 days, fed by both sexes. 1 brood per year.
- **POPULATION** Fairly common and widespread. Casual in the West in migration.
- **CONSERVATION** Neotropical migrant. Infrequent host to cowbird's eggs. Decline due to possible loss of South American wintering habitat.

Similar Birds

WESTERN WOOD-PEWEE
Ranges barely overlap; very similar in size and appearance; duskier and darker overall; darker lower mandible; voice is different.

EASTERN PHOEBE
Slightly larger; paler whitish to yellow underparts; lacks wing bars; both mandibles dark; pumps tail up and down while perched, especially upon landing; voice differs.

Flight Pattern
Rather slow fluttering direct flight on shallowly beating wings. Sallies forth to catch insects in midair, returning to perch.

Nest Identification	
Shape ⬤ Location 🪹 🌿	Grass, plant fibers, and spider web, covered with thick layer of lichens • fork of tree or saddled on horizontal branch, 15–50 feet above ground • built by female • 2–4 whitish eggs, with brown blotches and purple, often wreathed at large end; oval to short ovate, 0.7 x 0.5 inches.

Plumage Sexes similar	Habitat 🌾 🪵	Migration Migratory	Weight 0.5 ounce

DATE _____ TIME_____ LOCATION _____

Family TYRANNIDAE	Species *Empidonax flaviventris*	Length 5.5 inches	Wingspan 8.5 inches

YELLOW-BELLIED FLYCATCHER

Once you spot this small bird, its yellowish underparts from chin to undertail coverts make it easy to identify because it is the only eastern Empidonax with a yellow throat. Voice and habitat also are key to clinching the identification. It usually stays hidden low in trees, shrubs, or thickets, but making various squeaking or kissing sounds on the back of your hand may lure it from its hiding place. This flycatcher is credited with eating more ants than any other empid.

- **SONG** Often silent in migration. Slurred and explosive pse-ek! Also makes a per-WEE, reminiscent of a pewee's short song, and a shrill chiu.
- **BEHAVIOR** Secretive and quiet. Stays low in thickets near the ground and inside foliage in wet swampy woods. Eats a variety of insects, including beetles, moths, tent caterpillars, flies, ants, and some spiders. May subsist on mountain ash during severe weather. As it gives its single strong note it flutters its wings and jerks its head and tail as if the vocal effort was so strenuous as to cause the shudder.
- **BREEDING** Monogamous. Solitary.
- **NESTING** Incubation 12–14 days by female. Altricial young fed by both sexes. First flight at 13–14 days. 1 brood per year.
- **POPULATION** Common to fairly common. Stable.
- **CONSERVATION** Neotropical migrant. Occasionally parasitized by Brown-headed Cowbird.

large head
broad yellow eye ring
olive upperparts
pale orange lower mandible
yellow throat
olive wash on breast
2 whitish wing bars
yellow underparts
short tail

Similar Birds

CORDILLERAN FLYCATCHER Teardrop-shaped eye ring; less contrasting wings and wing bars; darker brown upperparts; proportionally longer tail; different voice.

ACADIAN FLYCATCHER Whitish gray throat; buff to white wash on wing bars; larger bill is yellowish below; yellow wash on belly and undertail coverts; proportionally longer tail; different voice.

Flight Pattern
Weak fluttering flight with shallow rapid wing beats. Sallies from perch to hawk insects and returns to same or nearby perch.

Nest Identification	
Shape	Location	Twigs, rootlets, weeds, and moss • lined with thin rootlets, grass, and fresh leaves • atop hillock of moss or on upturned stumps among roots of fallen trees, 0–2 feet above ground • built by female • 3–5 white eggs with light brown dots that become heavier near larger end; oval to short oval, 0.7 by 0.5 inches.

Plumage Sexes similar	Habitat	Migration Migratory	Weight 0.4 ounce

DATE _____ TIME_____ LOCATION _____

Family TYRANNIDAE	Species *Empidonax virescens*	Length 5.75 inches	Wingspan 8.75 inches

ACADIAN FLYCATCHER

Its scientific genus name, which means "mosquito king," widely misses the mark in describing this bird's feeding habits, but it is an apt description of the small size of a flycatcher that lords over a realm of small insects. It is the only Empidonax flycatcher to breed in the deep southern states of North America, where it rules in heavily wooded deciduous bottomlands, swamps, and riparian thickets, and in the wooded ravines of drier uplands. Like other empids it is best known by its voice.

• **SONG** Soft call of *peace* or *peeet*. Its explosive *PIZ-zza!!* sounds like a bird sneezing. On territory, males utter a mechanical *ti, ti, ti, ti* as they move from one perch to the next beneath the canopy.

• **BEHAVIOR** Solitary. Easily overlooked except for its occasional vocalizations. Perches in shade on lower to mid-level branches in thick trees to search for food, then dashes out to snatch insect. Eats wide variety of flying insects. Frequents wet areas in open woodlands where it aggressively drives away larger birds and other intruders from the breeding territory.

• **BREEDING** Monogamous.

• **NESTING** Incubation 13–15 days by female. Young altricial; fed by both sexes, but more by female. First flight at 13–15 days; male may feed fledglings while female starts second clutch. 2 broods per year.

• **POPULATION** Common; range expanding in Northeast.

• **CONSERVATION** Neotropical migrant. Frequently nest parasitized by Brown-headed Cowbird.

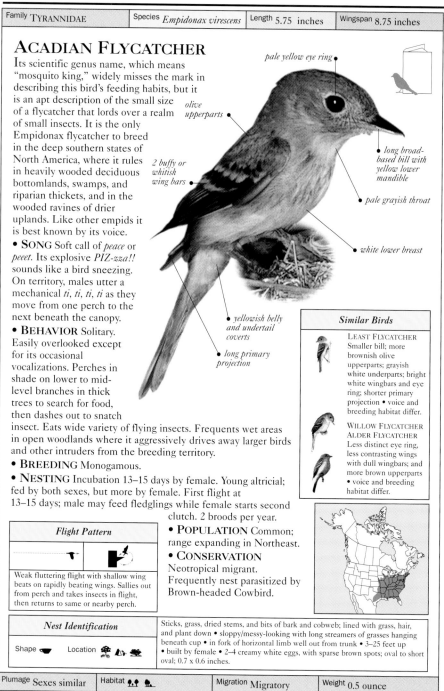

pale yellow eye ring

olive upperparts

2 buffy or whitish wing bars

long broad-based bill with yellow lower mandible

pale grayish throat

white lower breast

yellowish belly and undertail coverts

long primary projection

Similar Birds

LEAST FLYCATCHER
Smaller bill; more brownish olive upperparts; grayish white underparts; bright white wingbars and eye ring; shorter primary projection • voice and breeding habitat differ.

WILLOW FLYCATCHER
ALDER FLYCATCHER
Less distinct eye ring, less contrasting wings with dull wingbars; and more brown upperparts • voice and breeding habitat differ.

Flight Pattern

Weak fluttering flight with shallow wing beats on rapidly beating wings. Sallies out from perch and takes insects in flight, then returns to same or nearby perch.

Nest Identification

Shape ◥   Location 🪹 🌿 🌳

Sticks, grass, dried stems, and bits of bark and cobweb; lined with grass, hair, and plant down • sloppy/messy-looking with long streamers of grasses hanging beneath cup • in fork of horizontal limb well out from trunk • 3–25 feet up • built by female • 2–4 creamy white eggs, with sparse brown spots; oval to short oval; 0.7 x 0.6 inches.

Plumage Sexes similar	Habitat 🌿 🪨	Migration Migratory	Weight 0.5 ounce

DATE _____ TIME_____ LOCATION _____

| Family TYRANNIDAE | Species *Empidonax alnorum* | Length 5.75 inches | Wingspan 8–9 inches |

ALDER FLYCATCHER

Perhaps the most green-brown of the eastern empids, this bird was formerly known as Traill's Flycatcher, from which both it and the Willow Flycatcher were split into separate species in the 1970s. This shy bird is easily overlooked; during nesting season it stays hidden within the thick trees and shrubs of its alder swamp and wet meadow-thicket habitat. Occasionally it can be spotted dashing out of hiding to catch passing insects or perching conspicuously on an exposed branch to sing.

• **SONG** Raspy *fee-bee-o* or *way-bee-o* on breeding grounds. Also has call of bold *pep*.

• **BEHAVIOR** Male sings repeatedly for first 2 weeks after returning to territory in late spring, but after he bonds with female is largely silent. Stays low in thick vegetation, often hunting inside umbrella of thicket canopy. Perches in shrubs to spot prey, then catches it in flight. Eats wide variety of flying insects; gleans some from vegetation, including spiders and millipedes. Also feeds on some types of small berries.

• **BREEDING** Monogamous.

• **NESTING** Incubation 12–14 days by female. Altricial young. Fed by both sexes. First flight at 13–14 days. 1 brood per year.

• **POPULATION** Common and stable.

• **CONSERVATION** Neotropical migrant. Occasionally nest parasitized by Brown-headed Cowbird.

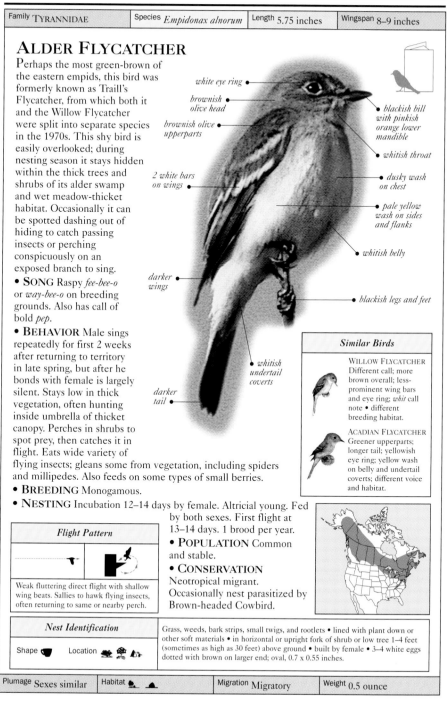

white eye ring
brownish olive head
brownish olive upperparts
2 white bars on wings
darker wings
darker tail
whitish undertail coverts
blackish bill with pinkish orange lower mandible
whitish throat
dusky wash on chest
pale yellow wash on sides and flanks
whitish belly
blackish legs and feet

Similar Birds

WILLOW FLYCATCHER Different call; more brown overall; less-prominent wing bars and eye ring; *whit* call note • different breeding habitat.

ACADIAN FLYCATCHER Greener upperparts; longer tail; yellowish eye ring; yellow wash on belly and undertail coverts; different voice and habitat.

Flight Pattern	
Weak fluttering direct flight with shallow wing beats. Sallies to hawk flying insects, often returning to same or nearby perch.	

Nest Identification	
Shape	Location	Grass, weeds, bark strips, small twigs, and rootlets • lined with plant down or other soft materials • in horizontal or upright fork of shrub or low tree 1–4 feet (sometimes as high as 30 feet) above ground • built by female • 3–4 white eggs dotted with brown on larger end; oval, 0.7 x 0.55 inches.

| Plumage Sexes similar | Habitat | Migration Migratory | Weight 0.5 ounce |

DATE _____ TIME_____ LOCATION _____

Family TYRANNIDAE	Species *Empidonax traillii*	Length 5.75 inches	Wingspan 8–9 inches

WILLOW FLYCATCHER

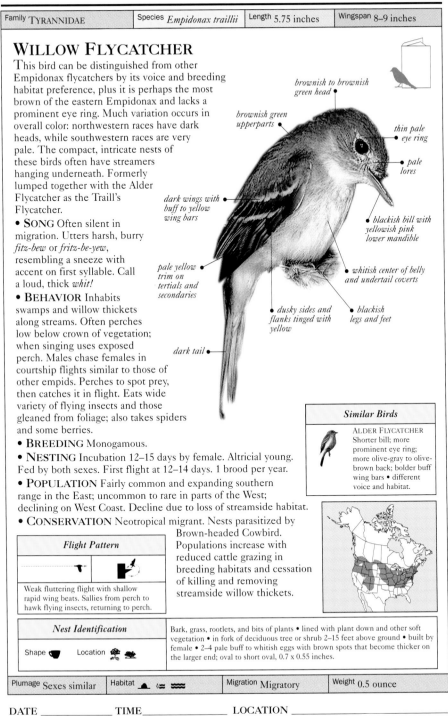

This bird can be distinguished from other Empidonax flycatchers by its voice and breeding habitat preference, plus it is perhaps the most brown of the eastern Empidonax and lacks a prominent eye ring. Much variation occurs in overall color: northwestern races have dark heads, while southwestern races are very pale. The compact, intricate nests of these birds often have streamers hanging underneath. Formerly lumped together with the Alder Flycatcher as the Traill's Flycatcher.

brownish to brownish green head

brownish green upperparts

thin pale eye ring

pale lores

blackish bill with yellowish pink lower mandible

dark wings with buff to yellow wing bars

whitish center of belly and undertail coverts

pale yellow trim on tertials and secondaries

dusky sides and flanks tinged with yellow

blackish legs and feet

dark tail

• **SONG** Often silent in migration. Utters harsh, burry *fitz-bew* or *fritz-be-yew*, resembling a sneeze with accent on first syllable. Call a loud, thick *whit!*

• **BEHAVIOR** Inhabits swamps and willow thickets along streams. Often perches low below crown of vegetation; when singing uses exposed perch. Males chase females in courtship flights similar to those of other empids. Perches to spot prey, then catches it in flight. Eats wide variety of flying insects and those gleaned from foliage; also takes spiders and some berries.

• **BREEDING** Monogamous.

• **NESTING** Incubation 12–15 days by female. Altricial young. Fed by both sexes. First flight at 12–14 days. 1 brood per year.

• **POPULATION** Fairly common and expanding southern range in the East; uncommon to rare in parts of the West; declining on West Coast. Decline due to loss of streamside habitat.

• **CONSERVATION** Neotropical migrant. Nests parasitized by Brown-headed Cowbird. Populations increase with reduced cattle grazing in breeding habitats and cessation of killing and removing streamside willow thickets.

Similar Birds

ALDER FLYCATCHER
Shorter bill; more prominent eye ring; more olive-gray to olive-brown back; bolder buff wing bars • different voice and habitat.

Flight Pattern

Weak fluttering flight with shallow rapid wing beats. Sallies from perch to hawk flying insects, returning to perch.

Nest Identification

Shape ⬤ Location 🌳🌿

Bark, grass, rootlets, and bits of plants • lined with plant down and other soft vegetation • in fork of deciduous tree or shrub 2–15 feet above ground • built by female • 2–4 pale buff to whitish eggs with brown spots that become thicker on the larger end; oval to short oval, 0.7 x 0.55 inches.

Plumage Sexes similar	Habitat 🔺 🌾 〰️	Migration Migratory	Weight 0.5 ounce

DATE _____ TIME_____ LOCATION _____

Family TYRANNIDAE	Species *Empidonax minimus*	Length 5.25 inches	Wingspan 7.5–8.5 inches

LEAST FLYCATCHER

large head

short triangular bill

white eye ring

whitish throat

pale lower mandible with dusky tip

gray wash on breast

olive-green to brown upperparts

paler underparts

white wing bars

short primary projection

pale yellow belly

pale yellow undertail coverts

A common summer breeding resident in North America and the smallest of the eastern empids, the Least Flycatcher is perhaps the most often-encountered small flycatcher in the East. During breeding season the male makes a noisy territorial display, calling *chee-BECK* more than sixty times per minute while chasing other flycatchers in its territory. Note its small size, small bill, brown to olive wash on the upperparts, and conspicuous eye ring and wing bars.

• **SONG** Sings raspy repetitive *chee-BECK*. Call is piercing *whitt-whitt-whitt*.
• **BEHAVIOR** Active, often changing perches. Flicks tail and wings a lot; jerks tail strongly upward. Chases female in courtship; chases ecologically similar American Redstart out of nesting territory. Perches to spot prey, then catches it in the air while flying. Also gleans insects from branches and foliage. Eats wide variety of insects, some spiders, and a few berries and seeds.
• **BREEDING** Monogamous. Sometimes in loose colonies.
• **NESTING** Incubation 13–15 days by female. Altricial young stay in nest 12–17 days. Fed by both sexes. 1–2 broods per year.
• **POPULATION** Common and widespread but declining in parts of range.
• **CONSERVATION** Neotropical migrant. Uncommon host to cowbird. Declining population noted by National Audubon Society.

Similar Birds

WILLOW, ALDER, AND ACADIAN FLYCATCHERS
Larger; larger bills; greener upperparts; longer primary extensions; different voices • Willow Flycatcher has less prominent eye ring but similar *whit* call note.

DUSKY FLYCATCHER
Slightly longer, narrower bill; longer tail; grayer throat; less contrast in wings; more narrow eye ring; different song.

HAMMOND'S FLYCATCHER
Small narrow bill; part of lower mandible is orangish; gray throat; darker olive-gray breast; more distinct teardrop-shaped eye ring; long primary projection; different voice.

Flight Pattern

Weak fluttering direct flight with shallow wing beats. Sallies to take insects in flight and returns to same or nearby perch.

Nest Identification

Shape   Location

Grass, bark strips, twigs, lichens, and plant fibers; bound by spider or caterpillar webs • in fork of tree or shrub 2–60 feet above ground • built by female • 3–6 creamy white eggs; ovate, 0.6 x 0.5 inches.

Plumage Sexes similar	Habitat	Migration Migratory	Weight 0.4 ounce

DATE _____ TIME_____ LOCATION _____

Family TYRANNIDAE	Species *Empidonax hammondii*	Length 5.5 inches	Wingspan 9 inches

HAMMOND'S FLYCATCHER

This small bird avoids competition for nest sites and food by living higher on mountains in open coniferous forests and nesting at higher elevations and farther north than most other *Empidonax* flycatchers. Spending much of its day perched high in the trees, this rather large-headed, short-tailed empid has a relatively horizontal stance, with the tail on the same plane as the body or slightly cocked. It often shows a small patch of orangish color at the base of the lower mandible.
• **SONG** Often silent for long periods of time. Low, rapid, hoarse, sharp two-syllable *sill-it* or *chi-pit* and low-pitched, rough *greeep* or *pweeet*. Call is raspy, sharp *peet*.
• **BEHAVIOR** Active, flicking tail frequently and often flicking wings at same time. Perches in tree to spot prey, then quickly catches it in flight. Eats wide variety of flying insects and others it gleans from foliage.
• **BREEDING** Monogamous.
• **NESTING** Incubation 12–16 days by female. Altricial young stay in nest 16–18 days. Fed by both sexes. 1 brood per year.
• **POPULATION** Common and widespread. Casual in East.
• **CONSERVATION** Neotropical migrant. Vulnerable to loss of habitat from logging of montane coniferous forests.

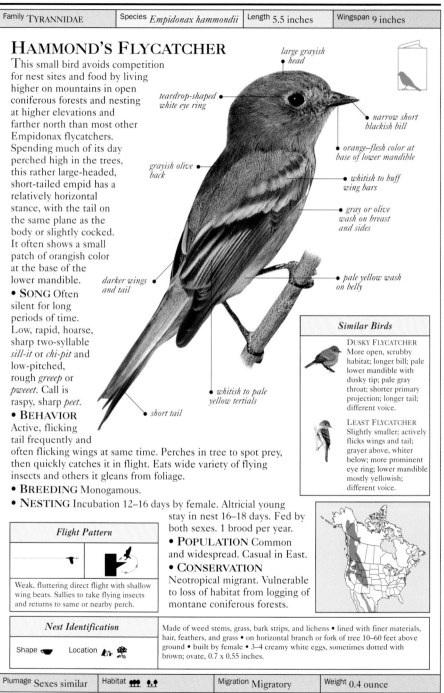

large grayish head
teardrop-shaped white eye ring
narrow short blackish bill
orange–flesh color at base of lower mandible
grayish olive back
whitish to buff wing bars
gray or olive wash on breast and sides
darker wings and tail
pale yellow wash on belly
whitish to pale yellow tertials
short tail

Similar Birds

DUSKY FLYCATCHER
More open, scrubby habitat; longer bill; pale lower mandible with dusky tip; pale gray throat; shorter primary projection; longer tail; different voice.

LEAST FLYCATCHER
Slightly smaller; actively flicks wings and tail; grayer above, whiter below; more prominent eye ring; lower mandible mostly yellowish; different voice.

Flight Pattern
Weak, fluttering direct flight with shallow wing beats. Sallies to take flying insects and returns to same or nearby perch.

Nest Identification	
Shape ⌒ Location 🌿 🪹	Made of weed stems, grass, bark strips, and lichens • lined with finer materials, hair, feathers, and grass • on horizontal branch or fork of tree 10–60 feet above ground • built by female • 3–4 creamy white eggs, sometimes dotted with brown; ovate, 0.7 x 0.55 inches.

Plumage Sexes similar	Habitat 🌳 🌾	Migration Migratory	Weight 0.4 ounce

DATE _____ TIME_____ LOCATION _____

Family TYRANNIDAE	Species *Empidonax wrightii*	Length 6 inches	Wingspan 9.5 inches

GRAY FLYCATCHER

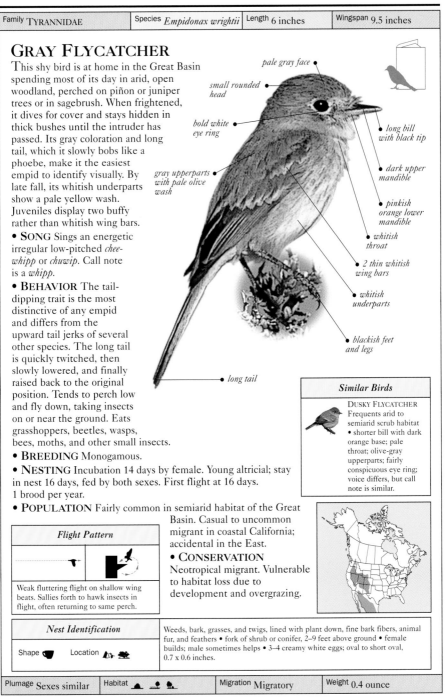

pale gray face

small rounded head

bold white eye ring

gray upperparts with pale olive wash

long bill with black tip

dark upper mandible

pinkish orange lower mandible

whitish throat

2 thin whitish wing bars

whitish underparts

blackish feet and legs

long tail

This shy bird is at home in the Great Basin spending most of its day in arid, open woodland, perched on piñon or juniper trees or in sagebrush. When frightened, it dives for cover and stays hidden in thick bushes until the intruder has passed. Its gray coloration and long tail, which it slowly bobs like a phoebe, make it the easiest empid to identify visually. By late fall, its whitish underparts show a pale yellow wash. Juveniles display two buffy rather than whitish wing bars.

• SONG Sings an energetic irregular low-pitched *chee-whipp* or *chuwip*. Call note is a *whipp*.

• BEHAVIOR The tail-dipping trait is the most distinctive of any empid and differs from the upward tail jerks of several other species. The long tail is quickly twitched, then slowly lowered, and finally raised back to the original position. Tends to perch low and fly down, taking insects on or near the ground. Eats grasshoppers, beetles, wasps, bees, moths, and other small insects.

• BREEDING Monogamous.

• NESTING Incubation 14 days by female. Young altricial; stay in nest 16 days, fed by both sexes. First flight at 16 days. 1 brood per year.

• POPULATION Fairly common in semiarid habitat of the Great Basin. Casual to uncommon migrant in coastal California; accidental in the East.

• CONSERVATION Neotropical migrant. Vulnerable to habitat loss due to development and overgrazing.

Similar Birds

DUSKY FLYCATCHER
Frequents arid to semiarid scrub habitat • shorter bill with dark orange base; pale throat; olive-gray upperparts; fairly conspicuous eye ring; voice differs, but call note is similar.

Flight Pattern

Weak fluttering flight on shallow wing beats. Sallies forth to hawk insects in flight, often returning to same perch.

Nest Identification

Shape

Location

Weeds, bark, grasses, and twigs, lined with plant down, fine bark fibers, animal fur, and feathers • fork of shrub or conifer, 2–9 feet above ground • female builds; male sometimes helps • 3–4 creamy white eggs; oval to short oval, 0.7 x 0.6 inches.

Plumage Sexes similar	Habitat	Migration Migratory	Weight 0.4 ounce

DATE _____ TIME_____ LOCATION _____

| Family TYRANNIDAE | Species *Empidonax oberholseri* | Length 5.75 inches | Wingspan 8–9 inches |

DUSKY FLYCATCHER

This bird prefers to breed and nest in the open woodlands and brushlands of high mountain chaparrals of western North America. It is similar to Hammond's Flycatcher but stays lower in elevation and less sheltered in trees, outside the dense spruce-fir forests preferred by Hammond's. It is intermediate between the Hammond's and Gray Flycatchers in body size, bill size, and tail length, and sometimes shows a yellowish wash on its underparts.

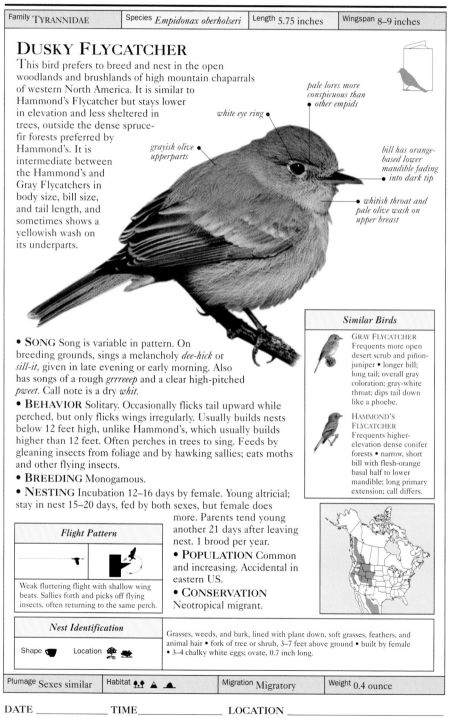

pale lores more conspicuous than other empids

white eye ring

grayish olive upperparts

bill has orange-based lower mandible fading into dark tip

whitish throat and pale olive wash on upper breast

• **SONG** Song is variable in pattern. On breeding grounds, sings a melancholy *dee-hick* or *sill-it*, given in late evening or early morning. Also has songs of a rough *grrreeep* and a clear high-pitched *pweet*. Call note is a dry *whit*.
• **BEHAVIOR** Solitary. Occasionally flicks tail upward while perched, but only flicks wings irregularly. Usually builds nests below 12 feet high, unlike Hammond's, which usually builds higher than 12 feet. Often perches in trees to sing. Feeds by gleaning insects from foliage and by hawking sallies; eats moths and other flying insects.
• **BREEDING** Monogamous.
• **NESTING** Incubation 12–16 days by female. Young altricial; stay in nest 15–20 days, fed by both sexes, but female does more. Parents tend young another 21 days after leaving nest. 1 brood per year.
• **POPULATION** Common and increasing. Accidental in eastern US.
• **CONSERVATION** Neotropical migrant.

Similar Birds

GRAY FLYCATCHER
Frequents more open desert scrub and piñon-juniper • longer bill; long tail; overall gray coloration; gray-white throat; dips tail down like a phoebe.

HAMMOND'S FLYCATCHER
Frequents higher-elevation dense conifer forests • narrow, short bill with flesh-orange basal half to lower mandible; long primary extension; call differs.

Flight Pattern

Weak fluttering flight with shallow wing beats. Sallies forth and picks off flying insects, often returning to the same perch.

Nest Identification

Shape ⬦   Location 🌿 🌳

Grasses, weeds, and bark, lined with plant down, soft grasses, feathers, and animal hair • fork of tree or shrub, 3–7 feet above ground • built by female • 3–4 chalky white eggs; ovate, 0.7 inch long.

| Plumage Sexes similar | Habitat 🌾 ⛰ 🏔 | Migration Migratory | Weight 0.4 ounce |

DATE _____ TIME_____ LOCATION _____

Family TYRANNIDAE	Species *Empidonax difficilis*	Length 5.5 inches	Wingspan 8.5 inches

PACIFIC-SLOPE FLYCATCHER

Formerly lumped together with the Cordilleran Flycatcher as one species; they were called the Western Flycatcher. It is impossible to distinguish the two species in the field except by voice and breeding range. This common forest inhabitant often is spotted perched in deep shade, singing repetitive notes and catching insects in midair. In winter it migrates to western and southern Mexico. This empid has a big head, teardrop-shaped eye ring, brownish green upperparts, and a yellow wash on its underparts.

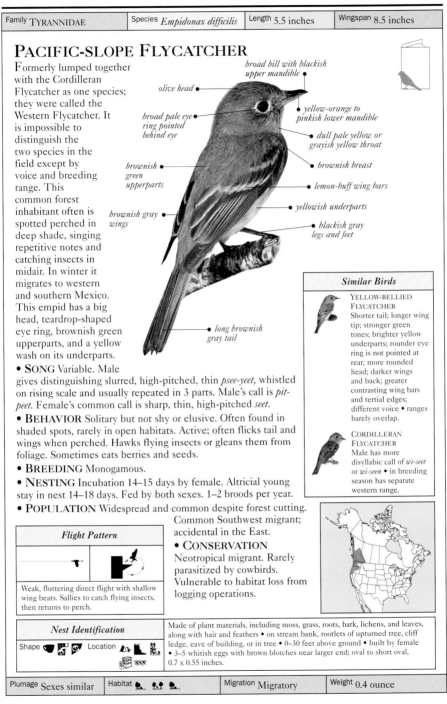

broad bill with blackish upper mandible

olive head

broad pale eye ring pointed behind eye

yellow-orange to pinkish lower mandible

dull pale yellow or grayish yellow throat

brownish green upperparts

brownish breast

lemon-buff wing bars

brownish gray wings

yellowish underparts

blackish gray legs and feet

long brownish gray tail

Similar Birds

YELLOW-BELLIED FLYCATCHER
Shorter tail; longer wing tip; stronger green tones; brighter yellow underparts; rounder eye ring is not pointed at rear; more rounded head; darker wings and back; greater contrasting wing bars and tertial edges; different voice • ranges barely overlap.

CORDILLERAN FLYCATCHER
Male has more disyllabic call of *wi-seet* or *wi-seen* • in breeding season has separate western range.

• **SONG** Variable. Male gives distinguishing slurred, high-pitched, thin *psee-yeet*, whistled on rising scale and usually repeated in 3 parts. Male's call is *pit-peet*. Female's common call is sharp, thin, high-pitched *seet*.

• **BEHAVIOR** Solitary but not shy or elusive. Often found in shaded spots, rarely in open habitats. Active; often flicks tail and wings when perched. Hawks flying insects or gleans them from foliage. Sometimes eats berries and seeds.

• **BREEDING** Monogamous.

• **NESTING** Incubation 14–15 days by female. Altricial young stay in nest 14–18 days. Fed by both sexes. 1–2 broods per year.

• **POPULATION** Widespread and common despite forest cutting. Common Southwest migrant; accidental in the East.

• **CONSERVATION** Neotropical migrant. Rarely parasitized by cowbirds. Vulnerable to habitat loss from logging operations.

Flight Pattern

Weak, fluttering direct flight with shallow wing beats. Sallies to catch flying insects, then returns to perch.

Nest Identification

Shape ◗ ▨ ◨   Location ▲ ▙ ▥ ▦ ▨

Made of plant materials, including moss, grass, roots, bark, lichens, and leaves, along with hair and feathers • on stream bank, rootlets of upturned tree, cliff ledge, eave of building, or in tree • 0–30 feet above ground • built by female • 3–5 whitish eggs with brown blotches near larger end; oval to short oval, 0.7 x 0.55 inches.

Plumage Sexes similar	Habitat 🌲 🌿 🌲	Migration Migratory	Weight 0.4 ounce

DATE _____ TIME_____ LOCATION _____

Family TYRANNIDAE	Species *Empidonax occidentalis*	Length 5.5 inches	Wingspan 8.5 nches

CORDILLERAN FLYCATCHER

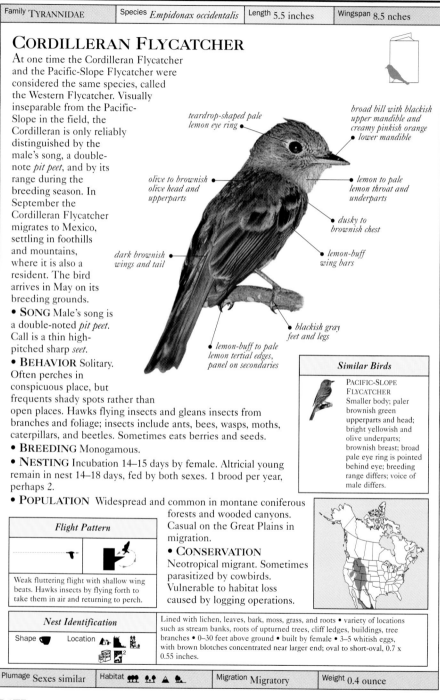

At one time the Cordilleran Flycatcher and the Pacific-Slope Flycatcher were considered the same species, called the Western Flycatcher. Visually inseparable from the Pacific-Slope in the field, the Cordilleran is only reliably distinguished by the male's song, a double-note *pit peet*, and by its range during the breeding season. In September the Cordilleran Flycatcher migrates to Mexico, settling in foothills and mountains, where it is also a resident. The bird arrives in May on its breeding grounds.

teardrop-shaped pale lemon eye ring

broad bill with blackish upper mandible and creamy pinkish orange lower mandible

olive to brownish olive head and upperparts

lemon to pale lemon throat and underparts

dusky to brownish chest

dark brownish wings and tail

lemon-buff wing bars

blackish gray feet and legs

lemon-buff to pale lemon tertial edges, panel on secondaries

• **SONG** Male's song is a double-noted *pit peet*. Call is a thin high-pitched sharp *seet*.
• **BEHAVIOR** Solitary. Often perches in conspicuous place, but frequents shady spots rather than open places. Hawks flying insects and gleans insects from branches and foliage; insects include ants, bees, wasps, moths, caterpillars, and beetles. Sometimes eats berries and seeds.
• **BREEDING** Monogamous.
• **NESTING** Incubation 14–15 days by female. Altricial young remain in nest 14–18 days, fed by both sexes. 1 brood per year, perhaps 2.
• **POPULATION** Widespread and common in montane coniferous forests and wooded canyons. Casual on the Great Plains in migration.
• **CONSERVATION** Neotropical migrant. Sometimes parasitized by cowbirds. Vulnerable to habitat loss caused by logging operations.

Similar Birds

PACIFIC-SLOPE FLYCATCHER
Smaller body; paler brownish green upperparts and head; bright yellowish and olive underparts; brownish breast; broad pale eye ring is pointed behind eye; breeding range differs; voice of male differs.

Flight Pattern

Weak fluttering flight with shallow wing beats. Hawks insects by flying forth to take them in air and returning to perch.

Nest Identification	Lined with lichen, leaves, bark, moss, grass, and roots • variety of locations such as stream banks, roots of upturned trees, cliff ledges, buildings, tree branches • 0–30 feet above ground • built by female • 3–5 whitish eggs, with brown blotches concentrated near larger end; oval to short-oval, 0.7 x 0.55 inches.
Shape 🥣 Location 🔺	

Plumage Sexes similar	Habitat 🌲 🌿 ⛰ 🍂	Migration Migratory	Weight 0.4 ounce

DATE _____ TIME_____ LOCATION _____

Family TYRANNIDAE	Species *Empidonax fulvifrons*	Length 4.5–5 inches	Wingspan 7.5–8 inches

BUFF-BREASTED FLYCATCHER

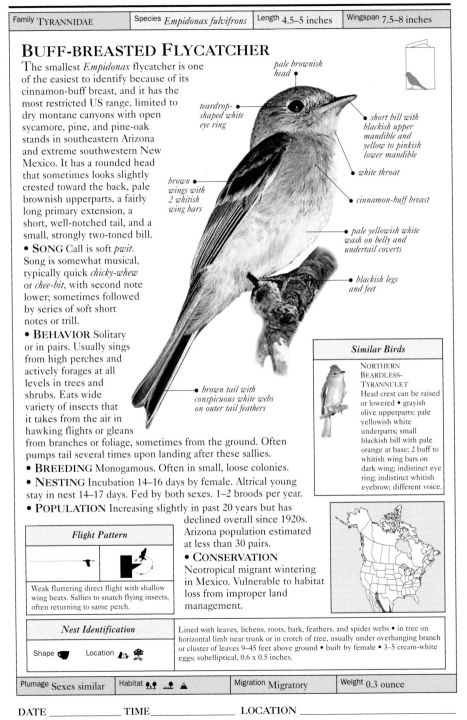

The smallest *Empidonax* flycatcher is one of the easiest to identify because of its cinnamon-buff breast, and it has the most restricted US range, limited to dry montane canyons with open sycamore, pine, and pine-oak stands in southeastern Arizona and extreme southwestern New Mexico. It has a rounded head that sometimes looks slightly crested toward the back, pale brownish upperparts, a fairly long primary extension, a short, well-notched tail, and a small, strongly two-toned bill.

pale brownish head

teardrop-shaped white eye ring

short bill with blackish upper mandible and yellow to pinkish lower mandible

white throat

brown wings with 2 whitish wing bars

cinnamon-buff breast

pale yellowish white wash on belly and undertail coverts

blackish legs and feet

- **SONG** Call is soft *pwit*. Song is somewhat musical, typically quick *chicky-whew* or *chee-bit*, with second note lower; sometimes followed by series of soft short notes or trill.
- **BEHAVIOR** Solitary or in pairs. Usually sings from high perches and actively forages at all levels in trees and shrubs. Eats wide variety of insects that it takes from the air in hawking flights or gleans from branches or foliage, sometimes from the ground. Often pumps tail several times upon landing after these sallies.

brown tail with conspicuous white webs on outer tail feathers

- **BREEDING** Monogamous. Often in small, loose colonies.
- **NESTING** Incubation 14–16 days by female. Altricial young stay in nest 14–17 days. Fed by both sexes. 1–2 broods per year.
- **POPULATION** Increasing slightly in past 20 years but has declined overall since 1920s. Arizona population estimated at less than 30 pairs.
- **CONSERVATION** Neotropical migrant wintering in Mexico. Vulnerable to habitat loss from improper land management.

Similar Birds

NORTHERN BEARDLESS-TYRANNULET
Head crest can be raised or lowered • grayish olive upperparts; pale yellowish white underparts; small blackish bill with pale orange at base; 2 buff to whitish wing bars on dark wing; indistinct eye ring; indistinct whitish eyebrow; different voice.

Flight Pattern

Weak fluttering direct flight with shallow wing beats. Sallies to snatch flying insects, often returning to same perch.

Nest Identification

Shape — Location —

Lined with leaves, lichens, roots, bark, feathers, and spider webs • in tree on horizontal limb near trunk or in crotch of tree, usually under overhanging branch or cluster of leaves 9–45 feet above ground • built by female • 3–5 cream-white eggs; subelliptical, 0.6 x 0.5 inches.

Plumage Sexes similar	Habitat	Migration Migratory	Weight 0.3 ounce

DATE _____ TIME_____ LOCATION _____

Family TYRANNIDAE	Species *Sayornis nigricans*	Length 6–7 inches	Wingspan 10.5–11 inches

BLACK PHOEBE

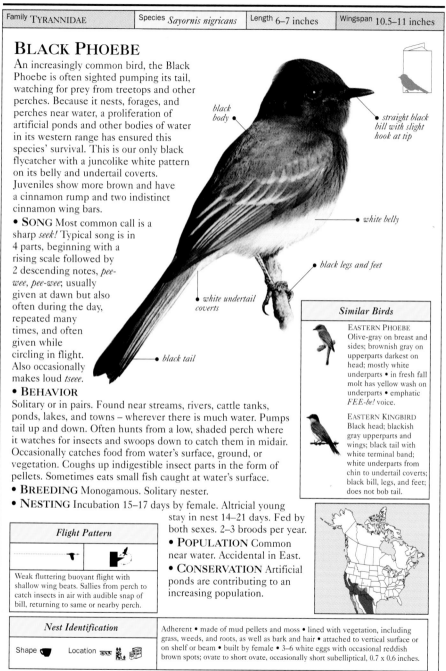

An increasingly common bird, the Black Phoebe is often sighted pumping its tail, watching for prey from treetops and other perches. Because it nests, forages, and perches near water, a proliferation of artificial ponds and other bodies of water in its western range has ensured this species' survival. This is our only black flycatcher with a juncolike white pattern on its belly and undertail coverts. Juveniles show more brown and have a cinnamon rump and two indistinct cinnamon wing bars.

black body

straight black bill with slight hook at tip

white belly

black legs and feet

white undertail coverts

black tail

• **SONG** Most common call is a sharp *seek!* Typical song is in 4 parts, beginning with a rising scale followed by 2 descending notes, *pee-wee, pee-wee*; usually given at dawn but also often during the day, repeated many times, and often given while circling in flight. Also occasionally makes loud *tseee*.

• **BEHAVIOR** Solitary or in pairs. Found near streams, rivers, cattle tanks, ponds, lakes, and towns – wherever there is much water. Pumps tail up and down. Often hunts from a low, shaded perch where it watches for insects and swoops down to catch them in midair. Occasionally catches food from water's surface, ground, or vegetation. Coughs up indigestible insect parts in the form of pellets. Sometimes eats small fish caught at water's surface.

• **BREEDING** Monogamous. Solitary nester.

• **NESTING** Incubation 15–17 days by female. Altricial young stay in nest 14–21 days. Fed by both sexes. 2–3 broods per year.

• **POPULATION** Common near water. Accidental in East.

• **CONSERVATION** Artificial ponds are contributing to an increasing population.

Similar Birds

EASTERN PHOEBE
Olive-gray on breast and sides; brownish gray on upperparts darkest on head; mostly white underparts • in fresh fall molt has yellow wash on underparts • emphatic *FEE-be!* voice.

EASTERN KINGBIRD
Black head; blackish gray upperparts and wings; black tail with white terminal band; white underparts from chin to undertail coverts; black bill, legs, and feet; does not bob tail.

Flight Pattern

Weak fluttering buoyant flight with shallow wing beats. Sallies from perch to catch insects in air with audible snap of bill, returning to same or nearby perch.

Nest Identification

Shape ◣   Location ▨ ⛰ 🏚

Adherent • made of mud pellets and moss • lined with vegetation, including grass, weeds, and roots, as well as bark and hair • attached to vertical surface or on shelf or beam • built by female • 3–6 white eggs with occasional reddish brown spots; ovate to short ovate, occasionally short subelliptical, 0.7 x 0.6 inches.

Plumage Sexes similar	Habitat ≈≈ ⏝ ⏝	Migration Most do not migrate	Weight 0.7 ounce

DATE _____ TIME_____ LOCATION _____

Family TYRANNIDAE	Species *Sayornis phoebe*	Length 7 inches	Wingspan 11.5 inches

EASTERN PHOEBE

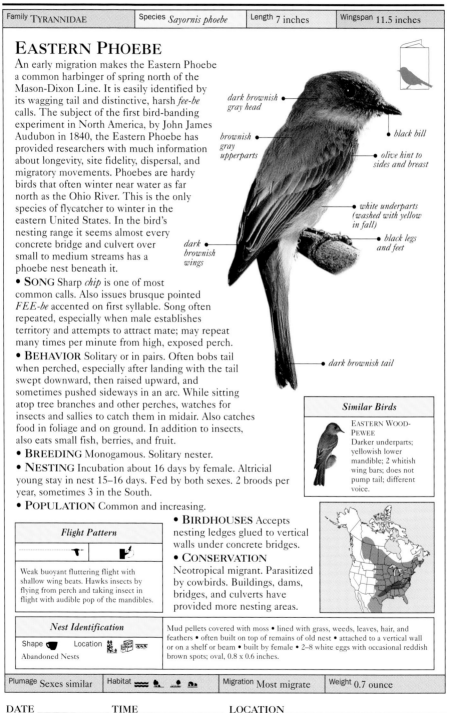

An early migration makes the Eastern Phoebe a common harbinger of spring north of the Mason-Dixon Line. It is easily identified by its wagging tail and distinctive, harsh *fee-be* calls. The subject of the first bird-banding experiment in North America, by John James Audubon in 1840, the Eastern Phoebe has provided researchers with much information about longevity, site fidelity, dispersal, and migratory movements. Phoebes are hardy birds that often winter near water as far north as the Ohio River. This is the only species of flycatcher to winter in the eastern United States. In the bird's nesting range it seems almost every concrete bridge and culvert over small to medium streams has a phoebe nest beneath it.

dark brownish gray head

brownish gray upperparts

black bill

olive hint to sides and breast

white underparts (washed with yellow in fall)

black legs and feet

dark brownish wings

dark brownish tail

- **SONG** Sharp *chip* is one of most common calls. Also issues brusque pointed *FEE-be* accented on first syllable. Song often repeated, especially when male establishes territory and attempts to attract mate; may repeat many times per minute from high, exposed perch.
- **BEHAVIOR** Solitary or in pairs. Often bobs tail when perched, especially after landing with the tail swept downward, then raised upward, and sometimes pushed sideways in an arc. While sitting atop tree branches and other perches, watches for insects and sallies to catch them in midair. Also catches food in foliage and on ground. In addition to insects, also eats small fish, berries, and fruit.
- **BREEDING** Monogamous. Solitary nester.
- **NESTING** Incubation about 16 days by female. Altricial young stay in nest 15–16 days. Fed by both sexes. 2 broods per year, sometimes 3 in the South.
- **POPULATION** Common and increasing.
- **BIRDHOUSES** Accepts nesting ledges glued to vertical walls under concrete bridges.
- **CONSERVATION** Neotropical migrant. Parasitized by cowbirds. Buildings, dams, bridges, and culverts have provided more nesting areas.

Similar Birds

EASTERN WOOD-PEWEE Darker underparts; yellowish lower mandible; 2 whitish wing bars; does not pump tail; different voice.

Flight Pattern

Weak buoyant fluttering flight with shallow wing beats. Hawks insects by flying from perch and taking insect in flight with audible pop of the mandibles.

Nest Identification

Shape   Location

Abandoned Nests

Mud pellets covered with moss • lined with grass, weeds, leaves, hair, and feathers • often built on top of remains of old nest • attached to a vertical wall or on a shelf or beam • built by female • 2–8 white eggs with occasional reddish brown spots; oval, 0.8 x 0.6 inches.

Plumage Sexes similar	Habitat	Migration Most migrate	Weight 0.7 ounce

DATE _____ TIME_____ LOCATION _____

Family TYRANNIDAE	Species *Sayornis saya*	Length 7.5 inches	Wingspan 12.5 inches

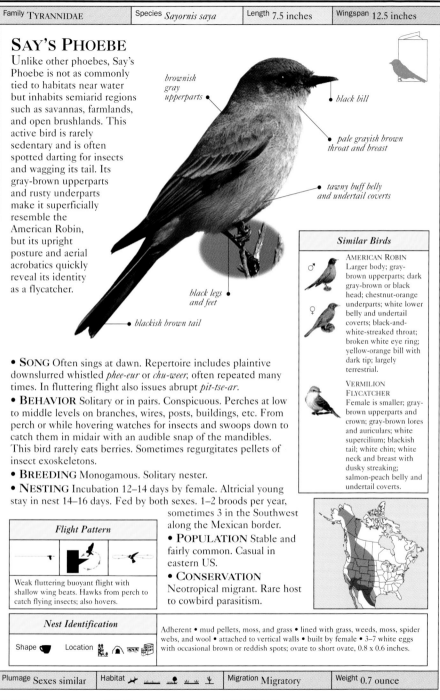

SAY'S PHOEBE

Unlike other phoebes, Say's Phoebe is not as commonly tied to habitats near water but inhabits semiarid regions such as savannas, farmlands, and open brushlands. This active bird is rarely sedentary and is often spotted darting for insects and wagging its tail. Its gray-brown upperparts and rusty underparts make it superficially resemble the American Robin, but its upright posture and aerial acrobatics quickly reveal its identity as a flycatcher.

brownish gray upperparts

black bill

pale grayish brown throat and breast

tawny buff belly and undertail coverts

black legs and feet

blackish brown tail

Similar Birds

AMERICAN ROBIN
♂ Larger body; gray-brown upperparts; dark gray-brown or black head; chestnut-orange underparts; white lower belly and undertail
♀ coverts; black-and-white-streaked throat; broken white eye ring; yellow-orange bill with dark tip; largely terrestrial.

VERMILION FLYCATCHER
Female is smaller; gray-brown upperparts and crown; gray-brown lores and auriculars; white supercilium; blackish tail; white chin; white neck and breast with dusky streaking; salmon-peach belly and undertail coverts.

• **SONG** Often sings at dawn. Repertoire includes plaintive downslurred whistled *phee-eur* or *chu-weer*, often repeated many times. In fluttering flight also issues abrupt *pit-tse-ar*.

• **BEHAVIOR** Solitary or in pairs. Conspicuous. Perches at low to middle levels on branches, wires, posts, buildings, etc. From perch or while hovering watches for insects and swoops down to catch them in midair with an audible snap of the mandibles. This bird rarely eats berries. Sometimes regurgitates pellets of insect exoskeletons.

• **BREEDING** Monogamous. Solitary nester.

• **NESTING** Incubation 12–14 days by female. Altricial young stay in nest 14–16 days. Fed by both sexes. 1–2 broods per year, sometimes 3 in the Southwest along the Mexican border.

• **POPULATION** Stable and fairly common. Casual in eastern US.

• **CONSERVATION** Neotropical migrant. Rare host to cowbird parasitism.

Flight Pattern

Weak fluttering buoyant flight with shallow wing beats. Hawks from perch to catch flying insects; also hovers.

Nest Identification

Shape | Location

Adherent • mud pellets, moss, and grass • lined with grass, weeds, moss, spider webs, and wool • attached to vertical walls • built by female • 3–7 white eggs with occasional brown or reddish spots; ovate to short ovate, 0.8 x 0.6 inches.

Plumage Sexes similar	Habitat	Migration Migratory	Weight 0.7 ounce

DATE _____ TIME_____ LOCATION _____

Family TYRANNIDAE	Species *Pyrocephalus rubinus*	Length 6 inches	Wingspan 9.5 inches

VERMILION FLYCATCHER

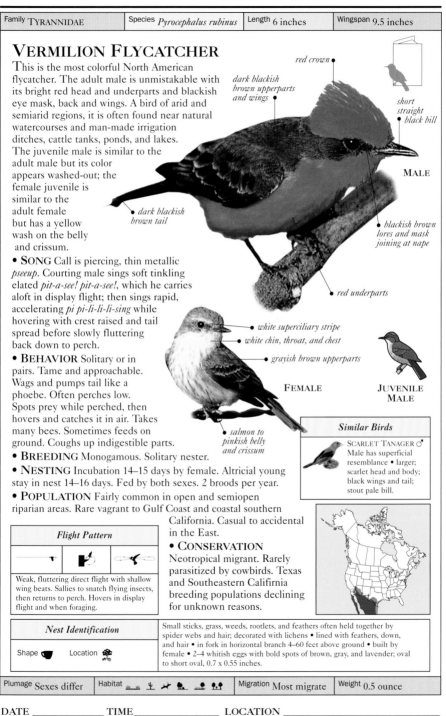

This is the most colorful North American flycatcher. The adult male is unmistakable with its bright red head and underparts and blackish eye mask, back and wings. A bird of arid and semiarid regions, it is often found near natural watercourses and man-made irrigation ditches, cattle tanks, ponds, and lakes. The juvenile male is similar to the adult male but its color appears washed-out; the female juvenile is similar to the adult female but has a yellow wash on the belly and crissum.

red crown

dark blackish brown upperparts and wings

short straight black bill

MALE

dark blackish brown tail

blackish brown lores and mask joining at nape

• **SONG** Call is piercing, thin metallic *pseeup*. Courting male sings soft tinkling elated *pit-a-see! pit-a-see!*, which he carries aloft in display flight; then sings rapid, accelerating *pi pi-li-li-li-sing* while hovering with crest raised and tail spread before slowly fluttering back down to perch.

red underparts

white superciliary stripe

white chin, throat, and chest

grayish brown upperparts

FEMALE

JUVENILE MALE

• **BEHAVIOR** Solitary or in pairs. Tame and approachable. Wags and pumps tail like a phoebe. Often perches low. Spots prey while perched, then hovers and catches it in air. Takes many bees. Sometimes feeds on ground. Coughs up indigestible parts.

salmon to pinkish belly and crissum

Similar Birds

SCARLET TANAGER ♂
Male has superficial resemblance • larger; scarlet head and body; black wings and tail; stout pale bill.

• **BREEDING** Monogamous. Solitary nester.
• **NESTING** Incubation 14–15 days by female. Altricial young stay in nest 14–16 days. Fed by both sexes. 2 broods per year.
• **POPULATION** Fairly common in open and semiopen riparian areas. Rare vagrant to Gulf Coast and coastal southern California. Casual to accidental in the East.

• **CONSERVATION** Neotropical migrant. Rarely parasitized by cowbirds. Texas and Southeastern Califirnia breeding populations declining for unknown reasons.

Flight Pattern

Weak, fluttering direct flight with shallow wing beats. Sallies to snatch flying insects, then returns to perch. Hovers in display flight and when foraging.

Nest Identification	
Shape	Location

Small sticks, grass, weeds, rootlets, and feathers often held together by spider webs and hair; decorated with lichens • lined with feathers, down, and hair • in fork in horizontal branch 4–60 feet above ground • built by female • 2–4 whitish eggs with bold spots of brown, gray, and lavender; oval to short oval, 0.7 x 0.55 inches.

Plumage Sexes differ	Habitat	Migration Most migrate	Weight 0.5 ounce

DATE _____ TIME_____ LOCATION _____

Family TYRANNIDAE	Species *Myiarchus tuberculifer*	Length 6.5–7 inches	Wingspan 11 inches

DUSKY-CAPPED FLYCATCHER

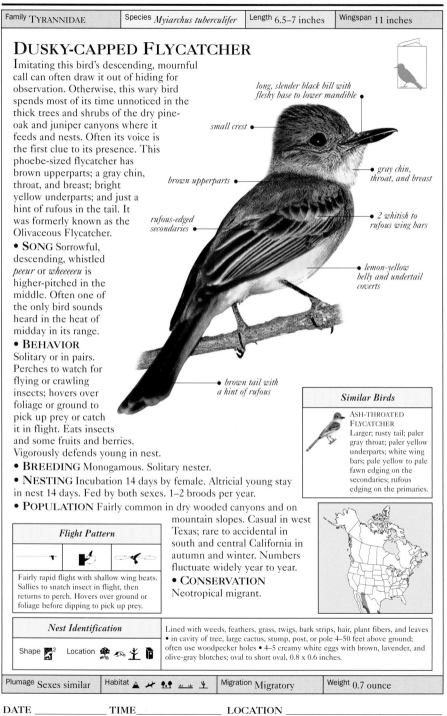

Imitating this bird's descending, mournful call can often draw it out of hiding for observation. Otherwise, this wary bird spends most of its time unnoticed in the thick trees and shrubs of the dry pine-oak and juniper canyons where it feeds and nests. Often its voice is the first clue to its presence. This phoebe-sized flycatcher has brown upperparts; a gray chin, throat, and breast; bright yellow underparts; and just a hint of rufous in the tail. It was formerly known as the Olivaceous Flycatcher.

long, slender black bill with fleshy base to lower mandible

small crest

brown upperparts

gray chin, throat, and breast

rufous-edged secondaries

2 whitish to rufous wing bars

lemon-yellow belly and undertail coverts

brown tail with a hint of rufous

• **SONG** Sorrowful, descending, whistled *peeur* or *wheeeeeu* is higher-pitched in the middle. Often one of the only bird sounds heard in the heat of midday in its range.

• **BEHAVIOR** Solitary or in pairs. Perches to watch for flying or crawling insects; hovers over foliage or ground to pick up prey or catch it in flight. Eats insects and some fruits and berries. Vigorously defends young in nest.

• **BREEDING** Monogamous. Solitary nester.

• **NESTING** Incubation 14 days by female. Altricial young stay in nest 14 days. Fed by both sexes. 1–2 broods per year.

• **POPULATION** Fairly common in dry wooded canyons and on mountain slopes. Casual in west Texas; rare to accidental in south and central California in autumn and winter. Numbers fluctuate widely year to year.

• **CONSERVATION** Neotropical migrant.

Similar Birds

ASH-THROATED FLYCATCHER
Larger; rusty tail; paler gray throat; paler yellow underparts; white wing bars; pale yellow to pale fawn edging on the secondaries; rufous edging on the primaries.

Flight Pattern

Fairly rapid flight with shallow wing beats. Sallies to snatch insect in flight, then returns to perch. Hovers over ground or foliage before dipping to pick up prey.

Nest Identification

Shape [ ] Location [ ]

Lined with weeds, feathers, grass, twigs, bark strips, hair, plant fibers, and leaves • in cavity of tree, large cactus, stump, post, or pole 4–50 feet above ground; often use woodpecker holes • 4–5 creamy white eggs with brown, lavender, and olive-gray blotches; oval to short oval, 0.8 x 0.6 inches.

Plumage Sexes similar	Habitat	Migration Migratory	Weight 0.7 ounce

DATE _____ TIME_____ LOCATION _____

| Family TYRANNIDAE | Species *Myiarchus cinerascens* | Length 8.5 inches | Wingspan 14 inches |

ASH-THROATED FLYCATCHER

This bird inhabits a wide range of habitats, from desert scrub below sea level to mountain regions of oak and piñon-juniper more than 9,000 feet high. It has the typical color pattern of *Myiarchus* flycatchers, with grayish brown upperparts, gray from the chin to lower breast, yellowish underparts, and rufous in the long tail. The visual key to its identity lies in the paleness of the underparts, which include a whitish throat and pale yellowish belly and undertail coverts.

grayish brown head

grayish brown upperparts

grayish brown wings

stout black bill

silvery white throat

pale gray breast

2 white wing bars

pale yellowish belly and undertail coverts

black legs and feet

rufous wash on inner webs of tail

• **SONG** Most often a coarse *pwrrit*, like a referee's whistle, and a short *puip* or *huit*. On breeding grounds sings a rolling nasal *ka-brik, ka-brik*. Dawn song is varied arrangement of the calls.

• **BEHAVIOR** Solitary or in pairs. Seeks prey while perched, then hovers above and drops down on it or sallies from perch to catch it in flight. When hawking often does not return to same perch. Sometimes feeds from ground. Eats variety of insects, spiders, and caterpillars; also fruit, berries, and small lizards. Occasionally defends territory from large birds passing through, including hawks. Sometimes usurps nesting cavities from woodpeckers, forcing them to begin another hole elsewhere.

• **BREEDING** Monogamous. Solitary nester.

• **NESTING** Incubation 15 days by female. Altricial young stay in nest 14–16 days. Fed by both sexes. 1–2 broods per year.

• **POPULATION** Common to fairly common in wide variety of habitats. Rare to accidental in fall and winter in the East.

• **BIRDHOUSES** Uses bluebird nesting boxes and other nesting boxes with sufficient-sized openings to allow them access.

• **CONSERVATION** Stable and increasing in some areas. Neotropical migrant.

Similar Birds

NUTTING'S FLYCATCHER
Darker yellow belly; more olive-brown upperparts; dark color on outer webs of outer tail feathers does not extend across tips; orange mouth lining; different voice
• accidental in winter in southeastern Arizona.

DUSKY-CAPPED FLYCATCHER
Smaller; brighter lemon-yellow underparts; rufous-edged secondaries; tail largely lacks rufous; different voice • only in the West

Flight Pattern

Fairly strong flight with shallow wing beats. Sallies from perch to snatch insects in flight. Sometimes hovers above foliage or ground before dipping to catch prey.

Nest Identification

Shape __2__   Location __

Made of weeds, grass, twigs, and rootlets • often lined with hair and feathers • in tree cavity, man-made boxes, and woodpecker holes in trees, poles, and posts 3–20 feet above ground • built by both sexes • 3–7 creamy white eggs blotched with brown and lavender; oval to short oval, 0.9 x 0.7 inches.

| Plumage Sexes similar | Habitat | Migration Migratory | Weight 1.0 ounce |

DATE _____ TIME_____ LOCATION _____

Family TYRANNIDAE	Species *Myiarchus nuttingi*	Length 7.25 inches	Wingspan 12 inches

NUTTING'S FLYCATCHER

On rare occasion, this native Mexican bird has found its way in winter to the dry arid regions of southeastern Arizona. This flycatcher is difficult to distinguish from other similar *Myiarchus* flycatchers, but often it can be identified by the sound of its call. In Mexico and Central America, the bird is uncommon to fairly common in the lowlands and foothills in arid to semiarid scrubby woodlands and thorn forests. The best visual mark of distinction is the orange mouth lining, a characteristic almost impossible to see in the field.

- **SONG** Nutting's Flycatcher sings a sharp chattering *wheep, wheep,* or *wheek, wheek.* This bird also has a repetitious *ki, di-di-dir* sound.
- **BEHAVIOR** Solitary or in pairs. This flycatcher frequents the interiors and the edges of deciduous woodlots and it also spends its time in second growth, from the low to the middle levels. It can be seen sallying and hovering within foliage to catch insects for food or to snatch some berries; less often it is seen hawking insects in flight.
- **BREEDING** Monogamous. Solitary.
- **NESTING** The breeding biology of Nutting's Flycatcher is poorly known, but it is assumed to be similar to others in its genus. Incubation 14 days by female. Young altricial; stay in nest 14–16 days, fed by both sexes. 1–2 broods per year.
- **POPULATION** Accidental to southeastern Arizona in the US.

darker crown sometimes tinged with cinnamon

olive-brown upperparts

pale gray throat and breast

2 white wing bars

wing coverts and secondaries broadly edged buffy white

cinnamon-rufous-edged primaries

yellow belly and undertail coverts

dusky central tail feathers; other tail feathers with inner webs rufous

Similar Birds

ASH-THROATED FLYCATCHER
Gray-brown overall; paler yellow belly; pale gray throat and breast; creamy pink-colored inside of mouth; voice differs.

Flight Pattern

Fairly strong flight on rapidly beating wings. Hovers and dips to pick up prey; may hawk in flight and return to perch.

Nest Identification	
Shape	Location	Cavity lined with grasses, weeds, hair, twigs, rootlets, and feathers • tree, pole, or post; old woodpecker hole • 1–20 feet above ground • built by both sexes • 3–5 creamy white eggs, heavily blotched and streaked with reddish brown, purple, and black; oval to short oval, 0.8 x 0.6 inches.

Plumage Sexes similar	Habitat	Migration Nonmigratory	Weight 0.8 ounce

| Family TYRANNIDAE | Species *Myiarchus crinitus* | Length 8.5 inches | Wingspan 12–14 inches |

GREAT CRESTED FLYCATCHER

This big eastern flycatcher with a rusty tail and shaggy crest stays hidden in tall trees, but its coarse song is heard throughout the forest. Although similar in size to the Eastern Kingbird, the Great Crested Flycatcher prefers thickly wooded areas. Males defend their large territories by battling in the air with other males, clawing one another and sometimes pulling out feathers. Like some other members of its genus, it often tops off the nest with a discarded snakeskin, but in today's throwaway society it more readily finds cellophane and plastic. Perched birds show two white wing bars and cinnamon-rufous-edged primaries.

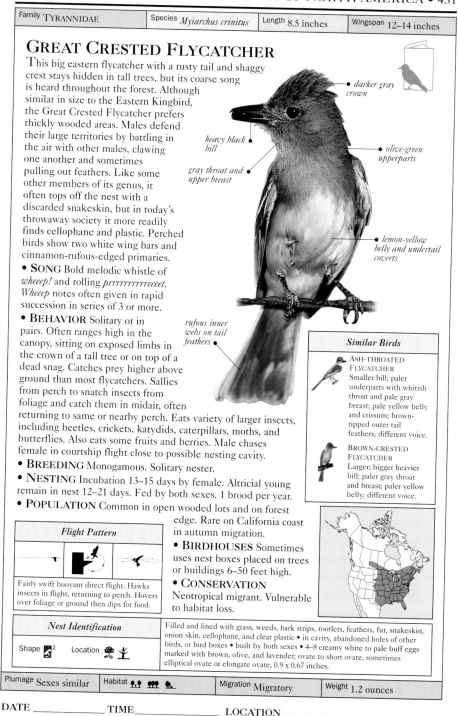

darker gray crown

heavy black bill

olive-green upperparts

gray throat and upper breast

lemon-yellow belly and undertail coverts

rufous inner webs on tail feathers

• **SONG** Bold melodic whistle of *wheeep!* and rolling *prrrrrrrrrrreeeet*. *Wheeep* notes often given in rapid succession in series of 3 or more.

• **BEHAVIOR** Solitary or in pairs. Often ranges high in the canopy, sitting on exposed limbs in the crown of a tall tree or on top of a dead snag. Catches prey higher above ground than most flycatchers. Sallies from perch to snatch insects from foliage and catch them in midair, often returning to same or nearby perch. Eats variety of larger insects, including beetles, crickets, katydids, caterpillars, moths, and butterflies. Also eats some fruits and berries. Male chases female in courtship flight close to possible nesting cavity.

• **BREEDING** Monogamous. Solitary nester.

• **NESTING** Incubation 13–15 days by female. Altricial young remain in nest 12–21 days. Fed by both sexes. 1 brood per year.

• **POPULATION** Common in open wooded lots and on forest edge. Rare on California coast in autumn migration.

• **BIRDHOUSES** Sometimes uses nest boxes placed on trees or buildings 6–50 feet high.

• **CONSERVATION** Neotropical migrant. Vulnerable to habitat loss.

Similar Birds

ASH-THROATED FLYCATCHER
Smaller bill; paler underparts with whitish throat and pale gray breast; pale yellow belly and crissum; brown-tipped outer tail feathers; different voice.

BROWN-CRESTED FLYCATCHER
Larger; bigger heavier bill; paler gray throat and breast; paler yellow belly; different voice.

Flight Pattern		

Fairly swift buoyant direct flight. Hawks insects in flight, returning to perch. Hovers over foliage or ground then dips for food.

Nest Identification	
Shape	Location	Filled and lined with grass, weeds, bark strips, rootlets, feathers, fur, snakeskin, onion skin, cellophane, and clear plastic • in cavity, abandoned holes of other birds, or bird boxes • built by both sexes • 4–8 creamy white to pale buff eggs marked with brown, olive, and lavender; ovate to short ovate, sometimes elliptical ovate or elongate ovate, 0.9 x 0.67 inches.

| Plumage Sexes similar | Habitat | Migration Migratory | Weight 1.2 ounces |

DATE _____ TIME_____ LOCATION _____

Family TYRANNIDAE	Species *Myiarchus tyrannulus*	Length 8.75 inches	Wingspan 12–14 inches

BROWN-CRESTED FLYCATCHER

This flycatcher makes its home in the sycamore canyons, mountain woodlands, saguaro desert, or any arid country where the trees are large enough for its nesting holes. Like other flycatchers the males aggressively defend their territory during breeding season, often attacking other birds with their claws and pulling out feathers. Their victims may be other flycatchers, woodpeckers, or wrens, all potential threats to take over the nesting cavity. When excited it may raise its bushy crest.

- **SONG** Rough loud *come HERE, come HERE* or *whit-will-do, whit-will-do*! Also makes sharp calls of *bew, pwit,* or *purreeet.*
- **BEHAVIOR** Solitary or in pairs. Hawks flying insects or gleans them from foliage or ground. Occasionally catches and eats hummingbirds. Also takes small lizards, berries, and fruits. Hovers and plucks prey from trees and shrubs. Perches to eat fruits and berries.
- **BEHAVIOR** Monogamous. Solitary nester. Very defensive around nest cavity, driving other birds away.
- **NESTING** Incubation 13–15 days by female. Altricial young stay in nest 12–21 days. Fed by both sexes. 1 brood per year.
- **POPULATION** Fairly common. Casual to the Gulf Coast and Florida.
- **CONSERVATION** A neotropical migrant that winters in Mexico.

bushy crest

darkest coloring is on head

long thick dark bill is often fleshy at base

olive-brown upperparts

pale grayish throat and chest

2 white wing bars

pale lemon-yellow belly and undertail coverts

rufous in primaries

rufous on inner webs of outer tail feathers

Similar Birds

ASH-THROATED FLYCATCHER
Smaller; smaller bill; paler yellow underparts; less olive on back; dusky brown of outer tail feathers crosses tip of tail; different voice.

GREAT CRESTED FLYCATCHER
Deeper, brighter yellow belly and crissum; darker gray throat and chest; different voice.

Flight Pattern

Purposeful buoyant rapid wing beats. Sallies to take insects in air and returns to perch. Also hovers and dips for prey.

Nest Identification

Shape | Location

Lined with plant fibers, animal hair, and feathers; often adds snakeskin, onion skin, or clear plastic • in holes in giant cactus, tree, man-made structure, or abandoned woodpecker holes, 5–30 feet above ground • built by both sexes • 3–6 white to pale buff eggs with brown and lavender blotches; oval to short oval, 1 x 0.8 inches.

Plumage Sexes similar	Habitat	Migration Migratory	Weight 1.5 ounces

DATE _____ TIME_____ LOCATION _____

| Family TYRANNIDAE | Species *Pitangus sulphuratus* | Length 9.75 inches | Wingspan 16 inches |

GREAT KISKADEE

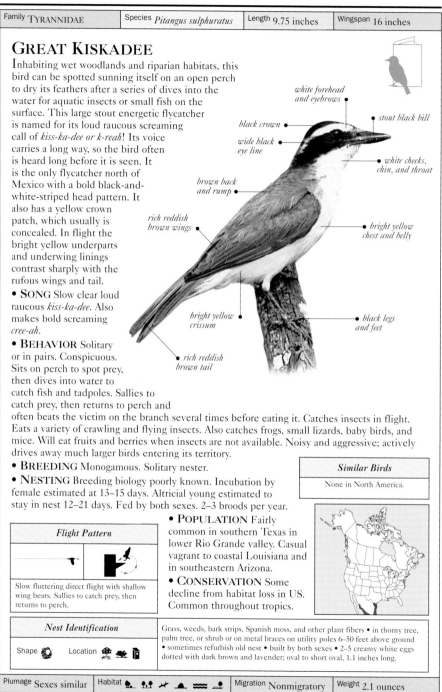

Inhabiting wet woodlands and riparian habitats, this bird can be spotted sunning itself on an open perch to dry its feathers after a series of dives into the water for aquatic insects or small fish on the surface. This large stout energetic flycatcher is named for its loud raucous screaming call of *kiss-ka-dee* or *k-reah*! Its voice carries a long way, so the bird often is heard long before it is seen. It is the only flycatcher north of Mexico with a bold black-and-white-striped head pattern. It also has a yellow crown patch, which usually is concealed. In flight the bright yellow underparts and underwing linings contrast sharply with the rufous wings and tail.

white forehead and eyebrows

black crown

stout black bill

wide black eye line

white cheeks, chin, and throat

brown back and rump

rich reddish brown wings

bright yellow chest and belly

• **SONG** Slow clear loud raucous *kiss-ka-dee*. Also makes bold screaming *cree-ah*.

bright yellow crissum

black legs and feet

• **BEHAVIOR** Solitary or in pairs. Conspicuous. Sits on perch to spot prey, then dives into water to catch fish and tadpoles. Sallies to catch prey, then returns to perch and often beats the victim on the branch several times before eating it. Catches insects in flight. Eats a variety of crawling and flying insects. Also catches frogs, small lizards, baby birds, and mice. Will eat fruits and berries when insects are not available. Noisy and aggressive; actively drives away much larger birds entering its territory.

rich reddish brown tail

• **BREEDING** Monogamous. Solitary nester.

• **NESTING** Breeding biology poorly known. Incubation by female estimated at 13–15 days. Altricial young estimated to stay in nest 12–21 days. Fed by both sexes. 2–3 broods per year.

Similar Birds
None in North America.

• **POPULATION** Fairly common in southern Texas in lower Rio Grande valley. Casual vagrant to coastal Louisiana and in southeastern Arizona.

• **CONSERVATION** Some decline from habitat loss in US. Common throughout tropics.

Flight Pattern

Slow fluttering direct flight with shallow wing beats. Sallies to catch prey, then returns to perch.

Nest Identification

Shape ●   Location 🌳 🌿 ▯

Grass, weeds, bark strips, Spanish moss, and other plant fibers • in thorny tree, palm tree, or shrub or on metal braces on utility poles 6–50 feet above ground • sometimes refurbish old nest • built by both sexes • 2–5 creamy white eggs dotted with dark brown and lavender; oval to short oval, 1.1 inches long.

| Plumage Sexes similar | Habitat 🐾 🏕 🦅 🏔 〜 ⛰ | Migration Nonmigratory | Weight 2.1 ounces |

DATE _____ TIME_____ LOCATION _____

Family TYRANNIDAE	Species *Myiodynastes luteiventris*	Length 8.5 inches	Wingspan 14.5 inches

SULPHUR-BELLIED FLYCATCHER

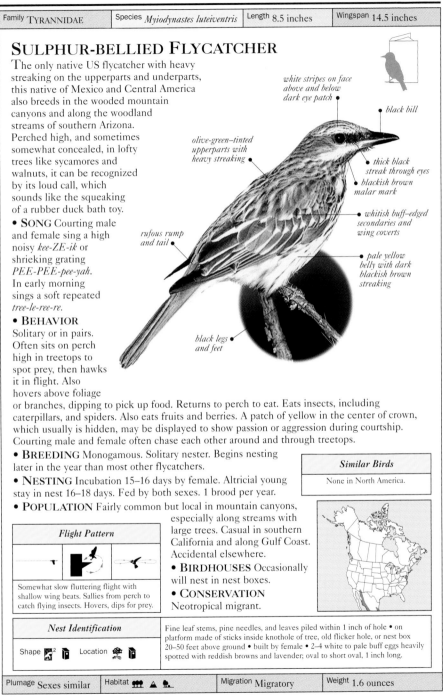

The only native US flycatcher with heavy streaking on the upperparts and underparts, this native of Mexico and Central America also breeds in the wooded mountain canyons and along the woodland streams of southern Arizona. Perched high, and sometimes somewhat concealed, in lofty trees like sycamores and walnuts, it can be recognized by its loud call, which sounds like the squeaking of a rubber duck bath toy.

white stripes on face above and below dark eye patch

black bill

olive-green–tinted upperparts with heavy streaking

thick black streak through eyes

blackish brown malar mark

whitish buff–edged secondaries and wing coverts

• **SONG** Courting male and female sing a high noisy *kee-ZE-ik* or shrieking grating *PEE-PEE-pee-yah.* In early morning sings a soft repeated *tree-le-ree-re.*

rufous rump and tail

pale yellow belly with dark blackish brown streaking

• **BEHAVIOR** Solitary or in pairs. Often sits on perch high in treetops to spot prey, then hawks it in flight. Also hovers above foliage

black legs and feet

or branches, dipping to pick up food. Returns to perch to eat. Eats insects, including caterpillars, and spiders. Also eats fruits and berries. A patch of yellow in the center of crown, which usually is hidden, may be displayed to show passion or aggression during courtship. Courting male and female often chase each other around and through treetops.

• **BREEDING** Monogamous. Solitary nester. Begins nesting later in the year than most other flycatchers.

• **NESTING** Incubation 15–16 days by female. Altricial young stay in nest 16–18 days. Fed by both sexes. 1 brood per year.

• **POPULATION** Fairly common but local in mountain canyons, especially along streams with large trees. Casual in southern California and along Gulf Coast. Accidental elsewhere.

• **BIRDHOUSES** Occasionally will nest in nest boxes.

• **CONSERVATION** Neotropical migrant.

Similar Birds
None in North America.

Flight Pattern

Somewhat slow fluttering flight with shallow wing beats. Sallies from perch to catch flying insects. Hovers, dips for prey.

Nest Identification

Shape — Location —

Fine leaf stems, pine needles, and leaves piled within 1 inch of hole • on platform made of sticks inside knothole of tree, old flicker hole, or nest box 20–50 feet above ground • built by female • 2–4 white to pale buff eggs heavily spotted with reddish browns and lavender; oval to short oval, 1 inch long.

Plumage Sexes similar	Habitat	Migration Migratory	Weight 1.6 ounces

DATE _____ TIME_____ LOCATION _____

Family TYRANNIDAE	Species *Tyrannus melancholicus*	Length 8–9.25 inches	Wingspan 15–16 inches

TROPICAL KINGBIRD

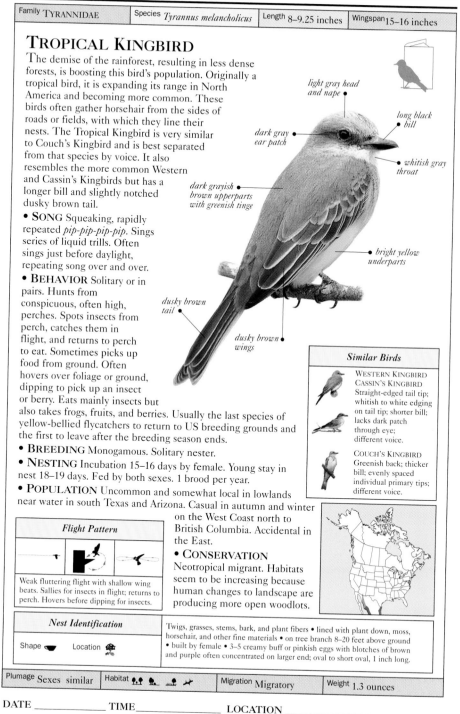

The demise of the rainforest, resulting in less dense forests, is boosting this bird's population. Originally a tropical bird, it is expanding its range in North America and becoming more common. These birds often gather horsehair from the sides of roads or fields, with which they line their nests. The Tropical Kingbird is very similar to Couch's Kingbird and is best separated from that species by voice. It also resembles the more common Western and Cassin's Kingbirds but has a longer bill and slightly notched dusky brown tail.

light gray head and nape

long black bill

dark gray ear patch

whitish gray throat

dark grayish brown upperparts with greenish tinge

bright yellow underparts

dusky brown tail

dusky brown wings

- **SONG** Squeaking, rapidly repeated *pip-pip-pip-pip*. Sings series of liquid trills. Often sings just before daylight, repeating song over and over.
- **BEHAVIOR** Solitary or in pairs. Hunts from conspicuous, often high, perches. Spots insects from perch, catches them in flight, and returns to perch to eat. Sometimes picks up food from ground. Often hovers over foliage or ground, dipping to pick up an insect or berry. Eats mainly insects but also takes frogs, fruits, and berries. Usually the last species of yellow-bellied flycatchers to return to US breeding grounds and the first to leave after the breeding season ends.
- **BREEDING** Monogamous. Solitary nester.
- **NESTING** Incubation 15–16 days by female. Young stay in nest 18–19 days. Fed by both sexes. 1 brood per year.
- **POPULATION** Uncommon and somewhat local in lowlands near water in south Texas and Arizona. Casual in autumn and winter on the West Coast north to British Columbia. Accidental in the East.
- **CONSERVATION** Neotropical migrant. Habitats seem to be increasing because human changes to landscape are producing more open woodlots.

Similar Birds

WESTERN KINGBIRD
CASSIN'S KINGBIRD
Straight-edged tail tip; whitish to white edging on tail tip; shorter bill; lacks dark patch through eye; different voice.

COUCH'S KINGBIRD
Greenish back; thicker bill; evenly spaced individual primary tips; different voice.

Flight Pattern

Weak fluttering flight with shallow wing beats. Sallies for insects in flight; returns to perch. Hovers before dipping for insects.

Nest Identification

Shape

Location

Twigs, grasses, stems, bark, and plant fibers • lined with plant down, moss, horsehair, and other fine materials • on tree branch 8–20 feet above ground • built by female • 3–5 creamy buff or pinkish eggs with blotches of brown and purple often concentrated on larger end; oval to short oval, 1 inch long.

Plumage Sexes similar	Habitat	Migration Migratory	Weight 1.3 ounces

DATE _____ TIME_____ LOCATION _____

Family TYRANNIDAE	Species *Tyrannus couchii*	Length 8–9.25 inches	Wingspan 15–16 inches

COUCH'S KINGBIRD

This bird is very similar to the Tropical Kingbird but has subtle differences in plumage and bill size. In fact, it was once considered a race of the Tropical Kingbird, but in the 1980s it was declared a separate species. Tropical and Couch's Kingbirds do not readily hybridize. Its breeding range in the United States is restricted to southern Texas, and it is best distinguished in the field by voice. Although primarily nonmigratory, birds in the northernmost parts of the breeding range are migratory.

- **SONG** A high, trilled, nasal *breeeear* and a single-note or repeated *kip*. Predawn song is a series of rich whistles with abrupt inflections, *s'wee-s'wee-s'wee s'wee-I-chu*.
- **BEHAVIOR** Solitary or in pairs. Sometimes gregarious in winter. Perches and forages in middle to high levels. Sits on perch to spot prey. Sallies out to catch insects in midair. Hovers over foliage or ground, dipping down to pick up insects and berries. Eats various flying and crawling insects, also berries and fruits.
- **BREEDING** Monogamous. Solitary.
- **NESTING** Breeding biology poorly known. Incubation by female estimated at 14–16 days. Young altricial; fed by both sexes. First flight at 18–20 days. 1 brood per year.
- **POPULATION** Common in lower Rio Grande Valley in summer; uncommon in winter. Casual to the Gulf Coast in fall and winter.
- **CONSERVATION** Neotropical migrant. Increasing in range and in numbers.

light gray face and nape

long stout black bill

dark gray ear patch

whitish throat

greenish gray back

dark grayish brown wings

bright yellow underparts

black legs and feet

dark grayish brown tail, slightly notched

Similar Birds

TROPICAL KINGBIRD Grayer back; longer, thinner bill; unevenly staggered tips of primaries; voice differs.

WESTERN KINGBIRD CASSIN'S KINGBIRD Smaller thinner bills; indistinct, lighter gray ear patches; squared tips of tails; voices differ.

Flight Pattern

Slow fluttering flight on shallow wing beats. Sallies to take insects in flight, returns to perch. Hovers down for insects.

Nest Identification

Shape ⌣   Location 🪺 🌿

Twigs, leaves, Spanish moss, weeds, and bark strips, with lining of finer materials • on tree limb, 8–25 feet high • built by female • 3–5 pinkish to warm buff eggs, with brown and lavender blotches; ovate to long ovate, subelliptical to long elliptical; 1.0 x 0.7 inches.

Plumage Sexes similar	Habitat 🌳 🌾 🏞	Migration Northern birds migrate	Weight 1.6 ounces

DATE _____ TIME _____ LOCATION _____

| Family TYRANNIDAE | Species *Tyrannus vociferans* | Length 8–9 inches | Wingspan 15–16.5 inches |

CASSIN'S KINGBIRD

The loud morning song of the male can be heard through the canyons in the foothills covered with oak-piñon and pine-juniper-sycamore woodlands on the lower slopes of the mountains where this bird makes its home. This flycatcher eats more berries and fruit, in addition to its diet of insects, than any other North American kingbird. Darker on the head, back, and breast than the very similar and more widespread Western Kingbird, this bird has a pale tip on its squared tail. Cassin's Kingbird often inhabits higher altitudes than the Western Kingbird.

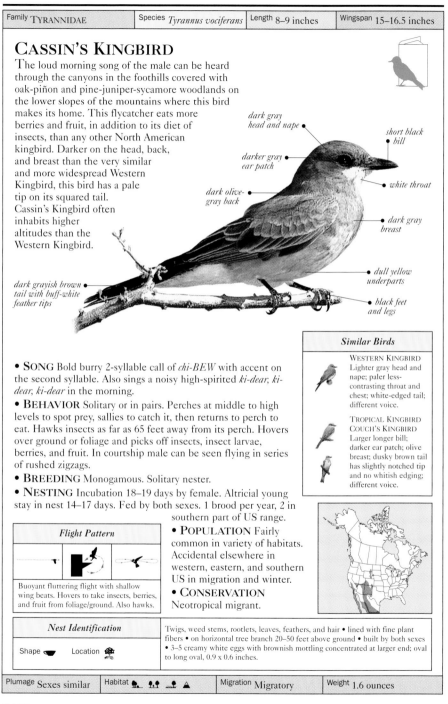

dark gray head and nape

short black bill

darker gray ear patch

dark olive-gray back

white throat

dark gray breast

dull yellow underparts

dark grayish brown tail with buff-white feather tips

black feet and legs

• **SONG** Bold burry 2-syllable call of *chi-BEW* with accent on the second syllable. Also sings a noisy high-spirited *ki-dear, ki-dear, ki-dear* in the morning.
• **BEHAVIOR** Solitary or in pairs. Perches at middle to high levels to spot prey, sallies to catch it, then returns to perch to eat. Hawks insects as far as 65 feet away from its perch. Hovers over ground or foliage and picks off insects, insect larvae, berries, and fruit. In courtship male can be seen flying in series of rushed zigzags.
• **BREEDING** Monogamous. Solitary nester.
• **NESTING** Incubation 18–19 days by female. Altricial young stay in nest 14–17 days. Fed by both sexes. 1 brood per year, 2 in southern part of US range.
• **POPULATION** Fairly common in variety of habitats. Accidental elsewhere in western, eastern, and southern US in migration and winter.
• **CONSERVATION** Neotropical migrant.

Similar Birds

WESTERN KINGBIRD
Lighter gray head and nape; paler less-contrasting throat and chest; white-edged tail; different voice.

TROPICAL KINGBIRD
COUCH'S KINGBIRD
Larger longer bill; darker ear patch; olive breast; dusky brown tail has slightly notched tip and no whitish edging; different voice.

Flight Pattern

Buoyant fluttering flight with shallow wing beats. Hovers to take insects, berries, and fruit from foliage/ground. Also hawks.

Nest Identification

Shape ◡ Location 🪹

Twigs, weed stems, rootlets, leaves, feathers, and hair • lined with fine plant fibers • on horizontal tree branch 20–50 feet above ground • built by both sexes • 3–5 creamy white eggs with brownish mottling concentrated at larger end; oval to long oval, 0.9 x 0.6 inches.

| Plumage Sexes similar | Habitat 🌳 🌿 🌲 🏔 | Migration Migratory | Weight 1.6 ounces |

DATE _____ TIME_____ LOCATION _____

Family TYRANNIDAE	Species *Tyrannus crassirostris*	Length 9.5 inches	Wingspan 15–16 inches

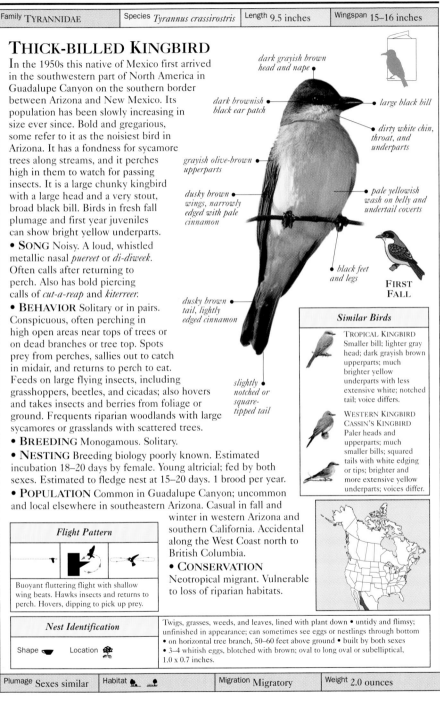

THICK-BILLED KINGBIRD

In the 1950s this native of Mexico first arrived in the southwestern part of North America in Guadalupe Canyon on the southern border between Arizona and New Mexico. Its population has been slowly increasing in size ever since. Bold and gregarious, some refer to it as the noisiest bird in Arizona. It has a fondness for sycamore trees along streams, and it perches high in them to watch for passing insects. It is a large chunky kingbird with a large head and a very stout, broad black bill. Birds in fresh fall plumage and first year juveniles can show bright yellow underparts.

dark grayish brown head and nape

dark brownish black ear patch

large black bill

dirty white chin, throat, and underparts

grayish olive-brown upperparts

dusky brown wings, narrowly edged with pale cinnamon

pale yellowish wash on belly and undertail coverts

black feet and legs

FIRST FALL

dusky brown tail, lightly edged cinnamon

- **SONG** Noisy. A loud, whistled metallic nasal *pureet* or *di-diweek*. Often calls after returning to perch. Also has bold piercing calls of *cut-a-reap* and *kiterreer*.
- **BEHAVIOR** Solitary or in pairs. Conspicuous, often perching in high open areas near tops of trees or on dead branches or tree top. Spots prey from perches, sallies out to catch in midair, and returns to perch to eat. Feeds on large flying insects, including grasshoppers, beetles, and cicadas; also hovers and takes insects and berries from foliage or ground. Frequents riparian woodlands with large sycamores or grasslands with scattered trees.
- **BREEDING** Monogamous. Solitary.
- **NESTING** Breeding biology poorly known. Estimated incubation 18–20 days by female. Young altricial; fed by both sexes. Estimated to fledge nest at 15–20 days. 1 brood per year.
- **POPULATION** Common in Guadalupe Canyon; uncommon and local elsewhere in southeastern Arizona. Casual in fall and winter in western Arizona and southern California. Accidental along the West Coast north to British Columbia.
- **CONSERVATION** Neotropical migrant. Vulnerable to loss of riparian habitats.

slightly notched or square-tipped tail

Similar Birds

TROPICAL KINGBIRD
Smaller bill; lighter gray head; dark grayish brown upperparts; much brighter yellow underparts with less extensive white; notched tail; voice differs.

WESTERN KINGBIRD
CASSIN'S KINGBIRD
Paler heads and upperparts; much smaller bills; squared tails with white edging or tips; brighter and more extensive yellow underparts; voices differ.

Flight Pattern

Buoyant fluttering flight with shallow wing beats. Hawks insects and returns to perch. Hovers, dipping to pick up prey.

Nest Identification

Shape ⌒   Location 🕸

Twigs, grasses, weeds, and leaves, lined with plant down • untidy and flimsy; unfinished in appearance; can sometimes see eggs or nestlings through bottom • on horizontal tree branch, 50–60 feet above ground • built by both sexes • 3–4 whitish eggs, blotched with brown; oval to long oval or subelliptical, 1.0 x 0.7 inches.

Plumage Sexes similar	Habitat 🌳 🌿	Migration Migratory	Weight 2.0 ounces

DATE _____ TIME_____ LOCATION _____

Family TYRANNIDAE	Species *Tyrannus verticalis*	Length 8.75 inches	Wingspan 15–16 inches

WESTERN KINGBIRD

The most common and well-known kingbird in the West has easily adapted to the ongoing development of its habitat. It even takes advantage of it by using telephone poles and other artificial structures as nesting areas and fences and utility wires as hunting perches. Often found in urban areas, it is more gregarious than any other kingbird, with two or more pairs occasionally nesting in the same tree. Aggressive, it also is known for its tenacity for chasing hawks, crows, ravens, and other large birds away from its nesting territory. It can be distinguished from other large flycatchers and kingbirds by the black tail with white edging on each side. A red-orange crown patch usually is concealed.

pale ashy gray head, neck, and breast

dark thin gray eye patch

olive-green tinted back

small black bill

bright lemon-yellow underparts

black legs and feet

dark brownish black wings contrasted with paler back

black squared tail with white edges

• **SONG** Call is a rather quiet clipped *bek*. Has an abrasive and bickering chatter of *ker-er-ip, ker-er-ip, pree pree pr-prrr*.

• **BEHAVIOR** Solitary or in pairs or small groups. Gregarious in winter. Conspicuous. Hunts from open perches at low, middle, and high levels. Sits on perch to spot prey, flies out to catch in midair, and returns to perch to eat. Often hovers above foliage or ground and dips down to pick up food. Feeds on various insects, fruits, and berries. Male performs hectic courtship flight, darting upward into air, fluttering, vibrating feathers, and delivering trilling song.

• **BREEDING** Monogamous. Solitary. Sometimes found in loose semicolonies.

• **NESTING** Incubation 18–19 days by female. Young stay in nest 16–17 days, fed by both sexes. 1–2 broods per year.

• **POPULATION** Common in semiarid open country. Range has expanded during the 20th century as expansion of agriculture has created more suitable nesting and foraging areas. Some winter in southern Florida. Accidental in fall migration to New England and the Atlantic Coast.

• **CONSERVATION** Neotropical migrant.

Similar Birds

CASSIN'S KINGBIRD
Darker gray head, breast, and neck; darker olive-brown back; pale buffy white tips on dusky brown tail feathers; whiter throat; voice differs.

TROPICAL AND COUCH'S KINGBIRDS
Larger, longer bills; darker ear patches; darker upperparts; yellow of underparts extends upward to throats; slightly notched tails; voices differ.

Flight Pattern

Buoyant fluttering flight on shallow wing beats. Sallies for insects in flight, returns to perch. Hovers over prey and dips down.

Nest Identification

Shape [symbol] Location [symbols]

Grass, weeds, twigs, and plant fibers, lined with finer materials, including hair, plant down, and cotton • near trunk on horizontal limb or fork of tree, 8–40 feet above ground • sometimes on brace or cross-arm of utility pole, church steeple, or other man-made structure • built by both sexes • 3–7 whitish eggs, heavily blotched with brown, lavender, and black; oval to short oval, 1.0 x 0.6 inches.

Plumage Sexes similar	Habitat [symbols]	Migration Migratory	Weight 1.4 ounces

DATE _____ TIME_____ LOCATION _____

Family TYRANNIDAE	Species *Tyrannus tyrannus*	Length 8.5 inches	Wingspan 14–15 inches

EASTERN KINGBIRD

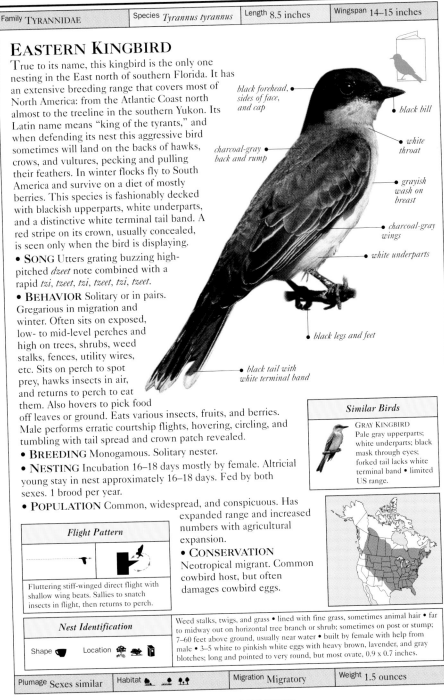

True to its name, this kingbird is the only one nesting in the East north of southern Florida. It has an extensive breeding range that covers most of North America: from the Atlantic Coast north almost to the treeline in the southern Yukon. Its Latin name means "king of the tyrants," and when defending its nest this aggressive bird sometimes will land on the backs of hawks, crows, and vultures, pecking and pulling their feathers. In winter flocks fly to South America and survive on a diet of mostly berries. This species is fashionably decked with blackish upperparts, white underparts, and a distinctive white terminal tail band. A red stripe on its crown, usually concealed, is seen only when the bird is displaying.

- **SONG** Utters grating buzzing high-pitched *dzeet* note combined with a rapid *tzi, tzeet, tzi, tzeet, tzi, tzeet.*
- **BEHAVIOR** Solitary or in pairs. Gregarious in migration and winter. Often sits on exposed, low- to mid-level perches and high on trees, shrubs, weed stalks, fences, utility wires, etc. Sits on perch to spot prey, hawks insects in air, and returns to perch to eat them. Also hovers to pick food off leaves or ground. Eats various insects, fruits, and berries. Male performs erratic courtship flights, hovering, circling, and tumbling with tail spread and crown patch revealed.
- **BREEDING** Monogamous. Solitary nester.
- **NESTING** Incubation 16–18 days mostly by female. Altricial young stay in nest approximately 16–18 days. Fed by both sexes. 1 brood per year.
- **POPULATION** Common, widespread, and conspicuous. Has expanded range and increased numbers with agricultural expansion.
- **CONSERVATION** Neotropical migrant. Common cowbird host, but often damages cowbird eggs.

black forehead, sides of face, and cap

black bill

white throat

charcoal-gray back and rump

grayish wash on breast

charcoal-gray wings

white underparts

black legs and feet

black tail with white terminal band

Similar Birds

GRAY KINGBIRD
Pale gray upperparts; white underparts; black mask through eyes; forked tail lacks white terminal band • limited US range.

Flight Pattern

Fluttering stiff-winged direct flight with shallow wing beats. Sallies to snatch insects in flight, then returns to perch.

Nest Identification

Shape   Location

Weed stalks, twigs, and grass • lined with fine grass, sometimes animal hair • far to midway out on horizontal tree branch or shrub; sometimes on post or stump; 7–60 feet above ground, usually near water • built by female with help from male • 3–5 white to pinkish white eggs with heavy brown, lavender, and gray blotches; long and pointed to very round, but most ovate, 0.9 x 0.7 inches.

Plumage Sexes similar	Habitat	Migration Migratory	Weight 1.5 ounces

DATE _____ TIME _____ LOCATION _____

Family TYRANNIDAE	Species *Tyrannus forficatus*	Length 11.5–15 inches	Wingspan 14.25–15.5 inches

SCISSOR-TAILED FLYCATCHER

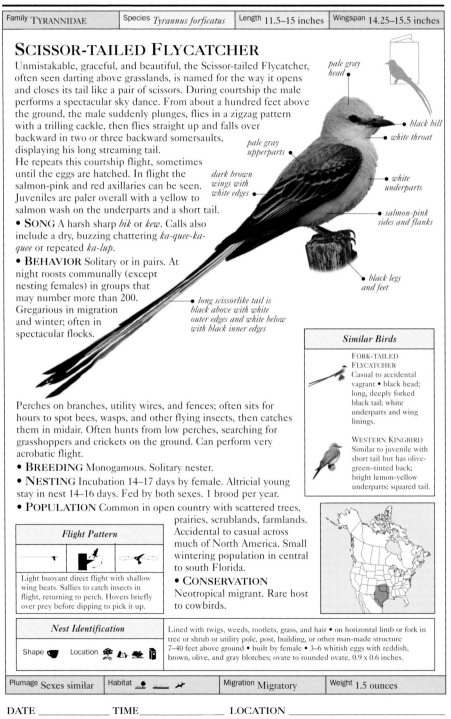

Unmistakable, graceful, and beautiful, the Scissor-tailed Flycatcher, often seen darting above grasslands, is named for the way it opens and closes its tail like a pair of scissors. During courtship the male performs a spectacular sky dance. From about a hundred feet above the ground, the male suddenly plunges, flies in a zigzag pattern with a trilling cackle, then flies straight up and falls over backward in two or three backward somersaults, displaying his long streaming tail. He repeats this courtship flight, sometimes until the eggs are hatched. In flight the salmon-pink and red axillaries can be seen. Juveniles are paler overall with a yellow to salmon wash on the underparts and a short tail.

pale gray head

black bill

white throat

pale gray upperparts

dark brown wings with white edges

white underparts

salmon-pink sides and flanks

• **SONG** A harsh sharp *bik* or *kew*. Calls also include a dry, buzzing chattering *ka-quee-ka-quee* or repeated *ka-lup*.

• **BEHAVIOR** Solitary or in pairs. At night roosts communally (except nesting females) in groups that may number more than 200. Gregarious in migration and winter; often in spectacular flocks.

black legs and feet

long scissorlike tail is black above with white outer edges and white below with black inner edges

Perches on branches, utility wires, and fences; often sits for hours to spot bees, wasps, and other flying insects, then catches them in midair. Often hunts from low perches, searching for grasshoppers and crickets on the ground. Can perform very acrobatic flight.

• **BREEDING** Monogamous. Solitary nester.

• **NESTING** Incubation 14–17 days by female. Altricial young stay in nest 14–16 days. Fed by both sexes. 1 brood per year.

• **POPULATION** Common in open country with scattered trees, prairies, scrublands, farmlands. Accidental to casual across much of North America. Small wintering population in central to south Florida.

• **CONSERVATION** Neotropical migrant. Rare host to cowbirds.

Similar Birds

FORK-TAILED FLYCATCHER
Casual to accidental vagrant • black head; long, deeply forked black tail; white underparts and wing linings.

WESTERN KINGBIRD
Similar to juvenile with short tail but has olive-green–tinted back; bright lemon-yellow underparts; squared tail.

Flight Pattern

Light buoyant direct flight with shallow wing beats. Sallies to catch insects in flight, returning to perch. Hovers briefly over prey before dipping to pick it up.

Nest Identification
Shape ⬤ Location 🌲 🏠 🌿 📦	Lined with twigs, weeds, rootlets, grass, and hair • on horizontal limb or fork in tree or shrub or utility pole, post, building, or other man-made structure 7–40 feet above ground • built by female • 3–6 whitish eggs with reddish, brown, olive, and gray blotches; ovate or rounded ovate, 0.9 x 0.6 inches.

Plumage Sexes similar	Habitat ⬤ ▬ ⤳	Migration Migratory	Weight 1.5 ounces

DATE _____ TIME_____ LOCATION _____

Family TYRANNIDAE	Species *Pachyramphus aglaiae*	Length 6.5–7.25 inches	Wingspan 11.5 inches

ROSE-THROATED BECARD

The brilliant rose-colored throat of the male helps distinguish this stocky big-headed flycatcher. Often nesting on or very near the same site year after year, it may take weeks to build its huge globular nest, which is 1–2.5 feet in size and hangs from the tip of a drooping tree branch high above the ground or over water. A native of Mexico and Central America, its range includes parts of southeast Arizona and southeast Texas. The race occurring in Texas is darker overall; males have blackish upperparts and dark gray underparts, and the rose patch on the throat is much reduced or absent. Texas females have a sooty black crown and deeper buff to tawny cinnamon underparts. Juveniles are similar to adult females.

blackish cap and nape, extending down to eyes

rose or rose-pink patch on lower throat and upper breast

gray upperparts

pale gray underparts

MALE

- **SONG** Call is a sad downslurred whistled *tseeoou*, often preceded by a reedy chatter. Alarm note is a soft *peek*. Has a rarely heard song at dawn, which is plaintive, reedy, and long-continued, *wheeuu-whyeeeuur, wheeuu-whyeeeuur.*

gray to dark gray crown

ocher-buff hind collar

- **BEHAVIOR** Solitary or in pairs. After nesting season may join mixed-species foraging flocks. Sits quietly, almost motionless, hidden in foliage on branch at middle levels in clearing, opening, or forest edge, watching for insects. Easily overlooked. Catches insects in flight. Eats insects, their larvae, and some wild fruits and berries. Also frequents canopy.

pale buff underparts

grayish brown or cinnamon upperparts

FEMALE

- **BREEDING** Monogamous. Solitary.

- **NESTING** Breeding biology poorly known. Estimated incubation 15–17 days by female. Young altricial; brooded by female; stay in nest 19–21 days, fed by both sexes. Has 1 brood per year.

Similar Birds

None in North American range.

- **POPULATION** Casual to rare in southeastern Arizona and in the lower Rio Grande Valley area of Texas.

- **CONSERVATION** Neotropical migrant. Rare host to cowbird parasitism.

Flight Pattern

Weak flights, often of short duration, with rapid shallow wing beats. Sallies forth to take insects in flight or off foliage.

Nest Identification

Shape 🪺   Location 🐾

Lichen, bark, vine, pine needles, spider web, and feathers, lined with finer materials • hangs from branch of tree, 13–70 feet above ground • built by both sexes, but female does most • 2–6 white or creamy white eggs, with brown blotches; short subelliptical, 0.9 x 0.7 inches.

Plumage Sexes differ	Habitat 🔺 🏕 🪵	Migration US birds migrate	Weight 1.1 ounces

DATE _____ TIME_____ LOCATION _____

Family LANIIDAE	Species *Lanius ludovicianus*	Length 9 inches	Wingspan 12.5–13 inches

LOGGERHEAD SHRIKE

This large-headed bird with whitish underparts is one of two shrike species that nest and breed in North America. Known as the "Butcher Bird" across its range, this adept hunter usually perches in the open to watch for prey. It has the unusual behavior of caching the bodies of its prey by suspending them impaled on a plant spine or the barbed wire of a fence. The caches may serve as larder for future use, to soften the food for easier rendering, or to passively advertise the presence of the territory and its owner. Juveniles have brownish upperparts and more distinctly barred underparts.

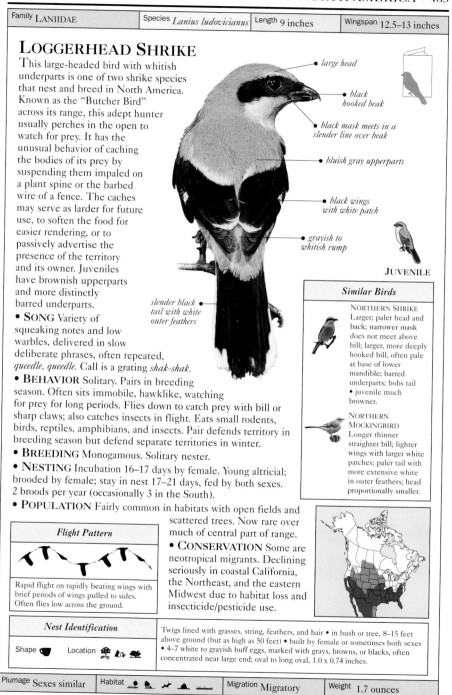

large head

black hooked beak

black mask meets in a slender line over beak

bluish gray upperparts

black wings with white patch

grayish to whitish rump

slender black tail with white outer feathers

JUVENILE

- **SONG** Variety of squeaking notes and low warbles, delivered in slow deliberate phrases, often repeated, *queedle, queedle.* Call is a grating *shak-shak*.
- **BEHAVIOR** Solitary. Pairs in breeding season. Often sits immobile, hawklike, watching for prey for long periods. Flies down to catch prey with bill or sharp claws; also catches insects in flight. Eats small rodents, birds, reptiles, amphibians, and insects. Pair defends territory in breeding season but defend separate territories in winter.
- **BREEDING** Monogamous. Solitary nester.
- **NESTING** Incubation 16–17 days by female. Young altricial; brooded by female; stay in nest 17–21 days, fed by both sexes. 2 broods per year (occasionally 3 in the South).
- **POPULATION** Fairly common in habitats with open fields and scattered trees. Now rare over much of central part of range.
- **CONSERVATION** Some are neotropical migrants. Declining seriously in coastal California, the Northeast, and the eastern Midwest due to habitat loss and insecticide/pesticide use.

Similar Birds

NORTHERN SHRIKE
Larger; paler head and back; narrower mask does not meet above bill; larger, more deeply hooked bill, often pale at base of lower mandible; barred underparts; bobs tail • juvenile much browner.

NORTHERN MOCKINGBIRD
Longer thinner straighter bill; lighter wings with larger white patches; paler tail with more extensive white in outer feathers; head proportionally smaller.

Flight Pattern
Rapid flight on rapidly beating wings with brief periods of wings pulled to sides. Often flies low across the ground.

Nest Identification	
Shape Location	Twigs lined with grasses, string, feathers, and hair • in bush or tree, 8–15 feet above ground (but as high as 50 feet) • built by female or sometimes both sexes • 4–7 white to grayish buff eggs, marked with grays, browns, or blacks, often concentrated near large end; oval to long oval, 1.0 x 0.74 inches.

Plumage Sexes similar	Habitat	Migration Migratory	Weight 1.7 ounces

DATE _____ TIME_____ LOCATION _____

Family LANIIDAE	Species *Lanius excubitor*	Length 9–10 inches	Wingspan 13.5–16.5 inches

NORTHERN SHRIKE

white feathering above bill

black eye patch

pale gray upperparts and head

large hooked bill, often with pale base to lower mandible

whitish underparts with faint barring

FIRST WINTER

JUVENILE

Perched high in the treetops, this robin-sized bird acts as a sentry, often uttering loud warning calls to other birds as it scans the landscape for prey. The larger and more northerly distributed of the two shrikes that nest and breed in North America, it is aggressive and will attack Blue Jays or other birds larger than itself, especially in defending its caches. Irruptive movements south in the winter seem to be correlated with the availability of prey species, especially small mammals. In flight the white wing patches, white rump, and white outer tail feathers contrast against the black wings and tail. The female is similar to the male but duller and sometimes more brown. Young birds are browner than adults and have heavier barring on their underparts.

• **SONG** Sings a low disjointed jerky thrasherlike song of clear notes and phrases, some musical, interspersed with grating shrieks. Call is a *shak-shak*. Also imitates calls of other birds.

• **BEHAVIOR** Solitary. Pairs in breeding season. Hunts in daytime. Perches in prominent lookout to spot prey; catches prey with beak, stuns it, and often impales it on sharp thorns or branches until ready to eat. Caches food for later use in this manner. Feeds on small mammals, mostly rodents, small birds, and insects. Aggressive in pursuit of prey. White in tail and white wing patches flash in flight.

• **BREEDING** Monogamous. Solitary nester.

• **NESTING** Incubation 15–16 days by female. Young altricial; brooded by female; stay in nest 20 days, fed by both sexes. First flight at about 20 days, but fed by both sexes for 10 more days or longer. 1 brood per year.

• **POPULATION** Uncommon in taiga (boreal forest) in clearings, open areas, and edges.

• **FEEDERS** Raw hamburger, suet. Also hunts feeder visitors.

Similar Birds

LOGGERHEAD SHRIKE Smaller; darker head and back; gray to white rump; wider mask extending above eye and across bill; smaller and less strongly hooked black bill; gray underparts with very faint or no barring • juveniles are gray-brown and lightly barred.

Flight Pattern

Swift undulating flight on shallow rapid wing beats, often low to the ground.

Nest Identification

Shape | Location

Sticks lined with feathers, hair, and fine materials • in tree or shrub, 12–20 feet above ground • built by both sexes • 4–9 grayish or greenish white eggs, heavily blotched with olive, brown, and lavender; oval to long oval, 1.1 x 0.8 inches.

Plumage Sexes similar	Habitat	Migration Migratory	Weight 2.3 ounces

DATE _____ TIME_____ LOCATION _____

Family VIREONIDAE	Species *Vireo griseus*	Length 5 inches	Wingspan 8 inches

WHITE-EYED VIREO

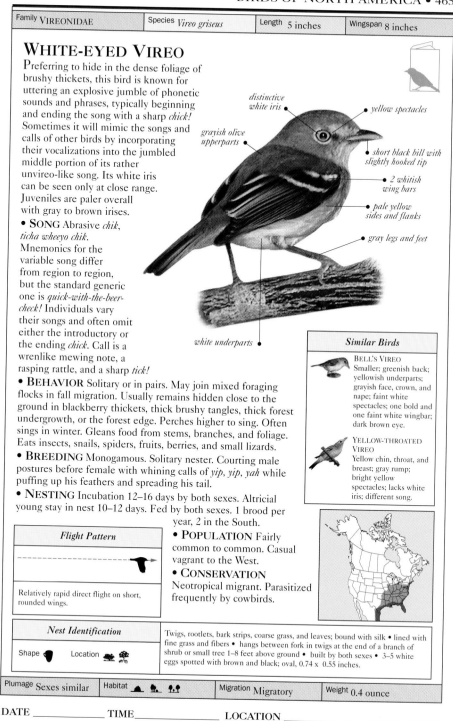

Preferring to hide in the dense foliage of brushy thickets, this bird is known for uttering an explosive jumble of phonetic sounds and phrases, typically beginning and ending the song with a sharp *chick!* Sometimes it will mimic the songs and calls of other birds by incorporating their vocalizations into the jumbled middle portion of its rather unvireo-like song. Its white iris can be seen only at close range. Juveniles are paler overall with gray to brown irises.

distinctive white iris

yellow spectacles

grayish olive upperparts

short black bill with slightly hooked tip

2 whitish wing bars

pale yellow sides and flanks

gray legs and feet

white underparts

- **SONG** Abrasive *chik, ticha wheeyo chik.* Mnemonics for the variable song differ from region to region, but the standard generic one is *quick-with-the-beer-check!* Individuals vary their songs and often omit either the introductory or the ending *chick.* Call is a wrenlike mewing note, a rasping rattle, and a sharp *tick!*
- **BEHAVIOR** Solitary or in pairs. May join mixed foraging flocks in fall migration. Usually remains hidden close to the ground in blackberry thickets, thick brushy tangles, thick forest undergrowth, or the forest edge. Perches higher to sing. Often sings in winter. Gleans food from stems, branches, and foliage. Eats insects, snails, spiders, fruits, berries, and small lizards.
- **BREEDING** Monogamous. Solitary nester. Courting male postures before female with whining calls of *yip, yip, yah* while puffing up his feathers and spreading his tail.
- **NESTING** Incubation 12–16 days by both sexes. Altricial young stay in nest 10–12 days. Fed by both sexes. 1 brood per year, 2 in the South.
- **POPULATION** Fairly common to common. Casual vagrant to the West.
- **CONSERVATION** Neotropical migrant. Parasitized frequently by cowbirds.

Similar Birds

BELL'S VIREO
Smaller; greenish back; yellowish underparts; grayish face, crown, and nape; faint white spectacles; one bold and one faint white wingbar; dark brown eye.

YELLOW-THROATED VIREO
Yellow chin, throat, and breast; gray rump; bright yellow spectacles; lacks white iris; different song.

Flight Pattern

Relatively rapid direct flight on short, rounded wings.

Nest Identification

Shape •   Location 🌿 🌳

Twigs, rootlets, bark strips, coarse grass, and leaves; bound with silk • lined with fine grass and fibers • hangs between fork in twigs at the end of a branch of shrub or small tree 1–8 feet above ground • built by both sexes • 3–5 white eggs spotted with brown and black; oval, 0.74 x 0.55 inches.

Plumage Sexes similar	Habitat 🌲 🌳 🌾	Migration Migratory	Weight 0.4 ounce

DATE _____ TIME_____ LOCATION _____

| Family VIREONIDAE | Species *Vireo bellii* | Length 4.75 inches | Wingspan 7–8 inches |

BELL'S VIREO

This small plain bird is the western counterpart of the White-eyed Vireo. It is a frequent victim of the Brown-headed Cowbird, which often lays eggs in its nest – the vireo often responds by building a new floor in the nest, covering the cowbird's eggs and its own. Although these birds actively forage during the day they are most often detected by their frequent singing. Overall plumage varies across its range, from the eastern and midwestern birds, which have greenish upperparts and yellowish underparts, to the West Coast race, which has gray upperparts and whitish underparts.

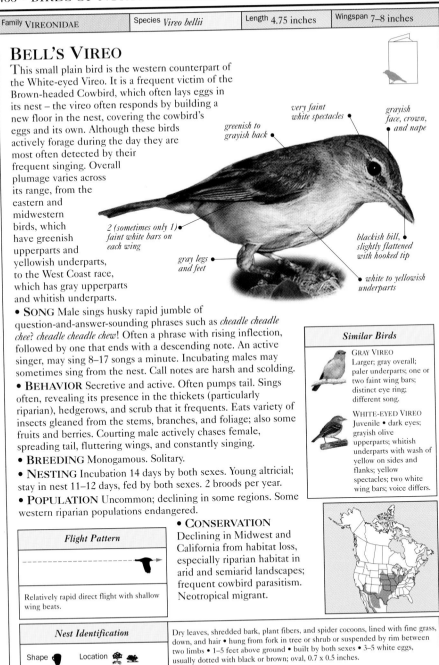

very faint white spectacles

greenish to grayish back

grayish face, crown, and nape

2 (sometimes only 1) faint white bars on each wing

gray legs and feet

blackish bill, slightly flattened with hooked tip

white to yellowish underparts

• **SONG** Male sings husky rapid jumble of question-and-answer-sounding phrases such as *cheadle cheadle chee? cheadle cheadle chew*! Often a phrase with rising inflection, followed by one that ends with a descending note. An active singer, may sing 8–17 songs a minute. Incubating males may sometimes sing from the nest. Call notes are harsh and scolding.
• **BEHAVIOR** Secretive and active. Often pumps tail. Sings often, revealing its presence in the thickets (particularly riparian), hedgerows, and scrub that it frequents. Eats variety of insects gleaned from the stems, branches, and foliage; also some fruits and berries. Courting male actively chases female, spreading tail, fluttering wings, and constantly singing.
• **BREEDING** Monogamous. Solitary.
• **NESTING** Incubation 14 days by both sexes. Young altricial; stay in nest 11–12 days, fed by both sexes. 2 broods per year.
• **POPULATION** Uncommon; declining in some regions. Some western riparian populations endangered.

Similar Birds

GRAY VIREO
Larger; gray overall; paler underparts; one or two faint wing bars; distinct eye ring; different song.

WHITE-EYED VIREO
Juvenile • dark eyes; grayish olive upperparts; whitish underparts with wash of yellow on sides and flanks; yellow spectacles; two white wing bars; voice differs.

• **CONSERVATION** Declining in Midwest and California from habitat loss, especially riparian habitat in arid and semiarid landscapes; frequent cowbird parasitism. Neotropical migrant.

Flight Pattern
Relatively rapid direct flight with shallow wing beats.

Nest Identification	
Shape	Location	Dry leaves, shredded bark, plant fibers, and spider cocoons, lined with fine grass, down, and hair • hung from fork in tree or shrub or suspended by rim between two limbs • 1–5 feet above ground • built by both sexes • 3–5 white eggs, usually dotted with black or brown; oval, 0.7 x 0.5 inches.

| Plumage Sexes similar | Habitat | Migration Migratory | Weight 0.3 ounce |

DATE _____ TIME_____ LOCATION _____

Family VIREONIDAE	Species *Vireo atricapillus*	Length 4.5 inches	Wingspan 8 inches

BLACK-CAPPED VIREO

The Black-capped Vireo is a federally listed endangered species. Difficult to spot because it forages among oak-scrub and dense thickets, it is a persistent singer often detected by its song. The male's black cap and broken white spectacles are distinctive. Females can be identified by the slate-gray cap; juvenile females have more buff-colored plumage. In the fall, this bird migrates southwest, wintering along the western coast of Mexico.

• **SONG** Persistent hurried series of twittering insistent 2- or 3-note phrases suggestive of *come here, right-now-quick!* Call note is *ji-dit*, similar to Ruby-crowned Kinglet.

• **BEHAVIOR** Solitary or in pairs. Secretive. Searches restlessly for food in deep cover among trees and thickets, looking for insects, their eggs, and larvae. Also eats small spiders and small fruits and berries. During fluttering display flight, male sings courtship song to female or follows her, singing and spreading tail.

• **BREEDING** Monogamous. Solitary.

• **NESTING** Incubation 14–17 days by both sexes; female at night and both sexes alternating during day. Young altricial; stay in nest 10–12 days, fed by both sexes. 2 broods per year.

• **POPULATION** Endangered. Uncommon to fairly common and local. Extirpated over much of its former range.

• **CONSERVATION** Cowbird brood parasitism a factor, with more than 90 percent of vireo nests parasitized in some areas, such as the Edwards Plateau in Texas. An additional known factor is the loss of oak-juniper habitat, primarily due to the development of land.

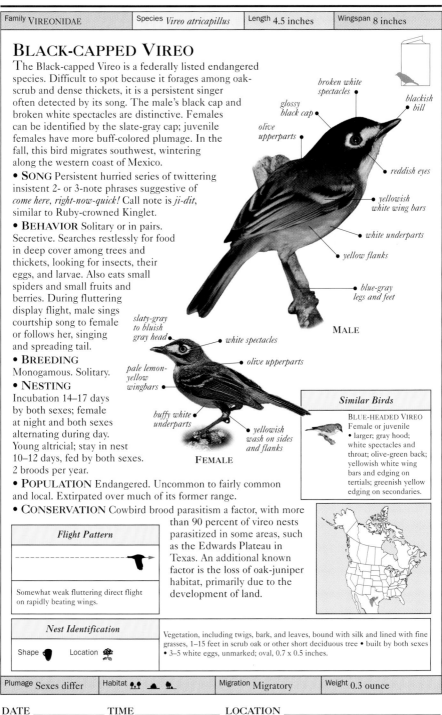

broken white spectacles
glossy black cap
blackish bill
olive upperparts
reddish eyes
yellowish white wing bars
white underparts
yellow flanks
blue-gray legs and feet

MALE

slaty-gray to bluish gray head
white spectacles
olive upperparts
pale lemon-yellow wingbars
buffy white underparts
yellowish wash on sides and flanks

FEMALE

Similar Birds

BLUE-HEADED VIREO
Female or juvenile
• larger; gray hood; white spectacles and throat; olive-green back; yellowish white wing bars and edging on tertials; greenish yellow edging on secondaries.

Flight Pattern
Somewhat weak fluttering direct flight on rapidly beating wings.

Nest Identification	
Shape ● Location ✿	Vegetation, including twigs, bark, and leaves, bound with silk and lined with fine grasses, 1–15 feet in scrub oak or other short deciduous tree • built by both sexes • 3–5 white eggs, unmarked; oval, 0.7 x 0.5 inches.

Plumage Sexes differ	Habitat	Migration Migratory	Weight 0.3 ounce

DATE _____ TIME_____ LOCATION _____

Family VIREONIDAE	Species *Vireo vicinior*	Length 5.5 inches	Wingspan 8.75 inches

GRAY VIREO

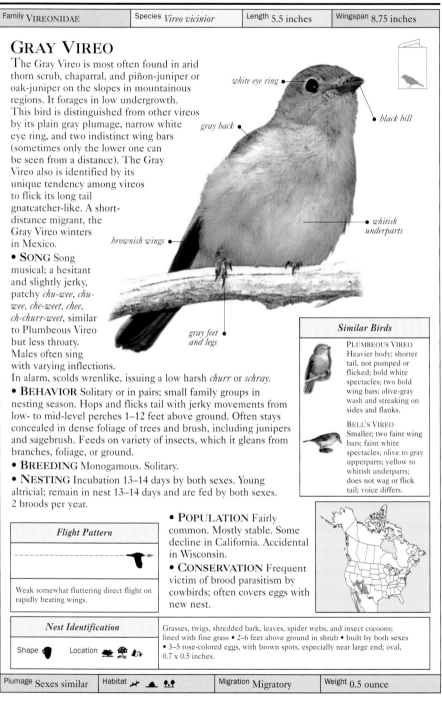

The Gray Vireo is most often found in arid thorn scrub, chaparral, and piñon-juniper or oak-juniper on the slopes in mountainous regions. It forages in low undergrowth. This bird is distinguished from other vireos by its plain gray plumage, narrow white eye ring, and two indistinct wing bars (sometimes only the lower one can be seen from a distance). The Gray Vireo also is identified by its unique tendency among vireos to flick its long tail gnatcatcher-like. A short-distance migrant, the Gray Vireo winters in Mexico.

white eye ring

black bill

gray back

whitish underparts

brownish wings

gray feet and legs

• **SONG** Song musical; a hesitant and slightly jerky, patchy *chu-wee, chu-wee, che-weet, chee, ch-churr-weet*, similar to Plumbeous Vireo but less throaty. Males often sing with varying inflections. In alarm, scolds wrenlike, issuing a low harsh *churr* or *schray*.

• **BEHAVIOR** Solitary or in pairs; small family groups in nesting season. Hops and flicks tail with jerky movements from low- to mid-level perches 1–12 feet above ground. Often stays concealed in dense foliage of trees and brush, including junipers and sagebrush. Feeds on variety of insects, which it gleans from branches, foliage, or ground.

• **BREEDING** Monogamous. Solitary.

• **NESTING** Incubation 13–14 days by both sexes. Young altricial; remain in nest 13–14 days and are fed by both sexes. 2 broods per year.

Similar Birds

PLUMBEOUS VIREO
Heavier body; shorter tail, not pumped or flicked; bold white spectacles; two bold wing bars; olive-gray wash and streaking on sides and flanks.

BELL'S VIREO
Smaller; two faint wing bars; faint white spectacles; olive to gray upperparts; yellow to whitish underparts; does not wag or flick tail; voice differs.

• **POPULATION** Fairly common. Mostly stable. Some decline in California. Accidental in Wisconsin.

• **CONSERVATION** Frequent victim of brood parasitism by cowbirds; often covers eggs with new nest.

Flight Pattern

Weak somewhat fluttering direct flight on rapidly beating wings.

Nest Identification

Shape ● Location

Grasses, twigs, shredded bark, leaves, spider webs, and insect cocoons; lined with fine grass • 2–6 feet above ground in shrub • built by both sexes • 3–5 rose-colored eggs, with brown spots, especially near large end; oval, 0.7 x 0.5 inches.

Plumage Sexes similar	Habitat	Migration Migratory	Weight 0.5 ounce

DATE _____ TIME_____ LOCATION _____

Family VIREONIDAE	Species *Vireo flavifrons*	Length 5.5 inches	Wingspan 9.5 inches

YELLOW-THROATED VIREO

Considered the most brilliantly colored vireo, this bird is most often observed in deciduous forests. Its characteristic song is a series of short phrases similar in pattern to several other vireos in its range but with long pauses between phrases and a coarse quality.

• SONG Burry series of 2-note or sometimes 3-note phrases with hesitantly long pauses between them sounding like *three-EIGHT, three-EIGHT . . . three-EIGHT*, repeated with the pattern and quality of a Blue-headed Vireo with a sore throat. Calls harsh, nasal, accelerating, rapid series of *cheh, cheh, cheh* notes.

yellow spectacles

olive-green head

olive-green upperparts

slightly hooked black bill

bright yellow throat, chin, and breast

2 white wing bars

white belly, flanks, and crissum

brownish black wings

brownish black tail

gray legs and feet

• BEHAVIOR Solitary or in pairs. In autumn migration may form mixed foraging flocks. Generally forages in treetops, eating mostly insects. Also eats some small fruits and berries. In courtship male performs nest-building display, singing and crouching before female. He often begins several nests in his territory before pairing.

• BREEDING Monogamous. Solitary nester.

• NESTING Incubation 14 days by both sexes. Altricial young stay in nest 14 days. Fed by both sexes. 1 brood per year.

• POPULATION Fairly common and stable overall but declining in the Northeast (particularly in areas with insecticide spraying of shade trees) and increasing in the upper Midwest. Rare vagrant in the West; casual in winter in south Florida.

• CONSERVATION Neotropical migrant. Common brood parasite host for Brown-headed Cowbird; sometimes builds second floor to cover its own eggs as well as cowbird's.

Similar Birds

PINE WARBLER
Slender, pointed bill; slightly notched tail; yellow chin and throat; yellow breast and sides with dusky streaking; thin, broken yellow eye ring; narrow yellow superciliary mark; thin, straight black bill; white tail spots.

Flight Pattern
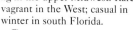
Relatively weak fluttering direct flight with rapid wing beats.

Nest Identification	
Shape ♥ Location 🪺	Grass covered with lichens • lined with grass, shredded bark, spider webs, and cocoons • in deciduous trees 3–60 feet above ground • built by both sexes • 3–5 white to pinkish white eggs with brown spots, especially near large end; oval, 0.7 x 0.5 inches.

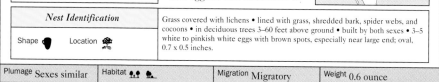

Plumage Sexes similar	Habitat 🌳 🌲	Migration Migratory	Weight 0.6 ounce

DATE _____ TIME_____ LOCATION _____

Family VIREONIDAE	Species *Vireo plumbeus*	Length 5.25 inches	Wingspan 8.5 inches

PLUMBEOUS VIREO

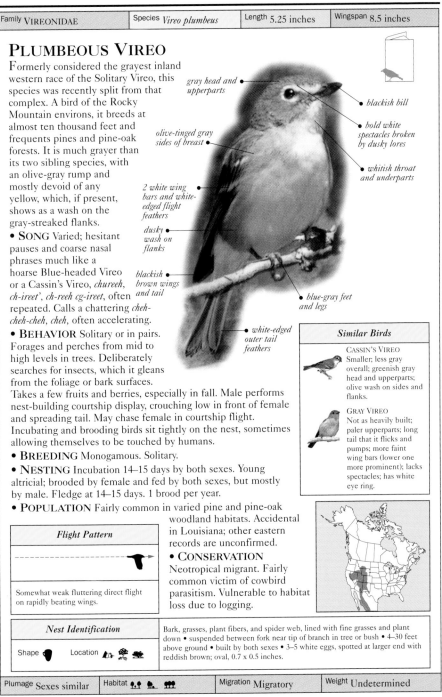

Formerly considered the grayest inland western race of the Solitary Vireo, this species was recently split from that complex. A bird of the Rocky Mountain environs, it breeds at almost ten thousand feet and frequents pines and pine-oak forests. It is much grayer than its two sibling species, with an olive-gray rump and mostly devoid of any yellow, which, if present, shows as a wash on the gray-streaked flanks.

gray head and upperparts

blackish bill

bold white spectacles broken by dusky lores

olive-tinged gray sides of breast

whitish throat and underparts

2 white wing bars and white-edged flight feathers

dusky wash on flanks

blackish brown wings and tail

blue-gray feet and legs

white-edged outer tail feathers

- **SONG** Varied; hesitant pauses and coarse nasal phrases much like a hoarse Blue-headed Vireo or a Cassin's Vireo, *chureeh, ch-ireet', ch-reeh cg-ireet*, often repeated. Calls a chattering *cheh-cheh-cheh, cheh*, often accelerating.
- **BEHAVIOR** Solitary or in pairs. Forages and perches from mid to high levels in trees. Deliberately searches for insects, which it gleans from the foliage or bark surfaces. Takes a few fruits and berries, especially in fall. Male performs nest-building courtship display, crouching low in front of female and spreading tail. May chase female in courtship flight. Incubating and brooding birds sit tightly on the nest, sometimes allowing themselves to be touched by humans.
- **BREEDING** Monogamous. Solitary.
- **NESTING** Incubation 14–15 days by both sexes. Young altricial; brooded by female and fed by both sexes, but mostly by male. Fledge at 14–15 days. 1 brood per year.
- **POPULATION** Fairly common in varied pine and pine-oak woodland habitats. Accidental in Louisiana; other eastern records are unconfirmed.
- **CONSERVATION** Neotropical migrant. Fairly common victim of cowbird parasitism. Vulnerable to habitat loss due to logging.

Similar Birds

CASSIN'S VIREO
Smaller; less gray overall; greenish gray head and upperparts; olive wash on sides and flanks.

GRAY VIREO
Not as heavily built; paler upperparts; long tail that it flicks and pumps; more faint wing bars (lower one more prominent); lacks spectacles; has white eye ring.

Flight Pattern

Somewhat weak fluttering direct flight on rapidly beating wings.

Nest Identification

Shape ◗ Location 🌳 🌲 🌳

Bark, grasses, plant fibers, and spider web, lined with fine grasses and plant down • suspended between fork near tip of branch in tree or bush • 4–30 feet above ground • built by both sexes • 3–5 white eggs, spotted at larger end with reddish brown; oval, 0.7 x 0.5 inches.

Plumage Sexes similar	Habitat 🌾 🌿 🌳	Migration Migratory	Weight Undetermined

DATE _____ TIME _____ LOCATION _____

Family VIREONIDAE	Species *Vireo cassinii*	Length 5 inches	Wingspan 8.5 inches

CASSIN'S VIREO

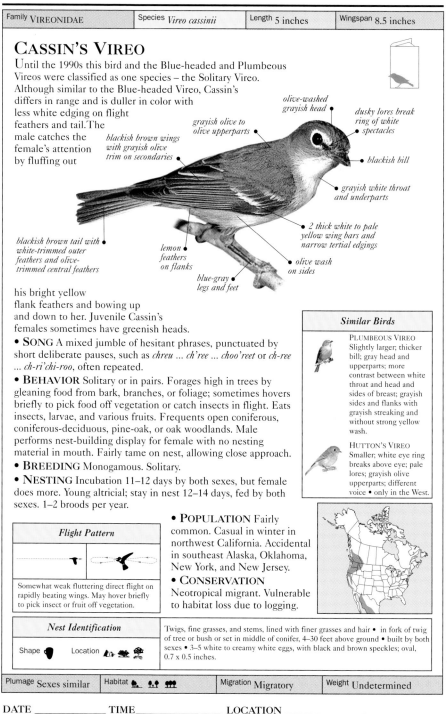

Until the 1990s this bird and the Blue-headed and Plumbeous Vireos were classified as one species – the Solitary Vireo. Although similar to the Blue-headed Vireo, Cassin's differs in range and is duller in color with less white edging on flight feathers and tail. The male catches the female's attention by fluffing out

olive-washed grayish head

dusky lores break ring of white spectacles

grayish olive to olive upperparts

blackish brown wings with grayish olive trim on secondaries

blackish bill

grayish white throat and underparts

blackish brown tail with white-trimmed outer feathers and olive-trimmed central feathers

lemon feathers on flanks

2 thick white to pale yellow wing bars and narrow tertial edgings

olive wash on sides

blue-gray legs and feet

his bright yellow flank feathers and bowing up and down to her. Juvenile Cassin's females sometimes have greenish heads.

• **SONG** A mixed jumble of hesitant phrases, punctuated by short deliberate pauses, such as *chreu ... ch'ree ... choo'reet* or *ch-ree ... ch-ri'chi-roo*, often repeated.

• **BEHAVIOR** Solitary or in pairs. Forages high in trees by gleaning food from bark, branches, or foliage; sometimes hovers briefly to pick food off vegetation or catch insects in flight. Eats insects, larvae, and various fruits. Frequents open coniferous, coniferous-deciduous, pine-oak, or oak woodlands. Male performs nest-building display for female with no nesting material in mouth. Fairly tame on nest, allowing close approach.

• **BREEDING** Monogamous. Solitary.

• **NESTING** Incubation 11–12 days by both sexes, but female does more. Young altricial; stay in nest 12–14 days, fed by both sexes. 1–2 broods per year.

• **POPULATION** Fairly common. Casual in winter in northwest California. Accidental in southeast Alaska, Oklahoma, New York, and New Jersey.

• **CONSERVATION** Neotropical migrant. Vulnerable to habitat loss due to logging.

Similar Birds

PLUMBEOUS VIREO
Slightly larger; thicker bill; gray head and upperparts; more contrast between white throat and head and sides of breast; grayish sides and flanks with grayish streaking and without strong yellow wash.

HUTTON'S VIREO
Smaller; white eye ring breaks above eye; pale lores; grayish olive upperparts; different voice • only in the West.

Flight Pattern

Somewhat weak fluttering direct flight on rapidly beating wings. May hover briefly to pick insect or fruit off vegetation.

Nest Identification

Shape

Location

Twigs, fine grasses, and stems, lined with finer grasses and hair • in fork of twig of tree or bush or set in middle of conifer, 4–30 feet above ground • built by both sexes • 3–5 white to creamy white eggs, with black and brown speckles; oval, 0.7 x 0.5 inches.

Plumage Sexes similar	Habitat	Migration Migratory	Weight Undetermined

DATE _____ TIME_____ LOCATION _____

Family VIREONIDAE	Species *Vireo solitarius*	Length 5.25 inches	Wingspan 8.5 inches

BLUE-HEADED VIREO

This bird makes its home in the thick coniferous and mixed coniferous-deciduous forests of Canada and the eastern United States, where it breeds southward through the southern Appalachians. The Appalachian race is larger, with a bluish gray back and the

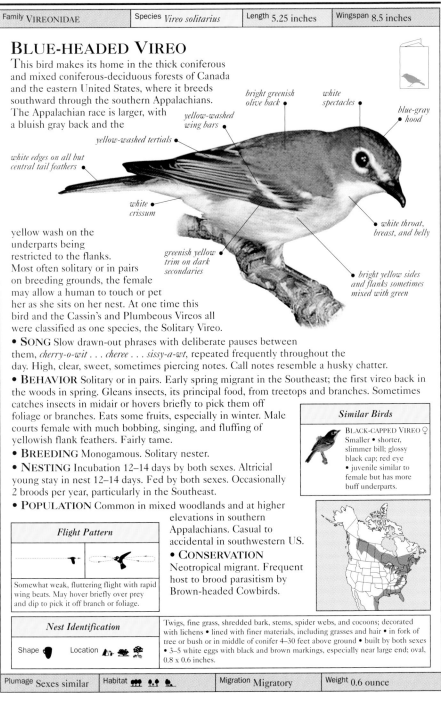

bright greenish olive back

white spectacles

blue-gray hood

yellow-washed wing bars

yellow-washed tertials

white edges on all but central tail feathers

white crissum

white throat, breast, and belly

yellow wash on the underparts being restricted to the flanks. Most often solitary or in pairs on breeding grounds, the female may allow a human to touch or pet her as she sits on her nest. At one time this bird and the Cassin's and Plumbeous Vireos all were classified as one species, the Solitary Vireo.

greenish yellow trim on dark secondaries

bright yellow sides and flanks sometimes mixed with green

• **SONG** Slow drawn-out phrases with deliberate pauses between them, *cherry-o-wit . . . cheree . . . sissy-a-wt*, repeated frequently throughout the day. High, clear, sweet, sometimes piercing notes. Call notes resemble a husky chatter.

• **BEHAVIOR** Solitary or in pairs. Early spring migrant in the Southeast; the first vireo back in the woods in spring. Gleans insects, its principal food, from treetops and branches. Sometimes catches insects in midair or hovers briefly to pick them off foliage or branches. Eats some fruits, especially in winter. Male courts female with much bobbing, singing, and fluffing of yellowish flank feathers. Fairly tame.

• **BREEDING** Monogamous. Solitary nester.

• **NESTING** Incubation 12–14 days by both sexes. Altricial young stay in nest 12–14 days. Fed by both sexes. Occasionally 2 broods per year, particularly in the Southeast.

• **POPULATION** Common in mixed woodlands and at higher elevations in southern Appalachians. Casual to accidental in southwestern US.

• **CONSERVATION** Neotropical migrant. Frequent host to brood parasitism by Brown-headed Cowbirds.

Similar Birds
BLACK-CAPPED VIREO ♀ Smaller • shorter, slimmer bill; glossy black cap; red eye • juvenile similar to female but has more buff underparts.

Flight Pattern
Somewhat weak, fluttering flight with rapid wing beats. May hover briefly over prey and dip to pick it off branch or foliage.

Nest Identification	Twigs, fine grass, shredded bark, stems, spider webs, and cocoons; decorated with lichens • lined with finer materials, including grasses and hair • in fork of tree or bush or in middle of conifer 4–30 feet above ground • built by both sexes • 3–5 white eggs with black and brown markings, especially near large end; oval, 0.8 x 0.6 inches.
Shape 🥚 Location 🌳 🌿 🌲	

Plumage Sexes similar	Habitat 🌳 🌾 🌲	Migration Migratory	Weight 0.6 ounce

DATE _____ TIME_____ LOCATION _____

| Family VIREONIDAE | Species *Vireo huttoni* | Length 4.75–5 inches | Wingspan 7–8 inches |

HUTTON'S VIREO

This small, kingletlike vireo actively forages high in the treetops, where it can be easily overlooked save for its very vocal nature. It may rapidly repeat the same song hundreds of times within a short period. Its olive-tinged plumage serves as a camouflage in the southwestern mountains and Pacific coastal woodlands where this bird makes its home. The West Coast race has greener upperparts than the interior southwestern race, which has grayer plumage.

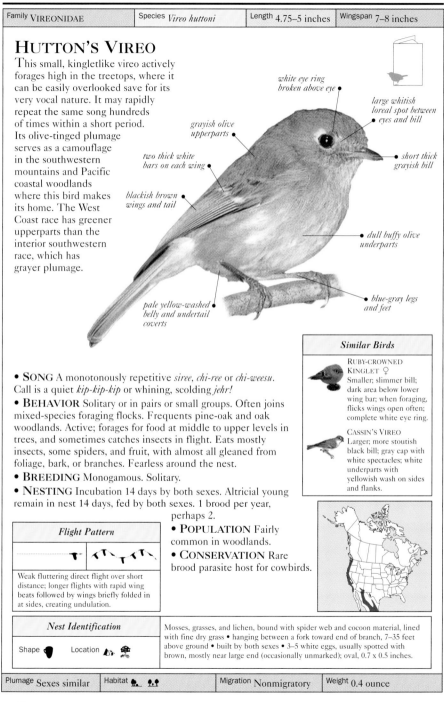

white eye ring broken above eye

large whitish loreal spot between eyes and bill

grayish olive upperparts

two thick white bars on each wing

short thick grayish bill

blackish brown wings and tail

dull buffy olive underparts

pale yellow-washed belly and undertail coverts

blue-gray legs and feet

Similar Birds

RUBY-CROWNED KINGLET ♀
Smaller; slimmer bill; dark area below lower wing bar; when foraging, flicks wings open often; complete white eye ring.

CASSIN'S VIREO
Larger; more stoutish black bill; gray cap with white spectacles; white underparts with yellowish wash on sides and flanks.

• **SONG** A monotonously repetitive *siree, chi-ree* or *chi-weesu*. Call is a quiet *kip-kip-kip* or whining, scolding *jehr!*
• **BEHAVIOR** Solitary or in pairs or small groups. Often joins mixed-species foraging flocks. Frequents pine-oak and oak woodlands. Active; forages for food at middle to upper levels in trees, and sometimes catches insects in flight. Eats mostly insects, some spiders, and fruit, with almost all gleaned from foliage, bark, or branches. Fearless around the nest.
• **BREEDING** Monogamous. Solitary.
• **NESTING** Incubation 14 days by both sexes. Altricial young remain in nest 14 days, fed by both sexes. 1 brood per year, perhaps 2.
• **POPULATION** Fairly common in woodlands.
• **CONSERVATION** Rare brood parasite host for cowbirds.

Flight Pattern

Weak fluttering direct flight over short distance; longer flights with rapid wing beats followed by wings briefly folded in at sides, creating undulation.

Nest Identification

Shape Location

Mosses, grasses, and lichen, bound with spider web and cocoon material, lined with fine dry grass • hanging between a fork toward end of branch, 7–35 feet above ground • built by both sexes • 3–5 white eggs, usually spotted with brown, mostly near large end (occasionally unmarked); oval, 0.7 x 0.5 inches.

| Plumage Sexes similar | Habitat | Migration Nonmigratory | Weight 0.4 ounce |

DATE _____ TIME_____ LOCATION _____

Family VIREONIDAE	Species *Vireo gilvus*	Length 5–5.5 inches	Wingspan 8.75 inches

WARBLING VIREO

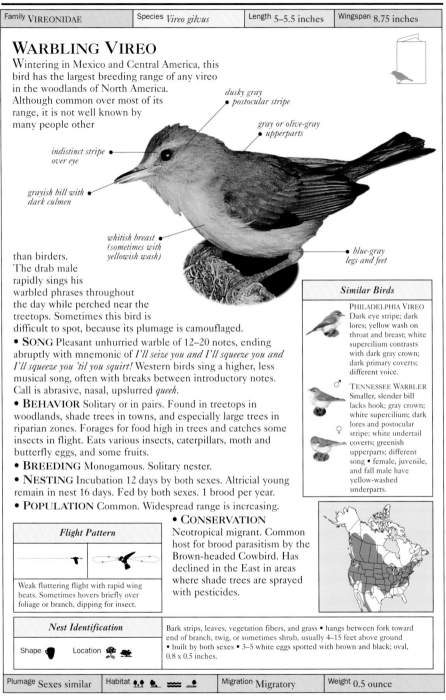

Wintering in Mexico and Central America, this bird has the largest breeding range of any vireo in the woodlands of North America. Although common over most of its range, it is not well known by many people other

dusky gray postocular stripe

gray or olive-gray upperparts

indistinct stripe over eye

grayish bill with dark culmen

whitish breast (sometimes with yellowish wash)

than birders. The drab male rapidly sings his warbled phrases throughout the day while perched near the treetops. Sometimes this bird is difficult to spot, because its plumage is camouflaged.

blue-gray legs and feet

• **SONG** Pleasant unhurried warble of 12–20 notes, ending abruptly with mnemonic of *I'll seize you and I'll squeeze you and I'll squeeze you 'til you squirt!* Western birds sing a higher, less musical song, often with breaks between introductory notes. Call is abrasive, nasal, upslurred *queeh*.

• **BEHAVIOR** Solitary or in pairs. Found in treetops in woodlands, shade trees in towns, and especially large trees in riparian zones. Forages for food high in trees and catches some insects in flight. Eats various insects, caterpillars, moth and butterfly eggs, and some fruits.

• **BREEDING** Monogamous. Solitary nester.

• **NESTING** Incubation 12 days by both sexes. Altricial young remain in nest 16 days. Fed by both sexes. 1 brood per year.

• **POPULATION** Common. Widespread range is increasing.

• **CONSERVATION** Neotropical migrant. Common host for brood parasitism by the Brown-headed Cowbird. Has declined in the East in areas where shade trees are sprayed with pesticides.

Similar Birds

PHILADELPHIA VIREO
Dark eye stripe; dark lores; yellow wash on throat and breast; white supercilium contrasts with dark gray crown; dark primary coverts; different voice.

TENNESSEE WARBLER
Smaller, slender bill lacks hook; gray crown; white supercilium; dark lores and postocular stripe; white undertail coverts; greenish upperparts; different song • female, juvenile, and fall male have yellow-washed underparts.

Flight Pattern

Weak fluttering flight with rapid wing beats. Sometimes hovers briefly over foliage or branch, dipping for insect.

Nest Identification

Shape ◖ Location 🌿 🌳

Bark strips, leaves, vegetation fibers, and grass • hangs between fork toward end of branch, twig, or sometimes shrub, usually 4–15 feet above ground • built by both sexes • 3–5 white eggs spotted with brown and black; oval, 0.8 x 0.5 inches.

Plumage Sexes similar	Habitat 🌿 🌲 〰 🍃	Migration Migratory	Weight 0.5 ounce

DATE _____ TIME_____ LOCATION _____

Family VIREONIDAE	Species *Vireo philadelphicus*	Length 4.75–5.25 inches	Wingspan 8–9 inches

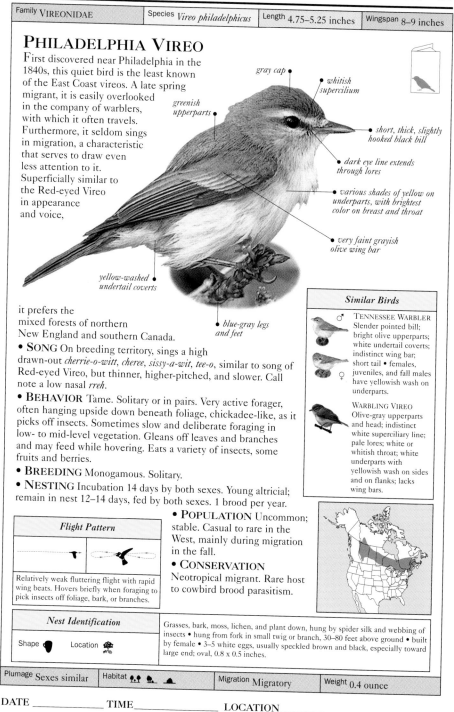

PHILADELPHIA VIREO

First discovered near Philadelphia in the 1840s, this quiet bird is the least known of the East Coast vireos. A late spring migrant, it is easily overlooked in the company of warblers, with which it often travels. Furthermore, it seldom sings in migration, a characteristic that serves to draw even less attention to it. Superficially similar to the Red-eyed Vireo in appearance and voice,

gray cap

greenish upperparts

whitish supercilium

short, thick, slightly hooked black bill

dark eye line extends through lores

various shades of yellow on underparts, with brightest color on breast and throat

very faint grayish olive wing bar

yellow-washed undertail coverts

blue-gray legs and feet

it prefers the mixed forests of northern New England and southern Canada.

- **SONG** On breeding territory, sings a high drawn-out *cherrie-o-witt, cheree, sissy-a-wit, tee-o*, similar to song of Red-eyed Vireo, but thinner, higher-pitched, and slower. Call note a low nasal *rreh*.
- **BEHAVIOR** Tame. Solitary or in pairs. Very active forager, often hanging upside down beneath foliage, chickadee-like, as it picks off insects. Sometimes slow and deliberate foraging in low- to mid-level vegetation. Gleans off leaves and branches and may feed while hovering. Eats a variety of insects, some fruits and berries.
- **BREEDING** Monogamous. Solitary.
- **NESTING** Incubation 14 days by both sexes. Young altricial; remain in nest 12–14 days, fed by both sexes. 1 brood per year.
- **POPULATION** Uncommon; stable. Casual to rare in the West, mainly during migration in the fall.
- **CONSERVATION** Neotropical migrant. Rare host to cowbird brood parasitism.

Similar Birds

TENNESSEE WARBLER ♂ Slender pointed bill; bright olive upperparts; white undertail coverts; indistinct wing bar; short tail • females, juveniles, and fall males have yellowish wash on underparts.

WARBLING VIREO Olive-gray upperparts and head; indistinct white superciliary line; pale lores; white or whitish throat; white underparts with yellowish wash on sides and on flanks; lacks wing bars.

Flight Pattern

Relatively weak fluttering flight with rapid wing beats. Hovers briefly when foraging to pick insects off foliage, bark, or branches.

Nest Identification

Shape ● Location ⬡

Grasses, bark, moss, lichen, and plant down, hung by spider silk and webbing of insects • hung from fork in small twig or branch, 30–80 feet above ground • built by female • 3–5 white eggs, usually speckled brown and black, especially toward large end; oval, 0.8 x 0.5 inches.

Plumage Sexes similar	Habitat ♠♣ ♠. ▲	Migration Migratory	Weight 0.4 ounce

DATE _____ TIME_____ LOCATION _____

| Family VIREONIDAE | Species *Vireo olivaceus* | Length 6 inches | Wingspan 10 inches |

RED-EYED VIREO

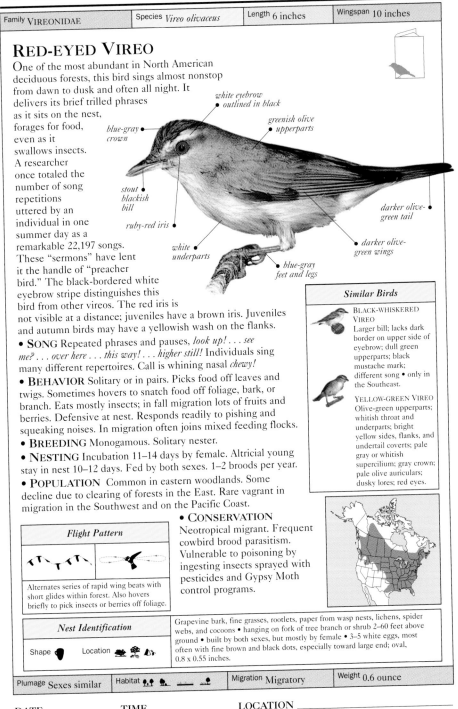

One of the most abundant in North American deciduous forests, this bird sings almost nonstop from dawn to dusk and often all night. It delivers its brief trilled phrases as it sits on the nest, forages for food, even as it swallows insects. A researcher once totaled the number of song repetitions uttered by an individual in one summer day as a remarkable 22,197 songs. These "sermons" have lent it the handle of "preacher bird." The black-bordered white eyebrow stripe distinguishes this bird from other vireos. The red iris is not visible at a distance; juveniles have a brown iris. Juveniles and autumn birds may have a yellowish wash on the flanks.

white eyebrow outlined in black

greenish olive upperparts

blue-gray crown

stout blackish bill

ruby-red iris

darker olive-green tail

white underparts

darker olive-green wings

blue-gray feet and legs

- **SONG** Repeated phrases and pauses, *look up! . . . see me? . . . over here . . . this way! . . . higher still!* Individuals sing many different repertoires. Call is whining nasal *chewy!*
- **BEHAVIOR** Solitary or in pairs. Picks food off leaves and twigs. Sometimes hovers to snatch food off foliage, bark, or branch. Eats mostly insects; in fall migration lots of fruits and berries. Defensive at nest. Responds readily to pishing and squeaking noises. In migration often joins mixed feeding flocks.
- **BREEDING** Monogamous. Solitary nester.
- **NESTING** Incubation 11–14 days by female. Altricial young stay in nest 10–12 days. Fed by both sexes. 1–2 broods per year.
- **POPULATION** Common in eastern woodlands. Some decline due to clearing of forests in the East. Rare vagrant in migration in the Southwest and on the Pacific Coast.
- **CONSERVATION** Neotropical migrant. Frequent cowbird brood parasitism. Vulnerable to poisoning by ingesting insects sprayed with pesticides and Gypsy Moth control programs.

Similar Birds

BLACK-WHISKERED VIREO
Larger bill; lacks dark border on upper side of eyebrow; dull green upperparts; black mustache mark; different song • only in the Southeast.

YELLOW-GREEN VIREO
Olive-green upperparts; whitish throat and underparts; bright yellow sides, flanks, and undertail coverts; pale gray or whitish supercilium; gray crown; pale olive auriculars; dusky lores; red eyes.

Flight Pattern

Alternates series of rapid wing beats with short glides within forest. Also hovers briefly to pick insects or berries off foliage.

Nest Identification

Shape | Location

Grapevine bark, fine grasses, rootlets, paper from wasp nests, lichens, spider webs, and cocoons • hanging on fork of tree branch or shrub 2–60 feet above ground • built by both sexes, but mostly by female • 3–5 white eggs, most often with fine brown and black dots, especially toward large end; oval, 0.8 x 0.55 inches.

| Plumage Sexes similar | Habitat | Migration Migratory | Weight 0.6 ounce |

Family VIREONIDAE	Species *Vireo flavoviridis*	Length 6 inches	Wingspan 10 inches

YELLOW-GREEN VIREO

Very similar to the Red-eyed Vireo and recently split from it to restore it as a separate species, this native of Mexico has become a rare breeding bird in southern Texas and is being seen more often in southern California in the fall and along the Gulf Coast in spring. It shows extensively yellow-green upperparts (including a face with strong yellow sides), flanks, and undertail coverts, as well as a dull olive crown with more obscure head striping than the Red-eyed Vireo and inconspicuous or absent dark bordering lines.

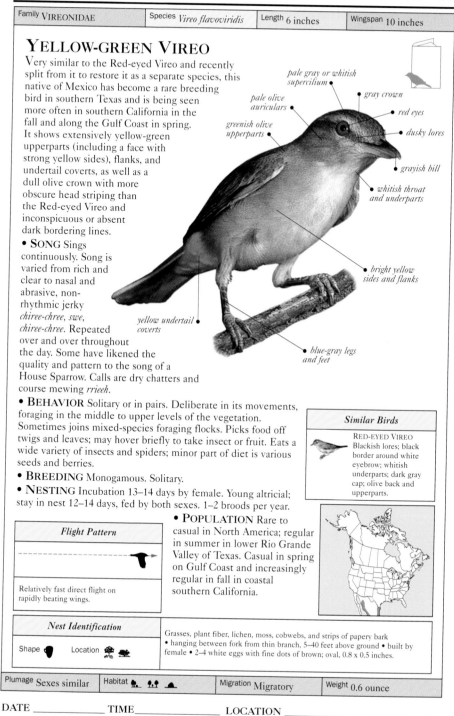

pale gray or whitish supercilium

gray crown

pale olive auriculars

red eyes

greenish olive upperparts

dusky lores

grayish bill

whitish throat and underparts

bright yellow sides and flanks

yellow undertail coverts

blue-gray legs and feet

• **SONG** Sings continuously. Song is varied from rich and clear to nasal and abrasive, non-rhythmic jerky *chiree-chree, swe, chiree-chree.* Repeated over and over throughout the day. Some have likened the quality and pattern to the song of a House Sparrow. Calls are dry chatters and course mewing *rrieeh.*

• **BEHAVIOR** Solitary or in pairs. Deliberate in its movements, foraging in the middle to upper levels of the vegetation. Sometimes joins mixed-species foraging flocks. Picks food off twigs and leaves; may hover briefly to take insect or fruit. Eats a wide variety of insects and spiders; minor part of diet is various seeds and berries.

• **BREEDING** Monogamous. Solitary.

• **NESTING** Incubation 13–14 days by female. Young altricial; stay in nest 12–14 days, fed by both sexes. 1–2 broods per year.

Similar Birds

RED-EYED VIREO
Blackish lores; black border around white eyebrow; whitish underparts; dark gray cap; olive back and upperparts.

• **POPULATION** Rare to casual in North America; regular in summer in lower Rio Grande Valley of Texas. Casual in spring on Gulf Coast and increasingly regular in fall in coastal southern California.

Flight Pattern

Relatively fast direct flight on rapidly beating wings.

Nest Identification

Shape ●   Location 🌳 🌿

Grasses, plant fiber, lichen, moss, cobwebs, and strips of papery bark • hanging between fork from thin branch, 5–40 feet above ground • built by female • 2–4 white eggs with fine dots of brown; oval, 0.8 x 0.5 inches.

Plumage Sexes similar	Habitat 🌱 🌿 ⛰	Migration Migratory	Weight 0.6 ounce

DATE _____ TIME_____ LOCATION _____

Family CORVIDAE	Species *Perisoreus canadensis*	Length 11.5 inches	Wingspan 16–17 inches

GRAY JAY

Sometimes called the "camp robber," the Gray Jay is known for its bold behavior. Often observed at cabins and campsites, it will steal food and nonedible items. With its large salivary glands, it secretes mucous that allows it to store food by sticking it on twigs, pine needles, and tree branches. Several geographical races exist across its coast-to-coast range. These races vary most noticeably in the extent of the dark patch on the nape and crown, from almost none in the Rocky Mountain races to extensive patches in the races inhabiting the northwest coast. Juveniles are entirely sooty gray with a whitish mustache. Although nonmigratory, birds practice some altitudinal migration in winter.

black head patch

pale gray head

dark smoky gray upperparts

short black bill

white throat

gray breast

dark smoky gray wings and tail

gray underparts range from pale to dark depending on race

• **SONG** Has a large repertoire of calls, including a fluted *wheeoo* and a low *chuck*. Calls also include a bold hawklike whistle, as well as a *cla-cla-cla-cla-cla*. Sometimes mimics hawk cries and songs sung by small birds.

black legs and feet

JUVENILE

• **BEHAVIOR** Tame, bold, and curious. Caches food. Omnivorous. Eats mice, eggs, and young of other birds. Takes a variety of insects, carrion, camp food, seeds, nuts, and berries. Shows no fear of humans and comes close to snatch food and other objects. Males engage in courtship feeding of females.
• **BREEDING** Monogamous. Small colonies.
• **NESTING** Incubation 16–18 days by female. Young altricial; stay in nest 15–21 days, fed by both sexes. 1 brood per year.
• **POPULATION** Common to fairly common in conifer and mixed-conifer forests. Declining in some areas due to timber harvesting. Casual in winter in midwestern and northeastern states just south of breeding range.

Similar Birds

CLARK'S NUTCRACKER Chunky; medium gray upperparts and underparts; short white tail with black central feathers; black wings with white secondaries creating patch on inner wing in flight; entirely gray head; white eye ring; long black bill.

• **FEEDERS** Will attend feeders with corn, suet, and sunflower seeds.
• **CONSERVATION** Vulnerable to habitat loss from logging operations as well as forest fragmentation.

Flight Pattern

Light buoyant flight on steady wing beats; often glides between perches within or between trees and from perch to ground.

Nest Identification	Lined with moss, grass, sticks, bark, feathers, and fur, fastened together with spider webs and insect cocoons • on horizontal branch near trunk or in crotch of tree, 4–30 feet above ground but can be up to 85 feet • built by both sexes • 2–5 grayish white, pale green, pale gray, sometimes white eggs, with fine olive-buff, brown, or gray spots; oval, 1.2 x 0.8 inches.
Shape	
Location	

Plumage Sexes similar	Habitat	Migration Nonmigratory	Weight 2.6 ounces

DATE _____ TIME_____ LOCATION _____

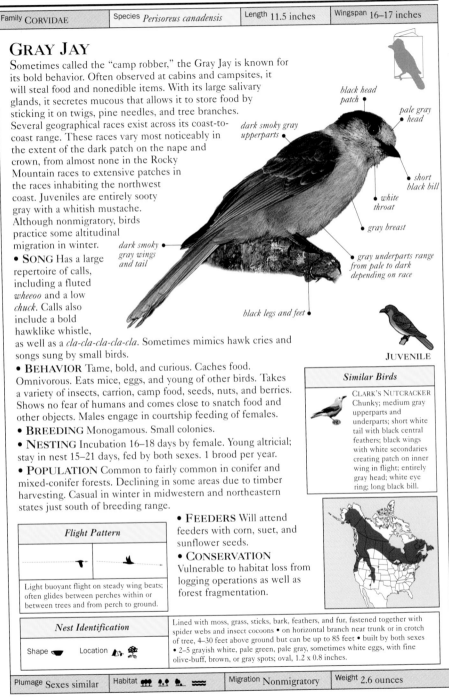

Family CORVIDAE	Species *Cyanocitta stelleri*	Length 11.5 inches	Wingspan 17 inches

STELLER'S JAY

Recognized as the only crested jay in the West, Steller's Jay is named after Arctic explorer Georg Wilhelm Steller, who discovered this bird on the Alaska coast in 1741. The darkest jay in North America, it has a black head and crest and a sooty black back and breast. The extent of black on the body is variable among local populations, as is the amount of blue or white striping on the head or throat.

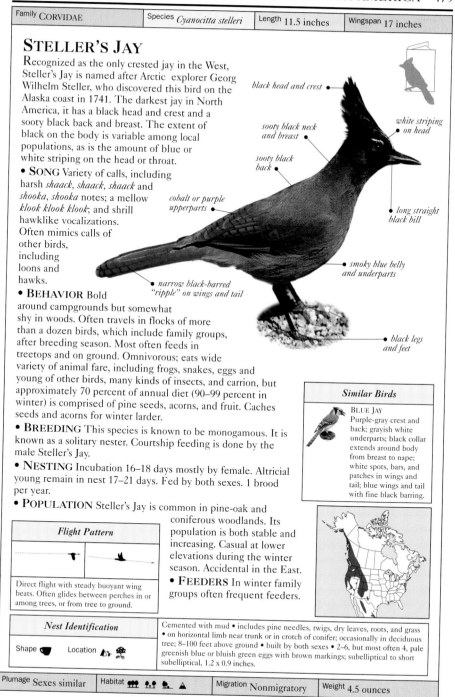

black head and crest

sooty black neck and breast

white striping on head

sooty black back

cobalt or purple upperparts

long straight black bill

smoky blue belly and underparts

narrow black-barred "ripple" on wings and tail

black legs and feet

• **SONG** Variety of calls, including harsh *shaack, shaack, shaack* and *shooka, shooka* notes; a mellow *klook klook klook*; and shrill hawklike vocalizations. Often mimics calls of other birds, including loons and hawks.

• **BEHAVIOR** Bold around campgrounds but somewhat shy in woods. Often travels in flocks of more than a dozen birds, which include family groups, after breeding season. Most often feeds in treetops and on ground. Omnivorous; eats wide variety of animal fare, including frogs, snakes, eggs and young of other birds, many kinds of insects, and carrion, but approximately 70 percent of annual diet (90–99 percent in winter) is comprised of pine seeds, acorns, and fruit. Caches seeds and acorns for winter larder.

• **BREEDING** This species is known to be monogamous. It is known as a solitary nester. Courtship feeding is done by the male Steller's Jay.

• **NESTING** Incubation 16–18 days mostly by female. Altricial young remain in nest 17–21 days. Fed by both sexes. 1 brood per year.

• **POPULATION** Steller's Jay is common in pine-oak and coniferous woodlands. Its population is both stable and increasing. Casual at lower elevations during the winter season. Accidental in the East.

• **FEEDERS** In winter family groups often frequent feeders.

Similar Birds

BLUE JAY
Purple-gray crest and back; grayish white underparts; black collar extends around body from breast to nape; white spots, bars, and patches in wings and tail; blue wings and tail with fine black barring.

Flight Pattern

Direct flight with steady buoyant wing beats. Often glides between perches in or among trees, or from tree to ground.

Nest Identification

Shape ☕   Location 🌲🌳

Cemented with mud • includes pine needles, twigs, dry leaves, roots, and grass • on horizontal limb near trunk or in crotch of conifer; occasionally in deciduous tree; 8–100 feet above ground • built by both sexes • 2–6, but most often 4, pale greenish blue or bluish green eggs with brown markings; subelliptical to short subelliptical, 1.2 x 0.9 inches.

Plumage Sexes similar	Habitat	Migration Nonmigratory	Weight 4.5 ounces

DATE _____ TIME_____ LOCATION _____

Family CORVIDAE	Species *Cyanocitta cristata*	Length 11 inches	Wingspan 16 inches

BLUE JAY

Once considered primarily a forest dweller, the Blue Jay has adapted to cities, parks, gardens, and forest fragmentation. Some populations remain in locales year-round, while more northern ones migrate south in flocks of 50–100. Common despite clear-cutting in eastern forests, its range is expanding northwest. It is easily recognized by its large size; blue-purple upperparts, wings, and tail; and jaunty bluish purple crest.

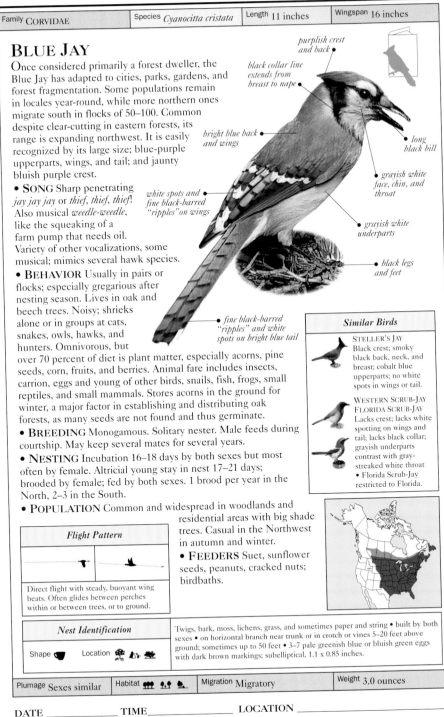

purplish crest and back

black collar line extends from breast to nape

bright blue back and wings

long black bill

grayish white face, chin, and throat

white spots and fine black-barred "ripples" on wings

grayish white underparts

black legs and feet

fine black-barred "ripples" and white spots on bright blue tail

- **SONG** Sharp penetrating *jay jay jay* or *thief, thief, thief*! Also musical *weedle-weedle*, like the squeaking of a farm pump that needs oil. Variety of other vocalizations, some musical; mimics several hawk species.
- **BEHAVIOR** Usually in pairs or flocks; especially gregarious after nesting season. Lives in oak and beech trees. Noisy; shrieks alone or in groups at cats, snakes, owls, hawks, and hunters. Omnivorous, but over 70 percent of diet is plant matter, especially acorns, pine seeds, corn, fruits, and berries. Animal fare includes insects, carrion, eggs and young of other birds, snails, fish, frogs, small reptiles, and small mammals. Stores acorns in the ground for winter, a major factor in establishing and distributing oak forests, as many seeds are not found and thus germinate.
- **BREEDING** Monogamous. Solitary nester. Male feeds during courtship. May keep several mates for several years.
- **NESTING** Incubation 16–18 days by both sexes but most often by female. Altricial young stay in nest 17–21 days; brooded by female; fed by both sexes. 1 brood per year in the North, 2–3 in the South.
- **POPULATION** Common and widespread in woodlands and residential areas with big shade trees. Casual in the Northwest in autumn and winter.
- **FEEDERS** Suet, sunflower seeds, peanuts, cracked nuts; birdbaths.

Similar Birds

STELLER'S JAY
Black crest; smoky black back, neck, and breast; cobalt blue upperparts; no white spots in wings or tail.

WESTERN SCRUB-JAY
FLORIDA SCRUB-JAY
Lacks crest; lacks white spotting on wings and tail; lacks black collar; grayish underparts contrast with gray-streaked white throat • Florida Scrub-Jay restricted to Florida.

Flight Pattern

Direct flight with steady, buoyant wing beats. Often glides between perches within or between trees, or to ground.

Nest Identification

Shape ▰ Location 🪹 🌳 🌲

Twigs, bark, moss, lichens, grass, and sometimes paper and string • built by both sexes • on horizontal branch near trunk or in crotch or vines 5–20 feet above ground; sometimes up to 50 feet • 3–7 pale greenish blue or bluish green eggs with dark brown markings; subelliptical, 1.1 x 0.85 inches.

Plumage Sexes similar	Habitat 🌳 🌿 🪨	Migration Migratory	Weight 3.0 ounces

DATE _____ TIME_____ LOCATION _____

Family CORVIDAE	Species *Aphelocoma insularis*	Length 12 inches	Wingspan 16 inches

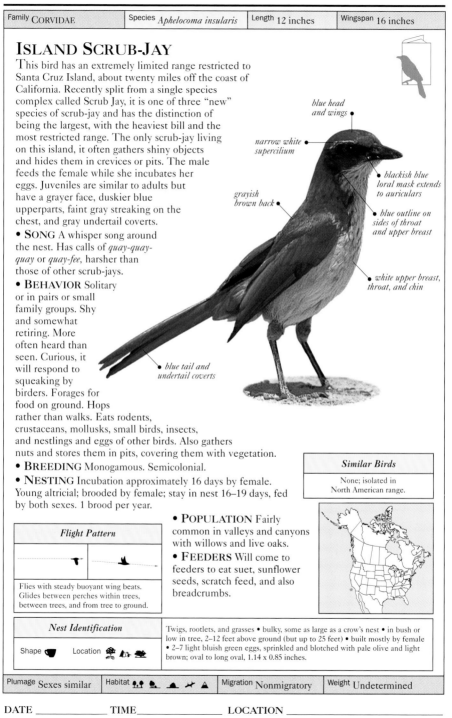

ISLAND SCRUB-JAY

This bird has an extremely limited range restricted to Santa Cruz Island, about twenty miles off the coast of California. Recently split from a single species complex called Scrub Jay, it is one of three "new" species of scrub-jay and has the distinction of being the largest, with the heaviest bill and the most restricted range. The only scrub-jay living on this island, it often gathers shiny objects and hides them in crevices or pits. The male feeds the female while she incubates her eggs. Juveniles are similar to adults but have a grayer face, duskier blue upperparts, faint gray streaking on the chest, and gray undertail coverts.

• **SONG** A whisper song around the nest. Has calls of *quay-quay-quay* or *quay-fee*, harsher than those of other scrub-jays.

• **BEHAVIOR** Solitary or in pairs or small family groups. Shy and somewhat retiring. More often heard than seen. Curious, it will respond to squeaking by birders. Forages for food on ground. Hops rather than walks. Eats rodents, crustaceans, mollusks, small birds, insects, and nestlings and eggs of other birds. Also gathers nuts and stores them in pits, covering them with vegetation.

• **BREEDING** Monogamous. Semicolonial.

• **NESTING** Incubation approximately 16 days by female. Young altricial; brooded by female; stay in nest 16–19 days, fed by both sexes. 1 brood per year.

blue head and wings

narrow white supercilium

grayish brown back

blackish blue loral mask extends to auriculars

blue outline on sides of throat and upper breast

white upper breast, throat, and chin

blue tail and undertail coverts

Similar Birds

None; isolated in North American range.

• **POPULATION** Fairly common in valleys and canyons with willows and live oaks.

• **FEEDERS** Will come to feeders to eat suet, sunflower seeds, scratch feed, and also breadcrumbs.

Flight Pattern

Flies with steady buoyant wing beats. Glides between perches within trees, between trees, and from tree to ground.

Nest Identification	
Shape	Location

Twigs, rootlets, and grasses • bulky, some as large as a crow's nest • in bush or low in tree, 2–12 feet above ground (but up to 25 feet) • built mostly by female • 2–7 light bluish green eggs, sprinkled and blotched with pale olive and light brown; oval to long oval, 1.14 x 0.85 inches.

Plumage Sexes similar	Habitat	Migration Nonmigratory	Weight Undetermined

DATE _____ TIME_____ LOCATION _____

| Family CORVIDAE | Species *Aphelocoma californica* | Length 11 inches | Wingspan 16 inches |

WESTERN SCRUB-JAY

Until recently the Western, Island, and Florida Scrub-Jays were considered races of one species, the Scrub Jay. The Western Scrub-Jay has a large range over varying habitats, and the several races currently accepted show some differences in plumage, including intensity of blue upperparts, color of crissum, and size of bill. This tame, bold bird serves as a major disperser of oak forests because of its habit of caching acorns in the earth for winter stores. Found near urban areas, it will sometimes take food from the hand of a human.

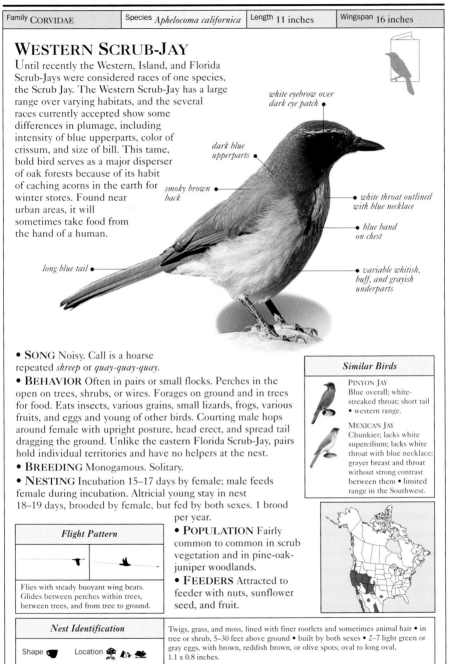

white eyebrow over dark eye patch

dark blue upperparts

smoky brown back

long blue tail

white throat outlined with blue necklace

blue band on chest

variable whitish, buff, and grayish underparts

• **SONG** Noisy. Call is a hoarse repeated *shreep* or *quay-quay-quay*.
• **BEHAVIOR** Often in pairs or small flocks. Perches in the open on trees, shrubs, or wires. Forages on ground and in trees for food. Eats insects, various grains, small lizards, frogs, various fruits, and eggs and young of other birds. Courting male hops around female with upright posture, head erect, and spread tail dragging the ground. Unlike the eastern Florida Scrub-Jay, pairs hold individual territories and have no helpers at the nest.
• **BREEDING** Monogamous. Solitary.
• **NESTING** Incubation 15–17 days by female; male feeds female during incubation. Altricial young stay in nest 18–19 days, brooded by female, but fed by both sexes. 1 brood per year.
• **POPULATION** Fairly common to common in scrub vegetation and in pine-oak-juniper woodlands.
• **FEEDERS** Attracted to feeder with nuts, sunflower seed, and fruit.

Similar Birds

PINYON JAY
Blue overall; white-streaked throat; short tail • western range.

MEXICAN JAY
Chunkier; lacks white supercilium; lacks white throat with blue necklace; grayer breast and throat without strong contrast between them • limited range in the Southwest.

Flight Pattern

Flies with steady buoyant wing beats. Glides between perches within trees, between trees, and from tree to ground.

Nest Identification

Shape   Location

Twigs, grass, and moss, lined with finer rootlets and sometimes animal hair • in tree or shrub, 5–30 feet above ground • built by both sexes • 2–7 light green or gray eggs, with brown, reddish brown, or olive spots; oval to long oval, 1.1 x 0.8 inches.

| Plumage Sexes similar | Habitat | Migration Nonmigratory | Weight 2.8 ounces |

DATE _____ TIME_____ LOCATION _____

Family CORVIDAE	Species *Aphelocoma ultramarina*	Length 11 inches	Wingspan 15 inches

MEXICAN JAY

Traveling in clamoring flocks of 6–20 birds, Mexican Jays are often observed mobbing hawks and occasionally snakes or less common predators such as bobcats and foxes. Offspring often live with relatives for several years and help care for the young, which usually are produced in only one or two nests of the clan. Considered one of the most sedentary birds in North America, the Mexican Jay rarely journeys beyond its immediate breeding territory. It is a fairly common resident of oak and pine-oak forests in foothills, canyons, and mountains from 2,000 to 9,000 feet. The Arizona race has pale blue plumage, while the Texas race shows medium blue plumage. Juveniles have grayish blue upperparts, gray underparts, and a yellow bill. It was formerly known as the Gray-breasted Jay.

blackish lores and around eyes

light to medium blue upperparts

stout black bill

gray back with brown central patch

grayish white underparts

black legs and feet

long blue tail

• **SONG** Raucous ringing *weenk*, often heard in a series. Calls also include a *wait-wait-wait* and a soft *coo*.
• **BEHAVIOR** Gregarious. Tame. Travels in flocks of 5–20 or more birds, many of whom are related. Flocks made up of 2 breeding pairs and others that assist in nest building, feeding young, and territorial defense. Eats acorns as staple food but also takes wild fruit, various insects, carrion, and eggs and young of smaller birds.
• **BREEDING** Monogamous. Gregarious. Cooperative.
• **NESTING** Incubation 16–18 days by female. Altricial young remain in nest 24–25 days. Young are fed by both sexes as well as by other birds. 1 brood per year.

Similar Birds

WESTERN SCRUB-JAY
White throat outlined by blue necklace; white eyebrow; more slender body • deeper blue upperparts than Arizona race of Mexican Jay.

• **POPULATION** Fairly common to common in montane pine-oak canyons of the Southwest.
• **CONSERVATION** Depends on mature pine-oak forests; vulnerable to habitat loss.

Flight Pattern
Slow steady buoyant wing beats. Glides between perches within trees, between trees, and from trees to ground.

Nest Identification	Lined with fine grass, hair, twigs, and roots • on horizontal branch or in crotch of oak, or sometimes conifer, 6–30 feet above ground • built by both sexes and other birds • 4–7 pale green eggs with green markings; subelliptical to long, 1.2 x 0.8 inches.
Shape ⬤ Location 🌲 🏕	

Plumage Sexes differ	Habitat 🌿 🌲 ⛰ ✈	Migration Nonmigratory	Weight 4.3 ounces

DATE _____ TIME _____ LOCATION _____

| Family CORVIDAE | Species *Gymnorhinus cyanocephalus* | Length 10.5 inches | Wingspan 15 inches |

PINYON JAY

Flying in huge flocks sometimes numbering
into the hundreds, or as many as a thousand, in
spring, autumn, and winter, these birds appear
to be migrating but are traveling from the desert
9,000 feet up the mountains in search of piñon
nuts and other food. In the highly organized
colonies, feeding flocks leave several birds to act
as sentries, which sound warning calls when an
intruder approaches. Adults are proportioned
like a small blue crow with a long bill and
short tail. Juveniles are similar to adults
but duller overall.

• **SONG** Noisy. Warning call of *crauk-crauk*. High nasal caw, *kaa-eh*, with
lower second note. Also makes
various high-pitched jaylike mews,
caws, and chatters.

• **BEHAVIOR** Gregarious.
Crowlike in behavior; walks,
hops, and forages on ground
as well as in trees. Nests in
colonies of up to 150 birds,
travels in large foraging
flocks of up to a thousand
birds, and roosts communally
in nonbreeding season.
Mostly forages in mountains
in bands of conifers, especially
piñon pines, at elevations of
3,000–8,000 feet. Eats piñon
nuts and other pine seeds, grass
seeds, berries, fruit, grain, insects, and eggs and young of small
birds. Will boldly approach human habitations for food scraps.

• **BREEDING** Monogamous. Colonial.

• **NESTING** Incubation 16–17 days by female. Altricial young
stay in nest 21 days. Fed by both sexes. 1–2 broods per year.

• **POPULATION** Common in piñon-juniper habitat in high
plateaus and interior mountains.
Stable, though numbers
drastically fluctuate.

• **CONSERVATION**
Dependent on piñon-juniper
woodlands; vulnerable to
habitat loss.

long pointed black bill

blue throat with white streaks

blue overall

black legs

blue tail

Similar Birds

WESTERN SCRUB-JAY
Longer tail; grayish
white underparts; white
throat outlined with
blue necklace; brown
back patch.

STELLER'S JAY
Crested; blackish
underparts; blue
upperparts.

Flight Pattern

Buoyant, steady direct flight with deep
wing beats.

| Nest Identification | | Sticks, crumbled bark, grasses, stems, roots, bits of hair, and paper • sometimes 3 nests in 1 tree; on branch or fork of tree 3–25 feet above ground • built by both sexes • 3–5 bluish white or greenish white eggs; subelliptical to long oval, 1.2 x 0.8 inches. |
| Shape | Location | |

| Plumage Sexes similar | Habitat | Migration Nonmigratory | Weight 3.6 ounces |

DATE _____ TIME_____ LOCATION _____

Family CORVIDAE	Species *Nucifraga columbiana*	Length 12.5 inches	Wingspan 18 inches

CLARK'S NUTCRACKER

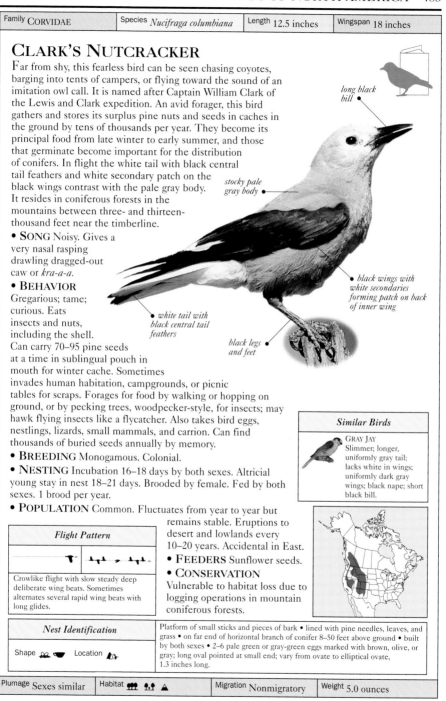

Far from shy, this fearless bird can be seen chasing coyotes, barging into tents of campers, or flying toward the sound of an imitation owl call. It is named after Captain William Clark of the Lewis and Clark expedition. An avid forager, this bird gathers and stores its surplus pine nuts and seeds in caches in the ground by tens of thousands per year. They become its principal food from late winter to early summer, and those that germinate become important for the distribution of conifers. In flight the white tail with black central tail feathers and white secondary patch on the black wings contrast with the pale gray body. It resides in coniferous forests in the mountains between three- and thirteen-thousand feet near the timberline.

long black bill

stocky pale gray body

black wings with white secondaries forming patch on back of inner wing

white tail with black central tail feathers

black legs and feet

• **SONG** Noisy. Gives a very nasal rasping drawling dragged-out caw or *kra-a-a.*

• **BEHAVIOR** Gregarious; tame; curious. Eats insects and nuts, including the shell. Can carry 70–95 pine seeds at a time in sublingual pouch in mouth for winter cache. Sometimes invades human habitation, campgrounds, or picnic tables for scraps. Forages for food by walking or hopping on ground, or by pecking trees, woodpecker-style, for insects; may hawk flying insects like a flycatcher. Also takes bird eggs, nestlings, lizards, small mammals, and carrion. Can find thousands of buried seeds annually by memory.

• **BREEDING** Monogamous. Colonial.

• **NESTING** Incubation 16–18 days by both sexes. Altricial young stay in nest 18–21 days. Brooded by female. Fed by both sexes. 1 brood per year.

• **POPULATION** Common. Fluctuates from year to year but remains stable. Eruptions to desert and lowlands every 10–20 years. Accidental in East.

• **FEEDERS** Sunflower seeds.

• **CONSERVATION** Vulnerable to habitat loss due to logging operations in mountain coniferous forests.

Similar Birds

GRAY JAY
Slimmer; longer, uniformly gray tail; lacks white in wings; uniformly dark gray wings; black nape; short black bill.

Flight Pattern

Crowlike flight with slow steady deep deliberate wing beats. Sometimes alternates several rapid wing beats with long glides.

Nest Identification

Shape Location

Platform of small sticks and pieces of bark • lined with pine needles, leaves, and grass • on far end of horizontal branch of conifer 8–50 feet above ground • built by both sexes • 2–6 pale green or gray-green eggs marked with brown, olive, or gray; long oval pointed at small end; vary from ovate to elliptical ovate, 1.3 inches long.

Plumage Sexes similar	Habitat	Migration Nonmigratory	Weight 5.0 ounces

DATE _____ TIME _____ LOCATION _____

Family CORVIDAE	Species *Pica hudsonia*	Length 17.5–22 inches	Wingspan 24 inches

BLACK-BILLED MAGPIE

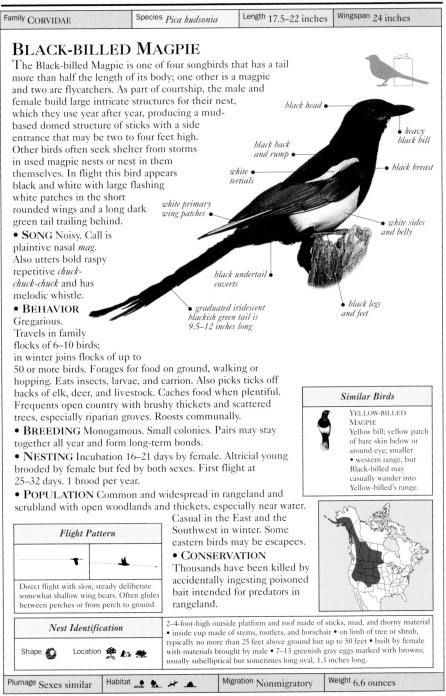

The Black-billed Magpie is one of four songbirds that has a tail more than half the length of its body; one other is a magpie and two are flycatchers. As part of courtship, the male and female build large intricate structures for their nest, which they use year after year, producing a mud-based domed structure of sticks with a side entrance that may be two to four feet high. Other birds often seek shelter from storms in used magpie nests or nest in them themselves. In flight this bird appears black and white with large flashing white patches in the short rounded wings and a long dark green tail trailing behind.

- **SONG** Noisy. Call is plaintive nasal *mag.* Also utters bold raspy repetitive *chuck-chuck-chuck* and has melodic whistle.
- **BEHAVIOR** Gregarious. Travels in family flocks of 6–10 birds; in winter joins flocks of up to 50 or more birds. Forages for food on ground, walking or hopping. Eats insects, larvae, and carrion. Also picks ticks off backs of elk, deer, and carrion. Caches food when plentiful. Frequents open country with brushy thickets and scattered trees, especially riparian groves. Roosts communally.
- **BREEDING** Monogamous. Small colonies. Pairs may stay together all year and form long-term bonds.
- **NESTING** Incubation 16–21 days by female. Altricial young brooded by female but fed by both sexes. First flight at 25–32 days. 1 brood per year.
- **POPULATION** Common and widespread in rangeland and scrubland with open woodlands and thickets, especially near water. Casual in the East and Southwest in winter. Some eastern birds may be escapees.
- **CONSERVATION** Thousands have been killed by accidentally ingesting poisoned bait intended for predators in rangeland.

black head
heavy black bill
black back and rump
black breast
white tertials
white primary wing patches
white sides and belly
black undertail coverts
graduated iridescent blackish green tail is 9.5–12 inches long
black legs and feet

Similar Birds

YELLOW-BILLED MAGPIE
Yellow bill; yellow patch of bare skin below or around eye; smaller • western range, but Black-billed may casually wander into Yellow-billed's range.

Flight Pattern

Direct flight with slow, steady deliberate somewhat shallow wing beats. Often glides between perches or from perch to ground.

Nest Identification

Shape

Location

2–4-foot-high outside platform and roof made of sticks, mud, and thorny material • inside cup made of stems, rootlets, and horsehair • on limb of tree or shrub, typically no more than 25 feet above ground but up to 50 feet • built by female with materials brought by male • 7–13 greenish gray eggs marked with browns; usually subelliptical but sometimes long oval, 1.3 inches long.

Plumage Sexes similar	Habitat	Migration Nonmigratory	Weight 6.6 ounces

DATE _____ TIME_____ LOCATION _____

| Family CORVIDAE | Species *Pica nuttalli* | Length 16.5 inches | Wingspan 22 inches |

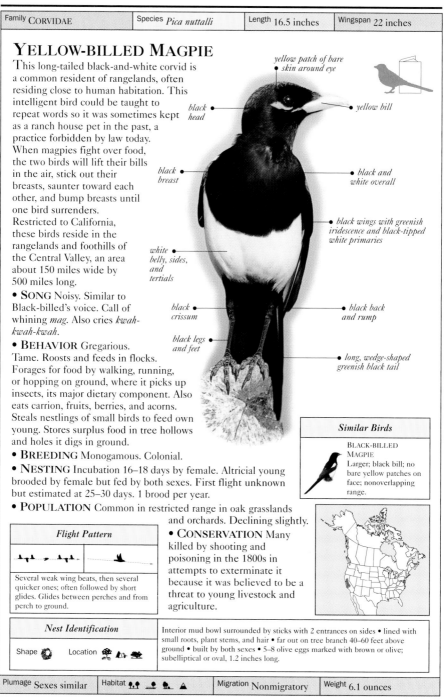

YELLOW-BILLED MAGPIE

This long-tailed black-and-white corvid is a common resident of rangelands, often residing close to human habitation. This intelligent bird could be taught to repeat words so it was sometimes kept as a ranch house pet in the past, a practice forbidden by law today. When magpies fight over food, the two birds will lift their bills in the air, stick out their breasts, saunter toward each other, and bump breasts until one bird surrenders. Restricted to California, these birds reside in the rangelands and foothills of the Central Valley, an area about 150 miles wide by 500 miles long.

yellow patch of bare skin around eye

black head

yellow bill

black breast

black and white overall

black wings with greenish iridescence and black-tipped white primaries

white belly, sides, and tertials

black crissum

black back and rump

black legs and feet

long, wedge-shaped greenish black tail

• SONG Noisy. Similar to Black-billed's voice. Call of whining *mag*. Also cries *kwah-kwah-kwah*.

• BEHAVIOR Gregarious. Tame. Roosts and feeds in flocks. Forages for food by walking, running, or hopping on ground, where it picks up insects, its major dietary component. Also eats carrion, fruits, berries, and acorns. Steals nestlings of small birds to feed own young. Stores surplus food in tree hollows and holes it digs in ground.

• BREEDING Monogamous. Colonial.

• NESTING Incubation 16–18 days by female. Altricial young brooded by female but fed by both sexes. First flight unknown but estimated at 25–30 days. 1 brood per year.

• POPULATION Common in restricted range in oak grasslands and orchards. Declining slightly.

• CONSERVATION Many killed by shooting and poisoning in the 1800s in attempts to exterminate it because it was believed to be a threat to young livestock and agriculture.

Similar Birds

BLACK-BILLED MAGPIE
Larger; black bill; no bare yellow patches on face; nonoverlapping range.

Flight Pattern

Several weak wing beats, then several quicker ones; often followed by short glides. Glides between perches and from perch to ground.

Nest Identification

Shape Location

Interior mud bowl surrounded by sticks with 2 entrances on sides • lined with small roots, plant stems, and hair • far out on tree branch 40–60 feet above ground • built by both sexes • 5–8 olive eggs marked with brown or olive; subelliptical or oval, 1.2 inches long.

| Plumage Sexes similar | Habitat | Migration Nonmigratory | Weight 6.1 ounces |

DATE _____ TIME_____ LOCATION _____

Family CORVIDAE	Species *Corvus brachyrhynchos*	Length 17.5 inches	Wingspan 33–40 inches

AMERICAN CROW

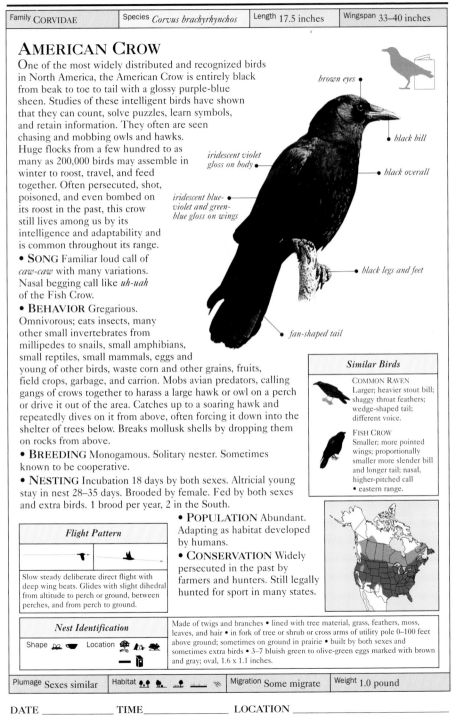

One of the most widely distributed and recognized birds in North America, the American Crow is entirely black from beak to toe to tail with a glossy purple-blue sheen. Studies of these intelligent birds have shown that they can count, solve puzzles, learn symbols, and retain information. They often are seen chasing and mobbing owls and hawks. Huge flocks from a few hundred to as many as 200,000 birds may assemble in winter to roost, travel, and feed together. Often persecuted, shot, poisoned, and even bombed on its roost in the past, this crow still lives among us by its intelligence and adaptability and is common throughout its range.

brown eyes

iridescent violet gloss on body

iridescent blue-violet and green-blue gloss on wings

black bill

black overall

black legs and feet

fan-shaped tail

- **SONG** Familiar loud call of *caw-caw* with many variations. Nasal begging call like *uh-uah* of the Fish Crow.
- **BEHAVIOR** Gregarious. Omnivorous; eats insects, many other small invertebrates from millipedes to snails, small amphibians, small reptiles, small mammals, eggs and young of other birds, waste corn and other grains, fruits, field crops, garbage, and carrion. Mobs avian predators, calling gangs of crows together to harass a large hawk or owl on a perch or drive it out of the area. Catches up to a soaring hawk and repeatedly dives on it from above, often forcing it down into the shelter of trees below. Breaks mollusk shells by dropping them on rocks from above.
- **BREEDING** Monogamous. Solitary nester. Sometimes known to be cooperative.
- **NESTING** Incubation 18 days by both sexes. Altricial young stay in nest 28–35 days. Brooded by female. Fed by both sexes and extra birds. 1 brood per year, 2 in the South.
- **POPULATION** Abundant. Adapting as habitat developed by humans.
- **CONSERVATION** Widely persecuted in the past by farmers and hunters. Still legally hunted for sport in many states.

Similar Birds

COMMON RAVEN
Larger; heavier stout bill; shaggy throat feathers; wedge-shaped tail; different voice.

FISH CROW
Smaller; more pointed wings; proportionally smaller more slender bill and longer tail; nasal, higher-pitched call
• eastern range.

Flight Pattern

Slow steady deliberate direct flight with deep wing beats. Glides with slight dihedral from altitude to perch or ground, between perches, and from perch to ground.

Nest Identification

Shape — Location —

Made of twigs and branches • lined with tree material, grass, feathers, moss, leaves, and hair • in fork of tree or shrub or cross arms of utility pole 0–100 feet above ground; sometimes on ground in prairie • built by both sexes and sometimes extra birds • 3–7 bluish green to olive-green eggs marked with brown and gray; oval, 1.6 x 1.1 inches.

Plumage Sexes similar	Habitat	Migration Some migrate	Weight 1.0 pound

DATE _____ TIME_____ LOCATION _____

Family CORVIDAE	Species *Corvus caurinus*	Length 16 inches	Wingspan 30–36 inches

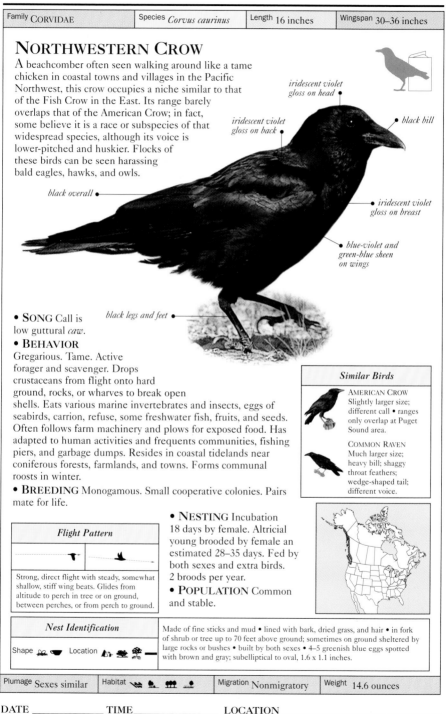

NORTHWESTERN CROW

A beachcomber often seen walking around like a tame chicken in coastal towns and villages in the Pacific Northwest, this crow occupies a niche similar to that of the Fish Crow in the East. Its range barely overlaps that of the American Crow; in fact, some believe it is a race or subspecies of that widespread species, although its voice is lower-pitched and huskier. Flocks of these birds can be seen harassing bald eagles, hawks, and owls.

iridescent violet gloss on head

iridescent violet gloss on back

black bill

black overall

iridescent violet gloss on breast

blue-violet and green-blue sheen on wings

black legs and feet

- **SONG** Call is low guttural *caw*.
- **BEHAVIOR** Gregarious. Tame. Active forager and scavenger. Drops crustaceans from flight onto hard ground, rocks, or wharves to break open shells. Eats various marine invertebrates and insects, eggs of seabirds, carrion, refuse, some freshwater fish, fruits, and seeds. Often follows farm machinery and plows for exposed food. Has adapted to human activities and frequents communities, fishing piers, and garbage dumps. Resides in coastal tidelands near coniferous forests, farmlands, and towns. Forms communal roosts in winter.
- **BREEDING** Monogamous. Small cooperative colonies. Pairs mate for life.
- **NESTING** Incubation 18 days by female. Altricial young brooded by female an estimated 28–35 days. Fed by both sexes and extra birds. 2 broods per year.
- **POPULATION** Common and stable.

Similar Birds

AMERICAN CROW
Slightly larger size; different call • ranges only overlap at Puget Sound area.

COMMON RAVEN
Much larger size; heavy bill; shaggy throat feathers; wedge-shaped tail; different voice.

Flight Pattern

Strong, direct flight with steady, somewhat shallow, stiff wing beats. Glides from altitude to perch in tree or on ground, between perches, or from perch to ground.

Nest Identification

Shape ☂ ⌣ Location ⛺ ⚘ 🌳 —

Made of fine sticks and mud • lined with bark, dried grass, and hair • in fork of shrub or tree up to 70 feet above ground; sometimes on ground sheltered by large rocks or bushes • built by both sexes • 4–5 greenish blue eggs spotted with brown and gray; subelliptical to oval, 1.6 x 1.1 inches.

Plumage Sexes similar	Habitat 🌊 🐚 🌿 ⚓	Migration Nonmigratory	Weight 14.6 ounces

DATE _____ TIME_____ LOCATION _____

Family CORVIDAE	Species *Corvus cryptoleucus*	Length 19.5 inches	Wingspan 38 inches

CHIHUAHUAN RAVEN

Sometimes called the White-necked Raven, this bird has white bases on the back of the neck and lower throat feathers that show only when ruffled by the wind or when the bird becomes agitated. Highly adventuresome, these birds sometimes dive into rotating air masses or dust devils and allow themselves to be taken for an upward ride. A small raven of arid grasslands, scrublands, and desert, it uses the endless strings of utility poles crossing the barren landscapes it inhabits as lookout stations, resting places, and nesting locations, placing nests high on the cross-arms of the poles.

black overall with purple gloss

heavy bill

black legs and feet

wedge-shaped tail

• **SONG** Call is drawling *crooaak*. Utters guttural *quark, quark* as a warning call.
• **BEHAVIOR** Gregarious. Active forager and scavenger. Eats wide variety of insects, insect larvae, spiders, worms, snails, earthworms, small mammals, lizards, eggs and young of other birds, carrion, grains, nuts, corn, cactus fruit, and scraps of human food. Breeds late in season, timing nesting with food availability. Forms flocks soon after nesting season that may become enormous, numbering in the thousands before winter. Male ruffles neck feathers in courtship display and engages in acrobatic aerial display for female. Then male and female sit next to each other and rub bills, bow to one another, and raise wings.
• **BREEDING** Monogamous. Colonial.
• **NESTING** Incubation 18–21 days by both sexes. Altricial young stay in nest 30 days. Brooded by female. Fed by both sexes. 1 brood per year.
• **POPULATION** Common to fairly common in arid to semiarid grassland, rangeland, and desert.

Similar Birds

COMMON RAVEN
Larger; heavier bill; longer tail; pale gray bases on upper neck and throat feathers.

AMERICAN CROW
Smaller; smaller bill; fan-shaped tail; dark gray bases on neck and throat feathers; different call.

• **CONSERVATION** Formerly highly persecuted by ranchers and farmers who considered them pests or threats to livestock; they were systematically shot and poisoned by the thousands in control programs.

Flight Pattern

Alternates between several deep wing beats and short to long glides; glides from altitude to ground or perch. Soars effortlessly on thermals and updrafts.

Nest Identification

Shape ᴗᴗ ◡ Location 🌲 🌿 📦

Prickly sticks and sometimes barbed wire • lined with bark chips, grass, hair, and bits of refuse • in fork of tree or shrub 9–40 feet above ground; sometimes on man-made structures such as windmills or utility poles • built by female • 3–8 pale or grayish green eggs with lilac and brown markings; subelliptical to long oval, 1.8 x 1.3 inches.

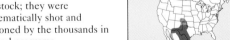

Plumage Sexes similar	Habitat	Migration Most do not migrate	Weight 1.2 pounds

DATE _____ TIME_____ LOCATION _____

Family CORVIDAE	Species *Corvus corax*	Length 24–26 inches	Wingspan 46–56 inches

COMMON RAVEN

This magnificent flier is the aerial equal of hawks and falcons and is the largest passerine, or perching bird, in North America. If any bird truly enjoys flying to the point of playing in the air, it must be this raven. Intelligent resourceful hunters and scavengers, groups of these birds have been observed working together to capture prey that is too large for one bird to conquer. It is a revered totem and spirit to many Native Americans. Adults are glossy black overall, with a huge "Roman nose," and shaggy throat feathers that can be elevated or sleeked down. The female is similar to the male but smaller.

nostrils hidden by stiff tufts of feathers extending about a third of the way out the bill

black overall with iridescent purple and violet sheen

long heavy bill

long wedge-shaped tail with long central tail feathers

black legs and feet

• **SONG** Variety of vocalizations, some quite musical, but most often a croaking drawling *croooaaak* or *cur-ruk* or metallic *tok.*
• **BEHAVIOR** Tame. Quick learner. Solitary or in pairs or small groups. Gregarious in winter, when it may occur in large foraging flocks and nightly communal roosts. Active forager, scavenger, and hunter. Omnivorous; eats wide variety of small invertebrates, from tadpoles and shellfish to worms and insects. Also takes many small vertebrates, including minnows, eggs and young of other birds, and rodents, as well as carrion and refuse. Elaborate courtship flight with great display of acrobatics and pair flying, male above female, wing-tip to wing-tip and heads touching.
• **BREEDING** Monogamous. Solitary; small, loose colonies in the North. Mates for life.
• **NESTING** Incubation 18–21 days by female. Altricial young stay in nest 38–44 days. Brooded by female. Fed by both sexes. 1 brood per year.

Similar Birds

AMERICAN CROW
Smaller; smaller bill; lacks shaggy throat feathers; fan-shaped tail; different call.

CHIHUAHUAN RAVEN
Smaller; shorter bill and wings; nasal bristles extend farther out on culmen; white-based neck and throat feathers.

• **POPULATION** Common. Expanding in California; also in Appalachians into areas where birds had been extirpated.
• **CONSERVATION** In past was shot, trapped, and poisoned for alleged damage to wild game and domesticated animals.

Flight Pattern

Strong flight, often rising in circles. Alternates deep wing beats with long glides or soaring on flat wings like a hawk. Soars on thermals and updrafts.

Nest Identification

Shape   Location

Branches and sticks on outside; cup made of small sticks • lined with bark chips, animal hair, sheep's wool, lichens, moss, seaweed, and grass • on cliff near water, in mountains, or in fork of tree 45–80 feet above ground • built by both sexes • 3–7 greenish or gray-green eggs with brown or olive spots; subelliptical to long oval, 2 x 1.4 inches.

Plumage Sexes similar	Habitat	Migration Nonmigratory	Weight 2.7 pounds

DATE _____ TIME_____ LOCATION _____

Family ALAUDIDAE	Species *Alauda arvensis*	Length 7.25 inches	Wingspan 13 inches

SKY LARK

This European native was introduced to Vancouver Island, British Columbia, in the early 1900s. It has established a population there and in the open fields and meadows of nearby San Juan Island, Washington. Like most larks this bird seldom perches in trees but walks on the ground. Although it looks like just a small brown bird on the ground, its song-flight displays during courtship are spectacular. The male pursues the female to great heights in a towering flight, hovering or circling while singing a continuous eruption of warbles and trills in sustained runs.

small crest

buff eyebrows

slim pale bill

brown upperparts with heavy blackish brown streaking

brownish black streaking on breast and sides

white outer tail feathers

buff-white underparts

pinkish legs and feet

- **SONG** Flies in circle or hovers high in air while singing an ongoing melody of complex gurgles, whistles, and trills. Ventriloquial. Call is gurgling bubbly *cherru*p.
- **BEHAVIOR** Solitary or in pairs. May form small flocks in winter. On ground has horizontal, head-down posture. Forages for food on ground by walking and running; does not hop. Eats mostly seeds, grains, and insects. Most often seen when flushed from roadside or grasses; rises with white tail edging and white secondary tips flashing. In courtship male runs around female, lifting his crest and tail and letting his wings fall limp.
- **BREEDING** Monogamous.
- **NESTING** Incubation 11–12 days by female. Altricial young stay in nest 9–10 days. Brooded by female. Fed by both sexes. 2 broods per year.
- **POPULATION** Vancouver Island population gradually declining. Common in Hawaii. Accidental in winter on Pacific Coast to northern California. Siberian race rare in migration on Aleutians.

Similar Birds

HORNED LARK
Juvenile lacks crest; white spots and streaking on upperparts; black tail with white outer feathers; lacks white trailing edge on secondaries.

AMERICAN PIPIT
Grayish upperparts; buff underparts with brownish streaking; black tail with white outer tail feathers; lacks crest and white secondary tips; bobs tail continuously.

Flight Pattern

Moderately swift flight with rapid wing beats. Hovers while skylarking in territory at great heights, then glides to ground.

Nest Identification

Shape ⌣ ⬭   Location ▬ ⋰⋰

Lined with roots, grass, and occasionally hair • on ground in open field • built by female • 3–7 grayish white eggs with olive or brown blotches; subelliptical, 1 inch long.

Plumage Sexes similar	Habitat ⋯ ⬆	Migration Nonmigratory	Weight 1.5 ounces

DATE _____ TIME_____ LOCATION _____

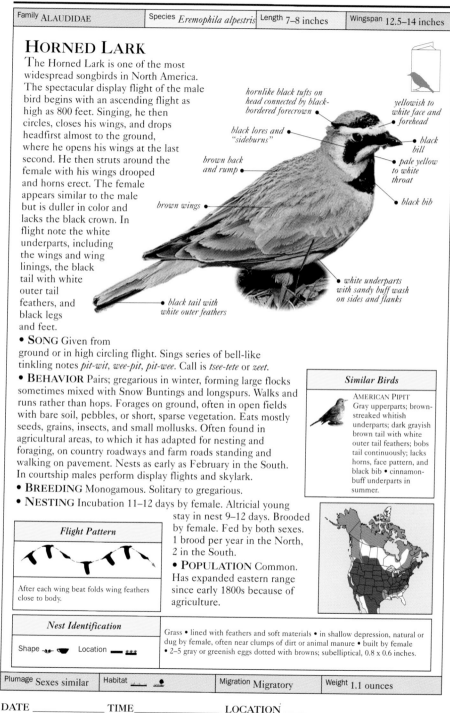

Family ALAUDIDAE	Species *Eremophila alpestris*	Length 7–8 inches	Wingspan 12.5–14 inches

HORNED LARK

The Horned Lark is one of the most widespread songbirds in North America. The spectacular display flight of the male bird begins with an ascending flight as high as 800 feet. Singing, he then circles, closes his wings, and drops headfirst almost to the ground, where he opens his wings at the last second. He then struts around the female with his wings drooped and horns erect. The female appears similar to the male but is duller in color and lacks the black crown. In flight note the white underparts, including the wings and wing linings, the black tail with white outer tail feathers, and black legs and feet.

hornlike black tufts on head connected by black-bordered forecrown

yellowish to white face and forehead

black lores and "sideburns"

black bill

brown back and rump

pale yellow to white throat

brown wings

black bib

black tail with white outer feathers

white underparts with sandy buff wash on sides and flanks

• **SONG** Given from ground or in high circling flight. Sings series of bell-like tinkling notes *pit-wit, wee-pit, pit-wee*. Call is *tsee-tete* or *zeet*.

• **BEHAVIOR** Pairs; gregarious in winter, forming large flocks sometimes mixed with Snow Buntings and longspurs. Walks and runs rather than hops. Forages on ground, often in open fields with bare soil, pebbles, or short, sparse vegetation. Eats mostly seeds, grains, insects, and small mollusks. Often found in agricultural areas, to which it has adapted for nesting and foraging, on country roadways and farm roads standing and walking on pavement. Nests as early as February in the South. In courtship males perform display flights and skylark.

• **BREEDING** Monogamous. Solitary to gregarious.

• **NESTING** Incubation 11–12 days by female. Altricial young stay in nest 9–12 days. Brooded by female. Fed by both sexes. 1 brood per year in the North, 2 in the South.

• **POPULATION** Common. Has expanded eastern range since early 1800s because of agriculture.

Similar Birds

AMERICAN PIPIT
Gray upperparts; brown-streaked whitish underparts; dark grayish brown tail with white outer tail feathers; bobs tail continuously; lacks horns, face pattern, and black bib • cinnamon-buff underparts in summer.

Flight Pattern

After each wing beat folds wing feathers close to body.

Nest Identification

Shape ⚲ ⚬   Location ▬ ⋯

Grass • lined with feathers and soft materials • in shallow depression, natural or dug by female, often near clumps of dirt or animal manure • built by female • 2–5 gray or greenish eggs dotted with browns; subelliptical, 0.8 x 0.6 inches.

Plumage Sexes similar	Habitat	Migration Migratory	Weight 1.1 ounces

DATE _____ TIME_____ LOCATION _____

| Family HIRUNDINIDAE | Species *Progne subis* | Length 7.25–8.5 inches | Wingspan 15.5–16.75 inches |

PURPLE MARTIN

Colonies once nested in holes in tall dead trees and saguaro cacti. Today the largest North American swallow usually nests in man-made multidwelling martin houses, sometimes with hundreds of pairs nesting together. Martin houses were inspired by the Native American custom of placing empty gourds on tall poles to attract the Purple Martin for aesthetic reasons and to reduce the insect population around villages and crops. Juvenile males have browner upperparts with whitish bellies and some purple sheen to their bodies. Juvenile females are brown overall with whitish bellies. A long-distant migrant, it winters from Venezuela to southeastern Brazil.

MALE

• dark iridescent purplish blue overall

FIRST SPRING MALE

• **SONG** A variety of rich low-pitched liquid gurgling notes and chirruping, mixed with cackling and varying in pitch. Songs often given predawn and in flight.

• **BEHAVIOR** In pairs or colonies. In fall, communal migratory and roosting flocks may number in the tens of thousands. Mostly catches and eats insects in flight, but also forages on ground. Nesting birds will eat broken eggshells placed for them. Frequents open country, rural agricultural areas, especially near water, and urban/suburban areas.

• **BREEDING** Monogamous. Colonial.

• **NESTING** Incubation 15–18 days by female. Young altricial; brooded by female; stay in nest 26–31 days, fed by both sexes. 1–3 broods per year.

• **POPULATION** Common; declining, especially in the West.

• **BIRDHOUSES** Man-made martin houses and gourds.

• **CONSERVATION** Neotropical migrant. National Audubon Society Blue List. Practice of removing dead cavity-filled trees, especially in riparian areas, has reduced nesting sites. Introduced European Starling and House Sparrow compete for nesting cavities.

bluish gray upperparts •

grayish to whitish lower breast and belly •

• forked tail

FEMALE

forked tail •

Similar Birds

TREE SWALLOW Smaller; entire underparts are bright white with no grayish tone; dark glossy blue-green upperparts • juveniles and first spring adults have browner upperparts.

GRAY-BREASTED MARTIN ♂ Smaller; gray-brown face, throat, and flanks; dusky gray-brown underparts; dark bluish upperparts; cleft tail • eastern range.

Flight Pattern

Strong graceful flight with few rapid wing beats followed by long glides. Often flies in circles while gliding.

Nest Identification

Shape

Location

Grasses, leaves, mud, feathers, and bits of debris • in martin houses, old woodpecker holes in trees and cacti, or in ridges in cliffs or large rocks • 5–20 feet above ground • built by both sexes • 3–8 plain white eggs; oval to long oval, 0.96 x 0.68 inches.

| Plumage Sexes differ | Habitat | Migration Migratory | Weight 1.7 ounces |

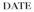

DATE _____ TIME_____ LOCATION _____

Family HIRUNDINIDAE	Species *Tachycineta bicolor*	Length 5.75 inches	Wingspan 12.5 inches

TREE SWALLOW

The Tree Swallow is equally common in open fields, marshes, or towns. This bird's ability to adapt to its ever-changing environment has led to its abundant and widespread population. Migrating in huge flocks during the day, it is one of the first swallows to travel to its summer home in upper North America. Many winter on the southern Atlantic Coast, Gulf Coast, and in Florida. In flight it shows dark upperparts, white underparts, triangular wings with greenish underwing linings, and a notched tail. Juveniles have dusky brown upperparts and often a dusky wash on the breast.

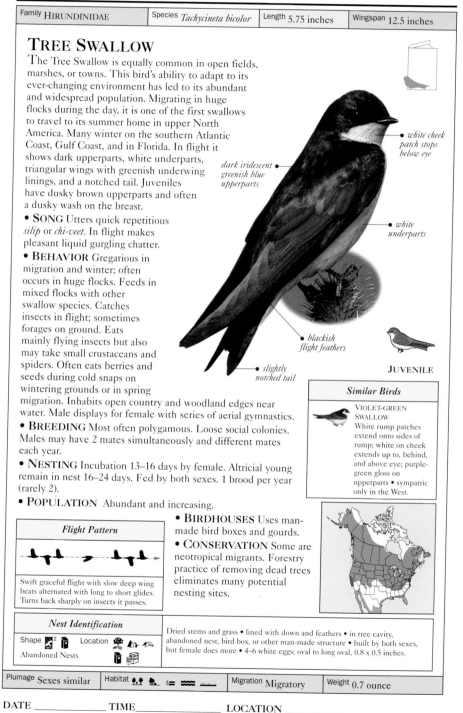

dark iridescent greenish blue upperparts

white cheek patch stops below eye

white underparts

blackish flight feathers

slightly notched tail

JUVENILE

- **SONG** Utters quick repetitious *silip* or *chi-veet*. In flight makes pleasant liquid gurgling chatter.
- **BEHAVIOR** Gregarious in migration and winter; often occurs in huge flocks. Feeds in mixed flocks with other swallow species. Catches insects in flight; sometimes forages on ground. Eats mainly flying insects but also may take small crustaceans and spiders. Often eats berries and seeds during cold snaps on wintering grounds or in spring migration. Inhabits open country and woodland edges near water. Male displays for female with series of aerial gymnastics.
- **BREEDING** Most often polygamous. Loose social colonies. Males may have 2 mates simultaneously and different mates each year.
- **NESTING** Incubation 13–16 days by female. Altricial young remain in nest 16–24 days. Fed by both sexes. 1 brood per year (rarely 2).
- **POPULATION** Abundant and increasing.
- **BIRDHOUSES** Uses man-made bird boxes and gourds.
- **CONSERVATION** Some are neotropical migrants. Forestry practice of removing dead trees eliminates many potential nesting sites.

Similar Birds

VIOLET-GREEN SWALLOW
White rump patches extend onto sides of rump; white on cheek extends up to, behind, and above eye; purple-green gloss on upperparts • sympatric only in the West.

Flight Pattern

Swift graceful flight with slow deep wing beats alternated with long to short glides. Turns back sharply on insects it passes.

Nest Identification

Shape [icons] Location [icons]
Abandoned Nests [icons]

Dried stems and grass • lined with down and feathers • in tree cavity, abandoned nest, bird box, or other man-made structure • built by both sexes, but female does more • 4–6 white eggs; oval to long oval, 0.8 x 0.5 inches.

Plumage Sexes similar	Habitat [icons]	Migration Migratory	Weight 0.7 ounce

DATE _____ TIME_____ LOCATION _____

| Family HIRUNDINIDAE | Species *Tachycineta thalassina* | Length 5–5.25 inches | Wingspan 11–12 inches |

VIOLET-GREEN SWALLOW

The gloss of brilliant greens and purples that shows on its head, back, and rump in bright sunlight and the white patches on the sides of its rump that show in flight set this bird apart from its cousin, the Tree Swallow, with which it often closely associates. Its historical choice for nesting sites is in dead trees of partially cleared forests or abandoned woodpecker holes. Females show duller upperparts than males. Juveniles have gray-brown upperparts without

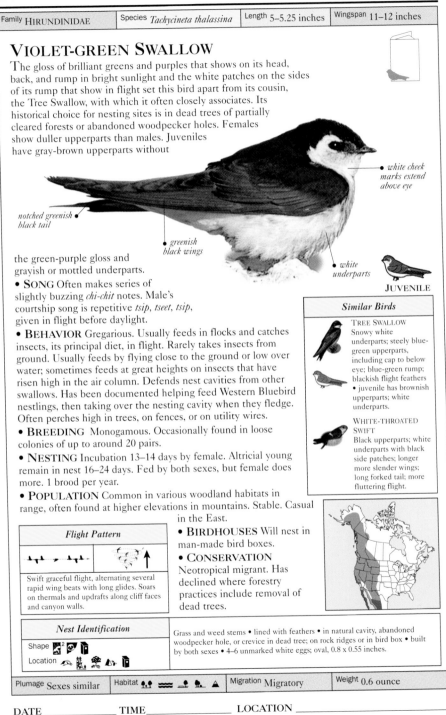

white cheek marks extend above eye

notched greenish black tail

greenish black wings

white underparts

JUVENILE

the green-purple gloss and grayish or mottled underparts.

• **SONG** Often makes series of slightly buzzing *chi-chit* notes. Male's courtship song is repetitive *tsip, tseet, tsip,* given in flight before daylight.

• **BEHAVIOR** Gregarious. Usually feeds in flocks and catches insects, its principal diet, in flight. Rarely takes insects from ground. Usually feeds by flying close to the ground or low over water; sometimes feeds at great heights on insects that have risen high in the air column. Defends nest cavities from other swallows. Has been documented helping feed Western Bluebird nestlings, then taking over the nesting cavity when they fledge. Often perches high in trees, on fences, or on utility wires.

• **BREEDING** Monogamous. Occasionally found in loose colonies of up to around 20 pairs.

• **NESTING** Incubation 13–14 days by female. Altricial young remain in nest 16–24 days. Fed by both sexes, but female does more. 1 brood per year.

• **POPULATION** Common in various woodland habitats in range, often found at higher elevations in mountains. Stable. Casual in the East.

Similar Birds

TREE SWALLOW
Snowy white underparts; steely blue-green upperparts, including cap to below eye; blue-green rump; blackish flight feathers • juvenile has brownish upperparts; white underparts.

WHITE-THROATED SWIFT
Black upperparts; white underparts with black side patches; longer more slender wings; long forked tail; more fluttering flight.

• **BIRDHOUSES** Will nest in man-made bird boxes.

• **CONSERVATION** Neotropical migrant. Has declined where forestry practices include removal of dead trees.

Flight Pattern	

Swift graceful flight, alternating several rapid wing beats with long glides. Soars on thermals and updrafts along cliff faces and canyon walls.

Nest Identification	
Shape	Grass and weed stems • lined with feathers • in natural cavity, abandoned woodpecker hole, or crevice in dead tree; on rock ridges or in bird box • built by both sexes • 4–6 unmarked white eggs; oval, 0.8 x 0.55 inches.
Location	

| Plumage Sexes similar | Habitat | Migration Migratory | Weight 0.6 ounce |

DATE _____ TIME_____ LOCATION _____

Family HIRUNDINIDAE	Species *Stelgidopteryx serripennis*	Length 5.5 inches	Wingspan 11–12 inches

NORTHERN ROUGH-WINGED SWALLOW

This bird is named for the tiny hooks found on its outer primary feathers. Their function is unknown, but they may produce a sound during courtship display. The male and female use their feet to dig nesting burrows, some as long as six feet, depending on the nature of the soil, but most are nine to twenty-eight inches deep. Since it is highly adaptable this bird has a wide breeding range. Juveniles are similar to adults but show more cinnamon tones in their upperparts and have cinnamon wing bars.

short black bill

light gray-brown wash on chin, throat, and upper breast

medium brown upperparts

- **SONG** Usually remains silent, but sometimes utters harsh, buzzing *quiz-z-zeeitp* or *zzrrit.*
- **BEHAVIOR** Solitary or in pairs or small flocks. Gregarious in migration. Catches and consumes a variety of flying insects while in flight. Also occasionally takes insects from ground. Often feeds low over open landscapes or water and sometimes feeds along with other species of swallows. Quickly adapted nesting to utilize crevices in rock cuts along interstate highways. During courtship male chases female, flying with white undertail coverts spread along sides of tail.

dark brownish black wings and wing linings

dull white underparts

slightly forked dark brownish black tail

- **BREEDING** Monogamous. Solitary or in small colonies.
- **NESTING** Incubation 12 days by female. Altricial young remain in nest 19–21 days. Fed by both sexes. 1 brood per year.
- **POPULATION** Common and increasing.
- **BIRDHOUSES** Will nest in some types of man-made structures but has not been recorded to use nest boxes.
- **CONSERVATION** Neotropical migrant.

Similar Birds

BANK SWALLOW Smaller; darker brown upperparts; dark brown breast band; snow-white underparts; faster wing beats with quick changes of direction.

Flight Pattern

Swift graceful flight with several deep slow wing beats, pulling back wings after each stroke, then a short to long glide.

Nest Identification

Shape   Location

No nest materials except a few bark chips, grass, and leaves • on bank, sides of rough cliff, highway/railroad rock cuts, or building or in abandoned burrows, drain pipes, or sewer pipes • dug by both sexes • 4–8 plain white eggs; long oval, 0.7 x 0.5 inches.

Plumage Sexes similar	Habitat	Migration Migratory	Weight 0.6 ounce

DATE _____ TIME_____ LOCATION _____

Family HIRUNDINIDAE	Species *Riparia riparia*	Length 4.75 inches	Wingspan 10–11 inches

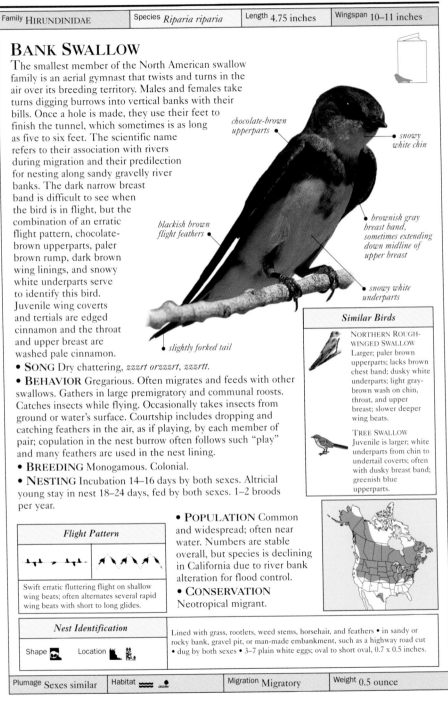

BANK SWALLOW

The smallest member of the North American swallow family is an aerial gymnast that twists and turns in the air over its breeding territory. Males and females take turns digging burrows into vertical banks with their bills. Once a hole is made, they use their feet to finish the tunnel, which sometimes is as long as five to six feet. The scientific name refers to their association with rivers during migration and their predilection for nesting along sandy gravelly river banks. The dark narrow breast band is difficult to see when the bird is in flight, but the combination of an erratic flight pattern, chocolate-brown upperparts, paler brown rump, dark brown wing linings, and snowy white underparts serve to identify this bird. Juvenile wing coverts and tertials are edged cinnamon and the throat and upper breast are washed pale cinnamon.

chocolate-brown upperparts

snowy white chin

blackish brown flight feathers

brownish gray breast band, sometimes extending down midline of upper breast

snowy white underparts

slightly forked tail

• **SONG** Dry chattering, *zzzrt orzzzrt, zzzrtt.*
• **BEHAVIOR** Gregarious. Often migrates and feeds with other swallows. Gathers in large premigratory and communal roosts. Catches insects while flying. Occasionally takes insects from ground or water's surface. Courtship includes dropping and catching feathers in the air, as if playing, by each member of pair; copulation in the nest burrow often follows such "play" and many feathers are used in the nest lining.
• **BREEDING** Monogamous. Colonial.
• **NESTING** Incubation 14–16 days by both sexes. Altricial young stay in nest 18–24 days, fed by both sexes. 1–2 broods per year.

Similar Birds

NORTHERN ROUGH-WINGED SWALLOW
Larger; paler brown upperparts; lacks brown chest band; dusky white underparts; light gray-brown wash on chin, throat, and upper breast; slower deeper wing beats.

TREE SWALLOW
Juvenile is larger; white underparts from chin to undertail coverts; often with dusky breast band; greenish blue upperparts.

• **POPULATION** Common and widespread; often near water. Numbers are stable overall, but species is declining in California due to river bank alteration for flood control.
• **CONSERVATION** Neotropical migrant.

Flight Pattern
Swift erratic fluttering flight on shallow wing beats; often alternates several rapid wing beats with short to long glides.

Nest Identification	
Shape ⬛ Location ⬛ ⬛	Lined with grass, rootlets, weed stems, horsehair, and feathers • in sandy or rocky bank, gravel pit, or man-made embankment, such as a highway road cut • dug by both sexes • 3–7 plain white eggs; oval to short oval, 0.7 x 0.5 inches.

Plumage Sexes similar	Habitat 〰〰 ⬩	Migration Migratory	Weight 0.5 ounce

DATE _____ TIME_____ LOCATION _____

Family HIRUNDINIDAE	Species *Petrochelidon pyrrhonota*	Length 5.5 inches	Wingspan 12 inches

CLIFF SWALLOW

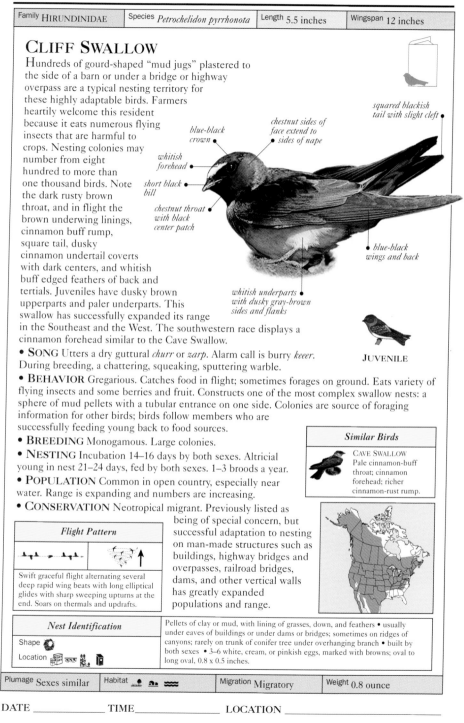

Hundreds of gourd-shaped "mud jugs" plastered to the side of a barn or under a bridge or highway overpass are a typical nesting territory for these highly adaptable birds. Farmers heartily welcome this resident because it eats numerous flying insects that are harmful to crops. Nesting colonies may number from eight hundred to more than one thousand birds. Note the dark rusty brown throat, and in flight the brown underwing linings, cinnamon buff rump, square tail, dusky cinnamon undertail coverts with dark centers, and whitish buff edged feathers of back and tertials. Juveniles have dusky brown upperparts and paler underparts. This swallow has successfully expanded its range in the Southeast and the West. The southwestern race displays a cinnamon forehead similar to the Cave Swallow.

blue-black crown
whitish forehead
short black bill
chestnut throat with black center patch
chestnut sides of face extend to sides of nape
squared blackish tail with slight cleft
blue-black wings and back
whitish underparts with dusky gray-brown sides and flanks

JUVENILE

• **SONG** Utters a dry guttural *churr* or *zarp*. Alarm call is burry *keeer*. During breeding, a chattering, squeaking, sputtering warble.

• **BEHAVIOR** Gregarious. Catches food in flight; sometimes forages on ground. Eats variety of flying insects and some berries and fruit. Constructs one of the most complex swallow nests: a sphere of mud pellets with a tubular entrance on one side. Colonies are source of foraging information for other birds; birds follow members who are successfully feeding young back to food sources.

• **BREEDING** Monogamous. Large colonies.

• **NESTING** Incubation 14–16 days by both sexes. Altricial young in nest 21–24 days, fed by both sexes. 1–3 broods a year.

• **POPULATION** Common in open country, especially near water. Range is expanding and numbers are increasing.

• **CONSERVATION** Neotropical migrant. Previously listed as being of special concern, but successful adaptation to nesting on man-made structures such as buildings, highway bridges and overpasses, railroad bridges, dams, and other vertical walls has greatly expanded populations and range.

Similar Birds
CAVE SWALLOW Pale cinnamon-buff throat; cinnamon forehead; richer cinnamon-rust rump.

Flight Pattern
Swift graceful flight alternating several deep rapid wing beats with long elliptical glides with sharp sweeping upturns at the end. Soars on thermals and updrafts.

Nest Identification	
Shape	Pellets of clay or mud, with lining of grasses, down, and feathers • usually under eaves of buildings or under dams or bridges; sometimes on ridges of canyons; rarely on trunk of conifer tree under overhanging branch • built by both sexes • 3–6 white, cream, or pinkish eggs, marked with browns; oval to long oval, 0.8 x 0.5 inches.
Location	

Plumage Sexes similar	Habitat	Migration Migratory	Weight 0.8 ounce

DATE _____ TIME_____ LOCATION _____

Family HIRUNDINIDAE	Species *Petrochelidon fulva*	Length 5.5 inches	Wingspan 12 inches

CAVE SWALLOW

This bird plasters its cuplike nests to the sides of caves, but it has adapted to man-made structures and now also uses buildings, bridges, culverts, and even drainage pipes. A native of Mexico and the West Indies, in North America two races nest, one in the Southwest and one in Florida. One of the most visited colonies is established in the entrance to Carlsbad Caverns. Similar in appearance to the Cliff Swallow, it

cinnamon forehead

blue-black upperparts with whitish buff streaks on back

whitish buff edging to tertials

cinnamon-buff throat extends around neck as a collar

chestnut rump

blackish flight feathers

whitish underparts with rufous wash on breast and sides

squared tail

dusky cinnamon undertail coverts with dark centers

JUVENILE

often nests with them, and with Barn Swallows. In flight it shows brownish underwing linings. The southwestern race of the Cliff Swallow has the cinnamon forehead but has a dark throat.

- **SONG** Series of dry warbling buzzy chatters; sometimes calls *chu-chu* or *zweih*.
- **BEHAVIOR** Gregarious. Eats insects caught in flight. Builds a complex nest: a sphere constructed of mud pellets with a tubular entrance on one side. Colonies often active on same site year after year and may repair and reuse old nests.
- **BREEDING** Monogamous. Colonial.
- **NESTING** Incubation 15–18 days by both sexes. Young altricial; remain in nest 21–33 days, fed by both sexes. Has 2 broods per year.

Similar Birds

CLIFF SWALLOW
Pale whitish to buff forehead; dark rusty brown throat with black center patch; pale cinnamon-buff rump • southwestern race has cinnamon forehead.

- **POPULATION** Fairly common but somewhat local. Expanding range and increasing in number. Casual in Northeast.
- **CONSERVATION** Neotropical migrant.

Flight Pattern

Swift graceful flight, alternating several rapid deep wing beats with long elliptical glides ending on sharp sweeping upturns. Soars on winds and thermals.

Nest Identification

Shape

Location

Pellets of clay and mud with lining of grasses and a few feathers • plastered to sides of caves, sinkholes, bridges, culverts, buildings, or even drainage pipes • built by both sexes • 3–5 white eggs, marked with browns; oval to long oval, 0.8 x 0.5 inches.

Plumage Sexes similar	Habitat	Migration Migratory	Weight 0.7 ounce

DATE _____ TIME_____ LOCATION _____

Family HIRUNDINIDAE	Species *Hirundo rustica*	Length 6.75–7.5 inches	Wingspan 12.5–13.5 inches

BARN SWALLOW

Since early colonial times this bird has been a welcome presence on farms because it eats many crop-destroying insects. Usually nesting inside of barns or other buildings, it is the only North American swallow with buffy to cinnamon underparts and underwing linings and a white-spotted deeply forked tail. The female is similar to the male but most often is duller in color. Juveniles have shorter forked tails and creamy white underparts. The most wide-ranging swallow in the world, it is cosmopolitan, found breeding or wintering on almost all continents.

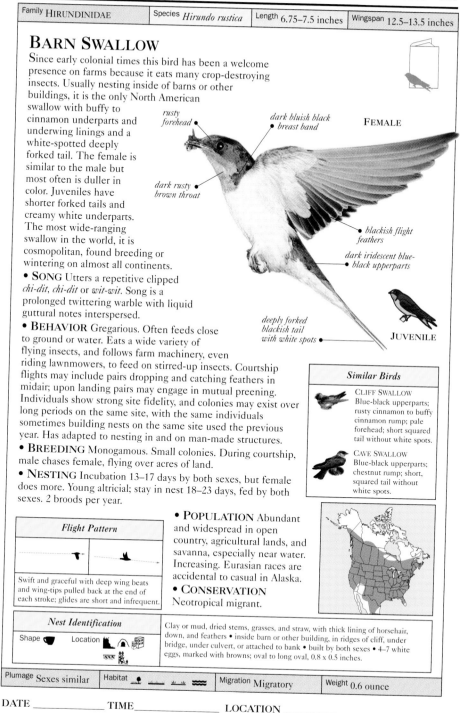

rusty forehead

dark bluish black breast band

FEMALE

dark rusty brown throat

blackish flight feathers

dark iridescent blue-black upperparts

deeply forked blackish tail with white spots

JUVENILE

• **SONG** Utters a repetitive clipped *chi-dit, chi-dit* or *wit-wit*. Song is a prolonged twittering warble with liquid guttural notes interspersed.
• **BEHAVIOR** Gregarious. Often feeds close to ground or water. Eats a wide variety of flying insects, and follows farm machinery, even riding lawnmowers, to feed on stirred-up insects. Courtship flights may include pairs dropping and catching feathers in midair; upon landing pairs may engage in mutual preening. Individuals show strong site fidelity, and colonies may exist over long periods on the same site, with the same individuals sometimes building nests on the same site used the previous year. Has adapted to nesting in and on man-made structures.
• **BREEDING** Monogamous. Small colonies. During courtship, male chases female, flying over acres of land.
• **NESTING** Incubation 13–17 days by both sexes, but female does more. Young altricial; stay in nest 18–23 days, fed by both sexes. 2 broods per year.

Similar Birds

CLIFF SWALLOW
Blue-black upperparts; rusty cinnamon to buffy cinnamon rump; pale forehead; short squared tail without white spots.

CAVE SWALLOW
Blue-black upperparts; chestnut rump; short, squared tail without white spots.

Flight Pattern

Swift and graceful with deep wing beats and wing-tips pulled back at the end of each stroke; glides are short and infrequent.

• **POPULATION** Abundant and widespread in open country, agricultural lands, and savanna, especially near water. Increasing. Eurasian races are accidental to casual in Alaska.
• **CONSERVATION** Neotropical migrant.

Nest Identification	
Shape	Location

Clay or mud, dried stems, grasses, and straw, with thick lining of horsehair, down, and feathers • inside barn or other building, in ridges of cliff, under bridge, under culvert, or attached to bank • built by both sexes • 4–7 white eggs, marked with browns; oval to long oval, 0.8 x 0.5 inches.

Plumage Sexes similar	Habitat	Migration Migratory	Weight 0.6 ounce

DATE _____ TIME_____ LOCATION _____

Family PARIDAE	Species *Poecile carolinensis*	Length 4.75 inches	Wingspan 7.5 inches

CAROLINA CHICKADEE

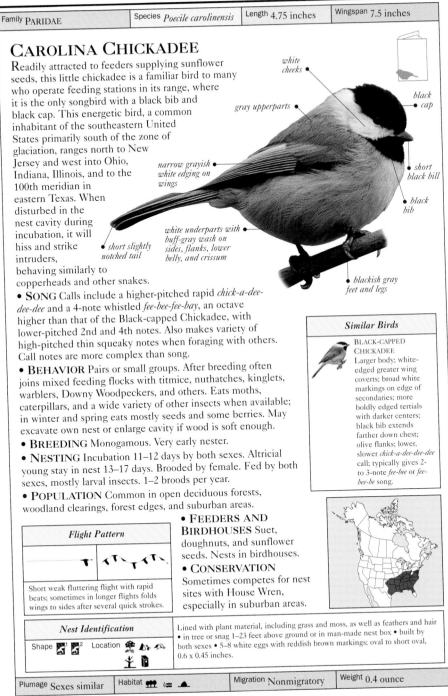

Readily attracted to feeders supplying sunflower seeds, this little chickadee is a familiar bird to many who operate feeding stations in its range, where it is the only songbird with a black bib and black cap. This energetic bird, a common inhabitant of the southeastern United States primarily south of the zone of glaciation, ranges north to New Jersey and west into Ohio, Indiana, Illinois, and to the 100th meridian in eastern Texas. When disturbed in the nest cavity during incubation, it will hiss and strike intruders, behaving similarly to copperheads and other snakes.

white cheeks

gray upperparts

black cap

narrow grayish white edging on wings

short black bill

black bib

short slightly notched tail

white underparts with buff-gray wash on sides, flanks, lower belly, and crissum

blackish gray feet and legs

• **SONG** Calls include a higher-pitched rapid *chick-a-dee-dee-dee* and a 4-note whistled *fee-bee-fee-bay*, an octave higher than that of the Black-capped Chickadee, with lower-pitched 2nd and 4th notes. Also makes variety of high-pitched thin squeaky notes when foraging with others. Call notes are more complex than song.

• **BEHAVIOR** Pairs or small groups. After breeding often joins mixed feeding flocks with titmice, nuthatches, kinglets, warblers, Downy Woodpeckers, and others. Eats moths, caterpillars, and a wide variety of other insects when available; in winter and spring eats mostly seeds and some berries. May excavate own nest or enlarge cavity if wood is soft enough.

• **BREEDING** Monogamous. Very early nester.

• **NESTING** Incubation 11–12 days by both sexes. Altricial young stay in nest 13–17 days. Brooded by female. Fed by both sexes, mostly larval insects. 1–2 broods per year.

• **POPULATION** Common in open deciduous forests, woodland clearings, forest edges, and suburban areas.

• **FEEDERS AND BIRDHOUSES** Suet, doughnuts, and sunflower seeds. Nests in birdhouses.

• **CONSERVATION** Sometimes competes for nest sites with House Wren, especially in suburban areas.

Similar Birds

BLACK-CAPPED CHICKADEE Larger body; white-edged greater wing coverts; broad white markings on edge of secondaries; more boldly edged tertials with darker centers; black bib extends farther down chest; olive flanks; lower, slower *chick-a-dee-dee-dee* call; typically gives 2- to 3-note *fee-bee* or *fee-bee-be* song.

Flight Pattern

Short weak fluttering flight with rapid beats; sometimes in longer flights folds wings to sides after several quick strokes.

Nest Identification

Shape | Location

Lined with plant material, including grass and moss, as well as feathers and hair • in tree or snag 1–23 feet above ground or in man-made nest box • built by both sexes • 5–8 white eggs with reddish brown markings; oval to short oval, 0.6 x 0.45 inches.

Plumage Sexes similar	Habitat	Migration Nonmigratory	Weight 0.4 ounce

DATE _____ TIME_____ LOCATION _____

Family PARIDAE	Species *Poecile atricapilla*	Length 5.5 inches	Wingspan 7.5–8.5 inches

BLACK-CAPPED CHICKADEE

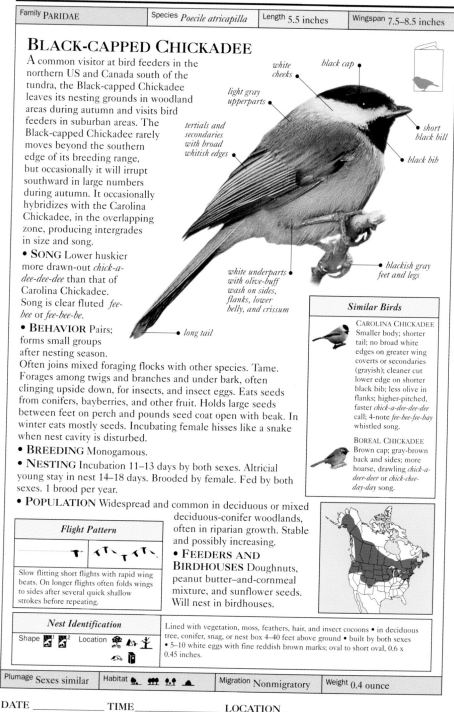

A common visitor at bird feeders in the northern US and Canada south of the tundra, the Black-capped Chickadee leaves its nesting grounds in woodland areas during autumn and visits bird feeders in suburban areas. The Black-capped Chickadee rarely moves beyond the southern edge of its breeding range, but occasionally it will irrupt southward in large numbers during autumn. It occasionally hybridizes with the Carolina Chickadee, in the overlapping zone, producing intergrades in size and song.

white cheeks
black cap
light gray upperparts
tertials and secondaries with broad whitish edges
short black bill
black bib
white underparts with olive-buff wash on sides, flanks, lower belly, and crissum
blackish gray feet and legs
long tail

- **SONG** Lower huskier more drawn-out *chick-a-dee-dee-dee* than that of Carolina Chickadee. Song is clear fluted *fee-bee* or *fee-bee-be*.
- **BEHAVIOR** Pairs; forms small groups after nesting season. Often joins mixed foraging flocks with other species. Tame. Forages among twigs and branches and under bark, often clinging upside down, for insects, and insect eggs. Eats seeds from conifers, bayberries, and other fruit. Holds large seeds between feet on perch and pounds seed coat open with beak. In winter eats mostly seeds. Incubating female hisses like a snake when nest cavity is disturbed.
- **BREEDING** Monogamous.
- **NESTING** Incubation 11–13 days by both sexes. Altricial young stay in nest 14–18 days. Brooded by female. Fed by both sexes. 1 brood per year.
- **POPULATION** Widespread and common in deciduous or mixed deciduous-conifer woodlands, often in riparian growth. Stable and possibly increasing.
- **FEEDERS AND BIRDHOUSES** Doughnuts, peanut butter–and-cornmeal mixture, and sunflower seeds. Will nest in birdhouses.

Similar Birds

CAROLINA CHICKADEE
Smaller body; shorter tail; no broad white edges on greater wing coverts or secondaries (grayish); cleaner cut lower edge on shorter black bib; less olive in flanks; higher-pitched, faster *chick-a-dee-dee-dee* call; 4-note *fee-bee-fee-bay* whistled song.

BOREAL CHICKADEE
Brown cap; gray-brown back and sides; more hoarse, drawling *chick-a-deer-deer* or *chick-chee-day-day* song.

Flight Pattern
Slow flitting short flights with rapid wing beats. On longer flights often folds wings to sides after several quick shallow strokes before repeating.

Nest Identification	
Shape	Location	Lined with vegetation, moss, feathers, hair, and insect cocoons • in deciduous tree, conifer, snag, or nest box 4–40 feet above ground • built by both sexes • 5–10 white eggs with fine reddish brown marks; oval to short oval, 0.6 x 0.45 inches.

Plumage Sexes similar	Habitat	Migration Nonmigratory	Weight 0.4 ounce

DATE _____ TIME_____ LOCATION _____

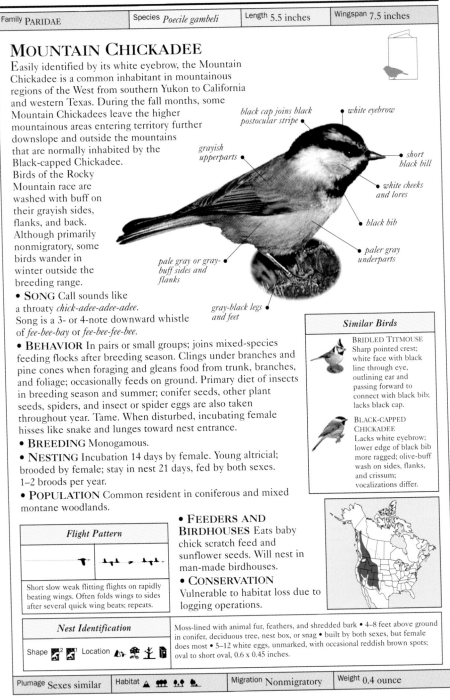

Family PARIDAE	Species *Poecile gambeli*	Length 5.5 inches	Wingspan 7.5 inches

MOUNTAIN CHICKADEE

Easily identified by its white eyebrow, the Mountain Chickadee is a common inhabitant in mountainous regions of the West from southern Yukon to California and western Texas. During the fall months, some Mountain Chickadees leave the higher mountainous areas entering territory further downslope and outside the mountains that are normally inhabited by the Black-capped Chickadee. Birds of the Rocky Mountain race are washed with buff on their grayish sides, flanks, and back. Although primarily nonmigratory, some birds wander in winter outside the breeding range.

black cap joins black postocular stripe
white eyebrow
grayish upperparts
short black bill
white cheeks and lores
black bib
paler gray underparts
pale gray or gray-buff sides and flanks
gray-black legs and feet

• **SONG** Call sounds like a throaty *chick-adee-adee-adee*. Song is a 3- or 4-note downward whistle of *fee-bee-bay* or *fee-bee-fee-bee*.

• **BEHAVIOR** In pairs or small groups; joins mixed-species feeding flocks after breeding season. Clings under branches and pine cones when foraging and gleans food from trunk, branches, and foliage; occasionally feeds on ground. Primary diet of insects in breeding season and summer; conifer seeds, other plant seeds, spiders, and insect or spider eggs are also taken throughout year. Tame. When disturbed, incubating female hisses like snake and lunges toward nest entrance.

• **BREEDING** Monogamous.

• **NESTING** Incubation 14 days by female. Young altricial; brooded by female; stay in nest 21 days, fed by both sexes. 1–2 broods per year.

• **POPULATION** Common resident in coniferous and mixed montane woodlands.

Similar Birds

BRIDLED TITMOUSE
Sharp pointed crest; white face with black line through eye, outlining ear and passing forward to connect with black bib; lacks black cap.

BLACK-CAPPED CHICKADEE
Lacks white eyebrow; lower edge of black bib more ragged; olive-buff wash on sides, flanks, and crissum; vocalizations differ.

• **FEEDERS AND BIRDHOUSES** Eats baby chick scratch feed and sunflower seeds. Will nest in man-made birdhouses.

• **CONSERVATION** Vulnerable to habitat loss due to logging operations.

Flight Pattern

Short slow weak flitting flights on rapidly beating wings. Often folds wings to sides after several quick wing beats; repeats.

Nest Identification	Moss-lined with animal fur, feathers, and shredded bark • 4–8 feet above ground in conifer, deciduous tree, nest box, or snag • built by both sexes, but female does most • 5–12 white eggs, unmarked, with occasional reddish brown spots; oval to short oval, 0.6 x 0.45 inches.
Shape Location	

Plumage Sexes similar	Habitat	Migration Nonmigratory	Weight 0.4 ounce

DATE _____ TIME _____ LOCATION _____

Family PARIDAE	Species *Poecile sclateri*	Length 5 inches	Wingspan 7.25 inches

MEXICAN CHICKADEE

The only chickadee in Mexico and in its very restricted US range, this bird is often observed in pairs or in small groups and occasionally in mixed-species flocks. A common resident in coniferous and mixed woodlands in mountains, populations of the Mexican Chickadee in Mexico may be vulnerable to diminishing habitat. Although

black cap
white cheeks
short black bill
black bib extending onto upper breast; whitish band below bib extends down center of belly
grayish upperparts
paler grayish underparts
dark gray sides, flanks, and undertail coverts
gray-black legs and feet

considered a mostly permanent resident, the Mexican Chickadee sometimes moves to lower elevations in the winter months.

• **SONG** Unlike other chickadees, the Mexican's songs are complex; short, clear to slightly burry trilled whistle of *chischu-wur* and a rich *cheelee*. Call includes husky buzzing notes of *chi-pi-tit*.

• **BEHAVIOR** In pairs or small groups. Joins mixed-species feeding flocks after breeding season. Clings under branches or pine cones when feeding, or gleans trunks, branches, and foliage for insects, spiders, egg cases, and seeds from conifers and other plants. Tame. Female sweeps nest entrance with crushed insects held in bill, presumably to deter nest predators.

• **BREEDING** Monogamous.

• **NESTING** Breeding biology poorly known. Estimated incubation 11–14 days by female. Young altricial; brooded by female; fledge nest in estimated 18–21 days, fed by both sexes. 1–2 broods per year.

• **POPULATION** Stable in limited US range.

• **CONSERVATION** Vulnerable to habitat loss of montane conifers due to logging operations, especially in Mexican range.

Similar Birds

BLACK-CAPPED CHICKADEE Smaller black bib does not reach breast; olive-buff wash on sides, flanks, and undertail coverts; more white edging on greater coverts, tertials, and secondaries; voice differs; ranges do not overlap.

MOUNTAIN CHICKADEE White eyebrow; pale gray sides, flanks, and crissum; shorter black bib does not extend onto breast; voice differs.

Flight Pattern

Short slow weak flitting flights on rapidly beating wings. Often folds wings to sides after several shallow strokes; repeated.

Nest Identification

Shape | Location

Fine grasses, bark strips, moss, and plant down, lined with animal fur • 5–45 feet above ground in snag or tree (mesic montane pine, spruce-fir, and pine-oak woodlands) • built by female • 5–8 white eggs, finely marked with reddish brown spots; ovate to elongate ovate, 0.6 x 0.45 inches.

Plumage Sexes similar	Habitat	Migration Nonmigratory	Weight 0.4 ounce

DATE _____ TIME _____ LOCATION _____

Family PARIDAE	Species *Poecile rufescens*	Length 4.75 inches	Wingspan 5.25 inches

CHESTNUT-BACKED CHICKADEE

Known for its richly colored plumage, the Chestnut-backed Chickadee is a common resident of humid coniferous forests along the Pacific Coast. Pairs defend their individual nesting areas but typically reside near other pairs, forming a loose colony. They often feed high in the trees in pairs or small family groups. The race along the central California coast from San Francisco southward displays very little chestnut on the sides and flanks, and the underparts are mostly gray.

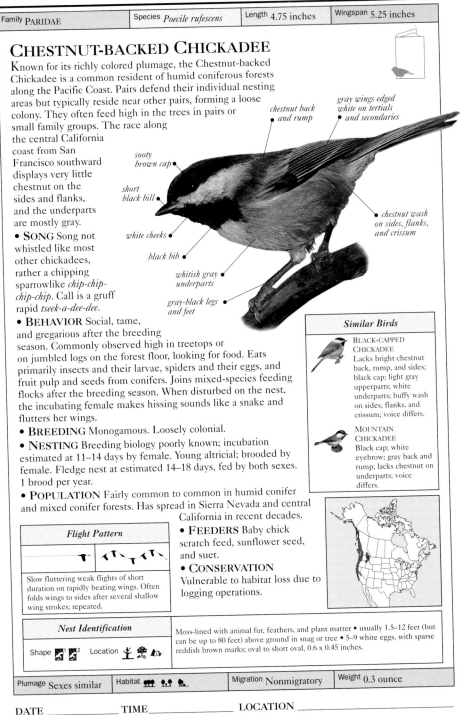

chestnut back and rump

gray wings edged white on tertials and secondaries

sooty brown cap

short black bill

white cheeks

black bib

whitish gray underparts

gray-black legs and feet

chestnut wash on sides, flanks, and crissum

- **SONG** Song not whistled like most other chickadees, rather a chipping sparrowlike *chip-chip-chip-chip*. Call is a gruff rapid *tseek-a-dee-dee*.
- **BEHAVIOR** Social, tame, and gregarious after the breeding season. Commonly observed high in treetops or on jumbled logs on the forest floor, looking for food. Eats primarily insects and their larvae, spiders and their eggs, and fruit pulp and seeds from conifers. Joins mixed-species feeding flocks after the breeding season. When disturbed on the nest, the incubating female makes hissing sounds like a snake and flutters her wings.
- **BREEDING** Monogamous. Loosely colonial.
- **NESTING** Breeding biology poorly known; incubation estimated at 11–14 days by female. Young altricial; brooded by female. Fledge nest at estimated 14–18 days, fed by both sexes. 1 brood per year.
- **POPULATION** Fairly common to common in humid conifer and mixed conifer forests. Has spread in Sierra Nevada and central California in recent decades.
- **FEEDERS** Baby chick scratch feed, sunflower seed, and suet.
- **CONSERVATION** Vulnerable to habitat loss due to logging operations.

Similar Birds

BLACK-CAPPED CHICKADEE Lacks bright chestnut back, rump, and sides; black cap; light gray upperparts; white underparts; buffy wash on sides, flanks, and crissum; voice differs.

MOUNTAIN CHICKADEE Black cap; white eyebrow; gray back and rump; lacks chestnut on underparts; voice differs.

Flight Pattern

Slow fluttering weak flights of short duration on rapidly beating wings. Often folds wings to sides after several shallow wing strokes; repeated.

Nest Identification

Shape | Location

Moss-lined with animal fur, feathers, and plant matter • usually 1.5–12 feet (but can be up to 80 feet) above ground in snag or tree • 5–9 white eggs, with sparse reddish brown marks; oval to short oval, 0.6 x 0.45 inches.

Plumage Sexes similar	Habitat	Migration Nonmigratory	Weight 0.3 ounce

DATE _____ TIME_____ LOCATION _____

Family PARIDAE	Species *Poecile hudsonica*	Length 5.5 inches	Wingspan 8 inches

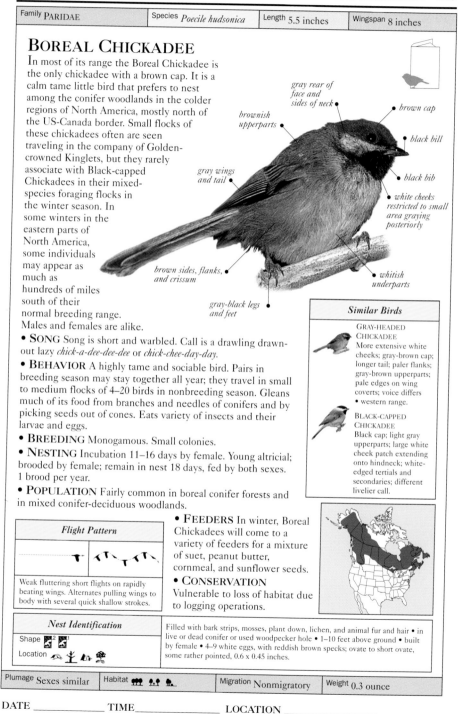

BOREAL CHICKADEE

In most of its range the Boreal Chickadee is the only chickadee with a brown cap. It is a calm tame little bird that prefers to nest among the conifer woodlands in the colder regions of North America, mostly north of the US-Canada border. Small flocks of these chickadees often are seen traveling in the company of Golden-crowned Kinglets, but they rarely associate with Black-capped Chickadees in their mixed-species foraging flocks in the winter season. In some winters in the eastern parts of North America, some individuals may appear as much as hundreds of miles south of their normal breeding range. Males and females are alike.

gray rear of face and sides of neck

brown cap

brownish upperparts

black bill

gray wings and tail

black bib

white cheeks restricted to small area graying posteriorly

brown sides, flanks, and crissum

whitish underparts

gray-black legs and feet

- **SONG** Song is short and warbled. Call is a drawling drawn-out lazy *chick-a-dee-dee-dee* or *chick-chee-day-day*.
- **BEHAVIOR** A highly tame and sociable bird. Pairs in breeding season may stay together all year; they travel in small to medium flocks of 4–20 birds in nonbreeding season. Gleans much of its food from branches and needles of conifers and by picking seeds out of cones. Eats variety of insects and their larvae and eggs.
- **BREEDING** Monogamous. Small colonies.
- **NESTING** Incubation 11–16 days by female. Young altricial; brooded by female; remain in nest 18 days, fed by both sexes. 1 brood per year.
- **POPULATION** Fairly common in boreal conifer forests and in mixed conifer-deciduous woodlands.

Similar Birds

GRAY-HEADED CHICKADEE
More extensive white cheeks; gray-brown cap; longer tail; paler flanks; gray-brown upperparts; pale edges on wing coverts; voice differs
- western range.

BLACK-CAPPED CHICKADEE
Black cap; light gray upperparts; large white cheek patch extending onto hindneck; white-edged tertials and secondaries; different livelier call.

- **FEEDERS** In winter, Boreal Chickadees will come to a variety of feeders for a mixture of suet, peanut butter, cornmeal, and sunflower seeds.
- **CONSERVATION** Vulnerable to loss of habitat due to logging operations.

Flight Pattern

Weak fluttering short flights on rapidly beating wings. Alternates pulling wings to body with several quick shallow strokes.

Nest Identification

Shape

Location

Filled with bark strips, mosses, plant down, lichen, and animal fur and hair • in live or dead conifer or used woodpecker hole • 1–10 feet above ground • built by female • 4–9 white eggs, with reddish brown specks; ovate to short ovate, some rather pointed, 0.6 x 0.45 inches.

Plumage Sexes similar	Habitat	Migration Nonmigratory	Weight 0.3 ounce

DATE _____ TIME_____ LOCATION _____

| Family PARIDAE | Species *Poecile cincta* | Length 5.5 inches | Wingspan 8 inches |

GRAY-HEADED CHICKADEE

Perhaps the hardiest of all chickadees, the Gray-headed Chickadee lives much farther north than the rest of its congeners, with only the Boreal Chickadee as a distant neighbor. This subarctic chickadee, formerly called the Siberian Tit, is a Eurasian native of Siberia and Alaska. Populations of the Gray-headed Chickadee are generally scarce and live primarily among scattered conifers and riparian willow and aspen thickets. The Gray-headed Chickadee is a permanent resident of the northern edges of the tree line and visits human habitations in winter, where it may dine on scraps of frozen meat.

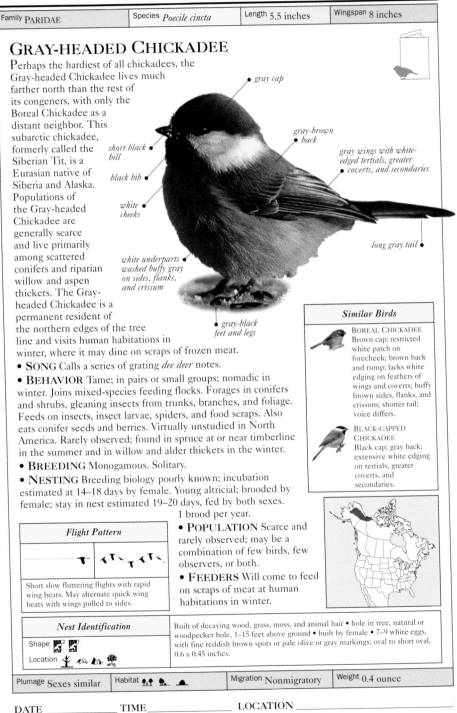

gray cap

gray-brown back

gray wings with white-edged tertials, greater coverts, and secondaries

short black bill

black bib

white cheeks

white underparts washed buffy gray on sides, flanks, and crissum

long gray tail

gray-black feet and legs

• **SONG** Calls a series of grating *dee deer* notes.
• **BEHAVIOR** Tame; in pairs or small groups; nomadic in winter. Joins mixed-species feeding flocks. Forages in conifers and shrubs, gleaning insects from trunks, branches, and foliage. Feeds on insects, insect larvae, spiders, and food scraps. Also eats conifer seeds and berries. Virtually unstudied in North America. Rarely observed; found in spruce at or near timberline in the summer and in willow and alder thickets in the winter.
• **BREEDING** Monogamous. Solitary.
• **NESTING** Breeding biology poorly known; incubation estimated at 14–18 days by female. Young altricial; brooded by female; stay in nest estimated 19–20 days, fed by both sexes. 1 brood per year.
• **POPULATION** Scarce and rarely observed; may be a combination of few birds, few observers, or both.
• **FEEDERS** Will come to feed on scraps of meat at human habitations in winter.

Similar Birds

BOREAL CHICKADEE Brown cap; restricted white patch on forecheek; brown back and rump; lacks white edging on feathers of wings and coverts; buffy brown sides, flanks, and crissum; shorter tail; voice differs.

BLACK-CAPPED CHICKADEE Black cap; gray back; extensive white edging on tertials, greater coverts, and secondaries.

Flight Pattern

Short slow fluttering flights with rapid wing beats. May alternate quick wing beats with wings pulled to sides.

Nest Identification

Shape

Location

Built of decaying wood, grass, moss, and animal hair • hole in tree, natural or woodpecker hole, 1–15 feet above ground • built by female • 7–9 white eggs, with fine reddish brown spots or pale olive or gray markings; oval to short oval, 0.6 x 0.45 inches.

| Plumage Sexes similar | Habitat | Migration Nonmigratory | Weight 0.4 ounce |

DATE _____ TIME_____ LOCATION _____

Family PARIDAE	Species *Baeolophus wollweberi*	Length 5.25 inches	Wingspan 7.5 inches

BRIDLED TITMOUSE

The Bridled Titmouse is a Mexican species whose range crosses the United States' border into the mountains of southeast Arizona and southwest New Mexico. A common bird within its range, the Bridled Titmouse enjoys a stable population, frequenting forests with oaks and pines or, occasionally, riparian areas with cottonwood-willow-mesquite associations. The black-and-white "bridled" face pattern is unmistakable when combined with the black-edged crest.

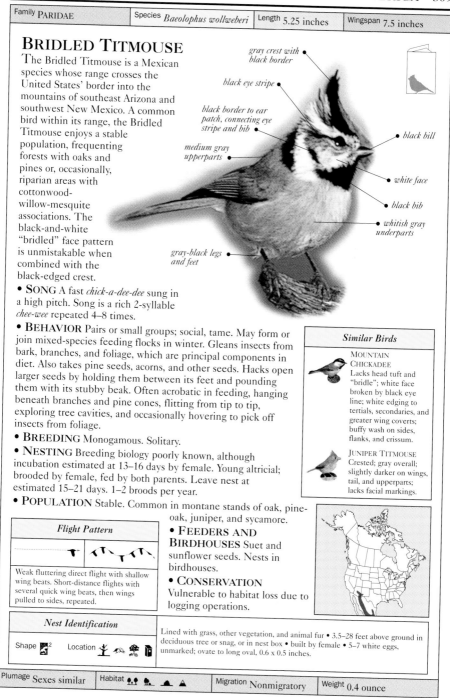

gray crest with black border

black eye stripe

black border to ear patch, connecting eye stripe and bib

medium gray upperparts

black bill

white face

black bib

whitish gray underparts

gray-black legs and feet

• **SONG** A fast *chick-a-dee-dee* sung in a high pitch. Song is a rich 2-syllable *chee-wee* repeated 4–8 times.

• **BEHAVIOR** Pairs or small groups; social, tame. May form or join mixed-species feeding flocks in winter. Gleans insects from bark, branches, and foliage, which are principal components in diet. Also takes pine seeds, acorns, and other seeds. Hacks open larger seeds by holding them between its feet and pounding them with its stubby beak. Often acrobatic in feeding, hanging beneath branches and pine cones, flitting from tip to tip, exploring tree cavities, and occasionally hovering to pick off insects from foliage.

• **BREEDING** Monogamous. Solitary.

• **NESTING** Breeding biology poorly known, although incubation estimated at 13–16 days by female. Young altricial; brooded by female, fed by both parents. Leave nest at estimated 15–21 days. 1–2 broods per year.

• **POPULATION** Stable. Common in montane stands of oak, pine-oak, juniper, and sycamore.

• **FEEDERS AND BIRDHOUSES** Suet and sunflower seeds. Nests in birdhouses.

• **CONSERVATION** Vulnerable to habitat loss due to logging operations.

Similar Birds

MOUNTAIN CHICKADEE Lacks head tuft and "bridle"; white face broken by black eye line; white edging to tertials, secondaries, and greater wing coverts; buffy wash on sides, flanks, and crissum.

JUNIPER TITMOUSE Crested; gray overall; slightly darker on wings, tail, and upperparts; lacks facial markings.

Flight Pattern

Weak fluttering direct flight with shallow wing beats. Short-distance flights with several quick wing beats, then wings pulled to sides, repeated.

Nest Identification

Shape   Location

Lined with grass, other vegetation, and animal fur • 3.5–28 feet above ground in deciduous tree or snag, or in nest box • built by female • 5–7 white eggs, unmarked; ovate to long oval, 0.6 x 0.5 inches.

Plumage Sexes similar	Habitat	Migration Nonmigratory	Weight 0.4 ounce

DATE _____ TIME _____ LOCATION _____

Family PARIDAE	Species *Baeolophus inornatus*	Length 5.25 inches	Wingspan 7.5 inches

OAK TITMOUSE

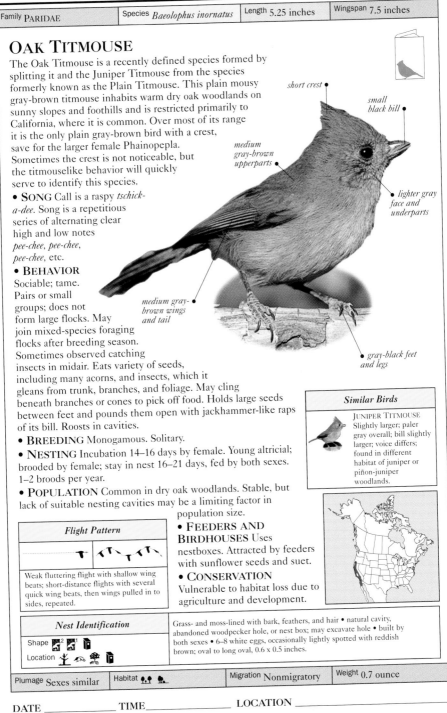

The Oak Titmouse is a recently defined species formed by splitting it and the Juniper Titmouse from the species formerly known as the Plain Titmouse. This plain mousy gray-brown titmouse inhabits warm dry oak woodlands on sunny slopes and foothills and is restricted primarily to California, where it is common. Over most of its range it is the only plain gray-brown bird with a crest, save for the larger female Phainopepla. Sometimes the crest is not noticeable, but the titmouselike behavior will quickly serve to identify this species.

short crest

small black bill

medium gray-brown upperparts

lighter gray face and underparts

• **SONG** Call is a raspy *tschick-a-dee.* Song is a repetitious series of alternating clear high and low notes *pee-chee, pee-chee, pee-chee,* etc.

• **BEHAVIOR** Sociable; tame. Pairs or small groups; does not form large flocks. May join mixed-species foraging flocks after breeding season. Sometimes observed catching insects in midair. Eats variety of seeds, including many acorns, and insects, which it gleans from trunk, branches, and foliage. May cling beneath branches or cones to pick off food. Holds large seeds between feet and pounds them open with jackhammer-like raps of its bill. Roosts in cavities.

medium gray-brown wings and tail

gray-black feet and legs

• **BREEDING** Monogamous. Solitary.

• **NESTING** Incubation 14–16 days by female. Young altricial; brooded by female; stay in nest 16–21 days, fed by both sexes. 1–2 broods per year.

• **POPULATION** Common in dry oak woodlands. Stable, but lack of suitable nesting cavities may be a limiting factor in population size.

• **FEEDERS AND BIRDHOUSES** Uses nestboxes. Attracted by feeders with sunflower seeds and suet.

• **CONSERVATION** Vulnerable to habitat loss due to agriculture and development.

Similar Birds

JUNIPER TITMOUSE
Slightly larger; paler gray overall; bill slightly larger; voice differs; found in different habitat of juniper or piñon-juniper woodlands.

Flight Pattern

Weak fluttering flight with shallow wing beats; short-distance flights with several quick wing beats, then wings pulled in to sides, repeated.

Nest Identification

Shape

Location

Grass- and moss-lined with bark, feathers, and hair • natural cavity, abandoned woodpecker hole, or nest box; may excavate hole • built by both sexes • 6–8 white eggs, occasionally lightly spotted with reddish brown; oval to long oval, 0.6 x 0.5 inches.

Plumage Sexes similar	Habitat	Migration Nonmigratory	Weight 0.7 ounce

DATE _____ TIME_____ LOCATION _____

Family PARIDAE	Species *Baeolophus griseus*	Length 5.5 inches	Wingspan 8 inches

JUNIPER TITMOUSE

Formerly the Juniper Titmouse and the very similar Oak Titmouse were lumped together as one species, the Plain Titmouse. The two "new" titmice's ranges overlap only in one small area of northern California. Only two other gray crested birds occur in the range of the Juniper Titmouse in the mountains of southeast Arizona and southwest New Mexico: the much larger female Phainopepla and the Bridled Titmouse, distinctively marked with its black-and-white face pattern. As its name implies, look for this plain titmouse in juniper or piñon-juniper woodlands, as well as in riparian woodlands and suburban shade trees.

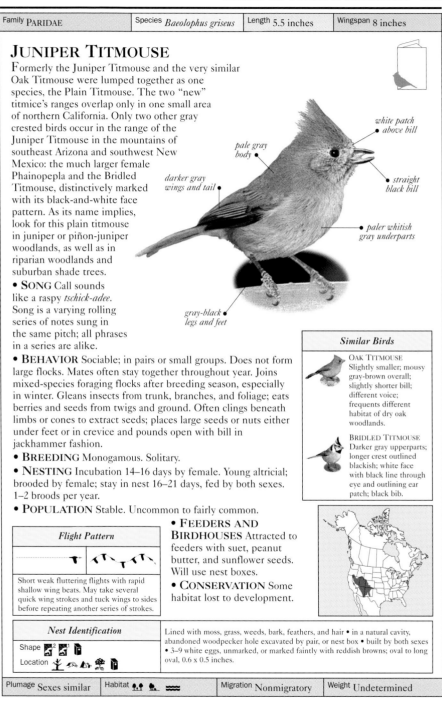

white patch above bill

pale gray body

darker gray wings and tail

straight black bill

paler whitish gray underparts

gray-black legs and feet

• **SONG** Call sounds like a raspy *tschick-adee*. Song is a varying rolling series of notes sung in the same pitch; all phrases in a series are alike.

• **BEHAVIOR** Sociable; in pairs or small groups. Does not form large flocks. Mates often stay together throughout year. Joins mixed-species foraging flocks after breeding season, especially in winter. Gleans insects from trunk, branches, and foliage; eats berries and seeds from twigs and ground. Often clings beneath limbs or cones to extract seeds; places large seeds or nuts either under feet or in crevice and pounds open with bill in jackhammer fashion.

• **BREEDING** Monogamous. Solitary.

• **NESTING** Incubation 14–16 days by female. Young altricial; brooded by female; stay in nest 16–21 days, fed by both sexes. 1–2 broods per year.

• **POPULATION** Stable. Uncommon to fairly common.

Similar Birds

OAK TITMOUSE
Slightly smaller; mousy gray-brown overall; slightly shorter bill; different voice; frequents different habitat of dry oak woodlands.

BRIDLED TITMOUSE
Darker gray upperparts; longer crest outlined blackish; white face with black line through eye and outlining ear patch; black bib.

• **FEEDERS AND BIRDHOUSES** Attracted to feeders with suet, peanut butter, and sunflower seeds. Will use nest boxes.

• **CONSERVATION** Some habitat lost to development.

Flight Pattern

Short weak fluttering flights with rapid shallow wing beats. May take several quick wing strokes and tuck wings to sides before repeating another series of strokes.

Nest Identification

Shape

Location

Lined with moss, grass, weeds, bark, feathers, and hair • in a natural cavity, abandoned woodpecker hole excavated by pair, or nest box • built by both sexes • 3–9 white eggs, unmarked, or marked faintly with reddish browns; oval to long oval, 0.6 x 0.5 inches.

Plumage Sexes similar	Habitat	Migration Nonmigratory	Weight Undetermined

DATE _____ TIME_____ LOCATION _____

Family PARIDAE	Species *Baeolophus bicolor*	Length 6.5 inches	Wingspan 10.75 inches

TUFTED TITMOUSE

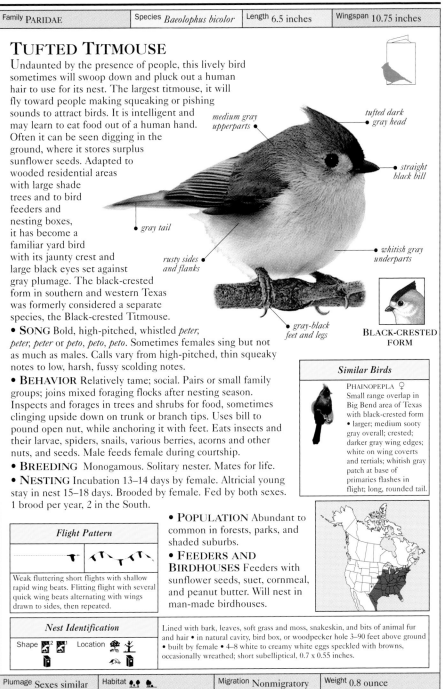

Undaunted by the presence of people, this lively bird sometimes will swoop down and pluck out a human hair to use for its nest. The largest titmouse, it will fly toward people making squeaking or pishing sounds to attract birds. It is intelligent and may learn to eat food out of a human hand. Often it can be seen digging in the ground, where it stores surplus sunflower seeds. Adapted to wooded residential areas with large shade trees and to bird feeders and nesting boxes, it has become a familiar yard bird with its jaunty crest and large black eyes set against gray plumage. The black-crested form in southern and western Texas was formerly considered a separate species, the Black-crested Titmouse.

medium gray upperparts

tufted dark gray head

straight black bill

gray tail

rusty sides and flanks

whitish gray underparts

gray-black feet and legs

BLACK-CRESTED FORM

• **SONG** Bold, high-pitched, whistled *peter, peter, peter* or *peto, peto, peto*. Sometimes females sing but not as much as males. Calls vary from high-pitched, thin squeaky notes to low, harsh, fussy scolding notes.

• **BEHAVIOR** Relatively tame; social. Pairs or small family groups; joins mixed foraging flocks after nesting season. Inspects and forages in trees and shrubs for food, sometimes clinging upside down on trunk or branch tips. Uses bill to pound open nut, while anchoring it with feet. Eats insects and their larvae, spiders, snails, various berries, acorns and other nuts, and seeds. Male feeds female during courtship.

• **BREEDING** Monogamous. Solitary nester. Mates for life.

• **NESTING** Incubation 13–14 days by female. Altricial young stay in nest 15–18 days. Brooded by female. Fed by both sexes. 1 brood per year, 2 in the South.

Similar Birds

PHAINOPEPLA ♀
Small range overlap in Big Bend area of Texas with black-crested form • larger; medium sooty gray overall; crested; darker gray wing edges; white on wing coverts and tertials; whitish gray patch at base of primaries flashes in flight; long, rounded tail.

• **POPULATION** Abundant to common in forests, parks, and shaded suburbs.

• **FEEDERS AND BIRDHOUSES** Feeders with sunflower seeds, suet, cornmeal, and peanut butter. Will nest in man-made birdhouses.

Flight Pattern
Weak fluttering short flights with shallow rapid wing beats. Flitting flight with several quick wing beats alternating with wings drawn to sides, then repeated.

Nest Identification	
Shape	Location	Lined with bark, leaves, soft grass and moss, snakeskin, and bits of animal fur and hair • in natural cavity, bird box, or woodpecker hole 3–90 feet above ground • built by female • 4–8 white to creamy white eggs speckled with browns, occasionally wreathed; short subelliptical, 0.7 x 0.55 inches.

Plumage Sexes similar	Habitat	Migration Nonmigratory	Weight 0.8 ounce

DATE _____ TIME_____ LOCATION _____

Family REMIZIDAE	Species *Auriparus flaviceps*	Length 4.5 inches	Wingspan 7 inches

VERDIN

Sometimes using as many as two thousand twigs, this tiny bird builds an elaborate sphere-shaped nest up to eight inches in diameter. The spherical nest has thick walls to insulate it from the hot desert sun and the cold desert nights. Nests built early in the season have their side entrances facing away from the cooling winds to conserve heat; those built later in the nesting season face the direction of the wind for its cooling breezes. As it often nests ten or more miles away from any water source, this bird eats fruit and insects to obtain needed moisture. Brownish gray juveniles lack the yellow head and chestnut shoulder patch of the adults and, except for their shorter tail, could be mistaken for a Bushtit.

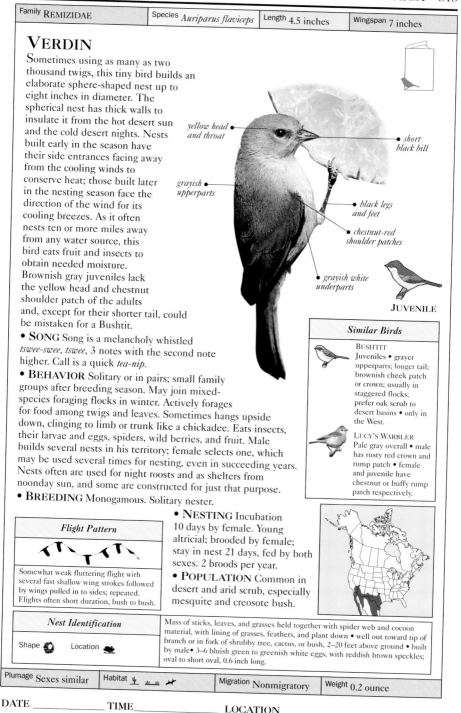

yellow head and throat

grayish upperparts

short black bill

black legs and feet

chestnut-red shoulder patches

grayish white underparts

JUVENILE

• **SONG** Song is a melancholy whistled *tswee-swee, tswee*, 3 notes with the second note higher. Call is a quick *tea-nip*.
• **BEHAVIOR** Solitary or in pairs; small family groups after breeding season. May join mixed-species foraging flocks in winter. Actively forages for food among twigs and leaves. Sometimes hangs upside down, clinging to limb or trunk like a chickadee. Eats insects, their larvae and eggs, spiders, wild berries, and fruit. Male builds several nests in his territory; female selects one, which may be used several times for nesting, even in succeeding years. Nests often are used for night roosts and as shelters from noonday sun, and some are constructed for just that purpose.
• **BREEDING** Monogamous. Solitary nester.
• **NESTING** Incubation 10 days by female. Young altricial; brooded by female; stay in nest 21 days, fed by both sexes. 2 broods per year.
• **POPULATION** Common in desert and arid scrub, especially mesquite and creosote bush.

Similar Birds

BUSHTIT
Juveniles • grayer upperparts; longer tail; brownish cheek patch or crown; usually in staggered flocks; prefer oak scrub to desert basins • only in the West.

LUCY'S WARBLER
Pale gray overall • male has rusty red crown and rump patch • female and juvenile have chestnut or buffy rump patch respectively.

Flight Pattern

Somewhat weak fluttering flight with several fast shallow wing strokes followed by wings pulled in to sides; repeated. Flights often short duration, bush to bush.

Nest Identification

Shape   Location

Mass of sticks, leaves, and grasses held together with spider web and cocoon material, with lining of grasses, feathers, and plant down • well out toward tip of branch or in fork of shrubby tree, cactus, or bush, 2–20 feet above ground • built by male• 3–6 bluish green to greenish white eggs, with reddish brown speckles; oval to short oval, 0.6 inch long.

Plumage Sexes similar	Habitat	Migration Nonmigratory	Weight 0.2 ounce

DATE _____ TIME_____ LOCATION _____

Family AEGITHALIDAE	Species *Psaltriparus minimus*	Length 4.5 inches	Wingspan 7 inches

BUSHTIT

Often observed traveling in flocks, the Bushtit is sociable toward other Bushtits and other birds, often joining mixed-species flocks or letting other groups of Bushtits forage through their nesting territories. Females have cream to yellowish eyes, distinguishing them from male and juvenile birds, which have dark brown eyes. Coastal birds have brown crowns; interior populations have gray crowns and brown cheeks. Southwest populations, in which some adult males have black masks, were formerly considered a separate species, the Black-eared Bushtit. Some birds may move downslope to lower elevations during winter months.

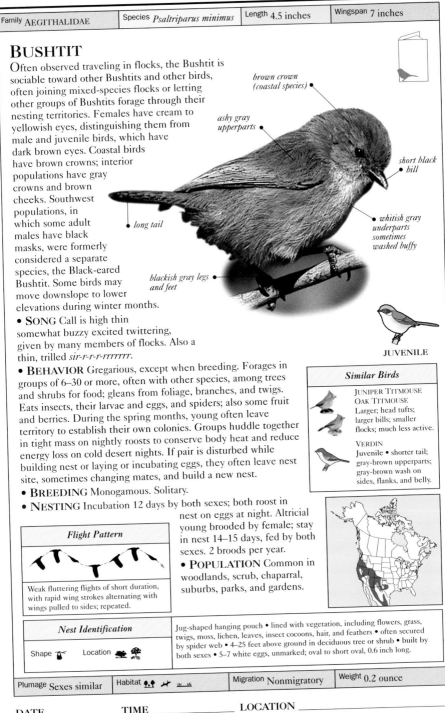

brown crown (coastal species)
ashy gray upperparts
short black bill
long tail
whitish gray underparts sometimes washed buffy
blackish gray legs and feet

JUVENILE

• **SONG** Call is high thin somewhat buzzy excited twittering, given by many members of flocks. Also a thin, trilled *sir-r-r-r-rrrrrrr*.
• **BEHAVIOR** Gregarious, except when breeding. Forages in groups of 6–30 or more, often with other species, among trees and shrubs for food; gleans from foliage, branches, and twigs. Eats insects, their larvae and eggs, and spiders; also some fruit and berries. During the spring months, young often leave territory to establish their own colonies. Groups huddle together in tight mass on nightly roosts to conserve body heat and reduce energy loss on cold desert nights. If pair is disturbed while building nest or laying or incubating eggs, they often leave nest site, sometimes changing mates, and build a new nest.
• **BREEDING** Monogamous. Solitary.
• **NESTING** Incubation 12 days by both sexes; both roost in nest on eggs at night. Altricial young brooded by female; stay in nest 14–15 days, fed by both sexes. 2 broods per year.
• **POPULATION** Common in woodlands, scrub, chaparral, suburbs, parks, and gardens.

Similar Birds

JUNIPER TITMOUSE
OAK TITMOUSE
Larger; head tufts; larger bills; smaller flocks; much less active.

VERDIN
Juvenile • shorter tail; gray-brown upperparts; gray-brown wash on sides, flanks, and belly.

Flight Pattern

Weak fluttering flights of short duration, with rapid wing strokes alternating with wings pulled to sides; repeated.

Nest Identification

Shape   Location

Jug-shaped hanging pouch • lined with vegetation, including flowers, grass, twigs, moss, lichen, leaves, insect cocoons, hair, and feathers • often secured by spider web • 4–25 feet above ground in deciduous tree or shrub • built by both sexes • 5–7 white eggs, unmarked; oval to short oval, 0.6 inch long.

Plumage Sexes similar	Habitat	Migration Nonmigratory	Weight 0.2 ounce

DATE _____ TIME_____ LOCATION _____

Family SITTIDAE	Species *Sitta canadensis*	Length 4.5 inches	Wingspan 8 inches

RED-BREASTED NUTHATCH

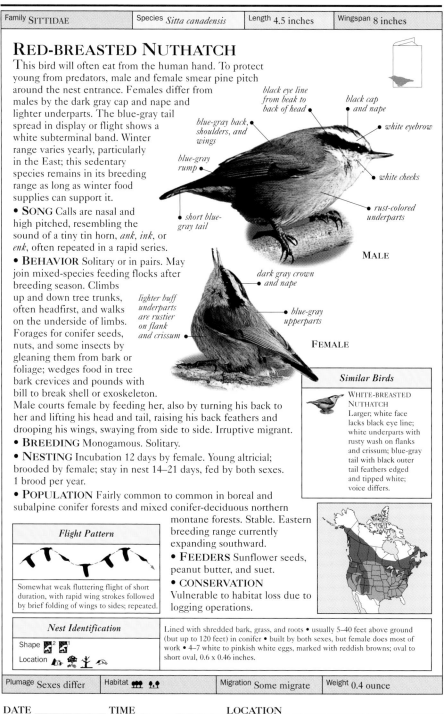

This bird will often eat from the human hand. To protect young from predators, male and female smear pine pitch around the nest entrance. Females differ from males by the dark gray cap and nape and lighter underparts. The blue-gray tail spread in display or flight shows a white subterminal band. Winter range varies yearly, particularly in the East; this sedentary species remains in its breeding range as long as winter food supplies can support it.

black eye line from beak to back of head

black cap and nape

white eyebrow

blue-gray back, shoulders, and wings

blue-gray rump

white cheeks

rust-colored underparts

short blue-gray tail

MALE

- **SONG** Calls are nasal and high pitched, resembling the sound of a tiny tin horn, *ank, ink,* or *enk,* often repeated in a rapid series.

dark gray crown and nape

lighter buff underparts are rustier on flank and crissum

blue-gray upperparts

FEMALE

- **BEHAVIOR** Solitary or in pairs. May join mixed-species feeding flocks after breeding season. Climbs up and down tree trunks, often headfirst, and walks on the underside of limbs. Forages for conifer seeds, nuts, and some insects by gleaning them from bark or foliage; wedges food in tree bark crevices and pounds with bill to break shell or exoskeleton. Male courts female by feeding her, also by turning his back to her and lifting his head and tail, raising his back feathers and drooping his wings, swaying from side to side. Irruptive migrant.

- **BREEDING** Monogamous. Solitary.

- **NESTING** Incubation 12 days by female. Young altricial; brooded by female; stay in nest 14–21 days, fed by both sexes. 1 brood per year.

- **POPULATION** Fairly common to common in boreal and subalpine conifer forests and mixed conifer-deciduous northern montane forests. Stable. Eastern breeding range currently expanding southward.

- **FEEDERS** Sunflower seeds, peanut butter, and suet.

- **CONSERVATION** Vulnerable to habitat loss due to logging operations.

Similar Birds

WHITE-BREASTED NUTHATCH Larger; white face lacks black eye line; white underparts with rusty wash on flanks and crissum; blue-gray tail with black outer tail feathers edged and tipped white; voice differs.

Flight Pattern

Somewhat weak fluttering flight of short duration, with rapid wing strokes followed by brief folding of wings to sides; repeated.

Nest Identification

Shape

Location

Lined with shredded bark, grass, and roots • usually 5–40 feet above ground (but up to 120 feet) in conifer • built by both sexes, but female does most of work • 4–7 white to pinkish white eggs, marked with reddish browns; oval to short oval, 0.6 x 0.46 inches.

Plumage Sexes differ	Habitat	Migration Some migrate	Weight 0.4 ounce

DATE _____ TIME _____ LOCATION _____

Family SITTIDAE	Species *Sitta carolinensis*	Length 5–6 inches	Wingspan 9–11 inches

WHITE-BREASTED NUTHATCH

The largest and most widespread of the North American nuthatches, this nimble bird can balance upside down on tree trunks, catch a falling nut in midair, and rapidly hop down skinny branches. In winter it joins mixed-species flocks and often feeds together in the same tree with chickadees, Downy Woodpeckers, and Brown Creepers. It is quick to accept bird feeders, and will often attempt to intimidate other avian visitors by spreading its wings and tail and swaying back and forth. Females in the Northeast have dark blue-gray crowns.

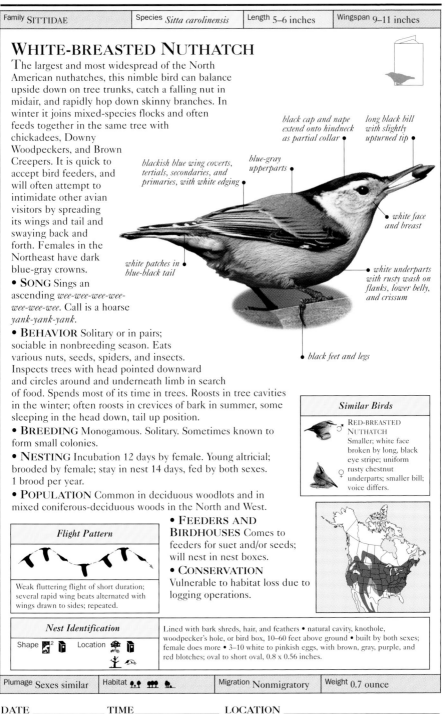

black cap and nape extend onto hindneck as partial collar

long black bill with slightly upturned tip

blue-gray upperparts

blackish blue wing coverts, tertials, secondaries, and primaries, with white edging

white face and breast

white patches in blue-black tail

white underparts with rusty wash on flanks, lower belly, and crissum

black feet and legs

• **SONG** Sings an ascending *wee-wee-wee-wee-wee-wee-wee*. Call is a hoarse *yank-yank-yank*.

• **BEHAVIOR** Solitary or in pairs; sociable in nonbreeding season. Eats various nuts, seeds, spiders, and insects. Inspects trees with head pointed downward and circles around and underneath limb in search of food. Spends most of its time in trees. Roosts in tree cavities in the winter; often roosts in crevices of bark in summer, some sleeping in the head down, tail up position.

• **BREEDING** Monogamous. Solitary. Sometimes known to form small colonies.

• **NESTING** Incubation 12 days by female. Young altricial; brooded by female; stay in nest 14 days, fed by both sexes. 1 brood per year.

• **POPULATION** Common in deciduous woodlots and in mixed coniferous-deciduous woods in the North and West.

Similar Birds

RED-BREASTED NUTHATCH Smaller; white face broken by long, black eye stripe; uniform rusty chestnut underparts; smaller bill; voice differs.

• **FEEDERS AND BIRDHOUSES** Comes to feeders for suet and/or seeds; will nest in nest boxes.

• **CONSERVATION** Vulnerable to habitat loss due to logging operations.

Flight Pattern

Weak fluttering flight of short duration; several rapid wing beats alternated with wings drawn to sides; repeated.

Nest Identification

Shape [icons]   Location [icons]

Lined with bark shreds, hair, and feathers • natural cavity, knothole, woodpecker's hole, or bird box, 10–60 feet above ground • built by both sexes; female does more • 3–10 white to pinkish eggs, with brown, gray, purple, and red blotches; oval to short oval, 0.8 x 0.56 inches.

Plumage Sexes similar	Habitat	Migration Nonmigratory	Weight 0.7 ounce

DATE _____ TIME_____ LOCATION _____

| Family SITTIDAE | Species *Sitta pygmaea* | Length 4.25 inches | Wingspan 8 inches |

PYGMY NUTHATCH

In the fall and winter, these nuthatches work through the treetops in loud flocks along with chickadees and titmice. At night, groups of as many as 100 birds will roost in a single cavity. This is the smallest of the North American nuthatches, and like all birds in its genus, it has long toes with sharp claws, allowing it to cling to tree trunks. Its small size, gray-brown cap, and a white spot on

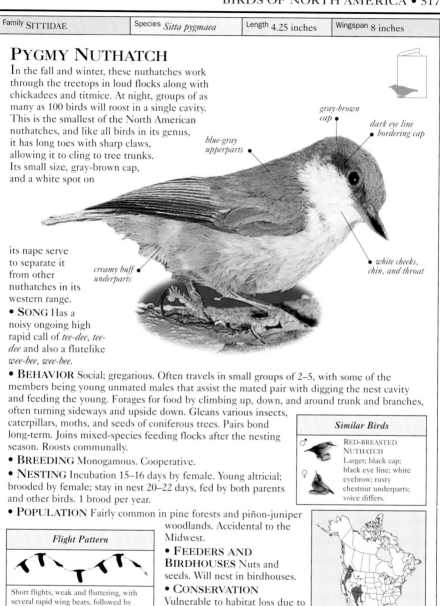

gray-brown cap

dark eye line bordering cap

blue-gray upperparts

creamy buff underparts

white cheeks, chin, and throat

its nape serve to separate it from other nuthatches in its western range.

• **SONG** Has a noisy ongoing high rapid call of *tee-dee, tee-dee* and also a flutelike *wee-bee, wee-bee*.

• **BEHAVIOR** Social; gregarious. Often travels in small groups of 2–5, with some of the members being young unmated males that assist the mated pair with digging the nest cavity and feeding the young. Forages for food by climbing up, down, and around trunk and branches, often turning sideways and upside down. Gleans various insects, caterpillars, moths, and seeds of coniferous trees. Pairs bond long-term. Joins mixed-species feeding flocks after the nesting season. Roosts communally.

• **BREEDING** Monogamous. Cooperative.

• **NESTING** Incubation 15–16 days by female. Young altricial; brooded by female; stay in nest 20–22 days, fed by both parents and other birds. 1 brood per year.

• **POPULATION** Fairly common in pine forests and piñon-juniper woodlands. Accidental to the Midwest.

• **FEEDERS AND BIRDHOUSES** Nuts and seeds. Will nest in birdhouses.

• **CONSERVATION** Vulnerable to habitat loss due to logging activities.

Similar Birds

♂ ♀ RED-BREASTED NUTHATCH
Larger; black cap; black eye line; white eyebrow; rusty chestnut underparts; voice differs.

Flight Pattern

Short flights, weak and fluttering, with several rapid wing beats, followed by wings pulled to sides; repeated.

Nest Identification

Shape ▨¹ ▨² ▯

Location 🏕 🌿 ⚱ ▯

Lined with leaves, shredded pinecones, plant down, fur, and feathers • in dead tree, old post, abandoned woodpecker hole, or nest box, 8–60 feet above ground • built by both parents and other birds • 4–9 white eggs, sparsely flecked with reddish brown; oval to short oval, 0.6 x 0.45 inches.

| Plumage Sexes similar | Habitat 🌳 🌾 🪵 | Migration Nonmigratory | Weight 0.4 ounce |

DATE _____ TIME_____ LOCATION _____

Family CERTHIIDAE	Species *Certhia americana*	Length 5.25 inches	Wingspan 7–8 inches

BROWN CREEPER

This tree-dwelling bird roosts by hanging onto a tree trunk or the side of a house with its sharp claws. Unlike the nuthatches, it does not move sideways or upside down when foraging for insects. Rather, it circles the tree in an upward direction, as if it were ascending a spiral staircase, or it takes a straighter path up, then drops to the base of a nearby tree and starts working its way up again. The long decurved bill is an efficient tool for picking insects out of bark crevices, and the stiff tail feathers prop the bird upright just as a woodpecker's tail does.

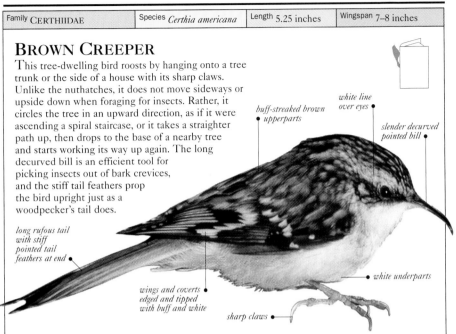

white line over eyes

buff-streaked brown upperparts

slender decurved pointed bill

long rufous tail with stiff pointed tail feathers at end

wings and coverts edged and tipped with buff and white

white underparts

sharp claws

- **SONG** Call is a soft musical *see-see-titi-see*, similar to that of the Golden-crowned Kinglet, but thinner. Call note is a soft thin *seee*.
- **BEHAVIOR** Solitary or in pairs. Tame. Often joins mixed-species foraging flocks in winter. Forages for food by spiraling up tree, but does not move down or sideways. Hops back occasionally, but then moves on up. Eats various insects, larvae, seeds, and some nuts. Well camouflaged and difficult to spot; often escapes predators by pressing its body tightly against tree, spreading wings and tail, and remaining motionless. Fledglings roost in tight circle with heads in center of ring.
- **BREEDING** Monogamous. Solitary nester.
- **NESTING** Incubation 13–17 days by female. Young altricial; brooded by female; stay in nest 13–16 days. Fed by both sexes. 1 brood per year.
- **POPULATION** Fairly common in pine, spruce-fir, mixed coniferous-deciduous, swampy forests; declining in some areas.
- **FEEDERS** Will come to feeders for mixture of nuts, peanut butter, suet, and cornmeal. Mixture can be put directly on tree trunk.
  - **CONSERVATION** Nesting area threatened due to cutting of forest habitat.

Flight Pattern
Strong direct flights of short duration with rapid shallow wing beats.

Nest Identification	Twigs, moss, conifer needles, pieces of bark, and silk, lined with shredded bark and feathers • in cavity of dead tree, or beneath piece of bark against tree, 5–50 feet above ground • built by both sexes; female does more • 4–8 white eggs, sparsely flecked with reddish brown and often wreathed; oval to short oval, 0.6 x 0.46 inches.
Shape ● Location	

Plumage Sexes similar	Habitat	Migration Migratory	Weight 0.3 ounce

DATE _____ TIME_____ LOCATION _____

| Family TROGLODYTIDAE | Species *Campylorhynchus brunneicapillus* | Length 8.5 inches | Wingspan 10.75 inches |

CACTUS WREN

The Arizona state bird often builds its domed nest in the heavily barbed cholla cactus, where its nestlings and eggs are protected from predators. Once the young leave the cactus, the old nests are maintained and used for a roosting area by the adult birds. The largest of the North American wrens, with its large size, long tail, and long, slightly decurved bill, actually is more suggestive of a small thrasher

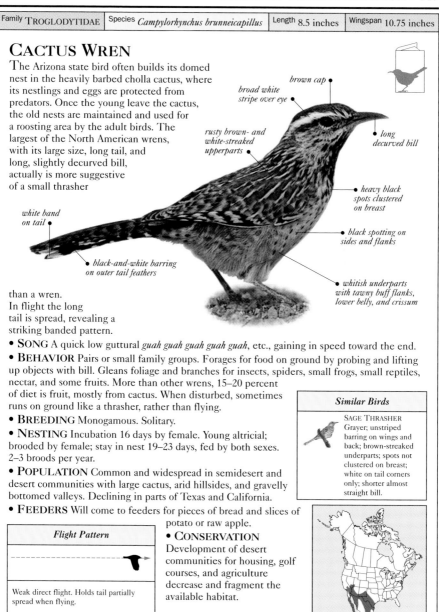

brown cap

broad white stripe over eye

rusty brown- and white-streaked upperparts

long decurved bill

heavy black spots clustered on breast

black spotting on sides and flanks

whitish underparts with tawny buff flanks, lower belly, and crissum

white band on tail

black-and-white barring on outer tail feathers

than a wren. In flight the long tail is spread, revealing a striking banded pattern.

• **SONG** A quick low guttural *guah guah guah guah guah*, etc., gaining in speed toward the end.

• **BEHAVIOR** Pairs or small family groups. Forages for food on ground by probing and lifting up objects with bill. Gleans foliage and branches for insects, spiders, small frogs, small reptiles, nectar, and some fruits. More than other wrens, 15–20 percent of diet is fruit, mostly from cactus. When disturbed, sometimes runs on ground like a thrasher, rather than flying.

• **BREEDING** Monogamous. Solitary.

• **NESTING** Incubation 16 days by female. Young altricial; brooded by female; stay in nest 19–23 days, fed by both sexes. 2–3 broods per year.

• **POPULATION** Common and widespread in semidesert and desert communities with large cactus, arid hillsides, and gravelly bottomed valleys. Declining in parts of Texas and California.

• **FEEDERS** Will come to feeders for pieces of bread and slices of potato or raw apple.

• **CONSERVATION** Development of desert communities for housing, golf courses, and agriculture decrease and fragment the available habitat.

Similar Birds

SAGE THRASHER
Grayer; unstriped barring on wings and back; brown-streaked underparts; spots not clustered on breast; white on tail corners only; shorter almost straight bill.

Flight Pattern

Weak direct flight. Holds tail partially spread when flying.

Nest Identification

Shape   Location

Stems, plant fibers, and grass, lined with feathers and fur • most often in cholla cactus; sometimes in prickly bush, old woodpecker hole, orange tree, or side of man-made structure • built by male • 2–7 pinkish eggs, speckled with brown; oval, 0.9 inch long.

| Plumage Sexes similar | Habitat | Migration Nonmigratory | Weight 1.4 ounces |

DATE _____ TIME_____ LOCATION _____

Family TROGLODYTIDAE	Species *Salpinctes obsoletus*	Length 6 inches	Wingspan 9 inches

ROCK WREN

This bird frequents more arid and barren terrain than its cousin, the Canyon Wren. Its grayish brown color serves as a camouflage, but the male often can be spotted when he hops to the top of a boulder to sing or to admonish intruders. The nest is built in a rock crevice, but a trail of tiny rocks leading to the opening is a clue to its location.

buffy white supercilium

grayish brown upperparts with white flecking

long slender bill

Individual males sing many variations of their songs and of those of neighboring males; some have more than 100 songs in their repertoire. When the black-barred cinnamon tail is flicked open it reveals a thick blackish subterminal band and buffy tips.

undertail coverts

cinnamon rump

fine-streaked white breast

cinnamon-buff wash on flanks and lightly barred

- **SONG** Sings a mix of buzzy trills, *keree-keree-keree, chair, chair, chair, deedle, deedle, deedle, tur, tur, tur, keree.* Call is a raspy *tic-keer.*
- **BEHAVIOR** Solitary or in pairs. Hops around, among, and between rocks. Bobs body and frequently cocks tail upward. Sings from conspicuous perches on rocks; forages for food around and between rocks. Eats insects, spiders, and various larvae. Often lines pathways to nests with hundreds of small pebbles and small animal bones.
- **BREEDING** Monogamous. Solitary nester.
- **NESTING** Breeding biology poorly known, but incubation estimated at 12–14 days by female. Young altricial; brooded by female; remain in nest estimated 14 days, fed by both sexes. 1–2 broods per year.
- **POPULATION** Fairly common in canyons, cliffs, and valleys with rocky outcroppings in arid and semiarid regions. Casual to accidental in fall and winter in the East.

Similar Birds

CANYON WREN
Bright white throat and upper breast; rich red-brown belly and underparts; rusty red upperparts; long slightly decurved bill.

Flight Pattern

Weak fluttering direct flights, often short, on shallowly beating wings.

Nest Identification	
Shape	Rootlets, grasses, and various stems, with lining of feathers, various hair, and fur • in ridges of rock, crevices, burrows, banks, or even buildings • usually hidden by pile of rocks • built by both sexes • 4–10 white eggs, lightly flecked with reddish brown; oval, 0.7 inch long.
Location	

Plumage Sexes similar	Habitat	Migration Migratory	Weight 0.6 ounce

DATE _____ TIME _____ LOCATION _____

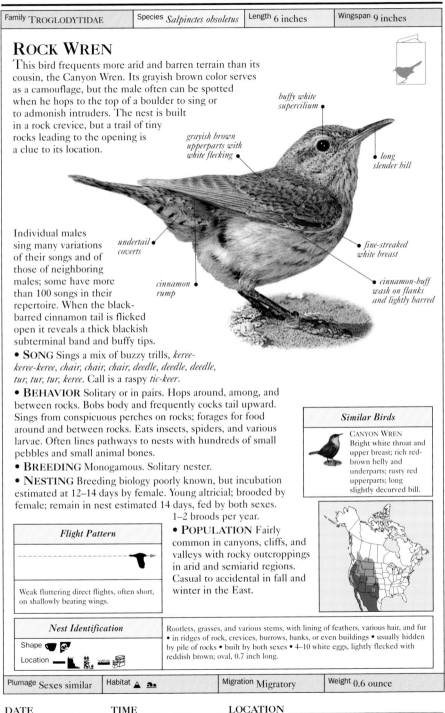

Family TROGLODYTIDAE	Species *Catherpes mexicanus*	Length 5.75 inches	Wingspan 7.5 inches

CANYON WREN

True to its name, this energetic bird historically makes its home among the canyons, rocks, and caves in western North America. Adapting to man and his buildings, this wren now often builds its nest in or on them, especially those made of stone. Often staying hidden, its bold white breast showing through the crevices

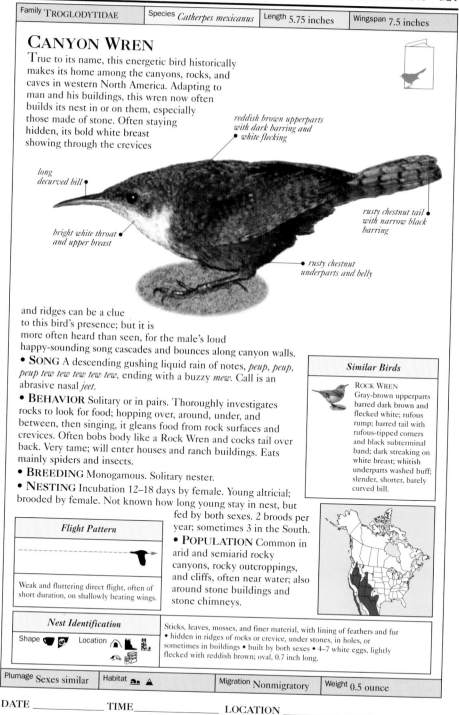

reddish brown upperparts with dark barring and white flecking

long decurved bill

bright white throat and upper breast

rusty chestnut tail with narrow black barring

rusty chestnut underparts and belly

and ridges can be a clue to this bird's presence; but it is more often heard than seen, for the male's loud happy-sounding song cascades and bounces along canyon walls.

• **SONG** A descending gushing liquid rain of notes, *peup, peup, peup tew tew tew tew tew*, ending with a buzzy *mew*. Call is an abrasive nasal *jeet*.

• **BEHAVIOR** Solitary or in pairs. Thoroughly investigates rocks to look for food; hopping over, around, under, and between, then singing, it gleans food from rock surfaces and crevices. Often bobs body like a Rock Wren and cocks tail over back. Very tame; will enter houses and ranch buildings. Eats mainly spiders and insects.

• **BREEDING** Monogamous. Solitary nester.

• **NESTING** Incubation 12–18 days by female. Young altricial; brooded by female. Not known how long young stay in nest, but fed by both sexes. 2 broods per year; sometimes 3 in the South.

• **POPULATION** Common in arid and semiarid rocky canyons, rocky outcroppings, and cliffs, often near water; also around stone buildings and stone chimneys.

Similar Birds

ROCK WREN
Gray-brown upperparts barred dark brown and flecked white; rufous rump; barred tail with rufous-tipped corners and black subterminal band; dark streaking on white breast; whitish underparts washed buff; slender, shorter, barely curved bill.

Flight Pattern

Weak and fluttering direct flight, often of short duration, on shallowly beating wings.

Nest Identification

Shape   Location

Sticks, leaves, mosses, and finer material, with lining of feathers and fur • hidden in ridges of rocks or crevice, under stones, in holes, or sometimes in buildings • built by both sexes • 4–7 white eggs, lightly flecked with reddish brown; oval, 0.7 inch long.

Plumage Sexes similar	Habitat	Migration Nonmigratory	Weight 0.5 ounce

DATE _____ TIME_____ LOCATION _____

Family TROGLODYTIDAE	Species *Thryothorus ludovicianus*	Length 5.5 inches	Wingspan 7.75 inches

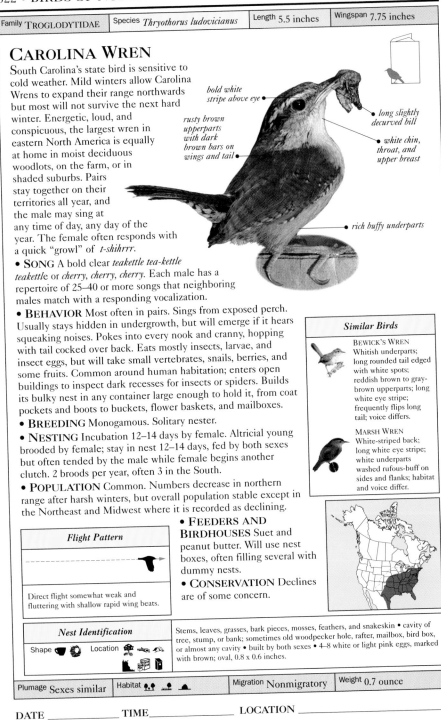

CAROLINA WREN

South Carolina's state bird is sensitive to cold weather. Mild winters allow Carolina Wrens to expand their range northwards but most will not survive the next hard winter. Energetic, loud, and conspicuous, the largest wren in eastern North America is equally at home in moist deciduous woodlots, on the farm, or in shaded suburbs. Pairs stay together on their territories all year, and the male may sing at any time of day, any day of the year. The female often responds with a quick "growl" of *t-shihrrr*.

bold white stripe above eye

rusty brown upperparts with dark brown bars on wings and tail

long slightly decurved bill

white chin, throat, and upper breast

rich buffy underparts

• **SONG** A bold clear *teakettle tea-kettle teakettle* or *cherry, cherry, cherry.* Each male has a repertoire of 25–40 or more songs that neighboring males match with a responding vocalization.

• **BEHAVIOR** Most often in pairs. Sings from exposed perch. Usually stays hidden in undergrowth, but will emerge if it hears squeaking noises. Pokes into every nook and cranny, hopping with tail cocked over back. Eats mostly insects, larvae, and insect eggs, but will take small vertebrates, snails, berries, and some fruits. Common around human habitation; enters open buildings to inspect dark recesses for insects or spiders. Builds its bulky nest in any container large enough to hold it, from coat pockets and boots to buckets, flower baskets, and mailboxes.

• **BREEDING** Monogamous. Solitary nester.

• **NESTING** Incubation 12–14 days by female. Altricial young brooded by female; stay in nest 12–14 days, fed by both sexes but often tended by the male while female begins another clutch. 2 broods per year, often 3 in the South.

• **POPULATION** Common. Numbers decrease in northern range after harsh winters, but overall population stable except in the Northeast and Midwest where it is recorded as declining.

• **FEEDERS AND BIRDHOUSES** Suet and peanut butter. Will use nest boxes, often filling several with dummy nests.

• **CONSERVATION** Declines are of some concern.

Similar Birds

BEWICK'S WREN Whitish underparts; long rounded tail edged with white spots; reddish brown to gray-brown upperparts; long white eye stripe; frequently flips long tail; voice differs.

MARSH WREN White-striped back; long white eye stripe; white underparts washed rufous-buff on sides and flanks; habitat and voice differ.

Flight Pattern

Direct flight somewhat weak and fluttering with shallow rapid wing beats.

Nest Identification

Shape — Location —

Stems, leaves, grasses, bark pieces, mosses, feathers, and snakeskin • cavity of tree, stump, or bank; sometimes old woodpecker hole, rafter, mailbox, bird box, or almost any cavity • built by both sexes • 4–8 white or light pink eggs, marked with brown; oval, 0.8 x 0.6 inches.

Plumage Sexes similar	Habitat	Migration Nonmigratory	Weight 0.7 ounce

DATE _____ TIME_____ LOCATION _____

Family TROGLODYTIDAE	Species *Thryomanes bewickii*	Length 5.25 inches	Wingspan 7.25 inches

BEWICK'S WREN

This bird ranges across most of the western United States eastward to the Appalachians. It usually builds its nest in natural cavities, but also will nest in mailboxes, baskets, cow skulls, or almost anything that provides shelter. A tame bird, it often resides near farms, homes, and small towns. For reasons still largely unknown, the Bewick's Wren is now rare in areas where it was once common. Since at least the 1960s, populations have seriously declined east of the Mississippi River. Color varies geographically from mousy gray-brown in the West to rusty brown in the East.

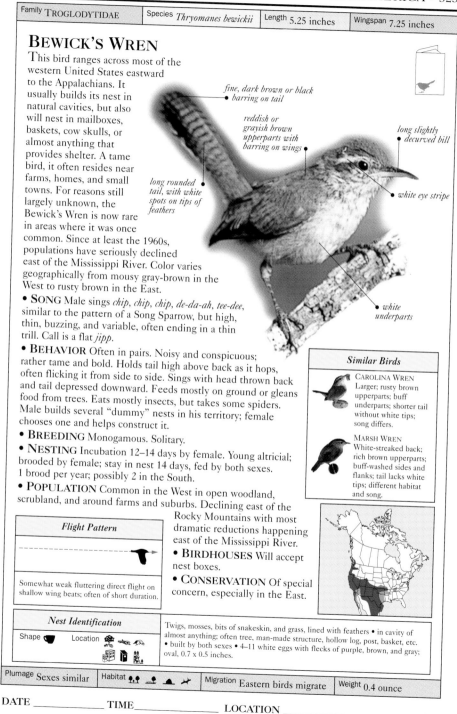

fine, dark brown or black barring on tail

reddish or grayish brown upperparts with barring on wings

long slightly decurved bill

long rounded tail, with white spots on tips of feathers

white eye stripe

white underparts

• **SONG** Male sings *chip, chip, chip, de-da-ah, tee-dee,* similar to the pattern of a Song Sparrow, but high, thin, buzzing, and variable, often ending in a thin trill. Call is a flat *jipp.*

• **BEHAVIOR** Often in pairs. Noisy and conspicuous; rather tame and bold. Holds tail high above back as it hops, often flicking it from side to side. Sings with head thrown back and tail depressed downward. Feeds mostly on ground or gleans food from trees. Eats mostly insects, but takes some spiders. Male builds several "dummy" nests in his territory; female chooses one and helps construct it.

• **BREEDING** Monogamous. Solitary.

• **NESTING** Incubation 12–14 days by female. Young altricial; brooded by female; stay in nest 14 days, fed by both sexes. 1 brood per year; possibly 2 in the South.

• **POPULATION** Common in the West in open woodland, scrubland, and around farms and suburbs. Declining east of the Rocky Mountains with most dramatic reductions happening east of the Mississippi River.

• **BIRDHOUSES** Will accept nest boxes.

• **CONSERVATION** Of special concern, especially in the East.

Similar Birds

CAROLINA WREN
Larger; rusty brown upperparts; buff underparts; shorter tail without white tips; song differs.

MARSH WREN
White-streaked back; rich brown upperparts; buff-washed sides and flanks; tail lacks white tips; different habitat and song.

Flight Pattern

Somewhat weak fluttering direct flight on shallow wing beats; often of short duration.

Nest Identification

Shape ☕   Location 🌳🏠🪵📦📮🐦🐎

Twigs, mosses, bits of snakeskin, and grass, lined with feathers • in cavity of almost anything; often tree, man-made structure, hollow log, post, basket, etc. • built by both sexes • 4–11 white eggs with flecks of purple, brown, and gray; oval, 0.7 x 0.5 inches.

Plumage Sexes similar	Habitat 🌾 🌿 ⛰ ✈	Migration Eastern birds migrate	Weight 0.4 ounce

DATE _____ TIME_____ LOCATION _____

Family TROGLODYTIDAE	Species *Troglodytes aedon*	Length 4.75 inches	Wingspan 6–7 inches

HOUSE WREN

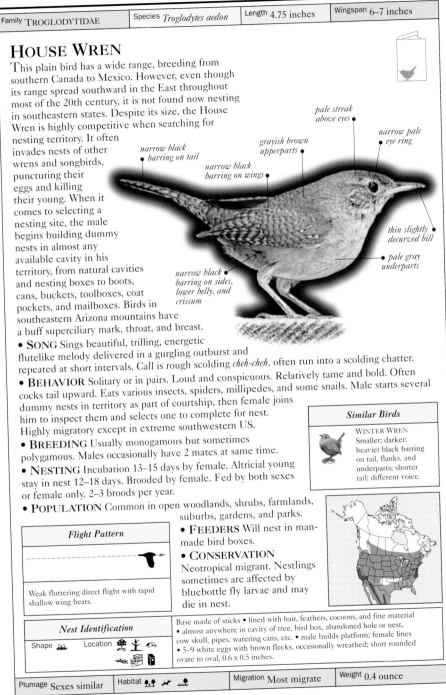

This plain bird has a wide range, breeding from southern Canada to Mexico. However, even though its range spread southward in the East throughout most of the 20th century, it is not found now nesting in southeastern states. Despite its size, the House Wren is highly competitive when searching for nesting territory. It often invades nests of other wrens and songbirds, puncturing their eggs and killing their young. When it comes to selecting a nesting site, the male begins building dummy nests in almost any available cavity in his territory, from natural cavities and nesting boxes to boots, cans, buckets, toolboxes, coat pockets, and mailboxes. Birds in southeastern Arizona mountains have a buff superciliary mark, throat, and breast.

pale streak above eyes

narrow pale eye ring

grayish brown upperparts

narrow black barring on tail

narrow black barring on wings

thin slightly decurved bill

pale gray underparts

narrow black barring on sides, lower belly, and crissum

- **SONG** Sings beautiful, trilling, energetic flutelike melody delivered in a gurgling outburst and repeated at short intervals. Call is rough scolding *cheh-cheh*, often run into a scolding chatter.
- **BEHAVIOR** Solitary or in pairs. Loud and conspicuous. Relatively tame and bold. Often cocks tail upward. Eats various insects, spiders, millipedes, and some snails. Male starts several dummy nests in territory as part of courtship, then female joins him to inspect them and selects one to complete for nest. Highly migratory except in extreme southwestern US.
- **BREEDING** Usually monogamous but sometimes polygamous. Males occasionally have 2 mates at same time.
- **NESTING** Incubation 13–15 days by female. Altricial young stay in nest 12–18 days. Brooded by female. Fed by both sexes or female only. 2–3 broods per year.
- **POPULATION** Common in open woodlands, shrubs, farmlands, suburbs, gardens, and parks.
- **FEEDERS** Will nest in man-made bird boxes.
- **CONSERVATION** Neotropical migrant. Nestlings sometimes are affected by bluebottle fly larvae and may die in nest.

Similar Birds

WINTER WREN Smaller; darker; heavier black barring on tail, flanks, and underparts; shorter tail; different voice.

Flight Pattern

Weak fluttering direct flight with rapid shallow wing beats.

Nest Identification

Shape ⌒⌒   Location 🌲 🪵 🐿️ 🏠 🗑️

Base made of sticks • lined with hair, feathers, cocoons, and fine material • almost anywhere in cavity of tree, bird box, abandoned hole or nest, cow skull, pipes, watering cans, etc. • male builds platform; female lines • 5–9 white eggs with brown flecks, occasionally wreathed; short rounded ovate to oval, 0.6 x 0.5 inches.

Plumage Sexes similar	Habitat 🌳 ✈ 🏞️	Migration Most migrate	Weight 0.4 ounce

DATE _____ TIME_____ LOCATION _____

Family TROGLODYTIDAE	Species *Troglodytes troglodytes*	Length 4 inches	Wingspan 6 inches

WINTER WREN

One of the smallest songbirds in North America, this short-tailed wren nests primarily in the coniferous forests of Canada and the northern US, but it also resides along the Pacific Coast from central California to the Aleutians, and in the Appalachians south to northern Georgia. It usually hides in thick undergrowth, but when excited it will fly up, perch, bob its head up and down, and deliver an alarm call or a rapid, cascading song that may last six to seven seconds and contain more than a hundred notes. This is the only member of the wren family found in Europe.

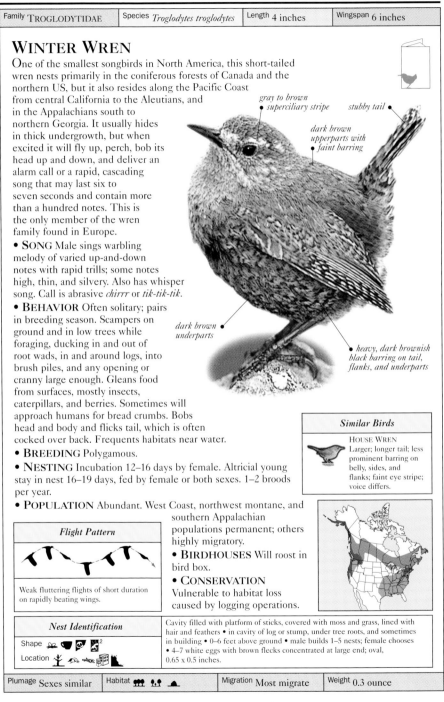

gray to brown superciliary stripe

stubby tail

dark brown upperparts with faint barring

dark brown underparts

heavy, dark brownish black barring on tail, flanks, and underparts

• **SONG** Male sings warbling melody of varied up-and-down notes with rapid trills; some notes high, thin, and silvery. Also has whisper song. Call is abrasive *chirrr* or *tik-tik-tik*.

• **BEHAVIOR** Often solitary; pairs in breeding season. Scampers on ground and in low trees while foraging, ducking in and out of root wads, in and around logs, into brush piles, and any opening or cranny large enough. Gleans food from surfaces, mostly insects, caterpillars, and berries. Sometimes will approach humans for bread crumbs. Bobs head and body and flicks tail, which is often cocked over back. Frequents habitats near water.

• **BREEDING** Polygamous.

• **NESTING** Incubation 12–16 days by female. Altricial young stay in nest 16–19 days, fed by female or both sexes. 1–2 broods per year.

• **POPULATION** Abundant. West Coast, northwest montane, and southern Appalachian populations permanent; others highly migratory.

• **BIRDHOUSES** Will roost in bird box.

• **CONSERVATION** Vulnerable to habitat loss caused by logging operations.

Similar Birds

HOUSE WREN
Larger; longer tail; less prominent barring on belly, sides, and flanks; faint eye stripe; voice differs.

Flight Pattern

Weak fluttering flights of short duration on rapidly beating wings.

Nest Identification

Shape
Location

Cavity filled with platform of sticks, covered with moss and grass, lined with hair and feathers • in cavity of log or stump, under tree roots, and sometimes in building • 0–6 feet above ground • male builds 1–5 nests; female chooses • 4–7 white eggs with brown flecks concentrated at large end; oval, 0.65 x 0.5 inches.

Plumage Sexes similar	Habitat	Migration Most migrate	Weight 0.3 ounce

DATE _____ TIME _____ LOCATION _____

| Family TROGLODYTIDAE | Species *Cistothorus platensis* | Length 4.5 inches | Wingspan 5.5–6 inches |

SEDGE WREN

Camouflaged by its plumage, this wren stays hidden in dense marsh grasses, except when it perches to sing, which it sometimes does at night. The female chooses one of several rather well-concealed nests built by the male, then lines it with materials of her choice. This wren ranges over much of the grasslands and marshlands of the central and north-central United States and south-central Canada, often going where the habitat is most suitable and often changing nesting areas from year to year.

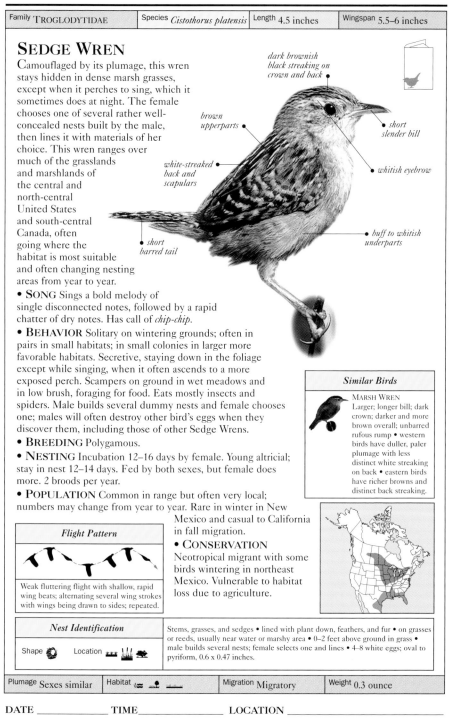

dark brownish black streaking on crown and back

brown upperparts

short slender bill

white-streaked back and scapulars

whitish eyebrow

short barred tail

buff to whitish underparts

• SONG Sings a bold melody of single disconnected notes, followed by a rapid chatter of dry notes. Has call of *chip-chip*.
• BEHAVIOR Solitary on wintering grounds; often in pairs in small habitats; in small colonies in larger more favorable habitats. Secretive, staying down in the foliage except while singing, when it often ascends to a more exposed perch. Scampers on ground in wet meadows and in low brush, foraging for food. Eats mostly insects and spiders. Male builds several dummy nests and female chooses one; males will often destroy other bird's eggs when they discover them, including those of other Sedge Wrens.
• BREEDING Polygamous.
• NESTING Incubation 12–16 days by female. Young altricial; stay in nest 12–14 days. Fed by both sexes, but female does more. 2 broods per year.
• POPULATION Common in range but often very local; numbers may change from year to year. Rare in winter in New Mexico and casual to California in fall migration.
• CONSERVATION Neotropical migrant with some birds wintering in northeast Mexico. Vulnerable to habitat loss due to agriculture.

Similar Birds

MARSH WREN
Larger; longer bill; dark crown; darker and more brown overall; unbarred rufous rump • western birds have duller, paler plumage with less distinct white streaking on back • eastern birds have richer browns and distinct back streaking.

Flight Pattern

Weak fluttering flight with shallow, rapid wing beats; alternating several wing strokes with wings being drawn to sides; repeated.

Nest Identification

Shape ⬤ Location ✦✦✦ ᴗᴗ ❧

Stems, grasses, and sedges • lined with plant down, feathers, and fur • on grasses or reeds, usually near water or marshy area • 0–2 feet above ground in grass • male builds several nests; female selects one and lines • 4–8 white eggs; oval to pyriform, 0.6 x 0.47 inches.

| Plumage Sexes similar | Habitat 〰️ 🌱 〰️ | Migration Migratory | Weight 0.3 ounce |

DATE _____ TIME_____ LOCATION _____

Family TROGLODYTIDAE	Species *Cistothorus palustris*	Length 4.5–5 inches	Wingspan 5.5–7 inches

MARSH WREN

This bird usually stays hidden, but its song can be heard over the reeds and cattails of the marshlands. The male builds several intricate globular-shaped nests, which have side doors; the female chooses one and adds the lining of shredded plants and feathers. The male often roosts in one of the dummy nests. Some males have more than one mate, with each one occupying a small section of his territory. The black-and-white streaking on the back of the Marsh Wren is less distinct in western birds.

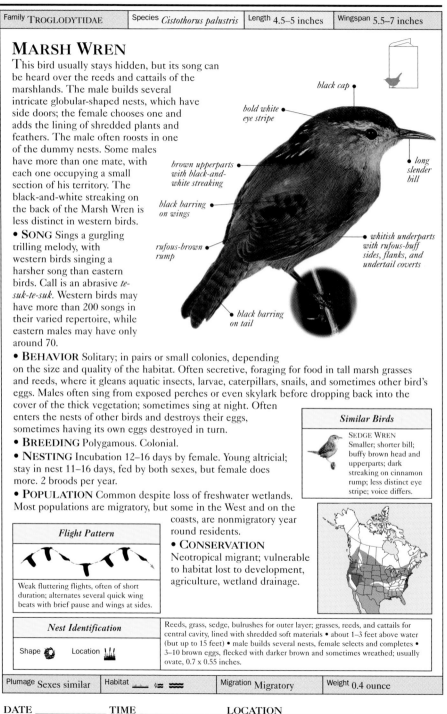

black cap

bold white eye stripe

brown upperparts with black-and-white streaking

black barring on wings

rufous-brown rump

long slender bill

whitish underparts with rufous-buff sides, flanks, and undertail coverts

black barring on tail

• **SONG** Sings a gurgling trilling melody, with western birds singing a harsher song than eastern birds. Call is an abrasive *te-suk-te-suk*. Western birds may have more than 200 songs in their varied repertoire, while eastern males may have only around 70.

• **BEHAVIOR** Solitary; in pairs or small colonies, depending on the size and quality of the habitat. Often secretive, foraging for food in tall marsh grasses and reeds, where it gleans aquatic insects, larvae, caterpillars, snails, and sometimes other bird's eggs. Males often sing from exposed perches or even skylark before dropping back into the cover of the thick vegetation; sometimes sing at night. Often enters the nests of other birds and destroys their eggs, sometimes having its own eggs destroyed in turn.

• **BREEDING** Polygamous. Colonial.

• **NESTING** Incubation 12–16 days by female. Young altricial; stay in nest 11–16 days, fed by both sexes, but female does more. 2 broods per year.

• **POPULATION** Common despite loss of freshwater wetlands. Most populations are migratory, but some in the West and on the coasts, are nonmigratory year round residents.

• **CONSERVATION** Neotropical migrant; vulnerable to habitat lost to development, agriculture, wetland drainage.

Similar Birds

SEDGE WREN
Smaller; shorter bill; buffy brown head and upperparts; dark streaking on cinnamon rump; less distinct eye stripe; voice differs.

Flight Pattern

Weak fluttering flights, often of short duration; alternates several quick wing beats with brief pause and wings at sides.

Nest Identification

Shape 🪺 Location 🌾

Reeds, grass, sedge, bulrushes for outer layer; grasses, reeds, and cattails for central cavity, lined with shredded soft materials • about 1–3 feet above water (but up to 15 feet) • male builds several nests, female selects and completes • 3–10 brown eggs, flecked with darker brown and sometimes wreathed; usually ovate, 0.7 x 0.55 inches.

Plumage Sexes similar	Habitat	Migration Migratory	Weight 0.4 ounce

DATE _____ TIME_____ LOCATION _____

Family CINCLIDAE	Species *Cinclus mexicanus*	Length 7.5 inches	Wingspan 9 inches

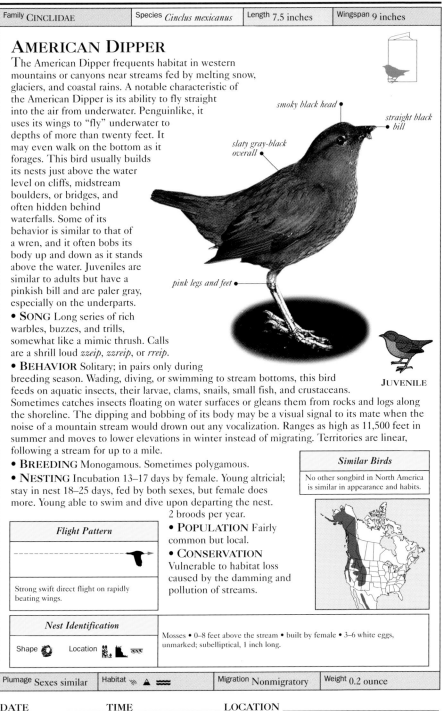

AMERICAN DIPPER

The American Dipper frequents habitat in western mountains or canyons near streams fed by melting snow, glaciers, and coastal rains. A notable characteristic of the American Dipper is its ability to fly straight into the air from underwater. Penguinlike, it uses its wings to "fly" underwater to depths of more than twenty feet. It may even walk on the bottom as it forages. This bird usually builds its nests just above the water level on cliffs, midstream boulders, or bridges, and often hidden behind waterfalls. Some of its behavior is similar to that of a wren, and it often bobs its body up and down as it stands above the water. Juveniles are similar to adults but have a pinkish bill and are paler gray, especially on the underparts.

smoky black head

straight black bill

slaty gray-black overall

pink legs and feet

JUVENILE

• SONG Long series of rich warbles, buzzes, and trills, somewhat like a mimic thrush. Calls are a shrill loud *zzeip, zzreip,* or *rreip.*
• BEHAVIOR Solitary; in pairs only during breeding season. Wading, diving, or swimming to stream bottoms, this bird feeds on aquatic insects, their larvae, clams, snails, small fish, and crustaceans. Sometimes catches insects floating on water surfaces or gleans them from rocks and logs along the shoreline. The dipping and bobbing of its body may be a visual signal to its mate when the noise of a mountain stream would drown out any vocalization. Ranges as high as 11,500 feet in summer and moves to lower elevations in winter instead of migrating. Territories are linear, following a stream for up to a mile.
• BREEDING Monogamous. Sometimes polygamous.
• NESTING Incubation 13–17 days by female. Young altricial; stay in nest 18–25 days, fed by both sexes, but female does more. Young able to swim and dive upon departing the nest. 2 broods per year.
• POPULATION Fairly common but local.
• CONSERVATION Vulnerable to habitat loss caused by the damming and pollution of streams.

Similar Birds

No other songbird in North America is similar in appearance and habits.

Flight Pattern

Strong swift direct flight on rapidly beating wings.

Nest Identification

Shape   Location

Mosses • 0–8 feet above the stream • built by female • 3–6 white eggs, unmarked; subelliptical, 1 inch long.

Plumage Sexes similar	Habitat	Migration Nonmigratory	Weight 0.2 ounce

DATE _____ TIME_____ LOCATION _____

Family REGULIDAE	Species *Regulus satrapa*	Length 4 inches	Wingspan 6.5–7 inches

GOLDEN-CROWNED KINGLET

Living in dense coniferous forests, this tiny bird's baseball-sized sphere-shaped nest is so small that its clutch of half-inch eggs must be laid in two layers. A tame bird, it will sometimes enter human habitations and not try to escape if held. It often feeds in mixed-species foraging flocks with woodpeckers, creepers, chickadees, nuthatches, and others. Females and juveniles have a yellow crown bordered by black.

• **SONG** Sings a song beginning with 3–4 high-pitched *tsee, tsee, tsee* notes, followed by a rapid trill. Call is a series of 3–4 high-pitched *tsee* notes.
• **BEHAVIOR** Solitary or in pairs. Tame. Flits wings as it hops along branches. Forages through dense foliage of trees to pick off food. Eats mainly insects, their eggs, and larvae; takes some seeds. Drinks tree sap, sometimes taking it from sapsucker drill wells. May hawk insects or hover briefly to glean them from trunk, branch, or foliage.
• **BREEDING** Monogamous. Solitary nester.
• **NESTING** Incubation 14–15 days by female. Young altricial; stay in nest 14–19 days, fed by both sexes. 1–2 broods per year.
• **POPULATION** Common in coniferous woodlands. Populations may drop after harsh cold seasons on winter range; long-term stable, with range expanding to northeast. Many populations nonmigratory.
• **CONSERVATION** Neotropical migrant. Vulnerable to habitat loss caused by logging, especially of mature coniferous forests.

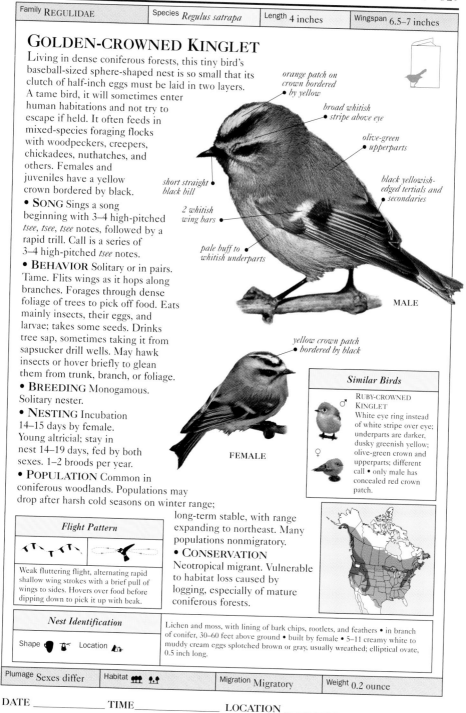

orange patch on crown bordered by yellow
broad whitish stripe above eye
olive-green upperparts
black yellowish-edged tertials and secondaries
short straight black bill
2 whitish wing bars
pale buff to whitish underparts
MALE

yellow crown patch bordered by black
FEMALE

Similar Birds
RUBY-CROWNED KINGLET
White eye ring instead of white stripe over eye; underparts are darker, dusky greenish yellow; olive-green crown and upperparts; different call • only male has concealed red crown patch.

Flight Pattern
Weak fluttering flight, alternating rapid shallow wing strokes with a brief pull of wings to sides. Hovers over food before dipping down to pick it up with beak.

Nest Identification
Shape — Location —
Lichen and moss, with lining of bark chips, rootlets, and feathers • in branch of conifer, 30–60 feet above ground • built by female • 5–11 creamy white to muddy cream eggs splotched brown or gray, usually wreathed; elliptical ovate, 0.5 inch long.

Plumage Sexes differ	Habitat	Migration Migratory	Weight 0.2 ounce

DATE _____ TIME _____ LOCATION _____

Family REGULIDAE	Species *Regulus calendula*	Length 4.25 inches	Wingspan 6.75–7.5 inches

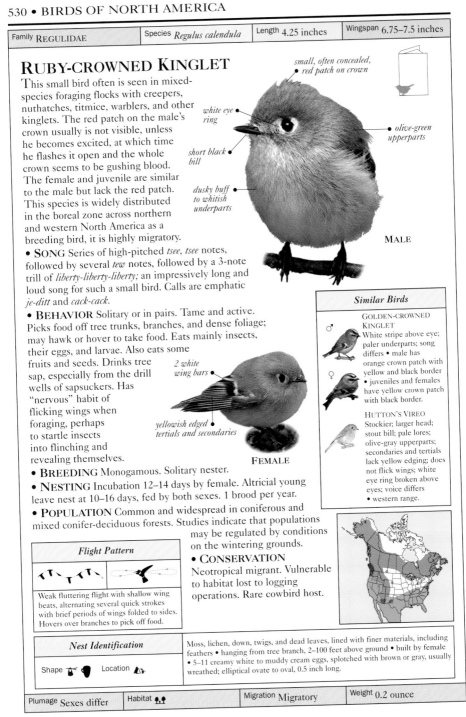

RUBY-CROWNED KINGLET

This small bird often is seen in mixed-species foraging flocks with creepers, nuthatches, titmice, warblers, and other kinglets. The red patch on the male's crown usually is not visible, unless he becomes excited, at which time he flashes it open and the whole crown seems to be gushing blood. The female and juvenile are similar to the male but lack the red patch. This species is widely distributed in the boreal zone across northern and western North America as a breeding bird, it is highly migratory.

small, often concealed, red patch on crown

white eye ring

short black bill

dusky buff to whitish underparts

olive-green upperparts

MALE

• **SONG** Series of high-pitched *tsee, tsee* notes, followed by several *tew* notes, followed by a 3-note trill of *liberty-liberty-liberty*; an impressively long and loud song for such a small bird. Calls are emphatic *je-ditt* and *cack-cack*.

• **BEHAVIOR** Solitary or in pairs. Tame and active. Picks food off tree trunks, branches, and dense foliage; may hawk or hover to take food. Eats mainly insects, their eggs, and larvae. Also eats some fruits and seeds. Drinks tree sap, especially from the drill wells of sapsuckers. Has "nervous" habit of flicking wings when foraging, perhaps to startle insects into flinching and revealing themselves.

2 white wing bars

yellowish edged tertials and secondaries

FEMALE

• **BREEDING** Monogamous. Solitary nester.

• **NESTING** Incubation 12–14 days by female. Altricial young leave nest at 10–16 days, fed by both sexes. 1 brood per year.

• **POPULATION** Common and widespread in coniferous and mixed conifer-deciduous forests. Studies indicate that populations may be regulated by conditions on the wintering grounds.

• **CONSERVATION** Neotropical migrant. Vulnerable to habitat lost to logging operations. Rare cowbird host.

Similar Birds

GOLDEN-CROWNED KINGLET
♂ White stripe above eye; paler underparts; song differs • male has orange crown patch with yellow and black border • juveniles and females have yellow crown patch with black border.
♀

HUTTON'S VIREO
Stockier; larger head; stout bill; pale lores; olive-gray upperparts; secondaries and tertials lack yellow edging; does not flick wings; white eye ring broken above eyes; voice differs • western range.

Flight Pattern

Weak fluttering flight with shallow wing beats, alternating several quick strokes with brief periods of wings folded to sides. Hovers over branches to pick off food.

Nest Identification

Shape   Location

Moss, lichen, down, twigs, and dead leaves, lined with finer materials, including feathers • hanging from tree branch, 2–100 feet above ground • built by female • 5–11 creamy white to muddy cream eggs, splotched with brown or gray, usually wreathed; elliptical ovate to oval, 0.5 inch long.

Plumage Sexes differ	Habitat	Migration Migratory	Weight 0.2 ounce

DATE _____ TIME_____ LOCATION _____

| Family SYLVIIDAE | Species *Locustella ochotensis* | Length 5.5–6 inches | Wingspan 9.5–10 inches |

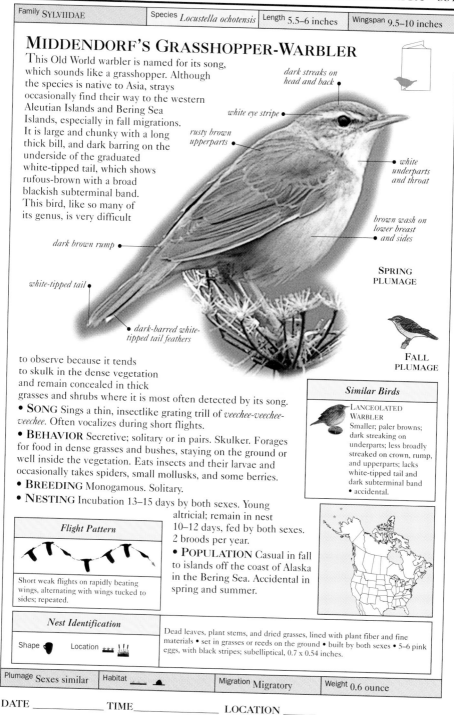

MIDDENDORF'S GRASSHOPPER-WARBLER

This Old World warbler is named for its song, which sounds like a grasshopper. Although the species is native to Asia, strays occasionally find their way to the western Aleutian Islands and Bering Sea Islands, especially in fall migrations. It is large and chunky with a long thick bill, and dark barring on the underside of the graduated white-tipped tail, which shows rufous-brown with a broad blackish subterminal band. This bird, like so many of its genus, is very difficult

dark streaks on head and back

white eye stripe

rusty brown upperparts

white underparts and throat

brown wash on lower breast and sides

SPRING PLUMAGE

dark brown rump

white-tipped tail

dark-barred white-tipped tail feathers

FALL PLUMAGE

to observe because it tends to skulk in the dense vegetation and remain concealed in thick grasses and shrubs where it is most often detected by its song.

• **SONG** Sings a thin, insectlike grating trill of *veechee-veechee-veechee*. Often vocalizes during short flights.

• **BEHAVIOR** Secretive; solitary or in pairs. Skulker. Forages for food in dense grasses and bushes, staying on the ground or well inside the vegetation. Eats insects and their larvae and occasionally takes spiders, small mollusks, and some berries.

• **BREEDING** Monogamous. Solitary.

• **NESTING** Incubation 13–15 days by both sexes. Young altricial; remain in nest 10–12 days, fed by both sexes. 2 broods per year.

• **POPULATION** Casual in fall to islands off the coast of Alaska in the Bering Sea. Accidental in spring and summer.

Similar Birds

LANCEOLATED WARBLER
Smaller; paler browns; dark streaking on underparts; less broadly streaked on crown, rump, and upperparts; lacks white-tipped tail and dark subterminal band • accidental.

Flight Pattern

Short weak flights on rapidly beating wings, alternating with wings tucked to sides; repeated.

Nest Identification

Shape   Location

Dead leaves, plant stems, and dried grasses, lined with plant fiber and fine materials • set in grasses or reeds on the ground • built by both sexes • 5–6 pink eggs, with black stripes; subelliptical, 0.7 x 0.54 inches.

| Plumage Sexes similar | Habitat | Migration Migratory | Weight 0.6 ounce |

DATE _____ TIME_____ LOCATION _____

Family SYLVIIDAE	Species *Phylloscopus fuscatus*	Length 4.5 inches	Wingspan 7.25 inches

DUSKY WARBLER

Its small size, dark brown plumage, and lack of wing bars set the Dusky Warbler apart from the other Old World warblers that have strayed to Alaska. While many of these warblers are somewhat similar in appearance, they are easily distinguished by song, and the vocalizations of this species are definitive. The small thin bill, oval-shaped in cross section, sets it apart from sparrows and buntings. In flight this bird shows a rounded straight tail and brownish white underparts. Although it is native to Eurasia, strays sometimes visit North America, and these birds have been spotted on the outer Aleutian Islands throughout the year and in the fall during migration on the southern coast of Alaska and as far as California.

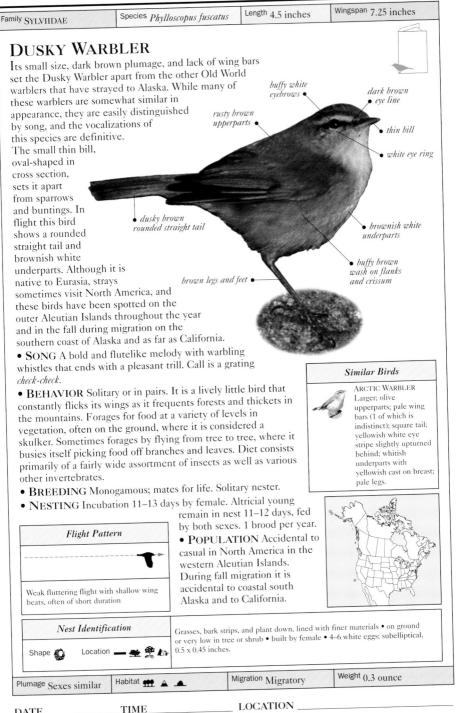

buffy white eyebrows

dark brown eye line

rusty brown upperparts

thin bill

white eye ring

dusky brown rounded straight tail

brownish white underparts

buffy brown wash on flanks and crissum

brown legs and feet

• **SONG** A bold and flutelike melody with warbling whistles that ends with a pleasant trill. Call is a grating *check-check*.

• **BEHAVIOR** Solitary or in pairs. It is a lively little bird that constantly flicks its wings as it frequents forests and thickets in the mountains. Forages for food at a variety of levels in vegetation, often on the ground, where it is considered a skulker. Sometimes forages by flying from tree to tree, where it busies itself picking food off branches and leaves. Diet consists primarily of a fairly wide assortment of insects as well as various other invertebrates.

• **BREEDING** Monogamous; mates for life. Solitary nester.

• **NESTING** Incubation 11–13 days by female. Altricial young remain in nest 11–12 days, fed by both sexes. 1 brood per year.

• **POPULATION** Accidental to casual in North America in the western Aleutian Islands. During fall migration it is accidental to coastal south Alaska and to California.

Similar Birds

ARCTIC WARBLER Larger; olive upperparts; pale wing bars (1 of which is indistinct); square tail; yellowish white eye stripe slightly upturned behind; whitish underparts with yellowish cast on breast; pale legs.

Flight Pattern

Weak fluttering flight with shallow wing beats, often of short duration

Nest Identification	
Shape	Location	Grasses, bark strips, and plant down, lined with finer materials • on ground or very low in tree or shrub • built by female • 4–6 white eggs; subelliptical, 0.5 x 0.45 inches.

Plumage Sexes similar	Habitat	Migration Migratory	Weight 0.3 ounce

DATE _____ TIME_____ LOCATION _____

Family SYLVIIDAE	Species *Phylloscopus borealis*	Length 5 inches	Wingspan 7.75 inches

ARCTIC WARBLER

This bird is the only Old World Warbler that nests in North America. After wintering in Asia it migrates across the Bering Strait and is a common summer visitor to western Alaska, where it builds its sphere-shaped nest on the ground, hidden in dense thickets of willow or birch. This very active bird resembles a vireo. A wing bar on the greater coverts varies in appearance, and a second wing bar on the median coverts is very faint.

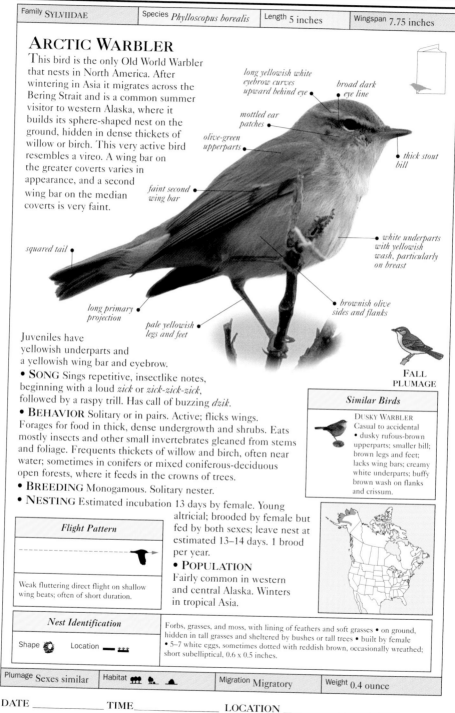

long yellowish white eyebrow curves upward behind eye

broad dark eye line

mottled ear patches

olive-green upperparts

thick stout bill

faint second wing bar

squared tail

white underparts with yellowish wash, particularly on breast

long primary projection

pale yellowish legs and feet

brownish olive sides and flanks

FALL PLUMAGE

Juveniles have yellowish underparts and a yellowish wing bar and eyebrow.

- **SONG** Sings repetitive, insectlike notes, beginning with a loud *zick* or *zick-zick-zick*, followed by a raspy trill. Has call of buzzing *dzik*.
- **BEHAVIOR** Solitary or in pairs. Active; flicks wings. Forages for food in thick, dense undergrowth and shrubs. Eats mostly insects and other small invertebrates gleaned from stems and foliage. Frequents thickets of willow and birch, often near water; sometimes in conifers or mixed coniferous-deciduous open forests, where it feeds in the crowns of trees.
- **BREEDING** Monogamous. Solitary nester.
- **NESTING** Estimated incubation 13 days by female. Young altricial; brooded by female but fed by both sexes; leave nest at estimated 13–14 days. 1 brood per year.
- **POPULATION** Fairly common in western and central Alaska. Winters in tropical Asia.

Similar Birds

DUSKY WARBLER
Casual to accidental
- dusky rufous-brown upperparts; smaller bill; brown legs and feet; lacks wing bars; creamy white underparts; buffy brown wash on flanks and crissum.

Flight Pattern

Weak fluttering direct flight on shallow wing beats; often of short duration.

Nest Identification	
Shape ⬡ Location ▬ ✱✱✱	Forbs, grasses, and moss, with lining of feathers and soft grasses • on ground, hidden in tall grasses and sheltered by bushes or tall trees • built by female • 5–7 white eggs, sometimes dotted with reddish brown, occasionally wreathed; short subelliptical, 0.6 x 0.5 inches.

Plumage Sexes similar	Habitat 🌾 🌳 ⛰	Migration Migratory	Weight 0.4 ounce

DATE _____ TIME_____ LOCATION _____

| Family SYLVIIDAE | Species *Polioptila caerulea* | Length 4.25 inches | Wingspan 5.75–6.5 inches |

BLUE-GRAY GNATCATCHER

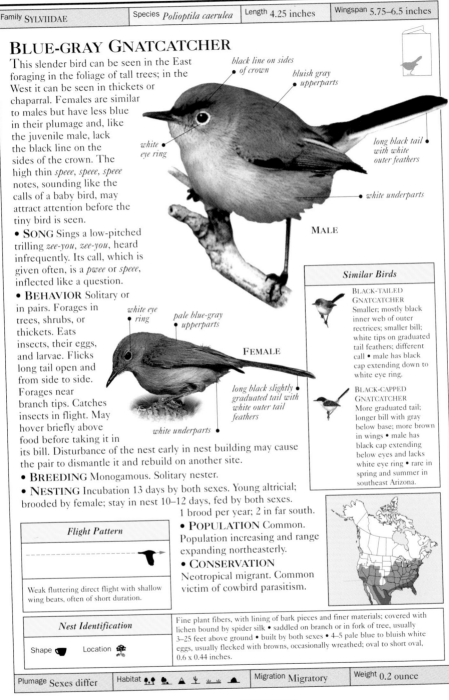

This slender bird can be seen in the East foraging in the foliage of tall trees; in the West it can be seen in thickets or chaparral. Females are similar to males but have less blue in their plumage and, like the juvenile male, lack the black line on the sides of the crown. The high thin *speee, speee, speee* notes, sounding like the calls of a baby bird, may attract attention before the tiny bird is seen.

black line on sides of crown

bluish gray upperparts

white eye ring

long black tail with white outer feathers

white underparts

MALE

• **SONG** Sings a low-pitched trilling *zee-you, zee-you*, heard infrequently. Its call, which is given often, is a *pwee* or *speee*, inflected like a question.

• **BEHAVIOR** Solitary or in pairs. Forages in trees, shrubs, or thickets. Eats insects, their eggs, and larvae. Flicks long tail open and from side to side. Forages near branch tips. Catches insects in flight. May hover briefly above food before taking it in its bill. Disturbance of the nest early in nest building may cause the pair to dismantle it and rebuild on another site.

white eye ring

pale blue-gray upperparts

FEMALE

long black slightly graduated tail with white outer tail feathers

white underparts

Similar Birds

BLACK-TAILED GNATCATCHER
Smaller; mostly black inner web of outer rectrices; smaller bill; white tips on graduated tail feathers; different call • male has black cap extending down to white eye ring.

BLACK-CAPPED GNATCATCHER
More graduated tail; longer bill with gray below base; more brown in wings • male has black cap extending below eyes and lacks white eye ring • rare in spring and summer in southeast Arizona.

• **BREEDING** Monogamous. Solitary nester.

• **NESTING** Incubation 13 days by both sexes. Young altricial; brooded by female; stay in nest 10–12 days, fed by both sexes. 1 brood per year; 2 in far south.

• **POPULATION** Common. Population increasing and range expanding northeasterly.

• **CONSERVATION** Neotropical migrant. Common victim of cowbird parasitism.

Flight Pattern
Weak fluttering direct flight with shallow wing beats, often of short duration.

Nest Identification	Fine plant fibers, with lining of bark pieces and finer materials; covered with lichen bound by spider silk • saddled on branch or in fork of tree, usually 3–25 feet above ground • built by both sexes • 4–5 pale blue to bluish white eggs, usually flecked with browns, occasionally wreathed; oval to short oval, 0.6 x 0.44 inches.
Shape ⌣ Location 🌲	

| Plumage Sexes differ | Habitat 🌿🌳🔥△⚓⚓⚓🌲 | Migration Migratory | Weight 0.2 ounce |

DATE _____ TIME_____ LOCATION _____

Family SYLVIIDAE	Species *Polioptila californica*	Length 4.25 inches	Wingspan 5.5–6 inches

CALIFORNIA GNATCATCHER

This bird was once classified in the same species with the Black-tailed Gnatcatcher, but the California Gnatcatcher is darker overall and has different vocalizations. Living in desert sage scrub growth, its range is limited to southwestern California and Baja. The northern race is federally listed as threatened due to habitat loss from housing development in scrub areas.

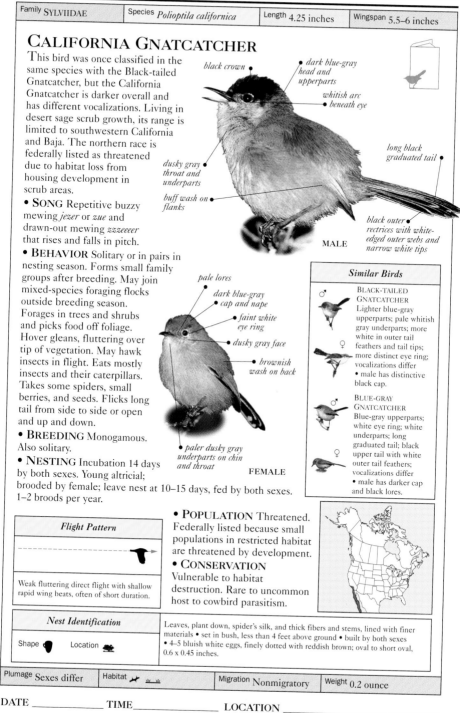

black crown

dark blue-gray head and upperparts

whitish arc beneath eye

long black graduated tail

dusky gray throat and underparts

buff wash on flanks

black outer rectrices with white-edged outer webs and narrow white tips

MALE

- **SONG** Repetitive buzzy mewing *jezer* or *zue* and drawn-out mewing *zzzeeeer* that rises and falls in pitch.
- **BEHAVIOR** Solitary or in pairs in nesting season. Forms small family groups after breeding. May join mixed-species foraging flocks outside breeding season. Forages in trees and shrubs and picks food off foliage. Hover gleans, fluttering over tip of vegetation. May hawk insects in flight. Eats mostly insects and their caterpillars. Takes some spiders, small berries, and seeds. Flicks long tail from side to side or open and up and down.
- **BREEDING** Monogamous. Also solitary.
- **NESTING** Incubation 14 days by both sexes. Young altricial; brooded by female; leave nest at 10–15 days, fed by both sexes. 1–2 broods per year.

pale lores

dark blue-gray cap and nape

faint white eye ring

dusky gray face

brownish wash on back

paler dusky gray underparts on chin and throat

FEMALE

Similar Birds

♂ **BLACK-TAILED GNATCATCHER** Lighter blue-gray upperparts; pale whitish gray underparts; more white in outer tail feathers and tail tips; more distinct eye ring; vocalizations differ
- male has distinctive black cap.

♀

♂ **BLUE-GRAY GNATCATCHER** Blue-gray upperparts; white eye ring; white underparts; long graduated tail; black upper tail with white outer tail feathers; vocalizations differ
- male has darker cap and black lores.

♀

Flight Pattern

Weak fluttering direct flight with shallow rapid wing beats, often of short duration.

- **POPULATION** Threatened. Federally listed because small populations in restricted habitat are threatened by development.
- **CONSERVATION** Vulnerable to habitat destruction. Rare to uncommon host to cowbird parasitism.

Nest Identification	
Shape 🪹 Location 🌳	Leaves, plant down, spider's silk, and thick fibers and stems, lined with finer materials • set in bush, less than 4 feet above ground • built by both sexes • 4–5 bluish white eggs, finely dotted with reddish brown; oval to short oval, 0.6 x 0.45 inches.

Plumage Sexes differ	Habitat 🦅 ⚘ ⚘	Migration Nonmigratory	Weight 0.2 ounce

DATE _____ TIME _____ LOCATION _____

Family SYLVIIDAE	Species *Polioptila melanura*	Length 4 inches	Wingspan 5.5–6 inches

BLACK-TAILED GNATCATCHER

This bird lives near desert gulches and scrub growth. The male's black cap sets it apart from similar gnatcatchers, with the exception of the Black-capped Gnatcatcher, which is rare and local in southeastern Arizona. Males have white outer webs on outer tail feathers and white terminal spots on graduated tail feathers. Females have a brown wash on their blue-gray upperparts, especially on the back, and, like the nonbreeding males, lack the black cap.

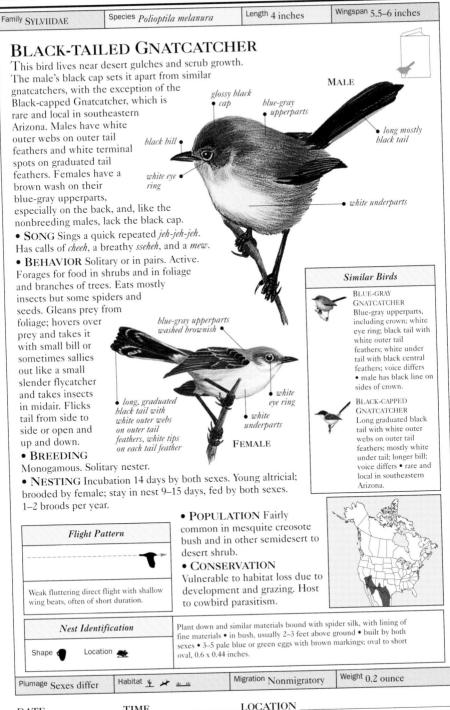

MALE

glossy black cap

blue-gray upperparts

black bill

white eye ring

long mostly black tail

white underparts

- **SONG** Sings a quick repeated *jeh-jeh-jeh*. Has calls of *cheeh*, a breathy *sseheh*, and a *mew*.
- **BEHAVIOR** Solitary or in pairs. Active. Forages for food in shrubs and in foliage and branches of trees. Eats mostly insects but some spiders and seeds. Gleans prey from foliage; hovers over prey and takes it with small bill or sometimes sallies out like a small slender flycatcher and takes insects in midair. Flicks tail from side to side or open and up and down.

blue-gray upperparts washed brownish

long, graduated black tail with white outer webs on outer tail feathers, white tips on each tail feather

white eye ring

white underparts

FEMALE

Similar Birds

BLUE-GRAY GNATCATCHER
Blue-gray upperparts, including crown; white eye ring; black tail with white outer tail feathers; white under tail with black central feathers; voice differs • male has black line on sides of crown.

BLACK-CAPPED GNATCATCHER
Long graduated black tail with white outer webs on outer tail feathers; mostly white under tail; longer bill; voice differs • rare and local in southeastern Arizona.

- **BREEDING** Monogamous. Solitary nester.
- **NESTING** Incubation 14 days by both sexes. Young altricial; brooded by female; stay in nest 9–15 days, fed by both sexes. 1–2 broods per year.

- **POPULATION** Fairly common in mesquite creosote bush and in other semidesert to desert shrub.
- **CONSERVATION** Vulnerable to habitat loss due to development and grazing. Host to cowbird parasitism.

Flight Pattern
Weak fluttering direct flight with shallow wing beats, often of short duration.

Nest Identification	Plant down and similar materials bound with spider silk, with lining of fine materials • in bush, usually 2–3 feet above ground • built by both sexes • 3–5 pale blue or green eggs with brown markings; oval to short oval, 0.6 x 0.44 inches.
Shape ● Location ♣	

Plumage Sexes differ	Habitat	Migration Nonmigratory	Weight 0.2 ounce

DATE _____ TIME_____ LOCATION _____

Family SYLVIIDAE	Species *Polioptila nigriceps*	Length 4.25 inches	Wingspan 5.75–6.5 inches

BLACK-CAPPED GNATCATCHER

A native of Mexico, this bird has extended its range on rare occasions into southeastern Arizona, where it has nested. Like many gnatcatchers, it often wags its tail from side to side. Females are similar to males but are duller in color and lack the black cap. Winter males also lack the black cap but often retain some black flecking on the head above the eye. The slender black bill of this species is longer than that of other North American gnatcatchers, and the shape of the tail is more graduated.

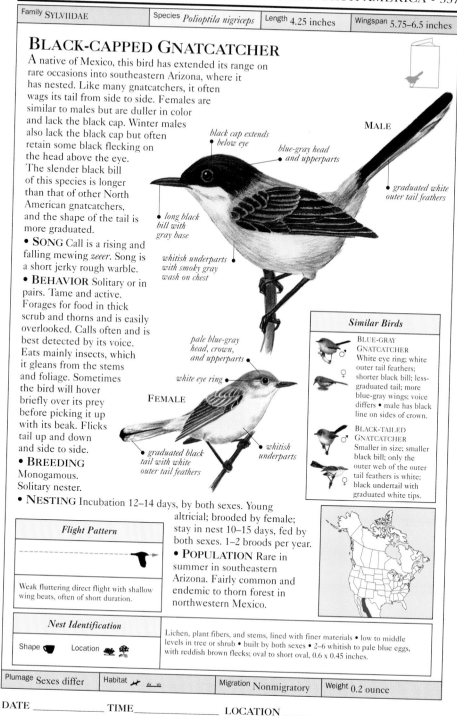

MALE

black cap extends below eye

blue-gray head and upperparts

graduated white outer tail feathers

long black bill with gray base

whitish underparts with smoky gray wash on chest

• **SONG** Call is a rising and falling mewing *zeeer*. Song is a short jerky rough warble.
• **BEHAVIOR** Solitary or in pairs. Tame and active. Forages for food in thick scrub and thorns and is easily overlooked. Calls often and is best detected by its voice. Eats mainly insects, which it gleans from the stems and foliage. Sometimes the bird will hover briefly over its prey before picking it up with its beak. Flicks tail up and down and side to side.
• **BREEDING** Monogamous. Solitary nester.
• **NESTING** Incubation 12–14 days, by both sexes. Young altricial; brooded by female; stay in nest 10–15 days, fed by both sexes. 1–2 broods per year.
• **POPULATION** Rare in summer in southeastern Arizona. Fairly common and endemic to thorn forest in northwestern Mexico.

pale blue-gray head, crown, and upperparts

white eye ring

FEMALE

graduated black tail with white outer tail feathers

whitish underparts

Similar Birds

BLUE-GRAY GNATCATCHER ♂ ♀
White eye ring; white outer tail feathers; shorter black bill; less-graduated tail; more blue-gray wings; voice differs • male has black line on sides of crown.

BLACK-TAILED GNATCATCHER ♂ ♀
Smaller in size; smaller black bill; only the outer web of the outer tail feathers is white; black undertail with graduated white tips.

Flight Pattern

Weak fluttering direct flight with shallow wing beats, often of short duration.

Nest Identification

Shape 🍵   Location 🌳 🌿

Lichen, plant fibers, and stems, lined with finer materials • low to middle levels in tree or shrub • built by both sexes • 2–6 whitish to pale blue eggs, with reddish brown flecks; oval to short oval, 0.6 x 0.45 inches.

Plumage Sexes differ	Habitat 🪴 🌾 🌾	Migration Nonmigratory	Weight 0.2 ounce

DATE _____ TIME_____ LOCATION _____

Family MUSCICAPIDAE	Species *Ficedula parva*	Length 4.75 inches	Wingspan 7.5 inches

RED-BREASTED FLYCATCHER

One of the smallest Old World flycatchers, this Eurasian bird is an occasional visitor to the western Aleutians and St. Lawrence Island, Alaska. The female and juvenile male have a creamy wash on the throat and a gray wash on the breast. Both sexes have a white eye ring and a black tail with a white base to the outer tail feathers.

• **SONG** Sings a bold warbling trill *trrrrrt*. Has calls of a whistled *hu-lee, hu-lee* and a dry grating *zee-it*.

• **BEHAVIOR** Solitary or in pairs. Relatively tame. Frequents mature conifer and mixed conifer-deciduous forests. Eats insects. Perches low to spot prey, catches while in flight, and returns to perch to eat. Often flicks its tail erect when calling.

• **BREEDING** Monogamous. Solitary nester.

• **NESTING** Incubation 12 to 13 days by female. Altricial young brooded by female; stay in nest 12–15 days, fed by both sexes. 1 brood per year.

• **POPULATION** This bird is casual to accidental in North America in the western Aleutian Islands and on St. Lawrence Island, Alaska. In Eurasia it is a fairly common to uncommon bird frequenting forested areas.

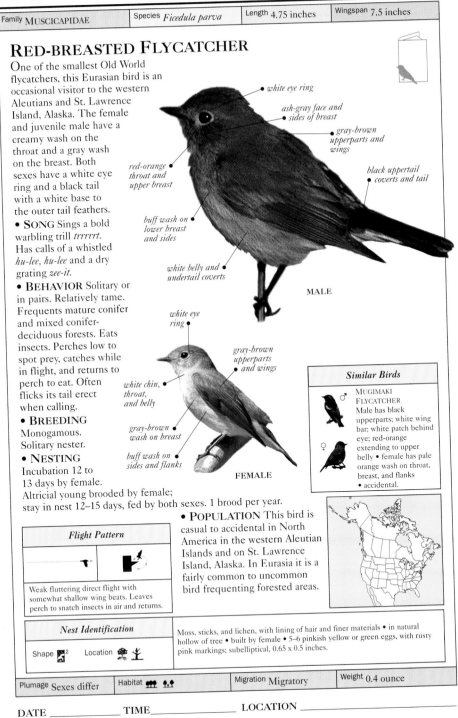

white eye ring

ash-gray face and sides of breast

gray-brown upperparts and wings

black uppertail coverts and tail

red-orange throat and upper breast

buff wash on lower breast and sides

white belly and undertail coverts

MALE

white eye ring

gray-brown upperparts and wings

white chin, throat, and belly

gray-brown wash on breast

buff wash on sides and flanks

FEMALE

Similar Birds

MUGIMAKI FLYCATCHER
Male has black upperparts; white wing bar; white patch behind eye; red-orange extending to upper belly • female has pale orange wash on throat, breast, and flanks • accidental.

Flight Pattern

Weak fluttering direct flight with somewhat shallow wing beats. Leaves perch to snatch insects in air and returns.

Nest Identification

Shape   Location

Moss, sticks, and lichen, with lining of hair and finer materials • in natural hollow of tree • built by female • 5–6 pinkish yellow or green eggs, with rusty pink markings; subelliptical, 0.65 x 0.5 inches.

Plumage Sexes differ	Habitat	Migration Migratory	Weight 0.4 ounce

DATE _____ TIME_____ LOCATION _____

Family MUSCICAPIDAE	Species *Muscicapa sibirica*	Length 5.25 inches	Wingspan 8.5 inches

SIBERIAN FLYCATCHER

This Old World flycatcher breeds and nests in the evergreen forests of Asia. Occasionally it has been observed in the western Aleutian Islands of Alaska. It is a small bird with a wide flat bill, typical of flycatchers, and a short straight tail. It has a partial whitish collar, a dark supraloral spot, and long projection of the primaries. In flight it shows dark centers on its undertail coverts. In the field it can be confused with the somewhat similar Gray-spotted and Asian Brown Flycatchers.

white eye ring

brownish supraloral spot

short bill

dark grayish brown upperparts

white throat with indistinct malar mark

partial whitish collar

indistinct pale wing bar

dark grayish brown wash on sides and flanks

long primary projection

• SONG The Siberian Flycatcher has a gentle *chirring* call.
• BEHAVIOR A solitary bird; or in pairs. Fairly tame and approachable. It tends to perch, immobile and erect, to spot prey, then fly out to catch it in flight and return to its perch to feed. Diet mostly insects. Occasionally this flycatcher will flick its wings while perched on an open exposed branch from which it does its hunting. This flycatcher is a fairly common bird in its native range in Siberia, where it inhabits mixed conifer woodlands on plains and hills.
• BREEDING Monogamous. Solitary nester.
• NESTING Incubation 11–13 days by female. Young altricial; brooded by female; stay in nest 13–15 days, fed by both sexes. 1 brood per year.
• POPULATION The Siberian Flycatcher is accidental to casual in North America in the western Aleutian Islands off the coast of Alaska.

Similar Birds

GRAY-SPOTTED FLYCATCHER
Larger; smaller head; whitish streaks on forehead; heavy brown streaking on white underparts; unmarked undertail coverts.

ASIAN BROWN FLYCATCHER
Larger bill with creamy pink base to lower mandible; paler supraloral area; shorter wings; paler upperparts; unmarked undertail coverts • accidental.

Flight Pattern

Weak fluttering direct flight with shallow wing beats; sallies forth to take insects in flight, returning to same or nearby perch.

Nest Identification
Shape ▼   Location ▲

Lichen with lining of larch needles • on tree branch or set in fork of tree • built by female • 4–5 green eggs, dotted with rusty brown; subelliptical, 0.6 x 0.45 inches.

Plumage Sexes similar	Habitat 🌲 🌿	Migration Migratory	Weight 0.4 ounce

DATE _____ TIME_____ LOCATION _____

| Family MUSCICAPIDAE | Species *Muscicapa griseisticta* | Length 6 inches | Wingspan 9 inches |

GRAY-SPOTTED FLYCATCHER

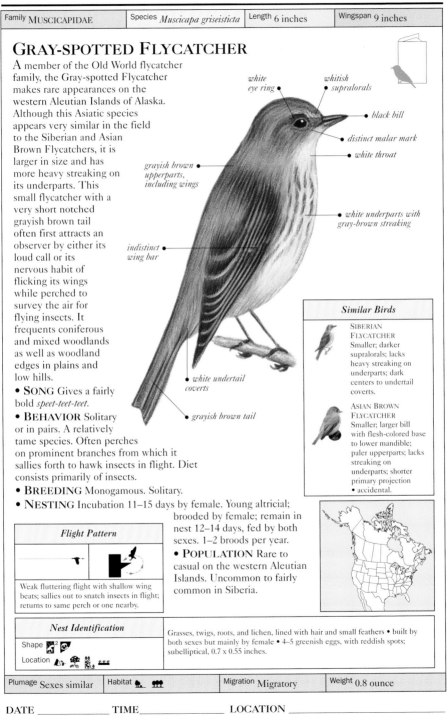

A member of the Old World flycatcher family, the Gray-spotted Flycatcher makes rare appearances on the western Aleutian Islands of Alaska. Although this Asiatic species appears very similar in the field to the Siberian and Asian Brown Flycatchers, it is larger in size and has more heavy streaking on its underparts. This small flycatcher with a very short notched grayish brown tail often first attracts an observer by either its loud call or its nervous habit of flicking its wings while perched to survey the air for flying insects. It frequents coniferous and mixed woodlands as well as woodland edges in plains and low hills.

white eye ring
whitish supralorals
black bill
distinct malar mark
white throat
grayish brown upperparts, including wings
white underparts with gray-brown streaking
indistinct wing bar
white undertail coverts
grayish brown tail

• **SONG** Gives a fairly bold *speet-teet-teet*.

• **BEHAVIOR** Solitary or in pairs. A relatively tame species. Often perches on prominent branches from which it sallies forth to hawk insects in flight. Diet consists primarily of insects.

• **BREEDING** Monogamous. Solitary.

• **NESTING** Incubation 11–15 days by female. Young altricial; brooded by female; remain in nest 12–14 days, fed by both sexes. 1–2 broods per year.

• **POPULATION** Rare to casual on the western Aleutian Islands. Uncommon to fairly common in Siberia.

Similar Birds

SIBERIAN FLYCATCHER Smaller; darker supralorals; lacks heavy streaking on underparts; dark centers to undertail coverts.

ASIAN BROWN FLYCATCHER Smaller; larger bill with flesh-colored base to lower mandible; paler upperparts; lacks streaking on underparts; shorter primary projection • accidental.

Flight Pattern

Weak fluttering flight with shallow wing beats; sallies out to snatch insects in flight; returns to same perch or one nearby.

Nest Identification

Shape

Location

Grasses, twigs, roots, and lichen, lined with hair and small feathers • built by both sexes but mainly by female • 4–5 greenish eggs, with reddish spots; subelliptical, 0.7 x 0.55 inches.

| Plumage Sexes similar | Habitat | Migration Migratory | Weight 0.8 ounce |

DATE _____ TIME_____ LOCATION _____

Family TURDIDAE	Species *Luscinia calliope*	Length 6 inches	Wingspan 10 inches

SIBERIAN RUBYTHROAT

Occasionally this native of Eurasia makes visits to the Aleutians and other islands off the Alaskan coast, and summer visits may indicate breeding pairs. It frequents trees with thick undergrowth, where it perches to sing its pleasant songs. Females are similar to males but are duller in color and do not have a red throat. Some adult females have pinkish throats and juveniles have buffy ones.

• **SONG** Has a bold flutelike call of *feeyoueet-feeyoueet*. Song is a variety of loud clicks and whistles.

• **BEHAVIOR** Solitary or found in pairs. Often cocks tail upward. Forages for food on ground and picks food off bushes. Feeds on insects, worms, and various wild berries. Frequents open grasslands with scattered thickets in winter as well as in migration. Tends to skulk in the more dense vegetation, which makes it difficult to locate.

• **BREEDING** Monogamous. Solitary nester.

• **NESTING** Incubation 14 days by female. Altricial young stay in nest 12 days, fed by both sexes. 1 brood per year.

• **POPULATION** Widely distributed breeder in Asia and eastern Europe; winters in southern Asia. Rare in North America but is an annual migrant through the western Aleutian and St. Lawrence Island. Summer records at Attu Island may indicate breeding. One record exists for Toronto, Ontario.

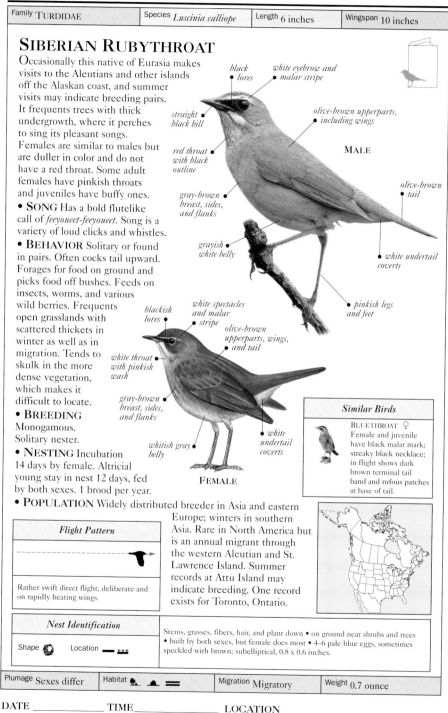

black lores

white eyebrow and malar stripe

olive-brown upperparts, including wings

straight black bill

red throat with black outline

MALE

olive-brown tail

gray-brown breast, sides, and flanks

grayish white belly

white undertail coverts

blackish lores

white spectacles and malar stripe

olive-brown upperparts, wings, and tail

pinkish legs and feet

white throat with pinkish wash

gray-brown breast, sides, and flanks

whitish gray belly

white undertail coverts

FEMALE

Similar Birds

BLUETHROAT ♀ Female and juvenile have black malar mark; streaky black necklace; in flight shows dark brown terminal tail band and rufous patches at base of tail.

Flight Pattern

Rather swift direct flight, deliberate and on rapidly beating wings.

Nest Identification

Shape —   Location —

Stems, grasses, fibers, hair, and plant down • on ground near shrubs and trees • built by both sexes, but female does most • 4–6 pale blue eggs, sometimes speckled with brown; subelliptical, 0.8 x 0.6 inches.

Plumage Sexes differ	Habitat	Migration Migratory	Weight 0.7 ounce

DATE _____ TIME_____ LOCATION _____

Family TURDIDAE	Species *Luscinia svecica*	Length 5.5 inches	Wingspan 9 inches

BLUETHROAT

This Eurasian bird has successfully established a breeding population in North America on the tundra of northern Alaska, and it is a regular migrant on St. Lawrence Island. It usually hides on the ground under dense thickets and trees, except when the male skylarks or flies to a high perch to sing. Females and juveniles have a pale throat with a black border. In all plumages, the bird can be identified in flight by the rufous patches at the base of the tail in combination with its dark brown terminal band.

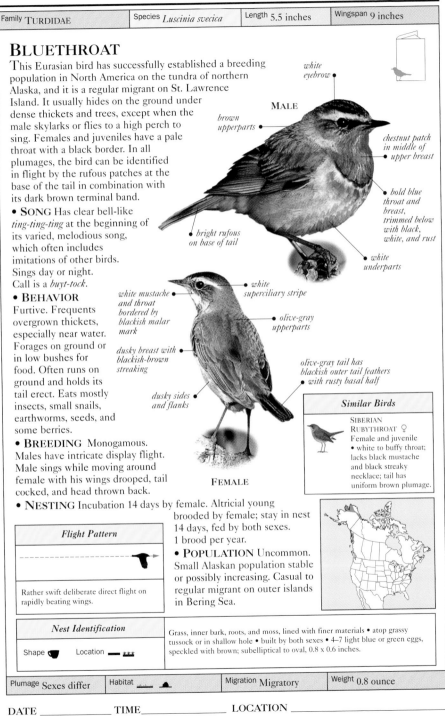

white eyebrow

MALE

brown upperparts

chestnut patch in middle of upper breast

bold blue throat and breast, trimmed below with black, white, and rust

bright rufous on base of tail

white underparts

white superciliary stripe

white mustache and throat bordered by blackish malar mark

olive-gray upperparts

dusky breast with blackish-brown streaking

olive-gray tail has blackish outer tail feathers with rusty basal half

dusky sides and flanks

FEMALE

- **SONG** Has clear bell-like *ting-ting-ting* at the beginning of its varied, melodious song, which often includes imitations of other birds. Sings day or night. Call is a *buyt-tock.*

- **BEHAVIOR** Furtive. Frequents overgrown thickets, especially near water. Forages on ground or in low bushes for food. Often runs on ground and holds its tail erect. Eats mostly insects, small snails, earthworms, seeds, and some berries.

- **BREEDING** Monogamous. Males have intricate display flight. Male sings while moving around female with his wings drooped, tail cocked, and head thrown back.

- **NESTING** Incubation 14 days by female. Altricial young brooded by female; stay in nest 14 days, fed by both sexes. 1 brood per year.

- **POPULATION** Uncommon. Small Alaskan population stable or possibly increasing. Casual to regular migrant on outer islands in Bering Sea.

Similar Birds

SIBERIAN RUBYTHROAT ♀
Female and juvenile
• white to buffy throat; lacks black mustache and black streaky necklace; tail has uniform brown plumage.

Flight Pattern

Rather swift deliberate direct flight on rapidly beating wings.

Nest Identification

Shape ◗   Location ▬ ▬

Grass, inner bark, roots, and moss, lined with finer materials • atop grassy tussock or in shallow hole • built by both sexes • 4–7 light blue or green eggs, speckled with brown; subelliptical to oval, 0.8 x 0.6 inches.

Plumage Sexes differ	Habitat ▬ ▲	Migration Migratory	Weight 0.8 ounce

DATE _____ TIME_____ LOCATION _____

Family TURDIDAE	Species *Tarsiger cyanurus*	Length 5–5.75 inches	Wingspan 8.5–9 inches

RED-FLANKED BLUETAIL

On rare occasions, vagrants of this sparrow-sized Eurasian native have been spotted on the outer Aleutian Islands and the Pribilofs, as well as once in California. It usually makes its home among thick forests of pine and deciduous trees, more often frequenting coniferous forests on hillsides near streams. Juveniles are similar to females in plumage. The blue plumage of the male is variable, and it takes several years for immature birds to attain the bright blue upperparts.

• **SONG** Clear single whistle or short monotonous warble. Sings from exposed perch high in tree, often at very top. Call is a *hueet* or a hoarse *keck-keck*.

• **BEHAVIOR** Solitary or in pairs or small flocks. Very active. Hops vigorously on ground while bobbing tail up and down. Forages on ground and in trees for insects and berries, which it gleans from branches or foliage. Found in forests with dense undergrowth.

• **BREEDING** Monogamous. Solitary.

• **NESTING** Incubation 12–15 days by female. Altricial young are brooded by female; stay in nest 12–15 days, fed by both sexes. 1–2 broods per year.

• **POPULATION** Accidental in North America in western Aleutians and Pribilof Islands. A single record exists from the Farallon Islands off California. Common in Siberia as a breeding bird.

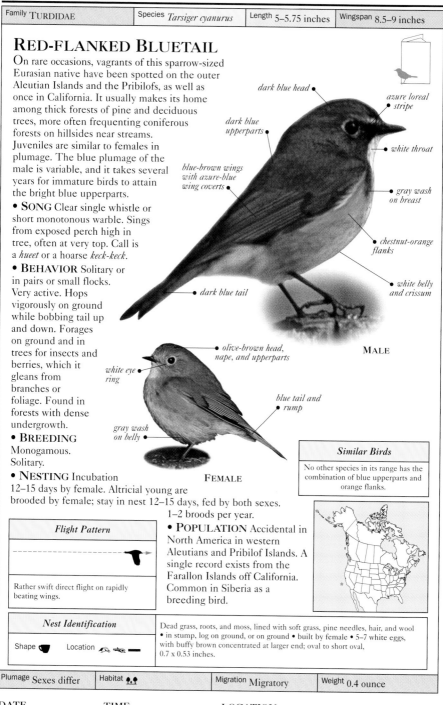

dark blue head

azure loreal stripe

dark blue upperparts

white throat

blue-brown wings with azure-blue wing coverts

gray wash on breast

chestnut-orange flanks

white belly and crissum

dark blue tail

MALE

olive-brown head, nape, and upperparts

white eye ring

blue tail and rump

gray wash on belly

FEMALE

Similar Birds

No other species in its range has the combination of blue upperparts and orange flanks.

Flight Pattern

Rather swift direct flight on rapidly beating wings.

Nest Identification

Shape   Location

Dead grass, roots, and moss, lined with soft grass, pine needles, hair, and wool • in stump, log on ground, or on ground • built by female • 5–7 white eggs, with buffy brown concentrated at larger end; oval to short oval, 0.7 x 0.53 inches.

Plumage Sexes differ	Habitat	Migration Migratory	Weight 0.4 ounce

DATE _____ TIME_____ LOCATION _____

Family TURDIDAE	Species *Oenanthe oenanthe*	Length 5.5–6 inches	Wingspan 10.5–11 inches

NORTHERN WHEATEAR

This long-distance flier begins its migratory route near Greenland and eventually reaches West Africa. During its courtship display, the male sings while flying upward, continues to sing while hovering, then sings with tail spread toward the female as it is gliding back down. Females and nonbreeding males are similar and show a white rump and tail base in flight.

• **SONG** Utters bossy *chack-chack* and whistled *hweet*. Song is often given in flight and imitates songs of other birds, combining call notes into a scratchy jumble of warbled notes.

• **BEHAVIOR** Solitary or in pairs. Bobs tail. Active; often nervously restless when foraging. Often makes short flights to hawk insects in air near ground. Picks food off trees and shrubs and forages on ground. Eats various insects, fruit, seeds, and small bulbs. Inhabits open, dry areas of tundra and mountain slopes, often near rocky areas. Often perches on rocks, trees, or posts.

• **BREEDING** Monogamous. Solitary nester.

• **NESTING** Incubation 14 days by both sexes, but female does more. Altricial young stay in nest 15–16 days; brooded by female; fed by both sexes. 1–2 broods per year.

• **POPULATION** Rare on Atlantic Coast primarily in autumn migration. Accidental elsewhere. Fairly common breeding bird in Greenland, Siberia, and arctic regions of Alaska and both eastern and western Canada.

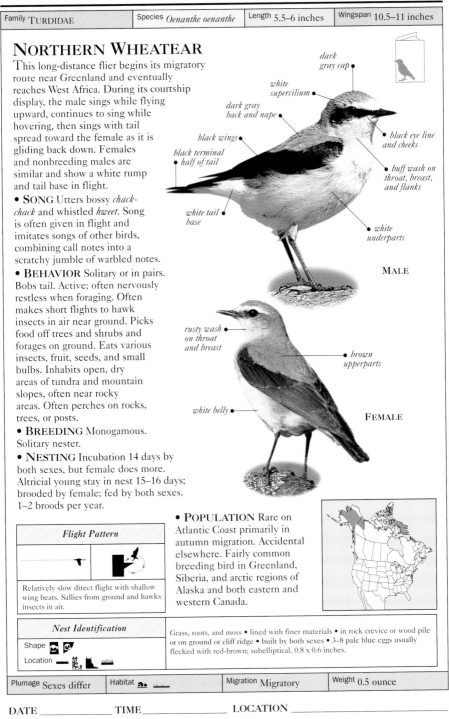

dark gray cap

white supercilium

dark gray back and nape

black wings

black terminal half of tail

black eye line and cheeks

buff wash on throat, breast, and flanks

white tail base

white underparts

MALE

rusty wash on throat and breast

brown upperparts

white belly

FEMALE

Flight Pattern

Relatively slow direct flight with shallow wing beats. Sallies from ground and hawks insects in air.

Nest Identification

Shape

Location

Grass, roots, and moss • lined with finer materials • in rock crevice or wood pile or on ground or cliff ridge • built by both sexes • 3–8 pale blue eggs usually flecked with red-brown; subelliptical, 0.8 x 0.6 inches.

Plumage Sexes differ	Habitat	Migration Migratory	Weight 0.5 ounce

Family TURDIDAE	Species Saxicola torquata	Length 5.25 inches	Wingspan 8.5 inches

STONECHAT

This native of Eurasia makes its home either in open meadows with brushy areas or at the edges of marshes, where it often perches conspicuously on low bushes. Occasionally Stonechats have been observed on islands near the Alaska coast and once on Grand Manan Island off New Brunswick. Males in flight show a whitish rump, which contrasts with the black tail and blackish back, and a white spot shows on the inner coverts at the base of the upper wing. Females in flight also show a white rump and uppertail coverts. Juveniles appear similar to females but have white shoulder patches and pale buffy rump patches.

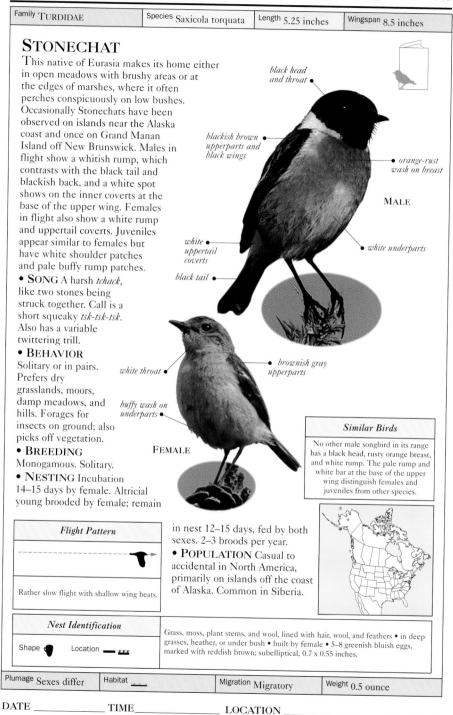

black head and throat

blackish brown upperparts and black wings

orange-rust wash on breast

MALE

white uppertail coverts

black tail

white underparts

• **SONG** A harsh *tchack*, like two stones being struck together. Call is a short squeaky *tsk-tsk-tsk*. Also has a variable twittering trill.
• **BEHAVIOR** Solitary or in pairs. Prefers dry grasslands, moors, damp meadows, and hills. Forages for insects on ground; also picks off vegetation.
• **BREEDING** Monogamous. Solitary.
• **NESTING** Incubation 14–15 days by female. Altricial young brooded by female; remain

white throat

brownish gray upperparts

buffy wash on underparts

FEMALE

Similar Birds

No other male songbird in its range has a black head, rusty orange breast, and white rump. The pale rump and white bar at the base of the upper wing distinguish females and juveniles from other species.

in nest 12–15 days, fed by both sexes. 2–3 broods per year.
• **POPULATION** Casual to accidental in North America, primarily on islands off the coast of Alaska. Common in Siberia.

Flight Pattern
Rather slow flight with shallow wing beats.

Nest Identification	
Shape	Location ▬ ✦✦✦

Grass, moss, plant stems, and wool, lined with hair, wool, and feathers • in deep grasses, heather, or under bush • built by female • 5–8 greenish bluish eggs, marked with reddish brown; subelliptical, 0.7 x 0.55 inches.

Plumage Sexes differ	Habitat ___	Migration Migratory	Weight 0.5 ounce

DATE _____ TIME_____ LOCATION _____

Family TURDIDAE	Species *Sialia sialis*	Length 7–7.75 inches	Wingspan 11.5–13 inches

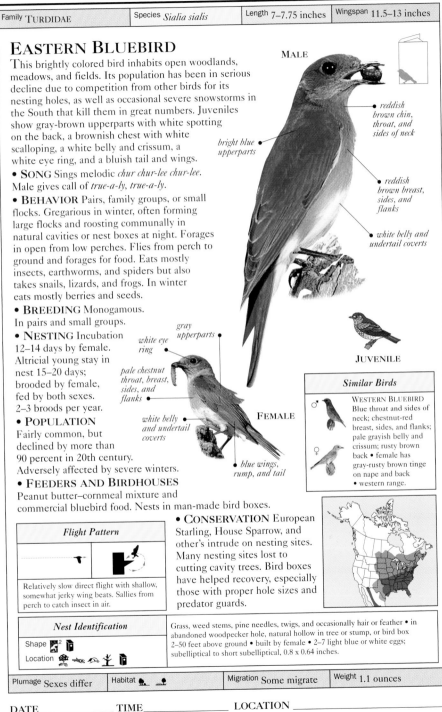

EASTERN BLUEBIRD

This brightly colored bird inhabits open woodlands, meadows, and fields. Its population has been in serious decline due to competition from other birds for its nesting holes, as well as occasional severe snowstorms in the South that kill them in great numbers. Juveniles show gray-brown upperparts with white spotting on the back, a brownish chest with white scalloping, a white belly and crissum, a white eye ring, and a bluish tail and wings.

MALE

- reddish brown chin, throat, and sides of neck
- bright blue upperparts
- reddish brown breast, sides, and flanks
- white belly and undertail coverts

- **SONG** Sings melodic *chur chur-lee chur-lee*. Male gives call of *true-a-ly, true-a-ly*.
- **BEHAVIOR** Pairs, family groups, or small flocks. Gregarious in winter, often forming large flocks and roosting communally in natural cavities or nest boxes at night. Forages in open from low perches. Flies from perch to ground and forages for food. Eats mostly insects, earthworms, and spiders but also takes snails, lizards, and frogs. In winter eats mostly berries and seeds.
- **BREEDING** Monogamous. In pairs and small groups.
- **NESTING** Incubation 12–14 days by female. Altricial young stay in nest 15–20 days; brooded by female, fed by both sexes. 2–3 broods per year.
- **POPULATION** Fairly common, but declined by more than 90 percent in 20th century. Adversely affected by severe winters.
- **FEEDERS AND BIRDHOUSES** Peanut butter–cornmeal mixture and commercial bluebird food. Nests in man-made bird boxes.
- **CONSERVATION** European Starling, House Sparrow, and other's intrude on nesting sites. Many nesting sites lost to cutting cavity trees. Bird boxes have helped recovery, especially those with proper hole sizes and predator guards.

- gray upperparts
- white eye ring
- pale chestnut throat, breast, sides, and flanks
- white belly and undertail coverts
- blue wings, rump, and tail

FEMALE

JUVENILE

Similar Birds

WESTERN BLUEBIRD
Blue throat and sides of neck; chestnut-red breast, sides, and flanks; pale grayish belly and crissum; rusty brown back • female has gray-rusty brown tinge on nape and back • western range.

Flight Pattern

Relatively slow direct flight with shallow, somewhat jerky wing beats. Sallies from perch to catch insect in air.

Nest Identification

Shape
Location

Grass, weed stems, pine needles, twigs, and occasionally hair or feather • in abandoned woodpecker hole, natural hollow in tree or stump, or bird box 2–50 feet above ground • built by female • 2–7 light blue or white eggs; subelliptical to short subelliptical, 0.8 x 0.64 inches.

Plumage Sexes differ	Habitat	Migration Some migrate	Weight 1.1 ounces

DATE _____ TIME_____ LOCATION _____

Family TURDIDAE	Species *Sialia mexicana*	Length 7–7.75 inches	Wingspan 11.5–13 inches

WESTERN BLUEBIRD

The Western Bluebird's brilliant blue throat distinguishes it from the Eastern Bluebird, and its chestnut-red underparts distinguish it from the Mountain Bluebird. In recent years its population has declined due to loss of habitat, especially large old trees, which it uses for nesting cavities. Bird boxes have been helpful but have not kept up with the loss of trees. Juveniles are brownish gray with white-spotted upperparts and underparts and bluish wings and tails.

- **SONG** Male's song is *f-few, f-few, faweee*. Also calls *pa-wee* or *mew*.
- **BEHAVIOR** In pairs or small family groups. More gregarious in winter. Often hunts from low perches from which it drops down on prey or hawks insects. Forages for food on ground and catches insects in flight. Eats insects, earthworms, spiders, and snails; in winter, principally feeds on various berries. Defends nesting cavity from other birds. Often roosts communally in winter, with many individuals sharing the same cavity for the night.
- **BREEDING** Monogamous. Solitary or small colonies.
- **NESTING** Incubation 13–14 days by female. Young altricial; brooded by female; leave nest in 15–22 days, fed by both sexes. 2 broods per year.
- **POPULATION** Common in open woodlands, riparian woodlands, cut-over woodlands, and farmlands; common in winter in deserts and semideserts.
- **FEEDERS AND BIRDHOUSES** Mealworms, peanut butter and suet mixture, cornmeal mixes, and commercial bluebird mixes. Currents, raisins, and soaked raisins are also favorites. Will nest in bird boxes.
- **CONSERVATION** Population declining due to loss of habitat and nesting sites because of competition from other songbirds.

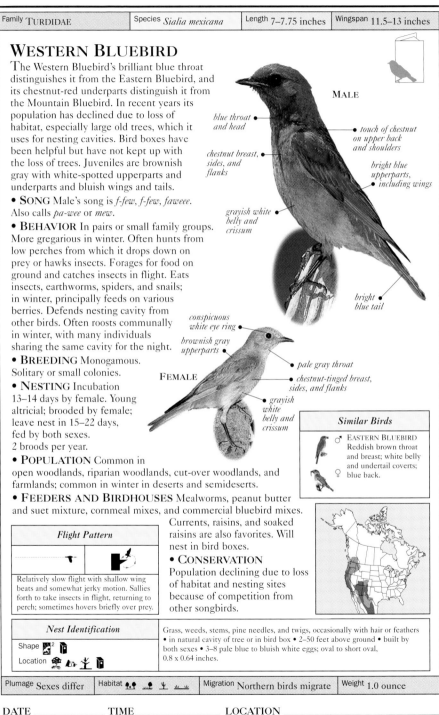

MALE

blue throat and head

touch of chestnut on upper back and shoulders

chestnut breast, sides, and flanks

bright blue upperparts, including wings

grayish white belly and crissum

bright blue tail

conspicuous white eye ring

brownish gray upperparts

FEMALE

pale gray throat

chestnut-tinged breast, sides, and flanks

grayish white belly and crissum

Similar Birds

♂ EASTERN BLUEBIRD Reddish brown throat and breast; white belly and undertail coverts; ♀ blue back.

Flight Pattern

Relatively slow flight with shallow wing beats and somewhat jerky motion. Sallies forth to take insects in flight, returning to perch; sometimes hovers briefly over prey.

Nest Identification	
Shape	Grass, weeds, stems, pine needles, and twigs, occasionally with hair or feathers • in natural cavity of tree or in bird box • 2–50 feet above ground • built by both sexes • 3–8 pale blue to bluish white eggs; oval to short oval, 0.8 x 0.64 inches.
Location	

Plumage Sexes differ	Habitat	Migration Northern birds migrate	Weight 1.0 ounce

DATE _____ TIME_____ LOCATION _____

| Family TURDIDAE | Species *Sialia currucoides* | Length 7–7.25 inches | Wingspan 11–12.75 inches |

MOUNTAIN BLUEBIRD

The overall brilliant blue coloring of the male sets it apart from other birds in its genus. Most often making its home in the tree-covered mountains and open landscapes of western North America, generally above seven thousand feet, it is considered to be at risk by conservationists due to its declining nesting habitat. In winter it descends to open lowlands and deserts. Juveniles are similar to females but with pale whitish streaking and spotting on the breast and sides.

• **SONG** Often silent. A low warbling *tru-lee*. Call is a *phew*.

• **BEHAVIOR** Solitary or in pairs or small family groups. Hovers more than other bluebirds, dropping on prey from above or pouncing on it from low perches. Catches insects in flight and forages on ground. Eats insects, caterpillars, and some fruits and berries. Eats mostly insects in summer.

• **BREEDING** Monogamous. Solitary nester.

• **NESTING** Incubation 13–14 days by female. Altricial young brooded by female first 6 days; stay in nest 22–23 days, fed by both sexes. 2 broods per year.

• **POPULATION** Fairly common but declined over much of its range in the 1900s due to loss of nesting cavities to other species. Casual in the East during migration and winter to north Atlantic seaboard.

• **BIRDHOUSES** Will nest in bird boxes.

• **CONSERVATION** Habitat loss is a concern.

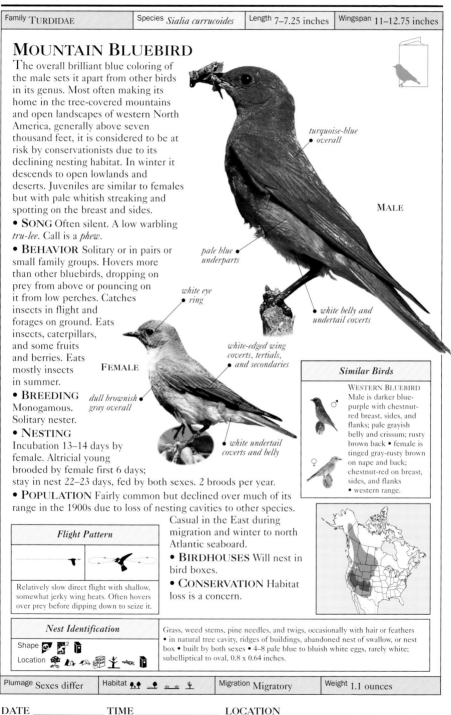

turquoise-blue overall

MALE

pale blue underparts

white eye ring

white belly and undertail coverts

FEMALE

dull brownish gray overall

white-edged wing coverts, tertials, and secondaries

white undertail coverts and belly

Similar Birds

WESTERN BLUEBIRD Male is darker blue-purple with chestnut-red breast, sides, and flanks; pale grayish belly and crissum; rusty brown back • female is tinged gray-rusty brown on nape and back; chestnut-red on breast, sides, and flanks • western range.

Flight Pattern

Relatively slow direct flight with shallow, somewhat jerky wing beats. Often hovers over prey before dipping down to seize it.

Nest Identification

Shape

Location

Grass, weed stems, pine needles, and twigs, occasionally with hair or feathers • in natural tree cavity, ridges of buildings, abandoned nest of swallow, or nest box • built by both sexes • 4–8 pale blue to bluish white eggs, rarely white; subelliptical to oval, 0.8 x 0.64 inches.

| Plumage Sexes differ | Habitat | Migration Migratory | Weight 1.1 ounces |

DATE _____ TIME_____ LOCATION _____

Family TURDIDAE	Species *Myadestes townsendi*	Length 8.5–9 inches	Wingspan 13–14.5 inches

TOWNSEND'S SOLITAIRE

Its beautiful prolonged song given from high up in the trees, is in marked contrast with the rather plain-looking plumage of this gray bird. Although it makes its home in the high mountains most of the year, during the winter season Townsend's Solitaire moves into the canyons, where it maintains a winter territory and protects a critical food supply. In flight the white outer tail feathers contrast with the inner black ones, and the bird shows white axillaries and a long buffy wing patch. Juveniles are dark brownish gray, with buffy and white scalloping on both the upperparts and underparts, as well as a buffy crissum and wing patch.

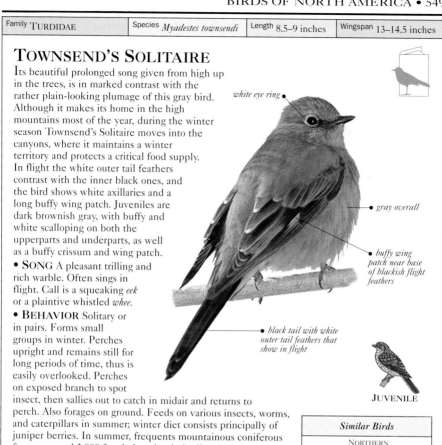

white eye ring

gray overall

buffy wing patch near base of blackish flight feathers

black tail with white outer tail feathers that show in flight

- **SONG** A pleasant trilling and rich warble. Often sings in flight. Call is a squeaking *eek* or a plaintive whistled *whee*.
- **BEHAVIOR** Solitary or in pairs. Forms small groups in winter. Perches upright and remains still for long periods of time, thus is easily overlooked. Perches on exposed branch to spot insect, then sallies out to catch in midair and returns to perch. Also forages on ground. Feeds on various insects, worms, and caterpillars in summer; winter diet consists principally of juniper berries. In summer, frequents mountainous coniferous forests around 3,000 feet below the timberline; in winter, descends to canyons with open juniper forests on lower slopes.
- **BREEDING** Monogamous. Solitary or small family groups.
- **NESTING** Incubation 14 days by both sexes, but female does more. Altricial young brooded by female; remain in nest 15–16 days, fed by both sexes. 1 brood per year (possibly 2 broods in the South).
- **POPULATION** Fairly common in montane coniferous forests. Casual to rare in winter in eastern North America.

JUVENILE

Similar Birds

NORTHERN MOCKINGBIRD
Superficial resemblance • paler gray overall; two whitish wing bars; white wing patch; faint eye stripe; longer bill.

Flight Pattern

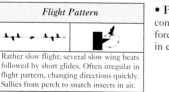

Rather slow flight; several slow wing beats followed by short glides. Often irregular in flight pattern, changing directions quickly. Sallies from perch to snatch insects in air.

Nest Identification	
Shape ⌒⌒ Location ▬ 🌿 🌿	Grass, roots, and moss, lined with fine materials • on ground, sheltered by overhanging branches, rocks, or natural overhang • built by both sexes • 3–8 pale blue eggs, usually unmarked, occasionally flecked with red-brown; oval, varying from short oval to long oval, 0.8 x 0.6 inches.

Plumage Sexes similar	Habitat 🌲 ⛰ 🌿 🍂 🌾	Migration Migratory	Weight 1.2 ounces

DATE _____ TIME_____ LOCATION _____

Family TURDIDAE	Species *Catharus fuscescens*	Length 7–7.5 inches	Wingspan 11–11.5 inches

VEERY

This bird is named for the lovely ethereal downward-slurring song of the male, which is heard at sunset, a repeated *veer-u*. It is one of the most splendid songs of any bird in North America. Its tawny and buff plumage serves as camouflage in the forest it calls home. The Veery is the least spotted of North America's brown-backed thrushes, with the western populations slightly more spotted than the eastern ones. This bird haunts shaded moist woodlands with dense to scattered understory.

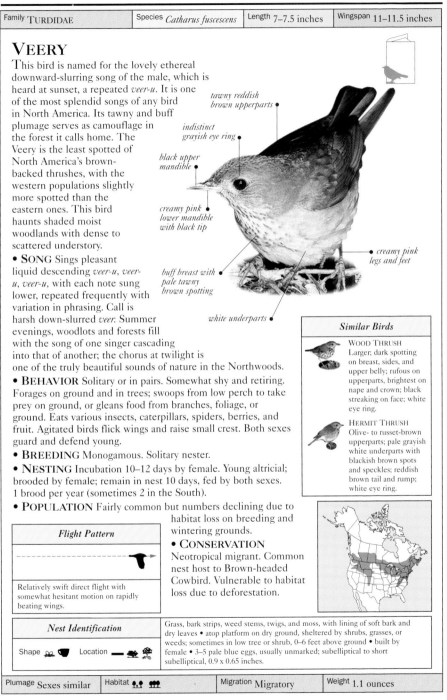

tawny reddish brown upperparts

indistinct grayish eye ring

black upper mandible

creamy pink lower mandible with black tip

buff breast with pale tawny brown spotting

white underparts

creamy pink legs and feet

• **SONG** Sings pleasant liquid descending *veer-u, veer-u, veer-u*, with each note sung lower, repeated frequently with variation in phrasing. Call is harsh down-slurred *veer*. Summer evenings, woodlots and forests fill with the song of one singer cascading into that of another; the chorus at twilight is one of the truly beautiful sounds of nature in the Northwoods.

• **BEHAVIOR** Solitary or in pairs. Somewhat shy and retiring. Forages on ground and in trees; swoops from low perch to take prey on ground, or gleans food from branches, foliage, or ground. Eats various insects, caterpillars, spiders, berries, and fruit. Agitated birds flick wings and raise small crest. Both sexes guard and defend young.

• **BREEDING** Monogamous. Solitary nester.

• **NESTING** Incubation 10–12 days by female. Young altricial; brooded by female; remain in nest 10 days, fed by both sexes. 1 brood per year (sometimes 2 in the South).

• **POPULATION** Fairly common but numbers declining due to habitat loss on breeding and wintering grounds.

• **CONSERVATION** Neotropical migrant. Common nest host to Brown-headed Cowbird. Vulnerable to habitat loss due to deforestation.

Similar Birds

WOOD THRUSH Larger; dark spotting on breast, sides, and upper belly; rufous on upperparts, brightest on nape and crown; black streaking on face; white eye ring.

HERMIT THRUSH Olive- to russet-brown upperparts; pale grayish white underparts with blackish brown spots and speckles; reddish brown tail and rump; white eye ring.

Flight Pattern

Relatively swift direct flight with somewhat hesitant motion on rapidly beating wings.

Nest Identification	Grass, bark strips, weed stems, twigs, and moss, with lining of soft bark and dry leaves • atop platform on dry ground, sheltered by shrubs, grasses, or weeds; sometimes in low tree or shrub, 0–6 feet above ground • built by female • 3–5 pale blue eggs, usually unmarked; subelliptical to short subelliptical, 0.9 x 0.65 inches.
Shape ⌣ ▽ Location ▬ 🌿 🌳	

Plumage Sexes similar	Habitat 🌱 🌿		Migration Migratory	Weight 1.1 ounces

DATE _____ TIME_____ LOCATION _____

Family TURDIDAE	Species *Catharus minimus*	Length 7–7.75 inches	Wingspan 11.5–13.5 inches

GRAY-CHEEKED THRUSH

This bird is a truly long-distance migrant. Each spring some of its population fly from southern Brazil to Alaska, across the Bering Strait, and on to their nesting grounds in eastern Siberia. Others spread across the arctic tundra and northern taiga from Alaska to Newfoundland. It has the most northern nesting range of any spotted thrush. In migration it can be found in almost any habitat from woodlots to city parks. The Newfoundland race has warmer-toned upperparts with a sepia back.

• **SONG** Male sings thin oboelike phrases, somewhat

inconspicuous gray eye ring

black upper mandible

olive-gray brown upperparts

black lower mandible with yellowish pink base

gray cheeks

pale buff wash on breast and throat, with black-brown spots

grayish white underparts

pink legs and feet

like the Veery, but middle phrases rise and first and last ones drop, *wheeoo-titi-wheeoo*. Call is a thin high abrasive *phreu*. Vocal at dawn and especially at dusk.

• **BEHAVIOR** Solitary or in pairs. Shy and retiring, often staying in the dense understory and thickets. More heard than seen. Feeds on spiders, caterpillars, earthworms, various insects, and even small crayfish. In fall migration, feeds more on berries and some fruits.

• **BREEDING** Monogamous. Solitary nester.

• **NESTING** Incubation 13–14 days by female. Young altricial; brooded by female; stay in nest 11–13 days. Fed by female. 1–2 broods per year.

• **POPULATION** Common; southern breeding populations declining due to loss of habitat.

• **CONSERVATION** Neotropical migrant. Vulnerable on both breeding grounds and wintering areas to habitat loss from logging operations and forest fragmentation.

Similar Birds

SWAINSON'S THRUSH
Conspicuous eye ring; browner upperparts; buffy lores, cheeks, throat, and upper breast; buffy underwing linings; different voice.

BICKNELL'S THRUSH
Formerly considered subspecies of Gray-cheeked Thrush
• smaller; warmer brown tones on upperparts, especially on tail and rump; more extensive yellow on lower mandible
• limited range in extreme northeast US
• best separated by voice.

Flight Pattern

Relatively swift direct flight with somewhat jerky wing strokes.

Nest Identification

Shape ☕   Location 🌲🌳🌿

Grass, sedge, bark, weed stems, twigs, and moss, with lining of grass, leaves, and fine rootlets • on low branch of tree or shrub, usually 0–10 feet above ground (but as high as 20 feet) • built by female • 3–6 greenish blue to pale blue eggs, most often speckled brown; oval to short oval, 0.9 x 0.65 inches.

Plumage Sexes similar	Habitat 🌾🌿 🏞️	Migration Migratory	Weight 1.2 ounces

DATE _____ TIME_____ LOCATION _____

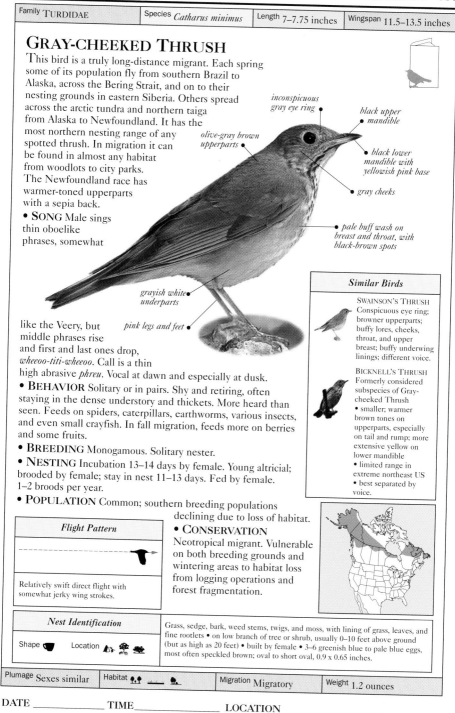

Family TURDIDAE	Species *Catharus ustulatus*	Length 7 inches	Wingspan 11.5 inches

SWAINSON'S THRUSH

Named for 19th-century British ornithologist William Swainson, this bird migrates through North America from its nesting grounds in Canada and mountainous eastern and western US to its winter home in the tropics. Migrating at night, flocks of these birds give plaintive, Spring Peeper-like calls in the darkness as they pass overhead. It often travels in mixed flocks with other thrushes, vireos, and wood warblers. In flight these birds show buff underwing linings.

prominent buff eye ring

buff-olive-brown upperparts

black bill with pinkish yellow base to lower mandible

buff cheeks, chin, and throat

buff breast with brownish spots

whitish gray underparts

pink legs and feet

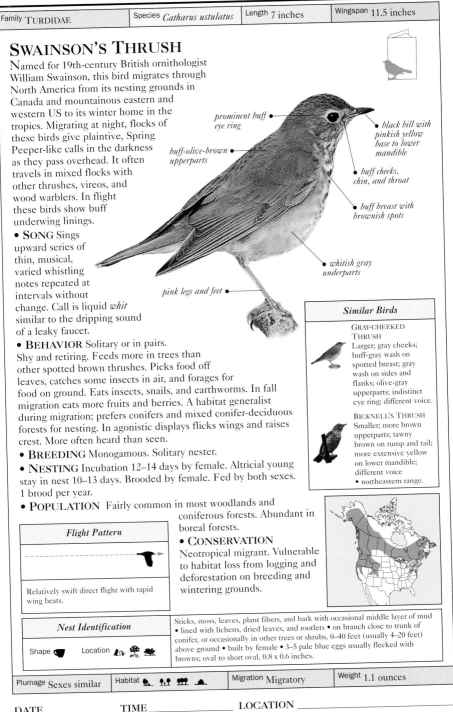

• **SONG** Sings upward series of thin, musical, varied whistling notes repeated at intervals without change. Call is liquid *whit* similar to the dripping sound of a leaky faucet.
• **BEHAVIOR** Solitary or in pairs. Shy and retiring. Feeds more in trees than other spotted brown thrushes. Picks food off leaves, catches some insects in air, and forages for food on ground. Eats insects, snails, and earthworms. In fall migration eats more fruits and berries. A habitat generalist during migration; prefers conifers and mixed conifer-deciduous forests for nesting. In agonistic displays flicks wings and raises crest. More often heard than seen.
• **BREEDING** Monogamous. Solitary nester.
• **NESTING** Incubation 12–14 days by female. Altricial young stay in nest 10–13 days. Brooded by female. Fed by both sexes. 1 brood per year.
• **POPULATION** Fairly common in most woodlands and coniferous forests. Abundant in boreal forests.
• **CONSERVATION** Neotropical migrant. Vulnerable to habitat loss from logging and deforestation on breeding and wintering grounds.

Similar Birds

GRAY-CHEEKED THRUSH
Larger; gray cheeks; buff-gray wash on spotted breast; gray wash on sides and flanks; olive-gray upperparts; indistinct eye ring; different voice.

BICKNELL'S THRUSH
Smaller; more brown upperparts; tawny brown on rump and tail; more extensive yellow on lower mandible; different voice
• northeastern range.

Flight Pattern

Relatively swift direct flight with rapid wing beats.

Nest Identification

Shape ☕   Location 🌲 🌿 🌳

Sticks, moss, leaves, plant fibers, and bark with occasional middle layer of mud • lined with lichens, dried leaves, and rootlets • on branch close to trunk of conifer, or occasionally in other trees or shrubs, 0–40 feet (usually 4–20 feet) above ground • built by female • 3–5 pale blue eggs usually flecked with browns; oval to short oval, 0.8 x 0.6 inches.

Plumage Sexes similar	Habitat 🌲 🌿 🌳 🏔	Migration Migratory	Weight 1.1 ounces

DATE _____ TIME_____ LOCATION _____

Family TURDIDAE	Species *Catharus guttatus*	Length 6.75 inches	Wingspan 11.5 inches

HERMIT THRUSH

Often considered to have one of the most beautiful songs of all North American birds, the Hermit Thrush lives in habitats with coniferous and deciduous trees and along forest edges. It is Vermont's state bird and the only brown-backed spotted thrush to winter in the US. Color variations exist across its broad breeding range: northern Pacific Coast races are smaller and darker with gray flanks; western mountain races are larger and paler also with gray flanks; and eastern races are brownish gray with buff-brown flanks.

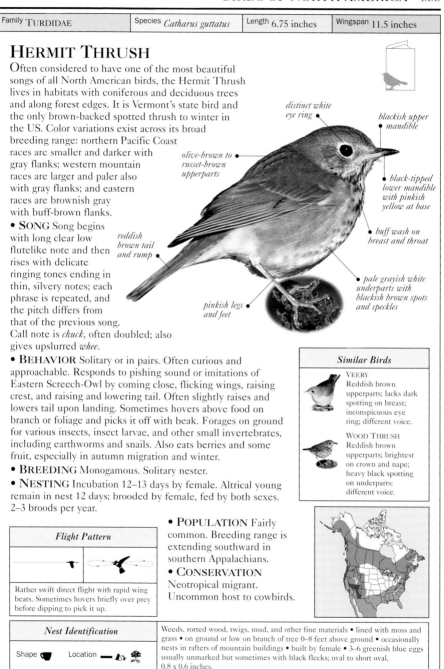

distinct white eye ring

blackish upper mandible

olive-brown to russet-brown upperparts

black-tipped lower mandible with pinkish yellow at base

buff wash on breast and throat

reddish brown tail and rump

pale grayish white underparts with blackish brown spots and speckles

pinkish legs and feet

• **SONG** Song begins with long clear low flutelike note and then rises with delicate ringing tones ending in thin, silvery notes; each phrase is repeated, and the pitch differs from that of the previous song. Call note is *chuck*, often doubled; also gives upslurred *whee*.

• **BEHAVIOR** Solitary or in pairs. Often curious and approachable. Responds to pishing sound or imitations of Eastern Screech-Owl by coming close, flicking wings, raising crest, and raising and lowering tail. Often slightly raises and lowers tail upon landing. Sometimes hovers above food on branch or foliage and picks it off with beak. Forages on ground for various insects, insect larvae, and other small invertebrates, including earthworms and snails. Also eats berries and some fruit, especially in autumn migration and winter.

• **BREEDING** Monogamous. Solitary nester.

• **NESTING** Incubation 12–13 days by female. Altrical young remain in nest 12 days; brooded by female, fed by both sexes. 2–3 broods per year.

• **POPULATION** Fairly common. Breeding range is extending southward in southern Appalachians.

• **CONSERVATION** Neotropical migrant. Uncommon host to cowbirds.

Similar Birds

VEERY
Reddish brown upperparts; lacks dark spotting on breast; inconspicuous eye ring; different voice.

WOOD THRUSH
Reddish brown upperparts; brightest on crown and nape; heavy black spotting on underparts; different voice.

Flight Pattern

Rather swift direct flight with rapid wing beats. Sometimes hovers briefly over prey before dipping to pick it up.

Nest Identification

Shape ⬤   Location ▬ ⬤ ⬤

Weeds, rotted wood, twigs, mud, and other fine materials • lined with moss and grass • on ground or low on branch of tree 0–8 feet above ground • occasionally nests in rafters of mountain buildings • built by female • 3–6 greenish blue eggs usually unmarked but sometimes with black flecks; oval to short oval, 0.8 x 0.6 inches.

Plumage Sexes similar	Habitat 🌲 🌿 🐾	Migration Most migrate	Weight 1.1 ounces

DATE _____ TIME _____ LOCATION _____

| Family TURDIDAE | Species *Hylocichla mustelina* | Length 7.75–8 inches | Wingspan 13–14 inches |

WOOD THRUSH

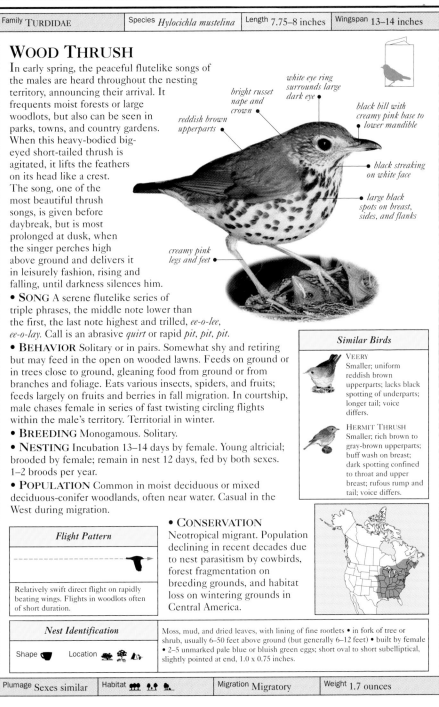

In early spring, the peaceful flutelike songs of the males are heard throughout the nesting territory, announcing their arrival. It frequents moist forests or large woodlots, but also can be seen in parks, towns, and country gardens. When this heavy-bodied big-eyed short-tailed thrush is agitated, it lifts the feathers on its head like a crest. The song, one of the most beautiful thrush songs, is given before daybreak, but is most prolonged at dusk, when the singer perches high above ground and delivers it in leisurely fashion, rising and falling, until darkness silences him.

white eye ring surrounds large dark eye

bright russet nape and crown

reddish brown upperparts

black bill with creamy pink base to lower mandible

black streaking on white face

large black spots on breast, sides, and flanks

creamy pink legs and feet

• **SONG** A serene flutelike series of triple phrases, the middle note lower than the first, the last note highest and trilled, *ee-o-lee, ee-o-lay.* Call is an abrasive *quirt* or rapid *pit, pit, pit.*

• **BEHAVIOR** Solitary or in pairs. Somewhat shy and retiring but may feed in the open on wooded lawns. Feeds on ground or in trees close to ground, gleaning food from ground or from branches and foliage. Eats various insects, spiders, and fruits; feeds largely on fruits and berries in fall migration. In courtship, male chases female in series of fast twisting circling flights within the male's territory. Territorial in winter.

• **BREEDING** Monogamous. Solitary.

• **NESTING** Incubation 13–14 days by female. Young altricial; brooded by female; remain in nest 12 days, fed by both sexes. 1–2 broods per year.

• **POPULATION** Common in moist deciduous or mixed deciduous-conifer woodlands, often near water. Casual in the West during migration.

Similar Birds

VEERY
Smaller; uniform reddish brown upperparts; lacks black spotting of underparts; longer tail; voice differs.

HERMIT THRUSH
Smaller; rich brown to gray-brown upperparts; buff wash on breast; dark spotting confined to throat and upper breast; rufous rump and tail; voice differs.

• **CONSERVATION** Neotropical migrant. Population declining in recent decades due to nest parasitism by cowbirds, forest fragmentation on breeding grounds, and habitat loss on wintering grounds in Central America.

Flight Pattern

Relatively swift direct flight on rapidly beating wings. Flights in woodlots often of short duration.

Nest Identification

Shape ☕   Location 🌳 🌿 🐦

Moss, mud, and dried leaves, with lining of fine rootlets • in fork of tree or shrub, usually 6–50 feet above ground (but generally 6–12 feet) • built by female • 2–5 unmarked pale blue or bluish green eggs; short oval to short subelliptical, slightly pointed at end, 1.0 x 0.75 inches.

| Plumage Sexes similar | Habitat 🌲 🌿 🌳 | Migration Migratory | Weight 1.7 ounces |

DATE _____ TIME_____ LOCATION _____

Family TURDIDAE	Species *Turdus obscurus*	Length 8.5 inches	Wingspan 12.5 inches

EYEBROWED THRUSH

Vagrants of this Asian thrush occasionally find their way to North America and have been recorded in northern Alaska, the western Aleutians, and the Pribilofs. It is a regular visitor each spring on the outer Aleutians. Females are similar to males but have a white throat with black streaking and are browner and duller overall.

• **SONG** Call is a high-pitched drawling *dzee*.

• **BEHAVIOR** Solitary or in pairs. Flocks in migration and winter. Relatively tame. Frequents mixed forests of birches, larches, and conifers, especially along water.

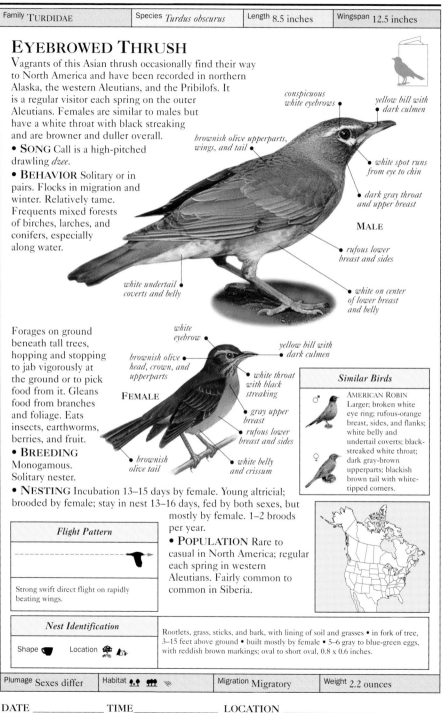

conspicuous white eyebrows

yellow bill with dark culmen

brownish olive upperparts, wings, and tail

white spot runs from eye to chin

dark gray throat and upper breast

MALE

rufous lower breast and sides

white undertail coverts and belly

white on center of lower breast and belly

Forages on ground beneath tall trees, hopping and stopping to jab vigorously at the ground or to pick food from it. Gleans food from branches and foliage. Eats insects, earthworms, berries, and fruit.

• **BREEDING** Monogamous. Solitary nester.

white eyebrow

brownish olive head, crown, and upperparts

FEMALE

yellow bill with dark culmen

white throat with black streaking

gray upper breast

rufous lower breast and sides

brownish olive tail

white belly and crissum

Similar Birds

AMERICAN ROBIN
Larger; broken white eye ring; rufous-orange breast, sides, and flanks; white belly and undertail coverts; black-streaked white throat; dark gray-brown upperparts; blackish brown tail with white-tipped corners.

• **NESTING** Incubation 13–15 days by female. Young altricial; brooded by female; stay in nest 13–16 days, fed by both sexes, but mostly by female. 1–2 broods per year.

• **POPULATION** Rare to casual in North America; regular each spring in western Aleutians. Fairly common to common in Siberia.

Flight Pattern
Strong swift direct flight on rapidly beating wings.

Nest Identification	
Shape	Location	Rootlets, grass, sticks, and bark, with lining of soil and grasses • in fork of tree, 3–15 feet above ground • built mostly by female • 5–6 gray to blue-green eggs, with reddish brown markings; oval to short oval, 0.8 x 0.6 inches.

Plumage Sexes differ	Habitat	Migration Migratory	Weight 2.2 ounces

DATE _____ TIME_____ LOCATION _____

Family TURDIDAE	Species *Turdus naumanni*	Length 9.5 inches	Wingspan 14.75–16.5 inches

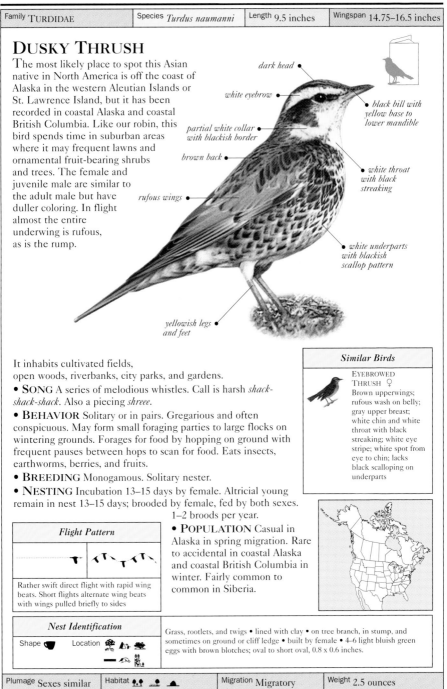

DUSKY THRUSH

The most likely place to spot this Asian native in North America is off the coast of Alaska in the western Aleutian Islands or St. Lawrence Island, but it has been recorded in coastal Alaska and coastal British Columbia. Like our robin, this bird spends time in suburban areas where it may frequent lawns and ornamental fruit-bearing shrubs and trees. The female and juvenile male are similar to the adult male but have duller coloring. In flight almost the entire underwing is rufous, as is the rump.

dark head •

• white eyebrow

• black bill with yellow base to lower mandible

partial white collar • with blackish border

brown back •

rufous wings •

• white throat with black streaking

• white underparts with blackish scallop pattern

• yellowish legs and feet

It inhabits cultivated fields, open woods, riverbanks, city parks, and gardens.

• **SONG** A series of melodious whistles. Call is harsh *shack-shack-shack*. Also a piecing *shreee*.

• **BEHAVIOR** Solitary or in pairs. Gregarious and often conspicuous. May form small foraging parties to large flocks on wintering grounds. Forages for food by hopping on ground with frequent pauses between hops to scan for food. Eats insects, earthworms, berries, and fruits.

• **BREEDING** Monogamous. Solitary nester.

• **NESTING** Incubation 13–15 days by female. Altricial young remain in nest 13–15 days; brooded by female, fed by both sexes. 1–2 broods per year.

• **POPULATION** Casual in Alaska in spring migration. Rare to accidental in coastal Alaska and coastal British Columbia in winter. Fairly common to common in Siberia.

Similar Birds

EYEBROWED THRUSH ♀
Brown upperwings; rufous wash on belly; gray upper breast; white chin and white throat with black streaking; white eye stripe; white spot from eye to chin; lacks black scalloping on underparts

Flight Pattern

Rather swift direct flight with rapid wing beats. Short flights alternate wing beats with wings pulled briefly to sides

Nest Identification

Shape ⌣   Location 🌿 🌳 🌲 — 🍃 🌳

Grass, rootlets, and twigs • lined with clay • on tree branch, in stump, and sometimes on ground or cliff ledge • built by female • 4–6 light bluish green eggs with brown blotches; oval to short oval, 0.8 x 0.6 inches.

Plumage Sexes similar	Habitat 🌾 🌿 🌲	Migration Migratory	Weight 2.5 ounces

DATE _____ TIME_____ LOCATION _____

Family TURDIDAE	Species *Turdus pilaris*	Length 10 inches	Wingspan 15–16 inches

FIELDFARE

In 1937 a flock of these European birds was migrating from Norway toward Britain when a storm blew them across the Atlantic Ocean; they made landfall in Greenland. A small but thriving nesting population has survived there, and vagrants sometimes make their way to Alaska and the northeastern part of North America. The Fieldfare differs from other thrushes by its gray head and rump contrasting with a rufous-brown back and black tail. In flight the underwing linings show white.

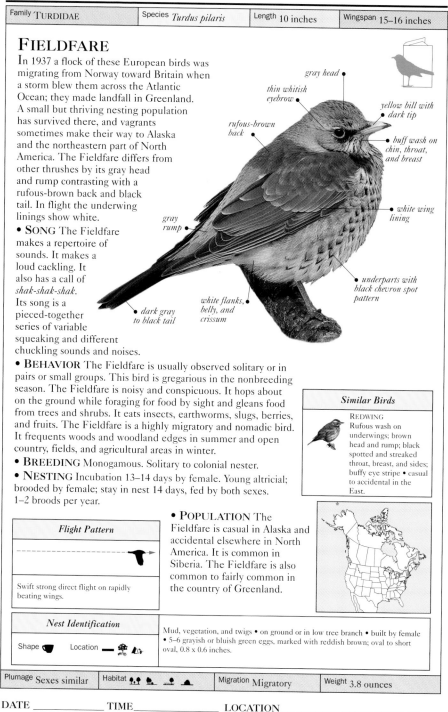

gray head

thin whitish eyebrow

rufous-brown back

yellow bill with dark tip

buff wash on chin, throat, and breast

white wing lining

gray rump

underparts with black chevron spot pattern

dark gray to black tail

white flanks, belly, and crissum

- **SONG** The Fieldfare makes a repertoire of sounds. It makes a loud cackling. It also has a call of *shak-shak-shak*. Its song is a pieced-together series of variable squeaking and different chuckling sounds and noises.
- **BEHAVIOR** The Fieldfare is usually observed solitary or in pairs or small groups. This bird is gregarious in the nonbreeding season. The Fieldfare is noisy and conspicuous. It hops about on the ground while foraging for food by sight and gleans food from trees and shrubs. It eats insects, earthworms, slugs, berries, and fruits. The Fieldfare is a highly migratory and nomadic bird. It frequents woods and woodland edges in summer and open country, fields, and agricultural areas in winter.
- **BREEDING** Monogamous. Solitary to colonial nester.
- **NESTING** Incubation 13–14 days by female. Young altricial; brooded by female; stay in nest 14 days, fed by both sexes. 1–2 broods per year.

Similar Birds

REDWING
Rufous wash on underwings; brown head and rump; black spotted and streaked throat, breast, and sides; buffy eye stripe • casual to accidental in the East.

- **POPULATION** The Fieldfare is casual in Alaska and accidental elsewhere in North America. It is common in Siberia. The Fieldfare is also common to fairly common in the country of Greenland.

Flight Pattern

Swift strong direct flight on rapidly beating wings.

Nest Identification

Shape | Location

Mud, vegetation, and twigs • on ground or in low tree branch • built by female • 5–6 grayish or bluish green eggs, marked with reddish brown; oval to short oval, 0.8 x 0.6 inches.

Plumage Sexes similar	Habitat	Migration Migratory	Weight 3.8 ounces

DATE _____ TIME_____ LOCATION _____

Family TURDIDAE	Species *Turdus rufopalliatus*	Length 9.5 inches	Wingspan 14.75–16.5 inches

RUFOUS-BACKED ROBIN

This native of Mexico is a casual but regular visitor to the Southwest. It is difficult to spot, however, because it frequents more dense forests and shrubs than the American Robin. It often forages in the treetops as well as on the ground. The female is similar to the male but has duller coloring. The juvenile has whitish to cinnamon underparts spotted with dark brown, a brown rump, and brown uppertail coverts.

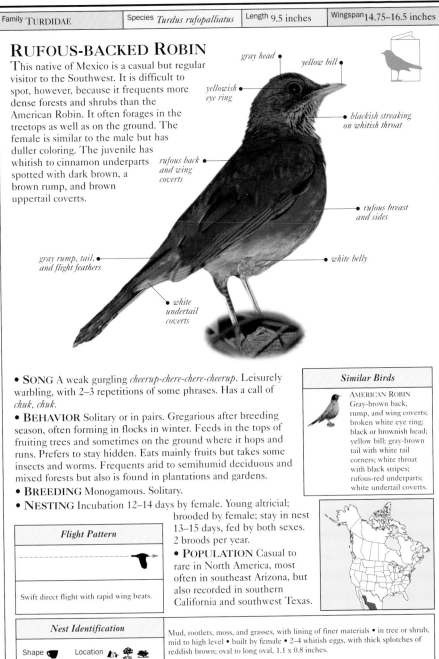

gray head

yellow bill

yellowish eye ring

blackish streaking on whitish throat

rufous back and wing coverts

rufous breast and sides

gray rump, tail, and flight feathers

white belly

white undertail coverts

- **SONG** A weak gurgling *cheerup-chere-chere-cheerup*. Leisurely warbling, with 2–3 repetitions of some phrases. Has a call of *chuk, chuk.*
- **BEHAVIOR** Solitary or in pairs. Gregarious after breeding season, often forming in flocks in winter. Feeds in the tops of fruiting trees and sometimes on the ground where it hops and runs. Prefers to stay hidden. Eats mainly fruits but takes some insects and worms. Frequents arid to semihumid deciduous and mixed forests but also is found in plantations and gardens.
- **BREEDING** Monogamous. Solitary.
- **NESTING** Incubation 12–14 days by female. Young altricial; brooded by female; stay in nest 13–15 days, fed by both sexes. 2 broods per year.
- **POPULATION** Casual to rare in North America, most often in southeast Arizona, but also recorded in southern California and southwest Texas.

Similar Birds

AMERICAN ROBIN
Gray-brown back, rump, and wing coverts; broken white eye ring; black or brownish head; yellow bill; gray-brown tail with white tail corners; white throat with black stripes; rufous-red underparts; white undertail coverts.

Flight Pattern

Swift direct flight with rapid wing beats.

Nest Identification

Shape

Location

Mud, rootlets, moss, and grasses, with lining of finer materials • in tree or shrub, mid to high level • built by female • 2–4 whitish eggs, with thick splotches of reddish brown; oval to long oval, 1.1 x 0.8 inches.

Plumage Sexes similar	Habitat	Migration Nonmigratory	Weight 2.7 ounces

DATE _____ TIME_____ LOCATION _____

Family TURDIDAE	Species *Turdus migratorius*	Length 10 inches	Wingspan 14–16 inches

AMERICAN ROBIN

In many areas this bird is considered a sign of spring, though it is a year-round resident in most of its US range. It is among the most common, widely distributed, and most well-known birds in North America. Juveniles are similar to adults but have heavily spotted underparts and white spotting and edging on the back and shoulders.

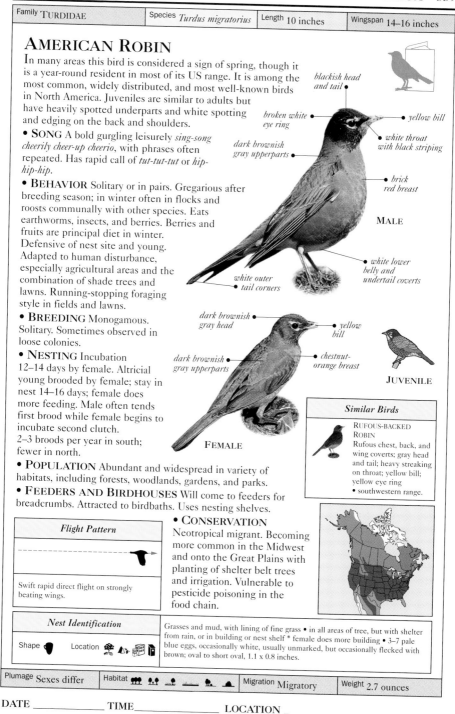

blackish head and tail

broken white eye ring

dark brownish gray upperparts

yellow bill

white throat with black striping

brick red breast

MALE

- **SONG** A bold gurgling leisurely *sing-song cheerily cheer-up cheerio*, with phrases often repeated. Has rapid call of *tut-tut-tut* or *hip-hip-hip*.

- **BEHAVIOR** Solitary or in pairs. Gregarious after breeding season; in winter often in flocks and roosts communally with other species. Eats earthworms, insects, and berries. Berries and fruits are principal diet in winter. Defensive of nest site and young. Adapted to human disturbance, especially agricultural areas and the combination of shade trees and lawns. Running-stopping foraging style in fields and lawns.

- **BREEDING** Monogamous. Solitary. Sometimes observed in loose colonies.

- **NESTING** Incubation 12–14 days by female. Altricial young brooded by female; stay in nest 14–16 days; female does more feeding. Male often tends first brood while female begins to incubate second clutch. 2–3 broods per year in south; fewer in north.

white outer tail corners

white lower belly and undertail coverts

dark brownish gray head

dark brownish gray upperparts

yellow bill

chestnut-orange breast

JUVENILE

FEMALE

- **POPULATION** Abundant and widespread in variety of habitats, including forests, woodlands, gardens, and parks.

- **FEEDERS AND BIRDHOUSES** Will come to feeders for breadcrumbs. Attracted to birdbaths. Uses nesting shelves.

Similar Birds

RUFOUS-BACKED ROBIN Rufous chest, back, and wing coverts; gray head and tail; heavy streaking on throat; yellow bill; yellow eye ring • southwestern range.

Flight Pattern
Swift rapid direct flight on strongly beating wings.

- **CONSERVATION** Neotropical migrant. Becoming more common in the Midwest and onto the Great Plains with planting of shelter belt trees and irrigation. Vulnerable to pesticide poisoning in the food chain.

Nest Identification	
Shape	Location	Grasses and mud, with lining of fine grass • in all areas of tree, but with shelter from rain, or in building or nest shelf * female does more building • 3–7 pale blue eggs, occasionally white, usually unmarked, but occasionally flecked with brown; oval to short oval, 1.1 x 0.8 inches.

Plumage Sexes differ	Habitat	Migration Migratory	Weight 2.7 ounces

DATE _____ TIME _____ LOCATION _____

Family TURDIDAE	Species *Ixoreus naevius*	Length 9.5 inches	Wingspan 14–16 inches

VARIED THRUSH

This uniquely colored thrush, unlike the American Robin, frequents dense damp coniferous and deciduous forests and undergrowth as well as suburban lawns. It usually feeds and spends time on the ground, except when the male perches to sing his somewhat eerie song. One of the most strikingly colored thrushes, it has orange underparts, wing bars, and eyebrows. Females have a dusky brown cast to the upperparts and a dusky brown breast band. Juveniles are similar to the female but have a scaly appearance to the neck and breast and have white underparts.

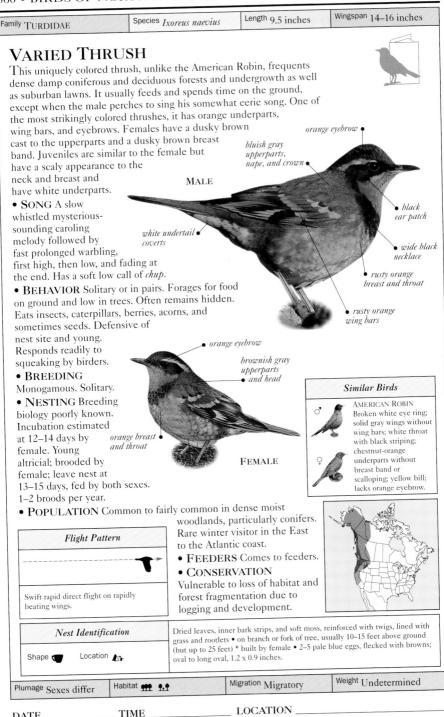

orange eyebrow

bluish gray upperparts, nape, and crown

MALE

black ear patch

white undertail coverts

wide black necklace

rusty orange breast and throat

rusty orange wing bars

orange eyebrow

brownish gray upperparts and head

orange breast and throat

FEMALE

• **SONG** A slow whistled mysterious-sounding caroling melody followed by fast prolonged warbling, first high, then low, and fading at the end. Has a soft low call of *chup*.

• **BEHAVIOR** Solitary or in pairs. Forages for food on ground and low in trees. Often remains hidden. Eats insects, caterpillars, berries, acorns, and sometimes seeds. Defensive of nest site and young. Responds readily to squeaking by birders.

• **BREEDING** Monogamous. Solitary.

• **NESTING** Breeding biology poorly known. Incubation estimated at 12–14 days by female. Young altricial; brooded by female; leave nest at 13–15 days, fed by both sexes. 1–2 broods per year.

• **POPULATION** Common to fairly common in dense moist woodlands, particularly conifers. Rare winter visitor in the East to the Atlantic coast.

• **FEEDERS** Comes to feeders.

• **CONSERVATION** Vulnerable to loss of habitat and forest fragmentation due to logging and development.

Similar Birds

♂ ♀ AMERICAN ROBIN Broken white eye ring; solid gray wings without wing bars; white throat with black striping; chestnut-orange underparts without breast band or scalloping; yellow bill; lacks orange eyebrow.

Flight Pattern

Swift rapid direct flight on rapidly beating wings.

Nest Identification	
Shape Location	Dried leaves, inner bark strips, and soft moss, reinforced with twigs, lined with grass and rootlets • on branch or fork of tree, usually 10–15 feet above ground (but up to 25 feet) • built by female • 2–5 pale blue eggs, flecked with browns; oval to long oval, 1.2 x 0.9 inches.

Plumage Sexes differ	Habitat	Migration Migratory	Weight Undetermined

DATE _____ TIME_____ LOCATION _____

Family TURDIDAE	Species *Ridgwayia pinicola*	Length 9.5 inches	Wingspan 14–16 inches

AZTEC THRUSH

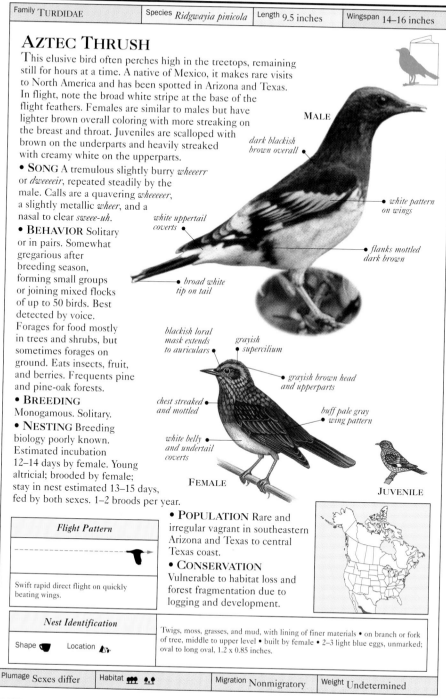

This elusive bird often perches high in the treetops, remaining still for hours at a time. A native of Mexico, it makes rare visits to North America and has been spotted in Arizona and Texas. In flight, note the broad white stripe at the base of the flight feathers. Females are similar to males but have lighter brown overall coloring with more streaking on the breast and throat. Juveniles are scalloped with brown on the underparts and heavily streaked with creamy white on the upperparts.

- **SONG** A tremulous slightly burry *wheeerr* or *dweeeeir*, repeated steadily by the male. Calls are a quavering *wheeeeer*, a slightly metallic *wheer*, and a nasal to clear *sweee-uh*.

- **BEHAVIOR** Solitary or in pairs. Somewhat gregarious after breeding season, forming small groups or joining mixed flocks of up to 50 birds. Best detected by voice. Forages for food mostly in trees and shrubs, but sometimes forages on ground. Eats insects, fruit, and berries. Frequents pine and pine-oak forests.

- **BREEDING** Monogamous. Solitary.

- **NESTING** Breeding biology poorly known. Estimated incubation 12–14 days by female. Young altricial; brooded by female; stay in nest estimated 13–15 days, fed by both sexes. 1–2 broods per year.

- **POPULATION** Rare and irregular vagrant in southeastern Arizona and Texas to central Texas coast.

- **CONSERVATION** Vulnerable to habitat loss and forest fragmentation due to logging and development.

MALE

dark blackish brown overall

white pattern on wings

flanks mottled dark brown

white uppertail coverts

broad white tip on tail

blackish loral mask extends to auriculars

grayish supercilium

grayish brown head and upperparts

chest streaked and mottled

buff pale gray wing pattern

white belly and undertail coverts

FEMALE

JUVENILE

Flight Pattern
Swift rapid direct flight on quickly beating wings.

Nest Identification	
Shape	Location	Twigs, moss, grasses, and mud, with lining of finer materials • on branch or fork of tree, middle to upper level • built by female • 2–3 light blue eggs, unmarked; oval to long oval, 1.2 x 0.85 inches.

Plumage Sexes differ	Habitat	Migration Nonmigratory	Weight Undetermined

DATE _____ TIME _____ LOCATION _____

Family TIMALIIDAE	Species *Chamaea fasciata*	Length 6.5 inches	Wingspan 9.75 inches

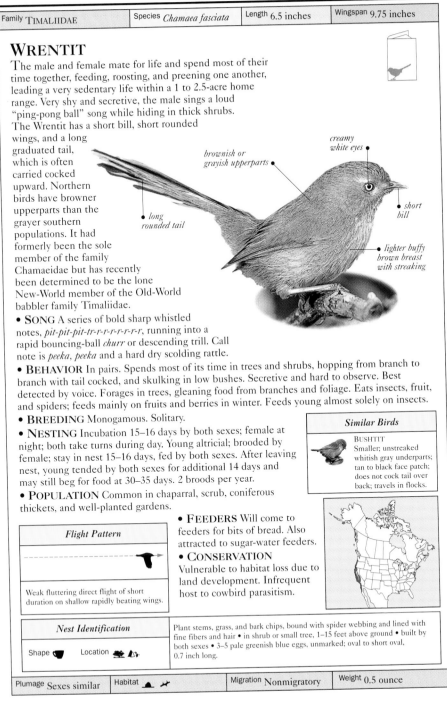

WRENTIT

The male and female mate for life and spend most of their time together, feeding, roosting, and preening one another, leading a very sedentary life within a 1 to 2.5-acre home range. Very shy and secretive, the male sings a loud "ping-pong ball" song while hiding in thick shrubs. The Wrentit has a short bill, short rounded wings, and a long graduated tail, which is often carried cocked upward. Northern birds have browner upperparts than the grayer southern populations. It had formerly been the sole member of the family Chamaeidae but has recently been determined to be the lone New-World member of the Old-World babbler family Timaliidae.

creamy white eyes

brownish or grayish upperparts

short bill

long rounded tail

lighter buffy brown breast with streaking

- **SONG** A series of bold sharp whistled notes, *pit-pit-pit-tr-r-r-r-r-r-r-r*, running into a rapid bouncing-ball *churr* or descending trill. Call note is *peeka, peeka* and a hard dry scolding rattle.
- **BEHAVIOR** In pairs. Spends most of its time in trees and shrubs, hopping from branch to branch with tail cocked, and skulking in low bushes. Secretive and hard to observe. Best detected by voice. Forages in trees, gleaning food from branches and foliage. Eats insects, fruit, and spiders; feeds mainly on fruits and berries in winter. Feeds young almost solely on insects.
- **BREEDING** Monogamous. Solitary.
- **NESTING** Incubation 15–16 days by both sexes; female at night; both take turns during day. Young altricial; brooded by female; stay in nest 15–16 days, fed by both sexes. After leaving nest, young tended by both sexes for additional 14 days and may still beg for food at 30–35 days. 2 broods per year.
- **POPULATION** Common in chaparral, scrub, coniferous thickets, and well-planted gardens.

Similar Birds
BUSHTIT Smaller; unstreaked whitish gray underparts; tan to black face patch; does not cock tail over back; travels in flocks.

- **FEEDERS** Will come to feeders for bits of bread. Also attracted to sugar-water feeders.
- **CONSERVATION** Vulnerable to habitat loss due to land development. Infrequent host to cowbird parasitism.

Flight Pattern
Weak fluttering direct flight of short duration on shallow rapidly beating wings.

Nest Identification	Plant stems, grass, and bark chips, bound with spider webbing and lined with fine fibers and hair • in shrub or small tree, 1–15 feet above ground • built by both sexes • 3–5 pale greenish blue eggs, unmarked; oval to short oval, 0.7 inch long.
Shape 🥄 Location 🪹 🌿	

Plumage Sexes similar	Habitat 🌲 ✈	Migration Nonmigratory	Weight 0.5 ounce

DATE _____ TIME_____ LOCATION _____

| Family MIMIDAE | Species *Dumetella carolinensis* | Length 8.5–9 inches | Wingspan 11–12 inches |

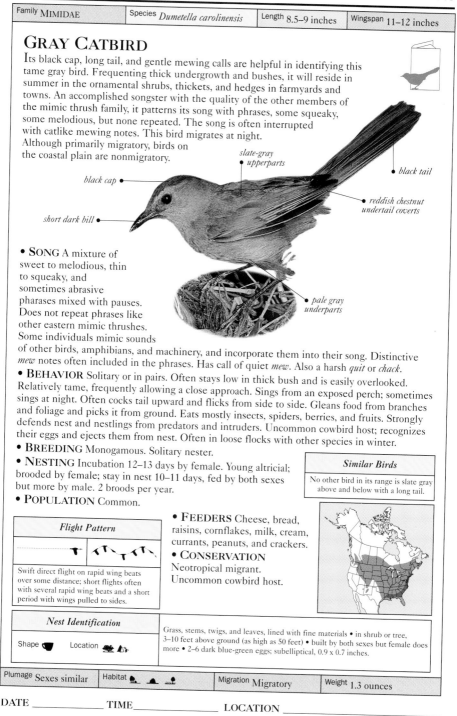

GRAY CATBIRD

Its black cap, long tail, and gentle mewing calls are helpful in identifying this tame gray bird. Frequenting thick undergrowth and bushes, it will reside in summer in the ornamental shrubs, thickets, and hedges in farmyards and towns. An accomplished songster with the quality of the other members of the mimic thrush family, it patterns its song with phrases, some squeaky, some melodious, but none repeated. The song is often interrupted with catlike mewing notes. This bird migrates at night. Although primarily migratory, birds on the coastal plain are nonmigratory.

slate-gray upperparts

black cap

black tail

reddish chestnut undertail coverts

short dark bill

• **SONG** A mixture of sweet to melodious, thin to squeaky, and sometimes abrasive phrases mixed with pauses. Does not repeat phrases like other eastern mimic thrushes. Some individuals mimic sounds

pale gray underparts

of other birds, amphibians, and machinery, and incorporate them into their song. Distinctive *mew* notes often included in the phrases. Has call of quiet *mew*. Also a harsh *quit* or *chack*.
• **BEHAVIOR** Solitary or in pairs. Often stays low in thick bush and is easily overlooked. Relatively tame, frequently allowing a close approach. Sings from an exposed perch; sometimes sings at night. Often cocks tail upward and flicks from side to side. Gleans food from branches and foliage and picks it from ground. Eats mostly insects, spiders, berries, and fruits. Strongly defends nest and nestlings from predators and intruders. Uncommon cowbird host; recognizes their eggs and ejects them from nest. Often in loose flocks with other species in winter.
• **BREEDING** Monogamous. Solitary nester.
• **NESTING** Incubation 12–13 days by female. Young altricial; brooded by female; stay in nest 10–11 days, fed by both sexes but more by male. 2 broods per year.
• **POPULATION** Common.

Similar Birds

No other bird in its range is slate gray above and below with a long tail.

• **FEEDERS** Cheese, bread, raisins, cornflakes, milk, cream, currants, peanuts, and crackers.
• **CONSERVATION** Neotropical migrant. Uncommon cowbird host.

Flight Pattern

Swift direct flight on rapid wing beats over some distance; short flights often with several rapid wing beats and a short period with wings pulled to sides.

Nest Identification

Shape Location

Grass, stems, twigs, and leaves, lined with fine materials • in shrub or tree, 3–10 feet above ground (as high as 50 feet) • built by both sexes but female does more • 2–6 dark blue-green eggs; subelliptical, 0.9 x 0.7 inches.

| Plumage Sexes similar | Habitat | Migration Migratory | Weight 1.3 ounces |

DATE _____ TIME_____ LOCATION _____

Family MIMIDAE	Species *Mimus polyglottos*	Length 10 inches	Wingspan 13–15 inches

NORTHERN MOCKINGBIRD

True to its scientific name, *polyglottos*, meaning "many tongued," this bird imitates dozens of other birds, as well as other animals, insects, machinery, and even musical instruments. Traditionally considered a southern bird, it has adapted to a wide range of habitats, from lush southern plantation gardens to dry cactus land. Although nonmigratory over most of its range, northernmost populations do migrate. When sparring with a rival or when in flight, the large white wing patches and the white outer tail feathers flash conspicuously. Juveniles have underparts spotted with gray-browns.

medium gray upperparts

2 white wing bars

short blackish bill

long blackish gray tail with white outer feathers

large white wing patches on blackish wings

gray-white underparts

- **SONG** Perches to sing a variety of original and imitative sounds, each repeated 3–5 (or more) times. Also has an evening "whisper song." Call is a bold abrasive *check*. Often flutters skyward while singing and tumbles back to perch. May sing well into the night or, on moonlit nights or under the glow of a security light, may sing all night.

JUVENILE

- **BEHAVIOR** Solitary or in pairs. Conspicuous. Forages on ground and in bushes and trees. Lifts wings straight up with a jerky snap to bring insects out of hiding. Eats various insects and fruit. Very defensive during breeding season, especially close to the nest or young. Will attack larger birds and mammals that come too near. Sexes defend separate winter feeding territory. Has adapted well to disturbed habitats created by man and thrives in suburbs, towns, villages, and farmlands.
- **BREEDING** Monogamous. Solitary nester. Long-term pair bonds. Males perform display where they face one another and hop sideways, trying to keep other birds out of territory.
- **NESTING** Incubation 12–13 days by female. Young altricial; brooded by female; stay in nest 11–13 days, fed by both sexes. 2–3 broods per year.

Similar Birds

BAHAMA MOCKINGBIRD
Larger; lacks white wing patches; browner upperparts; streaking on neck and flanks; white-tipped tail
• eastern range.

TOWNSEND'S SOLITAIRE
Darker gray; white eye ring; buff wing patches; shorter bill; white outer tail feathers.

- **POPULATION** Common. Range is expanding north, particularly to the Northeast. Casual north of the mapped distribution range, sometimes as far north as Alaska.
- **FEEDERS** Will come for bread, suet, and raisins.

Flight Pattern

Long flight is swift and strong on steadily beating wings. Shorter flights with several quick wing strokes alternated with wings pulled to sides; repeated.

Nest Identification

Shape ◥   Location 🌳🌳🌿

Sticks, stems, bits of fabric, dead leaves, and string, lined with finer materials • set in fork on branch of tree or shrub, usually 3–10 feet above ground • built by both sexes • 2–6 blue-green eggs, with splotches of brown; oval to short oval, occasionally short subelliptical, 1.0 x 0.8 inches.

Plumage Sexes similar	Habitat 🌿🌱🌊▫️🍃🌱	Migration Nonmigratory	Weight 1.7 ounces

DATE _____ TIME_____ LOCATION _____

Family MIMIDAE	Species *Oreoscoptes montanus*	Length 8.5 inches	Wingspan 11.5 inches

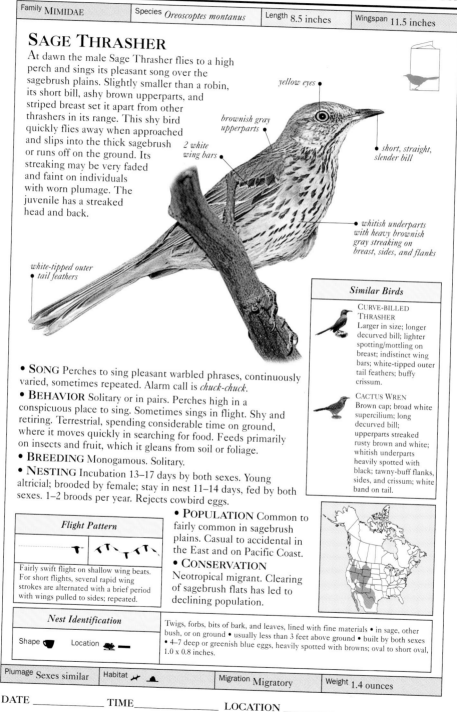

SAGE THRASHER

At dawn the male Sage Thrasher flies to a high perch and sings its pleasant song over the sagebrush plains. Slightly smaller than a robin, its short bill, ashy brown upperparts, and striped breast set it apart from other thrashers in its range. This shy bird quickly flies away when approached and slips into the thick sagebrush or runs off on the ground. Its streaking may be very faded and faint on individuals with worn plumage. The juvenile has a streaked head and back.

yellow eyes

brownish gray upperparts

2 white wing bars

short, straight, slender bill

whitish underparts with heavy brownish gray streaking on breast, sides, and flanks

white-tipped outer tail feathers

Similar Birds

CURVE-BILLED THRASHER
Larger in size; longer decurved bill; lighter spotting/mottling on breast; indistinct wing bars; white-tipped outer tail feathers; buffy crissum.

CACTUS WREN
Brown cap; broad white supercilium; long decurved bill; upperparts streaked rusty brown and white; whitish underparts heavily spotted with black; tawny-buff flanks, sides, and crissum; white band on tail.

• **SONG** Perches to sing pleasant warbled phrases, continuously varied, sometimes repeated. Alarm call is *chuck-chuck*.
• **BEHAVIOR** Solitary or in pairs. Perches high in a conspicuous place to sing. Sometimes sings in flight. Shy and retiring. Terrestrial, spending considerable time on ground, where it moves quickly in searching for food. Feeds primarily on insects and fruit, which it gleans from soil or foliage.
• **BREEDING** Monogamous. Solitary.
• **NESTING** Incubation 13–17 days by both sexes. Young altricial; brooded by female; stay in nest 11–14 days, fed by both sexes. 1–2 broods per year. Rejects cowbird eggs.

• **POPULATION** Common to fairly common in sagebrush plains. Casual to accidental in the East and on Pacific Coast.
• **CONSERVATION** Neotropical migrant. Clearing of sagebrush flats has led to declining population.

Flight Pattern

Fairly swift flight on shallow wing beats. For short flights, several rapid wing strokes are alternated with a brief period with wings pulled to sides; repeated.

Nest Identification

Shape ☕   Location 🪹 ▬

Twigs, forbs, bits of bark, and leaves, lined with fine materials • in sage, other bush, or on ground • usually less than 3 feet above ground • built by both sexes • 4–7 deep or greenish blue eggs, heavily spotted with browns; oval to short oval, 1.0 x 0.8 inches.

Plumage Sexes similar	Habitat 🌿 ⛰	Migration Migratory	Weight 1.4 ounces

DATE _____ TIME_____ LOCATION _____

Family MIMIDAE	Species *Toxostoma rufum*	Length 11.5 inches	Wingspan 12.5–14 inches

BROWN THRASHER

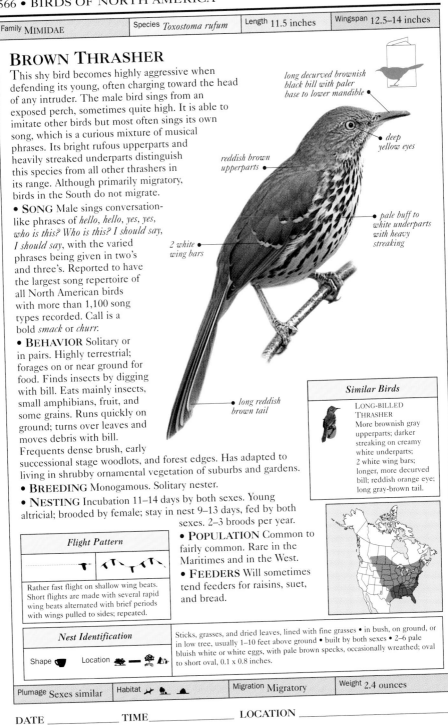

This shy bird becomes highly aggressive when defending its young, often charging toward the head of any intruder. The male bird sings from an exposed perch, sometimes quite high. It is able to imitate other birds but most often sings its own song, which is a curious mixture of musical phrases. Its bright rufous upperparts and heavily streaked underparts distinguish this species from all other thrashers in its range. Although primarily migratory, birds in the South do not migrate.

long decurved brownish black bill with paler base to lower mandible

deep yellow eyes

reddish brown upperparts

pale buff to white underparts with heavy streaking

2 white wing bars

• **SONG** Male sings conversation-like phrases of *hello, hello, yes, yes, who is this? Who is this? I should say, I should say,* with the varied phrases being given in two's and three's. Reported to have the largest song repertoire of all North American birds with more than 1,100 song types recorded. Call is a bold *smack* or *churr.*
• **BEHAVIOR** Solitary or in pairs. Highly terrestrial; forages on or near ground for food. Finds insects by digging with bill. Eats mainly insects, small amphibians, fruit, and some grains. Runs quickly on ground; turns over leaves and moves debris with bill. Frequents dense brush, early successional stage woodlots, and forest edges. Has adapted to living in shrubby ornamental vegetation of suburbs and gardens.
• **BREEDING** Monogamous. Solitary nester.
• **NESTING** Incubation 11–14 days by both sexes. Young altricial; brooded by female; stay in nest 9–13 days, fed by both sexes. 2–3 broods per year.

long reddish brown tail

Similar Birds

LONG-BILLED THRASHER More brownish gray upperparts; darker streaking on creamy white underparts; 2 white wing bars; longer, more decurved bill; reddish orange eye; long gray-brown tail.

• **POPULATION** Common to fairly common. Rare in the Maritimes and in the West.
• **FEEDERS** Will sometimes tend feeders for raisins, suet, and bread.

Flight Pattern

Rather fast flight on shallow wing beats. Short flights are made with several rapid wing beats alternated with brief periods with wings pulled to sides; repeated.

Nest Identification

Shape — Location

Sticks, grasses, and dried leaves, lined with fine grasses • in bush, on ground, or in low tree, usually 1–10 feet above ground • built by both sexes • 2–6 pale bluish white or white eggs, with pale brown specks, occasionally wreathed; oval to short oval, 0.1 x 0.8 inches.

Plumage Sexes similar	Habitat	Migration Migratory	Weight 2.4 ounces

DATE _____ TIME_____ LOCATION _____

Family MIMIDAE	Species *Toxostoma longirostre*	Length 11.5 inches	Wingspan 12.5–13.5 inches

LONG-BILLED THRASHER

This native of eastern Mexico and southern Texas is similar to the Brown Thrasher in habit and appearance, but it has a longer, more decurved bill. Its plumage is more gray, although the time of year and the extent of the bird's molt of the feathers also can affect color. Highly terrestrial, foraging on or near the ground, it flies to a high open perch to sing. This bird is most at home in the dense undergrowth of river-bottom forests but also is found in the cactus and mesquite of drier uplands.

• **SONG** Male perches to sing conversation-like phrases, similar to the Brown Thrasher, in doubles and triples. Various calls of *tsuck*, a soft *kleak*, and a bold flutelike *cheeooep*.

• **BEHAVIOR** Solitary or in pairs. Terrestrial. Somewhat shy, retreating when approached. Runs on ground; forages for food on ground and low in trees and shrubs. Often finds insects by digging in ground with bill. Eats mostly insects, small amphibians, and fruit. Maintains interspecific winter territories with Brown Thrasher when both are present.

• **BREEDING** Monogamous. Solitary.

• **NESTING** Incubation 13–14 days by both sexes. Altricial young brooded by female for just 2 days; leave nest at 12–14 days, fed by both sexes. 1–2 broods per year.

• **POPULATION** Common in brush and scrubland, bottomland willows, and dense forest habitat. Rare in western Texas. Accidental in New Mexico and Colorado.

• **CONSERVATION** Declining in southern Texas due to clearing of brushlands for development and agriculture. Common host to cowbird eggs.

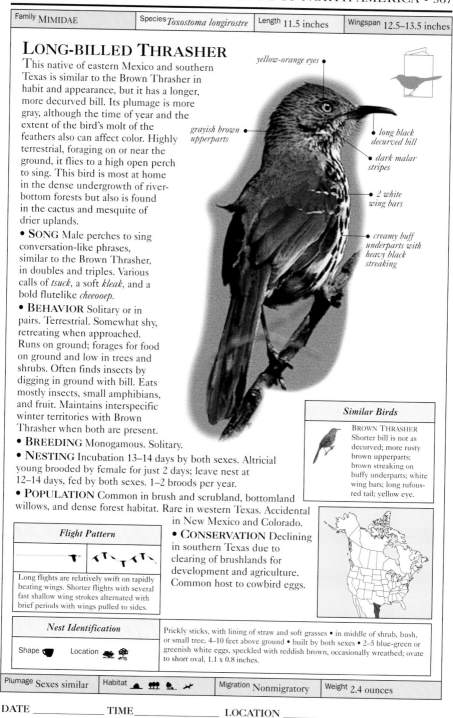

yellow-orange eyes

grayish brown upperparts

long black decurved bill

dark malar stripes

2 white wing bars

creamy buff underparts with heavy black streaking

Similar Birds

BROWN THRASHER Shorter bill is not as decurved; more rusty brown upperparts; brown streaking on buffy underparts; white wing bars; long rufous-red tail; yellow eye.

Flight Pattern

Long flights are relatively swift on rapidly beating wings. Shorter flights with several fast shallow wing strokes alternated with brief periods with wings pulled to sides.

Nest Identification

Shape ⬦   Location 🌿 🌳

Prickly sticks, with lining of straw and soft grasses • in middle of shrub, bush, or small tree, 4–10 feet above ground • built by both sexes • 2–5 blue-green or greenish white eggs, speckled with reddish brown, occasionally wreathed; ovate to short oval, 1.1 x 0.8 inches.

Plumage Sexes similar	Habitat	Migration Nonmigratory	Weight 2.4 ounces

DATE _____ TIME_____ LOCATION _____

Family MIMIDAE	Species *Toxostoma bendirei*	Length 9–10 inches	Wingspan 13–15 inches

BENDIRE'S THRASHER

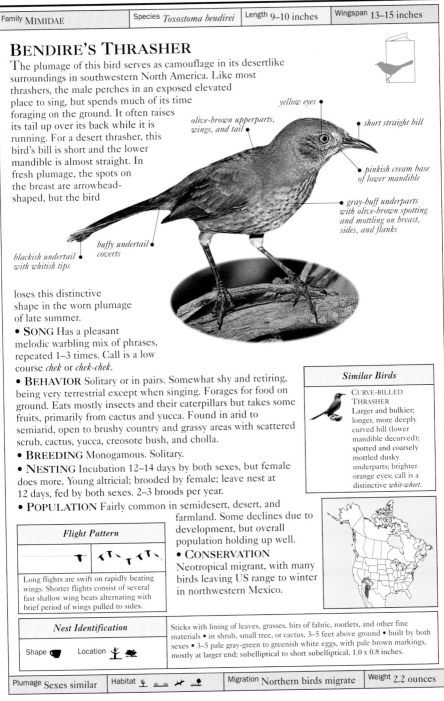

The plumage of this bird serves as camouflage in its desertlike surroundings in southwestern North America. Like most thrashers, the male perches in an exposed elevated place to sing, but spends much of its time foraging on the ground. It often raises its tail up over its back while it is running. For a desert thrasher, this bird's bill is short and the lower mandible is almost straight. In fresh plumage, the spots on the breast are arrowhead-shaped, but the bird

yellow eyes

olive-brown upperparts, wings, and tail

short straight bill

pinkish cream base of lower mandible

gray-buff underparts with olive-brown spotting and mottling on breast, sides, and flanks

blackish undertail with whitish tips

buffy undertail coverts

loses this distinctive shape in the worn plumage of late summer.

• **SONG** Has a pleasant melodic warbling mix of phrases, repeated 1–3 times. Call is a low course *chek* or *chek-chek*.

• **BEHAVIOR** Solitary or in pairs. Somewhat shy and retiring, being very terrestrial except when singing. Forages for food on ground. Eats mostly insects and their caterpillars but takes some fruits, primarily from cactus and yucca. Found in arid to semiarid, open to brushy country and grassy areas with scattered scrub, cactus, yucca, creosote bush, and cholla.

• **BREEDING** Monogamous. Solitary.

• **NESTING** Incubation 12–14 days by both sexes, but female does more. Young altricial; brooded by female; leave nest at 12 days, fed by both sexes. 2–3 broods per year.

• **POPULATION** Fairly common in semidesert, desert, and farmland. Some declines due to development, but overall population holding up well.

• **CONSERVATION** Neotropical migrant, with many birds leaving US range to winter in northwestern Mexico.

Similar Birds

CURVE-BILLED THRASHER
Larger and bulkier; longer, more deeply curved bill (lower mandible decurved); spotted and coarsely mottled dusky underparts; brighter orange eyes; call is a distinctive *whit-wheet*.

Flight Pattern

Long flights are swift on rapidly beating wings. Shorter flights consist of several fast shallow wing beats alternating with brief period of wings pulled to sides.

Nest Identification

Shape ☕ Location 🌱 🌲

Sticks with lining of leaves, grasses, bits of fabric, rootlets, and other fine materials • in shrub, small tree, or cactus, 3–5 feet above ground • built by both sexes • 3–5 pale gray-green to greenish white eggs, with pale brown markings, mostly at larger end; subelliptical to short subelliptical, 1.0 x 0.8 inches.

Plumage Sexes similar	Habitat 🌱 🌿 🌿 ✈ ⚓	Migration Northern birds migrate	Weight 2.2 ounces

DATE _____ TIME_____ LOCATION _____

Family MIMIDAE	Species *Toxostoma curvirostre*	Length 11 inches	Wingspan 14 inches

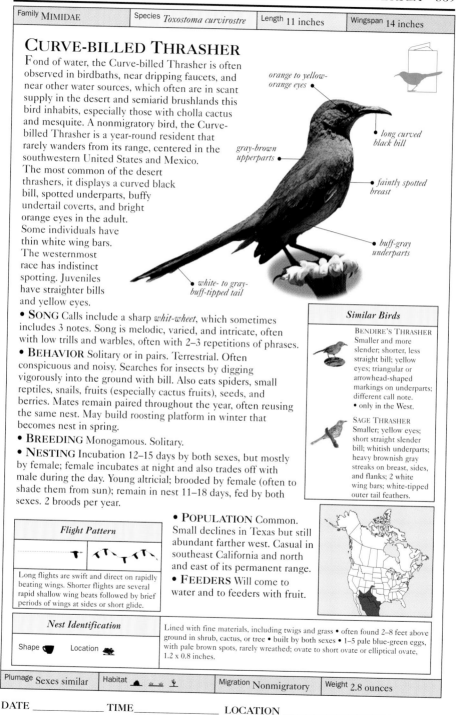

CURVE-BILLED THRASHER

Fond of water, the Curve-billed Thrasher is often observed in birdbaths, near dripping faucets, and near other water sources, which often are in scant supply in the desert and semiarid brushlands this bird inhabits, especially those with cholla cactus and mesquite. A nonmigratory bird, the Curve-billed Thrasher is a year-round resident that rarely wanders from its range, centered in the southwestern United States and Mexico. The most common of the desert thrashers, it displays a curved black bill, spotted underparts, buffy undertail coverts, and bright orange eyes in the adult. Some individuals have thin white wing bars. The westernmost race has indistinct spotting. Juveniles have straighter bills and yellow eyes.

orange to yellow-orange eyes

long curved black bill

gray-brown upperparts

faintly spotted breast

buff-gray underparts

white- to gray-buff-tipped tail

- **SONG** Calls include a sharp *whit-wheet*, which sometimes includes 3 notes. Song is melodic, varied, and intricate, often with low trills and warbles, often with 2–3 repetitions of phrases.
- **BEHAVIOR** Solitary or in pairs. Terrestrial. Often conspicuous and noisy. Searches by digging vigorously into the ground with bill. Also eats spiders, small reptiles, snails, fruits (especially cactus fruits), seeds, and berries. Mates remain paired throughout the year, often reusing the same nest. May build roosting platform in winter that becomes nest in spring.
- **BREEDING** Monogamous. Solitary.
- **NESTING** Incubation 12–15 days by both sexes, but mostly by female; female incubates at night and also trades off with male during the day. Young altricial; brooded by female (often to shade them from sun); remain in nest 11–18 days, fed by both sexes. 2 broods per year.

Similar Birds

BENDIRE'S THRASHER Smaller and more slender; shorter, less straight bill; yellow eyes; triangular or arrowhead-shaped markings on underparts; different call note.
- only in the West.

SAGE THRASHER Smaller; yellow eyes; short straight slender bill; whitish underparts; heavy brownish gray streaks on breast, sides, and flanks; 2 white wing bars; white-tipped outer tail feathers.

- **POPULATION** Common. Small declines in Texas but still abundant farther west. Casual in southeast California and north and east of its permanent range.
- **FEEDERS** Will come to water and to feeders with fruit.

Flight Pattern

Long flights are swift and direct on rapidly beating wings. Shorter flights are several rapid shallow wing beats followed by brief periods of wings at sides or short glide.

Nest Identification

Shape   Location

Lined with fine materials, including twigs and grass • often found 2–8 feet above ground in shrub, cactus, or tree • built by both sexes • 1–5 pale blue-green eggs, with pale brown spots, rarely wreathed; ovate to short ovate or elliptical ovate, 1.2 x 0.8 inches.

Plumage Sexes similar	Habitat	Migration Nonmigratory	Weight 2.8 ounces

DATE _____ TIME_____ LOCATION _____

Family MIMIDAE	Species *Toxostoma redivivum*	Length 11–13 inches	Wingspan 14–16 inches

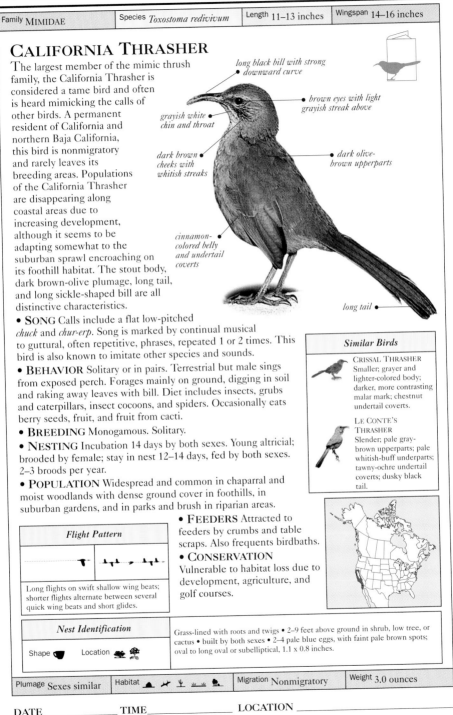

CALIFORNIA THRASHER

The largest member of the mimic thrush family, the California Thrasher is considered a tame bird and often is heard mimicking the calls of other birds. A permanent resident of California and northern Baja California, this bird is nonmigratory and rarely leaves its breeding areas. Populations of the California Thrasher are disappearing along coastal areas due to increasing development, although it seems to be adapting somewhat to the suburban sprawl encroaching on its foothill habitat. The stout body, dark brown-olive plumage, long tail, and long sickle-shaped bill are all distinctive characteristics.

long black bill with strong downward curve

brown eyes with light grayish streak above

grayish white chin and throat

dark brown cheeks with whitish streaks

dark olive-brown upperparts

cinnamon-colored belly and undertail coverts

long tail

• **SONG** Calls include a flat low-pitched *chuck* and *chur-erp*. Song is marked by continual musical to guttural, often repetitive, phrases, repeated 1 or 2 times. This bird is also known to imitate other species and sounds.

• **BEHAVIOR** Solitary or in pairs. Terrestrial but male sings from exposed perch. Forages mainly on ground, digging in soil and raking away leaves with bill. Diet includes insects, grubs and caterpillars, insect cocoons, and spiders. Occasionally eats berry seeds, fruit, and fruit from cacti.

• **BREEDING** Monogamous. Solitary.

• **NESTING** Incubation 14 days by both sexes. Young altricial; brooded by female; stay in nest 12–14 days, fed by both sexes. 2–3 broods per year.

• **POPULATION** Widespread and common in chaparral and moist woodlands with dense ground cover in foothills, in suburban gardens, and in parks and brush in riparian areas.

• **FEEDERS** Attracted to feeders by crumbs and table scraps. Also frequents birdbaths.

• **CONSERVATION** Vulnerable to habitat loss due to development, agriculture, and golf courses.

Similar Birds

CRISSAL THRASHER Smaller; grayer and lighter-colored body; darker, more contrasting malar mark; chestnut undertail coverts.

LE CONTE'S THRASHER Slender; pale gray-brown upperparts; pale whitish-buff underparts; tawny-ochre undertail coverts; dusky black tail.

Flight Pattern

Long flights on swift shallow wing beats; shorter flights alternate between several quick wing beats and short glides.

Nest Identification

Shape ◗ Location 🌿 🌳

Grass-lined with roots and twigs • 2–9 feet above ground in shrub, low tree, or cactus • built by both sexes • 2–4 pale blue eggs, with faint pale brown spots; oval to long oval or subelliptical, 1.1 x 0.8 inches.

Plumage Sexes similar	Habitat 🔺 ✈ ⚓ 🌾 🏠	Migration Nonmigratory	Weight 3.0 ounces

DATE _____ TIME_____ LOCATION _____

Family MIMIDAE	Species *Toxostoma crissale*	Length 11.5 inches	Wingspan 13.5 inches

CRISSAL THRASHER

A common resident of southwestern deserts, the Crissal Thrasher is shy and stays hidden in dense underbrush. Like other thrashers, the male sings a musical varied song, often delivered from a high perch, concealed in vegetation. The common name refers to the crissal area or crissum, the rich chestnut undertail coverts, which helps distinguish this thrasher from other thrashers, along with the

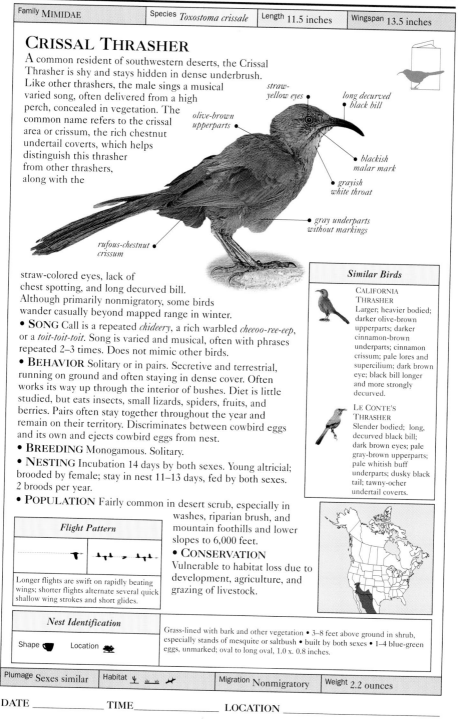

straw-yellow eyes

long decurved black bill

olive-brown upperparts

blackish malar mark

grayish white throat

gray underparts without markings

rufous-chestnut crissum

straw-colored eyes, lack of chest spotting, and long decurved bill. Although primarily nonmigratory, some birds wander casually beyond mapped range in winter.

• **SONG** Call is a repeated *chideery*, a rich warbled *cheeoo-ree-eep*, or a *toit-toit-toit*. Song is varied and musical, often with phrases repeated 2–3 times. Does not mimic other birds.

• **BEHAVIOR** Solitary or in pairs. Secretive and terrestrial, running on ground and often staying in dense cover. Often works its way up through the interior of bushes. Diet is little studied, but eats insects, small lizards, spiders, fruits, and berries. Pairs often stay together throughout the year and remain on their territory. Discriminates between cowbird eggs and its own and ejects cowbird eggs from nest.

• **BREEDING** Monogamous. Solitary.

• **NESTING** Incubation 14 days by both sexes. Young altricial; brooded by female; stay in nest 11–13 days, fed by both sexes. 2 broods per year.

• **POPULATION** Fairly common in desert scrub, especially in washes, riparian brush, and mountain foothills and lower slopes to 6,000 feet.

• **CONSERVATION** Vulnerable to habitat loss due to development, agriculture, and grazing of livestock.

Similar Birds

CALIFORNIA THRASHER Larger; heavier bodied; darker olive-brown upperparts; darker cinnamon-brown underparts; cinnamon crissum; pale lores and supercilium; dark brown eye; black bill longer and more strongly decurved.

LE CONTE'S THRASHER Slender bodied; long, decurved black bill; dark brown eyes; pale gray-brown upperparts; pale whitish buff underparts; dusky black tail; tawny-ocher undertail coverts.

Flight Pattern

Longer flights are swift on rapidly beating wings; shorter flights alternate several quick shallow wing strokes and short glides.

Nest Identification

Shape ☕ Location 🌿

Grass-lined with bark and other vegetation • 3–8 feet above ground in shrub, especially stands of mesquite or saltbush • built by both sexes • 1–4 blue-green eggs, unmarked; oval to long oval, 1.0 x 0.8 inches.

Plumage Sexes similar	Habitat 🌱 🌾 🌾 ✈	Migration Nonmigratory	Weight 2.2 ounces

DATE _____ TIME_____ LOCATION _____

Family MIMIDAE	Species *Toxostoma lecontei*	Length 10–11 inches	Wingspan 12–13 inches

LE CONTE'S THRASHER

brown eyes

long decurved black bill

pale gray-brown upperparts

unmarked breast

slender body

tawny ocher undertail coverts

pale whitish buff underparts

dusky black tail

Most often inhabiting the hottest lowest deserts of the Southwest around sparse vegetation, Le Conte's Thrasher is distinguished by its pale plumage, the lightest in color among all the "curve-billed" thrashers and often closely matching the surrounding soils. Le Conte's Thrasher is identified by its pale gray-brown upperparts and buff-white underparts. A difficult bird to observe on the ground, it always seems to be running away with the dusky black tail cocked high, keeping the shrubbery between itself and the observer. Just after daylight, the male selects an exposed perch for singing, which offers the best opportunity for observation.

- **SONG** Calls include an ascending *tweep* or *ch-reeip*. Some of the shorter calls suggest a House Finch. Usually heard at dawn and dusk, song is a loud and musical warbling, somewhat robinlike, with some repeated phrases. Does not mimic.
- **BEHAVIOR** Solitary or in pairs. Terrestrial, shy, and elusive. Digs into ground and turns over vegetation and pebbles with bill. Eats insects, including their larvae; also feeds on spiders, fruits (especially of cactus), and berries. Runs rapidly on ground with dark tail held high.
- **BREEDING** Monogamous. Solitary.
- **NESTING** Incubation 15 days by both sexes. Young altricial; brooded by female; stay in nest 13–17 days, fed by both sexes. 2–3 broods per year.

Similar Birds

CALIFORNIA THRASHER
Larger in size; darker stockier body; olive-brown upperparts; cinnamon-brown underparts; long heavy decurved bill; tawny buff undertail coverts.

CRISSAL THRASHER
Darker overall; straw-yellow eyes; rufous-chestnut crissum; dusky malar mark.

- **POPULATION** Uncommon in low desert scrub, especially with creosote bushes. Declining in areas where desert has been converted into farmland.
- **CONSERVATION** Vulnerable to habitat loss due to development and agriculture.

Flight Pattern

Short flights with shallow wing beats; sometimes alternates several quick wing beats with period of wings drawn to sides.

Nest Identification

Shape   Location

Lined with flower clusters, feathers, sticks, and twigs; unique double lining • 2–4 feet above ground in shrub • built by both sexes • 2–4 blue-green eggs, usually with pale brown spots at larger end; subelliptical to short subelliptical, 1.1 x 0.8 inches.

Plumage Sexes similar	Habitat ⚊ ↗	Migration Nonmigratory	Weight 2.2 ounces

DATE _____ TIME_____ LOCATION _____

Family STURNIDAE	Species *Sturnus vulgaris*	Length 8.5 inches	Wingspan 15.5 inches

EUROPEAN STARLING

This chunky Eurasian species was introduced to North America in 1890 in New York City's Central Park and has become so well established that large flocks have in some cases become a nuisance, roosting in cities and towns from coast to coast and north into Canada to the tree line. Tenacious in nature, this bird competes with native species such as woodpeckers, flycatchers, and bluebirds for nesting holes. This bird's winter plumage shows white specks and its yellow bill becomes a dull gray. Juveniles are sooty gray-brown overall with pale streaking on the underparts and a dull brown bill.

buffy tips and edging to feathers of back and mantle

short tail

long pointed yellow bill

black overall with iridescent sheen of purple and green

• **SONG** Sings various trilling melodies, clear whistles, clatters, and twitters in groups. Imitates songs of other birds, including Eastern Wood-Pewee and Northern Bobwhite, as well as mechanical sounds. Also has a flutelike *pheeEW*. Singing male often stands erect and flaps wings vigorously in display.

• **BEHAVIOR** Solitary or in pairs in breeding season. Juveniles form foraging flocks. Gregarious after breeding season, forming flocks with juveniles for foraging and roosting. Joins other species in winter roosts, which may number more than a million birds. Most often feeds in open areas, primarily on the ground. Eats various insects, fruits, and grains. The muscles that open its bill are stronger than those that close it, a unique trait that allows this bird to insert its bill in vegetation or into the ground and then pry it open to reveal food.

JUVENILE

• **BREEDING** Monogamous. Often forms loose colonies. Some individual males polygynous. Aggressive in claiming nesting chambers.

• **NESTING** Incubation 12–14 days by both sexes, but female does more. Young altricial; brooded by female; stay in nest 18–21 days, fed by both sexes. First flight at about 26 days. 2–3 broods per year.

• **POPULATION** Common. Stable over most of continent; perhaps still expanding range north and south.

Similar Birds

No native species of blackbird has yellow bill; short tail; chunky body; buffy streaking on back and wing coverts; and a notched tail.

• **FEEDERS AND BIRDHOUSES** Will come for bread, peanut butter, suet, and small seeds. Uses bluebird-sized or larger nest boxes.

• **CONSERVATION** Conservation laws in the US do not protect nongame, non-native species.

Flight Pattern

Strong swift direct flight on rapidly beating wings.

Nest Identification	Grass, twigs, forbs, rootlets, and straw • in natural hollow of tree, bird box, crevice in man-made structure, or abandoned woodpecker hole, 10–25 feet above ground (but up to 60 feet) • built by both sexes • 4–8 pale bluish or greenish white eggs, usually unmarked, but sometimes marked with browns; short oval to long oval, 1.2 x 0.8 inches.
Shape	
Location	

Plumage Sexes similar	Habitat	Migration Northern birds migrate	Weight 3.0 ounces

DATE _____ TIME_____ LOCATION _____

| Family STURNIDAE | Species *Acridotheres cristatellus* | Length 9.75–10.5 inches | Wingspan 16–18 inches |

CRESTED MYNA

Originally a native of Southeast Asia, this bird was introduced in Vancouver, British Columbia, in 1897, and its population rose to a few thousand birds in the 1920s. Today, it has declined to only a few hundred birds, perhaps due to the unsuitable climate and competition for nesting holes with recently arrived and expanding populations of the European Starling. The Crested Myna is a short-tailed starling with a stocky body set off by a white wing patch and short brushy crest. In flight the large white wing patches show in bold contrast to the glossy black body.

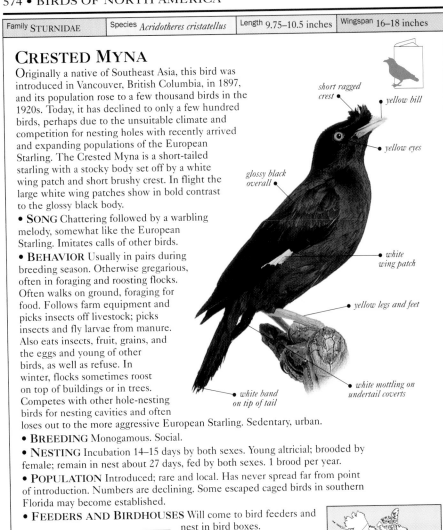

short ragged crest

yellow bill

yellow eyes

glossy black overall

white wing patch

yellow legs and feet

white mottling on undertail coverts

white band on tip of tail

• **SONG** Chattering followed by a warbling melody, somewhat like the European Starling. Imitates calls of other birds.

• **BEHAVIOR** Usually in pairs during breeding season. Otherwise gregarious, often in foraging and roosting flocks. Often walks on ground, foraging for food. Follows farm equipment and picks insects off livestock; picks insects and fly larvae from manure. Also eats insects, fruit, grains, and the eggs and young of other birds, as well as refuse. In winter, flocks sometimes roost on top of buildings or in trees. Competes with other hole-nesting birds for nesting cavities and often loses out to the more aggressive European Starling. Sedentary, urban.

• **BREEDING** Monogamous. Social.

• **NESTING** Incubation 14–15 days by both sexes. Young altricial; brooded by female; remain in nest about 27 days, fed by both sexes. 1 brood per year.

• **POPULATION** Introduced; rare and local. Has never spread far from point of introduction. Numbers are declining. Some escaped caged birds in southern Florida may become established.

• **FEEDERS AND BIRDHOUSES** Will come to bird feeders and nest in bird boxes.

• **CONSERVATION** Introduced species without the protections given to native species. Losing nesting cavities to other introduced species.

Flight Pattern
Swift direct flight with powerful rapid wing strokes.

Nest Identification	Grass, forbs, rootlets, paper, and snakeskin • in cavity of tree, bird box, or under eave of building • built by both sexes • 4–7 shiny greenish blue eggs; short oval to long oval, 1.2 inches long.
Shape	Location

| Plumage Sexes similar | Habitat | Migration Nonmigratory | Weight 4.0 ounces |

DATE _____ TIME_____ LOCATION _____

Family PRUNELLIDAE	Species *Prunella montanella*	Length 5.5 inches	Wingspan 9 inches

SIBERIAN ACCENTOR

Strays of this Eurasian species sometimes can be spotted in Alaska or along the northern Pacific coast of North America, usually in fall or winter. A shy bird, it stays hidden among dense coniferous trees and shrubs in the mountains, where it feeds on the ground. Note the rusty brown upperparts, grayish rump, and the tawny buff underparts

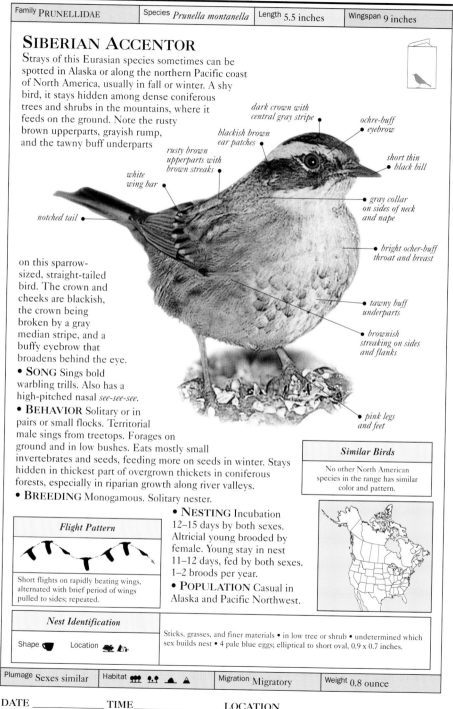

dark crown with central gray stripe

ochre-buff eyebrow

blackish brown ear patches

rusty brown upperparts with brown streaks

short thin black bill

white wing bar

gray collar on sides of neck and nape

notched tail

bright ocher-buff throat and breast

tawny buff underparts

brownish streaking on sides and flanks

pink legs and feet

on this sparrow-sized, straight-tailed bird. The crown and cheeks are blackish, the crown being broken by a gray median stripe, and a buffy eyebrow that broadens behind the eye.

• **SONG** Sings bold warbling trills. Also has a high-pitched nasal *see-see-see*.

• **BEHAVIOR** Solitary or in pairs or small flocks. Territorial male sings from treetops. Forages on ground and in low bushes. Eats mostly small invertebrates and seeds, feeding more on seeds in winter. Stays hidden in thickest part of overgrown thickets in coniferous forests, especially in riparian growth along river valleys.

• **BREEDING** Monogamous. Solitary nester.

• **NESTING** Incubation 12–15 days by both sexes. Altricial young brooded by female. Young stay in nest 11–12 days, fed by both sexes. 1–2 broods per year.

• **POPULATION** Casual in Alaska and Pacific Northwest.

Similar Birds

No other North American species in the range has similar color and pattern.

Flight Pattern

Short flights on rapidly beating wings, alternated with brief period of wings pulled to sides; repeated.

Nest Identification

Shape ◗   Location 🌿 🌳

Sticks, grasses, and finer materials • in low tree or shrub • undetermined which sex builds nest • 4 pale blue eggs; elliptical to short oval, 0.9 x 0.7 inches.

Plumage Sexes similar	Habitat 🌳 🌿 🏔 ⛰	Migration Migratory	Weight 0.8 ounce

DATE _____ TIME _____ LOCATION _____

Family MOTACILLIDAE	Species *Motacilla flava*	Length 6.5 inches	Wingspan 9 inches

YELLOW WAGTAIL

Primarily a Eurasian species, this bird is one of two wagtails that summer and nest in North America. It is a small sparrow-sized bird with a long tail, which it pumps up and down as it walks, and it frequents wet meadows and river banks, where it often perches on grass stems or trees. The white outer tail feathers are obvious in flight, as is the inner white bar on the wing. The female is similar to the male but duller in color. The juvenile has brownish upperparts and ocher-white underparts with a blackish brown breast band and malar marks.

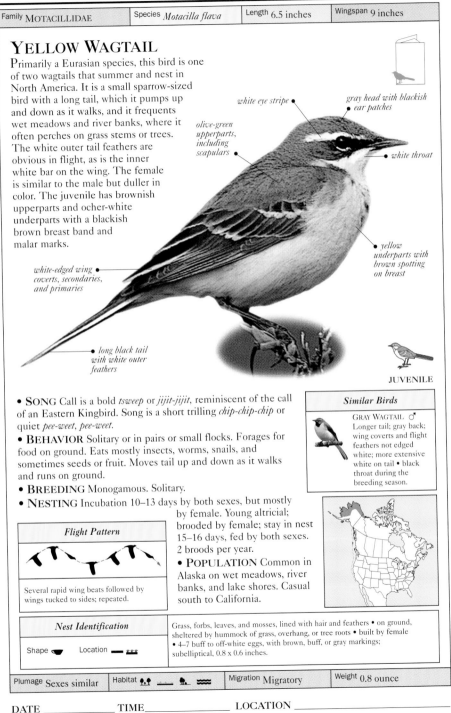

white eye stripe

gray head with blackish ear patches

olive-green upperparts, including scapulars

white throat

yellow underparts with brown spotting on breast

white-edged wing coverts, secondaries, and primaries

long black tail with white outer feathers

JUVENILE

- **SONG** Call is a bold *tsweep* or *jijit-jijit*, reminiscent of the call of an Eastern Kingbird. Song is a short trilling *chip-chip-chip* or quiet *pee-weet, pee-weet.*
- **BEHAVIOR** Solitary or in pairs or small flocks. Forages for food on ground. Eats mostly insects, worms, snails, and sometimes seeds or fruit. Moves tail up and down as it walks and runs on ground.
- **BREEDING** Monogamous. Solitary.
- **NESTING** Incubation 10–13 days by both sexes, but mostly by female. Young altricial; brooded by female; stay in nest 15–16 days, fed by both sexes. 2 broods per year.
- **POPULATION** Common in Alaska on wet meadows, river banks, and lake shores. Casual south to California.

Similar Birds

GRAY WAGTAIL ♂ Longer tail; gray back; wing coverts and flight feathers not edged white; more extensive white on tail • black throat during the breeding season.

Flight Pattern

Several rapid wing beats followed by wings tucked to sides; repeated.

Nest Identification

Shape ⌣   Location ▬ ♣♣♣

Grass, forbs, leaves, and mosses, lined with hair and feathers • on ground, sheltered by hummock of grass, overhang, or tree roots • built by female • 4–7 buff to off-white eggs, with brown, buff, or gray markings; subelliptical, 0.8 x 0.6 inches.

Plumage Sexes similar	Habitat	Migration Migratory	Weight 0.8 ounce

DATE _____ TIME_____ LOCATION _____

Family MOTACILLIDAE	Species *Motacilla cinerea*	Length 7–7.75 inches	Wingspan 10–10.5 inches

GRAY WAGTAIL

The long tail of this bird, which is longer than its body, sets it apart from other birds in its family that visit North America. Usually found along streams and rivers in Eurasia, strays sometimes visit the outer islands of Alaska and once California. The female bird and nonbreeding male have a whitish rather than a blackish throat and buffy yellow underparts. Juveniles may be yellow only on the undertail coverts. In flight the white bar on the inner wing and the white outer tail feathers contrast with the yellow-green rump, yellow uppertail coverts, and the blackish color of the greater secondary coverts, secondaries, and rectrices.

• **SONG** Song is 3 or 4 notes, *tsee-tsee-tsee*. Has call of *chink*, *chink* or *tisk*, *tisk*.

• **BEHAVIOR** Solitary or in pairs. Conspicuous; pumps tail up and down as it walks. Frequents open areas and rocky shorelines along fast-flowing streams. Forages on ground and wades into streams. Eats insects and snails.

• **BREEDING** Monogamous. Solitary.

• **NESTING** Incubation 11–14 days, usually by female, but male will assist. Altricial young brooded by female; stay in nest 11–12 days, fed by both sexes. 1–2 broods per year.

• **POPULATION** Rare to casual spring migrant on western Aleutians, the Pribilofs, and St. Lawrence Island, Alaska. Accidental in California.

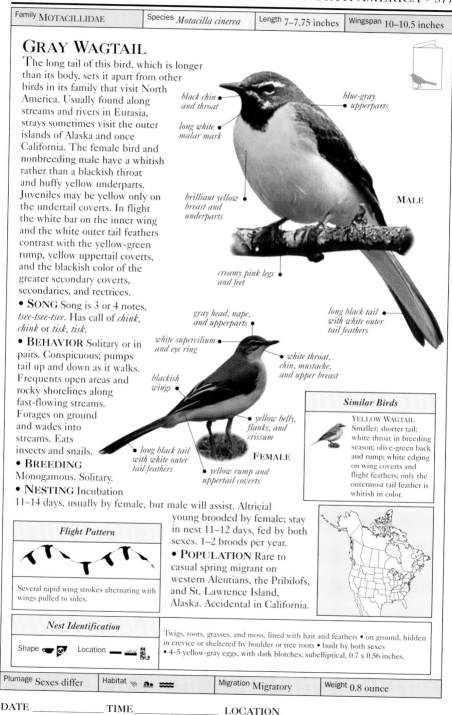

black chin and throat

long white malar mark

blue-gray upperparts

brilliant yellow breast and underparts

MALE

creamy pink legs and feet

long black tail with white outer tail feathers

gray head, nape, and upperparts

white supercilium and eye ring

blackish wings

white throat, chin, mustache, and upper breast

yellow belly, flanks, and crissum

FEMALE

long black tail with white outer tail feathers

yellow rump and uppertail coverts

Similar Birds

YELLOW WAGTAIL
Smaller; shorter tail; white throat in breeding season; olive-green back and rump; white edging on wing coverts and flight feathers; only the outermost tail feather is whitish in color.

Flight Pattern

Several rapid wing strokes alternating with wings pulled to sides.

Nest Identification

Shape — Location ——

Twigs, roots, grasses, and moss, lined with hair and feathers • on ground, hidden in crevice or sheltered by boulder or tree roots • built by both sexes • 4–5 yellow-gray eggs, with dark blotches; subelliptical, 0.7 x 0.56 inches.

Plumage Sexes differ	Habitat	Migration Migratory	Weight 0.8 ounce

DATE _____ TIME_____ LOCATION _____

Family MOTACILLIDAE	Species *Motacilla alba*	Length 6.5–7.25 inches	Wingspan 8.5–10 inches

WHITE WAGTAIL

This Eurasian bird has a small but stable
nesting population in Alaska and
Greenland. Like most wagtails, it wags
its long black tail, with white outer tail
feathers, up and down and bobs its
head while walking. Highly
adaptable, it will nest under eaves
of houses, on bridges, and ivy-
covered walls, as well as
natural cavities of cliffs and
banks. The adult female is
similar to the male.
Wintering adults have less
extensive black on the
chin, throat, and breast,
and juveniles have
mostly white underparts.

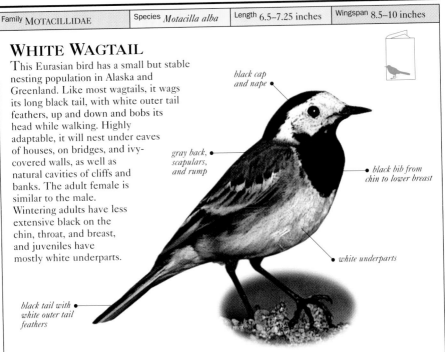

*black cap
and nape*

*gray back,
scapulars,
and rump*

*black bib from
chin to lower breast*

white underparts

*black tail with
white outer tail
feathers*

• **SONG** Sings an energetic trilling twitter with notes similar to
its call notes, which sound like *chizzik-chizzik*.
• **BEHAVIOR** Solitary or in pairs; in flocks in migration and
winter. Forages for food on ground, on and around rocks, and in
shallow water. Eats mostly insects and snails. Frequents
wetlands, shores of lakes, ponds, rivers, and inhabited areas,
including agricultural areas.
• **BREEDING** Monogamous. Solitary. Courting male chases
female until she notices him, then he shows off his shining
black neck.
• **NESTING** Incubation 12–14 days by both sexes, but female
does more. Young altricial; brooded by female; stay in nest
14–16 days, fed by both sexes.
1–2 broods per year.
• **POPULATION** Small
Alaskan population is fairly
common and stable. Casual in
North America on the West
Coast; accidental in the East.

Similar Birds

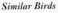

BLACK-BACKED
WAGTAIL
In flight, shows mostly
white wings with black
tips to outer primaries
• breeding adult has
black back • winter
adult has black U-
shaped patch
encircling breast from
side of head.

Flight Pattern

Several rapid wing beats alternated with
wings drawn to sides; repeated.

Nest Identification	
Shape ⌣ Location 🏔️ 🪨 🏠 〰️ ▬ 🪨	Grass, forbs, leaves, roots, twigs, lichen, and moss, lined with grass, hair, and feathers • in cavity or ridge of cliff, bank, bridge, or building, 3–10 feet above ground • sometimes on ground sheltered by grassy tussock or tree roots • built by female • 4–8 grayish or bluish white eggs, with gray or brown speckles; subelliptical, 0.8 x 0.6 inches.

Plumage Sexes similar	Habitat 🪨 〰️ ⚓ 〰️	Migration Migratory	Weight 0.7 ounce

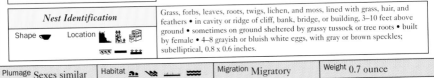

DATE _____ TIME_____ LOCATION _____

Family MOTACILLIDAE	Species *Motacilla lugens*	Length 7.25 inches	Wingspan 10 inches

BLACK-BACKED WAGTAIL

This slender long-tailed native of Asia reaches the Western Hemisphere by making regular spring and summer visits to the western Aleutian Islands. Occasionally these birds also nest in the Aleutians. Although the Black-backed Wagtail is very similar to the White Wagtail in appearance, its upperparts are black instead of gray when the bird is in breeding plumage. The long tail is black with white outer tail feathers, which is conspicuous in flight, as are the almost entirely white wings. Winter plumage shows a white throat with a black necklace. Juveniles resemble adults but are gray without black markings on head, upperparts, or breast. This bird frequents wetlands, river banks, and lake shores.

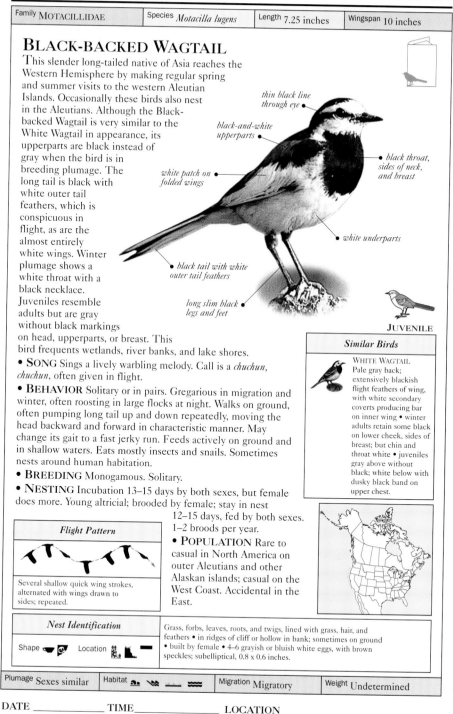

thin black line through eye

black-and-white upperparts

white patch on folded wings

black throat, sides of neck, and breast

white underparts

black tail with white outer tail feathers

long slim black legs and feet

JUVENILE

- **SONG** Sings a lively warbling melody. Call is a *chuchun, chuchun*, often given in flight.
- **BEHAVIOR** Solitary or in pairs. Gregarious in migration and winter, often roosting in large flocks at night. Walks on ground, often pumping long tail up and down repeatedly, moving the head backward and forward in characteristic manner. May change its gait to a fast jerky run. Feeds actively on ground and in shallow waters. Eats mostly insects and snails. Sometimes nests around human habitation.
- **BREEDING** Monogamous. Solitary.
- **NESTING** Incubation 13–15 days by both sexes, but female does more. Young altricial; brooded by female; stay in nest 12–15 days, fed by both sexes. 1–2 broods per year.
- **POPULATION** Rare to casual in North America on outer Aleutians and other Alaskan islands; casual on the West Coast. Accidental in the East.

Similar Birds

WHITE WAGTAIL
Pale gray back; extensively blackish flight feathers of wing, with white secondary coverts producing bar on inner wing • winter adults retain some black on lower cheek, sides of breast; but chin and throat white • juveniles gray above without black; white below with dusky black band on upper chest.

Flight Pattern

Several shallow quick wing strokes, alternated with wings drawn to sides; repeated.

Nest Identification

Shape ⌒ 🥚   Location 🪨 🛏 ▬

Grass, forbs, leaves, roots, and twigs, lined with grass, hair, and feathers • in ridges of cliff or hollow in bank; sometimes on ground • built by female • 4–6 grayish or bluish white eggs, with brown speckles; subelliptical, 0.8 x 0.6 inches.

Plumage Sexes similar	Habitat 🪨 🌾 ▬ ≈	Migration Migratory	Weight Undetermined

DATE _____ TIME_____ LOCATION _____

Family MOTACILLIDAE	Species *Anthus hodgsoni*	Length 6 inches	Wingspan 10 inches

OLIVE-BACKED PIPIT

This Asian species sometimes strays to the islands off the west coast of Alaska. Males sing from the tops of conifers. Like all pipits, it spends much of its time walking around on the ground, moving its tail up and down. The combination of its olive back with faint streaking, the two-toned eyebrow (orange-buff in front and whitish behind), and the broken eye stripe bordering the dusky ear spot set this bird apart from its close cousin, the Tree Pipit. In its native Eurasia this bird frequents woods in open grassy areas and hills, especially along rivers and bogs, and spruce-fir forests.

• **SONG** Metallic *seep-seep-sia-sia*. Call is a nasal *tsee*. Notes often given in flight.

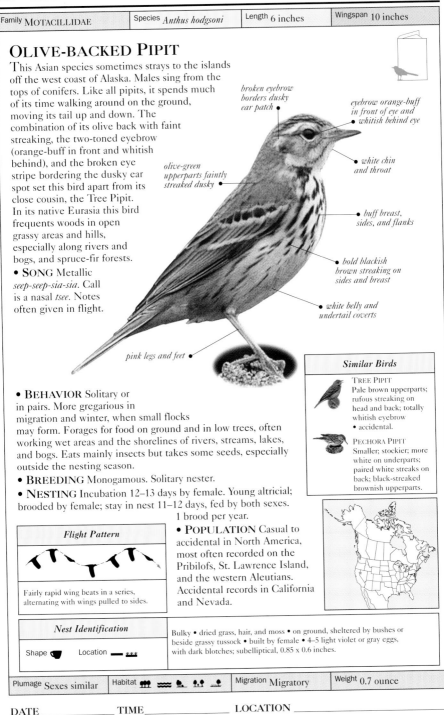

broken eyebrow borders dusky ear patch •

eyebrow orange-buff in front of eye and • whitish behind eye

olive-green upperparts faintly streaked dusky •

• white chin and throat

• buff breast, sides, and flanks

• bold blackish brown streaking on sides and breast

• white belly and undertail coverts

• pink legs and feet

• **BEHAVIOR** Solitary or in pairs. More gregarious in migration and winter, when small flocks may form. Forages for food on ground and in low trees, often working wet areas and the shorelines of rivers, streams, lakes, and bogs. Eats mainly insects but takes some seeds, especially outside the nesting season.

• **BREEDING** Monogamous. Solitary nester.

• **NESTING** Incubation 12–13 days by female. Young altricial; brooded by female; stay in nest 11–12 days, fed by both sexes. 1 brood per year.

• **POPULATION** Casual to accidental in North America, most often recorded on the Pribilofs, St. Lawrence Island, and the western Aleutians. Accidental records in California and Nevada.

Similar Birds

TREE PIPIT
Pale brown upperparts; rufous streaking on head and back; totally whitish eyebrow • accidental.

PECHORA PIPIT
Smaller; stockier; more white on underparts; paired white streaks on back; black-streaked brownish upperparts.

Flight Pattern

Fairly rapid wing beats in a series, alternating with wings pulled to sides.

Nest Identification

Shape ◖   Location ▬ ▪▪▪

Bulky • dried grass, hair, and moss • on ground, sheltered by bushes or beside grassy tussock • built by female • 4–5 light violet or gray eggs, with dark blotches; subelliptical, 0.85 x 0.6 inches.

Plumage Sexes similar	Habitat 🌳 〰 🪨 🌿 🌱	Migration Migratory	Weight 0.7 ounce

DATE _____ TIME_____ LOCATION _____

Family MOTACILLIDAE	Species *Anthus gustavi*	Length 5.5–6 inches	Wingspan 9.5–10.5 inches

PECHORA PIPIT

This bird takes its name from the Pechora River Valley in northeastern Russia, where it breeds and nests. A shy bird, it usually stays hidden in dense thickets and remains quiet if it is flushed. Strays have made rare visits to the Aleutians and St. Lawrence Island, Alaska.

heavily streaked blackish brown upperparts

2 white streaks down each side of back

indistinct buffy white eye line

2 white wing bars

white belly and outer tail feathers

heavy black streaking on breast, sides, and flanks

yellowish wash on breast and sides

long curved back claw

A retiring species, it is easily overlooked on the brushy tundra and taiga bogs and swamps that it frequents. The heavy streaking on the back suggests a juvenile Red-throated Pipit, but the whiter underparts and the double white stripes on each side of the back are distinguishing characteristics.

• **SONG** Often silent, even when flushed. Call is a harsh *pit*, *pipit*, or *pwit*, usually given 3 times. Usually sings while flying in courtship and territory displays.

• **BEHAVIOR** Solitary or in pairs. Secretive. Forages for food on ground and in low trees and bushes. Often frequents dense wet areas such as northern bogs and swamps. May bob tail as it walks. Eats mainly insects, particularly in the breeding season; takes some seeds in migration and on wintering grounds.

• **BREEDING** Monogamous. Solitary nester.

• **NESTING** Incubation 12–13 days by female. Young altricial; brooded by female; stay in nest 12–14 days, fed by both sexes. 1 brood per year.

• **POPULATION** Casual to accidental in North America in the western Aleutians and St. Lawrence Island, Alaska.

Similar Birds

TREE PIPIT
Olive-gray upperparts; rufous streaking on head and back; whitish eyebrow • accidental.

OLIVE-BACKED PIPIT
Lightly streaked, greenish olive upperparts; eyebrow is orange-buff in front of eye and whitish behind; broken eye stripe borders dark ear spot.

Flight Pattern

Fairly swift rapid wing beats in a series, alternating with wings pulled to sides; repeated.

Nest Identification

Shape 🥣   Location ▬ ☘☘☘

Grass and plant material, lined with small leaves • on ground, often sheltered by tree roots, grassy tussock, or shrubs • built by female • 4–6 gray or greenish eggs with dark spots; subelliptical, 0.84 x 0.6 inches.

Plumage Sexes similar	Habitat 🌿🌿 🌲 ▬	Migration Migratory	Weight 0.7 ounce

DATE _____ TIME _____ LOCATION _____

Family MOTACILLIDAE	Species *Anthus cervinus*	Length 6 inches	Wingspan 10 inches

RED-THROATED PIPIT

This bird takes its name from its reddish head, throat, and breast in breeding season. A mainly Eurasian species, it breeds in extreme western Alaska and off-shore islands and occurs rarely as a migrant in California. The head and breast of both the female and nonbreeding male are duller in color. Juveniles and some adult females show no red and have heavily streaked and spotted underparts. Winter males usually retain some reddish pink on their cheeks.

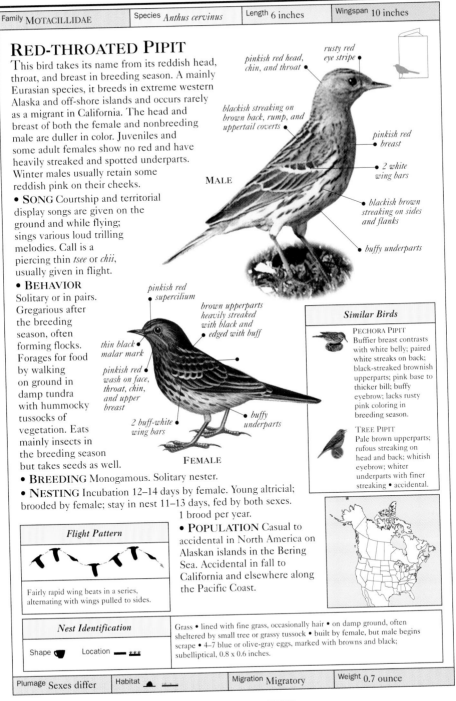

pinkish red head, chin, and throat

rusty red eye stripe

blackish streaking on brown back, rump, and uppertail coverts

pinkish red breast

2 white wing bars

MALE

blackish brown streaking on sides and flanks

buffy underparts

• **SONG** Courtship and territorial display songs are given on the ground and while flying; sings various loud trilling melodies. Call is a piercing thin *tsee* or *chii*, usually given in flight.

• **BEHAVIOR** Solitary or in pairs. Gregarious after the breeding season, often forming flocks. Forages for food by walking on ground in damp tundra with hummocky tussocks of vegetation. Eats mainly insects in the breeding season but takes seeds as well.

pinkish red supercilium

brown upperparts heavily streaked with black and edged with buff

thin black malar mark

pinkish red wash on face, throat, chin, and upper breast

2 buff-white wing bars

buffy underparts

FEMALE

Similar Birds

PECHORA PIPIT
Buffier breast contrasts with white belly; paired white streaks on back; black-streaked brownish upperparts; pink base to thicker bill; buffy eyebrow; lacks rusty pink coloring in breeding season.

TREE PIPIT
Pale brown upperparts; rufous streaking on head and back; whitish eyebrow; whiter underparts with finer streaking • accidental.

• **BREEDING** Monogamous. Solitary nester.

• **NESTING** Incubation 12–14 days by female. Young altricial; brooded by female; stay in nest 11–13 days, fed by both sexes. 1 brood per year.

• **POPULATION** Casual to accidental in North America on Alaskan islands in the Bering Sea. Accidental in fall to California and elsewhere along the Pacific Coast.

Flight Pattern

Fairly rapid wing beats in a series, alternating with wings pulled to sides.

Nest Identification	
Shape	Location	Grass • lined with fine grass, occasionally hair • on damp ground, often sheltered by small tree or grassy tussock • built by female, but male begins scrape • 4–7 blue or olive-gray eggs, marked with browns and black; subelliptical, 0.8 x 0.6 inches.

Plumage Sexes differ	Habitat	Migration Migratory	Weight 0.7 ounce

| Family MOTACILLIDAE | Species *Anthus rubescens* | Length 6.5 inches | Wingspan 10–11 inches |

AMERICAN PIPIT

This sparrow-sized bird spends most of its time on the open ground, where it runs and walks, rather than hops. Like many of the pipits, the male has a dramatic song flight in which he flies to a height of 50 to 200 feet then floats down with feet dangling below and tail cocked upward, all the while continuing to sing. The American Pipit's breeding ranges extend from alpine tundra in the high mountains of the western US to arctic tundra across the top of the continent. Winter birds have browner upperparts and they have more heavily streaked underparts.

slim blackish bill

grayish brown upperparts

buffy wing bars on dark gray wings

buff underparts with faint brown streaking

white outer tail feathers

black legs and feet

• **SONG** A repetitive rapid series of notes, *chee-chee-chee* or *cheedal-cheedal-cheedal*. Call sounds like *wit, wit* or *pip-pit* and is most often given in flight.

• **BEHAVIOR** Solitary or in pairs; gregarious after breeding season, forming flocks that may be very large and mixed with other species, including Horned Larks and longspurs. Walks on ground, often bobbing its head while pumping tail up and down or wagging it. Forages in foliage, grass, and soil. Also wades into shallow waters to pick food from surface. Eats insects and their larvae, seeds, small mollusks, and crustaceans. Alpine species may escape severe weather by moving down mountain slopes to warmer valleys.

• **BREEDING** Monogamous. Solitary nester. Male has courtship song flight.

• **NESTING** Incubation 13–15 days by female. Young altricial; brooded by female; stay in nest 13–15 days, when they can make short flight. Fed by both sexes. 1 brood per year.

• **POPULATION** Common and widespread in tundra and alpine tundra; in winter, in fields and on beaches.

• **CONSERVATION** Neotropical migrant. Vulnerable to habitat loss on wintering grounds as well as foraging areas in migration.

Similar Birds

SPRAGUE'S PIPIT Buff- and blackish-streaked upperparts; dark eye on pale buff face with pale eye ring; pinkish to yellow legs and feet; slender yellowish bill; white underparts with deeper buff on lightly streaked breast; does not pump tail.

Flight Pattern

Swift flight on series of rapidly beating wings, alternated with wings pulled to sides; repeated.

Nest Identification

Shape　Location

Often no nest materials; sometimes sticks and grass, occasionally with lining of small amount of mammal hair • sheltered by bank, rocks, or hillock • built by female • 3–7 grayish white eggs, with brown splotches; subelliptical, 0.8 x 0.6 inches.

| Plumage Sexes similar | Habitat | Migration Migratory | Weight 0.8 ounce |

DATE _____ TIME_____ LOCATION _____

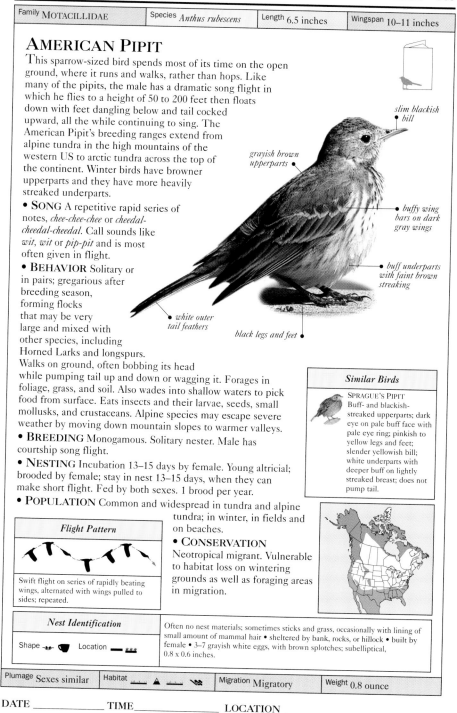

| Family MOTACILLIDAE | Species *Anthus spragueii* | Length 6.5 inches | Wingspan 10–11 inches |

SPRAGUE'S PIPIT

Because its plumage serves as camouflage in the prairie grasses, this bird is hard to spot. When frightened, it often chooses to run or freeze, rather than fly. Olive-tan upperparts are edged with buff on the coverts, flight feathers, and back, creating a scaly appearance. Dark eyes encircled by thin eye rings stand out in sharp contrast to a buffy face. In flight, white outer feathers are evident on the mostly black tail. Unlike the American Pipit, it does not bob or wag its tail when it walks.

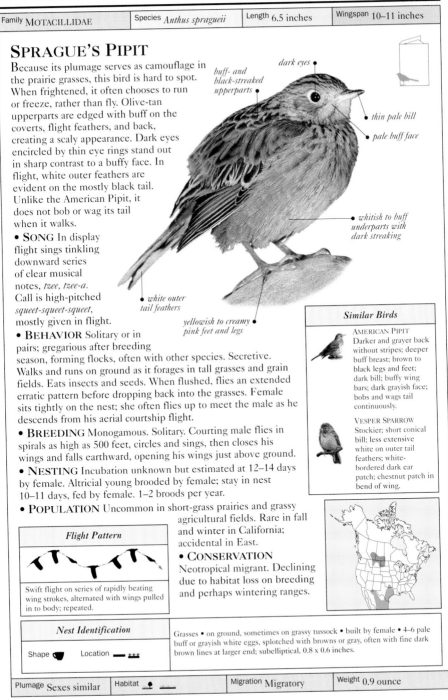

dark eyes

buff- and black-streaked upperparts

thin pale bill

pale buff face

whitish to buff underparts with dark streaking

white outer tail feathers

yellowish to creamy pink feet and legs

- **SONG** In display flight sings tinkling downward series of clear musical notes, *tzee, tzee-a.* Call is high-pitched *squeet-squeet-squeet*, mostly given in flight.

- **BEHAVIOR** Solitary or in pairs; gregarious after breeding season, forming flocks, often with other species. Secretive. Walks and runs on ground as it forages in tall grasses and grain fields. Eats insects and seeds. When flushed, flies an extended erratic pattern before dropping back into the grasses. Female sits tightly on the nest; she often flies up to meet the male as he descends from his aerial courtship flight.

- **BREEDING** Monogamous. Solitary. Courting male flies in spirals as high as 500 feet, circles and sings, then closes his wings and falls earthward, opening his wings just above ground.

- **NESTING** Incubation unknown but estimated at 12–14 days by female. Altricial young brooded by female; stay in nest 10–11 days, fed by female. 1–2 broods per year.

- **POPULATION** Uncommon in short-grass prairies and grassy agricultural fields. Rare in fall and winter in California; accidental in East.

- **CONSERVATION** Neotropical migrant. Declining due to habitat loss on breeding and perhaps wintering ranges.

Similar Birds

AMERICAN PIPIT
Darker and grayer back without stripes; deeper buff breast; brown to black legs and feet; dark bill; buffy wing bars; dark grayish face; bobs and wags tail continuously.

VESPER SPARROW
Stockier; short conical bill; less extensive white on outer tail feathers; white-bordered dark ear patch; chestnut patch in bend of wing.

Flight Pattern

Swift flight on series of rapidly beating wing strokes, alternated with wings pulled in to body; repeated.

Nest Identification

Shape ● Location ▬ ✴✴✴

Grasses • on ground, sometimes on grassy tussock • built by female • 4–6 pale buff or grayish white eggs, splotched with browns or gray, often with fine dark brown lines at larger end; subelliptical, 0.8 x 0.6 inches.

| Plumage Sexes similar | Habitat | Migration Migratory | Weight 0.9 ounce |

DATE _____ TIME _____ LOCATION _____

Family BOMBYCILLIDAE	Species *Bombycilla garrulus*	Length 8.25 inches	Wingspan 13–14 inches

BOHEMIAN WAXWING

True to its name, this bird is highly nomadic and travels in flocks over a wide range in search of abundant food sources, particularly berries, which make up its principal diet. In winter it often is attracted to berries and fruits produced by ornamental plantings in towns and residential areas, and flocks may appear as if from nowhere, lingering until the larder is stripped. Gray underparts with cinnamon undertail coverts distinguish it from the smaller Cedar Waxwing. Like its more widespread relative its tail is yellow tipped. In flight it shows a white patch at the base of the primaries. Juveniles have heavily streaked underparts and whitish throats.

long grayish cinnamon crest

narrow black mask with white lower border

grayish upperparts with more brown on the back and head

black chin

usually waxy red tips on secondaries

gray underparts

white markings on grayish wings with red and yellow borders

cinnamon undertail coverts

blackish gray tail with yellow trim

JUVENILE

- **SONG** While flying, utters continuous twittering and chatter. Call is an abrasive *scree* or *zirrrr.*
- **BEHAVIOR** In pairs or small groups during breeding season; gregarious rest of year, forming flocks. Usually feeds close to other birds on ground and in trees. Perches to spot insects, then hawks them in flight. Eats fruit, berries, and insects. Drinks sap. Very tame. Southward eruptions are unpredictable and varied, often tied to crashes in food sources in breeding range.
- **BREEDING** Monogamous. Colonial.
- **NESTING** Incubation 14–15 days by female. Young altricial; brooded by female; stay in nest 13–18 days, fed by both sexes. 1 brood per year.
- **POPULATION** Fairly common to uncommon in mixed conifer and open coniferous woodlands and muskeg; widespread in range in winter.
- **FEEDERS** Comes to feeders for dried fruits and berries.
- **CONSERVATION** Vulnerable to habitat loss due to logging in coniferous forests.

Similar Birds

CEDAR WAXWING
Smaller; browner upperparts; yellow on belly; white undertail coverts; lacks yellow and white bars and spots on wings.

Flight Pattern
Strong rapid flight with a series of rapid wing beats alternating with wings pulled briefly to sides. Hawks for insects.

Nest Identification	
Shape ⬤ ▬ Location 🌲	Sticks, lichen, stems, and grass; lined with mosses and fine materials • far out on horizontal limb, 4–50 feet above ground • built by both sexes • 2–6 pale bluish gray eggs, splotched and marked with black, especially at larger end; oval, 1.0 x 0.7 inches.

Plumage Sexes similar	Habitat 🌳 🌿	Migration Migratory	Weight 2.0 ounces

DATE _____ TIME_____ LOCATION _____

Family BOMBYCILLIDAE	Species *Bombycilla cedrorum*	Length 7 inches	Wingspan 11–12.25 inches

CEDAR WAXWING

Named for the red waxlike tips on its secondaries, this social bird travels in large flocks in the nonbreeding season and may even nest in loose colonies. The purpose of the "red wax" is long-debated, but younger birds do not have it and the older birds that do often choose each other as mates and produce more young than the younger pairs. At times this bird may become so intoxicated on overripe fruit that it cannot fly. Females are similar to males but show a brownish rather than a blackish throat (a difficult field mark that can be observed only at close hand). Juveniles have streaked upperparts and underparts.

brownish head and back

long brownish crest

narrow black mask bordered white below

blackish throat

brownish breast, sides, and wing coverts

light yellow belly

red waxy tips on secondary flight feathers of older birds

gray rump and uppertail coverts

white undertail coverts

yellow trim on end of gray-black tail

JUVENILE

- **SONG** Call is thin, high-pitched warbled *zeeee* or *zeeeet*, more protracted just before leaving perch; may call constantly in flight.
- **BEHAVIOR** In pairs or in small to large flocks. Gregarious, especially in migration and winter. Tame and sociable. Feeds close to other birds in trees or on ground. Eats fruit, flower petals, and insects; drinks sap. Several may sit on a wire or branch and pass a piece of fruit back and forth, beak to beak. Hawks insects, particularly mayfly hatches and those of similar species, especially along streams.
- **BREEDING** Monogamous. Solitary to colonial. During courtship, male and female will sit together and pass flower petals back and forth, share food, and rub bills.
- **NESTING** Incubation 12–16 days by both sexes. Young altricial; brooded by female; stay in nest 14–18 days, fed by both sexes. 1–2 broods per year.
- **POPULATION** Fairly common to uncommon in woodland, forest edge, farmlands with fruit trees, towns, and suburbs.
- **FEEDERS** Raisins and berries; attracted to birdbaths.
- **CONSERVATION** Neotropical migrant. Not a common cowbird host; often rejects or damages its eggs.

Similar Birds

BOHEMIAN WAXWING Larger; grayer; cinnamon undertail coverts; white and yellow spots and bars on wings; white bar at base of primaries on folded wing shows as white patch in flight.

Flight Pattern

Strong rapid flight with several quick wing strokes alternating with brief periods of wings pulled to sides; repeated.

Nest Identification	Sticks, mosses, and grass, lined with fine grass, moss, rootlets, hair, and pine needles •on limb or in fork of conifer or deciduous tree, 6–60 feet above ground • built by both sexes • 2–6 pale bluish gray eggs, dotted with black and brown; oval, 0.8 x 0.6 inches.
Shape ⬯ ☕ Location 🌳 🌲	

Plumage Sexes similar	Habitat 🌿 🌳	Migration Migratory	Weight 1.1 ounces

DATE _____ TIME_____ LOCATION _____

Family PTILOGONATIDAE	Species *Phainopepla nitens*	Length 7.75 inches	Wingspan 11.5 inches

PHAINOPEPLA

This may be the only North American bird that nests in two different regions during the same breeding season. The early nest of the breeding season is usually in the desert. Then, as the desert warms with the season, the Phainopepla moves to a higher, more moist habitat and nests again. These highly nomadic birds survive by following the crops of mistletoe and other berries. The glossy black-crested males flash a white wing patch at the base of the primaries in flight; the slate-gray juveniles and females show a pale gray one.

• **SONG** Sings a short trilling somewhat liquid whistle of *tlee-oo-eee*, which is not often heard. Has mellow call of *whew* or *werp?*

• **BEHAVIOR** Solitary or in pairs or loose groups. Forages for food in trees, bushes, and, rarely, on ground. Catches insects in flight, similar to flycatcher. Eats mistletoe and various other berries; defends food trees and shrubs from other birds. Also eats spiders and flower petals. May hover over food and pick it up. Male has courtship display in which he flies 300 feet or so and zigzags or circles above his territory; sometimes other males join in above their own territories. Sometimes wanders beyond breeding range after nesting season.

• **BREEDING** Monogamous. Solitary or in small colonies.

• **NESTING** Incubation 14 days by both sexes. Young altricial; brooded by female; stay in nest 19–20 days, fed by both sexes. 1–2 broods per year.

• **POPULATION** Fairly common to common in desert scrub, mesquite brushland, and semiarid and riparian woodland and oak foothills. Accidental in the East.

• **CONSERVATION** Vulnerable to habitat loss due to development and agriculture, also cutting of mesquite for charcoal in Mexico.

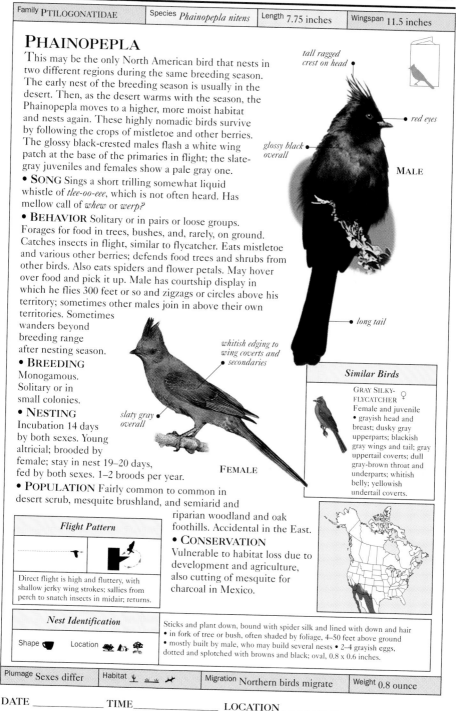

tall ragged crest on head

red eyes

glossy black overall

MALE

long tail

whitish edging to wing coverts and secondaries

slaty gray overall

FEMALE

Similar Birds

GRAY SILKY-FLYCATCHER ♀
Female and juvenile
• grayish head and breast; dusky gray upperparts; blackish gray wings and tail; gray uppertail coverts; dull gray-brown throat and underparts; whitish belly; yellowish undertail coverts.

Flight Pattern
Direct flight is high and fluttery, with shallow jerky wing strokes; sallies from perch to snatch insects in midair; returns.

Nest Identification	
Shape	Location

Sticks and plant down, bound with spider silk and lined with down and hair • in fork of tree or bush, often shaded by foliage, 4–50 feet above ground • mostly built by male, who may build several nests • 2–4 grayish eggs, dotted and splotched with browns and black; oval, 0.8 x 0.6 inches.

Plumage Sexes differ	Habitat	Migration Northern birds migrate	Weight 0.8 ounce

DATE _____ TIME _____ LOCATION _____

Family PEUCEDRAMIDAE	Species *Peucedramus taeniatus*	Length 5.25 inches	Wingspan 8.5 inches

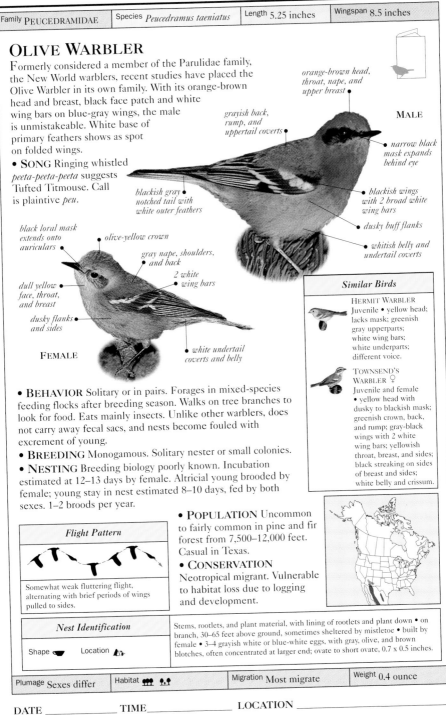

OLIVE WARBLER

Formerly considered a member of the Parulidae family, the New World warblers, recent studies have placed the Olive Warbler in its own family. With its orange-brown head and breast, black face patch and white wing bars on blue-gray wings, the male is unmistakeable. White base of primary feathers shows as spot on folded wings.

• **SONG** Ringing whistled *peeta-peeta-peeta* suggests Tufted Titmouse. Call is plaintive *peu*.

orange-brown head, throat, nape, and upper breast

grayish back, rump, and uppertail coverts

MALE

narrow black mask expands behind eye

blackish gray notched tail with white outer feathers

blackish wings with 2 broad white wing bars

dusky buff flanks

whitish belly and undertail coverts

black loral mask extends onto auriculars

olive-yellow crown

gray nape, shoulders, and back

2 white wing bars

dull yellow face, throat, and breast

dusky flanks and sides

FEMALE

white undertail coverts and belly

Similar Birds

HERMIT WARBLER
Juvenile • yellow head; lacks mask; greenish gray upperparts; white wing bars; white underparts; different voice.

TOWNSEND'S WARBLER ♀
Juvenile and female • yellow head with dusky to blackish mask; greenish crown, back, and rump; gray-black wings with 2 white wing bars; yellowish throat, breast, and sides; black streaking on sides of breast and sides; white belly and crissum.

• **BEHAVIOR** Solitary or in pairs. Forages in mixed-species feeding flocks after breeding season. Walks on tree branches to look for food. Eats mainly insects. Unlike other warblers, does not carry away fecal sacs, and nests become fouled with excrement of young.
• **BREEDING** Monogamous. Solitary nester or small colonies.
• **NESTING** Breeding biology poorly known. Incubation estimated at 12–13 days by female. Altricial young brooded by female; young stay in nest estimated 8–10 days, fed by both sexes. 1–2 broods per year.

• **POPULATION** Uncommon to fairly common in pine and fir forest from 7,500–12,000 feet. Casual in Texas.
• **CONSERVATION** Neotropical migrant. Vulnerable to habitat loss due to logging and development.

Flight Pattern

Somewhat weak fluttering flight, alternating with brief periods of wings pulled to sides.

Nest Identification

Shape ⌣ Location 🌲

Stems, rootlets, and plant material, with lining of rootlets and plant down • on branch, 30–65 feet above ground, sometimes sheltered by mistletoe • built by female • 3–4 grayish white or blue-white eggs, with gray, olive, and brown blotches, often concentrated at larger end; ovate to short ovate, 0.7 x 0.5 inches.

Plumage Sexes differ	Habitat 🌲 🌿	Migration Most migrate	Weight 0.4 ounce

DATE _____ TIME_____ LOCATION _____

Family PARULIDAE	Species *Vermivora pinus*	Length 4.75 inches	Wingspan 6.75–7.5 inches

BLUE-WINGED WARBLER

Except when the male perches high to sing, this unobtrusive, deliberate bird usually forages low, amid brushy overgrown fields and thickets. It often interbreeds with the Golden-winged Warbler, producing the fertile hybrids known as Lawrence's Warbler and Brewster's Warbler. The female is similar to the male but duller in color and has less yellow on her crown. When its range overlaps that of the Golden-winged Warbler, it tends to displace it.

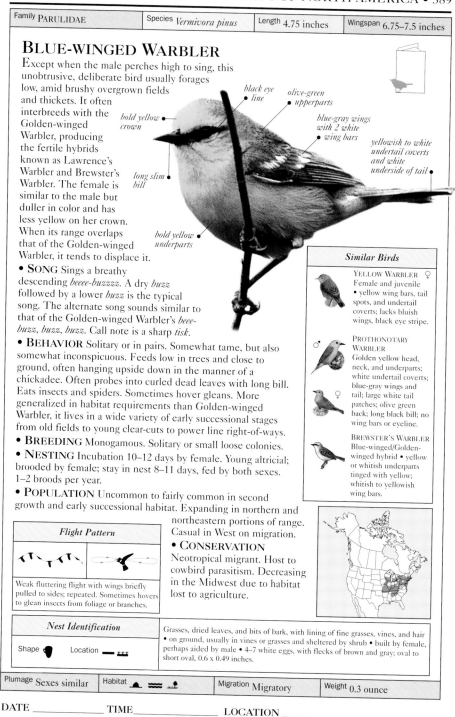

black eye line
olive-green upperparts
bold yellow crown
blue-gray wings with 2 white wing bars
yellowish to white undertail coverts and white underside of tail
long slim bill
bold yellow underparts

- **SONG** Sings a breathy descending *beeee-buzzzz*. A dry *buzz* followed by a lower *buzz* is the typical song. The alternate song sounds similar to that of the Golden-winged Warbler's *beee-buzz, buzz, buzz*. Call note is a sharp *tisk*.
- **BEHAVIOR** Solitary or in pairs. Somewhat tame, but also somewhat inconspicuous. Feeds low in trees and close to ground, often hanging upside down in the manner of a chickadee. Often probes into curled dead leaves with long bill. Eats insects and spiders. Sometimes hover gleans. More generalized in habitat requirements than Golden-winged Warbler, it lives in a wide variety of early successional stages from old fields to young clear-cuts to power line right-of-ways.
- **BREEDING** Monogamous. Solitary or small loose colonies.
- **NESTING** Incubation 10–12 days by female. Young altricial; brooded by female; stay in nest 8–11 days, fed by both sexes. 1–2 broods per year.
- **POPULATION** Uncommon to fairly common in second growth and early successional habitat. Expanding in northern and northeastern portions of range. Casual in West on migration.
- **CONSERVATION** Neotropical migrant. Host to cowbird parasitism. Decreasing in the Midwest due to habitat lost to agriculture.

Similar Birds

YELLOW WARBLER ♀
Female and juvenile
• yellow wing bars, tail spots, and undertail coverts; lacks bluish wings, black eye stripe.

PROTHONOTARY WARBLER ♂
Golden yellow head, neck, and underparts; white undertail coverts; blue-gray wings and tail; large white tail patches; olive green back; long black bill; no wing bars or eyeline. ♀

BREWSTER'S WARBLER
Blue-winged/Golden-winged hybrid • yellow or whitish underparts tinged with yellow; whitish to yellowish wing bars.

Flight Pattern

Weak fluttering flight with wings briefly pulled to sides; repeated. Sometimes hovers to glean insects from foliage or branches.

Nest Identification

Shape 🔻   Location ▬ ✱✱✱

Grasses, dried leaves, and bits of bark, with lining of fine grasses, vines, and hair • on ground, usually in vines or grasses and sheltered by shrub • built by female, perhaps aided by male • 4–7 white eggs, with flecks of brown and gray; oval to short oval, 0.6 x 0.49 inches.

Plumage Sexes similar	Habitat ▲ ≈ ⚲	Migration Migratory	Weight 0.3 ounce

DATE _____ TIME _____ LOCATION _____

Family PARULIDAE	Species *Vermivora peregrina*	Length 4.75 inches	Wingspan 7.5–8 inches

TENNESSEE WARBLER

Despite its name, this short-tailed plump-bodied warbler nests almost entirely in Canada and is found in Tennessee only during migration. Fall adults and juveniles are similar to females but have a yellowish wash on the underparts, except for the undertail coverts, which are almost always white.

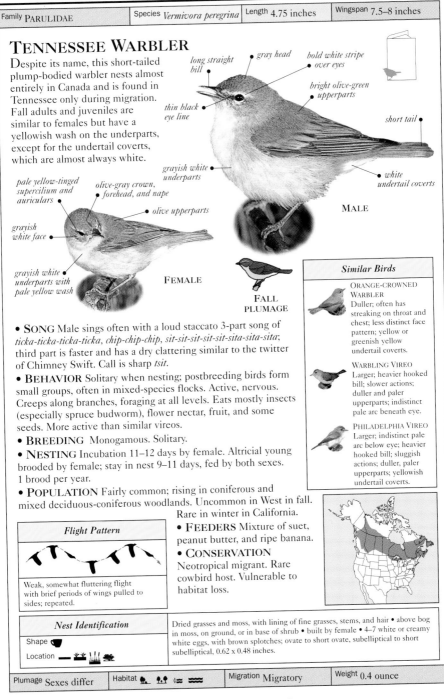

long straight bill

gray head

bold white stripe over eyes

bright olive-green upperparts

thin black eye line

short tail

grayish white underparts

white undertail coverts

MALE

pale yellow-tinged supercilium and auriculars

olive-gray crown, forehead, and nape

olive upperparts

grayish white face

grayish white underparts with pale yellow wash

FEMALE

FALL PLUMAGE

Similar Birds

ORANGE-CROWNED WARBLER
Duller; often has streaking on throat and chest; less distinct face pattern; yellow or greenish yellow undertail coverts.

WARBLING VIREO
Larger; heavier hooked bill; slower actions; duller and paler upperparts; indistinct pale arc beneath eye.

PHILADELPHIA VIREO
Larger; indistinct pale arc below eye; heavier hooked bill; sluggish actions; duller, paler upperparts; yellowish undertail coverts.

• **SONG** Male sings often with a loud staccato 3-part song of *ticka-ticka-ticka-ticka, chip-chip-chip, sit-sit-sit-sit-sit-sita-sita-sita*; third part is faster and has a dry clattering similar to the twitter of Chimney Swift. Call is sharp *tsit*.
• **BEHAVIOR** Solitary when nesting; postbreeding birds form small groups, often in mixed-species flocks. Active, nervous. Creeps along branches, foraging at all levels. Eats mostly insects (especially spruce budworm), flower nectar, fruit, and some seeds. More active than similar vireos.
• **BREEDING** Monogamous. Solitary.
• **NESTING** Incubation 11–12 days by female. Altricial young brooded by female; stay in nest 9–11 days, fed by both sexes. 1 brood per year.
• **POPULATION** Fairly common; rising in coniferous and mixed deciduous-coniferous woodlands. Uncommon in West in fall. Rare in winter in California.
• **FEEDERS** Mixture of suet, peanut butter, and ripe banana.
• **CONSERVATION** Neotropical migrant. Rare cowbird host. Vulnerable to habitat loss.

Flight Pattern

Weak, somewhat fluttering flight with brief periods of wings pulled to sides; repeated.

Nest Identification	
Shape	Dried grasses and moss, with lining of fine grasses, stems, and hair • above bog in moss, on ground, or in base of shrub • built by female • 4–7 white or creamy white eggs, with brown splotches; ovate to short ovate, subelliptical to short subelliptical, 0.62 x 0.48 inches.
Location	

Plumage Sexes differ	Habitat	Migration Migratory	Weight 0.4 ounce

DATE _____ TIME_____ LOCATION _____

| Family PARULIDAE | Species *Vermivora celata* | Length 4.75–5 inches | Wingspan 7–8 inches |

ORANGE-CROWNED WARBLER

The brownish orange head patch for which this warbler is named is rarely noticeable unless the bird is frightened or agitated. It most often lives and nests in thick foliage close to the ground, but the male perches at the tops of tall trees to sing. Considerable color variation in this widely distributed species ranges from dull greenish birds in the East to brighter yellow birds in the West. The female

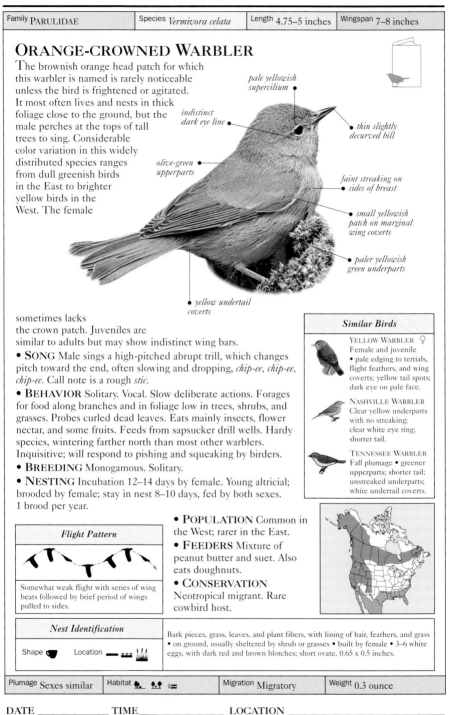

pale yellowish supercilium

indistinct dark eye line

thin slightly decurved bill

olive-green upperparts

faint streaking on sides of breast

small yellowish patch on marginal wing coverts

paler yellowish green underparts

yellow undertail coverts

sometimes lacks the crown patch. Juveniles are similar to adults but may show indistinct wing bars.

• **SONG** Male sings a high-pitched abrupt trill, which changes pitch toward the end, often slowing and dropping, *chip-ee, chip-ee, chip-ee.* Call note is a rough *stic.*
• **BEHAVIOR** Solitary. Vocal. Slow deliberate actions. Forages for food along branches and in foliage low in trees, shrubs, and grasses. Probes curled dead leaves. Eats mainly insects, flower nectar, and some fruits. Feeds from sapsucker drill wells. Hardy species, wintering farther north than most other warblers. Inquisitive; will respond to pishing and squeaking by birders.
• **BREEDING** Monogamous. Solitary.
• **NESTING** Incubation 12–14 days by female. Young altricial; brooded by female; stay in nest 8–10 days, fed by both sexes. 1 brood per year.

Similar Birds

YELLOW WARBLER ♀
Female and juvenile
• pale edging to tertials, flight feathers, and wing coverts; yellow tail spots; dark eye on pale face.

NASHVILLE WARBLER
Clear yellow underparts with no streaking; clear white eye ring; shorter tail.

TENNESSEE WARBLER
Fall plumage • greener upperparts; shorter tail; unstreaked underparts; white undertail coverts.

• **POPULATION** Common in the West; rarer in the East.
• **FEEDERS** Mixture of peanut butter and suet. Also eats doughnuts.
• **CONSERVATION** Neotropical migrant. Rare cowbird host.

Flight Pattern

Somewhat weak flight with series of wing beats followed by brief period of wings pulled to sides.

Nest Identification

Shape ☕   Location ▬ ✶✶✶ ⱬⱬⱬ

Bark pieces, grass, leaves, and plant fibers, with lining of hair, feathers, and grass • on ground, usually sheltered by shrub or grasses • built by female • 3–6 white eggs, with dark red and brown blotches; short ovate, 0.65 x 0.5 inches.

| Plumage Sexes similar | Habitat 🐿 🐾 ≈ | Migration Migratory | Weight 0.3 ounce |

DATE _____ TIME_____ LOCATION _____

| Family PARULIDAE | Species *Vermivora ruficapilla* | Length 4.75 inches | Wingspan 7.25–7.75 inches |

NASHVILLE WARBLER

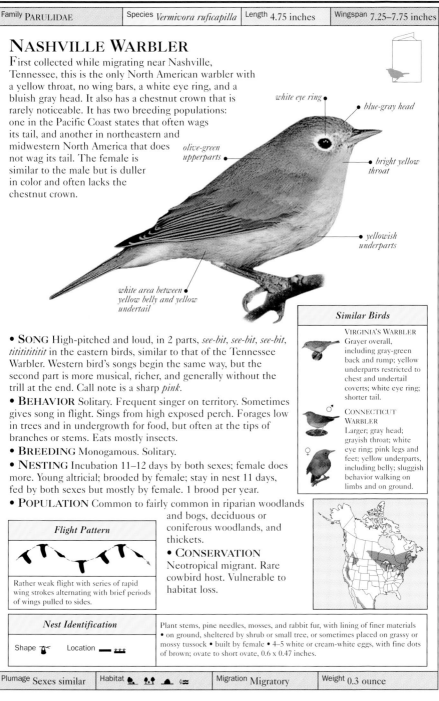

First collected while migrating near Nashville, Tennessee, this is the only North American warbler with a yellow throat, no wing bars, a white eye ring, and a bluish gray head. It also has a chestnut crown that is rarely noticeable. It has two breeding populations: one in the Pacific Coast states that often wags its tail, and another in northeastern and midwestern North America that does not wag its tail. The female is similar to the male but is duller in color and often lacks the chestnut crown.

white eye ring

blue-gray head

olive-green upperparts

bright yellow throat

yellowish underparts

white area between yellow belly and yellow undertail

- **SONG** High-pitched and loud, in 2 parts, *see-bit, see-bit, see-bit, tititititit* in the eastern birds, similar to that of the Tennessee Warbler. Western bird's songs begin the same way, but the second part is more musical, richer, and generally without the trill at the end. Call note is a sharp *pink*.
- **BEHAVIOR** Solitary. Frequent singer on territory. Sometimes gives song in flight. Sings from high exposed perch. Forages low in trees and in undergrowth for food, but often at the tips of branches or stems. Eats mostly insects.
- **BREEDING** Monogamous. Solitary.
- **NESTING** Incubation 11–12 days by both sexes; female does more. Young altricial; brooded by female; stay in nest 11 days, fed by both sexes but mostly by female. 1 brood per year.
- **POPULATION** Common to fairly common in riparian woodlands and bogs, deciduous or coniferous woodlands, and thickets.
- **CONSERVATION** Neotropical migrant. Rare cowbird host. Vulnerable to habitat loss.

Similar Birds

VIRGINIA'S WARBLER
Grayer overall, including gray-green back and rump; yellow underparts restricted to chest and undertail coverts; white eye ring; shorter tail.

CONNECTICUT WARBLER
Larger; gray head; grayish throat; white eye ring; pink legs and feet; yellow underparts, including belly; sluggish behavior walking on limbs and on ground.

Flight Pattern

Rather weak flight with series of rapid wing strokes alternating with brief periods of wings pulled to sides.

Nest Identification

Shape _____   Location _____

Plant stems, pine needles, mosses, and rabbit fur, with lining of finer materials • on ground, sheltered by shrub or small tree, or sometimes placed on grassy or mossy tussock • built by female • 4–5 white or cream-white eggs, with fine dots of brown; ovate to short ovate, 0.6 x 0.47 inches.

| Plumage Sexes similar | Habitat | Migration Migratory | Weight 0.3 ounce |

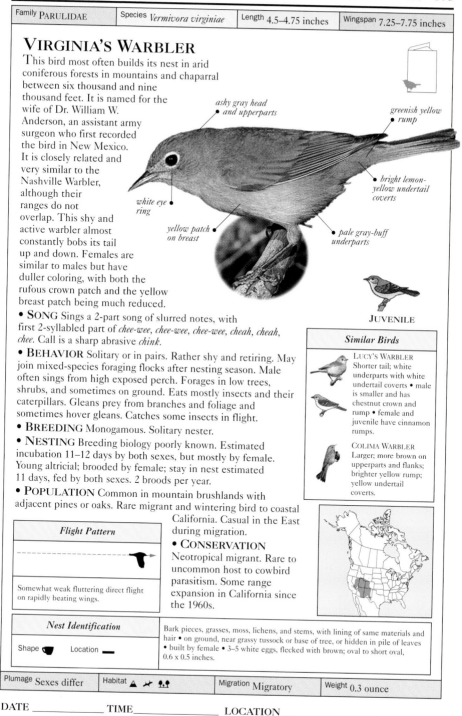

| Family PARULIDAE | Species *Vermivora virginiae* | Length 4.5–4.75 inches | Wingspan 7.25–7.75 inches |

VIRGINIA'S WARBLER

This bird most often builds its nest in arid coniferous forests in mountains and chaparral between six thousand and nine thousand feet. It is named for the wife of Dr. William W. Anderson, an assistant army surgeon who first recorded the bird in New Mexico. It is closely related and very similar to the Nashville Warbler, although their ranges do not overlap. This shy and active warbler almost constantly bobs its tail up and down. Females are similar to males but have duller coloring, with both the rufous crown patch and the yellow breast patch being much reduced.

ashy gray head and upperparts

greenish yellow rump

bright lemon-yellow undertail coverts

white eye ring

yellow patch on breast

pale gray-buff underparts

JUVENILE

• **SONG** Sings a 2-part song of slurred notes, with first 2-syllabled part of *chee-wee, chee-wee, chee-wee, cheah, cheah, chee.* Call is a sharp abrasive *chink.*

• **BEHAVIOR** Solitary or in pairs. Rather shy and retiring. May join mixed-species foraging flocks after nesting season. Male often sings from high exposed perch. Forages in low trees, shrubs, and sometimes on ground. Eats mostly insects and their caterpillars. Gleans prey from branches and foliage and sometimes hover gleans. Catches some insects in flight.

• **BREEDING** Monogamous. Solitary nester.

• **NESTING** Breeding biology poorly known. Estimated incubation 11–12 days by both sexes, but mostly by female. Young altricial; brooded by female; stay in nest estimated 11 days, fed by both sexes. 2 broods per year.

• **POPULATION** Common in mountain brushlands with adjacent pines or oaks. Rare migrant and wintering bird to coastal California. Casual in the East during migration.

• **CONSERVATION** Neotropical migrant. Rare to uncommon host to cowbird parasitism. Some range expansion in California since the 1960s.

Similar Birds

LUCY'S WARBLER Shorter tail; white underparts with white undertail coverts • male is smaller and has chestnut crown and rump • female and juvenile have cinnamon rumps.

COLIMA WARBLER Larger; more brown on upperparts and flanks; brighter yellow rump; yellow undertail coverts.

Flight Pattern

Somewhat weak fluttering direct flight on rapidly beating wings.

Nest Identification

Shape ⌣   Location ▬

Bark pieces, grasses, moss, lichens, and stems, with lining of same materials and hair • on ground, near grassy tussock or base of tree, or hidden in pile of leaves • built by female • 3–5 white eggs, flecked with brown; oval to short oval, 0.6 x 0.5 inches.

| Plumage Sexes differ | Habitat ▲ ⋟ ♠♠ | Migration Migratory | Weight 0.3 ounce |

DATE _____ TIME_____ LOCATION _____

Family PARULIDAE	Species *Vermivora crissalis*	Length 5.5 inches	Wingspan 8.5 inches

COLIMA WARBLER

This large warbler is a native of Mexico but has a breeding range in southwestern Texas and makes its summer home in the high mountain canyon oak forests of the Chisos Mountains in Big Bend National Park. This trusting bird is similar to Virginia's Warbler but is larger, longer tailed, has browner upperparts and underparts, and rarely bobs its tail. The female is similar to the male, and juveniles are similar to adults but have buffy wing bars, pale yellow uppertail coverts, and little or no rufous on the crown.

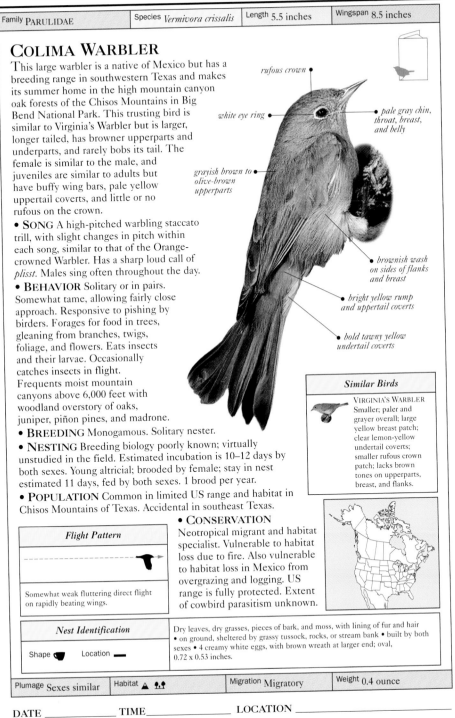

rufous crown

white eye ring

pale gray chin, throat, breast, and belly

grayish brown to olive-brown upperparts

brownish wash on sides of flanks and breast

bright yellow rump and uppertail coverts

bold tawny yellow undertail coverts

• **SONG** A high-pitched warbling staccato trill, with slight changes in pitch within each song, similar to that of the Orange-crowned Warbler. Has a sharp loud call of *plisst*. Males sing often throughout the day.

• **BEHAVIOR** Solitary or in pairs. Somewhat tame, allowing fairly close approach. Responsive to pishing by birders. Forages for food in trees, gleaning from branches, twigs, foliage, and flowers. Eats insects and their larvae. Occasionally catches insects in flight. Frequents moist mountain canyons above 6,000 feet with woodland overstory of oaks, juniper, piñon pines, and madrone.

• **BREEDING** Monogamous. Solitary nester.

• **NESTING** Breeding biology poorly known; virtually unstudied in the field. Estimated incubation is 10–12 days by both sexes. Young altricial; brooded by female; stay in nest estimated 11 days, fed by both sexes. 1 brood per year.

• **POPULATION** Common in limited US range and habitat in Chisos Mountains of Texas. Accidental in southeast Texas.

Similar Birds

VIRGINIA'S WARBLER Smaller; paler and grayer overall; large yellow breast patch; clear lemon-yellow undertail coverts; smaller rufous crown patch; lacks brown tones on upperparts, breast, and flanks.

• **CONSERVATION** Neotropical migrant and habitat specialist. Vulnerable to habitat loss due to fire. Also vulnerable to habitat loss in Mexico from overgrazing and logging. US range is fully protected. Extent of cowbird parasitism unknown.

Flight Pattern

Somewhat weak fluttering direct flight on rapidly beating wings.

Nest Identification	Dry leaves, dry grasses, pieces of bark, and moss, with lining of fur and hair • on ground, sheltered by grassy tussock, rocks, or stream bank • built by both sexes • 4 creamy white eggs, with brown wreath at larger end; oval, 0.72 x 0.53 inches.
Shape 🥚 Location ▬	

Plumage Sexes similar	Habitat ▲ 🌿	Migration Migratory	Weight 0.4 ounce

DATE _____ TIME_____ LOCATION _____

| Family PARULIDAE | Species *Vermivora luciae* | Length 4.25 inches | Wingspan 7 inches |

LUCY'S WARBLER

Distinguished from similar birds by its reddish rump, Lucy's Warbler is the only wood warbler to nest in the desert of southwestern North America and the only western warbler to nest in crevices and tree cavities. It was named for the daughter of Spencer F. Baird, secretary of the Smithsonian Institution. A small pale plain gray bird, it is kinglet-sized and has a chestnut crown, chestnut uppertail coverts, and a habit of constantly bobbing its tail.

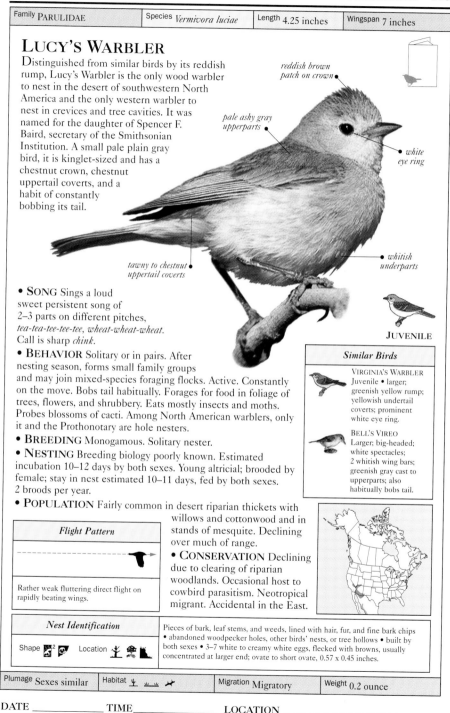

reddish brown patch on crown

pale ashy gray upperparts

white eye ring

tawny to chestnut uppertail coverts

whitish underparts

JUVENILE

- **SONG** Sings a loud sweet persistent song of 2–3 parts on different pitches, *tea-tea-tee-tee-tee, wheat-wheat-wheat.* Call is sharp *chink.*
- **BEHAVIOR** Solitary or in pairs. After nesting season, forms small family groups and may join mixed-species foraging flocks. Active. Constantly on the move. Bobs tail habitually. Forages for food in foliage of trees, flowers, and shrubbery. Eats mostly insects and moths. Probes blossoms of cacti. Among North American warblers, only it and the Prothonotary are hole nesters.
- **BREEDING** Monogamous. Solitary nester.
- **NESTING** Breeding biology poorly known. Estimated incubation 10–12 days by both sexes. Young altricial; brooded by female; stay in nest estimated 10–11 days, fed by both sexes. 2 broods per year.
- **POPULATION** Fairly common in desert riparian thickets with willows and cottonwood and in stands of mesquite. Declining over much of range.
- **CONSERVATION** Declining due to clearing of riparian woodlands. Occasional host to cowbird parasitism. Neotropical migrant. Accidental in the East.

Similar Birds

VIRGINIA'S WARBLER Juvenile • larger; greenish yellow rump; yellowish undertail coverts; prominent white eye ring.

BELL'S VIREO Larger; big-headed; white spectacles; 2 whitish wing bars; greenish gray cast to upperparts; also habitually bobs tail.

Flight Pattern

Rather weak fluttering direct flight on rapidly beating wings.

Nest Identification

Shape | Location

Pieces of bark, leaf stems, and weeds, lined with hair, fur, and fine bark chips • abandoned woodpecker holes, other birds' nests, or tree hollows • built by both sexes • 3–7 white to creamy white eggs, flecked with browns, usually concentrated at larger end; ovate to short ovate, 0.57 x 0.45 inches.

| Plumage Sexes similar | Habitat | Migration Migratory | Weight 0.2 ounce |

DATE _____ TIME _____ LOCATION _____

Family PARULIDAE	Species *Parula superciliosa*	Length 4.25 inches	Wingspan 7 inches

CRESCENT-CHESTED WARBLER

On rare occasion this tiny Mexican bird visits North America and has been spotted in southeastern Arizona and Big Bend National Park, Texas. The combination of the bold white eyebrow and yellow underparts, gray head, and greenish back is definitive among North American warblers. The female is similar to the male, but the crescent on her breast is a very pale washed-out chestnut. The southwestern spring and fall records are from pine-oak woodlands in mountain canyons, while the one wintering bird was found in willow-riparian area. The juvenile male is similar to the adult female, while the juvenile female may lack the chestnut on her breast.

conspicuous white eyebrow widens behind eye

bluish gray head

olive-green back

yellow chin, throat, and breast

chestnut crescent on breast

white belly, flanks, and undertail coverts

• **SONG** An insectlike dry buzz of *dzzzzzzzzzr* or *zzirrrrrrrrrr*. Call is a soft, somewhat abrasive *sik* or *ship*.

• **BEHAVIOR** Solitary or in pairs. More gregarious in winter, joining mixed-species flocks to feed. Forages for food in middle to upper level of trees, with rather slow deliberate actions. Gleans from twigs and foliage, often picking food from the undersides of leaves. Hangs chickadee-like beneath leaves and branches to examine surfaces for prey. Eats mostly insects but also takes some berries and fruits.

• **BREEDING** Monogamous. Solitary.

• **NESTING** Breeding biology poorly known; incubation estimated at 12–14 days by female. Young altricial; brooded by female; stay in nest estimated 8–10 days, fed by both sexes. 1–2 broods per year.

Similar Birds

TROPICAL PARULA
Black lores; 2 bold white wing bars; bluish gray head, wings, rump, and tail; greenish back; whitish undertail coverts; bright yellow underparts; lacks white supercilium; lacks crescent on chest
• uncommon in south Texas.

• **POPULATION** Casual to accidental in North America in mountains of southeastern Arizona and Chisos Mountains of southwestern Texas. Generally uncommon in Mexico, ranging within 200 miles of Arizona border.

Flight Pattern

Weak flight of short duration on rapidly beating wings, alternating with brief periods of wings pulled to sides.

Nest Identification

Shape ◖   Location ▬ ▬ ⸭⸭⸭ ▮

Moss, grass, and conifer needles, with lining of finer materials • atop grassy tussock or sheltered by hill or bank on or near the ground • female is believed to build nest without help from the male • 3 plain white eggs; oval to short oval, 0.7 x 0.5 inches.

Plumage Sexes similar	Habitat 🌿 🌱 ⛰	Migration Nonmigratory	Weight 0.3 ounce

DATE _____ TIME_____ LOCATION _____

Family PARULIDAE	Species *Dendroica petechia*	Length 5 inches	Wingspan 7.75 inches

YELLOW WARBLER

This plump-bodied bird has a wider range than any other North American warbler, nesting from Canada to Mexico and from the Pacific to the Atlantic Coasts. A habitat generalist, like many warblers, it feeds harmful leaf-eating caterpillars to its nestlings. When a cowbird invades and lays eggs in this warbler's nest, the female builds a roof over all of the eggs, both hers and the brood parasite's, and often lays a new set on the "new" nest floor. As many as six stories have been found in a single nest, each floor containing entombed cowbird eggs. Bright red streaking on the male's underparts distinguishes him from the female and all other North American warblers. Females may have faint reddish streaking on their underparts. Juveniles resemble adult females.

bright yellow head

dark eye contrasts with yellow face

short tail with yellow edging on feathers

yellowish overall

MALE

bright yellow underparts with reddish streaking

• **SONG** Sings a swift warbling *sweet-sweet, I'm-so-sweet* or *tseet-tseet-tseet-titi-deet*, bouncy and variable. Similar to some songs of Chestnut-sided Warbler and American Redstart.

• **BEHAVIOR** Solitary or in pairs. Tame and conspicuous. Active. Forages in bushes, shrubs, or trees. Gleans food from branches and foliage; sometimes hawks insects. Eats mostly insects, larvae, and some fruit.

• **BREEDING** Monogamous. Solitary.

• **NESTING** Incubation 11–12 days by female. Altricial young brooded by female; stay in nest 9–12 days, fed by both sexes. 1–2 broods per year.

• **POPULATION** Common and widespread in riparian thickets, second-growth woodlands, gardens, orchards, and wetlands.

yellow wing bars and edging

yellowish olive back, wings, and tail

FEMALE

Similar Birds

WILSON'S WARBLER ♀
Female and juvenile
• longer darker tail; lacks yellow tail spots; more uniform olive-green coloring on upperparts; no wing bars; female may show trace of dark cap.

ORANGE-CROWNED WARBLER
Olive-green overall; paler underparts with dusky streaking; uniform dark tail without pale edging or spots; lacks wing bars.

• **CONSERVATION** Neotropical migrant. Common host to cowbird parasitism. Vulnerable to habitat loss, especially in riparian areas, and to herbicide spraying of willow thickets for grazing.

Flight Pattern
Weak, fluttering flight with brief periods of wings drawn to sides. Sallies out to snatch insects in air and returns to perch.

Nest Identification	
Shape Location	Strongly built from plant material, grasses, moss, lichen, and fur, bound with spider's silk and cocoon material; lined with fine materials • in fork of tree or bush, 6–14 feet high (but up to 60 feet) • built mostly by female; male watches • 3–6 grayish, green, or bluish white eggs, splotched with grays, olives, and browns, wreathed at large end; oval to short oval, 0.7 x 0.5 inches.

Plumage Sexes differ	Habitat	Migration Migratory	Weight 0.3 ounce

DATE _____ TIME_____ LOCATION _____

Family PARULIDAE	Species *Dendroica pensylvanica*	Length 5–5.25 inches	Wingspan 7.5–8.25 inches

CHESTNUT-SIDED WARBLER

The only North American warbler with pure white underparts in all seasons, this bird most often lives in second-growth deciduous woodlands. An active feeder, it often cocks its tail high above its back, exposing a white crissum. Birds in fall plumage have a white eye ring on a gray face, a green crown, and creamy yellow wing bars; males have chestnut on the sides and black streaking on a green back.

light olive-green upperparts with black streaking

yellow crown

black lores and eye stripe

2 pale yellow wing bars

black malar mark

rich chestnut sides

MALE

slate-blue legs and feet

white underparts

- **SONG** High-pitched *please-please-pleased-to-meetcha.* Alternate or "second" song lacks strong up-and-down slurred notes at the end and is similar to that of the Yellow Warbler, *deet-deet-deet-titi-deet.* Call is a husky slurred *chip.*

- **BEHAVIOR** Solitary or in pairs. Tame and active. Singing male is conspicuous on territory. Picks food off leaves of trees and forages on ground. Catches insects in flight. Eats insects, caterpillars, seeds, and berries.

greenish upperparts with black streaking

2 yellowish white wing bars

yellow-green forehead and crown

FALL PLUMAGE

blackish gray lores, malar, and postocular stripe

less chestnut on sides

- **BREEDING** Monogamous. Solitary.

- **NESTING** Incubation 11–13 days by female. Altricial young brooded by female; remain in nest 10–12 days, fed by both sexes. 1–2 broods per year.

FEMALE

Similar Birds

All plumages are distinctive and if seen well are not likely to be confused with any other warbler.

- **POPULATION** Fairly common to common in brushy thickets, second-growth deciduous woodlands, brushy old fields, and young clear-cuts. Rare migrant in West.

- **CONSERVATION** Neotropical migrant. Vulnerable to habitat loss through natural succession processes. Rare in the early 1800s, but became increasingly common as eastern forests were cut, and brushy, early succession-stage woody habitats emerged. Declining in some areas as current forests mature.

Flight Pattern

Weak fluttering flight with brief periods of wings drawn to sides. Sallies forth to snatch insects in air, returning to perch.

Nest Identification

Shape ◗   Location 🌿 🌳

Bark chips, vines, and plant material, with lining of animal hair and grasses • in fork of small tree or shrub, or in blackberry thicket, 1–4 feet above ground • built by female • 3–5 white to greenish white or creamy white eggs, with purple and brown blotches; oval to short oval, 0.66 x 0.5 inches.

Plumage Sexes differ	Habitat 🌿 🌾	Migration Migratory	Weight 0.4 ounce

DATE _____ TIME_____ LOCATION _____

Family PARULIDAE	Species *Dendroica magnolia*	Length 5 inches	Wingspan 7.75 inches

MAGNOLIA WARBLER

Often fanning its tail to show its broad white subterminal band and yellow rump, this bird nests in damp coniferous forests. The tail from below is white at the base with a black terminal band. From above, the white band is interrupted in the middle. Females are similar but show two white wing bars and sometimes a white eye ring during their first spring; a black loral mask may extend onto auriculars.
Juveniles and fall-plumaged birds have gray heads with white eye rings, greenish gray upperparts with black streaking on the males, black streaking on the sides and flanks of males, and faint streaking on the flanks of females.

blackish upperparts

white wing patch

broad white eyebrow

broken white eye ring

dark blackish streaking on breast, sides, and flanks

MALE

yellow underparts

olive-tinged gray crown and hindneck

white supercilium and eye ring

black-spotted yellow-olive back

gray wings with 2 white wing bars

yellow underparts with black streaking

white undertail coverts

FALL PLUMAGE

FIRST SPRING FEMALE

- **SONG** Brief high-pitched *wee-o, wee-o, wee-chew* or *weety-weety-weeteeo*, 2 or 3 slurred phrases with an ending note higher in pitch, emphatic and down-slurred. Call is distinctive nasal dry chip *tzek*.
- **BEHAVIOR** Solitary or in pairs. Tame and active. Males sing from conspicuous perches or while foraging. Often spreading tail, busily gleans insects from branches and foliage; occasionally hawks them in flight. Eats insects, larvae, caterpillars, and spiders.
- **BREEDING** Monogamous. Solitary.
- **NESTING** Incubation 11–13 days by female. Altricial young brooded by female; stay in nest 8–10 days, fed by both sexes. 1 brood per year.
- **POPULATION** Fairly common to common; slight decline in parts of Appalachians, increase in southern Appalachians and in New England. Casual in winter in Florida. Rare migrant in West.
- **CONSERVATION** Neotropical migrant. Vulnerable to habitat loss. Loss of eastern spruce-fir forests to adelgids and air pollution is causing a decline in numbers.

Similar Birds

PRAIRIE WARBLER
Fall • yellowish supercilium; has only arc beneath eye; olive-green rump; uniform olive-green tail; lacks grayish white breast band; pumps tail.

Flight Pattern

Weak fluttering flight with brief periods of wings drawn to sides. Sallies forth to take insects in flight, returning to perch.

Nest Identification

Shape 🥣 Location 🌿 🌲

Grasses and sticks, lined with rootlets • on horizontal branch, usually 1–15 feet above ground • built by both sexes • 3–5 white, creamy white, or greenish white eggs, with brown dots or splotches, sometimes wreathed at larger end; subelliptical to short subelliptical, 0.64 x 0.48 inches.

Plumage Sexes differ	Habitat 🌾 🌲	Migration Migratory	Weight 0.3 ounce

DATE _____ TIME_____ LOCATION _____

Family PARULIDAE	Species *Dendroica tigrina*	Length 4.75 inches	Wingspan 7 inches

CAPE MAY WARBLER

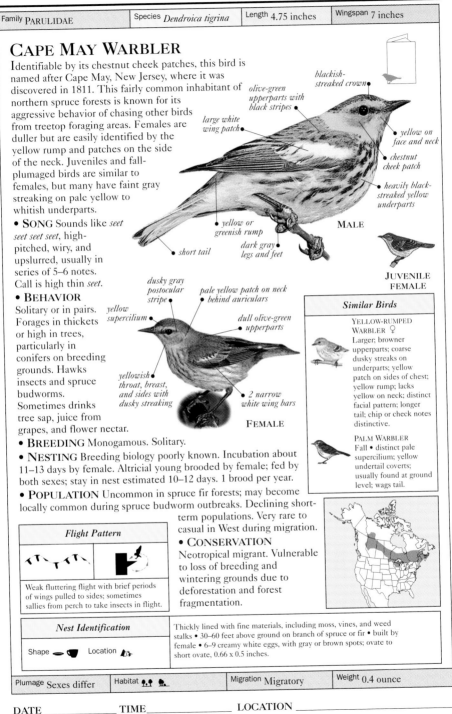

Identifiable by its chestnut cheek patches, this bird is named after Cape May, New Jersey, where it was discovered in 1811. This fairly common inhabitant of northern spruce forests is known for its aggressive behavior of chasing other birds from treetop foraging areas. Females are duller but are easily identified by the yellow rump and patches on the side of the neck. Juveniles and fall-plumaged birds are similar to females, but many have faint gray streaking on pale yellow to whitish underparts.

olive-green upperparts with black stripes
large white wing patch
blackish-streaked crown
yellow on face and neck
chestnut cheek patch
heavily black-streaked yellow underparts
yellow or greenish rump
short tail
dark gray legs and feet
MALE

JUVENILE FEMALE

- **SONG** Sounds like *seet seet seet seet*, high-pitched, wiry, and upslurred, usually in series of 5–6 notes. Call is high thin *seet*.

- **BEHAVIOR** Solitary or in pairs. Forages in thickets or high in trees, particularly in conifers on breeding grounds. Hawks insects and spruce budworms. Sometimes drinks tree sap, juice from grapes, and flower nectar.

dusky gray postocular stripe
pale yellow patch on neck behind auriculars
yellow supercilium
dull olive-green upperparts
yellowish throat, breast, and sides with dusky streaking
2 narrow white wing bars
FEMALE

Similar Birds

YELLOW-RUMPED WARBLER ♀
Larger; browner upperparts; coarse dusky streaks on underparts; yellow patch on sides of chest; yellow rump; lacks yellow on neck; distinct facial pattern; longer tail; chip or check notes distinctive.

PALM WARBLER
Fall • distinct pale supercilium; yellow undertail coverts; usually found at ground level; wags tail.

- **BREEDING** Monogamous. Solitary.

- **NESTING** Breeding biology poorly known. Incubation about 11–13 days by female. Altricial young brooded by female; fed by both sexes; stay in nest estimated 10–12 days. 1 brood per year.

- **POPULATION** Uncommon in spruce fir forests. Declining short-term populations. Very rare to casual in West during migration.

- **CONSERVATION** Neotropical migrant. Vulnerable to loss of breeding and wintering grounds due to deforestation and forest fragmentation.

Flight Pattern

Weak fluttering flight with brief periods of wings pulled to sides; sometimes sallies from perch to take insects in flight.

Nest Identification	
Shape	Location	Thickly lined with fine materials, including moss, vines, and weed stalks • 30–60 feet above ground on branch of spruce or fir • built by female • 6–9 creamy white eggs, with gray or brown spots; ovate to short ovate, 0.66 x 0.5 inches.

Plumage Sexes differ	Habitat	Migration Migratory	Weight 0.4 ounce

DATE _____ TIME_____ LOCATION _____

Family PARULIDAE	Species *Dendroica caerulescens*	Length 5.25 inches	Wingspan 7–7.5 inches

BLACK-THROATED BLUE WARBLER

Easily identified by its deep blue-gray back, white underparts, and white wing patch, this common migratory bird can be seen across eastern North America every spring and fall. Its nesting ranges from southern Canada through the Appalachians to northern Georgia. Females differ from their mates more than any of the wood warblers, with brownish olive to gray upperparts, whitish supercilium, and small white patch at the base of the primaries. Juvenile females sometimes lack the white patch.

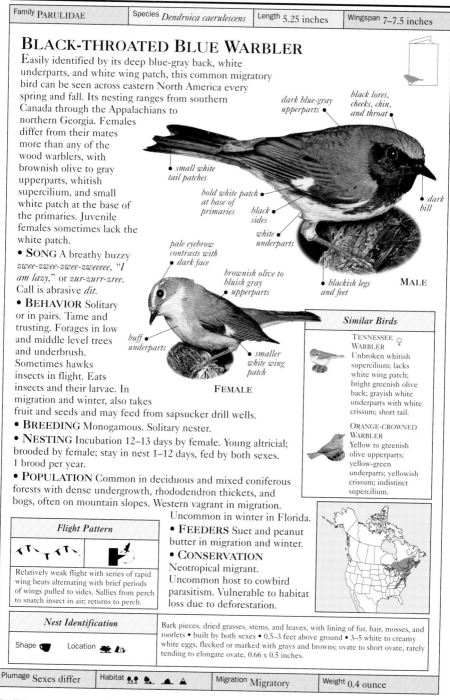

dark blue-gray upperparts

black lores, cheeks, chin, and throat

small white tail patches

bold white patch at base of primaries

black sides

dark bill

pale eyebrow contrasts with dark face

white underparts

brownish olive to bluish gray upperparts

blackish legs and feet

MALE

buff underparts

smaller white wing patch

FEMALE

- **SONG** A breathy buzzy *zwee-zwee-zwee-zweeeee*, "*I am lazy*," or *zur-zurr-zree*. Call is abrasive *dit*.
- **BEHAVIOR** Solitary or in pairs. Tame and trusting. Forages in low and middle level trees and underbrush. Sometimes hawks insects in flight. Eats insects and their larvae. In migration and winter, also takes fruit and seeds and may feed from sapsucker drill wells.
- **BREEDING** Monogamous. Solitary nester.
- **NESTING** Incubation 12–13 days by female. Young altricial; brooded by female; stay in nest 1–12 days, fed by both sexes. 1 brood per year.
- **POPULATION** Common in deciduous and mixed coniferous forests with dense undergrowth, rhododendron thickets, and bogs, often on mountain slopes. Western vagrant in migration. Uncommon in winter in Florida.
- **FEEDERS** Suet and peanut butter in migration and winter.
- **CONSERVATION** Neotropical migrant. Uncommon host to cowbird parasitism. Vulnerable to habitat loss due to deforestation.

Similar Birds

TENNESSEE WARBLER ♀
Unbroken whitish supercilium; lacks white wing patch; bright greenish olive back; grayish white underparts with white crissum; short tail.

ORANGE-CROWNED WARBLER
Yellow to greenish olive upperparts; yellow-green underparts; yellowish crissum; indistinct supercilium.

Flight Pattern

Relatively weak flight with series of rapid wing beats alternating with brief periods of wings pulled to sides. Sallies from perch to snatch insect in air; returns to perch.

Nest Identification

Shape ☕   Location 🌿 🌲

Bark pieces, dried grasses, stems, and leaves, with lining of fur, hair, mosses, and rootlets • built by both sexes • 0.5–3 feet above ground • 3–5 white to creamy white eggs, flecked or marked with grays and browns; ovate to short ovate, rarely tending to elongate ovate, 0.66 x 0.5 inches.

Plumage Sexes differ	Habitat 🌿🌱 🌲 🔺 🔺	Migration Migratory	Weight 0.4 ounce

DATE _____ TIME_____ LOCATION _____

| Family PARULIDAE | Species *Dendroica coronata* | Length 5.5 inches | Wingspan 8.5 inches |

YELLOW-RUMPED WARBLER

In the East this is the most prevalent migrating warbler, and in winter it is the most abundant in North America. Plumage varies with geography. In the West the group known as Audubon's Warbler has a yellow throat and broken white eye ring. The northern and eastern group known as the Myrtle Warbler has white eyebrows, a white arc beneath the eye, and white on the throat and both sides of the neck. Until recently these groups were considered two species, but they interbreed where their ranges overlap and have been classified as geographic races of one species. Juveniles are similar to winter adults.

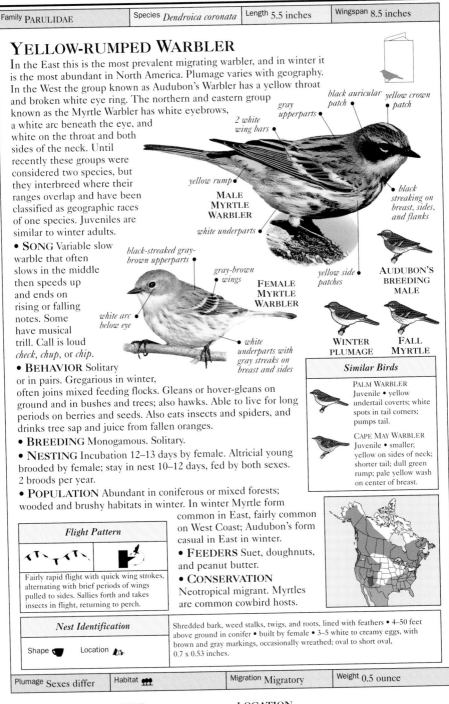

black auricular patch • yellow crown patch

gray upperparts •

2 white wing bars •

yellow rump •

MALE MYRTLE WARBLER

white underparts •

• black streaking on breast, sides, and flanks

black-streaked gray-brown upperparts •

gray-brown wings •

FEMALE MYRTLE WARBLER

white arc below eye •

yellow side patches •

AUDUBON'S BREEDING MALE

• white underparts with gray streaks on breast and sides

WINTER PLUMAGE

FALL MYRTLE

- **SONG** Variable slow warble that often slows in the middle then speeds up and ends on rising or falling notes. Some have musical trill. Call is loud *check, chup,* or *chip.*
- **BEHAVIOR** Solitary or in pairs. Gregarious in winter, often joins mixed feeding flocks. Gleans or hover-gleans on ground and in bushes and trees; also hawks. Able to live for long periods on berries and seeds. Also eats insects and spiders, and drinks tree sap and juice from fallen oranges.
- **BREEDING** Monogamous. Solitary.
- **NESTING** Incubation 12–13 days by female. Altricial young brooded by female; stay in nest 10–12 days, fed by both sexes. 2 broods per year.
- **POPULATION** Abundant in coniferous or mixed forests; wooded and brushy habitats in winter. In winter Myrtle form common in East, fairly common on West Coast; Audubon's form casual in East in winter.
- **FEEDERS** Suet, doughnuts, and peanut butter.
- **CONSERVATION** Neotropical migrant. Myrtles are common cowbird hosts.

Similar Birds

PALM WARBLER Juvenile • yellow undertail coverts; white spots in tail corners; pumps tail.

CAPE MAY WARBLER Juvenile • smaller; yellow on sides of neck; shorter tail; dull green rump; pale yellow wash on center of breast.

Flight Pattern

Fairly rapid flight with quick wing strokes, alternating with brief periods of wings pulled to sides. Sallies forth and takes insects in flight, returning to perch.

| Nest Identification | Shredded bark, weed stalks, twigs, and roots, lined with feathers • 4–50 feet above ground in conifer • built by female • 3–5 white to creamy eggs, with brown and gray markings, occasionally wreathed; oval to short oval, 0.7 x 0.53 inches. |
| Shape 🐦 Location 🐦 | |

| Plumage Sexes differ | Habitat 🌳 | Migration Migratory | Weight 0.5 ounce |

Family PARULIDAE	Species *Dendroica nigrescens*	Length 4.75–5 inches	Wingspan 7.5–8 inches

BLACK-THROATED GRAY WARBLER

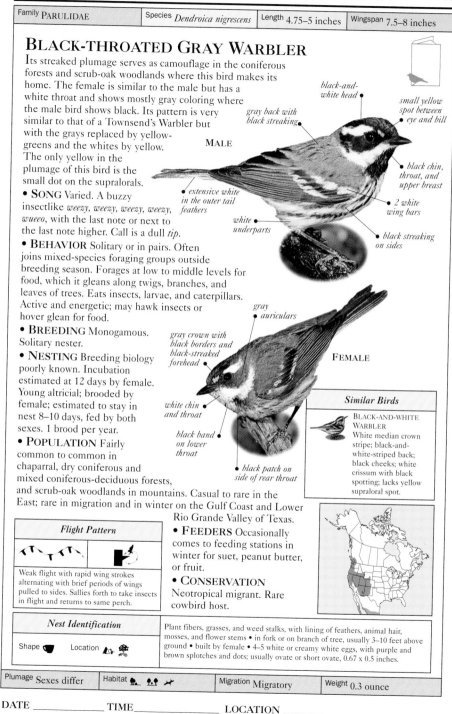

Its streaked plumage serves as camouflage in the coniferous forests and scrub-oak woodlands where this bird makes its home. The female is similar to the male but has a white throat and shows mostly gray coloring where the male bird shows black. Its pattern is very similar to that of a Townsend's Warbler but with the grays replaced by yellow-greens and the whites by yellow. The only yellow in the plumage of this bird is the small dot on the supralorals.

- **SONG** Varied. A buzzy insectlike *weezy, weezy, weezy, weezy, wueeo*, with the last note or next to the last note higher. Call is a dull *tip*.
- **BEHAVIOR** Solitary or in pairs. Often joins mixed-species foraging groups outside breeding season. Forages at low to middle levels for food, which it gleans along twigs, branches, and leaves of trees. Eats insects, larvae, and caterpillars. Active and energetic; may hawk insects or hover glean for food.
- **BREEDING** Monogamous. Solitary nester.
- **NESTING** Breeding biology poorly known. Incubation estimated at 12 days by female. Young altricial; brooded by female; estimated to stay in nest 8–10 days, fed by both sexes. 1 brood per year.
- **POPULATION** Fairly common to common in chaparral, dry coniferous and mixed coniferous-deciduous forests, and scrub-oak woodlands in mountains. Casual to rare in the East; rare in migration and in winter on the Gulf Coast and Lower Rio Grande Valley of Texas.
- **FEEDERS** Occasionally comes to feeding stations in winter for suet, peanut butter, or fruit.
- **CONSERVATION** Neotropical migrant. Rare cowbird host.

black-and-white head

small yellow spot between eye and bill

gray back with black streaking

MALE

black chin, throat, and upper breast

extensive white in the outer tail feathers

2 white wing bars

white underparts

black streaking on sides

gray auriculars

gray crown with black borders and black-streaked forehead

FEMALE

white chin and throat

black band on lower throat

black patch on side of rear throat

Similar Birds

BLACK-AND-WHITE WARBLER
White median crown stripe; black-and-white-striped back; black cheeks; white crissum with black spotting; lacks yellow supraloral spot.

Flight Pattern

Weak flight with rapid wing strokes alternating with brief periods of wings pulled to sides. Sallies forth to take insects in flight and returns to same perch.

Nest Identification

Shape [icon]   Location [icons]

Plant fibers, grasses, and weed stalks, with lining of feathers, animal hair, mosses, and flower stems • in fork or on branch of tree, usually 3–10 feet above ground • built by female • 4–5 white or creamy white eggs, with purple and brown splotches and dots; usually ovate or short ovate, 0.67 x 0.5 inches.

Plumage Sexes differ	Habitat [icons]	Migration Migratory	Weight 0.3 ounce

DATE _____ TIME_____ LOCATION _____

Family PARULIDAE	Species *Dendroica chrysoparia*	Length 4.75–5 inches	Wingspan 7.5–8 inches

GOLDEN-CHEEKED WARBLER

Now endangered, this habitat specialist of "cedar breaks," Ashe juniper and oaks, breeds only on or near the Edwards Plateau in Texas and winters in Mexico and Central America. From the mature Ashe juniper the female strips bark and binds it with spider webs to camouflage the outside of its nest. The male sings sunrise to sunset from high conspicuous perches on its nesting territory. Females have white throats and underparts. Juveniles have olive upperparts streaked with black and streaked sides to their throats.

• **SONG** 4–5 harsh buzzy notes, *bzzz-layzee-dayzee* or *tweeah-tweeah-tweesy*. Call is *tip*.

• **BEHAVIOR** Solitary or in pairs. Clings chickadee-like under branches as it forages. Gleans food from foliage, stems, and twigs. Eats mostly insects. Feeds at heights of 30 feet or less, hunting in middle to lower levels. Outside breeding season joins mixed foraging flocks. Returns to breeding grounds in mid-March and males begin territorial songs.

• **BREEDING** Monogamous and solitary.

• **NESTING** Incubation 12 days by female. Young altricial; brooded by female; stay in nest 9 days, fed by both sexes. 1 brood per year.

• **POPULATION** Rare; limited to hill country of central Texas.

• **CONSERVATION** Federally endangered. One of the rarest songbirds in North America. Vulnerable to Blue Jay predation, cowbird parasitism, and habitat destruction. Neotropical migrant.

black crown
golden cheeks with black outline
black eye line
black upperparts
2 white wing bars
black chin, throat, and bib
black streaking on sides
white underparts

MALE

dark olive-green upperparts and crown with black streaking
2 white wing bars
blackish eye line
streaky blackish bib
black streaks on sides
light golden cheeks without outline

FEMALE

Similar Birds

BLACK-THROATED GREEN WARBLER ♀ Juvenile female • olive cap; unstreaked olive-green upperparts; olive auricular patch; greenish olive rump.

Flight Pattern

Weak flight with rapid wing strokes alternating with brief periods of wings pulled to sides.

Nest Identification	Bark pieces, grasses, spider's silk, and rootlets, with lining of feathers and hair • in fork of tree, usually 15–20 feet above ground • built by female • 3–5 white to creamy white eggs, with brown and gray dots and flecks; generally ovate to short ovate, 0.75 x 0.5 inches.
Shape	Location

Plumage Sexes differ	Habitat	Migration Migratory	Weight 0.4 ounce

DATE _____ TIME_____ LOCATION _____

| Family PARULIDAE | Species *Dendroica virens* | Length 4.75–5 inches | Wingspan 7.5–8 inches |

BLACK-THROATED GREEN WARBLER

Like many in its family, the individual Black-throated Green Warbler sings two different songs, but in two different contexts: one in the vicinity of the female or nest and the other near the territorial boundaries or when stimulated by another male. It is the only warbler in eastern North America with bold yellow cheeks. The female is similar to the male but shows fewer black streaks on the sides of her body, less black on her throat, and has a yellowish chin and upper throat. The juvenile is similar to the female but has a white throat and lacks the black on its breast.

olive-green auricular patch

yellow- and olive-green upperparts with black streaking on back

MALE

bright yellow forehead and sides of face

yellow wash on flanks

black chin, throat, and upper breast

2 white wing bars

white underparts

black streaking on flanks and sides

yellowish chin

FEMALE

black throat veiled with whitish feather tips

- **SONG** A throaty *trees-trees-whispering-trees* (the territorial/male interaction song) and a hoarse *zay-zay-zay-zoo-zeee* (the pair bonding/nest vicinity song). Call is a flat soft *tsip*.
- **BEHAVIOR** Solitary or in pairs. Forages at mid-level in vegetation and in the interior of branches, usually not at the tips. Gleans from twigs and foliage; hover-gleans and may hawk flying prey. Eats adult insects, caterpillars, larvae, and some berries, particularly in migration.
- **BREEDING** Monogamous. Solitary.
- **NESTING** Incubation 12 days by female. Young altricial; brooded by female; remain in nest 8–10 days, fed by both sexes, but female does more. 1–2 broods per year.
- **POPULATION** Fairly common in a variety of habitats of conifer, mixed deciduous-conifer, and deciduous woodlands. Some winter regularly in southern Florida; casual to accidental in the West. Numbers decreasing in the Great Lakes areas and in parts of New England.
- **CONSERVATION** Neotropical migrant. Vulnerable to habitat loss. Rare host to cowbird parasitism.

Similar Birds

GOLDEN-CHEEKED WARBLER
♂ Gray to black upperparts with black streaking; black or black-streaked crown; yellow face; black eye line connected to the dark color of nape; ♀ black ear patch; white crissum • restricted rang in Texas.

Flight Pattern	

Somewhat weak flight with rapid wing strokes, alternating with brief periods of wings pulled to sides. Sallies from perch, takes insect in air, and returns to perch.

Nest Identification	
Shape ⬤ Location 🌿 🌲	Dead grasses, plant fibers, and stems, with lining of animal hair, flower stems, and feathers • usually in crotch of small or large evergreen or in hardwood tree on horizontal branch, 3–80 feet above ground • built by both sexes • 3–5 gray-white or creamy white eggs, with brown and purple dots and blotches, often wreathed; oval to short oval, 0.65 x 0.5 inches.

| Plumage Sexes differ | Habitat 🌿 🌲 | Migration Migratory | Weight 0.3 ounce |

DATE _____ TIME_____ LOCATION _____

| Family PARULIDAE | Species *Dendroica townsendi* | Length 4.75–5 inches | Wingspan 7.5–8 inches |

TOWNSEND'S WARBLER

The western counterpart of the Black-throated Green Warbler nests in high pines and spruces of the Pacific Northwest. The bright yellow underparts and yellow face with black cheek patch are difficult to see because the bird forages and sings in the tops of the mature conifers. Townsend's Warbler often hybridizes with the Hermit Warbler where ranges overlap.

blackish ear patch with wide yellow trim

olive-green upperparts with black streaks

dark blackish crown

2 white wing bars

black chin, throat, and upper breast

- **SONG** Variable. Raspy high *weezy, weezy, weezy, tweea*, rising in pitch but dropping at the end. Call is high sharp *tsik*.

white in outer 2–3 tail feathers

white belly

yellow breast

yellowish sides with black streaking

- **BEHAVIOR** Solitary or in pairs. Gregarious after breeding season; joins mixed-species foraging flocks. Aggressive toward

olive crown with black streaking

narrow black streaking on back

2 thin white wing bars

yellow chin and throat

olive cheeks

MALE

necklace of black streaks on lower throat

other species. Sometimes hover-gleans from branches and foliage. Eats insects, caterpillars, and spiders.

thin black streaks on sides and flanks

FEMALE

- **BREEDING** Monogamous. Solitary.
- **NESTING** Breeding biology poorly known. Incubation estimated at 12 days by female. Altricial young brooded by female; stay in nest estimated 8–12 days. Fed by both sexes; female may do more. 1 brood per year.
- **POPULATION** Fairly common in coniferous and mixed coniferous-deciduous forests. Casual to accidental in winter and in migration in the East. May be increasing slightly and expanding range southward in Washington and Oregon.

Similar Birds

BLACK-THROATED GREEN WARBLER Yellow cheeks and face without dark ear patches; whitish chest; olive back with black streaking; yellowish wash on undertail coverts • eastern breeding range has almost no overlap.

HERMIT WARBLER Lacks black cheeks and crown; yellow restricted to breast and sides; fine black streaking on sides and flanks.

- **FEEDERS** Mixture of peanut butter, cheese, and marshmallows.
- **CONSERVATION** Neotropical migrant. Degree of cowbird parasitism unknown. Subject to forest fragmentation by logging.

Flight Pattern
Relatively weak flight on rapidly beating wings, alternating with brief periods of wings pulled to sides; repeated.

Nest Identification	Bark pieces, plant fibers, lichens, grasses, and cocoon materials, with lining of feathers and animal hair • across limb of conifer, high above ground • built by both sexes • 3–5 white eggs, with fine dots of brown; short ovate, 0.7 x 0.5 inches.
Shape ⬩ Location ▲	

| Plumage Sexes differ | Habitat 🌲 🌿 | Migration Migratory | Weight 0.3 ounce |

Family PARULIDAE	Species *Dendroica occidentalis*	Length 5 inches	Wingspan 7.75 inches

HERMIT WARBLER

This bird is difficult to spot because it spends its time in the tops of tall fir and pine trees. It exhibits a marked partiality to conifers when foraging and nesting. Sometimes it can be drawn into the open when it hears a call or imitation of the Saw-whet Owl. This warbler generally has gray upperparts and white underparts with a brilliant yellow face. Males have a black throat. Females are similar to males but have a yellow chin and little or no black on the throat. Juveniles are similar to females; juvenile females have more olive to the upperparts.

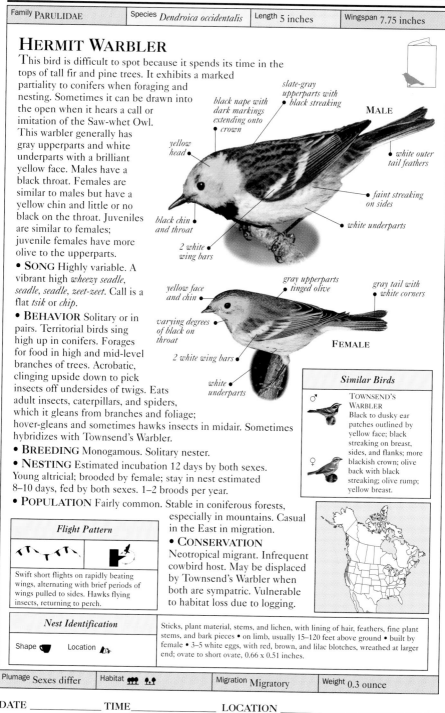

slate-gray
upperparts with
black streaking

black nape with
dark markings
extending onto
crown

MALE

yellow
head

white outer
tail feathers

faint streaking
on sides

black chin
and throat

white underparts

2 white
wing bars

gray upperparts
tinged olive

gray tail with
white corners

yellow face
and chin

varying degrees
of black on
throat

FEMALE

2 white wing bars

white
underparts

• **SONG** Highly variable. A vibrant high *wheezy seadle, seadle, seadle, zeet-zeet*. Call is a flat *tsik* or *chip*.

• **BEHAVIOR** Solitary or in pairs. Territorial birds sing high up in conifers. Forages for food in high and mid-level branches of trees. Acrobatic, clinging upside down to pick insects off undersides of twigs. Eats adult insects, caterpillars, and spiders, which it gleans from branches and foliage; hover-gleans and sometimes hawks insects in midair. Sometimes hybridizes with Townsend's Warbler.

• **BREEDING** Monogamous. Solitary nester.

• **NESTING** Estimated incubation 12 days by both sexes. Young altricial; brooded by female; stay in nest estimated 8–10 days, fed by both sexes. 1–2 broods per year.

• **POPULATION** Fairly common. Stable in coniferous forests, especially in mountains. Casual in the East in migration.

• **CONSERVATION** Neotropical migrant. Infrequent cowbird host. May be displaced by Townsend's Warbler when both are sympatric. Vulnerable to habitat loss due to logging.

Similar Birds

♂ TOWNSEND'S WARBLER Black to dusky ear patches outlined by yellow face; black streaking on breast, sides, and flanks; more blackish crown; olive back with black streaking; olive rump; ♀ yellow breast.

Flight Pattern

Swift short flights on rapidly beating wings, alternating with brief periods of wings pulled to sides. Hawks flying insects, returning to perch.

Nest Identification

Shape 🥄　　Location 🌲

Sticks, plant material, stems, and lichen, with lining of hair, feathers, fine plant stems, and bark pieces • on limb, usually 15–120 feet above ground • built by female • 3–5 white eggs, with red, brown, and lilac blotches, wreathed at larger end; ovate to short ovate, 0.66 x 0.51 inches.

Plumage Sexes differ	Habitat 🌳 🌿	Migration Migratory	Weight 0.3 ounce

DATE _____ TIME _____ LOCATION _____

Family PARULIDAE	Species *Dendroica fusca*	Length 5 inches	Wingspan 8 inches

BLACKBURNIAN WARBLER

Head and throat glowing like embers, the males are unmistakable. Juveniles and fall males are similar. It frequents coniferous or mixed deciduous-conifer forests in most of its breeding range; in the Appalachians, it is also found in lower drier forests of pine-oak-hickory.

• **SONG** Thin high-pitched ascending trill in 2–3 parts, ending with upslurred note that some people cannot hear: *seep seep seep seep titi zeeeeee*. Call is rich *tsip*.

• **BEHAVIOR** Solitary or in pairs. May join mixed foraging flocks after breeding. Gleans prey from branches, twigs, and foliage in treetops. Sometimes catches

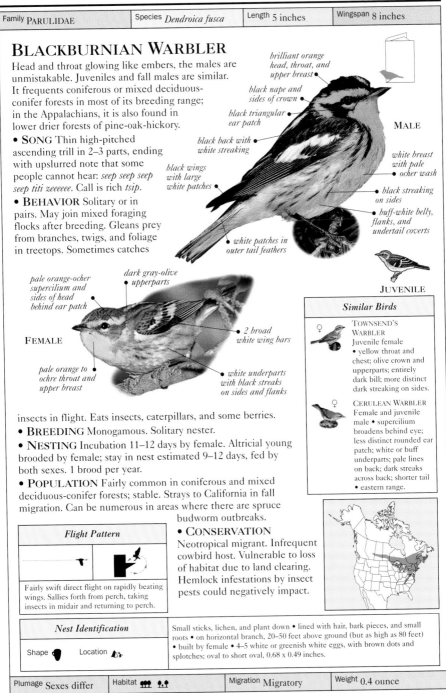

brilliant orange head, throat, and upper breast

black nape and sides of crown

black triangular ear patch

black back with white streaking

black wings with large white patches

white patches in outer tail feathers

MALE

white breast with pale ocher wash

black streaking on sides

buff-white belly, flanks, and undertail coverts

dark gray-olive upperparts

pale orange-ocher supercilium and sides of head behind ear patch

FEMALE

pale orange to ochre throat and upper breast

2 broad white wing bars

white underparts with black streaks on sides and flanks

JUVENILE

Similar Birds

♀ **TOWNSEND'S WARBLER**
Juvenile female • yellow throat and chest; olive crown and upperparts; entirely dark bill; more distinct dark streaking on sides.

♀ **CERULEAN WARBLER**
Female and juvenile male • supercilium broadens behind eye; less distinct rounded ear patch; white or buff underparts; pale lines on back; dark streaks across back; shorter tail • eastern range.

insects in flight. Eats insects, caterpillars, and some berries.

• **BREEDING** Monogamous. Solitary nester.

• **NESTING** Incubation 11–12 days by female. Altricial young brooded by female; stay in nest estimated 9–12 days, fed by both sexes. 1 brood per year.

• **POPULATION** Fairly common in coniferous and mixed deciduous-conifer forests; stable. Strays to California in fall migration. Can be numerous in areas where there are spruce budworm outbreaks.

• **CONSERVATION** Neotropical migrant. Infrequent cowbird host. Vulnerable to loss of habitat due to land clearing. Hemlock infestations by insect pests could negatively impact.

Flight Pattern

Fairly swift direct flight on rapidly beating wings. Sallies forth from perch, taking insects in midair and returning to perch.

Nest Identification	
Shape Location	Small sticks, lichen, and plant down • lined with hair, bark pieces, and small roots • on horizontal branch, 20–50 feet above ground (but as high as 80 feet) • built by female • 4–5 white or greenish white eggs, with brown dots and splotches; oval to short oval, 0.68 x 0.49 inches.

Plumage Sexes differ	Habitat	Migration Migratory	Weight 0.4 ounce

DATE _____ TIME_____ LOCATION _____

Family PARULIDAE	Species *Dendroica dominica*	Length 5.25 inches	Wingspan 8.5 inches

YELLOW-THROATED WARBLER

Some of these birds frequent the old oak trees of the Southeast and Mississippi Valley, where Spanish moss is abundant. Their habitat varies regionally from tall swampy bottomland hardwoods, to oak-pine woods on ridges, to lowland pine forests, to sycamores in riparian corridors. In all habitats, this long-billed warbler sings loudly from the tops of trees, and can be identified by the black face set off by a bold white supercilium and bright yellow chin and throat. The female is similar to the male but duller and has fewer black markings. Most migrate but southern populations are sedentary.

black-and-white head with white patch on sides of neck

white or yellow supraloral

white arc under eye, white stripe over eye

long black bill

blue-gray upperparts

bright yellow chin, throat, and breast

2 white wing bars

white underparts

black stripes on sides of breast, sides, and flanks

large white tail spots

• **SONG** Loud descending series of 3–4 measured whistles, followed by 2–3 weaker notes and more rapid notes, ending with sharper ascending note, *tweede-tweede-tweede-tweede-dee-da-m-deet*. Call note is high soft *tsip*.

• **BEHAVIOR** Solitary or in pairs. Somewhat sluggish and deliberate. Joins mixed-species feeding flocks after breeding season. Creeps along inner branches, twigs, and in foliage, foraging generally in the upper parts of trees; however, sometimes lower and even on the ground. Uses long bill and behavior similar to that of Brown Creeper to extract insects from bark crevices and pick them from the surface. Also catches insects in flight. Eats insects, caterpillars, and spiders.

• **BREEDING** Monogamous. Solitary nester.

• **NESTING** Breeding biology poorly known. Incubation by female estimated at 12–13 days. Altricial young brooded by female; stay in nest estimated 10 days, fed by female (possibly some by male). 1–2 broods per year.

• **POPULATION** Fairly common in habitat. Stable overall; some expansion in the Northeast and noted decline in the Florida Panhandle and southern Alabama. Casual in the West during fall migration; rare to casual in southeastern Canada during spring migration.

Similar Birds

BLACKBURNIAN WARBLER
Juvenile fall male
• shorter bill; yellow-orange throat and supercilium; yellow patch on side of head; blackish back with white stripes; 2 white wing bars; dusky streaks on sides and flanks.

• **FEEDERS** Bread crumbs and suet.

• **CONSERVATION** Neotropical migrant. Infrequent cowbird host. Vulnerable to habitat loss due to logging, land clearing, and development.

Flight Pattern

Fairly swift flight of short duration on rapidly beating wings. Sallies forth from perch, taking insects in air, and returns to perch.

Nest Identification

Shape
Location

Plant down, stems, grasses, and cocoon material, with lining of feathers and fine plant material • tucked into Spanish moss or on or near end of branch, 10–100 feet above ground • built mostly by female • 4–5 grayish white or greenish white eggs, with lavender, reddish, and grayish flecks and splotches; subelliptical to short subelliptical, 0.68 x 0.51 inches.

Plumage Sexes similar	Habitat	Migration Migratory	Weight 0.3 ounce

DATE _____ TIME_____ LOCATION _____

Family PARULIDAE	Species *Dendroica graciae*	Length 4.75 inches	Wingspan 7.75 inches

GRACE'S WARBLER

This energetic bird makes its summer home in the mountain pine and pine-oak forests of southwestern North America. Because it feeds in the tops of tall pine trees, it often is difficult to spot. Females are similar to males but duller in color and with more brown on the upperparts. In appearance and habitat this species is the western counterpart of the

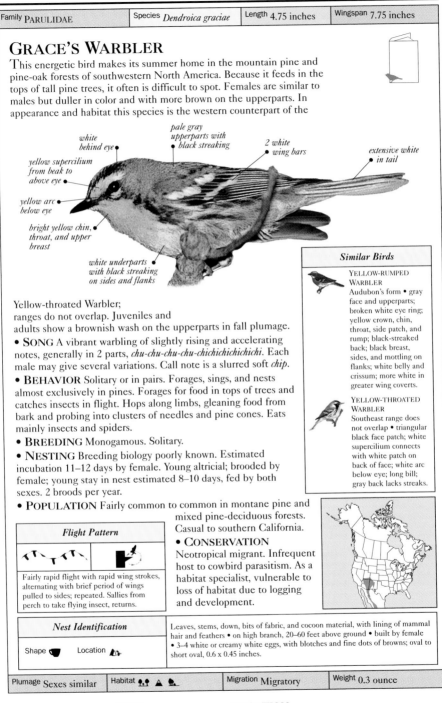

white behind eye

pale gray upperparts with black streaking

2 white wing bars

extensive white in tail

yellow supercilium from beak to above eye

yellow arc below eye

bright yellow chin, throat, and upper breast

white underparts with black streaking on sides and flanks

Similar Birds

YELLOW-RUMPED WARBLER
Audubon's form • gray face and upperparts; broken white eye ring; yellow crown, chin, throat, side patch, and rump; black-streaked back; black breast, sides, and mottling on flanks; white belly and crissum; more white in greater wing coverts.

YELLOW-THROATED WARBLER
Southeast range does not overlap • triangular black face patch; white supercilium connects with white patch on back of face; white arc below eye; long bill; gray back lacks streaks.

Yellow-throated Warbler; ranges do not overlap. Juveniles and adults show a brownish wash on the upperparts in fall plumage.

• **SONG** A vibrant warbling of slightly rising and accelerating notes, generally in 2 parts, *chu-chu-chu-chu-chichichichichichi*. Each male may give several variations. Call note is a slurred soft *chip*.

• **BEHAVIOR** Solitary or in pairs. Forages, sings, and nests almost exclusively in pines. Forages for food in tops of trees and catches insects in flight. Hops along limbs, gleaning food from bark and probing into clusters of needles and pine cones. Eats mainly insects and spiders.

• **BREEDING** Monogamous. Solitary.

• **NESTING** Breeding biology poorly known. Estimated incubation 11–12 days by female. Young altricial; brooded by female; young stay in nest estimated 8–10 days, fed by both sexes. 2 broods per year.

• **POPULATION** Fairly common to common in montane pine and mixed pine-deciduous forests. Casual to southern California.

• **CONSERVATION** Neotropical migrant. Infrequent host to cowbird parasitism. As a habitat specialist, vulnerable to loss of habitat due to logging and development.

Flight Pattern
Fairly rapid flight with rapid wing strokes, alternating with brief period of wings pulled to sides; repeated. Sallies from perch to take flying insect, returns.

Nest Identification	
Shape ◖ Location ⚑	Leaves, stems, down, bits of fabric, and cocoon material, with lining of mammal hair and feathers • on high branch, 20–60 feet above ground • built by female • 3–4 white or creamy white eggs, with blotches and fine dots of browns; oval to short oval, 0.6 x 0.45 inches.

Plumage Sexes similar	Habitat 🐦 ▲ 🌲	Migration Migratory	Weight 0.3 ounce

DATE _____ TIME _____ LOCATION _____

Family PARULIDAE	Species *Dendroica pinus*	Length 5.25 inches	Wingspan 8.5 inches

PINE WARBLER

True to its name, the long-tailed somewhat heavy-billed Pine Warbler inhabits open pine tree groves, where it conceals its nest among needles near the branch tips. It is distinguished from other warblers by its tendency to winter throughout much of its breeding range. Males and females are similar, both showing a white belly and undertail coverts, although females are duller in color with less yellow on their breasts. Juveniles have brownish to brownish olive upperparts with white wing bars, and underparts varying from white to yellowish with a brownish wash on the flanks.

blackish eye line
yellow line over eyes
large bill
yellow chin and throat
greenish olive upperparts with no streaking
yellow breast has dark streaks on sides
2 white wing bars
long tail projects beyond undertail coverts
white belly and undertail coverts
white patches at ends of 2 outer tail feathers

JUVENILE FEMALE

- **SONG** Twittering musical trill similar to Chipping Sparrow but varying in speed, loudness, and pitch. Call is slurred *tsup*.
- **BEHAVIOR** Solitary or in pairs. Very vocal. Gregarious in winter; often joins mixed feeding flocks. Gleans food by creeping slowly and deliberately along branches, usually high in trees, but sometimes lower, even on ground. Often flies from tree to tree, diving for passing insects. Eats insects, caterpillars, and spiders. Also eats seeds, wild grapes, and some berries. Aggressive toward other species sharing same pine habitat.
- **BREEDING** Monogamous. Solitary.
- **NESTING** Incubation 10 days by both sexes. Young altricial; brooded by female; leave nest within 10 days, fed by both sexes. 2–3 broods per year in the South, 1 brood per year in the North.
- **POPULATION** Fairly common to common. Stable or increasing slightly, but some decline in coastal New England and Great Lakes region due to clearing of pines. Subject to loss in severe winters. Increases occur as pines mature. Casual in West.
- **FEEDERS** Peanut butter and cornmeal mixture.
- **CONSERVATION** Neotropical migrant. Infrequent host to cowbird parasitism. Vulnerable to fragmentation and clearing of pine forests.

Similar Birds

YELLOW-THROATED VIREO
Heavier hooked bill; yellow spectacles; white belly and flanks; no streaking on sides or breast; gray rump and crissum; no white in tail corners; sluggish.

BAY-BREASTED WARBLER
BLACKPOLL WARBLER
Basic plumage • black streaking on back; much less white in tail corners; shorter tails with less extension from undertail coverts; paler cheeks contrast less with throat color.

Flight Pattern

Weak flight, rapid wing beats alternated with brief period of wings pulled to sides. Sallies out to take flying insects, returns.

Nest Identification

Shape / Location

Lined with feathers, weeds, grass, bark, pine needles, twigs, and spider webs • built on or near end of limb, 10–135 feet above ground • built by female • 3–5 off-white eggs, with brown specks near larger end; oval to short oval, 0.7 x 0.5 inches.

Plumage Sexes similar	Habitat	Migration Northern birds migrate	Weight 0.4 ounce

DATE _____ TIME_____ LOCATION _____

Family PARULIDAE	Species *Dendroica palmarum*	Length 5.25 inches	Wingspan 8.5 inches

PALM WARBLER

This inhabitant of northern bogs pumps its tail up and down more than any other warbler. Two subspecies occur: the eastern form with strongly washed yellow underparts and the western form with whitish underparts with stronger streaking. Both nest on knolls of moss at the foot of small spruce or pine trees. A medium-distance migrant, the Palm Warbler winters in the South and frequents open habitats such as cultivated fields, marshes, pastures, parks, and gardens. Some winter in open pine woods or along their edges. The species is associated with palms only on some of its wintering areas and shows no inclination to seek them out. Fall adults and juveniles are drab, washed out, and lack the chestnut cap.

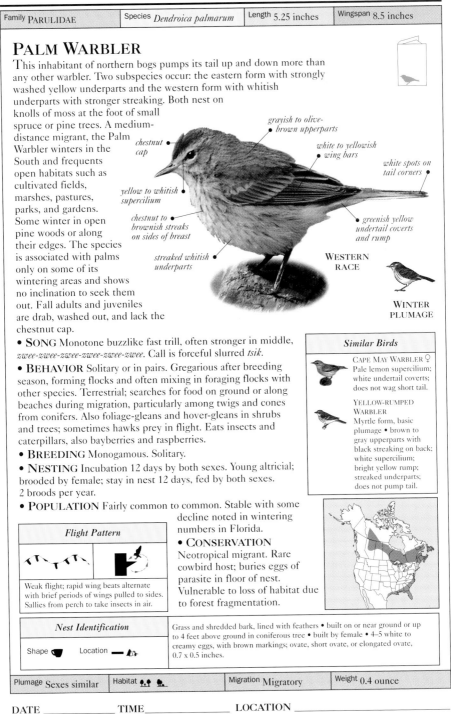

grayish to olive-brown upperparts

chestnut cap

white to yellowish wing bars

white spots on tail corners

yellow to whitish supercilium

chestnut to brownish streaks on sides of breast

greenish yellow undertail coverts and rump

streaked whitish underparts

WESTERN RACE

WINTER PLUMAGE

- **SONG** Monotone buzzlike fast trill, often stronger in middle, *zwee-zwee-zwee-zwee-zwee-zwee*. Call is forceful slurred *tsik*.
- **BEHAVIOR** Solitary or in pairs. Gregarious after breeding season, forming flocks and often mixing in foraging flocks with other species. Terrestrial; searches for food on ground or along beaches during migration, particularly among twigs and cones from conifers. Also foliage-gleans and hover-gleans in shrubs and trees; sometimes hawks prey in flight. Eats insects and caterpillars, also bayberries and raspberries.
- **BREEDING** Monogamous. Solitary.
- **NESTING** Incubation 12 days by both sexes. Young altricial; brooded by female; stay in nest 12 days, fed by both sexes. 2 broods per year.
- **POPULATION** Fairly common to common. Stable with some decline noted in wintering numbers in Florida.
- **CONSERVATION** Neotropical migrant. Rare cowbird host; buries eggs of parasite in floor of nest. Vulnerable to loss of habitat due to forest fragmentation.

Similar Birds

CAPE MAY WARBLER ♀
Pale lemon supercilium; white undertail coverts; does not wag short tail.

YELLOW-RUMPED WARBLER
Myrtle form, basic plumage • brown to gray upperparts with black streaking on back; white supercilium; bright yellow rump; streaked underparts; does not pump tail.

Flight Pattern

Weak flight; rapid wing beats alternate with brief periods of wings pulled to sides. Sallies from perch to take insects in air.

Nest Identification	
Shape 〰 Location ▬ 🐦	Grass and shredded bark, lined with feathers • built on or near ground or up to 4 feet above ground in coniferous tree • built by female • 4–5 white to creamy eggs, with brown markings; ovate, short ovate, or elongated ovate, 0.7 x 0.5 inches.

Plumage Sexes similar	Habitat 🌿🌿 🌾	Migration Migratory	Weight 0.4 ounce

DATE _____ TIME_____ LOCATION _____

Family PARULIDAE	Species *Dendroica castanea*	Length 5.5 inches	Wingspan 8.5 inches

BAY-BREASTED WARBLER

The male's warm chestnut and creamy markings help identify this native of northern coniferous forests. It is one of the largest warblers. Females are duller and have a gray rump. Juveniles and winter adults have olive upperparts with streaking

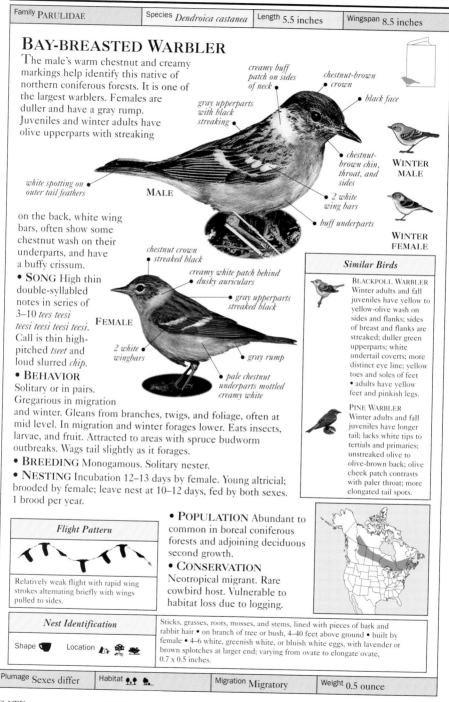

creamy buff patch on sides of neck

chestnut-brown crown

black face

gray upperparts with black streaking

white spotting on outer tail feathers

MALE

chestnut-brown chin, throat, and sides

WINTER MALE

2 white wing bars

buff underparts

WINTER FEMALE

on the back, white wing bars, often show some chestnut wash on their underparts, and have a buffy crissum.

chestnut crown streaked black

creamy white patch behind dusky auriculars

gray upperparts streaked black

FEMALE

2 white wingbars

gray rump

pale chestnut underparts mottled creamy white

- **SONG** High thin double-syllabled notes in series of 3–10 *tees teesi teesi teesi teesi teesi*. Call is thin high-pitched *tseet* and loud slurred *chip*.

- **BEHAVIOR** Solitary or in pairs. Gregarious in migration and winter. Gleans from branches, twigs, and foliage, often at mid level. In migration and winter forages lower. Eats insects, larvae, and fruit. Attracted to areas with spruce budworm outbreaks. Wags tail slightly as it forages.

- **BREEDING** Monogamous. Solitary nester.

- **NESTING** Incubation 12–13 days by female. Young altricial; brooded by female; leave nest at 10–12 days, fed by both sexes. 1 brood per year.

Similar Birds

BLACKPOLL WARBLER Winter adults and fall juveniles have yellow-olive wash on sides and flanks; sides of breast and flanks are streaked; duller green upperparts; white undertail coverts; more distinct eye line; yellow toes and soles of feet • adults have yellow feet and pinkish legs.

PINE WARBLER Winter adults and fall juveniles have longer tail; lacks white tips to tertials and primaries; unstreaked olive to olive-brown back; olive cheek patch contrasts with paler throat; more elongated tail spots.

- **POPULATION** Abundant to common in boreal coniferous forests and adjoining deciduous second growth.

- **CONSERVATION** Neotropical migrant. Rare cowbird host. Vulnerable to habitat loss due to logging.

Flight Pattern

Relatively weak flight with rapid wing strokes alternating briefly with wings pulled to sides.

Nest Identification	
Shape	Location	Sticks, grasses, roots, mosses, and stems, lined with pieces of bark and rabbit hair • on branch of tree or bush, 4–40 feet above ground • built by female • 4–6 white, greenish white, or bluish white eggs, with lavender or brown splotches at larger end; varying from ovate to elongate ovate, 0.7 x 0.5 inches.

Plumage Sexes differ	Habitat	Migration Migratory	Weight 0.5 ounce

DATE _____ TIME_____ LOCATION _____

Family PARULIDAE	Species *Dendroica striata*	Length 5.25 inches	Wingspan 8.5 inches

BLACKPOLL WARBLER

This summer resident of Canadian boreal forests migrates more than twenty-five hundred miles in the fall, flying nonstop over water to winter in northern South America. Juveniles and fall adults have streaked greenish upperparts; a pale greenish yellow wash on the face, throat, and breast; a white belly and crissum; legs that are pale pinkish on the front and back but dark on the sides; and yellow soles.

black cap

bold black streaks on gray back

white cheeks

black malar mark

MALE

2 white wing bars

WINTER PLUMAGE

white underparts with black-streaked sides and flanks

pink legs and feet

- **SONG** Mechanical series of high thin *tseet* notes that begin softly and get louder and more intense; may contain 10–20 notes. Much variation between individuals. Call is sharp loud *chip*.

dusky eye line and gray-buff supercilium

grayish head and neck

olive-gray crown

FEMALE

white underparts

blackish streaked throat, sides, and flanks

- **BEHAVIOR** Solitary or in pairs. Sluggish and deliberate. Forages low to high in migration, but stays in middle to upper levels on breeding grounds. Catches insects in air or combs leaves and twigs for food. Eats insects, caterpillars, cankerworms, spiders and their eggs, and pokeberries.
- **BREEDING** Monogamous. Polygynous. Females breed with the territory-holding male on the previous year's nesting site.
- **NESTING** Incubation 12 days by female. Altricial young brooded by female; stay in nest 11–12 days, fed by both sexes. 1–2 broods per year.

Similar Birds

♂
♀
BAY-BREASTED WARBLER
Juvenile and fall adult
• bulkier; brighter green upperparts; thicker wing bars; little or no streaking on underparts; many show buff sides and/or flanks; creamy undertail coverts; gray legs and feet.

PINE WARBLER
Larger bill; unstreaked olive upperparts; shorter undertail coverts make tail look longer; more white in tail corners; brown legs and feet.

BLACK-AND-WHITE WARBLER
Black-and-white-striped crown; black back with white stripes; black spotting and streaking on undertail coverts; black legs and feet
• male has black throat and cheeks.

- **POPULATION** Abundant in northern boreal coniferous forests. May be declining in southern part of breeding range.
- **CONSERVATION** Neotropical migrant. Vulnerable to habitat loss from logging and forest fragmentation.

Flight Pattern
Fairly swift direct flight on rapidly beating wings.

Nest Identification	Lined with spruce sprigs, twigs, bark, dried grass, feathers, weeds, moss, and lichen • on branch near trunk, 2–33 feet above ground • built by female • 3–5 white to off-white eggs, with brown or lavender markings, occasionally wreathed; oval to long oval, 0.72 x 0.53 inches.
Shape 🥄 Location 🔺	

Plumage Sexes differ	Habitat 🌿 🌱	Migration Migratory	Weight 0.5 ounce

DATE _____ TIME _____ LOCATION _____

Family PARULIDAE	Species *Mniotilta varia*	Length 5 inches	Wingspan 8.5–9 inches

BLACK-AND-WHITE WARBLER

This mostly black-and-white striped bird feeds nuthatch-style, moving up and down the trunks of trees and crawling over and under branches, a foraging behavior unlike any other warbler. It is one of the earliest warblers to return to the breeding grounds in early spring, because its bark-gleaning foraging habit does not require it to linger on wintering grounds until the leaves begin to develop. Females are similar to males but have cream-colored flanks and creamy whitish rather than black cheeks. Juveniles are similar to females.

bold black-and-white stripes on head and most of body

distinctive white stripe over and under each eye

slightly curved slim bill

black cheeks and throat

2 white wing bars

white belly

JUVENILE

• **SONG** Repetitive thin high-pitched series of 6–10 *wee-sea, wee-sea* notes like the sound of a turning squeaky wheel. Sometimes a trill is added as an ending to the cadence. Has call of an abrasive *chip* or *tink*, and a *seap*.

• **BEHAVIOR** Solitary or in pairs. Probes into bark crevices with long bill; does not prop body on tree with tail as do woodpeckers and creepers. Eats adult insects, caterpillars, and spiders. Occasionally hawks and hover-gleans. If flushed from ground nest, female performs distraction display, dragging wings with tail spread.

• **BREEDING** Monogamous. Solitary.

• **NESTING** Incubation 10–12 days by female. Young altricial; brooded by female; remain in nest 8–12 days but still not able to fly well; fed by both sexes. 1–2 broods per year.

• **POPULATION** Widespread in mature and second-growth deciduous or mixed deciduous-conifer woodlands with large trees. Declining in the Midwest and Great Lakes region because of habitat loss and cowbird parasitism. Vagrant in the West during migration as far north as Alaska.

Similar Birds

BLACK-THROATED GRAY WARBLER
Small yellow spot between eye and bill; blackish crown; gray back with black streaking; white undertail coverts; lacks central crown stripe.

BLACKPOLL WARBLER ♂
Black crown; white cheeks; gray back with black streaking; white throat; white undertail coverts.

• **CONSERVATION** Neotropical migrant. Common host to cowbird eggs. Vulnerable to forest fragmentation and habitat loss due to logging operations in mature forests.

Flight Pattern

Relatively weak flight with rapid wing strokes alternating with brief periods of wings pulled to sides; repeated.

Nest Identification

Shape 🥣   Location ▬ 🐦 🐦

Grasses, bark pieces, dead leaves, rootlets, and pine needles, lined with moss and mammal hair • on ground, near base of tree or bush, or in small hollow of rock, stump, or log • built by female • 4–6 creamy white or white eggs, flecked with brown; short subelliptical to subelliptical, 0.67 x 0.52 inches.

Plumage Sexes similar	Habitat 🌲 🌳	Migration Migratory	Weight 0.4 ounce

DATE _____ TIME_____ LOCATION _____

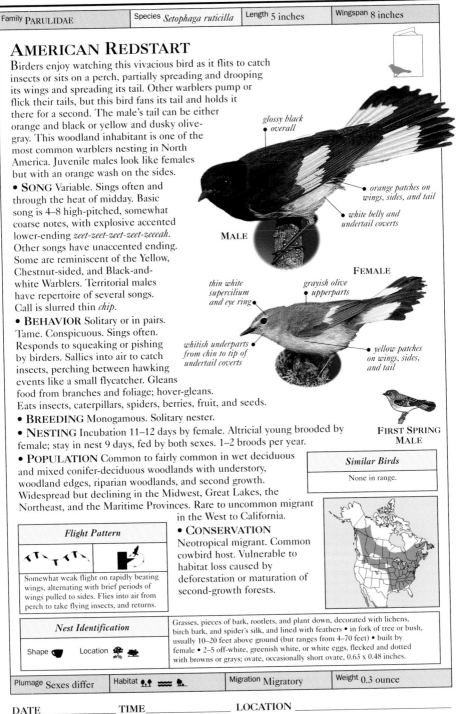

Family PARULIDAE	Species *Setophaga ruticilla*	Length 5 inches	Wingspan 8 inches

AMERICAN REDSTART

Birders enjoy watching this vivacious bird as it flits to catch insects or sits on a perch, partially spreading and drooping its wings and spreading its tail. Other warblers pump or flick their tails, but this bird fans its tail and holds it there for a second. The male's tail can be either orange and black or yellow and dusky olive-gray. This woodland inhabitant is one of the most common warblers nesting in North America. Juvenile males look like females but with an orange wash on the sides.

glossy black overall

orange patches on wings, sides, and tail

white belly and undertail coverts

MALE

- **SONG** Variable. Sings often and through the heat of midday. Basic song is 4–8 high-pitched, somewhat coarse notes, with explosive accented lower-ending *zeet-zeet-zeet-zeet-zeeeah.* Other songs have unaccented ending. Some are reminiscent of the Yellow, Chestnut-sided, and Black-and-white Warblers. Territorial males have repertoire of several songs. Call is slurred thin *chip.*

FEMALE

thin white supercilium and eye ring

grayish olive upperparts

whitish underparts from chin to tip of undertail coverts

yellow patches on wings, sides, and tail

- **BEHAVIOR** Solitary or in pairs. Tame. Conspicuous. Sings often. Responds to squeaking or pishing by birders. Sallies into air to catch insects, perching between hawking events like a small flycatcher. Gleans food from branches and foliage; hover-gleans. Eats insects, caterpillars, spiders, berries, fruit, and seeds.

- **BREEDING** Monogamous. Solitary nester.

- **NESTING** Incubation 11–12 days by female. Altricial young brooded by female; stay in nest 9 days, fed by both sexes. 1–2 broods per year.

FIRST SPRING MALE

- **POPULATION** Common to fairly common in wet deciduous and mixed conifer-deciduous woodlands with understory, woodland edges, riparian woodlands, and second growth. Widespread but declining in the Midwest, Great Lakes, the Northeast, and the Maritime Provinces. Rare to uncommon migrant in the West to California.

Similar Birds
None in range.

- **CONSERVATION** Neotropical migrant. Common cowbird host. Vulnerable to habitat loss caused by deforestation or maturation of second-growth forests.

Flight Pattern
Somewhat weak flight on rapidly beating wings, alternating with brief periods of wings pulled to sides. Flies into air from perch to take flying insects, and returns.

Nest Identification	
Shape	Location	Grasses, pieces of bark, rootlets, and plant down, decorated with lichens, birch bark, and spider's silk, and lined with feathers • in fork of tree or bush, usually 10–20 feet above ground (but ranges from 4–70 feet) • built by female • 2–5 off-white, greenish white, or white eggs, flecked and dotted with browns or grays; ovate, occasionally short ovate, 0.63 x 0.48 inches.

Plumage Sexes differ	Habitat	Migration Migratory	Weight 0.3 ounce

DATE _____ TIME_____ LOCATION _____

Family PARULIDAE	Species *Seiurus aurocapillus*	Length 6 inches	Wingspan 9 inches

OVENBIRD

In the leaf litter under tall deciduous trees, the female bird builds a small oven-shaped nest with a side entrance. Unlike many warblers, it does not often forage in live vegetation; instead it walks on the ground, foraging among the leaf litter and twigs, its wings partially drooped and its tail cocked upward and sometimes quickly raised and slowly lowered. It is sometimes called the Wood Wagtail because it moves its tail up and down. Most singing is done from an elevated perch, and the song of one territorial male initiates a response song from each neighbor, which in turn stimulates another to do so, until a wave of Ovenbird songs sweeps across the woodlot.

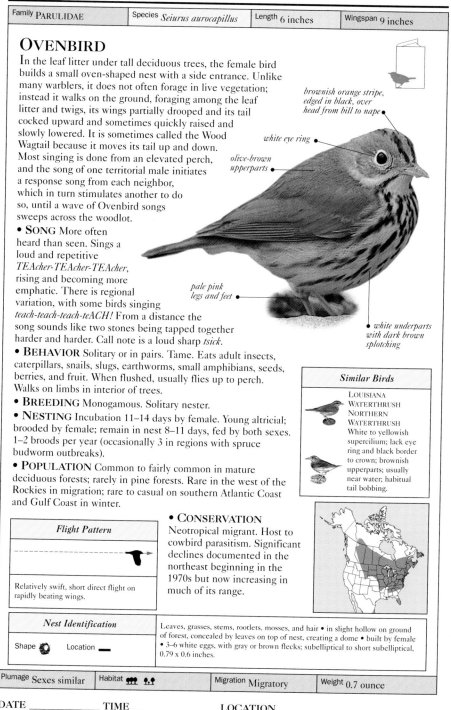

brownish orange stripe, edged in black, over head from bill to nape

white eye ring

olive-brown upperparts

pale pink legs and feet

white underparts with dark brown splotching

• **SONG** More often heard than seen. Sings a loud and repetitive *TEAcher-TEAcher-TEAcher*, rising and becoming more emphatic. There is regional variation, with some birds singing *teach-teach-teach-teACH!* From a distance the song sounds like two stones being tapped together harder and harder. Call note is a loud sharp *tsick*.

• **BEHAVIOR** Solitary or in pairs. Tame. Eats adult insects, caterpillars, snails, slugs, earthworms, small amphibians, seeds, berries, and fruit. When flushed, usually flies up to perch. Walks on limbs in interior of trees.

• **BREEDING** Monogamous. Solitary nester.

• **NESTING** Incubation 11–14 days by female. Young altricial; brooded by female; remain in nest 8–11 days, fed by both sexes. 1–2 broods per year (occasionally 3 in regions with spruce budworm outbreaks).

• **POPULATION** Common to fairly common in mature deciduous forests; rarely in pine forests. Rare in the west of the Rockies in migration; rare to casual on southern Atlantic Coast and Gulf Coast in winter.

• **CONSERVATION** Neotropical migrant. Host to cowbird parasitism. Significant declines documented in the northeast beginning in the 1970s but now increasing in much of its range.

Similar Birds
LOUISIANA WATERTHRUSH NORTHERN WATERTHRUSH White to yellowish supercilium; lack eye ring and black border to crown; brownish upperparts; usually near water; habitual tail bobbing.

Flight Pattern
Relatively swift, short direct flight on rapidly beating wings.

Nest Identification	
Shape ⬤ Location ▬	Leaves, grasses, stems, rootlets, mosses, and hair • in slight hollow on ground of forest, concealed by leaves on top of nest, creating a dome • built by female • 3–6 white eggs, with gray or brown flecks; subelliptical to short subelliptical, 0.79 x 0.6 inches.

Plumage Sexes similar	Habitat 🌳 🌿	Migration Migratory	Weight 0.7 ounce

DATE _____ TIME_____ LOCATION _____

Family PARULIDAE	Species *Seiurus noveboracensis*	Length 5.75 inches	Wingspan 8.75 inches

NORTHERN WATERTHRUSH

Northern lakeshores, slow-running streams, and bogs are the most common habitats of the Northern Waterthrush. Walking, rather than hopping, along the ground, the Northern Waterthrush often is observed repeatedly bobbing the rear part of its body and its tail while searching for food. An early migrant, the Northern Waterthrush generally begins traveling southward by mid-July.

whitish to pale yellow supercilium

olive-brown to gray-brown upperparts

heavily streaked throat, upper breast, and sides

whitish to pale yellow underparts

• **SONG** Begins with loud insistent notes, tapering to rapidly whistled lower tones, *twit twit twit twit sweet sweet sweet chew chew chew*, with the individual notes grouped in series of 3's and 4's. Call is a very loud ringing metallic *chink*.

• **BEHAVIOR** Solitary or in pairs. Terrestrial but often sings from elevated perches and walks, bobbing, on branches. Forages on ground by picking up leaves with its bill and tossing them aside or turning them over. Eats aquatic and terrestrial adult insects, caterpillars, and case worms; also sometimes slugs, mollusks, crustaceans, and small fish. Frequents areas with dense shrub and slowly moving or still water.

• **BREEDING** Monogamous. Solitary.

• **NESTING** Breeding biology poorly known. Estimated incubation 13 days by female. Young altricial; brooded by female; stay in nest estimated 10 days, fed by both sexes. 1 brood per year.

• **POPULATION** Generally common in wooded swamps, forests with standing water, bogs, and thickets with slowly running or standing water. Rare to uncommon in migration in the Southwest to California. Rare to casual in winter in the US, except for southern Florida where it is uncommon.

• **CONSERVATION** Neotropical migrant. Uncommon host to cowbird parasitism. Some declines in southern portions of breeding range and increases in New England portions. Vulnerable to habitat loss due to deforestation and drainage.

Similar Birds

LOUISIANA WATERTHRUSH Longer stouter bill; white supercilium broadens behind eye; fewer and less-contrasting streaks on underparts; unmarked white throat; contrasting pinkish buff wash on flanks; bright pink legs and feet; more deliberate and exaggerated tail bobbing with a circular body motion; song differs.

Flight Pattern

Fairly swift direct flight for short distances on rapidly beating wings.

Nest Identification	
Shape 🥄 Location 🐾 🪨	Lined with grass, animal hair, moss, twigs, pine needles, bark strips, and roots • often built in moss-covered stumps near water • 0–2 feet above ground • built by female • 3–6 cream or buff-white eggs, with brown or gray spots or speckles; ovate to short ovate, 0.8 x 0.57 inches.

Plumage Sexes similar	Habitat	Migration Migratory	Weight 0.8 ounce

DATE _____ TIME_____ LOCATION _____

| Family PARULIDAE | Species *Seiurus motacilla* | Length 6 inches | Wingspan 9 inches |

LOUISIANA WATERTHRUSH

The less common of the two waterthrush species frequents fast-running streams and floodplain river swamps, where it hides its nests on streamside banks, under tree roots, or in rock crevices. This bird has a nesting range from Minnesota to New England and as far south as Texas and Georgia. In spring it is one of the earliest warblers to arrive on the nesting grounds and one of the first to depart in late summer and early fall.

darker crown

long stout bill

broad gray-buff stripe broadens behind eye and becomes white

olive-gray to olive-brown upperparts

unstreaked white chin and throat

olive-striped breast, sides, and flanks

white or buff-white underparts

pinkish buff flanks contrast with white underparts

bright pink legs and feet

• **SONG** Loud and clear, beginning with 3–4 high-pitched downslurred notes, followed by a brief rapid medley of jumbled notes that cascade up and down prior to fading away, *SWEER SWEER SWEER chee chi-wit-it chit swee-yuu.* The combination of slurred opening notes and ending twittering is diagnostic. Call is a loud bright *chik.*

• **BEHAVIOR** Solitary or in pairs. Sings on ground or from elevated perch in trees. Bobs rear and tail while walking. Terrestrial, primarily foraging on ground, along stream banks, on rocks and logs in water, and in the stream shallows. Bobs up and down while foraging, much like a sandpiper, with a slow circular exaggerated motion. Dines on adult aquatic and terrestrial insects, caterpillars, mollusks, snails, and small fish. Territories are linear along stream.

• **BREEDING** Monogamous. Solitary.

• **NESTING** Incubation 12–14 days by female. Young altricial; brooded by female; remain in nest 9–10 days, fed by both sexes. 1 brood per year.

• **POPULATION** Uncommon to fairly common. Restricted habitat specialist along fast-flowing streams within woodlands, often in mountains or hilly terrain, or in floodplain forests and swamps in lower country. Casual in the West during the migration season.

Similar Birds

NORTHERN WATERTHRUSH
Narrow buff to white eye stripes of uniform color and width; smaller bill; streaked and spotted throat; pale yellow to white underparts with darker, more uniform streaking; olive-brown to gray-brown upperparts; dull pink legs and feet; different voice.

• **CONSERVATION** Neotropical migrant. Frequent host to cowbird parasitism. Deforestation and stream siltation negatively impact both breeding and wintering areas.

Flight Pattern
Swift short direct flights on rapidly beating wings.

Nest Identification	Lined with roots, fern stems, grass, animal fur, dead leaves, moss, and twigs • 0–2 feet above ground, on bank, rock crevice, or roots of tree, no further than 3–6 feet from water • built by both sexes, but female does more • 4–6 white or cream-colored eggs, with brown and gray specks or blotches; oval to short oval, 0.78 x 0.6 inches.
Shape ⬤ Location ━━ 🪵	

| Plumage Sexes similar | Habitat | Migration Migratory | Weight 0.7 ounce |

| Family PARULIDAE | Species *Oporornis formosus* | Length 5.25 inches | Wingspan 8.25 inches |

KENTUCKY WARBLER

This retiring, short-tailed chunky bird is named for the
state where it was first encountered, but it is common
throughout most of the damp shaded woodlands in
southeastern North America. The female is especially
wary and will sometimes abandon her nest if she is
threatened. She appears similar to the male, but her
black areas are duller. Juvenile females have dark
olive plumage in place of black.

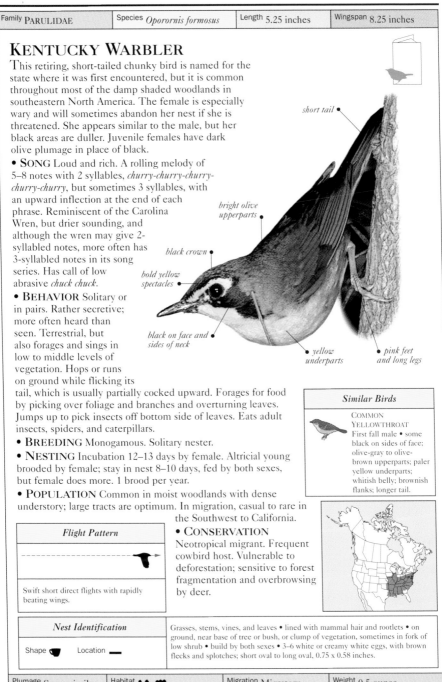

short tail

bright olive
upperparts

black crown

bold yellow
spectacles

black on face and
sides of neck

yellow
underparts

pink feet
and long legs

• **SONG** Loud and rich. A rolling melody of
5–8 notes with 2 syllables, *churry-churry-churry-
churry-churry*, but sometimes 3 syllables, with
an upward inflection at the end of each
phrase. Reminiscent of the Carolina
Wren, but drier sounding, and
although the wren may give 2-
syllabled notes, more often has
3-syllabled notes in its song
series. Has call of low
abrasive *chuck chuck*.

• **BEHAVIOR** Solitary or
in pairs. Rather secretive;
more often heard than
seen. Terrestrial, but
also forages and sings in
low to middle levels of
vegetation. Hops or runs
on ground while flicking its
tail, which is usually partially cocked upward. Forages for food
by picking over foliage and branches and overturning leaves.
Jumps up to pick insects off bottom side of leaves. Eats adult
insects, spiders, and caterpillars.

• **BREEDING** Monogamous. Solitary nester.

• **NESTING** Incubation 12–13 days by female. Altricial young
brooded by female; stay in nest 8–10 days, fed by both sexes,
but female does more. 1 brood per year.

• **POPULATION** Common in moist woodlands with dense
understory; large tracts are optimum. In migration, casual to rare in
the Southwest to California.

• **CONSERVATION**
Neotropical migrant. Frequent
cowbird host. Vulnerable to
deforestation; sensitive to forest
fragmentation and overbrowsing
by deer.

Similar Birds

COMMON
YELLOWTHROAT
First fall male • some
black on sides of face;
olive-gray to olive-
brown upperparts; paler
yellow underparts;
whitish belly; brownish
flanks; longer tail.

Flight Pattern

Swift short direct flights with rapidly
beating wings.

Nest Identification

Shape | Location

Grasses, stems, vines, and leaves • lined with mammal hair and rootlets • on
ground, near base of tree or bush, or clump of vegetation, sometimes in fork of
low shrub • build by both sexes • 3–6 white or creamy white eggs, with brown
flecks and splotches; short oval to long oval, 0.75 x 0.58 inches.

| Plumage Sexes similar | Habitat | Migration Migratory | Weight 0.5 ounce |

DATE _____ TIME_____ LOCATION _____

Family PARULIDAE	Species *Oporornis agilis*	Length 5.5 inches	Wingspan 8.75 inches

CONNECTICUT WARBLER

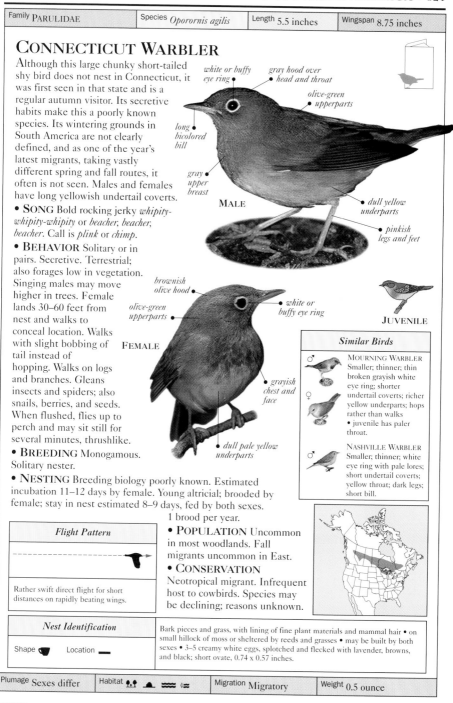

Although this large chunky short-tailed shy bird does not nest in Connecticut, it was first seen in that state and is a regular autumn visitor. Its secretive habits make this a poorly known species. Its wintering grounds in South America are not clearly defined, and as one of the year's latest migrants, taking vastly different spring and fall routes, it often is not seen. Males and females have long yellowish undertail coverts.

white or buffy eye ring

gray hood over head and throat

olive-green upperparts

long bicolored bill

gray upper breast

MALE

dull yellow underparts

pinkish legs and feet

• **SONG** Bold rocking jerky *whipity-whipity-whipity* or *beacher, beacher, beacher*. Call is *plink* or *chimp*.

• **BEHAVIOR** Solitary or in pairs. Secretive. Terrestrial; also forages low in vegetation. Singing males may move higher in trees. Female lands 30–60 feet from nest and walks to conceal location. Walks with slight bobbing of tail instead of hopping. Walks on logs and branches. Gleans insects and spiders; also snails, berries, and seeds. When flushed, flies up to perch and may sit still for several minutes, thrushlike.

brownish olive hood

olive-green upperparts

white or buffy eye ring

JUVENILE

FEMALE

grayish chest and face

Similar Birds

MOURNING WARBLER Smaller; thinner; thin broken grayish white eye ring; shorter undertail coverts; richer yellow underparts; hops rather than walks • juvenile has paler throat.

NASHVILLE WARBLER Smaller; thinner; white eye ring with pale lores; short undertail coverts; yellow throat; dark legs; short bill.

dull pale yellow underparts

• **BREEDING** Monogamous. Solitary nester.

• **NESTING** Breeding biology poorly known. Estimated incubation 11–12 days by female. Young altricial; brooded by female; stay in nest estimated 8–9 days, fed by both sexes. 1 brood per year.

• **POPULATION** Uncommon in most woodlands. Fall migrants uncommon in East.

• **CONSERVATION** Neotropical migrant. Infrequent host to cowbirds. Species may be declining; reasons unknown.

Flight Pattern
Rather swift direct flight for short distances on rapidly beating wings.

Nest Identification	
Shape	Location	Bark pieces and grass, with lining of fine plant materials and mammal hair • on small hillock of moss or sheltered by reeds and grasses • may be built by both sexes • 3–5 creamy white eggs, splotched and flecked with lavender, browns, and black; short ovate, 0.74 x 0.57 inches.

Plumage Sexes differ	Habitat	Migration Migratory	Weight 0.5 ounce

DATE _____ TIME_____ LOCATION _____

Family PARULIDAE	Species *Oporornis philadelphia*	Length 5.25 inches	Wingspan 8.25 inches

MOURNING WARBLER

The eastern counterpart to MacGillivray's Warbler was named for the way its black breast and gray hood resemble a person in mourning. Usually skulking in the undergrowth of damp woodlands, the male will fly up from the bushes to sing and is more often heard than seen. The female is similar to the male but has a paler dusky hood, light grayish throat, and a more distinct eye ring. Juveniles have pale yellowish throats and broken thin white eye rings. Traveling over eastern Mexico, this bird circumnavigates the western Gulf of Mexico, making it one of the latest spring migrants of all North American warblers.

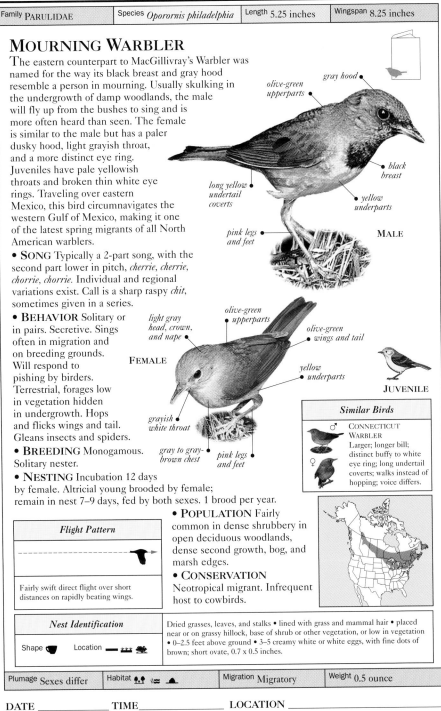

gray hood

olive-green upperparts

black breast

long yellow undertail coverts

yellow underparts

pink legs and feet

MALE

• **SONG** Typically a 2-part song, with the second part lower in pitch, *cherrie, cherrie, chorrie, chorrie.* Individual and regional variations exist. Call is a sharp raspy *chit,* sometimes given in a series.

• **BEHAVIOR** Solitary or in pairs. Secretive. Sings often in migration and on breeding grounds. Will respond to pishing by birders. Terrestrial, forages low in vegetation hidden in undergrowth. Hops and flicks wings and tail. Gleans insects and spiders.

• **BREEDING** Monogamous. Solitary nester.

• **NESTING** Incubation 12 days by female. Altricial young brooded by female; remain in nest 7–9 days, fed by both sexes. 1 brood per year.

olive-green upperparts

light gray head, crown, and nape

olive-green wings and tail

FEMALE

yellow underparts

JUVENILE

grayish white throat

gray to gray-brown chest

pink legs and feet

Similar Birds

♂ **CONNECTICUT WARBLER** Larger; longer bill; distinct buffy to white eye ring; long undertail coverts; walks instead of hopping; voice differs.
♀

• **POPULATION** Fairly common in dense shrubbery in open deciduous woodlands, dense second growth, bog, and marsh edges.

• **CONSERVATION** Neotropical migrant. Infrequent host to cowbirds.

Flight Pattern
Fairly swift direct flight over short distances on rapidly beating wings.

Nest Identification	Dried grasses, leaves, and stalks • lined with grass and mammal hair • placed near or on grassy hillock, base of shrub or other vegetation, or low in vegetation • 0–2.5 feet above ground • 3–5 creamy white or white eggs, with fine dots of brown; short ovate, 0.7 x 0.5 inches.
Shape ▽ Location ▬ ✿✿✿ 🌿	

Plumage Sexes differ	Habitat 🐾 🌾 🏔	Migration Migratory	Weight 0.5 ounce

DATE _____ TIME_____ LOCATION _____

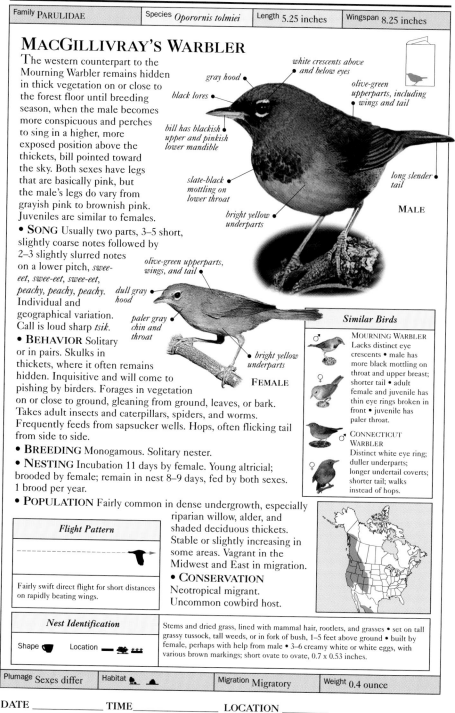

Family PARULIDAE	Species *Oporornis tolmiei*	Length 5.25 inches	Wingspan 8.25 inches

MacGillivray's Warbler

The western counterpart to the Mourning Warbler remains hidden in thick vegetation on or close to the forest floor until breeding season, when the male becomes more conspicuous and perches to sing in a higher, more exposed position above the thickets, bill pointed toward the sky. Both sexes have legs that are basically pink, but the male's legs do vary from grayish pink to brownish pink. Juveniles are similar to females.

white crescents above and below eyes

gray hood

black lores

olive-green upperparts, including wings and tail

bill has blackish upper and pinkish lower mandible

slate-black mottling on lower throat

long slender tail

bright yellow underparts

MALE

• **SONG** Usually two parts, 3–5 short, slightly coarse notes followed by 2–3 slightly slurred notes on a lower pitch, *swee-eet, swee-eet, swee-eet, peachy, peachy, peachy.* Individual and geographical variation. Call is loud sharp *tsik.*

olive-green upperparts, wings, and tail

dull gray hood

paler gray chin and throat

bright yellow underparts

FEMALE

• **BEHAVIOR** Solitary or in pairs. Skulks in thickets, where it often remains hidden. Inquisitive and will come to pishing by birders. Forages in vegetation on or close to ground, gleaning from ground, leaves, or bark. Takes adult insects and caterpillars, spiders, and worms. Frequently feeds from sapsucker wells. Hops, often flicking tail from side to side.

• **BREEDING** Monogamous. Solitary nester.

• **NESTING** Incubation 11 days by female. Young altricial; brooded by female; remain in nest 8–9 days, fed by both sexes. 1 brood per year.

• **POPULATION** Fairly common in dense undergrowth, especially riparian willow, alder, and shaded deciduous thickets. Stable or slightly increasing in some areas. Vagrant in the Midwest and East in migration.

• **CONSERVATION** Neotropical migrant. Uncommon cowbird host.

Similar Birds

MOURNING WARBLER Lacks distinct eye crescents • male has more black mottling on throat and upper breast; shorter tail • adult female and juvenile has thin eye rings broken in front • juvenile has paler throat.

CONNECTICUT WARBLER Distinct white eye ring; duller underparts; longer undertail coverts; shorter tail; walks instead of hops.

Flight Pattern
Fairly swift direct flight for short distances on rapidly beating wings.

Nest Identification	
Shape	Location	Stems and dried grass, lined with mammal hair, rootlets, and grasses • set on tall grassy tussock, tall weeds, or in fork of bush, 1–5 feet above ground • built by female, perhaps with help from male • 3–6 creamy white or white eggs, with various brown markings; short ovate to ovate, 0.7 x 0.53 inches.

Plumage Sexes differ	Habitat	Migration Migratory	Weight 0.4 ounce

DATE _____ TIME_____ LOCATION _____

| Family PARULIDAE | Species *Geothlypis trichas* | Length 5 inches | Wingspan 8 inches |

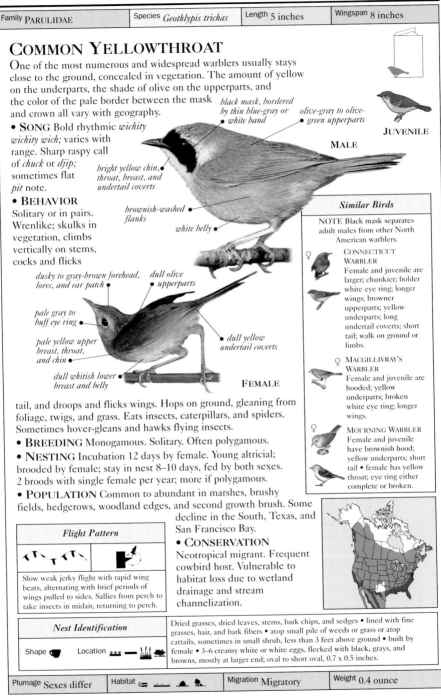

COMMON YELLOWTHROAT

One of the most numerous and widespread warblers usually stays close to the ground, concealed in vegetation. The amount of yellow on the underparts, the shade of olive on the upperparts, and the color of the pale border between the mask and crown all vary with geography.

black mask, bordered by thin blue-gray or white band

olive-gray to olive-green upperparts

JUVENILE

MALE

- **SONG** Bold rhythmic *wichity wichity wich*; varies with range. Sharp raspy call of *chuck* or *djip*; sometimes flat *pit* note.

bright yellow chin, throat, breast, and undertail coverts

- **BEHAVIOR** Solitary or in pairs. Wrenlike; skulks in vegetation, climbs vertically on stems, cocks and flicks

brownish-washed flanks

white belly

Similar Birds

NOTE Black mask separates adult males from other North American warblers.

♀ CONNECTICUT WARBLER
Female and juvenile are larger; chunkier; bolder white eye ring; longer wings; browner upperparts; yellow underparts; long undertail coverts; short tail; walk on ground or limbs.

dusky to gray-brown forehead, lores, and ear patch

dull olive upperparts

pale gray to buff eye ring

pale yellow upper breast, throat, and chin

dull yellow undertail coverts

dull whitish lower breast and belly

FEMALE

♀ MACGILLIVRAY'S WARBLER
Female and juvenile are hooded; yellow underparts; broken white eye ring; longer wings.

♀ MOURNING WARBLER
Female and juvenile have brownish hood; yellow underparts; short tail • female has yellow throat; eye ring either complete or broken.

tail, and droops and flicks wings. Hops on ground, gleaning from foliage, twigs, and grass. Eats insects, caterpillars, and spiders. Sometimes hover-gleans and hawks flying insects.
- **BREEDING** Monogamous. Solitary. Often polygamous.
- **NESTING** Incubation 12 days by female. Young altricial; brooded by female; stay in nest 8–10 days, fed by both sexes. 2 broods with single female per year; more if polygamous.
- **POPULATION** Common to abundant in marshes, brushy fields, hedgerows, woodland edges, and second growth brush. Some decline in the South, Texas, and San Francisco Bay.
- **CONSERVATION** Neotropical migrant. Frequent cowbird host. Vulnerable to habitat loss due to wetland drainage and stream channelization.

Flight Pattern	
Slow weak jerky flight with rapid wing beats, alternating with brief periods of wings pulled to sides. Sallies from perch to take insects in midair, returning to perch.	

Nest Identification	Dried grasses, dried leaves, stems, bark chips, and sedges • lined with fine grasses, hair, and bark fibers • atop small pile of weeds or grass or atop cattails, sometimes in small shrub, less than 3 feet above ground • built by female • 3–6 creamy white or white eggs, flecked with black, grays, and browns, mostly at larger end; oval to short oval, 0.7 x 0.5 inches.
Shape ⬤ Location ⬚⬚⬚ ▬ 𝄢	

| Plumage Sexes differ | Habitat ⬚ ⬚ ▲ ⬚ | Migration Migratory | Weight 0.4 ounce |

DATE _____ TIME_____ LOCATION _____

Family PARULIDAE	Species *Wilsonia citrina*	Length 5.25 inches	Wingspan 8 inches

HOODED WARBLER

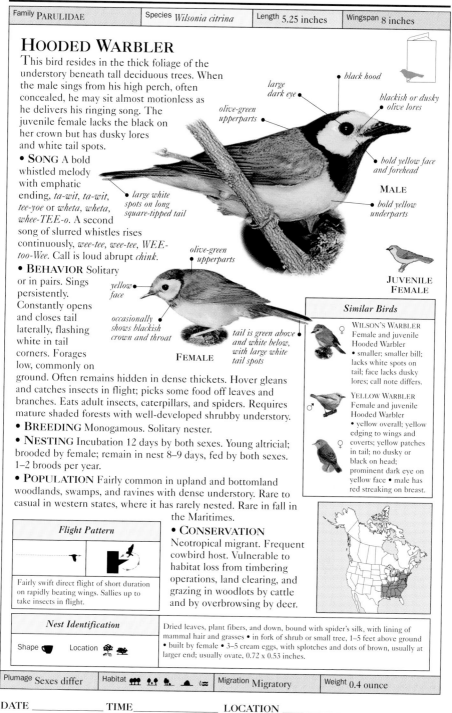

This bird resides in the thick foliage of the understory beneath tall deciduous trees. When the male sings from his high perch, often concealed, he may sit almost motionless as he delivers his ringing song. The juvenile female lacks the black on her crown but has dusky lores and white tail spots.

black hood

large dark eye

olive-green upperparts

blackish or dusky olive lores

bold yellow face and forehead

MALE

bold yellow underparts

• **SONG** A bold whistled melody with emphatic ending, *ta-wit, ta-wit, tee-yoe* or *wheta, wheta, whee-TEE-o*. A second song of slurred whistles rises continuously, *wee-tee, wee-tee, WEE-too-Wee*. Call is loud abrupt *chink*.

large white spots on long square-tipped tail

olive-green upperparts

JUVENILE FEMALE

• **BEHAVIOR** Solitary or in pairs. Sings persistently. Constantly opens and closes tail laterally, flashing white in tail corners. Forages low, commonly on

yellow face

occasionally shows blackish crown and throat

tail is green above and white below, with large white tail spots

FEMALE

ground. Often remains hidden in dense thickets. Hover gleans and catches insects in flight; picks some food off leaves and branches. Eats adult insects, caterpillars, and spiders. Requires mature shaded forests with well-developed shrubby understory.

• **BREEDING** Monogamous. Solitary nester.

• **NESTING** Incubation 12 days by both sexes. Young altricial; brooded by female; remain in nest 8–9 days, fed by both sexes. 1–2 broods per year.

• **POPULATION** Fairly common in upland and bottomland woodlands, swamps, and ravines with dense understory. Rare to casual in western states, where it has rarely nested. Rare in fall in the Maritimes.

Similar Birds

WILSON'S WARBLER Female and juvenile Hooded Warbler • smaller; smaller bill; lacks white spots on tail; face lacks dusky lores; call note differs.

YELLOW WARBLER Female and juvenile Hooded Warbler • yellow overall; yellow edging to wings and coverts; yellow patches in tail; no dusky or black on head; prominent dark eye on yellow face • male has red streaking on breast.

• **CONSERVATION** Neotropical migrant. Frequent cowbird host. Vulnerable to habitat loss from timbering operations, land clearing, and grazing in woodlots by cattle and by overbrowsing by deer.

Flight Pattern

Fairly swift direct flight of short duration on rapidly beating wings. Sallies up to take insects in flight.

Nest Identification

Shape   Location

Dried leaves, plant fibers, and down, bound with spider's silk, with lining of mammal hair and grasses • in fork of shrub or small tree, 1–5 feet above ground • built by female • 3–5 cream eggs, with splotches and dots of brown, usually at larger end; usually ovate, 0.72 x 0.53 inches.

Plumage Sexes differ	Habitat	Migration Migratory	Weight 0.4 ounce

Family PARULIDAE	Species *Wilsonia pusilla*	Length 4.75 inches	Wingspan 7.5 inches

WILSON'S WARBLER

Making its home in the thick damp woodlands and bogs of western North America, this active warbler has a wide nesting range, from Alaska to New Mexico, in the boreal forest from the Pacific to the Atlantic coast in Canada, and south into the New England states. The female is similar to the male but lacks the black cap or has only a light gray-black wash on her crown. Juvenile females lack the black crown altogether.

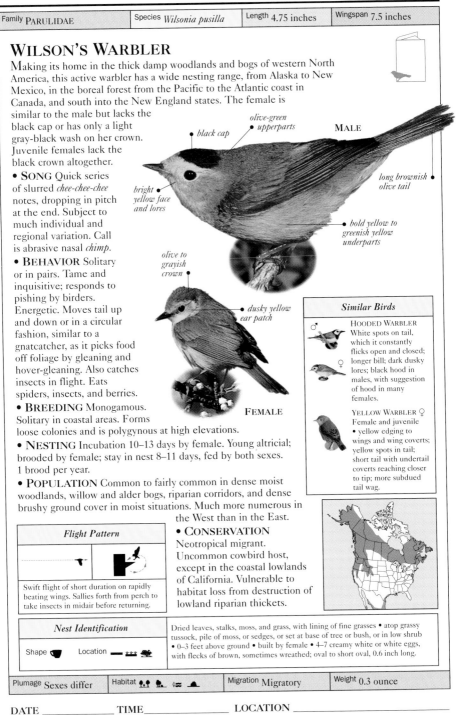

olive-green
upperparts

black cap

MALE

long brownish
olive tail

bright
yellow face
and lores

bold yellow to
greenish yellow
underparts

olive to
grayish
crown

dusky yellow
ear patch

FEMALE

- **SONG** Quick series of slurred *chee-chee-chee* notes, dropping in pitch at the end. Subject to much individual and regional variation. Call is abrasive nasal *chimp*.
- **BEHAVIOR** Solitary or in pairs. Tame and inquisitive; responds to pishing by birders. Energetic. Moves tail up and down or in a circular fashion, similar to a gnatcatcher, as it picks food off foliage by gleaning and hover-gleaning. Also catches insects in flight. Eats spiders, insects, and berries.
- **BREEDING** Monogamous. Solitary in coastal areas. Forms loose colonies and is polygynous at high elevations.
- **NESTING** Incubation 10–13 days by female. Young altricial; brooded by female; stay in nest 8–11 days, fed by both sexes. 1 brood per year.
- **POPULATION** Common to fairly common in dense moist woodlands, willow and alder bogs, riparian corridors, and dense brushy ground cover in moist situations. Much more numerous in the West than in the East.
- **CONSERVATION** Neotropical migrant. Uncommon cowbird host, except in the coastal lowlands of California. Vulnerable to habitat loss from destruction of lowland riparian thickets.

Similar Birds

HOODED WARBLER
White spots on tail, which it constantly flicks open and closed; longer bill; dark dusky lores; black hood in males, with suggestion of hood in many females.

YELLOW WARBLER ♀
Female and juvenile
• yellow edging to wings and wing coverts; yellow spots in tail; short tail with undertail coverts reaching closer to tip; more subdued tail wag.

Flight Pattern

Swift flight of short duration on rapidly beating wings. Sallies forth from perch to take insects in midair before returning.

Nest Identification

Shape ◖   Location ▬ ⟐ ♣

Dried leaves, stalks, moss, and grass, with lining of fine grasses • atop grassy tussock, pile of moss, or sedges, or set at base of tree or bush, or in low shrub • 0–3 feet above ground • built by female • 4–7 creamy white or white eggs, with flecks of brown, sometimes wreathed; oval to short oval, 0.6 inch long.

Plumage Sexes differ	Habitat	Migration Migratory	Weight 0.3 ounce

DATE _____ TIME_____ LOCATION _____

Family PARULIDAE	Species *Wilsonia canadensis*	Length 5–6 inches	Wingspan 7.5–8.75 inches

CANADA WARBLER

This bird sings frequently from the dense forest undergrowth it favors, or from an exposed perch just above it, with a jumbled warbling song that defies a fitting mnemonic. It actively forages for insects by flushing them from the foliage and chasing them. Males have been observed in "anticipatory feeding," offering insects to the unhatched eggs in the well-concealed nest on the ground. Canada Warblers are more often seen than heard on the breeding grounds, but a bird often will reveal itself, coming close to squeaking and pishing sounds made by birders. This early fall migrant heads southward before many other warblers begin their migrations. During migration they are often seen in pairs, and may be traveling with their mate of the season.

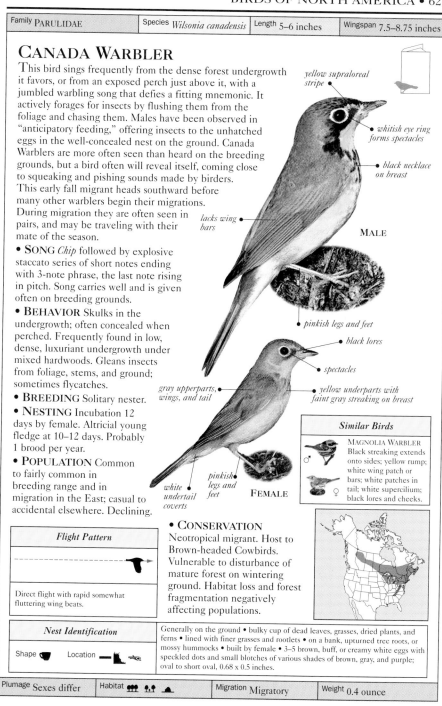

yellow supraloreal stripe

whitish eye ring forms spectacles

black necklace on breast

lacks wing bars

MALE

pinkish legs and feet

black lores

spectacles

gray upperparts, wings, and tail

yellow underparts with faint gray streaking on breast

pinkish legs and feet

white undertail coverts

FEMALE

- **SONG** *Chip* followed by explosive staccato series of short notes ending with 3-note phrase, the last note rising in pitch. Song carries well and is given often on breeding grounds.
- **BEHAVIOR** Skulks in the undergrowth; often concealed when perched. Frequently found in low, dense, luxuriant undergrowth under mixed hardwoods. Gleans insects from foliage, stems, and ground; sometimes flycatches.
- **BREEDING** Solitary nester.
- **NESTING** Incubation 12 days by female. Altricial young fledge at 10–12 days. Probably 1 brood per year.
- **POPULATION** Common to fairly common in breeding range and in migration in the East; casual to accidental elsewhere. Declining.

Similar Birds

MAGNOLIA WARBLER Black streaking extends onto sides; yellow rump; white wing patch or bars; white patches in tail; white supercilium; black lores and cheeks.

- **CONSERVATION** Neotropical migrant. Host to Brown-headed Cowbirds. Vulnerable to disturbance of mature forest on wintering ground. Habitat loss and forest fragmentation negatively affecting populations.

Flight Pattern

Direct flight with rapid somewhat fluttering wing beats.

Nest Identification

Shape 🍵   Location 🪵 🪹

Generally on the ground • bulky cup of dead leaves, grasses, dried plants, and ferns • lined with finer grasses and rootlets • on a bank, upturned tree roots, or mossy hummocks • built by female • 3–5 brown, buff, or creamy white eggs with speckled dots and small blotches of various shades of brown, gray, and purple; oval to short oval, 0.68 x 0.5 inches.

Plumage Sexes differ	Habitat 🌳 🌿 ⛰	Migration Migratory	Weight 0.4 ounce

DATE _____ TIME _____ LOCATION _____

Family PARULIDAE	Species *Cardellina rubrifrons*	Length 5 inches	Wingspan 7.5 inches

RED-FACED WARBLER

Sporting a scarlet and black face, this active bird is easily recognizable. A native of Mexico and Central America, it regularly nests in the high mountain forests of Arizona and New Mexico in conifers, oaks, and aspen at 6,400–8,000 feet, sometimes lower in shaded canyons. This inquisitive species comes readily to the squeaking and pishing of birders. When clinging chickadee-like upside down on trees, the white nape patch and white rump often are visible. The red on the face of the female is a little less bright than that of the male, and juveniles are similar to adults, just a little duller.

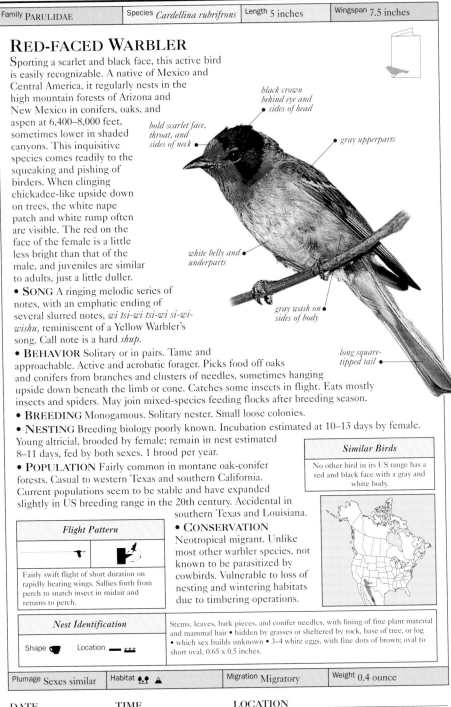

black crown behind eye and sides of head

bold scarlet face, throat, and sides of neck

gray upperparts

white belly and underparts

gray wash on sides of body

long square-tipped tail

• **SONG** A ringing melodic series of notes, with an emphatic ending of several slurred notes, *wi tsi-wi tsi-wi si-wi-wishu*, reminiscent of a Yellow Warbler's song. Call note is a hard *shup*.

• **BEHAVIOR** Solitary or in pairs. Tame and approachable. Active and acrobatic forager. Picks food off oaks and conifers from branches and clusters of needles, sometimes hanging upside down beneath the limb or cone. Catches some insects in flight. Eats mostly insects and spiders. May join mixed-species feeding flocks after breeding season.

• **BREEDING** Monogamous. Solitary nester. Small loose colonies.

• **NESTING** Breeding biology poorly known. Incubation estimated at 10–13 days by female. Young altricial, brooded by female; remain in nest estimated 8–11 days, fed by both sexes. 1 brood per year.

• **POPULATION** Fairly common in montane oak-conifer forests. Casual to western Texas and southern California. Current populations seem to be stable and have expanded slightly in US breeding range in the 20th century. Accidental in southern Texas and Louisiana.

• **CONSERVATION** Neotropical migrant. Unlike most other warbler species, not known to be parasitized by cowbirds. Vulnerable to loss of nesting and wintering habitats due to timbering operations.

Similar Birds

No other bird in its US range has a red and black face with a gray and white body.

Flight Pattern

Fairly swift flight of short duration on rapidly beating wings. Sallies forth from perch to snatch insect in midair and returns to perch.

Nest Identification

Shape 🪹   Location ▬ ✦✦✦

Stems, leaves, bark pieces, and conifer needles, with lining of fine plant material and mammal hair • hidden by grasses or sheltered by rock, base of tree, or log • which sex builds unknown • 3–4 white eggs, with fine dots of brown; oval to short oval, 0.65 x 0.5 inches.

Plumage Sexes similar	Habitat 🪶🌲 ▲	Migration Migratory	Weight 0.4 ounce

DATE _____ TIME _____ LOCATION _____

Family PARULIDAE	Species *Myioborus pictus*	Length 5.5 inches	Wingspan 8.5 inches

PAINTED REDSTART

Easily identified by its conspicuous scarlet breast and white wing patches, this native of Mexico and Central America also nests in the wooded pine-oak foothills and mountain canyons of the Southwest. It often spreads its tail and droops its wings while hopping over stumps and branches. In the dark shadowed habitats the redstart frequents, the resulting white flashes may attract the attention of the bird's mate, foraging nearby. The white flashes may also startle insects into revealing themselves as prey. In flight this bird shows a white crissum with black scalloping. Juveniles are duskier and lack the red underparts until early fall.

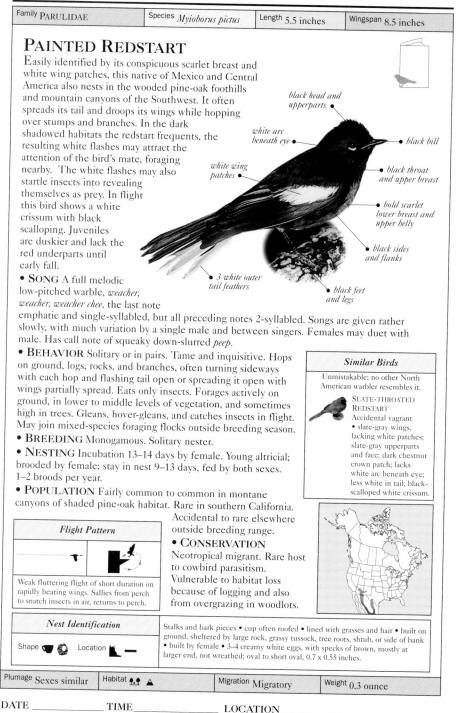

black head and upperparts

white arc beneath eye

white wing patches

black bill

black throat and upper breast

bold scarlet lower breast and upper belly

black sides and flanks

3 white outer tail feathers

black feet and legs

• **SONG** A full melodic low-pitched warble, *weacher, weacher, weacher chee*, the last note emphatic and single-syllabled, but all preceding notes 2-syllabled. Songs are given rather slowly, with much variation by a single male and between singers. Females may duet with male. Has call note of squeaky down-slurred *peep*.

• **BEHAVIOR** Solitary or in pairs. Tame and inquisitive. Hops on ground, logs, rocks, and branches, often turning sideways with each hop and flashing tail open or spreading it open with wings partially spread. Eats only insects. Forages actively on ground, in lower to middle levels of vegetation, and sometimes high in trees. Gleans, hover-gleans, and catches insects in flight. May join mixed-species foraging flocks outside breeding season.

• **BREEDING** Monogamous. Solitary nester.

• **NESTING** Incubation 13–14 days by female. Young altricial; brooded by female; stay in nest 9–13 days, fed by both sexes. 1–2 broods per year.

• **POPULATION** Fairly common to common in montane canyons of shaded pine-oak habitat. Rare in southern California. Accidental to rare elsewhere outside breeding range.

• **CONSERVATION** Neotropical migrant. Rare host to cowbird parasitism. Vulnerable to habitat loss because of logging and also from overgrazing in woodlots.

Similar Birds

Unmistakable; no other North American warbler resembles it.

SLATE-THROATED REDSTART Accidental vagrant • slate-gray wings, lacking white patches; slate-gray upperparts and face; dark chestnut crown patch; lacks white arc beneath eye; less white in tail; black-scalloped white crissum.

Flight Pattern

Weak fluttering flight of short duration on rapidly beating wings. Sallies from perch to snatch insects in air, returns to perch.

Nest Identification

Shape — Location —

Stalks and bark pieces • cup often roofed • lined with grasses and hair • built on ground, sheltered by large rock, grassy tussock, tree roots, shrub, or side of bank • built by female • 3–4 creamy white eggs, with specks of brown, mostly at larger end, not wreathed; oval to short oval, 0.7 x 0.55 inches.

Plumage Sexes similar	Habitat	Migration Migratory	Weight 0.3 ounce

DATE _____ TIME_____ LOCATION _____

Family PARULIDAE	Species *Euthlypis lachrymosa*	Length 5.75 inches	Wingspan 9 inches

FAN-TAILED WARBLER

A native of Mexico and northern Central America, this shy bird is a rare spring, summer, and fall visitor to southeastern Arizona. Unlike many of the warblers, it walks on the ground rather than hops, and it often wags its spread tail from side to side or bobs it up and down. This is a long-legged warbler with a long graduated white-tipped tail. There is little difference in plumages between the sexes. Juveniles are dark sooty gray overall with two thin white wing bars, a yellow crissum, and a pale yellow vent.

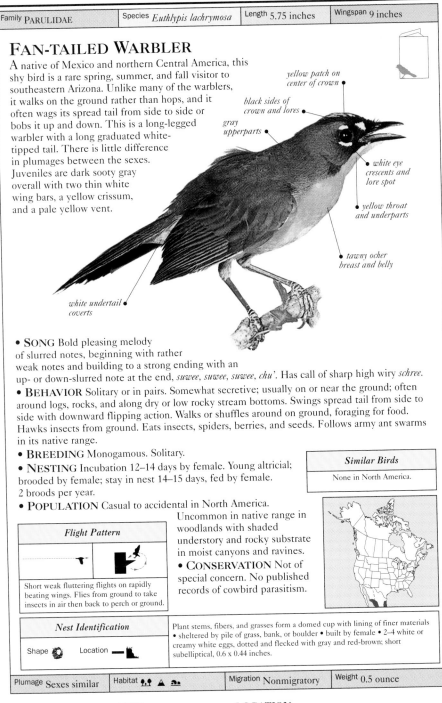

yellow patch on center of crown

black sides of crown and lores

gray upperparts

white eye crescents and lore spot

yellow throat and underparts

tawny ocher breast and belly

white undertail coverts

• **SONG** Bold pleasing melody of slurred notes, beginning with rather weak notes and building to a strong ending with an up- or down-slurred note at the end, *suwee, suwee, suwee, chu'*. Has call of sharp high wiry *schree*.
• **BEHAVIOR** Solitary or in pairs. Somewhat secretive; usually on or near the ground; often around logs, rocks, and along dry or low rocky stream bottoms. Swings spread tail from side to side with downward flipping action. Walks or shuffles around on ground, foraging for food. Hawks insects from ground. Eats insects, spiders, berries, and seeds. Follows army ant swarms in its native range.
• **BREEDING** Monogamous. Solitary.
• **NESTING** Incubation 12–14 days by female. Young altricial; brooded by female; stay in nest 14–15 days, fed by female. 2 broods per year.
• **POPULATION** Casual to accidental in North America. Uncommon in native range in woodlands with shaded understory and rocky substrate in moist canyons and ravines.
• **CONSERVATION** Not of special concern. No published records of cowbird parasitism.

Similar Birds
None in North America.

Flight Pattern
Short weak fluttering flights on rapidly beating wings. Flies from ground to take insects in air then back to perch or ground.

Nest Identification	Plant stems, fibers, and grasses form a domed cup with lining of finer materials • sheltered by pile of grass, bank, or boulder • built by female • 2–4 white or creamy white eggs, dotted and flecked with gray and red-brown; short subelliptical, 0.6 x 0.44 inches.
Shape ⬤ Location ▬	

Plumage Sexes similar	Habitat	Migration Nonmigratory	Weight 0.5 ounce

DATE _____ TIME_____ LOCATION _____

Family PARULIDAE	Species *Basileuterus rufifrons*	Length 5.25 inches	Wingspan 8 inches

RUFOUS-CAPPED WARBLER

Easily identifiable by its bold rufous cap, broad white eyebrow, and yellow throat, this endemic of Mexico and Guatemala is an infrequent visitor to southern and western Texas and southeastern Arizona. Like many warblers, it cocks its tail and tends to remain hidden in the dense undergrowth of woodlands. This warbler's tail is unusually long and slender and is waved in the manner of a gnatcatcher.

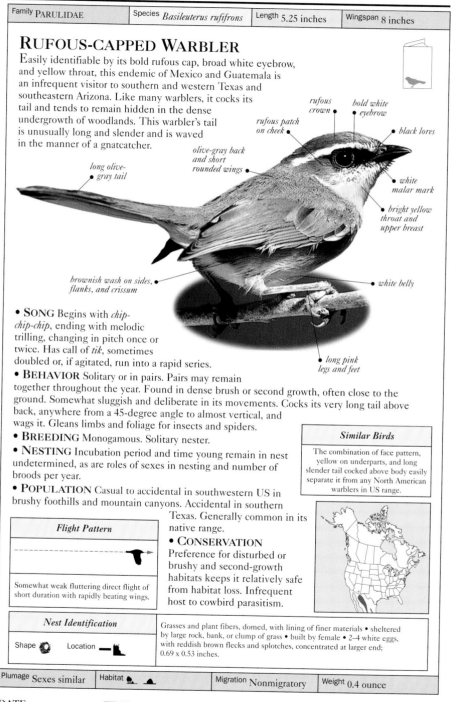

rufous crown

bold white eyebrow

rufous patch on cheek

black lores

olive-gray back and short rounded wings

long olive-gray tail

white malar mark

bright yellow throat and upper breast

brownish wash on sides, flanks, and crissum

white belly

long pink legs and feet

• **SONG** Begins with *chip-chip-chip*, ending with melodic trilling, changing in pitch once or twice. Has call of *tik*, sometimes doubled or, if agitated, run into a rapid series.

• **BEHAVIOR** Solitary or in pairs. Pairs may remain together throughout the year. Found in dense brush or second growth, often close to the ground. Somewhat sluggish and deliberate in its movements. Cocks its very long tail above back, anywhere from a 45-degree angle to almost vertical, and wags it. Gleans limbs and foliage for insects and spiders.

• **BREEDING** Monogamous. Solitary nester.

• **NESTING** Incubation period and time young remain in nest undetermined, as are roles of sexes in nesting and number of broods per year.

• **POPULATION** Casual to accidental in southwestern US in brushy foothills and mountain canyons. Accidental in southern Texas. Generally common in its native range.

• **CONSERVATION** Preference for disturbed or brushy and second-growth habitats keeps it relatively safe from habitat loss. Infrequent host to cowbird parasitism.

Similar Birds

The combination of face pattern, yellow on underparts, and long slender tail cocked above body easily separate it from any North American warblers in US range.

Flight Pattern

Somewhat weak fluttering direct flight of short duration with rapidly beating wings.

Nest Identification

Shape ⬤ Location ━━ 🪵

Grasses and plant fibers, domed, with lining of finer materials • sheltered by large rock, bank, or clump of grass • built by female • 2–4 white eggs, with reddish brown flecks and splotches, concentrated at larger end; 0.69 x 0.53 inches.

Plumage Sexes similar	Habitat	Migration Nonmigratory	Weight 0.4 ounce

DATE _____ TIME_____ LOCATION _____

Family PARULIDAE	Species *Icteria virens*	Length 7.25 inches	Wingspan 9–10 inches

YELLOW-BREASTED CHAT

The largest North American warbler is named for its song, which resembles bizarre loud chattering. The large size, stocky body, thick bill, and long tail are unusual for a warbler, yet DNA studies confirm its taxonomic placement within this family. Unlike other warblers, it often sings at night in addition to its daytime vocalizations, a trait shared with some of the mimic thrushes. The female is similar to the male but has gray lores.

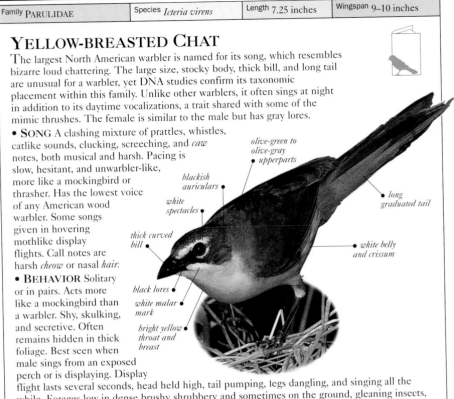

olive-green to olive-gray upperparts
blackish auriculars
white spectacles
thick curved bill
black lores
white malar mark
bright yellow throat and breast
long graduated tail
white belly and crissum

- **SONG** A clashing mixture of prattles, whistles, catlike sounds, clucking, screeching, and *caw* notes, both musical and harsh. Pacing is slow, hesitant, and unwarbler-like, more like a mockingbird or thrasher. Has the lowest voice of any American wood warbler. Some songs given in hovering mothlike display flights. Call notes are harsh *cheow* or nasal *hair*.
- **BEHAVIOR** Solitary or in pairs. Acts more like a mockingbird than a warbler. Shy, skulking, and secretive. Often remains hidden in thick foliage. Best seen when male sings from an exposed perch or is displaying. Display flight lasts several seconds, head held high, tail pumping, legs dangling, and singing all the while. Forages low in dense brushy shrubbery and sometimes on the ground, gleaning insects, larvae, berries, and fruits. The only warbler known to hold food in its feet.
- **BREEDING** Monogamous. Solitary nester or small colonies.
- **NESTING** Incubation 11–12 days by female. Altricial young brooded by female; stay in nest 8–11 days, fed by both sexes. 2 broods per year.
- **POPULATION** Common in dense thickets, brush, or scrub, especially along swamp margins and streams. Significant decline over much of its eastern range.
- **CONSERVATION** Neotropical migrant. Common host to Brown-headed Cowbird. Vulnerable to habitat loss due to land development and clearing, urbanization, and natural succession from old fields to maturation of forests.

Similar Birds

No similar species in North America.

Flight Pattern

Weak direct flights of short duration. In singing display, flies with legs dangling and wings flapping limply.

Nest Identification

Shape ☕   Location 🪶

Dried stems, leaves, grasses, and bark pieces, lined with soft grasses, stems, and leaves • in bush, vines, or thorny shrub, 2–8 feet above ground • built by female • 3–6 white or creamy white eggs, with flecks of rust or violet, concentrated at larger end; oval, 0.86 x 0.67 inches.

Plumage Sexes similar	Habitat 🌿 ⛰ 🌾	Migration Migratory	Weight 0.9 ounce

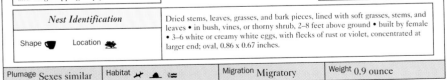

DATE _____ TIME_____ LOCATION _____

| Family THRAUPIDAE | Species *Piranga flava* | Length 8 inches | Wingspan 12.75 inches |

HEPATIC TANAGER

Named for the liver-red plumage of the male, this tropical bird has a small summer range in the southwestern mountain forests of North America. Not shy around humans, the male perches in tall trees to sing a sing-song series of musical phrases, similar to those of the Black-headed Grosbeak, but faster. The adult male retains his red plumage throughout the year. The combination of dark bill and dusky gray auriculars in both sexes are good field marks to separate them from other tanager species. Juveniles are similar to females but have paler underparts with buffy wing bars and are heavily streaked with brown.

grayish cheek patch

dark red to orange-red overall

blackish bill

grayish wash on back and flanks

MALE

• SONG Clear bold musical phrases in back-and-forth sing-song pattern. Call note is a loud *chip* or *chuck*, similar to the Hermit Thrush.
• BEHAVIOR Solitary or in pairs. Often joins mixed-species foraging flocks after the nesting season. Forages for food in upper foliage of tall trees where it gleans from branches, stems, and leaves. Sometimes catches insects in flight. Eats insects and fruit. Sings often and is often detected by calls or song. Restless and active. Often flies considerable distances, moving rapidly from one tree to the next or traveling all the way across mountain canyons.
• BREEDING Monogamous. In courtship display male moves head back and forth and lifts bill to sky, showing off his bright throat.
• NESTING Breeding biology poorly known. Estimated incubation 13–14 days by female. Young altricial; brooded by female; stay in nest estimated 13–15 days, fed by both sexes. 1 brood per year.

grayish cheek patch

olive-green upperparts

yellow underparts

grayish wash on flanks

FEMALE

Similar Birds

♂ SUMMER TANAGER Large yellow-brown bill; lacks grayish cheek patch • male displays brighter reds.

• POPULATION Uncommon to fairly common in pine and pine-oak in mountain canyons. Accidental on Gulf Coast.
• CONSERVATION Neotropical migrant. Rare host to cowbird parasitism.

Flight Pattern

Relatively swift direct flight on rapidly beating wings.

Nest Identification

Shape ⌣ Location ▲⬥ ❀

Forbs, grasses, stems, and flower petals with lining of soft grass • in fork, toward end of limb, 15–50 feet above ground • built mostly by female, but male may bring materials • 3–5 bluish greenish eggs with brownish markings, often wreathed; oval to short oval, 1.0 x 0.75 inches.

| Plumage Sexes differ | Habitat ▲ ⬩⬩ ⬩⬩ | Migration Migratory | Weight 1.3 ounces |

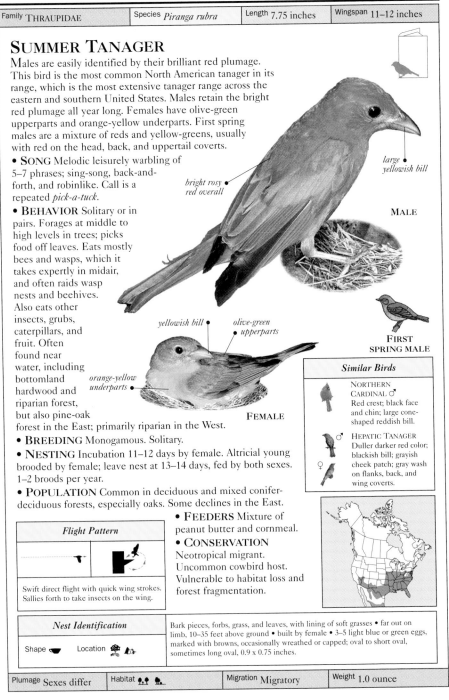

| Family THRAUPIDAE | Species *Piranga rubra* | Length 7.75 inches | Wingspan 11–12 inches |

SUMMER TANAGER

Males are easily identified by their brilliant red plumage. This bird is the most common North American tanager in its range, which is the most extensive tanager range across the eastern and southern United States. Males retain the bright red plumage all year long. Females have olive-green upperparts and orange-yellow underparts. First spring males are a mixture of reds and yellow-greens, usually with red on the head, back, and uppertail coverts.

• **SONG** Melodic leisurely warbling of 5–7 phrases; sing-song, back-and-forth, and robinlike. Call is a repeated *pick-a-tuck*.

• **BEHAVIOR** Solitary or in pairs. Forages at middle to high levels in trees; picks food off leaves. Eats mostly bees and wasps, which it takes expertly in midair, and often raids wasp nests and beehives. Also eats other insects, grubs, caterpillars, and fruit. Often found near water, including bottomland hardwood and riparian forest, but also pine-oak forest in the East; primarily riparian in the West.

large yellowish bill

MALE

bright rosy red overall

yellowish bill
olive-green upperparts

FIRST SPRING MALE

orange-yellow underparts

FEMALE

• **BREEDING** Monogamous. Solitary.

• **NESTING** Incubation 11–12 days by female. Altricial young brooded by female; leave nest at 13–14 days, fed by both sexes. 1–2 broods per year.

• **POPULATION** Common in deciduous and mixed conifer-deciduous forests, especially oaks. Some declines in the East.

• **FEEDERS** Mixture of peanut butter and cornmeal.

• **CONSERVATION** Neotropical migrant. Uncommon cowbird host. Vulnerable to habitat loss and forest fragmentation.

Similar Birds

NORTHERN CARDINAL ♂ Red crest; black face and chin; large cone-shaped reddish bill.

HEPATIC TANAGER Duller darker red color; blackish bill; grayish cheek patch; gray wash on flanks, back, and wing coverts.

Flight Pattern	

Swift direct flight with quick wing strokes. Sallies forth to take insects on the wing.

Nest Identification	
Shape	Location	Bark pieces, forbs, grass, and leaves, with lining of soft grasses • far out on limb, 10–35 feet above ground • built by female • 3–5 light blue or green eggs, marked with browns, occasionally wreathed or capped; oval to short oval, sometimes long oval, 0.9 x 0.75 inches.

| Plumage Sexes differ | Habitat | Migration Migratory | Weight 1.0 ounce |

DATE _____ TIME_____ LOCATION _____

| Family THRAUPIDAE | Species *Piranga olivacea* | Length 7 inches | Wingspan 11–12 inches |

SCARLET TANAGER

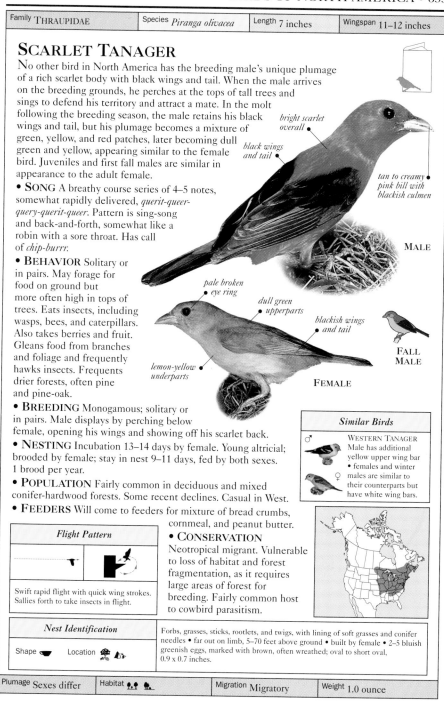

No other bird in North America has the breeding male's unique plumage of a rich scarlet body with black wings and tail. When the male arrives on the breeding grounds, he perches at the tops of tall trees and sings to defend his territory and attract a mate. In the molt following the breeding season, the male retains his black wings and tail, but his plumage becomes a mixture of green, yellow, and red patches, later becoming dull green and yellow, appearing similar to the female bird. Juveniles and first fall males are similar in appearance to the adult female.

bright scarlet overall

black wings and tail

tan to creamy pink bill with blackish culmen

MALE

- **SONG** A breathy course series of 4–5 notes, somewhat rapidly delivered, *querit-queer-query-querit-queer*. Pattern is sing-song and back-and-forth, somewhat like a robin with a sore throat. Has call of *chip-burr.*
- **BEHAVIOR** Solitary or in pairs. May forage for food on ground but more often high in tops of trees. Eats insects, including wasps, bees, and caterpillars. Also takes berries and fruit. Gleans food from branches and foliage and frequently hawks insects. Frequents drier forests, often pine and pine-oak.

pale broken eye ring

dull green upperparts

blackish wings and tail

FALL MALE

lemon-yellow underparts

FEMALE

- **BREEDING** Monogamous; solitary or in pairs. Male displays by perching below female, opening his wings and showing off his scarlet back.
- **NESTING** Incubation 13–14 days by female. Young altricial; brooded by female; stay in nest 9–11 days, fed by both sexes. 1 brood per year.
- **POPULATION** Fairly common in deciduous and mixed conifer-hardwood forests. Some recent declines. Casual in West.
- **FEEDERS** Will come to feeders for mixture of bread crumbs, cornmeal, and peanut butter.

- **CONSERVATION** Neotropical migrant. Vulnerable to loss of habitat and forest fragmentation, as it requires large areas of forest for breeding. Fairly common host to cowbird parasitism.

Similar Birds	
♂	WESTERN TANAGER Male has additional yellow upper wing bar
♀	• females and winter males are similar to their counterparts but have white wing bars.

Flight Pattern	
Swift rapid flight with quick wing strokes. Sallies forth to take insects in flight.	

Nest Identification	
Shape ⬛ Location 🪹 🌿	Forbs, grasses, sticks, rootlets, and twigs, with lining of soft grasses and conifer needles • far out on limb, 5–70 feet above ground • built by female • 2–5 bluish greenish eggs, marked with brown, often wreathed; oval to short oval, 0.9 x 0.7 inches.

| Plumage Sexes differ | Habitat 🌿 🌳 | Migration Migratory | Weight 1.0 ounce |

DATE _____ TIME_____ LOCATION _____

Family THRAUPIDAE	Species *Piranga ludoviciana*	Length 7.25 inches	Wingspan 11–12 inches

WESTERN TANAGER

One of only two North American tanagers with distinct wing bars, this bird frequents the coniferous forests of the western mountain region, where it is one of the most colorful species present. It has on rare occasions hybridized with its close cousin, the Scarlet Tanager. In the molt after the breeding season, the male's red head fades to a yellowish color with fine streaking on the crown. The female's olive-gray back contrasts sharply with the yellow-green rump, uppertail coverts, and nape. Juveniles resemble females but with head and body streaked dark brown.

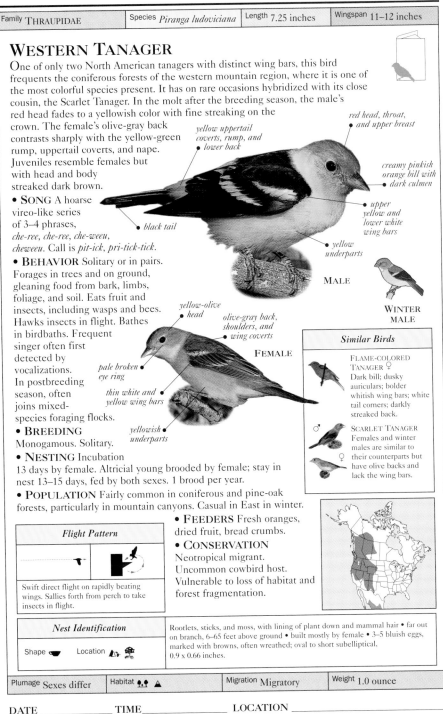

yellow uppertail coverts, rump, and lower back

red head, throat, and upper breast

creamy pinkish orange bill with dark culmen

upper yellow and lower white wing bars

yellow underparts

MALE

WINTER MALE

black tail

yellow-olive head

olive-gray back, shoulders, and wing coverts

FEMALE

pale broken eye ring

thin white and yellow wing bars

yellowish underparts

- **SONG** A hoarse vireo-like series of 3–4 phrases, *che-ree, che-ree, che-weeu, cheweeu.* Call is *pit-ick, pri-tick-tick.*
- **BEHAVIOR** Solitary or in pairs. Forages in trees and on ground, gleaning food from bark, limbs, foliage, and soil. Eats fruit and insects, including wasps and bees. Hawks insects in flight. Bathes in birdbaths. Frequent singer often first detected by vocalizations. In postbreeding season, often joins mixed-species foraging flocks.
- **BREEDING** Monogamous. Solitary.
- **NESTING** Incubation 13 days by female. Altricial young brooded by female; stay in nest 13–15 days, fed by both sexes. 1 brood per year.
- **POPULATION** Fairly common in coniferous and pine-oak forests, particularly in mountain canyons. Casual in East in winter.
- **FEEDERS** Fresh oranges, dried fruit, bread crumbs.
- **CONSERVATION** Neotropical migrant. Uncommon cowbird host. Vulnerable to loss of habitat and forest fragmentation.

Similar Birds

FLAME-COLORED TANAGER ♂ Dark bill; dusky auriculars; bolder whitish wing bars; white tail corners; darkly streaked back.

SCARLET TANAGER ♂ ♀ Females and winter males are similar to their counterparts but have olive backs and lack the wing bars.

Flight Pattern	

Swift direct flight on rapidly beating wings. Sallies forth from perch to take insects in flight.

Nest Identification	
Shape ⌒ Location 🔺 🌲	Rootlets, sticks, and moss, with lining of plant down and mammal hair • far out on branch, 6–65 feet above ground • built mostly by female • 3–5 bluish eggs, marked with browns, often wreathed; oval to short subelliptical, 0.9 x 0.66 inches.

Plumage Sexes differ	Habitat 🌿🌱 🔺	Migration Migratory	Weight 1.0 ounce

DATE _____ TIME_____ LOCATION _____

Family THRAUPIDAE	Species *Piranga bidentata*	Length 7.25 inches	Wingspan 11–12 inches

FLAME-COLORED TANAGER

A tropical species, this bird has visited the mountains of southwestern Texas on rare occasion and is casual in the mountains of southeastern Arizona, where it has nested. The orange-red color of the male combined with the blackish wings and tail, white wing bars and tertial spots, and black-streaked back are definitive. Juveniles have dark brown-streaked yellow underparts. The word *bidentata* in the scientific name refers to the visible "teeth" along the cutting edge of the upper mandible.

• **SONG** Trilling series of 3–5 burry vireo-like phrases, *chick-churee-chuwee*, similar to song of Western Tanager. Call is hard, rolled *pr-reck*.

• **BEHAVIOR** Solitary or in pairs. Joins mixed foraging flocks after breeding season. Forages from middle to high levels in trees. Eats insects and fruits. Gleans from branches and foliage. Occasionally hawks insects. Frequents humid coniferous, oak, and pine-oak forests in mountains.

• **BREEDING** Monogamous and solitary.

• **NESTING** Breeding biology poorly known. Estimated incubation 13–14 days by female. Young altricial; brooded by female; stay in nest 13–15 days, fed by both sexes. 1 brood per year.

• **POPULATION** Casual to southeastern Arizona. Accidental in southwest Texas.

• **CONSERVATION** Vulnerable to habitat loss and forest fragmentation. Extent of cowbird parasitism unknown.

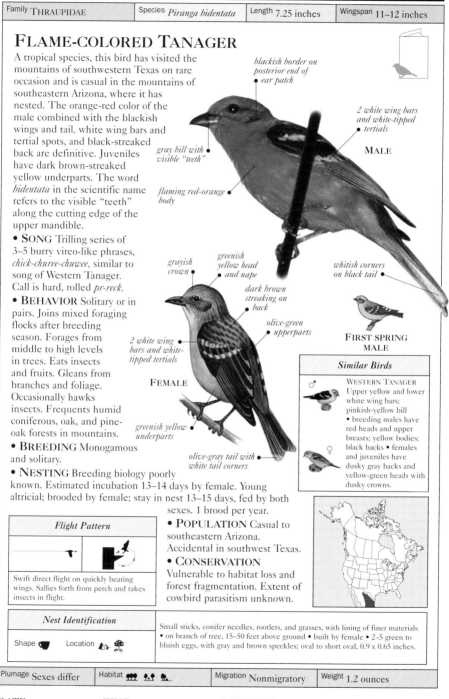

blackish border on posterior end of ear patch

2 white wing bars and white-tipped tertials

MALE

gray bill with visible "teeth"

flaming red-orange body

grayish crown

greenish yellow head and nape

dark brown streaking on back

olive-green upperparts

whitish corners on black tail

FIRST SPRING MALE

2 white wing bars and white-tipped tertials

FEMALE

greenish yellow underparts

olive-gray tail with white tail corners

Similar Birds

♂ WESTERN TANAGER Upper yellow and lower white wing bars; pinkish-yellow bill • breeding males have red heads and upper breasts; yellow bodies; black backs • females and juveniles have dusky gray backs and yellow-green heads with dusky crowns.

Flight Pattern

Swift direct flight on quickly beating wings. Sallies forth from perch and takes insects in flight.

Nest Identification

Shape ⬱   Location 🌲 🌿

Small sticks, conifer needles, rootlets, and grasses, with lining of finer materials • on branch of tree, 15–50 feet above ground • built by female • 2–5 green to bluish eggs, with gray and brown speckles; oval to short oval, 0.9 x 0.65 inches.

Plumage Sexes differ	Habitat 🐾 🌿 🌳	Migration Nonmigratory	Weight 1.2 ounces

DATE _____ TIME _____ LOCATION _____

Family EMBERIZIDAE	Species *Pipilo chlorurus*	Length 7.25 inches	Wingspan 10 inches

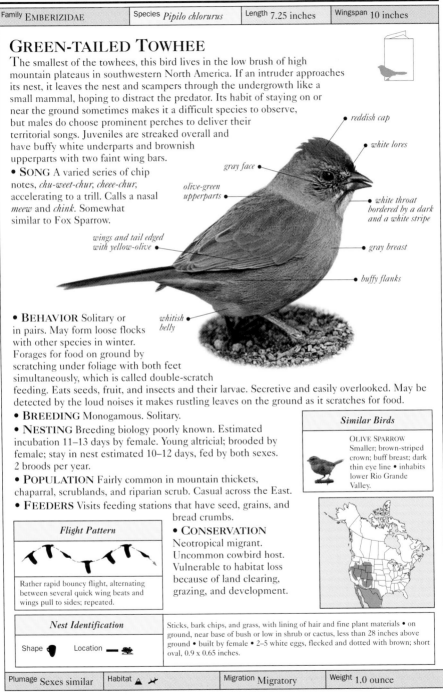

GREEN-TAILED TOWHEE

The smallest of the towhees, this bird lives in the low brush of high mountain plateaus in southwestern North America. If an intruder approaches its nest, it leaves the nest and scampers through the undergrowth like a small mammal, hoping to distract the predator. Its habit of staying on or near the ground sometimes makes it a difficult species to observe, but males do choose prominent perches to deliver their territorial songs. Juveniles are streaked overall and have buffy white underparts and brownish upperparts with two faint wing bars.

• **SONG** A varied series of chip notes, *chu-weet-chur, cheee-chur,* accelerating to a trill. Calls a nasal *meew* and *chink.* Somewhat similar to Fox Sparrow.

reddish cap

white lores

gray face

olive-green upperparts

white throat bordered by a dark and a white stripe

gray breast

buffy flanks

wings and tail edged with yellow-olive

• **BEHAVIOR** Solitary or in pairs. May form loose flocks with other species in winter. Forages for food on ground by scratching under foliage with both feet simultaneously, which is called double-scratch feeding. Eats seeds, fruit, and insects and their larvae. Secretive and easily overlooked. May be detected by the loud noises it makes rustling leaves on the ground as it scratches for food.

whitish belly

• **BREEDING** Monogamous. Solitary.
• **NESTING** Breeding biology poorly known. Estimated incubation 11–13 days by female. Young altricial; brooded by female; stay in nest estimated 10–12 days, fed by both sexes. 2 broods per year.
• **POPULATION** Fairly common in mountain thickets, chaparral, scrublands, and riparian scrub. Casual across the East.
• **FEEDERS** Visits feeding stations that have seed, grains, and bread crumbs.

Similar Birds

OLIVE SPARROW
Smaller; brown-striped crown; buff breast; dark thin eye line • inhabits lower Rio Grande Valley.

• **CONSERVATION**
Neotropical migrant. Uncommon cowbird host. Vulnerable to habitat loss because of land clearing, grazing, and development.

Flight Pattern
Rather rapid bouncy flight, alternating between several quick wing beats and wings pull to sides; repeated.

Nest Identification	Sticks, bark chips, and grass, with lining of hair and fine plant materials • on ground, near base of bush or low in shrub or cactus, less than 28 inches above ground • built by female • 2–5 white eggs, flecked and dotted with brown; short oval, 0.9 x 0.65 inches.
Shape ● Location ▬ ♣	

Plumage Sexes similar	Habitat ▲ ⤪	Migration Migratory	Weight 1.0 ounce

DATE _____ TIME_____ LOCATION _____

Family EMBERIZIDAE	Species *Pipilo maculatus*	Length 7–7.5 inches	Wingspan 10–11 inches

SPOTTED TOWHEE

This bird is the western counterpart of the Eastern Towhee, and until recently they were considered one species, the Rufous-sided Towhee. The white spotting on the upperparts, wings, and tail shows geographical variation. The white on the undersides of the tail corners flash in flight. Juveniles are brown with two white wing bars and darker brown streaking on the upperparts and underparts.

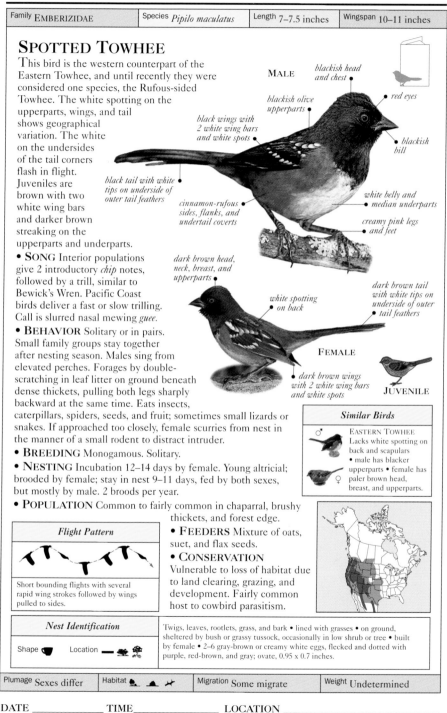

MALE

blackish head and chest

red eyes

blackish olive upperparts

black wings with 2 white wing bars and white spots

blackish bill

black tail with white tips on underside of outer tail feathers

cinnamon-rufous sides, flanks, and undertail coverts

white belly and median underparts

creamy pink legs and feet

dark brown head, neck, breast, and upperparts

white spotting on back

dark brown tail with white tips on underside of outer tail feathers

FEMALE

dark brown wings with 2 white wing bars and white spots

JUVENILE

• **SONG** Interior populations give 2 introductory *chip* notes, followed by a trill, similar to Bewick's Wren. Pacific Coast birds deliver a fast or slow trilling. Call is slurred nasal mewing *guee*.

• **BEHAVIOR** Solitary or in pairs. Small family groups stay together after nesting season. Males sing from elevated perches. Forages by double-scratching in leaf litter on ground beneath dense thickets, pulling both legs sharply backward at the same time. Eats insects, caterpillars, spiders, seeds, and fruit; sometimes small lizards or snakes. If approached too closely, female scurries from nest in the manner of a small rodent to distract intruder.

• **BREEDING** Monogamous. Solitary.

• **NESTING** Incubation 12–14 days by female. Young altricial; brooded by female; stay in nest 9–11 days, fed by both sexes, but mostly by male. 2 broods per year.

• **POPULATION** Common to fairly common in chaparral, brushy thickets, and forest edge.

• **FEEDERS** Mixture of oats, suet, and flax seeds.

• **CONSERVATION** Vulnerable to loss of habitat due to land clearing, grazing, and development. Fairly common host to cowbird parasitism.

Similar Birds

♂ **EASTERN TOWHEE** Lacks white spotting on back and scapulars • male has blacker upperparts • female has paler brown head, breast, and upperparts.
♀

Flight Pattern

Short bounding flights with several rapid wing strokes followed by wings pulled to sides.

Nest Identification

Shape   Location

Twigs, leaves, rootlets, grass, and bark • lined with grasses • on ground, sheltered by bush or grassy tussock, occasionally in low shrub or tree • built by female • 2–6 gray-brown or creamy white eggs, flecked and dotted with purple, red-brown, and gray; ovate, 0.95 x 0.7 inches.

Plumage Sexes differ	Habitat	Migration Some migrate	Weight Undetermined

DATE _____ TIME_____ LOCATION _____

Family EMBERIZIDAE	Species *Pipilo erythrophthalmus*	Length 7–7.5 inches	Wingspan 10–11 inches

EASTERN TOWHEE

Sometimes called a Ground Robin in the South, this is the eastern counterpart of the Spotted Towhee. Until recently these birds were classified as one species, the Rufous-sided Towhee. The two species hybridize where their ranges overlap along rivers in the Great Plains. The smaller Florida race has whitish eyes instead of red like most other races. In flight the white undertail corners flash conspicuously. Juveniles are brown overall with pale chins and dark streaking on underparts and upperparts.

black upperparts and hood

red eyes

MALE

white outer tail feathers

tawny buff undertail coverts

rufous sides

white underparts

distinct white patch at base of primaries and distinct white tertial edges

white outer tail feathers

brown upperparts and hood

tawny buff undertail coverts

rufous sides

white patch at base of primaries and white tertial edges

white underparts

FEMALE

JUVENILE

• **SONG** A clear whistled *drink-your-teeeaaa*, with the "tea" trilled. Much individual variation, with some birds leaving off the introductory note and some omitting the ending trill. Has calls of *toe-WHEEE* and *che-wink* or *wank*.

• **BEHAVIOR** Solitary or in pairs. Secretive; stays low in underbrush and on ground. Frequents brushy thickets, woodland edges, and riparian areas. Males are conspicuous when singing, often choosing an exposed perch. Usually detected by the rustle of dry leaves on ground; forages by double-scratching, pulling both legs sharply backward at once. Eats insects, caterpillars, small salamanders, fruits, and seeds.

• **BREEDING** Monogamous. Solitary. Courting male chases female and fans tail to show off white spots on outer feathers.

• **NESTING** Incubation 12–13 days by female. Young altricial; brooded by female; stay in nest 10–12 days, fed by both sexes, more by male. 2–3 broods per year.

• **POPULATION** Common to fairly common. Major decline in Northeast in last half of 20th century.

Similar Birds

SPOTTED TOWHEE
Extensive white spotting on back and scapulars • female shows darker browns on head, breast, and upperparts.

• **FEEDERS** Mixture of oats, suet, and seeds.

• **CONSERVATION** Declines in Northeast poorly understood; vulnerable to loss of habitat, clearing of land, development, and pesticides in food chain. Frequent cowbird host.

Flight Pattern

Short bouncy flights with tail spread; series of rapid wing beats alternating with wings pulled to sides; repeated.

Nest Identification

Shape | Location

Sticks, rootlets, grass, bark, and leaves, with lining of soft grasses • on ground, sheltered by grassy tussock or bush, occasionally in low bush or tree, 1–5 feet above ground (but up to 20 feet) • built by female • 2–6 creamy white or grayish eggs; oval, 0.9 x 0.66 inches.

Plumage Sexes differ	Habitat	Migration Northern birds migrate	Weight 1.5 ounces

DATE _____ TIME_____ LOCATION _____

Family EMBERIZIDAE	Species *Pipilo fuscus*	Length 8 inches	Wingspan 11–11.5 inches

CANYON TOWHEE

This sparrowlike bird was formerly lumped with the very similar California Towhee and together they were called the Brown Towhee. Now considered a separate species, the Canyon Towhee is paler with a more rufous cap and a dark central chest spot. Not as strongly territorial as the California Towhee, it shows little aggressive interactions when defending its nesting area. Juveniles are similar to adults but have streaked underparts, two cinnamon wing bars, and, darker streaked upperparts.

rufous cap

grayish overall

conspicuous buff eye ring

buff throat and upper breast

necklace of light dusky streaks

dark central chest spot

whitish patch on belly

cinnamon undertail coverts

long tail

• **SONG** 1–2 introductory chips, followed by series of accelerating chips, *chwee, chwee, chilly, chilly, chilly.* Call is nasal slurred *chedep* or *chee-yep;* also a light *ssip.*

• **BEHAVIOR** Solitary or in pairs. Often in small groups after breeding season. Stays low in brush or on ground. Hops rather than walks. Forages by double-scratching on ground in soil or leaf litter. Eats grain, insects, and seeds. Females sit tightly on nest, and, when flushed by intruder, scurry away with wings drooped like a small rodent to lure interloper from nest site.

• **BREEDING** Monogamous. Solitary nester. Pair mates for life.

• **NESTING** Incubation 11 days by female. Young altricial; brooded by female; stay in nest 8–9 days, fed by both sexes. 2–3 broods per year.

• **POPULATION** Common on the lower slopes of mountain canyons covered with brush, juniper, or piñon.

• **FEEDERS** Will come to feeders for seeds.

• **CONSERVATION** Uncommon host to parasitism by cowbirds.

Similar Birds

CALIFORNIA TOWHEE
Ranges do not overlap • brownish overall; longer tail; lacks spot between breast and belly; brownish crown contrasts little with head and nape; cinnamon lores contrast with face; dusky brown underparts.

ABERT'S TOWHEE
Cinnamon-brown upperparts; paler cinnamon undertail coverts and mottled cinnamon-brown spot between breast and belly; cinnamon-brown crown.

Flight Pattern

Short flights with rapidly beating wings alternating with wings pulled briefly in to sides.

Nest Identification

Shape [symbol]   Location [symbols]

Stems, grass, and sticks, with lining of leaves, bark pieces, and mammal hair • in thickest part of tree, usually 3–12 feet above ground • built mostly by female • 2–6 light green or blue eggs, with various splotches, dots, and flecks of black and brown; ovate, 0.92 x 0.68 inches.

Plumage Sexes similar	Habitat ▲ ▲	Migration Nonmigratory	Weight 1.6 ounces

DATE _____ TIME_____ LOCATION _____

Family EMBERIZIDAE	Species *Pipilo crissalis*	Length 9 inches	Wingspan 11.5–12.5 inches

CALIFORNIA TOWHEE

Formerly lumped with the Canyon Towhee as the Brown Towhee. The California Towhee is browner than the Canyon Towhee, has a less contrasting cap and lacks a dark central breast spot. Looking similar to a large sparrow, it hops rather than walks. These towhees mate for life, and the male guards the female while she feeds. After foraging separately, members of a mated pair repeatedly perform a display of sideways posturing and quick bowing movements. If the mate fails to respond to its partner's pair-reinforcement attempts, it is set upon as if it were a territorial intruder. Juveniles are similar to adults but have faintly streaked upperparts, dusky streaked underparts, and two cinnamon wing bars.

chestnut brown crown
buff lores
brownish gray overall
buff throat with conspicuous border of dark spots
cinnamon undertail coverts
long dark tail

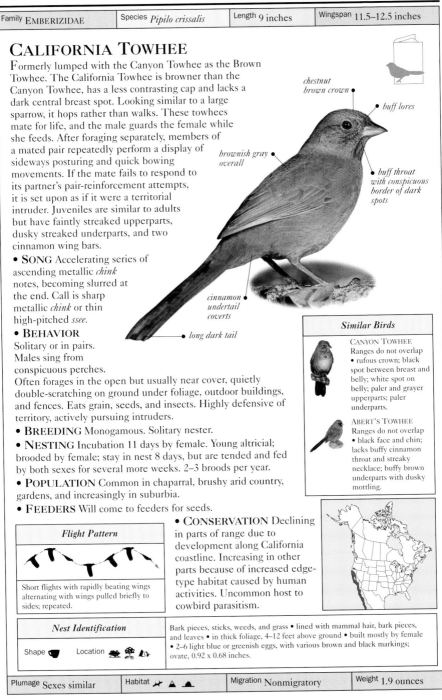

- **SONG** Accelerating series of ascending metallic *chink* notes, becoming slurred at the end. Call is sharp metallic *chink* or thin high-pitched *ssee*.
- **BEHAVIOR** Solitary or in pairs. Males sing from conspicuous perches. Often forages in the open but usually near cover, quietly double-scratching on ground under foliage, outdoor buildings, and fences. Eats grain, seeds, and insects. Highly defensive of territory, actively pursuing intruders.
- **BREEDING** Monogamous. Solitary nester.
- **NESTING** Incubation 11 days by female. Young altricial; brooded by female; stay in nest 8 days, but are tended and fed by both sexes for several more weeks. 2–3 broods per year.
- **POPULATION** Common in chaparral, brushy arid country, gardens, and increasingly in suburbia.
- **FEEDERS** Will come to feeders for seeds.
- **CONSERVATION** Declining in parts of range due to development along California coastline. Increasing in other parts because of increased edge-type habitat caused by human activities. Uncommon host to cowbird parasitism.

Similar Birds

CANYON TOWHEE
Ranges do not overlap • rufous crown; black spot between breast and belly; white spot on belly; paler and grayer upperparts; paler underparts.

ABERT'S TOWHEE
Ranges do not overlap • black face and chin; lacks buffy cinnamon throat and streaky necklace; buffy brown underparts with dusky mottling.

Flight Pattern

Short flights with rapidly beating wings alternating with wings pulled briefly to sides; repeated.

Nest Identification

Shape | Location | Bark pieces, sticks, weeds, and grass • lined with mammal hair, bark pieces, and leaves • in thick foliage, 4–12 feet above ground • built mostly by female • 2–6 light blue or greenish eggs, with various brown and black markings; ovate, 0.92 x 0.68 inches.

Plumage Sexes similar	Habitat	Migration Nonmigratory	Weight 1.9 ounces

DATE _____ TIME_____ LOCATION _____

Family EMBERIZIDAE	Species *Pipilo aberti*	Length 9.5 inches	Wingspan 12–13 inches

ABERT'S TOWHEE

This shy bird is difficult to spot as it hides in bushes or hops on the ground beneath desert scrub. It is particularly fond of riparian thickets. Its voice, however, provides a clue to its location, because it calls frequently. Like many of the towhees, the male and female mate for life. It can be distinguished from the similar California and Canyon Towhees by its black face and unstreaked breast. Juveniles are similar to adults but their underparts are paler and duller and are streaked dusky.

cinnamon gray-brown upperparts

black face

pale cinnamon-brown underparts, mottled dusky

cinnamon vent and undertail coverts

long tail, darker than upperparts

- **SONG** A series of 4–6 repetitive *peek* or *chip* notes, accelerating and dropping in pitch at the end, *chip, chip, chip, chip, chip, chee-chee-chee-chee-chee.* Call is a sharp thin slightly nasal *peek*, often repeated.

- **BEHAVIOR** Solitary or in pairs. Terrestrial. Somewhat shy and secretive. Forages for food by double-scratching on ground and in fallen leaves. Eats seeds, grains, and insects. Wary, often scoots for the cover of brush and stays hidden at the first sign of an intruder. Young hatch asynchronously, and both sexes selectively feed the larger nestlings, leading to brood reduction in nesting seasons when food supply is scarce.

- **BREEDING** Monogamous. Solitary.

- **NESTING** Incubation 14 days by female. Young altricial; brooded by female; stay in nest 12–13 days, fed by both sexes. 2 broods per year.

- **POPULATION** Common in brush in arid country and riparian thickets; declining in some regions.

- **CONSERVATION** Declines have been attributed to heavy parasitism by cowbirds as well as loss of habitat due to clearing of arid scrublands.

Similar Birds

CANYON TOWHEE
Ranges do not overlap • grayish upperparts, face, and sides; chestnut cap; dark chest spot; necklace of dusky streaks; buffy lores, chin, and throat; white belly.

CALIFORNIA TOWHEE
Brownish overall; warm brown crown; buff lores, chin, and throat; dusky necklace; pale eye ring.

Flight Pattern

Short flights with rapidly beating wings alternating with wings pulled briefly to sides; repeated.

Nest Identification

Shape

Location

Forbs, bark pieces, leaves, and vines • lined with dead grass and mammal hair • in tree or bush, usually 25–30 feet above ground • built by female • 2–5 pale bluish white eggs, with scattered marks of dark brown; ovate, 0.9 x 0.7 inches.

Plumage Sexes similar	Habitat	Migration Nonmigratory	Weight 1.7 ounces

DATE _____ TIME _____ LOCATION _____

Family EMBERIZIDAE	Species *Aimophila carpalis*	Length 5.75 inches	Wingspan 8.25 inches

RUFOUS-WINGED SPARROW

Primarily a native of Mexico, this sparrow has a small range in southern Arizona. In the spring it waits until after a substantial rainfall to build its nest, or if no rain, will delay nesting until the following spring. The male sings throughout the year, usually perched on a cactus or other low vegetation. It can be distinguished from other small sparrows in its range by the dark double stripes on the sides of its face. Juveniles are paler with less distinct face marking, buffy wing bars, and streaking on the breast and sides. Juveniles have a dark bill and brownish auriculars.

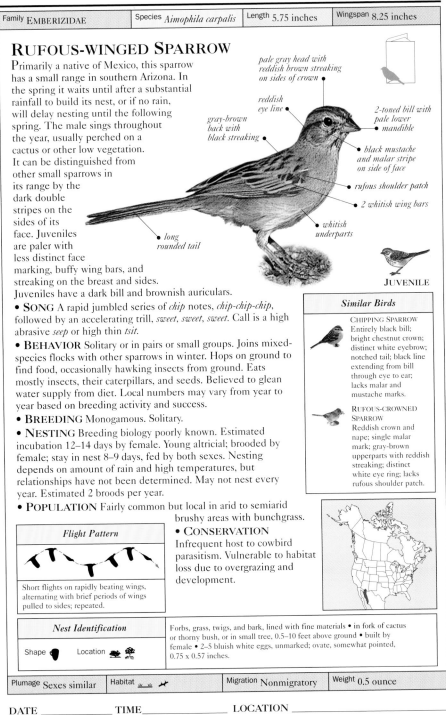

pale gray head with reddish brown streaking on sides of crown

reddish eye line

gray-brown back with black streaking

2-toned bill with pale lower mandible

black mustache and malar stripe on side of face

rufous shoulder patch

2 whitish wing bars

whitish underparts

long rounded tail

JUVENILE

• **SONG** A rapid jumbled series of *chip* notes, *chip-chip-chip*, followed by an accelerating trill, *sweet, sweet, sweet*. Call is a high abrasive *seep* or high thin *tsit*.

• **BEHAVIOR** Solitary or in pairs or small groups. Joins mixed-species flocks with other sparrows in winter. Hops on ground to find food, occasionally hawking insects from ground. Eats mostly insects, their caterpillars, and seeds. Believed to glean water supply from diet. Local numbers may vary from year to year based on breeding activity and success.

• **BREEDING** Monogamous. Solitary.

• **NESTING** Breeding biology poorly known. Estimated incubation 12–14 days by female. Young altricial; brooded by female; stay in nest 8–9 days, fed by both sexes. Nesting depends on amount of rain and high temperatures, but relationships have not been determined. May not nest every year. Estimated 2 broods per year.

• **POPULATION** Fairly common but local in arid to semiarid brushy areas with bunchgrass.

• **CONSERVATION** Infrequent host to cowbird parasitism. Vulnerable to habitat loss due to overgrazing and development.

Similar Birds

CHIPPING SPARROW
Entirely black bill; bright chestnut crown; distinct white eyebrow; notched tail; black line extending from bill through eye to ear; lacks malar and mustache marks.

RUFOUS-CROWNED SPARROW
Reddish crown and nape; single malar mark; gray-brown upperparts with reddish streaking; distinct white eye ring; lacks rufous shoulder patch.

Flight Pattern

Short flights on rapidly beating wings, alternating with brief periods of wings pulled to sides; repeated.

Nest Identification	Forbs, grass, twigs, and bark, lined with fine materials • in fork of cactus or thorny bush, or in small tree, 0.5–10 feet above ground • built by female • 2–5 bluish white eggs, unmarked; ovate, somewhat pointed, 0.75 x 0.57 inches.
Shape ◗ Location 🌳 🌳	

Plumage Sexes similar	Habitat ⸎ ⸎ ✈	Migration Nonmigratory	Weight 0.5 ounce

DATE _____ TIME_____ LOCATION _____

| Family EMBERIZIDAE | Species *Aimophila cassinii* | Length 6 inches | Wingspan 9 inches |

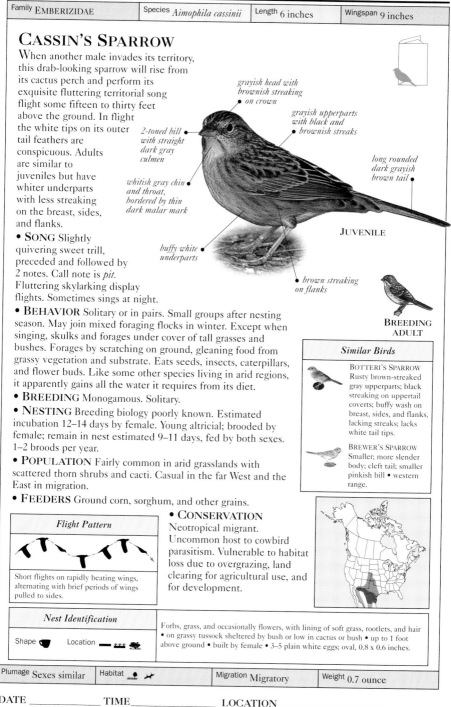

CASSIN'S SPARROW

When another male invades its territory, this drab-looking sparrow will rise from its cactus perch and perform its exquisite fluttering territorial song flight some fifteen to thirty feet above the ground. In flight the white tips on its outer tail feathers are conspicuous. Adults are similar to juveniles but have whiter underparts with less streaking on the breast, sides, and flanks.

grayish head with brownish streaking on crown

grayish upperparts with black and brownish streaks

2-toned bill with straight dark gray culmen

long rounded dark grayish brown tail

whitish gray chin and throat, bordered by thin dark malar mark

buffy white underparts

JUVENILE

brown streaking on flanks

BREEDING ADULT

- **SONG** Slightly quivering sweet trill, preceded and followed by 2 notes. Call note is *pit*. Fluttering skylarking display flights. Sometimes sings at night.
- **BEHAVIOR** Solitary or in pairs. Small groups after nesting season. May join mixed foraging flocks in winter. Except when singing, skulks and forages under cover of tall grasses and bushes. Forages by scratching on ground, gleaning food from grassy vegetation and substrate. Eats seeds, insects, caterpillars, and flower buds. Like some other species living in arid regions, it apparently gains all the water it requires from its diet.
- **BREEDING** Monogamous. Solitary.
- **NESTING** Breeding biology poorly known. Estimated incubation 12–14 days by female. Young altricial; brooded by female; remain in nest estimated 9–11 days, fed by both sexes. 1–2 broods per year.
- **POPULATION** Fairly common in arid grasslands with scattered thorn shrubs and cacti. Casual in the far West and the East in migration.
- **FEEDERS** Ground corn, sorghum, and other grains.

Similar Birds

BOTTERI'S SPARROW Rusty brown-streaked gray upperparts; black streaking on uppertail coverts; buffy wash on breast, sides, and flanks, lacking streaks; lacks white tail tips.

BREWER'S SPARROW Smaller; more slender body; cleft tail; smaller pinkish bill • western range.

- **CONSERVATION** Neotropical migrant. Uncommon host to cowbird parasitism. Vulnerable to habitat loss due to overgrazing, land clearing for agricultural use, and for development.

Flight Pattern

Short flights on rapidly beating wings, alternating with brief periods of wings pulled to sides.

Nest Identification

Shape ☕   Location ▬ ⬩⬩⬩ 🌿

Forbs, grass, and occasionally flowers, with lining of soft grass, rootlets, and hair • on grassy tussock sheltered by bush or low in cactus or bush • up to 1 foot above ground • built by female • 3–5 plain white eggs; oval, 0.8 x 0.6 inches.

| Plumage Sexes similar | Habitat 🌱 ⤴ | Migration Migratory | Weight 0.7 ounce |

DATE _____ TIME_____ LOCATION _____

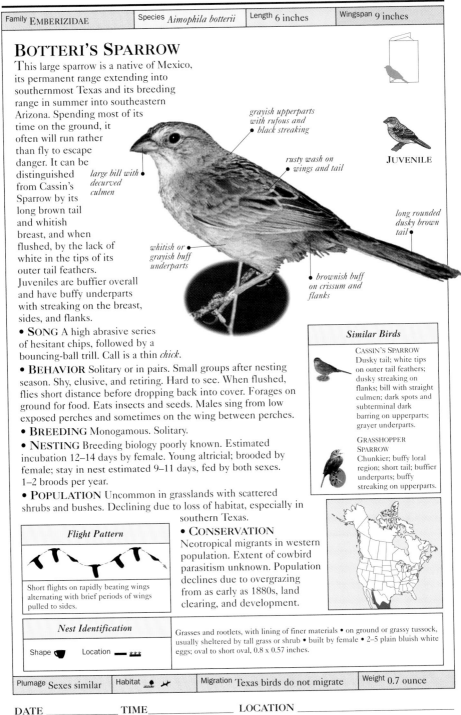

Family EMBERIZIDAE	Species *Aimophila botterii*	Length 6 inches	Wingspan 9 inches

BOTTERI'S SPARROW

This large sparrow is a native of Mexico, its permanent range extending into southernmost Texas and its breeding range in summer into southeastern Arizona. Spending most of its time on the ground, it often will run rather than fly to escape danger. It can be distinguished from Cassin's Sparrow by its long brown tail and whitish breast, and when flushed, by the lack of white in the tips of its outer tail feathers. Juveniles are buffier overall and have buffy underparts with streaking on the breast, sides, and flanks.

grayish upperparts with rufous and black streaking

rusty wash on wings and tail

JUVENILE

large bill with decurved culmen

long rounded dusky brown tail

whitish or grayish buff underparts

brownish buff on crissum and flanks

- **SONG** A high abrasive series of hesitant chips, followed by a bouncing-ball trill. Call is a thin *chick*.
- **BEHAVIOR** Solitary or in pairs. Small groups after nesting season. Shy, elusive, and retiring. Hard to see. When flushed, flies short distance before dropping back into cover. Forages on ground for food. Eats insects and seeds. Males sing from low exposed perches and sometimes on the wing between perches.
- **BREEDING** Monogamous. Solitary.
- **NESTING** Breeding biology poorly known. Estimated incubation 12–14 days by female. Young altricial; brooded by female; stay in nest estimated 9–11 days, fed by both sexes. 1–2 broods per year.
- **POPULATION** Uncommon in grasslands with scattered shrubs and bushes. Declining due to loss of habitat, especially in southern Texas.

Similar Birds

CASSIN'S SPARROW
Dusky tail; white tips on outer tail feathers; dusky streaking on flanks; bill with straight culmen; dark spots and subterminal dark barring on upperparts; grayer underparts.

GRASSHOPPER SPARROW
Chunkier; buffy loral region; short tail; buffier underparts; buffy streaking on upperparts.

- **CONSERVATION** Neotropical migrants in western population. Extent of cowbird parasitism unknown. Population declines due to overgrazing from as early as 1880s, land clearing, and development.

Flight Pattern
Short flights on rapidly beating wings alternating with brief periods of wings pulled to sides.

Nest Identification	
Shape	Location	Grasses and rootlets, with lining of finer materials • on ground or grassy tussock, usually sheltered by tall grass or shrub • built by female • 2–5 plain bluish white eggs; oval to short oval, 0.8 x 0.57 inches.

Plumage Sexes similar	Habitat	Migration Texas birds do not migrate	Weight 0.7 ounce

DATE _____ TIME_____ LOCATION _____

Family EMBERIZIDAE	Species *Aimophila ruficeps*	Length 6 inches	Wingspan 9 inches

RUFOUS-CROWNED SPARROW

The black "whisker" lines on each side of its face, white eye ring, and lack of a white supercilium distinguish this bird from the similar Chipping Sparrow. The wary Rufous-crowned Sparrow will run and hide from danger, rather than fly. Despite this tendency, the sparrow is often conspicuous and easily observed when not approached too closely. It will, however, come out into the open in response to a squeaking noise. Juveniles have buffier upperparts and underparts, with streaking on the breast, and often show two narrow white wing bars.

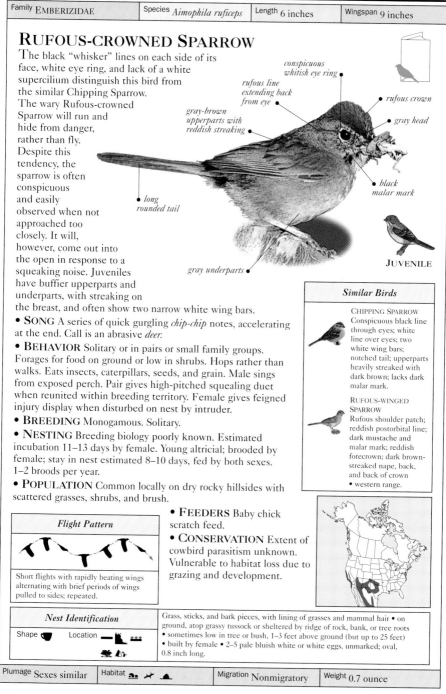

conspicuous whitish eye ring

rufous line extending back from eye

gray-brown upperparts with reddish streaking

rufous crown

gray head

black malar mark

long rounded tail

gray underparts

JUVENILE

• **SONG** A series of quick gurgling *chip-chip* notes, accelerating at the end. Call is an abrasive *deer*.
• **BEHAVIOR** Solitary or in pairs or small family groups. Forages for food on ground or low in shrubs. Hops rather than walks. Eats insects, caterpillars, seeds, and grain. Male sings from exposed perch. Pair gives high-pitched squealing duet when reunited within breeding territory. Female gives feigned injury display when disturbed on nest by intruder.
• **BREEDING** Monogamous. Solitary.
• **NESTING** Breeding biology poorly known. Estimated incubation 11–13 days by female. Young altricial; brooded by female; stay in nest estimated 8–10 days, fed by both sexes. 1–2 broods per year.
• **POPULATION** Common locally on dry rocky hillsides with scattered grasses, shrubs, and brush.
• **FEEDERS** Baby chick scratch feed.
• **CONSERVATION** Extent of cowbird parasitism unknown. Vulnerable to habitat loss due to grazing and development.

Similar Birds

CHIPPING SPARROW
Conspicuous black line through eyes; white line over eyes; two white wing bars; notched tail; upperparts heavily streaked with dark brown; lacks dark malar mark.

RUFOUS-WINGED SPARROW
Rufous shoulder patch; reddish postorbital line; dark mustache and malar mark; reddish forecrown; dark brown-streaked nape, back, and back of crown
• western range.

Flight Pattern

Short flights with rapidly beating wings alternating with brief periods of wings pulled to sides; repeated.

Nest Identification

Shape ☕ Location

Grass, sticks, and bark pieces, with lining of grasses and mammal hair • on ground, atop grassy tussock or sheltered by ridge of rock, bank, or tree roots • sometimes low in tree or bush, 1–3 feet above ground (but up to 25 feet) • built by female • 2–5 pale bluish white or white eggs, unmarked; oval, 0.8 inch long.

Plumage Sexes similar	Habitat	Migration Nonmigratory	Weight 0.7 ounce

DATE _____ TIME _____ LOCATION _____

Family EMBERIZIDAE	Species *Aimophila quinquestriata*	Length 6 inches	Wingspan 9 inches

FIVE-STRIPED SPARROW

This sparrow is named for the five white stripes on its head – one above each eye, mustache marks on both sides of the face, and one on the throat. A native of Mexico, its summer breeding range extends into a very small part of southern Arizona, where it is limited to steep rocky hillsides covered with a mixture of dense tall shrubs and grasses. Juveniles have a brownish head and upperparts, traces of the supercilium and mustache marks, dusky gray throat and underparts, and pale yellow median throat and belly.

white supercilium

dark brown upperparts, nape, and crown

white eye ring

white mustache mark

gray face

black stripe borders white throat

black spot at base of gray breast

white belly

gray sides, flanks, and undertail coverts

• **SONG** Brief trilled chipping phrase of *serr-it-chee-chee-it-ts-chee-chee-it-serr-serr*. Each successive song differs from the preceding one, and individual males may have more than 100 song types. Has a call of *sik* or a low clucking.

• **BEHAVIOR** Solitary or in pairs. May join mixed foraging flocks in winter. Forages on ground or low in shrubs and is easily overlooked. Sometimes male sings from ground while foraging, but often sings from exposed perch. Eats insects and seeds gleaned from ground or foliage. Defends territory against other species of sparrows, as well as other Five-striped males.

• **BREEDING** Monogamous. Solitary.

• **NESTING** Incubation 12–13 days by female. Young altricial; brooded by female; stay in nest 9–10 days, fed by both sexes. Male feeds and tends fledglings while female incubates second clutch. 1–3 broods per year.

Similar Birds

BLACK-THROATED SPARROW
Completely black chin, throat, and chest; 2 white stripes on each side of head; white underparts with brownish sides and flanks; brown upperparts; white outermost tail feathers and white tips to outer tail feathers.

SAGE SPARROW
White underparts; gray upperparts, including head; white eye ring; white supraloral area; white mustache bordered by black malar mark; black spot in center of breast; brown streaking on sides and flanks.

• **POPULATION** Uncommon and local in North America; limited breeding range in southern Arizona.

• **CONSERVATION** Neotropical migrant. Common host to cowbird parasitism.

Flight Pattern

Short flights with rapidly beating wings alternating with brief periods of wings pulled to sides.

Nest Identification

Shape ◗   Location ▬ ✶✶✶ ✿

Rootlets and grass, with lining of finer materials • atop grassy tussock, on ground, or low in bush, 0.5–4.5 feet above ground • built by female • 3–4 plain white eggs; oval, 0.8 x 0.6 inches.

Plumage Sexes similar	Habitat 🪶 ✈ ⚎ ⚎ 🏔 ▲	Migration US birds migrate	Weight 0.7 ounce

DATE _____ TIME_____ LOCATION _____

Family EMBERIZIDAE	Species *Spizella arborea*	Length 6.25 inches	Wingspan 9.75 inches

AMERICAN TREE SPARROW

After nesting near the frigid tundra regions, flocks of these sparrows migrate south and can be found primarily in the United States during the winter. Sometimes traveling in flocks of thirty-five to forty birds, but often smaller, they scout out food supplies and willingly come to outdoor feeders. Males often winter farther north than females and juveniles. Males sing during courtship and also to claim territory.

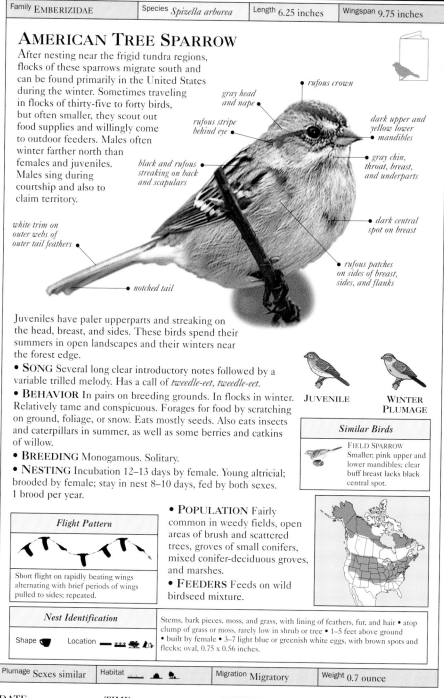

gray head and nape

rufous stripe behind eye

black and rufous streaking on back and scapulars

white trim on outer webs of outer tail feathers

notched tail

rufous crown

dark upper and yellow lower mandibles

gray chin, throat, breast, and underparts

dark central spot on breast

rufous patches on sides of breast, sides, and flanks

Juveniles have paler upperparts and streaking on the head, breast, and sides. These birds spend their summers in open landscapes and their winters near the forest edge.

- **SONG** Several long clear introductory notes followed by a variable trilled melody. Has a call of *tweedle-eet, tweedle-eet.*
- **BEHAVIOR** In pairs on breeding grounds. In flocks in winter. Relatively tame and conspicuous. Forages for food by scratching on ground, foliage, or snow. Eats mostly seeds. Also eats insects and caterpillars in summer, as well as some berries and catkins of willow.
- **BREEDING** Monogamous. Solitary.
- **NESTING** Incubation 12–13 days by female. Young altricial; brooded by female; stay in nest 8–10 days, fed by both sexes. 1 brood per year.

JUVENILE   WINTER PLUMAGE

Similar Birds

FIELD SPARROW
Smaller; pink upper and lower mandibles; clear buff breast lacks black central spot.

- **POPULATION** Fairly common in weedy fields, open areas of brush and scattered trees, groves of small conifers, mixed conifer-deciduous groves, and marshes.
- **FEEDERS** Feeds on wild birdseed mixture.

Flight Pattern

Short flight on rapidly beating wings alternating with brief periods of wings pulled to sides; repeated.

Nest Identification

Shape   Location

Stems, bark pieces, moss, and grass, with lining of feathers, fur, and hair • atop clump of grass or moss, rarely low in shrub or tree • 1–5 feet above ground • built by female • 3–7 light blue or greenish white eggs, with brown spots and flecks; oval, 0.75 x 0.56 inches.

Plumage Sexes similar	Habitat	Migration Migratory	Weight 0.7 ounce

DATE _____ TIME_____ LOCATION _____

Family EMBERIZIDAE	Species *Spizella passerina*	Length 5.5 inches	Wingspan 8–9 inches

CHIPPING SPARROW

Its bold chestnut cap, bordered by a long white superciliary stripe during breeding season, helps identify this tiny sparrow. Named for its song and call, it sings from its high perch during the day, and sometimes even at night, or calls as it forages for food in trees, gardens, and backyards. One of the tamest sparrows, it will take food from human hands. Juveniles lack the white eyebrow and

chestnut cap
gray nape and cheeks
white supercilium
black bill
light brown upperparts with black or brown streaking
black line extends from bill through eye to ear
long slightly notched tail
2 white wing bars
gray underparts
JUVENILE
WINTER PLUMAGE

Similar Birds

CLAY-COLORED SPARROW
Black-streaked brown crown with gray center stripe; buffy brown cheek patch bordered by dark postocular stripe and dark mustache mark; pale grayish eyebrow; whitish chin and submustachial stripe separated by buffy malar mark; whitish underparts with buffy wash on breast.

chestnut cap but have a streaked crown and nape, streaked underparts, and buffy wing bars. Winter birds have brown-streaked crowns, brown faces, and dark lores.

• **SONG** A repetitive series of trilled chip notes, *chip-chip-chip-chip-chip-chip-chip*, all the same pitch. Has a call of *seek*.

• **BEHAVIOR** Solitary or in pairs. In small family groups after breeding season. May join mixed-species foraging flocks in winter. Forages on ground and picks off foliage. Eats seeds, insects, their caterpillars, and spiders.

• **BREEDING** Monogamous. Solitary. A few males polygynous.

• **NESTING** Incubation 11–14 days by female. Young altricial; brooded by female; stay in nest 8–12 days, fed by both sexes. 2 broods per year.

• **POPULATION** Common and widespread in open mixed coniferous-deciduous forests, forest edges, gardens, lawns, and short-grass fields.

• **FEEDERS** Comes to feeders for breadcrumbs and seeds.

• **CONSERVATION** Neotropical migrant. Common host to cowbird parasitism.

Flight Pattern

Typically, short flights with rapidly beating wings alternating with brief periods of wings pulled to sides; repeated.

Nest Identification	Grass, forbs, weed stalks, and rootlets, with lining of mammal hair and grass • on branch or vine tangle, rarely on ground • most often 3–11 feet above ground (but up to 60 feet) • built by female • 2–5 bluish green eggs, marked with dark browns, blues, and blacks, often wreathed; subelliptical to short subelliptical, 0.7 x 0.5 inches.
Shape ⬩ Location ⛰ ⚘	

Plumage Sexes similar	Habitat 🏘 ⚘ 〰	Migration Migratory	Weight 0.4 ounce

DATE _____ TIME_____ LOCATION _____

Family EMBERIZIDAE	Species *Spizella pallida*	Length 5.5 inches	Wingspan 8 inches

CLAY-COLORED SPARROW

The male bird perches to claim its territory while singing its buzzy insectlike song across the grasslands. Wintering primarily in the highlands of central Mexico, this tiny bird flies north to summer in the prairies of Canada and the northern United States. In flight this frequent visitor to backyard feeders shows a dark buff rump. Juveniles have a gray nape, buffy brown cheek patch, and streaked underparts.

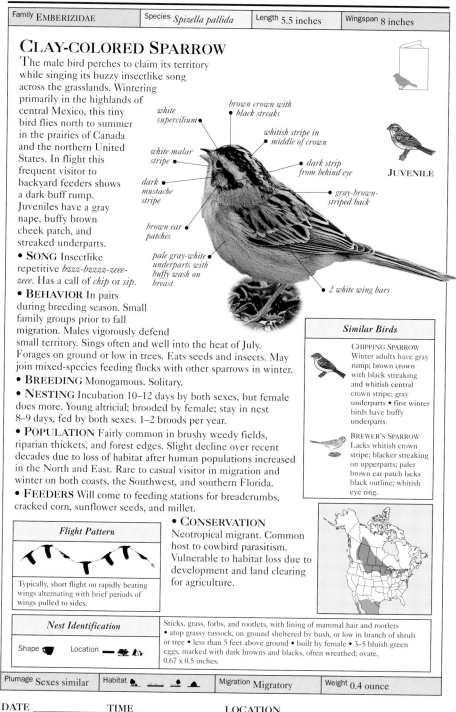

white supercilium

brown crown with black streaks

whitish stripe in middle of crown

white malar stripe

dark strip from behind eye

JUVENILE

dark mustache stripe

gray-brown-striped back

brown ear patches

pale gray-white underparts with buffy wash on breast

2 white wing bars

- **SONG** Insectlike repetitive *bzzz-bzzzz-zeee-zeee.* Has a call of *chip* or *sip.*
- **BEHAVIOR** In pairs during breeding season. Small family groups prior to fall migration. Males vigorously defend small territory. Sings often and well into the heat of July. Forages on ground or low in trees. Eats seeds and insects. May join mixed-species feeding flocks with other sparrows in winter.
- **BREEDING** Monogamous. Solitary.
- **NESTING** Incubation 10–12 days by both sexes, but female does more. Young altricial; brooded by female; stay in nest 8–9 days, fed by both sexes. 1–2 broods per year.
- **POPULATION** Fairly common in brushy weedy fields, riparian thickets, and forest edges. Slight decline over recent decades due to loss of habitat after human populations increased in the North and East. Rare to casual visitor in migration and winter on both coasts, the Southwest, and southern Florida.
- **FEEDERS** Will come to feeding stations for breadcrumbs, cracked corn, sunflower seeds, and millet.

Similar Birds

CHIPPING SPARROW
Winter adults have gray rump; brown crown with black streaking and whitish central crown stripe; gray underparts • first winter birds have buffy underparts.

BREWER'S SPARROW
Lacks whitish crown stripe; blacker streaking on upperparts; paler brown ear patch lacks black outline; whitish eye ring.

- **CONSERVATION** Neotropical migrant. Common host to cowbird parasitism. Vulnerable to habitat loss due to development and land clearing for agriculture.

Flight Pattern

Typically, short flight on rapidly beating wings alternating with brief periods of wings pulled to sides.

Nest Identification

Shape 🥄 Location 🌿 🔼

Sticks, grass, forbs, and rootlets, with lining of mammal hair and rootlets • atop grassy tussock, on ground sheltered by bush, or low in branch of shrub or tree • less than 5 feet above ground • built by female • 3–5 bluish green eggs, marked with dark browns and blacks, often wreathed; ovate, 0.67 x 0.5 inches.

Plumage Sexes similar	Habitat 🌾 ⬛ 🌿 🌱	Migration Migratory	Weight 0.4 ounce

Family EMBERIZIDAE	Species *Spizella breweri*	Length 5.5 inches	Wingspan 8 inches

BREWER'S SPARROW

At sunrise and just before sunset, countless territorial males sing continuous choruses, their buzzing trill spreading across the Great Basin of the western United States. The Timberline Sparrow, an isolated subspecies that nests above the timberline in the subalpine

brown crown with fine black streaking

pale brown ear patch with dark borders

brown upperparts with black streaking

grayish white eyebrow

pale lores

whitish eye ring

dark malar stripe

grayish white throat and underparts

dark brown wings with buff wing bars

zone of the Canadian Rockies north into southeastern Alaska, may be a separate species. Shy and wary on the nesting grounds, this sparrow is tame during other times of the year and often visits gardens and outdoor feeders. Juveniles are similar to adults but are buffier overall with streaked underparts; both juveniles and adults show a buffy brown rump.

JUVENILE

• **SONG** An insectlike long-continuing buzzing trill, with each sequence of the song given on different pitches, one sequence following another in long sessions without pauses. Call is *tsip*.

• **BEHAVIOR** Solitary or in pairs. In small family groups after breeding season. In winter, may join mixed-species foraging flocks with other sparrows and buntings. Forages on or near ground for food. Eats mostly insects in spring and summer. In fall and winter, eats mostly seeds. Found almost anywhere that sagebrush occurs. When disturbed by intruder, incubating or brooding female often runs rather than flies from nest.

• **BREEDING** Monogamous. Solitary.

• **NESTING** Incubation 11–13 days, mostly by female, but some by male. Young altricial; brooded by female; stay in nest 8–9 days, fed by both sexes. 1–2 broods per year.

• **POPULATION** Common in arid brushland, sagebrush flats, mountain meadows, and also in thickets. Accidental in the East.

• **FEEDERS** Will come for baby chick scratch feed.

• **CONSERVATION** Neotropical migrant. Infrequent host to cowbird parasitism.

Similar Birds

CHIPPING SPARROW
Winter • dark streaking on rufous crown; gray rump; bold white wing bars; less contrasting eyebrow stripe; lacks white eye ring and dark malar mark.

CLAY-COLORED SPARROW
Whitish or buffy white central stripe; buffier streaking on upperparts; buffier washes on underparts; gray nape; buffier cheek patch; lacks white eye ring.

Flight Pattern

Short flights with rapid wing beats alternating with brief periods of wings pulled to sides; repeated.

Nest Identification

Shape ⤴   Location 🌿 🌵 🪾

Forbs and dried grasses, with lining of rootlets and mammal hair • in bush or cactus • usually less than 4 feet above ground • built by female • 3–5 bluish green eggs, with dark brown dots and specks; subelliptical to ovate, 0.7 x 0.5 inches.

Plumage Sexes similar	Habitat 🪶 ⛰	Migration Migratory	Weight 0.5 ounce

Family EMBERIZIDAE	Species *Spizella pusilla*	Length 5.75 inches	Wingspan 8.5 inches

FIELD SPARROW

This sparrow stays near the ground in fields and open woodlands. When defending its nest, the male flies from tree to tree singing a melody that accelerates like the bouncing of a dropped rubber ball. The clearing of the primeval eastern forest provided thousands of acres of habitat ideally suited for this

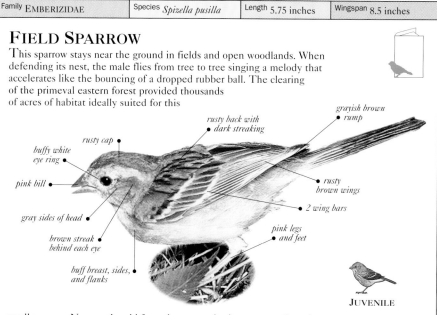

grayish brown rump

rusty back with dark streaking

rusty cap

buffy white eye ring

pink bill

gray sides of head

rusty brown wings

2 wing bars

brown streak behind each eye

pink legs and feet

buff breast, sides, and flanks

JUVENILE

small sparrow. Now, as the old farms become suburbs or succumb to the woodlots brought on by ecological succession, this bird is declining in this range.

• **SONG** A pleasant *seea-seea-seea-wee-wee-wee*, which begins with separate clear whistled notes and accelerates, either ascending, descending, or staying on the same pitch. Call is abrasive *chip*.

• **BEHAVIOR** Solitary or in pairs in breeding season. In small family flocks after nesting. In winter, forms flocks that may join mixed-species foraging flocks. Forages on ground or low in shrubbery for insects, caterpillars, seeds, and spiders. Tame and curious; responds to squeaking and pishing by birders.

• **BREEDING** Monogamous. Solitary.

• **NESTING** Incubation 10–17 days by female. Young altricial; brooded by female; stay in nest 7–8 days, fed by both sexes. Male tends and feeds fledglings while female incubates second clutch. 2–3 broods per year.

Similar Birds

CLAY-COLORED SPARROW
Brown crown with central stripe; buffy cheek patch; buffy brown malar mark; gray nape; buffy edges and streaks on upperparts; whitish underparts with buffy wash on chest and flanks; 2 buffy wing bars.

• **POPULATION** Fairly common in old fields, open brushy woodlands, thorn scrub, and forest edge. Casual in West. Uncommon in the Maritimes.

• **FEEDERS** Small grain.

• **CONSERVATION** Common host to cowbird parasitism.

Flight Pattern

Short flights with rapid wing beats alternating with brief periods of wings pulled to sides; repeated.

Nest Identification

Shape   Location

Fine grasses, leaves, and dried grass, with lining of mammal hair and rootlets • atop grassy tussock or clump of vegetation, sometimes in vine or bush • less than 3 feet above ground • built by female • 2–6 creamy pale greenish bluish white eggs, marked with browns, occasionally wreathed; short subelliptical, 0.7 x 0.53 inches.

Plumage Sexes similar	Habitat	Migration Northern birds migrate	Weight 0.4 ounce

Family EMBERIZIDAE	Species *Spizella atrogularis*	Length 5.75 inches	Wingspan 9 inches

BLACK-CHINNED SPARROW

The black chin of the breeding male combined with the rusty back and gray body set this bird apart from similar sparrows. Females are similar to males but have a plain gray head and underparts, sometimes with a trace of black on the chin. Juveniles are similar to females and winter birds, but have light streaking on their underparts and a brownish wash on their heads. Although primarily nonmigratory, birds in the northern parts of the range do migrate.

• SONG A series of 2 or more clear chips run into a bouncing-ball trill of *sweet-sweet-swee-I-iiiiiiiiir*, similar to the song of a Field Sparrow. Has a call of high thin *seep*.

• BEHAVIOR Solitary or in pairs. After breeding season and in winter, sometimes in small family groups. Shy and retiring. Male chooses prominent singing perch. Forages for food in brush and on ground. Eats insects and seeds. Little is known of its biology.

• BREEDING Monogamous. Loose colonial.

• NESTING Incubation 13 days, mostly by female. Young altricial; brooded by female; stay in nest estimated 8–12 days, fed by both sexes. 1–2 broods per year.

• POPULATION Uncommon and local in chaparral, sagebrush, and arid scrub on grassy slopes in foothills and mountains.

• CONSERVATION Neotropical migrant. Uncommon host to cowbird parasitism. Vulnerable to habitat loss because of development, land clearing, overgrazing, and fire retardation leading to maturing of chaparral habitat. Species requires open, early stage of post-fire chaparral habitat development.

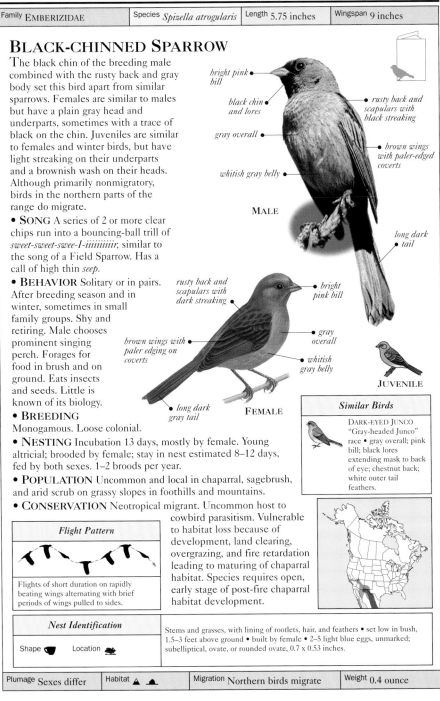

bright pink bill

black chin and lores

gray overall

whitish gray belly

rusty back and scapulars with black streaking

brown wings with paler-edged coverts

MALE

long dark tail

rusty back and scapulars with dark streaking

brown wings with paler edging on coverts

bright pink bill

gray overall

whitish gray belly

long dark gray tail

FEMALE

JUVENILE

Similar Birds

DARK-EYED JUNCO "Gray-headed Junco" race • gray overall; pink bill; black lores extending mask to back of eye; chestnut back; white outer tail feathers.

Flight Pattern

Flights of short duration on rapidly beating wings alternating with brief periods of wings pulled to sides.

Nest Identification	Stems and grasses, with lining of rootlets, hair, and feathers • set low in bush, 1.5–3 feet above ground • built by female • 2–5 light blue eggs, unmarked; subelliptical, ovate, or rounded ovate, 0.7 x 0.53 inches.
Shape ➥ Location ☙	

Plumage Sexes differ	Habitat ▲ ▲	Migration Northern birds migrate	Weight 0.4 ounce

DATE _____ TIME_____ LOCATION _____

Family EMBERIZIDAE	Species *Pooecetes gramineus*	Length 5.5–6.75 inches	Wingspan 10–11.25 inches

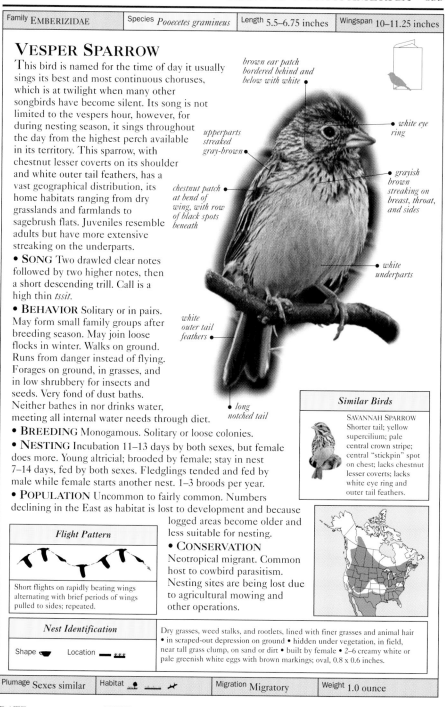

VESPER SPARROW

This bird is named for the time of day it usually sings its best and most continuous choruses, which is at twilight when many other songbirds have become silent. Its song is not limited to the vespers hour, however, for during nesting season, it sings throughout the day from the highest perch available in its territory. This sparrow, with chestnut lesser coverts on its shoulder and white outer tail feathers, has a vast geographical distribution, its home habitats ranging from dry grasslands and farmlands to sagebrush flats. Juveniles resemble adults but have more extensive streaking on the underparts.

brown ear patch bordered behind and below with white

white eye ring

upperparts streaked gray-brown

grayish brown streaking on breast, throat, and sides

chestnut patch at bend of wing, with row of black spots beneath

white underparts

• **SONG** Two drawled clear notes followed by two higher notes, then a short descending trill. Call is a high thin *tssit*.

• **BEHAVIOR** Solitary or in pairs. May form small family groups after breeding season. May join loose flocks in winter. Walks on ground. Runs from danger instead of flying. Forages on ground, in grasses, and in low shrubbery for insects and seeds. Very fond of dust baths. Neither bathes in nor drinks water, meeting all internal water needs through diet.

white outer tail feathers

long notched tail

• **BREEDING** Monogamous. Solitary or loose colonies.

• **NESTING** Incubation 11–13 days by both sexes, but female does more. Young altricial; brooded by female; stay in nest 7–14 days, fed by both sexes. Fledglings tended and fed by male while female starts another nest. 1–3 broods per year.

• **POPULATION** Uncommon to fairly common. Numbers declining in the East as habitat is lost to development and because logged areas become older and less suitable for nesting.

• **CONSERVATION** Neotropical migrant. Common host to cowbird parasitism. Nesting sites are being lost due to agricultural mowing and other operations.

Similar Birds

SAVANNAH SPARROW Shorter tail; yellow supercilium; pale central crown stripe; central "stickpin" spot on chest; lacks chestnut lesser coverts; lacks white eye ring and outer tail feathers.

Flight Pattern

Short flights on rapidly beating wings alternating with brief periods of wings pulled to sides; repeated.

Nest Identification

Shape   Location

Dry grasses, weed stalks, and rootlets, lined with finer grasses and animal hair • in scraped-out depression on ground • hidden under vegetation, in field, near tall grass clump, on sand or dirt • built by female • 2–6 creamy white or pale greenish white eggs with brown markings; oval, 0.8 x 0.6 inches.

Plumage Sexes similar	Habitat	Migration Migratory	Weight 1.0 ounce

DATE _____ TIME _____ LOCATION _____

Family EMBERIZIDAE	Species *Chondestes grammacus*	Length 5.75–6.75 inches	Wingspan 10.5–11 inches

LARK SPARROW

This sparrow, with its harlequin head pattern, has a lovely voice and sings from the ground, a perch, or while flying, sometimes even at night. Frequenting the open prairies and other open habitats, mostly west of the Mississippi River, it can be identified by the dark spot in the center of its breast and the long rounded tail with extensive white edging. Juveniles are similar to adults but more washed-out with an ill-defined head pattern, buffier coloration, dark brown streaking on the white throat, and white underparts with a buffy wash on the sides of the breast.

black, white, and chestnut-brown stripes on head

chestnut ear patches

white mustache

brown and black streaking on back

black malar mark

whitish underparts with buff wash on flanks

long rounded black tail with white edging

JUVENILE

- **SONG** Long, pleasant bubbling melody, beginning with 2 loud clear notes followed by series of chips, buzzes, and trills. Call is repetitive sharp metallic *tik*, often given in flight.
- **BEHAVIOR** Solitary or in pairs. Gregarious. Feeds in flocks, even during breeding season. Forages for food on ground and low in trees and shrubs. Eats seeds, insects, and caterpillars. Females on nest perform distraction display when disturbed, scurrying away with wings fluttering and tail spread. Prior to copulating, male often passes to female a twig or grass stem, which she holds.
- **BREEDING** Monogamous. Occasionally polygamous. Often in loose colonies. Male displays while swaggering on the ground in front of female, his tail spread, showing off its white feathers.
- **NESTING** Incubation 11–12 days by female. Young altricial; brooded by female; remain in nest 9–10 days, fed by both sexes. 1 brood per year.
- **POPULATION** Common in cultivated areas, fields, pastures, grassland, prairie, and savanna. Range has declined east of the Mississippi River due to loss of habitat. Casual to East coast.
- **FEEDERS** Small grains.
- **CONSERVATION** Neotropical migrant. Uncommon cowbird host. Vulnerable to habitat loss due to land clearing, development, overgrazing, and nest losses to agricultural operations.

Similar Birds
Head pattern is distinctive; not likely to be confused with other sparrows.

Flight Pattern
Short fluttering flight on rapidly beating wings alternating with brief periods of wings pulled to sides.

Nest Identification	
Shape ⏝ Location	Sticks, grass, and forbs • lined with rootlets and grasses • atop grassy tussock shaded by bush, or low in tree, sometimes in shrub or bush or in abandoned nest • 3–30 feet above ground • built by female • 3–6 creamy to grayish white eggs, marked with dark browns and blacks, often wreathed; oval, 0.8 x 0.62 inches.

Plumage Sexes similar	Habitat	Migration Migratory	Weight 1.0 ounce

DATE _____ TIME_____ LOCATION _____

Family EMBERIZIDAE	Species *Amphispiza bilineata*	Length 5.5 inches	Wingspan 8.5 inches

BLACK-THROATED SPARROW

Its bold black throat and the white stripes above its eye extending from its bill are good clues for identifying this sparrow. As long as it is able to get water from its diet, it thrives in the desert country, surviving long periods of time without drinking water. Accessible water is necessary, however, in the heat of the summer through autumn, until the rains begin and green vegetation develops. It has not adapted well to the transition of habitats as some of its range has been developed into suburbs. Juveniles lack the black chin, throat, and breast of adults and are streaked with brown on the breast and sides.

grayish head

white eyebrow

white mustache

brownish gray upperparts

black lores, chin, throat, and chest

whitish underparts

gray-buff wash on sides, flanks, and crissum

rounded black tail with white trim on outer tail feathers and white tips

JUVENILE

• **SONG** A high bell-like song with 2 introductory notes followed by a trill *queat-queat, toodle-oodle-oodle*; variable. Call is an abrasive *chip* or high sweet tinkling twitters.

• **BEHAVIOR** Solitary or in pairs. Sometimes forms small family groups after nesting season. Joins mixed-species foraging flocks in winter. Fairly tame and curious. Responds to pishing by birders. Forages for food on ground and in low vegetation. Eats seeds, spiders, and insects. Walks or runs, often with tail cocked upward. Timing of breeding varies annually, apparently based on seasonal rainfall amounts and food availability.

• **BREEDING** Monogamous. Solitary.

• **NESTING** Breeding biology poorly known. Estimated incubation 12–15 days by female. Young altricial; brooded by female; stay in nest estimated 10–11 days, fed by both sexes. 2 broods per year.

• **POPULATION** Fairly common in desert and semidesert scrub, especially on rocky uplands. Declining in some areas due to development of habitat. Accidental in the East.

• **CONSERVATION** Neotropical migrant. Uncommon host to cowbird parasitism. Vulnerable to habitat loss caused by combination of land clearing and development.

Similar Birds

SAGE SPARROW Juvenile similar to juvenile Black-throated Sparrow • white eyebrow stripe and white eye ring; sandy gray-brown crown, nape, and back; fine dusky streaks on chest; traces of central dark spot on chest; tail lacks white edging and tips; brown streaking on sides and flanks.

Flight Pattern

Typically, short-duration flights on rapidly beating wings alternating with brief periods of wings pulled to sides; repeated.

Nest Identification

Shape

Location

Forbs and grass, with lining of mammal hair and plant fibers • in middle of bush or cactus, less than 10 feet above ground • built by female • 2–4 plain white or pale blue eggs; oval, 0.7 x 0.52 inches.

Plumage Sexes similar	Habitat	Migration Northern birds migrate	Weight 0.5 ounce

DATE _____ TIME _____ LOCATION _____

Family EMBERIZIDAE	Species *Amphispiza belli*	Length 6.25 inches	Wingspan 8.25 inches

SAGE SPARROW

This shy sparrow of coastal California and the Great Basin area west of the Rocky Mountains most often skulks and hides under dense scrub. It often flicks its tail as it walks on the ground; when it runs, it usually holds its tail perpendicular to its back, wrenlike. Males perch to sing conspicuously on the top of a bush. The coastal subspecies Bell's Sparrow has much darker gray upperparts with more distinct facial markings than the paler interior race, with its sandier upperparts with faint streaking. Although the species is primarily migratory, the coastal race is not. Juveniles are duller overall and have more heavily streaked upperparts and underparts.

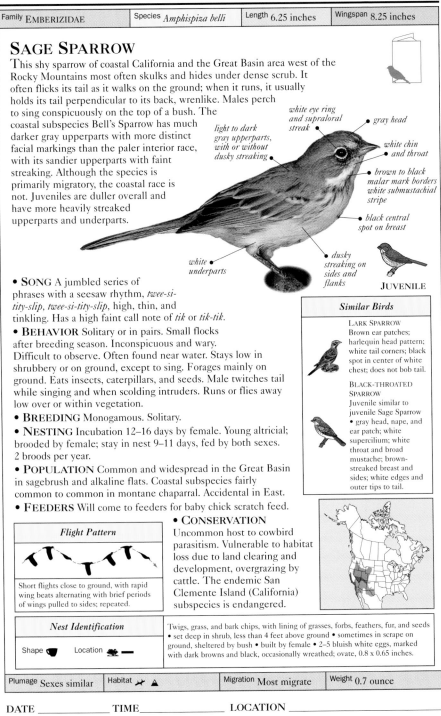

light to dark gray upperparts, with or without dusky streaking

white eye ring and supraloral streak

gray head

white chin and throat

brown to black malar mark borders white submustachial stripe

black central spot on breast

white underparts

dusky streaking on sides and flanks

JUVENILE

- **SONG** A jumbled series of phrases with a seesaw rhythm, *twee-si-tity-slip, twee-si-tity-slip*, high, thin, and tinkling. Has a high faint call note of *tik* or *tik-tik*.
- **BEHAVIOR** Solitary or in pairs. Small flocks after breeding season. Inconspicuous and wary. Difficult to observe. Often found near water. Stays low in shrubbery or on ground, except to sing. Forages mainly on ground. Eats insects, caterpillars, and seeds. Male twitches tail while singing and when scolding intruders. Runs or flies away low over or within vegetation.
- **BREEDING** Monogamous. Solitary.
- **NESTING** Incubation 12–16 days by female. Young altricial; brooded by female; stay in nest 9–11 days, fed by both sexes. 2 broods per year.
- **POPULATION** Common and widespread in the Great Basin in sagebrush and alkaline flats. Coastal subspecies fairly common to common in montane chaparral. Accidental in East.
- **FEEDERS** Will come to feeders for baby chick scratch feed.

Similar Birds

LARK SPARROW
Brown ear patches; harlequin head pattern; white tail corners; black spot in center of white chest; does not bob tail.

BLACK-THROATED SPARROW
Juvenile similar to juvenile Sage Sparrow • gray head, nape, and ear patch; white supercilium; white throat and broad mustache; brown-streaked breast and sides; white edges and outer tips to tail.

- **CONSERVATION** Uncommon host to cowbird parasitism. Vulnerable to habitat loss due to land clearing and development, overgrazing by cattle. The endemic San Clemente Island (California) subspecies is endangered.

Flight Pattern

Short flights close to ground, with rapid wing beats alternating with brief periods of wings pulled to sides; repeated.

Nest Identification

Shape   Location

Twigs, grass, and bark chips, with lining of grasses, forbs, feathers, fur, and seeds • set deep in shrub, less than 4 feet above ground • sometimes in scrape on ground, sheltered by bush • built by female • 2–5 bluish white eggs, marked with dark browns and black, occasionally wreathed; ovate, 0.8 x 0.65 inches.

Plumage Sexes similar	Habitat	Migration Most migrate	Weight 0.7 ounce

DATE _____ TIME_____ LOCATION _____

Family EMBERIZIDAE	Species *Calamospiza melanocorys*	Length 7 inches	Wingspan 11 inches

LARK BUNTING

In the spring hundreds of these birds fly in choreographed circles and shapes like a rolling wheel of birds. As they move across the prairie, birds from the rear fly to the front over birds settling into vegetation. They remain in flocks as they return to their nesting grounds on the sagebrush plains. Males and females have similar winter plumage, but males show black primaries. Juveniles are similar to winter adults. This is the state bird of Colorado.

• **SONG** Flutelike warbling melody of full whistles and trills. Often sings in groups. Call is *hoo-ee*.

• **BEHAVIOR** In pairs or flocks. Gregarious; in flocks most of year. Forages on ground and in low vegetation. Eats insects, caterpillars, and seeds. Territorial males ascend 20–30 feet with white wing patches flashing, pour out song, and descend with jerky butterfly movements to ground. Neighboring males often join in display flights.

• **BREEDING** Monogamous. Some are polygynous. Loose colonies. Displaying male fluffs out feathers and crest and sings.

• **NESTING** Incubation 11–12 days by female; some males help. Altricial young brooded by female; stay in nest 8–9 days, fed by both sexes. 2 broods per year.

• **POPULATION** Common in grasslands, dry plains, prairies, sagebrush flats, and meadows. Rare to casual on Pacific Coast in fall and winter. Casual in the East in fall and winter.

• **FEEDERS** Occasionally attends feeders that supply small grains and seeds.

• **CONSERVATION** Neotropical migrant. Uncommon host to cowbird parasitism. Historical population declines in northern and eastern parts of breeding range caused by loss of prairie habitat.

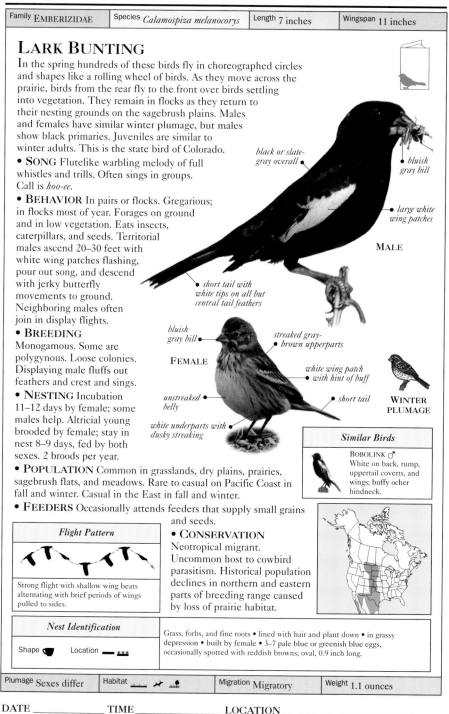

black or slate-gray overall
bluish gray bill
large white wing patches
MALE
short tail with white tips on all but central tail feathers

bluish gray bill
FEMALE
streaked gray-brown upperparts
white wing patch with hint of buff
unstreaked belly
short tail
white underparts with dusky streaking
WINTER PLUMAGE

Similar Birds
BOBOLINK ♂
White on back, rump, uppertail coverts, and wings; buffy ocher hindneck.

Flight Pattern
Strong flight with shallow wing beats alternating with brief periods of wings pulled to sides.

Nest Identification	
Shape 🥣 Location ▬ ✱✱✱	Grass, forbs, and fine roots • lined with hair and plant down • in grassy depression • built by female • 3–7 pale blue or greenish blue eggs, occasionally spotted with reddish browns; oval, 0.9 inch long.

Plumage Sexes differ	Habitat	Migration Migratory	Weight 1.1 ounces

DATE _____ TIME_____ LOCATION _____

Family EMBERIZIDAE	Species *Passerculus sandwichensis*	Length 5.25–6.25 inches	Wingspan 8–9.5 inches

SAVANNAH SPARROW

Named for the city in Georgia where it was first spotted, this bird has a wide range, living in grassy marshes and wet meadows to grasslands and cultivated grass to tundra. It also has considerable variation between the many races that make up the species. Like many sparrows, it spends most of its time on the ground; when disturbed, it scurries through the grasses, running mouselike rather than flying away. But if hard-pressed it flies up a short distance then drops back into the grasses.

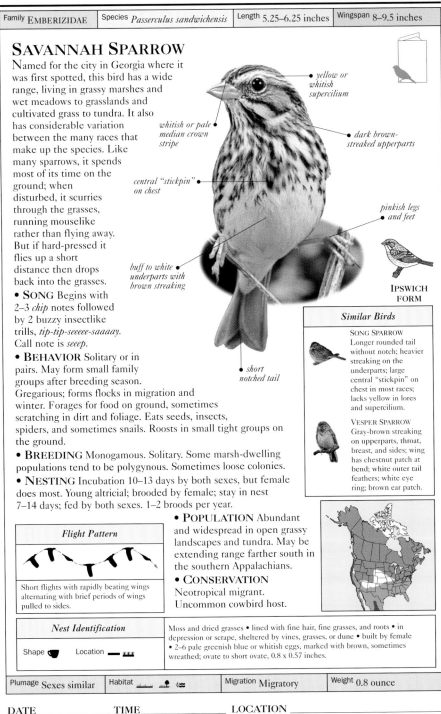

yellow or whitish supercilium

dark brown-streaked upperparts

whitish or pale median crown stripe

central "stickpin" on chest

pinkish legs and feet

buff to white underparts with brown streaking

short notched tail

IPSWICH FORM

- **SONG** Begins with 2–3 *chip* notes followed by 2 buzzy insectlike trills, *tip-tip-seeeee-saaaay*. Call note is *seeep*.
- **BEHAVIOR** Solitary or in pairs. May form small family groups after breeding season. Gregarious; forms flocks in migration and winter. Forages for food on ground, sometimes scratching in dirt and foliage. Eats seeds, insects, spiders, and sometimes snails. Roosts in small tight groups on the ground.
- **BREEDING** Monogamous. Solitary. Some marsh-dwelling populations tend to be polygynous. Sometimes loose colonies.
- **NESTING** Incubation 10–13 days by both sexes, but female does most. Young altricial; brooded by female; stay in nest 7–14 days; fed by both sexes. 1–2 broods per year.

Similar Birds

SONG SPARROW
Longer rounded tail without notch; heavier streaking on the underparts; large central "stickpin" on chest in most races; lacks yellow in lores and supercilium.

VESPER SPARROW
Gray-brown streaking on upperparts, throat, breast, and sides; wing has chestnut patch at bend; white outer tail feathers; white eye ring; brown ear patch.

- **POPULATION** Abundant and widespread in open grassy landscapes and tundra. May be extending range farther south in the southern Appalachians.
- **CONSERVATION** Neotropical migrant. Uncommon cowbird host.

Flight Pattern

Short flights with rapidly beating wings alternating with brief periods of wings pulled to sides.

Nest Identification

Shape   Location

Moss and dried grasses • lined with fine hair, fine grasses, and roots • in depression or scrape, sheltered by vines, grasses, or dune • built by female • 2–6 pale greenish blue or whitish eggs, marked with brown, sometimes wreathed; ovate to short ovate, 0.8 x 0.57 inches.

Plumage Sexes similar	Habitat	Migration Migratory	Weight 0.8 ounce

DATE _____ TIME_____ LOCATION _____

Family EMBERIZIDAE	Species *Ammodramus savannarum*	Length 4.75–5.5 inches	Wingspan 8–8.5 inches

GRASSHOPPER SPARROW

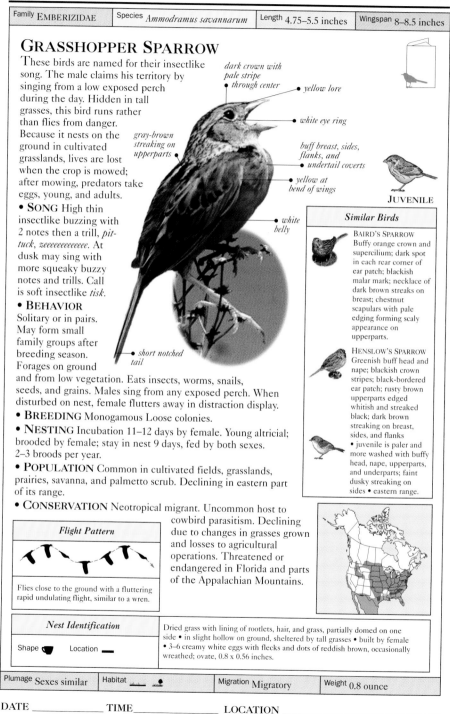

These birds are named for their insectlike song. The male claims his territory by singing from a low exposed perch during the day. Hidden in tall grasses, this bird runs rather than flies from danger. Because it nests on the ground in cultivated grasslands, lives are lost when the crop is mowed; after mowing, predators take eggs, young, and adults.

dark crown with pale stripe through center

yellow lore

white eye ring

gray-brown streaking on upperparts

buff breast, sides, flanks, and undertail coverts

yellow at bend of wings

white belly

JUVENILE

• **SONG** High thin insectlike buzzing with 2 notes then a trill, *pit-tuck, zeeeeeeeeeeee*. At dusk may sing with more squeaky buzzy notes and trills. Call is soft insectlike *tisk*.

• **BEHAVIOR** Solitary or in pairs. May form small family groups after breeding season. Forages on ground and from low vegetation. Eats insects, worms, snails, seeds, and grains. Males sing from any exposed perch. When disturbed on nest, female flutters away in distraction display.

short notched tail

• **BREEDING** Monogamous Loose colonies.

• **NESTING** Incubation 11–12 days by female. Young altricial; brooded by female; stay in nest 9 days, fed by both sexes. 2–3 broods per year.

• **POPULATION** Common in cultivated fields, grasslands, prairies, savanna, and palmetto scrub. Declining in eastern part of its range.

• **CONSERVATION** Neotropical migrant. Uncommon host to cowbird parasitism. Declining due to changes in grasses grown and losses to agricultural operations. Threatened or endangered in Florida and parts of the Appalachian Mountains.

Similar Birds

BAIRD'S SPARROW
Buffy orange crown and supercilium; dark spot in each rear corner of ear patch; blackish malar mark; necklace of dark brown streaks on breast; chestnut scapulars with pale edging forming scaly appearance on upperparts.

HENSLOW'S SPARROW
Greenish buff head and nape; blackish crown stripes; black-bordered ear patch; rusty brown upperparts edged whitish and streaked black; dark brown streaking on breast, sides, and flanks
• juvenile is paler and more washed with buffy head, nape, upperparts, and underparts; faint dusky streaking on sides • eastern range.

Flight Pattern

Flies close to the ground with a fluttering rapid undulating flight, similar to a wren.

Nest Identification

Shape 🥣   Location ▬

Dried grass with lining of rootlets, hair, and grass, partially domed on one side • in slight hollow on ground, sheltered by tall grasses • built by female • 3–6 creamy white eggs with flecks and dots of reddish brown, occasionally wreathed; ovate, 0.8 x 0.56 inches.

Plumage Sexes similar	Habitat ▬ ♣	Migration Migratory	Weight 0.8 ounce

DATE _____ TIME_____ LOCATION _____

Family EMBERIZIDAE	Species *Ammodramus bairdii*	Length 5.5 inches	Wingspan 8.5 inches

BAIRD'S SPARROW

On nesting grounds males establish territories by perching on a tussock or shrub and singing. In the 1870s this bird was one of the most abundant in the prairies of its region, but remnant populations now cling to the habitat remains. When frightened it scurries mouselike through the grass and hides. The best field marks on this elusive sparrow are the broad buff-ocher central crown stripe and the necklace of brownish black streaks across the chest.

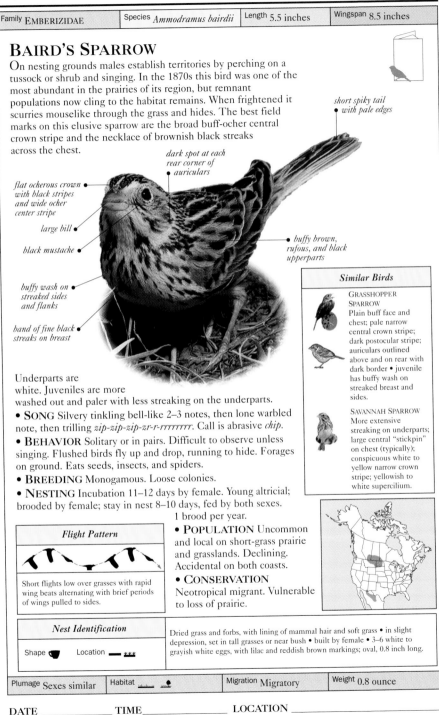

short spiky tail with pale edges

dark spot at each rear corner of auriculars

flat ocherous crown with black stripes and wide ocher center stripe

large bill

black mustache

buffy brown, rufous, and black upperparts

buffy wash on streaked sides and flanks

band of fine black streaks on breast

Similar Birds

GRASSHOPPER SPARROW
Plain buff face and chest; pale narrow central crown stripe; dark postocular stripe; auriculars outlined above and on rear with dark border • juvenile has buffy wash on streaked breast and sides.

SAVANNAH SPARROW
More extensive streaking on underparts; large central "stickpin" on chest (typically); conspicuous white to yellow narrow crown stripe; yellowish to white supercilium.

Underparts are white. Juveniles are more washed out and paler with less streaking on the underparts.

- **SONG** Silvery tinkling bell-like 2–3 notes, then lone warbled note, then trilling *zip-zip-zip-zr-r-rrrrrrrr*. Call is abrasive *chip*.
- **BEHAVIOR** Solitary or in pairs. Difficult to observe unless singing. Flushed birds fly up and drop, running to hide. Forages on ground. Eats seeds, insects, and spiders.
- **BREEDING** Monogamous. Loose colonies.
- **NESTING** Incubation 11–12 days by female. Young altricial; brooded by female; stay in nest 8–10 days, fed by both sexes. 1 brood per year.
- **POPULATION** Uncommon and local on short-grass prairie and grasslands. Declining. Accidental on both coasts.
- **CONSERVATION** Neotropical migrant. Vulnerable to loss of prairie.

Flight Pattern

Short flights low over grasses with rapid wing beats alternating with brief periods of wings pulled to sides.

Nest Identification

Shape 🥄   Location ▬ ▬▬

Dried grass and forbs, with lining of mammal hair and soft grass • in slight depression, set in tall grasses or near bush • built by female • 3–6 white to grayish white eggs, with lilac and reddish brown markings; oval, 0.8 inch long.

Plumage Sexes similar	Habitat ▬▬▬ ▴	Migration Migratory	Weight 0.8 ounce

DATE _____ TIME_____ LOCATION _____

Family EMBERIZIDAE	Species *Ammodramus leconteii*	Length 4.5–5.25 inches	Wingspan 6.5–7.25 inches

LE CONTE'S SPARROW

One of the smallest sparrows, this bird is most often found in prairie wetlands. A secretive bird, Le Conte's Sparrow often scurries mouselike in thick cover when flushed, rarely flying, and only a few feet at a time when it does. The species has declined in some parts of its range with the disappearance of damp fields and other similar habitats. This sparrow is a casual migrant in the Northeast and West, traveling only short distances off the main migration pathways. Juveniles are buffier overall and are heavily streaked on their underparts.

white central crown stripe

bright broad buff-orange eyebrows

chestnut streaks on nape

straw-colored streaks on back

thin bill

grayish ear patches

bristly tail

dark brown-streaked orange-buff breast and sides

• **SONG** Call resembles a short shrill grasshopper-like *buzz*. High-pitched and thin, it has a short squeaky introductory note followed by a buzzy trill and ending with a final *chip* note. Call note is a thin *tsip*.
• **BEHAVIOR** Solitary or in pairs. Secretive. Skulking. Walks and runs on ground to forage within matted vegetation, often in wet grasslands and bogs. In winter months, combs ground for seeds from grass and weeds. During summer, eats wide variety of insects, seeds, and spiders. Territorial male sings from exposed perch, with head pulled back and bill pointed skyward.
• **BREEDING** Monogamous. Solitary.
• **NESTING** Incubation 12–13 days by female. Young altricial; brooded by female; stay in nest estimated 8–10 days, fed by both sexes. 1–2 broods per year.
• **POPULATION** Fairly common and somewhat local in wet meadows, bog, and marsh edges. Declining in parts of range.

Similar Birds

NELSON'S SHARP-TAILED SPARROW
Broad blue-gray crown stripe; unstreaked blue-gray nape; less color contrast on upperparts; olive-brown body with whitish streaks; frequents marsh habitat.

GRASSHOPPER SPARROW
Whitish to buff eyebrows; brown, black, and buff nape; brown auricular patch with dark borders; whitish underparts with buffy wash on chest and sides; lacks streaks on breast and sides.

• **CONSERVATION**
Uncommon host to cowbird parasitism. Vulnerable to loss of habitat due to draining of wetlands and development of habitat for agriculture.

Flight Pattern

Alternates of rapid wing beats with brief periods of wings pulled to sides; flies short distances before dropping back into grass.

Nest Identification

Shape ▭   Location ▬ ⁂

Grass, rushes, and stems, lined with fine materials • usually on or near ground • built by female • 3–5 grayish white eggs with brown spots; ovate, 0.7 x 0.53 inches.

Plumage Sexes similar	Habitat	Migration Migratory	Weight 0.5 ounce

DATE _____ TIME _____ LOCATION _____

Family EMBERIZIDAE	Species *Ammodramus nelsoni*	Length 4.75 inches	Wingspan 7.25 inches

NELSON'S SHARP-TAILED SPARROW

Its streaked plumage serves as camouflage in the dense freshwater marsh grasses it inhabits in Canada, the northern prairie marshes of the US, and parts of Maine. When frightened, it scampers mouselike, with its head held low, and does not fly. It recently was determined to be a separate species from the Saltmarsh Sharp-tailed Sparrow; both were formerly lumped together under the name Sharp-tailed Sparrow. Adults show whitish or gray streaking on scapulars. Juveniles have buffer underparts and buffy heads without the gray auriculars and nape and lack streaking on the breast and flanks.

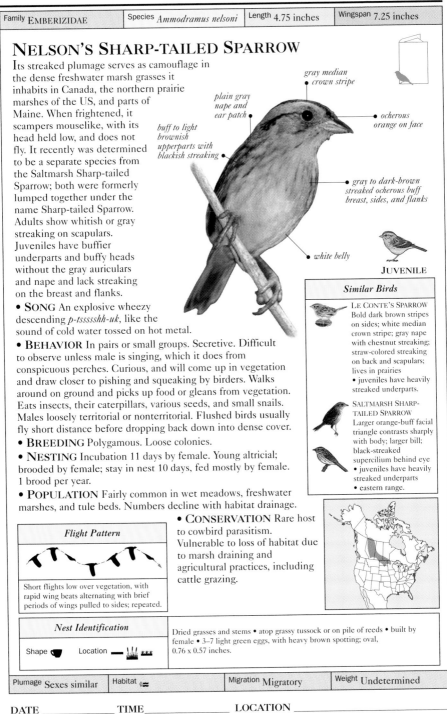

gray median crown stripe

plain gray nape and ear patch

buff to light brownish upperparts with blackish streaking

ocherous orange on face

gray to dark-brown streaked ocherous buff breast, sides, and flanks

white belly

JUVENILE

- **SONG** An explosive wheezy descending *p-tssssshh-uk*, like the sound of cold water tossed on hot metal.
- **BEHAVIOR** In pairs or small groups. Secretive. Difficult to observe unless male is singing, which it does from conspicuous perches. Curious, and will come up in vegetation and draw closer to pishing and squeaking by birders. Walks around on ground and picks up food or gleans from vegetation. Eats insects, their caterpillars, various seeds, and small snails. Males loosely territorial or nonterritorial. Flushed birds usually fly short distance before dropping back down into dense cover.
- **BREEDING** Polygamous. Loose colonies.
- **NESTING** Incubation 11 days by female. Young altricial; brooded by female; stay in nest 10 days, fed mostly by female. 1 brood per year.
- **POPULATION** Fairly common in wet meadows, freshwater marshes, and tule beds. Numbers decline with habitat drainage.

Similar Birds

LE CONTE'S SPARROW
Bold dark brown stripes on sides; white median crown stripe; gray nape with chestnut streaking; straw-colored streaking on back and scapulars; lives in prairies
- juveniles have heavily streaked underparts.

SALTMARSH SHARP-TAILED SPARROW
Larger orange-buff facial triangle contrasts sharply with body; larger bill; black-streaked supercilium behind eye
- juveniles have heavily streaked underparts
- eastern range.

- **CONSERVATION** Rare host to cowbird parasitism. Vulnerable to loss of habitat due to marsh draining and agricultural practices, including cattle grazing.

Flight Pattern

Short flights low over vegetation, with rapid wing beats alternating with brief periods of wings pulled to sides; repeated.

Nest Identification

Shape ☕   Location 🌾 ✸✸✸

Dried grasses and stems • atop grassy tussock or on pile of reeds • built by female • 3–7 light green eggs, with heavy brown spotting; oval, 0.76 x 0.57 inches.

Plumage Sexes similar	Habitat 🌾	Migration Migratory	Weight Undetermined

DATE _____ TIME_____ LOCATION _____

Family EMBERIZIDAE	Species *Passerella iliaca*	Length 6.75–7.5 inches	Wingspan 10.5–11.75 inches

FOX SPARROW

Named for its rufous coloring, particularly on the rump and tail, the Fox Sparrow is one of the largest of all sparrows. There is much variation in size and coloration over the wide breeding range. The most richly plumaged birds breed in the boreal forests from Alaska to Newfoundland and are the forms seen in winter in the southeastern US, such as the *P. i. zaboria* pictured here. In the western mountain races, birds have gray heads and backs, while northwestern Pacific coastal races are sooty brown with dark brown rumps and tails. While mostly solitary, this sparrow sometimes is observed associating with other sparrows. Migrates in late March and early November, generally traveling at night.

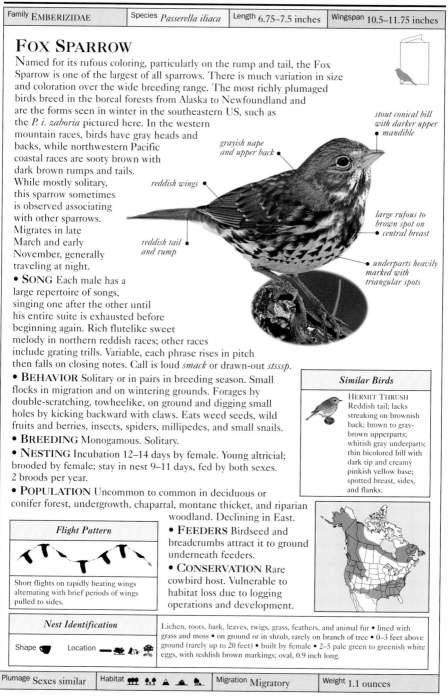

stout conical bill with darker upper mandible

grayish nape and upper back

reddish wings

reddish tail and rump

large rufous to brown spot on central breast

underparts heavily marked with triangular spots

• **SONG** Each male has a large repertoire of songs, singing one after the other until his entire suite is exhausted before beginning again. Rich flutelike sweet melody in northern reddish races; other races include grating trills. Variable, each phrase rises in pitch then falls on closing notes. Call is loud *smack* or drawn-out *stsssp*.

• **BEHAVIOR** Solitary or in pairs in breeding season. Small flocks in migration and on wintering grounds. Forages by double-scratching, towheelike, on ground and digging small holes by kicking backward with claws. Eats weed seeds, wild fruits and berries, insects, spiders, millipedes, and small snails.

• **BREEDING** Monogamous. Solitary.

• **NESTING** Incubation 12–14 days by female. Young altricial; brooded by female; stay in nest 9–11 days, fed by both sexes. 2 broods per year.

• **POPULATION** Uncommon to common in deciduous or conifer forest, undergrowth, chaparral, montane thicket, and riparian woodland. Declining in East.

• **FEEDERS** Birdseed and breadcrumbs attract it to ground underneath feeders.

• **CONSERVATION** Rare cowbird host. Vulnerable to habitat loss due to logging operations and development.

Similar Birds

HERMIT THRUSH Reddish tail; lacks streaking on brownish back; brown to gray-brown upperparts; whitish gray underparts; thin bicolored bill with dark tip and creamy pinkish yellow base; spotted breast, sides, and flanks.

Flight Pattern

Short flights on rapidly beating wings alternating with brief periods of wings pulled to sides.

Nest Identification

Shape ● Location ●

Lichen, roots, bark, leaves, twigs, grass, feathers, and animal fur • lined with grass and moss • on ground or in shrub, rarely on branch of tree • 0–3 feet above ground (rarely up to 20 feet) • built by female • 2–5 pale green to greenish white eggs, with reddish brown markings; oval, 0.9 inch long.

Plumage Sexes similar	Habitat	Migration Migratory	Weight 1.1 ounces

DATE _____ TIME_____ LOCATION _____

Family EMBERIZIDAE	Species *Melospiza melodia*	Length 5.75–7.5 inches	Wingspan 8.25–12.5 inches

SONG SPARROW

Even with its drab plumage, this bold songbird is easy to spot when it perches in the open, trilling its pleasant melody. In flight it pumps its tail up and down. Inhabiting a wide range, this bird is found throughout most of North America and is perhaps the continent's most variable species, with approximately thirty-one subspecies recognized. The Aleutian race, *M. m. maxima*, is so large and dark it looks like a different species. Because of the work of Ohio bird biologist Margaret Morse Nice, the biology of this bird may be the best-known of any songbird on the continent. Juveniles are similar to adults but appear buffier overall with finer streaking.

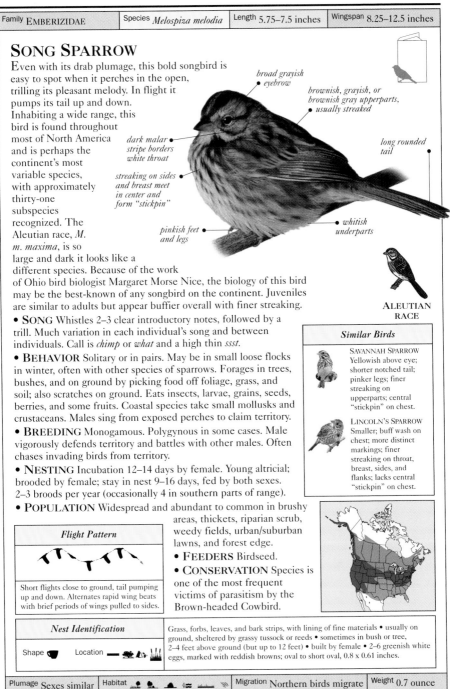

broad grayish eyebrow

brownish, grayish, or brownish gray upperparts, usually streaked

long rounded tail

dark malar stripe borders white throat

streaking on sides and breast meet in center and form "stickpin"

pinkish feet and legs

whitish underparts

ALEUTIAN RACE

• **SONG** Whistles 2–3 clear introductory notes, followed by a trill. Much variation in each individual's song and between individuals. Call is *chimp* or *what* and a high thin *ssst*.

• **BEHAVIOR** Solitary or in pairs. May be in small loose flocks in winter, often with other species of sparrows. Forages in trees, bushes, and on ground by picking food off foliage, grass, and soil; also scratches on ground. Eats insects, larvae, grains, seeds, berries, and some fruits. Coastal species take small mollusks and crustaceans. Males sing from exposed perches to claim territory.

• **BREEDING** Monogamous. Polygynous in some cases. Male vigorously defends territory and battles with other males. Often chases invading birds from territory.

• **NESTING** Incubation 12–14 days by female. Young altricial; brooded by female; stay in nest 9–16 days, fed by both sexes. 2–3 broods per year (occasionally 4 in southern parts of range).

• **POPULATION** Widespread and abundant to common in brushy areas, thickets, riparian scrub, weedy fields, urban/suburban lawns, and forest edge.

• **FEEDERS** Birdseed.

• **CONSERVATION** Species is one of the most frequent victims of parasitism by the Brown-headed Cowbird.

Similar Birds

SAVANNAH SPARROW
Yellowish above eye; shorter notched tail; pinker legs; finer streaking on upperparts; central "stickpin" on chest.

LINCOLN'S SPARROW
Smaller; buff wash on chest; more distinct markings; finer streaking on throat, breast, sides, and flanks; lacks central "stickpin" on chest.

Flight Pattern

Short flights close to ground, tail pumping up and down. Alternates rapid wing beats with brief periods of wings pulled to sides.

Nest Identification

Shape   Location

Grass, forbs, leaves, and bark strips, with lining of fine materials • usually on ground, sheltered by grassy tussock or reeds • sometimes in bush or tree, 2–4 feet above ground (but up to 12 feet) • built by female • 2–6 greenish white eggs, marked with reddish browns; oval to short oval, 0.8 x 0.61 inches.

Plumage Sexes similar	Habitat	Migration Northern birds migrate	Weight 0.7 ounce

DATE _____ TIME_____ LOCATION _____

Family EMBERIZIDAE	Species *Melospiza lincolnii*	Length 5.25–6 inches	Wingspan 7.25–8.75 inches

LINCOLN'S SPARROW

This inhabitant of northern bogs and mountain meadowlands is skittish, often raising its slight crest when disturbed. It is sometimes overlooked because of its furtive habits and similarity to the Song Sparrow, with which it may compete when nesting territories overlap. This sparrow can be distinguished by its sweet gurgling melody that sounds similar to that of a House Wren or Purple Finch, and by the buffy band crossing the chest and separating the white chin and throat from the white lower breast and belly. Juveniles are paler and buffier overall with more streaking on their underparts.

buff-colored wash on back and shoulders, with black streaking

buff-colored eye rings

broad gray eyebrows

buff wash on mustache

whitish chin and throat

rufous wings and wing coverts

buff wash and fine streaks on breast, sides, and flanks

rounded tail

unstreaked whitish belly

• **SONG** Features rapid bubbling trilled notes, with last notes harsher, louder, and lower in pitch, *chur-chur-chur-wee-wee-wee-wee-wah*. Alarm call is a flat-toned repetitious *tschup*. Calls also include a sharp buzzlike *zeee*.

• **BEHAVIOR** Solitary or in pairs. Sometimes joins mixed-species foraging flocks on wintering grounds. Secretive. Skulks low in thickets or on ground. Kicks backward with both feet like a towhee as it scratches among leaves on the ground; feeds on insects and small grains, as well as seeds from weeds and grasses. In migration, often found in brushy tangles near water. Often sings from a concealed perch during spring migration.

• **BREEDING** Monogamous. Solitary.

• **NESTING** Incubation 12–14 days by female. Young altricial; brooded by female; stay in nest 9–12 days, fed by both sexes. 1–2 broods per year.

• **POPULATION** Uncommon to fairly common in bogs, wet meadows, riparian thickets, and mountain meadows. Uncommon to fairly common in thickets and weedy fields in winter.

• **FEEDERS** Attracted by seed, particularly in migration.

• **CONSERVATION** Neotropical migrant. Rare host to cowbird parasitism. Vulnerable to loss of habitat because of logging operations and development.

Similar Birds

SONG SPARROW
Longer tail; thicker bill; thicker malar stripe; heavier streaking on underparts; central "stickpin" on chest; white underparts lack buffy wash on chest; brown upperparts with rufous and black streaking.

SWAMP SPARROW
Duller breast with thinner blurry streaks; gray head; rufous-brown crown with gray central stripe; unstreaked white throat; rufous wings and primary coverts.

Flight Pattern

Short flights with rapid wing beats alternating with brief periods of wings pulled to sides; repeated.

Nest Identification

Shape ☕   Location ✱✱✱ ▬

Grass or sedge lined, sometimes with hair • often built in grass, hollow depressions, or moss • built by female • 3–6 pale green to greenish white eggs, with reddish brown markings; oval to short oval, 0.8 x 0.6 inches.

Plumage Sexes similar	Habitat ▲ ▲ ▲ ⚟	Migration Migratory	Weight 0.8 ounce

DATE _____ TIME_____ LOCATION _____

Family EMBERIZIDAE	Species _Melospiza georgiana_	Length 4.75–5.75 inches	Wingspan 7.5–8 inches

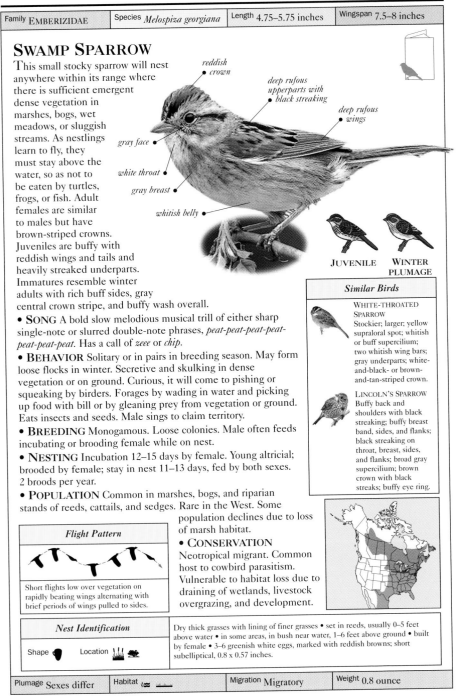

SWAMP SPARROW

This small stocky sparrow will nest anywhere within its range where there is sufficient emergent dense vegetation in marshes, bogs, wet meadows, or sluggish streams. As nestlings learn to fly, they must stay above the water, so as not to be eaten by turtles, frogs, or fish. Adult females are similar to males but have brown-striped crowns. Juveniles are buffy with reddish wings and tails and heavily streaked underparts. Immatures resemble winter adults with rich buff sides, gray central crown stripe, and buffy wash overall.

reddish crown

deep rufous upperparts with black streaking

deep rufous wings

gray face

white throat

gray breast

whitish belly

JUVENILE

WINTER PLUMAGE

- **SONG** A bold slow melodious musical trill of either sharp single-note or slurred double-note phrases, _peat-peat-peat-peat-peat-peat-peat_. Has a call of _zeee_ or _chip_.
- **BEHAVIOR** Solitary or in pairs in breeding season. May form loose flocks in winter. Secretive and skulking in dense vegetation or on ground. Curious, it will come to pishing or squeaking by birders. Forages by wading in water and picking up food with bill or by gleaning prey from vegetation or ground. Eats insects and seeds. Male sings to claim territory.
- **BREEDING** Monogamous. Loose colonies. Male often feeds incubating or brooding female while on nest.
- **NESTING** Incubation 12–15 days by female. Young altricial; brooded by female; stay in nest 11–13 days, fed by both sexes. 2 broods per year.
- **POPULATION** Common in marshes, bogs, and riparian stands of reeds, cattails, and sedges. Rare in the West. Some population declines due to loss of marsh habitat.
- **CONSERVATION** Neotropical migrant. Common host to cowbird parasitism. Vulnerable to habitat loss due to draining of wetlands, livestock overgrazing, and development.

Similar Birds

WHITE-THROATED SPARROW
Stockier; larger; yellow supraloral spot; whitish or buff supercilium; two whitish wing bars; gray underparts; white-and-black- or brown-and-tan-striped crown.

LINCOLN'S SPARROW
Buffy back and shoulders with black streaking; buffy breast band, sides, and flanks; black streaking on throat, breast, sides, and flanks; broad gray supercilium; brown crown with black streaks; buffy eye ring.

Flight Pattern

Short flights low over vegetation on rapidly beating wings alternating with brief periods of wings pulled to sides.

Nest Identification

Shape ● Location 🌾🪶

Dry thick grasses with lining of finer grasses • set in reeds, usually 0–5 feet above water • in some areas, in bush near water, 1–6 feet above ground • built by female • 3–6 greenish white eggs, marked with reddish browns; short subelliptical, 0.8 x 0.57 inches.

Plumage Sexes differ	Habitat 🌾 ⌇	Migration Migratory	Weight 0.8 ounce

DATE _____ TIME_____ LOCATION _____

Family EMBERIZIDAE	Species *Zonotrichia albicollis*	Length 6.25–7.5 inches	Wingspan 8.75–10 inches

WHITE-THROATED SPARROW

The song of the White-throated Sparrow is heard in the Canadian wilderness and in the northeastern US where it breeds in woodland undergrowth, clearings, and gardens. Distinguishing marks include a broad yellow eyebrow, or supraloral stripe in the front of the eye, which tapers to either white or tan, and a sharply outlined white throat. Although it is common and widespread, sightings of this bird are rare in the West.

black or brown borders crown stripes and eye line

rusty brown upperparts

yellow supraloral stripe

dark bill

white throat

2 white wing bars

grayish underparts with diffuse streaking

• **SONG** A thin whistle, starting with 2 single notes followed by 3 triple notes: *poor-sam-peabody, peabody, peabody* or *pure-sweet-Canada, Canada, Canada*. Calls include a grating *pink* and a drawled lisping *tseep*. Territorial birds often sing at night. Some black-and-white-striped females sing.

JUVENILE

TAN-STRIPED

• **BEHAVIOR** Solitary or in pairs. In winter joins flocks of other White-throats and mixed species. Hops on ground or forages in shrubs and trees. Scratches among leaves for food. Eats mostly weed seeds, fruit from trees, tree buds, and insects. May hawk insects in midair. Attracted by pishing and squeaking by birders. Two adult color morphs are based on head striping: black-and-white-striped and brown-and-tan-striped. Field studies show that white-striped males tend to mate with tan-striped females, and tan-striped males tend to mate with white-striped females.

• **BREEDING** Monogamous. Solitary.

• **NESTING** Incubation 11–14 days by female. Young altricial; brooded by female; stay in nest 7–12 days, fed by both sexes. 1–2 broods per year.

• **POPULATION** Common and widespread in conifer and mixed-conifer forest, forest edge and clearings, and thickets. Rare in the West.

• **FEEDERS** Seeds and grains.

• **CONSERVATION** Uncommon host to cowbird parasitism. Vulnerable to habitat loss due to logging.

Similar Birds

WHITE-CROWNED SPARROW
Black-and-white-striped crown; pink bill; lacks whitish throat contrasting with gray breast; lacks yellow supraloral spot; tertials lack bright rufous coloring.

HARRIS SPARROW
Winter adult and juvenile • slightly larger; pink bill; crown varies from tan with black stippling, to black with white spotting, to black; face buffy tan; chin varies from white to blackish; throat white, black-and-white, or black; blackish band crossing upper breast.

Flight Pattern

Relatively short flights with rapid wing beats alternating with brief periods of wings pulled to sides; repeated.

Nest Identification
Shape ◥ Location ❧ ▬

Lined with coarse grass, wood chips, twigs, pine needles, roots, and other fine materials • often found at edge of clearing • 0–3 feet above ground • built by female • 3–6 greenish, bluish, or cream-white eggs with reddish brown markings; subelliptical or long elliptical, 0.8 x 0.6 inches.

Plumage Sexes similar	Habitat 🌿 🪨 🌲 👥	Migration Migratory	Weight 0.9 ounce

Family EMBERIZIDAE	Species *Zonotrichia querula*	Length 6.75–7.75 inches	Wingspan 10.25–11.75 inches

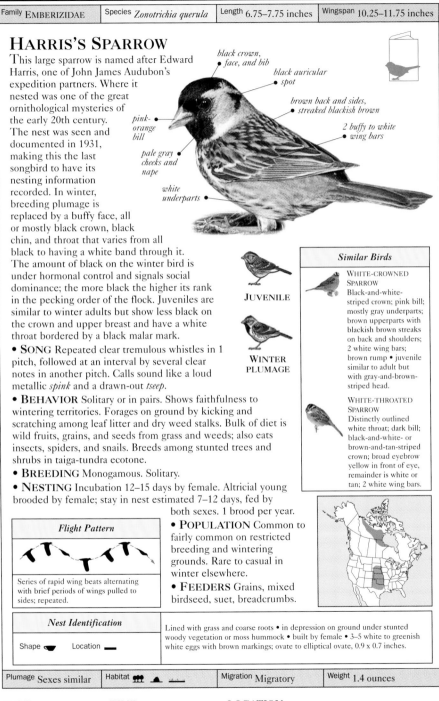

HARRIS'S SPARROW

This large sparrow is named after Edward Harris, one of John James Audubon's expedition partners. Where it nested was one of the great ornithological mysteries of the early 20th century. The nest was seen and documented in 1931, making this the last songbird to have its nesting information recorded. In winter, breeding plumage is replaced by a buffy face, all or mostly black crown, black chin, and throat that varies from all black to having a white band through it. The amount of black on the winter bird is under hormonal control and signals social dominance; the more black the higher its rank in the pecking order of the flock. Juveniles are similar to winter adults but show less black on the crown and upper breast and have a white throat bordered by a black malar mark.

black crown, face, and bib

black auricular spot

brown back and sides, streaked blackish brown

pink-orange bill

pale gray cheeks and nape

2 buffy to white wing bars

white underparts

JUVENILE

WINTER PLUMAGE

Similar Birds

WHITE-CROWNED SPARROW
Black-and-white-striped crown; pink bill; mostly gray underparts; brown upperparts with blackish brown streaks on back and shoulders; 2 white wing bars; brown rump • juvenile similar to adult but with gray-and-brown-striped head.

WHITE-THROATED SPARROW
Distinctly outlined white throat; dark bill; black-and-white- or brown-and-tan-striped crown; broad eyebrow yellow in front of eye, remainder is white or tan; 2 white wing bars.

• **SONG** Repeated clear tremulous whistles in 1 pitch, followed at an interval by several clear notes in another pitch. Calls sound like a loud metallic *spink* and a drawn-out *tseep*.

• **BEHAVIOR** Solitary or in pairs. Shows faithfulness to wintering territories. Forages on ground by kicking and scratching among leaf litter and dry weed stalks. Bulk of diet is wild fruits, grains, and seeds from grass and weeds; also eats insects, spiders, and snails. Breeds among stunted trees and shrubs in taiga-tundra ecotone.

• **BREEDING** Monogamous. Solitary.

• **NESTING** Incubation 12–15 days by female. Altricial young brooded by female; stay in nest estimated 7–12 days, fed by both sexes. 1 brood per year.

• **POPULATION** Common to fairly common on restricted breeding and wintering grounds. Rare to casual in winter elsewhere.

• **FEEDERS** Grains, mixed birdseed, suet, breadcrumbs.

Flight Pattern

Series of rapid wing beats alternating with brief periods of wings pulled to sides; repeated.

Nest Identification

Shape ◣   Location ▬

Lined with grass and coarse roots • in depression on ground under stunted woody vegetation or moss hummock • built by female • 3–5 white to greenish white eggs with brown markings; ovate to elliptical ovate, 0.9 x 0.7 inches.

Plumage Sexes similar	Habitat 🌳 🔺 〰	Migration Migratory	Weight 1.4 ounces

DATE _____ TIME_____ LOCATION _____

Family EMBERIZIDAE	Species *Zonotrichia leucophrys*	Length 6.5–7.5 inches	Wingspan 9.25–10.25 inches

WHITE-CROWNED SPARROW

This bold bird is easy to identify, with conspicuous black stripes on its white crown, a pink to dull yellow bill, and a pale gray throat. Like many sparrows, the male sings to claim its territory and duels to defend its ground. His songs may even continue into the night. As is usual with a wide geographical range, there is morphological and behavioral variation. The most striking subspecies differences include bill color and white versus black supralorals. Juveniles have heavily streaked underparts and a brown-and-buff-streaked head. Immatures have a brown-and-tan-striped head and unstreaked underparts.

white supercilium

black postocular stripe

brownish upperparts with blackish brown streaking

2 white wing bars

brownish wash on sides and flanks

white crown with bold black stripes

pink to dull yellow bill

whitish gray throat

grayish underparts become white on belly

JUVENILE

FIRST WINTER

• **SONG** A melancholy whistled *poor-wet-wetter-chee-zee*. Has call note of *pink* or sharp *tseek*.

• **BEHAVIOR** Solitary or in pairs. In small family groups after breeding season. Forms flocks in winter. Males sing from exposed perches; sometimes in spring on wintering grounds. Gleans food from vegetation; hops on ground and forages by scratching. Eats seeds, insects, caterpillars, and parts of plants.

• **BREEDING** Monogamous. Individuals in some nonmigratory populations may pair for life. Some polygynous.

• **NESTING** Incubation 11–14 days by female. Young altricial; brooded by female; stay in nest 7–12 days, fed by both sexes. Male continues to feed young while female starts another nest. 2–4 broods per year (largest number of broods in southern populations; 1 brood in far north).

• **POPULATION** Common to fairly common in woodlands, thickets, wet meadows, and chaparral.

• **FEEDERS** Baby chick scratch and seeds.

• **CONSERVATION** Neotropical migrant. Uncommon host to cowbird parasitism. Vulnerable in the West to habitat loss because of land development and logging.

Similar Birds

WHITE-THROATED SPARROW
More rufous-brown upperparts; mostly dark bill; well-defined white throat patch; yellow spot between eye and bill; gray underparts; two white wing bars; black-and-white- or brown-and-tan-striped cap.

HARRIS'S SPARROW
Winter adult and juvenile • slightly larger; pink bill; crown varies from tan with black stippling, to black with white spotting, to black; face buffy tan; chin varies from white to blackish; throat white, black-and-white, or black; blackish band crossing upper breast.

Flight Pattern

Short flights on rapidly beating wings alternating with brief periods of wings pulled to sides; repeated.

Nest Identification

Shape ◗ Location ▬ ✿✿✿ ▲▲

Grass, sticks, rootlets, and forbs • lined with soft grasses, feathers, and hair • on clump of grass or moss, sheltered by bush, or in small tree • 0–5 feet above ground (but up to 30 feet) • built by female • 2–6 light blue or green eggs marked with reddish browns; ovate to short ovate or long ovate, 0.8 x 0.6 inches.

Plumage Sexes similar	Habitat ▴▵ ▲ ▲ ▲	Migration Northern birds migrate	Weight 1.0 ounce

DATE _____ TIME_____ LOCATION _____

Family EMBERIZIDAE	Species *Zonotrichia atricapilla*	Length 7 inches	Wingspan 9.75 inches

GOLDEN-CROWNED SPARROW

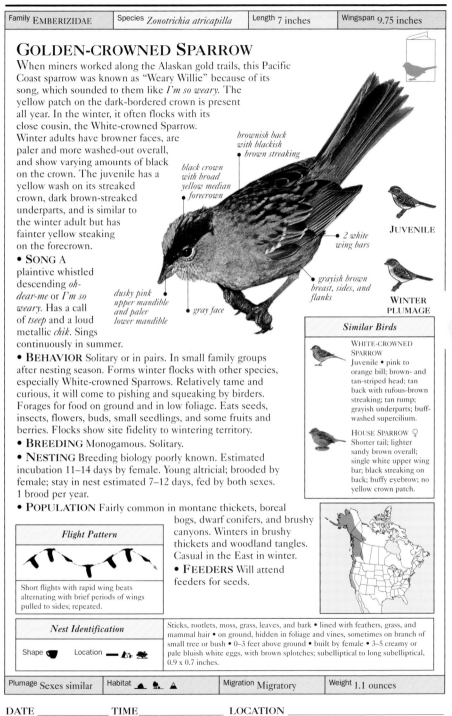

When miners worked along the Alaskan gold trails, this Pacific Coast sparrow was known as "Weary Willie" because of its song, which sounded to them like *I'm so weary*. The yellow patch on the dark-bordered crown is present all year. In the winter, it often flocks with its close cousin, the White-crowned Sparrow. Winter adults have browner faces, are paler and more washed-out overall, and show varying amounts of black on the crown. The juvenile has a yellow wash on its streaked crown, dark brown-streaked underparts, and is similar to the winter adult but has fainter yellow steaking on the forecrown.

brownish back with blackish brown streaking

black crown with broad yellow median forecrown

2 white wing bars

JUVENILE

grayish brown breast, sides, and flanks

WINTER PLUMAGE

• **SONG** A plaintive whistled descending *oh-dear-me* or *I'm so weary*. Has a call of *tseep* and a loud metallic *chik*. Sings continuously in summer.

dusky pink upper mandible and paler lower mandible

gray face

• **BEHAVIOR** Solitary or in pairs. In small family groups after nesting season. Forms winter flocks with other species, especially White-crowned Sparrows. Relatively tame and curious, it will come to pishing and squeaking by birders. Forages for food on ground and in low foliage. Eats seeds, insects, flowers, buds, small seedlings, and some fruits and berries. Flocks show site fidelity to wintering territory.

• **BREEDING** Monogamous. Solitary.

• **NESTING** Breeding biology poorly known. Estimated incubation 11–14 days by female. Young altricial; brooded by female; stay in nest estimated 7–12 days, fed by both sexes. 1 brood per year.

• **POPULATION** Fairly common in montane thickets, boreal bogs, dwarf conifers, and brushy canyons. Winters in brushy thickets and woodland tangles. Casual in the East in winter.

• **FEEDERS** Will attend feeders for seeds.

Similar Birds

WHITE-CROWNED SPARROW
Juvenile • pink to orange bill; brown- and tan-striped head; tan back with rufous-brown streaking; tan rump; grayish underparts; buff-washed supercilium.

HOUSE SPARROW ♀
Shorter tail; lighter sandy brown overall; single white upper wing bar; black streaking on back; buffy eyebrow; no yellow crown patch.

Flight Pattern

Short flights with rapid wing beats alternating with brief periods of wings pulled to sides; repeated.

Nest Identification

Shape ⬦   Location ▬ ⏶ ❧

Sticks, rootlets, moss, grass, leaves, and bark • lined with feathers, grass, and mammal hair • on ground, hidden in foliage and vines, sometimes on branch of small tree or bush • 0–3 feet above ground • built by female • 3–5 creamy or pale bluish white eggs, with brown splotches; subelliptical to long subelliptical, 0.9 x 0.7 inches.

Plumage Sexes similar	Habitat ▲ ❧. ▲	Migration Migratory	Weight 1.1 ounces

DATE _____ TIME_____ LOCATION _____

Family EMBERIZIDAE	Species *Junco hyemalis*	Length 5.75–6.5 inches	Wingspan 9.25–10 inches

DARK-EYED JUNCO

In 1973 the American Ornithologists' Union grouped under one heading what was once considered five different junco species. Thus, the Dark-eyed Junco is composed of geographic races that differ in color and range but are closely related and have similar habits. All races of the species complex have white outer tail feathers; a black, gray, or brown hood; and white lower breast, belly, and undertail coverts. All have similar songs; all but one have a pink bill. Females tend to be paler and sometimes browner on the back. Juveniles have streaked upperparts and underparts.

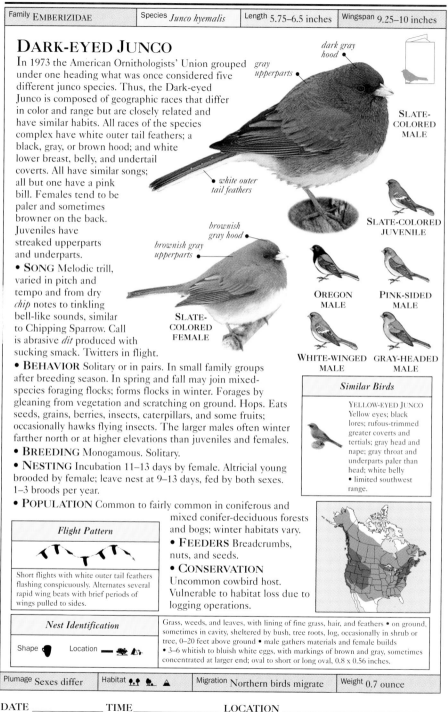

dark gray hood

gray upperparts

SLATE-COLORED MALE

white outer tail feathers

SLATE-COLORED JUVENILE

brownish gray hood

brownish gray upperparts

OREGON MALE

PINK-SIDED MALE

SLATE-COLORED FEMALE

WHITE-WINGED MALE

GRAY-HEADED MALE

- **SONG** Melodic trill, varied in pitch and tempo and from dry *chip* notes to tinkling bell-like sounds, similar to Chipping Sparrow. Call is abrasive *dit* produced with sucking smack. Twitters in flight.
- **BEHAVIOR** Solitary or in pairs. In small family groups after breeding season. In spring and fall may join mixed-species foraging flocks; forms flocks in winter. Forages by gleaning from vegetation and scratching on ground. Hops. Eats seeds, grains, berries, insects, caterpillars, and some fruits; occasionally hawks flying insects. The larger males often winter farther north or at higher elevations than juveniles and females.
- **BREEDING** Monogamous. Solitary.
- **NESTING** Incubation 11–13 days by female. Altricial young brooded by female; leave nest at 9–13 days, fed by both sexes. 1–3 broods per year.
- **POPULATION** Common to fairly common in coniferous and mixed conifer-deciduous forests and bogs; winter habitats vary.
- **FEEDERS** Breadcrumbs, nuts, and seeds.
- **CONSERVATION** Uncommon cowbird host. Vulnerable to habitat loss due to logging operations.

Similar Birds

YELLOW-EYED JUNCO Yellow eyes; black lores; rufous-trimmed greater coverts and tertials; gray head and nape; gray throat and underparts paler than head; white belly
- limited southwest range.

Flight Pattern

Short flights with white outer tail feathers flashing conspicuously. Alternates several rapid wing beats with brief periods of wings pulled to sides.

Nest Identification

Shape   Location

Grass, weeds, and leaves, with lining of fine grass, hair, and feathers • on ground, sometimes in cavity, sheltered by bush, tree roots, log, occasionally in shrub or tree, 0–20 feet above ground • male gathers materials and female builds
• 3–6 whitish to bluish white eggs, with markings of brown and gray, sometimes concentrated at larger end; oval to short or long oval, 0.8 x 0.56 inches.

Plumage Sexes differ	Habitat	Migration Northern birds migrate	Weight 0.7 ounce

DATE _____ TIME_____ LOCATION _____

| Family EMBERIZIDAE | Species *Junco phaeonotus* | Length 6.25 inches | Wingspan 9.75 inches |

YELLOW-EYED JUNCO

The only junco with yellow eyes found in North America, this primarily Mexican bird has a small range in the mountains of Arizona and New Mexico. The male sings while courting the female, fanning his tail, alternately dragging it and holding it upright, and swaggering around the female. Usually residing in mountains above six thousand feet in pine-oak and coniferous forests, some birds move to lower elevations in the winter. The white outer tail feathers are conspicuous in flight. Juvenile birds have dusky eyes and dusky-streaked heads, upperparts, and underparts.

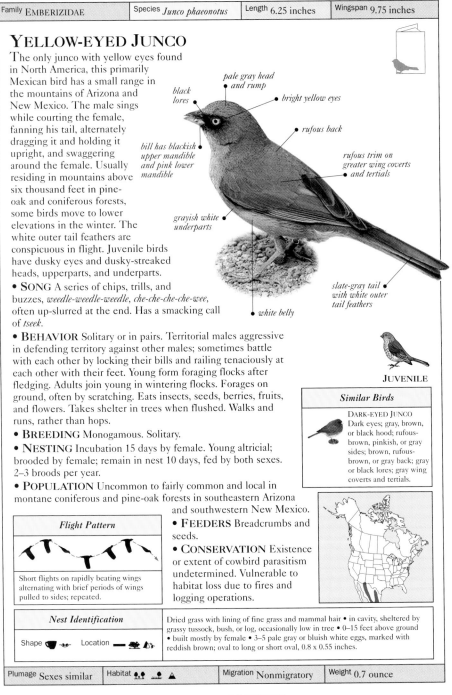

- **SONG** A series of chips, trills, and buzzes, *weedle-weedle-weedle, che-che-che-che-wee,* often up-slurred at the end. Has a smacking call of *tseek.*
- **BEHAVIOR** Solitary or in pairs. Territorial males aggressive in defending territory against other males; sometimes battle with each other by locking their bills and railing tenaciously at each other with their feet. Young form foraging flocks after fledging. Adults join young in wintering flocks. Forages on ground, often by scratching. Eats insects, seeds, berries, fruits, and flowers. Takes shelter in trees when flushed. Walks and runs, rather than hops.
- **BREEDING** Monogamous. Solitary.
- **NESTING** Incubation 15 days by female. Young altricial; brooded by female; remain in nest 10 days, fed by both sexes. 2–3 broods per year.
- **POPULATION** Uncommon to fairly common and local in montane coniferous and pine-oak forests in southeastern Arizona and southwestern New Mexico.
- **FEEDERS** Breadcrumbs and seeds.
- **CONSERVATION** Existence or extent of cowbird parasitism undetermined. Vulnerable to habitat loss due to fires and logging operations.

JUVENILE

Similar Birds

DARK-EYED JUNCO Dark eyes; gray, brown, or black hood; rufous-brown, pinkish, or gray sides; brown, rufous-brown, or gray back; gray or black lores; gray wing coverts and tertials.

Flight Pattern

Short flights on rapidly beating wings alternating with brief periods of wings pulled to sides; repeated.

Nest Identification

Shape — Location —

Dried grass with lining of fine grass and mammal hair • in cavity, sheltered by grassy tussock, bush, or log, occasionally low in tree • 0–15 feet above ground • built mostly by female • 3–5 pale gray or bluish white eggs, marked with reddish brown; oval to long or short oval, 0.8 x 0.55 inches.

| Plumage Sexes similar | Habitat | Migration Nonmigratory | Weight 0.7 ounce |

DATE _____ TIME_____ LOCATION _____

Family EMBERIZIDAE	Species *Calcarius mccownii*	Length 6 inches	Wingspan 10 inches

McCOWN'S LONGSPUR

During years of heavy rainfall, this inhabitant of arid short-grass plains will desert its nesting grounds. A monogamous species, males and females are often together, walking side by side. Winter males are similar to breeding females but show deeper chestnut in the median coverts and more black in the breast band. Winter females are buffy with broad buffy eyebrows. Juveniles are paler with a scaly-backed look and streaked heads and underparts. All plumages show a white tail with a black inverted T-shaped pattern.

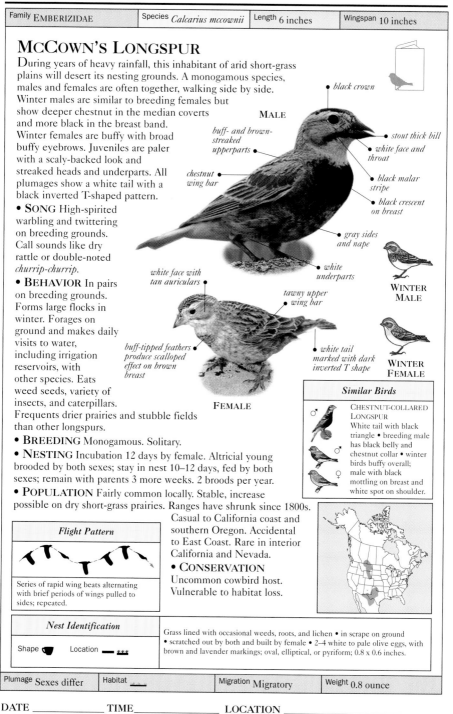

MALE

- black crown
- buff- and brown-streaked upperparts
- stout thick bill
- white face and throat
- chestnut wing bar
- black malar stripe
- black crescent on breast
- gray sides and nape
- white underparts

WINTER MALE

- white face with tan auriculars
- tawny upper wing bar
- buff-tipped feathers produce scalloped effect on brown breast
- white tail marked with dark inverted T shape

FEMALE

WINTER FEMALE

- **SONG** High-spirited warbling and twittering on breeding grounds. Call sounds like dry rattle or double-noted *churrip-churrip*.
- **BEHAVIOR** In pairs on breeding grounds. Forms large flocks in winter. Forages on ground and makes daily visits to water, including irrigation reservoirs, with other species. Eats weed seeds, variety of insects, and caterpillars. Frequents drier prairies and stubble fields than other longspurs.
- **BREEDING** Monogamous. Solitary.
- **NESTING** Incubation 12 days by female. Altricial young brooded by both sexes; stay in nest 10–12 days, fed by both sexes; remain with parents 3 more weeks. 2 broods per year.
- **POPULATION** Fairly common locally. Stable, increase possible on dry short-grass prairies. Ranges have shrunk since 1800s. Casual to California coast and southern Oregon. Accidental to East Coast. Rare in interior California and Nevada.
- **CONSERVATION** Uncommon cowbird host. Vulnerable to habitat loss.

Similar Birds

♂ ♂ ♀ **CHESTNUT-COLLARED LONGSPUR** White tail with black triangle • breeding male has black belly and chestnut collar • winter birds buffy overall; male with black mottling on breast and white spot on shoulder.

Flight Pattern

Series of rapid wing beats alternating with brief periods of wings pulled to sides; repeated.

Nest Identification

Shape ◖ Location ▬ ✷✷✷

Grass lined with occasional weeds, roots, and lichen • in scrape on ground • scratched out by both and built by female • 2–4 white to pale olive eggs, with brown and lavender markings; oval, elliptical, or pyriform; 0.8 x 0.6 inches.

Plumage Sexes differ	Habitat ▬▬	Migration Migratory	Weight 0.8 ounce

DATE _____ TIME_____ LOCATION _____

| Family EMBERIZIDAE | Species *Calcarius lapponicus* | Length 6–7 inches | Wingspan 10.5–11.75 inches |

LAPLAND LONGSPUR

In winter this bird is commonly in the company of Horned Larks, Snow Buntings, and other longspurs on barren snow-swept fields throughout the north and central US, sometimes in large flocks. Resembling a House Sparrow, it is seen often. In all plumages the outer two tail feathers are partly white and partly black. Females are duller in color with rufous greater wing coverts and edging on the tertials, and a bold dark triangle outlines buff ear patches. Juveniles are similar to females but with heavy streaking on the head, back, and underparts.

• **SONG** Liquid warbling Bobolink-like song given in flight. Call is melodious *tee-lee-oo* or *tee-dle* or dry rattling *drit-ri-it.*

• **BEHAVIOR** In pairs or small family groups in summer. Forages on ground for insects and spiders; also eats seeds from grass and sedges; mostly weed seeds in winter. Migrates in flocks in late fall and early spring. Flocks number in the thousands on US wintering grounds. Courting tundra male may sing while chasing female on ground; gives skylarking flight song, rising from ground in front of female, singing above her, and gliding back down with tail and wings spread.

• **BREEDING** Monogamous. Solitary.

• **NESTING** Incubation 10–14 days by female. Young altricial; brooded by female; stay in nest 8–10 days, fed by both sexes. Fledglings are divided equally between the sexes; each tends its half of the brood. 1 brood per year.

• **POPULATION** Common to abundant on arctic tundra in summer; prairies, grassy fields, stubble fields, and dune areas along shorelines. Widespread.

black crown, lores, cheeks, throat, and breast
reddish brown nape
broad white stripe extends from eye to sides of breast
white underparts with black streaking on sides and flanks

MALE

blackish brown crown
tan auriculars bordered blackish
broad white supercilium
chestnut nape with blackish streaking

FEMALE

WINTER MALE **WINTER FEMALE**

Similar Birds

SMITH'S LONGSPUR ♂
Winter • rich buff nape and underparts; thin dusky streaking on underparts; white shoulder patch, often hidden; 2 white outer tail feathers tipped black on distal third of outer web; small thin bill; buffy supercilium. ♀

Flight Pattern

Rapid wing beats alternating with brief periods of wings pulled to sides.

Nest Identification	
Shape ◖ Location ▬	Fine grass and feathers • lined with grass and moss • in scrape or shallow depression • built by female • 4–7 greenish white to pale gray-green eggs, with brown and black markings; elliptical to oval, 0.8 x 0.6 inches.

| Plumage Sexes differ | Habitat | Migration Migratory | Weight 1.0 ounce |

DATE _____ TIME_____ LOCATION _____

Family EMBERIZIDAE	Species *Calcarius pictus*	Length 5.75–6.5 inches	Wingspan 10–11 inches

SMITH'S LONGSPUR

This bird is most often observed during winter months, foraging in pastures and other open areas, including airports, in the Midwest and farther south. Winter flocks often do not closely associate with other foraging longspurs, pipits, or Horned Larks. Smith's Longspur is not wary and allows close approach, but if pushed to flight the birds fly up in a zigzag, giving clicking call notes. The white outer tail feathers bordering the black tail are conspicuous in flight.

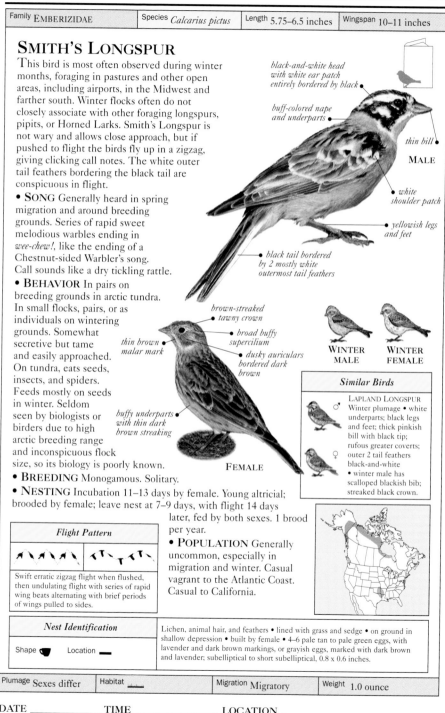

black-and-white head with white ear patch entirely bordered by black

buff-colored nape and underparts

thin bill

MALE

white shoulder patch

yellowish legs and feet

black tail bordered by 2 mostly white outermost tail feathers

- **SONG** Generally heard in spring migration and around breeding grounds. Series of rapid sweet melodious warbles ending in *wee-chew!*, like the ending of a Chestnut-sided Warbler's song. Call sounds like a dry tickling rattle.

- **BEHAVIOR** In pairs on breeding grounds in arctic tundra. In small flocks, pairs, or as individuals on wintering grounds. Somewhat secretive but tame and easily approached. On tundra, eats seeds, insects, and spiders. Feeds mostly on seeds in winter. Seldom seen by biologists or birders due to high arctic breeding range and inconspicuous flock size, so its biology is poorly known.

brown-streaked tawny crown

broad buffy supercilium

thin brown malar mark

dusky auriculars bordered dark brown

buffy underparts with thin dark brown streaking

FEMALE

WINTER MALE

WINTER FEMALE

Similar Birds

♂ LAPLAND LONGSPUR Winter plumage • white underparts; black legs and feet; thick pinkish bill with black tip; rufous greater coverts; outer 2 tail feathers black-and-white

♀ • winter male has scalloped blackish bib; streaked black crown.

- **BREEDING** Monogamous. Solitary.
- **NESTING** Incubation 11–13 days by female. Young altricial; brooded by female; leave nest at 7–9 days, with flight 14 days later, fed by both sexes. 1 brood per year.
- **POPULATION** Generally uncommon, especially in migration and winter. Casual vagrant to the Atlantic Coast. Casual to California.

Flight Pattern

Swift erratic zigzag flight when flushed, then undulating flight with series of rapid wing beats alternating with brief periods of wings pulled to sides.

Nest Identification

Shape ◗ Location ▬

Lichen, animal hair, and feathers • lined with grass and sedge • on ground in shallow depression • built by female • 4–6 pale tan to pale green eggs, with lavender and dark brown markings, or grayish eggs, marked with dark brown and lavender; subelliptical to short subelliptical, 0.8 x 0.6 inches.

Plumage Sexes differ	Habitat ▬▬	Migration Migratory	Weight 1.0 ounce

DATE _____ TIME_____ LOCATION _____

Family EMBERIZIDAE	Species *Calcarius ornatus*	Length 5.75–6.5 inches	Wingspan 10–10.75 inches

CHESTNUT-COLLARED LONGSPUR

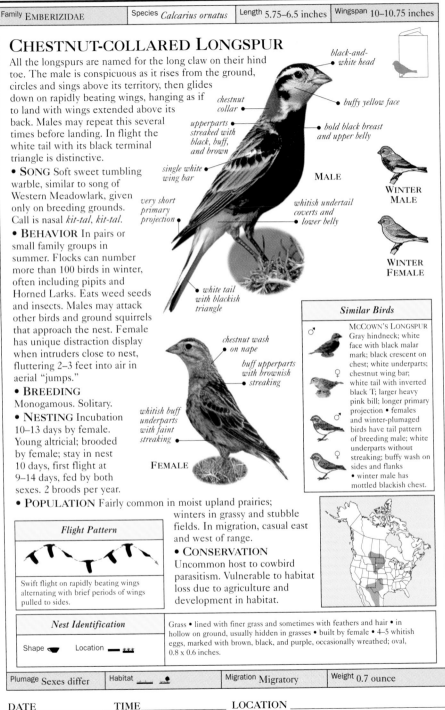

All the longspurs are named for the long claw on their hind toe. The male is conspicuous as it rises from the ground, circles and sings above its territory, then glides down on rapidly beating wings, hanging as if to land with wings extended above its back. Males may repeat this several times before landing. In flight the white tail with its black terminal triangle is distinctive.

- **SONG** Soft sweet tumbling warble, similar to song of Western Meadowlark, given only on breeding grounds. Call is nasal *kit-tal, kit-tal.*
- **BEHAVIOR** In pairs or small family groups in summer. Flocks can number more than 100 birds in winter, often including pipits and Horned Larks. Eats weed seeds and insects. Males may attack other birds and ground squirrels that approach the nest. Female has unique distraction display when intruders come close to nest, fluttering 2–3 feet into air in aerial "jumps."
- **BREEDING** Monogamous. Solitary.
- **NESTING** Incubation 10–13 days by female. Young altricial; brooded by female; stay in nest 10 days, first flight at 9–14 days, fed by both sexes. 2 broods per year.
- **POPULATION** Fairly common in moist upland prairies; winters in grassy and stubble fields. In migration, casual east and west of range.
- **CONSERVATION** Uncommon host to cowbird parasitism. Vulnerable to habitat loss due to agriculture and development in habitat.

black-and-white head

chestnut collar

upperparts streaked with black, buff, and brown

single white wing bar

very short primary projection

buffy yellow face

bold black breast and upper belly

MALE

whitish undertail coverts and lower belly

white tail with blackish triangle

WINTER MALE

WINTER FEMALE

chestnut wash on nape

buff upperparts with brownish streaking

whitish buff underparts with faint streaking

FEMALE

Similar Birds

♂ McCOWN'S LONGSPUR Gray hindneck; white face with black malar mark; black crescent on chest; white underparts.
♀ chestnut wing bar; white tail with inverted black T; larger heavy pink bill; longer primary projection • females and winter-plumaged birds have tail pattern of breeding male; white underparts without streaking; buffy wash on sides and flanks • winter male has mottled blackish chest.

Flight Pattern

Swift flight on rapidly beating wings alternating with brief periods of wings pulled to sides.

Nest Identification	Grass • lined with finer grass and sometimes with feathers and hair • in hollow on ground, usually hidden in grasses • built by female • 4–5 whitish eggs, marked with brown, black, and purple, occasionally wreathed; oval, 0.8 x 0.6 inches.
Shape ⌣ Location ▬ ꞏꞏꞏ	

Plumage Sexes differ	Habitat ▬ ♠	Migration Migratory	Weight 0.7 ounce

DATE _____ TIME_____ LOCATION _____

Family EMBERIZIDAE	Species *Emberiza rustica*	Length 5.75–6 inches	Wingspan 9–9.5 inches

RUSTIC BUNTING

This bird is a native of Eurasia and visits the Aleutians and other islands in the Bering Sea regularly during migration. It is casual along the Pacific Coast to California. Females and winter males are similar to breeding males but have a chestnut rump, brown crown, brown cheeks, a pale spot at the end of the ear patch, and white underparts streaked with brown. Juveniles are similar to females but are duller overall and have darker brown streaking.

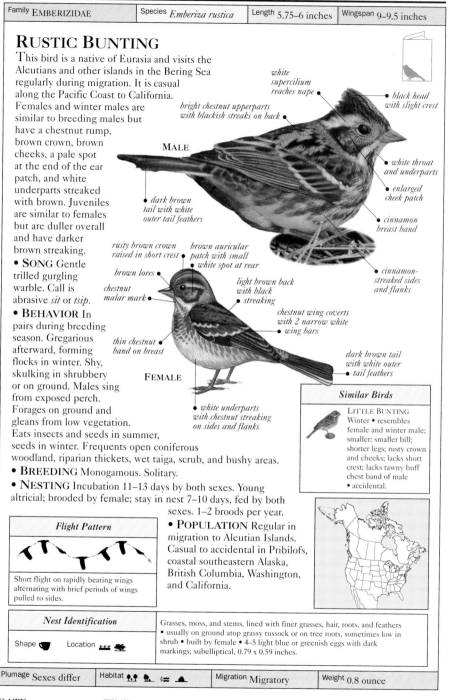

white supercilium reaches nape

bright chestnut upperparts with blackish streaks on back

black head with slight crest

MALE

white throat and underparts

enlarged cheek patch

cinnamon breast band

dark brown tail with white outer tail feathers

cinnamon-streaked sides and flanks

rusty brown crown raised in short crest

brown auricular patch with small white spot at rear

brown lores

light brown back with black streaking

chestnut malar mark

chestnut wing coverts with 2 narrow white wing bars

thin chestnut band on breast

dark brown tail with white outer tail feathers

FEMALE

white underparts with chestnut streaking on sides and flanks

• **SONG** Gentle trilled gurgling warble. Call is abrasive *sit* or *tsip*.

• **BEHAVIOR** In pairs during breeding season. Gregarious afterward, forming flocks in winter. Shy, skulking in shrubbery or on ground. Males sing from exposed perch. Forages on ground and gleans from low vegetation. Eats insects and seeds in summer, seeds in winter. Frequents open coniferous woodland, riparian thickets, wet taiga, scrub, and bushy areas.

• **BREEDING** Monogamous. Solitary.

• **NESTING** Incubation 11–13 days by both sexes. Young altricial; brooded by female; stay in nest 7–10 days, fed by both sexes. 1–2 broods per year.

• **POPULATION** Regular in migration to Aleutian Islands. Casual to accidental in Pribilofs, coastal southeastern Alaska, British Columbia, Washington, and California.

Similar Birds

LITTLE BUNTING
Winter • resembles female and winter male; smaller; smaller bill; shorter legs; rusty crown and cheeks; lacks short crest; lacks tawny buff chest band of male • accidental.

Flight Pattern

Short flight on rapidly beating wings alternating with brief periods of wings pulled to sides.

Nest Identification	
Shape ◣ Location ••• 🌳	Grasses, moss, and stems, lined with finer grasses, hair, roots, and feathers • usually on ground atop grassy tussock or on tree roots, sometimes low in shrub • built by female • 4–5 light blue or greenish eggs with dark markings; subelliptical, 0.79 x 0.59 inches.

Plumage Sexes differ	Habitat 🌿🌿 🦅 ⬚ ⛰	Migration Migratory	Weight 0.8 ounce

DATE _____ TIME_____ LOCATION _____

Family EMBERIZIDAE	Species *Emberiza aureola*	Length 5.5 inches	Wingspan 9 inches

YELLOW-BREASTED BUNTING

The bold chestnut breast band, midway between the black face and white shoulder patch, is conspicuous against the yellow underparts of this bunting. A Eurasian native; stragglers occasionally visit the western Aleutians in spring migration. The male's chestnut breast band, white shoulder patches, and white outer tail feathers are conspicuous in flight. The male's molt to basic plumage leaves him similar in appearance to the female, with dark brown streaking on his brown back and streaking on the sides and flanks of his yellow underparts. He retains, however, a mostly chestnut crown and nape, a broken chestnut breast band, and a streaky black face. Juveniles are similar to females but have yellow washes on their whitish underparts and more extensively streaked underparts.

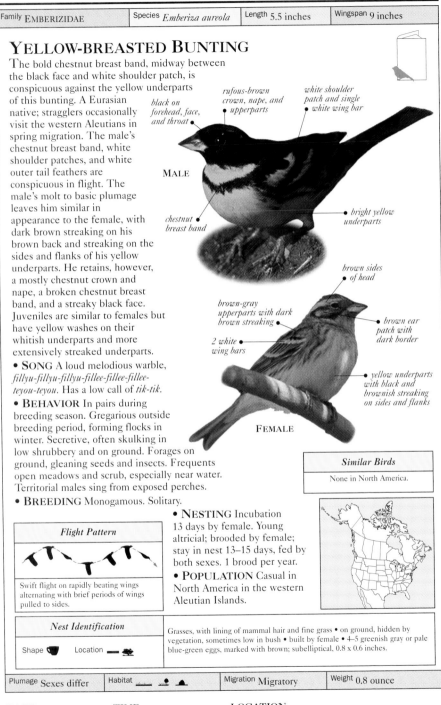

rufous-brown crown, nape, and upperparts

white shoulder patch and single white wing bar

black on forehead, face, and throat

MALE

chestnut breast band

bright yellow underparts

brown sides of head

brown-gray upperparts with dark brown streaking

brown ear patch with dark border

2 white wing bars

yellow underparts with black and brownish streaking on sides and flanks

FEMALE

- **SONG** A loud melodious warble, *fillyu-fillyu-fillyu-fillee-fillee-fillee-teyou-teyou*. Has a low call of *tik-tik*.
- **BEHAVIOR** In pairs during breeding season. Gregarious outside breeding period, forming flocks in winter. Secretive, often skulking in low shrubbery and on ground. Forages on ground, gleaning seeds and insects. Frequents open meadows and scrub, especially near water. Territorial males sing from exposed perches.
- **BREEDING** Monogamous. Solitary.
- **NESTING** Incubation 13 days by female. Young altricial; brooded by female; stay in nest 13–15 days, fed by both sexes. 1 brood per year.
- **POPULATION** Casual in North America in the western Aleutian Islands.

Similar Birds
None in North America.

Flight Pattern

Swift flight on rapidly beating wings alternating with brief periods of wings pulled to sides.

Nest Identification

Shape • Location

Grasses, with lining of mammal hair and fine grass • on ground, hidden by vegetation, sometimes low in bush • built by female • 4–5 greenish gray or pale blue-green eggs, marked with brown; subelliptical, 0.8 x 0.6 inches.

Plumage Sexes differ	Habitat	Migration Migratory	Weight 0.8 ounce

DATE _____ TIME_____ LOCATION _____

Family EMBERIZIDAE	Species *Emberiza schoeniclus*	Length 6–7.25 inches	Wingspan 9–10 inches

REED BUNTING

Vagrants of this Eurasian species are sometimes observed on the western islands of the Aleutians. This bird constantly flicks its tail up and down as it forages and hops through the reed beds and thickets of freshwater or saltwater marshes. Alternate-plumaged males in flight show a black hood broken only by a white mustache and bordered by a complete white collar. Their rusty chestnut shoulder patches contrast with the browner back, and the blackish brown tail is bordered by white outer tail feathers and tail corners. All individuals show white outer tail feathers when flying. Winter and juvenile males show a brown triangular patch on the throat and upper breast.

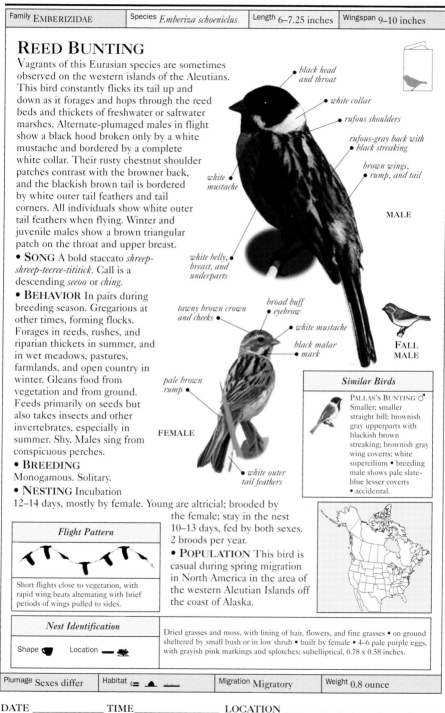

black head and throat

white collar

rufous shoulders

rufous-gray back with black streaking

brown wings, rump, and tail

MALE

white mustache

white belly, breast, and underparts

• **SONG** A bold staccato *shreep-shreep-teeree-tititick*. Call is a descending *seeoo* or *ching*.

• **BEHAVIOR** In pairs during breeding season. Gregarious at other times, forming flocks. Forages in reeds, rushes, and riparian thickets in summer, and in wet meadows, pastures, farmlands, and open country in winter. Gleans food from vegetation and from ground. Feeds primarily on seeds but also takes insects and other invertebrates, especially in summer. Shy. Males sing from conspicuous perches.

• **BREEDING** Monogamous. Solitary.

• **NESTING** Incubation 12–14 days, mostly by female. Young are altricial; brooded by

tawny brown crown and cheeks

broad buff eyebrow

white mustache

black malar mark

FALL MALE

pale brown rump

FEMALE

white outer tail feathers

Similar Birds

PALLAS'S BUNTING ♂ Smaller; smaller straight bill; brownish gray upperparts with blackish brown streaking; brownish gray wing coverts; white supercilium • breeding male shows pale slate-blue lesser coverts • accidental.

the female; stay in the nest 10–13 days, fed by both sexes. 2 broods per year.

• **POPULATION** This bird is casual during spring migration in North America in the area of the western Aleutian Islands off the coast of Alaska.

Flight Pattern
Short flights close to vegetation, with rapid wing beats alternating with brief periods of wings pulled to sides.

Nest Identification	
Shape ◗ Location ▬ ✿	Dried grasses and moss, with lining of hair, flowers, and fine grasses • on ground sheltered by small bush or in low shrub • built by female • 4–6 pale purple eggs, with grayish pink markings and splotches; subelliptical, 0.78 x 0.58 inches.

Plumage Sexes differ	Habitat 〜 ▲ 〜	Migration Migratory	Weight 0.8 ounce

DATE _____ TIME _____ LOCATION _____

Family EMBERIZIDAE	Species *Plectrophenax nivalis*	Length 6.25–7.25 inches	Wingspan 12–13 inches

SNOW BUNTING

This bird can survive temperatures as low as fifty-eight degrees below zero and often tunnels in the snow in the shelter of grass tussocks or shrubs to keep warm. When seen in flight from below, it often appears completely white, like a large snowflake. Males have a white rump. Nonbreeding females have a cinnamon rump and shoulders.

• **SONG** Series of bold repetitive high trilling musical notes. Sings only on breeding grounds, usually in fluttering display flight and from the ground. Call is whistling *teu*.

• **BEHAVIOR** In pairs on breeding grounds. Fledged young quickly form foraging flocks when independent of parental care. Gregarious after breeding, often roosting, traveling, and feeding in large flocks. Frequently bathes in snow. Forages on ground for seeds, insects, and caterpillars. Coastal birds also feed on small crustaceans and mollusks. Joins other open-landscape bird species in winter, including Lapland Longspurs and Horned Larks.

• **BREEDING** Monogamous. Pairs.

• **NESTING** Incubation 10–16 days by female. Young altricial; brooded by female; stay in nest 10–17 days, fed by both sexes. 1 brood per year; birds in the southern limits of range occasionally have 2 broods.

• **POPULATION** Fairly common in summer on arctic rocky shores, dry tundra, cliffs, and talus slopes; winters in stubble fields, grassy fields, and on coastal beaches and around sand dunes.

• **BIRDHOUSES** Will build nest in birdhouses.

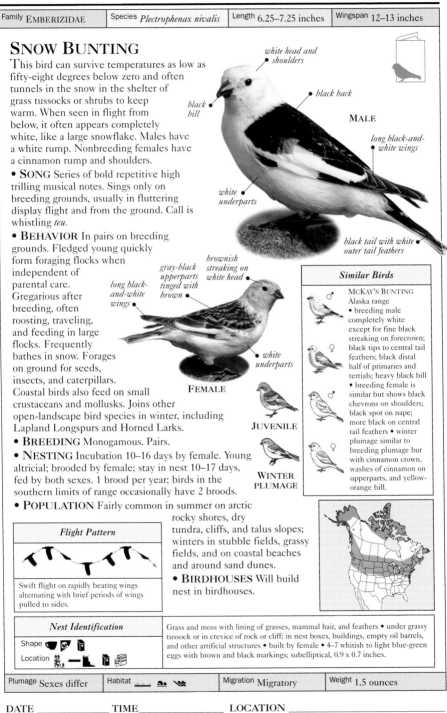

white head and shoulders

black bill

black back

MALE

long black-and-white wings

white underparts

black tail with white outer tail feathers

long black-and-white wings

gray-black upperparts tinged with brown

brownish streaking on white head

white underparts

FEMALE

JUVENILE

WINTER PLUMAGE

Similar Birds

♂ MCKAY'S BUNTING
Alaska range
• breeding male completely white except for fine black streaking on forecrown; black tips to central tail feathers; black distal half of primaries and tertials; heavy black bill
• breeding female is similar but shows black chevrons on shoulders; black spot on nape; more black on central tail feathers • winter plumage similar to breeding plumage but with cinnamon crown, washes of cinnamon on upperparts, and yellow-orange bill.

Flight Pattern

Swift flight on rapidly beating wings alternating with brief periods of wings pulled to sides.

Nest Identification

Shape

Location

Grass and moss with lining of grasses, mammal hair, and feathers • under grassy tussock or in crevice of rock or cliff; in nest boxes, buildings, empty oil barrels, and other artificial structures • built by female • 4–7 whitish to light blue-green eggs with brown and black markings; subelliptical, 0.9 x 0.7 inches.

Plumage Sexes differ	Habitat	Migration Migratory	Weight 1.5 ounces

DATE _____ TIME_____ LOCATION _____

Family EMBERIZIDAE	Species *Plectrophenax hyperboreus*	Length 6.25–7.25 inches	Wingspan 12–13 inches

McKay's Bunting

Said to be the whitest of all North American songbirds, this bird is closely related to the Snow Bunting, and some consider it to be part of the same species. It has a limited breeding range of only a few Bering Sea islands (Hall and St. Matthew and rarely on St. Paul in the Pribilofs or on St. Lawrence). It winters on the western and southeastern coasts of Alaska. Winter-plumaged birds have yellow-orange bills with black tips and cinnamon-washed crowns, napes, auriculars, and upperparts.

• SONG A loud trilled flutelike warbling, similar to the Snow Bunting's song. Call is abrasive *tew*.

• BEHAVIOR In pairs during breeding season. Gregarious at other times. Male performs courtship flights, skylarking in circles over female. Also sings from perches or from ground. Forages on ground. Eats seeds, spiders, flowers, leaflets, and insects. Breeds on shores of tundra pools, rocky ground, and beaches.

• BREEDING Monogamous and solitary.

• NESTING Incubation 10–16 days by female. Young altricial; brooded by female; stay in nest 10–17 days, fed by both sexes. 2 broods per year.

• POPULATION Uncommon to fairly common on breeding islands. Uncommon in winter in coastal Alaska. Accidental south to Oregon.

• BIRDHOUSES Nest boxes.

• CONSERVATION Seriously threatened by native and introduced predators on its nesting islands.

bright white overall

black distal half of primaries

black tertials

black tips to central tail feathers

large black bill

black legs and feet

MALE

bill has blackish upper mandible and paler dusky lower mandible

fine black streaking on crown and nape

black chevron streaking on back and shoulders

primaries have white base

black alula

FEMALE

more extensive black in central tail feathers

WINTER MALE

WINTER FEMALE

Similar Birds

♂ SNOW BUNTING Breeding adults have black or smoky gray back; more black on wings and tail • winter plumage shows more black on wings and tail; more black streaking on upperparts; more extensive cinnamon wash on underparts; cinnamon on crown, auriculars, nape, and back • basic-plumaged female also shows cinnamon rump.

♀

Flight Pattern

Swift flight with series of rapid wing beats alternating with brief periods of wings pulled to sides.

Nest Identification

Shape

Location

Grass with lining of finer grasses • in rock crevice, building, nest box, or on ground under grass tussock or moss hummock • built by female • 3–5 pale green eggs with spots of pale brown; oval to subelliptical, 0.9 x 0.7 inches.

Plumage Sexes differ	Habitat	Migration Migratory	Weight 1.9 ounces

DATE _____ TIME_____ LOCATION _____

Family CARDINALIDAE	Species *Cardinalis cardinalis*	Length 7.5–9.25 inches	Wingspan 10–12 inches

NORTHERN CARDINAL

The official bird of seven US states sings a variety of cheerful melodies year-round. The male fights other birds to defend his territory and sometimes tries to attack his own reflection in windows, automobile mirrors, chrome, and hubcaps. Having adapted to suburban areas, these birds visit backyard feeders regularly and sometimes take food from the hand. Juveniles resemble the adult female but have a blackish instead of reddish bill.

• **SONG** Variable. Variety of gurgling and clear whistled melodies. More than 25 different songs. Best-known phrases include *whoit cheer, whoit cheer, cheer-cheer-cheer; cheer; whoit-whoit-whoit-whoit; wheat-wheat-wheat-wheat;* and *bir-dy, bir-dy, bir-dy, bir-dy.* Female in courtship duets with male after territory is established and prior to nesting. Call is abrasive metallic *chip* or *pik.*

• **BEHAVIOR** Solitary or in pairs during breeding season. Gregarious at other times, forming flocks in winter or joining mixed-species foraging flocks. Forages in trees, bushes, and on ground. Eats insects, seeds, grains, fruits, and snails. Drinks sap from holes drilled by sapsuckers. Hops rather than walks on ground.

• **BREEDING** Monogamous. Solitary. Male feeds female during courtship and while incubating.

• **NESTING** Incubation 12–13 days, mostly by female. Young altricial; brooded by female; stay in nest 9–11 days, fed by both sexes. Male may continue to tend fledglings while female begins incubating new set of eggs. 2–4 broods per year.

• **POPULATION** Abundant and widespread in woodland edges, undergrowth, thickets, and residential areas. Range has expanded north in the last century, partly due to increase of feeding stations. Casual in West.

• **FEEDERS** Cracked corn, sunflower seeds, birdseed. Will bathe in birdbaths.

• **CONSERVATION** Common cowbird host, especially in the central portion of its range.

accentuated crest

black mask through eyes

cone-shaped reddish bill

black patch at base of bill extends onto throat

red overall

MALE

red tip

dusky lores and patch at base of bill

buffy golden brown head and underparts

buffy olive upperparts

FEMALE

buff-brown underparts

red wash on wings and tail

JUVENILE

Similar Birds

PYRRHULOXIA ♀
Resembles female and juvenile Northern Cardinal; stubby sharply curved yellowish bill; red eye ring; red tip to long gray crest; grayish upperparts; red edging to primaries; reddish wash on throat and underparts.

Flight Pattern

Short flight just above vegetation or below canopy; rapidly beating wings alternate with brief periods of wings pulled to sides.

Nest Identification

Shape ◣   Location 🌳🌿🌲

Twigs, weeds, grass, bark strips, and leaves • lined with hair and grass • in fork of low tree or bush or set in tangled twigs or vines • usually less than 5 feet above ground (but up to 15 feet) • built by female • 3–4 pale greenish, bluish, or grayish eggs with dots and flecks of gray, purple, and brown; oval, 1.0 x 0.7 inches.

Plumage Sexes differ	Habitat 🌿 🌱 🌾	Migration Nonmigratory	Weight 1.6 ounces

DATE _____ TIME_____ LOCATION _____

Family CARDINALIDAE	Species *Cardinalis sinuatus*	Length 8.75 inches	Wingspan 11.25 inches

PYRRHULOXIA

This long-crested bird of southwestern North America and Mexico looks like a gray cardinal with a parrotlike bill. Both the male and female aggressively defend their two- to three-acre territory until it is established, whereupon it becomes the duty of the male to maintain it. The female is similar to the male but has a buffy gray breast, a red tip to her gray crest, red washes on her throat and the midline of her breast and belly, and red edging to her primaries. In winter the yellow bill of both sexes turns grayish yellow. In flight the underwing coverts flash red.

• **SONG** Varied series of rich loud whistles, *chewee, chewee, chewee; wheet-wheet-wheet,* very similar to Northern Cardinal. Call is sharp metallic *plik* or *chink.*

• **BEHAVIOR** Solitary or in pairs during breeding season. Gregarious at other times, forming flocks in winter. Often joins mixed-species foraging flocks in winter. Forages for food in trees, bushes, and on ground but spends much time on ground, where it hops instead of walks. Eats flower spikes, various fruits, berries, seeds, insects, and larvae. Male sings from exposed perch.

• **BREEDING** Monogamous. Solitary.

• **NESTING** Incubation 14 days by female. Young altricial; brooded by female; leave nest at 10–11 days, fed by both sexes. 1 brood per year.

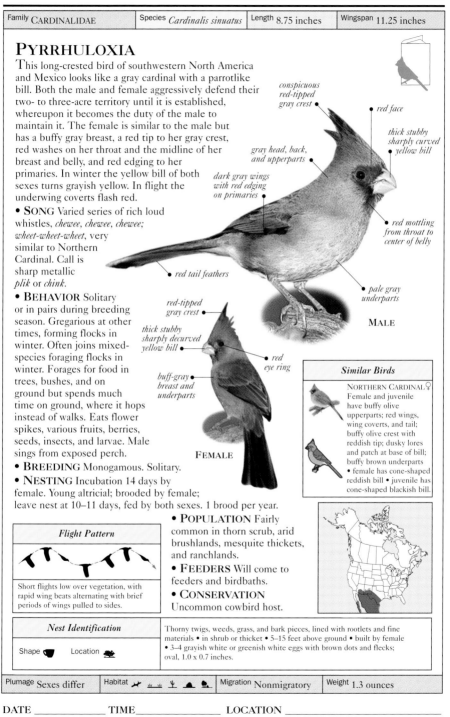

conspicuous red-tipped gray crest

red face

thick stubby sharply curved yellow bill

gray head, back, and upperparts

dark gray wings with red edging on primaries

red mottling from throat to center of belly

red tail feathers

pale gray underparts

MALE

red-tipped gray crest

thick stubby sharply decurved yellow bill

buff-gray breast and underparts

red eye ring

FEMALE

Similar Birds

NORTHERN CARDINAL.♀ Female and juvenile have buffy olive upperparts; red wings, wing coverts, and tail; buffy olive crest with reddish tip; dusky lores and patch at base of bill; buffy brown underparts • female has cone-shaped reddish bill • juvenile has cone-shaped blackish bill.

• **POPULATION** Fairly common in thorn scrub, arid brushlands, mesquite thickets, and ranchlands.

• **FEEDERS** Will come to feeders and birdbaths.

• **CONSERVATION** Uncommon cowbird host.

Flight Pattern

Short flights low over vegetation, with rapid wing beats alternating with brief periods of wings pulled to sides.

Nest Identification

Shape ❤   Location 🌳

Thorny twigs, weeds, grass, and bark pieces, lined with rootlets and fine materials • in shrub or thicket • 5–15 feet above ground • built by female • 3–4 grayish white or greenish white eggs with brown dots and flecks; oval, 1.0 x 0.7 inches.

Plumage Sexes differ	Habitat 🦌 ⚘ ⚘ 🌿 🌲 🏔	Migration Nonmigratory	Weight 1.3 ounces

DATE _____ TIME_____ LOCATION _____

Family CARDINALIDAE	Species *Pheucticus chrysopeplus*	Length 8.5–9.25 inches	Wingspan 12–13 inches

YELLOW GROSBEAK

This bright yellow-and-black bird looks like a large American Goldfinch or an oriole, but the heavy dark bill is definitive of a grosbeak. Native to western Mexico, vagrants sometimes visit southeastern Arizona in summer, where they frequent riparian areas and canyons. Juveniles resemble adult females but have a pale lemon-yellow throat and underparts.

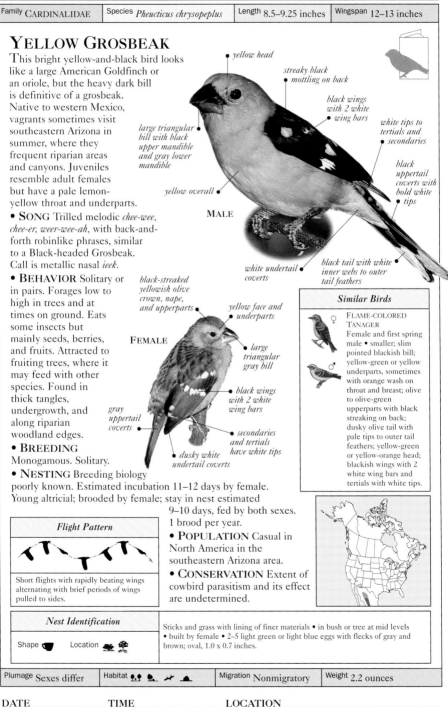

yellow head

streaky black mottling on back

black wings with 2 white wing bars

white tips to tertials and secondaries

black uppertail coverts with bold white tips

large triangular bill with black upper mandible and gray lower mandible

yellow overall

MALE

• **SONG** Trilled melodic *chee-wee, chee-er, weer-wee-ah*, with back-and-forth robinlike phrases, similar to a Black-headed Grosbeak. Call is metallic nasal *ieek*.

white undertail coverts

black tail with white inner webs to outer tail feathers

• **BEHAVIOR** Solitary or in pairs. Forages low to high in trees and at times on ground. Eats some insects but mainly seeds, berries, and fruits. Attracted to fruiting trees, where it may feed with other species. Found in thick tangles, undergrowth, and along riparian woodland edges.

black-streaked yellowish olive crown, nape, and upperparts

yellow face and underparts

FEMALE

large triangular gray bill

black wings with 2 white wing bars

gray uppertail coverts

secondaries and tertials have white tips

dusky white undertail coverts

• **BREEDING** Monogamous. Solitary.

• **NESTING** Breeding biology poorly known. Estimated incubation 11–12 days by female. Young altricial; brooded by female; stay in nest estimated 9–10 days, fed by both sexes. 1 brood per year.

Similar Birds

FLAME-COLORED TANAGER
Female and first spring male • smaller; slim pointed blackish bill; yellow-green or yellow underparts, sometimes with orange wash on throat and breast; olive to olive-green upperparts with black streaking on back; dusky olive tail with pale tips to outer tail feathers; yellow-green or yellow-orange head; blackish wings with 2 white wing bars and tertials with white tips.

• **POPULATION** Casual in North America in the southeastern Arizona area.

• **CONSERVATION** Extent of cowbird parasitism and its effect are undetermined.

Flight Pattern
Short flights with rapidly beating wings alternating with brief periods of wings pulled to sides.

Nest Identification	
Shape ⌣ Location 🌳🌿	Sticks and grass with lining of finer materials • in bush or tree at mid levels • built by female • 2–5 light green or light blue eggs with flecks of gray and brown; oval, 1.0 x 0.7 inches.

Plumage Sexes differ	Habitat 🌾🐦🦆✈🏔	Migration Nonmigratory	Weight 2.2 ounces

DATE _____ TIME_____ LOCATION _____

Family CARDINALIDAE	Species *Pheucticus ludovicianus*	Length 7–8.5 inches	Wingspan 12–13 inches

ROSE-BREASTED GROSBEAK

This bird's clear notes are delivered in robinlike phrases, but the song is sweet. Males sing constantly, even while sparring to win a female. In flight the male shows rosy red wing linings and white rump; females flash yellow wing linings. First fall males have less streaking on underparts than females, buffy wash across the breast, and rose-red wing linings. First spring males are similar to adult males but with brown edges to the black plumage.

- **SONG** Rich warbled melodious phrases interspersed with call notes. Squeaky abrasive call, *eek*.
- **BEHAVIOR** Solitary or in pairs in breeding season. Flocks in migration and winter. Forages in trees, shrubs, and on ground. Eats seeds, insects, caterpillars, tree flowers, fruits, and berries. Hover gleans high in trees at branch tips; females more often than males.
- **BREEDING** Monogamous. Solitary. Male and female rub bills to display affection during courtship.
- **NESTING** Incubation 13–14 days by both sexes. Altricial young brooded by both sexes, more by female; stay in nest 9–12 days, fed by both sexes. Male may tend while female begins second nesting. 1–2 broods per year.
- **POPULATION** Common to fairly common in deciduous forest, woodland, and second growth. Rare migrant in West. Rare to accidental in winter on southern California coast.
- **FEEDERS** Use increases during migration.
- **CONSERVATION** Neotropical migrant. Common cowbird host. Vulnerable to habitat loss due to logging.

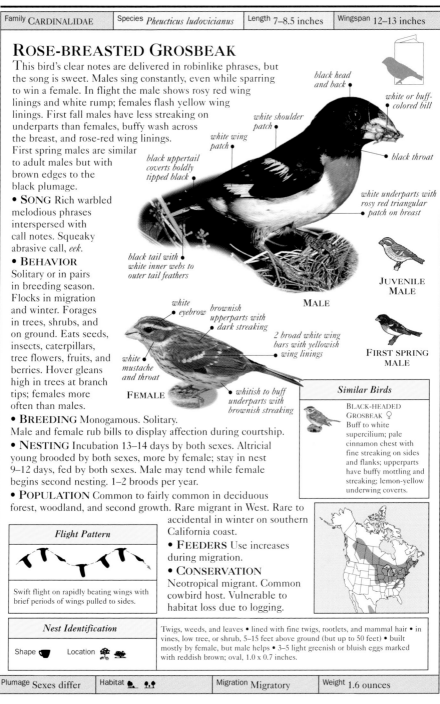

black head and back

white or buff-colored bill

white shoulder patch

white wing patch

black uppertail coverts boldly tipped black

black throat

white underparts with rosy red triangular patch on breast

black tail with white inner webs to outer tail feathers

MALE

JUVENILE MALE

white eyebrow

brownish upperparts with dark streaking

2 broad white wing bars with yellowish wing linings

FIRST SPRING MALE

white mustache and throat

FEMALE

whitish to buff underparts with brownish streaking

Similar Birds

BLACK-HEADED GROSBEAK ♀
Buff to white supercilium; pale cinnamon chest with fine streaking on sides and flanks; upperparts have buffy mottling and streaking; lemon-yellow underwing coverts.

Flight Pattern
Swift flight on rapidly beating wings with brief periods of wings pulled to sides.

Nest Identification	
Shape ▭ Location ❀ ❁	Twigs, weeds, and leaves • lined with fine twigs, rootlets, and mammal hair • in vines, low tree, or shrub, 5–15 feet above ground (but up to 50 feet) • built mostly by female, but male helps • 3–5 light greenish or bluish eggs marked with reddish brown; oval, 1.0 x 0.7 inches.

Plumage Sexes differ	Habitat 🌿 🌳	Migration Migratory	Weight 1.6 ounces

DATE _____ TIME_____ LOCATION _____

Family CARDINALIDAE	Species *Pheucticus melanocephalus*	Length 7–8.5 inches	Wingspan 12–13 inches

BLACK-HEADED GROSBEAK

Easily observed in western woodlands, this tame bird attends feeders and sometimes takes food from the hand. Both sexes aggressively defend their territory from other grosbeaks. Lemon wing linings are conspicuous in flight. First fall males have rich cinnamon-buff underparts, blackish brown cheek patches, white eyebrow and mustache, and white tips to tertials.

• **SONG** Rich back-and-forth series of warbled phrases, robinlike. Similar to Rose-breasted Grosbeak but lower pitched. Female sings less with more variations. Call is high squeaky *plik*.

• **BEHAVIOR** Solitary or in pairs in breeding season. Gregarious in migration and winter; may form flocks. Forages in trees, bushes, and on ground. Eats seeds, insects, caterpillars, berries, and fruits. Some hybridize with Rose-breasted Grosbeak where ranges overlap in Great Plains. Both sexes may sing "whisper" songs while incubating and brooding.

• **BREEDING** Monogamous. Solitary.

• **NESTING** Incubation 12–14 days by both sexes. Altricial young brooded by both sexes, more by female; stay in nest 11–12 days, fed by both sexes. 1 brood per year.

• **POPULATION** Common to fairly common in open woodlands, especially pine-oak and oak, forest edge, and riparian woodlands. Casual in migration and winter to the Midwest and the East.

• **FEEDERS** Various seeds.

• **CONSERVATION** Neotropical migrant. Uncommon cowbird host. Vulnerable to habitat loss due to logging and fires.

black head

cinnamon-orange hind collar and postocular stripe

large dark conical bill

black upperparts with brown edging to feathers

MALE

2 white wing bars

white patch at base of primaries

cinnamon rump

cinnamon underparts

black tail with white inner webs to outer tail feathers

brown head and upperparts with dark streaking

white median crown stripe

white supercilium and mustache

2 white wing bars

pale cinnamon throat and underparts

JUVENILE MALE

lemon wash on belly

white undertail coverts

fine brown streaks on sides and flanks

FEMALE

Similar Birds

ROSE-BREASTED GROSBEAK ♀ Heavier streaked white to buffy underparts; darker upperparts; brown edging to feathers on back; gray to pale creamy pink bill; paler upper mandible.

Flight Pattern

Short flights with rapid wing beats alternating with brief periods of wings pulled to sides.

Nest Identification

Shape ☕ Location 🌿 🌳

Sticks, weeds, rootlets, and pine needles, lined with finer materials • in dense part of tree or shrub, usually near water, about 4–25 feet above ground • built by female • 3–4 light greenish or bluish eggs dotted with reddish brown; oval, 1.0 x 0.7 inches.

Plumage Sexes differ	Habitat 🌿🌳	Migration Migratory	Weight 1.5 ounces

DATE _____ TIME_____ LOCATION _____

Family CARDINALIDAE	Species *Guiraca caerulea*	Length 6.25–7.5 inches	Wingspan 10.5–11.5 inches

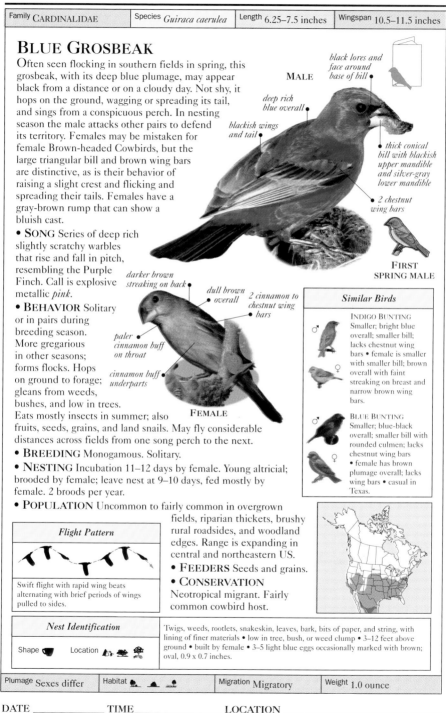

BLUE GROSBEAK

Often seen flocking in southern fields in spring, this grosbeak, with its deep blue plumage, may appear black from a distance or on a cloudy day. Not shy, it hops on the ground, wagging or spreading its tail, and sings from a conspicuous perch. In nesting season the male attacks other pairs to defend its territory. Females may be mistaken for female Brown-headed Cowbirds, but the large triangular bill and brown wing bars are distinctive, as is their behavior of raising a slight crest and flicking and spreading their tails. Females have a gray-brown rump that can show a bluish cast.

• **SONG** Series of deep rich slightly scratchy warbles that rise and fall in pitch, resembling the Purple Finch. Call is explosive metallic *pink*.

• **BEHAVIOR** Solitary or in pairs during breeding season. More gregarious in other seasons; forms flocks. Hops on ground to forage; gleans from weeds, bushes, and low in trees. Eats mostly insects in summer; also fruits, seeds, grains, and land snails. May fly considerable distances across fields from one song perch to the next.

• **BREEDING** Monogamous. Solitary.

• **NESTING** Incubation 11–12 days by female. Young altricial; brooded by female; leave nest at 9–10 days, fed mostly by female. 2 broods per year.

• **POPULATION** Uncommon to fairly common in overgrown fields, riparian thickets, brushy rural roadsides, and woodland edges. Range is expanding in central and northeastern US.

• **FEEDERS** Seeds and grains.

• **CONSERVATION** Neotropical migrant. Fairly common cowbird host.

MALE

black lores and face around base of bill

deep rich blue overall

blackish wings and tail

thick conical bill with blackish upper mandible and silver-gray lower mandible

2 chestnut wing bars

FIRST SPRING MALE

darker brown streaking on back

dull brown overall

2 cinnamon to chestnut wing bars

paler cinnamon buff on throat

cinnamon buff underparts

FEMALE

Similar Birds

INDIGO BUNTING Smaller; bright blue overall; smaller bill; lacks chestnut wing bars • female is smaller with smaller bill; brown overall with faint streaking on breast and narrow brown wing bars.

BLUE BUNTING Smaller; blue-black overall; smaller bill with rounded culmen; lacks chestnut wing bars • female has brown plumage overall; lacks wing bars • casual in Texas.

Flight Pattern
Swift flight with rapid wing beats alternating with brief periods of wings pulled to sides.

Nest Identification	
Shape	Location	Twigs, weeds, rootlets, snakeskin, leaves, bark, bits of paper, and string, with lining of finer materials • low in tree, bush, or weed clump • 3–12 feet above ground • built by female • 3–5 light blue eggs occasionally marked with brown; oval, 0.9 x 0.7 inches.

Plumage Sexes differ	Habitat	Migration Migratory	Weight 1.0 ounce

DATE _____ TIME_____ LOCATION _____

Family CARDINALIDAE	Species *Passerina amoena*	Length 5.25–5.75 inches	Wingspan 8–9 inches

LAZULI BUNTING

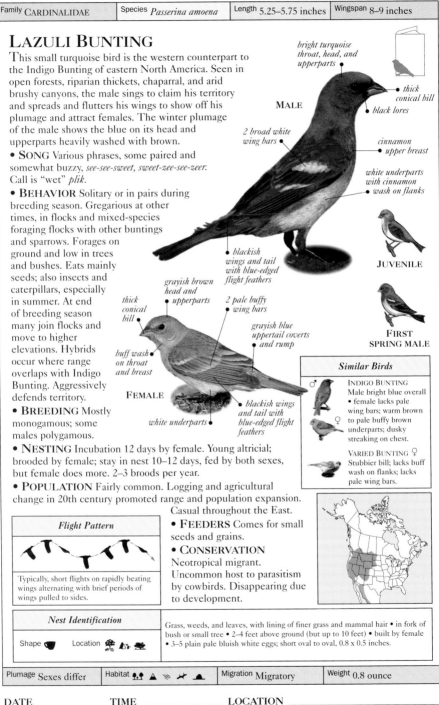

This small turquoise bird is the western counterpart to the Indigo Bunting of eastern North America. Seen in open forests, riparian thickets, chaparral, and arid brushy canyons, the male sings to claim his territory and spreads and flutters his wings to show off his plumage and attract females. The winter plumage of the male shows the blue on its head and upperparts heavily washed with brown.

• **SONG** Various phrases, some paired and somewhat buzzy, *see-see-sweet, sweet-zee-see-zeer.* Call is "wet" *plik.*

• **BEHAVIOR** Solitary or in pairs during breeding season. Gregarious at other times, in flocks and mixed-species foraging flocks with other buntings and sparrows. Forages on ground and low in trees and bushes. Eats mainly seeds; also insects and caterpillars, especially in summer. At end of breeding season many join flocks and move to higher elevations. Hybrids occur where range overlaps with Indigo Bunting. Aggressively defends territory.

• **BREEDING** Mostly monogamous; some males polygamous.

• **NESTING** Incubation 12 days by female. Young altricial; brooded by female; stay in nest 10–12 days, fed by both sexes, but female does more. 2–3 broods per year.

• **POPULATION** Fairly common. Logging and agricultural change in 20th century promoted range and population expansion. Casual throughout the East.

• **FEEDERS** Comes for small seeds and grains.

• **CONSERVATION** Neotropical migrant. Uncommon host to parasitism by cowbirds. Disappearing due to development.

bright turquoise throat, head, and upperparts

thick conical bill

black lores

MALE

2 broad white wing bars

cinnamon upper breast

white underparts with cinnamon wash on flanks

JUVENILE

blackish wings and tail with blue-edged flight feathers

grayish brown head and upperparts

2 pale buffy wing bars

grayish blue uppertail coverts and rump

thick conical bill

buff wash on throat and breast

FEMALE

blackish wings and tail with blue-edged flight feathers

white underparts

FIRST SPRING MALE

Similar Birds

♂ **INDIGO BUNTING** Male bright blue overall • female lacks pale wing bars; warm brown to pale buffy brown underparts; dusky streaking on chest. ♀

VARIED BUNTING ♀ Stubbier bill; lacks buff wash on flanks; lacks pale wing bars.

Flight Pattern

Typically, short flights on rapidly beating wings alternating with brief periods of wings pulled to sides.

Nest Identification

Shape ▬   Location 🌳 🔺 🌳

Grass, weeds, and leaves, with lining of finer grass and mammal hair • in fork of bush or small tree • 2–4 feet above ground (but up to 10 feet) • built by female • 3–5 plain pale bluish white eggs; short oval to oval, 0.8 x 0.5 inches.

Plumage Sexes differ	Habitat 👥 🔺 🌿 ✈ 🌲	Migration Migratory	Weight 0.8 ounce

DATE _____ TIME_____ LOCATION _____

Family CARDINALIDAE	Species *Passerina cyanea*	Length 5.25–5.75 inches	Wingspan 8–9 inches

INDIGO BUNTING

The male's distinctive plumage looks blue in sunlight and almost black in shade or backlighting. Populations are expanding with the creation of disturbed habitat after logging, highway and power line construction, and farmland abandonment. Its breeding range now includes much of the Southwest.

• **SONG** Series of varied measured strident phrases, usually paired, *sweet-sweet, sweeter-sweeter, here-here*, often with an added trilled ending. Call is a "wet" *spit* or *plik*.

• **BEHAVIOR** Solitary or in pairs during breeding season. Gregarious at other times; in flocks in winter, often with other buntings, sparrows, and finches. Forages in trees, shrubs, and on ground. Eats variety of insects and larvae, especially in summer; also dandelion seeds, weed seeds, grass seeds, small grains, and wild berries. Males defensive of territory; often engage in colorful chases with other males.

• **BREEDING** Monogamous. Solitary. Some males polygynous when outnumbered by females.

• **NESTING** Incubation 12–14 days by female. Young altricial; brooded by female; leave nest at 9–12 days, fed mostly by female; some males bring food. 2 broods per year.

• **POPULATION** Fairly common to common. Abundant in some deciduous forest edges, old fields, clearings, and agricultural areas. Expanding.

• **FEEDERS** Comes for small seeds and grains.

• **CONSERVATION** Neotropical migrant. Common host to cowbird parasitism. Some habitat loss due to maturation of cut-over forests.

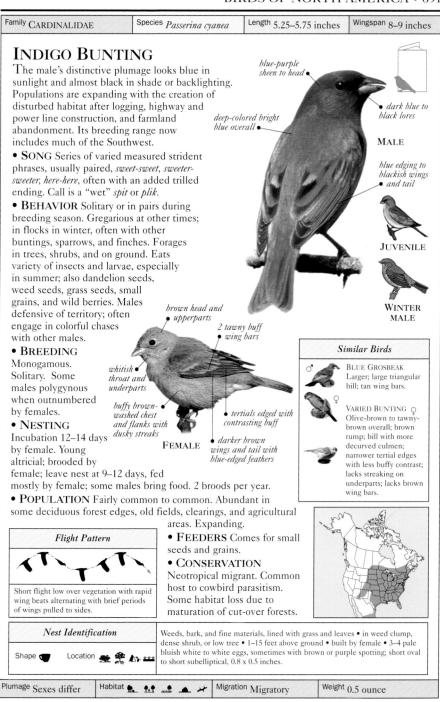

blue-purple sheen to head

dark blue to black lores

deep-colored bright blue overall

MALE

blue edging to blackish wings and tail

JUVENILE

WINTER MALE

brown head and upperparts

2 tawny buff wing bars

whitish throat and underparts

buffy brown-washed chest and flanks with dusky streaks

tertials edged with contrasting buff

darker brown wings and tail with blue-edged feathers

FEMALE

Similar Birds

♂ **BLUE GROSBEAK** Larger; large triangular bill; tan wing bars.

♀ **VARIED BUNTING** ♀ Olive-brown to tawny-brown overall; brown rump; bill with more decurved culmen; narrower tertial edges with less buffy contrast; lacks streaking on underparts; lacks brown wing bars.

Flight Pattern
Short flight low over vegetation with rapid wing beats alternating with brief periods of wings pulled to sides.

Nest Identification	Weeds, bark, and fine materials, lined with grass and leaves • in weed clump, dense shrub, or low tree • 1–15 feet above ground • built by female • 3–4 pale bluish white to white eggs, sometimes with brown or purple spotting; short oval to short subelliptical, 0.8 x 0.5 inches.
Shape ▽ Location 🌿 🌳 🔺 ⛺	

Plumage Sexes differ	Habitat 🌿 🌾 🔻 🔺 ✹	Migration Migratory	Weight 0.5 ounce

DATE _____ TIME_____ LOCATION _____

Family CARDINALIDAE	Species *Passerina versicolor*	Length 5–5.5 inches	Wingspan 8–8.5 inches

VARIED BUNTING

If this bird is seen in the open on a sunny day, the exquisite colors in the male's breeding plumage are striking: varied reds, violet-blues, deep purples, and blacks. When seen from a distance or in poor light, however, it appears black overall. In the molt to basic plumage following the breeding season, males show brownish rather than plum-colored plumage, and the red nape is faded and washed with browns, while the forecrown, face, and rump retain some blue. Juveniles resemble females but show narrow buff wing bars and a brighter brown body.

• **SONG** Various high-pitched slightly scratchy thin warbles similar to the song of the Painted Bunting. Call is a "wet" *spik*.

• **BEHAVIOR** Solitary or in pairs during breeding season. Solitary or in small groups at other times. Shy and secretive. Remains hidden in thickets close to ground and often distances itself from human habitation. Forages in low dense vegetation or on ground. Takes some insects but major diet is seeds. Bonded pairs spend much time together. Male sings from exposed perch. Natural history is poorly studied.

• **BREEDING** Monogamous. Solitary.

• **NESTING** Breeding biology poorly known. Incubation 12–13 days by female. Young altricial; brooded by female; stay in nest estimated 12 days, fed by both sexes. 1–2 broods per year.

• **POPULATION** Common locally in mesquite chaparral, dry washes, and arid thorn scrub, often near water.

• **CONSERVATION** Neotropical migrant. Rare host to cowbird parasitism. Vulnerable to habitat loss from agriculture and development.

slightly curved grayish bill

deep red nape

blue-edged black wings and tail

deep violet-blue face, crown, and hind collar

royal blue rump

plum-purple throat, breast, and back

deep purple on lower belly and undertail coverts

MALE

gray-brown upperparts

slightly curved grayish bill

faint bluish sheen on wings and tail

pale buff underparts

FEMALE

WINTER PLUMAGE

Similar Birds

LAZULI BUNTING ♀
Gray-brown head and upperparts; white underparts; buffy wash on throat and breast; gray-blue rump; 2 narrow buffy white wing bars.

INDIGO BUNTING ♀
Brown head and upperparts; blue-tinged rump; tertials edged with buff; 2 tawny buff wing bars; whitish throat and underparts; chest and flanks washed buffy brown with dusky streaks.

Flight Pattern

Short flights close to vegetation, with rapid wing beats alternating with brief periods of wings pulled to sides.

Nest Identification

Shape ☕   Location 🌿 🌳 🔺

Stalks, grass, cotton, snakeskin, and paper, with lining of rootlets, grass, and hair • in fork of low tree or bush, usually 2–10 feet above ground • built by both sexes • 3–4 white to light blue eggs, characteristically unmarked; short to oval subelliptical, 0.7 x 0.5 inches.

Plumage Sexes differ	Habitat 🔺 ✈ ᵐ ᵐ 🔺	Migration Migratory	Weight 0.4 ounce

DATE _____ TIME_____ LOCATION _____

Family CARDINALIDAE	Species *Passerina ciris*	Length 5–5.5 inches	Wingspan 8–8.5 inches

PAINTED BUNTING

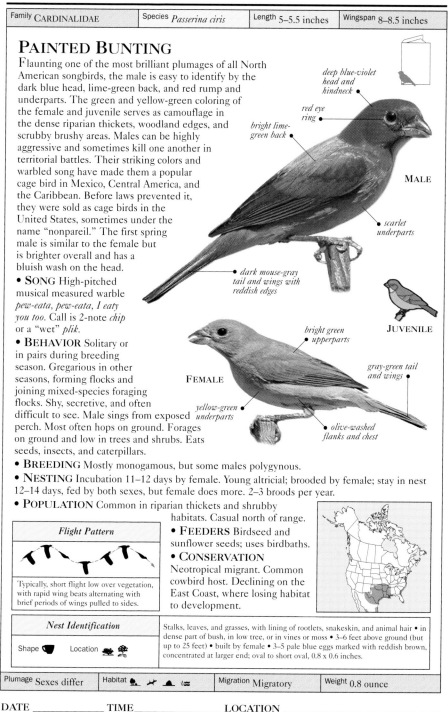

Flaunting one of the most brilliant plumages of all North American songbirds, the male is easy to identify by the dark blue head, lime-green back, and red rump and underparts. The green and yellow-green coloring of the female and juvenile serves as camouflage in the dense riparian thickets, woodland edges, and scrubby brushy areas. Males can be highly aggressive and sometimes kill one another in territorial battles. Their striking colors and warbled song have made them a popular cage bird in Mexico, Central America, and the Caribbean. Before laws prevented it, they were sold as cage birds in the United States, sometimes under the name "nonpareil." The first spring male is similar to the female but is brighter overall and has a bluish wash on the head.

deep blue-violet head and hindneck

red eye ring

bright lime-green back

MALE

scarlet underparts

dark mouse-gray tail and wings with reddish edges

JUVENILE

bright green upperparts

gray-green tail and wings

FEMALE

yellow-green underparts

olive-washed flanks and chest

• **SONG** High-pitched musical measured warble *pew-eata, pew-eata, I eaty you too.* Call is 2-note *chip* or a "wet" *plik.*

• **BEHAVIOR** Solitary or in pairs during breeding season. Gregarious in other seasons, forming flocks and joining mixed-species foraging flocks. Shy, secretive, and often difficult to see. Male sings from exposed perch. Most often hops on ground. Forages on ground and low in trees and shrubs. Eats seeds, insects, and caterpillars.

• **BREEDING** Mostly monogamous, but some males polygynous.

• **NESTING** Incubation 11–12 days by female. Young altricial; brooded by female; stay in nest 12–14 days, fed by both sexes, but female does more. 2–3 broods per year.

• **POPULATION** Common in riparian thickets and shrubby habitats. Casual north of range.

• **FEEDERS** Birdseed and sunflower seeds; uses birdbaths.

• **CONSERVATION** Neotropical migrant. Common cowbird host. Declining on the East Coast, where losing habitat to development.

Flight Pattern
Typically, short flight low over vegetation, with rapid wing beats alternating with brief periods of wings pulled to sides.

Nest Identification	
Shape ▼ Location 🌳 🌿	Stalks, leaves, and grasses, with lining of rootlets, snakeskin, and animal hair • in dense part of bush, in low tree, or in vines or moss • 3–6 feet above ground (but up to 25 feet) • built by female • 3–5 pale blue eggs marked with reddish brown, concentrated at larger end; oval to short oval, 0.8 x 0.6 inches.

Plumage Sexes differ	Habitat 🌳 🌾 🌲 〰	Migration Migratory	Weight 0.8 ounce

DATE _____ TIME _____ LOCATION _____

Family CARDINALIDAE	Species *Spiza americana*	Length 6–7 inches	Wingspan 9–11 inches

DICKCISSEL

This bird is named for its song of *dick-dick-dick-cissel*. Often flying in flocks over grassy prairies, the Dickcissel, with its black bib and yellow breast, looks like a small meadowlark. Females are similar to males but lack the black bib and have duller chestnut wing patches.

- **SONG** Staccato *dick-dick-dick-cissel*. Has an insectlike call of *bzzrrrt*.
- **BEHAVIOR** Solitary or in pairs during breeding season. Gregarious at other times, forming wintering flocks numbering thousands of birds. Joins communal roosts after breeding season. Male sings from exposed perches and in flight. Forages on ground. Eats grains, seeds, and insects.
- **BREEDING** Polygamous, although some birds are monogamous.
- **NESTING** Incubation 12–13 days by female. Altricial young brooded by female; stay in nest 7–10 days, fed by female. 1–2 broods per year.
- **POPULATION** Common to abundant in grasslands, meadows, savannas, and fields. Local and irregular east of Appalachians. Rare in migration on Atlantic and Pacific Coasts. Casual in winter in the East.
- **FEEDERS** Birds in northern part of range come to feeders.

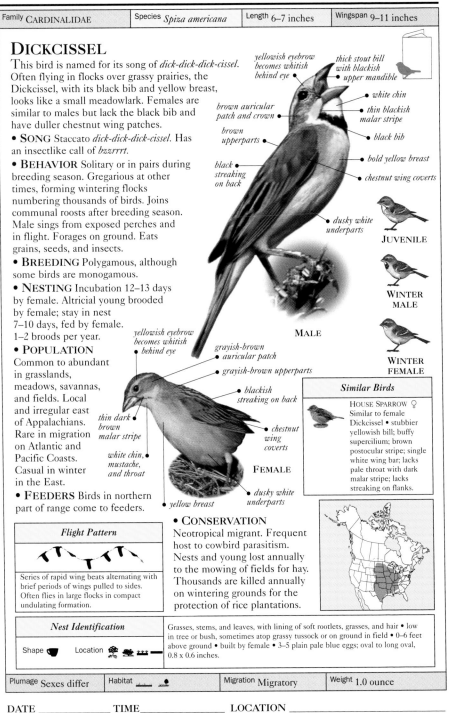

yellowish eyebrow becomes whitish behind eye

thick stout bill with blackish upper mandible

white chin

brown auricular patch and crown

thin blackish malar stripe

brown upperparts

black bib

black streaking on back

bold yellow breast

chestnut wing coverts

dusky white underparts

JUVENILE

WINTER MALE

MALE

yellowish eyebrow becomes whitish behind eye

grayish-brown auricular patch

grayish-brown upperparts

blackish streaking on back

thin dark brown malar stripe

chestnut wing coverts

white chin, mustache, and throat

FEMALE

dusky white underparts

yellow breast

WINTER FEMALE

Similar Birds

HOUSE SPARROW ♀
Similar to female Dickcissel • stubbier yellowish bill; buffy supercilium; brown postocular stripe; single white wing bar; lacks pale throat with dark malar stripe; lacks streaking on flanks.

- **CONSERVATION** Neotropical migrant. Frequent host to cowbird parasitism. Nests and young lost annually to the mowing of fields for hay. Thousands are killed annually on wintering grounds for the protection of rice plantations.

Flight Pattern

Series of rapid wing beats alternating with brief periods of wings pulled to sides. Often flies in large flocks in compact undulating formation.

Nest Identification

Shape ☕ Location 🐜 🌿 •••

Grasses, stems, and leaves, with lining of soft rootlets, grasses, and hair • low in tree or bush, sometimes atop grassy tussock or on ground in field • 0–6 feet above ground • built by female • 3–5 plain pale blue eggs; oval to long oval, 0.8 x 0.6 inches.

Plumage Sexes differ	Habitat	Migration Migratory	Weight 1.0 ounce

DATE _____ TIME_____ LOCATION _____

Family ICTERIDAE	Species *Dolichonyx oryzivorus*	Length 6.25–8 inches	Wingspan 10.25–12.5 inches

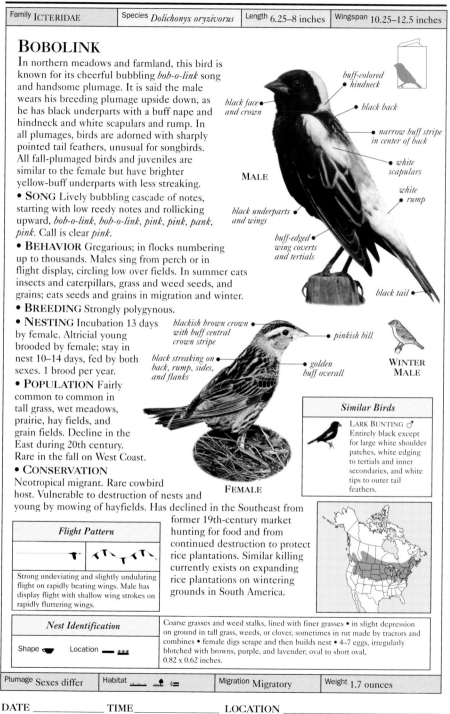

BOBOLINK

In northern meadows and farmland, this bird is known for its cheerful bubbling *bob-o-link* song and handsome plumage. It is said the male wears his breeding plumage upside down, as he has black underparts with a buff nape and hindneck and white scapulars and rump. In all plumages, birds are adorned with sharply pointed tail feathers, unusual for songbirds. All fall-plumaged birds and juveniles are similar to the female but have brighter yellow-buff underparts with less streaking.

• **SONG** Lively bubbling cascade of notes, starting with low reedy notes and rollicking upward, *bob-o-link, bob-o-link, pink, pink, pank, pink*. Call is clear *pink*.

• **BEHAVIOR** Gregarious; in flocks numbering up to thousands. Males sing from perch or in flight display, circling low over fields. In summer eats insects and caterpillars, grass and weed seeds, and grains; eats seeds and grains in migration and winter.

• **BREEDING** Strongly polygynous.

• **NESTING** Incubation 13 days by female. Altricial young brooded by female; stay in nest 10–14 days, fed by both sexes. 1 brood per year.

• **POPULATION** Fairly common to common in tall grass, wet meadows, prairie, hay fields, and grain fields. Decline in the East during 20th century. Rare in the fall on West Coast.

• **CONSERVATION** Neotropical migrant. Rare cowbird host. Vulnerable to destruction of nests and young by mowing of hayfields. Has declined in the Southeast from former 19th-century market hunting for food and from continued destruction to protect rice plantations. Similar killing currently exists on expanding rice plantations on wintering grounds in South America.

buff-colored hindneck

black face and crown

black back

narrow buff stripe in center of back

white scapulars

white rump

MALE

black underparts and wings

buff-edged wing coverts and tertials

black tail

blackish brown crown with buff central crown stripe

pinkish bill

black streaking on back, rump, sides, and flanks

golden buff overall

WINTER MALE

FEMALE

Similar Birds

LARK BUNTING ♂ Entirely black except for large white shoulder patches, white edging to tertials and inner secondaries, and white tips to outer tail feathers.

Flight Pattern

Strong undeviating and slightly undulating flight on rapidly beating wings. Male has display flight with shallow wing strokes on rapidly fluttering wings.

Nest Identification	Coarse grasses and weed stalks, lined with finer grasses • in slight depression on ground in tall grass, weeds, or clover, sometimes in rut made by tractors and combines • female digs scrape and then builds nest • 4–7 eggs, irregularly blotched with browns, purple, and lavender; oval to short oval, 0.82 x 0.62 inches.
Shape ⬦ Location ▬ ▴▴▴	

Plumage Sexes differ	Habitat	Migration Migratory	Weight 1.7 ounces

DATE _____ TIME_____ LOCATION _____

Family ICTERIDAE	Species *Agelaius phoeniceus*	Length 7.5–9.5 inches	Wingspan 12–14.5 inches

RED-WINGED BLACKBIRD

Believed one of the most numerous land birds in North America, the Red-winged Blackbird is known for aggressively defending its territory from intruders. Many geographical races exist across its extensive range. Females, identifiable by dark brown upperparts and heavily streaked underparts, sometimes show a red tinge on wing coverts, chin, and throat. Males resemble females at a year old but have less streaking and some red on their epaulettes; they develop glossy black plumage after their second year.

red shoulder patches (epaulettes) with broad buff-yellow distal tips

black overall, including wings and tail

MALE

• **SONG** Gurgling reedy *konk-la-ree* or *gurr-ga-leee*. Calls: low *clack*, sharp nasal *deekk*, and metallic *tiink*.

• **BEHAVIOR** Gregarious. Small breeding colonies in summer. Winter flocks often segregated by sex and age. Runs or hops while foraging on ground. Eats mostly seeds, grains, berries, and wild fruit; in summer also eats insects, caterpillars, grubs, spiders, mollusks, and snails. Male's social dominance is proportional to amount of red displayed.

brown crown

dusky tan face

broad dusky tan supercilium

FIRST YEAR MALE

• **BREEDING** Colonial. Some males polygynous.

• **NESTING** Incubation 11–12 days by female. Altricial young brooded by female; stay in nest 10–14 days, fed mostly by female. 2–3 broods per year.

thin brown malar mark

dark brown postocular stripe

brown upperparts with dark streaks

2 thin tan wing bars

dusky white underparts heavily streaked with brown

FEMALE

Similar Birds

♂ TRICOLORED BLACKBIRD Longer, more slender body • male's red epaulettes have whitish borders • females have darker bodies; heavier streaks on underparts; blackish bellies; lack chestnut and buff edges to upperparts; lack pink coloring on throat • West Coast only.

• **POPULATION** Abundant to common in fields, riparian thickets and scrub, freshwater and brackish marshes.

• **FEEDERS** Breadcrumbs and birdseed.

• **CONSERVATION** Vulnerable to pesticides in food chain and to habitat loss due to the drainage of wetlands. Nests and young are destroyed by mowing operations.

Flight Pattern
Strong flight on rapidly beating wings; displaying males fly with slow stiff shallow wing beats with epaulettes raised.

Nest Identification	
Shape ◗	Dried cattail leaves and sedges, lined with fine grasses and rushes • fastened to stalks or twigs with plant fibers • in cattails, bushes, trees, dense grass, or on ground, preferably near or over water • built by female • 3–5 (usually 4) pale blue-green eggs spotted or with zigzag lines of black, browns, and purple; oval, 0.97 x 0.75 inches.
Location	

Plumage Sexes differ	Habitat	Migration Migratory	Weight 2.3 ounces

DATE _____ TIME_____ LOCATION _____

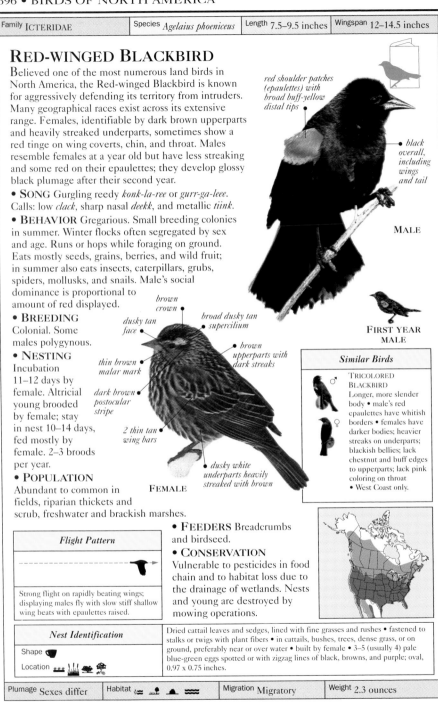

Family ICTERIDAE	Species *Agelaius tricolor*	Length 7.5–9 inches	Wingspan 12–13.5 inches

TRICOLORED BLACKBIRD

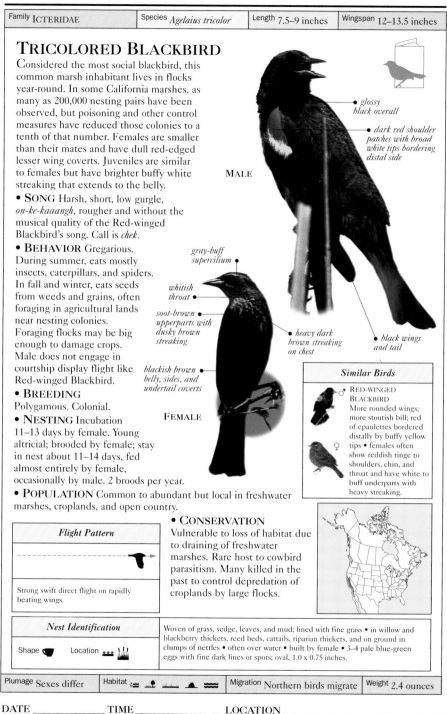

Considered the most social blackbird, this common marsh inhabitant lives in flocks year-round. In some California marshes, as many as 200,000 nesting pairs have been observed, but poisoning and other control measures have reduced those colonies to a tenth of that number. Females are smaller than their mates and have dull red-edged lesser wing coverts. Juveniles are similar to females but have brighter buffy white streaking that extends to the belly.

• **SONG** Harsh, short, low gurgle, *on-ke-kaaangh*, rougher and without the musical quality of the Red-winged Blackbird's song. Call is *chek*.

• **BEHAVIOR** Gregarious. During summer, eats mostly insects, caterpillars, and spiders. In fall and winter, eats seeds from weeds and grains, often foraging in agricultural lands near nesting colonies. Foraging flocks may be big enough to damage crops. Male does not engage in courtship display flight like Red-winged Blackbird.

• **BREEDING** Polygamous. Colonial.

• **NESTING** Incubation 11–13 days by female. Young altricial; brooded by female; stay in nest about 11–14 days, fed almost entirely by female, occasionally by male. 2 broods per year.

• **POPULATION** Common to abundant but local in freshwater marshes, croplands, and open country.

• **CONSERVATION** Vulnerable to loss of habitat due to draining of freshwater marshes. Rare host to cowbird parasitism. Many killed in the past to control depredation of croplands by large flocks.

MALE

glossy black overall

dark red shoulder patches with broad white tips bordering distal side

gray-buff supercilium

whitish throat

soot-brown upperparts with dusky brown streaking

blackish brown belly, sides, and undertail coverts

FEMALE

heavy dark brown streaking on chest

black wings and tail

Similar Birds

♂ RED-WINGED BLACKBIRD More rounded wings; more stoutish bill; red of epaulettes bordered distally by buffy yellow tips • females often show reddish tinge to shoulders, chin, and throat and have white to buff underparts with heavy streaking.

Flight Pattern
Strong swift direct flight on rapidly beating wings.

Nest Identification	
Shape ⬤ Location ▦ ⌇	Woven of grass, sedge, leaves, and mud; lined with fine grass • in willow and blackberry thickets, reed beds, cattails, riparian thickets, and on ground in clumps of nettles • often over water • built by female • 3–4 pale blue-green eggs with fine dark lines or spots; oval, 1.0 x 0.75 inches.

Plumage Sexes differ	Habitat	Migration Northern birds migrate	Weight 2.4 ounces

DATE _____ TIME_____ LOCATION _____

Family ICTERIDAE	Species *Sturnella magna*	Length 9–11 inches	Wingspan 13.5–17 inches

EASTERN MEADOWLARK

A common inhabitant of fields and meadows, the Eastern Meadowlark often is observed flicking its tail open and shut while walking through grass and weeds and along roadsides. Clearing of forests in eastern North America has led to the expansion of its breeding range. Fall-plumaged birds show narrow buffy mottling in the black breast band and a buffy wash on the face, supercilium, flanks, and undertail coverts. Juveniles have black spotting on the chest, sides, and flanks.

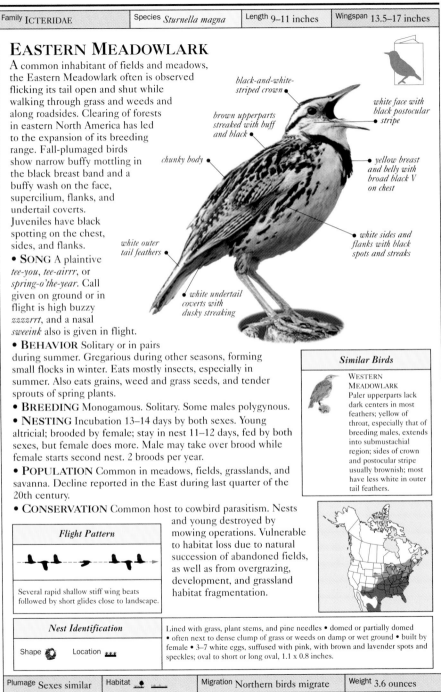

black-and-white-striped crown

brown upperparts streaked with buff and black

chunky body

white face with black postocular stripe

yellow breast and belly with broad black V on chest

white sides and flanks with black spots and streaks

white outer tail feathers

white undertail coverts with dusky streaking

• **SONG** A plaintive *tee-you, tee-airrr*, or *spring-o'the-year*. Call given on ground or in flight is high buzzy *zzzzrrt*, and a nasal *sweeink* also is given in flight.

• **BEHAVIOR** Solitary or in pairs during summer. Gregarious during other seasons, forming small flocks in winter. Eats mostly insects, especially in summer. Also eats grains, weed and grass seeds, and tender sprouts of spring plants.

• **BREEDING** Monogamous. Solitary. Some males polygynous.

• **NESTING** Incubation 13–14 days by both sexes. Young altricial; brooded by female; stay in nest 11–12 days, fed by both sexes, but female does more. Male may take over brood while female starts second nest. 2 broods per year.

• **POPULATION** Common in meadows, fields, grasslands, and savanna. Decline reported in the East during last quarter of the 20th century.

• **CONSERVATION** Common host to cowbird parasitism. Nests and young destroyed by mowing operations. Vulnerable to habitat loss due to natural succession of abandoned fields, as well as from overgrazing, development, and grassland habitat fragmentation.

Similar Birds

WESTERN MEADOWLARK
Paler upperparts lack dark centers in most feathers; yellow of throat, especially that of breeding males, extends into submustachial region; sides of crown and postocular stripe usually brownish; most have less white in outer tail feathers.

Flight Pattern

Several rapid shallow stiff wing beats followed by short glides close to landscape.

Nest Identification	
Shape ⬤ Location ▪▪▪	Lined with grass, plant stems, and pine needles • domed or partially domed • often next to dense clump of grass or weeds on damp or wet ground • built by female • 3–7 white eggs, suffused with pink, with brown and lavender spots and speckles; oval to short or long oval, 1.1 x 0.8 inches.

Plumage Sexes similar	Habitat ♠ ⸏⸏	Migration Northern birds migrate	Weight 3.6 ounces

DATE _____ TIME_____ LOCATION _____

Family ICTERIDAE	Species *Sturnella neglecta*	Length 9–11 inches	Wingspan 13.5–17 inches

WESTERN MEADOWLARK

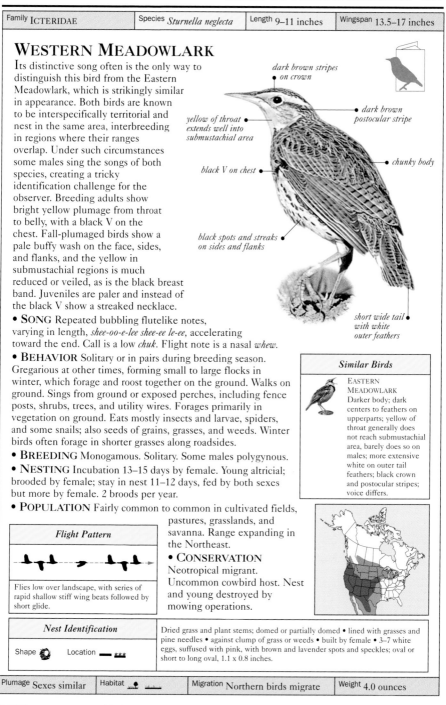

Its distinctive song often is the only way to distinguish this bird from the Eastern Meadowlark, which is strikingly similar in appearance. Both birds are known to be interspecifically territorial and nest in the same area, interbreeding in regions where their ranges overlap. Under such circumstances some males sing the songs of both species, creating a tricky identification challenge for the observer. Breeding adults show bright yellow plumage from throat to belly, with a black V on the chest. Fall-plumaged birds show a pale buffy wash on the face, sides, and flanks, and the yellow in submustachial regions is much reduced or veiled, as is the black breast band. Juveniles are paler and instead of the black V show a streaked necklace.

dark brown stripes on crown

yellow of throat extends well into submustachial area

dark brown postocular stripe

chunky body

black V on chest

black spots and streaks on sides and flanks

short wide tail with white outer feathers

• **SONG** Repeated bubbling flutelike notes, varying in length, *shee-oo-e-lee shee-ee le-ee*, accelerating toward the end. Call is a low *chuk*. Flight note is a nasal *whew*.

• **BEHAVIOR** Solitary or in pairs during breeding season. Gregarious at other times, forming small to large flocks in winter, which forage and roost together on the ground. Walks on ground. Sings from ground or exposed perches, including fence posts, shrubs, trees, and utility wires. Forages primarily in vegetation on ground. Eats mostly insects and larvae, spiders, and some snails; also seeds of grains, grasses, and weeds. Winter birds often forage in shorter grasses along roadsides.

• **BREEDING** Monogamous. Solitary. Some males polygynous.

• **NESTING** Incubation 13–15 days by female. Young altricial; brooded by female; stay in nest 11–12 days, fed by both sexes but more by female. 2 broods per year.

• **POPULATION** Fairly common to common in cultivated fields, pastures, grasslands, and savanna. Range expanding in the Northeast.

• **CONSERVATION** Neotropical migrant. Uncommon cowbird host. Nest and young destroyed by mowing operations.

Similar Birds

EASTERN MEADOWLARK Darker body; dark centers to feathers on upperparts; yellow of throat generally does not reach submustachial area, barely does so on males; more extensive white on outer tail feathers; black crown and postocular stripes; voice differs.

Flight Pattern

Flies low over landscape, with series of rapid shallow stiff wing beats followed by short glide.

Nest Identification

Shape   Location ▬ ☘☘

Dried grass and plant stems; domed or partially domed • lined with grasses and pine needles • against clump of grass or weeds • built by female • 3–7 white eggs, suffused with pink, with brown and lavender spots and speckles; oval or short to long oval, 1.1 x 0.8 inches.

Plumage Sexes similar	Habitat	Migration Northern birds migrate	Weight 4.0 ounces

DATE _____ TIME_____ LOCATION _____

Family ICTERIDAE	Species *Xanthocephalus xanthocephalus*	Length 8.75–11 inches	Wingspan 14–17 inches

YELLOW-HEADED BLACKBIRD

Brilliant yellow plumage and white wing patches contrasting with its all-black body make this robin-sized marsh bird easy to identify. Often nesting in colonies, it is highly aggressive in defending its grounds and will attack other birds and even human intruders, especially if young are in the nest. The song of the male is considered by many to be the poorest vocalization of any North American songbird. Males are larger than females, and the white wing patch is conspicuous in flight. Juveniles show dark brown upperparts with cinnamon-buff edging to the body feathers, pale buff underparts with a cinnamon wash on the flanks, an ocherous buff head and breast, a whitish throat, and dusky brown auriculars.

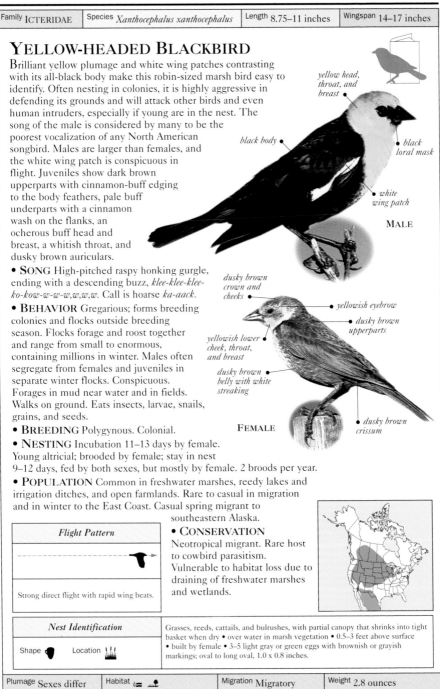

yellow head, throat, and breast

black body

black loral mask

white wing patch

MALE

dusky brown crown and cheeks

yellowish eyebrow

dusky brown upperparts

yellowish lower cheek, throat, and breast

dusky brown belly with white streaking

dusky brown crissum

FEMALE

• **SONG** High-pitched raspy honking gurgle, ending with a descending buzz, *klee-klee-klee-ko-kow-w-w-w,w,w,w.* Call is hoarse *ka-aack.*

• **BEHAVIOR** Gregarious; forms breeding colonies and flocks outside breeding season. Flocks forage and roost together and range from small to enormous, containing millions in winter. Males often segregate from females and juveniles in separate winter flocks. Conspicuous. Forages in mud near water and in fields. Walks on ground. Eats insects, larvae, snails, grains, and seeds.

• **BREEDING** Polygynous. Colonial.

• **NESTING** Incubation 11–13 days by female. Young altricial; brooded by female; stay in nest 9–12 days, fed by both sexes, but mostly by female. 2 broods per year.

• **POPULATION** Common in freshwater marshes, reedy lakes and irrigation ditches, and open farmlands. Rare to casual in migration and in winter to the East Coast. Casual spring migrant to southeastern Alaska.

• **CONSERVATION** Neotropical migrant. Rare host to cowbird parasitism. Vulnerable to habitat loss due to draining of freshwater marshes and wetlands.

Flight Pattern
Strong direct flight with rapid wing beats.

Nest Identification	
Shape ● Location ⋔	Grasses, reeds, cattails, and bulrushes, with partial canopy that shrinks into tight basket when dry • over water in marsh vegetation • 0.5–3 feet above surface • built by female • 3–5 light gray or green eggs with brownish or grayish markings; oval to long oval, 1.0 x 0.8 inches.

Plumage Sexes differ	Habitat	Migration Migratory	Weight 2.8 ounces

DATE _____ TIME_____ LOCATION _____

Family ICTERIDAE	Species *Euphagus carolinus*	Length 8.25–9.75 inches	Wingspan 13–15 inches

RUSTY BLACKBIRD

This bird is named for the rusty wash on its fall and winter plumage. Only birds in juvenile plumage have dark eyes; older birds in immature plumage have yellow eyes like adults. Juvenile plumage resembles that of winter adults. Fall males have a blackish loral mask that contrasts with the rufous wash on the rest of the plumage. The fall female has a gray rump and cinnamon-gray supercilium and underparts. Flying in large flocks from their wintering grounds, these birds will swoop down to forage behind tractors and plows.

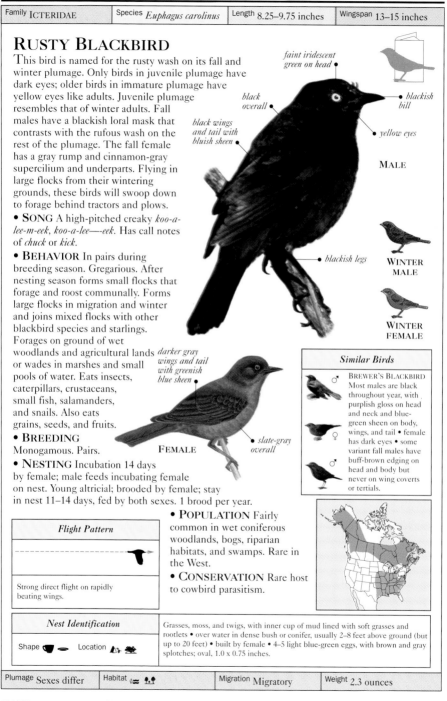

faint iridescent green on head

black overall

black wings and tail with bluish sheen

blackish bill

yellow eyes

MALE

blackish legs

WINTER MALE

WINTER FEMALE

• **SONG** A high-pitched creaky *koo-a-lee-m-eek, koo-a-lee—eek*. Has call notes of *chuck* or *kick*.

• **BEHAVIOR** In pairs during breeding season. Gregarious. After nesting season forms small flocks that forage and roost communally. Forms large flocks in migration and winter and joins mixed flocks with other blackbird species and starlings. Forages on ground of wet woodlands and agricultural lands or wades in marshes and small pools of water. Eats insects, caterpillars, crustaceans, small fish, salamanders, and snails. Also eats grains, seeds, and fruits.

• **BREEDING** Monogamous. Pairs.

• **NESTING** Incubation 14 days by female; male feeds incubating female on nest. Young altricial; brooded by female; stay in nest 11–14 days, fed by both sexes. 1 brood per year.

darker gray wings and tail with greenish blue sheen

slate-gray overall

FEMALE

Similar Birds

♂ BREWER'S BLACKBIRD Most males are black throughout year, with purplish gloss on head and neck and blue-green sheen on body, wings, and tail • female has dark eyes • some variant fall males have buff-brown edging on head and body but never on wing coverts or tertials.

♀

♂

• **POPULATION** Fairly common in wet coniferous woodlands, bogs, riparian habitats, and swamps. Rare in the West.

• **CONSERVATION** Rare host to cowbird parasitism.

Flight Pattern
Strong direct flight on rapidly beating wings.

Nest Identification	
Shape 🥚 ⌣ Location 🌿 🌲	Grasses, moss, and twigs, with inner cup of mud lined with soft grasses and rootlets • over water in dense bush or conifer, usually 2–8 feet above ground (but up to 20 feet) • built by female • 4–5 light blue-green eggs, with brown and gray splotches; oval, 1.0 x 0.75 inches.

Plumage Sexes differ	Habitat 〰 🏕	Migration Migratory	Weight 2.3 ounces

DATE _____ TIME _____ LOCATION _____

Family ICTERIDAE	Species *Euphagus cyanocephalus*	Length 8.75–10.25 inches	Wingspan 14–16 inches

BREWER'S BLACKBIRD

Huge flocks can be seen flying over farm fields during plowing season, and the species has expanded its range and abundance with the spread of agriculture. One of the most common blackbirds, the male's plumage remains glossy black year-round. In fall, some males acquire buffy edging on the head and body feathers but never on the wing coverts or tertials. Juveniles resemble females but lack the green sheen on wings and tail.

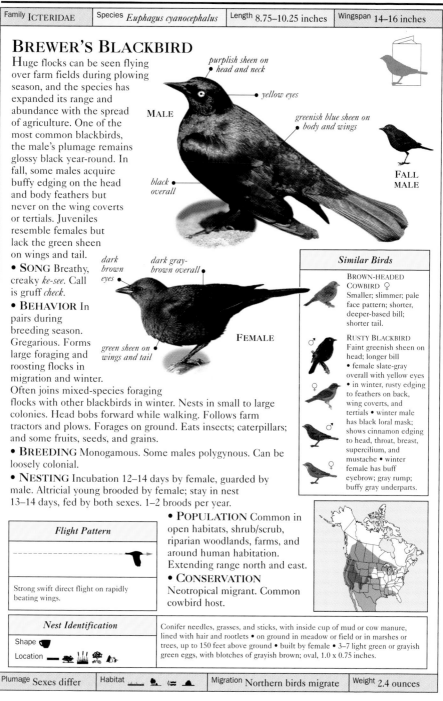

purplish sheen on head and neck

yellow eyes

MALE

greenish blue sheen on body and wings

FALL MALE

black overall

dark brown eyes

dark gray-brown overall

FEMALE

green sheen on wings and tail

• **SONG** Breathy, creaky *ke-see.* Call is gruff *check.*
• **BEHAVIOR** In pairs during breeding season. Gregarious. Forms large foraging and roosting flocks in migration and winter. Often joins mixed-species foraging flocks with other blackbirds in winter. Nests in small to large colonies. Head bobs forward while walking. Follows farm tractors and plows. Forages on ground. Eats insects; caterpillars; and some fruits, seeds, and grains.
• **BREEDING** Monogamous. Some males polygynous. Can be loosely colonial.
• **NESTING** Incubation 12–14 days by female, guarded by male. Altricial young brooded by female; stay in nest 13–14 days, fed by both sexes. 1–2 broods per year.

Similar Birds

BROWN-HEADED COWBIRD ♀
Smaller; slimmer; pale face pattern; shorter, deeper-based bill; shorter tail.

RUSTY BLACKBIRD
Faint greenish sheen on head; longer bill • female slate-gray overall with yellow eyes • in winter, rusty edging to feathers on back, wing coverts, and tertials • winter male has black loral mask; shows cinnamon edging to head, throat, breast, supercilium, and mustache • winter female has buff eyebrow; gray rump; buffy gray underparts.

• **POPULATION** Common in open habitats, shrub/scrub, riparian woodlands, farms, and around human habitation. Extending range north and east.
• **CONSERVATION** Neotropical migrant. Common cowbird host.

Flight Pattern
Strong swift direct flight on rapidly beating wings.

Nest Identification	
Shape	Conifer needles, grasses, and sticks, with inside cup of mud or cow manure, lined with hair and rootlets • on ground in meadow or field or in marshes or trees, up to 150 feet above ground • built by female • 3–7 light green or grayish green eggs, with blotches of grayish brown; oval, 1.0 x 0.75 inches.
Location	

Plumage Sexes differ	Habitat	Migration Northern birds migrate	Weight 2.4 ounces

DATE _____ TIME_____ LOCATION _____

| Family ICTERIDAE | Species *Quiscalus quiscula* | Length 11–13.5 inches | Wingspan 17–18.5 inches |

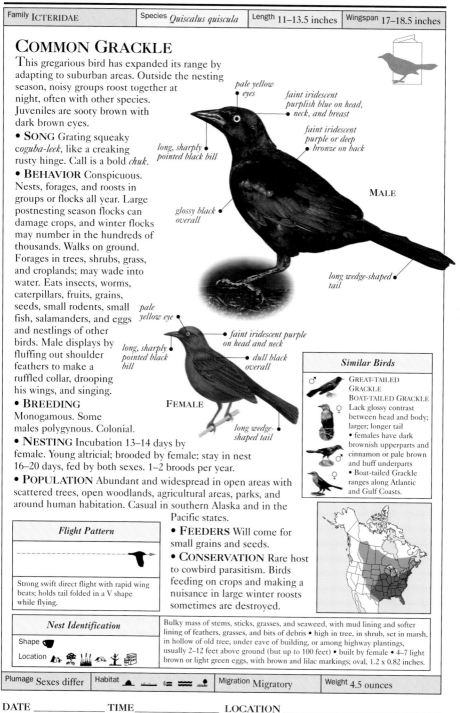

COMMON GRACKLE

This gregarious bird has expanded its range by adapting to suburban areas. Outside the nesting season, noisy groups roost together at night, often with other species. Juveniles are sooty brown with dark brown eyes.

pale yellow eyes

faint iridescent purplish blue on head, neck, and breast

faint iridescent purple or deep bronze on back

long, sharply pointed black bill

• **SONG** Grating squeaky *coguba-leek*, like a creaking rusty hinge. Call is a bold *chuk*.

• **BEHAVIOR** Conspicuous. Nests, forages, and roosts in groups or flocks all year. Large postnesting season flocks can damage crops, and winter flocks may number in the hundreds of thousands. Walks on ground. Forages in trees, shrubs, grass, and croplands; may wade into water. Eats insects, worms, caterpillars, fruits, grains, seeds, small rodents, small fish, salamanders, and eggs and nestlings of other birds. Male displays by fluffing out shoulder feathers to make a ruffled collar, drooping his wings, and singing.

glossy black overall

MALE

long wedge-shaped tail

pale yellow eye

faint iridescent purple on head and neck

long, sharply pointed black bill

dull black overall

• **BREEDING** Monogamous. Some males polygynous. Colonial.

FEMALE

long wedge-shaped tail

• **NESTING** Incubation 13–14 days by female. Young altricial; brooded by female; stay in nest 16–20 days, fed by both sexes. 1–2 broods per year.

• **POPULATION** Abundant and widespread in open areas with scattered trees, open woodlands, agricultural areas, parks, and around human habitation. Casual in southern Alaska and in the Pacific states.

• **FEEDERS** Will come for small grains and seeds.

• **CONSERVATION** Rare host to cowbird parasitism. Birds feeding on crops and making a nuisance in large winter roosts sometimes are destroyed.

Similar Birds

♂ GREAT-TAILED GRACKLE
BOAT-TAILED GRACKLE
♀ Lack glossy contrast between head and body; larger; longer tail
• females have dark brownish upperparts and cinnamon or pale brown and buff underparts
• Boat-tailed Grackle ranges along Atlantic and Gulf Coasts.

Flight Pattern

Strong swift direct flight with rapid wing beats; holds tail folded in a V shape while flying.

Nest Identification

Shape

Location

Bulky mass of stems, sticks, grasses, and seaweed, with mud lining and softer lining of feathers, grasses, and bits of debris • high in tree, in shrub, set in marsh, in hollow of old tree, under eave of building, or among highway plantings, usually 2–12 feet above ground (but up to 100 feet) • built by female • 4–7 light brown or light green eggs, with brown and lilac markings; oval, 1.2 x 0.82 inches.

| Plumage Sexes differ | Habitat | Migration Migratory | Weight 4.5 ounces |

DATE _____ TIME_____ LOCATION _____

Family ICTERIDAE	Species *Quiscalus mexicanus*	Length 10.5–18.5 inches	Wingspan 13.5–25 inches

GREAT-TAILED GRACKLE

The Great-tailed and Boat-tailed Grackles were once considered to be one species. Although these birds nest closely in coastal eastern Texas and western Louisiana, they do not interbreed. This bird often walks on the ground with its large keel-shaped tail cocked over its back. Walking in the open, males turn like weathervanes when a strong gust of wind strikes their tails. Males are larger than females. Juveniles are similar to females with a grayish brown belly but with streaked underparts and dark eyes.

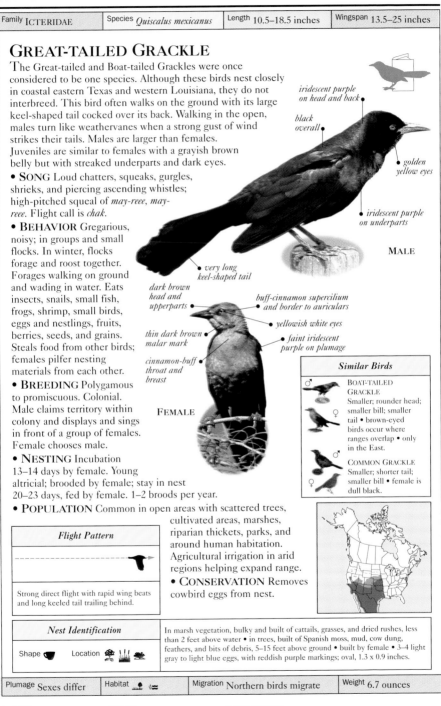

iridescent purple on head and back

black overall

golden yellow eyes

iridescent purple on underparts

MALE

very long keel-shaped tail

dark brown head and upperparts

buff-cinnamon supercilium and border to auriculars

yellowish white eyes

thin dark brown malar mark

faint iridescent purple on plumage

cinnamon-buff throat and breast

FEMALE

- **SONG** Loud chatters, squeaks, gurgles, shrieks, and piercing ascending whistles; high-pitched squeal of *may-reee, may-reee*. Flight call is *chak*.
- **BEHAVIOR** Gregarious, noisy; in groups and small flocks. In winter, flocks forage and roost together. Forages walking on ground and wading in water. Eats insects, snails, small fish, frogs, shrimp, small birds, eggs and nestlings, fruits, berries, seeds, and grains. Steals food from other birds; females pilfer nesting materials from each other.
- **BREEDING** Polygamous to promiscuous. Colonial. Male claims territory within colony and displays and sings in front of a group of females. Female chooses male.
- **NESTING** Incubation 13–14 days by female. Young altricial; brooded by female; stay in nest 20–23 days, fed by female. 1–2 broods per year.
- **POPULATION** Common in open areas with scattered trees, cultivated areas, marshes, riparian thickets, parks, and around human habitation. Agricultural irrigation in arid regions helping expand range.
- **CONSERVATION** Removes cowbird eggs from nest.

Similar Birds

♂ BOAT-TAILED GRACKLE
Smaller; rounder head; smaller bill; smaller ♀ tail • brown-eyed birds occur where ranges overlap • only in the East.

♂ COMMON GRACKLE
Smaller; shorter tail; smaller bill • female is ♀ dull black.

Flight Pattern

Strong direct flight with rapid wing beats and long keeled tail trailing behind.

Nest Identification

Shape 🍵   Location 🌿 🌾 🪻

In marsh vegetation, bulky and built of cattails, grasses, and dried rushes, less than 2 feet above water • in trees, built of Spanish moss, mud, cow dung, feathers, and bits of debris, 5–15 feet above ground • built by female • 3–4 light gray to light blue eggs, with reddish purple markings; oval, 1.3 x 0.9 inches.

Plumage Sexes differ	Habitat 🌱 🌾	Migration Northern birds migrate	Weight 6.7 ounces

DATE _____ TIME_____ LOCATION _____

Family ICTERIDAE	Species *Molothrus aeneus*	Length 6.5–8.75 inches	Wingspan 10–13 inches

BRONZED COWBIRD

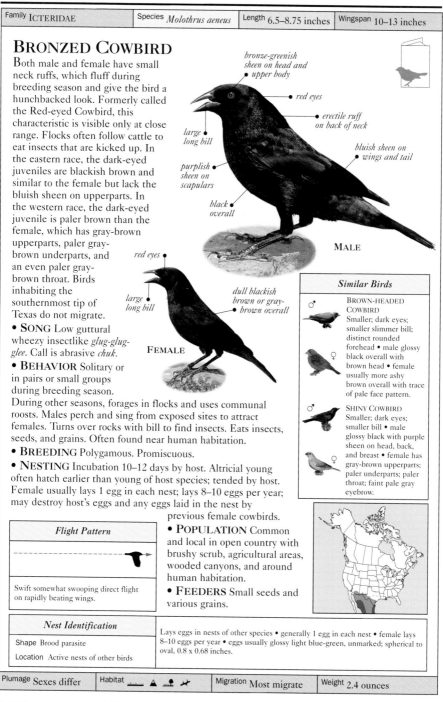

Both male and female have small neck ruffs, which fluff during breeding season and give the bird a hunchbacked look. Formerly called the Red-eyed Cowbird, this characteristic is visible only at close range. Flocks often follow cattle to eat insects that are kicked up. In the eastern race, the dark-eyed juveniles are blackish brown and similar to the female but lack the bluish sheen on upperparts. In the western race, the dark-eyed juvenile is paler brown than the female, which has gray-brown upperparts, paler gray-brown underparts, and an even paler gray-brown throat. Birds inhabiting the southernmost tip of Texas do not migrate.

bronze-greenish sheen on head and upper body

red eyes

erectile ruff on back of neck

bluish sheen on wings and tail

large long bill

purplish sheen on scapulars

black overall

MALE

red eyes

large long bill

dull blackish brown or gray-brown overall

FEMALE

• **SONG** Low guttural wheezy insectlike *glug-glug-glee*. Call is abrasive *chuk*.
• **BEHAVIOR** Solitary or in pairs or small groups during breeding season. During other seasons, forages in flocks and uses communal roosts. Males perch and sing from exposed sites to attract females. Turns over rocks with bill to find insects. Eats insects, seeds, and grains. Often found near human habitation.
• **BREEDING** Polygamous. Promiscuous.
• **NESTING** Incubation 10–12 days by host. Altricial young often hatch earlier than young of host species; tended by host. Female usually lays 1 egg in each nest; lays 8–10 eggs per year; may destroy host's eggs and any eggs laid in the nest by previous female cowbirds.

Similar Birds

♂ **BROWN-HEADED COWBIRD** Smaller; dark eyes; smaller slimmer bill; distinct rounded forehead • male glossy black overall with brown head • female ♀ usually more ashy brown overall with trace of pale face pattern.

♂ **SHINY COWBIRD** Smaller; dark eyes; smaller bill • male glossy black with purple sheen on head, back, and breast • female ♀ has gray-brown upperparts; paler underparts; paler throat; faint pale gray eyebrow.

• **POPULATION** Common and local in open country with brushy scrub, agricultural areas, wooded canyons, and around human habitation.
• **FEEDERS** Small seeds and various grains.

Flight Pattern
Swift somewhat swooping direct flight on rapidly beating wings.

Nest Identification	
Shape Brood parasite	Lays eggs in nests of other species • generally 1 egg in each nest • female lays 8–10 eggs per year • eggs usually glossy light blue-green, unmarked; spherical to oval, 0.8 x 0.68 inches.
Location Active nests of other birds	

Plumage Sexes differ	Habitat	Migration Most migrate	Weight 2.4 ounces

DATE _____ TIME_____ LOCATION _____

Family ICTERIDAE	Species *Molothrus ater*	Length 7–8.25 inches	Wingspan 11.75–13.75 inches

BROWN-HEADED COWBIRD

This common cowbird travels and roosts in large flocks with other blackbirds after breeding season; winter mixed-species flocks can number in the millions. Originally of the Great Plains, where it associated with bison, this species has expanded its range east and west, with the fragmentation of the eastern forest and the increase in range cattle and ranching. Like all cowbirds it is a brood parasite and lays its eggs in the nests of other birds. Juveniles resemble females but are paler overall; upperparts have pale edging, giving a scaly effect; underparts are streaky and throats gray-white.

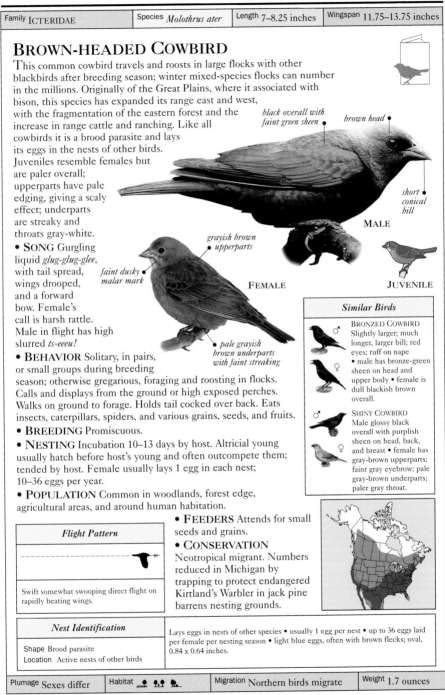

black overall with faint green sheen

brown head

short conical bill

MALE

grayish brown upperparts

faint dusky malar mark

FEMALE

JUVENILE

pale grayish brown underparts with faint streaking

• **SONG** Gurgling liquid *glug-glug-glee*, with tail spread, wings drooped, and a forward bow. Female's call is harsh rattle. Male in flight has high slurred *ts-eeeu!*

• **BEHAVIOR** Solitary, in pairs, or small groups during breeding season; otherwise gregarious, foraging and roosting in flocks. Calls and displays from the ground or high exposed perches. Walks on ground to forage. Holds tail cocked over back. Eats insects, caterpillars, spiders, and various grains, seeds, and fruits.

• **BREEDING** Promiscuous.

• **NESTING** Incubation 10–13 days by host. Altricial young usually hatch before host's young and often outcompete them; tended by host. Female usually lays 1 egg in each nest; 10–36 eggs per year.

• **POPULATION** Common in woodlands, forest edge, agricultural areas, and around human habitation.

Similar Birds

♂ **BRONZED COWBIRD** Slightly larger; much longer, larger bill; red eyes; ruff on nape
♀ • male has bronze-green sheen on head and upper body • female is dull blackish brown overall.

♂ **SHINY COWBIRD** Male glossy black overall with purplish sheen on head, back, and breast • female has gray-brown upperparts; faint gray eyebrow; pale gray-brown underparts; paler gray throat.

• **FEEDERS** Attends for small seeds and grains.

• **CONSERVATION** Neotropical migrant. Numbers reduced in Michigan by trapping to protect endangered Kirtland's Warbler in jack pine barrens nesting grounds.

Flight Pattern
Swift somewhat swooping direct flight on rapidly beating wings.

Nest Identification	
Shape Brood parasite Location Active nests of other birds	Lays eggs in nests of other species • usually 1 egg per nest • up to 36 eggs laid per female per nesting season • light blue eggs, often with brown flecks; oval, 0.84 x 0.64 inches.

Plumage Sexes differ	Habitat	Migration Northern birds migrate	Weight 1.7 ounces

DATE _____ TIME_____ LOCATION _____

Family ICTERIDAE	Species *Icterus spurius*	Length 6–7.75 inches	Wingspan 9.25–10.25 inches

ORCHARD ORIOLE

This small oriole with its burnt-orange underparts is found in most of eastern North America in summer. It spends most of its time in trees in suburban and rural open stands and is often unwary when approached. Juveniles resemble females, and first spring males are similar to females but have a black chin and throat. Leaves breeding grounds in early fall.

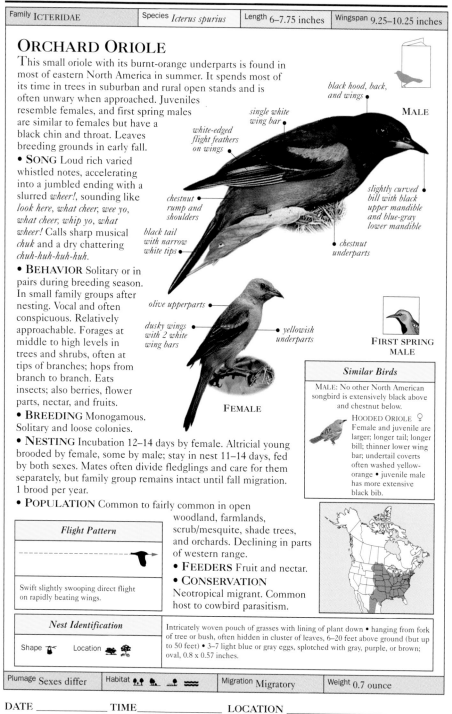

single white wing bar

white-edged flight feathers on wings

black hood, back, and wings

MALE

slightly curved bill with black upper mandible and blue-gray lower mandible

chestnut rump and shoulders

black tail with narrow white tips

chestnut underparts

• **SONG** Loud rich varied whistled notes, accelerating into a jumbled ending with a slurred *wheer!*, sounding like *look here, what cheer, wee yo, what cheer, whip yo, what wheer!* Calls sharp musical *chuk* and a dry chattering *chuh-huh-huh-huh.*

• **BEHAVIOR** Solitary or in pairs during breeding season. In small family groups after nesting. Vocal and often conspicuous. Relatively approachable. Forages at middle to high levels in trees and shrubs, often at tips of branches; hops from branch to branch. Eats insects; also berries, flower parts, nectar, and fruits.

olive upperparts

dusky wings with 2 white wing bars

yellowish underparts

FIRST SPRING MALE

FEMALE

Similar Birds

MALE: No other North American songbird is extensively black above and chestnut below.

HOODED ORIOLE ♀ Female and juvenile are larger; longer tail; longer bill; thinner lower wing bar; undertail coverts often washed yellow-orange • juvenile male has more extensive black bib.

• **BREEDING** Monogamous. Solitary and loose colonies.

• **NESTING** Incubation 12–14 days by female. Altricial young brooded by female, some by male; stay in nest 11–14 days, fed by both sexes. Mates often divide fledglings and care for them separately, but family group remains intact until fall migration. 1 brood per year.

• **POPULATION** Common to fairly common in open woodland, farmlands, scrub/mesquite, shade trees, and orchards. Declining in parts of western range.

• **FEEDERS** Fruit and nectar.

• **CONSERVATION** Neotropical migrant. Common host to cowbird parasitism.

Flight Pattern	
Swift slightly swooping direct flight on rapidly beating wings.	

Nest Identification	
Shape 🦅 Location 🌳 🌳	Intricately woven pouch of grasses with lining of plant down • hanging from fork of tree or bush, often hidden in cluster of leaves, 6–20 feet above ground (but up to 50 feet) • 3–7 light blue or gray eggs, splotched with gray, purple, or brown; oval, 0.8 x 0.57 inches.

Plumage Sexes differ	Habitat 🌾 🌳 🌿 〰️	Migration Migratory	Weight 0.7 ounce

DATE _____ TIME_____ LOCATION _____

Family ICTERIDAE	Species *Icterus cucullatus*	Length 7–8 inches	Wingspan 11.25–12 inches

HOODED ORIOLE

This bird flits from treetop to treetop and sometimes hangs upside down like a chickadee. It is associated with palm trees in its breeding range, most often nesting in them. The breeding male's orange-yellow head, black lores and bib, and white wing bars are distinctive. There is color variation in the males of different races, ranging from bright orange to bright yellow. Juveniles are similar to adult females. First spring males resemble females but have black lores and bib.

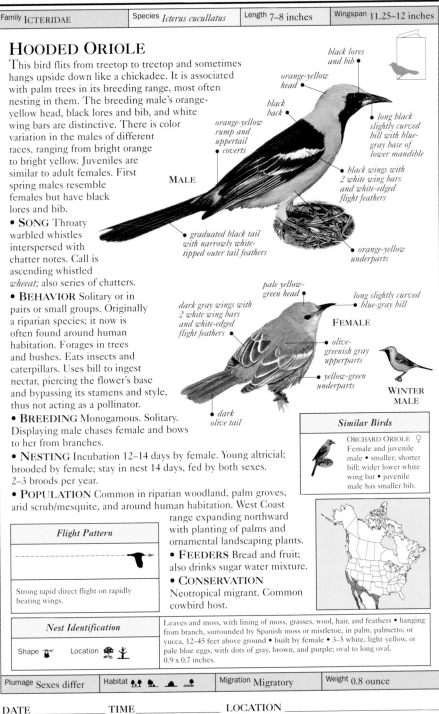

black lores and bib

orange-yellow head

black back

orange-yellow rump and uppertail coverts

long black slightly curved bill with blue-gray base of lower mandible

black wings with 2 white wing bars and white-edged flight feathers

MALE

orange-yellow underparts

graduated black tail with narrowly white-tipped outer tail feathers

pale yellow-green head

long slightly curved blue-gray bill

dark gray wings with 2 white wing bars and white-edged flight feathers

FEMALE

olive-greenish gray upperparts

yellow-green underparts

WINTER MALE

dark olive tail

• **SONG** Throaty warbled whistles interspersed with chatter notes. Call is ascending whistled *wheat;* also series of chatters.

• **BEHAVIOR** Solitary or in pairs or small groups. Originally a riparian species; it now is often found around human habitation. Forages in trees and bushes. Eats insects and caterpillars. Uses bill to ingest nectar, piercing the flower's base and bypassing its stamens and style, thus not acting as a pollinator.

• **BREEDING** Monogamous. Solitary. Displaying male chases female and bows to her from branches.

• **NESTING** Incubation 12–14 days by female. Young altricial; brooded by female; stay in nest 14 days, fed by both sexes. 2–3 broods per year.

• **POPULATION** Common in riparian woodland, palm groves, arid scrub/mesquite, and around human habitation. West Coast range expanding northward with planting of palms and ornamental landscaping plants.

• **FEEDERS** Bread and fruit; also drinks sugar water mixture.

• **CONSERVATION** Neotropical migrant. Common cowbird host.

Similar Birds

ORCHARD ORIOLE ♀
Female and juvenile male • smaller; shorter bill • wider lower white wing bar • juvenile male has smaller bib.

Flight Pattern

Strong rapid direct flight on rapidly beating wings.

Nest Identification

Shape | Location

Leaves and moss, with lining of moss, grasses, wool, hair, and feathers • hanging from branch, surrounded by Spanish moss or mistletoe, in palm, palmetto, or yucca, 12–45 feet above ground • built by female • 3–5 white, light yellow, or pale blue eggs, with dots of gray, brown, and purple; oval to long oval, 0.9 x 0.7 inches.

Plumage Sexes differ	Habitat	Migration Migratory	Weight 0.8 ounce

DATE _____ TIME_____ LOCATION _____

Family ICTERIDAE	Species *Icterus pustulatus*	Length 7.5–9 inches	Wingspan 12–13.5 inches

STREAK-BACKED ORIOLE

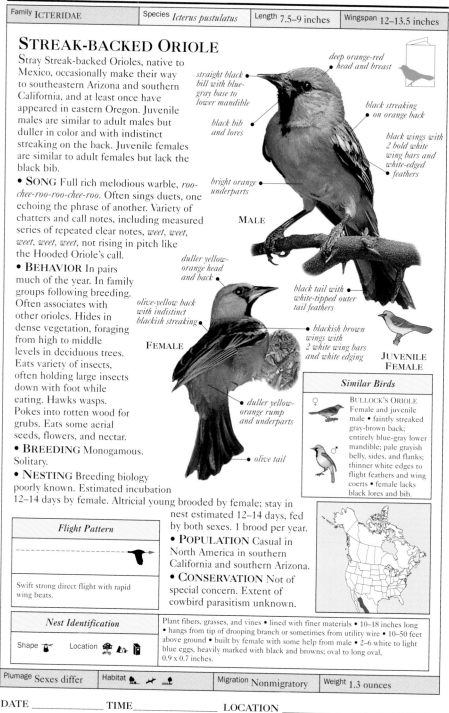

Stray Streak-backed Orioles, native to Mexico, occasionally make their way to southeastern Arizona and southern California, and at least once have appeared in eastern Oregon. Juvenile males are similar to adult males but duller in color and with indistinct streaking on the back. Juvenile females are similar to adult females but lack the black bib.

• **SONG** Full rich melodious warble, *roo-chee-roo-roo-chee-roo*. Often sings duets, one echoing the phrase of another. Variety of chatters and call notes, including measured series of repeated clear notes, *weet, weet, weet, weet, weet*, not rising in pitch like the Hooded Oriole's call.

• **BEHAVIOR** In pairs much of the year. In family groups following breeding. Often associates with other orioles. Hides in dense vegetation, foraging from high to middle levels in deciduous trees. Eats variety of insects, often holding large insects down with foot while eating. Hawks wasps. Pokes into rotten wood for grubs. Eats some aerial seeds, flowers, and nectar.

• **BREEDING** Monogamous. Solitary.

• **NESTING** Breeding biology poorly known. Estimated incubation 12–14 days by female. Altricial young brooded by female; stay in nest estimated 12–14 days, fed by both sexes. 1 brood per year.

• **POPULATION** Casual in North America in southern California and southern Arizona.

• **CONSERVATION** Not of special concern. Extent of cowbird parasitism unknown.

deep orange-red head and breast

straight black bill with blue-gray base to lower mandible

black bib and lores

black streaking on orange back

black wings with 2 bold white wing bars and white-edged feathers

bright orange underparts

MALE

duller yellow-orange head and back

olive-yellow back with indistinct blackish streaking

FEMALE

black tail with white-tipped outer tail feathers

blackish brown wings with 2 white wing bars and white edging

JUVENILE FEMALE

duller yellow-orange rump and underparts

olive tail

Similar Birds

♀

BULLOCK'S ORIOLE
Female and juvenile male • faintly streaked gray-brown back; entirely blue-gray lower mandible; pale grayish belly, sides, and flanks; thinner white edges to flight feathers and wing coerts • female lacks black lores and bib.

♂

Flight Pattern
Swift strong direct flight with rapid wing beats.

Nest Identification	
Shape 🌿 Location 🌳 🌲 🎋	Plant fibers, grasses, and vines • lined with finer materials • 10–18 inches long • hangs from tip of drooping branch or sometimes from utility wire • 10–50 feet above ground • built by female with some help from male • 2–6 white to light blue eggs, heavily marked with black and browns; oval to long oval, 0.9 x 0.7 inches.

Plumage Sexes differ	Habitat 🌳 ✈ 🌊	Migration Nonmigratory	Weight 1.3 ounces

DATE _____ TIME_____ LOCATION _____

Family ICTERIDAE	Species *Icterus galbula*	Length 7–8.25 inches	Wingspan 11.25–12.5 inches

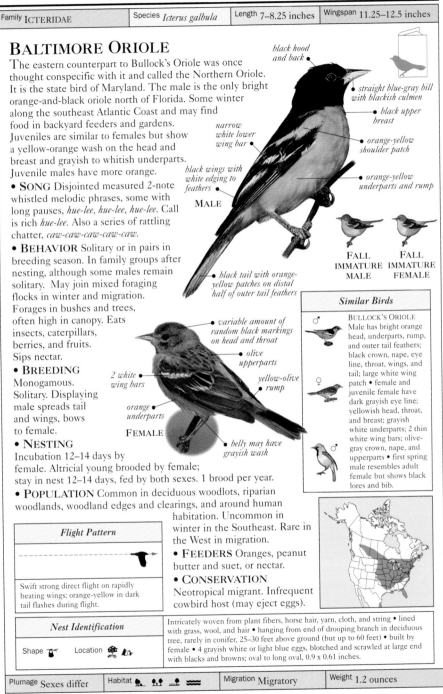

BALTIMORE ORIOLE

The eastern counterpart to Bullock's Oriole was once thought conspecific with it and called the Northern Oriole. It is the state bird of Maryland. The male is the only bright orange-and-black oriole north of Florida. Some winter along the southeast Atlantic Coast and may find food in backyard feeders and gardens. Juveniles are similar to females but show a yellow-orange wash on the head and breast and grayish to whitish underparts. Juvenile males have more orange.

- **SONG** Disjointed measured 2-note whistled melodic phrases, some with long pauses, *hue-lee, hue-lee, hue-lee*. Call is rich *hue-lee*. Also a series of rattling chatter, *caw-caw-caw-caw-caw*.

- **BEHAVIOR** Solitary or in pairs in breeding season. In family groups after nesting, although some males remain solitary. May join mixed foraging flocks in winter and migration. Forages in bushes and trees, often high in canopy. Eats insects, caterpillars, berries, and fruits. Sips nectar.

- **BREEDING** Monogamous. Solitary. Displaying male spreads tail and wings, bows to female.

- **NESTING** Incubation 12–14 days by female. Altricial young brooded by female; stay in nest 12–14 days, fed by both sexes. 1 brood per year.

- **POPULATION** Common in deciduous woodlots, riparian woodlands, woodland edges and clearings, and around human habitation. Uncommon in winter in the Southeast. Rare in the West in migration.

- **FEEDERS** Oranges, peanut butter and suet, or nectar.

- **CONSERVATION** Neotropical migrant. Infrequent cowbird host (may eject eggs).

black hood and back

straight blue-gray bill with blackish culmen

black upper breast

orange-yellow shoulder patch

orange-yellow underparts and rump

narrow white lower wing bar

black wings with white edging to feathers

MALE

black tail with orange-yellow patches on distal half of outer tail feathers

FALL IMMATURE MALE

FALL IMMATURE FEMALE

variable amount of random black markings on head and throat

olive upperparts

yellow-olive rump

2 white wing bars

orange underparts

FEMALE

belly may have grayish wash

Similar Birds

BULLOCK'S ORIOLE Male has bright orange head, underparts, rump, and outer tail feathers; black crown, nape, eye line, throat, wings, and tail; large white wing patch • female and juvenile female have dark grayish eye line; yellowish head, throat, and breast; grayish white underparts; 2 thin white wing bars; olive-gray crown, nape, and upperparts • first spring male resembles adult female but shows black lores and bib.

Flight Pattern
Swift strong direct flight on rapidly beating wings; orange-yellow in dark tail flashes during flight.

Nest Identification	
Shape	Location

Intricately woven from plant fibers, horse hair, yarn, cloth, and string • lined with grass, wool, and hair • hanging from end of drooping branch in deciduous tree, rarely in conifer, 25–30 feet above ground (but up to 60 feet) • built by female • 4 grayish white or light blue eggs, blotched and scrawled at large end with blacks and browns; oval to long oval, 0.9 x 0.61 inches.

Plumage Sexes differ	Habitat	Migration Migratory	Weight 1.2 ounces

DATE _____ TIME_____ LOCATION _____

Family ICTERIDAE	Species *Icterus bullockii*	Length 7–8.25 inches	Wingspan 11.25–12.5 inches

BULLOCK'S ORIOLE

Once considered the same species as the Baltimore Oriole, with which it hybridizes in the Great Plains, this bird was formerly called the Northern Oriole. The bright orange male differs from other orioles in its face pattern and in its large white wing patches that flash in flight.

black cap, nape, bib, and eye stripe

straight blue-gray bill with blackish culmen

black back

MALE

orange face

black tail with orange outer tail feathers

black wings with large white patch and edging to feathers

orange rump

orange underparts

gray legs and feet

FIRST SPRING MALE

olive-brown crown and nape

dusky eye line

yellow face, throat, and breast

olive-brown back and wings

blackish brown wings with 2 white wing bars

olive tail

FEMALE

buffy gray belly and rump, sometimes washed yellow-orange

- **SONG** Measured clear whistled single and double notes with some gruff or scratchy notes. Has rough nasal call of *cheah*, given singly or in series. Also has a loud rattle.

- **BEHAVIOR** Solitary or in pairs during breeding season. In small family groups after nesting. Pairs spend much time together and both will attack predators. Noisy and conspicuous. Frequents river valley and agricultural areas. Forages in trees and bushes. Sips nectar. Eats insects, caterpillars, berries, and fruit.

- **BREEDING** Monogamous; also solitary.

- **NESTING** Incubation 12–14 days by female. Young altricial; brooded by female; stay in nest 12–4 days, fed by both sexes. 1 brood per year.

- **POPULATION** Common in open areas with shade trees and in foothill oak forests. Uncommon in winter in southern California; casual vagrant to the East in migration and winter.

- **FEEDERS** Suet, sliced orange, and nectar water.

- **CONSERVATION** Neotropical migrant. Frequent host to cowbird parasitism. Range increasing near man-made watercourses planted with shrubs and trees.

Similar Birds

BALTIMORE ORIOLE ♂
Male has hooded appearance due to more extensive black on head and throat; orange upper wing bar; white lower wing bar; orange distal half to outer tail feathers • female shows various degrees of black, olive, and orange on head; lacks eye stripe; orange or orange-washed underparts. ♀

Flight Pattern

Swift strong direct flight with rapid wing beats.

Nest Identification

Shape ⌇ Location 🌳 🌲

Plant fiber, horse hair, string, and bark, with lining of moss, plant down, wool, and hair • hanging from end of branch, often in cottonwood or willow, or in clump of mistletoe, 6–15 feet above ground • built by female, with some help from male • 4–5 light blue or pale gray eggs with dots of brown, gray, or black, scrawled with purplish black line; oval to long oval, 0.93 x 0.63 inches.

Plumage Sexes differ	Habitat 🌳 🌿 ⛰ 🌾	Migration Migratory	Weight 1.2 ounces

DATE _____ TIME_____ LOCATION _____

Family ICTERIDAE	Species *Icterus parisorum*	Length 7.5–9 inches	Wingspan 10–13.5 inches

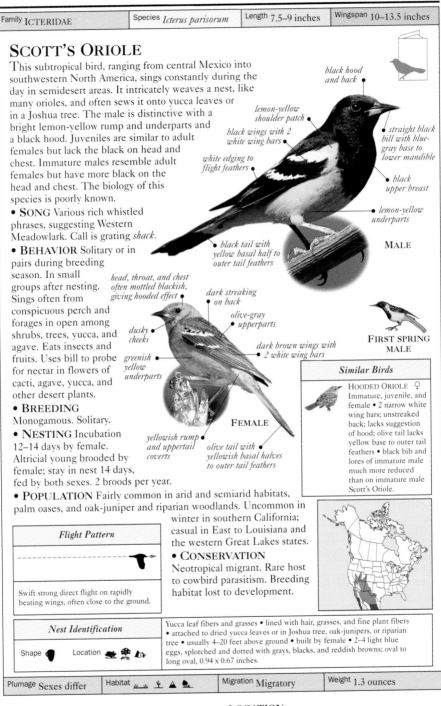

SCOTT'S ORIOLE

This subtropical bird, ranging from central Mexico into southwestern North America, sings constantly during the day in semidesert areas. It intricately weaves a nest, like many orioles, and often sews it onto yucca leaves or in a Joshua tree. The male is distinctive with a bright lemon-yellow rump and underparts and a black hood. Juveniles are similar to adult females but lack the black on head and chest. Immature males resemble adult females but have more black on the head and chest. The biology of this species is poorly known.

• **SONG** Various rich whistled phrases, suggesting Western Meadowlark. Call is grating *shack*.

• **BEHAVIOR** Solitary or in pairs during breeding season. In small groups after nesting. Sings often from conspicuous perch and forages in open among shrubs, trees, yucca, and agave. Eats insects and fruits. Uses bill to probe for nectar in flowers of cacti, agave, yucca, and other desert plants.

• **BREEDING** Monogamous. Solitary.

• **NESTING** Incubation 12–14 days by female. Altricial young brooded by female; stay in nest 14 days, fed by both sexes. 2 broods per year.

• **POPULATION** Fairly common in arid and semiarid habitats, palm oases, and oak-juniper and riparian woodlands. Uncommon in winter in southern California; casual in East to Louisiana and the western Great Lakes states.

• **CONSERVATION** Neotropical migrant. Rare host to cowbird parasitism. Breeding habitat lost to development.

black hood and back

lemon-yellow shoulder patch

black wings with 2 white wing bars

white edging to flight feathers

straight black bill with blue-gray base to lower mandible

black upper breast

lemon-yellow underparts

MALE

black tail with yellow basal half to outer tail feathers

head, throat, and chest often mottled blackish, giving hooded effect

dark streaking on back

olive-gray upperparts

dusky cheeks

greenish yellow underparts

dark brown wings with 2 white wing bars

FIRST SPRING MALE

yellowish rump and uppertail coverts

olive tail with yellowish basal halves to outer tail feathers

FEMALE

Similar Birds

HOODED ORIOLE ♀
Immature, juvenile, and female • 2 narrow white wing bars; unstreaked back; lacks suggestion of hood; olive tail lacks yellow base to outer tail feathers • black bib and lores of immature male much more reduced than on immature male Scott's Oriole.

Flight Pattern

Swift strong direct flight on rapidly beating wings, often close to the ground.

Nest Identification	Yucca leaf fibers and grasses • lined with hair, grasses, and fine plant fibers • attached to dried yucca leaves or in Joshua tree, oak-junipers, or riparian tree • usually 4–20 feet above ground • built by female • 2–4 light blue eggs, splotched and dotted with grays, blacks, and reddish browns; oval to long oval, 0.94 x 0.67 inches.
Shape ◗ Location 🌳 🌿 ⛰	

Plumage Sexes differ	Habitat �‧ ⚘ ♇ ▲ 🐾	Migration Migratory	Weight 1.3 ounces

DATE _____ TIME_____ LOCATION _____

| Family FRINGILLIDAE | Species *Fringilla montifringilla* | Length 5.5–6.25 inches | Wingspan 8.5–10 inches |

BRAMBLING

This Eurasian native occasionally makes visits during migration to the western islands of Alaska. It is casual in the fall and winter across coastal and southern Canada and the northern US to California. Females are similar to males in fresh fall plumage but are duller in color with an olive-brown head and back. Winter males have orange-buff shoulders and chests, a white shoulder bar, and black spotting on the flanks. In flight the long white wing stripe and white rump are distinctive. Juveniles are similar to adult females but are paler with heavier streaking on the back.

• **SONG** Bold grating *dzhweeeeee*. Flight call is nasal *check-check-check*. Call is harsh *tweerk*.

• **BEHAVIOR** Solitary or in pairs while nesting, but in flocks for rest of year; joins mixed foraging flocks in winter. Forages in trees, bushes, and on ground. Eats seeds and insects in summer; seeds in winter. Nests in northern forests with birch trees. Winters in woodlands and weedy fields.

• **BREEDING** Monogamous. Stays in pairs.

• **NESTING** Incubation 11–12 days by female. Young altricial; brooded by female; stay in nest 11–13 days, fed by both sexes. 1–2 broods per year.

• **POPULATION** Rare to casual except western islands in Bering Sea, where it is fairly common in spring migration; has nested at least once on Attu Island. Scattered fall and winter records from coast to coast in southern Canada and northern US to California.

• **FEEDERS** Will come to feeders for sunflower seeds.

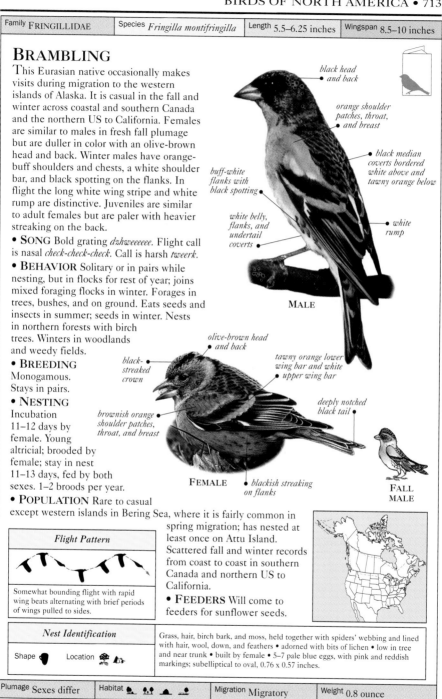

black head and back

orange shoulder patches, throat, and breast

black median coverts bordered white above and tawny orange below

buff-white flanks with black spotting

white belly, flanks, and undertail coverts

white rump

MALE

olive-brown head and back

black-streaked crown

tawny orange lower wing bar and white upper wing bar

brownish orange shoulder patches, throat, and breast

deeply notched black tail

FEMALE

blackish streaking on flanks

FALL MALE

Flight Pattern
Somewhat bounding flight with rapid wing beats alternating with brief periods of wings pulled to sides.

Nest Identification	Grass, hair, birch bark, and moss, held together with spiders' webbing and lined with hair, wool, down, and feathers • adorned with bits of lichen • low in tree and near trunk • built by female • 5–7 pale blue eggs, with pink and reddish markings; subelliptical to oval, 0.76 x 0.57 inches.
Shape ● Location 🌲 🪴	

| Plumage Sexes differ | Habitat 🌿 🌿 🌳 🌱 | Migration Migratory | Weight 0.8 ounce |

DATE _____ TIME_____ LOCATION _____

Family FRINGILLIDAE	Species *Leucosticte tephrocotis*	Length 5.75–6 inches	Wingspan 9–9.5 inches

GRAY-CROWNED ROSY-FINCH

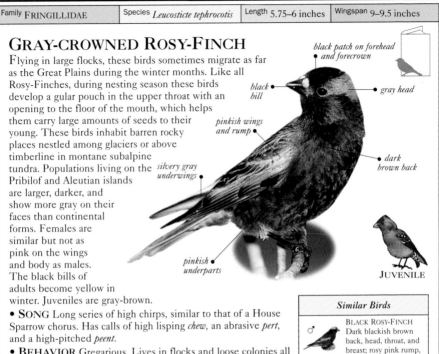

Flying in large flocks, these birds sometimes migrate as far as the Great Plains during the winter months. Like all Rosy-Finches, during nesting season these birds develop a gular pouch in the upper throat with an opening to the floor of the mouth, which helps them carry large amounts of seeds to their young. These birds inhabit barren rocky places nestled among glaciers or above timberline in montane subalpine tundra. Populations living on the Pribilof and Aleutian islands are larger, darker, and show more gray on their faces than continental forms. Females are similar but not as pink on the wings and body as males. The black bills of adults become yellow in winter. Juveniles are gray-brown.

black patch on forehead and forecrown
gray head
black bill
pinkish wings and rump
silvery gray underwings
dark brown back
pinkish underparts

JUVENILE

• **SONG** Long series of high chirps, similar to that of a House Sparrow chorus. Has calls of high lisping *chew*, an abrasive *pert*, and a high-pitched *peent*.

• **BEHAVIOR** Gregarious. Lives in flocks and loose colonies all year. Males weakly territorial. Forages in shrubs, grasses, and on ground, hunting in crevices, among rocks, around tundra and snow pools, and along glaciers. Walks rather than hops. Eats mostly seeds but actively takes insects, sometimes hawking them in flight. In many populations, males greatly outnumber females, and competition during courtship can be vigorous. Mountain populations descend to lower elevations in winter.

• **BREEDING** Monogamous. Colonial. Female chooses territory while male follows and defends her from other birds.

• **NESTING** Incubation 12–14 days by female. Young altricial; brooded by female; stay in nest 16–22 days, fed by both sexes. 1 brood in the mountains; 2 broods elsewhere.

Similar Birds

♂ ♀ BLACK ROSY-FINCH
Dark blackish brown back, head, throat, and breast; rosy pink rump, wing patch, and underparts; black forehead and forecrown; gray head band • only in the West.

♂ ♀ BROWN-CAPPED ROSY-FINCH
Dark brown cap; rich brown back, nape, face, throat, and chest; reddish pink underparts, wing patch, rump and uppertail coverts • western range.

• **POPULATION** Common and widespread in Alaska and northwestern Canada. Locally common on alpine tundra over remaining range. Casual in winter to the Midwest and southern California; accidental to Ontario, Quebec, and Maine.

Flight Pattern

Somewhat bounding flight with several rapid wing beats alternating with brief period of wings pulled to sides.

Nest Identification

Shape 🥣   Location 🌿🏚🏔

Grass, rootlets, lichen, and moss, lined with fine grass, plant down, and occasionally feathers • in ridges of rocks and cliffs, sometimes in cave or eave of building • built by female • 4–5 white eggs, occasionally dotted with reddish brown; short pyriform, 0.9 x 0.61 inches.

Plumage Sexes differ	Habitat ▲ ᴸ ⚬	Migration Some migrate	Weight Undetermined

DATE _____ TIME_____ LOCATION _____

Family FRINGILLIDAE	Species *Leucosticte atrata*	Length 6 inches	Wingspan 9.5 inches

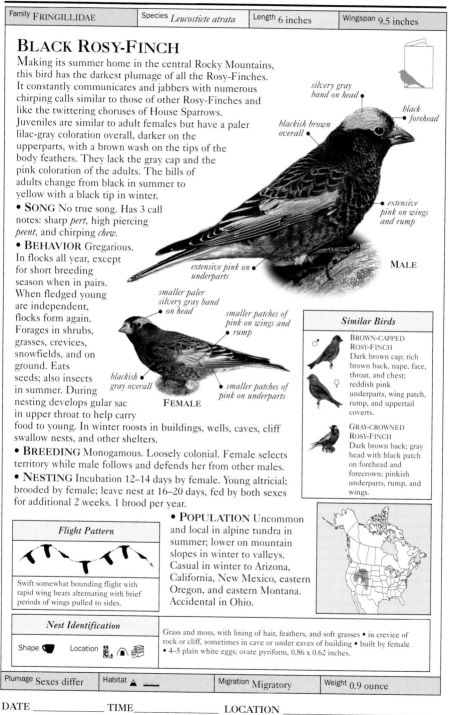

BLACK ROSY-FINCH

Making its summer home in the central Rocky Mountains, this bird has the darkest plumage of all the Rosy-Finches. It constantly communicates and jabbers with numerous chirping calls similar to those of other Rosy-Finches and like the twittering choruses of House Sparrows. Juveniles are similar to adult females but have a paler lilac-gray coloration overall, darker on the upperparts, with a brown wash on the tips of the body feathers. They lack the gray cap and the pink coloration of the adults. The bills of adults change from black in summer to yellow with a black tip in winter.

- **SONG** No true song. Has 3 call notes: sharp *pert*, high piercing *peent*, and chirping *chew*.
- **BEHAVIOR** Gregarious. In flocks all year, except for short breeding season when in pairs. When fledged young are independent, flocks form again. Forages in shrubs, grasses, crevices, snowfields, and on ground. Eats seeds; also insects in summer. During nesting develops gular sac in upper throat to help carry food to young. In winter roosts in buildings, wells, caves, cliff swallow nests, and other shelters.
- **BREEDING** Monogamous. Loosely colonial. Female selects territory while male follows and defends her from other males.
- **NESTING** Incubation 12–14 days by female. Young altricial; brooded by female; leave nest at 16–20 days, fed by both sexes for additional 2 weeks. 1 brood per year.

silvery gray band on head

black forehead

blackish brown overall

extensive pink on wings and rump

extensive pink on underparts

MALE

smaller paler silvery gray band on head

smaller patches of pink on wings and rump

blackish gray overall

smaller patches of pink on underparts

FEMALE

Similar Birds

♂ **BROWN-CAPPED ROSY-FINCH** Dark brown cap; rich brown back, nape, face, throat, and chest; ♀ reddish pink underparts, wing patch, rump, and uppertail coverts.

GRAY-CROWNED ROSY-FINCH Dark brown back; gray head with black patch on forehead and forecrown; pinkish underparts, rump, and wings.

- **POPULATION** Uncommon and local in alpine tundra in summer; lower on mountain slopes in winter to valleys. Casual in winter to Arizona, California, New Mexico, eastern Oregon, and eastern Montana. Accidental in Ohio.

Flight Pattern

Swift somewhat bounding flight with rapid wing beats alternating with brief periods of wings pulled to sides.

Nest Identification

Shape 🍵   Location 🌿 🏠 🏢

Grass and moss, with lining of hair, feathers, and soft grasses • in crevice of rock or cliff, sometimes in cave or under eaves of building • built by female • 4–5 plain white eggs; ovate pyriform, 0.86 x 0.62 inches.

Plumage Sexes differ	Habitat ▲	Migration Migratory	Weight 0.9 ounce

DATE _____ TIME_____ LOCATION _____

Family FRINGILLIDAE	Species *Leucosticte australis*	Length 6 inches	Wingspan 9.5 inches

BROWN-CAPPED ROSY-FINCH

These birds roost in winter with other species of Rosy-Finches, totaling as many as a thousand birds in old mud nests of Cliff Swallows or in crevices of cliffs. A bird of high mountain subalpine tundra, mainly in the Colorado Rockies, it is reluctant to leave its high altitudes, even in winter, migrating down the slopes often no farther than the five-thousand-foot level. Females are drab brown with a wash of red on the lesser wing coverts and rump. Juveniles are similar to females but lack pink on the shoulders and rump. The bills of all adults are black in summer and yellow with a black tip in winter.

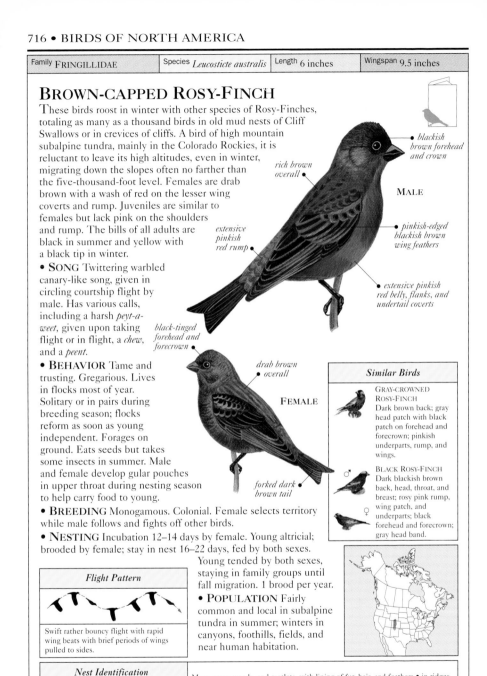

blackish brown forehead and crown

rich brown overall

MALE

pinkish-edged blackish brown wing feathers

extensive pinkish red rump

extensive pinkish red belly, flanks, and undertail coverts

black-tinged forehead and forecrown

drab brown overall

FEMALE

forked dark brown tail

- **SONG** Twittering warbled canary-like song, given in circling courtship flight by male. Has various calls, including a harsh *peyt-a-weet*, given upon taking flight or in flight, a *chew*, and a *peent*.
- **BEHAVIOR** Tame and trusting. Gregarious. Lives in flocks most of year. Solitary or in pairs during breeding season; flocks reform as soon as young independent. Forages on ground. Eats seeds but takes some insects in summer. Male and female develop gular pouches in upper throat during nesting season to help carry food to young.
- **BREEDING** Monogamous. Colonial. Female selects territory while male follows and fights off other birds.
- **NESTING** Incubation 12–14 days by female. Young altricial; brooded by female; stay in nest 16–22 days, fed by both sexes. Young tended by both sexes, staying in family groups until fall migration. 1 brood per year.
- **POPULATION** Fairly common and local in subalpine tundra in summer; winters in canyons, foothills, fields, and near human habitation.

Similar Birds

GRAY-CROWNED ROSY-FINCH
Dark brown back; gray head patch with black patch on forehead and forecrown; pinkish underparts, rump, and wings.

BLACK ROSY-FINCH
Dark blackish brown back, head, throat, and breast; rosy pink rump, wing patch, and underparts; black forehead and forecrown; gray head band.

Flight Pattern

Swift rather bouncy flight with rapid wing beats with brief periods of wings pulled to sides.

Nest Identification

Shape ☕ Location 🪨 🏠 🏚️

Moss, grass, weeds, and rootlets, with lining of fur, hair, and feathers • in ridges of cliffs, in rock crevices, or sometimes in cave or under eaves of building • built by female • 3–5 plain white eggs; ovate pyriform, 0.85 x 0.61 inches.

Plumage Sexes differ	Habitat ▲ ⌂ ⛰ ▲	Migration Migratory	Weight 0.9 ounce

DATE _____ TIME_____ LOCATION _____

Family FRINGILLIDAE	Species *Pinicola enucleator*	Length 9–9.75 inches	Wingspan 13.75–15 inches

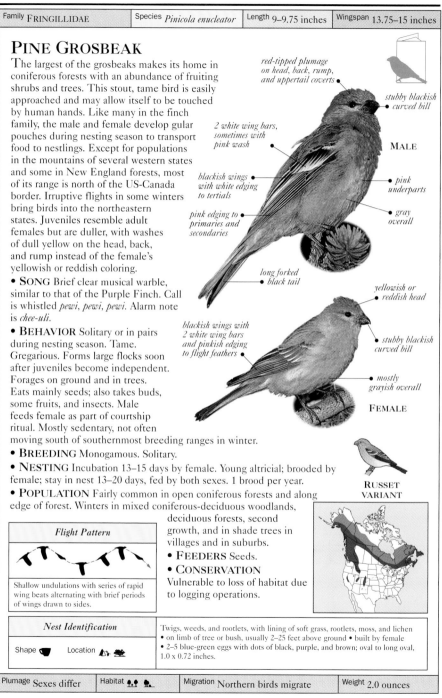

PINE GROSBEAK

The largest of the grosbeaks makes its home in coniferous forests with an abundance of fruiting shrubs and trees. This stout, tame bird is easily approached and may allow itself to be touched by human hands. Like many in the finch family, the male and female develop gular pouches during nesting season to transport food to nestlings. Except for populations in the mountains of several western states and some in New England forests, most of its range is north of the US-Canada border. Irruptive flights in some winters bring birds into the northeastern states. Juveniles resemble adult females but are duller, with washes of dull yellow on the head, back, and rump instead of the female's yellowish or reddish coloring.

- **SONG** Brief clear musical warble, similar to that of the Purple Finch. Call is whistled *pewi, pewi, pewi*. Alarm note is *chee-uli*.

- **BEHAVIOR** Solitary or in pairs during nesting season. Tame. Gregarious. Forms large flocks soon after juveniles become independent. Forages on ground and in trees. Eats mainly seeds; also takes buds, some fruits, and insects. Male feeds female as part of courtship ritual. Mostly sedentary, not often moving south of southernmost breeding ranges in winter.

- **BREEDING** Monogamous. Solitary.

- **NESTING** Incubation 13–15 days by female. Young altricial; brooded by female; stay in nest 13–20 days, fed by both sexes. 1 brood per year.

- **POPULATION** Fairly common in open coniferous forests and along edge of forest. Winters in mixed coniferous-deciduous woodlands, deciduous forests, second growth, and in shade trees in villages and in suburbs.

- **FEEDERS** Seeds.

- **CONSERVATION** Vulnerable to loss of habitat due to logging operations.

red-tipped plumage on head, back, rump, and uppertail coverts

stubby blackish curved bill

MALE

2 white wing bars, sometimes with pink wash

blackish wings with white edging to tertials

pink edging to primaries and secondaries

pink underparts

gray overall

long forked black tail

yellowish or reddish head

stubby blackish curved bill

blackish wings with 2 white wing bars and pinkish edging to flight feathers

mostly grayish overall

FEMALE

RUSSET VARIANT

Flight Pattern	
Shallow undulations with series of rapid wing beats alternating with brief periods of wings drawn to sides.	

Nest Identification	
Shape ◥ Location 🌿 🌲	Twigs, weeds, and rootlets, with lining of soft grass, rootlets, moss, and lichen • on limb of tree or bush, usually 2–25 feet above ground • built by female • 2–5 blue-green eggs with dots of black, purple, and brown; oval to long oval, 1.0 x 0.72 inches.

Plumage Sexes differ	Habitat 🐦 🌲	Migration Northern birds migrate	Weight 2.0 ounces

DATE _____ TIME_____ LOCATION _____

Family FRINGILLIDAE	Species *Carpodacus purpureus*	Length 5.5–6.25 inches	Wingspan 9.25–10.5 inches

PURPLE FINCH

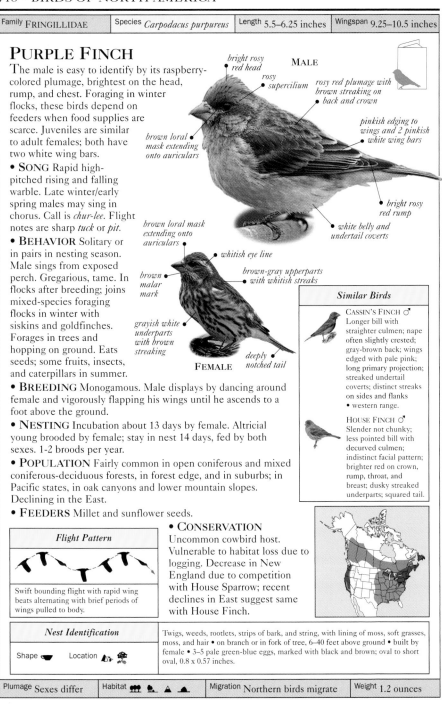

The male is easy to identify by its raspberry-colored plumage, brightest on the head, rump, and chest. Foraging in winter flocks, these birds depend on feeders when food supplies are scarce. Juveniles are similar to adult females; both have two white wing bars.

MALE

bright rosy red head

rosy supercilium

rosy red plumage with brown streaking on back and crown

pinkish edging to wings and 2 pinkish white wing bars

brown loral mask extending onto auriculars

bright rosy red rump

white belly and undertail coverts

brown loral mask extending onto auriculars

whitish eye line

brown-gray upperparts with whitish streaks

brown malar mark

grayish white underparts with brown streaking

deeply notched tail

FEMALE

- **SONG** Rapid high-pitched rising and falling warble. Late winter/early spring males may sing in chorus. Call is *chur-lee*. Flight notes are sharp *tuck* or *pit*.
- **BEHAVIOR** Solitary or in pairs in nesting season. Male sings from exposed perch. Gregarious, tame. In flocks after breeding; joins mixed-species foraging flocks in winter with siskins and goldfinches. Forages in trees and hopping on ground. Eats seeds; some fruits, insects, and caterpillars in summer.
- **BREEDING** Monogamous. Male displays by dancing around female and vigorously flapping his wings until he ascends to a foot above the ground.
- **NESTING** Incubation about 13 days by female. Altricial young brooded by female; stay in nest 14 days, fed by both sexes. 1-2 broods per year.
- **POPULATION** Fairly common in open coniferous and mixed coniferous-deciduous forests, in forest edge, and in suburbs; in Pacific states, in oak canyons and lower mountain slopes. Declining in the East.
- **FEEDERS** Millet and sunflower seeds.

Similar Birds

CASSIN'S FINCH ♂
Longer bill with straighter culmen; nape often slightly crested; gray-brown back; wings edged with pale pink; long primary projection; streaked undertail coverts; distinct streaks on sides and flanks
• western range.

HOUSE FINCH ♂
Slender not chunky; less pointed bill with decurved culmen; indistinct facial pattern; brighter red on crown, rump, throat, and breast; dusky streaked underparts; squared tail.

- **CONSERVATION** Uncommon cowbird host. Vulnerable to habitat loss due to logging. Decrease in New England due to competition with House Sparrow; recent declines in East suggest same with House Finch.

Flight Pattern
Swift bounding flight with rapid wing beats alternating with brief periods of wings pulled to body.

Nest Identification	Twigs, weeds, rootlets, strips of bark, and string, with lining of moss, soft grasses, moss, and hair • on branch or in fork of tree, 6–40 feet above ground • built by female • 3–5 pale green-blue eggs, marked with black and brown; oval to short oval, 0.8 x 0.57 inches.
Shape ⌒ Location 🌲🌳	

Plumage Sexes differ	Habitat 🌾 🌿 🔺 🔺	Migration Northern birds migrate	Weight 1.2 ounces

DATE _____ TIME_____ LOCATION _____

Family FRINGILLIDAE	Species *Carpodacus cassinii*	Length 6 inches	Wingspan 9.75 inches

CASSIN'S FINCH

Inhabiting the coniferous mountain forests of the West, these birds move in autumn with their young to lower elevations for the winter. Females have pale coloring and streaked undertail coverts that help distinguish them from other similar finches. In summer, this bird occurs at higher elevations than the Purple and House Finches. Juveniles closely resemble adult females

• **SONG** Long rich warbling, variable in pattern and length. Calls are clear *cheep, cheep, cheep* and *kee-up*, and a 3-syllabled flight note of *tee-dee-yip*.

• **BEHAVIOR** Solitary or in pairs during nesting season; forms family groups after breeding. Gregarious and tame. Forages on ground and high in trees; eats conifer seeds and buds, some insects in summer. Frequents salt licks and gathers at salted roadsides in winter. Nests in different sites each year.

• **BREEDING** Monogamous. Semicolonial.

• **NESTING** Incubation 12–14 days by female. Young altricial; brooded by female; stay in nest 14 days, fed by both sexes. 2 broods per year.

• **POPULATION** Fairly common in high montane open coniferous forests. In winter in deciduous woodlands, brushy scrublands, and second growth. Casual in winter to the West Coast and east to Minnesota, Oklahoma, and central Texas.

• **FEEDERS** Seeds.

• **CONSERVATION** Neotropical migrant. Rare cowbird host. Vulnerable to loss of habitat due to logging.

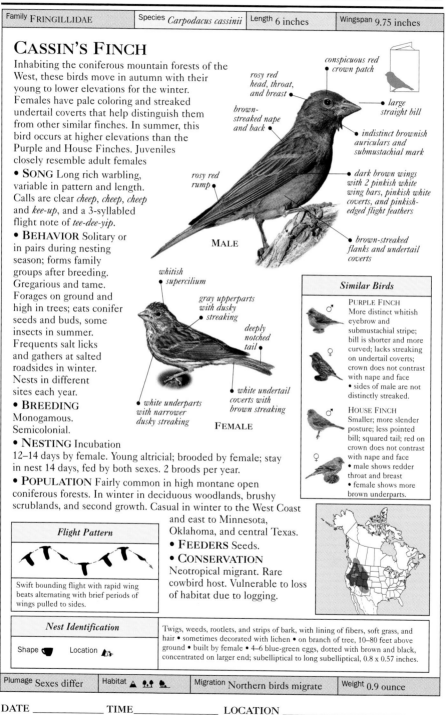

conspicuous red crown patch

rosy red head, throat, and breast

brown-streaked nape and back

large straight bill

indistinct brownish auriculars and submustachial mark

rosy red rump

dark brown wings with 2 pinkish white wing bars, pinkish white coverts, and pinkish-edged flight feathers

MALE

brown-streaked flanks and undertail coverts

whitish supercilium

gray upperparts with dusky streaking

deeply notched tail

white undertail coverts with brown streaking

white underparts with narrower dusky streaking

FEMALE

Similar Birds

PURPLE FINCH ♂
More distinct whitish eyebrow and submustachial stripe; bill is shorter and more curved; lacks streaking on undertail coverts; crown does not contrast with nape and face
• sides of male are not distinctly streaked. ♀

HOUSE FINCH ♂
Smaller; more slender posture; less pointed bill; squared tail; red on crown does not contrast with nape and face
• male shows redder throat and breast
• female shows more brown underparts. ♀

Flight Pattern
Swift bounding flight with rapid wing beats alternating with brief periods of wings pulled to sides.

Nest Identification	Twigs, weeds, rootlets, and strips of bark, with lining of fibers, soft grass, and hair • sometimes decorated with lichen • on branch of tree, 10–80 feet above ground • built by female • 4–6 blue-green eggs, dotted with brown and black, concentrated on larger end; subelliptical to long subelliptical, 0.8 x 0.57 inches.
Shape ◥ Location ▲	

Plumage Sexes differ	Habitat ▲ ♣♣ ♠	Migration Northern birds migrate	Weight 0.9 ounce

| Family FRINGILLIDAE | Species *Carpodacus mexicanus* | Length 6 inches | Wingspan 9.75 inches |

HOUSE FINCH

Originally confined to the West, this finch was called a Linnet and introduced as a cage bird on Long Island, New York, in the 1940s. It became abundant in the East, surpassing the House Sparrow. Today, it is among the most widely distributed songbird species in North America. It often feeds with the Purple Finch, especially in winter. Some male variants are orange or yellow instead of red. Juveniles resemble adult females.

• **SONG** Varied rich high-pitched scratchy warble composed chiefly of 3-note phrases; many end with rising inflections. Both sexes sing, but male's song is longer, more complex, and more frequent. Call is nasal *chee* or *chee-wheet;* in flight a sharp nasal *nyee-ah.*

• **BEHAVIOR** Solitary or in pairs during nesting season. Gregarious. Forms small family groups when young become independent. Larger foraging flocks in winter may join with other finches. Actively forages on ground, in fields, and in suburban areas. Eats mostly seeds but in summer takes insects and fruits. Drinks maple sap. Males are conspicuous and sing often. Studies indicate that the redder the male's plumage, the more desirable he is to females.

• **BREEDING** Monogamous. Solitary.

• **NESTING** Incubation 12–14 days by female. Altricial young brooded by female; stay in nest 11–19 days, fed by both sexes. 1–3 broods per year.

• **POPULATION** Abundant over much of North America in a wide variety of habitats, from arid scrub, wooded canyons, cultivated fields, and open woodlands to suburban yards and urban areas.

• **FEEDERS** Thistle, millet, sunflower, and other seeds.

• **CONSERVATION** Rare cowbird host in the West; fairly common host in the East.

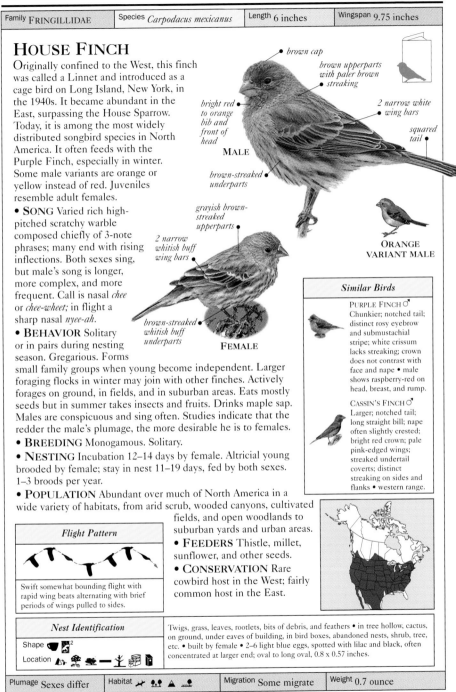

brown cap

brown upperparts with paler brown streaking

2 narrow white wing bars

squared tail

bright red to orange bib and front of head

MALE

brown-streaked underparts

grayish brown-streaked upperparts

2 narrow whitish buff wing bars

brown-streaked whitish buff underparts

FEMALE

ORANGE VARIANT MALE

Similar Birds

PURPLE FINCH ♂
Chunkier; notched tail; distinct rosy eyebrow and submustachial stripe; white crissum lacks streaking; crown does not contrast with face and nape • male shows raspberry-red on head, breast, and rump.

CASSIN'S FINCH ♂
Larger; notched tail; long straight bill; nape often slightly crested; bright red crown; pale pink-edged wings; streaked undertail coverts; distinct streaking on sides and flanks • western range.

Flight Pattern

Swift somewhat bounding flight with rapid wing beats alternating with brief periods of wings pulled to sides.

Nest Identification

Shape

Location

Twigs, grass, leaves, rootlets, bits of debris, and feathers • in tree hollow, cactus, on ground, under eaves of building, in bird boxes, abandoned nests, shrub, tree, etc. • built by female • 2–6 light blue eggs, spotted with lilac and black, often concentrated at larger end; oval to long oval, 0.8 x 0.57 inches.

| Plumage Sexes differ | Habitat | Migration Some migrate | Weight 0.7 ounce |

DATE _____ TIME_____ LOCATION _____

Family FRINGILLIDAE	Species *Loxia curvirostra*	Length 5.5–6.5 inches	Wingspan 10–10.75 inches

RED CROSSBILL

Crossbills take their name from the overlapping tips of the upper and lower mandibles. A resident of evergreen forests, they insert the crossed mandibles into conifer cones, forcing the scales apart while the tongue scoops the seed into the mouth. Nestlings have straight mandibles that cross gradually about three weeks out of the nest. Having abundant food year-round, this species begins nesting as early as January. Juveniles have weakly crossed mandibles, gray-olive upperparts heavily streaked dark brown, dark brown-streaked whitish underparts with yellowish wash, and buff-yellow rump. Subspecies of this bird vary in size, bill size, and vocalizations and may represent up to nine separate species.

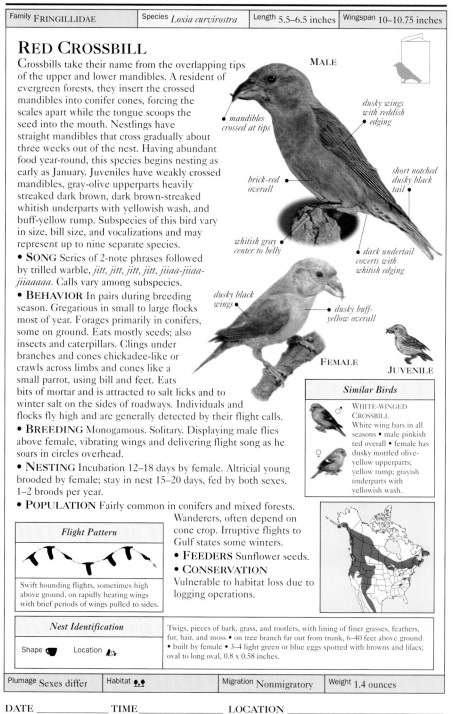

MALE

mandibles crossed at tips

dusky wings with reddish edging

brick-red overall

short notched dusky black tail

whitish gray center to belly

dark undertail coverts with whitish edging

dusky black wings

dusky buff-yellow overall

FEMALE

JUVENILE

• **SONG** Series of 2-note phrases followed by trilled warble, *jitt, jitt, jitt, jitt, jiiaa-jiiaa-jiiaaaaa*. Calls vary among subspecies.

• **BEHAVIOR** In pairs during breeding season. Gregarious in small to large flocks most of year. Forages primarily in conifers, some on ground. Eats mostly seeds; also insects and caterpillars. Clings under branches and cones chickadee-like or crawls across limbs and cones like a small parrot, using bill and feet. Eats bits of mortar and is attracted to salt licks and to winter salt on the sides of roadways. Individuals and flocks fly high and are generally detected by their flight calls.

• **BREEDING** Monogamous. Solitary. Displaying male flies above female, vibrating wings and delivering flight song as he soars in circles overhead.

• **NESTING** Incubation 12–18 days by female. Altricial young brooded by female; stay in nest 15–20 days, fed by both sexes. 1–2 broods per year.

• **POPULATION** Fairly common in conifers and mixed forests. Wanderers, often depend on cone crop. Irruptive flights to Gulf states some winters.

• **FEEDERS** Sunflower seeds.

• **CONSERVATION** Vulnerable to habitat loss due to logging operations.

Similar Birds

WHITE-WINGED CROSSBILL
White wing bars in all seasons • male pinkish red overall • female has dusky mottled olive-yellow upperparts; yellow rump; grayish underparts with yellowish wash.

Flight Pattern

Swift bounding flights, sometimes high above ground, on rapidly beating wings with brief periods of wings pulled to sides.

Nest Identification

Shape ⬥ Location 🔺

Twigs, pieces of bark, grass, and rootlets, with lining of finer grasses, feathers, fur, hair, and moss • on tree branch far out from trunk, 6–40 feet above ground • built by female • 3–4 light green or blue eggs spotted with browns and lilacs; oval to long oval, 0.8 x 0.58 inches.

Plumage Sexes differ	Habitat ♠,♦	Migration Nonmigratory	Weight 1.4 ounces

DATE _____ TIME_____ LOCATION _____

Family FRINGILLIDAE	Species *Loxia leucoptera*	Length 6–6.75 inches	Wingspan 9.5–10.5 inches

WHITE-WINGED CROSSBILL

Frequenting a northern range, White-winged Crossbills rarely are observed in large numbers in the US, except during food shortages and periods of overpopulation. Males are bright pink with a dusky band on the lower back, but plumage pales during winter months. Juveniles resemble adult females but are buffy tan overall with heavy brown streaking.

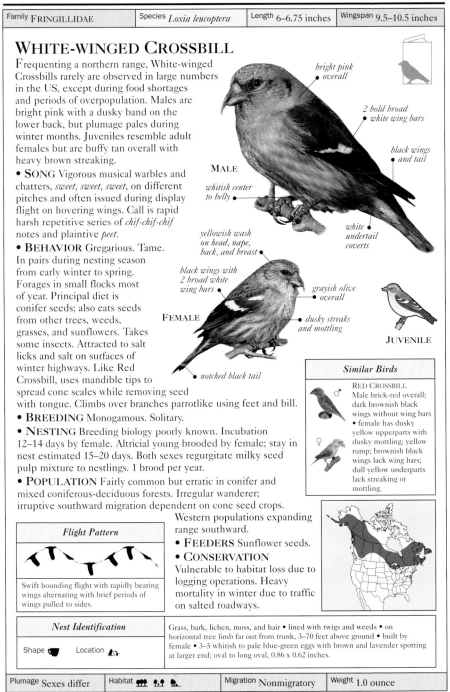

bright pink overall

2 bold broad white wing bars

black wings and tail

MALE

whitish center to belly

white undertail coverts

yellowish wash on head, nape, back, and breast

black wings with 2 broad white wing bars

FEMALE

grayish olive overall

dusky streaks and mottling

JUVENILE

notched black tail

• **SONG** Vigorous musical warbles and chatters, *sweet, sweet, sweet*, on different pitches and often issued during display flight on hovering wings. Call is rapid harsh repetitive series of *chif-chif-chif* notes and plaintive *peet*.
• **BEHAVIOR** Gregarious. Tame. In pairs during nesting season from early winter to spring. Forages in small flocks most of year. Principal diet is conifer seeds; also eats seeds from other trees, weeds, grasses, and sunflowers. Takes some insects. Attracted to salt licks and salt on surfaces of winter highways. Like Red Crossbill, uses mandible tips to spread cone scales while removing seed with tongue. Climbs over branches parrotlike using feet and bill.
• **BREEDING** Monogamous. Solitary.
• **NESTING** Breeding biology poorly known. Incubation 12–14 days by female. Altricial young brooded by female; stay in nest estimated 15–20 days. Both sexes regurgitate milky seed pulp mixture to nestlings. 1 brood per year.
• **POPULATION** Fairly common but erratic in conifer and mixed coniferous-deciduous forests. Irregular wanderer; irruptive southward migration dependent on cone seed crops. Western populations expanding range southward.
• **FEEDERS** Sunflower seeds.
• **CONSERVATION** Vulnerable to habitat loss due to logging operations. Heavy mortality in winter due to traffic on salted roadways.

Similar Birds

RED CROSSBILL
Male brick-red overall; dark brownish black wings without wing bars
• female has dusky yellow upperparts with dusky mottling; yellow rump; brownish black wings lack wing bars; dull yellow underparts lack streaking or mottling.

Flight Pattern

Swift bounding flight with rapidly beating wings alternating with brief periods of wings pulled to sides.

Nest Identification

Shape   Location

Grass, bark, lichen, moss, and hair • lined with twigs and weeds • on horizontal tree limb far out from trunk, 3–70 feet above ground • built by female • 3–5 whitish to pale blue-green eggs with brown and lavender spotting at larger end; oval to long oval, 0.86 x 0.62 inches.

Plumage Sexes differ	Habitat	Migration Nonmigratory	Weight 1.0 ounce

DATE _____ TIME _____ LOCATION _____

Family FRINGILLIDAE	Species *Carduelis flammea*	Length 5–5.5 inches	Wingspan 8.25–9 inches

COMMON REDPOLL

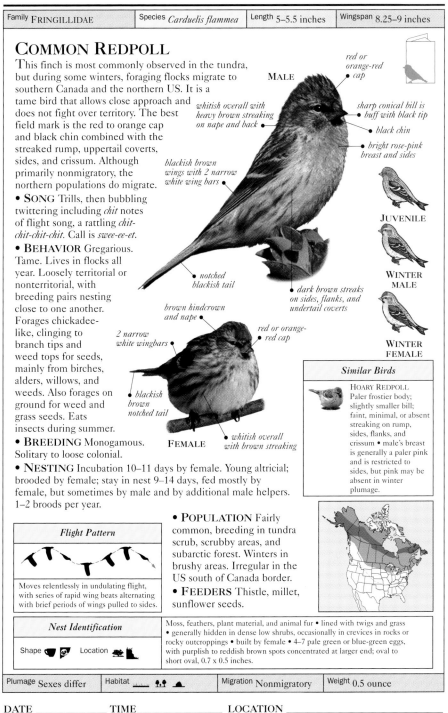

This finch is most commonly observed in the tundra, but during some winters, foraging flocks migrate to southern Canada and the northern US. It is a tame bird that allows close approach and does not fight over territory. The best field mark is the red to orange cap and black chin combined with the streaked rump, uppertail coverts, sides, and crissum. Although primarily nonmigratory, the northern populations do migrate.

MALE

red or orange-red cap

whitish overall with heavy brown streaking on nape and back

sharp conical bill is buff with black tip

black chin

bright rose-pink breast and sides

blackish brown wings with 2 narrow white wing bars

JUVENILE

- **SONG** Trills, then bubbling twittering including *chit* notes of flight song, a rattling *chit-chit-chit-chit*. Call is *swee-ee-et*.
- **BEHAVIOR** Gregarious. Tame. Lives in flocks all year. Loosely territorial or nonterritorial, with breeding pairs nesting close to one another. Forages chickadee-like, clinging to branch tips and weed tops for seeds, mainly from birches, alders, willows, and weeds. Also forages on ground for weed and grass seeds. Eats insects during summer.
- **BREEDING** Monogamous. Solitary to loose colonial.
- **NESTING** Incubation 10–11 days by female. Young altricial; brooded by female; stay in nest 9–14 days, fed mostly by female, but sometimes by male and by additional male helpers. 1–2 broods per year.

notched blackish tail

dark brown streaks on sides, flanks, and undertail coverts

WINTER MALE

brown hindcrown and nape

red or orange-red cap

2 narrow white wingbars

WINTER FEMALE

blackish brown notched tail

FEMALE

whitish overall with brown streaking

Similar Birds

HOARY REDPOLL
Paler frostier body; slightly smaller bill; faint, minimal, or absent streaking on rump, sides, flanks, and crissum • male's breast is generally a paler pink and is restricted to sides, but pink may be absent in winter plumage.

- **POPULATION** Fairly common, breeding in tundra scrub, scrubby areas, and subarctic forest. Winters in brushy areas. Irregular in the US south of Canada border.
- **FEEDERS** Thistle, millet, sunflower seeds.

Flight Pattern

Moves relentlessly in undulating flight, with series of rapid wing beats alternating with brief periods of wings pulled to sides.

Nest Identification

Shape   Location

Moss, feathers, plant material, and animal fur • lined with twigs and grass • generally hidden in dense low shrubs, occasionally in crevices in rocks or rocky outcroppings • built by female • 4–7 pale green or blue-green eggs, with purplish to reddish brown spots concentrated at larger end; oval to short oval, 0.7 x 0.5 inches.

Plumage Sexes differ	Habitat	Migration Nonmigratory	Weight 0.5 ounce

DATE _____ TIME_____ LOCATION _____

Family FRINGILLIDAE	Species *Carduelis hornemanni*	Length 5–5.75 inches	Wingspan 8.5–9.25 inches

HOARY REDPOLL

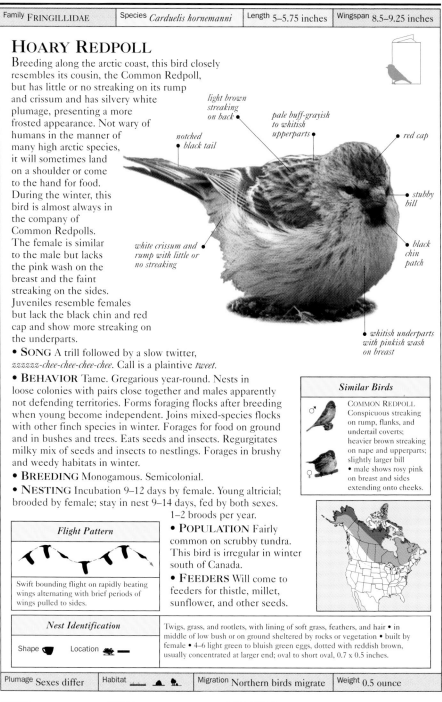

Breeding along the arctic coast, this bird closely resembles its cousin, the Common Redpoll, but has little or no streaking on its rump and crissum and has silvery white plumage, presenting a more frosted appearance. Not wary of humans in the manner of many high arctic species, it will sometimes land on a shoulder or come to the hand for food. During the winter, this bird is almost always in the company of Common Redpolls. The female is similar to the male but lacks the pink wash on the breast and the faint streaking on the sides. Juveniles resemble females but lack the black chin and red cap and show more streaking on the underparts.

light brown streaking on back

pale buff-grayish to whitish upperparts

notched black tail

red cap

stubby bill

white crissum and rump with little or no streaking

black chin patch

whitish underparts with pinkish wash on breast

• SONG A trill followed by a slow twitter, *zzzzzz-chee-chee-chee-chee*. Call is a plaintive *tweet*.

• BEHAVIOR Tame. Gregarious year-round. Nests in loose colonies with pairs close together and males apparently not defending territories. Forms foraging flocks after breeding when young become independent. Joins mixed-species flocks with other finch species in winter. Forages for food on ground and in bushes and trees. Eats seeds and insects. Regurgitates milky mix of seeds and insects to nestlings. Forages in brushy and weedy habitats in winter.

• BREEDING Monogamous. Semicolonial.

• NESTING Incubation 9–12 days by female. Young altricial; brooded by female; stay in nest 9–14 days, fed by both sexes. 1–2 broods per year.

Similar Birds

♂ COMMON REDPOLL
Conspicuous streaking on rump, flanks, and undertail coverts; heavier brown streaking on nape and upperparts; slightly larger bill
♀ • male shows rosy pink on breast and sides extending onto cheeks.

Flight Pattern

Swift bounding flight on rapidly beating wings alternating with brief periods of wings pulled to sides.

• POPULATION Fairly common on scrubby tundra. This bird is irregular in winter south of Canada.

• FEEDERS Will come to feeders for thistle, millet, sunflower, and other seeds.

Nest Identification

Shape ❤ Location 🌿 ▬

Twigs, grass, and rootlets, with lining of soft grass, feathers, and hair • in middle of low bush or on ground sheltered by rocks or vegetation • built by female • 4–6 light green to bluish green eggs, dotted with reddish brown, usually concentrated at larger end; oval to short oval, 0.7 x 0.5 inches.

Plumage Sexes differ	Habitat 〰️ ▲ 🏔️	Migration Northern birds migrate	Weight 0.5 ounce

DATE _____ TIME_____ LOCATION _____

Family FRINGILLIDAE	Species *Carduelis pinus*	Length 4.5–5.25 inches	Wingspan 8.5–9 inches

PINE SISKIN

In fall and winter this is a common visitor to northern forests, where it forages in flocks that may include several thousand birds. When food is scarce these daytime migrants may travel as far south as Florida and central Mexico, flying in tightly formed flocks. In flight the yellow wing stripe at the base of the flight feathers and the yellow base to the outer tail feathers are conspicuous. Females are similar to males but with more washed-out yellow plumage. Juveniles resemble females but show a yellowish wash overall.

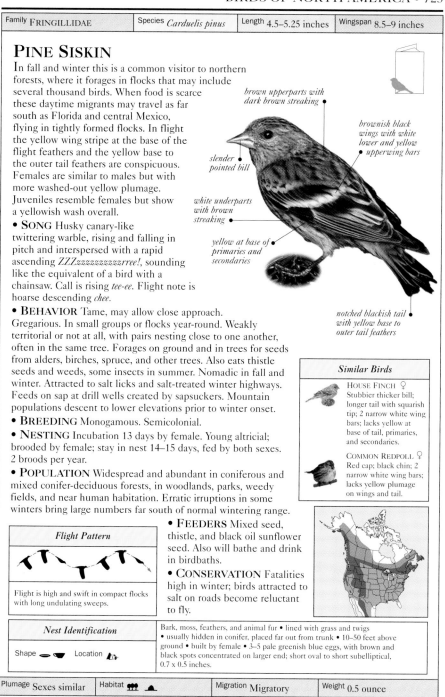

brown upperparts with dark brown streaking •

brownish black wings with white lower and yellow • upperwing bars

slender • pointed bill

white underparts with brown streaking •

yellow at base of • primaries and secondaries

notched blackish tail • with yellow base to outer tail feathers

• **SONG** Husky canary-like twittering warble, rising and falling in pitch and interspersed with a rapid ascending *ZZZzzzzzzzzzzrree!*, sounding like the equivalent of a bird with a chainsaw. Call is rising *tee-ee*. Flight note is hoarse descending *chee*.

• **BEHAVIOR** Tame, may allow close approach. Gregarious. In small groups or flocks year-round. Weakly territorial or not at all, with pairs nesting close to one another, often in the same tree. Forages on ground and in trees for seeds from alders, birches, spruce, and other trees. Also eats thistle seeds and weeds, some insects in summer. Nomadic in fall and winter. Attracted to salt licks and salt-treated winter highways. Feeds on sap at drill wells created by sapsuckers. Mountain populations descent to lower elevations prior to winter onset.

• **BREEDING** Monogamous. Semicolonial.

• **NESTING** Incubation 13 days by female. Young altricial; brooded by female; stay in nest 14–15 days, fed by both sexes. 2 broods per year.

• **POPULATION** Widespread and abundant in coniferous and mixed conifer-deciduous forests, in woodlands, parks, weedy fields, and near human habitation. Erratic irruptions in some winters bring large numbers far south of normal wintering range.

Similar Birds

HOUSE FINCH ♀
Stubbier thicker bill; longer tail with squarish tip; 2 narrow white wing bars; lacks yellow at base of tail, primaries, and secondaries.

COMMON REDPOLL ♀
Red cap; black chin; 2 narrow white wing bars; lacks yellow plumage on wings and tail.

• **FEEDERS** Mixed seed, thistle, and black oil sunflower seed. Also will bathe and drink in birdbaths.

• **CONSERVATION** Fatalities high in winter; birds attracted to salt on roads become reluctant to fly.

Flight Pattern
Flight is high and swift in compact flocks with long undulating sweeps.

Nest Identification	Bark, moss, feathers, and animal fur • lined with grass and twigs • usually hidden in conifer, placed far out from trunk • 10–50 feet above ground • built by female • 3–5 pale greenish blue eggs, with brown and black spots concentrated on larger end; short oval to short subelliptical, 0.7 x 0.5 inches.
Shape ⌒ ◡ Location ▲	

Plumage Sexes similar	Habitat 🐦 ▲	Migration Migratory	Weight 0.5 ounce

DATE _____ TIME_____ LOCATION _____

Family FRINGILLIDAE	Species *Carduelis psaltria*	Length 4.5 inches	Wingspan 8 inches

LESSER GOLDFINCH

Smaller than the American Goldfinch, this bird is welcome in the Southwest because of its pleasant song and the amount of weed seeds it consumes. It can be distinguished from other goldfinches by the white patch at the base of the primaries, which shows as a white wing stripe in flight. All adult males have a black crown, but the color of the back varies with range: black-backed birds in the East and green-backed birds in the West. Juvenile males are similar to females but have a black forehead and black streaking on the crown.

black cap
dark greenish olive upperparts
long conical blackish bill
GREEN-BACKED MALE
white wing bar
conspicuous white wing patch at base of primaries
bright yellow-green underparts
black wings with white edges to tertials
yellow undertail coverts
JUVENILE MALE
FEMALE
greenish olive upperparts
BLACK-BACKED MALE
blackish wings with 2 white wing bars
dull yellowish green underparts
white tips to tertials and white base to primaries
notched blackish tail

- **SONG** Complex warbling twittering exuberant series of *swee* notes. Call is mewing *tee-yee* and drawn-out nasal *zweeir*.
- **BEHAVIOR** In pairs or small flocks. Gregarious. Forages in flocks in brush, shrubs, and weedy fields. Frequents birdbaths and faucets. Eats weed seeds, other seeds, and insects.
- **BREEDING** Monogamous. Pairs stay together in winter; may mate for life. Male displays with singing flight song; feeds female during courtship.
- **NESTING** Late nester. Incubation 12 days by female, fed by male. Altricial young brooded by female; stay in nest 11–15 days. Both sexes feed regurgitated milky seed pulp. 1–2 broods per year.
- **POPULATION** Common in open habitats with scattered trees, brush fields, and woodland borders, especially near water and near human habitation. Casual in the Great Plains. Accidental in the East.
- **FEEDERS** Thistle, mixed seeds, and sunflower seeds.
- **CONSERVATION** Rare cowbird host.

Similar Birds

♂ ♀ AMERICAN GOLDFINCH Larger; stubby pinkish bill; whitish undertail coverts; blackish wings with 2 whitish to buff wing bars and white edging to tertials and secondaries; lacks white patch across base of primaries • in winter has brownish upperparts; grayish white underparts with buff wash on flanks.

Flight Pattern

High bouncy swift flight with rapid wing beats alternating with brief periods of wings pulled to sides.

Nest Identification

Shape 🥄   Location 🌳 🌲 🌾

Plant fibers, grasses, and bark pieces, with lining of feathers, cotton, and plant down • usually cradled across limb of tree or bush or occasionally set in tall weeds • 2–30 feet above ground • built by female • 3–6 light blue eggs, usually unmarked; ovate to rounded ovate, 0.61 x 0.45 inches.

Plumage Sexes differ	Habitat 🌾 🌿 🌳	Migration Northern birds migrate	Weight 0.3 ounce

DATE _____ TIME_____ LOCATION _____

Family FRINGILLIDAE	Species *Carduelis lawrencei*	Length 4.75 inches	Wingspan 8.25 inches

LAWRENCE'S GOLDFINCH

Nomadic because they require freshwater for drinking and bathing, these small birds inhabit some of the most arid country occupied by any goldfinch species. Their range is limited to the valleys of southern California and northern Baja California. Large yellow wing patches are conspicuous in flight.

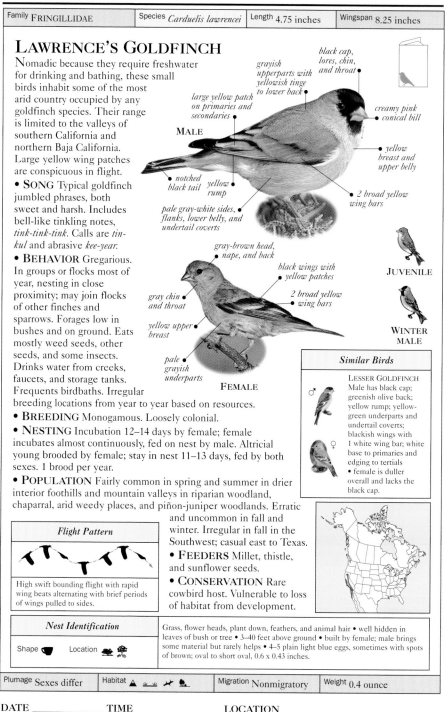

grayish upperparts with yellowish tinge to lower back

black cap, lores, chin, and throat

large yellow patch on primaries and secondaries

MALE

creamy pink conical bill

yellow breast and upper belly

notched black tail

yellow rump

2 broad yellow wing bars

pale gray-white sides, flanks, lower belly, and undertail coverts

gray-brown head, nape, and back

JUVENILE

black wings with yellow patches

gray chin and throat

2 broad yellow wing bars

yellow upper breast

WINTER MALE

pale grayish underparts

FEMALE

- **SONG** Typical goldfinch jumbled phrases, both sweet and harsh. Includes bell-like tinkling notes, *tink-tink-tink*. Calls are *tin-kul* and abrasive *kee-year.*
- **BEHAVIOR** Gregarious. In groups or flocks most of year, nesting in close proximity; may join flocks of other finches and sparrows. Forages low in bushes and on ground. Eats mostly weed seeds, other seeds, and some insects. Drinks water from creeks, faucets, and storage tanks. Frequents birdbaths. Irregular breeding locations from year to year based on resources.
- **BREEDING** Monogamous. Loosely colonial.
- **NESTING** Incubation 12–14 days by female; female incubates almost continuously, fed on nest by male. Altricial young brooded by female; stay in nest 11–13 days, fed by both sexes. 1 brood per year.
- **POPULATION** Fairly common in spring and summer in drier interior foothills and mountain valleys in riparian woodland, chaparral, arid weedy places, and piñon-juniper woodlands. Erratic and uncommon in fall and winter. Irregular in fall in the Southwest; casual east to Texas.
- **FEEDERS** Millet, thistle, and sunflower seeds.
- **CONSERVATION** Rare cowbird host. Vulnerable to loss of habitat from development.

Similar Birds

LESSER GOLDFINCH Male has black cap; greenish olive back; yellow rump; yellow-green underparts and undertail coverts; blackish wings with 1 white wing bar; white base to primaries and edging to tertials • female is duller overall and lacks the black cap.

Flight Pattern

High swift bounding flight with rapid wing beats alternating with brief periods of wings pulled to sides.

Nest Identification

Shape   Location

Grass, flower heads, plant down, feathers, and animal hair • well hidden in leaves of bush or tree • 3–40 feet above ground • built by female; male brings some material but rarely helps • 4–5 plain light blue eggs, sometimes with spots of brown; oval to short oval, 0.6 x 0.43 inches.

Plumage Sexes differ	Habitat	Migration Nonmigratory	Weight 0.4 ounce

DATE _____ TIME_____ LOCATION _____

Family FRINGILLIDAE	Species *Carduelis tristis*	Length 5 inches	Wingspan 8.75–9 inches

AMERICAN GOLDFINCH

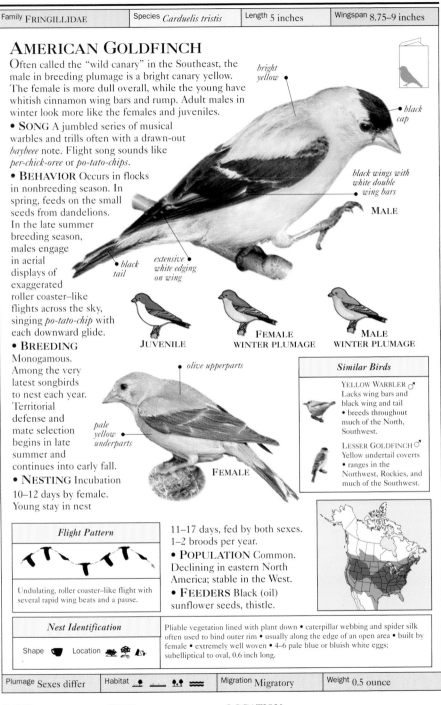

Often called the "wild canary" in the Southeast, the male in breeding plumage is a bright canary yellow. The female is more dull overall, while the young have whitish cinnamon wing bars and rump. Adult males in winter look more like the females and juveniles.

• **SONG** A jumbled series of musical warbles and trills often with a drawn-out *baybee* note. Flight song sounds like *per-chick-oree* or *po-tato-chips*.

• **BEHAVIOR** Occurs in flocks in nonbreeding season. In spring, feeds on the small seeds from dandelions. In the late summer breeding season, males engage in aerial displays of exaggerated roller coaster–like flights across the sky, singing *po-tato-chip* with each downward glide.

• **BREEDING** Monogamous. Among the very latest songbirds to nest each year. Territorial defense and mate selection begins in late summer and continues into early fall.

• **NESTING** Incubation 10–12 days by female. Young stay in nest

bright yellow

black cap

black wings with white double wing bars

MALE

black tail

extensive white edging on wing

JUVENILE

FEMALE
WINTER PLUMAGE

MALE
WINTER PLUMAGE

olive upperparts

pale yellow underparts

FEMALE

Similar Birds

YELLOW WARBLER ♂
Lacks wing bars and black wing and tail • breeds throughout much of the North, Southwest.

LESSER GOLDFINCH ♂
Yellow undertail coverts • ranges in the Northwest, Rockies, and much of the Southwest.

Flight Pattern

Undulating, roller coaster–like flight with several rapid wing beats and a pause.

11–17 days, fed by both sexes. 1–2 broods per year.

• **POPULATION** Common. Declining in eastern North America; stable in the West.

• **FEEDERS** Black (oil) sunflower seeds, thistle.

Nest Identification

Shape ⬤ Location 🌿 🌳 🔻

Pliable vegetation lined with plant down • caterpillar webbing and spider silk often used to bind outer rim • usually along the edge of an open area • built by female • extremely well woven • 4–6 pale blue or bluish white eggs; subelliptical to oval, 0.6 inch long.

Plumage Sexes differ	Habitat	Migration Migratory	Weight 0.5 ounce

DATE _____ TIME_____ LOCATION _____

Family FRINGILLIDAE	Species *Carduelis sinica*	Length 6 inches	Wingspan 9.25 inches

ORIENTAL GREENFINCH

This Eurasian bird is a rare migratory visitor to the outer Aleutians and Pribilofs off mainland Alaska. Conspicuous in flight are the broad yellow stripe at the base of the primaries and secondaries and the yellow base of the outer tail feathers. Females are similar to males but duller in color with a brownish head. Juveniles resemble adult females but have a buffy wash on the underparts and brown-streaked upperparts and underparts.

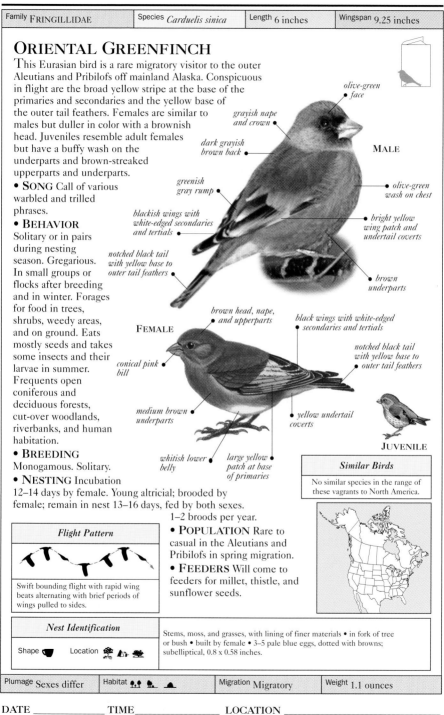

olive-green face

grayish nape and crown

dark grayish brown back

MALE

greenish gray rump

olive-green wash on chest

blackish wings with white-edged secondaries and tertials

bright yellow wing patch and undertail coverts

notched black tail with yellow base to outer tail feathers

brown underparts

brown head, nape, and upperparts

black wings with white-edged secondaries and tertials

FEMALE

notched black tail with yellow base to outer tail feathers

conical pink bill

medium brown underparts

yellow undertail coverts

JUVENILE

whitish lower belly

large yellow patch at base of primaries

• **SONG** Call of various warbled and trilled phrases.

• **BEHAVIOR** Solitary or in pairs during nesting season. Gregarious. In small groups or flocks after breeding and in winter. Forages for food in trees, shrubs, weedy areas, and on ground. Eats mostly seeds and takes some insects and their larvae in summer. Frequents open coniferous and deciduous forests, cut-over woodlands, riverbanks, and human habitation.

• **BREEDING** Monogamous. Solitary.

• **NESTING** Incubation 12–14 days by female. Young altricial; brooded by female; remain in nest 13–16 days, fed by both sexes. 1–2 broods per year.

• **POPULATION** Rare to casual in the Aleutians and Pribilofs in spring migration.

• **FEEDERS** Will come to feeders for millet, thistle, and sunflower seeds.

Similar Birds
No similar species in the range of these vagrants to North America.

Flight Pattern

Swift bounding flight with rapid wing beats alternating with brief periods of wings pulled to sides.

Nest Identification

Shape 🍵   Location 🌿 🌳 🌲

Stems, moss, and grasses, with lining of finer materials • in fork of tree or bush • built by female • 3–5 pale blue eggs, dotted with browns; subelliptical, 0.8 x 0.58 inches.

Plumage Sexes differ	Habitat 🌾 🌳 ⛰	Migration Migratory	Weight 1.1 ounces

DATE _____ TIME_____ LOCATION _____

Family FRINGILLIDAE	Species *Pyrrhula pyrrhula*	Length 6.5 inches	Wingspan 10 inches

EURASIAN BULLFINCH

This brightly colored visitor from Eurasia occasionally is recorded in the spring on the western Alaskan islands and in winter on mainland coastal Alaska. A stocky big-headed bird with a short bill, it most often remains hidden in dense forests or thickets in the summer but is conspicuous in the fall and winter, when it forms flocks and becomes highly nomadic. The peculiar profile is distinctive in that the culmen forms a continuous arc with the crown and nape. In flight the contrasting white stripe on the black wing and the white rump are conspicuous on both sexes. The juvenile resembles the female but shows a brown cap and face.

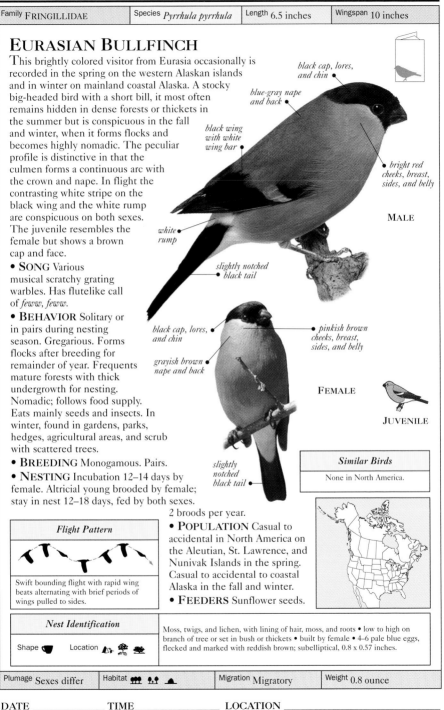

black cap, lores, and chin

blue-gray nape and back

black wing with white wing bar

bright red cheeks, breast, sides, and belly

MALE

white rump

slightly notched black tail

black cap, lores, and chin

grayish brown nape and back

pinkish brown cheeks, breast, sides, and belly

FEMALE

JUVENILE

slightly notched black tail

• **SONG** Various musical scratchy grating warbles. Has flutelike call of *feww, feww.*

• **BEHAVIOR** Solitary or in pairs during nesting season. Gregarious. Forms flocks after breeding for remainder of year. Frequents mature forests with thick undergrowth for nesting. Nomadic; follows food supply. Eats mainly seeds and insects. In winter, found in gardens, parks, hedges, agricultural areas, and scrub with scattered trees.

• **BREEDING** Monogamous. Pairs.

• **NESTING** Incubation 12–14 days by female. Altricial young brooded by female; stay in nest 12–18 days, fed by both sexes. 2 broods per year.

• **POPULATION** Casual to accidental in North America on the Aleutian, St. Lawrence, and Nunivak Islands in the spring. Casual to accidental to coastal Alaska in the fall and winter.

• **FEEDERS** Sunflower seeds.

Similar Birds
None in North America.

Flight Pattern

Swift bounding flight with rapid wing beats alternating with brief periods of wings pulled to sides.

Nest Identification	
Shape ☕ Location 🌿 🏵 🌳	Moss, twigs, and lichen, with lining of hair, moss, and roots • low to high on branch of tree or set in bush or thickets • built by female • 4–6 pale blue eggs, flecked and marked with reddish brown; subelliptical, 0.8 x 0.57 inches.

Plumage Sexes differ	Habitat 🐛 🏵 🔺	Migration Migratory	Weight 0.8 ounce

DATE _____ TIME_____ LOCATION _____

Family FRINGILLIDAE	Species *Coccothraustes vespertinus*	Length 7.75–8.5 inches	Wingspan 13–13.75 inches

EVENING GROSBEAK

Since the late 19th century the breeding range of this chunky bird has expanded eastward, supported by seed from new trees and by increased feeding stations. Fall migratory patterns are erratic; birds only leave breeding ranges when food supplies fail or populations become sizeable. Flocks may arrive in a region one winter and not return the next. In flight the short notched tail and large wing patches are distinctive.

• **SONG** Series of clipped warbled phrases, ending in shrill whistled note. Calls are loud piercing *clee-ip*, *peeer* and *chirp*. Flocks sound like chorus of amplified House Sparrows.

• **BEHAVIOR** Gregarious. Tame. Noisy. In groups and flocks during breeding season; pairs nest closely. Eats insects, including spruce budworm, while nesting; also eats buds, sap, and seeds from trees and shrubs; fruits and berries. In winter looks for salt and drinks water from melting snow.

• **BREEDING** Monogamous. Semicolonial.

• **NESTING** Incubation 11–14 days by female; male feeds incubating female on nest. Young altricial; brooded by female; stay in nest 13–14 days, fed by both sexes. 1–2 broods per year.

• **POPULATION** Fairly common in breeding season in conifers and mixed woodlots; in mountains in West. Irregular in winter in woodlots, parks, second growth, suburban areas.

• **FEEDERS** Sunflower seeds; frequents birdbaths.

• **CONSERVATION** Rare cowbird host. Many killed on salt-treated highways in winter.

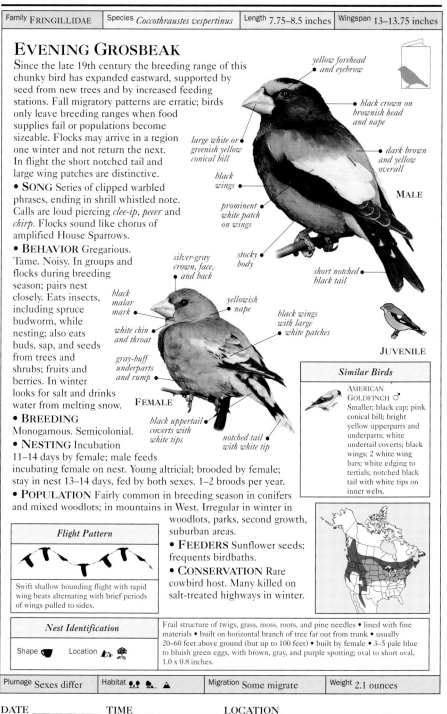

yellow forehead and eyebrow

black crown on brownish head and nape

large white or greenish yellow conical bill

dark brown and yellow overall

black wings

MALE

prominent white patch on wings

stocky body

short notched black tail

silver-gray crown, face, and back

black malar mark

yellowish nape

black wings with large white patches

JUVENILE

white chin and throat

gray-buff underparts and rump

FEMALE

black uppertail coverts with white tips

notched tail with white tip

Similar Birds

AMERICAN GOLDFINCH ♂ Smaller; black cap; pink conical bill; bright yellow upperparts and underparts; white undertail coverts; black wings; 2 white wing bars; white edging to tertials; notched black tail with white tips on inner webs.

Flight Pattern	

Swift shallow bounding flight with rapid wing beats alternating with brief periods of wings pulled to sides.

Nest Identification	
Shape Location	Frail structure of twigs, grass, moss, roots, and pine needles • lined with fine materials • built on horizontal branch of tree far out from trunk • usually 20–60 feet above ground (but up to 100 feet) • built by female • 3–5 pale blue to bluish green eggs, with brown, gray, and purple spotting; oval to short oval, 1.0 x 0.8 inches.

Plumage Sexes differ	Habitat	Migration Some migrate	Weight 2.1 ounces

DATE _____ TIME _____ LOCATION _____

Family FRINGILLIDAE	Species *Coccothraustes coccothraustes*	Length 7 inches	Wingspan 13 inches

HAWFINCH

This stocky thick-necked bird makes its home in Europe and Asia but occasionally crosses over the Bering Strait to the western islands and west coast of Alaska. The adult's massive blue-gray bill turns yellow in winter. In its undulating flight, it looks dumpy overhead, and the white wing patches and short white-tipped tail are conspicuous. Females are similar to males but appear duller in color, with more gray on the wings and brown underparts. Juveniles have yellow bills, gray-brown upperparts, and buffy brown underparts with dusky mottling and streaking.

tawny buff head

gray neck

dark chestnut-brown back, rump, and uppertail coverts

huge conical bill

bold blue-black wings with white shoulder patches

black chin, throat, and loral mask

gray malar mark

short white-tipped brown tail

pinkish brown underparts

• **SONG** Soft high-pitched squeaky warble. Call is a high-pitched sibilant *tseep.* Flight note, frequently given loudly, is an explosive *tick.* Often first detected by *tick* note.

• **BEHAVIOR** In pairs during nesting season. Gregarious. In family groups or small flocks following breeding season. Often flocks in trees and stays hidden in the foliage. Forages for food on ground and in the canopies of trees. Has a waddling type of walk that resembles the shuffle of a parrot. Eats mostly large tree seeds but also some fruits and insects. Nomadic, this bird follows the food supply.

• **BREEDING** Monogamous. Solitary.

• **NESTING** Incubation 9–14 days, mostly by female. Young altricial; brooded by female; stay in nest 10–14 days, tended by both sexes. 1 brood per year.

• **POPULATION** Rare to casual in North America on the Aleutians, Pribilofs, and St. Lawrence Islands and in western Alaska.

• **FEEDERS** Will come to feeders for sunflower seeds.

• **CONSERVATION** Vulnerable to habitat loss due to logging operations.

Similar Birds
None among vagrants to or residents of North America.

Flight Pattern

Swift bounding flight with rapid wing beats alternating with brief periods of wings pulled to sides.

Nest Identification

Shape ▬   Location 🌲

Roots, twigs, and lichen, with lining of plant fibers, hair, and rootlets • low in tree, 6–18 feet above ground • built by female • 3–7 greenish eggs with blackish brown markings, sometimes concentrated at larger end; subelliptical, 0.95 x 0.68 inches.

Plumage Sexes differ	Habitat	Migration Migratory	Weight 1.9 ounces

DATE _____ TIME_____ LOCATION _____

Family PASSERIDAE	Species *Passer domesticus*	Length 5.5–6.5 inches	Wingspan 9.5–10 inches

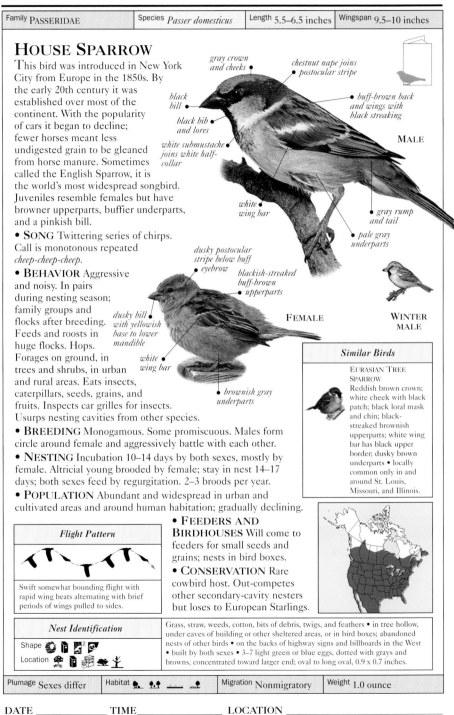

HOUSE SPARROW

This bird was introduced in New York City from Europe in the 1850s. By the early 20th century it was established over most of the continent. With the popularity of cars it began to decline; fewer horses meant less undigested grain to be gleaned from horse manure. Sometimes called the English Sparrow, it is the world's most widespread songbird. Juveniles resemble females but have browner upperparts, buffier underparts, and a pinkish bill.

gray crown and cheeks

chestnut nape joins postocular stripe

black bill

black bib and lores

white submustache joins white half-collar

buff-brown back and wings with black streaking

MALE

white wing bar

gray rump and tail

pale gray underparts

• **SONG** Twittering series of chirps. Call is monotonous repeated *cheep-cheep-cheep.*

• **BEHAVIOR** Aggressive and noisy. In pairs during nesting season; family groups and flocks after breeding. Feeds and roosts in huge flocks. Hops. Forages on ground, in trees and shrubs, in urban and rural areas. Eats insects, caterpillars, seeds, grains, and fruits. Inspects car grilles for insects. Usurps nesting cavities from other species.

dusky postocular stripe below buff eyebrow

blackish-streaked buff-brown upperparts

dusky bill with yellowish base to lower mandible

white wing bar

brownish gray underparts

FEMALE

WINTER MALE

pale gray underparts

• **BREEDING** Monogamous. Some promiscuous. Males form circle around female and aggressively battle with each other.

• **NESTING** Incubation 10–14 days by both sexes, mostly by female. Altricial young brooded by female; stay in nest 14–17 days; both sexes feed by regurgitation. 2–3 broods per year.

• **POPULATION** Abundant and widespread in urban and cultivated areas and around human habitation; gradually declining.

Similar Birds

EURASIAN TREE SPARROW
Reddish brown crown; white cheek with black patch; black loral mask and chin; black-streaked brownish upperparts; white wing bar has black upper border; dusky brown underparts • locally common only in and around St. Louis, Missouri, and Illinois.

Flight Pattern

Swift somewhat bounding flight with rapid wing beats alternating with brief periods of wings pulled to sides.

• **FEEDERS AND BIRDHOUSES** Will come to feeders for small seeds and grains; nests in bird boxes.

• **CONSERVATION** Rare cowbird host. Out-competes other secondary-cavity nesters but loses to European Starlings.

Nest Identification	
Shape	Grass, straw, weeds, cotton, bits of debris, twigs, and feathers • in tree hollow, under eaves of building or other sheltered areas, or in bird boxes; abandoned nests of other birds • on the backs of highway signs and billboards in the West • built by both sexes • 3–7 light green or blue eggs, dotted with grays and browns, concentrated toward larger end; oval to long oval, 0.9 x 0.7 inches.
Location	

Plumage Sexes differ	Habitat	Migration Nonmigratory	Weight 1.0 ounce

DATE _____ TIME _____ LOCATION _____

ACCIDENTAL SPECIES

Because birds are so mobile some individuals occasionally are recorded great distances from their normal ranges. These rare birds – rare because they are geographically misplaced – create some of the most exciting experiences for birders when they are discovered, and the news of their presence often spreads quickly. Included here is a list of these accidental species and those occurrences that have been reliably documented in the area covered by this field guide. Some of the following occurrences are recorded in general terms, such as the Pacific Coast, while others are specific to states or provinces, such as California (CA) or Alberta (AB); still others cite a geographic area within a state or province, such as the Aleutian Islands (Is.), in Alaska (AK). These records are provided as listed by the American Ornithologists Union (AOU) *Check-list of North American Birds*, 7th edition, with multiple locations separated by semicolons.

Shy Albatross, *Thalassarche cauta*: Pacific Coast; WA.

Light-mantled Albatross, *Phoebetria palpebrata:* CA.

Wandering Albatross, *Diomedea exulans*: Pacific Coast; CA.

Short-tailed Albatross, *Phoebastria albatrus*: Gulf of Alaska; AK; off coast of BC, WA, and CA.

Manx Shearwater, *Puffinus puffinus*: Pacific Coast; WA; CA.

Wilson's Storm-Petrel, *Oceanites oceanicus*: Pacific Coast; WA; OR.

White-tailed Tropicbird, *Phaethon lepturus*: south CA; AZ.

Red-billed Tropicbird, *Phaethon aethereus*: south CA coast; WA; AZ.

Great Frigatebird, *Fregata minor*: OK; CA.

Yellow Bittern, *Ixobrychus sinensis*: Aleutian Is., AK.

Chinese Egret, *Egretta eulophotes*: Aleutian Is., AK.

Reddish Egret, *Egretta rufescens*: NV; AZ; CO; west TX.

Chinese Pond-Heron, *Ardeola bacchus*: St. Paul Is. and Pribilof Is., AK.

Yellow-crowned Night-Heron, *Nyctanassa violacea*: accidental to casual in northeast TX.

Lesser White-fronted Goose, *Anser erythropus*: Attu Is., AK.

Garganey, *Anas querquedula*: BC; AB; SK; CA; AZ; north TX; OK.

Smew, *Mergellus albellus*: WA; CA.

Swallow-tailed Kite, *Elanoides forficatus*: NM; east CO; south SK.

King Rail, *Rallus elegans*: SD; IA; KS; southwest TX; CO; ND.

Purple Gallinule, *Porphyrula martinica*: CA; NV; UT; WY.

Eurasian Coot, *Fulica atra*: Pribilof Is., AK.

Common Crane, *Grus grus*: Fairbanks, AK; AB; NE; NM.

European Golden-Plover, *Pluvialis apricaria*: Point Barrow, AK.

Collared Plover, *Charadrius collaris*: Uvalde, TX.

Black-winged Stilt, *Himantopus himantopus*: Aleutian Is., AK.

Common Greenshank, *Tringa nebularia*: Aleutian Is. and Pribilof Is., AK.

Marsh Sandpiper, *Tringa stagnatilis*: Aleutian Is., AK.

Green Sandpiper, *Tringa ochropus*: Aleutian Is. and St. Lawrence Is., AK.

Terek Sandpiper, *Xenus cinereus*: Aleutian Is., St. Lawrence Is., and south AK.

Little Curlew, *Numenius minutus*: Santa Maria Valley, CA; St. Lawrence Is., AK.

Temminck's Stint, *Calidris temminckii*: Aleutian Is. and Pribilof Is., AK; BC; WA.

Spoonbill Sandpiper, *Eurynorhynchus pygmeus*: Aleutian Is. and northwest AK; coastal BC.

Broad-billed Sandpiper, *Limicola falcinellus*: Aleutian Is., AK.

Ruff, *Philomachus pugnax*: Aleutian Is., Pribilof Is., and southwest AK; BC; CA; AZ; AB; SK; MB.

Jack Snipe, *Lymnocryptes minimus*: Pribilof Is., AK; CA.

Pin-tailed Snipe, *Gallinago stenura*: west Aleutian Is., AK.

Oriental Pratincole, *Glareola maldivarum*: Aleutian Is. and St. Lawrence Is., AK.

Black-headed Gull, *Larus ridibundus*: Aleutian Is., Pribilof Is., and central AK; Pacific Coast from south-central AK to south CA; northeast CO; TX.

Band-tailed Gull, *Larus belcheri*: CA coast.

Sandwich Tern, *Sterna sandvicensis*: south CA coast.

Sooty Tern, *Sterna fuscata*: CA; west TX.

White-winged Tern, *Chlidonias leucopterus*: Aleutian Is. and west AK; Pacific Coast from AK to south CA.

Red-billed Pigeon, *Columba flavirostris*: south TX.

Oriental Turtle-Dove, *Streptopelia orientalis*: Aleutian Is. and Pribilof Is., AK; BC.

Oriental Scops-Owl, *Otus sunia*: Aleutian Is. and Amchitka Is., AK.

Jungle Nightjar, *Caprimulgus indicus*: AK.

White-collared Swift, *Streptoprocne zonaris*: northwest CA.

Common Swift, *Apus apus*: Pribilof Is., AK.

Buff-bellied Hummingbird, *Amazilia yucatanensis*: northwest and central TX.

Cinnamon Hummingbird, *Amazilia rutila*: south AZ; southwest NM.

Bumblebee Hummingbird, *Atthis heloisa*: south AZ.

Eurasian Hoopoe, *Upupa epops*: west AK.

Eurasian Wryneck, *Jynx torquilla*: Wales, AK.

Great Spotted Woodpecker, *Dendrocopos major*: Aleutian Is., AK.

Tufted Flycatcher, *Mitrephanes phaeocercus*: Big Bend, TX.

Gray Kingbird, *Tyrannus dominicensis*: Vancouver Is., BC.

Fork-tailed Flycatcher, *Tyrannus savana*: AB; ID; CA.

Brown Shrike, *Lanius cristatus*: Aleutian Is., St. Lawrence Is., and south AK coast; CA.

Common House-Martin, *Delichon urbica*: Pribilof Is. and Nome, AK.

Lanceolated Warbler, *Locustella lanceolata*: Aleutian Is., AK; Farallon Is., CA.

Wood Warbler, *Phylloscopus sibilatrix*: Aleutian Is., AK.

Narcissus Flycatcher, *Ficedula narcissina*: Aleutian Is., AK.

Mugimaki Flycatcher, *Ficedula mugimaki*: Aleutian Is., AK.

Asian Brown Flycatcher, *Muscicapa dauurica*: Aleutian Is., AK.

Siberian Blue Robin, *Luscinia cyane*: Aleutian Is., AK.

Blue Mockingbird, *Melanotis caerulescens*: south AZ.

Tree Pipit, *Anthus trivialis*: Cape Prince of Wales, AK.

Gray Silky-flycatcher, *Ptilogonys cinereus*: southwest TX.

Golden-winged Warbler, *Vermivora chrysoptera*: OR; CA; AZ; CO; NM; MB; SK.

Northern Parula, *Parula americana*: CA; AZ; NM; WY; SK.

Tropical Parula, *Parula pitiayumi*: AZ.

Prairie Warbler, *Dendroica discolor*: south AK coast; OR; NV; NM; AZ; MT; WY.

Cerulean Warbler, *Dendroica cerulea*: southeast NE; east OK; north-central TX; CA; AZ; CO; NM.

Prothonotary Warbler, *Protonotaria citrea*: CA coast; WA; OR; NV.

Worm-eating Warbler, *Helmitheros vermivorus*: CO.

Swainson's Warbler, *Limnothlypis swainsonii*: east CO; south NE; AZ.

Slate-throated Redstart, *Myioborus miniatus*: southeast NM; south AZ.

Worthen's Sparrow, *Spizella wortheni*: Silver City, NM.

Henslow's Sparrow, *Ammodramus henslowii*: central KS; southwest TX.

Pine Bunting, *Emberiza leucocephalos*: Aleutian Is., AK.

Little Bunting, *Emberiza pusilla*: Aleutian Is. and St. Lawrence Is., AK; Point Loma, CA.

Yellow-throated Bunting, *Emberiza elegans*: Attu Island, AK.

Gray Bunting, *Emberiza variabilis*: Aleutian Is., AK.

Pallas's Bunting, *Emberiza pallasi*: Barrow, AK.

Shiny Cowbird, *Molothrus bonariensis*: OK; central TX.

Black-vented Oriole, *Icterus wagleri*: Patagonia, AZ; southwest TX.

Common Rosefinch, *Carpodacus erythrinus*: west Aleutian Is., St. Lawrence Is., and Pribilof Is., AK.

Eurasian Siskin, *Carduelis spinus*: Aleutian Is., AK.

GLOSSARY

• **AERIE**
A nest located on a cliff or high place, usually built by a raptor, a bird of prey.

• **AGAVE**
A desert plant with a spikelike flower, similar to a Yucca plant.

• **AIR SAC**
A series of thin-walled sacs, typically eight or nine (but ranging from six to fourteen, depending on the species) that in conjunction with the paired lungs comprise the bird's respiratory system.

• **ALAR BAR**
A contrasting line (bar) of plumage beginning in the alar region of the wing (where the wing bends at the wrist and on the leading edge) and running from that point at an angle toward the bird's body, stopping where the back of the wing joins the body. The effect is a patch or line of feathers that differ from the color of the wing feathers around it, thus producing a visible bar on the top of the wing. Sometimes the bar runs from the alula to the base of the wing on the front side (leading edge).

• **ALTERNATE PLUMAGE**
See Breeding Plumage.

• **ALTITUDINAL MOVEMENTS**
(Vertical migrations) A bird's regular seasonal vertical movement, often from the mountaintops in summer to lower regions or valleys during winter, with a return to higher elevations the following spring.

• **ALTRICIAL**
Term for young birds that hatch in a helpless state, usually naked with eyes closed, and are totally dependent on the parents.

• **ALULA**
A small group of feathers that protrude from the outermost joint of the wing. It has its own group of muscles and moves independently from the flight feathers. By adjusting the angle of the alula, the bird is able to regulate the air flow over the top of the wing, allowing it to alight or land at slower speeds without stalling.

• **ANHEDRAL**
The downward curve of a bird's wings when in flight.

• **ARBOREAL**
A tree-dwelling bird.

• **AURICULARS**
Feathers along the sides of the ears, often called ear coverts or ear patches.

• **AXILLARIES**
Rigid feathers along the underside of the wings where they connect to the body, corresponding to the underarm area in a human.

• **BASIC PLUMAGE**
See Winter Plumage.

• **BREEDING PLUMAGE**
(Alternate plumage) Seasonal alterations in appearance to attract birds of the opposite sex, such as changes in color or the addition of ornamental ruffs. This is accomplished by a feather molt from the basic, or winter, plumage.

• **CAMBIUM**
Plant tissue near the inner bark of a tree that produces lateral growth.

• **CATKIN**
A spike of flowers such as those found on a willow or birch tree.

• **CERE**
The fleshy area on top of the base of the upper bill that contains the nostrils. Present on the bills of some bird species, particularly among birds of prey.

• **CLUTCH**
The total number of eggs laid during a single nesting period; some birds lay several clutches in a nesting season.

• **COLONIAL**
The pattern of nesting close together with birds of the same species. Sometimes only a few nests packed close together constitute a colony, but some may hold hundreds or thousands of nesting pairs.

• **CONSPECIFIC**
Birds that are members of the same species.

• **CONGENERS**
Distinct bird species that are related to one another by being in the same genus.

• **COVERTS**
A covering of feathers overlaying the upper and lower part of the wings, covering the bases of the flight feathers (wing coverts); also on top of the tail feathers (uppertail coverts and undertail coverts).

• **CRECHE**
An aggregation of hatchlings of a nesting colony, living together while they are in a dependent state and fed and tended by the adult birds.

• **CREPUSCULAR**
Birds that feed and are active during twilight hours.

- **CRISSUM**
Feathers covering the base of the undertail, usually a different color from the rest of the underparts. Also called undertail coverts.
- **CROP**
Where food is stored in the esophagus for later digestion, or to be regurgitated and fed to hatchlings. Some birds, such as pigeons and doves, have a two-chambered crop that produces special milk to nourish their young.
- **CROWN**
Top of the head between the forehead and the back of the head or occiput.
- **CULMEN**
Top ridge of the upper mandible, darker on some birds than the side of the bill.
- **DABBLING**
Method of surface feeding by a relatively short-necked short-legged duck. It tips up the tail and body, then dips its bill and neck into water. These ducks are called dabblers. See Tipping-up.
- **DECURVED**
Sloped downward, usually referring to the bill.
- **DETRITUS**
Small particles of dead organic matter.
- **DIHEDRAL**
Wings held in a shallow V while bird is in flight.
- **DISTAL BAND**
A strip of color near the end of the tail, end of wing, or on the lower part of the leg.
- **DIURNAL**
Birds that feed and are active during the day.
- **ECLIPSE PLUMAGE**
Dull-colored plumage, similar to that of the female, into which many male ducks briefly molt in summer.

- **EXTIRPATED**
Exterminated or destroyed from a part of a species range.
- **EYE RING**
A circle around the eye, usually of a contrasting color.
- **EYE STRIPE OR EYEBROW**
See Supercilium.
- **FIELD MARKS**
Plumage or anatomical features of a bird that help to distinguish it from other similar species.
- **FLASHMARK**
Color or marking on plumage that is visible only when the bird is in flight.
- **FLEDGE**
The act of a young bird (nestling) leaving the nest. Also fledging.
- **FLEDGLING**
A young bird that has feathers and is old enough to have left the nest but is still dependent on adult birds for care and feeding.
- **GONYS**
A ridge on the lower mandible of a gull that causes the midline to appear angled. Sometimes shows a red patch during breeding season.
- **GORGET**
A small iridescent patch on the throat of a hummingbird.
- **GULAR SAC**
A large or small pouch in the upper throat that helps a bird regulate body temperature and sometimes holds undigested food. In a few species, such as the Magnificent Frigatebird, the pouch greatly expands for courtship display.
- **HAWKING**
The act of catching prey, usually insects, in flight. Generally done with the bill. Typical of flycatchers.

- **HERONRY**
(Rookery) The colonial nesting site for herons, egrets, and ibises.
- **HINDNECK**
The bird's nape or back of the neck.
- **HUMERAL**
The patch of feathers overlying the bone near the upperwing or shoulder area.
- **JIZZ**
The abstract combination of a bird's posture, plumage pattern, shape, size, and behavior that allows an experienced birder to recognize a species instantly without further examination.
- **LAMELLAE**
Miniature ridges inside the bill of a duck or water bird that resemble the teeth of a comb and serve as a strainer during feeding.
- **LARDER**
A place where a shrike impales and stores its prey on sharp branches or wire.
- **LEK**
A communal gathering place during breeding season where males of some species of birds display to attract the females. It contains numerous territories, each guarded by a different male.
- **LORES**
Space between the eyes and the base of the upper part of the bill on the side of the bird's face.
- **MALAR**
Refers to the cheek area along the side of the face. Field mark here is called malar mark or malar stripe.
- **MANDIBLE**
The lower half of the bill. Maxilla is the upper half; both halves collectively are called mandibles.

• **MANTLE**
The feathers covering the back and upperwing coverts; feathers of the back and folded wings.

• **MANUS**
The portion of a bird's wing that corresponds to the hand of a human. The fused bones of the palm and reduced digits bear the primary feathers and the alula.

• **MELANISTIC**
A bird that has a surplus of dark pigment in its plumage.

• **MIMIC THRUSH**
A member of the family Mimidae, which includes thrashers, catbirds, and mockingbirds.

• **MORPH**
When birds of the same species have two or more different colored plumages, that are independant of season, sex, age, or breeding. Color phases may or may not be related to range and climate.

• **NEOTROPICAL**
The New World tropical region that encompasses the northern portion of the Mexican rain forest and the Caribbean islands, and extends to the nontropical regions of South America.

• **NEW WORLD**
Earth's Western Hemisphere; includes North, South, and Central America.

• **NOCTURNAL**
Birds that feed and are active at night.

• **NON-PASSERINE**
Any of the birds that are not Passerines, which are the songbirds or perching birds. Includes loons, waterfowl, owls, shorebirds, hawks, woodpeckers, and doves.

• **NUCHAL PATCH**
A patch of contrasting color located on the back of the bird's neck or nape.

• **OCCIPITAL PATCH**
A patch of color located high on the back of the head. Higher on the head than the nuchal patch.

• **OCCIPUT**
The area on the back of a bird's head between the nape and the crown.

• **OCOTILLO**
A spiny desert shrub with red flower clusters at the tips of its branches.

• **OLD WORLD**
Earth's Eastern Hemisphere; Europe, Asia, and Africa.

• **ORBITAL RING**
See Eye Ring.

• **PALEARCTIC**
Faunal region surrounded by the Atlantic, Arctic, and Pacific Oceans; encompasses Asia north of the Himalayas, Europe, and Africa north of the Sahara desert.

• **PASSERINES**
Any of the birds belonging to the order Passeriforms, which comprise more than fifty percent of the world's birds. Highly evolved, these birds are able to sing and have three forward-pointing toes adapted for perching.

• **PEEP**
Birder's name for a group of small, similar-looking sandpipers; may have been derived from their high-pitched calls.

• **PELAGIC**
Birds that spend most of their time at sea and rarely are seen from shore.

• **PIEBALD**
Plumage that shows two contrasting colors.

• **PISHING**
Sound produced by birders to attract birds; made by clinching the teeth together and forcing air out through the teeth and lips to create a noise that sounds like *pish-pish-pish*.

• **POLYANDROUS**
When female bird has two or more mates; female often larger, has brighter plumage, and defends her territory. Male of the species usually incubates and tends young.

• **POLYGYNOUS**
When a male bird takes two or more mates.

• **POLYGAMOUS**
When both male and female of a species may take two or more mates.

• **POSTOCULAR STRIPE**
A line that leads from behind the bird's eye to the auricular or ear patch.

• **PRECOCIAL**
Term for young birds that hatch with their eyes open, are down-covered, and are able to leave the nest within two days of hatching. These hatchlings may be either partially or not at all dependent on the parents for care and feeding.

• **PRIMARIES**
One of two sets of flight feathers, or remiges, located distally to the secondaries and joined to the manus of the wing.

• **PROMISCUOUS**
Birds, male or female, that come together solely for mating purposes and leave within a few hours to mate with other birds.

• **PYRIFORM**
Pear-shaped; often used to describe shape of egg.

- **RAPTORS**
A name applied to birds of prey – the hawks, falcons, eagles, kites, and owls.

- **RECTRICES**
The principal feathers that make up the tail. They range in number from eight to twenty-four, but the average in songbirds is twelve.

- **REMIGES**
Refers to flight feathers – primaries, secondaries, and tertials.

- **RIPARIAN**
Located on or near a river bank, stream bank, or other body of water.

- **SCAPULARS**
Feathers joined to the shoulder area of the bird and covering the top of the folded wing.

- **SECONDARIES**
One of two sets of flight feathers located between the body and the primaries and joined to the part of the wing that corresponds to the forearm of a human.

- **SEMIALTRICIAL**
Term for young birds that hatch with eyes either open or closed, are down-covered, and are incapable of leaving the nest; fed by parents.

- **SEMICOLONIAL**
Nesting pattern in which several birds of the same species nest close to one another, often within sight of each other's nests and do not behave aggressively toward one another.

- **SEMIPRECOCIAL**
Term for young birds that hatch with eyes open, are down-covered, and able to leave the nest soon after hatching, but remain in nest and are fed by parents.

- **SKYLARKING**
Elaborate territorial display flight given by a male songbird. It sings and often flutters in circles before swooping back to earth.

- **SPATULATE**
A long rounded spoonlike shape; sometimes used to describe bill or tail.

- **SPECULUM**
A small area of contrasting iridescent feathers located on the secondary feathers of the wings. Often seen in ducks.

- **SQUEAKING**
Sound produced by birders to attract birds; made by pursing the lips tightly together and sucking air in to make a high-pitched sound. This can be amplified by placing the lips on the back of the hand and sucking in a kissing fashion.

- **SUPERCILIUM**
Line above each eye; an eyebrow. Also called a superciliary stripe.

- **SUPERSPECIES**
Closely related species that are often separated from each other by geographic barriers. Without these barriers the two species probably would interbreed and become one.

- **SYMPATRIC**
Birds that inhabit the same range but remain distinct and separate species.

- **TAIGA**
Subarctic coniferous forests.

- **TARSUS**
The top of the foot behind the toes, often called the shank. Usually either bare or covered with scales, plates, or sometimes feathers.

- **TERTIALS**
The group of secondary feathers closest to the body; often a contrasting color.

- **TIPPING-UP**
Method of surface feeding by a duck, goose, or swan in which it raises its tail and dips its bill, head, and neck into the water. See Dabbling.

- **TOTIPALMATE**
All four toes joined together by webbing.

- **TYMPANI**
(Tympaniform membranes) Valves in the vocal organ of a bird that produce sound.

- **UNDERPARTS**
The plumage and coloring on the breast, belly, sides, flanks, and undertail coverts.

- **UPPERPARTS**
The plumage and coloring on the nape, back, shoulders, rump, and upper part of tail.

- **VANE**
Contoured flight feather that acts as a propeller. It consists of a central shaft surrounded by an inner and outer web.

- **VENT**
The opening of the cloaca, or anus; sometimes refers to a contrasting patch of feathers in this area.

- **WATTLE**
Fleshy piece of brightly colored skin that hangs from the lower bill; associated with turkeys and some chickens.

- **WILDTYPE**
A biological term based in genetics that describes the form that most individuals in a wild population take; description includes shape, color, patterns, and size.

- **WINGSTRIP**
A distinct line on the wing, usually of a contrasting color.

- **WINTER PLUMAGE**
(Basic plumage) Seasonal alteration in a bird's appearance produced by the fall molt.

INDEX

References to full-page species profiles are shown in boldface type. All of the rare birds that occasionally appear in the region covered by this book are not shown in full-page profiles, but additional information on accidental species is located on pp. 734–35. The common and scientific names of these birds are followed by an **A** in this index. An **E** denotes a species that does not range west of the 100th meridian, the line of demarcation used in creating this book. More information on these species can be found in the DK Smithsonian Handbooks: *Birds of North America, Eastern Region*.

ACKNOWLEDGMENTS

The author would like to dedicate this book to his father, Fred J. Alsop, Jr., and thank his wife, Cathi Alsop, for her support during the writing of this book and for editing the final proofs of the range maps.

Southern Lights would like to thank: Ron Austing for photo coordination; Kristi Tipton for research on species profiles and range maps; Sandra Porter, Kristy Cuccini, Kelly Buford, and Anne Esquivel for species profile research; Mark Dennis, Martin Copeland, and Fergus Muir, DK Picture Library, for photo and illustration research; Jenny Cromie and Nina Costopoulos for editorial assistance; Holly Cross and R. Clay White for copyediting; Denise McIntyre and Rebecca Benton for proofreading; Marianne Thomas, Melissa Givens, George Griswold III, Jim Larussa, Will McCalley, Rick Tucker, and Christana Laycock for graphic assistance; Catherine O'Hare, Michelle Boylan, Taylor Rogers, Brad Reisinger, and Beth Brown for administrative support; and Charles (Chuck) Hunter of the US Fish and Wildlife Service, John C. Sterling, and Joseph DiCostanzo of the American Museum of Natural History, for manuscript review and commentary.

651, 653, 655, 656, 657, 660, 661, 665, 667, 668, 670, 671, 676*t*, 676*b*, 677*t*, 684*t*, 684*b*, 687*t*, 687*b*, 689*t*, 689*b*, 691*t*, 693*t*, 693*b*, 694*t*, 695*b*, 696*t*, 696*b*, 698, 702*t*, 706*t*, 706*b*, 707*t*, 707*b*, 708*b*, 710*t*, 718*t*, 718*b*, 720*t*, 720*b*, 722*t*, 722*b*, 728*t*, 728*b*, 731*t*, 731*b*, 733*b*.
Rick & Nora Bowers 50, 51, 105, 112, 127*b*, 144*t*, 178, 189*b*, 278, 328, 354, 355, 377, 386*t*, 386*b*, 388, 392, 406*t*, 406*b*, 433, 467*b*, 499, 500, 507, 594, 595, 631, 633*t*, 641, 648, 662, 686*b*.
Cornell Laboratory of Ornithology/Allen Brooks 37*t*; L. Page Brown 166; Lang Elliott 723*b*; George Sutton 35*t*. **Mike Danzenbaker** 58, 59, 61, 65, 74, 78, 104, 117*t*, 117*b*, 122, 136*t*, 136*b*, 150*t*, 156, 157, 177, 198, 216*t*, 216*b*, 219, 222, 225, 233, 234, 238, 239, 246, 253, 258, 259, 260, 273, 286, 293, 294, 302, 325, 326, 336, 361, 374, 375, 391*b*, 396*t*, 401*t*, 401*b*, 407, 416, 430, 431, 435, 439, 455, 489, 492, 496, 504, 528, 531, 541*t*, 543*b*, 545*t*, 545*b*, 556, 560*t*, 568, 570, 572, 577*b*, 578, 579, 588*t*, 608*b*, 629, 644, 647, 679*t*, 681*t*, 681*b*, 686*t*, 692*b*, 697*t*, 697*b*, 702*b*, 724, 727*t*, 730*b*, 732. **DK Picture Library**/Dennis Avon 202*t*, 340, 574; Mike Dunning 155; Frank Greenaway 172, 180; Cyril Laubscher 94, 100, 106, 173, 200*t*, 228, 730*t*, 733*t*; Karl & Steve Maslowski 445, 460, 503, 518, 529*b*, 546*t*, 548*b*, 666, 669, 695*t*; Jane Miller 209; Kim Taylor 121*t*, 121*b*; Jerry Young 174b, 359*b*. **Frank Lane Picture Agency**/Yuri Artukhin 581; Richard Brooks 538*b*, 713*b*; A. R. Hamblin 347; H. Hautala 423; Steve McCutcheon 621*b*; Mark Newman 212; P. Reynolds 319; Roger Tidman 538*t*; R. Van Nostrand 372; Roger Wilmshurst 184*t*, 184*b*, 557; Martin Withers 352. **Kevin T. Karlson** 45, 79, 84*b*, 89, 111, 113, 116*t*, 123*b*, 124*b*, 125*t*, 125*b*, 128*t*, 128*b*, 132*b*, 134*t*, 134*b*, 139*b*, 143*b*, 144*b*, 160, 164, 191*t*, 191*b*, 193*b*, 206, 227, 231, 232, 277*b*, 279, 291, 305, 337, 338, 343*t*, 343*b*, 344, 389*t*, 402*b*, 475, 482, 490, 529*t*, 583, 587*t*, 590*t*, 590*b*, 599*b*, 600*b*, 618, 645, 659*b*, 663, 678*b*. **Brian E. Small** 43, 53, 62, 63, 71, 77, 80, 82, 83*t*, 90, 96, 108, 116*b*, 119*b*, 126*b*, 135*b*, 140*t*, 153, 154, 162, 167, 168, 170, 179, 187*t*, 193*t*, 194, 195, 200*b*, 203*b*, 204, 205, 213, 221, 224, 237, 249, 251, 252, 255, 256, 257, 261, 265, 267, 269, 275*t*, 275*b*, 283, 292, 295, 304, 311, 329, 342, 357, 369, 389*b*, 390*t*, 390*b*, 393*t*, 395*b*, 398*t*, 398*b*, 399*t*, 399*b*, 402*t*, 403*b*, 404*t*, 404*b*, 413*t*, 413*b*, 415, 417*t*, 418, 421, 422, 424, 428, 438, 440, 441, 442, 443, 446, 448, 449, 452, 454, 456, 457, 458, 461,

467*t*, 468, 469, 470, 471, 473, 478, 481, 484, 485, 486, 491, 494*t*, 494*b*, 498, 505, 506, 510, 511, 514, 517, 520, 533, 534*b*, 535*t*, 535*b*, 547*t*, 547*b*, 548*t*, 549, 551, 558, 560*b*, 562, 565, 571, 575, 582*t*, 585, 587*b*, 588*b*, 593, 603*t*, 603*b*, 605*b*, 606*t*, 606*b*, 607*t*, 607*b*, 610, 613*b*, 614*t*, 614*b*, 616*t*, 616*b*, 623*t*, 623*b*, 626*t*, 628, 633*b*, 636*t*, 636*b*, 639*b*, 642, 646, 652, 654*t*, 658, 659*t*, 664, 672, 675*t*, 675*b*, 677*b*, 678*t*, 682*b*, 685*t*, 685*b*, 688*t*, 688*b*, 690*t*, 690*b*, 691*b*, 692*t*, 703*t*, 705*t*, 705*b*, 708*t*, 710*b*, 711*t*, 711*b*, 712*t*, 712*b*, 714, 715*b*, 717*t*, 717*b*, 719*t*, 719*b*, 721*t*, 726*t*, 726*b*, 727*b*. **Tom Vezo** 7*b*, 38, 40, 41, 44, 46, 48, 49, 52, 81, 102, 103, 110, 140*b*, 141*t*, 141*b*, 142*t*, 142*b*, 143*t*, 163, 174*t*, 187*b*, 190*t*, 190*b*, 199, 203*t*, 215*t*, 215*b*, 243, 247, 248, 254, 266, 272, 276*t*, 276*b*, 280, 281, 284, 285, 287, 289, 296, 297, 298, 300, 301, 303, 306, 310, 313, 317, 318, 351, 391*t*, 409, 411, 417*b*, 444, 447*t*, 447*b*, 453, 459, 479, 483, 487, 509, 523, 525, 542*t*, 542*b*, 544*t*, 544*b*, 553, 567, 576, 626*b*, 639*t*, 643, 682*t*, 699, 700*t*, 700*b*, 704*t*, 704*b*. **Vireo**/ Lance Beeny 188; J. D. Bland 183; R. & N. Bowers 521, 637, 709*t*; B. Chudleigh 244; H. Clarke 384, 450; Rob Curtis 462*t*, 462*b*, 621*t*; R. & S. Day 196, 694*b*; J. Dunning 630; H. & J. Eriksen 723*t*; M. Gage 268; W. Greene 186; C. H. Greenewalt 314; D. Hill 42; M. Lockwood 604*t*; A. Morris 131*t*, 131*b*, 308, 701*t*; J. P. Myers 264; T. Pederson 346; R. L. Pitman 327, 332; D. Roby & K. Brink 316; S. & S. Rucker 604*b*; K. Schafer 230; T. Shimba 57, 577*t*, 580; D. Tipling 508, 532, 543*t*, 680*t*, 680*b*, 713*t*, 729*t*; D. True 387*t*; T. J. Ulrich 379, 715*t*; Doug Wechsler 348, 477, 555*t*; D. & M. Zimmerman 70, 561*t*. **Richard Wagner** 397*t*, 410*t*, 410*b*, 674. **Kenny Walters** 27*b*, 29*b*, 33*b*.